ST/ESA/STAT/SER.G/63 (Vol. I)

Department of Economic and Social Affairs
Statistics Division

2014
International Trade Statistics Yearbook

Volume I
Trade by Country

United Nations
New York, 2015

DEPARTMENT OF ECONOMIC AND SOCIAL AFFAIRS

The Department of Economic and Social Affairs of the United Nations Secretariat is a vital interface between global policies in the economic, social and environmental spheres and national action. The Department works in three main interlinked areas: (i) it compiles, generates and analyses a wide range of economic, social and environmental data and information on which Member States of the United Nations draw to review common problems and to take stock of policy options; (ii) it facilitates the negotiations of Member States in many intergovernmental bodies on joint courses of action to address ongoing or emerging global challenges; and (iii) it advises interested Governments on the ways and means of translating policy frameworks developed in United Nations conferences and summits into programmes at the country level and, through technical assistance, helps build national capacities.

NOTE

Symbols of United Nations documents are composed of capital letters combined with figures.

The designations employed and the presentation of material in this publication do not imply the expression of any opinion whatsoever on the part of the Secretariat of the United Nations concerning the legal status of any country, territory, city or area, or of its authorities, or concerning the delimitation of its frontiers or boundaries.

Where the designation "country or area" appears in this publication, it covers countries, territories, cities or areas. In previous issues of this publication, where the designation "country" appears in the headings of tables, it should be interpreted to cover countries, territories, cities or areas.

In some tables, the designation "developed" economies is intended for statistical convenience and does not necessarily express a judgement about the stage reached by a particular country or area in the development process.

ST/ESA/STAT/SER.G/63 Vol. I

UNITED NATIONS PUBLICATION
Sales No. E.15.XVII.11 H

ISBN 978-92-1-161598-2
eISBN 978-92-1-057406-8
ISSN 1010-447X

Enquiries should be directed to
Sales and Marketing Section
Outreach Division
Department of Public Information
United Nations
New York 10017
USA

E-mail: publications@un.org
Internet: http://unp.un.org

Copyright © United Nations, 2015
All rights reserved

PREFACE

The *2014 International Trade Statistics Yearbook* (2014 ITSY) is the sixty-third edition of this yearbook. Its objective is to inform about the detailed merchandise and services imports and exports of individual countries (areas) by commodity and service category and by partner country (volume I), the world trade in individual commodities (3-digit SITC groups) (volume II) and total world merchandise trade - up to the year 2014. The two volumes are prepared at different points in time during 2015: *Volume I - Trade by Country* is made electronically available in June, and *Volume II - Trade by Commodity,* in December, as the preparation of the tables in Volume II requires additional country data which, normally, become available later in the year.

Beginning with 2013 edition, trade in services data was introduced to the *International Trade Statistics Yearbook: Volume I - Trade by Country*. Therefore, the content and format of the yearbook were redesigned to take into account new additions of graphs/tables and analytical text. The data used in the tables and graphs of the yearbook are taken at a specific time (end of May 2015) from the publicly available UN Comtrade (http://comtrade.un.org) and UN Service Trade (http://unstats.un.org/unsd/servicetrade) databases. Users are advised to visit these databases for additional and more current information as they are continuously updated.

The *International Trade Statistics Yearbook* is prepared by the Trade Statistics Branch of the Statistics Division, Department of Economic and Social Affairs of the United Nations Secretariat. Under the general supervision of the Chief of Branch, Ronald Jansen, the programme manager is Markie Muryawan and the chief editor is Habibur Rahman Khan, assisted by Marjorie Imperial-Damaso. Bekuretsion Amdemariam has the leading role in the processing of the data for UN Comtrade and Htu Aung for UN Service Trade. Habibur Rahman Khan, Kenneth Iversen, Daniel Eshetie, Nancy Snyder, Karoly Kovacs, and Markie Muryawan provided valuable contribution to the inclusion of trade in services data and the improvement of production processes. However, all staffs of the branch are involved in the generation of the data and the review/validation of the yearbook. Markie Muryawan, Salomon Cameo and Luis Gonzalez Morales developed the original software which is maintained by Daniel Eshetie and Salomon Cameo.

Comments and feedback on the yearbook are welcome. They may be sent to comtrade@un.org / tradeserv@un.org or to United Nations Statistics Division, Trade Statistics Branch, New York, New York 10017, USA.

TABLE OF CONTENTS

	Page
Introduction	vii
Concepts and definitions of International Merchandise Trade Statistics	viii
Concepts and definitions of Statistics of International Trade in Services	x
Description of world trade tables in part 1 (Tables A and D)	xiv
Description of tables and graphs of Country profiles in part 2	xv
Sources	xvii
Method of Estimation	xvii
Conversion of classification	xviii
Currency conversion and Period	xix
Country Nomenclature and Country Grouping	xix
Abbreviations and Explanation of symbols	xxiii
Disclaimer	xxiv
Contact	xxiv
Part 1: World Trade Tables	1
Total merchandise trade by regions and countries or areas (Table A)	2
World merchandise exports by provenance and destination (Table D)	20
Part 2: Country Trade Profiles	57
Countries (or areas)	58
European Union	396

Part 2: COUNTRY TRADE PROFILES

	Page		Page		Page
Afghanistan	58	Bangladesh	82	Brazil	104
Albania	60	Barbados	84	Brunei Darussalam	106
Algeria	62	Belarus	86	Bulgaria	108
Antigua and Barbuda	64	Belgium	88	Burkina Faso	110
Argentina	66	Belize	90	Burundi	112
Armenia	68	Benin	92	Cabo Verde	114
Aruba	70	Bermuda	94	Cambodia	116
Australia	72	Bhutan	96	Cameroon	118
Austria	74	Bolivia (Plurinational State of)	98	Canada	120
Azerbaijan	76			Central African Republic	122
Bahamas	78	Bosnia and Herzegovina	100	Chile	124
Bahrain	80	Botswana	102	China	126

	Page		Page		Page
China, Hong Kong Special Administrative Region	128	Iran (Islamic Republic of)	198	Nepal	270
China, Macao Special Administrative Region	130	Ireland	200	Netherlands	272
		Israel	202	New Caledonia	274
Colombia	132	Italy	204	New Zealand	276
Congo	134	Jamaica	206	Nicaragua	278
Cook Islands	136	Japan	208	Niger	280
Costa Rica	138	Jordan	210	Nigeria	282
Côte d'Ivoire	140	Kazakhstan	212	Norway, including Svalbard and Jan Mayen Islands	284
Croatia	142	Kenya	214		
Cyprus	144	Kiribati	216	Oman	286
Czech Republic	146	Korea, Republic of	218	Pakistan	288
Denmark	148	Kuwait	220	Panama	290
Dominica	150	Kyrgyzstan	222	Papua New Guinea	292
Dominican Republic	152	Latvia	224	Paraguay	294
Ecuador	154	Lesotho	226	Peru	296
Egypt	156	Lebanon	228	Philippines	298
El Salvador	158	Libya	230	Poland	300
Estonia	160	Lithuania	232	Portugal	302
Ethiopia	162	Luxembourg	234	Qatar	304
Fiji	164	Madagascar	236	Republic of Moldova	306
Finland	166	Malawi	238	Romania	308
France including Monaco	168	Malaysia	240	Russian Federation	310
		Maldives	242	Rwanda	312
French Polynesia	170	Mali	244	Saint Kitts and Nevis	314
Gambia	172	Malta	246	Saint Vincent and the Grenadines	316
Georgia	174	Mauritania	248		
Germany	176	Mauritius	250	Samoa	318
Ghana	178	Mexico	252	Sao Tome and Principe	320
Greece	180	Micronesia, Federated States of	254	Saudi Arabia	322
Greenland	182			Senegal	324
Guatemala	184	Mongolia	256	Serbia	334
Guyana	186	Montenegro	258	Singapore	336
Honduras	188	Montserrat	260	Slovakia	338
Hungary	190	Morocco	262	Slovenia	340
Iceland	192	Mozambique	264	Solomon Islands	334
India	194	Myanmar	266	South Africa	336
Indonesia	196	Namibia	268	Spain	338

	Page
Sri Lanka	340
State of Palestine	342
Sudan	344
Suriname	346
Sweden	348
Switzerland-Liechtenstein	350
Syrian Arab Republic	352
Thailand	354
The former Yugoslav Republic of Macedonia	356
Togo	358
Tonga	360
Trinidad and Tobago	362
Tunisia	364
Turkey	366
Turks and Caicos Islands	368
Uganda	370
Ukraine	372
United Arab Emirates	374
United Kingdom	376
United Republic of Tanzania	378
United States of America, including Puerto Rico and US Virgin Islands	380
Uruguay	382
Vanuatu	384
Venezuela (Bolivarian Republic of)	386
Viet Nam	388
Yemen	390
Zambia	392
Zimbabwe	394
European Union (28 member states)	396

INTRODUCTION

1. The *International Trade Statistics Yearbook: Volume I - Trade by Country*, provides an overview of the latest trends of trade in goods and services of most countries and areas in the world. The publication is aimed at both specialist trade data users and common audience at large. The presented data, charts and analyses will benefit policy makers, government agencies, non-government organizations, civil society organizations, journalists, academics, researchers, students, businesses and anyone who is interested in trade issues.

2. The main content of the yearbook is divided into two parts. Part 1 consists of two detailed world data tables on merchandise trade. One presents total merchandise imports and exports by countries, areas and regions in a time series up to the latest year, the other shows world merchandise exports by group of commodity and by provenance and destination in many smaller time series sub-tables. Part 2 contains the country trade profiles for most countries and areas in the world. The profiles offer an insight into the merchandise and services trade performance of individual countries and areas by means of brief descriptive text, concise data tables and charts using latest available data. For further information on data availability, please see the sources section of this Introduction.

3. The yearbook is also made available online at the publications repository of the UN Statistics Division (http://unstats.un.org/unsd/pubs). For more detailed and latest available data, please consult UN Comtrade (http://comtrade.un.org) and UN ServiceTrade (http://unstats.un.org/unsd/servicetrade), which are the sources of the information presented in the yearbook, and which are continuously updated.

Concepts and definitions of International Merchandise Trade Statistics

4. The merchandise trade data in this Yearbook have been compiled by national statistical authorities largely complying with the United Nations recommended *International Merchandise Trade Statistics, Concepts and Definitions 2010* (IMTS 2010).[1] The main elements of the concepts and definitions are:

    i. <u>Coverage</u>: As a general guideline, it is recommended that international merchandise trade statistics record all goods which add to or subtract from the stock of material resources of a country by entering (imports) or leaving (exports) its economic territory. The general guideline is subject to the clarifications provided in IMTS 2010, in particular, to the specific guidelines in chapter 1 concerning the inclusion or exclusion of certain categories of goods.

    ii. <u>Time of recording</u>: As a general guideline, it is recommended that goods be recorded at the time when they enter or leave the economic territory of a country.

    iii. <u>Statistical territory</u>: The statistical territory of a country is the territory with respect to which trade data are being compiled. The definition of the statistical territory may or may not coincide with the economic territory of a country or its customs territory, depending on the availability of data sources and other considerations. It follows that when the statistical territory of a country and its economic territory differ, international merchandise trade statistics do not provide a complete record of inward and outward flows of goods.

    iv. <u>Trade systems</u>: Depending on what parts of the economic territory are included in the statistical territory, the trade data-compilation system adopted by a country (its trade system) may be referred to as general or special.

a) The general trade system is in use when the statistical territory coincides with the economic territory. Consequently, it is recommended that the statistical territory of a country applying the general trade system comprises all applicable territorial elements. In this case, imports include goods entering the free circulation area, premises for inward processing, industrial free zones, premises for customs warehousing or commercial free zones and exports include goods leaving those territorial elements;

b) The special trade system is in use when the statistical territory comprises only a particular part of the economic territory, so that certain flows of goods which are in the scope of IMTS 2010 are not included in either import or export statistics of the compiling country. The strict definition of the special trade system is in use when the statistical territory comprises only the free circulation area, that is, the part within which goods "may be

---

[1] At its forty-first session, held from 23 to 26 February 2010, the Statistical Commission adopted the revised recommendations "International merchandise trade statistics: concepts and definitions 2010" (IMTS 2010) which provide very important amendments while retaining the existing conceptual framework contained in the previous recommendations. The publication is available under Statistical Papers, Series M No. 52, Rev.3 (United Nations publication, Sales No. E.10.XVII.13) and electronically at: http://unstats.un.org/unsd/pubs/gesgrid.asp?id=449.

disposed of without customs restriction". Consequently, in such a case, imports include only goods entering the free circulation area of a compiling country and exports include only goods leaving the free circulation area of a compiling country.

c) The relaxed definition of the special trade system is in use when (a) goods that enter a country for, or leave it after, inward processing, as well as (b) goods that enter or leave an industrial free zone, are also recorded and included in international merchandise trade statistics

    v.   <u>Classification</u>: It is recommended that countries use the *Harmonized Commodity Description and Coding System* (HS) for the collection, compilation and dissemination of international merchandise trade statistics as suggested by the Statistical Commission at its twenty-seventh session (22 February to 3 March 1993).[2] The Harmonized System was adopted by the Customs Co-operation Council in June 1983, and the International Convention on the Harmonized System (HS Convention) entered into force on 1 January 1988 (HS 1988).[3] In accordance with the preamble to the HS Convention, which recognized the importance of ensuring that the HS be kept up to date in the light of changes in technology or in patterns of international trade, the HS is regularly reviewed and revised. The fifth edition, HS 2012, came into effect 1 January 2012.[4] The *Standard International Trade Classification (SITC)*[5] which was in the past used by countries in data compilation and reporting has been recognized for its continued use in analysis.[6]

    vi.   <u>Valuation:</u> At its fifteenth session, in 1953, the Economic and Social Council, taking the view that trade statistics must reflect economic realities, recommended that the Governments of Member States of the United Nations, wherever possible, use transaction values in the compilation of their national statistics of external trade or, when national practices are based on other values, endeavour to provide supplementary statistical data based on transaction values (Economic and Social Council resolution 469 B (XV)). To promote the comparability of international merchandise trade statistics and taking into account the commercial and data reporting practices of the majority of countries, it is recommended that: (a) The statistical value of imported goods be a CIF-type value; (b) The statistical value of exported goods be an FOB-type value; however, countries are encouraged to compile FOB-type value of imported goods as supplementary information. FOB-type values include the transaction value of the goods and the value of services performed to deliver goods to the border of the exporting country. CIF-type values include the transaction value of the goods, the value of services performed to deliver goods to the border of the exporting country and the value of the

---

[2] See Official Records of the Economic and Social Council, 1993, Supplement No. 6 (E/1993/26), para. 162 (d).
[3] See Customs Co-operation Council, The Harmonized Commodity Description and Coding System, Brussels, 1989.
[4] See World Customs Organization, Harmonized Commodity Description and Coding System, Fifth Edition (2012), Brussels 2010.
[5] Standard International Trade Classification, Original, Statistical Papers, Series M No.10, Second Edition, 1951 (United Nations publication, Sales No. E.51.XVII.1); subsequent editions are published as United Nations publications under Series M No.34.
[6] See Official Records of the Economic and Social Council, 1999, Supplement No. 4 (E/1993/24), para. 24 (c).

services performed to deliver the goods from the border of the exporting country to the border of the importing country.

    vii.   <u>Partner country</u>: It is recommended that in the case of imports, the country of origin be recorded; and that in the case of exports, the country of last known destination be recorded. The country of origin of a good (for imports) is determined by rules of origin established by each country. The country of last known destination is the last country - as far as it is known at the time of exportation - to which goods are to be delivered, irrespective of where they have been initially dispatched to and whether or not, on their way to that last country, they are subject to any commercial transactions or other operations which change their legal status. Further, it is recommended that country of consignment be recorded for imports as the second partner country attribution, alongside country of origin; the compilation of export statistics on the country of consignment basis is only encouraged, depending on a country's needs and circumstances.

5.   The pages containing the country profiles (Part 2 of this publication) indicate the trade system, valuation and partner attribution each country is following. For more detailed information on national practices in the compilation and dissemination of international merchandise trade data please go to http://unstats.un.org/unsd/tradereport/introduction_MM.asp.

Concepts and definitions of Statistics of International Trade in Services

6.   The trade in services data in this Yearbook have been compiled by national statistical authorities or central banks largely complying with the *Manual on Statistics of International Trade in Services 2010* (MSITS 2010).[7]

7.   The main elements of the concepts and definitions of MSITS 2010 are:

    i.   <u>Definitions</u>: In general, MSITS 2010 respects the 2008 SNA use of the term services, which is defined as follows (2008 SNA, para. 6.17):

a) Services are the result of a production activity that changes the conditions of the consuming units, or facilitates the exchange of products or financial assets. These types of service may be described as change-effecting services and margin services, respectively. Change-effecting services are outputs produced to order and typically consist of changes in the conditions of the consuming units realized by the activities of producers at the demand of the consumers. They can also be referred to as "transformation services". Change-effecting services are not separate entities over which ownership rights can be established. They cannot be traded separately from their

---

[7] At its forty-first session, held from 23 to 26 February 2010, the Statistical Commission adopted the revised "Manual on Statistics of International Trade in Services" (MSITS 2010), which sets out an internationally agreed framework for the compilation and reporting of statistics of international trade in services and align with the revisions of well-established revised international statistical standards. The publication is available under Statistical Papers, Series M No. 86, Rev.1 (United Nations publication, Sales No.E.10.XVII.14) and electronically at http://unstats.un.org/unsd/tradeserv/TFSITS/msits2010.htm.

production. By the time their production is completed, they must have been provided to the consumers.

b) MSITS 2010 defines "international trade in services" as trade in services between residents and non-residents of an economy, as well as the supply of services through foreign affiliates established abroad and the supply of services through the presence of foreign individuals, either as foreign service suppliers themselves or as employees of a foreign service supplier.

Importantly, the services data included in this Yearbook only reflect trade in services between residents and non-residents.

    ii.   <u>Concept and definition of residence</u>: The residence of an institutional unit is the economic territory with which it has the strongest connection, constituting its centre of predominant economic interest. Each institutional unit is a resident of one and only one economic territory, as determined by its centre of predominant economic interest. An institutional unit is resident in an economic territory when there exists, within the economic territory, some location, dwelling, place of production, or other premises on which or from which the unit engages and intends to continue engaging, either indefinitely or over a finite but long period of time, in economic activities and transactions on a significant scale. The location need not be fixed as long as it remains within the economic territory. Actual or intended location for one year or more is used as an operational criterion. While the choice of one year as a specific period is somewhat arbitrary, it is adopted to eliminate uncertainty and facilitate international consistency. More specific criteria for determining residence are given in the MSITS 2010.

    iii.   <u>Valuation</u>: The market price is used as the basis for valuation of transactions in international trade in services. Market prices for transactions are defined as amounts of money that willing buyers pay to acquire something from willing sellers. The exchanges are made between independent parties and based on commercial considerations only and are sometimes called "at arm's length" transactions. These transactions will generally be valued at the actual price agreed between the supplier and the consumer.

    iv.   <u>Time of recording of transactions</u>: The appropriate time for recording transactions in services is when they are delivered or received (the "accruals basis"). Some services, such as certain transport or hotel services are provided within a discrete period, in which case there is no problem in determining the time of recording. Other services are supplied or take place on a continuous basis, for example, construction, operating leasing and insurance services. When construction takes place with a prior contract of sale, the ownership of the structure is effectively transferred progressively as the work proceeds. When services are provided over a period of time (such as freight, insurance and construction), there may be advance payments or settlements at later dates for such services. The provision of services should be recorded on an accrual basis in each accounting period, that is to say it should be recorded when the service is rendered and not when the payment occurs.

v. <u>Framework and scope</u>: MSITS 2010 recommends that the Sixth Edition of the Balance of Payments and International Investment Position Manual (BPM6)[8] recommendations on the principles of recording (regarding residence, valuation, time of recording, currency of recording and conversion) should be followed. The Extended Balance of Payments Services Classification (EBOPS) is a more detailed classification than that of BPM5 for international trade in services between residents and non-residents, by breaking down a number of the BPM5 service items. The main components of the EBOPS classification are presented in paragraph 7.vii below.

vi. <u>Partner country</u>: It is recommended that the breakdown by partner economy for services transactions between residents and non-residents be recorded, the aim being to report partner detail, first, at the level of services trade as a whole and, second, for each of the main types of services in EBOPS and (as a longer-term goal) for the more detailed EBOPS items. Partner country data for trade in services are not included in this publication, as most countries do not currently compile these data by partner country.

vii. <u>Classification</u>: In 1996, OECD and Eurostat, in consultation with IMF, developed for use by their members a more detailed classification than that presented in the IMF's Balance of Payments Manual (BPM5) for international trade in services between residents and non-residents, by breaking down a number of the BPM5 service items. This more detailed classification is termed the Extended Balance of Payments Services Classification (EBOPS). The EBOPS classification was published in 2002 in the MSITS 2002 and was subsequently revised to the EBOPS 2010 classification, as published in the MSITS 2010. The services data in this Yearbook follow the EBOPS 2002 classification (which corresponds to the BPM5 recommendations) due to the fact that most countries have not yet transitioned to the EBOPS 2010 classification (which corresponds to the BPM6 recommendations).

The 11 main EBOPS 2002 standard services components (as presented in the MSITS 2002) are:[9]

a) Transportation: covers all transportation services that are performed by residents of one economy for those of another and that involve the carriage of passengers, the movement of goods (freight), rentals (charters) of carriers with crew, and related supporting and auxiliary services. Some related items that are excluded from transportation services are freight insurance (included in insurance services); goods procured in ports by non-resident carriers and repairs of transportation equipment (both are treated as goods, not services); repairs of railway facilities, harbours and airfield facilities (included in

---

[8] International Monetary Fund. *Sixth Edition of the Balance of Payments Manual (BPM6)*. 2009. http://www.imf.org/external/pubs/ft/bop/2007/pdf/bpm6.pdf. The previous edition of this manual was the *Fifth Edition of the Balance of Payments Manual (BPM5)*, which was published in 1992. https://www.imf.org/external/pubs/ft/bopman/bopman.pdf.

[9] The full detailed EBOPS 2002 classification is available as an on-line annex to the MSITS 2002. http://unstats.un.org/unsd/tradekb/Attachment358.aspx.

construction services); and rentals or charters of carriers without crew (included in operational leasing services).

b) Travel: covers primarily the goods and services acquired from an economy by travelers during visits of less than one year to that economy. Includes business and personal travel, which includes health-related expenditure (total expenditure by those travelling for medical reasons), education-related expenditure (i.e., total expenditure by students), and all other personal travel expenditure.

c) Communications services: covers postal and courier services (which cover the pick-up, transport and delivery of letters, newspapers, periodicals, brochures, other printed matter, parcels and packages, including post office counter and mailbox rental services) and telecommunications services (which cover the transmission of sound, images or other information by telephone, telex, telegram, radio and television cable and broadcasting, satellite, electronic mail, facsimile services etc., including business network services, teleconferencing and support services). It does not include the value of the information transported. Also included are cellular telephone services, Internet backbone services and on-line access services, including provision of access to the Internet.

d) Construction services: covers work performed on construction projects and installation by employees of an enterprise in locations outside the territory of an enterprise.

e) Insurance services: covers the provision of various types of insurance to non-residents by resident insurance enterprises, and vice versa. These services are estimated or valued by the service charges included in total premiums rather than by the total value of the premiums.

f) Financial services: covers financial intermediation and auxiliary services, except those of life insurance enterprises and pension funds (which are included in life insurance and pension funding) and other insurance services that are conducted between residents and non-residents. Such services may be provided by banks, stock exchanges, factoring enterprises, credit card enterprises and other enterprises.

g) Computer and information services: covers hardware and software-related services and data-processing services; news agency services include the provision of news, photographs, and feature articles to the media; and database services and web search portals (search engine services that find internet addresses for clients who input keyword queries).

h) Royalties and license fees: covers international payments and receipts of franchising fees and the royalties paid for the use of registered trademarks and international payments and receipts for the authorised use of intangible, non-produced, non-financial assets and proprietary rights (such as patents, copyrights and industrial processes and designs) and with the use, through licensing agreements, of produced originals or prototypes (such as manuscripts, computer programs, and cinematographic works and sound recordings).

i) Other business services: covers merchanting, other trade-related services, operational leasing services, legal services, accounting, auditing, bookkeeping and tax consulting services, business and management consulting and public relations services, advertising, market research and public opinion polling, research and development, architectural, engineering and other technical services, waste treatment and de-pollution, agricultural, mining, and other on-site processing services, other business services, and services between related enterprises, not included elsewhere (n.i.e.).

j) Personal, cultural, and recreational services: covers services and associated fees related to the production of motion pictures (on film or videotape), radio and television programmes (live or on tape) and musical recordings services, as well as those services associated with museums, libraries, archives and other cultural, sporting and recreational activities.

k) Government services, not included elsewhere (n.i.e.): covers government transactions (including those of international organizations) not contained in the other components of EBOPS as defined above. Included are all transactions (in both goods and services) by embassies, consulates, military units and defence agencies with residents of economies in which the embassies, consulates, military units and defence agencies are located and all transactions with other economies. Excluded are transactions with residents of the home economies represented by the embassies, consulates, military units and defence agencies, and transactions in the commissaries, post exchanges and these embassies and consulates.

Description of world trade tables of part 1 (Tables A and D)

8.   Table A: Total merchandise trade by regions and countries or areas in U.S. dollars: It provides a breakdown of merchandise imports, exports and trade balance for world, regional groupings, selected economic and/or trade groupings and individual countries or areas.

9.   Table D: World merchandise exports by provenance and destination in U.S. dollars: In addition to total, table D also provides details by SITC sections or groupings of sections by regions and countries or areas (brief description of SITC sections can be found in the country profiles in Part 2).

10.   The totals of imports and exports presented in table A on the one hand and table D and the country profiles on the other hand are not necessarily identical as IFS and UN Comtrade are based on different data collection systems with different aims, procedures, timetable and sources for update and maintenance. Nevertheless, discrepancies are in general minor and usually do not affect the overall comparability of information provided in these tables. A systematic comparison of the figures from both sources (which includes the description of known and relevant conceptual differences) is available at http://unstats.un.org/unsd/trade/imts/annual%20totals.htm. Overall, the discrepancy in the world total or world aggregate of exports in table A and table D is around 1.0 percent or less in average, which is minor, given the differences between the two sources.

11.   A slightly different version of Table A containing quarterly and monthly data is published on a monthly basis as table 34 in the *United Nations Monthly Bulletin of Statistics*

(MBS). Updated, although different versions of Table D, are published as table 40, 41 and 42 in the July, September and November editions of the MBS. An updated version of these tables will be published in Volume 2 of the 2014 ITSY which will be produced later this year.

Description of tables and graphs of Country profiles in part 2

12. Part 2 contains detailed data for individual countries or areas. In addition, given the economic importance of the European Union (EU), separate pages have been included for the external trade of the EU (with its 28 members) as a whole.

13. Not all countries have data up to 2014 and not all countries have data for imports and exports for all years. The inclusion of a country (or area) in part 2 requires that at least some data are available for any year from 2010 onwards. Depending on the availability of data the following tables and graphs usually appear for each country or area:

14. Graph 1: Total merchandise trade, by value: This graph presents the trend of merchandise imports, exports and trade balance over the last 14 years.

15. Graph 2: Total services trade, by value: This graph presents the trend of services imports, exports and trade balance over the last 14 years.

16. Graph 3: Exports of services by EBOPS category: This graph presents the shares of total exports of services accounted for by each service category for the latest year such data are available.

17. Graph 4: Merchandise trade balance by MDG Regions: This graph presents, in the most recent year for which information on exports and imports are available, the trade balance by regions. The regional groupings were created for the purpose of this publication and are presented in paragraph 38.

18. Graph 5: Partner concentration of merchandise trade: This graph shows the partner concentration of imports and exports for the latest available year. Graph presents the top 25 partners which usually account for a very large share of exports or imports for most countries. On the horizontal axis from the center to the right are the cumulative percent of exports and from the center to the left the cumulative percent of imports. On the vertical axis is the cumulative number of partners ranked by total value of exports and imports in a decreasing order. So, on each side, the first bar represents share accounted for by the largest partner; second bar represents share accounted for by the largest two partners and so on.

19. Graph 5 also presents the Herfindahl-Hirschman (HH) Index for imports and exports which is a measure of concentration. In the case of exports (imports), the HH index is the sum of squares of the partner's share of total exports (imports):

$$HH\ Index = \sum_{i=1}^{n}\left(\frac{X_i}{X}\right)^2$$

20. n is the number of trading partners for exports (imports) and X_i is the value of exports (imports) to partner country i and X is the total value of exports (imports). The lower the HH index, the lower the partner concentration, and vice versa. If there is only one trading partner the HH index would equal 1.[10]

21. It should be noted that the HH index for a given country's exports (imports) depends on the distribution of share of exports (imports) among its partners. Hence a country with few major partners might have a lower HH index value, indicating low concentration, than a country with more partners if the former has its trade more evenly distributed among its partners than the latter.

22. <u>Graph 6: Imports of services by EBOPS category:</u> This graph presents the shares of total imports of services accounted for by each service category for the latest year such data are available.

23. <u>Table 1 and table 4: Top 10 export and import commodities:</u> These tables present the top 10 commodities in terms of 4-digit HS headings for exports and imports, respectively, using the aggregate of trade values for the last three reporting years as available. For countries which reported the last three years of data in HS 2012, the data in these tables follow HS 2012. For most other countries, the data in these tables are presented in HS 2007, with data for some years converted from HS 2012 into HS 2007 as required (see paragraph 33). For a few countries, the table contains data according to the HS 2002, HS 1996 or even HS 1992. For the convenience of users, the last column shows the SITC group (3 digits) that corresponds to the HS heading. The SITC group is identified based on the correlation and conversion tables between HS and SITC, Rev 3.[11]

24. In addition to trade values, the table 1 and table 4 also present unit values. Unit values are expressed in U.S. dollars (US$) per unit (kg, unit, Megawatt-hours (Mwh), pair, litre, carat etc.). The calculation of unit values on the heading level requires the availability of value and quantity information for all of the underlying detailed data (6-digit subheadings). In some cases, the quantity information for some sub-headings was estimated, to the extent possible (see paragraph 32) and thus the unit value for the heading appears in italics. If quantity information appears incorrect it is not shown.

25. <u>Table 2 and table 3: Merchandise Exports and Imports by SITC sections:</u> These tables show the structure of exports and imports in 2014 (or the latest available year) by SITC sections in terms of value, share of the total, growth in respect to the previous year and annual average growth for the last four years which is calculated as the geometric mean.

---

[10] For the application of HH index to measure partner concentration in merchandise trade, no thresholds are known to be established. Users might wish to define a specific limit of the HH index to indicate low concentration and a limit to indicate high concentration. However, based on the analyses of the data presented in the yearbook, following thresholds were applied to determine level of concentration of merchandise trade, both exports and imports: HH < 0.15 → Diversified; 0.15 < HH < 0.25 → Moderately concentrated; HH > 0.25 → Highly concentrated.

[11] The conversion tables are available on the website of UNSD at http://unstats.un.org/unsd/trade/methodology%20imts.htm.

Sources

26. Data on the total merchandise imports and exports of countries (or areas) presented in world table A are mainly taken from *International Financial Statistics* (IFS) published monthly by the International Monetary Fund (IMF). They are supplemented with data from other sources such as national publications and websites and the *United Nations Monthly Bulletin of Statistics Questionnaire* for the following countries: Andorra, Bermuda, Cayman Islands, Cuba, Gibraltar, Montenegro (beginning 2006), Niue, Russian Federation (beginning 1994), Serbia and Montenegro (before 2006), State of Palestine, Turkmenistan, Turks and Caicos, Tuvalu and Uzbekistan. Data on world merchandise exports by provenance and destination presented in world table D are derived from UN Comtrade data supplemented by estimated data for non-available countries and areas.

27. The data in the country profiles in part 2 of the publication (country trade profiles) are obtained from data directly submitted by countries to the United Nations Statistics Division (UNSD). All data published in the country profiles is available in UN Comtrade (http://comtrade.un.org) and UN ServiceTrade (http://unstats.un.org/unsd/servicetrade).

28. In some cases, original countries data are received via international and regional partner organizations, such as the Organization for Economic Co-operation and Development (OECD), the Food and Agriculture Organization of the United Nations (FAO), the International Monetary Fund (IMF), the International Trade Centre (ITC), the Caribbean Community (CARICOM) Secretariat, the Common Market of Eastern and Southern Africa (COMESA), the Economic Community of West African States (ECOWAS) and the UN regional commissions such as the Economic Commission for Latin America and the Caribbean (ECLAC) and the Economic and Social Commission for Western Asia (ESCWA). Data for the European Union (EU-28) is received from the Statistical Office of the European Union (Eurostat).

29. Table A shows data as available by end of May 2015 and table D uses data as available on UN Comtrade by end of May 2015. The country tables and graphs contain data available in UN Comtrade and UN ServiceTrade by end of May 2015.

Method of Estimation

30. Estimates for missing data in Table A are made in order to arrive at regional totals, but estimated data are not shown. The estimation process is automated using quarterly year-on-year growth rates for the extrapolation of missing quarterly data, unless quarterly data can be estimated using available monthly data within the quarter. Regional totals containing estimated data are printed in bold. Estimates are reviewed and adjusted where necessary.

31. Data for missing reporters in Table D are estimated either through the extrapolation of the data of the two adjacent years, or, if this is not possible, through the use of the data reported by the trading partners, that is, through mirror data. Mirror statistics are also used in case the partner distribution or confidential data make it necessary to adjust the reported data. All estimates are reviewed and adjusted where necessary.

32.   For part 2, the country trade profiles, modifications to the received data are only made in cases where the provided data are obviously incomplete, in particular in the case of unreported petroleum oils exports in merchandise data. Quantity information that is missing or does not comply with the World Customs Organization's recommendations are estimated and flagged in UN Comtrade accordingly. For data processed before June 2009 some quantity information that were identified as 'extreme' – meaning far outside a pre-defined 'normal' range – were replaced in UN Comtrade with estimates. The estimation of quantities is either based on the country's own data or uses standard unit values (SUVs) which are derived from the available information for all countries in the previous year.

Conversion of classification

33.   Conversion of classification for merchandise data: All countries follow recommendation to report their detailed merchandise trade data according to the Harmonized Commodity Description and Coding System (HS) (see paragraph 4.C.v). In order to provide comparable time series data in UN Comtrade for all countries, the data reported in the latest HS classification is converted into earlier versions of the HS, and to corresponding or earlier versions of the Standard International Trade Classification (SITC).[12] The latest edition of the HS classification was its fifth and was released in 2012. The commodities in this publication are mostly presented according to the one-digit sections of SITC, Rev.3 as the SITC sections provide a limited set of economically meaningful main categories.[13] In addition, data according to SITC, Rev.3 is available for long time series. In two tables, commodities are presented in terms of four-digit headings of the HS, often according to the 2012 version of HS but in many cases also in earlier HS versions.[14] The HS headings provide a meaningful description of traded commodities at a relatively detailed level and also allow the presentation of quantity information.

34.   Conversion of classification for trade in services data: For services data, most countries are still compiling data according to the EBOPS 2002 classification and, therefore, all services data presented in this Yearbook are presented according to this classification. For the cases in which a country has transitioned to the EBOPS 2010 classification (as presented in MSTIS 2010) and did not provide UNSD with data based on EBOPS 2002, and for those countries for which the IMF is the only data source,[15] the data were converted to the EBOPS 2002 classification in order to maintain consistency across countries. The conversion was based on the IMF's BPM5-

---

[12] Detailed information on the data conversions used for UN Comtrade can be found on the website of the United Nations Statistics Division at:
http://unstats.un.org/unsd/trade/conversions/HS%20Correlation%20and%20Conversion%20tables.htm.
[13] Standard International Trade Classification, Revision 3, Statistical Papers, Series M No.34/Rev.3, (United Nations publication, Sales No. E.86.XVII.12). SITC, Revision 4 was accepted by the United Nations Statistical Commission at its thirty-seventh session in March 2006 (see Official Records of the Economic and Social Council, 2006, Supplement No. 4, (E/CN.3/2006/32), chapter III, para. 26 (b)). Yet, it will require several years until a time series of data according to SITC, Revision 4 will be sufficiently long for publication.
[14] World Customs Organization, Harmonized Commodity Description and Coding System, Fourth Edition (2007) (HS 2007); World Customs Organization, Harmonized Commodity Description and Coding System, Third Edition (2002) (HS 2002); World Customs Organization, Harmonized Commodity Description and Coding System, Second Edition (1996) (HS 1996); World Customs Organization, Harmonized Commodity Description and Coding System (1992) (HS 1992).
[15] The IMF is only presenting data on a BPM6 basis (which corresponds to the EBOPS 2010 classification) for data from 2009 onwards.

to-BPM6 Conversion Matrix (available at http://www.imf.org/external/pubs/ft/bop/2008/08-10b.pdf).

Currency conversion and Period

35. Currency conversion: For both merchandise and trade in services data in this publication, conversion of values from national currencies into United States dollars is done by means of currency conversion factors based on official exchange rates. Values in currencies subject to fluctuation are converted into United States dollars using weighted average exchange rates specially calculated for this purpose. The weighted average exchange rate for a given currency for a given year is the component monthly factors, furnished by the International Monetary Fund in its IFS publication, weighted by the value of the relevant trade in each month; a monthly factor is the exchange rate (or the simple average rate) in effect during that month. These factors are applied to total imports and exports and to the trade in individual commodities with individual countries. The conversion factors applied to the data presented in table A are published quarterly in the *UN Monthly Bulletin of Statistics* (http://unstats.un.org/unsd/mbs/default.aspx) and are also available at: http://unstats.un.org/unsd/trade/data/tables.asp. For data published on UN Comtrade the applied conversion factors are available in a country's metadata on UN Comtrade.

36. Period: Generally, data refer to calendar years; however, for those countries which report according to some other reference year, the data are presented in the calendar year which covers the majority of the reference year used by the country.

Country Nomenclature and Country Grouping

37. Country nomenclature: The naming of countries (or areas) in this publication follows in general the *United Nations Standard Country or Area Codes for Statistical Use*.[16] The names and composition of countries as reporter are changing over time. Also, countries rarely follow the identical nomenclature in the recording of partner information. For example when former geographical entities commonly referred to in national statistics have changed, countries may introduce the corresponding changes in their statistics at different times. In this publication, wherever possible, areas of the world have been designated the names they currently bear.

It should be noted that, in this publication:

    i. Data published for China exclude those for Taiwan Province of China. Data representing the trade with Taiwan Province, which may have been reported by any reporting country or area, are included in the grouping Asia, nes. For statistical purposes, data for China also do not include those for Hong Kong Special Administrative Region and Macao Special Administrative Region.

    ii. Beginning 1 January 2000, Botswana, Lesotho, Namibia, South Africa and Swaziland provide their international trade statistics separately.

---

[16] Standard Country or Area Codes for Statistical Use, Series M No. 49, Rev.4, (United Nations publication, Sales No. M.98.XVII.9). The latest information is available online at: http://unstats.un.org/unsd/methods/m49/m49.htm.

iii. On 4 February 2003, the official name of the Federal Republic of Yugoslavia has been changed to Serbia and Montenegro.

iv. On 3 June 2006, Serbia and Montenegro formally dissolved into two independent countries: Montenegro and Serbia.

v. On 10 October 2010 the federation of the Netherlands Antilles was formally dissolved. The former Dutch Caribbean dependency ceased to exist with a change of the five islands' constitutional status. Under the new political structure, Curaçao and Sint Maarten (Dutch part) have become autonomous countries within the Kingdom of the Netherlands, joining Aruba, which gained the status in 1986. The islands of the remaining territorial grouping, alternately known as Bonaire, Sint Eustatius and Saba or the BES islands, are special municipalities and part of the country of the Netherlands and overseas territories of the European Union. For statistical purposes, the data for the Netherlands do not include the BES islands. Data referring to Netherlands Antilles (as a partner) prior to 2011 refer to the former territory which included Curaçao, Sint Maarten (Dutch part), Bonaire, Sint Eustatius and Saba.

vi. On 9 July 2011, Sudan formally dissolved into two independent countries: Sudan and South Sudan. Data provided for Sudan prior to 1 January 2012 refer to the former Sudan (including South Sudan). Data referring to Sudan (as a partner) for 2012 are attributed to Sudan excluding South Sudan.

vii. From January 2013 onwards, Saint Berthélemy is no longer part of customs territory of France, therefore it is recognised as a separate statistical area both as reporter and partner. Whereas from January 2014 onwards, Mayotte became part of statistical area of France and it is no longer shown either as a reporter or a partner.

38. <u>Regional groupings</u>: This publication uses the earlier version of regional groupings of the Millennium Development Goal (MDG) Indicator Database which are shown below (for their composition, see table A and http://comtrade.un.org/pb/groupings.aspx). The category 'Other' applies only to the presentation of data by trading partner and consists of Antarctica, Bunkers, Free Zones, 'Special Categories' (confidential partner) and Areas nes.:

    World
    Developed Countries
      - Asia-Pacific
      - Europe
      - North America
    South-eastern Europe
    Commonwealth of Independent States
      - CIS Europe
      - CIS Asia
    Northern Africa
    Sub-Saharan Africa
    Latin America & the Caribbean
      - Caribbean
      - Latin America
    Eastern Asia
    Southern Asia
    South-eastern Asia
    Western Asia
    Oceania
    Other

39. <u>Aggregations</u>: All regional aggregations are calculated as the sum of their components. This also includes the regional and world totals presented in table A (in bold) and table D. The figures for the country groupings aim to always reflect the composition of the grouping of the latest year published.

40. <u>Additional country groupings</u>: The composition of the additional country groupings which are used in world table A is as follows:

ANCOM-Andean Common Market
Bolivia (Plurinational State of), Colombia, Ecuador and Peru

APEC-Asian-Pacific Economic Co-operation
Australia, Brunei Darussalam, Canada, Chile, China, Hong Kong Special Administrative Region of China, Indonesia, Japan, Malaysia, Mexico, New Zealand, Papua New Guinea, Peru, Philippines, Republic of Korea, Russian Federation, Singapore, Taiwan Province of China, Thailand, United States of America and Viet Nam

ASEAN-Association of South-East Asian Nations
Brunei Darussalam, Cambodia, Indonesia, Lao People's Democratic Republic, Malaysia, Myanmar, Philippines, Singapore, Thailand and Viet Nam

CACM-Central American Common Market
Costa Rica, El Salvador, Guatemala, Honduras and Nicaragua

CARICOM-Caribbean Community and Common Market
Antigua and Barbuda, Bahamas (member of the Community only), Barbados, Belize, Dominica, Grenada, Guyana, Haiti, Jamaica, Montserrat, Saint Kitts and Nevis, Saint Lucia, Saint Vincent and the Grenadines, Suriname, Trinidad and Tobago

COMESA-Common Market for Eastern and Southern Africa
Burundi, Comoros, Democratic Republic of the Congo, Djibouti, Egypt, Eritrea, Ethiopia, Kenya, Libya, Madagascar, Malawi, Mauritius, Rwanda, Seychelles, Sudan, Swaziland, Uganda, Zambia and Zimbabwe

ECOWAS - Economic Community of West African States
Benin, Burkina Faso, Cape Verde, Cote d'Ivoire, Gambia, Ghana, Guinea, Guinea-Bissau, Liberia, Mali, Niger, Nigeria, Senegal, Sierra Leone and Togo

EFTA - European Free Trade Association
Iceland, Liechtenstein, Norway and Switzerland

EMCCA – Economic and Monetary Community of Central Africa
Cameroon, Central African Republic, Chad, Congo, Equatorial Guinea and Gabon

EU-28 - European Union 28
Austria, Belgium, Bulgaria, Croatia, Cyprus, Czech Republic, Denmark, Estonia, Finland, France, Germany, Greece, Hungary, Ireland, Italy, Latvia, Lithuania, Luxembourg, Malta, Netherlands, Poland, Portugal, Romania, Spain, Slovakia, Slovenia, Sweden and United Kingdom.

EU-27 - European Union 27
Austria, Belgium, Bulgaria, Cyprus, Czech Republic, Denmark, Estonia, Finland, France, Germany, Greece, Hungary, Ireland, Italy, Latvia, Lithuania, Luxembourg, Malta, Netherlands, Poland, Portugal, Romania, Spain, Slovakia, Slovenia, Sweden and United Kingdom.

EU-25 - European Union 25
Austria, Belgium, Denmark, Finland, France, Germany, Greece, Ireland, Italy, Luxembourg, Netherlands, Portugal, Spain, Sweden and United Kingdom (EU15) plus Czech Republic, Estonia, Hungary, Latvia, Lithuania, Malta, Poland, Slovakia, Slovenia, and Cyprus

EU-15 – European Union 15
Austria, Belgium, Denmark, Finland, France, Germany, Greece, Ireland, Italy, Luxembourg, Netherlands, Portugal, Spain, Sweden, United Kingdom.

LAIA - Latin American Integration Association (formerly Latin American Free Trade Association)
Argentina, Bolivia (Plurinational State of), Brazil, Chile, Colombia, Cuba, Ecuador, Mexico, Paraguay, Peru, Uruguay and Venezuela (Bolivarian Republic of)

LDC - Least developed countries
Afghanistan, Angola, Bangladesh, Benin, Bhutan, Burkina Faso, Burundi, Cambodia, Central African Republic, Chad, Comoros, Democratic Republic of the Congo, Djibouti, Equatorial Guinea, Eritrea, Ethiopia, Gambia, Guinea, Guinea-Bissau, Haiti, Kiribati, Lao People's Democratic Republic, Lesotho, Liberia, Madagascar, Malawi, Mali, Mauritania, Mozambique, Myanmar, Nepal, Niger, Rwanda, Samoa, Sao Tome and Principe, Senegal, Sierra Leone, Solomon Islands, Somalia, Sudan, Timor-Leste, Togo, Tuvalu, Uganda, United Republic of Tanzania, Vanuatu, Yemen and Zambia

MERCOSUR-Mercado Comun Sud-Americano
Argentina, Brazil, Paraguay, Uruguay and Venezuela

NAFTA-Northern American Free Trade Area
Canada, Mexico and United States of America

OECD-Organization for Economic Cooperation and Development
Australia, Austria, Belgium, Canada, Chile, Czech Republic, Denmark, Estonia, Finland, France, Germany, Greece, Hungary, Iceland, Ireland, Israel, Italy, Japan, Luxembourg, Mexico, Netherlands, New Zealand, Norway, Poland, Portugal, Republic of Korea, Slovakia, Slovenia, Spain, Sweden, Switzerland, Turkey, United Kingdom and United States of America

OPEC-Organization of Petroleum Exporting Countries
Algeria, Angola, Ecuador, Iran (Islamic Republic of), Iraq, Kuwait, Libya, Nigeria, Qatar, Saudi Arabia, United Arab Emirates and Venezuela (Bolivarian Republic of).

Abbreviations and Explanation of symbols

Names of some countries (or areas) or groups of countries (or areas) and of some commodities or groups of commodities have been abbreviated. Exact titles of countries or commodities can be found in various editions of the following publications:

- (i) Standard Country or Area Codes for Statistical Use
- (ii) Standard International Trade Classification (SITC)
- (iii) Harmonized Commodity Description and Coding System (HS)

In addition, the following abbreviations and symbols are used in this publication:

Not available	(na)
Not available	blank
Not available	...
Not applicable	–
Not applicable	.
Magnitude of less than half the unit used	0 or 0.0
More than 100,000 percent	>
Thousand	thsd
Million	mln
Billion	bln
Weight (kilograms)	kg
Megawatt-hours	Mwh
Average	Avg.
Not elsewhere specified	nes
U.S. dollar	US$
Imports	Imp
Exports	Exp
Balance	Bal
General trade system	G
Special trade system	S
Cost, insurance and freight	CIF
Free on board	FOB
Not included elsewhere	n.i.e.
(Royalties and) license (fees)	lic.

Disclaimer

The tables, graphs and text contained in this publication are provided only for illustration and despite all efforts might contain errors. When using this data users are advised to verify the latest information on UN Comtrade and UN ServiceTrade which is the source of this data.

Contact

This yearbook has been produced by the Trade Statistics Branch of the United Nations Statistics Division/ Department of Economic and Social Affairs. For questions or comments please contact us at:

Trade Statistics Branch
United Nations Statistics Division
2 United Nations Plaza, DC2-1540
New York, New York 10017
e-mail (merchandise): comtrade@un.org
e-mail (services): tradeserv@un.org

http://unstats.un.org/unsd/trade

2014
INTERNATIONAL TRADE
STATISTICS YEARBOOK

VOLUME I
TRADE BY COUNTRY

PART 1 – WORLD TRADE TABLES

Total merchandise trade by regions and countries or areas in U.S. dollars (Table A)

World merchandise exports by provenance and destination in U.S. dollars (Table D)

Total merchandise trade by regions and countries or areas (Table A)
Imports CIF, exports FOB and balance: million U.S. dollars
Commerce total de marchandises par régions et pays ou zones (Tableau A)
Importations CIF, exportations FOB, et balance : en millions de dollars E.-U.

Country or Area - Pays ou Zone	IMP EXP BAL	G/S	2000	2006	2007	2008	2009	2010	2011	2012	2013	2014
World	IMP		**6517703**	**12195963**	**14032553**	**16221474**	**12488612**	**15152112**	**18074317**	**18121894**	**18405296**	**18609905**
Monde	EXP		**6356560**	**11973699**	**13793581**	**16013161**	**12407649**	**15099379**	**18025336**	**18076241**	**18460736**	**18809670**
	BAL		**-161144**	**-222263**	**-238972**	**-208313**	**-80964**	**-52734**	**-48981**	**-45654**	**55440**	**199765**
Developed Countries[1,2]	IMP		**4494093**	**7827827**	**8805633**	**9837858**	**7404215**	**8627296**	**10094814**	**9855081**	**9864713**	**10008200**
Pays Developpés[1,2]	EXP		**4131930**	**6951124**	**7952604**	**8872791**	**6879564**	**7995822**	**9292737**	**9070940**	**9198936**	**9334619**
	BAL		**-362163**	**-876703**	**-853029**	**-965066**	**-524651**	**-631474**	**-802077**	**-784142**	**-665777**	**-673581**
Asia-Pacific	IMP		461429	738776	808813	987974	734728	917455	1125802	1173988	1105373	1082019
Asie-Pacifique	EXP		557030	792911	883403	1000104	759544	1014394	1131781	1092678	1008667	973091
	BAL		95601	54134	74590	12129	24816	96939	5980	-81309	-96705	-108928
Australia[3]	IMP	G	67704	132504	157687	191312	158919	193201	234357	250560	232595	227629
Australie[3]	EXP	G	63878	123285	141091	187150	153966	212337	271733	256675	252981	241181
	BAL		-3827	-9219	-16596	-4162	-4953	19136	37376	6115	20385	13552
Japan	IMP	G	379490	579603	619662	762626	550550	692435	854098	885610	832424	811882
Japon	EXP	G	479274	646755	714211	782049	580719	769772	822564	798621	714613	690273
	BAL		99783	67151	94549	19422	30169	77337	-31534	-86989	-117811	-121609
New Zealand	IMP	G	14235	26669	31463	34036	25259	31819	37346	37818	40354	42507
Nouvelle-Zélande	EXP	G	13879	22871	28102	30905	24859	32285	37484	37383	41074	41637
	BAL		-356	-3798	-3362	-3131	-401	466	138	-435	720	-870
Europe	IMP		2533386	4818709	5593484	6269011	4740532	5345998	6249100	5879215	5965085	**6046165**
Europe	EXP		2515996	4743462	5500188	6128233	4749484	5314924	6227864	5976989	6152001	**6267113**
	BAL		-17390	-75247	-93296	-140778	8951	-31074	-21236	97774	186916	**220948**
Andorra	IMP	S	1021	1780	1917	1931	1589	1518	1596	1396	1455	1556
Andorre	EXP	S	45	150	127	96	63	54	77	68	99	98
	BAL		-975	-1630	-1790	-1835	-1526	-1464	-1519	-1327	-1356	-1458
Austria	IMP	S	68986	130945	156760	176172	136081	150601	182340	169657	172596	171389
Autriche	EXP	S	64167	130376	157317	173397	130791	144889	169519	158821	166546	169188
	BAL		-4819	-570	557	-2775	-5290	-5712	-12821	-10836	-6050	-2201
Belgium	IMP	S	176992	352968	413074	466437	354666	391333	466833	439492	451921	451373
Belgique	EXP	S	187876	366758	431850	471932	371397	407055	475981	446637	467831	469036
	BAL		10884	13790	18776	5494	16731	15721	9148	7145	15910	17663
Croatia	IMP	G	7887	21488	25830	30728	21203	20051	22708	20762	20961	22523
Croatie	EXP	G	4432	10376	12364	14112	10474	11806	13375	12347	11928	13686
	BAL		-3455	-11112	-13465	-16617	-10729	-8244	-9333	-8415	-9033	-8837
Czech Republic	IMP	S	33934	93453	118467	142172	105256	126600	152122	141515	144320	152171
République tchèque	EXP	S	29057	95165	122760	146406	113175	133020	162897	157167	162302	173853
	BAL		-4877	1712	4293	4234	7920	6420	10775	15652	17983	21682
Denmark	IMP	S	44364	84220	97366	109158	80372	83170	96431	92295	98374	99126
Danemark	EXP	S	50390	90660	101599	115929	91817	95758	111900	106125	111351	110490
	BAL		6025	6440	4233	6772	11445	12589	15469	13830	12977	11364
Estonia	IMP	S	4236	11882	15064	16058	10151	12282	17757	17797	18142	17992
Estonie	EXP	S	3166	8759	10960	12468	9058	11607	16724	16083	16291	15931
	BAL		-1070	-3123	-4105	-3590	-1094	-675	-1033	-1714	-1851	-2061
Faeroe Islands	IMP	G	532	790	1016	988	783	780	986	1144	1110	...
Iles Féroé	EXP	G	472	651	746	852	762	839	1007	945	1080	...
	BAL		-60	-139	-270	-136	-22	59	20	-199	-29	...
Finland	IMP	G	33900	69448	81756	92160	60866	68773	84235	76558	77579	76464
Finlande	EXP	G	45482	77287	90092	96890	62872	69492	79126	73114	74433	74112
	BAL		11582	7839	8336	4730	2005	719	-5108	-3444	-3146	-2351

Total merchandise trade by regions and countries or areas (Table A)
Imports CIF, exports FOB and balance: million U.S. dollars
Commerce total de marchandises par régions et pays ou zones (Tableau A)
Importations CIF, exportations FOB, et balance : en millions de dollars E.-U.

Country or Area - Pays ou Zone	IMP EXP BAL	G/S	2000	2006	2007	2008	2009	2010	2011	2012	2013	2014
France	IMP	S	310831	546505	631447	715783	560484	608652	712895	666751	671355	660871
France	EXP	S	298765	490702	550458	608942	476098	516955	585313	558490	568023	567015
	BAL		-12066	-55803	-80989	-106840	-84386	-91697	-127582	-108260	-103332	-93856
Germany	IMP	S	495450	922381	1055997	1186681	926154	1056170	1256168	1164626	1192751	1217949
Allemagne	EXP	S	550223	1122112	1323818	1451390	1120666	1261577	1476955	1408370	1451631	1505467
	BAL		54773	199731	267822	264709	194512	205408	220787	243744	258880	287518
Gibraltar	IMP		480	639	796	769	679	627	703	605	748	...
Gibraltar	EXP		126	242	304	281	266	259	246	253	279	...
	BAL		-354	-397	-492	-488	-413	-368	-457	-353	-469	...
Greece	IMP	S	28323	66376	82521	95740	72636	67328	67468	63380	62084	63279
Grèce	EXP	S	10965	21733	26660	31431	24657	27991	33836	35485	36269	35810
	BAL		-17359	-44643	-55861	-64309	-47979	-39337	-33633	-27895	-25815	-27469
Hungary	IMP	S	31955	77206	94397	106380	78034	87612	100989	94282	99091	103942
Hongrie	EXP	S	28016	74217	93985	107465	84586	94759	110897	103047	108426	110905
	BAL		-3939	-2989	-412	1085	6552	7147	9908	8765	9335	6963
Iceland	IMP	G	2591	5078	6097	5614	3604	3920	4833	4772	4787	5240
Islande	EXP	G	1891	3242	4342	5191	4057	4604	5344	5064	4990	4980
	BAL		-700	-1836	-1755	-423	453	685	510	292	204	-261
Ireland	IMP	G	51444	76432	87049	84932	62595	60686	67167	63228	65997	70766
Irlande	EXP	G	77097	109005	122252	127050	119264	118951	127012	117770	115334	118635
	BAL		25653	32573	35203	42118	56669	58265	59845	54542	49336	47869
Italy	IMP	S	238021	442599	511870	563436	414725	486968	558813	489096	477292	470382
Italie	EXP	S	239902	417219	500239	544962	406685	446852	523283	501534	517628	528035
	BAL		1881	-25379	-11631	-18474	-8040	-40116	-35530	12438	40336	57653
Latvia	IMP	S	3187	11430	15182	15775	9346	11143	15442	16078	16781	16713
Lettonie	EXP	S	1867	5893	7892	9278	7174	8850	11995	12683	13317	13575
	BAL		-1320	-5538	-7290	-6497	-2173	-2292	-3446	-3395	-3464	-3137
Lithuania	IMP	G	5219	19413	24445	31295	18341	23385	31811	31988	34814	35218
Lituanie	EXP	G	3548	14153	17162	23770	16496	20726	28077	29625	32604	32396
	BAL		-1671	-5259	-7283	-7525	-1845	-2658	-3733	-2363	-2210	-2822
Luxembourg	IMP	S	10707	19737	22572	25828	19246	21738	26312	24180	23912	23545
Luxembourg	EXP	S	7833	13993	16359	17734	12905	14293	16798	13989	14086	15069
	BAL		-2875	-5744	-6213	-8094	-6342	-7444	-9515	-10190	-9826	-8476
Malta	IMP	G	3400	4073	4508	5744	4845	5735	7415	7923	7479	8122
Malte	EXP	G	2443	2705	2985	3609	2921	3721	5284	5697	5182	4836
	BAL		-957	-1368	-1523	-2135	-1924	-2014	-2131	-2226	-2297	-3286
Netherlands	IMP	S	198926	358510	421092	495056	382278	440024	507759	501163	507478	507005
Pays-Bas	EXP	S	213425	399635	472660	545897	431695	492742	569513	554699	567674	574206
	BAL		14499	41125	51568	50840	49418	52718	61754	53536	60196	67201
Norway	IMP	G	34395	64272	80378	90293	68970	77326	90787	87316	89988	88053
Norvège	EXP	G	60064	122112	136371	171764	116778	130669	160305	161026	153188	142301
	BAL		25669	57840	55992	81471	47808	53344	69518	73710	63201	54247
Poland	IMP	S	48970	127260	162437	204873	149723	178149	206844	196198	205174	219859
Pologne	EXP	S	31684	110941	138756	168674	136786	159829	187151	183523	202107	216666
	BAL		-17285	-16319	-23680	-36200	-12938	-18320	-19693	-12675	-3067	-3193
Portugal	IMP	S	38196	65639	76376	94726	71742	75576	82481	72306	75066	77745
Portugal	EXP	S	23280	42906	50246	57558	44350	48738	59608	58255	62841	64058
	BAL		-14916	-22734	-26129	-37168	-27393	-26838	-22872	-14051	-12225	-13687

Total merchandise trade by regions and countries or areas (Table A)
Imports CIF, exports FOB and balance: million U.S. dollars
Commerce total de marchandises par régions et pays ou zones (Tableau A)
Importations CIF, exportations FOB, et balance : en millions de dollars E.-U.

Country or Area - Pays ou Zone	IMP EXP BAL	G/S	2000	2006	2007	2008	2009	2010	2011	2012	2013	2014
Slovakia	IMP	S	13413	47310	62102	74034	56898	66110	81505	79077	83632	82042
Slovaquie	EXP	S	11889	41939	57765	70982	55553	64012	79011	79882	85244	85923
	BAL		-1524	-5371	-4337	-3052	-1345	-2098	-2494	805	1612	3882
Slovenia	IMP	S	10116	23032	29499	33991	24085	26305	31405	28392	29380	30189
Slovénie	EXP	S	8732	21293	26857	29600	22646	24717	29242	27080	28629	30672
	BAL		-1384	-1739	-2642	-4391	-1439	-1588	-2163	-1312	-751	483
Spain	IMP	S	152901	326046	384956	417049	290744	315548	362835	325836	333932	351452
Espagne	EXP	S	113348	213350	248917	277695	220848	246274	298458	286219	310996	318860
	BAL		-39553	-112697	-136038	-139353	-69897	-69274	-64377	-39618	-22936	-32592
Sweden	IMP	G	73328	127648	153463	168993	120262	148474	174730	164113	159665	159535
Suède	EXP	G	87737	147899	168979	183907	131042	158090	187243	172725	167620	162589
	BAL		14409	20251	15516	14914	10780	9616	12513	8612	7955	3054
Switzerland	IMP	S	76104	132030	153181	173686	147894	166924	196790	188618	191705	195988
Suisse	EXP	S	74867	141679	164809	191813	166847	185790	223225	213982	217079	229310
	BAL		-1237	9649	11627	18127	18953	18866	26435	25364	25374	33322
United Kingdom	IMP	G	333579	588118	621869	642529	486279	562493	638940	648671	645516	663718
Royaume-Uni	EXP	G	283206	446312	440556	467157	356758	410006	478460	476284	476991	477934
	BAL		-50373	-141806	-181312	-175372	-129521	-152487	-160480	-172387	-168525	-185785
North America	**IMP**		**1499277**	**2270342**	**2403337**	**2580873**	**1928954**	**2363843**	**2719913**	**2801878**	**2794255**	**2880017**
Amérique du Nord	**EXP**		**1058904**	**1414752**	**1569013**	**1744455**	**1370536**	**1666503**	**1933092**	**2001272**	**2038268**	**2094415**
	BAL		**-440373**	**-855590**	**-834324**	**-836418**	**-558418**	**-697339**	**-786820**	**-800606**	**-755987**	**-785601**
Bermuda	IMP	G	720	1094	1167	1159	1064	988	916	910	980	962
Bermudes	EXP	G	...	27	27	24	29	15	13	11	11	...
	BAL		...	-1067	-1140	-1135	-1035	-973	-903	-899	-969	...
Canada[3]	IMP	G	238811	350259	380701	408827	321247	392119	451246	462423	461925	465908
Canada[3]	EXP	G	276641	388315	420293	456419	314002	387481	452132	454833	458397	469980
	BAL		37830	38056	39593	47593	-7245	-4638	886	-7590	-3528	4072
Greenland	IMP	G	363	618	678	895	742	808	915	850	780	...
Groenland	EXP	G	272	396	431	487	360	380	475	480	490	...
	BAL		-92	-222	-247	-407	-382	-428	-441	-370	-290	...
United States[4]	IMP	G	1259300	1918080	2020400	2169490	1605300	1969180	2265890	2336520	2329060	2410440
Etats-Unis[4]	EXP	G	781918	1025970	1148200	1287440	1056040	1278490	1480290	1545710	1579050	1623410
	BAL		-477382	-892110	-872200	-882050	-549260	-690690	-785600	-790810	-750010	-787030
South-Eastern Europe	IMP		29538	103569	140118	170987	116966	125313	154685	145618	152512	**159022**
Europe du Sud-est	EXP		19549	60952	76657	93954	76969	89828	115549	107523	122767	**129401**
	BAL		-9989	-42617	-63462	-77033	-39996	-35486	-39136	-38095	-29745	**-29621**
Albania	IMP	G	1091	3058	4188	5251	4550	4406	5396	4882	4902	5230
Albanie	EXP	G	261	798	1078	1355	1091	1545	1951	1968	2332	2431
	BAL		-829	-2261	-3110	-3896	-3459	-2861	-3445	-2914	-2571	-2799
Bosnia and Herzegovina	IMP	S	3083	7345	9772	12282	8794	9204	11047	10018	10303	10988
Bosnie-Herzégovine	EXP	S	1067	3323	4166	5066	3939	4802	5850	5160	5688	5893
	BAL		-2017	-4023	-5606	-7217	-4856	-4402	-5196	-4858	-4615	-5095
Bulgaria	IMP	S	6505	23270	30086	37018	23552	25473	32579	32712	34350	...
Bulgarie	EXP	S	4809	15101	18575	22485	16378	20571	28222	26670	29492	...
	BAL		-1696	-8168	-11511	-14532	-7175	-4902	-4357	-6042	-4858	...
Montenegro	IMP	S	.	1838	2855	3748	2313	2186	2544	2309	2354	2369
Monténégro	EXP	S	.	557	624	617	388	437	632	471	498	447
	BAL		.	-1282	-2231	-3131	-1926	-1749	-1912	-1838	-1856	-1921

Total merchandise trade by regions and countries or areas (Table A)
Imports CIF, exports FOB and balance: million U.S. dollars
Commerce total de marchandises par régions et pays ou zones (Tableau A)
Importations CIF, exportations FOB, et balance : en millions de dollars E.-U.

Country or Area - Pays ou Zone	IMP EXP BAL	G/S	2000	2006	2007	2008	2009	2010	2011	2012	2013	2014
Romania	IMP	S	13055	51106	69602	82965	54256	61885	76251	70260	73452	77882
Roumanie	EXP	S	10367	32336	40042	49539	40621	49357	62659	57904	65881	69891
	BAL		-2688	-18770	-29560	-33426	-13635	-12528	-13592	-12355	-7571	-7991
Serbia	IMP	S	.	13188	18400	22880	18462	16686	19862	18927	20551	20437
Serbie	EXP	S	.	6437	8817	10971	11862	9766	11779	11348	14609	14813
	BAL		.	-6752	-9584	-11908	-6599	-6920	-8082	-7579	-5942	-5624
Serbia and Montenegro[5]	IMP	S	3711	.	.	.	.	.	.	.	.	.
Serbie et Monténégro[5]	EXP	S	1723	.	.	.	.	.	.	.	.	.
	BAL		-1988	.	.	.	.	.	.	.	.	.
TFYR Macedonia	IMP	S	2094	3763	5216	6843	5038	5474	7007	6511	6600	7228
L'ex-Ry de Macédoine	EXP	S	1323	2401	3356	3920	2692	3351	4455	4002	4267	4875
	BAL		-771	-1362	-1860	-2923	-2346	-2123	-2552	-2509	-2333	-2353
CIS	IMP		**70777**	**253434**	**352604**	**470011**	**304021**	**385468**	**510031**	**530549**	**536000**	**480391**
CEI	EXP		**143257**	**418466**	**497669**	**707830**	**440357**	**575065**	**761791**	**777493**	**762057**	**720048**
	BAL		**72480**	**165033**	**145065**	**237818**	**136337**	**189597**	**251760**	**246943**	**226057**	**239657**
Asia	IMP		**13519**	**45544**	**59849**	**73095**	**59330**	**56331**	**70856**	**80124**	**95596**	**93325**
Asie	EXP		**17794**	**58070**	**70828**	**139120**	**76419**	**99167**	**133280**	**135078**	**131847**	**129305**
	BAL		**4275**	**12527**	**10978**	**66025**	**17089**	**42836**	**62424**	**54954**	**36251**	**35980**
Armenia	IMP	S	882	2194	3282	4427	3303	3783	4196	4267	4386	4402
Arménie	EXP	S	294	1004	1219	1057	698	1011	1316	1428	1479	1519
	BAL		-588	-1190	-2063	-3370	-2605	-2771	-2881	-2839	-2907	-2882
Azerbaijan	IMP	G	1172	5267	5714	7170	6123	6601	9756	9653	10713	9188
Azerbaïdjan	EXP	G	1745	6372	6058	47756	14701	21360	26571	23908	23975	21829
	BAL		573	1105	345	40586	8578	14760	16815	14255	13263	12641
Georgia	IMP	G	710	3675	5212	6302	4500	5257	7065	8049	8026	8593
Géorgie	EXP	G	324	936	1232	1495	1134	1677	2189	2375	2909	2861
	BAL		-386	-2738	-3980	-4806	-3367	-3580	-4876	-5674	-5117	-5732
Kazakhstan	IMP	G	5040	24120	33260	38452	28409	24024	30000	35307	45966	41213
Kazakhstan	EXP	G	8812	38762	48351	71971	43196	57244	83316	88575	81912	78238
	BAL		3772	14642	15091	33519	14787	33220	53316	53268	35945	37025
Kyrgyzstan	IMP	S	558	1931	2789	4072	3040	3223	4261	5374	6070	5732
Kirghizistan	EXP	S	511	891	1321	1856	1673	1756	1979	1683	1791	1650
	BAL		-47	-1040	-1468	-2217	-1367	-1467	-2282	-3691	-4279	-4082
Tajikistan	IMP	G	675	1723	2455	3270	2569	2658	3186	3779	4121	4669
Tadjikistan	EXP	G	784	1399	1468	1406	1010	1196	1256	1358	1163	1078
	BAL		109	-324	-987	-1864	-1559	-1462	-1931	-2421	-2958	-3590
Uzbekistan	IMP	G	2697	4380	4848	7076	9023	8386	9953	...	13799	...
Ouzbékistan	EXP	G	2817	5617	8029	10369	10735	11587	13254	...	15087	...
	BAL		120	1237	3181	3293	1712	3201	3301	...	1288	...
Europe	IMP		57259	207890	292755	396916	244691	329137	439175	450426	440404	387067
Europe	EXP		125463	360396	426842	568710	363939	475898	628511	642415	630210	590743
	BAL		68205	152506	134087	171794	119248	146761	189336	191989	189805	203677
Belarus	IMP	G	8646	22351	28693	39381	28569	34884	45771	46404	42999	40788
Bélarus	EXP	G	7326	19734	24275	32571	21304	25284	41419	46060	37232	36392
	BAL		-1320	-2618	-4418	-6811	-7265	-9601	-4352	-345	-5766	-4396
Republic of Moldova	IMP	G	776	2693	3690	4899	3278	3855	5191	5213	5493	5317
République de Moldova	EXP	G	472	1050	1340	1591	1283	1542	2217	2162	2399	2340
	BAL		-305	-1643	-2350	-3308	-1995	-2314	-2975	-3051	-3094	-2978

Total merchandise trade by regions and countries or areas (Table A)
Imports CIF, exports FOB and balance: million U.S. dollars
Commerce total de marchandises par régions et pays ou zones (Tableau A)
Importations CIF, exportations FOB, et balance : en millions de dollars E.-U.

Country or Area - Pays ou Zone	IMP EXP BAL	G/S	2000	2006	2007	2008	2009	2010	2011	2012	2013	2014
Russian Federation	IMP	G	33880	137807	199754	267101	167411	229655	305605	314150	314967	286669
Fédération de Russie	EXP	G	103093	301244	351930	467581	301656	397668	516481	525383	527266	497909
	BAL		69213	163437	152176	200480	134245	168013	210877	211233	212299	211240
Ukraine	IMP	G	13956	45039	60618	85535	45433	60742	82608	84658	76946	54293
Ukraine	EXP	G	14573	38368	49296	66967	39696	51405	68394	68810	63312	54103
	BAL		617	-6671	-11322	-18568	-5737	-9337	-14214	-15848	-13634	-190
Northern Africa	IMP		**46956**	**86800**	**112469**	**164473**	**146452**	**161273**	**182446**	**206871**	**210902**	**224748**
Afrique du nord	EXP		**49865**	**131233**	**153521**	**207537**	**134078**	**164438**	**161581**	**199525**	**176950**	**161345**
	BAL		**2909**	**44433**	**41051**	**43064**	**-12374**	**3165**	**-20864**	**-7346**	**-33952**	**-63403**
Algeria	IMP	S	9172	20985	27525	39578	39333	40228	47279	50352	54965	58367
Algérie	EXP	S	22019	52760	59761	79587	45240	57786	73661	72857	65555	61413
	BAL		12848	31775	32236	40010	5907	17558	26383	22505	10590	3046
Egypt[6,7]	IMP	G	13963	20722	27063	48775	44946	52923	58903	65774	59662	...
Egypte[6,7]	EXP	G	4675	13694	16200	26246	23062	26438	30528	29409	28493	...
	BAL		-9288	-7028	-10863	-22528	-21884	-26485	-28376	-36365	-31169	...
Libya	IMP	G	3703	6053	6753	9116	10037	10506	7999	22996	27012	
Libye	EXP	G	10137	40333	47048	62031	37265	46016	18015	58954	43989	
	BAL		6434	34280	40295	52915	27228	35510	10016	35959	16977	
Morocco	IMP	S	11534	23980	32010	42366	32881	35385	44294	43290	44934	45823
Maroc	EXP	S	7175	12744	15340	20345	14054	17765	21524	21291	21847	23678
	BAL		-4359	-11236	-16670	-22021	-18827	-17620	-22770	-21999	-23088	-22144
Tunisia	IMP	G	8567	15043	19101	24622	19241	22218	23958	24447	24317	24828
Tunisie	EXP	G	5850	11694	15163	19319	14449	16427	17847	17008	17061	16756
	BAL		-2717	-3349	-3938	-5303	-4791	-5791	-6111	-7439	-7256	-8072
Sub-Saharan Africa	IMP		**78799**	**200869**	**241129**	**295233**	**253331**	**291417**	**361242**	**356558**	**382277**	**417338**
Afrique subsaharienne	EXP		**93493**	**233167**	**278671**	**364649**	**259940**	**338291**	**430514**	**419761**	**422428**	**423265**
	BAL		**14694**	**32298**	**37542**	**69416**	**6609**	**46874**	**69272**	**63203**	**40151**	**5927**
Angola[3]	IMP	S	3040	11600	9617	14544	22548	16574	17330	22340	22670	28086
Angola[3]	EXP	S	7703	31084	43452	72179	40080	46437	65801	70088	67438	58935
	BAL		4663	19484	33835	57634	17533	29864	48471	47748	44768	30849
Benin	IMP	S	567	1228	2037	2290	1553	1494	2701	2202	2148	...
Bénin	EXP	S	392	741	1052	1285	423	437	1397	1402	1154	...
	BAL		-174	-487	-984	-1005	-1130	-1057	-1304	-800	-995	...
Botswana	IMP	G	2079	3076	4077	5232	4771	5666	7300	8114	7007	...
Botswana	EXP	G	2661	4509	5170	5077	3514	4692	5893	5971	7765	...
	BAL		581	1434	1093	-155	-1257	-975	-1407	-2143	758	...
Burkina Faso	IMP	G	608	1323	1685	2009	2084	2157	2574	3420	3499	...
Burkina Faso	EXP	G	213	588	623	693	868	1319	2353	2183	2161	...
	BAL		-395	-735	-1062	-1315	-1216	-837	-221	-1237	-1338	...
Burundi	IMP	S	148	431	319	402	402	509	752	751	811	704
Burundi	EXP	S	50	58	62	54	62	100	122	132	99	124
	BAL		-98	-372	-257	-348	-340	-409	-630	-619	-712	-581
Cabo Verde	IMP	G	237	543	753	819	709	743	947	766	727	...
Cabo Verde	EXP	G	11	21	19	32	35	45	69	53	69	...
	BAL		-227	-522	-734	-788	-674	-698	-878	-713	-658	...
Cameroon	IMP	S	1483	3161	4218	5376	4322	4847	6498	7101	7006	...
Cameroun	EXP	S	1823	3587	3622	4279	3391	3896	4597	4500	4204	...
	BAL		341	427	-596	-1097	-931	-952	-1901	-2602	-2802	...

Total merchandise trade by regions and countries or areas (Table A)
Imports CIF, exports FOB and balance: million U.S. dollars
Commerce total de marchandises par régions et pays ou zones (Tableau A)
Importations CIF, exportations FOB, et balance : en millions de dollars E.-U.

Country or Area - Pays ou Zone	IMP EXP BAL	G/S	2000	2006	2007	2008	2009	2010	2011	2012	2013	2014
Cent. Afr. Rep.	IMP	S	118	203	251	298	273	244	276	276	250	...
Rép. centrafricaine	EXP	S	163	158	181	150	81	91	116	112	140	...
	BAL		45	-44	-70	-149	-192	-153	-161	-163	-111	...
Chad	IMP	S	483	1346	1794	1906	2289	2507	2700	2600	2997	...
Tchad	EXP	S	236	3342	3653	4345	2636	3411	4599	3901	4496	...
	BAL		-248	1995	1859	2439	347	903	1899	1301	1498	...
Comoros	IMP	S	43	116	139	174	171	190	277	300	285	...
Comores	EXP	S	14	10	14	9	16	18	25	25	25	...
	BAL		-29	-106	-125	-165	-155	-172	-251	-275	-260	...
Congo	IMP	S	479	2073	2606	3142	2987	2987	5200	5200	5500	...
Congo	EXP	S	2489	6078	5635	8300	6100	8200	11500	11000	9800	...
	BAL		2010	4004	3029	5159	3113	5213	6300	5800	4300	...
Cote d'Ivoire	IMP	S	2485	5825	6694	7863	7023	7863	6714	9774	12898	...
Côte d'Ivoire	EXP	S	3611	8477	8692	10301	10326	10285	10928	10861	13748	...
	BAL		1127	2652	1998	2438	3303	2423	4214	1087	849	...
Dem. Rep. of the Congo	IMP	S	697	2740	2950	4300	3900	4500	5500	6100	6300	...
Rép. dém. du Congo	EXP	S	824	2320	2600	4400	3500	5300	6600	6300	6300	...
	BAL		126	-420	-350	100	-400	800	1100	200	0	...
Djibouti	IMP	G	207	336	473	574	451	420	511	580	560	...
Djibouti	EXP	G	32	55	58	69	77	100	93	95	120	...
	BAL		-175	-281	-415	-505	-373	-320	-418	-485	-440	...
Equatorial Guinea	IMP	G	451	2023	2369	3934	5205	5680	6014	5987	6990	...
Guinée équatoriale	EXP	G	1097	8218	10205	15996	9108	9964	13532	15467	13981	...
	BAL		646	6195	7836	12062	3903	4285	7518	9480	6990	...
Ethiopia	IMP	G	1261	5304	5797	8268	7644	8535	9016	12641	...	...
Ethiopie	EXP	G	482	1044	1282	1561	1522	2270	3671	4062	...	...
	BAL		-779	-4260	-4516	-6708	-6123	-6265	-5345	-8579	...	...
Gabon	IMP	S	996	1726	2155	2607	2514	2984	3666	3630	3886	...
Gabon	EXP	S	2605	5454	6302	9566	5451	8691	9768	7704	9514	...
	BAL		1610	3728	4147	6959	2937	5706	6102	4075	5628	...
Gambia	IMP	G	187	259	323	325	304	300	336	380	348	...
Gambie	EXP	G	15	11	13	14	15	15	11	18	8	...
	BAL		-172	-248	-310	-311	-289	-285	-325	-362	-340	...
Ghana	IMP	G	2974	6748	8057	10243	8038	11038	15967	17965	17759	...
Ghana	EXP	G	1317	3725	4322	5625	5840	7960	12784	11976	13691	...
	BAL		-1657	-3023	-3735	-4618	-2199	-3077	-3183	-5989	-4067	...
Guinea	IMP	S	612	900	1218	1366	1060	1405	2106	2300	2150	...
Guinée	EXP	S	666	900	1203	1342	1050	1471	1433	1400	1300	...
	BAL		54	0	-15	-24	-10	66	-673	-900	-850	...
Guinea-Bissau	IMP	G	60	110	110	199	202	197	260	250	240	...
Guinée-Bissau	EXP	G	62	74	107	128	120	120	230	130	210	...
	BAL		3	-36	-3	-71	-82	-77	-30	-120	-30	...
Kenya	IMP	G	3105	7311	8989	11080	10207	12074	14783	16288	16358	...
Kenya	EXP	G	1734	3437	4080	4975	4463	5149	5756	6127	5856	...
	BAL		-1372	-3874	-4910	-6105	-5743	-6925	-9027	-10162	-10503	...
Lesotho	IMP	G	809	1496	1741	1995	1973	2206	2591	2587	2284	...
Lesotho	EXP	G	221	689	770	883	723	801	1168	1099	934	...
	BAL		-589	-807	-971	-1113	-1250	-1404	-1422	-1489	-1350	...

Total merchandise trade by regions and countries or areas (Table A)
Imports CIF, exports FOB and balance: million U.S. dollars
Commerce total de marchandises par régions et pays ou zones (Tableau A)
Importations CIF, exportations FOB, et balance : en millions de dollars E.-U.

Country or Area - Pays ou Zone	IMP EXP BAL	G/S	2000	2006	2007	2008	2009	2010	2011	2012	2013	2014
Liberia	IMP	S	...	467	499	813	551	710	814	1076	1210	...
Libéria	EXP	S	...	158	200	242	149	222	367	459	540	...
	BAL		...	-309	-299	-571	-402	-488	-447	-617	-670	...
Madagascar	IMP	S	999	1744	2449	3843	3160	2546	2628	2486	3198	...
Madagascar	EXP	S	828	994	1371	1670	1095	1082	1249	1236	1947	...
	BAL		-171	-750	-1078	-2173	-2065	-1464	-1379	-1250	-1250	...
Malawi	IMP	G	533	1206	1380	1700	2096	2162	2426	2334	2831	...
Malawi	EXP	G	379	541	709	860	1080	1130	1398	1183	1196	...
	BAL		-153	-665	-671	-840	-1015	-1032	-1027	-1151	-1636	...
Mali	IMP	S	807	1819	2183	3343	2487	3430	3391	2940	3699	...
Mali	EXP	S	552	1559	1567	2082	1783	1996	2392	2163	2601	...
	BAL		-255	-260	-616	-1261	-704	-1434	-999	-776	-1098	...
Mauritania	IMP	S	354	1089	1428	1669	1337	1708	2453	2971	3975	3642
Mauritanie	EXP	S	343	1268	1356	1651	1407	1799	2458	2624	2685	2298
	BAL		-11	180	-72	-18	70	91	6	-347	-1290	-1344
Mauritius	IMP	G	2206	3627	3894	4655	3734	4387	5149	5355	5399	...
Maurice	EXP	G	1803	2329	2238	2386	1939	2262	2565	2649	2872	...
	BAL		-403	-1298	-1656	-2269	-1795	-2125	-2584	-2706	-2527	...
Mozambique	IMP	S	1158	2869	3210	4008	3764	4600	6306	6800	8600	...
Mozambique	EXP	S	364	2381	2650	2653	2147	3000	3604	4100	4300	...
	BAL		-794	-488	-560	-1355	-1617	-1600	-2702	-2700	-4300	...
Namibia	IMP	G	1539	3247	4544	5260	6464	6506	6620	7356	7568	...
Namibie	EXP	G	1317	3645	4466	5373	5122	5290	5362	5481	5740	...
	BAL		-222	397	-78	114	-1343	-1216	-1258	-1876	-1828	...
Niger	IMP	S	390	955	1163	1659	1502	2179	1814	1799	1909	...
Niger	EXP	S	284	507	664	902	593	642	903	1503	1613	...
	BAL		-107	-448	-499	-757	-909	-1537	-910	-296	-295	...
Nigeria	IMP	G	8721	26760	37576	42378	33906	44235	64105	35703	44598	...
Nigéria	EXP	G	20975	57444	65133	80615	56742	84000	114500	114000	...	...
	BAL		12254	30684	27557	38237	22836	39765	50395	78297	...	...
Rwanda	IMP	G	211	547	736	1131	1227	1401	1775	1999	2480	...
Rwanda	EXP	G	52	147	176	267	193	255	464	470	689	...
	BAL		-159	-400	-559	-865	-1035	-1146	-1311	-1529	-1792	...
Saint Helena[8]	IMP	G	10	15	16	16	16	...	...	...	...	...
Sainte-Hélèna[8]	EXP	G	0	0	0	0	1	...	...	...	...	...
	BAL		-10	-15	-15	-16	-16	...	...	...	...	...
Sao Tome and Principe	IMP	S	30	71	79	114	103	112	132	140	140	...
Sao Tomé-et-Principe	EXP	S	3	8	7	11	8	11	11	11	12	...
	BAL		-27	-63	-72	-103	-95	-101	-121	-129	-128	...
Senegal	IMP	G	1513	3444	4271	5706	4549	4442	5390	5883	6067	...
Sénégal	EXP	G	921	1556	1652	2007	1906	2059	2432	2382	2440	...
	BAL		-592	-1888	-2618	-3699	-2643	-2383	-2958	-3501	-3627	...
Seychelles	IMP	G	343	758	861	1106	807	989	1049	1074	1098	...
Seychelles	EXP	G	193	380	356	437	402	400	483	497	578	...
	BAL		-150	-378	-506	-668	-405	-589	-566	-577	-520	...
Sierra Leone	IMP	S	149	389	445	534	521	771	1715	1604	1780	...
Sierra Leone	EXP	S	13	231	245	216	233	319	317	1081	1893	...
	BAL		-136	-158	-199	-319	-287	-452	-1398	-523	113	...

Total merchandise trade by regions and countries or areas (Table A)
Imports CIF, exports FOB and balance: million U.S. dollars
Commerce total de marchandises par régions et pays ou zones (Tableau A)
Importations CIF, exportations FOB, et balance : en millions de dollars E.-U.

Country or Area - Pays ou Zone	IMP EXP BAL	G/S	2000	2006	2007	2008	2009	2010	2011	2012	2013	2014
South Africa[3,9]	IMP	G	26795	67644	79873	94901	64439	80132	99714	101415	101263	99924
Afrique du Sud[3,9]	EXP	G	29987	58197	69787	84488	62627	81827	96931	87385	83540	91191
	BAL		3192	-9447	-10086	-10413	-1812	1695	-2783	-14030	-17723	-8733
Sudan[10]	IMP	G	1553	8074	8450	9352	9691	10045	9236	9230	9918	...
Soudan[10]	EXP	G	1807	5657	8866	11671	8257	11404	9689	4067	7086	...
	BAL		254	-2417	416	2319	-1434	1360	453	-5164	-2832	...
Swaziland	IMP	G	1039	1918	1853	1665	1617	1710	1940	1946	...	...
Swaziland	EXP	G	903	1779	1885	1681	1479	1557	1901	1897	...	...
	BAL		-137	-139	33	16	-138	-153	-39	-49	...	...
Togo	IMP	S	562	1091	1243	1499	1951	996	1800	1793	2108	...
Togo	EXP	S	362	634	700	901	811	641	1100	997	1048	...
	BAL		-200	-457	-543	-598	-1140	-356	-700	-796	-1059	...
Uganda	IMP	G	1511	2555	3497	4559	4265	4709	4565	5230	4927	...
Ouganda	EXP	G	469	1188	2003	2717	3004	3115	2399	2861	2847	...
	BAL		-1043	-1367	-1494	-1841	-1261	-1594	-2166	-2369	-2080	...
United Rep. of Tanzania	IMP	G	1523	4246	5337	7081	6296	7708	10702	11266	12235	...
Rép.-Unie de Tanzanie	EXP	G	663	1736	2022	2674	2367	3522	4392	5075	5043	...
	BAL		-860	-2510	-3315	-4407	-3929	-4186	-6310	-6191	-7191	...
Zambia	IMP	S	997	3086	4033	5017	3827	5319	7173	8000	10165	...
Zambie	EXP	S	681	3828	4641	5187	4389	7207	9009	8550	10596	...
	BAL		-316	742	608	170	562	1888	1837	550	431	...
Zimbabwe	IMP	G	1861	2300	2550	2950	2900	3800	4400	4400	4300	...
Zimbabwe	EXP	G	1923	2000	2400	2200	2269	3199	3512	3800	3552	...
	BAL		62	-300	-150	-750	-631	-601	-888	-600	-748	...
Latin America & The Caribbean	IMP		**376134**	**614285**	**733270**	**896727**	**673752**	**855961**	**1048634**	**1077587**	**1117529**	**1115359**
Amérique latine et les Caraïbes	EXP		**355954**	**670245**	**759828**	**888668**	**680162**	**861934**	**1074334**	**1086531**	**1090802**	**1068154**
	BAL		**-20181**	**55961**	**26557**	**-8059**	**6410**	**5974**	**25700**	**8944**	**-26727**	**-47205**
The Caribbean	IMP		**26914**	**44074**	**50404**	**61394**	**48543**	**50664**	**57049**	**56360**	**53460**	**52711**
Les Caraïbes	EXP		**11431**	**23738**	**24777**	**30405**	**19530**	**22196**	**29568**	**29994**	**31458**	**33297**
	BAL		**-15483**	**-20336**	**-25628**	**-30990**	**-29013**	**-28468**	**-27480**	**-26366**	**-22002**	**-19414**
Anguilla	IMP	S	99	143	248	272	169	157	153	150	145	...
Anguilla	EXP	S	4	13	9	11	23	12	16	8	4	...
	BAL		-95	-130	-239	-260	-146	-145	-137	-142	-141	...
Antigua and Barbuda	IMP	G	338	671	727	806	699	501	471	535	515	...
Antigua-et-Barbuda	EXP	G	42	164	174	92	206	35	29	29	32	...
	BAL		-296	-507	-553	-713	-493	-466	-442	-506	-483	...
Aruba	IMP	S	835	1041	1114	1134	1149	1069	1283	1258	1303	...
Aruba	EXP	S	173	109	98	100	136	125	151	173	167	...
	BAL		-662	-932	-1016	-1034	-1013	-945	-1132	-1085	-1136	...
Bahamas[11]	IMP	G	2074	2401	2449	2354	2699	2863	3411	3658	3276	...
Bahamas[11]	EXP	G	576	674	485	560	585	621	727	829	715	...
	BAL		-1498	-1726	-1965	-1794	-2114	-2241	-2684	-2829	-2561	...
Barbados	IMP	G	1156	1586	1709	1879	1471	1562	1805	1806	1759	...
Barbade	EXP	G	272	385	419	445	369	429	465	570	463	...
	BAL		-884	-1201	-1291	-1433	-1102	-1133	-1340	-1236	-1296	...
Cayman Islands	IMP	G	693	1048	1029	1078	893	828	911	910	929	...
Îles Caïmanes	EXP	G	4	17	21	15	19	13	22	20	30	...
	BAL		-689	-1032	-1008	-1064	-874	-815	-890	-890	-899	...

Total merchandise trade by regions and countries or areas (Table A)
Imports CIF, exports FOB and balance: million U.S. dollars
Commerce total de marchandises par régions et pays ou zones (Tableau A)
Importations CIF, exportations FOB, et balance : en millions de dollars E.-U.

Country or Area - Pays ou Zone	IMP EXP BAL	G/S	2000	2006	2007	2008	2009	2010	2011	2012	2013	2014
Cuba	IMP	S	3363	10174	10889	14249	...	...	...	...	...	...
Cuba	EXP	S	1219	2980	3998	3680	...	...	...	...	...	...
	BAL		-2144	-7194	-6892	-10570	...	...	...	...	...	...
Dominica	IMP	S	148	167	196	247	225	224	226	208	203	...
Dominique	EXP	S	54	42	38	40	34	37	29	36	38	...
	BAL		-95	-124	-158	-207	-191	-187	-197	-173	-165	...
Dominican Republic[3,12]	IMP	G	6416	8745	11289	14020	10057	12885	14522	14939	13876	...
République dominicaine[3,12]	EXP	G	966	1931	2635	2394	1690	2711	3678	4129	4482	...
	BAL		-5450	-6814	-8654	-11626	-8367	-10174	-10845	-10810	-9394	...
Grenada	IMP	S	246	331	365	377	293	317	329	336	368	...
Grenade	EXP	S	78	25	33	30	29	24	28	35	33	...
	BAL		-168	-305	-332	-347	-264	-293	-302	-301	-336	...
Haiti	IMP	G	1040	1879	1681	2310	2121	3147	3018	3170	3400	...
Haïti	EXP	G	313	480	522	475	576	579	767	814	885	...
	BAL		-727	-1399	-1159	-1835	-1546	-2568	-2251	-2356	-2516	...
Jamaica	IMP	G	3302	5314	6394	7734	4860	5201	6489	6485	6200	...
Jamaïque	EXP	G	1295	1874	2070	2542	1319	1331	1603	1709	1574	...
	BAL		-2007	-3440	-4324	-5192	-3540	-3870	-4886	-4776	-4626	...
Montserrat	IMP	S	...	30	30	38	30	29	33	35	40	...
Montserrat	EXP	S	...	1	3	4	3	1	2	2	2	...
	BAL		...	-29	-27	-34	-26	-28	-31	-34	-38	...
Neth. Antilles[13]	IMP	S	2862	2209	2549	3079	2607	2687	...	...	...	...
Antilles néer.[13]	EXP	S	2009	695	676	1088	810	811	...	...	...	...
	BAL		-853	-1515	-1872	-1991	-1797	-1876	...	...	...	...
Saint Kitts-Nevis	IMP	S	196	250	272	325	302	228	248	226	249	...
Saint-Kitts-et-Nevis	EXP	S	29	35	32	43	43	45	34	50	50	...
	BAL		-167	-214	-241	-282	-260	-183	-214	-176	-199	...
Saint Lucia	IMP	S	355	592	635	657	539	601	670	683	598	...
Sainte-Lucie	EXP	S	47	98	107	145	163	228	256	156	171	...
	BAL		-308	-494	-528	-512	-376	-373	-414	-527	-427	...
Saint Vincent-Grenadines	IMP	S	148	269	327	373	334	345	332	357	378	...
St.Vincent-Grenadines	EXP	S	50	38	48	52	50	44	39	44	48	...
	BAL		-97	-231	-279	-321	-284	-301	-293	-314	-330	...
Trinidad and Tobago	IMP	S	3308	6484	7662	9596	6953	6483	9976	9400	8799	...
Trinité-et-Tobago	EXP	S	4274	14159	13393	18663	9140	10188	14842	13100	12700	...
	BAL		966	7675	5731	9067	2187	3705	4866	3700	3902	...
Turks and Caicos Islands	IMP	G	149	498	581	591	375	302	...	...	...	...
Îles Turques et Caïques	EXP	G	9	18	16	25	21	16	...	...	...	...
	BAL		-140	-480	-564	-566	-355	-286	...	...	...	...
Latin America	IMP		**349220**	**570211**	**682866**	**835333**	**625209**	**805297**	**991585**	**1021226**	**1064069**	**1062647**
Amérique latine	EXP		**344523**	**646507**	**735051**	**858264**	**660632**	**839739**	**1044765**	**1056537**	**1059344**	**1034857**
	BAL		**-4698**	**76296**	**52185**	**22931**	**35423**	**34442**	**53180**	**35311**	**-4725**	**-27791**
Argentina	IMP	S	25154	34158	44707	57413	39105	48048	74319	68505	74002	65249
Argentine	EXP	S	26341	46568	55779	70588	56065	64722	84269	75219	83026	71936
	BAL		1187	12410	11072	13175	16961	16674	9950	6713	9024	6687
Belize	IMP	G	524	676	684	837	669	709	831	882	930	...
Belize	EXP	G	218	266	254	290	224	280	340	340	315	...
	BAL		-306	-410	-430	-547	-445	-430	-491	-541	-616	...

Total merchandise trade by regions and countries or areas (Table A)
Imports CIF, exports FOB and balance: million U.S. dollars
Commerce total de marchandises par régions et pays ou zones (Tableau A)
Importations CIF, exportations FOB, et balance : en millions de dollars E.-U.

Country or Area - Pays ou Zone	IMP EXP BAL	G/S	2000	2006	2007	2008	2009	2010	2011	2012	2013	2014
Bolivia (Plurinational State of)	IMP	G	1830	2814	3457	5081	4545	5590	7927	8578	9338	10421
Bolivie (État plurinational de)	EXP	G	1230	3875	4458	7058	4918	6179	8107	10312	11189	12266
	BAL		-600	1060	1001	1977	373	589	179	1733	1851	1845
Brazil	IMP	G	58643	95838	126645	182377	133673	191537	236946	228377	244677	237531
Brésil	EXP	G	55119	137807	160649	197942	152995	201915	256040	242580	242179	225102
	BAL		-3524	41969	34004	15565	19322	10378	19094	14203	-2498	-12429
Chile	IMP	S	18507	38406	47164	61903	41364	57928	73545	79080	80443	72433
Chili	EXP	S	19210	58680	67666	66456	51963	68996	80027	79712	77877	74547
	BAL		703	20274	20502	4553	10599	11068	6482	632	-2566	2113
Colombia	IMP	G	11539	26046	33164	39320	32898	40683	54675	58633	59397	64060
Colombie	EXP	G	13043	24388	29786	38265	32784	39710	56507	59573	58657	54788
	BAL		1505	-1658	-3378	-1055	-114	-973	1832	941	-740	-9272
Costa Rica	IMP	S	6389	11520	12957	15366	11460	13557	16218	17513	17923	17229
Costa Rica	EXP	S	5850	8216	9376	9575	8711	9343	10238	11151	11542	11217
	BAL		-539	-3305	-3582	-5791	-2750	-4214	-5980	-6362	-6381	-6012
Ecuador	IMP	G	3721	12114	13565	18852	15090	20591	24286	25304	27146	27740
Equateur	EXP	G	4927	12728	13852	18818	13863	17415	22345	23765	24848	25732
	BAL		1206	615	287	-34	-1227	-3176	-1941	-1539	-2298	-2007
El Salvador	IMP	S	4948	7628	8677	9754	7255	8548	10118	10270	10772	10513
El Salvador	EXP	S	2941	3513	3977	4579	3797	4472	4979	5340	5491	5273
	BAL		-2006	-4115	-4700	-5175	-3457	-4077	-5139	-4929	-5281	-5240
Guatemala	IMP	S	5171	10157	11861	12835	10066	12051	14518	14873	14368	14921
Guatemala	EXP	S	2711	3665	4489	5412	3835	5907	7201	7139	6975	7366
	BAL		-2460	-6492	-7371	-7423	-6232	-6145	-7317	-7734	-7392	-7555
Guyana	IMP	S	582	889	1059	1312	1161	1397	1763	1997	1750	...
Guyana	EXP	S	502	588	679	795	763	880	1116	1415	1380	...
	BAL		-80	-301	-381	-518	-398	-517	-647	-581	-370	...
Honduras	IMP	S	2980	5695	6762	8831	6133	7079	8953	9464	9169	...
Honduras	EXP	S	1297	2054	2120	2883	2304	2712	3892	4427	3923	...
	BAL		-1682	-3641	-4642	-5948	-3829	-4367	-5060	-5037	-5246	...
Mexico[3,14]	IMP	G	174500	256130	283264	310561	234385	301482	350856	370746	381202	399977
Mexique[3,14]	EXP	G	166368	250441	272055	291827	229683	298138	349569	370889	380107	397658
	BAL		-8132	-5689	-11209	-18734	-4702	-3344	-1287	143	-1095	-2319
Nicaragua	IMP	G	1805	3000	3579	4300	3438	4229	5180	5847	5647	...
Nicaragua	EXP	G	643	1027	1194	1473	1393	1845	2294	2644	2408	...
	BAL		-1163	-1973	-2385	-2827	-2045	-2384	-2886	-3204	-3239	...
Panama	IMP	S	3379	4831	6872	9050	7801	9145	11342	12633	...	...
Panama	EXP	S	859	1093	1164	1247	948	832	785	...	...	...
	BAL		-2519	-3738	-5709	-7803	-6853	-8313	-10556	...	...	...
Paraguay	IMP	S	2193	6090	5859	9033	6940	10040	12317	11502	12142	12169
Paraguay	EXP	S	2200	3472	4724	6407	5080	6517	7776	7282	9432	9655
	BAL		7	-2618	-1136	-2626	-1860	-3524	-4540	-4220	-2710	-2513
Peru[3]	IMP	S	7407	14897	19580	28373	21006	28818	37112	41089	42199	...
Pérou[3]	EXP	S	6955	23830	27882	31529	26885	35565	46118	45600	41484	37841
	BAL		-452	8933	8301	3157	5879	6747	9005	4510	-715	...
Suriname	IMP	G	243	894	1111	1518	1356	1380	1667	1755	2141	1982
Suriname	EXP	G	395	1123	1287	1668	1393	1851	2345	2525	2358	2113
	BAL		152	229	177	149	37	471	677	769	217	131

Total merchandise trade by regions and countries or areas (Table A)
Imports CIF, exports FOB and balance: million U.S. dollars
Commerce total de marchandises par régions et pays ou zones (Tableau A)
Importations CIF, exportations FOB, et balance : en millions de dollars E.-U.

Country or Area - Pays ou Zone	IMP EXP BAL	G/S	2000	2006	2007	2008	2009	2010	2011	2012	2013	2014
Uruguay	IMP	G	3466	4757	5726	8943	6209	8619	10623	10642	10990	10901
Uruguay	EXP	G	2295	3953	4485	6421	5417	6707	7997	8601	8844	9475
	BAL		-1171	-804	-1241	-2523	-792	-1912	-2626	-2041	-2146	-1425
Venezuela (Bolivarian Rep. of)	IMP	G	16213	33616	46097	49602	40597	33815	38346	43501	46363	...
Venezuela (Rép. bolivarienne)	EXP	G	31413	59208	69165	95021	57603	65745	92811	97340	86700	...
	BAL		15200	25592	23068	45419	17006	31930	54465	53840	40337	...
Eastern Asia	IMP		**742209**	**1646399**	**1909513**	**2206817**	**1857749**	**2516769**	**3048702**	**3130285**	**3278284**	**3323104**
Asie Orientale	EXP		**774892**	**1840231**	**2185425**	**2473784**	**2091251**	**2714089**	**3197937**	**3346975**	**3540640**	**3710419**
	BAL		**32683**	**193831**	**275912**	**266968**	**233502**	**197320**	**149236**	**216689**	**262355**	**387315**
China	IMP	S	225024	791797	956233	1131620	1004170	1396200	1742850	1817780	1950380	1960290
Chine	EXP	S	249203	969380	1217790	1428660	1201790	1578270	1899180	2048940	2210250	2342290
	BAL		24179	177583	261557	297040	197620	182070	156330	231160	259870	382000
China, Hong Kong SAR	IMP	G	212805	334681	367647	388505	347311	433111	483633	504405	523558	544112
Chine, Hong Kong RAS	EXP	G	201860	316816	344509	362675	318510	390143	428732	442799	458959	473659
	BAL		-10945	-17865	-23138	-25830	-28801	-42968	-54901	-61606	-64599	-70453
China, Macao SAR	IMP	G	2255	4565	5366	5365	4622	5513	7769	8877	10141	11262
Chine, Macao RAS	EXP	G	2539	2557	2543	1997	961	870	869	1021	1138	1241
	BAL		284	-2008	-2823	-3368	-3661	-4643	-6899	-7856	-9002	-10021
Korea, Republic of	IMP	G	160479	309350	356852	435275	323085	425212	524413	519585	515585	525514
Corée, République de	EXP	G	172272	325468	371492	422007	363534	466384	555216	547879	559632	572665
	BAL		11793	16118	14640	-13268	40449	41172	30803	28294	44047	47151
Mongolia	IMP	G	615	1486	2117	3616	2131	3278	6527	6739	6355	5237
Mongolie	EXP	G	536	1543	1889	2539	1903	2899	4780	4385	4273	5775
	BAL		-79	57	-228	-1077	-229	-379	-1747	-2354	-2082	538
Southern Asia	IMP		94740	280721	343079	465685	379516	505555	639137	657589	625197	**626166**
Asie Méridionale	EXP		91012	233539	271120	350844	282590	373614	491233	452037	461496	**480489**
	BAL		-3728	-47181	-71959	-114841	-96926	-131941	-147904	-205553	-163701	**-145676**
Afghanistan	IMP	G	1176	2582	2819	3020	3336	5154	6390	6200	5400	...
Afghanistan	EXP	G	137	408	497	540	403	388	376	350	500	...
	BAL		-1039	-2174	-2322	-2480	-2933	-4766	-6014	-5850	-4900	...
Bangladesh	IMP	G	8358	14964	17263	22473	20631	26071	33978	34133	33576	...
Bangladesh	EXP	G	4787	9103	10233	11777	12443	14195	19807	25113	27033	...
	BAL		-3572	-5861	-7030	-10695	-8188	-11877	-14171	-9020	-6543	...
Bhutan	IMP	G	235	419	526	543	529	854	1052	992	911	...
Bhoutan	EXP	G	127	414	675	520	495	641	678	535	544	...
	BAL		-108	-5	148	-23	-34	-213	-374	-457	-367	...
India[15]	IMP	G	51563	178485	229349	321025	257200	350192	464507	489689	465529	461448
Inde[15]	EXP	G	42378	121812	150160	194816	164912	226334	302892	296827	314809	319751
	BAL		-9185	-56674	-79189	-126210	-92288	-123858	-161615	-192863	-150720	-141697
Iran (Islamic Rep. of)[16,17]	IMP	S	14347	40772	45000	57401	50768	65404	61760	56500	49000	...
Iran (Rép. islamique d')[16,17]	EXP	S	28345	77012	83000	113668	78830	101316	130500	95500	82000	...
	BAL		13998	36240	38000	56267	28062	35912	68740	39000	33000	...
Maldives	IMP	G	389	923	1092	1382	963	1091	1465	1554	1733	1993
Maldives	EXP	G	76	135	108	126	76	74	127	162	167	145
	BAL		-313	-788	-984	-1256	-886	-1017	-1338	-1393	-1567	-1848
Nepal	IMP	G	1526	2488	3139	3562	4392	5495	5762	6499	6428	...
Népal	EXP	G	700	838	870	937	823	950	917	960	926	...
	BAL		-826	-1650	-2269	-2625	-3569	-4545	-4845	-5539	-5502	...

Total merchandise trade by regions and countries or areas (Table A)
Imports CIF, exports FOB and balance: million U.S. dollars
Commerce total de marchandises par régions et pays ou zones (Tableau A)
Importations CIF, exportations FOB, et balance : en millions de dollars E.-U.

Country or Area - Pays ou Zone	IMP EXP BAL	G/S	2000	2006	2007	2008	2009	2010	2011	2012	2013	2014
Pakistan	IMP	G	10864	29828	32590	42327	31648	37783	43955	42920	44647	45758
Pakistan	EXP	G	9028	16932	17838	20323	17523	21410	25383	22807	25121	25697
	BAL		-1836	-12896	-14752	-22003	-14125	-16373	-18572	-20114	-19526	-20061
Sri Lanka	IMP	G	6281	10259	11301	13953	10049	13512	20268	19102	17973	...
Sri Lanka	EXP	G	5433	6886	7740	8137	7085	8307	10553	9784	10397	...
	BAL		-848	-3373	-3560	-5816	-2965	-5205	-9715	-9318	-7576	...
South-eastern Asia	IMP		379470	689652	774039	939039	728238	955444	**1151184**	1226957	**1243719**	**1236772**
Asie du Sud-est	EXP		429596	770419	865146	988287	813295	1049884	**1232085**	1252265	**1271511**	**1315905**
	BAL		50126	80767	91106	49248	85057	94440	**80901**	25308	**27791**	**79133**
Brunei Darussalam	IMP	S	1107	1679	2101	2572	2449	3365	...	3563	...	...
Brunéi Darussalam	EXP	S	3907	7634	7693	10322	7200	9172	...	12982	...	...
	BAL		2801	5956	5592	7750	4751	5808	...	9418	...	...
Cambodia	IMP	S	1424	4749	5300	6508	5830	6791	9300	11000	13000	...
Cambodge	EXP	S	1123	3800	4400	4708	4196	5143	6950	8200	9100	...
	BAL		-302	-949	-900	-1800	-1634	-1648	-2350	-2800	-3900	...
Indonesia	IMP	S	43075	80650	93101	127538	93786	135323	176881	190992	186351	178182
Indonésie	EXP	S	65404	103528	118014	139606	119646	158074	200587	188516	182659	176341
	BAL		22329	22878	24913	12068	25860	22751	23706	-2476	-3692	-1841
Lao P.Dem.R.	IMP	S	535	1060	1067	1405	1461	2060	2404	3055	3020	...
Rép. dém. populaire lao	EXP	S	330	882	842	1085	1053	1746	2190	2271	2264	...
	BAL		-205	-177	-225	-320	-408	-314	-215	-784	-756	...
Malaysia	IMP	G	81963	131085	146171	156348	123757	164622	187473	196393	205898	208874
Malaisie	EXP	G	98229	160571	175966	199414	157244	198612	228086	227538	228331	234139
	BAL		16266	29486	29795	43066	33487	33990	40613	31145	22434	25265
Myanmar	IMP	G	2371	2538	3247	4256	4348	4760	9019	9151	12043	16226
Myanmar	EXP	G	1620	4539	6253	6882	6662	8661	9238	8877	11233	9183
	BAL		-751	2001	3006	2626	2314	3901	219	-274	-810	-7043
Philippines	IMP	G	36887	54077	57708	60491	45856	58533	64097	65845	65048	67085
Philippines	EXP	G	37767	47427	50518	49462	38421	51541	48316	52071	53885	61812
	BAL		880	-6651	-7190	-11030	-7436	-6992	-15781	-13773	-11163	-5273
Singapore	IMP	G	134546	238711	263155	319781	245785	310791	365770	379723	373016	366247
Singapour	EXP	G	137806	271809	299270	338176	269832	351867	409503	408393	410250	409769
	BAL		3259	33098	36115	18396	24048	41076	43733	28670	37234	43522
Thailand	IMP	S	61923	130606	141294	179168	134734	185121	229137	251464	249652	228200
Thaïlande	EXP	S	68963	130563	153858	175897	151910	193366	220221	227883	224863	225239
	BAL		7039	-43	12563	-3270	17176	8245	-8916	-23581	-24789	-2961
Timor-Leste	IMP	S	.	88	199	258	283	298	337	670	844	...
Timor-Leste	EXP	S	.	61	19	49	35	42	53	77	51	...
	BAL		.	-27	-180	-209	-248	-256	-283	-593	-793	...
Viet Nam	IMP	G	15638	44410	60697	80714	69949	83779	104041	115101	131260	148770
Viet Nam	EXP	G	14447	39606	48313	62685	57096	71658	94518	115458	132478	149565
	BAL		-1191	-4804	-12384	-18029	-12853	-12121	-9523	357	1218	795
Western Asia	IMP		**198063**	**479796**	**606001**	757727	609870	710884	864244	915190	972312	**995394**
Asie Occidentale	EXP		**261901**	**655780**	**742941**	1054195	740948	925948	1255259	1351546	1402153	**1454939**
	BAL		**63838**	**175984**	**136939**	296468	131078	215064	391015	436356	429842	**459544**
Bahrain	IMP	G	4633	10515	11488	10800	7300	9800	12730	14900	13000	...
Bahreïn	EXP	G	6194	12200	13634	17316	11874	15400	19650	20500	17500	...
	BAL		1561	1685	2146	6516	4574	5600	6920	5600	4500	...

Total merchandise trade by regions and countries or areas (Table A)
Imports CIF, exports FOB and balance: million U.S. dollars
Commerce total de marchandises par régions et pays ou zones (Tableau A)
Importations CIF, exportations FOB, et balance : en millions de dollars E.-U.

Country or Area - Pays ou Zone	IMP EXP BAL	G/S	2000	2006	2007	2008	2009	2010	2011	2012	2013	2014
Cyprus	IMP	G	3846	6951	8687	10873	7937	8647	8723	7381	6388	6754
Chypre	EXP	G	951	1153	1254	1755	1352	1507	1960	1829	2075	1916
	BAL		-2895	-5798	-7433	-9118	-6585	-7139	-6763	-5552	-4313	-4838
Iraq	IMP		...	...	...	33000	37000	43915	49000	57000	61000	...
Iraq	EXP		...	...	...	61273	41929	52483	83300	94400	89550	...
	BAL		...	...	...	28273	4929	8567	34300	37400	28550	...
Israel[18]	IMP	S	31404	50334	59039	67656	49278	61209	75830	75392	74861	...
Israël[18]	EXP	S	31404	46789	54065	60825	47934	58392	67648	63191	66607	68553
	BAL		0	-3544	-4973	-6831	-1344	-2817	-8182	-12201	-8254	...
Jordan	IMP	G	4597	11447	13511	16764	14534	15085	18463	20691	21701	22952
Jordanie	EXP	G	1899	5175	5725	7788	6531	7023	7964	7926	7896	8376
	BAL		-2698	-6272	-7786	-8976	-8002	-8062	-10499	-12765	-13804	-14576
Kuwait	IMP	S	7157	17243	21353	24840	19891	22691	25144	27259	29313	...
Koweït	EXP	S	19434	55081	61483	87538	54012	66619	102078	118912	115105	...
	BAL		12278	37838	40130	62699	34121	43927	76934	91653	85792	...
Lebanon	IMP	G	6230	9647	12251	16754	16574	18460	20165	21287	21236	...
Liban	EXP	G	715	2814	3574	4454	4187	5021	4267	4485	4059	...
	BAL		-5515	-6833	-8677	-12300	-12387	-13439	-15898	-16802	-17176	...
Oman	IMP	G	5040	10915	15978	22925	17865	19775	23620	29447	34333	...
Oman	EXP	G	11319	21585	24136	37719	28053	36601	47092	53174	56429	...
	BAL		6279	10670	8158	14795	10188	16827	23472	23727	22096	...
Qatar	IMP	S	3252	16441	23430	27900	24922	23240	22333	25223	27038	...
Qatar	EXP	S	11594	34052	44456	67307	48007	74800	114448	132985	136855	...
	BAL		8342	17611	21027	39407	23085	51560	92115	107761	109817	...
Saudi Arabia	IMP	S	30197	69800	90215	115133	95544	106864	131587	155592	163902	...
Arabie saoudite	EXP	S	77480	211306	233300	313427	192296	251147	364699	388400	375934	...
	BAL		47283	141506	143086	198294	96752	144283	233112	232808	212032	...
State of Palestine	IMP	S	2383	2759	3284	3466	3601	3959	4374	4697	4580	5055
État de Palestine	EXP	S	401	367	513	558	518	576	746	782	839	865
	BAL		-1982	-2392	-2771	-2908	-3082	-3383	-3628	-3915	-3740	-4190
Syrian Arab Rep.	IMP	S	4055	11488	14655	18105	15291	16950	16400	7800	5800	...
République arabe syrienne	EXP	S	4674	10919	11546	15410	10855	14000	10700	4000	3000	...
	BAL		620	-569	-3109	-2695	-4436	-2950	-5700	-3800	-2800	...
Turkey	IMP	S	54503	139576	170063	201964	140928	185544	240842	236545	251661	242183
Turquie	EXP	S	27775	85535	107272	132027	102143	113883	134907	152462	151803	157642
	BAL		-26728	-54041	-62791	-69937	-38785	-71661	-105935	-84083	-99858	-84541
United Arab Emirates	IMP	G	35009	100057	132500	177000	150000	165000	205000	220000	245000	...
Emirats arabes unis	EXP	G	49835	142505	154000	239213	185000	220000	285000	300000	365000	...
	BAL		14827	42448	21500	62213	35000	55000	80000	80000	120000	...
Yemen	IMP	S	2327	6081	8513	10548	9206	9746	10034	11975	12500	...
Yémen	EXP	S	3795	6653	6299	7584	6256	8497	10801	8500	9500	...
	BAL		1469	572	-2215	-2964	-2949	-1249	766	-3475	-3000	...
Oceania	IMP		**6924**	**12611**	**14697**	**16917**	**14503**	**16731**	**19199**	**19607**	**21851**	**23412**
Océanie	EXP		**5111**	**8542**	**10001**	**10622**	**8494**	**10465**	**12316**	**11646**	**10997**	**11087**
	BAL		**-1813**	**-4068**	**-4697**	**-6295**	**-6009**	**-6266**	**-6883**	**-7962**	**-10854**	**-12325**
American Samoa[19]	IMP	S	506	579	650	680	600	550	700	690	...	...
Samoa américaines[19]	EXP	S	346	439	450	570	470	300	280	300	...	...
	BAL		-160	-141	-200	-110	-130	-250	-420	-390	...	...

Total merchandise trade by regions and countries or areas (Table A)
Imports CIF, exports FOB and balance: million U.S. dollars
Commerce total de marchandises par régions et pays ou zones (Tableau A)
Importations CIF, exportations FOB, et balance : en millions de dollars E.-U.

Country or Area - Pays ou Zone	IMP EXP BAL	G/S	2000	2006	2007	2008	2009	2010	2011	2012	2013	2014
Cook Islands Iles Cook	IMP EXP BAL	G G	50 9 -41	100 3 -96	107 5 -102	111 4 -107	72 3 -69	81 5 -76	84 3 -81	90 5 -85	150 6 -145	... ...
Fiji Fidji	IMP EXP BAL	G G	857 539 -318	1804 693 -1111	1801 755 -1046	2265 922 -1343	1441 631 -811	1817 842 -975	2182 1070 -1112	2254 1224 -1030	2822 1107 -1715	3257 1375 -1882
French Polynesia Polynésie française	IMP EXP BAL	S S	905 200 -705	1656 235 -1420	1863 197 -1667	2187 195 -1991	1732 148 -1584	1740 153 -1587	1796 168 -1628	1706 139 -1567	1801 152 -1649	1760 170 -1590
Guam Guam	IMP EXP BAL	G G	... ...	501 53 -448	688 91 -596	649 105 -544	635 51 -584	698 46 -652	708 55 -653	693 46 -647	687 45 -642	... 41 ...
Kiribati Kiribati	IMP EXP BAL	G G	39 4 -36	62 6 -56	70 10 -60	75 8 -68	67 6 -61	73 4 -69	92 9 -83	100 6 -94	112 8 -105	... ...
Marshall Islands Iles Marshall	IMP EXP BAL	G G	55 9 -46	... ...	... ...	... ...	... ...	... ...	... ...	... ...	... ...	... ...
Micronesia[3] Micronésie[3]	IMP EXP BAL	S S	... ...	138 9 -129	146 16 -130	160 21 -139	171 18 -153	168 23 -145	188 43 -145	194 52 -142	188 35 -153	... ...
New Caledonia Nouvelle-Calédonie	IMP EXP BAL	S S	922 606 -317	2117 1349 -768	2809 2104 -705	3233 1300 -1933	2574 993 -1581	3312 1493 -1820	3698 1661 -2037	3245 1321 -1923	3240 1196 -2044	... ...
Niue Nioué	IMP EXP BAL	G G	2 0 -2	4 1 -2	7 3 -4	8 0 -8	6	... ...	... ...	... ...	... ...	... ...
Palau Palaos	IMP EXP BAL	S S	123	... ...	108	130	94	103	125	136	145	162 ... ...
Papua New Guinea Papouasie-Nouvelle-Guinée	IMP EXP BAL	G G	1151 2068 917	2287 4167 1880	2945 4684 1738	3547 5714 2167	3198 4404 1206	3950 5742 1792	4887 6908 2021	5500 6328 828	... 5951 ...	... ...
Samoa Samoa	IMP EXP BAL	S S	90 14 -76	219 11 -208	227 15 -212	249 11 -238	204 12 -193	278 13 -264	319 17 -302	308 34 -274	326 24 -302	... ...
Solomon Islands Iles Salomon	IMP EXP BAL	S S	92 69 -23	217 121 -95	287 165 -123	329 210 -119	270 163 -107	300 221 -79	474 411 -64	500 470 -30	530 440 -90	... ...
Tonga Tonga	IMP EXP BAL	G G	69 9 -60	116 10 -107	143 9 -134	168 10 -158	145 8 -137	159 8 -151	193 17 -176	199 17 -182	198 22 -176	... ...
Tuvalu Tuvalu	IMP EXP BAL	G G	5 0 -5	13 0 -13	16 0 -16	... ...	... ...	... ...	... ...	... ...	... ...	... ...
Vanuatu Vanuatu	IMP EXP BAL	G G	87 26 -61	217 49 -168	231 50 -180	314 57 -257	294 57 -237	285 49 -237	305 67 -238	296 55 -241	311 39 -273	311 63 -248

Total merchandise trade by regions and countries or areas (Table A)
Imports CIF, exports FOB and balance: million U.S. dollars
Commerce total de marchandises par régions et pays ou zones (Tableau A)
Importations CIF, exportations FOB, et balance : en millions de dollars E.-U.

Country or Area - Pays ou Zone	IMP EXP BAL	G/S	2000	2006	2007	2008	2009	2010	2011	2012	2013	2014
Non Petrol. Export[20] Pétrole N. Compris[20]	IMP EXP BAL		... 102397 ...	... 68523 ...	... 63510 ...	... 58864 ...	... 54558 ...	... 50567 ...	... 46868 ...	... 43440 ...	... 40262 ...	... 37317 ...
Additional Country Groupings												
ANCOM ANCOM	IMP EXP BAL		24496 26154 1658	55871 64821 8950	69767 75978 6212	91626 95671 4045	73539 78449 4911	95681 98869 3188	124001 133077 9076	133604 139249 5645	138080 136177 -1903	142988 130627 -12361
APEC CEAP	IMP EXP BAL		3308360 3110918 -197442	5776652 5442019 -334633	6427228 6209913 -217315	7360477 7051036 -309441	5694102 5633051 -61051	7348142 7230203 -117939	8777401 8468346 -309055	9099053 8694620 -404433	9196121 8861947 -334174	9270822 9076046 -194776
ASEAN ANASE	IMP EXP BAL		379470 429596 50126	689565 770359 80794	773840 865127 91287	938781 988238 49457	727955 813260 85305	955146 1049842 94696	1150848 1232032 81184	1226287 1252188 25901	1242876 1271460 28584	1235847 1315890 80042
CACM MCAC	IMP EXP BAL		21293 13442 -7850	37999 18475 -19524	43836 21156 -22680	51085 23921 -27164	38353 20040 -18313	45464 24279 -21186	54987 28604 -26383	57967 30701 -27266	57879 30340 -27539	57914 30648 -27265
CARICOM CARICOM	IMP EXP BAL		13681 8146 -5535	22432 19953 -2479	25302 19543 -5759	30362 25844 -4518	23710 14895 -8815	24987 16573 -8414	31270 22622 -8648	31532 21652 -9880	30606 20763 -9842	29467 19834 -9632
COMESA COMESA	IMP EXP BAL		34753 27001 -7753	69425 79805 10380	82897 96002 13105	119508 128432 8924	112081 94087 -17994	127911 117015 -10897	139492 97493 -41999	169160 132327 -36833	174900 120681 -54219	192111 107443 -84669
ECOWAS CEDEAO	IMP EXP BAL		20021 29437 9416	51861 76625 24764	68256 86193 17937	81046 106386 25339	66441 80893 14452	81958 111531 29574	110633 151216 40583	87856 150610 62754	101140 153912 52772	118406 157449 39044
EMCCA CEMAC	IMP EXP BAL		4010 8414 4404	10531 26836 16305	13392 29598 16206	17263 42636 25373	17589 26767 9177	19249 34252 15002	24354 44112 19758	24794 42684 17890	26630 42135 15504	28063 39163 11099
LAIA ALAI	IMP EXP BAL		329913 331178 1265	539871 629024 89153	646990 715662 68672	794758 835258 40500	596085 642519 46433	767217 817386 50169	941855 1018486 76631	966960 1029157 62197	1008667 1034382 25715	1006964 1012286 5322
LDCs PMA	IMP EXP BAL		41663 33172 -8491	101493 99460 -2033	116771 125396 8625	151557 174145 22588	151657 123407 -28250	166483 151954 -14529	199349 196227 -3122	218203 202086 -16117	237514 211286 -26228	262909 208388 -54521
MERCOSUR MERCOSUR	IMP EXP BAL		105669 117368 11699	174459 251009 76549	229034 294802 65768	307369 376379 69010	226523 277160 50637	292060 345606 53546	372551 448894 76343	362527 431021 68495	388174 430181 42007	371765 397051 25286
NAFTA ALENA	IMP EXP BAL		1672611 1224927 -447684	2524469 1664726 -859743	2684365 1840548 -843816	2888878 2035686 -853191	2160932 1599725 -561207	2662781 1964109 -698672	3067992 2281991 -786001	3169689 2371432 -798257	3172187 2417554 -754633	3276325 2491048 -785277
OECD OCDE	IMP EXP BAL		4910594 4535681 -374913	8560007 7683400 -876606	9646085 8783053 -863032	10825430 9793339 -1032091	8134061 7636170 -497891	9592888 8954827 -638062	11276863 10419372 -857491	11053598 10222726 -830872	11081848 10369652 -712196	11235691 10538588 -697104
OPEC OPEP	IMP EXP BAL		137962 298292 160330	371983 793159 421176	474666 896334 421669	609344 1290678 681334	539635 850867 311232	593064 1083764 490700	694168 1467159 772991	741770 1567202 825431	798007 1564410 766402	865433 1594195 728763

Total merchandise trade by regions and countries or areas (Table A)
Imports CIF, exports FOB and balance: million U.S. dollars
Commerce total de marchandises par régions et pays ou zones (Tableau A)
Importations CIF, exportations FOB, et balance : en millions de dollars E.-U.

Country or Area - Pays ou Zone	IMP EXP BAL	G/S	2000	2006	2007	2008	2009	2010	2011	2012	2013	2014
EU28	IMP		2441670	4695447	5458473	6126585	4602759	5190907	6070956	5705716	5789483	**5872893**
UE28	EXP		2394656	4523977	5253360	5832014	4519062	5064143	5930500	5682054	5872733	**5991804**
	BAL		-47013	-171470	-205113	-294571	-83697	-126764	-140456	-23662	83250	**118911**
Extra-EU28[21,22]	IMP		913310	1714282	1985545	2336609	1721874	2029009	2405295	2311903	2234492	2233121
Extra-UE28[21,22]	EXP		781270	1448509	1694259	1928718	1527320	1791433	2161865	2162563	2305992	2259968
	BAL		-132040	-265774	-291287	-407891	-194554	-237576	-243430	-149340	71500	26847
Memorandum Items												
World excluding intra-EU28 trade	IMP		**4989344**	**9214798**	**10559626**	**12431498**	**9607728**	**11990215**	**14408656**	**14728081**	**14850305**	**14970133**
Monde excl. le intra-UE28 com.	EXP		**4743173**	**8898231**	**10234480**	**12109865**	**9415907**	**11826668**	**14256701**	**14556749**	**14893995**	**15077834**
	BAL		**-246171**	**-316567**	**-325146**	**-321633**	**-191821**	**-163546**	**-151955**	**-171332**	**43690**	**107701**
World excluding intra-EU28 trade as percent of World	IMP		77	76	75	77	77	79	80	81	81	80
Monde excl. le intra-UE28 com.comme pour cent du Monde	EXP		75	74	74	76	76	78	79	81	81	80

Total merchandise trade by regions and countries or areas (Table A)
Imports CIF, exports FOB and balance: million U.S. dollars

Commerce total de marchandises par régions et pays ou zones (Tableau A)
Importations CIF, exportations FOB, et balance: en millions de dollars E.-U.

General notes:

For further information on Sources, Method of Estimation, Currency Conversion, Period, Country Nomenclature and Country Grouping of this table, as well as for a brief table description, please see the Introduction.

1. This classification is intended for statistical convenience and does not, necessarily, express a judgement about the stage reached by a particular country in the development process.
2. Developed Economies of America, Europe, and the Asia-Pacific region.
3. Imports FOB.
4. Including the trade of the U.S. Virgin Islands and Puerto Rico but excluding shipments of merchandise between the United States and its other possessions (Guam and American Samoa). Data include imports and exports of non-monetary gold.
5. Beginning 2006, data for Serbia and Montenegro is reported separately.
6. Prior to 2008, special trade.
7. Imports exclude petroleum imported without stated value. Exports cover domestic exports.
8. Year ending 31 March of the following year.
9. Exports include gold.
10. Including South Sudan.
11. Trade statistics exclude certain oil and chemical products.
12. Export and import values exclude trade in the processing zone.
13. The Netherlands Antilles was dissolved on October 10, 2010. Beginning 2011, data are reported separately for Curaçao, Sint Maarten (Dutch part), Bonaire, Saint Eustatius and Saba.
14. Trade data include maquiladoras and exclude goods from customs-bonded warehouses. Total exports include revaluation and exports of silver.
15. Excluding military goods, fissionable materials, bunkers, ships, and aircraft.
16. Data include oil and gas.The value of oil exports and total exports are rough estimates based on information published in various petroleum industry journals.
17. Year ending 20 March of the year stated.
18. Imports and exports net of returned goods. The figures also exclude Judea and Samaria and the Gaza area.
19. Year ending 30 September of the years stated.
20. Data refer to total exports less petroleum exports of Asia Middle East countries where petroleum, in this case, is the sum of SITC groups 333, 334 and 335.
21. Excluding intra-EU trade.
22. In the year 2000, the trade values refer to extra-EU27.

Remarque générale:

Pour plus d'information en ce qui concerne les sources, la méthode d'estimation, taux d'exchange, période, nomenclature des pays et groupement de pays, ainsi que pour une brève description de ce tableau, veuillez voir l'introduction.

1. Cette classification est utilisée pour plus de commodité dans la présentation des statistiques et n'implique pas nécessairement un jugement quant au stade de développement auquel est parvenu un pays donné.
2. Économies développées de l'Amérique, de l'Europe, et de la région Asie-Pacifique.
3. Importations FOB.
4. Y compris le commerce des Iles Vierges américaines et de Porto Rico mais non compris les échanges de marchandise, entre les Etats-Unis et leurs autres possessions (Guam et Samoa américaines). Les données comprennent les importations et exportations d'or non-monétaire.
5. Depuis début 2006, les données relatives à la Serbie et au Monténégro sont déclarées séparément.
6. Avant 2008, commerce special.
7. Non compris le pétrole brute dont la valeur des importations ne sont pas stipulée. Les exportations sont les exportations d'intérieur.
8. Année finissant le 31 mars de l'année suivante.
9. Les exportations comprennent l'or.
10. Y compris Soudan du Sud.
11. Les statistiques commerciales font exclusion de certains produits pétroliers et chimiques.
12. Les valeurs à l'exportation et à l'importation excluent le commerce de la zone de transformation.
13. Les Antilles néerlandaises ont été dissoutes le 10 Octobre 2010. A partir de 2011, les données sont présentées séparément pour Curaçao, Saint-Martin (partie néerlandaise), Bonaire, Saint-Eustache et Saba.
14. Les statistiques du commerce extérieur comprennent maquiladoras et ne comprennent pas les marchandises provenant des entrepôts en douane. Les exportations comprennent la réévaluation et les données sur les exportations d'argent.
15. À l'exclusion des marchandises militaires, des matières fissibles, des soutes, des bateaux, et de l'avion.
16. Les données comprennent le pétrole et le gaz. La valeur des exportations de pétrole et des exportations totales sont des évaluations grossières basées sur l'information publiée à divers journaux d'industrie de pétrole.
17. Année finissant le 20 mars de l'année indiquée.
18. Importations et exportations nets, ne comprennant pas les marchandises retournées. Sont également exclues les données de la Judée et de Samaria et ainsi que la zone de Gaza.
19. Année finissant le 30 septembre de l'année indiquée.
20. Les données se rapportent aux exportations totales moins les exportations pétrolières de Moyen-Orient d'Asie. Dans ce cas, le pétrole est la somme des groupes CTCI 333, 334 et 335.
21. Non compris le commerce d'intra-UE.
22. En l'année 2000, les valeurs du commerce se réfèrent à extra-UE27.

World merchandise exports by provenance and destination (Table D)

In million U.S. dollars f.o.b.

| Exports from | Year | World 1/ Monde 1/ | Developed economies 2/ Économies développées 2/ |||||| Commonwealth of Independent States Communauté d'Etats Indépendants ||
| | | | Asia-Pacific Asie-Pacifique || Europe || North America Amérique du Nord || | |
			Total	Total Japan/Japon	Total	Germany/Allemagne	Total	U.S.A./É.-U.	Total	Europe
					Total trade (SITC, Rev. 3, 0-9)						
World 1/	2000	6352789	4389700	413826 337473	2563283	476749	1412591	1176816	77233	65071
	2011	18088851	9854507	927548 682192	6385260	1144259	2541699	2032211	542241	447995
	2012	18178451	9668963	962706 705151	6064631	1089111	2641626	2111006	562266	456706
	2013	18671463	9827498	937876 688637	6224906	1123004	2664716	2119534	574451	457963
	2014	18857242	10048805	1021464 768573	6279611	1145284	2747730	2206610	523196	408964
Developed Economies - Asia-Pacific 2/	2000	556339	283778	30765 14422	93424	21063	159589	150831	1004	824
	2011	1130240	373487	91009 54805	130828	26071	151650	140669	15265	13870
	2012	1092168	364316	88355 52281	108421	23072	167539	155029	15874	14309
	2013	1006696	328645	80520 47093	91820	21052	156305	146044	14213	12576
	2014	965926	320045	76586 45578	90057	20636	153401	143807	12085	10376
Japan	2000	479276	243818	9835 .	83786	19997	150197	142480	793	624
	2011	823184	262233	19739 .	105874	23503	136621	127675	13754	12530
	2012	798620	259334	20385 .	86581	20796	152368	142085	14587	13203
	2013	715097	238107	19161 .	75694	18959	143252	134540	13036	11583
	2014	683846	229219	16538 .	74729	18857	137952	129951	11122	9583
Developed Economies - Europe 2/	2000	2526900	2122782	63491 46070	1802303	345338	256987	232390	31182	28101
	2011	6244489	4766004	128469 77533	4186428	817587	451107	401681	214870	195206
	2012	5995519	4500640	130648 79987	3908545	785960	461447	415027	223522	203158
	2013	6292284	4712895	130100 79457	4110044	818568	472750	422441	231144	208055
	2014	6320795	4768737	126485 78860	4145597	833688	496654	449087	197356	175686
France	2000	295345	239365	6445 4983	204528	44461	28392	25937	2392	1952
	2011	585724	425863	14979 9080	374299	97949	36585	32552	13009	11925
	2012	558461	398133	13801 9507	346411	92317	37922	34123	14719	13361
	2013	567988	406238	13292 9026	353231	93525	39714	35765	13666	11799
	2014	566656	408722	13132 9056	355259	93804	40331	36382	12084	10293
Germany	2000	549607	458641	15684 12137	382583	.	60374	56393	8923	8069
	2011	1482202	1085941	34224 21400	938202	.	113515	103075	66060	60460
	2012	1416184	1019921	35520 22186	860790	.	123611	112086	66735	61246
	2013	1458647	1051362	35870 22938	884132	.	131360	117840	66630	60596
	2014	1511137	1102788	34637 22790	928524	.	139628	127969	53260	47918
Developed Economies - North America 2/	2000	1057790	699129	86693 71335	193928	31336	418508	241623	3504	2715
	2011	1930848	1068634	110248 76937	345170	52639	613216	331765	14739	12250
	2012	2000392	1090297	117136 80393	342418	51756	630743	338266	17383	14551
	2013	2035439	1088720	106709 75468	334877	50176	647134	346198	17975	14788
	2014	2096502	1130392	109465 76661	344644	51812	676284	363228	17093	13467
United States	2000	780332	436300	79685 65252	179776	29242	176839	.	3325	2563
	2011	1479730	678910	97169 66160	300433	48779	281308	.	12823	10583
	2012	1545565	696763	104354 70043	300096	48355	292313	.	15318	12745
	2013	1578001	693652	94396 65143	298526	46945	300731	.	16135	13229
	2014	1622657	716541	97801 66963	306007	49110	312733	.	15580	12174
South-Eastern Europe	2000	19514	13492	50 37	12585	2634	857	764	813	674
	2011	115518	76671	354 276	74345	18610	1972	1627	6855	5886
	2012	107446	69938	405 314	67472	16854	2062	1761	6668	5617
	2013	122785	80838	451 359	78034	20166	2353	2072	8106	7069
	2014	127811	85738	451 334	82877	21797	2411	2120	7500	6479
Commonwealth of Independent States	2000	143026	80597	2952 2936	70384	10998	7261	5771	28974	24052
	2011	762951	403236	18890 18730	360628	28930	23718	20192	162832	128402
	2012	777877	415189	21854 21547	373118	30620	20217	16448	158836	118701
	2013	760955	412689	25833 25319	369698	28376	17158	13793	151087	107134
	2014	716695	389480	27791 27332	348332	25761	13357	11939	135364	93312
Russian Federation 4/	2000	103093	65496	2771 2764	57875	9232	4850	4648	13824	10807
	2011	512936	297617	17484 17413	264274	22766	15859	15288	89460	67139
	2012	522256	310593	19904 19789	277500	24039	13188	12843	85377	60031
	2013	525658	318603	24343 23939	282689	22886	11572	11101	82672	53336
	2014	494867	305273	26574 26192	267916	21466	10783	10337	72062	44381

For general note and footnotes see end of table

Les exportations de marchandises du monde par provenance et destination (Tableau D)

En millions de dollars E.-U. f.o.b.

← Exportations vers

South-Eastern Europe Europe du Sud-Est	Northern Africa Afrique septentrionale	Sub-Saharan Africa Afrique subsaharienne	Latin America and the Caribbean Amérique latine et Caraïbes	Eastern Asia Asie orientale	Southern Asia Asie méridionale	South-eastern Asia Asie du Sud-Est	Western Asia Asie occidentale	Oceania Océanie	Other 3/ Autres 3/	Année	Exportations en provence de ↓
\multicolumn{11}{c}{**Commerce total (CTCI, Rev. 3, 0-9)**}	
27384	54352	74643	363601	700278	81709	355975	191771	6355	29786	2000	Monde 1/
146394	200104	380794	1105929	3132449	561669	1091860	784857	33914	254132	2011	
140402	217174	397665	1144108	3273678	554113	1180950	819836	31523	187775	2012	
143854	222787	419622	1127010	3449517	552673	1236857	891574	31910	193711	2013	
155894	224676	442829	1115639	3352907	595086	1325723	943937	32560	95991	2014	
153	1694	4909	22054	140231	6988	78409	13637	2260	1223	2000	Economies développées - Asie-Pacifique 2/
613	3728	14673	47317	440408	35367	154294	34944	7312	2832	2011	
631	4358	13622	45255	408941	30358	159487	38983	7788	2555	2012	
546	3663	12174	37487	401183	23108	138226	37762	6144	3545	2013	
669	3880	11076	34805	372165	22669	134838	40206	6015	7474	2014	
108	1196	3721	20779	124536	4751	68494	10619	460	0	2000	Japon
565	2365	10811	42231	322669	16698	123072	26196	2589	...	2011	
470	3013	9884	41088	293380	14536	129394	30310	2624	...	2012	
411	2418	8968	34412	265544	11749	110974	27839	1638	...	2013	
464	2319	8049	31690	252818	12077	103951	30187	1950	0	2014	
19337	29952	31465	57255	78361	22286	40579	83738	1260	8705	2000	Economies développées - Europe 2/
94329	83993	108196	155320	328722	87040	104578	261254	3337	36847	2011	
90403	92064	105101	164774	325649	73612	113692	259173	3364	43525	2012	
97690	98263	109933	166539	348062	69628	118035	289065	3789	47241	2013	
104150	98986	107839	157375	372165	68977	114197	284289	4221	42503	2014	
1282	9180	7741	7237	9366	2416	4752	10136	822	658	2000	France
5569	21936	17597	15348	33539	7316	14914	27655	1853	1127	2011	
5392	20927	15593	16084	34443	6210	18081	25935	1617	1325	2012	
5975	20739	16237	17563	33997	5160	19032	26597	2077	706	2013	
6199	20113	16373	15468	36237	5427	17704	25903	1779	646	2014	
4185	4001	5607	13858	21330	4087	9799	17506	132	1537	2000	Allemagne
19915	10320	18784	40939	124083	22059	27631	63769	309	2393	2011	
19443	10630	17759	42389	118615	19107	29208	63993	450	7936	2012	
20650	11480	18279	43497	124689	17147	29548	69817	362	5187	2013	
23382	12240	18189	41272	137546	17572	29960	69364	917	4645	2014	
562	5660	6348	174597	88921	5586	48918	23864	393	308	2000	Economies développées - Amérique du Nord 2/
1799	12935	23295	378973	237370	32734	81431	77732	976	231	2011	
1688	11779	24927	412434	242858	30049	80521	87315	1128	12	2012	
1645	12470	26462	421349	261875	30117	84298	89728	771	28	2013	
1892	13907	28140	436187	263515	29793	84288	90469	803	22	2014	
509	5028	5928	170376	83248	4635	47368	22928	378	307	2000	Etats-Unis
1437	11509	21102	364814	210382	28320	76434	72895	880	225	2011	
1334	10247	22610	398448	215745	26403	75521	82143	1034	...	2012	
1407	10977	24052	408196	232281	26335	78980	85296	690	...	2013	
1636	12551	25390	423419	236866	25617	78944	85389	723	0	2014	
2212	358	156	160	218	139	76	1700	1	188	2000	Europe du Sud-Est
14752	1709	1155	664	1936	1101	354	9963	21	338	2011	
13023	2271	1207	839	2451	891	392	9253	87	425	2012	
13251	3102	1182	1319	2791	865	921	10087	46	277	2013	
13750	3393	1078	1129	2525	902	1247	10074	15	460	2014	
2633	1375	554	5982	9118	2984	1713	9071	4	19	2000	Communauté d'Etats Indépendants
16856	8904	3213	11173	78062	18107	11488	40177	13	8892	2011	
17620	12784	3239	9781	83680	19203	11650	44411	100	1385	2012	
12764	9815	3308	10212	87169	16342	15434	41025	19	1089	2013	
15145	10422	2979	9281	80887	17403	14406	40032	19	1276	2014	
1822	746	344	4307	6980	1896	1120	6556	2	0	2000	Fédération de Russie 4/
10387	6144	1764	7508	53245	8904	7664	22148	10	8085	2011	
11225	7873	1612	6843	56993	10681	7130	23654	90	184	2012	
7800	5406	1668	8168	59974	9343	8415	23542	16	50	2013	
7922	4815	1578	7600	56830	8822	7889	22014	15	48	2014	

Voir la fin du tableau pour la remarque générale et les notes.

World merchandise exports by provenance and destination (Table D)

In million U.S. dollars f.o.b.

Exports from	Year	World 1/ Monde 1/	Developed economies 2/ Économies développées 2/ Total	Asia-Pacific Asie-Pacifique Total	Japan Japon	Europe Total	Germany Allemagne	North America Amérique du Nord Total	U.S.A. É.-U.	Commonwealth of Independent States Communauté d'États Indépendants Total	Europe
					Total trade (SITC, Rev. 3, 0-9) [cont.]						
Northern Africa	2000	50201	41077	490	424	35543	3933	5043	4216	101	81
	2011	162531	114679	1086	858	90230	3986	23363	18660	874	816
	2012	198662	145341	2337	2157	121784	4435	21220	15532	840	656
	2013	177793	127397	3188	2255	109917	9102	14292	10524	847	697
	2014	163037	114682	2149	2037	102627	6756	9906	7730	883	840
Sub-Saharan Africa	2000	94703	59330	2642	2069	34067	3114	22621	21647	239	191
	2011	455500	211208	18289	11178	119859	10942	73060	65541	1114	955
	2012	457628	205147	18139	12621	129162	9271	57846	51425	1163	971
	2013	402964	172488	17238	12202	118222	8919	37028	32387	1218	1064
	2014	413901	179786	16511	10524	127750	9688	35525	30438	1236	1109
South Africa	2000	26298	15850	1873	1362	10968	1902	3009	2788	79	33
	2011	107946	41837	8565	7625	24445	5738	8828	8205	379	357
	2012	98872	35097	6721	5736	20020	4069	8356	7833	508	460
	2013	95112	33749	6527	5613	19963	3842	7259	6889	527	460
	2014	90612	34098	5829	4869	20962	4235	7307	6582	499	461
Latin America and the Caribbean	2000	353078	265627	8570	7727	43901	6927	213157	206833	1330	1280
	2011	1093017	608314	30122	26154	151277	22306	426916	384389	9192	8493
	2012	1096865	623765	28850	24686	143382	19823	451534	407404	9013	8249
	2013	1094458	627258	27409	23530	135818	17580	464031	409976	9298	8309
	2014	1077729	633468	25594	21618	129375	17094	478499	426727	9875	8964
Brazil	2000	55119	33697	2852	2481	16230	2520	14614	14048	522	487
	2011	256039	97906	10377	9487	57434	9310	30095	26951	5176	4670
	2012	242580	93433	8556	7991	52992	7657	31885	28801	4351	3851
	2013	242178	88573	8496	7972	50975	6905	29102	26395	4162	3504
	2014	225098	83533	7227	6738	45022	6965	31284	28932	4538	4106
Eastern Asia	2000	776206	410958	101770	90091	125356	27229	183831	173168	4994	3848
	2011	3222721	1275588	280429	223552	496705	104412	498454	460408	85963	62088
	2012	3396494	1280550	290196	227960	462088	92424	528266	487973	96059	69061
	2013	3613890	1296681	283874	221402	464467	90394	548340	506633	104292	74913
	2014	3760876	1367289	286465	221761	499668	95967	581156	538593	106777	76577
China	2000	249203	142806	45499	41654	41976	9278	55331	52156	3183	2411
	2011	1898388	896344	185915	148269	359795	76400	350633	325011	67227	46853
	2012	2048782	911389	193226	151627	337391	69213	380772	352438	75653	52425
	2013	2209007	931031	191818	150133	340740	67343	398473	369064	83517	58425
	2014	2342343	992282	193296	149410	371686	72703	427300	397105	85740	60007
Southern Asia	2000	91623	54957	8456	7729	28990	3824	17511	16422	1896	1243
	2011	493516	163166	10217	7130	105564	14307	47385	44090	6004	3799
	2012	446154	155731	11488	7797	91925	12865	52318	48842	5733	3805
	2013	482859	170896	12304	8722	99507	14337	59084	55232	5990	4081
	2014	477411	160157	19274	15435	83484	14397	57399	53843	6330	4438
South-Eastern Asia	2000	426829	218844	69522	57853	65445	12034	83877	80866	606	556
	2011	1244372	428339	175186	128239	140214	25283	112939	105932	6742	6128
	2012	1254007	430037	179372	127942	134431	24425	116234	109323	7018	6333
	2013	1272620	427994	173884	123500	130781	25872	123329	115706	7685	6827
	2014	1270307	429046	172754	123175	131945	26562	124347	116438	7571	6696
Western Asia	2000	251583	136106	36650	35897	56362	8137	43094	42034	2575	1496
	2011	1222641	359247	59413	55961	182242	18833	117592	56937	17780	10093
	2012	1345830	383093	70875	66599	180358	17283	131859	63646	20150	11289
	2013	1398000	375202	72702	68358	179954	18038	122546	58169	22587	12442
	2014	1455408	464413	154442	144230	191589	20739	118382	62257	21116	11013
Oceania	2000	4996	3024	1775	881	995	184	254	251	14	10
	2011	10505	5935	3837	838	1771	353	327	320	11	10
	2012	9411	4919	3052	869	1525	322	342	329	8	6
	2013	10720	5793	3663	971	1766	424	365	360	10	8
	2014	10844	5574	3497	1027	1667	387	410	402	9	7

For general note and footnotes see end of table

Les exportations de marchandises du monde par provenance et destination (Tableau D)

En millions de dollars E.-U. f.o.b.

⟵ Exportations vers

South-Eastern Europe Europe du Sud-Est	Northern Africa Afrique septentrionale	Sub-Saharan Africa Afrique subsaharienne	Latin America and the Caribbean Amérique latine et Caraïbes	Eastern Asia Asie orientale	Southern Asia Asie méridionale	South-eastern Asia Asie du Sud-Est	Western Asia Asie occidentale	Oceania Océanie	Other 3/ Autres 3/	Année	Exportations en provence de
	Commerce total (CTCI, Rev. 3, 0-9) [suite]
92	1179	336	2058	315	793	277	3122	1	849	2000	Afrique septentrionale
432	6111	4268	6381	6009	7523	1666	12436	43	2110	2011	
515	8241	4074	6649	10405	6170	1929	12312	4	2182	2012	
651	8826	3910	5321	7403	5564	2085	13844	3	1942	2013	
717	8529	3992	5288	6470	4368	3175	13052	3	1878	2014	
65	421	12379	2545	9488	5264	1955	2155	40	821	2000	Afrique subsaharienne
217	5843	78261	26161	77166	31626	9005	11406	1557	1934	2011	
708	2893	82946	21509	79472	35886	11089	13355	545	2916	2012	
479	1309	83705	13826	74289	29310	11740	12585	727	1289	2013	
625	1223	86283	16403	69742	30746	13096	12560	679	1522	2014	
30	91	4142	576	2657	531	739	1012	6	587	2000	Afrique du sud
87	531	26097	2195	19535	9185	3508	4014	22	555	2011	
93	558	27071	2052	17649	7307	4050	3558	58	871	2012	
84	535	26829	1700	19060	5062	3583	3452	32	500	2013	
68	401	27209	1370	14731	5048	2845	3740	48	556	2014	
324	1359	1679	61878	8864	2275	2795	2808	18	4122	2000	Amérique latine et Caraïbes
2206	10656	12023	240836	126045	14707	18839	19670	75	30454	2011	
2058	9972	12258	231257	139004	19536	26954	19288	61	3699	2012	
2154	9871	9676	218481	151645	18958	24347	19812	41	2917	2013	
1999	9646	8770	199619	141462	20809	27053	19189	42	5797	2014	
129	506	888	13886	2603	621	926	1338	4	...	2000	Brésil
839	5407	7177	58027	53526	6714	9796	11437	32	1	2011	
817	5555	7055	51023	50333	8798	10587	10598	24	4	2012	
765	5019	6474	54634	56915	6077	9214	10317	19	9	2013	
635	4811	5284	47042	49948	7438	11524	10328	17	0	2014	
688	3065	8358	25191	220123	13062	68294	18703	1258	1511	2000	Asie orientale
6811	21573	74969	173826	990123	129147	323549	125212	11639	4321	2011	
6059	27012	78182	183995	1082640	121928	371269	136349	8710	3741	2012	
6244	27541	86815	182689	1198808	127288	419757	147808	11886	4081	2013	
7187	30395	98544	186526	1183036	150990	451822	162636	11892	3783	2014	
356	1410	3602	7125	62121	4510	17341	6683	65	2	2000	Chine
5360	16636	56302	121082	394265	86063	170146	81714	3248	1	2011	
4890	20558	64612	134484	456791	82048	204337	90746	3275	...	2012	
4937	21765	70897	133232	525547	89284	244087	101780	2929	...	2013	
5722	24223	81627	135094	519029	110175	272116	113647	2688	...	2014	
47	2674	2178	1888	13195	3406	3781	7558	33	10	2000	Asie méridionale
658	8273	21866	14441	109388	27929	39572	73393	203	28623	2011	
623	8333	24619	16482	88400	27028	36421	74654	174	7956	2012	
737	8251	31292	16979	85281	32263	41302	77615	165	12089	2013	
1047	5539	31668	16852	86222	48365	33705	84876	150	2500	2014	
156	1009	4131	6782	75803	11386	98150	8580	996	386	2000	Asie du Sud-est
901	11096	21187	36669	317648	66603	310981	35115	7114	1977	2011	
764	5887	25092	36006	315083	60664	325434	38327	7720	1974	2012	
809	6004	25591	36946	324912	61163	330370	42000	7345	1802	2013	
807	5831	25668	36485	326411	60194	327366	41742	7541	1645	2014	
1112	5607	2113	2934	55140	7528	10745	16833	9	10881	2000	Asie occidentale
6819	25278	17632	14033	418248	109679	35167	83552	1229	133979	2011	
6308	31578	22328	14984	493837	128549	41411	86411	1437	115745	2012	
6881	33671	25486	15698	504696	137758	49499	110234	558	115730	2013	
7905	32923	36735	15528	446544	139595	119738	144793	690	25428	2014	
2	0	37	277	499	12	284	2	83	764	2000	Océanie
1	5	56	135	1324	106	937	5	396	1594	2011	
1	3	69	142	1258	239	701	5	405	1660	2012	
1	2	88	164	1403	310	843	9	415	1681	2013	
1	2	59	161	1763	274	793	18	489	1702	2014	

Voir la fin du tableau pour la remarque générale et les notes.

World merchandise exports by provenance and destination (Table D)

In million U.S. dollars f.o.b.

Exports from	Year	World 1/ Monde 1/	Developed economies 2/ Économies développées 2/							Commonwealth of Independent States Communauté d'Etats Indépendants	
			Total	Asia-Pacific Asie-Pacifique		Europe		North America Amérique du Nord		Total	Europe
				Total	Japan Japon	Total	Germany Allemagne	Total	U.S.A. É.-U.		
Food, beverages and tobacco (SITC, Rev. 3, 0 and 1)												
World 1/	2000	387083	271655	40631	36967	175536	32533	55488	44009	9849	8642
	2011	1164234	691247	74045	59808	487108	83598	130094	98722	51527	43199
	2012	1176549	680436	75063	60186	471174	80505	134199	101349	54740	44441
	2013	1256526	725059	73155	57055	510880	86948	141024	106943	59071	47525
	2014	1286588	742636	73195	56262	519933	88674	149508	114286	54320	42631
Developed Economies - Asia-Pacific 2/	2000	19827	9694	4285	3289	2443	277	2967	2615	52	44
	2011	51717	19094	9316	5678	4640	565	5138	4435	758	642
	2012	52653	18479	8972	5281	3981	473	5526	4821	697	558
	2013	54669	17947	8455	4667	4121	505	5371	4695	744	613
	2014	58672	20111	8425	4566	4315	458	7371	6574	551	412
Japan	2000	2088	612	72	.	107	14	432	395	9	9
	2011	4487	1028	95	.	205	32	728	682	38	38
	2012	4432	1035	106	.	186	35	744	695	31	31
	2013	4447	1025	104	.	199	42	722	671	37	36
	2014	4536	1099	106	.	219	32	774	716	45	41
Developed Economies - Europe 2/	2000	178437	151894	5172	4319	136289	26443	10433	8969	3784	3519
	2011	500649	409551	10249	7186	377380	67041	21921	18191	18487	17393
	2012	489975	397099	10285	6964	364244	65006	22571	18753	19187	17950
	2013	536512	434690	10770	7116	399814	71639	24107	20080	21084	19702
	2014	545265	440915	11465	7579	404065	71759	25386	21331	16926	15388
France	2000	31410	26548	981	902	23387	4572	2180	1853	351	335
	2011	70078	52767	1618	1342	47213	7856	3936	3170	990	919
	2012	66853	50771	1752	1423	44928	7288	4091	3318	1056	971
	2013	71698	54041	1798	1404	47933	7682	4310	3498	1128	1031
	2014	69131	52259	1813	1403	46031	7417	4415	3668	926	813
Germany	2000	21712	18446	290	250	17384	.	772	696	643	595
	2011	75568	63905	1165	813	60427	.	2313	1984	3271	2972
	2012	72829	60754	945	555	57581	.	2228	1881	3114	2811
	2013	79208	66229	906	514	62980	.	2342	1970	2940	2656
	2014	81132	67720	1123	700	64270	.	2327	1980	2231	1953
Developed Economies - North America 2/	2000	63390	38861	13367	12830	6717	914	18777	10624	986	886
	2011	141576	69809	17949	16066	11623	1468	40237	18957	2255	1994
	2012	141974	71758	17565	15474	11061	1426	43132	20389	2899	2518
	2013	151746	75004	16148	14033	12828	1714	46028	22061	2234	1886
	2014	160325	79693	17315	15024	14207	1836	48171	23467	1590	1319
United States	2000	47084	25762	11994	11534	5619	835	8149	.	955	858
	2011	107718	45934	15502	13890	9217	1312	21214	.	1614	1396
	2012	106859	46511	14993	13165	8880	1292	22638	.	2150	1817
	2013	114158	48162	13742	11873	10596	1589	23824	.	1693	1408
	2014	119864	50511	14881	12838	11175	1681	24455	.	1100	870
South-Eastern Europe	2000	1232	651	17	12	588	125	45	39	75	57
	2011	10359	5494	54	35	5300	624	139	115	451	403
	2012	10843	5568	89	66	5343	595	136	113	470	443
	2013	12941	6190	69	44	5943	639	177	147	575	532
	2014	13390	6434	73	40	6181	670	180	148	787	726
Commonwealth of Independent States	2000	3234	704	150	145	519	90	35	32	2090	1698
	2011	27366	3788	260	252	3412	313	116	98	13182	8407
	2012	36968	5699	501	486	5067	361	132	113	15985	9528
	2013	37264	5650	574	547	4937	449	139	120	18147	10822
	2014	36783	5654	310	284	5188	488	155	134	17099	9749
Russian Federation 4/	2000	1016	394	140	137	231	34	23	21	379	91
	2011	10082	1461	226	221	1183	109	53	44	2127	810
	2012	14132	1872	268	265	1550	141	54	45	4053	1353
	2013	13709	1774	224	218	1485	138	65	52	4732	1656
	2014	12945	1676	212	206	1403	130	61	49	4469	1564

For general note and footnotes see end of table

Les exportations de marchandises du monde par provenance et destination (Tableau D)

En millions de dollars E.-U. f.o.b.

← Exportations vers

South-Eastern Europe Europe du Sud-Est	Northern Africa Afrique septentrionale	Sub-Saharan Africa Afrique subsaharienne	Latin America and the Caribbean Amérique latine et Caraïbes	Eastern Asia Asie orientale	Southern Asia Asie méridionale	South-eastern Asia Asie du Sud-Est	Western Asia Asie occidentale	Oceania Océanie	Other 3/ Autres 3/	Année	Exportations en provence de ↓
	**Produits alimentaires, boisson et tabac (CTCI, Rev. 3, 0 et 1)**	
2492	7298	8256	22253	23731	5197	16016	17781	793	1762	2000	Monde 1/
13225	28414	43972	69730	89095	25267	71749	74685	2423	2901	2011	
13185	29426	46414	73945	97169	26498	75809	72433	2612	3882	2012	
13953	29065	48883	74900	107000	28452	83304	80800	2573	3465	2013	
14610	31029	48161	76440	114921	27320	88883	82687	2581	2999	2014	
5	393	392	490	3377	879	3002	991	454	98	2000	Economies développées -
13	1179	1189	1254	11630	1745	9153	4483	1102	117	2011	Asie-Pacifique 2/
7	1158	1253	1111	12433	2083	9444	4159	1211	619	2012	
6	990	1504	1080	14981	1551	9379	4511	1172	804	2013	
6	1357	1306	891	16086	1645	10567	4905	1146	100	2014	
0	0	18	23	1135	6	205	26	56	0	2000	Japon
0	7	40	35	2483	11	737	71	36	...	2011	
0	7	56	23	2360	20	787	72	41	...	2012	
0	31	45	24	2338	14	825	76	33	...	2013	
1	27	44	16	2370	16	798	88	33	...	2014	
1688	2963	3064	3113	2851	484	2053	5467	136	941	2000	Economies développées -
8328	8883	10815	6267	13080	1590	6512	16185	382	570	2011	Europe 2/
8201	8015	11024	6551	13389	2179	7009	16294	368	659	2012	
9175	8852	12137	7037	14824	1923	7788	17744	390	867	2013	
9579	10189	12471	7361	17635	2585	8201	18114	408	880	2014	
79	984	883	429	542	106	406	968	112	2	2000	France
348	4629	2604	770	3344	217	1731	2352	303	24	2011	
391	3122	2648	774	3311	209	1880	2374	279	38	2012	
389	3537	2921	896	3458	156	2038	2794	296	43	2013	
394	3699	2764	749	3425	167	2086	2309	312	39	2014	
193	367	112	203	255	126	188	974	1	204	2000	Allemagne
1264	520	884	416	1362	290	609	3008	3	37	2011	
1252	613	713	386	1660	610	724	2913	3	87	2012	
1445	739	935	465	1774	478	803	3253	4	143	2013	
1546	845	889	532	2245	939	918	3110	4	153	2014	
73	1936	805	9298	5475	785	2248	2770	78	74	2000	Economies développées -
119	3369	3357	26721	19557	2385	7266	6470	159	108	2011	Amérique du Nord 2/
162	2355	3056	27675	19589	2224	7074	5018	162	1	2012	
166	2737	3197	29824	22051	2618	8154	5586	166	9	2013	
136	2695	3001	32524	22790	2906	8827	5969	178	16	2014	
71	1499	658	8266	4943	268	1952	2558	77	74	2000	Etats-Unis
90	2856	2749	24284	17006	989	6381	5564	146	104	2011	
144	1575	2451	25250	17343	1082	6142	4063	149	...	2012	
133	1987	2434	27052	19595	1215	7019	4713	155	...	2013	
116	1908	2161	29579	20396	1289	7823	4817	164	...	2014	
284	44	6	3	4	34	5	114	1	13	2000	Europe du Sud-Est
2810	249	48	20	84	32	23	1125	0	23	2011	
2874	455	58	18	129	115	34	1100	0	23	2012	
2662	1176	66	16	360	109	100	1671	0	16	2013	
2876	1138	123	23	228	70	138	1546	0	27	2014	
27	17	15	7	160	30	2	167	...	15	2000	Communauté d'Etats
181	2532	615	115	2223	843	72	3639	0	176	2011	Indépendants
217	4241	695	142	2647	1595	115	5533	0	97	2012	
210	2452	1018	234	3004	1475	423	4557	0	93	2013	
220	2658	925	218	3334	1686	421	4437	2	128	2014	
6	6	0	1	155	7	1	67	...	0	2000	Fédération de Russie 4/
107	1482	576	64	2089	137	19	1923	0	97	2011	
127	1920	327	105	2212	631	26	2840	0	18	2012	
105	877	621	197	2514	472	141	2262	0	14	2013	
99	828	586	186	2374	446	133	2136	0	13	2014	

Voir la fin du tableau pour la remarque générale et les notes.

World merchandise exports by provenance and destination (Table D)

In million U.S. dollars f.o.b.

Exports from	Year	World 1/ Monde 1/	Developed economies 2/ Total	Asia-Pacific Total	Japan Japon	Europe Total	Germany Allemagne	North America Total	U.S.A. É.-U.	CIS Total	CIS Europe
					Food, beverages and tobacco (SITC, Rev. 3, 0 and 1) [cont.]						
Northern Africa	2000	2277	1661	281	279	1299	71	81	58	63	63
	2011	9184	4196	139	130	3819	212	237	180	669	649
	2012	8527	3816	158	149	3433	254	225	174	487	476
	2013	9723	4258	174	162	3813	214	271	209	584	574
	2014	9941	4366	192	182	3904	248	270	208	665	654
Sub-Saharan Africa	2000	10482	6448	512	439	5322	615	613	537	105	103
	2011	36327	16446	804	595	13530	1470	2112	1837	452	394
	2012	40343	18159	951	780	14326	1338	2882	2611	479	400
	2013	37082	16435	991	785	13740	1205	1703	1422	517	449
	2014	40414	18082	786	614	15244	1321	2052	1737	523	454
South Africa	2000	2168	1261	176	144	923	69	161	110	8	7
	2011	8620	2854	289	182	2254	244	311	191	191	185
	2012	8293	2701	274	169	2086	216	341	214	182	176
	2013	9003	3247	482	349	2412	248	353	216	209	205
	2014	9172	3082	314	208	2392	232	376	236	190	184
Latin America and the Caribbean	2000	47177	31343	2605	2313	13659	2245	15080	14395	1096	1082
	2011	168284	85603	7724	6775	39947	6594	37931	35141	7293	6967
	2012	169857	82150	7738	6786	37187	5871	37225	34638	6916	6520
	2013	175121	84994	8008	7007	37208	5156	39779	37434	6873	6352
	2014	174665	86191	6977	5809	37390	6081	41823	39398	7445	6887
Brazil	2000	10142	6609	710	514	4599	667	1300	1179	471	460
	2011	58415	23427	2890	2668	15964	2900	4573	3792	4410	4166
	2012	57354	21630	2886	2748	14964	2486	3780	3044	3537	3246
	2013	57396	21110	2822	2693	14609	2106	3679	3036	3402	3038
	2014	53971	19611	2265	2121	13724	2701	3622	3019	3789	3436
Eastern Asia	2000	21062	11179	7892	7697	1446	308	1841	1605	297	254
	2011	69229	28872	14052	12758	6706	1454	8115	7091	2710	2258
	2012	71868	29943	15052	13750	6329	1468	8562	7454	2786	2298
	2013	75457	29137	13895	12564	6743	1458	8499	7441	2977	2435
	2014	80096	29498	13846	12474	6949	1540	8702	7593	3168	2569
China	2000	13027	7217	4960	4877	1214	296	1044	910	189	162
	2011	52771	24192	10901	9947	6369	1425	6921	6077	2406	2010
	2012	54667	25005	11801	10847	5938	1416	7267	6357	2449	2011
	2013	58335	24830	11208	10172	6351	1423	7272	6393	2657	2171
	2014	61797	25090	11097	10030	6562	1504	7431	6515	2828	2287
Southern Asia	2000	8330	3483	853	787	1687	280	944	859	627	469
	2011	37474	8383	1478	1202	4753	664	2152	1892	1850	1250
	2012	39148	8189	1247	950	4694	542	2247	1983	1592	1099
	2013	46695	9715	1311	1000	5446	615	2958	2619	1661	1131
	2014	44413	10333	1133	790	5895	822	3305	2923	1760	1325
South-Eastern Asia	2000	23692	12540	5244	4705	3056	465	4240	3874	168	159
	2011	80880	31849	11350	8800	9637	1538	10862	9802	1196	1060
	2012	82700	31487	11848	9138	9333	1700	10306	9249	1100	968
	2013	83704	32466	12114	8791	9653	1719	10699	9608	1182	1058
	2014	83966	31863	11910	8493	9417	1681	10537	9441	1163	1041
Western Asia	2000	7475	2824	147	100	2321	624	356	328	508	307
	2011	29751	7238	372	194	5942	1422	923	747	2214	1776
	2012	30307	7228	398	227	5791	1303	1039	845	2135	1677
	2013	34195	7673	404	226	6200	1415	1070	889	2484	1963
	2014	37171	8561	507	270	6752	1566	1303	1085	2635	2100
Oceania	2000	469	374	107	52	191	76	76	75	0	0
	2011	1437	926	298	137	418	233	210	207	9	9
	2012	1388	862	258	135	386	169	217	206	7	6
	2013	1417	899	242	111	434	222	223	220	10	8
	2014	1488	937	257	136	427	203	253	248	9	7

For general note and footnotes see end of table

Les exportations de marchandises du monde par provenance et destination (Tableau D)

En millions de dollars E.-U. f.o.b.

← Exportations vers

South-Eastern Europe Europe du Sud-Est	Northern Africa Afrique septentrio-nale	Sub-Saharan Africa Afrique subsahari-enne	Latin America and the Caribbean Amérique latine et Caraïbes	Eastern Asia Asie orientale	Southern Asia Asie méridionale	South-eastern Asia Asie du Sud-Est	Western Asia Asie occidentale	Oceania Océanie	Other 3/ Autres 3/	Année	Exportations en provence de ↓
			Produits alimentaires, boisson et tabac (CTCI, Rev. 3, 0 et 1) [suite]								
10	169	84	5	11	2	10	238	1	24	2000	Afrique septentrionale
61	913	900	42	38	112	81	2045	2	126	2011	
36	887	904	56	48	94	106	2006	1	86	2012	
50	1014	1048	56	77	82	116	2325	2	110	2013	
58	1036	1002	60	105	110	139	2290	2	109	2014	
22	203	1983	79	234	458	186	717	6	43	2000	Afrique subsaharienne
50	580	10572	1377	1149	1979	1415	2151	55	101	2011	
149	635	11512	2150	926	2137	1733	2384	12	65	2012	
119	570	12171	342	1029	1915	1578	2346	18	43	2013	
198	627	12262	306	1314	2601	2097	2326	10	67	2014	
4	8	536	11	103	65	36	130	0	7	2000	Afrique du sud
3	14	3826	432	593	76	195	428	6	3	2011	
3	27	3866	357	392	63	236	442	7	16	2012	
2	24	4078	137	479	56	280	476	5	11	2013	
8	29	4096	53	698	85	352	553	5	21	2014	
167	811	566	8780	1541	396	736	1499	12	230	2000	Amérique latine et Caraïbes
745	7112	5793	30631	10391	3680	7067	9668	24	278	2011	
729	7679	5844	32653	12130	3847	7883	9719	23	283	2012	
735	7011	4773	32398	14304	3477	9362	10808	20	367	2013	
679	7091	3972	31225	13327	4102	10277	9852	21	483	2014	
85	185	264	1061	372	139	250	705	0	...	2000	Brésil
526	4019	3803	5425	4744	2833	2913	6305	10	...	2011	
419	4421	3547	5564	5803	3180	3131	6110	8	4	2012	
436	3603	3180	5851	6935	2751	3667	6455	7	0	2013	
376	3268	2629	5885	5608	2892	4200	5706	6	...	2014	
26	145	346	185	6265	195	2052	310	34	28	2000	Asie orientale
113	634	1750	1858	17141	1186	12884	1863	206	11	2011	
102	634	1826	1922	18152	1108	13276	1825	281	13	2012	
97	687	2083	2192	19507	1046	15642	1820	256	11	2013	
93	662	2194	1976	22070	1152	17101	1879	292	12	2014	
26	142	295	145	3365	152	1242	247	5	...	2000	Chine
108	596	1603	1742	10657	985	8977	1419	87	...	2011	
97	571	1653	1775	11645	907	9113	1350	101	...	2012	
93	645	1880	2076	12956	954	10712	1428	104	...	2013	
87	623	1984	1849	14650	1074	11971	1506	134	...	2014	
11	225	185	86	415	802	619	1874	2	1	2000	Asie méridionale
53	822	2739	298	1663	6106	5351	10177	20	12	2011	
60	1026	4184	325	1984	6194	6215	9355	9	15	2012	
66	1078	4466	340	1946	8853	8095	10431	13	31	2013	
57	1168	3825	384	2208	7393	7624	9593	12	55	2014	
36	127	651	150	3275	655	4999	976	46	70	2000	Asie du Sud-est
151	1008	4576	977	11742	3396	20996	3731	325	933	2011	
138	1168	4280	1160	13688	2489	21998	3793	368	1030	2012	
156	1023	4134	1181	14507	2517	21727	3734	377	703	2013	
150	1021	4784	1231	15207	2112	22094	3295	364	680	2014	
143	266	151	58	102	478	71	2659	0	217	2000	Asie occidentale
599	1130	1613	165	323	2211	671	13148	3	434	2011	
509	1171	1774	178	1976	2431	679	11245	4	976	2012	
510	1475	2286	200	333	2881	683	15265	5	400	2013	
557	1387	2293	239	500	953	1126	18478	6	435	2014	
0	...	7	0	21	0	32	0	24	10	2000	Océanie
1	3	4	5	72	1	258	1	145	10	2011	
1	0	2	4	77	3	244	1	171	16	2012	
1	0	2	2	77	3	257	1	154	10	2013	
1	0	2	2	115	4	270	2	139	7	2014	

Voir la fin du tableau pour la remarque générale et les notes.

World merchandise exports by provenance and destination (Table D)

In million U.S. dollars f.o.b.

| Exports from | Year | World 1/ Monde 1/ | Developed economies 2/ Économies développées 2/ ||||||| Commonwealth of Independent States Communauté d'Etats Indépendants ||
| | | | Total | Asia-Pacific Asie-Pacifique || Europe || North America Amérique du Nord || | |
				Total	Japan Japon	Total	Germany Allemagne	Total	U.S.A. É.-U.	Total	Europe
Crude materials (excluding fuels), oils, fats (SITC, Rev. 3, 2 and 4)												
World 1/	2000	213020	135131	21273	19728	83983	15224	29875	23140	3273	2923
	2011	893598	374383	61504	57336	255185	47104	57694	43495	16345	14103
	2012	843949	342878	54692	50869	230286	44185	57900	44401	16996	13628
	2013	842411	332140	53357	49903	224629	43277	54155	41452	17278	14114
	2014	822773	330462	51075	47342	222042	41474	57345	43681	16301	12886
Developed Economies - Asia-Pacific 2/	2000	17277	6994	3049	2577	2422	328	1523	1155	175	174
	2011	113893	22324	15921	15142	4414	928	1989	1296	727	697
	2012	105350	19799	13292	12645	4427	1003	2080	1409	565	548
	2013	114849	18041	12588	11979	3656	775	1798	1366	402	374
	2014	104463	16093	11106	10386	3312	756	1675	1422	429	417
Japan	2000	3369	747	30	.	437	96	280	268	5	4
	2011	12369	1816	42	.	1077	227	698	676	77	67
	2012	13453	1950	35	.	1050	308	865	847	87	80
	2013	12528	1635	34	.	898	238	703	686	76	67
	2014	11468	1523	29	.	732	220	762	740	84	74
Developed Economies - Europe 2/	2000	61182	51586	1529	1332	47688	9926	2369	2050	811	783
	2011	199151	150935	2754	2244	143562	30417	4619	3896	3865	3670
	2012	186643	139118	2379	1922	131914	28803	4825	4092	4119	3874
	2013	186778	139717	2629	2144	131855	29242	5233	4351	4252	3972
	2014	183803	139916	2495	1971	131665	28123	5757	4714	3425	3110
France	2000	6036	5195	62	54	4960	957	173	159	43	39
	2011	17407	14505	92	72	14115	2959	298	274	211	204
	2012	15292	12518	92	70	12037	2681	390	353	221	212
	2013	14614	11859	84	64	11420	2313	355	324	271	257
	2014	14339	11768	96	71	11299	2128	373	335	171	161
Germany	2000	9272	7481	98	75	7114	.	269	236	175	169
	2011	33158	26710	236	170	25373	.	1101	992	815	778
	2012	29946	23596	185	119	22362	.	1049	947	821	780
	2013	28680	22610	215	153	21328	.	1067	978	728	692
	2014	28412	22876	195	136	21597	.	1084	980	566	506
Developed Economies - North America 2/	2000	53039	35036	6987	6666	10335	1651	17714	12780	60	49
	2011	141887	53670	9241	8670	21228	2971	23201	14330	279	245
	2012	140922	49271	8794	8244	18004	3407	22473	14153	418	331
	2013	134214	49162	9136	8617	17460	3022	22565	14768	570	513
	2014	134546	51551	9034	8459	18144	2605	24373	16047	504	466
United States	2000	30471	15489	4053	3903	6505	965	4931	.	55	43
	2011	97215	26529	4554	4247	13106	2209	8869	.	258	227
	2012	96233	23533	4095	3776	11121	2591	8318	.	390	304
	2013	90239	23204	4343	4042	11067	2343	7795	.	548	494
	2014	90636	24508	4626	4288	11558	2019	8324	.	475	438
South-Eastern Europe	2000	1742	850	9	8	826	121	15	5	105	105
	2011	9754	4972	185	185	4701	588	85	15	71	64
	2012	7939	3754	183	182	3463	415	109	21	74	71
	2013	8901	4559	227	227	4235	520	97	30	66	62
	2014	7992	4086	159	156	3871	678	56	40	75	70
Commonwealth of Independent States	2000	9211	4881	597	597	4196	456	88	78	1629	1362
	2011	39443	11674	528	524	10929	825	217	204	7285	5724
	2012	40656	11420	451	433	10783	686	186	180	7864	5251
	2013	38718	11401	658	643	10531	739	212	196	7772	5417
	2014	36603	10863	622	614	10015	727	226	211	7288	4738
Russian Federation 4/	2000	4752	2850	588	587	2214	173	48	40	338	229
	2011	18054	6510	475	475	5856	437	179	168	1345	424
	2012	18783	6072	404	404	5512	405	156	151	2858	1052
	2013	18172	6158	552	551	5411	348	194	180	2973	1208
	2014	17160	5815	522	520	5110	329	183	170	2808	1140

For general note and footnotes see end of table

Les exportations de marchandises du monde par provenance et destination (Tableau D)

En millions de dollars E.-U. f.o.b.

← Exportations vers

South-Eastern Europe Europe du Sud-Est	Northern Africa Afrique septentrionale	Sub-Saharan Africa Afrique subsaharienne	Latin America and the Caribbean Amérique latine et Caraïbes	Eastern Asia Asie orientale	Southern Asia Asie méridionale	South-eastern Asia Asie du Sud-Est	Western Asia Asie occidentale	Oceania Océanie	Other 3/ Autres 3/	Année	Exportations en provence de ↓
	Matières brutes (sauf combustibles), huiles et graisses (CTCI, Rev. 3, 2 et 4)										
1140	2698	3042	10287	32716	6966	9135	6392	83	2156	2000	Monde 1/
8203	13999	14751	34556	304975	44638	42011	38340	279	1118	2011	
7622	12825	14040	33339	291847	45645	41114	36075	290	1279	2012	
7972	11995	13988	31067	309108	41924	39059	35797	273	1811	2013	
7943	11717	14431	31203	286752	45937	40565	35436	294	1732	2014	
56	116	351	117	6159	678	1505	377	29	721	2000	Economies développées -
16	27	931	389	80028	3042	4173	2014	106	116	2011	Asie-Pacifique 2/
124	57	674	311	73798	3312	4474	1998	111	127	2012	
110	72	785	268	84994	2749	4838	2365	99	125	2013	
163	99	912	220	76923	2675	5399	1351	101	98	2014	
1	3	41	33	1879	111	525	22	1	...	2000	Japon
8	14	183	79	8333	249	1523	85	1	...	2011	
11	8	199	97	9119	245	1642	89	4	...	2012	
19	7	210	111	8509	222	1635	101	2	...	2013	
16	4	223	100	7404	249	1740	124	2	...	2014	
397	1141	627	613	2814	636	651	1535	11	360	2000	Economies développées -
3688	3822	1821	1852	18532	4290	2426	7669	24	226	2011	Europe 2/
3413	4428	1939	2013	16841	4163	2478	7912	23	196	2012	
3729	4139	1887	2101	17541	3243	2371	7534	29	235	2013	
3715	4397	1691	1916	15171	3676	2129	7566	22	179	2014	
16	118	62	61	280	115	29	109	7	0	2000	France
105	380	117	112	1214	204	212	332	14	1	2011	
93	354	123	126	1047	174	217	397	16	6	2012	
110	318	117	179	1085	133	203	315	13	9	2013	
106	302	123	123	1096	138	226	264	12	10	2014	
95	91	101	110	601	125	140	206	1	146	2000	Allemagne
311	334	407	343	2397	605	382	851	0	1	2011	
363	532	386	352	2097	601	384	814	0	1	2012	
356	457	290	347	2232	462	410	785	0	1	2013	
372	537	237	329	1847	493	383	771	0	2	2014	
26	190	314	5427	8312	522	1923	975	21	232	2000	Economies développées -
220	2246	782	14630	52978	3572	6668	6673	48	122	2011	Amérique du Nord 2/
223	2278	743	14410	57778	2980	6547	6245	30	0	2012	
97	1762	654	13635	54123	2610	6715	4846	40	...	2013	
112	1738	601	14473	50662	3093	7133	4622	57	0	2014	
21	165	250	5057	6440	360	1472	911	19	232	2000	Etats-Unis
40	1851	575	12963	41047	2648	5731	5406	45	122	2011	
46	1984	560	12605	43798	2316	5756	5225	19	...	2012	
36	1502	530	12241	39934	2093	5816	4302	33	...	2013	
45	1552	471	13118	37948	2295	6040	4130	54	0	2014	
231	122	2	8	102	6	3	310	0	3	2000	Europe du Sud-Est
1537	180	223	11	495	150	7	2087	0	20	2011	
1224	187	274	17	538	46	12	1782	0	31	2012	
1175	186	252	14	702	110	32	1769	0	36	2013	
1138	197	208	8	532	178	29	1502	0	37	2014	
128	270	6	47	1247	175	62	767	0	0	2000	Communauté d'Etats
807	1385	181	268	12181	2242	146	3262	1	12	2011	Indépendants
673	1854	123	275	11854	2772	259	3561	0	0	2012	
808	1371	72	190	11036	2423	360	3286	0	0	2013	
762	1170	107	186	10317	2476	327	3107	0	0	2014	
23	190	1	12	973	45	21	300	0	0	2000	Fédération de Russie 4/
100	843	62	161	6912	540	106	1464	1	12	2011	
197	945	71	160	5827	598	184	1872	0	0	2012	
213	748	21	117	5671	497	183	1591	0	0	2013	
201	706	20	110	5355	469	173	1503	0	0	2014	

Voir la fin du tableau pour la remarque générale et les notes.

World merchandise exports by provenance and destination (Table D)

In million U.S. dollars f.o.b.

Exports from	Year	World 1/ Monde 1/	Developed economies 2/ — Total	Asia-Pacific Total	Japan Japon	Europe Total	Germany Allemagne	North America Total	U.S.A. É.-U.	CIS Total	CIS Europe

Crude materials (excluding fuels), oils, fats (SITC, Rev. 3, 2 and 4) [cont.]

Exports from	Year	World	Total	Asia-Pac Total	Japan	Europe Total	Germany	N.Am Total	U.S.A.	CIS Total	CIS Europe
Northern Africa	2000	1414	946	61	24	773	42	111	102	12	12
	2011	5701	2608	156	39	1846	149	606	594	67	65
	2012	5322	2357	116	22	1619	122	622	599	75	70
	2013	4654	2342	92	26	1682	116	568	537	33	29
	2014	4560	2428	99	28	1713	136	616	583	35	30
Sub-Saharan Africa	2000	7512	4531	521	506	3478	555	532	471	14	14
	2011	45002	19076	2171	2098	14090	1460	2815	2223	451	403
	2012	47517	18267	2004	1869	14200	1600	2062	1551	385	306
	2013	42442	14499	1709	1628	10662	1244	2128	1626	404	378
	2014	42501	14809	1773	1708	10702	1488	2334	1529	449	412
South Africa	2000	2693	1932	411	400	1205	338	315	306	8	8
	2011	18776	5734	1573	1527	3666	542	496	452	67	67
	2012	16943	5134	1338	1292	3034	308	762	735	84	74
	2013	17538	4975	1237	1198	3041	284	697	678	86	78
	2014	15297	4609	1251	1211	2559	364	799	574	114	99
Latin America and the Caribbean	2000	25161	15222	2677	2602	7717	1255	4828	4006	149	149
	2011	155405	56035	14884	14106	29902	5758	11249	9062	931	825
	2012	142733	49617	13438	12817	25499	4870	10679	8514	921	845
	2013	147780	47894	12465	11999	25163	4430	10265	8085	1217	1080
	2014	141058	46407	11633	11118	23315	3769	11458	9097	1614	1414
Brazil	2000	9140	6169	900	881	4222	771	1047	980	12	12
	2011	75880	24734	5210	5003	16701	2443	2822	1961	347	269
	2012	65790	20170	3666	3627	13786	1796	2718	1945	206	181
	2013	71528	20962	3813	3778	14234	2146	2915	2195	127	100
	2014	65951	19141	3104	3073	12445	1758	3592	2802	374	373
Eastern Asia	2000	11347	4318	1979	1894	1470	229	869	814	91	88
	2011	34374	12132	4345	4024	4910	1075	2877	2511	492	457
	2012	32183	10862	3840	3549	3996	893	3025	2660	450	412
	2013	31576	10448	3538	3257	4021	955	2889	2588	411	367
	2014	34314	10985	3660	3369	4281	1005	3044	2741	438	390
China	2000	4575	2767	1241	1205	1051	169	475	454	56	53
	2011	15546	7613	2285	2083	3381	795	1947	1737	323	296
	2012	14925	7173	2226	2061	2792	681	2155	1927	288	256
	2013	15192	6975	2102	1931	2811	695	2062	1891	244	213
	2014	16504	7359	2143	1965	3038	729	2178	2011	268	235
Southern Asia	2000	2568	1238	295	276	655	103	288	276	92	72
	2011	21494	5299	548	465	2594	449	2157	2089	188	117
	2012	23729	8933	704	547	2212	444	6016	5853	236	182
	2013	20467	5528	710	615	1915	385	2903	2784	217	156
	2014	19614	5151	681	581	1992	428	2477	2329	202	165
South-Eastern Asia	2000	18168	7767	3106	2833	3213	376	1448	1324	71	69
	2011	109912	31416	10063	9286	13661	2081	7692	7103	1604	1542
	2012	93509	25329	8759	8066	10992	1575	5579	5156	1553	1480
	2013	91618	23762	8702	8038	9928	1408	5132	4789	1575	1506
	2014	88595	23479	8766	8101	9690	1279	5023	4691	1512	1442
Western Asia	2000	2650	1083	115	110	885	111	83	73	61	47
	2011	14691	2707	126	109	2404	288	177	162	384	294
	2012	14706	2706	151	121	2324	244	230	199	336	259
	2013	17079	3092	217	178	2530	282	344	315	359	259
	2014	21781	3054	320	256	2449	333	285	259	327	231
Oceania	2000	1750	679	348	304	325	70	6	6	3	0
	2011	2891	1536	582	444	945	115	9	8	2	...
	2012	2740	1445	580	452	852	122	13	13	0	0
	2013	3333	1696	686	552	990	161	20	19	0	0
	2014	2943	1640	727	596	893	146	20	19	0	0

For general note and footnotes see end of table

Les exportations de marchandises du monde par provenance et destination (Tableau D)

En millions de dollars E.-U. f.o.b.

← Exportations vers

South-Eastern Europe Europe du Sud-Est	Northern Africa Afrique septentrionale	Sub-Saharan Africa Afrique subsaharienne	Latin America and the Caribbean Amérique latine et Caraïbes	Eastern Asia Asie orientale	Southern Asia Asie méridionale	South-eastern Asia Asie du Sud-Est	Western Asia Asie occidentale	Oceania Océanie	Other 3/ Autres 3/	Année	Exportations en provence de ↓
	**Matières brutes (sauf combustibles), huiles et graisses (CTCI, Rev. 3, 2 et 4)** *[suite]*
35	45	13	89	63	63	32	106	0	9	2000	Afrique septentrionale
78	466	229	350	442	586	163	671	0	42	2011	
97	346	204	309	414	665	186	592	0	77	2012	
61	224	197	209	359	430	215	565	0	19	2013	
59	289	181	213	316	429	127	465	0	19	2014	
19	113	1005	116	755	327	374	228	1	28	2000	Afrique subsaharienne
79	190	4823	673	14538	1767	2135	1152	30	87	2011	
356	145	4837	1803	14648	2660	2635	1433	3	345	2012	
156	117	4969	268	15902	1779	2738	1594	10	6	2013	
213	125	4931	366	14929	2365	2692	1600	15	6	2014	
10	6	112	23	358	62	154	29	0	0	2000	Afrique du sud
21	18	732	132	10185	713	953	217	2	0	2011	
15	16	739	112	8504	1231	901	202	1	5	2012	
8	28	680	89	9718	837	884	228	1	3	2013	
4	30	708	128	7598	1346	496	250	12	1	2014	
145	361	222	3381	3244	1370	669	389	1	7	2000	Amérique latine et Caraïbes
1136	2790	952	12527	66032	5643	4381	4732	2	245	2011	
1008	1517	806	11244	62941	6373	4196	3838	3	270	2012	
1234	2121	555	11478	68723	5660	4147	3567	3	1183	2013	
1078	1551	612	10927	62830	6642	4391	3770	2	1233	2014	
41	196	50	682	1211	328	210	241	1	...	2000	Brésil
243	994	261	3148	38540	1283	2594	3733	0	...	2011	
235	781	220	2307	34428	1407	3068	2967	1	...	2012	
274	956	184	2458	40350	941	2692	2584	1	...	2013	
196	827	205	2369	35874	1174	2936	2854	1	...	2014	
7	33	46	98	5248	440	948	116	1	1	2000	Asie orientale
123	216	396	938	11787	2254	4761	1271	4	0	2011	
94	221	400	840	11356	1979	4926	1049	5	0	2012	
119	224	407	825	11362	1967	4779	1029	5	0	2013	
117	195	500	909	12418	2144	5383	1218	6	0	2014	
6	18	23	42	1000	251	360	52	0	...	2000	Chine
113	176	194	591	2740	1180	1800	814	2	...	2011	
84	179	192	478	2962	990	1891	686	2	...	2012	
106	189	200	486	3394	984	1950	664	1	...	2013	
104	158	288	563	3487	1128	2306	842	2	...	2014	
6	31	39	55	491	212	224	179	0	0	2000	Asie méridionale
26	136	189	244	10293	2186	1871	1052	1	9	2011	
29	120	190	229	8767	2263	1807	1150	2	4	2012	
27	145	217	220	8233	2508	1708	1644	3	18	2013	
31	155	227	189	7993	2362	1672	1599	8	26	2014	
41	202	375	281	4015	2228	2373	794	15	4	2000	Asie du Sud-est
239	2269	3990	2425	34093	16414	14349	3034	53	27	2011	
171	1424	3594	1626	28648	15619	12852	2584	83	26	2012	
144	1338	3672	1590	31064	15453	10335	2584	73	27	2013	
133	1324	3672	1504	29639	14717	9986	2535	66	28	2014	
49	73	35	55	159	300	142	617	0	75	2000	Asie occidentale
254	270	233	144	2903	2405	457	4722	1	212	2011	
211	243	257	145	3637	2602	423	3931	10	204	2012	
311	294	319	119	4248	2723	437	5015	0	161	2013	
424	476	788	155	4449	4935	966	6102	0	105	2014	
1	...	7	1	106	7	228	...	3	714	2000	Océanie
0	1	1	106	673	88	474	1	10	0	2011	
0	3	0	117	627	210	319	0	19	0	2012	
0	2	0	149	821	270	384	0	11	0	2013	
0	1	0	136	573	244	331	0	16	0	2014	

Voir la fin du tableau pour la remarque générale et les notes.

World merchandise exports by provenance and destination (Table D)

In million U.S. dollars f.o.b.

Exports from	Year	World 1/ Monde 1/	Developed economies 2/ Total	Asia-Pacific Total	Japan Japon	Europe Total	Germany Allemagne	North America Total	U.S.A. É.-U.	CIS Total	CIS Europe
					Mineral fuels and related materials (SITC. Rev. 3, 3)						
World 1/	2000	656661	442341	71797	66623	222568	29298	147976	137266	11165	9697
	2011	3148739	1625307	197583	163131	974805	90464	452919	339100	57108	52086
	2012	3320984	1686722	217348	181677	1026586	94734	442788	322854	69092	58858
	2013	3272486	1658899	213950	178094	1029224	117265	415725	284263	61566	50250
	2014	3282734	1635297	299845	259211	938211	101090	397241	272034	56800	45949
Developed Economies - Asia-Pacific 2/	2000	15224	7843	5798	5119	901	85	1144	1143	7	7
	2011	94060	40094	33937	29532	5132	325	1025	987	69	68
	2012	88097	38156	34040	30389	3255	158	862	853	68	65
	2013	83321	36401	32428	27684	3174	108	799	750	70	65
	2014	81159	34229	31447	27556	2241	94	541	539	143	141
Japan	2000	1520	518	83	.	40	4	395	394	7	7
	2011	16293	3330	2267	.	332	5	731	692	69	68
	2012	13434	2434	1706	.	113	9	614	606	68	65
	2013	16682	4809	3385	.	660	10	764	715	67	64
	2014	15886	3218	2566	.	181	11	472	469	68	66
Developed Economies - Europe 2/	2000	131109	119060	136	102	101983	20560	16941	13150	384	367
	2011	507878	425796	758	683	385683	61582	39356	32684	3532	3003
	2012	531776	432542	1212	1067	396509	65619	34821	31588	4195	3685
	2013	556346	453659	1120	1003	419907	84504	32632	28369	5084	4513
	2014	496657	403409	1582	1484	374134	73896	27693	24427	5761	5326
France	2000	8183	7258	28	13	6660	1009	570	561	16	15
	2011	26610	20216	26	23	18570	2291	1619	1405	17	16
	2012	24831	18718	77	73	16920	1729	1721	1592	86	84
	2013	22236	17650	107	71	16091	1420	1452	1389	30	26
	2014	21984	17477	20	16	16209	1453	1248	1193	37	30
Germany	2000	7757	5384	13	9	4961	.	410	406	35	33
	2011	33312	31630	52	34	31254	.	323	281	475	408
	2012	38362	36369	45	25	36100	.	224	174	573	503
	2013	41244	39072	45	23	38849	.	177	141	915	837
	2014	40510	37091	40	19	36836	.	216	142	2324	2252
Developed Economies - North America 2/	2000	49686	41512	1485	1328	2019	97	38009	35232	8	8
	2011	245253	160154	5274	4787	31512	1594	123367	105397	1113	1045
	2012	253699	162147	4985	4533	32426	1175	124736	106342	601	568
	2013	268511	173436	4553	4120	31818	944	137064	112368	507	495
	2014	285413	187298	4181	3735	29926	750	153191	120407	446	433
United States	2000	13340	5570	1001	845	1793	80	2776	.	8	7
	2011	129233	49609	2988	2517	28653	1347	17968	.	1088	1021
	2012	137340	50888	3074	2627	29420	1054	18393	.	569	537
	2013	148278	57271	3031	2602	29548	862	24692	.	457	446
	2014	157024	62378	3163	2721	26445	673	32771	.	409	397
South-Eastern Europe	2000	1442	243	...	.	231	6	12	12	225	152
	2011	9305	3328	0	0	3256	213	72	71	1595	1098
	2012	9230	3141	0	0	3021	145	121	121	1598	1018
	2013	10104	3297	0	0	3264	242	33	33	2031	1482
	2014	9204	2225	0	0	2224	189	2	2	1483	1008
Commonwealth of Independent States	2000	62947	41876	302	302	40040	3736	1534	215	10357	9053
	2011	461773	319358	15078	15078	289216	19675	15064	12245	49567	46016
	2012	480061	318922	16980	16936	291310	20952	10631	7720	61404	52740
	2013	478366	327700	21748	21419	298295	19995	7656	5162	52685	43013
	2014	453882	308563	24209	23898	279793	17657	4561	3914	47629	38283
Russian Federation 4/	2000	52166	36681	302	302	36076	3554	303	189	6979	6287
	2011	346530	246261	15078	15078	221443	17461	9740	9395	33869	32190
	2012	368853	249610	16948	16936	226592	18304	6070	6052	49428	42768
	2013	372036	261517	21616	21288	235710	17369	4191	4135	42769	34900
	2014	351322	251701	23999	23689	223744	16402	3958	3904	34526	26972

For general note and footnotes see end of table

Les exportations de marchandises du monde par provenance et destination (Tableau D)

En millions de dollars E.-U. f.o.b.

⟵ Exportations vers

South-Eastern Europe Europe du Sud-Est	Northern Africa Afrique septentrio- nale	Sub-Saharan Africa Afrique subsahari- enne	Latin America and the Caribbean Amérique latine et Caraïbes	Eastern Asia Asie orientale	Southern Asia Asie méridionale	South-eastern Asia Asie du Sud-Est	Western Asia Asie occidentale	Oceania Océanie	Other 3/ Autres 3/	Année	Exportations en provence de
	**Combustibles minéraux et produits assimilés (CTCI, Rev. 3, 3)**
3229	7442	5814	33958	88961	11856	25830	12504	1115	12445	2000	Monde 1/
20930	36691	54018	189192	694521	119170	184694	68124	6523	92459	2011	
22749	43940	61699	191806	770377	125526	208115	78136	6189	56633	2012	
17120	43212	64059	167109	780521	119800	214074	77796	4965	63364	2013	
19567	37602	79634	172185	705333	168729	272527	82778	5028	47256	2014	
0	8	65	320	3610	499	1633	112	421	706	2000	Economies développées -
0	1	456	2398	29282	8389	11774	362	712	524	2011	Asie-Pacifique 2/
0	1	265	1917	28115	6408	10050	326	842	1950	2012	
1	1	245	872	28438	5072	9282	159	706	2073	2013	
1	1	157	1482	29583	5049	9217	166	717	416	2014	
...	0	2	42	701	27	220	4	0	...	2000	Japon
0	1	84	668	6443	213	5369	79	38	...	2011	
0	1	23	622	6042	429	3752	28	37	...	2012	
0	1	84	103	7351	231	3961	62	13	...	2013	
0	1	51	351	8006	210	3712	78	190	...	2014	
784	1350	1171	767	506	436	286	1985	6	4375	2000	Economies développées -
5216	7901	17324	7742	3435	1072	3096	15182	75	17507	2011	Europe 2/
6143	14122	17024	9598	9700	1007	4827	17059	77	15482	2012	
5679	13751	17627	10021	7862	533	4642	16345	18	21125	2013	
5505	11675	17335	7211	7854	553	4199	15990	12	17152	2014	
8	212	257	130	23	21	19	204	3	34	2000	France
43	878	2031	462	113	193	127	1841	4	684	2011	
29	1555	1464	366	86	263	66	1689	4	505	2012	
32	742	1397	265	153	26	121	1642	5	172	2013	
26	643	1939	224	254	27	108	1210	4	36	2014	
22	10	35	117	35	12	13	38	0	2056	2000	Allemagne
102	31	290	124	198	63	72	277	0	50	2011	
80	33	212	252	225	59	75	351	60	73	2012	
92	45	201	124	264	51	77	290	0	113	2013	
129	38	103	191	298	45	73	177	0	42	2014	
73	105	134	6228	821	97	419	287	2	0	2000	Economies développées -
268	1759	1844	60587	8290	1992	5121	4123	2	0	2011	Amérique du Nord 2/
315	1466	1980	69194	8076	1904	5030	2923	63	1	2012	
178	2134	3464	69916	8436	1492	5200	3720	28	...	2013	
301	2506	3740	75706	6420	1493	4640	2854	8	0	2014	
61	96	125	6142	582	85	418	251	2	...	2000	Etats-Unis
268	1707	1838	59152	4726	1883	5114	3848	2	...	2011	
273	1389	1977	68014	4642	1731	5025	2769	63	...	2012	
155	2132	3461	69213	5520	1270	5133	3638	28	...	2013	
256	2499	3738	74771	4537	1252	4544	2631	8	...	2014	
661	13	65	17	0	1	12	186	...	19	2000	Europe du Sud-Est
2494	188	139	7	4	72	36	1399	2	39	2011	
2019	324	325	5	1	60	71	1657	1	27	2012	
1864	326	343	2	2	40	431	1722	1	45	2013	
1861	463	153	2	1	31	737	2182	1	65	2014	
1626	28	22	4633	697	252	464	2990	1	2	2000	Communauté d'Etats
12712	2137	320	2624	48545	3853	6682	15612	0	362	2011	Indépendants
14053	2483	185	1426	53205	3583	6704	17533	80	483	2012	
9178	2282	211	2290	56381	2455	9596	15367	0	222	2013	
11609	2985	193	1799	51497	4095	9467	15685	0	360	2014	
1407	24	15	3416	590	15	428	2611	0	0	2000	Fédération de Russie 4/
9124	1834	251	2048	36271	1114	4950	10684	0	124	2011	
9779	1997	175	831	40253	837	3943	11771	80	149	2012	
6382	1669	189	1748	41731	621	4665	10726	...	19	2013	
6583	1576	178	1651	39883	586	4492	10129	...	18	2014	

Voir la fin du tableau pour la remarque générale et les notes.

World merchandise exports by provenance and destination (Table D)

In million U.S. dollars f.o.b.

Exports from	Year	World 1/ Monde 1/	Developed economies 2/ Total	Asia-Pacific Total	Japan Japon	Europe Total	Germany Allemagne	North America Total	U.S.A. É.-U.	CIS Total	CIS Europe
										Commonwealth of Independent States	

Mineral fuels and related materials (SITC. Rev. 3, 3) [cont.]

Exports from	Year	World	Dev. Total	Asia-Pac Total	Japan	Europe Total	Germany	N.America Total	U.S.A.	CIS Total	Europe
Northern Africa	2000	34262	28468	95	95	24088	2706	4285	3508	10	0
	2011	102592	80021	547	547	58995	1095	20479	15912	9	1
	2012	141277	112958	1906	1873	92629	1772	18423	12979	127	1
	2013	119023	93965	2807	1981	79919	6396	11239	8113	115	1
	2014	103510	79902	1742	1742	71326	3968	6834	5280	50	49
Sub-Saharan Africa	2000	45406	27747	229	193	9483	279	18035	17379	3	3
	2011	243472	119112	8453	2440	52679	2778	57980	51949	1	1
	2012	243408	118636	9925	5593	65064	2449	43647	38549	1	1
	2013	199970	93647	9417	5470	59315	2694	24915	21399	1	1
	2014	205875	95580	8761	4279	64017	2717	22802	19328	43	43
South Africa	2000	2664	1005	72	36	902	32	31	29	0	0
	2011	11334	1814	109	81	1633	168	73	73	0	0
	2012	11296	1468	72	58	1272	59	124	124	1	1
	2013	10108	1425	63	54	1237	53	126	123	0	0
	2014	9507	1798	29	21	1517	72	251	239	42	42
Latin America and the Caribbean	2000	62261	43938	434	371	3985	406	39519	38681	2	1
	2011	222416	123438	507	507	20922	77	102008	83410	36	7
	2012	256111	129454	1155	1155	24344	185	103955	82758	16	5
	2013	236340	126146	1160	1150	24364	612	100623	69134	9	9
	2014	220158	111538	1019	1019	22455	419	88064	59179	10	10
Brazil	2000	908	600	0	0	66	6	533	529	...	...
	2011	26791	10437	0	0	3918	31	6518	5866	...	...
	2012	26469	11098	31	31	4601	66	6466	5736	0	0
	2013	17822	7720	11	1	3425	111	4284	3704	0	0
	2014	20650	6571	0	0	2816	72	3755	3608	0	...
Eastern Asia	2000	19504	7958	5952	5704	452	46	1553	1477	97	78
	2011	105877	24310	14516	11932	5592	592	4202	4002	654	539
	2012	113215	25724	15886	11514	5122	551	4716	4517	568	460
	2013	113940	26581	16067	10621	5456	426	5059	4853	615	433
	2014	116300	26758	16485	10451	5149	377	5123	4956	607	373
China	2000	7855	3226	2080	1973	436	46	711	689	70	51
	2011	32274	6642	3438	3087	1988	497	1216	1067	447	352
	2012	31013	6185	2823	2472	1915	549	1447	1308	382	295
	2013	33786	5479	2105	1829	1879	423	1496	1307	443	286
	2014	34446	5139	2175	1446	1520	374	1444	1294	429	221
Southern Asia	2000	26801	16067	5325	5313	10595	184	147	147	11	3
	2011	150234	38783	2596	2446	34637	368	1550	1474	104	11
	2012	122537	30429	3423	3164	25783	10	1224	1222	75	11
	2013	128429	32445	3595	3504	25040	39	3810	3747	67	12
	2014	124905	21216	10804	10437	5893	30	4518	4517	222	12
South-Eastern Asia	2000	45412	18800	16753	13540	405	19	1643	1637	2	2
	2011	231230	67149	60289	40805	4109	48	2751	2659	34	29
	2012	229142	66891	61133	40562	3384	63	2374	2146	49	44
	2013	221356	59266	53720	35161	2296	39	3250	3069	67	64
	2014	214171	58378	52665	34252	2554	45	3158	2983	67	64
Western Asia	2000	161909	88235	34694	34557	28386	1172	25155	24686	58	22
	2011	774120	223762	55627	54374	83071	2117	85065	28312	393	267
	2012	851951	247678	66659	64849	83740	1656	97279	34060	389	259
	2013	856268	232300	67279	65925	76375	1265	88647	27264	314	163
	2014	970994	306148	146896	140307	78499	947	80753	26501	339	207
Oceania	2000	699	595	595	0	0	.	0	0	...	...
	2011	530	1	1	.	0	0	0	0	0	0
	2012	481	44	44	42	0	0	0	0	...	...
	2013	512	57	57	55	0	0	0	0	...	...
	2014	506	52	51	50	0	0	0	0	...	...

For general note and footnotes see end of table

Les exportations de marchandises du monde par provenance et destination (Tableau D)

En millions de dollars E.-U. f.o.b.

← Exportations vers

South-Eastern Europe Europe du Sud-Est	Northern Africa Afrique septentrionale	Sub-Saharan Africa Afrique subsaharienne	Latin America and the Caribbean Amérique latine et Caraïbes	Eastern Asia Asie orientale	Southern Asia Asie méridionale	South-eastern Asia Asie du Sud-Est	Western Asia Asie occidentale	Oceania Océanie	Other 3/ Autres 3/	Année	Exportations en provence de
\multicolumn{12}{c}{Combustibles minéraux et produits assimiles (CTCI, Rev. 3, 3) [suite]}
35	472	59	1830	167	173	173	2219	...	656	2000	Afrique septentrionale
6	2315	224	4642	5119	4432	842	3546	40	1395	2011	
5	3254	425	4778	9420	3603	1123	4030	...	1554	2012	
95	4160	297	3492	6629	3620	1361	3960	0	1330	2013	
187	3915	609	3365	5711	2239	2485	3773	0	1274	2014	
9	37	3646	1794	6329	4023	787	293	28	711	2000	Afrique subsaharienne
21	4418	20300	22455	49513	20520	3292	1364	1417	1060	2011	
30	950	22686	15951	51608	25919	4177	1555	460	1434	2012	
34	48	20069	11863	45370	21713	4808	1469	228	720	2013	
37	119	22338	14499	42778	22338	5494	1511	291	845	2014	
2	35	580	45	129	83	42	168	1	573	2000	Afrique du sud
20	9	3165	373	2144	1934	528	812	2	533	2011	
22	38	3171	256	1695	2059	840	1012	17	717	2012	
27	23	3435	300	1437	1815	505	716	2	422	2013	
6	110	3290	187	350	2168	404	663	22	468	2014	
3	1	92	15544	438	209	176	105	0	1751	2000	Amérique latine et Caraïbes
...	32	864	69794	21258	3870	1299	1363	10	453	2011	
0	83	1036	70030	36961	7618	8835	1512	6	559	2012	
0	21	147	52893	41388	7755	5983	1056	0	943	2013	
0	21	417	52088	38616	7828	6295	1481	2	1862	2014	
...	...	25	238	36	1	8	0	...	...	2000	Brésil
...	0	73	8840	4884	1705	804	48	...	...	2011	
0	...	67	5625	4848	3432	1261	137	1	0	2012	
...	0	54	3638	4051	1587	736	35	0	...	2013	
...	0	60	7075	3485	2348	1062	49	1	...	2014	
10	7	77	363	6606	489	2581	66	133	1116	2000	Asie orientale
45	28	1821	5971	32918	2329	31917	1375	819	3688	2011	
6	21	1681	5943	33166	1926	38581	1554	948	3096	2012	
0	145	2387	4020	31436	2080	40870	1712	971	3123	2013	
8	143	2622	3543	31411	2899	42326	1799	958	3226	2014	
10	6	59	209	2528	334	1360	53	0	...	2000	Chine
45	27	772	4078	10898	812	7706	622	223	...	2011	
6	18	713	4251	10539	409	7461	797	252	...	2012	
0	11	763	3230	11246	1000	10465	856	293	...	2013	
8	4	952	2734	11000	1806	11197	916	262	...	2014	
0	2008	8	679	7173	155	487	212	0	0	2000	Asie méridionale
21	4417	5245	5143	53798	3821	14050	12650	35	12168	2011	
16	3450	6089	5433	38463	2821	12057	16519	1	7184	2012	
14	3194	9451	3846	33461	2704	12639	19659	5	10944	2013	
3	662	10871	4446	41904	16495	7711	20562	1	813	2014	
3	9	28	78	13054	1725	11077	110	523	3	2000	Asie du Sud-est
9	135	1570	483	61296	15083	81241	875	2772	582	2011	
13	43	2147	244	56410	12216	86450	1188	2877	615	2012	
0	223	2855	533	52381	12800	88353	1637	2525	717	2013	
0	223	2899	539	50324	12770	84271	1638	2536	526	2014	
25	3405	446	1706	49457	3799	7735	3937	...	3106	2000	Asie occidentale
136	13359	3911	7331	380886	53737	25318	10274	550	54462	2011	
149	17743	7854	7269	445190	58463	30183	12281	740	24013	2012	
77	16927	6963	7360	468656	59535	30873	10990	367	21905	2013	
54	14889	18301	7501	399160	92940	95645	15137	365	20515	2014	
0	...	0	...	101	0	2	...	1	0	2000	Océanie
...	...	0	15	178	0	27	...	88	220	2011	
...	...	2	17	61	0	28	...	94	235	2012	
...	...	0	3	82	1	37	0	115	218	2013	
...	...	0	5	74	0	38	0	136	201	2014	

Voir la fin du tableau pour la remarque générale et les notes.

World merchandise exports by provenance and destination (Table D)

In million U.S. dollars f.o.b.

Exports from	Year	World 1/ Monde 1/	Developed economies 2/ — Total	Asia-Pacific Total	Japan Japon	Europe Total	Germany Allemagne	North America Total	U.S.A. É.-U.	CIS Total	CIS Europe
					Chemicals (SITC, Rev. 3, 5)						
World 1/	2000	565919	375650	29177	21235	260900	42877	85574	66221	7293	6108
	2011	1931460	1141086	88523	62960	820486	142867	232077	186276	54780	47830
	2012	1900749	1100703	87822	61602	781764	137156	231117	184429	59403	50331
	2013	1959823	1130102	83558	58172	814084	142841	232460	185070	64002	53865
	2014	2003400	1152422	82828	57511	829279	144536	240315	192498	60109	50032
Developed Economies - Asia-Pacific 2/	2000	39061	14664	1393	353	6096	976	7176	6972	23	19
	2011	94250	22554	2711	568	9883	2074	9959	9679	187	179
	2012	89464	21631	2579	584	9065	1848	9987	9703	191	179
	2013	85259	20662	2354	549	8202	1748	10107	9764	200	192
	2014	80954	20132	2237	567	7880	1708	10015	9747	201	191
Japan	2000	35160	12405	386	.	5500	899	6520	6354	22	18
	2011	84507	18269	572	.	8893	1860	8804	8625	179	172
	2012	78940	17200	490	.	7949	1573	8761	8589	179	169
	2013	75823	16498	424	.	7236	1522	8838	8610	180	173
	2014	72246	16108	364	.	6998	1512	8746	8566	180	171
Developed Economies - Europe 2/	2000	317313	260845	11710	8572	212446	36797	36689	33954	4360	4031
	2011	1002351	793079	31313	21440	658240	122087	103526	94394	35547	32876
	2012	967319	756032	31367	21645	620779	117638	103887	94388	36204	33168
	2013	1023375	795800	30957	21054	660284	122958	104559	93773	39549	36001
	2014	1038604	808401	28277	18829	670137	123825	109987	99765	36736	33230
France	2000	40440	32870	1270	908	27982	5990	3618	3362	530	469
	2011	100571	73639	3837	2970	63001	13748	6801	5965	3317	3060
	2012	97808	70990	3493	2691	60749	13141	6749	5951	3219	2936
	2013	101349	72277	3209	2400	62603	13895	6465	5633	3698	3350
	2014	100776	71878	2785	2015	62524	13746	6569	5844	3418	3051
Germany	2000	69666	53574	3003	2398	43606	.	6964	6328	1211	1124
	2011	213341	162725	6429	4752	139701	.	16595	15080	9365	8728
	2012	204297	153160	6456	4763	127328	.	19376	17890	9740	9021
	2013	216625	161825	6590	4838	134201	.	21034	19355	10416	9638
	2014	224614	169746	6742	4945	139484	.	23520	21749	9399	8677
Developed Economies - North America 2/	2000	94865	61283	8502	6582	24815	2845	27966	12116	312	267
	2011	246465	139608	16720	12707	61601	8168	61287	29122	1363	1271
	2012	243992	137536	17176	13132	60931	7939	59429	27212	1431	1310
	2013	246501	137491	15378	11405	61241	7628	60872	27967	1543	1381
	2014	249755	141133	16045	12095	63057	7869	62031	28222	1263	1083
United States	2000	80057	48161	8179	6371	24133	2719	15849	.	302	260
	2011	207030	106512	16109	12386	58245	7790	32158	.	1297	1211
	2012	206944	106380	16637	12842	57532	7545	32211	.	1374	1257
	2013	208624	105564	14883	11151	57781	7204	32899	.	1473	1317
	2014	211762	108809	15042	11329	59963	7605	33804	.	1204	1031
South-Eastern Europe	2000	1338	541	2	2	513	46	26	26	148	138
	2011	8162	4112	19	13	3800	1144	293	291	1042	956
	2012	7825	3917	20	13	3625	1174	272	263	1081	981
	2013	8401	4391	25	15	4189	1420	177	173	1217	1096
	2014	8789	4698	21	13	4489	1553	188	180	1217	1082
Commonwealth of Independent States	2000	8543	4570	35	33	3211	283	1324	1291	1360	838
	2011	39351	14176	171	101	11938	854	2068	1746	7346	5944
	2012	43743	16115	186	60	13919	725	2010	1636	10556	7656
	2013	37199	12093	158	70	10061	842	1874	1513	10737	7650
	2014	35522	11700	149	70	10043	819	1507	1228	9958	6961
Russian Federation 4/	2000	6181	3740	23	21	2535	218	1183	1165	607	189
	2011	21792	8467	112	71	7076	553	1279	1168	3457	2896
	2012	24610	8517	103	34	7272	486	1142	1054	5858	3958
	2013	23533	8703	75	27	7508	569	1120	1004	6383	4272
	2014	22222	8219	71	25	7090	537	1058	948	6027	4034

For general note and footnotes see end of table

Les exportations de marchandises du monde par provenance et destination (Tableau D)

En millions de dollars E.-U. f.o.b.

← Exportations vers

South-Eastern Europe Europe du Sud-Est	Northern Africa Afrique septentrio-nale	Sub-Saharan Africa Afrique subsahari-enne	Latin America and the Caribbean Amérique latine et Caraïbes	Eastern Asia Asie orientale	Southern Asia Asie méridionale	South-eastern Asia Asie du Sud-Est	Western Asia Asie occidentale	Oceania Océanie	Other 3/ Autres 3/	Année	Exportations en provence de ↓
\multicolumn{11}{c}{Produits chimiques (CTCI, Rev. 3, 5)}	
2699	4509	7655	39047	68018	8957	27494	16979	324	7294	2000	Monde 1/
17821	18411	35060	138434	277536	60515	102142	73386	1531	10758	2011	
17495	20158	35749	144297	273221	58427	106419	72844	1629	10404	2012	
19157	22339	40627	147446	270406	60481	116308	83859	1127	3967	2013	
19724	23066	42309	148850	277998	64496	119741	89653	1200	3831	2014	
2	52	161	1390	16114	491	5662	301	95	107	2000	Economies développées -
36	93	508	1442	54410	1714	12028	982	268	27	2011	Asie-Pacifique 2/
33	82	385	1482	51412	1626	11287	1035	278	22	2012	
31	81	310	1352	49480	1403	10571	885	273	11	2013	
37	89	293	1401	45520	1535	10587	891	251	16	2014	
2	45	105	1298	15458	446	5143	230	6	...	2000	Japon
32	84	289	1128	52026	1254	10426	813	6	...	2011	
26	69	229	1150	48442	1174	9650	813	8	...	2012	
26	67	220	1029	46953	1084	9041	719	6	...	2013	
30	70	216	1097	43475	1204	9147	713	6	...	2014	
2196	3328	3857	9213	8702	2805	4847	10664	146	6351	2000	Economies développées -
13854	10868	12382	29878	39646	10835	15393	38025	389	2456	2011	Europe 2/
13608	11850	12322	32089	39360	9813	15756	37387	381	2518	2012	
14965	13028	13243	34152	42626	9974	16636	40481	386	2536	2013	
15246	13399	13563	34451	45411	10380	16865	40971	436	2745	2014	
193	1065	1052	1207	1065	286	690	1358	122	2	2000	France
978	2972	3132	3569	4093	1051	2869	4607	332	11	2011	
907	3114	3168	3779	4076	966	2762	4487	298	43	2012	
1058	3367	3530	4282	4435	991	2699	4676	312	24	2013	
1098	3398	3154	4534	4598	1045	2662	4664	308	18	2014	
423	372	617	2378	2718	681	1316	2344	6	4026	2000	Allemagne
2400	1431	2245	7588	12564	3054	3776	8007	8	178	2011	
2465	1481	2026	8092	12732	2794	3786	7845	7	169	2012	
2712	1594	2110	8418	13756	2812	3923	8879	11	169	2013	
2914	1609	2361	8160	14455	2952	4108	8757	7	146	2014	
19	215	666	17202	9182	676	3844	1453	13	0	2000	Economies développées -
73	849	1994	51215	30630	5216	10705	4788	25	0	2011	Amérique du Nord 2/
69	920	2127	53517	28851	4110	10238	5157	36	0	2012	
93	957	2106	55329	29118	3843	10609	5378	35	0	2013	
111	956	2088	55344	29519	3753	10014	5541	33	0	2014	
17	207	648	16767	8305	619	3605	1413	12	...	2000	Etats-Unis
67	830	1823	49312	28557	4729	9280	4602	21	...	2011	
65	902	1947	51540	27078	3765	8895	4977	23	...	2012	
89	938	1967	53412	27079	3435	9446	5193	29	...	2013	
102	942	1933	53628	27481	3330	8983	5326	24	...	2014	
223	21	21	18	9	19	19	262	0	57	2000	Europe du Sud-Est
1686	79	79	137	75	159	67	722	1	5	2011	
1584	126	63	148	90	85	40	685	1	4	2012	
1712	119	70	55	93	81	42	616	0	5	2013	
1766	86	58	65	106	131	59	590	0	13	2014	
65	78	40	548	1031	245	118	488	1	1	2000	Communauté d'Etats
452	255	541	5199	5660	2400	1366	1879	2	75	2011	Indépendants
426	223	824	4347	5556	2460	1306	1881	0	49	2012	
446	277	785	3462	4925	1329	986	2107	0	51	2013	
418	171	648	3368	4971	1099	1144	1996	1	48	2014	
38	48	16	378	889	159	62	243	1	0	2000	Fédération de Russie 4/
198	74	194	3049	3009	1309	816	1195	0	26	2011	
267	76	468	2887	3021	1580	784	1145	0	6	2012	
335	111	449	2595	2280	682	577	1410	...	8	2013	
316	105	424	2450	2153	644	545	1331	...	8	2014	

Voir la fin du tableau pour la remarque générale et les notes.

World merchandise exports by provenance and destination (Table D)

In million U.S. dollars f.o.b.

Exports from	Year	World 1/ Monde 1/	Total	Asia-Pacific Total	Japan Japon	Europe Total	Germany Allemagne	North America Total	U.S.A. É.-U.	CIS Total	CIS Europe
					Chemicals (SITC, Rev. 3, 5) [cont.]						
Northern Africa	2000	2350	1095	25	2	1015	49	55	54	3	3
	2011	11302	4369	102	22	3792	84	475	464	40	30
	2012	11695	4395	28	6	3910	138	458	430	47	35
	2013	10656	3936	18	10	3635	42	284	274	25	18
	2014	11319	4607	19	10	4272	93	316	299	31	22
Sub-Saharan Africa	2000	2847	946	141	79	445	64	361	330	38	38
	2011	11642	2959	339	233	1432	152	1188	1164	52	52
	2012	12046	2972	597	473	1382	109	993	961	41	40
	2013	11631	2546	285	103	1402	152	859	811	46	45
	2014	11944	2976	220	85	1754	334	1002	948	51	50
South Africa	2000	2055	874	137	79	382	57	355	324	1	0
	2011	7229	2264	333	232	951	133	980	967	12	12
	2012	7349	2312	590	467	933	78	788	772	5	5
	2013	6857	1757	281	103	795	87	681	660	7	6
	2014	7042	2074	217	84	1100	281	757	735	6	5
Latin America and the Caribbean	2000	16624	7477	325	259	2088	315	5064	4945	12	11
	2011	59570	26835	1295	1073	9161	889	16379	15678	75	69
	2012	56239	23877	923	682	8270	704	14684	14041	73	63
	2013	55138	22776	860	564	7127	742	14788	14120	79	73
	2014	54431	22662	849	581	7555	795	14258	13612	89	80
Brazil	2000	3565	1471	157	141	649	152	665	641	3	3
	2011	15055	6626	582	509	3458	476	2586	2491	19	18
	2012	15004	6816	434	373	2980	323	3401	3315	23	21
	2013	14268	6148	328	281	2835	313	2984	2898	26	24
	2014	13221	5290	327	278	2587	304	2376	2287	43	41
Eastern Asia	2000	45641	11728	4104	3441	4184	868	3439	3221	444	368
	2011	236096	66146	23263	18346	23583	4735	19300	17995	5145	4032
	2012	232345	63041	21103	16074	22041	4119	19897	18565	5364	4162
	2013	243656	62881	19570	15133	23236	4201	20075	18696	5794	4414
	2014	260441	67022	20438	15701	24942	4448	21641	20156	6021	4674
China	2000	12098	6060	1714	1493	2570	645	1775	1661	131	93
	2011	114723	46294	13765	11024	18423	3731	14107	13140	3539	2772
	2012	113522	43570	12106	8894	17083	3251	14381	13432	3836	2942
	2013	119566	43841	11424	8422	17573	3319	14844	13836	4278	3238
	2014	134486	47728	12338	8918	19127	3538	16263	15160	4474	3474
Southern Asia	2000	5035	1853	171	102	1150	223	532	480	233	152
	2011	41838	13585	945	547	7160	1232	5480	5132	1369	900
	2012	42498	14909	1063	636	7132	1312	6714	6261	1312	916
	2013	46689	16982	1172	711	8408	1541	7401	6943	1414	1018
	2014	47713	16187	1083	641	7753	1382	7351	6978	1226	884
South-Eastern Asia	2000	21083	6188	2395	1681	2423	199	1369	1309	43	41
	2011	106000	31687	10944	7703	15815	587	4928	4659	353	298
	2012	108643	31938	11344	7864	15655	557	4939	4673	333	283
	2013	106897	26844	11030	7773	10728	560	5086	4892	334	292
	2014	107379	27504	11381	8148	10819	574	5305	4852	341	307
Western Asia	2000	11203	4458	374	128	2513	213	1571	1522	315	201
	2011	74204	21825	561	206	14070	858	7194	5952	2260	1222
	2012	84581	24166	1295	351	15025	869	7846	6296	2770	1538
	2013	83968	23451	1549	672	15528	975	6375	6141	3063	1684
	2014	96089	25144	1892	672	16541	1108	6711	6511	2974	1467
Oceania	2000	16	2	1	0	1	0	0	0	...	...
	2011	229	151	140	0	10	4	1	1	0	0
	2012	360	174	142	82	30	24	2	2	0	0
	2013	454	249	203	113	43	32	2	2	0	0
	2014	459	256	217	99	37	29	2	2	0	0

For general note and footnotes see end of table

Les exportations de marchandises du monde par provenance et destination (Tableau D)

En millions de dollars E.-U. f.o.b.

← Exportations vers

South-Eastern Europe Europe du Sud-Est	Northern Africa Afrique septentrionale	Sub-Saharan Africa Afrique subsaharienne	Latin America and the Caribbean Amérique latine et Caraïbes	Eastern Asia Asie orientale	Southern Asia Asie méridionale	South-eastern Asia Asie du Sud-Est	Western Asia Asie occidentale	Oceania Océanie	Other 3/ Autres 3/	Année	Exportations en provence de ↓
\multicolumn{11}{c}{Produits chimiques (CTCI, Rev. 3, 5)[suite]}	
9	172	44	118	32	545	42	255	0	34	2000	Afrique septentrionale
132	671	634	1183	126	2242	184	1583	0	139	2011	
206	968	768	1384	210	1654	147	1802	0	112	2012	
237	813	760	1414	87	1274	69	1931	0	109	2013	
181	758	816	1512	67	1351	65	1822	0	109	2014	
5	9	1245	105	116	233	72	69	0	6	2000	Afrique subsaharienne
5	73	6214	397	434	834	323	310	5	34	2011	
20	66	6358	426	547	667	512	404	4	30	2012	
18	49	6875	389	428	564	382	310	2	22	2013	
18	52	6579	339	553	604	450	301	2	19	2014	
5	9	658	101	114	160	70	62	0	1	2000	Afrique du sud
5	42	3256	337	380	395	273	258	3	6	2011	
1	31	3316	365	399	240	352	303	3	21	2012	
1	22	3489	366	352	289	316	247	1	11	2013	
2	21	3442	277	378	214	363	258	2	7	2014	
2	19	147	8269	362	66	162	83	0	24	2000	Amérique latine et Caraïbes
27	123	576	28258	2121	337	526	469	1	220	2011	
30	129	545	27737	2146	342	589	480	1	290	2012	
27	114	492	27714	2056	402	610	617	0	251	2013	
21	131	517	27206	2129	411	549	458	0	256	2014	
1	10	88	1693	156	21	80	40	0	...	2000	Brésil
2	53	404	6499	855	147	219	229	1	...	2011	
2	59	334	6345	868	115	196	246	1	0	2012	
3	46	310	6202	821	176	261	270	0	5	2013	
2	50	260	6021	894	204	219	237	0	...	2014	
42	205	628	1318	23683	1634	5179	760	17	3	2000	Asie orientale
407	1751	5219	12328	90192	19824	26842	8143	95	5	2011	
432	1883	5470	13263	86325	19563	28810	8065	125	5	2012	
451	1985	6278	14765	90164	20253	31636	9306	137	5	2013	
485	2200	7090	16037	92624	23472	34905	10417	164	6	2014	
23	91	219	511	2632	779	1356	290	6	...	2000	Chine
289	1018	3709	8529	18225	14198	14061	4800	59	...	2011	
304	1113	3965	9461	17086	13636	15511	4959	82	...	2012	
295	1200	4625	10708	17610	14005	17493	5424	87	...	2013	
325	1386	5395	11947	19272	17018	20391	6438	112	...	2014	
8	65	352	280	647	512	519	561	4	0	2000	Asie méridionale
102	534	3377	2454	6759	4572	3846	5003	24	213	2011	
137	617	3532	2818	5864	4118	4296	4817	23	56	2012	
205	702	4475	2794	5920	4597	4541	4854	28	178	2013	
212	649	4411	2818	8321	5125	3983	4741	27	13	2014	
14	55	275	232	6051	1229	6582	369	43	1	2000	Asie du Sud-est
44	300	1500	4325	28952	7155	29014	2414	223	34	2011	
39	285	1605	4720	30026	6944	30378	2094	243	39	2012	
41	294	1655	4051	31612	7475	32238	2088	232	32	2013	
39	285	1611	4097	31404	7715	32137	1983	230	32	2014	
113	291	211	354	2089	501	445	1714	0	711	2000	Asie occidentale
1005	2815	2024	1616	18531	5226	1816	9066	469	7550	2011	
912	3010	1738	2367	22720	7044	3027	9037	512	7278	2012	
933	3921	3564	1970	13776	9284	7946	15286	6	767	2013	
1189	4290	4630	2211	17247	8920	8944	19941	25	575	2014	
0	0	7	0	0	0	3	...	4	0	2000	Océanie
...	...	12	3	1	1	32	1	28	0	2011	
0	...	13	0	113	1	33	0	25	0	2012	
0	...	15	0	119	1	43	0	27	0	2013	
0	...	5	1	125	0	39	0	32	1	2014	

Voir la fin du tableau pour la remarque générale et les notes.

World merchandise exports by provenance and destination (Table D)

In million U.S. dollars f.o.b.

Exports from	Year	World 1/ Monde 1/	Developed economies 2/ Économies développées 2/ Total	Asia-Pacific Asie-Pacifique Total	Japan Japon	Europe Total	Germany Allemagne	North America Amérique du Nord Total	U.S.A. É.-U.	Commonwealth of Independent States Communauté d'Etats Indépendants Total	Europe
Manufactured goods classified chiefly by material (SITC, Rev. 3, 6)
World 1/	2000	864884	568460	40337	30998	366073	71059	162050	130369	10940	8871
	2011	2333930	1280716	103218	72541	893887	178255	283611	228387	70720	55214
	2012	2229619	1181075	96738	65466	796121	155660	288216	231050	79857	58719
	2013	2274351	1186962	94673	62597	802935	157828	289354	233985	83177	59748
	2014	2319555	1224173	96540	64887	824392	161931	303240	247071	75184	53438
Developed Economies - Asia-Pacific 2/	2000	56349	18597	3849	1803	5456	1114	9292	8625	158	116
	2011	129563	28095	6706	2521	9171	1696	12219	11329	1323	1156
	2012	123177	27405	5947	2058	8622	1418	12837	11844	1468	1280
	2013	111365	24183	5331	1738	7665	1265	11187	10400	1609	1358
	2014	99306	22579	5634	2388	6245	1028	10700	9964	1292	1066
Japan	2000	46676	13690	850	.	4552	1022	8288	7686	157	115
	2011	109689	20516	1864	.	7822	1606	10830	10023	1309	1145
	2012	105772	20610	1735	.	7206	1349	11669	10737	1452	1268
	2013	94294	17683	1580	.	5891	1181	10212	9478	1594	1346
	2014	82448	15625	1311	.	4870	967	9443	8779	1279	1056
Developed Economies - Europe 2/	2000	389015	325035	7268	4783	285846	59601	31921	29032	4806	4377
	2011	898077	700463	12162	6742	643555	140234	44746	39434	25415	23195
	2012	812253	622982	10648	5974	568301	122260	44034	39229	24400	22315
	2013	829772	630047	10486	5582	576978	124996	42582	38122	25231	23027
	2014	833687	642625	10217	5753	584990	127257	47418	42830	22286	19986
France	2000	41170	35053	654	444	31193	7735	3206	2793	205	180
	2011	70050	54569	1053	671	50021	13718	3496	3112	952	840
	2012	62636	48366	1009	636	43774	11673	3582	3201	809	728
	2013	61940	47455	869	477	43004	11705	3581	3206	778	691
	2014	62090	48176	797	473	43406	11792	3973	3570	625	542
Germany	2000	76521	63845	1352	846	56559	.	5935	5391	1276	1198
	2011	198933	157153	2506	1387	142973	.	11674	10580	7026	6601
	2012	178993	139397	2397	1287	125578	.	11422	10430	6253	5805
	2013	181344	140372	2443	1231	126528	.	11401	10374	6062	5594
	2014	184583	144667	2280	1296	130404	.	11983	10929	5339	4890
Developed Economies - North America 2/	2000	111200	77822	5107	4207	13184	1973	59531	34995	124	99
	2011	195517	116093	6578	4367	27035	4225	82480	43918	655	549
	2012	193819	113898	6669	4186	25688	3837	81540	41676	675	558
	2013	196272	112346	6478	4161	25144	3530	80724	41867	738	615
	2014	202374	114385	6317	4049	26606	3903	81462	42681	779	649
United States	2000	71990	40258	4380	3549	11348	1845	24529	.	112	89
	2011	139414	66008	5725	3715	21730	3993	38553	.	547	462
	2012	141623	66853	5941	3710	21057	3667	39855	.	567	462
	2013	144848	65963	5849	3684	21271	3356	38843	.	623	516
	2014	150283	67399	5711	3593	22917	3699	38770	.	686	565
South-Eastern Europe	2000	4672	3293	9	7	2958	442	327	279	107	89
	2011	24837	16454	22	9	15862	3465	570	394	1077	1036
	2012	21808	13889	29	11	13311	2683	548	440	1036	976
	2013	23011	15003	37	21	14452	3435	513	405	1244	1163
	2014	23343	15756	85	66	14989	2988	681	525	1044	962
Commonwealth of Independent States	2000	27524	14483	1243	1239	10728	1615	2513	2426	4228	3246
	2011	96461	42396	2462	2411	35390	5456	4544	4442	19238	14977
	2012	102091	43156	2992	2933	35282	5099	4881	4734	26144	17703
	2013	92911	38059	2021	1992	31397	4066	4641	4434	26064	16408
	2014	86665	36161	1943	1924	29670	3959	4548	4333	22792	14055
Russian Federation 4/	2000	18349	11959	1176	1174	8853	1330	1930	1887	1126	399
	2011	50474	29777	1319	1305	25172	3427	3286	3231	4876	2843
	2012	57214	32063	1731	1719	26511	3476	3821	3722	10899	5338
	2013	53831	28754	1466	1453	23568	3146	3720	3554	11691	5112
	2014	50834	27153	1384	1372	22256	2971	3512	3356	11041	4827

For general note and footnotes see end of table

Les exportations de marchandises du monde par provenance et destination (Tableau D)

En millions de dollars E.-U. f.o.b.

← Exportations vers

South-Eastern Europe Europe du Sud-Est	Northern Africa Afrique septentrio-nale	Sub-Saharan Africa Afrique subsahari-enne	Latin America and the Caribbean Amérique latine et Caraïbes	Eastern Asia Asie orientale	Southern Asia Asie méridionale	South-eastern Asia Asie du Sud-Est	Western Asia Asie occidentale	Oceania Océanie	Other 3/ Autres 3/	Année	Exportations en provence de ↓
\multicolumn{12}{c}{Articles manufacturés classés principalement d'après la matière première (CTCI, Rev. 3, 6)}
6496	9118	11570	47769	109879	18142	42194	36491	1019	2807	2000	Monde 1/
29240	32672	55931	132973	299086	112683	156730	152625	2310	8243	2011	
26449	35408	59520	137275	282288	103703	166194	149286	2383	6181	2012	
28017	37073	64720	136709	282973	113047	177227	156897	1900	5649	2013	
30149	38712	65596	137712	283554	107736	186288	164356	1824	4271	2014	
6	153	545	1540	21930	1109	10186	1524	317	285	2000	Economies développées - Asie-Pacifique 2/
114	456	1280	4253	56467	4051	28048	4720	691	63	2011	
81	425	1323	4192	48794	3644	29622	5495	672	56	2012	
42	427	1477	4173	44258	3291	26733	4532	594	46	2013	
49	483	1122	4144	36964	3316	24193	4603	506	55	2014	
6	150	429	1446	19458	961	8894	1421	64	...	2000	Japon
112	339	1030	3770	50804	3567	23780	4357	105	...	2011	
77	359	1035	3966	44551	3279	25073	5259	111	...	2012	
39	386	1275	4017	39040	2959	22914	4296	91	...	2013	
45	414	981	3983	32546	2931	20217	4370	58	0	2014	
4904	5803	3785	6690	10369	6568	4383	14766	159	1747	2000	Economies développées - Europe 2/
19687	16492	11645	17568	33854	22758	11150	35306	326	3414	2011	
18083	16751	12343	18134	32502	19109	11288	33825	323	2512	2012	
19319	17274	12548	18491	34413	20221	12388	37035	283	2523	2013	
21023	17506	11992	17511	33149	18132	11099	35802	284	2278	2014	
247	1711	670	619	814	243	357	1144	103	4	2000	France
1004	2956	1593	1420	2577	1092	880	2791	187	29	2011	
887	2783	1502	1378	2420	949	733	2619	170	19	2012	
962	2697	1426	1571	2543	639	741	2934	172	22	2013	
1006	2684	1576	1370	2474	625	656	2687	173	38	2014	
1158	761	652	1783	2199	610	950	2114	10	1163	2000	Allemagne
4081	1485	1852	4909	9229	2679	2969	7018	36	497	2011	
3656	1395	1771	4865	8990	2598	2950	6705	23	390	2012	
3865	1326	1801	4855	9405	1976	3408	7700	20	552	2013	
4485	1377	1899	4409	9885	1846	2659	7587	24	408	2014	
24	187	591	21581	5485	516	2135	2709	25	0	2000	Economies développées - Amérique du Nord 2/
114	597	1516	39661	16564	5755	3942	10572	48	0	2011	
83	415	1585	42891	15869	4597	3837	9903	67	0	2012	
98	430	1903	44074	16382	5790	3986	10465	60	0	2013	
122	462	2343	45742	17556	5655	4024	11272	33	0	2014	
20	139	569	20958	4946	431	1954	2581	24	...	2000	Etats-Unis
80	465	1366	37749	14546	5034	3666	9910	42	...	2011	
68	356	1462	40936	14269	3999	3573	9481	60	...	2012	
84	353	1519	42328	15004	5171	3714	10035	55	...	2013	
105	372	1764	44004	16136	5089	3818	10881	29	...	2014	
462	83	27	82	64	29	16	492	0	16	2000	Europe du Sud-Est
3405	398	103	90	616	181	48	2459	1	6	2011	
3045	326	57	176	963	122	55	2134	0	5	2012	
3046	374	77	192	849	100	95	2007	0	24	2013	
2911	410	86	207	734	88	65	2037	0	6	2014	
549	670	232	540	3145	826	845	2004	1	0	2000	Communauté d'Etats Indépendants
1877	1038	899	1182	7443	6089	2261	13961	6	72	2011	
1214	1483	839	1110	7736	3932	1925	14538	10	5	2012	
1137	1860	800	1162	6552	2902	1311	13054	6	3	2013	
1160	2188	701	1121	6128	2881	977	12548	6	3	2014	
160	310	122	368	2218	603	455	1027	...	0	2000	Fédération de Russie 4/
549	445	209	608	3272	4125	1007	5529	5	70	2011	
386	559	175	723	3293	2835	1043	5226	8	4	2012	
334	549	173	896	3141	2031	671	5584	6	2	2013	
315	518	163	846	2966	1918	634	5273	6	2	2014	

Voir la fin du tableau pour la remarque générale et les notes.

World merchandise exports by provenance and destination (Table D)

In million U.S. dollars f.o.b.

Exports from	Year	World 1/ Monde 1/	Developed economies 2/ Total (Asia-Pacific)	Asia-Pacific Total	Japan Japon	Europe Total	Germany Allemagne	North America Total	U.S.A. É.-U.	CIS Total	CIS Europe
Manufactured goods classified chiefly by material (SITC, Rev. 3, 6) [cont.]											
Northern Africa	2000	1898	1326	21	18	1193	68	112	104	8	1
	2011	9645	4481	34	21	4024	313	423	393	63	57
	2012	9106	3794	31	20	3368	281	396	367	68	59
	2013	8806	3593	30	19	3191	225	372	346	42	35
	2014	8388	3704	30	18	3317	244	358	332	38	33
Sub-Saharan Africa	2000	14234	9952	785	669	8089	262	1077	979	7	7
	2011	54615	32311	5416	5220	22948	1505	3947	3889	52	31
	2012	50621	27029	3604	3431	20025	1230	3400	3311	36	34
	2013	52321	27277	3739	3608	20383	1190	3154	3073	47	41
	2014	53051	28000	3672	3188	21117	1230	3211	3088	41	39
South Africa	2000	7487	4495	649	539	2888	176	958	862	2	2
	2011	28782	17519	5296	5124	8870	1423	3354	3302	28	26
	2012	23585	12985	3466	3309	6571	1064	2947	2864	33	31
	2013	23644	12913	3444	3322	6745	984	2724	2675	41	38
	2014	22679	11779	2856	2729	6269	1013	2654	2582	37	36
Latin America and the Caribbean	2000	42090	27538	1561	1446	6859	560	19117	18506	15	13
	2011	116655	57247	3387	2484	18026	1931	35834	34384	110	78
	2012	107227	54070	2955	1698	14115	1410	37001	35548	164	111
	2013	102423	51439	2221	1445	12093	943	37125	35734	173	130
	2014	103135	53691	2435	1549	13045	1165	38211	36768	169	93
Brazil	2000	11043	6548	666	612	2768	273	3114	2909	5	5
	2011	28753	14013	1168	1085	6429	1215	6415	6157	38	37
	2012	26626	12969	1057	958	5238	842	6674	6416	40	38
	2013	24903	12045	988	920	4603	460	6455	6275	78	73
	2014	26579	13898	1024	947	5548	680	7325	7112	63	38
Eastern Asia	2000	132035	46466	12332	10252	13552	2451	20582	18744	644	459
	2011	494374	174576	44225	33799	66010	11169	64341	57400	16393	10630
	2012	502334	173730	42296	31169	62527	10325	68908	61413	18645	11691
	2013	524946	173484	40186	28613	62128	10577	71170	63695	20515	12839
	2014	569782	185984	41396	29599	68211	11460	76376	68386	19740	12937
China	2000	42546	19264	5932	5145	6238	1178	7093	6500	332	189
	2011	319564	123326	27868	20426	49621	8762	45838	40554	14593	9235
	2012	334162	122405	27203	18747	46115	8275	49088	43273	16726	10167
	2013	361782	125175	26382	17859	46924	8448	51870	45989	18452	11265
	2014	401765	135926	27267	18566	52417	9257	56242	49869	17609	11306
Southern Asia	2000	24542	13637	1216	876	6243	1135	6177	5787	248	136
	2011	96585	34489	2071	1153	17991	2836	14428	13671	1063	518
	2012	86340	31723	2197	1081	15195	2451	14330	13507	1022	598
	2013	102507	37251	2311	1202	17653	2691	17287	16376	1087	698
	2014	94491	37002	2151	1125	18092	2612	16759	15883	1020	664
South-Eastern Asia	2000	34760	14652	6031	4932	4460	660	4161	3876	30	22
	2011	109629	34004	16816	13267	9455	1616	7734	7264	527	440
	2012	107108	33281	16809	12381	8352	1413	8121	7567	375	315
	2013	110724	35287	18686	13629	8232	1471	8369	7840	396	315
	2014	112019	34421	18022	13198	8145	1368	8253	7698	420	323
Western Asia	2000	25888	15273	733	609	7352	1172	7188	6965	563	305
	2011	104651	37261	882	295	24111	3809	12268	11793	4805	2548
	2012	111389	34229	931	371	21141	3251	12157	11349	5824	3078
	2013	116554	36656	1075	450	23415	3438	12165	11627	6030	3121
	2014	130438	47654	2735	1890	29746	4718	15173	14493	5563	2632
Oceania	2000	678	386	183	155	153	7	51	50	0	0
	2011	3321	2845	2459	252	309	0	77	76	0	0
	2012	2346	1888	1631	153	194	0	63	63	...	...
	2013	2739	2338	2069	136	203	0	65	65	0	0
	2014	2875	2211	1903	140	218	0	90	90	0	0

For general note and footnotes see end of table

Les exportations de marchandises du monde par provenance et destination (Tableau D)

En millions de dollars E.-U. f.o.b.

← Exportations vers

South-Eastern Europe Europe du Sud-Est	Northern Africa Afrique septentrio-nale	Sub-Saharan Africa Afrique subsahari-enne	Latin America and the Caribbean Amérique latine et Caraïbes	Eastern Asia Asie orientale	Southern Asia Asie méridionale	South-eastern Asia Asie du Sud-Est	Western Asia Asie occidentale	Oceania Océanie	Other 3/ Autres 3/	Année	Exportations en provence de ↓
	**Articles manufacturés classés principalement d'après la matière première (CTCI, Rev. 3, 6)[suite]**
2	208	62	15	40	5	18	167	0	47	2000	Afrique septentrionale
28	1133	739	97	207	126	32	2652	0	87	2011	
38	1743	725	82	231	124	67	2146	1	87	2012	
36	1556	729	108	191	97	22	2331	0	101	2013	
31	1474	695	99	215	119	36	1878	1	99	2014	
4	23	1741	338	1022	157	390	586	1	14	2000	Afrique subsaharienne
20	113	9872	615	7191	785	698	2498	21	439	2011	
62	125	10449	573	7612	838	743	2851	28	275	2012	
68	80	11138	407	7487	959	1052	3491	21	295	2013	
75	86	11044	348	7491	1027	1492	3156	3	287	2014	
3	10	819	295	947	114	317	483	1	2	2000	Afrique du sud
13	28	5308	536	3383	465	563	931	3	5	2011	
3	20	5380	495	2735	341	556	988	24	26	2012	
8	19	5242	362	3213	282	612	913	19	17	2013	
16	20	5439	304	3231	279	508	1041	2	24	2014	
2	110	254	10543	2545	113	462	461	2	45	2000	Amérique latine et Caraïbes
83	269	1013	31882	21916	441	2295	1333	7	57	2011	
35	194	854	29284	18793	418	2166	1173	8	66	2012	
61	204	951	28198	17780	378	1844	1336	4	55	2013	
71	217	1138	26142	17602	461	2157	1434	6	45	2014	
1	69	138	3135	666	47	255	179	1	...	2000	Brésil
17	113	587	8982	3166	262	1198	374	4	...	2011	
12	69	446	8766	2604	224	1182	309	4	0	2012	
18	78	520	7882	2875	122	952	330	3	0	2013	
16	97	555	7239	2685	219	1200	604	4	...	2014	
153	769	2159	5197	52187	5024	13626	5345	374	90	2000	Asie orientale
1295	5871	18323	30707	105648	38736	68645	33725	453	2	2011	
1313	6874	20835	33436	99632	34382	77214	35719	539	14	2012	
1444	7269	23367	32236	100988	37810	88931	38357	535	9	2013	
1592	8170	25811	34116	105175	45515	101284	41796	592	9	2014	
68	375	1160	1430	13538	1247	3224	1881	28	...	2000	Chine
1048	5092	16859	24822	47914	22720	38912	23958	319	...	2011	
1081	6083	19353	27177	46295	21753	47582	25295	412	...	2012	
1218	6572	21833	26266	49032	24877	59667	28291	398	...	2013	
1360	7463	24191	27998	53299	31514	71078	30877	450	...	2014	
12	251	1020	434	3956	1012	1179	2777	10	5	2000	Asie méridionale
187	1217	4579	2796	17437	7090	4739	20812	30	2147	2011	
190	1280	4317	3097	17408	7144	4644	15096	36	383	2012	
219	1307	5070	3442	21491	7840	6360	17950	30	460	2013	
341	1381	4754	3833	19240	8020	5278	13473	38	110	2014	
11	247	670	605	6881	1588	8266	1691	115	1	2000	Asie du Sud-est
117	869	2094	2474	23518	6116	32959	6188	671	90	2011	
71	932	2045	2481	22757	5978	32660	5827	616	86	2012	
87	837	2253	2478	23846	6585	32777	5767	308	103	2013	
88	846	2189	2407	26361	6597	32493	5807	287	103	2014	
365	613	471	194	2009	1189	687	3969	0	556	2000	Asie occidentale
2313	4220	3837	1646	7844	20545	1901	18399	13	1865	2011	
2237	4861	4109	1819	9648	23395	1959	20579	41	2690	2012	
2460	5456	4353	1745	8488	27039	1711	20571	16	2029	2013	
2687	5489	3679	2037	12417	15906	3175	30543	13	1275	2014	
1	...	14	9	245	4	2	0	14	1	2000	Océanie
0	...	31	1	379	10	12	0	43	0	2011	
0	0	39	0	343	20	14	1	41	0	2012	
0	...	54	2	250	33	16	2	42	0	2013	
0	0	43	3	521	19	15	6	55	1	2014	

Voir la fin du tableau pour la remarque générale et les notes.

World merchandise exports by provenance and destination (Table D)

In million U.S. dollars f.o.b.

Exports from	Year	World 1/ Monde 1/	Developed economies 2/ Économies développées 2/ Total	Asia-Pacific Asie-Pacifique Total	Japan Japon	Europe Total	Germany Allemagne	North America Amérique du Nord Total	U.S.A. É.-U.	Commonwealth of Independent States Communauté d'Etats Indépendants Total	Europe
						Machinery and transport equipment (SITC, Rev. 3, 7)					
World 1/	2000	2619224	1799271	137022	102478	985942	188822	676307	554529	19728	15840
	2011	5805603	3080600	256893	161782	1864533	406571	959174	787409	184872	159065
	2012	5831735	3005882	276168	172529	1695243	375904	1034471	854072	207101	173814
	2013	6034610	3081529	269316	174048	1751848	383303	1060365	879065	204089	167925
	2014	6195205	3243478	270670	178713	1853521	408241	1119288	936921	179399	144244
Developed Economies - Asia-Pacific 2/	2000	338298	189906	9501	291	63126	14800	117279	110881	536	422
	2011	496280	181817	16665	233	64416	15284	100735	93415	11792	10793
	2012	492813	188957	18499	225	54595	13523	115864	107338	12423	11279
	2013	430090	172130	15489	204	47968	12058	108673	101536	10662	9553
	2014	416480	167886	14272	193	48873	12162	104741	98074	9086	7858
Japan	2000	329680	185109	7675	.	61931	14533	115503	109214	526	414
	2011	480313	174181	13209	.	62868	14982	98104	91039	11715	10728
	2012	476231	181269	15212	.	53111	13249	112945	104736	12354	11228
	2013	414378	164643	12381	.	46456	11812	105806	98909	10583	9501
	2014	400681	159971	11073	.	47149	11917	101749	95351	9023	7816
Developed Economies - Europe 2/	2000	1019028	835582	24275	16825	697326	127649	113981	104691	11248	9772
	2011	2183141	1539357	48599	23928	1322979	278524	167779	150960	98256	89140
	2012	2055749	1419219	51059	25886	1190639	257368	177521	160512	103936	94810
	2013	2146565	1483081	51566	27037	1244019	267648	187496	168422	102186	91838
	2014	2231168	1571564	49833	27547	1318236	285619	203495	184823	85281	75480
France	2000	132952	103387	1699	1089	86545	19223	15143	14101	962	653
	2011	220871	147846	5734	1829	127227	46398	14885	13824	6018	5552
	2012	214196	137648	4646	2308	117354	45484	15648	14624	7748	7052
	2013	216670	142086	4757	2583	120385	45840	16944	15750	6247	5113
	2014	217571	145586	5133	3043	123041	46581	17412	16134	5484	4488
Germany	2000	272345	223326	8768	6855	175308	.	39250	37072	4105	3664
	2011	696182	464166	18923	11084	377556	.	67687	61417	35744	32466
	2012	664782	436362	20861	12202	340055	.	75445	67989	36790	33734
	2013	683228	448406	21003	12917	346806	.	80596	71404	36056	32583
	2014	712647	476550	19563	12401	372222	.	84764	77666	27051	24152
Developed Economies - North America 2/	2000	523665	335332	36795	28250	99404	18363	199133	101693	1535	1086
	2011	610726	315699	29292	14372	79347	19916	207060	88537	6866	5488
	2012	651430	335664	34152	15700	78544	19932	222968	97842	8069	6653
	2013	648232	325336	28679	14743	76592	18361	220065	95424	8149	6608
	2014	670209	336593	29292	15161	82853	19118	224449	98321	7625	6029
United States	2000	412200	227821	35994	27866	94397	17580	97431	.	1458	1018
	2011	500949	217981	27776	13815	71746	18410	118459	.	5926	4706
	2012	532008	228823	32611	15150	71108	18597	125104	.	7114	5865
	2013	532729	221997	27335	14246	70040	17245	124622	.	7254	5882
	2014	551298	229715	27971	14647	75640	18147	126104	.	6924	5471
South-Eastern Europe	2000	2785	2115	3	0	2009	521	103	93	83	72
	2011	33408	25247	55	22	24615	8567	576	529	2122	1864
	2012	31144	23552	55	20	22900	8188	596	550	1846	1604
	2013	38264	29053	60	29	28002	9704	991	944	2278	2086
	2014	41060	32001	71	32	31017	11344	913	862	2289	2085
Commonwealth of Independent States	2000	10412	3197	38	34	2867	478	293	271	4443	3317
	2011	33975	5899	271	249	5092	987	536	479	21393	17584
	2012	43325	6844	354	313	5828	1229	662	606	28617	20127
	2013	42656	7039	268	248	6108	1279	663	618	27079	18138
	2014	38064	6997	245	234	6113	1267	639	587	22940	14422
Russian Federation 4/	2000	6422	2634	35	34	2410	387	189	179	1573	749
	2011	12537	3185	255	247	2538	466	392	362	4332	2991
	2012	18528	3359	324	308	2581	551	455	415	9535	4581
	2013	21398	4149	251	247	3365	755	534	498	11077	5185
	2014	20448	4036	237	233	3274	698	525	483	10429	4881

For general note and footnotes see end of table

Les exportations de marchandises du monde par provenance et destination (Tableau D)

En millions de dollars E.-U. f.o.b.

← Exportations vers

South-Eastern Europe Europe du Sud-Est	Northern Africa Afrique septentrio-nale	Sub-Saharan Africa Afrique subsahari-enne	Latin America and the Caribbean Amérique latine et Caraïbes	Eastern Asia Asie orientale	Southern Asia Asie méridionale	South-eastern Asia Asie du Sud-Est	Western Asia Asie occidentale	Oceania Océanie	Other 3/ Autres 3/	Année	Exportations en provence de ↓
	Machines et matériel de transport (CTCI, Rev. 3, 7)
7389	17507	28879	158707	287529	22804	198745	71470	2013	5181	2000	Monde 1/
40232	49703	128162	404123	1086656	137385	413799	254038	16867	9165	2011	
37609	57160	122316	414894	1121042	122579	450603	271757	13702	7090	2012	
41532	59562	132447	427590	1200672	118417	453734	293225	16203	5610	2013	
45618	62212	132334	407843	1213690	120078	463023	306403	16684	4442	2014	
76	919	3093	17123	67403	2899	46357	8977	622	389	2000	Economies développées -
395	1830	9416	34276	155454	10238	66281	20897	3843	43	2011	Asie-Pacifique 2/
348	2499	8697	32937	135948	8372	73948	24659	3998	26	2012	
319	1710	7391	27500	118546	6092	59601	23283	2822	36	2013	
378	1729	6650	24586	115756	6576	55535	25464	2764	69	2014	
74	909	2942	16949	66606	2790	45359	8114	304	0	2000	Japon
379	1801	8832	33833	153533	9983	64252	19432	2372	...	2011	
321	2457	7984	32414	134182	8139	71889	22832	2391	...	2012	
293	1667	6830	27085	116889	5913	57656	21356	1462	...	2013	
339	1690	6205	24155	114128	6414	53547	23575	1632	...	2014	
6113	11744	15238	29111	38549	8198	22947	36132	553	3614	2000	Economies développées -
30833	28930	42611	71141	169961	35008	50676	111812	1679	2877	2011	Europe 2/
29458	30027	39972	73138	161848	27354	56282	109268	1793	3454	2012	
32830	33360	41830	76928	170284	24770	56470	119919	2234	2674	2013	
35778	33785	40869	71375	185340	25394	55277	121329	2622	2554	2014	
536	4200	4160	4149	5250	1384	2817	5172	337	600	2000	France
2502	8146	6566	7525	17181	3675	7672	12755	696	287	2011	
2537	8201	5240	8126	18303	2937	10984	11466	558	449	2012	
2817	8173	5428	8814	16874	2528	11573	11029	977	124	2013	
2935	7430	5399	6985	18600	2669	10244	11410	647	182	2014	
1738	1857	3307	7626	12322	1917	5981	9509	102	555	2000	Allemagne
8799	5310	10730	23138	83991	12258	15855	35918	239	34	2011	
8648	5395	10459	24017	78602	9650	17559	36890	338	72	2012	
9121	6003	10881	24398	81754	8948	17180	39968	305	209	2013	
10565	6374	10710	22721	92220	8807	17407	39331	855	56	2014	
266	2440	3056	84864	48817	2259	32401	12523	171	1	2000	Economies développées -
685	2319	9684	137661	68399	8363	31968	28597	484	0	2011	Amérique du Nord 2/
573	3202	10771	150655	67173	6553	31756	36493	514	8	2012	
699	3455	10673	153752	74062	6978	29820	35071	236	1	2013	
792	4699	10500	155260	80885	6789	30433	36417	215	1	2014	
244	2348	2934	83422	47397	2166	32085	12159	164	1	2000	Etats-Unis
590	2046	8798	133654	65557	7724	30857	27385	431	...	2011	
492	2937	9685	146768	64593	5961	30361	34797	478	...	2012	
614	3126	9822	149884	71153	6556	28481	33642	199	...	2013	
715	4480	9582	152011	77800	6422	29013	34455	181	...	2014	
193	70	20	25	35	42	17	154	0	30	2000	Europe du Sud-Est
1599	568	529	360	590	417	143	1816	15	1	2011	
1346	797	403	430	651	409	136	1490	83	2	2012	
1649	823	321	983	709	352	187	1864	42	3	2013	
1776	940	368	758	778	302	177	1658	11	2	2014	
198	155	103	138	844	680	146	501	1	6	2000	Communauté d'Etats
613	513	267	841	1505	1740	616	519	4	65	2011	Indépendants
831	581	268	998	1753	2265	571	588	7	2	2012	
765	475	219	1011	2183	1914	1335	623	11	1	2013	
743	502	227	975	2085	1775	1249	561	10	1	2014	
165	100	84	117	765	568	115	294	1	6	2000	Fédération de Russie 4/
279	444	207	648	1255	1241	571	309	3	63	2011	
415	474	151	683	1519	1676	484	230	2	1	2012	
359	367	89	776	1613	1492	1160	306	10	0	2013	
357	347	86	763	1604	1403	1126	288	9	0	2014	

Voir la fin du tableau pour la remarque générale et les notes.

2014 International Trade Statistics Yearbook, Vol. I

World merchandise exports by provenance and destination (Table D)

In million U.S. dollars f.o.b.

			Developed economies 2/ / Économies développées 2/							Commonwealth of Independent States / Communauté d'Etats Indépendants	
				Asia-Pacific / Asie-Pacifique		Europe		North America / Amérique du Nord			
Exports from	Year	World 1/ Monde 1/	Total	Total	Japan Japon	Total	Germany Allemagne	Total	U.S.A. É.-U.	Total	Europe
---	---	---	---	---	---	---	---	---	---	---	---
Machinery and transport equipment (SITC, Rev. 3, 7)cont.]												
Northern Africa	2000	1754	1566	1	1	1559	277	6	5	1	1
	2011	11184	8653	95	92	8327	1077	230	228	17	7
	2012	11121	8608	86	79	8292	1014	230	224	23	6
	2013	12558	9746	52	49	9441	1183	253	251	33	28
	2014	13696	9996	54	49	9683	1162	260	258	49	39
Sub-Saharan Africa	2000	5308	3385	403	155	2340	969	642	609	15	14
	2011	29496	11187	960	503	6728	2673	3499	3235	97	68
	2012	28823	10622	928	412	6354	2183	3340	3132	201	171
	2013	31035	9216	991	553	5490	2069	2734	2624	173	142
	2014	31653	10115	1148	627	6473	2191	2494	2276	111	99
South Africa	2000	4570	3150	390	143	2156	950	604	577	14	14
	2011	18970	9583	923	475	5483	2633	3177	2929	76	64
	2012	19088	8360	892	395	4473	2106	2995	2823	188	160
	2013	17873	7690	940	539	4362	1999	2387	2311	159	129
	2014	18693	8368	1106	610	5170	2122	2093	1904	100	90
Latin America and the Caribbean	2000	122150	108687	764	615	6608	1776	101316	98437	19	18
	2011	248884	184248	1981	989	15858	6108	166409	159009	613	488
	2012	264485	201234	2176	1203	16726	5781	182332	175284	782	645
	2013	281668	213906	2284	1085	16818	4520	194805	188012	819	585
	2014	286853	231461	2314	1301	13397	3803	215750	208216	488	429
Brazil	2000	15416	8675	358	290	3065	497	5252	5157	3	3
	2011	38812	11059	434	169	5744	1662	4881	4576	251	141
	2012	38251	12475	319	135	6599	1514	5557	5289	435	327
	2013	44217	14272	435	249	8053	1173	5784	5527	441	226
	2014	33089	12818	403	262	5130	880	7286	7031	237	191
Eastern Asia	2000	347614	188125	37112	32788	64658	14462	86355	82182	1052	698
	2011	1607373	618728	111119	86838	249702	53281	257907	240608	35689	28306
	2012	1671093	615849	118498	93313	226121	46842	271230	252965	42156	32627
	2013	1784498	623865	118253	94235	223738	45126	281874	262763	42454	32497
	2014	1846839	663834	121045	96604	239606	48669	303182	283377	42377	32289
China	2000	82600	46255	10601	9716	16464	3921	19191	18323	325	217
	2011	902599	419563	73635	57896	174515	36998	171412	161871	22789	17893
	2012	965288	426072	79268	62662	159779	33007	187026	176118	27721	20981
	2013	1039527	431488	81346	65041	155907	30957	194236	183018	27873	21045
	2014	1071841	463617	83312	66585	168765	33904	211540	199913	27514	20702
Southern Asia	2000	3731	1696	150	102	1009	220	536	515	71	34
	2011	44613	15282	892	466	9195	1814	5194	4987	908	741
	2012	42021	14328	988	481	8653	1604	4687	4492	973	728
	2013	48153	15402	1122	614	9292	1685	4988	4769	881	704
	2014	50150	15264	1076	599	8771	1562	5416	5212	766	618
South-Eastern Asia	2000	225567	118401	27610	23208	38165	7455	52626	51240	145	131
	2011	422482	138457	46003	33712	50390	12685	42064	39716	2170	1999
	2012	449561	144966	48242	34474	49889	12607	46835	44775	2677	2421
	2013	470298	154513	49401	34811	55432	13731	49680	46965	3081	2620
	2014	476819	157685	50354	36072	56443	14450	50888	48185	2973	2503
Western Asia	2000	18758	11174	341	203	6813	1825	4020	3894	570	265
	2011	83672	35843	860	377	27819	5657	7164	5690	4949	2588
	2012	89870	35850	1004	421	26677	5632	8170	6319	5397	2742
	2013	100235	38031	999	439	28921	5939	8110	6706	6295	3125
	2014	91827	39897	825	294	32034	6894	7038	6710	5415	2394
Oceania	2000	154	106	29	4	59	28	18	17	10	10
	2011	370	186	100	3	65	0	21	18	0	0
	2012	302	187	128	1	26	0	34	33	0	0
	2013	359	211	153	1	26	1	33	32	0	0
	2014	387	184	141	1	21	0	22	22	0	0

For general note and footnotes see end of table

Les exportations de marchandises du monde par provenance et destination (Tableau D)

En millions de dollars E.-U. f.o.b.

← Exportations vers

South-Eastern Europe Europe du Sud-Est	Northern Africa Afrique septentrionale	Sub-Saharan Africa Afrique subsaharienne	Latin America and the Caribbean Amérique latine et Caraïbes	Eastern Asia Asie orientale	Southern Asia Asie méridionale	South-eastern Asia Asie du Sud-Est	Western Asia Asie occidentale	Oceania Océanie	Other 3/ Autres 3/	Année	Exportations en provence de ↓
	Machines et matériel de transport (CTCI, Rev. 3, 7)*[suite]*
0	62	28	0	1	3	1	66	0	26	2000	Afrique septentrionale
118	423	375	49	42	12	359	915	0	222	2011	
126	694	332	20	41	15	296	777	1	187	2012	
160	710	357	23	24	27	294	997	1	186	2013	
161	758	382	17	22	85	317	1725	1	182	2014	
4	25	1370	92	140	40	118	107	3	8	2000	Afrique subsaharienne
25	448	14679	530	1087	299	330	594	18	201	2011	
47	954	14632	511	515	290	343	574	37	97	2012	
42	427	18216	499	634	232	432	648	442	76	2013	
41	203	17983	478	476	245	537	1034	354	76	2014	
4	21	967	88	136	25	96	65	2	2	2000	Afrique du sud
22	410	7543	358	278	228	209	252	5	6	2011	
27	417	8451	445	400	211	247	261	5	78	2012	
21	408	7809	417	523	164	277	376	3	25	2013	
19	187	8066	385	366	186	428	560	3	25	2014	
3	47	290	11643	631	99	526	174	1	30	2000	Amérique latine et
198	306	2178	52950	3979	623	2561	1145	26	58	2011	Caraïbes
236	230	2184	49597	5242	692	2619	1608	14	46	2012	
76	220	1877	55281	5596	612	1888	1332	10	51	2013	
111	452	1568	41767	5828	578	2872	1669	9	51	2014	
1	41	254	6013	131	70	97	130	1	...	2000	Brésil
38	214	1448	22049	1242	396	1526	573	15	0	2011	
137	148	1544	19694	1510	372	1283	646	8	0	2012	
22	182	1477	25658	988	233	588	346	6	3	2013	
17	392	1101	15466	676	247	1580	552	3	...	2014	
234	1157	3449	11502	92408	4160	37352	7457	528	188	2000	Asie orientale
3597	9119	36082	89284	553500	53486	142135	56047	9687	19	2011	
2795	11765	31072	89742	604303	49229	158080	59726	6360	16	2012	
2948	11301	35157	91471	682508	48023	174525	62643	9567	35	2013	
3585	12831	38400	93645	672386	54776	186600	68888	9480	36	2014	
39	283	1034	2120	21483	1303	7934	1814	10	...	2000	Chine
2659	6035	22558	54113	230539	37663	73523	30779	2378	0	2011	
2097	7307	22619	58353	266916	34676	84396	32947	2185	...	2012	
2155	7574	25174	59245	317400	34170	96227	36382	1838	...	2013	
2654	8734	27596	59661	294623	39931	104657	41345	1509	...	2014	
3	69	319	127	156	335	461	493	1	1	2000	Asie méridionale
225	1032	4502	2195	1727	3132	7883	6968	67	693	2011	
144	1660	4741	2600	1585	3039	5934	6893	23	101	2012	
131	1563	5394	3332	2032	4309	6324	8499	28	257	2013	
275	1310	5654	3456	2176	6257	5836	9123	33	2	2014	
31	254	1346	3706	37735	3155	57988	2659	114	32	2000	Asie du Sud-est
278	1833	4015	12119	126763	14933	108395	12443	813	262	2011	
285	1694	4787	11567	134563	14332	117569	16260	737	124	2012	
326	1938	5458	13427	139872	13433	118739	18749	641	121	2013	
336	1817	4983	13071	142094	13446	120281	19085	868	180	2014	
268	563	567	375	809	934	418	2227	7	846	2000	Asie occidentale
1666	2381	3820	2714	3643	9131	2343	12286	174	4723	2011	
1421	3059	4444	2695	7407	10028	3014	13420	106	3029	2012	
1587	3581	5543	3377	4203	11674	4046	19594	137	2167	2013	
1642	3186	4747	2443	5824	3851	3839	19447	249	1288	2014	
0	...	1	1	2	0	13	0	13	10	2000	Océanie
0	0	5	4	7	2	109	0	56	0	2011	
0	0	11	4	12	1	57	1	28	0	2012	
0	0	11	7	20	1	73	2	33	1	2013	
0	0	3	12	39	6	70	2	69	1	2014	

Voir la fin du tableau pour la remarque générale et les notes.

World merchandise exports by provenance and destination (Table D)

In million U.S. dollars f.o.b.

Exports from	Year	World 1/ Monde 1/	Developed economies 2/ — Asia-Pacific Total	Asia-Pacific Japan	Developed — Europe Total	Europe Germany Allemagne	Developed — North America Total	North America U.S.A. É.-U.	CIS Total	CIS Europe

Miscellaneous manufactured articles (SITC, Rev. 3, 8)

Exports from	Year	World	DE Asia-Pac Total	Japan	DE Europe Total	Germany	DE N.Am Total	U.S.A.	CIS Total	CIS Europe
World 1/	2000	776537	590863	64443	53829	316302	67196	210118	183304	9404	8001
	2011	1902484	1229309	122139	91896	762242	150489	344929	295890	59648	45277
	2012	1971325	1216241	131913	99510	718660	140106	365668	313769	65016	49612
	2013	2071264	1273944	130067	96833	760575	147260	383302	330518	73718	56918
	2014	2165709	1333062	127051	92906	810926	155895	395085	342424	72920	54840
Developed Economies - Asia-Pacific 2/	2000	46250	23611	1476	127	8212	2530	13923	13423	60	51
	2011	72819	27430	3077	187	12189	3765	12165	11533	273	253
	2012	70374	25012	2734	204	10234	3213	12044	11431	323	296
	2013	62263	23042	2594	174	9165	2932	11283	10791	348	333
	2014	62416	23261	2566	183	9707	2891	10988	10513	305	285
Japan	2000	43292	21705	525	.	7829	2456	13351	12873	58	49
	2011	66077	22399	993	.	10614	3497	10792	10265	260	243
	2012	63824	20268	684	.	8841	2942	10742	10227	305	280
	2013	55894	18425	625	.	7872	2701	9927	9533	323	309
	2014	56029	18604	547	.	8450	2704	9608	9237	292	277
Developed Economies - Europe 2/	2000	288632	246096	10521	8421	201318	41326	34258	31916	4596	4268
	2011	684861	539832	19113	13312	466892	84887	53827	49573	25191	22264
	2012	657975	509270	20514	14383	432394	79230	56362	51959	26428	23418
	2013	703771	543117	20279	14063	462442	85633	60396	55936	28082	25109
	2014	739168	574375	20716	14368	489281	92013	64378	59697	24693	21928
France	2000	28497	23630	1558	1416	19052	3940	3020	2668	226	204
	2011	62546	48262	2087	1748	41464	7770	4712	4061	1241	1094
	2012	60025	45858	2229	1880	38760	7356	4869	4299	1281	1093
	2013	63882	48785	2143	1780	40918	7729	5724	5175	1253	1083
	2014	65520	50060	2192	1810	42554	7914	5313	4721	1171	966
Germany	2000	51366	43807	1667	1311	37120	.	5020	4704	988	898
	2011	151588	118008	3752	2590	103157	.	11099	10286	6931	6337
	2012	141435	107840	3866	2706	92735	.	11239	10387	7110	6531
	2013	148487	113071	3948	2767	97132	.	11991	11093	7102	6450
	2014	154688	119442	3941	2762	103283	.	12219	11339	5894	5267
Developed Economies - North America 2/	2000	111721	73202	11744	9881	26290	4281	35168	16863	271	219
	2011	163608	100165	14538	10467	40717	6720	44910	15982	934	796
	2012	171623	103316	15031	10791	42083	6777	46201	15443	1095	917
	2013	175912	104360	14610	10562	43779	7056	45972	15264	1237	1066
	2014	181915	107721	14091	9981	47127	7415	46502	15685	1233	1026
United States	2000	93184	55116	11494	9680	25322	4102	18299	.	237	190
	2011	143306	81886	14099	10248	38876	6443	28911	.	829	708
	2012	151507	85638	14573	10568	40321	6507	30744	.	968	814
	2013	156166	86833	14170	10337	41971	6796	30692	.	1099	948
	2014	161584	89783	13662	9756	45319	7170	30801	.	1137	949
South-Eastern Europe	2000	5919	5677	9	6	5347	1365	322	303	70	60
	2011	17121	15425	19	12	15210	3692	196	171	458	428
	2012	16069	14269	26	20	14000	3336	244	219	544	508
	2013	17739	15619	30	20	15291	3640	298	275	669	628
	2014	19265	17079	39	25	16740	3844	301	275	588	534
Commonwealth of Independent States	2000	3700	1869	6	6	1485	461	377	366	874	707
	2011	7811	2455	30	26	2258	698	168	151	3974	3356
	2012	11210	3455	100	96	2919	1364	436	416	5924	4314
	2013	12263	3120	162	158	2525	790	433	417	6547	4650
	2014	11788	3166	154	149	2547	773	465	447	6117	4327
Russian Federation 4/	2000	2063	973	5	5	735	130	233	228	223	87
	2011	2272	741	18	16	599	225	124	113	540	374
	2012	4855	1522	85	84	1038	517	398	382	1860	864
	2013	5830	1507	157	155	961	371	389	379	2126	955
	2014	5506	1423	149	146	907	350	367	358	2008	902

For general note and footnotes see end of table

Les exportations de marchandises du monde par provenance et destination (Tableau D)

En millions de dollars E.-U. f.o.b.

← Exportations vers

South-Eastern Europe Europe du Sud-Est	Northern Africa Afrique septentrionale	Sub-Saharan Africa Afrique subsaharienne	Latin America and the Caribbean Amérique latine et Caraïbes	Eastern Asia Asie orientale	Southern Asia Asie méridionale	South-eastern Asia Asie du Sud-Est	Western Asia Asie occidentale	Oceania Océanie	Other 3/ Autres 3/	Année	Exportations en provence de ↓
\multicolumn{12}{c}{Articles manifacturés divers (CTCI, Rev. 3, 8)}
3356	4480	6411	39248	70774	4458	24589	20265	620	2069	2000	Monde 1/
12269	11503	30572	92607	266725	30815	77575	87225	1328	2907	2011	
11540	13981	34298	97926	301174	31988	94279	100696	1493	2693	2012	
12502	15200	35394	96023	313051	35014	107275	104655	1451	3039	2013	
14014	15678	40425	96536	329375	34989	111903	111574	1423	3809	2014	
14	52	174	802	15385	388	4933	577	118	133	2000	Economies développées -
17	97	319	2274	31424	970	8806	917	281	11	2011	Asie-Pacifique 2/
20	90	291	2416	30955	1021	9083	838	314	10	2012	
16	79	242	1621	27279	840	7659	780	341	17	2013	
20	87	229	1606	27504	753	7533	815	283	20	2014	
12	51	135	765	14980	343	4673	551	20	...	2000	Japon
15	92	192	2192	30896	891	8309	817	13	...	2011	
18	85	184	2305	30404	903	8589	751	14	...	2012	
14	72	152	1519	26801	716	7188	671	13	...	2013	
18	82	154	1493	26989	667	7021	697	11	0	2014	
2800	2669	2338	5393	9423	1359	3371	8797	208	1582	2000	Economies développées -
8951	5303	6931	12474	40845	7033	9705	27771	358	467	2011	Europe 2/
8175	5474	6968	13102	42450	6067	10294	28911	344	492	2012	
8980	6158	7442	13654	45942	5509	11359	32243	349	936	2013	
9887	6228	7545	13715	49968	5461	11943	34065	380	909	2014	
184	765	524	431	1157	181	296	967	132	4	2000	France
504	1646	1191	1062	4195	651	1074	2403	274	42	2011	
456	1513	1109	1097	4428	481	1097	2382	259	65	2012	
505	1604	1100	1137	4742	482	1306	2603	266	100	2013	
536	1646	1097	1045	5013	499	1384	2686	289	93	2014	
366	283	418	1004	1617	294	717	1320	6	546	2000	Allemagne
1725	743	1456	3007	10378	1906	2075	5332	11	17	2011	
1572	782	1398	3099	10382	1651	2182	5400	12	7	2012	
1733	790	1456	3468	11304	1536	2250	5745	16	17	2013	
2007	831	1396	3269	11924	1557	2474	5868	11	16	2014	
35	510	453	21696	8326	463	4596	2132	38	0	2000	Economies développées -
160	522	1295	26269	19182	2735	5992	6291	63	0	2011	Amérique du Nord 2/
148	527	1284	28096	20574	2546	6483	7484	70	0	2012	
173	475	1343	28951	21538	2647	6901	8225	62	0	2013	
184	540	1372	30317	23459	2291	6846	7880	72	0	2014	
33	502	434	21555	8197	450	4561	2062	37	...	2000	Etats-Unis
144	493	1169	25693	18561	2633	5808	6030	59	...	2011	
133	499	1188	27535	19935	2463	6284	6801	64	...	2012	
157	435	1248	28425	20848	2559	6667	7839	57	...	2013	
168	502	1294	29714	22685	2219	6629	7385	68	...	2014	
125	2	4	2	2	1	0	31	0	3	2000	Europe du Sud-Est
777	45	10	34	72	42	22	234	0	2	2011	
756	52	15	41	78	45	27	240	1	3	2012	
873	90	24	50	76	35	23	278	0	2	2013	
922	97	28	59	115	44	29	299	0	4	2014	
19	18	30	20	503	217	31	118	0	0	2000	Communauté d'Etats
208	107	96	78	222	352	119	170	0	29	2011	Indépendants
164	67	43	109	549	475	144	267	0	13	2012	
177	37	92	89	608	471	369	740	1	14	2013	
202	34	89	84	572	430	348	731	0	14	2014	
11	9	23	12	492	213	29	76	0	0	2000	Fédération de Russie 4/
26	97	85	69	179	306	104	102	0	22	2011	
15	61	32	98	514	427	134	186	0	6	2012	
30	30	78	78	553	429	357	636	0	7	2013	
28	28	73	74	522	405	337	600	0	6	2014	

Voir la fin du tableau pour la remarque générale et les notes.

World merchandise exports by provenance and destination (Table D)

In million U.S. dollars f.o.b.

				Developed economies 2/ / Économies développées 2/						Commonwealth of Independent States / Communauté d'Etats Indépendants	
				Asia-Pacific / Asie-Pacifique		Europe		North America / Amérique du Nord			
Exports from	Year	World 1/ Monde 1/	Total	Total	Japan Japon	Total	Germany Allemagne	Total	U.S.A. É.-U.	Total	Europe
				Miscellaneous manufactured articles (SITC, Rev. 3, 8)*[cont.]*							
Northern Africa	2000	6113	5902	6	5	5598	719	297	290	0	0
	2011	11103	10072	13	7	9147	1055	912	890	10	8
	2012	10141	8918	13	7	8126	851	779	758	11	9
	2013	10330	8934	14	9	8114	924	806	788	14	12
	2014	10464	9112	13	8	8319	899	780	761	13	12
Sub-Saharan Africa	2000	3650	2659	40	19	1663	357	956	939	1	1
	2011	8868	3142	63	14	1867	446	1212	1128	8	6
	2012	7521	2862	64	11	1548	318	1251	1220	17	15
	2013	7852	3166	59	12	1724	321	1383	1347	10	7
	2014	8668	3651	66	14	2270	377	1315	1275	16	10
South Africa	2000	1101	790	29	14	556	276	204	200	0	0
	2011	3362	878	36	4	567	314	274	246	5	3
	2012	3175	827	40	4	492	209	294	285	15	13
	2013	3038	728	36	6	464	169	228	219	5	2
	2014	3033	596	38	7	402	144	156	148	9	4
Latin America and the Caribbean	2000	31074	27206	182	100	1133	309	25891	25695	6	6
	2011	53468	38573	314	192	2817	626	35443	34772	57	52
	2012	53778	42467	325	212	2819	548	39323	38495	65	58
	2013	55900	45460	314	188	2830	596	42316	41471	75	68
	2014	59979	49520	326	205	3038	588	46156	45287	57	50
Brazil	2000	3455	2315	52	34	590	135	1673	1624	3	3
	2011	4926	2063	78	37	1138	305	847	810	39	38
	2012	4770	1847	90	47	899	240	858	823	41	38
	2013	4523	1842	87	39	858	228	897	858	45	42
	2014	4500	1782	82	35	875	224	825	776	31	27
Eastern Asia	2000	195614	139894	31956	28206	38834	8849	69104	65047	2369	1902
	2011	637790	347094	67397	54428	138679	31877	141017	130287	24847	15842
	2012	714512	358855	72879	58213	134582	28167	151394	140036	26076	17403
	2013	754532	367289	71341	56248	138137	27534	157811	145816	31476	21892
	2014	793334	379541	68522	52736	148815	28344	162204	150557	34379	23307
China	2000	85989	57952	18935	17210	13990	3023	25027	23605	2080	1646
	2011	458568	267449	53009	42791	105423	24172	109017	100397	23106	14279
	2012	533788	280936	57792	45938	103749	22028	119395	110009	24249	15773
	2013	579090	293211	57250	44878	109282	22073	126680	116614	29561	20208
	2014	619237	307389	54961	41899	120241	23393	132187	122329	32610	21781
Southern Asia	2000	19529	16267	408	251	7344	1628	8515	8003	598	372
	2011	72074	46894	1663	837	28890	6908	16341	14768	505	252
	2012	75827	45689	1823	906	27392	6400	16474	14904	517	268
	2013	72721	50960	1976	975	30785	7146	18199	16472	657	361
	2014	79698	54606	2222	1142	34911	7526	17473	15903	1125	762
South-Eastern Asia	2000	49639	37092	7497	6365	11946	2503	17649	16911	118	106
	2011	129451	76636	15426	12140	26321	5283	34889	33008	800	718
	2012	135799	81195	17966	14464	25987	5843	37242	35224	874	789
	2013	145582	86459	18228	14226	28044	6278	40186	37980	963	913
	2014	145610	86209	17816	13851	28135	6512	40258	38025	1010	958
Western Asia	2000	13578	10576	123	87	6869	2863	3584	3475	442	309
	2011	42307	21507	423	273	17241	4532	3843	3622	2590	1301
	2012	45273	20847	373	203	16561	4057	3913	3660	3141	1616
	2013	51137	22325	383	199	17729	4412	4213	3957	3639	1877
	2014	52079	24736	449	246	20026	4710	4262	3995	3385	1641
Oceania	2000	1117	812	473	355	264	3	74	74	0	0
	2011	1202	83	64	1	14	0	5	4	0	0
	2012	1226	86	65	0	15	0	6	6	0	0
	2013	1260	93	77	0	11	0	5	5	0	0
	2014	1326	85	71	0	10	1	4	4	0	0

For general note and footnotes see end of table

Les exportations de marchandises du monde par provenance et destination (Tableau D)

En millions de dollars E.-U. f.o.b.

⟵ Exportations vers

South-Eastern Europe Europe du Sud-Est	Northern Africa Afrique septentrio-nale	Sub-Saharan Africa Afrique subsahari-enne	Latin America and the Caribbean Amérique latine et Caraïbes	Eastern Asia Asie orientale	Southern Asia Asie méridionale	South-eastern Asia Asie du Sud-Est	Western Asia Asie occidentale	Oceania Océanie	Other 3/ Autres 3/	Année	Exportations en provence de ↓
	**Articles manifacturés divers (CTCI, Rev. 3, 8) [suite]**
0	52	46	3	1	1	1	53	0	54	2000	Afrique septentrionale
7	181	222	19	35	12	4	442	0	98	2011	
8	310	234	20	38	11	4	511	0	76	2012	
11	315	234	19	35	8	5	669	0	86	2013	
10	272	232	18	33	11	5	672	0	84	2014	
0	4	826	18	16	8	17	92	1	7	2000	Afrique subsaharienne
5	14	5296	102	44	107	44	86	10	11	2011	
43	13	4255	89	53	52	52	68	1	15	2012	
40	12	4248	54	78	30	37	156	2	17	2013	
36	8	4459	65	79	39	58	170	3	85	2014	
0	3	231	10	10	6	15	33	1	1	2000	Afrique du sud
2	7	2264	25	16	73	35	53	2	3	2011	
22	10	2142	22	24	30	32	44	1	7	2012	
17	10	2093	28	18	9	14	104	1	10	2013	
12	6	2166	36	30	20	32	113	2	11	2014	
2	10	27	3588	97	18	41	48	1	29	2000	Amérique latine et Caraïbes
12	23	252	13789	283	55	149	161	3	111	2011	
15	23	387	9890	390	61	220	179	1	78	2012	
16	21	236	9149	384	70	204	228	2	55	2013	
18	31	259	9079	383	66	276	255	2	33	2014	
1	4	17	1022	30	13	20	30	0	...	2000	Brésil
9	14	225	2252	88	32	90	113	1	0	2011	
9	14	365	2167	79	36	94	118	1	...	2012	
10	16	209	2008	90	47	92	163	1	...	2013	
10	24	210	1981	98	34	155	174	1	0	2014	
215	740	1632	6514	32754	949	6154	4212	168	14	2000	Asie orientale
1226	3948	11324	32666	149738	10887	33275	22404	370	10	2011	
1313	5608	16877	38788	179124	12586	46699	28134	447	5	2012	
1168	5903	17087	36887	188885	15614	57321	32489	404	10	2013	
1289	6166	21875	35994	196540	20060	60920	36171	389	10	2014	
184	486	801	2665	17527	283	1857	2137	16	...	2000	Chine
1097	3690	10573	27184	72683	8438	24854	19312	179	1	2011	
1221	5286	16117	32988	100530	9676	37833	24710	241	...	2012	
1071	5574	16423	31220	112500	13294	47297	28734	207	...	2013	
1185	5854	21221	30340	120620	17704	50372	31721	221	...	2014	
7	23	240	213	337	195	256	1378	14	2	2000	Asie méridionale
44	113	1207	1280	2953	906	1498	16223	23	428	2011	
43	171	1394	1442	3518	1032	1273	20599	27	124	2012	
59	172	1843	1627	2825	1012	1417	12010	37	102	2013	
124	206	1915	1707	4328	1037	1535	12151	31	934	2014	
15	102	478	676	3729	624	5075	1660	60	7	2000	Asie du Sud-est
48	225	2576	3331	20401	2863	17392	4948	185	47	2011	
45	291	1400	3569	21055	2520	19440	5107	249	55	2012	
51	278	1197	3559	23366	2243	21267	5890	212	97	2013	
48	271	1174	3520	23468	2219	21533	5846	216	95	2014	
123	297	161	58	177	234	109	1166	0	237	2000	Asie occidentale
813	926	1041	292	1514	4850	550	7577	12	635	2011	
809	1356	1153	363	2377	5568	555	8355	15	734	2012	
937	1661	1402	363	2029	6534	705	10944	16	582	2013	
1274	1738	1246	373	2887	2579	867	12512	17	465	2014	
0	...	2	266	23	0	3	1	10	1	2000	Océanie
0	...	3	1	12	3	20	1	23	1057	2011	
0	0	1	1	14	3	6	3	23	1089	2012	
0	0	5	0	6	0	7	2	25	1121	2013	
0	0	3	0	36	0	9	7	29	1155	2014	

Voir la fin du tableau pour la remarque générale et les notes.

World merchandise exports by provenance and destination (Table D)

In million U.S. dollars f.o.b.

Exports from	Year	World 1/ Monde 1/	Developed economies 2/ — Total	Asia-Pacific Total	Asia-Pacific Japan	Europe Total	Europe Germany	North America Total	North America U.S.A.	CIS Total	CIS Europe
Commodities and transactions not classified elsewhere in the SITC (SITC, Rev. 3, 9)											
World 1/	2000	269462	189829	7682	4554	137751	42832	44396	37535	6255	1957
	2011	908803	432213	22578	12021	329295	47009	80340	52259	47055	31068
	2012	903541	464833	21686	12666	347517	73807	95630	68075	9961	7228
	2013	959993	443865	19775	11924	334892	49910	89198	59103	11806	7879
	2014	781279	388796	20489	12156	281999	48753	86308	58365	10217	7066
Developed Economies - Asia-Pacific 2/	2000	24052	12472	639	317	5871	977	5963	5828	13	10
	2011	77658	34461	1608	205	25560	1696	7293	7029	108	72
	2012	70240	23848	1178	153	15743	1507	6927	6537	112	84
	2013	64879	16240	1283	96	7869	1662	7087	6741	177	88
	2014	62475	15607	1137	154	7343	1616	7127	6803	152	84
Japan	2000	17490	9032	214	.	3389	974	5429	5296	10	9
	2011	49449	20694	698	.	14062	1294	5934	5673	105	69
	2012	42534	14570	418	.	8125	1331	6028	5647	110	83
	2013	41051	13389	626	.	6482	1453	6281	5938	176	86
	2014	40551	13070	542	.	6131	1495	6398	6094	151	83
Developed Economies - Europe 2/	2000	142183	119322	2654	1660	105916	39501	10753	9217	897	489
	2011	268381	205007	3527	2024	185860	34663	15621	12863	4418	3523
	2012	293830	235241	3028	2243	204989	62911	27224	24609	4980	3883
	2013	309165	237787	2268	1448	218904	37577	16614	14254	5931	4154
	2014	252441	189209	1895	1331	173925	36430	13389	12346	4228	3283
France	2000	6657	5424	194	157	4748	1034	482	440	59	57
	2011	17591	14058	531	426	12688	3208	839	741	262	240
	2012	16819	13263	502	425	11890	2967	872	785	299	285
	2013	15599	12085	325	246	10877	2941	883	790	261	248
	2014	15245	11519	296	225	10195	2774	1027	916	252	242
Germany	2000	40968	32604	131	106	31812	.	661	578	272	195
	2011	80120	60507	1160	569	56624	.	2723	2455	2435	2170
	2012	85540	66650	765	530	63256	.	2629	2388	2364	2092
	2013	79830	59777	719	495	56307	.	2751	2525	2411	2146
	2014	84550	61932	753	530	57665	.	3515	3184	2262	2027
Developed Economies - North America 2/	2000	50224	36083	2708	1591	11165	1213	22210	17321	208	103
	2011	185816	113437	10655	5500	72108	7578	30674	15492	1273	864
	2012	202933	116709	12764	8333	73681	7261	30264	15209	2194	1696
	2013	214051	111586	11727	7827	66014	7922	33844	16478	2996	2224
	2014	211965	112017	13190	8157	62723	8316	36104	18398	3655	2461
United States	2000	32007	18124	2589	1504	10659	1116	4876	.	197	98
	2011	154864	84451	10416	5341	58859	7273	15176	.	1263	853
	2012	173051	88137	12430	8205	60656	7102	15050	.	2187	1689
	2013	182960	84658	11043	7209	56252	7550	17363	.	2988	2217
	2014	180208	83438	12745	7792	52991	8116	17703	.	3645	2452
South-Eastern Europe	2000	385	121	1	0	113	8	8	8	1	0
	2011	2573	1641	0	0	1599	318	42	41	38	36
	2012	2589	1848	3	3	1809	320	36	35	19	16
	2013	3424	2727	2	2	2658	567	67	65	26	19
	2014	4770	3459	3	3	3366	530	90	88	17	13
Commonwealth of Independent States	2000	17456	5876	120	119	5502	481	254	246	4946	1277
	2011	56772	3488	90	90	2393	122	1004	828	40848	26395
	2012	19824	9579	290	289	8010	204	1278	1044	2343	1381
	2013	21579	7627	242	241	5845	218	1540	1334	2056	1035
	2014	17388	6376	159	159	4963	70	1255	1087	1541	778
Russian Federation 4/	2000	12145	3124	43	43	2983	9	98	95	3551	221
	2011	51194	1215	0	.	408	89	808	808	38915	24612
	2012	15281	7578	40	39	6445	159	1093	1021	887	117
	2013	17149	6041	0	.	4681	190	1359	1299	920	48
	2014	14429	5250	0	.	4133	49	1118	1069	755	60

For general note and footnotes see end of table

Les exportations de marchandises du monde par provenance et destination (Tableau D)

En millions de dollars E.-U. f.o.b.

⟵ Exportations vers

South-Eastern Europe Europe du Sud-Est	Northern Africa Afrique septentrionale	Sub-Saharan Africa Afrique subsaharienne	Latin America and the Caribbean Amérique latine et Caraïbes	Eastern Asia Asie orientale	Southern Asia Asie méridionale	South-eastern Asia Asie du Sud-Est	Western Asia Asie occidentale	Oceania Océanie	Other 3/ Autres 3/	Année	Exportations en provence de ↓
	Articles et transactions non classés ailleurs dans la CTCI (CTCI, Rev. 3, 9)
3045	963	2650	11753	16609	2889	11609	9335	189	14335	2000	Monde 1/
4247	8657	17978	43595	114632	30983	42271	36401	2513	128257	2011	
4419	4136	23252	49284	138153	39368	37951	38278	2967	90939	2012	
4158	4273	19451	46010	185731	35564	45925	57796	3420	101993	2013	
5400	4177	19703	44893	149223	25794	42464	69467	3372	17773	2014	
14	38	56	223	5818	98	4876	414	29	1	2000	Economies développées - Asie-Pacifique 2/
22	28	203	537	22743	5073	13210	667	169	437	2011	
18	30	388	517	29735	3727	10501	842	104	418	2012	
20	303	220	622	33206	2110	10162	1246	138	434	2013	
17	31	187	549	31925	1159	11489	864	93	402	2014	
14	38	50	223	4319	68	3474	251	11	0	2000	Japon
19	28	162	526	18151	529	8676	540	17	...	2011	
17	26	174	512	18281	347	8012	467	18	...	2012	
19	186	153	525	17662	611	7755	558	19	...	2013	
15	31	175	494	17900	386	7768	543	18	...	2014	
396	639	1174	1823	3863	1580	1916	3779	17	6775	2000	Economies développées - Europe 2/
3544	1759	4691	8178	9280	4386	5576	9176	105	12261	2011	
3988	1271	3482	9183	9107	3706	6402	7818	56	8596	2012	
3569	1633	3165	4001	14516	3481	6430	17016	103	11533	2013	
4545	1327	2357	3786	17589	2750	4474	10017	56	12104	2014	
19	125	133	210	235	80	139	214	7	11	2000	France
85	328	362	426	823	233	348	575	43	49	2011	
92	286	341	437	772	231	342	521	34	201	2012	
102	301	317	419	706	205	351	604	36	212	2013	
98	311	319	437	778	257	338	672	34	231	2014	
92	190	245	317	1089	210	238	502	6	5201	2000	Allemagne
1232	466	921	1412	3964	1214	1893	3359	12	2705	2011	
1408	400	796	1329	3926	1151	1549	3073	6	2890	2012	
1325	527	605	1422	4200	883	1496	3196	6	3983	2013	
1363	629	599	1650	4673	933	1938	3764	16	4791	2014	
45	77	329	8301	2504	268	1350	1015	44	0	2000	Economies développées - Amérique du Nord 2/
160	1275	2824	22229	21770	2716	9768	10218	147	0	2011	
116	616	3382	25996	24948	5136	9557	14092	186	3	2012	
142	521	3123	25868	36165	4138	12914	16437	145	17	2013	
133	312	4496	26821	32223	3813	12371	15914	207	4	2014	
42	72	311	8210	2437	257	1321	994	43	...	2000	États-Unis
157	1261	2784	22006	20382	2679	9595	10150	135	...	2011	
113	605	3340	25799	24089	5086	9486	14031	179	...	2012	
140	505	3071	25642	33147	4036	12705	15933	134	...	2013	
131	296	4447	26594	29884	3721	12095	15763	194	...	2014	
32	3	10	5	3	8	4	150	0	48	2000	Europe du Sud-Est
444	2	23	6	1	46	8	121	1	242	2011	
175	5	12	6	1	9	17	166	1	331	2012	
270	9	30	7	1	37	10	160	2	146	2013	
500	61	54	7	29	59	13	260	2	308	2014	
2523	78	24	50	1150	287	61	2461	0	1	2000	Communauté d'Etats Indépendants
6	937	295	866	283	588	226	1136	1	8100	2011	
43	1852	261	1373	381	2122	626	508	1	735	2012	
45	1062	110	1775	2480	3372	1054	1292	0	706	2013	
31	714	89	1531	1983	2961	472	967	0	721	2014	
2513	...	0	2	556	12	23	2363	...	...	2000	Fédération de Russie 4/
4	925	179	862	258	132	91	942	...	7670	2011	
40	1841	213	1357	353	2097	531	384	...	0	2012	
43	1055	49	1762	2472	3120	661	1027	...	...	2013	
23	707	47	1519	1973	2951	450	753	...	...	2014	

Voir la fin du tableau pour la remarque générale et les notes.

World merchandise exports by provenance and destination (Table D)

In million U.S. dollars f.o.b.

| | | | Developed economies 2/ / Économies développées 2/ ||||||| Commonwealth of Independent States / Communauté d'Etats Indépendants ||
| | | | | Asia-Pacific / Asie-Pacifique || Europe || North America / Amérique du Nord || ||
Exports from	Year	World 1/ Monde 1/	Total	Total	Japan Japon	Total	Germany Allemagne	Total	U.S.A. É.-U.	Total	Europe
\u00a0			**Commodities and transactions not classified elsewhere in the SITC (SITC, Rev. 3, 9) *[cont.]***									
Northern Africa	2000	135	114	1	1	17	0	95	95	2	0
	2011	1820	278	0	0	278	0	0	0	0	0
	2012	1474	495	0	0	408	2	87	0	0	0
	2013	2043	622	0	0	123	4	499	6	0	0
	2014	1158	567	1	0	95	7	471	9	1	1
Sub-Saharan Africa	2000	5263	3662	10	9	3248	14	404	402	55	9
	2011	26077	6975	84	76	6585	458	305	116	1	1
	2012	27349	6599	65	51	6262	44	272	90	2	2
	2013	20631	5703	47	43	5505	45	151	85	20	0
	2014	19795	6572	84	9	6173	30	315	258	1	1
South Africa	2000	3561	2344	8	8	1956	3	380	379	45	0
	2011	10873	1192	6	0	1022	281	163	45	0	0
	2012	9142	1311	48	40	1158	28	105	17	0	0
	2013	7051	1014	45	42	906	17	64	6	20	0
	2014	5190	1792	17	0	1554	6	221	165	1	1
Latin America and the Caribbean	2000	6543	4216	22	22	1853	60	2342	2166	31	0
	2011	68335	36335	30	28	14643	324	21662	12935	77	6
	2012	46436	40896	139	134	14422	454	26335	18126	76	2
	2013	40088	34643	98	91	10215	581	24330	15986	55	11
	2014	37451	31997	40	37	9179	473	22779	15171	4	2
Brazil	2000	1449	1310	9	9	270	19	1031	1030	25	0
	2011	7406	5549	15	15	4081	278	1452	1297	71	0
	2012	8315	6428	74	74	3925	389	2429	2232	69	0
	2013	7521	4473	10	10	2359	368	2104	1903	44	1
	2014	7137	4421	22	22	1896	345	2504	2298	2	1
Eastern Asia	2000	3390	1290	442	110	759	15	88	79	1	1
	2011	37609	3686	1509	1426	1504	217	673	492	33	23
	2012	58943	2514	636	376	1367	58	510	345	13	9
	2013	85285	2996	1024	730	1008	117	963	780	49	37
	2014	59770	3658	1070	826	1710	123	878	824	47	38
China	2000	514	64	37	36	13	0	15	14	0	...
	2011	2343	1266	1016	1014	76	20	175	168	23	16
	2012	1417	42	7	6	21	6	14	14	2	0
	2013	1729	32	1	1	15	5	15	15	9	0
	2014	2267	33	3	2	15	4	14	14	6	0
Southern Asia	2000	1087	715	37	22	306	50	372	355	15	4
	2011	29203	452	24	14	344	36	84	78	16	10
	2012	14055	1532	42	33	864	102	626	621	6	3
	2013	17197	2613	107	102	968	234	1537	1523	5	1
	2014	16426	399	122	120	177	35	99	98	8	8
South-Eastern Asia	2000	8509	3404	885	589	1777	358	742	695	27	25
	2011	54789	17142	4296	2525	10827	1445	2019	1721	58	42
	2012	47546	14949	3271	993	10840	666	838	532	58	31
	2013	42440	9397	2003	1071	6468	666	926	564	87	58
	2014	41748	9507	1840	1061	6742	653	925	563	85	58
Western Asia	2000	10122	2483	124	104	1222	155	1136	1093	58	38
	2011	99245	9103	561	132	7584	151	959	661	184	97
	2012	117753	10389	65	56	9098	272	1226	919	157	120
	2013	138564	11675	796	268	9257	310	1622	1270	402	250
	2014	55029	9219	818	295	5543	463	2858	2702	478	339
Oceania	2000	114	70	38	11	2	0	29	29	1	...
	2011	525	207	193	1	9	0	4	4	0	0
	2012	569	233	204	2	22	6	6	6	0	0
	2013	645	251	176	3	58	8	17	16	0	0
	2014	861	209	130	4	61	7	18	17	0	...

For general note and footnotes see end of table

Les exportations de marchandises du monde par provenance et destination (Tableau D)

En millions de dollars E.-U. f.o.b.

⟵ Exportations vers

South-Eastern Europe Europe du Sud-Est	Northern Africa Afrique septentrio-nale	Sub-Saharan Africa Afrique subsahari-enne	Latin America and the Caribbean Amérique latine et Caraïbes	Eastern Asia Asie orientale	Southern Asia Asie méridionale	South-eastern Asia Asie du Sud-Est	Western Asia Asie occidentale	Oceania Océanie	Other 3/ Autres 3/	Année	Exportations en provenance de ↓
\multicolumn{12}{c}{Articles et transactions non classés ailleurs dans la CTCI (CTCI, Rev. 3, 9) [suite]}
0	0	0	0	0	0	0	18	0	0	2000	Afrique septentrionale
0	9	946	0	1	1	1	583	0	...	2011	
0	39	482	0	2	4	0	448	...	4	2012	
0	34	289	1	2	26	2	1067	...	1	2013	
31	27	75	3	1	25	1	426	...	1	2014	
2	5	562	4	875	18	11	62	0	4	2000	Afrique subsaharienne
12	8	6505	13	3209	5336	767	3251	1	1	2011	
2	5	8216	6	3562	3321	894	4087	0	654	2012	
2	5	6021	4	3362	2118	713	2570	5	109	2013	
6	4	6688	2	2120	1527	275	2463	0	137	2014	
2	...	239	4	860	16	7	42	0	...	2000	Afrique du sud
0	4	3	0	2556	5301	753	1064	0	0	2011	
0	...	6	0	3500	3131	886	307	0	0	2012	
0	0	3	0	3320	1609	694	391	0	0	2013	
0	0	3	0	2081	750	261	302	0	0	2014	
0	0	80	130	4	4	22	49	0	2006	2000	Amérique latine et Caraïbes
4	1	395	1006	64	58	562	800	2	29031	2011	
6	116	601	822	399	185	446	779	5	2105	2012	
5	161	645	1371	1414	604	310	869	1	10	2013	
21	153	287	1185	745	720	235	269	0	1834	2014	
0	...	54	41	0	1	6	12	0	...	2000	Brésil
4	0	375	832	5	56	452	62	1	...	2011	
4	63	531	555	193	33	373	65	1	...	2012	
3	137	540	936	806	220	227	134	1	...	2013	
17	153	265	1005	629	320	172	152	0	...	2014	
1	10	20	14	971	171	402	437	2	71	2000	Asie orientale
5	6	52	68	29034	444	3069	382	4	826	2011	
5	6	21	56	50378	1156	3652	277	4	861	2012	
18	27	49	292	73956	494	6053	452	11	887	2013	
19	28	51	305	50302	973	3303	468	11	605	2014	
0	9	11	1	47	161	8	209	0	2	2000	Chine
0	1	33	23	609	66	311	9	0	...	2011	
...	1	1	1	818	2	549	2	...	...	2012	
0	0	1	0	1409	1	276	1	0	...	2013	
...	0	1	2	2079	1	143	2	...	...	2014	
0	2	15	14	18	183	38	84	0	1	2000	Asie méridionale
1	1	28	32	14759	115	335	507	3	12954	2011	
5	9	172	539	10812	418	195	224	52	90	2012	
16	91	375	1378	9374	440	218	2566	21	100	2013	
4	8	11	20	52	1676	66	13634	0	548	2014	
4	12	307	1054	1062	181	1789	320	80	268	2000	Asie du Sud-est
16	4457	865	10535	10883	644	6635	1481	2072	0	2011	
2	51	5235	10639	7935	566	4088	1475	2547	0	2012	
4	73	4368	10128	8263	656	4935	1552	2977	1	2013	
11	43	4356	10116	7912	618	4571	1553	2974	1	2014	
26	99	72	134	340	92	1139	545	1	5133	2000	Asie occidentale
33	177	1152	124	2604	11574	2110	8079	6	64098	2011	
60	135	1000	147	883	19019	1571	7562	8	76822	2012	
66	355	1056	564	2963	18088	3098	12569	10	87719	2013	
80	1467	1051	568	4061	9512	5175	22633	15	771	2014	
...	...	0	0	1	0	1	0	14	27	2000	Océanie
0	0	0	0	2	0	5	0	3	307	2011	
...	0	0	1	10	1	2	0	3	320	2012	
...	0	0	1	29	1	26	0	8	330	2013	
0	0	0	0	281	1	20	0	14	336	2014	

Voir la fin du tableau pour la remarque générale et les notes.

World merchandise exports by provenance and destination (Table D)
Les exportations de marchandises du monde par provenance et destination (Tableau D)

General note:

For further information on Sources, Method of Estimation, Currency Conversion, Period, Country Nomenclature and Country Grouping of this table, as well as for a brief table description, please see the Introduction

Footnotes:

1. Exports for which country of destination is not available are included in the totals for the 'World' and in region "Others" (see footnote number 3 for further explanation)

2. This classification is intended for statistical convenience and does not, necessarily, express a judgment about the stage reached by a particular country in the development process.

3. The region "Others" as destination for exports contains the following trading partners: Antarctica, bunkers, free zones, confidential and not elsewhere specified countries

Remarque générale:

Pour plus d'information en ce qui concerne les sources, la méthode d'estimation, taux d'exchange, période, nomenclature des pays et groupement de pays, ainsi que pour une brève description de ce tableau, veuillez voir l'Introduction

1. Exportations dont les pays de destination n'est pas disponible sont incluses dansles totaux pour le 'Monde ' et dans la région "les autres " (voir note n ° 3 pour plus d'explications)

2. Cette classification est utilisée pour plus de commodité dans la présentation des statistiques et n'implique pas nécessairement un jugement quant au stade de développement auquel est parvenuun pays donné.

3. La région "Autres" comme destination des exportations comprend les partenaires commerciaux suivants: Antarctique, combustibles de soute, zones franches, partenaires confidentiels ou non specifiés ailleurs

2014 INTERNATIONAL TRADE STATISTICS YEARBOOK

VOLUME I
TRADE BY COUNTRY

PART 2 – COUNTRY TRADE PROFILES

169 Countries (or areas)

European Union

Afghanistan

Goods Imports: CIF, by origin **Goods Exports:** FOB, by last known destination **Trade System:** General

Overview:
In 2014, the value of merchandise exports of Afghanistan increased moderately by 10.8 percent to reach 570.5 mln US$, while its merchandise imports decreased moderately by 10.0 percent to reach 7.7 bln US$ (see graph 1, table 2 and table 3). The merchandise trade balance recorded a large deficit of 7.1 bln US$ (see graph 1). The largest merchandise trade balance was with MDG Southern Asia at -2.6 bln US$ (see graph 4). Merchandise exports in Afghanistan were highly concentrated amongst partners; imports were also highly concentrated. The top 3 partners accounted for 80 percent or more of exports and 3 partners accounted for 80 percent or more of imports (see graph 5). In 2012, the value of exports of services of Afghanistan decreased moderately by 12.1 percent, reaching 3.1 bln US$, while its imports of services increased substantially by 73.8 percent and reached 2.2 bln US$ (see graph 2). There was a moderate trade in services surplus of 817.0 mln US$.

Graph 1: Total merchandise trade, by value
(Bln US$ by year)

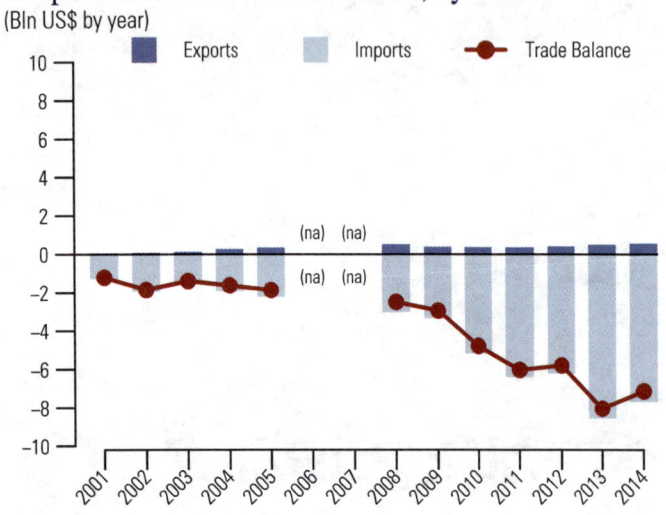

Graph 2: Total services trade, by value
(Bln US$ by year)

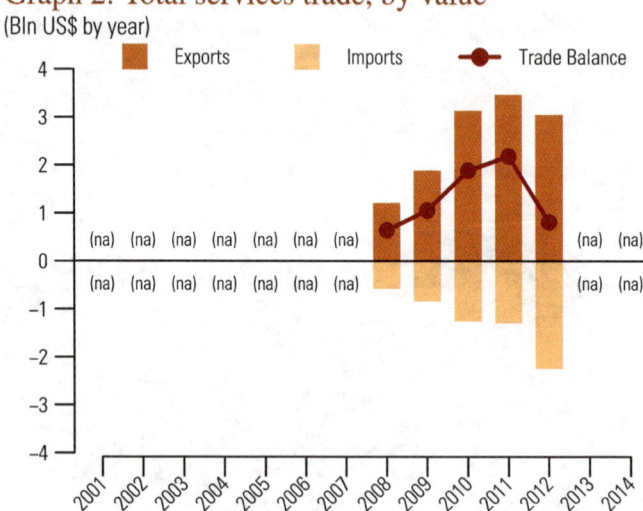

Exports Profile:
"Not classified elsewhere in the SITC" (SITC section 9), "Goods classified chiefly by material" (SITC section 6) and "Food, animals + beverages, tobacco" (SITC section 0+1) were the largest commodity groups for exports in 2014, representing respectively 70.7, 14.7 and 12.4 percent of exported goods (see table 2). From 2012 to 2014, the largest export commodity was "Commodities not specified according to kind" (HS code 9999) (see table 1). The top three destinations for merchandise exports were Pakistan, Areas nes and India, accounting for respectively 38.8, 27.7 and 22.0 percent of total exports. "Other business services" (EBOPS code 268) accounted for the largest share of exports of services in 2012 at 1.5 bln US$, followed by "Construction services" (EBOPS code 249) at 762.3 mln US$ and "Transportation" (EBOPS code 205) at 342.9 mln US$ (see graph 3).

Graph 3: Exports of services by EBOPS category
(% share in 2012)

- Other business (50.1 %)
- Construction (24.9 %)
- Transportation (11.2 %)
- Remaining (13.7 %)

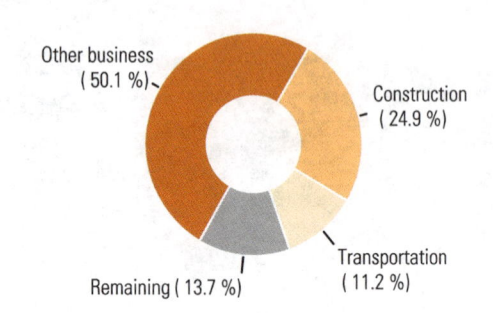

Table 1: Top 10 export commodities 2012 to 2014

HS code	4-digit heading of Harmonized System 2002	Value (million US$) 2012	2013	2014	Unit value 2012	2013	2014	Unit	SITC code
	All Commodities	428.9	515.0	570.5					
9999	Commodities not specified according to kind	280.3	371.3	403.6					931
5701	Carpets and other textile floor coverings, knotted	72.8	73.2	84.0	*107.9*	*103.2*	*103.5*	US$/m^2	659
0909	Seeds of anise, badian, fennel, coriander, cumin or caraway	54.1	61.1	70.8	3.3	4.0	3.4	US$/kg	075
1207	Other oil seeds and oleaginous fruits	20.6	9.1	11.9	1.6	1.1	1.5	US$/kg	222
0504	Guts, bladders and stomachs of animals (other than fish)	1.0	0.2	0.3	*3.4*	*3.3*	*3.9*	US$/kg	291

Source: UN Comtrade and UN ServiceTrade — 2014 International Trade Statistics Yearbook, Vol. I

Afghanistan

Services Imports and Exports: EBOPS 2002 categories

Table 2: Merchandise exports by SITC
(Value in million US$, growth and shares in percentage)

SITC	2014	Avg. Growth rates 2010-2014	2013-2014	2014 share
Total	570.5	10.1	10.8	100.0
0+1	70.8	-14.2	15.9	12.4
2+4	12.1	-34.9	30.4	2.1
6	84.0	2.5	14.7	14.7
9	403.6	37.2	8.7	70.7

Table 3: Merchandise imports by SITC
(Value in million US$, growth and shares in percentage)

SITC	2014	Avg. Growth rates 2010-2014	2013-2014	2014 share
Total	7697.2	10.5	-10.0	100.0
0+1	732.3	5.7	13.4	9.5
3	1488.6	8.5	2.5	19.3
5	91.8	2.7	-47.0	1.2
6	511.5	4.2	31.3	6.6
7	6.6	-62.6	2230.9	0.1
8	37.3	-28.0	3.4	0.5
9	4829.1	19.4	-17.6	62.7

SITC Legend

SITC Code	Description
Total	All commodities
0+1	Food, animals + beverages, tobacco
2+4	Crude materials + anim. & veg. oils
3	Mineral fuels, lubricants
5	Chemicals
6	Goods classified chiefly by material
7	Machinery and transport equipment
8	Miscellaneous manufactured articles
9	Not classified elsewhere in the SITC

Graph 4: Merchandise trade balance
(Bln US$ by MDG Regions in 2014)

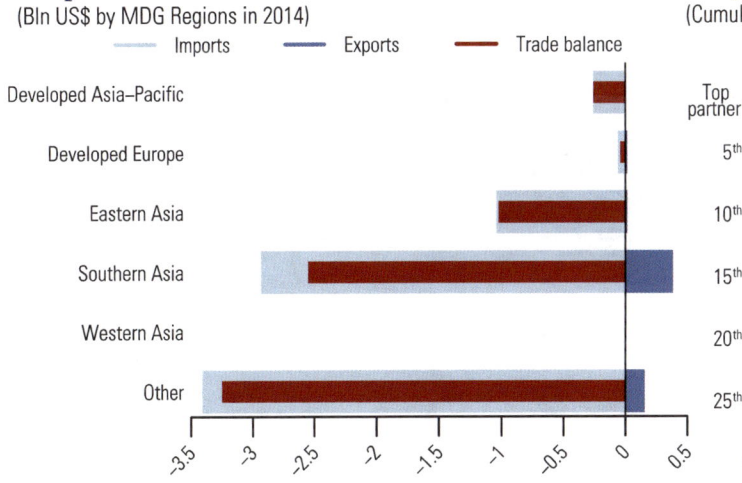

Graph 5: Partner concentration of merchandise trade
(Cumulative share by ranked partners in 2014)

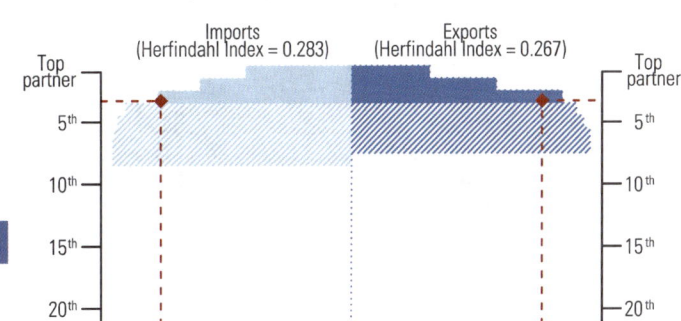

Imports (Herfindahl Index = 0.283)
Exports (Herfindahl Index = 0.267)

Graph 6: Imports of services by EBOPS category
(% share in 2012)

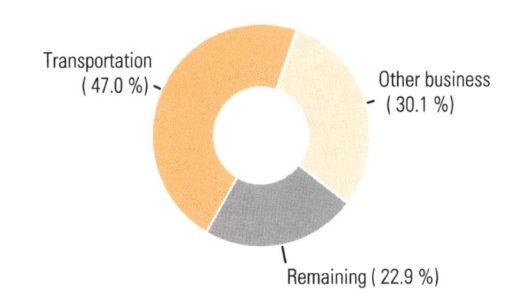

- Transportation (47.0 %)
- Other business (30.1 %)
- Remaining (22.9 %)

Imports Profile:

"Not classified elsewhere in the SITC" (SITC section 9), "Mineral fuels, lubricants" (SITC section 3) and "Food, animals + beverages, tobacco" (SITC section 0+1) were the largest commodity groups for imports in 2014, representing respectively 62.7, 19.3 and 9.5 percent of imported goods (see table 3). From 2012 to 2014, the largest import commodity was "Commodities not specified according to kind" (HS code 9999) (see table 4). The top three partners for merchandise imports were Areas nes, Pakistan and the Islamic Republic of Iran, accounting for respectively 58.3, 13.8 and 12.1 percent of total imports. "Transportation" (EBOPS code 205) accounted for the largest share of imports of services in 2012 at 1.1 bln US$, followed by "Other business services" (EBOPS code 268) at 674.3 mln US$ (see graph 6).

Table 4: Top 10 import commodities 2012 to 2014

HS code	4-digit heading of Harmonized System 2002	2012	2013	2014	2012	2013	2014	Unit	SITC code
	All Commodities	6205.0	8554.4	7697.2					
9999	Commodities not specified according to kind	4014.2	5857.5	4829.1					931
2703	Peat (including peat litter)	1517.5	1452.5	1488.6	0.8	0.5	1.6	US$/kg	322
1101	Wheat or meslin flour	175.5	429.1	498.9	0.3	0.3	0.3	US$/kg	046
5808	Braids in the piece; ornamental trimmings	110.2	151.4	295.9	22.0	24.1	24.2	US$/kg	656
6801	Setts, curbstones and flagstones, of natural stone (except slate)	163.3	219.7	160.3	0.1	0.1	0.1	US$/kg	661
0902	Tea, whether or not flavoured	69.1	151.1	111.7	1.3	1.5	1.1	US$/kg	074
3006	Pharmaceutical goods specified in Note 4 to this Chapter	36.0	139.6	68.4					541
1701	Cane or beet sugar and pure sucrose, in solid form	6.9	61.6	117.6	0.4	0.5	0.5	US$/kg	061
6206	Women's or girls' blouses, shirts and shirt-blouses	20.9	27.8	23.5	9.7	10.1	10.8	US$/unit	842
4012	Retreaded or used pneumatic tyres of rubber	31.1	10.2	29.2	40.4	39.3	35.5	US$/unit	625

2014 International Trade Statistics Yearbook, Vol. I — Source: UN Comtrade and UN ServiceTrade

Albania

Goods Imports: CIF, by origin   **Goods Exports:** FOB, by last known destination   **Trade System:** Special

Overview:
In 2014, the value of merchandise exports of Albania increased slightly by 4.3 percent to reach 2.4 bln US$, while its merchandise imports increased moderately by 7.2 percent to reach 5.2 bln US$ (see graph 1, table 2 and table 3). The merchandise trade balance recorded a large deficit of 2.8 bln US$ (see graph 1). The largest merchandise trade balance was with MDG Developed Europe at -1.4 bln US$ (see graph 4). Merchandise exports in Albania were highly concentrated amongst partners; imports were diversified. The top 6 partners accounted for 80 percent or more of exports and 14 partners accounted for 80 percent or more of imports (see graph 5). In 2013, the value of exports of services of Albania increased slightly by 2.8 percent, reaching 2.2 bln US$, while its imports of services increased substantially by 16.9 percent and reached 2.2 bln US$ (see graph 2). There was a relatively small trade in services surplus of 14.0 mln US$. See footnote*.

Graph 1: Total merchandise trade, by value
(Bln US$ by year)

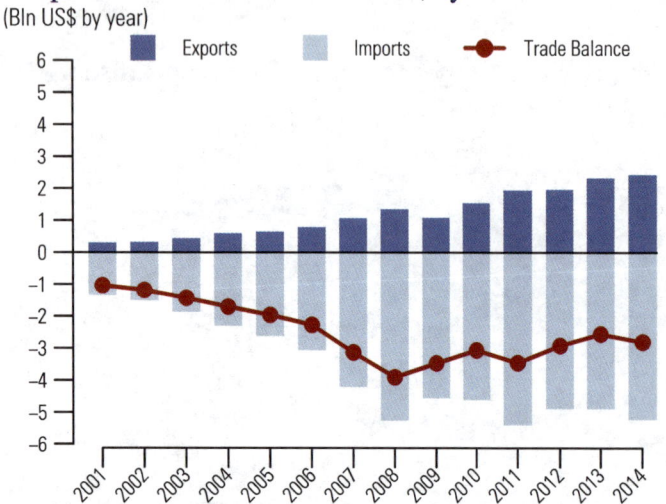

Graph 2: Total services trade, by value
(Bln US$ by year)

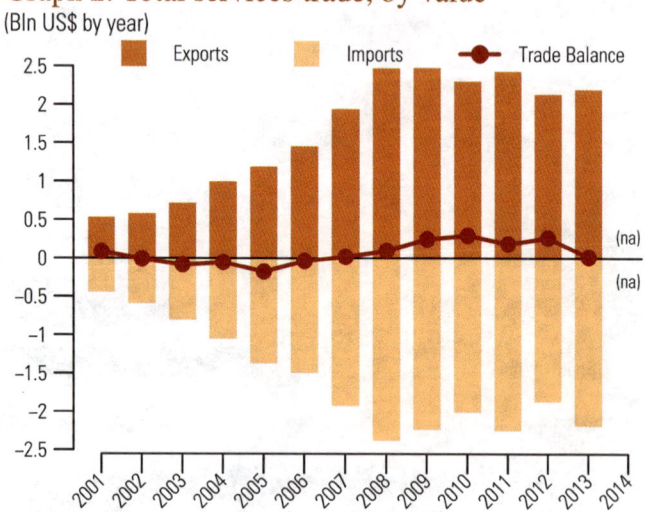

Exports Profile:
"Not classified elsewhere in the SITC" (SITC section 9), "Miscellaneous manufactured articles" (SITC section 8) and "Crude materials + anim. & veg. oils" (SITC section 2+4) were the largest commodity groups for exports in 2014, representing respectively 58.2, 26.6 and 5.6 percent of exported goods (see table 2). From 2012 to 2014, the largest export commodity was "Commodities not specified according to kind" (HS code 9999) (see table 1). The top three destinations for merchandise exports were Italy, Spain and Serbia, accounting for respectively 49.8, 8.4 and 8.1 percent of total exports. "Travel" (EBOPS code 236) accounted for the largest share of exports of services in 2013 at 1.5 bln US$, followed by "Transportation" (EBOPS code 205) at 357.0 mln US$ and "Communications services" (EBOPS code 245) at 178.0 mln US$ (see graph 3).

Graph 3: Exports of services by EBOPS category
(% share in 2013)

- Travel (66.9 %)
- Transportation (16.2 %)
- Communication (8.1 %)
- Remaining (8.8 %)

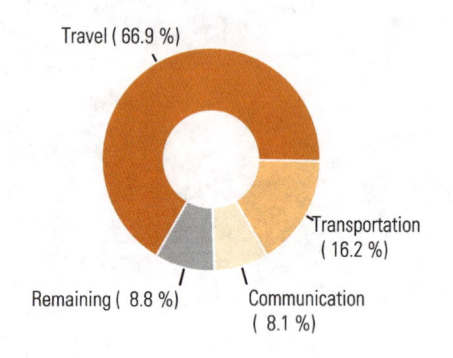

Table 1: Top 10 export commodities 2012 to 2014

HS code	4-digit heading of Harmonized System 2012	Value (million US$) 2012	2013	2014	Unit value 2012	2013	2014	Unit	SITC code
	All Commodities	1 967.9	2 331.5	2 430.7					
9999	Commodities not specified according to kind	4.5	1.5	1 415.0					931
2709	Petroleum oils and oils obtained from bituminous minerals, crude	492.9	658.0	...	0.5	0.5		US$/kg	333
6403	Footwear with outer soles of rubber, plastics, leather	141.9	156.8	151.9	17.3	18.2	17.8	US$/pair	851
6406	Parts of footwear	109.8	132.8	151.2	19.9	22.0	24.1	US$/kg	851
6203	Men's or boys'suits, ensembles, jackets, blazers, trousers	79.3	89.9	77.3	10.9	11.5	10.2	US$/unit	841
2610	Chromium ores and concentrates	49.1	91.1	74.0	0.1	0.1	0.2	US$/kg	287
7214	Other bars and rods of iron or non-alloy steel	78.5	123.0	...	0.6	0.6		US$/kg	676
2523	Portland cement, aluminous cement, slag cement	67.0	67.7	1.5	0.1	0.1	0.1	US$/kg	661
6205	Men's or boys'shirts	39.0	41.6	52.3	10.4	10.2	10.8	US$/unit	841
4819	Cartons, boxes, cases, bags and other packing containers, of paper	20.6	41.6	54.7	1.8	3.7	4.8	US$/kg	642

*In 2014, the reported share of non-standard HS codes increased significantly.

Albania

Services Imports and Exports: EBOPS 2002 categories

Table 2: Merchandise exports by SITC
(Value in million US$, growth and shares in percentage)

SITC	2014	Avg. Growth rates 2010-2014	2013-2014	2014 share
Total	2430.7	11.9	4.3	100.0
0+1	73.0	1.5	-29.7	3.0
2+4	136.6	-10.5	-46.1	5.6
3	38.1	-39.2	-94.7	1.6
5	6.5	-3.5	-63.0	0.3
6	95.5	-27.3	-78.6	3.9
7	19.2	-26.0	-75.4	0.8
8	646.7	3.1	-8.6	26.6
9	1415.0	318.6	61788.9	58.2

Table 3: Merchandise imports by SITC
(Value in million US$, growth and shares in percentage)

SITC	2014	Avg. Growth rates 2010-2014	2013-2014	2014 share
Total	5230.0	3.2	7.2	100.0
0+1	503.7	-10.1	-38.1	9.6
2+4	77.9	-22.5	-55.2	1.5
3	425.9	-9.5	-49.2	8.1
5	324.2	-8.6	-42.8	6.2
6	669.4	-12.0	-36.7	12.8
7	536.6	-11.5	-39.6	10.3
8	441.7	-4.1	-18.2	8.4
9	2250.6	431.8	86866.2	43.0

SITC Legend

SITC Code	Description
Total	All commodities
0+1	Food, animals + beverages, tobacco
2+4	Crude materials + anim. & veg. oils
3	Mineral fuels, lubricants
5	Chemicals
6	Goods classified chiefly by material
7	Machinery and transport equipment
8	Miscellaneous manufactured articles
9	Not classified elsewhere in the SITC

Graph 4: Merchandise trade balance
(Bln US$ by MDG Regions in 2014)

Graph 5: Partner concentration of merchandise trade
(Cumulative share by ranked partners in 2014)

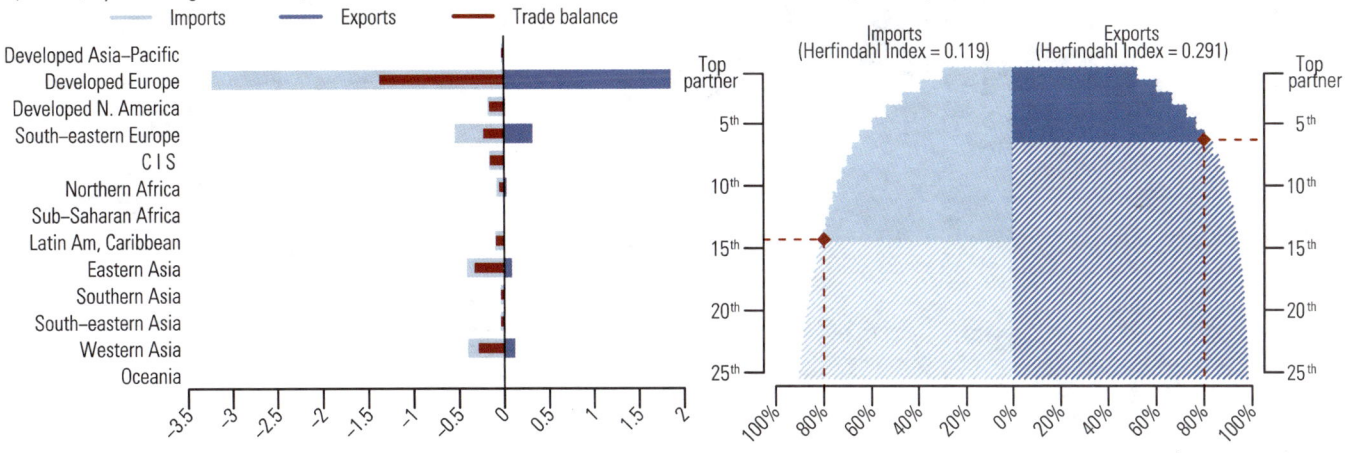

Imports (Herfindahl Index = 0.119)
Exports (Herfindahl Index = 0.291)

Graph 6: Imports of services by EBOPS category
(% share in 2013)

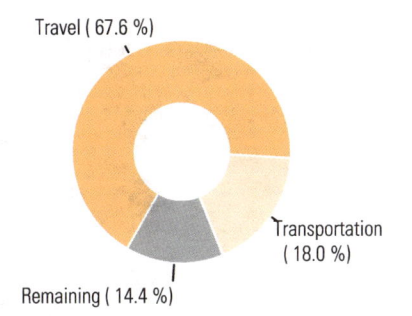

- Travel (67.6 %)
- Transportation (18.0 %)
- Remaining (14.4 %)

Imports Profile:

"Not classified elsewhere in the SITC" (SITC section 9), "Goods classified chiefly by material" (SITC section 6) and "Machinery and transport equipment" (SITC section 7) were the largest commodity groups for imports in 2014, representing respectively 43.0, 12.8 and 10.3 percent of imported goods (see table 3). From 2012 to 2014, the largest import commodity was "Commodities not specified according to kind" (HS code 9999) (see table 4). The top three partners for merchandise imports were Italy, Greece and China, accounting for respectively 31.5, 9.3 and 6.8 percent of total imports. "Travel" (EBOPS code 236) accounted for the largest share of imports of services in 2013 at 1.5 bln US$, followed by "Transportation" (EBOPS code 205) at 393.0 mln US$ (see graph 6).

Table 4: Top 10 import commodities 2012 to 2014

HS code	4-digit heading of Harmonized System 2012	Value (million US$) 2012	2013	2014	Unit value 2012	2013	2014	Unit	SITC code
	All Commodities	4879.8	4880.6	5230.0					
9999	Commodities not specified according to kind	3.5	2.3	2250.6					931
2710	Petroleum oils, other than crude	583.8	628.6	395.3	1.1	1.0	0.9	US$/kg	334
8703	Motor cars and other motor vehicles principally designed for the transport	212.1	191.9	183.4	0.5	3.2	2.3	thsd US$/unit	781
3004	Medicaments (excluding goods of heading 30.02, 30.05 or 30.06)	142.3	136.5	108.4	48.0	41.5	46.2	US$/kg	542
2716	Electrical energy	278.1	107.2	...	81.9	64.0		US$/MWh	351
4107	Leather further prepared after tanning or crusting	70.9	82.5	88.9	18.4	18.8	19.4	US$/kg	611
6406	Parts of footwear	64.2	73.3	76.2	8.4	8.8	8.4	US$/kg	851
1001	Wheat and meslin	88.8	81.0	41.3	0.3	0.3	0.3	US$/kg	041
2402	Cigars, cheroots, cigarillos and cigarettes	81.0	84.8	20.3	22.3	22.9	18.3	US$/kg	122
2711	Petroleum gases and other gaseous hydrocarbons	70.8	67.2	24.1	1.0	0.9	0.8	US$/kg	343

2014 International Trade Statistics Yearbook, Vol. I — Source: UN Comtrade and UN ServiceTrade

Algeria

Goods Imports: CIF, by origin | **Goods Exports:** FOB, by last known destination | **Trade System:** Special

Overview:
In 2014, the value of merchandise exports of Algeria decreased slightly by 4.2 percent to reach 63.2 bln US$, while its merchandise imports increased moderately by 6.8 percent to reach 58.6 bln US$ (see graph 1, table 2 and table 3). The merchandise trade balance recorded a relatively small surplus of 4.6 bln US$ (see graph 1). The largest merchandise trade balance was with MDG Developed Europe at 10.6 bln US$ (see graph 4). Merchandise exports in Algeria were diversified amongst partners; imports were also diversified. The top 11 partners accounted for 80 percent or more of exports and 19 partners accounted for 80 percent or more of imports (see graph 5). In 2012, the value of exports of services of Algeria increased moderately by 6.8 percent, reaching 4.0 bln US$, while its imports of services decreased substantially by 11.8 percent and reached 11.0 bln US$ (see graph 2). There was a large trade in services deficit of 7.0 bln US$.

Graph 1: Total merchandise trade, by value
(Bln US$ by year)

Graph 2: Total services trade, by value
(Bln US$ by year)

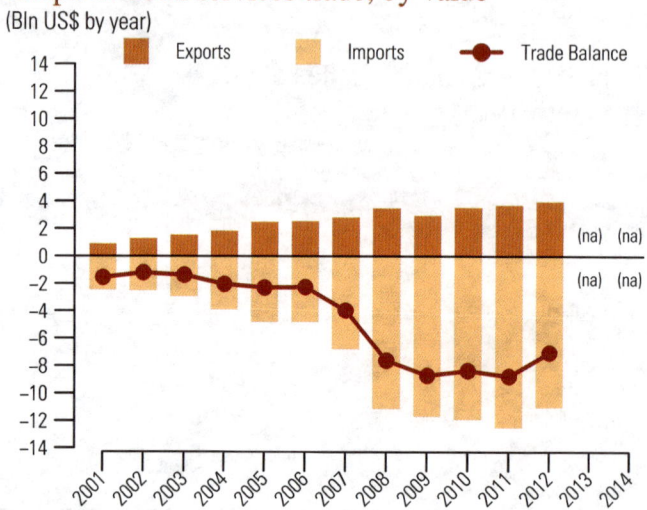

Exports Profile:
"Mineral fuels, lubricants" (SITC section 3), "Chemicals" (SITC section 5) and "Food, animals + beverages, tobacco" (SITC section 0+1) were the largest commodity groups for exports in 2014, representing respectively 97.4, 1.7 and 0.5 percent of exported goods (see table 2). From 2012 to 2014, the largest export commodity was "Petroleum oils and oils obtained from bituminous minerals, crude" (HS code 2709) (see table 1). The top three destinations for merchandise exports were Italy, Spain and the United States, accounting for respectively 14.4, 13.8 and 10.4 percent of total exports. "Other business services" (EBOPS code 268) accounted for the largest share of exports of services in 2012 at 2.1 bln US$, followed by "Transportation" (EBOPS code 205) at 732.5 mln US$ and "Financial services" (EBOPS code 260) at 272.8 mln US$ (see graph 3).

Graph 3: Exports of services by EBOPS category
(% share in 2012)

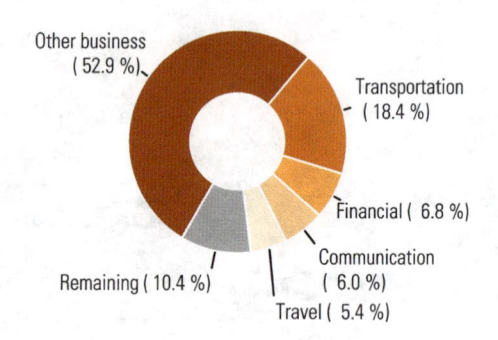

- Other business (52.9 %)
- Transportation (18.4 %)
- Financial (6.8 %)
- Communication (6.0 %)
- Travel (5.4 %)
- Remaining (10.4 %)

Table 1: Top 10 export commodities 2012 to 2014

HS code	4-digit heading of Harmonized System 2012	Value 2012	Value 2013	Value 2014	UV 2012	UV 2013	UV 2014	Unit	SITC code
	All Commodities	71 865.7	65 998.1	63 227.8					
2709	Petroleum oils and oils obtained from bituminous minerals, crude	32 879.4	30 380.1	24 376.9	0.9	0.8	0.8	US$/kg	333
2711	Petroleum gases and other gaseous hydrocarbons	27 001.3	25 676.5	24 144.3		0.5	0.7	US$/kg	343
2710	Petroleum oils, other than crude	9 921.6	7 769.5	12 091.1	0.9	0.8	0.8	US$/kg	334
2707	Oils and other products of high temperature coal tar	909.0	1 067.7	943.7	1.4	1.3	1.4	US$/kg	335
2814	Ammonia, anhydrous or in aqueous solution	420.8	303.9	570.9	0.6	0.5	0.5	US$/kg	522
1701	Cane or beet sugar and chemically pure sucrose, in solid form	208.0	272.5	229.4	0.7	0.6	0.5	US$/kg	061
2510	Natural calcium phosphates	152.9	96.7	96.5	0.1	0.1	0.1	US$/kg	272
3102	Mineral or chemical fertilisers, nitrogenous	9.3	38.4	294.0	0.2	0.3	0.3	US$/kg	562
2905	Acyclic alcohols and their derivatives	34.0	45.2	47.6	0.4		0.4	US$/kg	512
2902	Cyclic hydrocarbons	...	...	124.4			1.1	US$/kg	511

Source: UN Comtrade and UN ServiceTrade

Algeria

Services Imports and Exports: EBOPS 2002 categories

Table 2: Merchandise exports by SITC
(Value in million US$, growth and shares in percentage)

SITC	2014	Avg. Growth rates 2010-2014	2013-2014	2014 share
Total	63 227.8	2.6	-4.2	100.0
0+1	325.5	1.2	-19.0	0.5
2+4	112.2	1.9	-0.6	0.2
3	61 581.0	2.4	-5.1	97.4
5	1 098.5	37.0	147.4	1.7
6	90.8	-18.5	-21.3	0.1
7	14.2	0.1	-0.2	0.0
8	5.6	-12.7	-26.4	0.0

Table 3: Merchandise imports by SITC
(Value in million US$, growth and shares in percentage)

SITC	2014	Avg. Growth rates 2010-2014	2013-2014	2014 share
Total	58 618.1	9.3	6.8	100.0
0+1	10 877.6	16.1	15.4	18.6
2+4	1 961.2	6.0	-1.4	3.3
3	2 843.0	34.6	-33.7	4.9
5	6 832.9	11.3	9.6	11.7
6	10 976.4	2.8	15.8	18.7
7	22 245.9	7.4	9.9	38.0
8	2 879.9	16.0	-11.2	4.9
9	1.2	...	-62.6	0.0

SITC Legend

SITC Code	Description
Total	All commodities
0+1	Food, animals + beverages, tobacco
2+4	Crude materials + anim. & veg. oils
3	Mineral fuels, lubricants
5	Chemicals
6	Goods classified chiefly by material
7	Machinery and transport equipment
8	Miscellaneous manufactured articles
9	Not classified elsewhere in the SITC

Graph 4: Merchandise trade balance
(Bln US$ by MDG Regions in 2014)

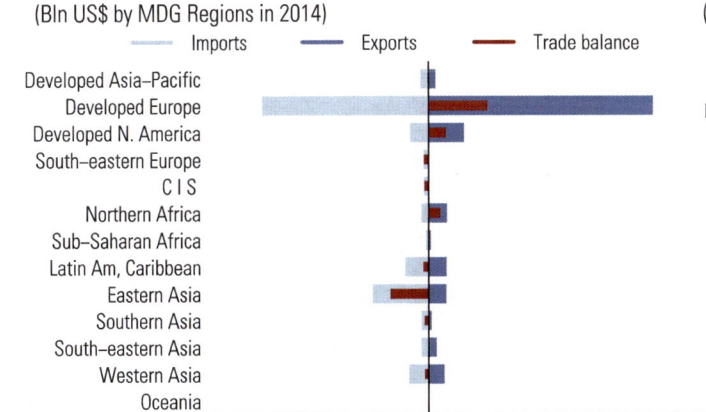

Graph 5: Partner concentration of merchandise trade
(Cumulative share by ranked partners in 2014)

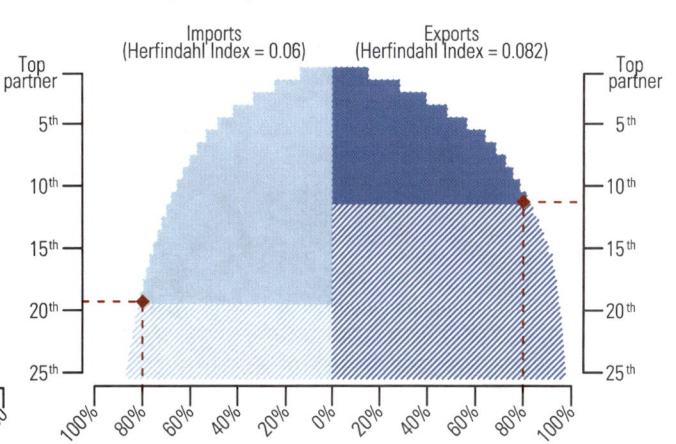

Imports (Herfindahl Index = 0.06)
Exports (Herfindahl Index = 0.082)

Graph 6: Imports of services by EBOPS category
(% share in 2012)

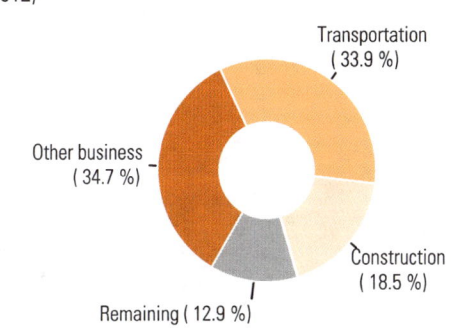

- Transportation (33.9 %)
- Other business (34.7 %)
- Construction (18.5 %)
- Remaining (12.9 %)

Imports Profile:

"Machinery and transport equipment" (SITC section 7), "Goods classified chiefly by material" (SITC section 6) and "Food, animals + beverages, tobacco" (SITC section 0+1) were the largest commodity groups for imports in 2014, representing respectively 38.0, 18.7 and 18.6 percent of imported goods (see table 3). From 2012 to 2014, the largest import commodity was "Motor cars and other motor vehicles principally designed for the transport" (HS code 8703) (see table 4). The top three partners for merchandise imports were China, France and Italy, accounting for respectively 12.8, 11.6 and 9.7 percent of total imports. "Other business services" (EBOPS code 268) accounted for the largest share of imports of services in 2012 at 3.8 bln US$, followed by "Transportation" (EBOPS code 205) at 3.7 bln US$ and "Construction services" (EBOPS code 249) at 2.0 bln US$ (see graph 6).

Table 4: Top 10 import commodities 2012 to 2014

HS code	4-digit heading of Harmonized System 2012	Value (million US$) 2012	2013	2014	Unit value 2012	2013	2014	Unit	SITC code
	All Commodities	50 369.4	54 910.0	58 618.1					
8703	Motor cars and other motor vehicles principally designed for the transport	3 908.7	3 728.7	2 965.5	9.9	10.5	*14.0*	thsd US$/unit	781
2710	Petroleum oils, other than crude	4 435.9	3 770.5	2 191.4	*0.8*	*1.0*	0.9	US$/kg	334
1001	Wheat and meslin	2 129.0	2 123.4	2 372.5	0.3	0.3	0.3	US$/kg	041
8704	Motor vehicles for the transport of goods	2 205.5	2 225.3	2 110.3	*706.4*	*289.8*		US$/unit	782
7214	Other bars and rods of iron or non-alloy steel	2 098.4	1 862.5	1 884.3	0.7	*0.6*	0.6	US$/kg	676
3004	Medicaments (excluding goods of heading 30.02, 30.05 or 30.06)	1 754.8	1 807.7	1 949.4	*54.9*	*64.6*	68.0	US$/kg	542
0402	Milk and cream, concentrated or containing added sugar	1 093.4	1 076.7	1 800.3	3.6	4.1	4.8	US$/kg	022
8411	Turbo-jets, turbo-propellers and other gas turbines	526.0	1 274.8	1 700.8					714
1005	Maize (corn)	941.9	892.6	977.3	0.3	0.3	0.2	US$/kg	044
1701	Cane or beet sugar and chemically pure sucrose, in solid form	960.9	881.8	840.9	*0.6*	0.5	0.4	US$/kg	061

Antigua and Barbuda

Goods Imports: CIF, by origin **Goods Exports:** FOB, by last known destination **Trade System:** General

Overview:

In 2014, the value of merchandise exports of Antigua and Barbuda decreased substantially by 29.9 percent to reach 23.1 mln US$, while its merchandise imports decreased substantially by 22.9 percent to reach 391.6 mln US$ (see graph 1, table 2 and table 3). The merchandise trade balance recorded a large deficit of 368.5 mln US$ (see graph 1). The largest merchandise trade balance was with MDG Developed North America at -192.5 mln US$ (see graph 4). Merchandise exports in Antigua and Barbuda were diversified amongst partners; imports were highly concentrated. The top 9 partners accounted for 80 percent or more of exports and 12 partners accounted for 80 percent or more of imports (see graph 5). In 2012, the value of exports of services of Antigua and Barbuda increased slightly by 0.2 percent, reaching 482.5 mln US$, while its imports of services decreased slightly by 3.2 percent and reached 204.1 mln US$ (see graph 2). There was a large trade in services surplus of 278.4 mln US$.

Graph 1: Total merchandise trade, by value
(Mln US$ by year)

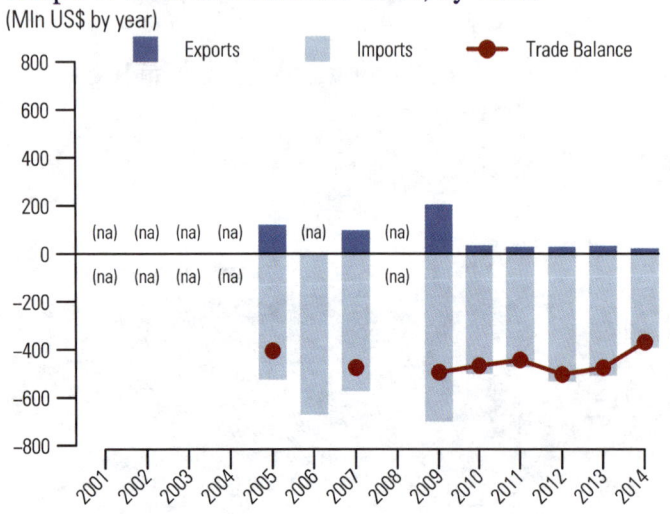

Graph 2: Total services trade, by value
(Mln US$ by year)

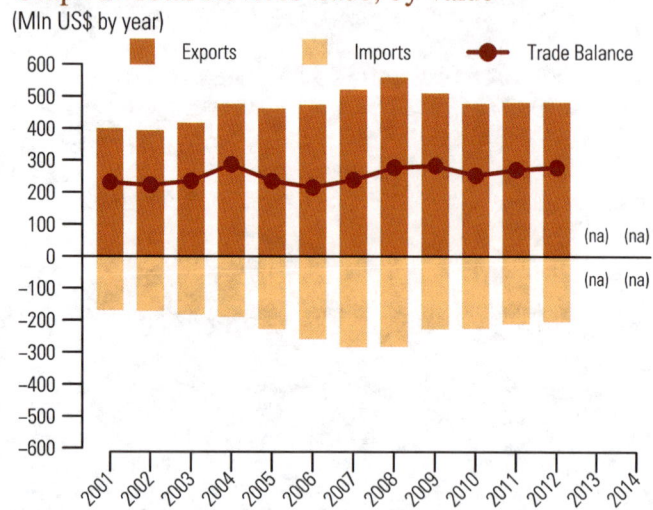

Exports Profile:

"Machinery and transport equipment" (SITC section 7), "Goods classified chiefly by material" (SITC section 6) and "Miscellaneous manufactured articles" (SITC section 8) were the largest commodity groups for exports in 2014, representing respectively 36.9, 33.9 and 9.2 percent of exported goods (see table 2). From 2012 to 2014, the largest export commodity was "Textile tarpaulin, sail, awning, tent, camping goods" (HS code 6306) (see table 1). The top three destinations for merchandise exports were the United States, the United Kingdom and Curaçao, accounting for respectively 24.0, 21.6 and 5.3 percent of total exports. "Travel" (EBOPS code 236) accounted for the largest share of exports of services in 2012 at 319.0 mln US$, followed by "Transportation" (EBOPS code 205) at 106.6 mln US$ and "Other business services" (EBOPS code 268) at 30.2 mln US$ (see graph 3).

Graph 3: Exports of services by EBOPS category
(% share in 2012)

- Travel (66.1 %)
- Transportation (22.1 %)
- Other business (6.3 %)
- Remaining (5.5 %)

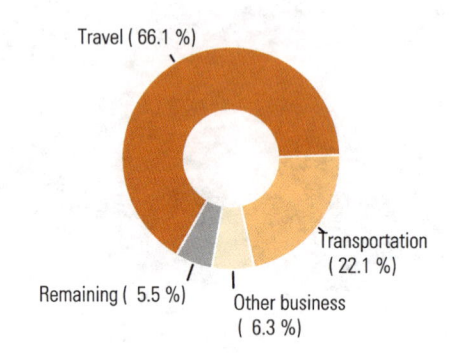

Table 1: Top 10 export commodities 2012 to 2014

HS code	4-digit heading of Harmonized System 1996	Value (million US$) 2012	2013	2014	Unit value 2012	2013	2014	Unit	SITC code
	All Commodities	29.0	32.9	23.1					
6306	Textile tarpaulin, sail, awning, tent, camping goods	7.4	9.4	5.1	104.6	97.5	45.9	US$/kg	658
2710	Oils petroleum, bituminous, distillates, except crude	0.5	4.1	1.0	25.8	0.0	2.0	US$/kg	334
8903	Yachts, pleasure, sports vessels, rowing boats, canoes	0.7	2.3	1.2	19.5	31.7		thsd US$/unit	793
2208	Liqueur, spirits and undenatured ethyl alcohol <80%	1.3	1.0	1.1	32.2	23.8	2.8	US$/litre	112
8525	Radio and TV transmitters, television cameras	2.4	0.9	0.1					764
7326	Articles of iron or steel nes	1.7	1.3	0.4	0.3	10.7	25.4	US$/kg	699
8803	Parts of aircraft, spacecraft, etc	0.2	0.1	2.4	137.5	975.2	454.8	US$/kg	792
7204	Ferrous waste or scrap, ingots or iron or steel	0.2	1.3	0.9	0.6	0.4	0.2	US$/kg	282
7113	Jewellery and parts, containing precious metal	1.2	0.3	0.7	14.2	26.2	19.9	thsd US$/kg	897
7010	Glass bottles, flasks, jars, phials, stoppers, etc	0.8	0.5	0.5	0.5	0.4	0.4	US$/kg	665

Antigua and Barbuda

Services Imports and Exports: EBOPS 2002 categories

Table 2: Merchandise exports by SITC
(Value in million US$, growth and shares in percentage)

SITC	2014	Avg. Growth rates 2010-2014	2013-2014	2014 share
Total	23.1	-9.8	-29.9	100.0
0+1	2.1	-4.7	4.9	9.0
2+4	1.0	89.7	-36.3	4.3
3	1.0	-5.3	-75.2	4.4
5	0.5	-11.1	-27.0	2.3
6	7.8	-5.1	-40.9	33.9
7	8.5	-10.4	11.2	36.9
8	2.1	-26.5	-41.4	9.2

Table 3: Merchandise imports by SITC
(Value in million US$, growth and shares in percentage)

SITC	2014	Avg. Growth rates 2010-2014	2013-2014	2014 share
Total	391.6	-6.0	-22.9	100.0
0+1	122.8	3.8	2.1	31.4
2+4	11.3	3.9	16.5	2.9
3	3.2	5.7	-98.1	0.8
5	31.9	-0.9	4.3	8.1
6	64.0	2.8	7.3	16.3
7	96.8	-0.5	47.3	24.7
8	61.6	3.4	15.6	15.7
9	0.0	-89.7	-95.2	0.0

SITC Legend

SITC Code	Description
Total	All commodities
0+1	Food, animals + beverages, tobacco
2+4	Crude materials + anim. & veg. oils
3	Mineral fuels, lubricants
5	Chemicals
6	Goods classified chiefly by material
7	Machinery and transport equipment
8	Miscellaneous manufactured articles
9	Not classified elsewhere in the SITC

Graph 4: Merchandise trade balance
(Mln US$ by MDG Regions in 2014)

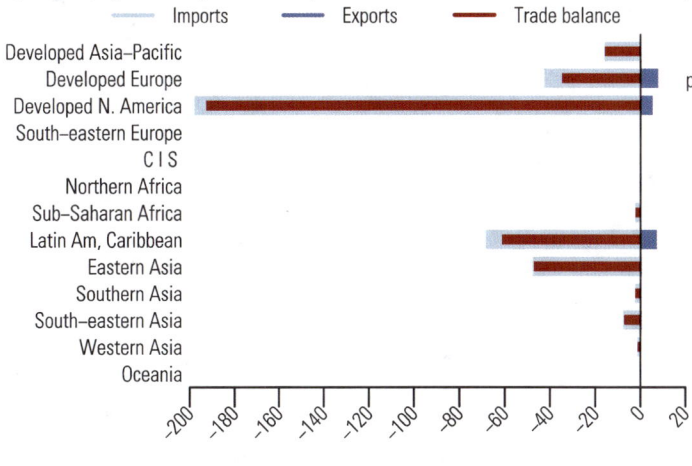

Graph 5: Partner concentration of merchandise trade
(Cumulative share by ranked partners in 2014)

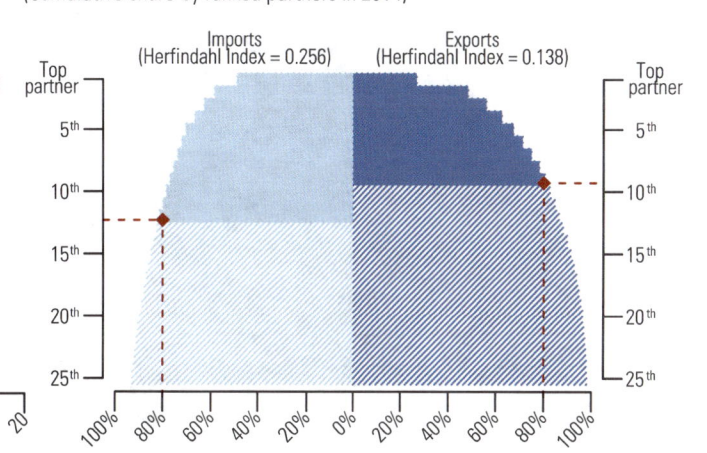

Imports (Herfindahl Index = 0.256)
Exports (Herfindahl Index = 0.138)

Graph 6: Imports of services by EBOPS category
(% share in 2012)

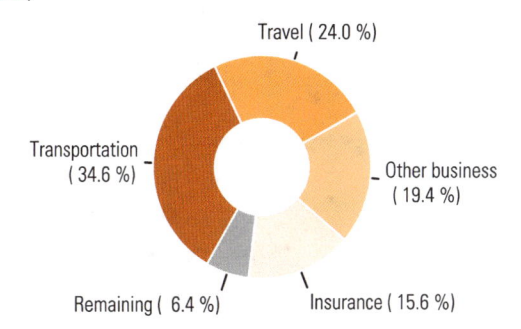

- Travel (24.0 %)
- Transportation (34.6 %)
- Other business (19.4 %)
- Insurance (15.6 %)
- Remaining (6.4 %)

Imports Profile:

"Food, animals + beverages, tobacco" (SITC section 0+1), "Machinery and transport equipment" (SITC section 7) and "Goods classified chiefly by material" (SITC section 6) were the largest commodity groups for imports in 2014, representing respectively 31.4, 24.7 and 16.3 percent of imported goods (see table 3). From 2012 to 2014, the largest import commodity was "Oils petroleum, bituminous, distillates, except crude" (HS code 2710) (see table 4). The top three partners for merchandise imports were the United States, Areas nes and China, accounting for respectively 37.8, 25.1 and 5.4 percent of total imports. "Transportation" (EBOPS code 205) accounted for the largest share of imports of services in 2012 at 70.5 mln US$, followed by "Travel" (EBOPS code 236) at 48.9 mln US$ and "Other business services" (EBOPS code 268) at 39.6 mln US$ (see graph 6).

Table 4: Top 10 import commodities 2012 to 2014

HS code	4-digit heading of Harmonized System 1996	Value (million US$) 2012	2013	2014	Unit value 2012	2013	2014	Unit	SITC code
	All Commodities	532.3	507.9	391.6					
2710	Oils petroleum, bituminous, distillates, except crude	195.7	168.3	3.1	1.5	1.3	0.2	US$/kg	334
8703	Motor vehicles for transport of persons (except buses)	13.7	15.7	25.0	11.2	13.9	15.1	thsd US$/unit	781
0207	Meat, edible offal of domestic poultry	12.5	12.4	12.1	1.5	2.1	2.1	US$/kg	012
2202	Waters, non-alcoholic sweetened or flavoured beverages	9.8	9.1	9.5	1.1	1.1	1.1	US$/litre	111
7113	Jewellery and parts, containing precious metal	8.1	7.8	8.9	2.7	2.3	2.8	thsd US$/kg	897
2106	Food preparations, nes	7.0	6.6	6.9	2.5	2.0	2.2	US$/kg	098
3004	Medicaments, therapeutic, prophylactic use, in dosage	6.9	6.3	5.8	27.5	33.2	26.5	US$/kg	542
6306	Textile tarpaulin, sail, awning, tent, camping goods	5.3	7.3	5.0	60.9	64.2	21.5	US$/kg	658
9403	Other furniture and parts thereof	4.6	4.4	6.6					821
8471	Automatic data processing machines (computers)	4.9	3.7	4.9			555.2	US$/unit	752

2014 International Trade Statistics Yearbook, Vol. I   Source: UN Comtrade and UN ServiceTrade

Argentina

| Goods Imports: CIF, by origin | Goods Exports: FOB, by last known destination | Trade System: Special |

Overview:
In 2014, the value of merchandise exports of Argentina decreased substantially by 10.8 percent to reach 68.3 bln US$, while its merchandise imports decreased substantially by 11.3 percent to reach 65.3 bln US$ (see graph 1, table 2 and table 3). The merchandise trade balance recorded a relatively small surplus of 3.0 bln US$ (see graph 1). The largest merchandise trade balance was with MDG Eastern Asia at -6.7 bln US$ (see graph 4). Merchandise exports in Argentina were diversified amongst partners; imports were also diversified. The top 28 partners accounted for 80 percent or more of exports and 15 partners accounted for 80 percent or more of imports (see graph 5). In 2013, the value of exports of services of Argentina decreased moderately by 6.3 percent, reaching 14.3 bln US$, while its imports of services increased slightly by 1.4 percent and reached 18.7 bln US$ (see graph 2). There was a moderate trade in services deficit of 4.3 bln US$.

Graph 1: Total merchandise trade, by value
(Bln US$ by year)

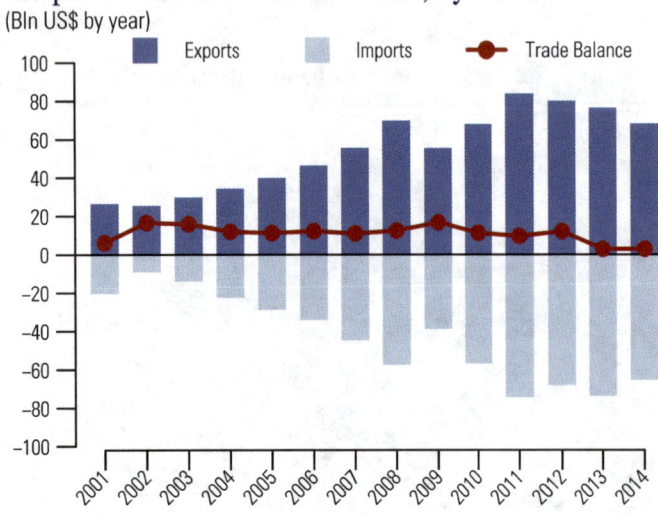

Graph 2: Total services trade, by value
(Bln US$ by year)

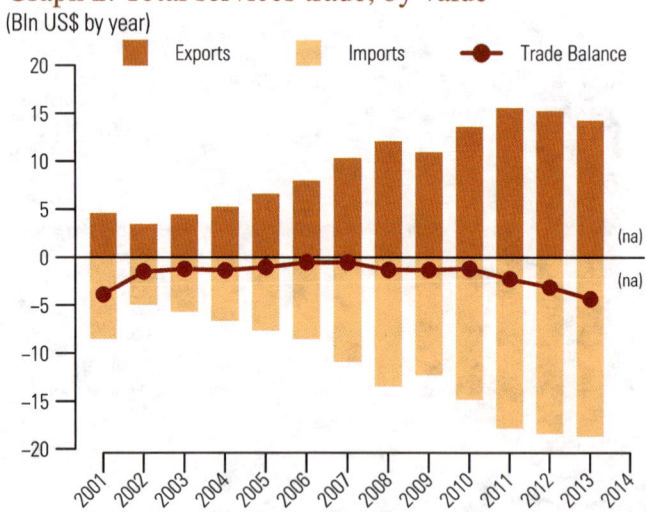

Exports Profile:
"Food, animals + beverages, tobacco" (SITC section 0+1), "Machinery and transport equipment" (SITC section 7) and "Crude materials + anim. & veg. oils" (SITC section 2+4) were the largest commodity groups for exports in 2014, representing respectively 42.2, 15.3 and 15.3 percent of exported goods (see table 2). From 2012 to 2014, the largest export commodity was "Oil-cake and other solid residues" (HS code 2304) (see table 1). The top three destinations for merchandise exports were Brazil, China and the United States, accounting for respectively 20.7, 6.7 and 5.5 percent of total exports. "Other business services" (EBOPS code 268) accounted for the largest share of exports of services in 2013 at 4.7 bln US$, followed by "Travel" (EBOPS code 236) at 4.3 bln US$ and "Transportation" (EBOPS code 205) at 2.6 bln US$ (see graph 3).

Graph 3: Exports of services by EBOPS category
(% share in 2013)

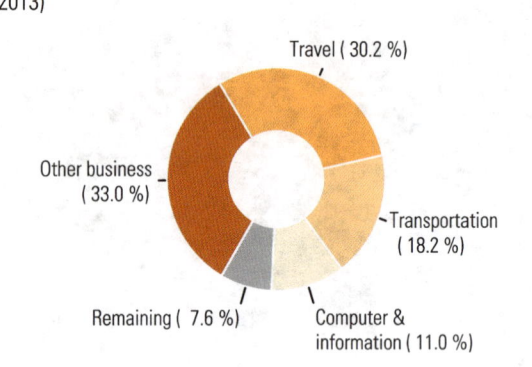

- Travel (30.2 %)
- Other business (33.0 %)
- Transportation (18.2 %)
- Computer & information (11.0 %)
- Remaining (7.6 %)

Table 1: Top 10 export commodities 2012 to 2014

HS code	4-digit heading of Harmonized System 2012	Value (million US$) 2012	2013	2014	Unit value 2012	2013	2014	Unit	SITC code
	All Commodities	80 246.1	76 633.9	68 335.1					
2304	Oil-cake and other solid residues	9 865.7	10 660.6	11 840.7	0.4	0.5	0.5	US$/kg	081
1005	Maize (corn)	4 841.1	5 848.0	3 524.7	0.3	0.3	0.2	US$/kg	044
1507	Soya-bean oil and its fractions	4 319.8	4 089.3	3 467.7	1.1	1.0	0.9	US$/kg	421
8704	Motor vehicles for the transport of goods	3 836.4	4 116.8	3 856.5	26.5	26.9	26.6	thsd US$/unit	782
8703	Motor cars and other motor vehicles principally designed for the transport	3 958.6	4 123.4	3 085.4	14.9	14.7	14.8	thsd US$/unit	781
1201	Soya beans, whether or not broken	3 191.6	4 089.4	3 776.8	0.5	0.5	0.5	US$/kg	222
9999	Commodities not specified according to kind	2 102.0	2 119.9	1 837.5					931
2709	Petroleum oils and oils obtained from bituminous minerals, crude	2 611.2	1 736.8	1 618.4	0.7	0.7	0.7	US$/kg	333
7108	Gold (including gold plated with platinum)	2 254.0	1 846.6	1 827.6	9.5	5.8		thsd US$/kg	971
1001	Wheat and meslin	2 952.0	725.4	603.6	0.3	0.3	0.3	US$/kg	041

Argentina

Services Imports and Exports: EBOPS 2002 categories

Table 2: Merchandise exports by SITC
(Value in million US$, growth and shares in percentage)

SITC	2014	Avg. Growth rates 2010-2014	Avg. Growth rates 2013-2014	2014 share
Total	68 335.1	0.1	-10.8	100.0
0+1	28 803.5	5.2	-9.2	42.2
2+4	10 424.3	-5.4	-11.0	15.3
3	3 197.1	-12.2	-10.1	4.7
5	6 459.5	2.3	1.7	9.5
6	4 655.1	-3.4	-5.1	6.8
7	10 487.1	-0.8	-23.1	15.3
8	643.4	-8.9	-18.1	0.9
9	3 665.2	2.9	-7.6	5.4

Table 3: Merchandise imports by SITC
(Value in million US$, growth and shares in percentage)

SITC	2014	Avg. Growth rates 2010-2014	Avg. Growth rates 2013-2014	2014 share
Total	65 323.4	3.6	-11.3	100.0
0+1	1 510.8	1.8	-3.5	2.3
2+4	2 060.9	0.7	-2.2	3.2
3	11 019.0	25.2	1.1	16.9
5	11 638.1	3.4	-3.5	17.8
6	7 088.3	-0.7	-8.2	10.9
7	27 265.3	0.2	-20.3	41.7
8	4 033.8	0.7	-9.4	6.2
9	707.1	14.2	8.5	1.1

SITC Legend

SITC Code	Description
Total	All commodities
0+1	Food, animals + beverages, tobacco
2+4	Crude materials + anim. & veg. oils
3	Mineral fuels, lubricants
5	Chemicals
6	Goods classified chiefly by material
7	Machinery and transport equipment
8	Miscellaneous manufactured articles
9	Not classified elsewhere in the SITC

Graph 4: Merchandise trade balance
(Bln US$ by MDG Regions in 2014)

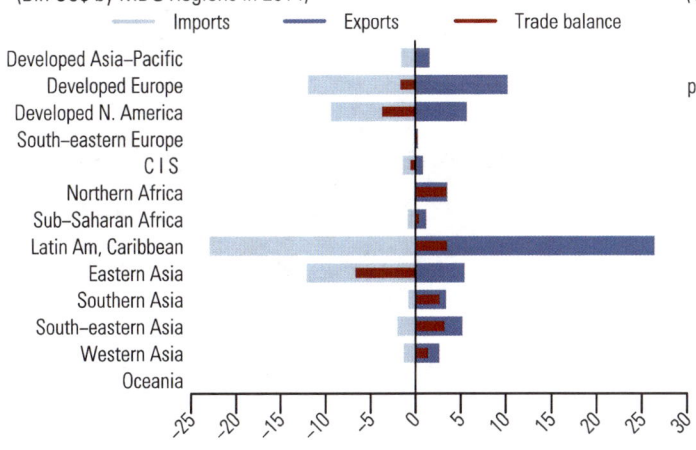

Graph 5: Partner concentration of merchandise trade
(Cumulative share by ranked partners in 2014)

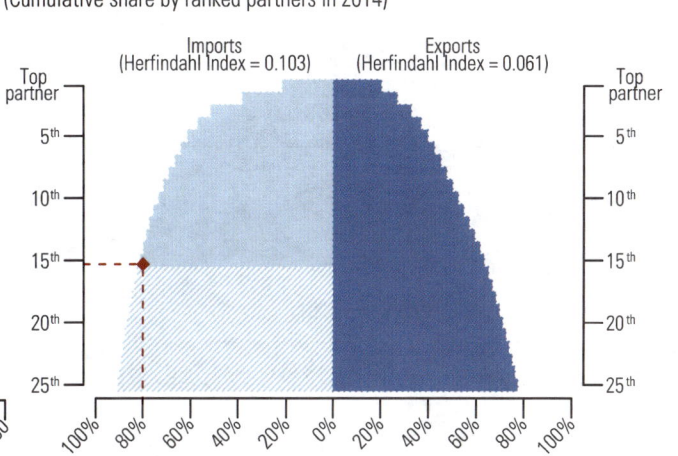

Imports (Herfindahl Index = 0.103)
Exports (Herfindahl Index = 0.061)

Graph 6: Imports of services by EBOPS category
(% share in 2013)

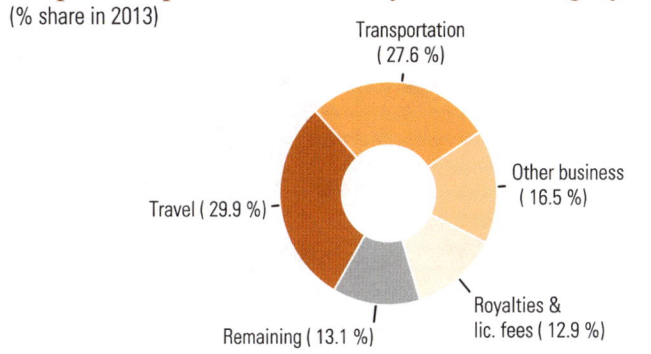

- Transportation (27.6 %)
- Travel (29.9 %)
- Remaining (13.1 %)
- Royalties & lic. fees (12.9 %)
- Other business (16.5 %)

Imports Profile:

"Machinery and transport equipment" (SITC section 7), "Chemicals" (SITC section 5) and "Mineral fuels, lubricants" (SITC section 3) were the largest commodity groups for imports in 2014, representing respectively 41.7, 17.8 and 16.9 percent of imported goods (see table 3). From 2012 to 2014, the largest import commodity was "Motor cars and other motor vehicles principally designed for the transport" (HS code 8703) (see table 4). The top three partners for merchandise imports were Brazil, China and the United States, accounting for respectively 24.7, 15.4 and 12.3 percent of total imports. "Travel" (EBOPS code 236) accounted for the largest share of imports of services in 2013 at 5.6 bln US$, followed by "Transportation" (EBOPS code 205) at 5.1 bln US$ and "Other business services" (EBOPS code 268) at 3.1 bln US$ (see graph 6).

Table 4: Top 10 import commodities 2012 to 2014

HS code	4-digit heading of Harmonized System 2012	2012	2013	2014	2012	2013	2014	Unit	SITC code
	All Commodities	68 020.0	73 655.5	65 323.4					
8703	Motor cars and other motor vehicles principally designed for the transport	5 359.8	7 064.4	3 567.8	11.7	12.5	12.2	thsd US$/unit	781
2711	Petroleum gases and other gaseous hydrocarbons	3 809.2	5 023.7	5 911.1	0.6	0.7	0.7	US$/kg	343
2710	Petroleum oils, other than crude	4 068.0	5 010.4	4 080.7	1.0	1.0	0.9	US$/kg	334
8708	Parts and accessories of the motor vehicles of headings 87.01 to 87.05	3 972.5	4 054.3	3 163.5	8.9	8.9	8.9	US$/kg	784
8517	Electrical apparatus for line telephony or line telegraphy	2 395.4	2 615.9	2 034.4					764
8704	Motor vehicles for the transport of goods	1 176.9	1 410.8	941.4	22.0	22.5	23.1	thsd US$/unit	782
3004	Medicaments (excluding goods of heading 30.02, 30.05 or 30.06)	1 129.1	1 126.0	1 081.3	64.6	60.2	55.7	US$/kg	542
3002	Human blood; animal blood prepared for therapeutic uses	751.9	843.5	855.9	512.3	593.0	776.4	US$/kg	541
8802	Other aircraft (for example, helicopters, aeroplanes); spacecraft	983.0	579.3	828.1	4.6	6.6	10.8	mln US$/unit	792
8471	Automatic data processing machines and units thereof	779.9	817.1	659.2	54.0	48.7	52.8	US$/unit	752

2014 International Trade Statistics Yearbook, Vol. I   Source: UN Comtrade and UN ServiceTrade

Armenia

Goods Imports: CIF, by origin **Goods Exports:** FOB, by last known destination **Trade System:** General

Overview:
In 2014, the value of merchandise exports of Armenia increased slightly by 1.5 percent to reach 1.5 bln US$, while its merchandise imports decreased slightly by 2.3 percent to reach 4.2 bln US$ (see graph 1, table 2 and table 3). The merchandise trade balance recorded a large deficit of 2.7 bln US$ (see graph 1). The largest merchandise trade balance was with MDG CIS at -966.4 mln US$ (see graph 4). Merchandise exports in Armenia were diversified amongst partners; imports were also diversified. The top 10 partners accounted for 80 percent or more of exports and 18 partners accounted for 80 percent or more of imports (see graph 5). In 2013, the value of exports of services of Armenia increased moderately by 5.5 percent, reaching 1.1 bln US$, while its imports of services increased slightly by 2.3 percent and reached 1.2 bln US$ (see graph 2). There was a relatively small trade in services deficit of 114.6 mln US$.

Graph 1: Total merchandise trade, by value
(Bln US$ by year)

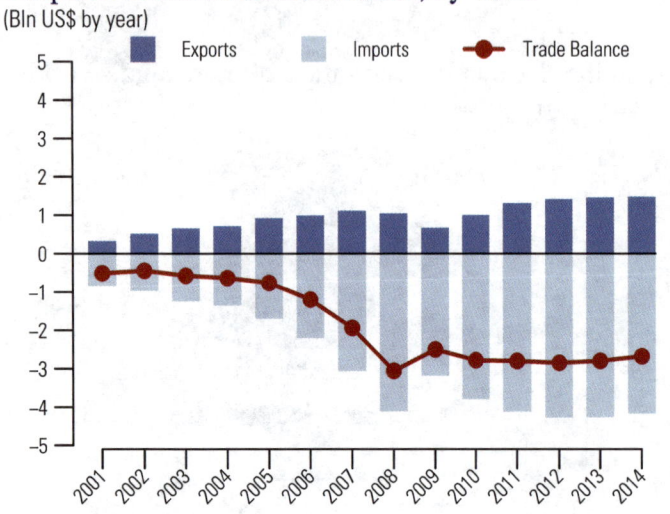

Graph 2: Total services trade, by value
(Bln US$ by year)

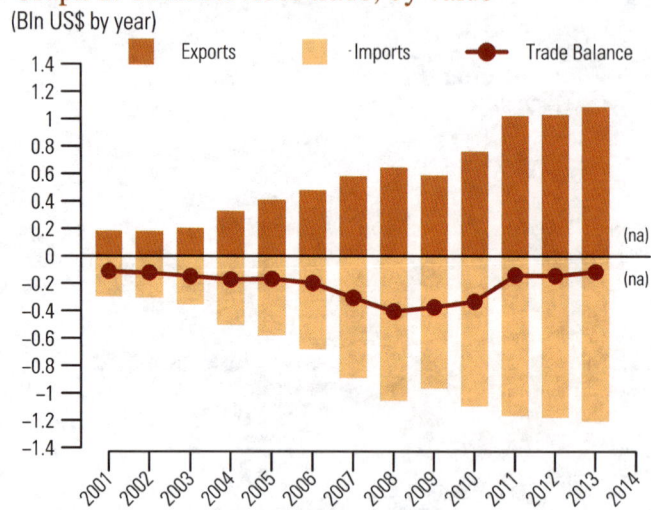

Exports Profile:
"Goods classified chiefly by material" (SITC section 6), "Food, animals + beverages, tobacco" (SITC section 0+1) and "Crude materials + anim. & veg. oils" (SITC section 2+4) were the largest commodity groups for exports in 2014, representing respectively 30.0, 27.5 and 20.5 percent of exported goods (see table 2). From 2012 to 2014, the largest export commodity was "Copper ores and concentrates" (HS code 2603) (see table 1). The top three destinations for merchandise exports were the Russian Federation, Germany and Bulgaria, accounting for respectively 20.8, 9.0 and 8.4 percent of total exports. "Travel" (EBOPS code 236) accounted for the largest share of exports of services in 2013 at 458.0 mln US$, followed by "Construction services" (EBOPS code 249) at 222.3 mln US$ and "Transportation" (EBOPS code 205) at 173.6 mln US$ (see graph 3).

Graph 3: Exports of services by EBOPS category
(% share in 2013)

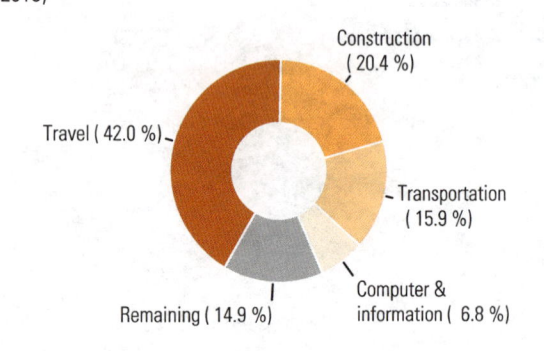

- Travel (42.0 %)
- Construction (20.4 %)
- Transportation (15.9 %)
- Computer & information (6.8 %)
- Remaining (14.9 %)

Table 1: Top 10 export commodities 2012 to 2014

HS code	4-digit heading of Harmonized System 2007	Value (million US$) 2012	2013	2014	Unit value 2012	2013	2014	Unit	SITC code
	All Commodities...	1 428.1	1 467.8	1 490.2					
2603	Copper ores and concentrates....................................	227.6	279.9	235.9	1.7	1.6	1.3	US$/kg	283
2208	Alcohol of a strength by volume of less than 80 % vol.....	164.8	186.2	163.7	11.5	13.2	12.5	US$/litre	112
7202	Ferro-alloys..	106.8	102.4	109.7	18.3	15.4	16.9	US$/kg	671
7102	Diamonds, whether or not worked, but not mounted or set..	79.1	88.1	118.0	582.3			US$/carat	667
7402	Unrefined copper; copper anodes for electrolytic refining...	104.8	90.2	71.8	10.6	8.3	7.3	US$/kg	682
2716	Electrical energy...	95.2	78.0	81.3	56.3	59.4	61.9	US$/MWh	351
7607	Aluminium foil (whether or not printed or backed with paper, paperboard..........	81.1	80.4	88.5	3.1	3.0	2.9	US$/kg	684
7108	Gold (including gold plated with platinum).....................	77.5	73.6	81.9	33.3	26.8	22.6	thsd US$/kg	971
2402	Cigars, cheroots, cigarillos and cigarettes.....................	41.8	68.0	115.9	8.9	10.2	11.0	US$/kg	122
8802	Other aircraft (for example, helicopters, aeroplanes); spacecraft............	48.7	22.6	1.7	48.7	7.5	1.7	mln US$/unit	792

Source: UN Comtrade and UN ServiceTrade

Armenia

Services Imports and Exports: EBOPS 2002 categories

Table 2: Merchandise exports by SITC
(Value in million US$, growth and shares in percentage)

SITC	2014	Avg. Growth rates 2010-2014	Avg. Growth rates 2013-2014	2014 share
Total	1 490.2	10.2	1.5	100.0
0+1	409.1	27.2	5.1	27.5
2+4	304.9	3.6	-5.7	20.5
3	90.3	22.0	2.2	6.1
5	20.1	12.8	-20.1	1.3
6	446.8	1.4	3.8	30.0
7	25.9	-5.6	-43.0	1.7
8	107.4	34.5	16.9	7.2
9	85.6	15.4	16.2	5.7

Table 3: Merchandise imports by SITC
(Value in million US$, growth and shares in percentage)

SITC	2014	Avg. Growth rates 2010-2014	Avg. Growth rates 2013-2014	2014 share
Total	4 159.5	2.4	-2.3	100.0
0+1	743.3	4.7	-4.6	17.9
2+4	122.8	6.8	9.2	3.0
3	814.0	5.3	-13.2	19.6
5	447.6	6.1	-0.4	10.8
6	828.5	3.3	9.9	19.9
7	695.4	-4.6	-6.1	16.7
8	342.4	4.3	9.7	8.2
9	165.4	-4.5	-2.9	4.0

SITC Legend

SITC Code	Description
Total	All commodities
0+1	Food, animals + beverages, tobacco
2+4	Crude materials + anim. & veg. oils
3	Mineral fuels, lubricants
5	Chemicals
6	Goods classified chiefly by material
7	Machinery and transport equipment
8	Miscellaneous manufactured articles
9	Not classified elsewhere in the SITC

Graph 4: Merchandise trade balance
(Bln US$ by MDG Regions in 2014)

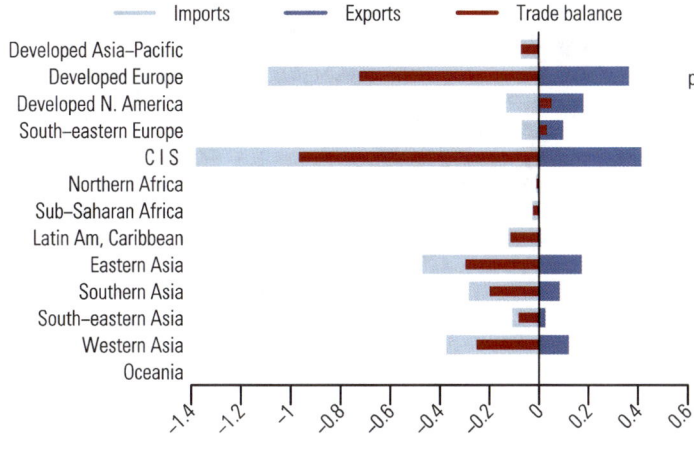

Graph 5: Partner concentration of merchandise trade
(Cumulative share by ranked partners in 2014)

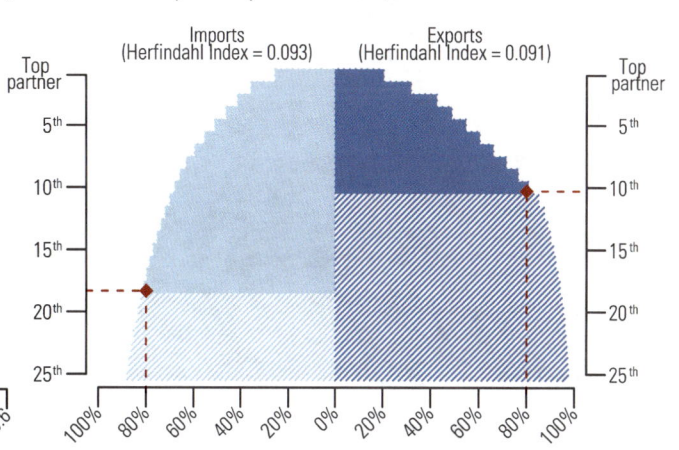

Imports (Herfindahl Index = 0.093)
Exports (Herfindahl Index = 0.091)

Graph 6: Imports of services by EBOPS category
(% share in 2013)

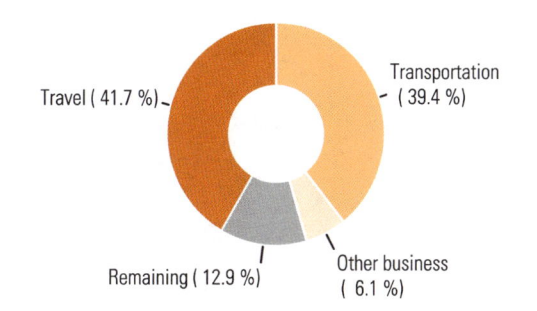

- Travel (41.7 %)
- Transportation (39.4 %)
- Remaining (12.9 %)
- Other business (6.1 %)

Imports Profile:

"Goods classified chiefly by material" (SITC section 6), "Mineral fuels, lubricants" (SITC section 3) and "Food, animals + beverages, tobacco" (SITC section 0+1) were the largest commodity groups for imports in 2014, representing respectively 19.9, 19.6 and 17.9 percent of imported goods (see table 3). From 2012 to 2014, the largest import commodity was "Petroleum gases and other gaseous hydrocarbons" (HS code 2711) (see table 4). The top three partners for merchandise imports were the Russian Federation, China and Turkey, accounting for respectively 25.4, 9.4 and 5.2 percent of total imports. "Travel" (EBOPS code 236) accounted for the largest share of imports of services in 2013 at 502.5 mln US$, followed by "Transportation" (EBOPS code 205) at 474.9 mln US$ and "Other business services" (EBOPS code 268) at 73.6 mln US$ (see graph 6).

Table 4: Top 10 import commodities 2012 to 2014

HS code	4-digit heading of Harmonized System 2007	Value 2012	Value 2013	Value 2014	Unit value 2012	Unit value 2013	Unit value 2014	Unit	SITC code
	All Commodities	4266.9	4256.2	4159.5					
2711	Petroleum gases and other gaseous hydrocarbons	520.3	575.6	467.3	0.3	0.3	0.3	US$/kg	343
2710	Petroleum oils, other than crude	360.5	341.6	321.2	1.0	1.0	1.0	US$/kg	334
7108	Gold (including gold plated with platinum)	74.0	168.6	145.1	53.7	43.9	40.8	thsd US$/kg	971
7102	Diamonds, whether or not worked, but not mounted or set	96.8	116.4	148.3	361.2			US$/carat	667
1001	Wheat and meslin	131.8	108.7	100.8	0.3	0.3	0.3	US$/kg	041
3004	Medicaments (excluding goods of heading 30.02, 30.05 or 30.06)	94.6	109.6	101.0	78.3	80.8	75.8	US$/kg	542
9999	Commodities not specified according to kind	186.6	1.8	20.3					931
8703	Motor cars and other motor vehicles principally designed for the transport	60.3	61.6	60.8	15.7	17.3	19.5	thsd US$/unit	781
8517	Electrical apparatus for line telephony or line telegraphy	69.4	48.9	59.2					764
7601	Unwrought aluminium	63.4	53.3	57.7	2.1	2.1	2.1	US$/kg	684

2014 International Trade Statistics Yearbook, Vol. I   Source: UN Comtrade and UN ServiceTrade

Aruba

Goods Imports: CIF, by origin **Goods Exports: FOB, by last known destination** **Trade System: General**

Overview:
In 2014, the value of merchandise exports of Aruba decreased substantially by 30.7 percent to reach 116.2 mln US$, while its merchandise imports decreased slightly by 1.5 percent to reach 1.3 bln US$ (see graph 1, table 2 and table 3). The merchandise trade balance recorded a large deficit of 1.2 bln US$ (see graph 1). The largest merchandise trade balance was with MDG Developed North America at -699.9 mln US$ (see graph 4). Merchandise exports in Aruba were moderately concentrated amongst partners; imports were highly concentrated. The top 4 partners accounted for 80 percent or more of exports and 5 partners accounted for 80 percent or more of imports (see graph 5). In 2013, the value of exports of services of Aruba increased moderately by 7.1 percent, reaching 1.9 bln US$, while its imports of services increased slightly by 3.6 percent and reached 848.6 mln US$ (see graph 2). There was a large trade in services surplus of 1.0 bln US$.

Graph 1: Total merchandise trade, by value
(Bln US$ by year)

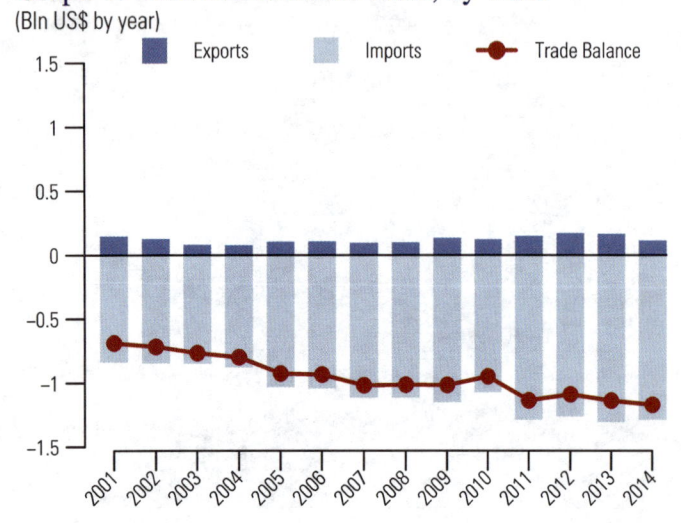

Graph 2: Total services trade, by value
(Bln US$ by year)

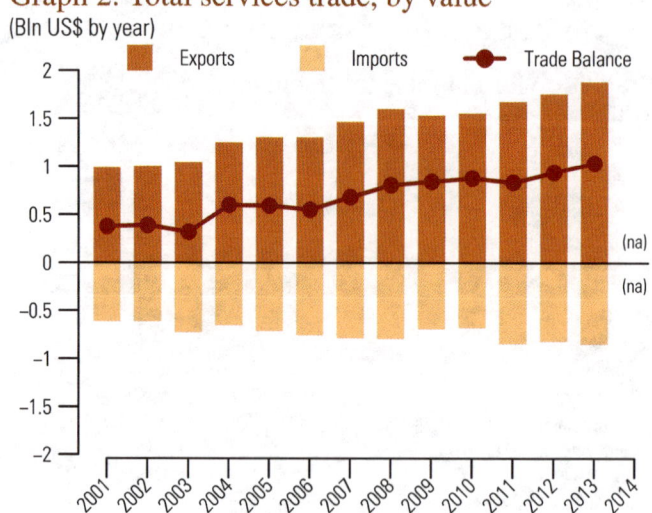

Exports Profile:
"Food, animals + beverages, tobacco" (SITC section 0+1), "Miscellaneous manufactured articles" (SITC section 8) and "Machinery and transport equipment" (SITC section 7) were the largest commodity groups for exports in 2014, representing respectively 68.1, 9.2 and 9.1 percent of exported goods (see table 2). From 2012 to 2014, the largest export commodity was "Alcohol of a strength by volume of less than 80 % vol" (HS code 2208) (see table 1). The top three destinations for merchandise exports were Colombia, the Bolivarian Republic of Venezuela and Curaçao, accounting for respectively 36.3, 18.8 and 14.0 percent of total exports. "Travel" (EBOPS code 236) accounted for the largest share of exports of services in 2013 at 1.5 bln US$, followed by "Other business services" (EBOPS code 268) at 236.9 mln US$ (see graph 3).

Graph 3: Exports of services by EBOPS category
(% share in 2013)

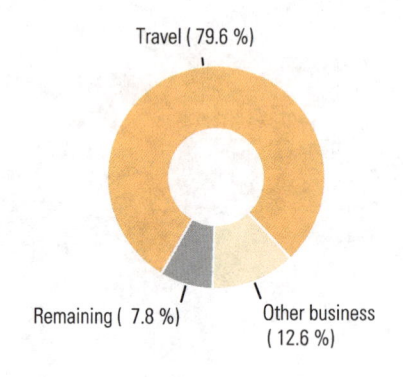

Travel (79.6 %)
Remaining (7.8 %)
Other business (12.6 %)

Table 1: Top 10 export commodities 2012 to 2014

HS code	4-digit heading of Harmonized System 2007	Value (million US$) 2012	2013	2014	Unit value 2012	2013	2014	Unit	SITC code
	All Commodities	173.1	167.8	116.2					
2208	Alcohol of a strength by volume of less than 80 % vol	70.0	78.4	61.2	11.5	12.6	14.3	US$/litre	112
2402	Cigars, cheroots, cigarillos and cigarettes	56.0	44.8	15.7	10.9	11.5	10.0	US$/kg	122
7113	Articles of jewellery and parts thereof, of precious metal	4.4	8.4	3.8	1.9	5.3	5.0	thsd US$/kg	897
9999	Commodities not specified according to kind	3.9	3.9	2.9					931
7204	Ferrous waste and scrap; remelting scrap ingots of iron or steel	2.2	2.7	2.8	0.2	0.2	0.3	US$/kg	282
7108	Gold (including gold plated with platinum)	3.4	2.3	0.0	5.0	12.0	0.2	thsd US$/kg	971
3303	Perfumes and toilet waters	1.9	1.6	1.3	40.8	52.6	34.7	US$/kg	553
7305	Other tubes and pipes (for example, welded, riveted or similarly closed)	2.9	0.5	0.0	2.5	1.9	2.3	US$/kg	679
2204	Wine of fresh grapes, including fortified wines	1.7	1.0	0.7	3.6	2.9	3.5	US$/litre	112
4202	Trunks, suit-cases, vanity-cases, executive-cases, brief-cases	0.4	0.7	1.7					831

Aruba

Services Imports and Exports: EBOPS 2002 categories

Table 2: Merchandise exports by SITC
(Value in million US$, growth and shares in percentage)

SITC	2014	Avg. Growth rates 2010-2014	Avg. Growth rates 2013-2014	2014 share
Total	116.2	-1.7	-30.7	100.0
0+1	79.2	-6.2	-36.7	68.1
2+4	3.2	63.0	-1.0	2.7
3	0.3	20.9	4884.3	0.2
5	5.3	17.1	-6.4	4.6
6	4.0	6.4	-21.5	3.5
7	10.6	21.9	12.3	9.1
8	10.7	14.4	-17.8	9.2
9	3.0	-10.0	-52.6	2.5

Table 3: Merchandise imports by SITC
(Value in million US$, growth and shares in percentage)

SITC	2014	Avg. Growth rates 2010-2014	Avg. Growth rates 2013-2014	2014 share
Total	1 284.1	4.6	-1.5	100.0
0+1	351.8	1.2	-13.5	27.4
2+4	22.6	4.2	4.9	1.8
3	93.0	7.4	-1.0	7.2
5	114.7	3.5	11.2	8.9
6	133.9	5.1	-4.8	10.4
7	261.0	7.0	8.1	20.3
8	286.4	5.7	2.0	22.3
9	20.7	30.4	34.9	1.6

SITC Legend

SITC Code	Description
Total	All commodities
0+1	Food, animals + beverages, tobacco
2+4	Crude materials + anim. & veg. oils
3	Mineral fuels, lubricants
5	Chemicals
6	Goods classified chiefly by material
7	Machinery and transport equipment
8	Miscellaneous manufactured articles
9	Not classified elsewhere in the SITC

Graph 4: Merchandise trade balance
(Mln US$ by MDG Regions in 2014)

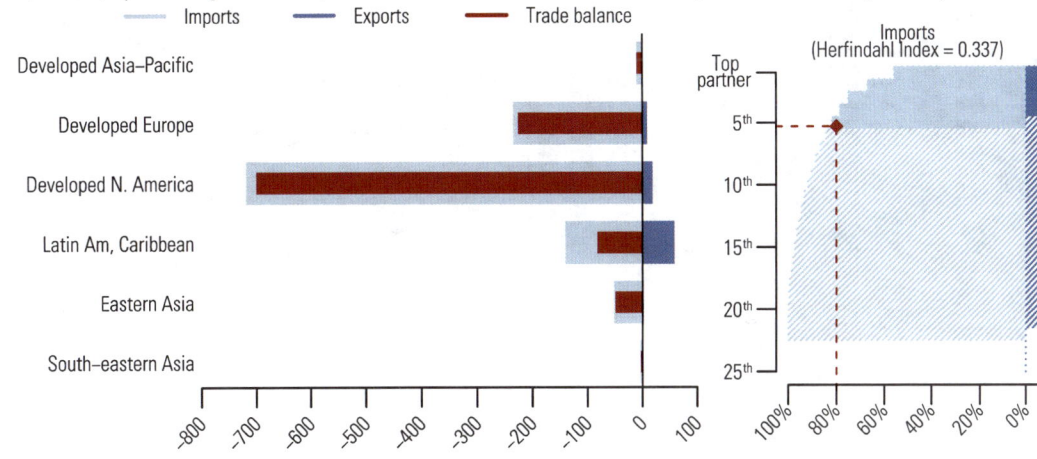

Graph 5: Partner concentration of merchandise trade
(Cumulative share by ranked partners in 2014)

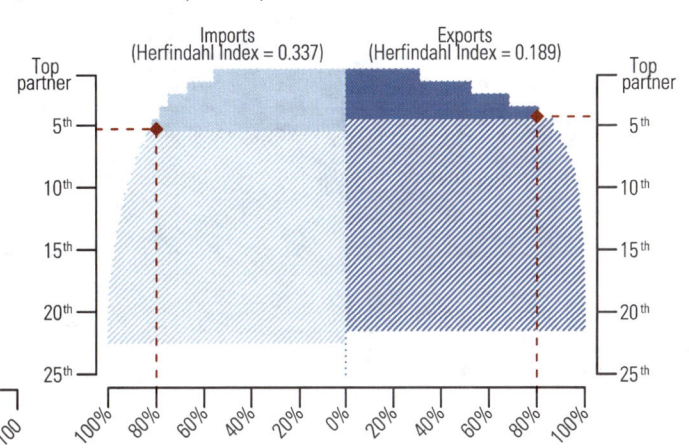

Imports (Herfindahl Index = 0.337)
Exports (Herfindahl Index = 0.189)

Graph 6: Imports of services by EBOPS category
(% share in 2013)

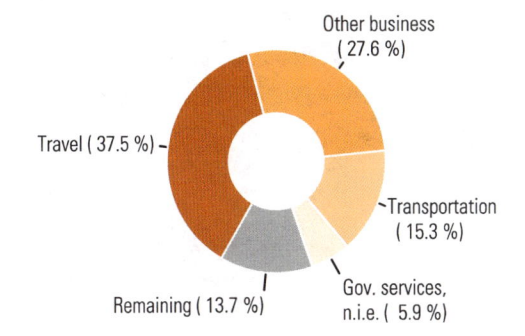

- Other business (27.6 %)
- Travel (37.5 %)
- Transportation (15.3 %)
- Gov. services, n.i.e. (5.9 %)
- Remaining (13.7 %)

Imports Profile:

"Food, animals + beverages, tobacco" (SITC section 0+1), "Miscellaneous manufactured articles" (SITC section 8) and "Machinery and transport equipment" (SITC section 7) were the largest commodity groups for imports in 2014, representing respectively 27.4, 22.3 and 20.3 percent of imported goods (see table 3). From 2012 to 2014, the largest import commodity was "Petroleum oils, other than crude" (HS code 2710) (see table 4). The top three partners for merchandise imports were the United States, the Netherlands and Areas nes, accounting for respectively 50.7, 11.3 and 10.0 percent of total imports. "Travel" (EBOPS code 236) accounted for the largest share of imports of services in 2013 at 318.4 mln US$, followed by "Other business services" (EBOPS code 268) at 234.1 mln US$ and "Transportation" (EBOPS code 205) at 130.2 mln US$ (see graph 6).

Table 4: Top 10 import commodities 2012 to 2014

HS code	4-digit heading of Harmonized System 2007	Value (million US$) 2012	2013	2014	Unit value 2012	2013	2014	Unit	SITC code
	All Commodities	1 259.8	1 303.3	1 284.1					
2710	Petroleum oils, other than crude	94.8	86.2	91.2	1.0	1.0	1.0	US$/kg	334
2208	Alcohol of a strength by volume of less than 80 % vol	77.9	97.6	61.0	9.2	12.6	12.5	US$/litre	112
8703	Motor cars and other motor vehicles principally designed for the transport	47.8	51.4	51.1	15.9	15.5	14.7	thsd US$/unit	781
7113	Articles of jewellery and parts thereof, of precious metal	38.0	46.6	44.4	2.2	3.0	1.0	thsd US$/kg	897
2402	Cigars, cheroots, cigarillos and cigarettes	61.8	43.5	16.4	11.9	11.6	10.3	US$/kg	122
8517	Electrical apparatus for line telephony or line telegraphy	21.1	29.5	28.0					764
9102	Wrist-watches, pocket-watches and other watches, of base metal	20.2	15.7	18.3					885
3004	Medicaments (excluding goods of heading 30.02, 30.05 or 30.06)	19.0	15.2	18.7	51.2	49.1	39.8	US$/kg	542
9403	Other furniture and parts thereof	13.1	18.6	20.5					821
9101	Wrist-watches, pocket-watches and other watches, precious metal	14.8	18.6	17.0					885

2014 International Trade Statistics Yearbook, Vol. I   Source: UN Comtrade and UN ServiceTrade

Australia

Goods Imports: FOB, by origin **Goods Exports:** FOB, by last known destination **Trade System:** General

Overview:
In 2014, the value of merchandise exports of Australia decreased slightly by 4.6 percent to reach 240.4 bln US$, while its merchandise imports decreased slightly by 2.1 percent to reach 227.5 bln US$ (see graph 1, table 2 and table 3). The merchandise trade balance recorded a relatively small surplus of 12.9 bln US$ in 2014, down slightly from the surplus of 19.7 bln US$ in 2013 (see graph 1). The largest merchandise trade balance was with MDG Eastern Asia at 45.6 bln US$ (see graph 4). Merchandise exports in Australia were moderately concentrated amongst partners; imports were diversified. The top 11 partners accounted for 80 percent or more of exports and 17 partners accounted for 80 percent or more of imports (see graph 5). In 2013, the value of exports of services of Australia increased slightly by 0.5 percent, reaching 53.4 bln US$, while its imports of services increased slightly by 2.6 percent and reached 66.6 bln US$ (see graph 2). There was a moderate trade in services deficit of 13.1 bln US$.

Graph 1: Total merchandise trade, by value
(Bln US$ by year)

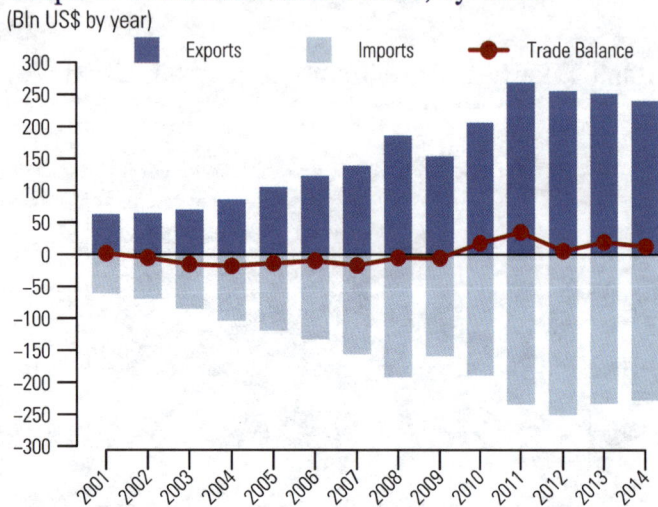

Graph 2: Total services trade, by value
(Bln US$ by year)

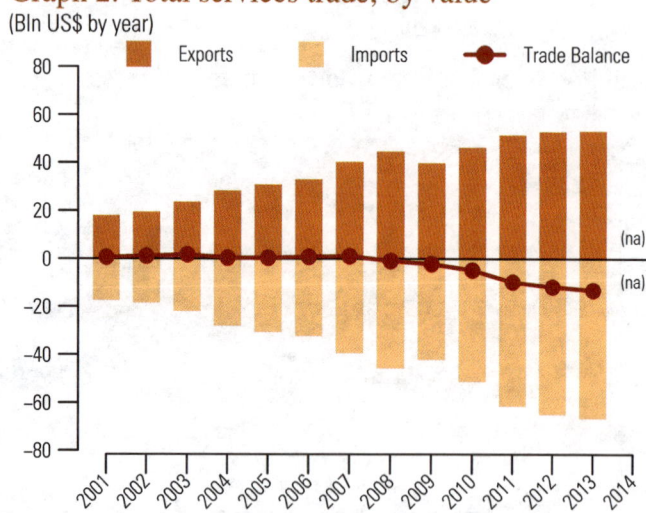

Exports Profile:
"Crude materials + anim. & veg. oils" (SITC section 2+4), "Mineral fuels, lubricants" (SITC section 3) and "Food, animals + beverages, tobacco" (SITC section 0+1) were the largest commodity groups for exports in 2014, representing respectively 36.6, 26.6 and 12.4 percent of exported goods (see table 2). From 2012 to 2014, the largest export commodity was "Iron ores and concentrates, including roasted iron pyrites" (HS code 2601), despite a drop of 10.5 percent in 2014 (see table 1). The top three destinations for merchandise exports were China, Japan and the Republic of Korea, accounting for respectively 32.7, 16.6 and 7.5 percent of total exports. "Travel" (EBOPS code 236) accounted for the largest share of exports of services in 2013 at 31.0 bln US$, followed by "Other business services" (EBOPS code 268) at 9.2 bln US$ and "Transportation" (EBOPS code 205) at 4.9 bln US$ (see graph 3).

Graph 3: Exports of services by EBOPS category
(% share in 2013)

- Travel (58.0 %)
- Other business (17.2 %)
- Transportation (9.1 %)
- Remaining (15.7 %)

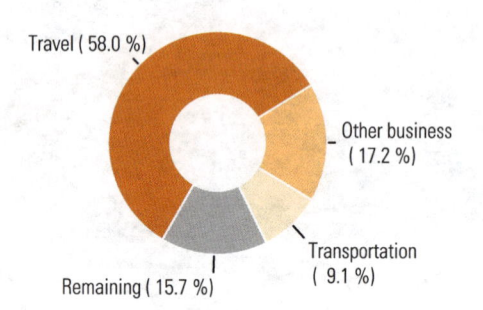

Table 1: Top 10 export commodities 2012 to 2014

HS code	4-digit heading of Harmonized System 2012	Value (million US$) 2012	2013	2014	Unit value 2012	2013	2014	Unit	SITC code
	All Commodities	256 242.9	252 155.1	240 444.7					
2601	Iron ores and concentrates, including roasted iron pyrites	56 726.9	67 209.0	60 174.4	0.1	0.1	0.1	US$/kg	281
2701	Coal; briquettes, ovoids and similar solid fuels manufactured from coal	42 699.3	38 423.5	34 430.8	0.1	0.1	0.1	US$/kg	321
2711	Petroleum gases and other gaseous hydrocarbons	15 165.8	15 255.0	17 154.0		0.6	0.7	US$/kg	343
7108	Gold (including gold plated with platinum)	16 033.9	13 385.9	12 031.1		42.4	38.2	thsd US$/kg	971
2709	Petroleum oils and oils obtained from bituminous minerals, crude	11 317.6	8 675.4	9 633.2	0.8	0.9	0.8	US$/kg	333
9999	Commodities not specified according to kind	9 782.5	8 648.1	7 947.9					931
1001	Wheat and meslin	6 759.5	5 875.6	5 343.4	0.3	0.3	0.3	US$/kg	041
2818	Artificial corundum, whether or not chemically defined	5 331.4	5 338.2	5 270.6	0.3	0.3	0.3	US$/kg	522
2603	Copper ores and concentrates	5 467.3	4 968.5	4 911.3	2.7	2.3	2.2	US$/kg	283
0202	Meat of bovine animals, frozen	2 963.6	3 566.5	4 676.6	3.9	4.0	4.5	US$/kg	011

Australia

Services Imports and Exports: EBOPS 2002 categories

Table 2: Merchandise exports by SITC
(Value in million US$, growth and shares in percentage)

SITC	2014	Avg. Growth rates 2010-2014	Avg. Growth rates 2013-2014	2014 share
Total	240 444.7	3.9	-4.6	100.0
0+1	29 926.3	9.4	6.1	12.4
2+4	87 932.0	7.1	-9.4	36.6
3	63 956.0	1.7	-1.9	26.6
5	6 616.8	-2.1	-12.0	2.8
6	13 823.3	0.3	-1.4	5.7
7	13 237.5	4.8	0.5	5.5
8	4 861.7	2.7	-0.2	2.0
9	20 091.0	-3.3	-8.9	8.4

Table 3: Merchandise imports by SITC
(Value in million US$, growth and shares in percentage)

SITC	2014	Avg. Growth rates 2010-2014	Avg. Growth rates 2013-2014	2014 share
Total	227 544.2	4.8	-2.1	100.0
0+1	13 421.7	9.6	6.5	5.9
2+4	3 193.0	5.5	14.3	1.4
3	36 235.1	8.7	-10.9	15.9
5	22 406.1	2.7	-1.9	9.8
6	25 941.6	6.0	1.2	11.4
7	85 032.2	3.5	-3.9	37.4
8	31 322.5	6.3	4.3	13.8
9	9 992.1	-3.9	6.1	4.4

SITC Legend

SITC Code	Description
Total	All commodities
0+1	Food, animals + beverages, tobacco
2+4	Crude materials + anim. & veg. oils
3	Mineral fuels, lubricants
5	Chemicals
6	Goods classified chiefly by material
7	Machinery and transport equipment
8	Miscellaneous manufactured articles
9	Not classified elsewhere in the SITC

Graph 4: Merchandise trade balance
(Bln US$ by MDG Regions in 2014)

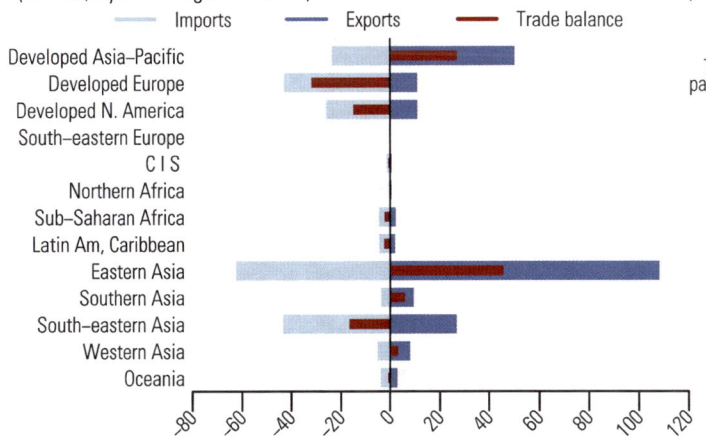

Graph 5: Partner concentration of merchandise trade
(Cumulative share by ranked partners in 2014)

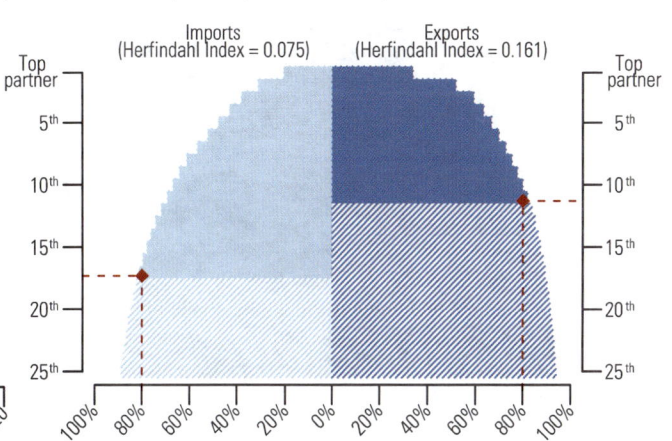

Imports (Herfindahl Index = 0.075)
Exports (Herfindahl Index = 0.161)

Graph 6: Imports of services by EBOPS category
(% share in 2013)

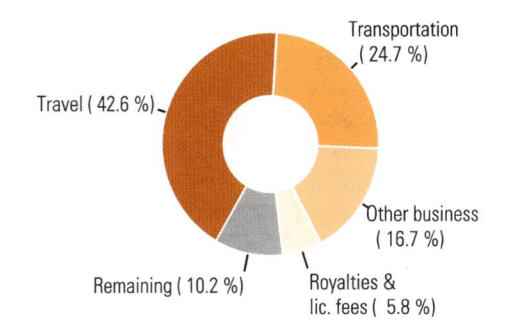

- Transportation (24.7 %)
- Travel (42.6 %)
- Other business (16.7 %)
- Royalties & lic. fees (5.8 %)
- Remaining (10.2 %)

Imports Profile:

"Machinery and transport equipment" (SITC section 7), "Mineral fuels, lubricants" (SITC section 3) and "Miscellaneous manufactured articles" (SITC section 8) were the largest commodity groups for imports in 2014, representing respectively 37.4, 15.9 and 13.8 percent of imported goods (see table 3). From 2012 to 2014, the largest import commodity was "Petroleum oils and oils obtained from bituminous minerals, crude" (HS code 2709) (see table 4). The top three partners for merchandise imports were China, the United States and Japan, accounting for respectively 19.4, 10.9 and 7.5 percent of total imports. "Travel" (EBOPS code 236) accounted for the largest share of imports of services in 2013 at 28.4 bln US$, followed by "Transportation" (EBOPS code 205) at 16.4 bln US$ and "Other business services" (EBOPS code 268) at 11.1 bln US$ (see graph 6).

Table 4: Top 10 import commodities 2012 to 2014

HS code	4-digit heading of Harmonized System 2012	Value 2012	Value 2013	Value 2014	Unit value 2012	Unit value 2013	Unit value 2014	Unit	SITC code
	All Commodities	250 464.8	232 481.3	227 544.2					
2709	Petroleum oils and oils obtained from bituminous minerals, crude	22 349.4	19 494.4	18 305.8	0.9	0.9	0.8	US$/kg	333
8703	Motor cars and other motor vehicles principally designed for the transport	17 518.0	17 646.8	15 849.9	20.4	19.4	19.2	thsd US$/unit	781
2710	Petroleum oils, other than crude	16 440.2	17 592.8	16 866.4		0.9	0.9	US$/kg	334
3004	Medicaments (excluding goods of heading 30.02, 30.05 or 30.06)	8 396.7	7 488.5	6 707.5		131.1	116.6	US$/kg	542
8517	Electrical apparatus for line telephony or line telegraphy	6 986.7	6 898.3	7 064.8					764
8471	Automatic data processing machines and units thereof	6 968.4	6 657.9	6 549.6	267.4	284.1	273.5	US$/unit	752
8704	Motor vehicles for the transport of goods	8 688.8	6 037.3	5 260.9		27.3	25.8	thsd US$/unit	782
9999	Commodities not specified according to kind	5 856.0	4 782.3	6 375.6					931
7108	Gold (including gold plated with platinum)	5 940.3	4 389.0	3 439.5		32.0	29.4	thsd US$/kg	971
4011	New pneumatic tyres, of rubber	3 103.9	2 589.6	2 213.9	134.8	114.5	98.9	US$/unit	625

2014 International Trade Statistics Yearbook, Vol. I — Source: UN Comtrade and UN ServiceTrade

Austria

Goods Imports: CIF, by origin   **Goods Exports: FOB, by last known destination**   **Trade System: Special**

Overview:

In 2013, the value of merchandise exports of Austria increased slightly by 4.7 percent to reach 166.3 bln US$, while its merchandise imports increased slightly by 2.2 percent to reach 173.4 bln US$ (see graph 1, table 2 and table 3). The merchandise trade balance recorded a relatively small deficit of 7.1 bln US$ (see graph 1). The largest merchandise trade balance was with MDG Developed Europe at -10.7 bln US$ (see graph 4). Merchandise exports in Austria were diversified amongst partners; imports were moderately concentrated. The top 18 partners accounted for 80 percent or more of exports and 15 partners accounted for 80 percent or more of imports (see graph 5). In 2013, the value of exports of services of Austria increased moderately by 7.3 percent, reaching 64.9 bln US$, while its imports of services increased moderately by 7.3 percent and reached 45.5 bln US$ (see graph 2). There was a moderate trade in services surplus of 19.4 bln US$.

Graph 1: Total merchandise trade, by value
(Bln US$ by year)

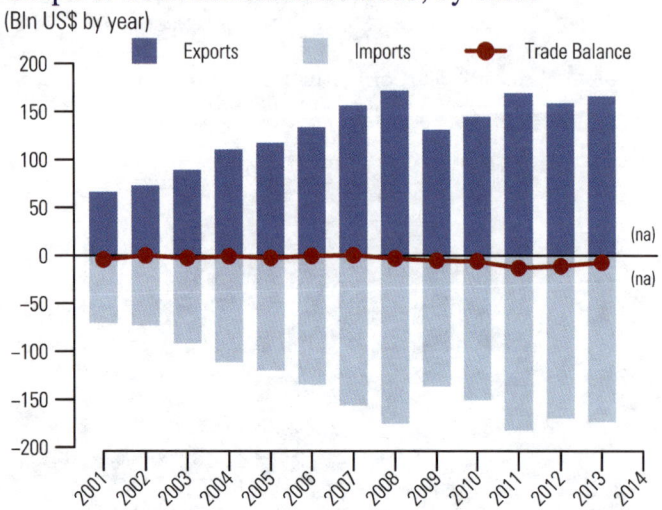

Graph 2: Total services trade, by value
(Bln US$ by year)

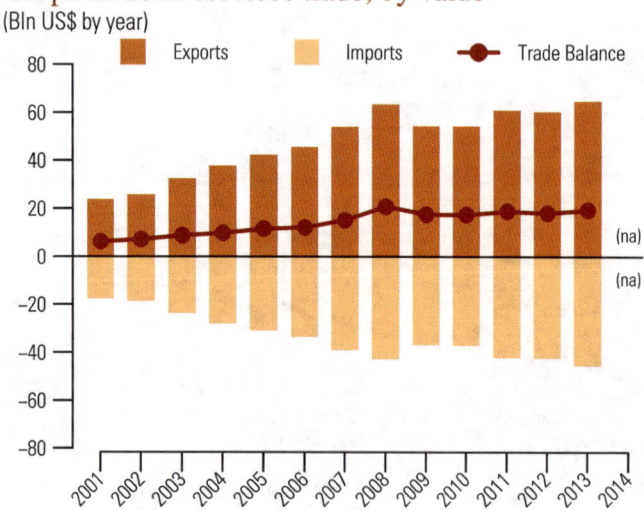

Exports Profile:

"Machinery and transport equipment" (SITC section 7), "Goods classified chiefly by material" (SITC section 6) and "Chemicals" (SITC section 5) were the largest commodity groups for exports in 2013, representing respectively 39.3, 21.0 and 11.9 percent of exported goods (see table 2). From 2011 to 2013, the largest export commodity was "Commodities not specified according to kind" (HS code 9999) (see table 1). The top three destinations for merchandise exports were Germany, Italy and Switzerland, accounting for respectively 30.1, 6.8 and 5.3 percent of total exports. "Travel" (EBOPS code 236) accounted for the largest share of exports of services in 2012 at 18.9 bln US$, followed by "Other business services" (EBOPS code 268) at 18.5 bln US$ and "Transportation" (EBOPS code 205) at 13.8 bln US$ (see graph 3).

Graph 3: Exports of services by EBOPS category
(% share in 2012)

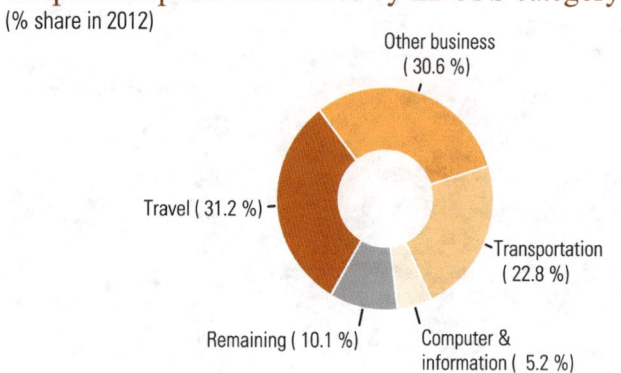

- Other business (30.6 %)
- Travel (31.2 %)
- Transportation (22.8 %)
- Computer & information (5.2 %)
- Remaining (10.1 %)

Table 1: Top 10 export commodities 2011 to 2013

HS code	4-digit heading of Harmonized System 2007	Value (million US$) 2011	2012	2013	Unit value 2011	2012	2013	Unit	SITC code
	All Commodities	169 511.4	158 821.0	166 271.4					
9999	Commodities not specified according to kind	6 639.7	6 228.7	6 388.2					931
3004	Medicaments (excluding goods of heading 30.02, 30.05 or 30.06)	5 907.9	5 320.4	5 510.0	74.6	69.6	54.9	US$/kg	542
8703	Motor cars and other motor vehicles principally designed for the transport	5 300.2	4 921.6	5 734.1	26.2		20.6	thsd US$/unit	781
8708	Parts and accessories of the motor vehicles of headings 87.01 to 87.05	4 792.4	4 556.3	4 728.7	11.3	9.4	10.2	US$/kg	784
8408	Compression-ignition internal combustion piston engines	2 780.5	2 518.7	2 763.5	4.2			thsd US$/unit	713
8407	Spark-ignition reciprocating or rotary internal combustion piston engines	3 307.9	2 378.8	2 123.8	2.7			thsd US$/unit	713
3002	Human blood; animal blood prepared for therapeutic uses	2 275.3	2 400.5	2 650.7	359.0	379.9	384.8	US$/kg	541
2710	Petroleum oils, other than crude	2 123.4	2 342.4	2 267.3	1.0	1.1		US$/kg	334
2202	Waters with added sugar	2 029.9	1 955.6	1 819.4	1.6		1.5	US$/litre	111
8504	Electrical transformers, static converters	1 986.9	1 693.4	1 628.6					771

Source: UN Comtrade and UN ServiceTrade

Austria

Services Imports and Exports: EBOPS 2002 categories

Table 2: Merchandise exports by SITC
(Value in million US$, growth and shares in percentage)

SITC	2013	Avg. Growth rates 2009-2013	Avg. Growth rates 2012-2013	2013 share
Total	166 271.4	6.1	4.7	100.0
0+1	11 514.3	5.5	7.5	6.9
2+4	4 605.6	6.9	6.0	2.8
3	4 491.7	-0.2	-22.8	2.7
5	19 818.4	6.7	5.5	11.9
6	34 856.3	5.5	1.0	21.0
7	65 407.5	7.3	8.4	39.3
8	18 221.8	3.6	7.7	11.0
9	7 355.9	7.2	-0.6	4.4

Table 3: Merchandise imports by SITC
(Value in million US$, growth and shares in percentage)

SITC	2013	Avg. Growth rates 2009-2013	Avg. Growth rates 2012-2013	2013 share
Total	173 357.5	6.2	2.2	100.0
0+1	12 211.7	5.7	7.5	7.0
2+4	8 252.7	9.5	-3.2	4.8
3	19 598.4	8.3	-11.9	11.3
5	22 251.7	7.0	6.8	12.8
6	26 300.9	6.1	0.9	15.2
7	57 501.7	6.4	6.3	33.2
8	23 993.2	3.8	4.1	13.8
9	3 247.2	-0.5	-7.0	1.9

SITC Legend

SITC Code	Description
Total	All commodities
0+1	Food, animals + beverages, tobacco
2+4	Crude materials + anim. & veg. oils
3	Mineral fuels, lubricants
5	Chemicals
6	Goods classified chiefly by material
7	Machinery and transport equipment
8	Miscellaneous manufactured articles
9	Not classified elsewhere in the SITC

Graph 4: Merchandise trade balance
(Bln US$ by MDG Regions in 2013)

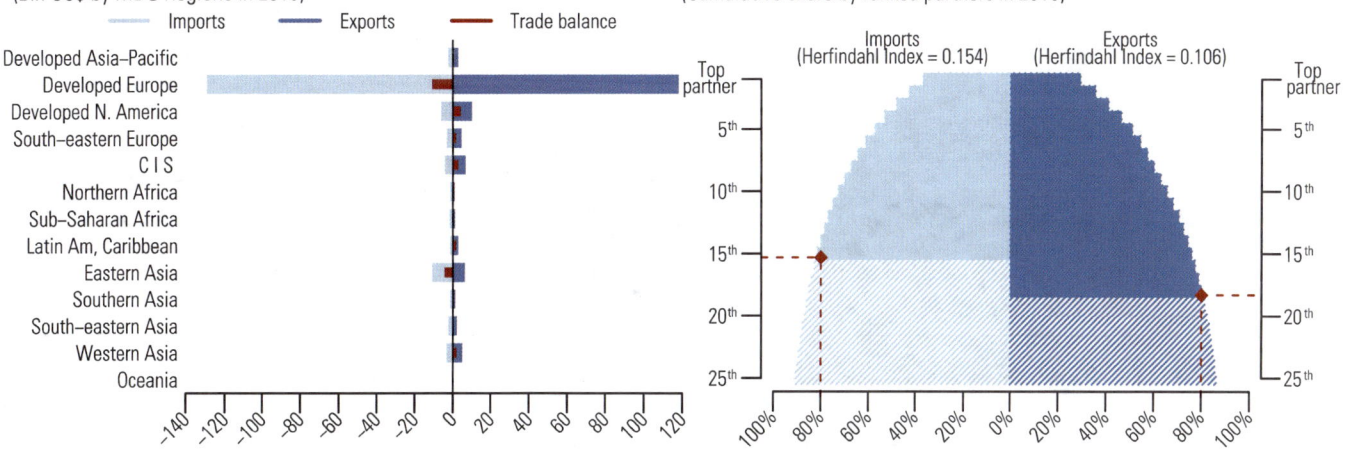

Graph 5: Partner concentration of merchandise trade
(Cumulative share by ranked partners in 2013)

Imports (Herfindahl Index = 0.154)
Exports (Herfindahl Index = 0.106)

Graph 6: Imports of services by EBOPS category
(% share in 2012)

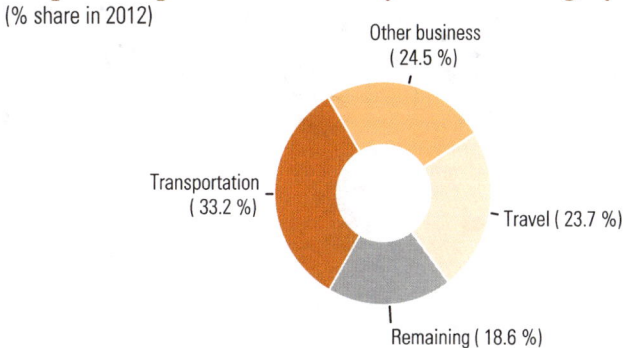

- Other business (24.5 %)
- Transportation (33.2 %)
- Travel (23.7 %)
- Remaining (18.6 %)

Imports Profile:

"Machinery and transport equipment" (SITC section 7), "Goods classified chiefly by material" (SITC section 6) and "Miscellaneous manufactured articles" (SITC section 8) were the largest commodity groups for imports in 2013, representing respectively 33.2, 15.2 and 13.8 percent of imported goods (see table 3). From 2011 to 2013, the largest import commodity was "Motor cars and other motor vehicles principally designed for the transport" (HS code 8703) (see table 4). The top three partners for merchandise imports were Germany, Italy and Switzerland, accounting for respectively 37.3, 6.2 and 5.4 percent of total imports. "Transportation" (EBOPS code 205) accounted for the largest share of imports of services in 2012 at 14.1 bln US$, followed by "Other business services" (EBOPS code 268) at 10.4 bln US$ and "Travel" (EBOPS code 236) at 10.1 bln US$ (see graph 6).

Table 4: Top 10 import commodities 2011 to 2013

HS code	4-digit heading of Harmonized System 2007	Value 2011	Value 2012	Value 2013	Unit 2011	Unit 2012	Unit 2013	Unit	SITC code
	All Commodities	182 349.8	169 663.2	173 357.5					
8703	Motor cars and other motor vehicles principally designed for the transport	9 674.0	8 632.3	8 762.6	22.5		18.9	thsd US$/unit	781
2710	Petroleum oils, other than crude	7 016.3	7 330.6	6 015.7	1.1	1.1		US$/kg	334
2709	Petroleum oils and oils obtained from bituminous minerals, crude	6 176.5	6 357.4	6 534.0	0.8	0.9	0.8	US$/kg	333
2711	Petroleum gases and other gaseous hydrocarbons	5 267.7	5 655.5	4 311.7	0.6	0.6	0.6	US$/kg	343
8708	Parts and accessories of the motor vehicles of headings 87.01 to 87.05	4 927.2	4 488.5	4 644.3	9.7	9.1	9.6	US$/kg	784
3004	Medicaments (excluding goods of heading 30.02, 30.05 or 30.06)	3 496.4	3 283.0	3 495.7	66.4	56.5	68.1	US$/kg	542
7108	Gold (including gold plated with platinum)	3 250.7	2 577.6	2 468.9	50.3		44.6	thsd US$/kg	971
2937	Hormones, prostaglandins, thromboxanes and leukotrienes	2 283.0	2 635.2	3 104.0	185.5			thsd US$/kg	541
8517	Electrical apparatus for line telephony or line telegraphy	2 278.7	2 486.3	2 610.2					764
8409	Parts suitable for use with the engines of heading 84	2 396.5	2 098.0	2 180.4	13.5	12.4	12.4	US$/kg	713

2014 International Trade Statistics Yearbook, Vol. I   Source: UN Comtrade and UN ServiceTrade

Azerbaijan

Goods Imports: CIF, by origin **Goods Exports:** FOB, by last known destination **Trade System:** General

Overview:
In 2014, the value of merchandise exports of Azerbaijan decreased moderately by 9.0 percent to reach 21.8 bln US$, while its merchandise imports decreased substantially by 14.7 percent to reach 9.2 bln US$ (see graph 1, table 2 and table 3). The merchandise trade balance recorded a large surplus of 12.6 bln US$ (see graph 1). The largest merchandise trade balance was with MDG Developed Europe at 8.5 bln US$ (see graph 4). Merchandise exports in Azerbaijan were diversified amongst partners; imports were also diversified. The top 13 partners accounted for 80 percent or more of exports and 14 partners accounted for 80 percent or more of imports (see graph 5). In 2012, the value of exports of services of Azerbaijan increased substantially by 57.4 percent, reaching 4.3 bln US$, while its imports of services increased substantially by 26.1 percent and reached 7.2 bln US$ (see graph 2). There was a moderate trade in services deficit of 2.9 bln US$.

Graph 1: Total merchandise trade, by value
(Bln US$ by year)

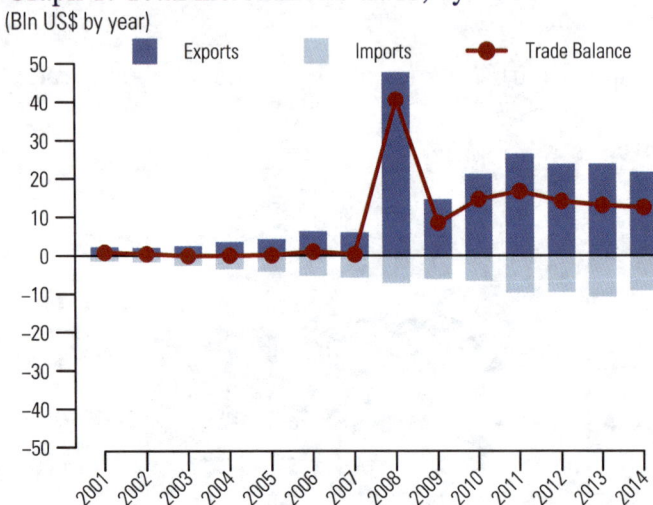

Graph 2: Total services trade, by value
(Bln US$ by year)

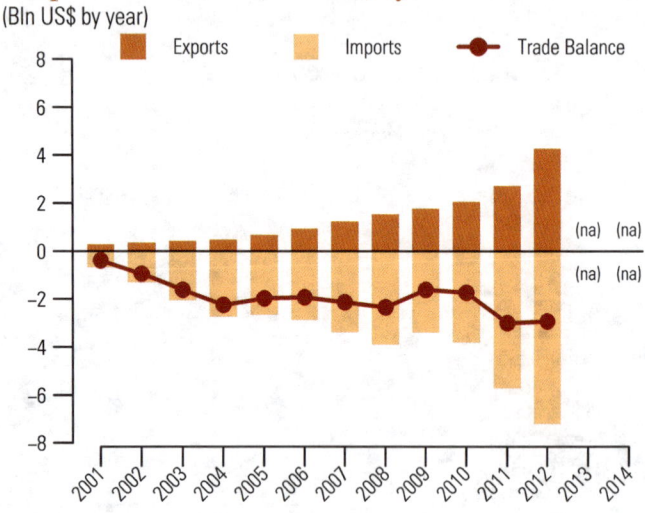

Exports Profile:
"Mineral fuels, lubricants" (SITC section 3), "Food, animals + beverages, tobacco" (SITC section 0+1) and "Chemicals" (SITC section 5) were the largest commodity groups for exports in 2014, representing respectively 92.8, 3.2 and 1.1 percent of exported goods (see table 2). From 2012 to 2014, the largest export commodity was "Petroleum oils and oils obtained from bituminous minerals, crude" (HS code 2709) (see table 1). The top three destinations for merchandise exports were Italy, Indonesia and Israel, accounting for respectively 23.5, 9.4 and 6.8 percent of total exports. "Travel" (EBOPS code 236) accounted for the largest share of exports of services in 2012 at 2.4 bln US$, followed by "Transportation" (EBOPS code 205) at 740.3 mln US$ and "Other business services" (EBOPS code 268) at 625.6 mln US$ (see graph 3).

Graph 3: Exports of services by EBOPS category
(% share in 2012)

- Travel (56.8 %)
- Transportation (17.3 %)
- Other business (14.6 %)
- Construction (5.7 %)
- Remaining (5.5 %)

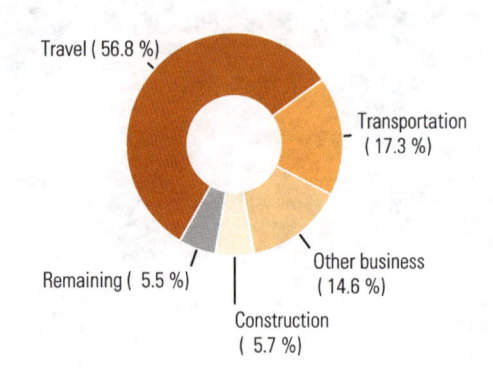

Table 1: Top 10 export commodities 2012 to 2014

HS code	4-digit heading of Harmonized System 2012	Value (million US$) 2012	2013	2014	Unit value 2012	2013	2014	Unit	SITC code
	All Commodities	23827.2	23904.1	21751.7					
2709	Petroleum oils and oils obtained from bituminous minerals, crude	20232.6	20244.1	18404.9	0.8	0.8	0.8	US$/kg	333
2710	Petroleum oils, other than crude	1321.2	1208.5	1365.0	0.8	0.7	0.6	US$/kg	334
2711	Petroleum gases and other gaseous hydrocarbons	661.6	732.6	325.0	0.3	0.3	0.2	US$/kg	343
1701	Cane or beet sugar and chemically pure sucrose, in solid form	214.2	243.6	221.2	1.0	1.0	1.0	US$/kg	061
9999	Commodities not specified according to kind	21.8	131.5	175.3					931
0810	Other fruit, fresh	103.5	87.8	72.2	0.8	0.8	1.0	US$/kg	057
7601	Unwrought aluminium	94.5	81.9	80.3	1.6	1.5	1.5	US$/kg	684
3901	Polymers of ethylene, in primary forms	61.6	75.8	104.6	1.1	1.2	1.2	US$/kg	571
1516	Animal or vegetable fats and oils	74.7	72.8	59.5	2.5	2.5	2.3	US$/kg	431
0802	Other nuts, fresh or dried, whether or not shelled or peeled	45.9	45.2	68.8	4.4	4.3	5.7	US$/kg	057

Source: UN Comtrade and UN ServiceTrade

Azerbaijan

Services Imports and Exports: EBOPS 2002 categories

Table 2: Merchandise exports by SITC
(Value in million US$, growth and shares in percentage)

SITC	2014	Avg. Growth rates 2010-2014	2013-2014	2014 share
Total	21 751.7	0.6	-9.0	100.0
0+1	692.9	12.2	0.5	3.2
2+4	172.4	-0.8	-25.0	0.8
3	20 177.2	0.1	-9.2	92.8
5	231.1	15.4	31.7	1.1
6	200.9	4.1	-24.6	0.9
7	87.2	-20.5	-46.7	0.4
8	14.8	-9.5	-18.1	0.1
9	175.3	92.9	33.3	0.8

Table 3: Merchandise imports by SITC
(Value in million US$, growth and shares in percentage)

SITC	2014	Avg. Growth rates 2010-2014	2013-2014	2014 share
Total	9 178.6	8.6	-14.7	100.0
0+1	1 451.6	6.5	-1.5	15.8
2+4	220.6	-4.4	-46.6	2.4
3	297.1	41.7	109.8	3.2
5	865.7	10.3	-6.8	9.4
6	1 807.7	6.1	-9.1	19.7
7	3 462.1	6.5	-17.4	37.7
8	615.7	12.1	-8.9	6.7
9	458.0	80.2	-51.9	5.0

SITC Legend

SITC Code	Description
Total	All commodities
0+1	Food, animals + beverages, tobacco
2+4	Crude materials + anim. & veg. oils
3	Mineral fuels, lubricants
5	Chemicals
6	Goods classified chiefly by material
7	Machinery and transport equipment
8	Miscellaneous manufactured articles
9	Not classified elsewhere in the SITC

Graph 4: Merchandise trade balance
(Bln US$ by MDG Regions in 2014)

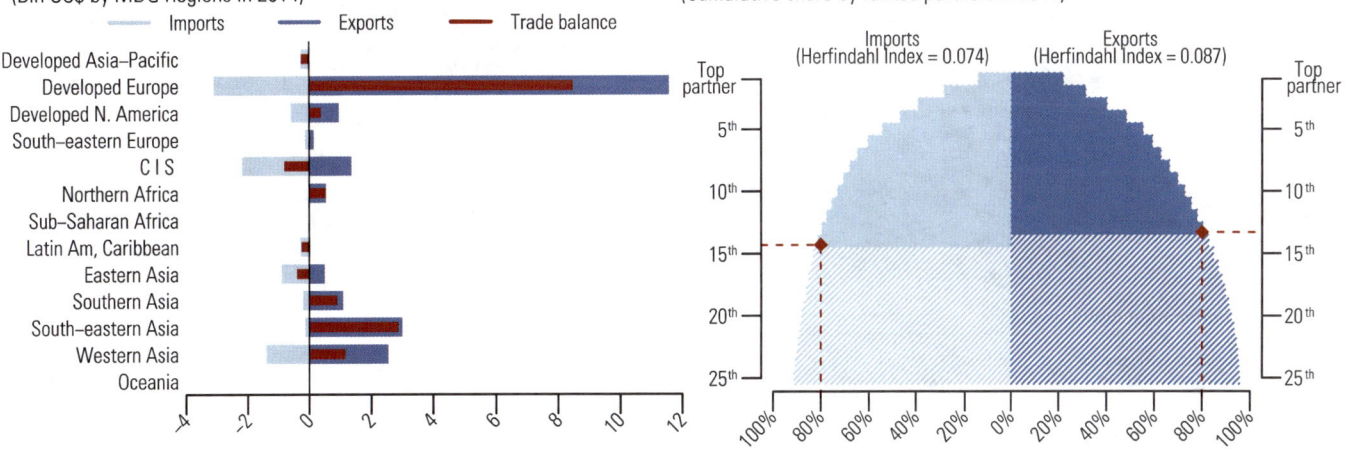

Graph 5: Partner concentration of merchandise trade
(Cumulative share by ranked partners in 2014)

Imports (Herfindahl Index = 0.074)
Exports (Herfindahl Index = 0.087)

Graph 6: Imports of services by EBOPS category
(% share in 2012)

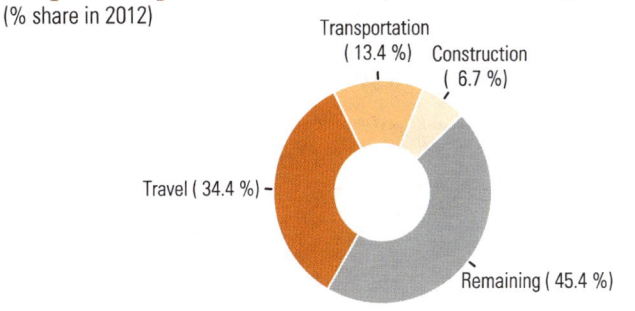

- Transportation (13.4 %)
- Construction (6.7 %)
- Travel (34.4 %)
- Remaining (45.4 %)

Imports Profile:

"Machinery and transport equipment" (SITC section 7), "Goods classified chiefly by material" (SITC section 6) and "Food, animals + beverages, tobacco" (SITC section 0+1) were the largest commodity groups for imports in 2014, representing respectively 37.7, 19.7 and 15.8 percent of imported goods (see table 3). From 2012 to 2014, the largest import commodity was "Motor cars and other motor vehicles principally designed for the transport" (HS code 8703) (see table 4). The top three partners for merchandise imports were Turkey, the Russian Federation and the United Kingdom, accounting for respectively 14.5, 14.2 and 9.5 percent of total imports. "Travel" (EBOPS code 236) accounted for the largest share of imports of services in 2012 at 2.5 bln US$, followed by "Transportation" (EBOPS code 205) at 968.4 mln US$ and "Construction services" (EBOPS code 249) at 485.2 mln US$ (see graph 6).

Table 4: Top 10 import commodities 2012 to 2014

HS code	4-digit heading of Harmonized System 2012	2012	2013	2014	2012	2013	2014	Unit	SITC code
	All Commodities	9641.7	10763.4	9178.6					
8703	Motor cars and other motor vehicles principally designed for the transport	547.2	556.3	472.6	10.5	8.2	12.3	thsd US$/unit	781
7108	Gold (including gold plated with platinum)	0.0	896.0	410.1		44.8	40.4	thsd US$/kg	971
2402	Cigars, cheroots, cigarillos and cigarettes	298.5	333.0	390.2	22.9	27.7	32.7	US$/kg	122
1001	Wheat and meslin	330.0	395.3	293.9	0.2	0.3	0.2	US$/kg	041
8802	Other aircraft (for example, helicopters, aeroplanes); spacecraft	341.0	420.3	15.0	11.0	22.1	5.0	mln US$/unit	792
8431	Parts suitable for use principally with the machinery of headings 84.25	189.3	222.9	243.2	18.5	16.2	25.8	US$/kg	723
3004	Medicaments (excluding goods of heading 30.02, 30.05 or 30.06)	209.5	214.2	195.9	16.5	14.4	12.6	US$/kg	542
7304	Tubes, pipes and hollow profiles, seamless, of iron (other than cast iron)	198.7	240.7	176.2	3.0	2.4	3.0	US$/kg	679
1701	Cane or beet sugar and chemically pure sucrose, in solid form	175.6	201.5	205.3	0.5	0.5	0.5	US$/kg	061
8481	Taps, cocks, valves and similar appliances for pipes, boiler shells	136.6	193.1	166.5	27.5	29.5	32.2	US$/kg	747

Source: UN Comtrade and UN ServiceTrade

Bahamas

Goods Imports: CIF, by n/a   **Goods Exports:** FOB, by n/a   **Trade System:** General

Overview:
In 2013, the value of merchandise exports of the Bahamas decreased slightly by 2.1 percent to reach 811.5 mln US$, while its merchandise imports decreased moderately by 7.7 percent to reach 3.4 bln US$ (see graph 1, table 2 and table 3). The merchandise trade balance recorded a large deficit of 2.6 bln US$ (see graph 1). The largest merchandise trade balance was with MDG Developed North America at -2.3 bln US$ (see graph 4). Merchandise exports in the Bahamas were highly concentrated amongst partners; imports were also highly concentrated. One partner accounted for 80 percent or more of exports and 1 partner accounted for 80 percent or more of imports (see graph 5). In 2012, the value of exports of services of the Bahamas increased moderately by 5.2 percent, reaching 2.8 bln US$, while its imports of services increased substantially by 19.0 percent and reached 1.5 bln US$ (see graph 2). There was a moderate trade in services surplus of 1.2 bln US$.

Graph 1: Total merchandise trade, by value
(Bln US$ by year)

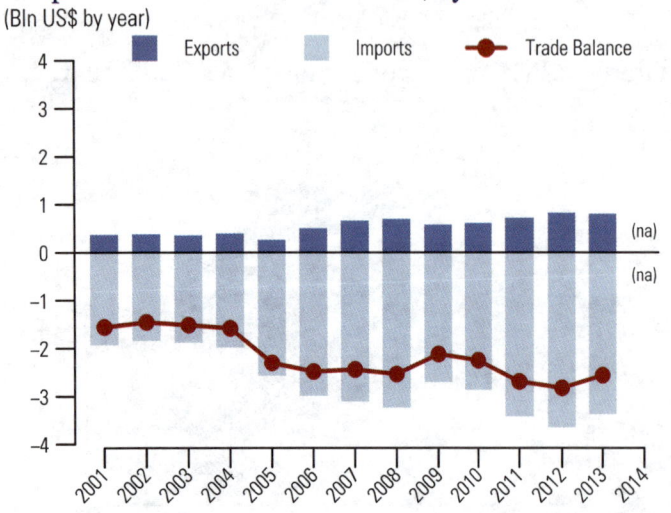

Graph 2: Total services trade, by value
(Bln US$ by year)

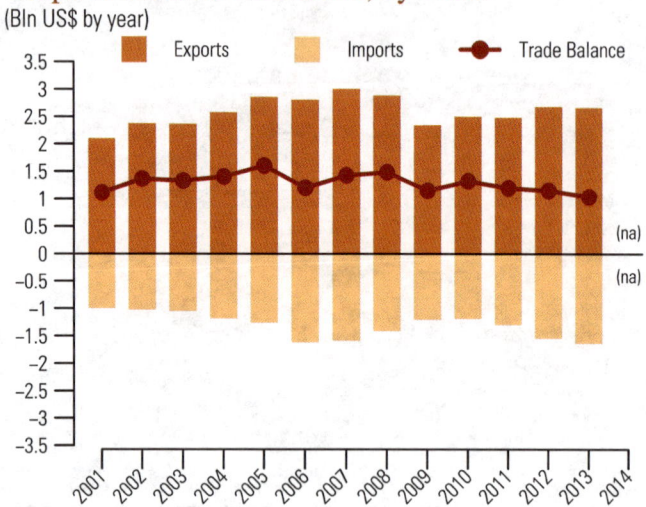

Exports Profile:
"Chemicals" (SITC section 5), "Mineral fuels, lubricants" (SITC section 3) and "Machinery and transport equipment" (SITC section 7) were the largest commodity groups for exports in 2013, representing respectively 36.3, 29.3 and 11.8 percent of exported goods (see table 2). From 2011 to 2013, the largest export commodity was "Petroleum oils, other than crude" (HS code 2710) (see table 1). The top three destinations for merchandise exports were the United States, France and the United Kingdom, accounting for respectively 81.3, 3.2 and 3.1 percent of total exports. "Travel" (EBOPS code 236) accounted for the largest share of exports of services in 2012 at 2.4 bln US$, followed by "Other business services" (EBOPS code 268) at 206.7 mln US$ (see graph 3).

Graph 3: Exports of services by EBOPS category
(% share in 2013)

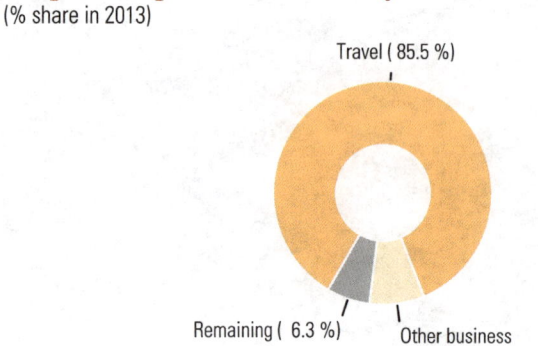

Travel (85.5 %)
Remaining (6.3 %)
Other business (8.2 %)

Table 1: Top 10 export commodities 2011 to 2013

HS code	4-digit heading of Harmonized System 2007	Value (million US$) 2011	2012	2013	Unit value 2011	2012	2013	Unit	SITC code
	All Commodities	726.9	828.7	811.5					
2710	Petroleum oils, other than crude	216.1	319.7	237.8					334
3903	Polymers of styrene, in primary forms	135.8	155.5	184.5	3.4	2.2	2.2	US$/kg	572
0306	Crustaceans, whether in shell or not	70.5	78.5	86.8	33.1	34.3	31.6	US$/kg	036
2933	Heterocyclic compounds with nitrogen hetero-atom(s) only	73.8	75.7	61.6	741.8	587.4	630.4	US$/kg	515
3303	Perfumes and toilet waters	32.9	38.7	34.5	*46.2*	83.1	72.9	US$/kg	553
8903	Yachts and other vessels for pleasure or sports; rowing boats and canoes	13.1	2.9	30.4	23.2	23.8	178.0	thsd US$/unit	793
2501	Salt (including table salt)	12.0	12.0	20.3	0.0	0.0	0.0	US$/kg	278
7326	Other articles of iron or steel	12.3	7.2	4.9	6.8	6.5	3.8	US$/kg	699
2517	Pebbles, gravel, broken or crushed stone	12.3	9.2	2.0	0.0	*0.0*	0.0	US$/kg	273
7204	Ferrous waste and scrap; remelting scrap ingots of iron or steel	9.1	7.3	5.9	5.7	2.2	9.3	US$/kg	282

Bahamas

Services Imports and Exports: EBOPS 2002 categories

Table 2: Merchandise exports by SITC
(Value in million US$, growth and shares in percentage)

SITC	2013	Avg. Growth rates 2009-2013	2012-2013	2013 share
Total	811.5	8.5	-2.1	100.0
0+1	93.0	8.2	11.5	11.5
2+4	34.2	-3.9	-7.2	4.2
3	237.8	20.7	-25.6	29.3
5	294.7	4.1	4.6	36.3
6	44.6	13.8	29.5	5.5
7	95.9	6.5	50.2	11.8
8	10.4	-4.7	18.2	1.3
9	0.9	252.1	4327.4	0.1

Table 3: Merchandise imports by SITC
(Value in million US$, growth and shares in percentage)

SITC	2013	Avg. Growth rates 2009-2013	2012-2013	2013 share
Total	3365.3	5.7	-7.7	100.0
0+1	531.8	2.2	-6.3	15.8
2+4	70.9	-1.3	-10.6	2.1
3	726.9	6.9	-16.9	21.6
5	380.7	8.8	-4.2	11.3
6	456.2	3.9	-11.8	13.6
7	657.5	5.6	-4.5	19.5
8	399.1	8.9	2.6	11.9
9	142.1	8.0	6.7	4.2

SITC Legend

SITC Code	Description
Total	All commodities
0+1	Food, animals + beverages, tobacco
2+4	Crude materials + anim. & veg. oils
3	Mineral fuels, lubricants
5	Chemicals
6	Goods classified chiefly by material
7	Machinery and transport equipment
8	Miscellaneous manufactured articles
9	Not classified elsewhere in the SITC

Graph 4: Merchandise trade balance
(Bln US$ by MDG Regions in 2013)

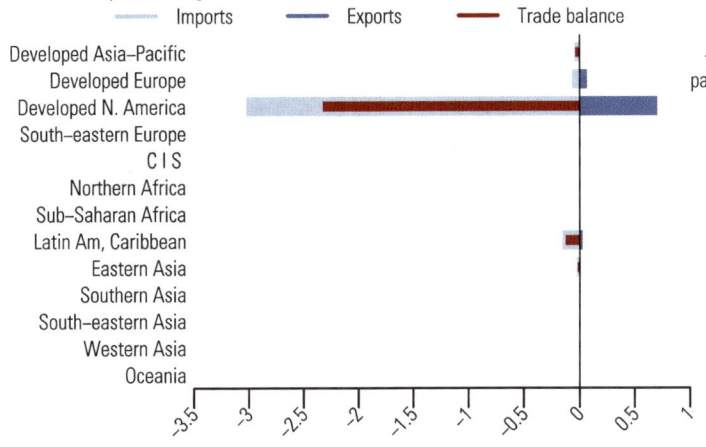

Graph 5: Partner concentration of merchandise trade
(Cumulative share by ranked partners in 2013)

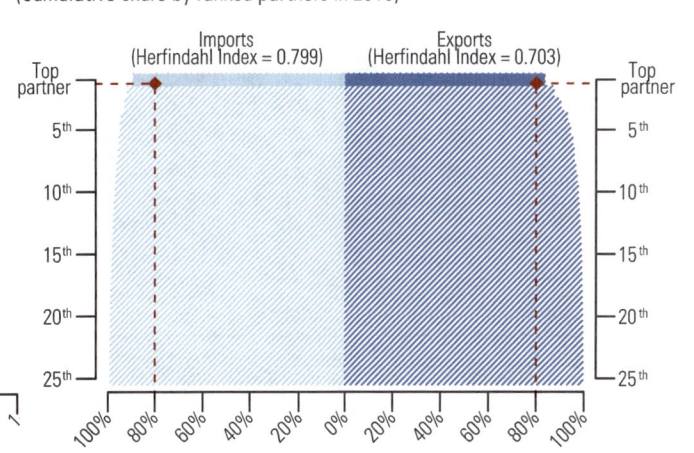

Imports (Herfindahl Index = 0.799)
Exports (Herfindahl Index = 0.703)

Graph 6: Imports of services by EBOPS category
(% share in 2013)

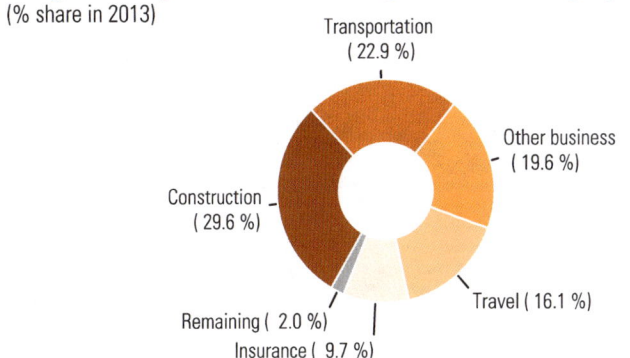

- Transportation (22.9 %)
- Other business (19.6 %)
- Construction (29.6 %)
- Remaining (2.0 %)
- Insurance (9.7 %)
- Travel (16.1 %)

Imports Profile:

"Mineral fuels, lubricants" (SITC section 3), "Machinery and transport equipment" (SITC section 7) and "Food, animals + beverages, tobacco" (SITC section 0+1) were the largest commodity groups for imports in 2013, representing respectively 21.6, 19.5 and 15.8 percent of imported goods (see table 3). From 2011 to 2013, the largest import commodity was "Petroleum oils, other than crude" (HS code 2710) (see table 4). The top three partners for merchandise imports were the United States, Trinidad and Tobago and Areas nes, accounting for respectively 87.5, 3.7 and 1.9 percent of total imports. "Transportation" (EBOPS code 205) accounted for the largest share of imports of services in 2012 at 388.3 mln US$, followed by "Other business services" (EBOPS code 268) at 370.3 mln US$ and "Travel" (EBOPS code 236) at 285.7 mln US$ (see graph 6).

Table 4: Top 10 import commodities 2011 to 2013

HS code	4-digit heading of Harmonized System 2007	Value (million US$) 2011	2012	2013	Unit value 2011	2012	2013	Unit	SITC code
	All Commodities	3410.3	3646.5	3365.3					
2710	Petroleum oils, other than crude	908.7	842.4	706.5					334
9999	Commodities not specified according to kind	131.2	133.2	142.1					931
8703	Motor cars and other motor vehicles principally designed for the transport	62.0	98.3	94.2	5.8	6.8	6.1	thsd US$/unit	781
3915	Waste, parings and scrap, of plastics	59.0	47.9	52.4	4.4	6.2	7.2	US$/kg	579
3303	Perfumes and toilet waters	49.3	51.8	43.3	25.0	25.5	20.7	US$/kg	553
2853	Other inorganic compounds	30.2	65.5	39.8	9.6	10.6	8.2	US$/kg	524
9403	Other furniture and parts thereof	44.8	47.6	40.2					821
3004	Medicaments (excluding goods of heading 30.02, 30.05 or 30.06)	55.9	30.4	27.6	41.6	37.7	37.9	US$/kg	542
7326	Other articles of iron or steel	43.3	37.6	24.1	7.4	5.1	5.3	US$/kg	699
7308	Structures (excluding prefabricated buildings of heading 94.06)	33.8	42.9	26.6	2.3	2.0	2.1	US$/kg	691

Bahrain

Goods Imports: CIF, by origin | **Goods Exports: FOB, by last known destination** | **Trade System: General**

Overview:
In 2012, the value of merchandise exports of Bahrain decreased substantially by 26.3 percent to reach 16.6 bln US$, while its merchandise imports decreased substantially by 19.2 percent to reach 14.2 bln US$ (see graph 1, table 2 and table 3). The merchandise trade balance recorded a relatively small surplus of 2.4 bln US$ (see graph 1). The largest merchandise trade balance was with MDG Western Asia at 1.9 bln US$ (see graph 4). Merchandise exports in Bahrain were highly concentrated amongst partners; imports were diversified. The top 5 partners accounted for 80 percent or more of exports and 13 partners accounted for 80 percent or more of imports (see graph 5). In 2012, the value of exports of services of Bahrain increased substantially by 146.6 percent, reaching 2.8 bln US$, while its imports of services increased substantially by 121.2 percent and reached 1.5 bln US$ (see graph 2). There was a large trade in services surplus of 1.3 bln US$.

Graph 1: Total merchandise trade, by value
(Bln US$ by year)

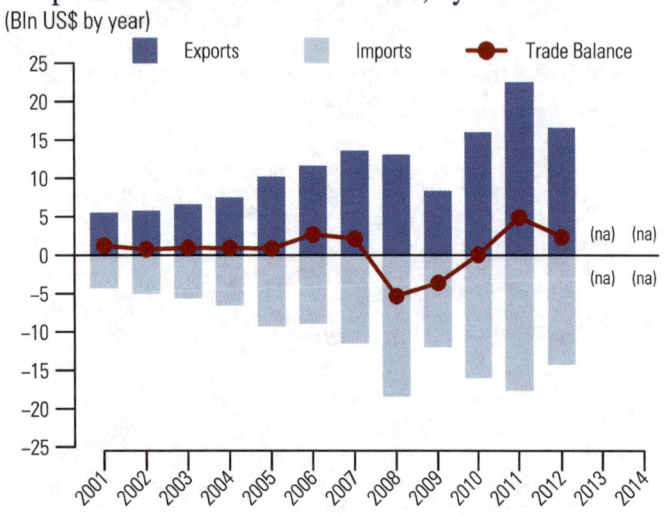

Graph 2: Total services trade, by value
(Bln US$ by year)

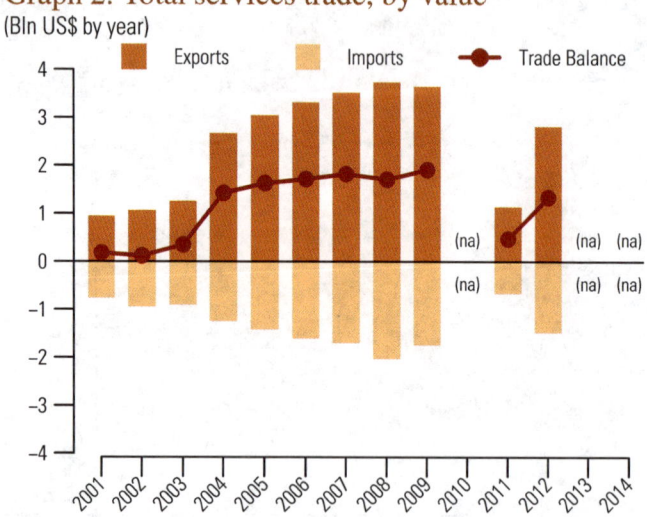

Exports Profile:
"Mineral fuels, lubricants" (SITC section 3), "Goods classified chiefly by material" (SITC section 6) and "Crude materials + anim. & veg. oils" (SITC section 2+4) were the largest commodity groups for exports in 2012, representing respectively 59.7, 15.5 and 8.8 percent of exported goods (see table 2). From 2010 to 2012, the largest export commodity was "Petroleum oils, other than crude" (HS code 2710) (see table 1). The top three destinations for merchandise exports were Areas nes, Saudi Arabia and Qatar, accounting for respectively 66.8, 8.5 and 3.7 percent of total exports. "Travel" (EBOPS code 236) accounted for the largest share of exports of services in 2012 at 1.1 bln US$, followed by "Transportation" (EBOPS code 205) at 691.5 mln US$ and "Communications services" (EBOPS code 245) at 638.3 mln US$ (see graph 3).

Graph 3: Exports of services by EBOPS category
(% share in 2012)

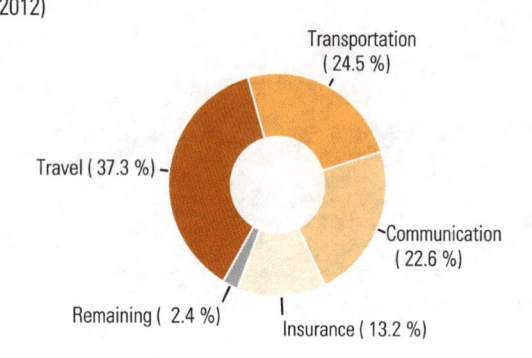

- Transportation (24.5 %)
- Travel (37.3 %)
- Communication (22.6 %)
- Insurance (13.2 %)
- Remaining (2.4 %)

Table 1: Top 10 export commodities 2010 to 2012

HS code	4-digit heading of Harmonized System 2007	Value (million US$) 2010	2011	2012	Unit value 2010	2011	2012	Unit	SITC code
	All Commodities	16059.2	22561.9	16621.2					
2710	Petroleum oils, other than crude	11507.9	15526.1	9888.5	0.7	0.8	1.1	US$/kg	334
2601	Iron ores and concentrates, including roasted iron pyrites	1187.3	2611.2	1368.6	0.2	0.2	0.2	US$/kg	281
7604	Aluminium bars, rods and profiles	825.4	1030.2	1301.4	2.4	2.6	2.6	US$/kg	684
7606	Aluminium plates, sheets and strip, of a thickness exceeding 0.2 mm	480.5	535.3	164.3	2.8	3.4	3.0	US$/kg	684
8703	Motor cars and other motor vehicles principally designed for the transport	171.4	253.8	290.0	32.4	30.5	27.7	thsd US$/unit	781
7614	Stranded wire, cables, plaited bands and the like, of aluminium	172.5	212.5	314.5	2.8	3.0	2.7	US$/kg	693
7605	Aluminium wire	165.8	222.2	173.3	2.5	2.8	2.5	US$/kg	684
0406	Cheese and curd	114.8	167.4	163.5	6.4	6.7	6.9	US$/kg	024
2106	Food preparations not elsewhere specified or included	110.4	128.5	155.3	3.2	3.2	3.4	US$/kg	098
2905	Acyclic alcohols and their derivatives	...	46.6	343.3		0.4	0.4	US$/kg	512

Source: UN Comtrade and UN ServiceTrade

Bahrain

Services Imports and Exports: EBOPS 2002 categories

Table 2: Merchandise exports by SITC
(Value in million US$, growth and shares in percentage)

SITC	2012	Avg. Growth rates 2008-2012	2011-2012	2012 share
Total	16621.2	6.2	-26.3	100.0
0+1	489.0	14.6	11.7	2.9
2+4	1455.1	22.0	-48.2	8.8
3	9926.0	3.4	-36.3	59.7
5	737.8	5.6	329.6	4.4
6	2569.8	4.7	-1.0	15.5
7	1124.2	20.3	42.5	6.8
8	317.5	13.9	86.3	1.9
9	1.7	-3.4	163.6	0.0

Table 3: Merchandise imports by SITC
(Value in million US$, growth and shares in percentage)

SITC	2012	Avg. Growth rates 2008-2012	2011-2012	2012 share
Total	14249.1	-6.2	-19.2	100.0
0+1	1484.5	7.3	4.6	10.4
2+4	1138.8	-2.6	-37.2	8.0
3	3970.9	-16.5	-48.7	27.9
5	859.5	5.3	3.5	6.0
6	1644.4	-6.9	0.8	11.5
7	4135.0	0.7	21.9	29.0
8	875.5	-0.2	7.9	6.1
9	140.4	21.5	29827.9	1.0

SITC Legend

SITC Code	Description
Total	All commodities
0+1	Food, animals + beverages, tobacco
2+4	Crude materials + anim. & veg. oils
3	Mineral fuels, lubricants
5	Chemicals
6	Goods classified chiefly by material
7	Machinery and transport equipment
8	Miscellaneous manufactured articles
9	Not classified elsewhere in the SITC

Graph 4: Merchandise trade balance
(Bln US$ by MDG Regions in 2012)

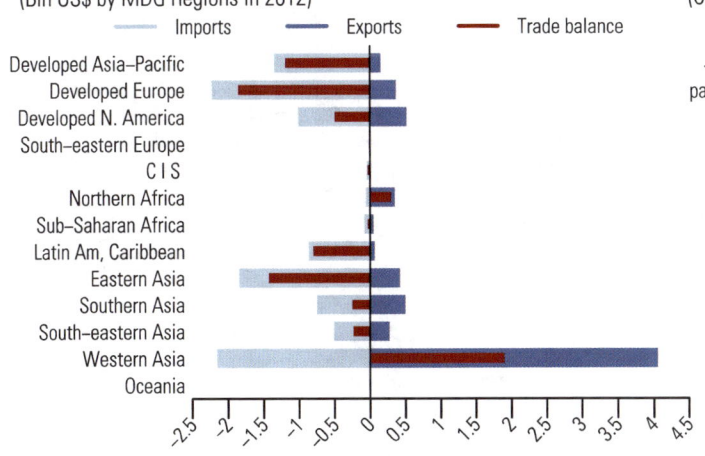

Graph 5: Partner concentration of merchandise trade
(Cumulative share by ranked partners in 2012)

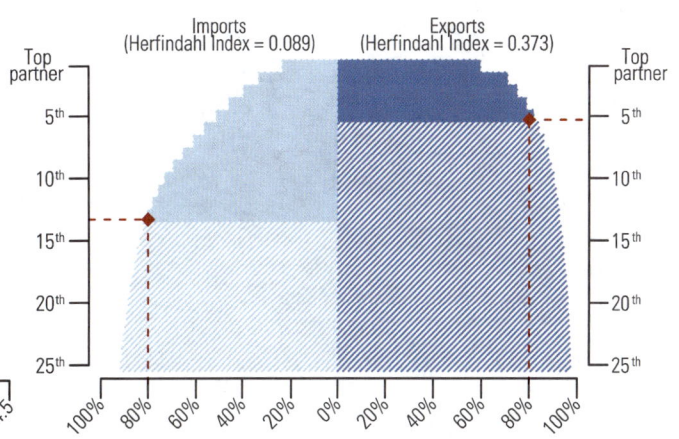

Imports (Herfindahl Index = 0.089)
Exports (Herfindahl Index = 0.373)

Graph 6: Imports of services by EBOPS category
(% share in 2012)

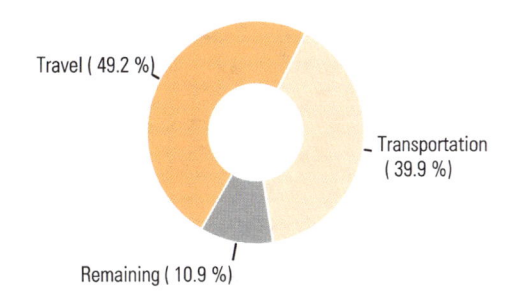

- Travel (49.2%)
- Transportation (39.9%)
- Remaining (10.9%)

Imports Profile:

"Machinery and transport equipment" (SITC section 7), "Mineral fuels, lubricants" (SITC section 3) and "Goods classified chiefly by material" (SITC section 6) were the largest commodity groups for imports in 2012, representing respectively 29.0, 27.9 and 11.5 percent of imported goods (see table 3). From 2010 to 2012, the largest import commodity was "Petroleum oils and oils obtained from bituminous minerals, crude" (HS code 2709) (see table 4). The top three partners for merchandise imports were Saudi Arabia, Areas nes and China, accounting for respectively 19.4, 19.3 and 8.2 percent of total imports. "Travel" (EBOPS code 236) accounted for the largest share of imports of services in 2012 at 728.7 mln US$, followed by "Transportation" (EBOPS code 205) at 590.4 mln US$ (see graph 6).

Table 4: Top 10 import commodities 2010 to 2012

HS code	4-digit heading of Harmonized System 2007	Value (million US$) 2010	2011	2012	Unit value 2010	2011	2012	Unit	SITC code
	All Commodities	16001.6	17643.3	14249.1					
2709	Petroleum oils and oils obtained from bituminous minerals, crude	5858.9	7469.5	3358.0	0.4	0.6	0.8	US$/kg	333
2601	Iron ores and concentrates, including roasted iron pyrites	1784.6	1349.6	671.2	0.4	0.3	0.2	US$/kg	281
8703	Motor cars and other motor vehicles principally designed for the transport	924.0	855.8	1304.6		23.1	24.4	thsd US$/unit	781
2818	Artificial corundum, whether or not chemically defined	433.8	241.3	145.4	0.5	0.5	0.3	US$/kg	285
8517	Electrical apparatus for line telephony or line telegraphy	142.2	230.4	315.2					764
2713	Petroleum coke and other residues	116.9	178.0	343.6	0.3	0.4	0.5	US$/kg	335
8471	Automatic data processing machines and units thereof	148.9	177.9	187.5	116.2	469.7	287.3	US$/unit	752
3004	Medicaments (excluding goods of heading 30.02, 30.05 or 30.06)	161.5	173.0	167.3	66.3	83.0	67.0	US$/kg	542
8544	Insulated (including enamelled or anodised) wire, cable	155.6	113.8	176.2	3.5	5.8	5.2	US$/kg	773
8504	Electrical transformers, static converters	221.2	92.9	48.3					771

2014 International Trade Statistics Yearbook, Vol. I — Source: UN Comtrade and UN ServiceTrade

Bangladesh

Goods Imports: CIF, by consignment **Goods Exports:** FOB, by last known destination **Trade System:** General

Overview:

In 2011, the value of merchandise exports of Bangladesh increased substantially by 26.4 percent to reach 24.3 bln US$, while its merchandise imports increased substantially by 35.1 percent to reach 41.2 bln US$ (see graph 1, table 2 and table 3). The merchandise trade balance recorded a moderate deficit of 16.9 bln US$ (see graph 1). The largest merchandise trade balance was with MDG South-eastern Asia at -15.9 bln US$ (see graph 4). Merchandise exports in Bangladesh were diversified amongst partners; imports were also diversified. The top 13 partners accounted for 80 percent or more of exports and 15 partners accounted for 80 percent or more of imports (see graph 5). In 2013, the value of exports of services of Bangladesh increased moderately by 9.6 percent, reaching 2.5 bln US$, while its imports of services increased substantially by 17.9 percent and reached 5.8 bln US$ (see graph 2). There was a large trade in services deficit of 3.3 bln US$.

Graph 1: Total merchandise trade, by value
(Bln US$ by year)

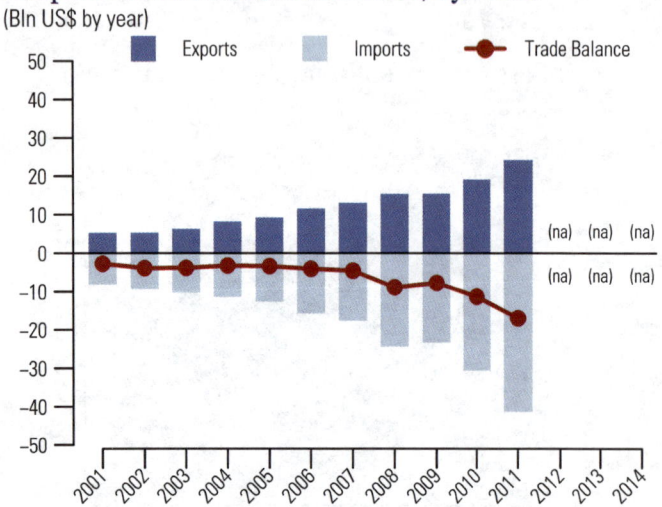

Graph 2: Total services trade, by value
(Bln US$ by year)

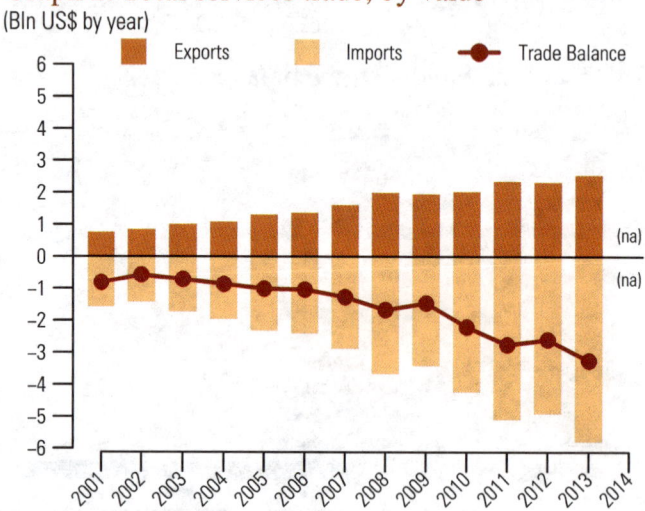

Exports Profile:

"Miscellaneous manufactured articles" (SITC section 8), "Goods classified chiefly by material" (SITC section 6) and "Food, animals + beverages, tobacco" (SITC section 0+1) were the largest commodity groups for exports in 2011, representing respectively 81.1, 9.8 and 3.8 percent of exported goods (see table 2). From 2009 to 2011, the largest export commodity was "T-shirts, singlets and other vests, knitted or crocheted" (HS code 6109) (see table 1). The top three destinations for merchandise exports were the United States, Germany and the United Kingdom, accounting for respectively 22.9, 14.6 and 9.3 percent of total exports. "Government services, n.i.e." (EBOPS code 291) accounted for the largest share of exports of services in 2013 at 1.1 bln US$, followed by "Transportation" (EBOPS code 205) at 492.0 mln US$ and "Other business services" (EBOPS code 268) at 370.0 mln US$ (see graph 3).

Graph 3: Exports of services by EBOPS category
(% share in 2013)

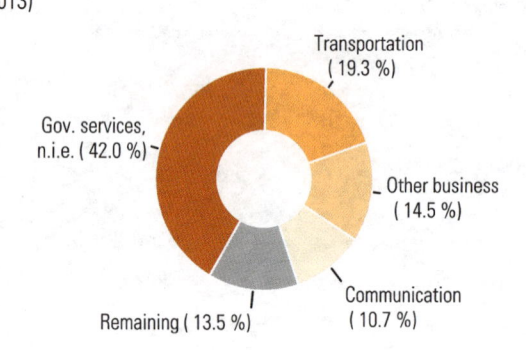

- Transportation (19.3%)
- Other business (14.5%)
- Communication (10.7%)
- Remaining (13.5%)
- Gov. services, n.i.e. (42.0%)

Table 1: Top 10 export commodities 2009 to 2011

HS code	4-digit heading of Harmonized System 2007	Value (million US$) 2009	2010	2011	Unit value 2009	2010	2011	Unit	SITC code
	All Commodities	15558.6	19231.0	24313.7					
6109	T-shirts, singlets and other vests, knitted or crocheted	3146.5	3845.5	4832.3	0.0	10.1	21.8	US$/unit	845
6203	Men's or boys' suits, ensembles, jackets, blazers, trousers	2954.3	3523.8	4545.9	5.2	11.4	25.1	US$/unit	841
6110	Jerseys, pullovers, cardigans, waist-coats and similar articles	1836.4	2073.7	2656.3	7.1	13.6	34.9	US$/unit	845
6204	Women's or girls' suits, ensembles, jackets, blazers, dresses, skirts	1299.6	1568.5	2076.1	5.6	13.3	27.6	US$/unit	842
6205	Men's or boys' shirts	950.2	1238.9	1705.6	5.5	13.5	31.4	US$/unit	841
6105	Men's or boys' shirts, knitted or crocheted	421.4	566.4	732.2	4.8	11.0	23.1	US$/unit	843
6302	Bed linen, table linen, toilet linen and kitchen linen	270.0	376.6	664.1	5.7	6.1	15.2	US$/kg	658
0306	Crustaceans, whether in shell or not	318.5	438.0	498.2	7.3	8.5	17.9	US$/kg	036
5307	Yarn of jute or of other textile bast fibres of heading 53.03	259.9	491.4	479.4	0.8	1.3	2.1	US$/kg	651
6103	Men's, boys' suits, jackets, trousers etc knitted or crocheted	300.8	300.7	424.2	5.4	10.8	25.2	US$/unit	843

Bangladesh

Services Imports and Exports: EBOPS 2002 categories

Table 2: Merchandise exports by SITC
(Value in million US$, growth and shares in percentage)

SITC	2011	Avg. Growth rates 2007-2011	Avg. Growth rates 2010-2011	2011 share
Total	24313.7	16.6	26.4	100.0
0+1	926.2	2.0	22.7	3.8
2+4	536.0	4.3	12.7	2.2
3	280.1	7.0	-22.3	1.2
5	171.0	-0.8	44.1	0.7
6	2387.6	14.1	20.4	9.8
7	282.8	-4.2	10.0	1.2
8	19730.1	19.4	29.1	81.1
9	0.0	-72.9	-83.4	0.0

Table 3: Merchandise imports by SITC
(Value in million US$, growth and shares in percentage)

SITC	2011	Avg. Growth rates 2007-2011	Avg. Growth rates 2010-2011	2011 share
Total	41221.7	23.7	35.1	100.0
0+1	4201.3	17.3	40.0	10.2
2+4	7169.8	20.4	42.3	17.4
3	3126.4	14.1	23.5	7.6
5	5073.0	24.5	40.2	12.3
6	10495.3	37.2	26.5	25.5
7	9370.1	23.2	43.0	22.7
8	1785.2	25.2	22.1	4.3
9	0.6	-78.3	94.7	0.0

SITC Legend

SITC Code	Description
Total	All commodities
0+1	Food, animals + beverages, tobacco
2+4	Crude materials + anim. & veg. oils
3	Mineral fuels, lubricants
5	Chemicals
6	Goods classified chiefly by material
7	Machinery and transport equipment
8	Miscellaneous manufactured articles
9	Not classified elsewhere in the SITC

Graph 4: Merchandise trade balance
(Bln US$ by MDG Regions in 2011)

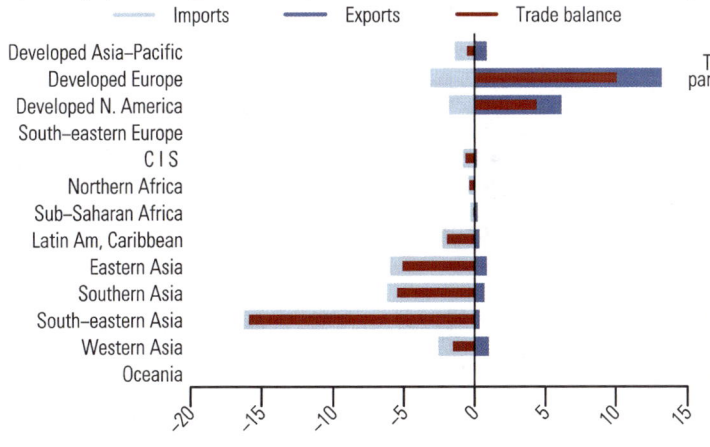

Graph 5: Partner concentration of merchandise trade
(Cumulative share by ranked partners in 2011)

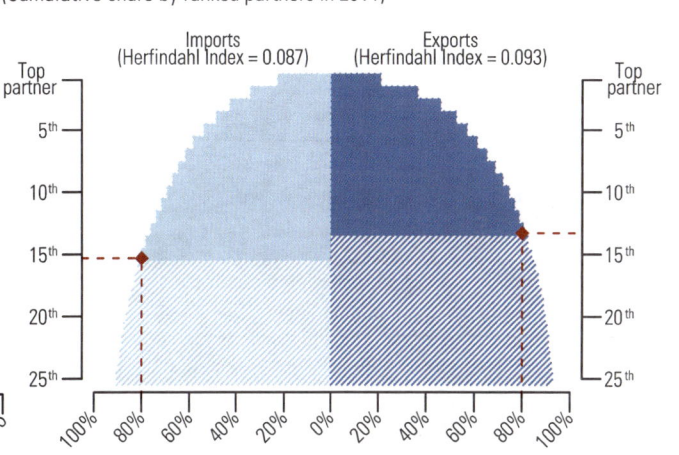

Imports (Herfindahl Index = 0.087)
Exports (Herfindahl Index = 0.093)

Graph 6: Imports of services by EBOPS category
(% share in 2013)

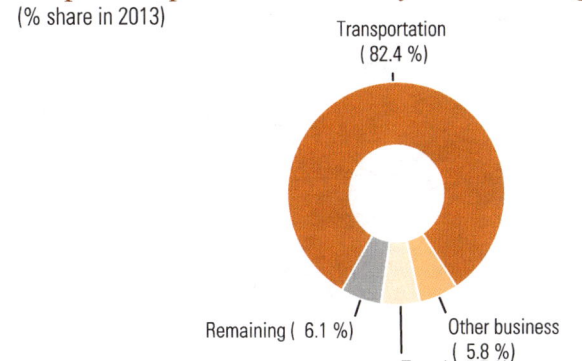

- Transportation (82.4 %)
- Remaining (6.1 %)
- Other business (5.8 %)
- Travel (5.7 %)

Imports Profile:

"Goods classified chiefly by material" (SITC section 6), "Machinery and transport equipment" (SITC section 7) and "Crude materials + anim. & veg. oils" (SITC section 2+4) were the largest commodity groups for imports in 2011, representing respectively 25.5, 22.7 and 17.4 percent of imported goods (see table 3). From 2009 to 2011, the largest import commodity was "Petroleum oils, other than crude" (HS code 2710) (see table 4). The top three partners for merchandise imports were China, Thailand and India, accounting for respectively 13.4, 12.4 and 11.1 percent of total imports. "Transportation" (EBOPS code 205) accounted for the largest share of imports of services in 2013 at 4.8 bln US$, followed by "Other business services" (EBOPS code 268) at 336.0 mln US$ and "Travel" (EBOPS code 236) at 331.0 mln US$ (see graph 6).

Table 4: Top 10 import commodities 2009 to 2011

HS code	4-digit heading of Harmonized System 2007	2009	2010	2011	2009	2010	2011	Unit	SITC code
	All Commodities	23245.0	30503.8	41221.7					
2710	Petroleum oils, other than crude	2316.6	2103.9	2739.3	0.4	0.5	0.5	US$/kg	334
5201	Cotton, not carded or combed	1143.1	1958.8	2393.5	1.4	2.0	3.4	US$/kg	263
1511	Palm oil and its fractions	1278.4	1460.1	2372.3	0.7	0.8	1.1	US$/kg	422
5208	Woven fabrics of cotton, containing 85 % or more by weight of cotton	680.9	957.5	1486.5	5.3	7.3	9.7	US$/kg	652
1001	Wheat and meslin	788.3	807.5	1004.8	0.3	0.3	0.4	US$/kg	041
1701	Cane or beet sugar and chemically pure sucrose, in solid form	584.0	731.5	1157.5	0.4	0.6	0.7	US$/kg	061
5209	Woven fabrics of cotton, containing 85 % or more by weight of cotton	575.7	740.9	1131.8	4.9	5.8	8.1	US$/kg	652
5205	Cotton yarn (other than sewing thread), containing 85 % or more	409.1	793.1	1130.9	2.7	3.8	5.1	US$/kg	651
1507	Soya-bean oil and its fractions	534.0	651.7	1109.4	0.8	0.9	1.3	US$/kg	421
2523	Portland cement, aluminous cement, slag cement	301.4	1322.1	561.7	0.0	0.2	0.1	US$/kg	661

2014 International Trade Statistics Yearbook, Vol. I — Source: UN Comtrade and UN ServiceTrade

Barbados

Goods Imports: CIF, by origin **Goods Exports:** FOB, by last known destination **Trade System:** General

Overview:
In 2014, the value of merchandise exports of Barbados increased slightly by 2.9 percent to reach 480.8 mln US$, while its merchandise imports decreased slightly by 1.6 percent to reach 1.7 bln US$ (see graph 1, table 2 and table 3). The merchandise trade balance recorded a large deficit of 1.3 bln US$ (see graph 1). The largest merchandise trade balance was with MDG Developed North America at -553.6 mln US$ (see graph 4). Merchandise exports in Barbados were diversified amongst partners; while imports were relatively concentrated. The top 11 partners accounted for 80 percent or more of exports and 11 partners accounted for 80 percent or more of imports (see graph 5). In 2010, the value of exports of services of Barbados increased substantially by 34.2 percent, reaching 569.0 mln US$, while its imports of services decreased slightly by 3.5 percent and reached 661.0 mln US$ (see graph 2). There was a relatively small trade in services deficit of 92.0 mln US$.

Graph 1: Total merchandise trade, by value
(Bln US$ by year)

Graph 2: Total services trade, by value
(Mln US$ by year)

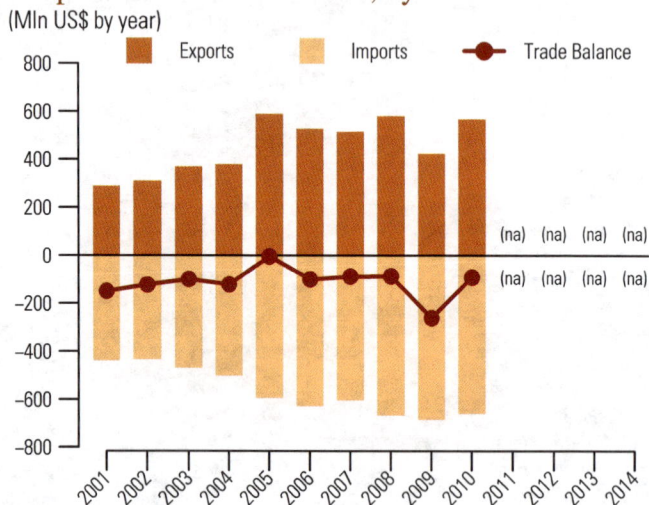

Exports Profile:
"Mineral fuels, lubricants" (SITC section 3), "Food, animals + beverages, tobacco" (SITC section 0+1) and "Miscellaneous manufactured articles" (SITC section 8) were the largest commodity groups for exports in 2014, representing respectively 29.7, 20.3 and 17.5 percent of exported goods (see table 2). From 2012 to 2014, the largest export commodity was "Petroleum oils, other than crude" (HS code 2710) (see table 1). The top three destinations for merchandise exports were Areas nes, the United States and Trinidad and Tobago, accounting for respectively 25.2, 20.8 and 11.8 percent of total exports. "Other business services" (EBOPS code 268) accounted for the largest share of exports of services in 2010 at 390.1 mln US$, followed by "Insurance services" (EBOPS code 253) at 52.0 mln US$ and "Government services, n.i.e." (EBOPS code 291) at 37.6 mln US$ (see graph 3).

Graph 3: Exports of services by EBOPS category
(% share in 2010)

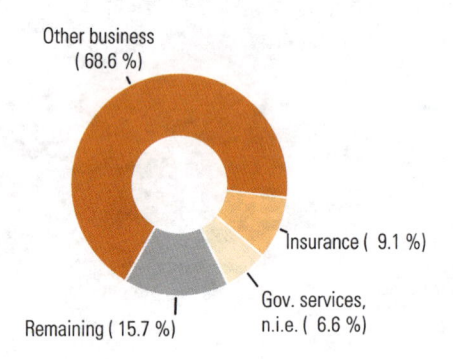

- Other business (68.6 %)
- Insurance (9.1 %)
- Gov. services, n.i.e. (6.6 %)
- Remaining (15.7 %)

Table 1: Top 10 export commodities 2012 to 2014

HS code	4-digit heading of Harmonized System 2002	Value (million US$) 2012	2013	2014	Unit value 2012	2013	2014	Unit	SITC code
	All Commodities	566.4	467.4	480.8					
2710	Petroleum oils, other than crude	137.2	128.1	116.3	1.1	1.0	1.0	US$/kg	334
3004	Medicaments (excluding goods of heading 30.02, 30.05 or 30.06)	68.5	45.9	45.9	61.3	1.5	35.4	US$/kg	542
2208	Alcohol of a strength by volume of less than 80 % vol	63.3	49.0	45.7	3.0	3.0	2.9	US$/litre	112
2709	Petroleum oils, crude	32.0	24.3	26.4	0.7	0.7	0.6	US$/kg	333
7113	Articles of jewellery and parts thereof, of precious metal	35.4	8.4	11.5		2.3	2.4	thsd US$/kg	897
2523	Portland cement, aluminous cement, slag cement	9.9	20.0	19.3	0.1	0.1	0.1	US$/kg	661
9021	Orthopaedic appliances, including crutches, surgical belts and trusses	12.8	17.6	16.0					899
4821	Paper or paperboard lables of all kinds, whether or not printed	10.3	12.2	12.1	22.4	25.3	21.9	US$/kg	892
1905	Bread, pastry, cakes, biscuits and other bakers' wares	9.4	9.2	11.7	3.4	3.6	3.2	US$/kg	048
1517	Margarine; edible mixtures	10.1	10.1	10.1	2.8	2.9	2.9	US$/kg	091

Source: UN Comtrade and UN ServiceTrade

Barbados

Services Imports and Exports: EBOPS 2002 categories

Table 2: Merchandise exports by SITC
(Value in million US$, growth and shares in percentage)

SITC	2014	Avg. Growth rates 2010-2014	Avg. Growth rates 2013-2014	2014 share
Total	480.8	11.3	2.9	100.0
0+1	97.4	2.5	1.4	20.3
2+4	7.0	4.0	10.9	1.5
3	142.8	623.3	-6.3	29.7
5	71.4	-5.5	-1.5	14.9
6	42.3	2.3	5.4	8.8
7	28.8	5.6	26.6	6.0
8	84.1	6.7	18.0	17.5
9	7.0	21.3	14.5	1.5

Table 3: Merchandise imports by SITC
(Value in million US$, growth and shares in percentage)

SITC	2014	Avg. Growth rates 2010-2014	Avg. Growth rates 2013-2014	2014 share
Total	1740.5	9.8	-1.6	100.0
0+1	320.4	3.5	-1.3	18.4
2+4	45.5	1.2	-0.6	2.6
3	444.7	118.6	-7.9	25.5
5	183.8	1.0	3.3	10.6
6	193.6	0.1	1.8	11.1
7	327.8	3.2	-0.3	18.8
8	217.8	3.4	3.3	12.5
9	6.8	5.1	-13.4	0.4

SITC Legend

SITC Code	Description
Total	All commodities
0+1	Food, animals + beverages, tobacco
2+4	Crude materials + anim. & veg. oils
3	Mineral fuels, lubricants
5	Chemicals
6	Goods classified chiefly by material
7	Machinery and transport equipment
8	Miscellaneous manufactured articles
9	Not classified elsewhere in the SITC

Graph 4: Merchandise trade balance
(Mln US$ by MDG Regions in 2014)

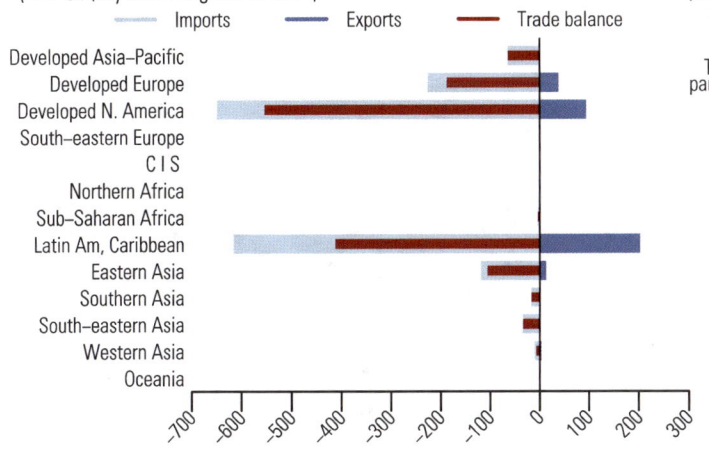

Graph 5: Partner concentration of merchandise trade
(Cumulative share by ranked partners in 2014)

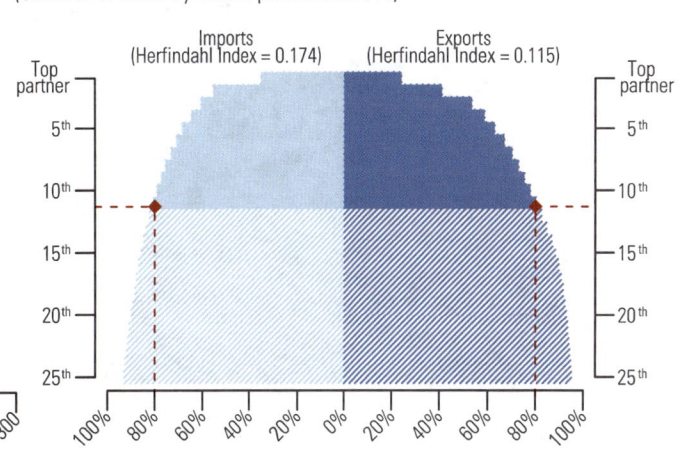

Imports (Herfindahl Index = 0.174)
Exports (Herfindahl Index = 0.115)

Graph 6: Imports of services by EBOPS category
(% share in 2010)

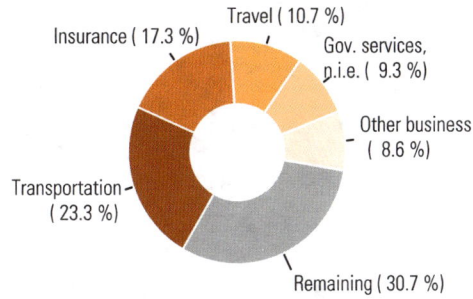

- Travel (10.7 %)
- Gov. services, p.i.e. (9.3 %)
- Other business (8.6 %)
- Remaining (30.7 %)
- Transportation (23.3 %)
- Insurance (17.3 %)

Imports Profile:

"Mineral fuels, lubricants" (SITC section 3), "Machinery and transport equipment" (SITC section 7) and "Food, animals + beverages, tobacco" (SITC section 0+1) were the largest commodity groups for imports in 2014, representing respectively 25.5, 18.8 and 18.4 percent of imported goods (see table 3). From 2012 to 2014, the largest import commodity was "Petroleum oils, other than crude" (HS code 2710) (see table 4). The top three partners for merchandise imports were the United States, Trinidad and Tobago and Suriname, accounting for respectively 33.0, 25.2 and 5.0 percent of total imports. "Transportation" (EBOPS code 205) accounted for the largest share of imports of services in 2010 at 154.2 mln US$, followed by "Insurance services" (EBOPS code 253) at 114.5 mln US$ and "Travel" (EBOPS code 236) at 70.9 mln US$ (see graph 6).

Table 4: Top 10 import commodities 2012 to 2014

HS code	4-digit heading of Harmonized System 2002	Value (million US$) 2012	2013	2014	Unit value 2012	2013	2014	Unit	SITC code
	All Commodities	1767.8	1768.7	1740.5					
2710	Petroleum oils, other than crude	533.9	462.9	426.6	0.9	0.8	0.8	US$/kg	334
3004	Medicaments (excluding goods of heading 30.02, 30.05 or 30.06)	58.0	60.1	66.1	34.2	30.9	33.0	US$/kg	542
8703	Motor cars and other motor vehicles principally designed for the transport	37.9	37.7	40.9	15.0	14.7	14.8	thsd US$/unit	781
8471	Automatic data processing machines and units thereof	24.3	27.0	25.8					752
8544	Insulated (including enamelled or anodised) wire, cable	11.3	18.3	25.7	9.2	14.3	17.7	US$/kg	773
7113	Articles of jewellery and parts thereof, of precious metal	18.4	17.1	19.8		3.1	2.9	thsd US$/kg	897
2106	Food preparations not elsewhere specified or included	17.2	18.2	18.3	3.3	2.8	0.4	US$/kg	098
3923	Articles for the conveyance or packing of goods, of plastics	17.3	17.8	17.8	3.3	1.4	3.4	US$/kg	893
2202	Waters with added sugar	16.6	16.9	15.0	0.9	0.9	0.9	US$/litre	111
8517	Electrical apparatus for line telephony or line telegraphy	10.6	19.7	17.6					764

2014 International Trade Statistics Yearbook, Vol. I   Source: UN Comtrade and UN ServiceTrade

Belarus

Goods Imports: CIF, by origin **Goods Exports:** FOB, by last known destination **Trade System:** General

Overview:
In 2014, the value of merchandise exports of Belarus decreased slightly by 2.2 percent to reach 36.4 bln US$, while its merchandise imports decreased moderately by 6.0 percent to reach 40.5 bln US$ (see graph 1, table 2 and table 3). The merchandise trade balance recorded a relatively small deficit of 4.1 bln US$ (see graph 1). The largest merchandise trade balance was with MDG CIS at -3.0 bln US$ (see graph 4). Merchandise exports in Belarus were moderately concentrated amongst partners; imports were highly concentrated. The top 9 partners accounted for 80 percent or more of exports and 9 partners accounted for 80 percent or more of imports (see graph 5). In 2013, the value of exports of services of Belarus increased substantially by 15.8 percent, reaching 6.9 bln US$, while its imports of services increased substantially by 15.1 percent and reached 4.5 bln US$ (see graph 2). There was a moderate trade in services surplus of 2.5 bln US$.

Graph 1: Total merchandise trade, by value
(Bln US$ by year)

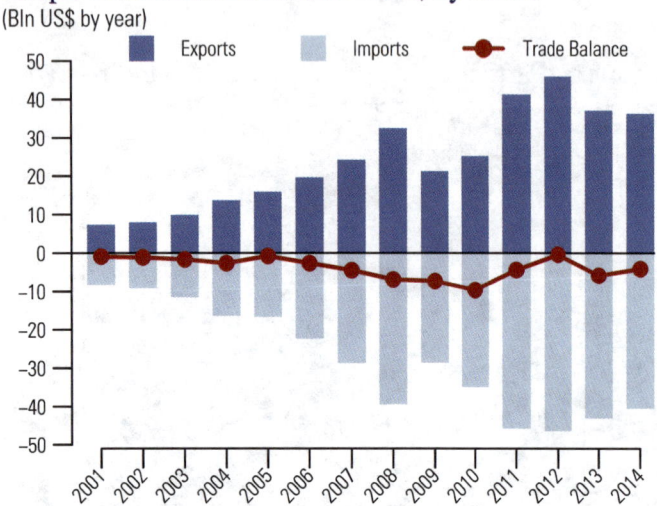

Graph 2: Total services trade, by value
(Bln US$ by year)

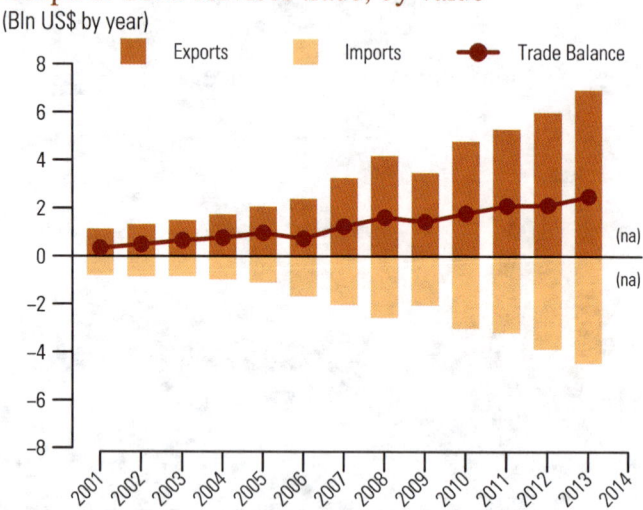

Exports Profile:
"Mineral fuels, lubricants" (SITC section 3), "Food, animals + beverages, tobacco" (SITC section 0+1) and "Machinery and transport equipment" (SITC section 7) were the largest commodity groups for exports in 2014, representing respectively 33.9, 14.2 and 13.9 percent of exported goods (see table 2). From 2012 to 2014, the largest export commodity was "Petroleum oils, other than crude" (HS code 2710) (see table 1). The top three destinations for merchandise exports were the Russian Federation, Ukraine and the Netherlands, accounting for respectively 40.1, 11.6 and 10.6 percent of total exports. "Transportation" (EBOPS code 205) accounted for the largest share of exports of services in 2013 at 3.8 bln US$, followed by "Construction services" (EBOPS code 249) at 906.3 mln US$ and "Travel" (EBOPS code 236) at 722.2 mln US$ (see graph 3).

Graph 3: Exports of services by EBOPS category
(% share in 2013)

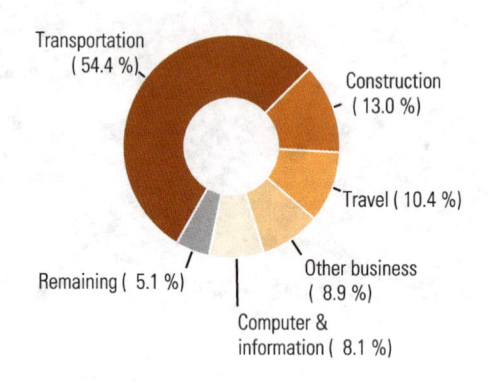

- Transportation (54.4 %)
- Construction (13.0 %)
- Travel (10.4 %)
- Other business (8.9 %)
- Computer & information (8.1 %)
- Remaining (5.1 %)

Table 1: Top 10 export commodities 2012 to 2014

HS code	4-digit heading of Harmonized System 2012	Value (million US$) 2012	2013	2014	Unit value 2012	2013	2014	Unit	SITC code
	All Commodities	46 059.9	37 203.0	36 389.4					
2710	Petroleum oils, other than crude	14 505.0	10 155.5	10 069.5	0.8	0.7	0.7	US$/kg	334
3104	Mineral or chemical fertilisers, potassic	2 662.4	2 052.4	2 684.3	0.4	0.4	0.3	US$/kg	562
9999	Commodities not specified according to kind	1 856.8	1 528.4	1 062.0					931
8704	Motor vehicles for the transport of goods	1 613.0	1 110.5	934.4	106.4	101.6	106.5	thsd US$/unit	782
2709	Petroleum oils and oils obtained from bituminous minerals, crude	1 288.1	1 241.3	1 124.3	0.8	0.8	0.7	US$/kg	333
8701	Tractors (other than tractors of heading 87.09)	1 437.4	1 076.3	847.8	21.6	19.7	18.4	thsd US$/unit	722
3814	Organic composite solvents and thinners	2 781.5	1.6	0.8	0.9	1.4	1.9	US$/kg	533
0402	Milk and cream, concentrated or containing added sugar	556.6	847.0	674.2	2.7	3.6	3.5	US$/kg	022
0406	Cheese and curd	580.2	649.4	797.8	4.3	4.6	4.8	US$/kg	024
4011	New pneumatic tyres, of rubber	705.1	610.9	387.0	165.3	141.8	101.4	US$/unit	625

Source: UN Comtrade and UN ServiceTrade

Belarus

Services Imports and Exports: EBOPS 2002 categories

Table 2: Merchandise exports by SITC
(Value in million US$, growth and shares in percentage)

SITC	2014	Avg. Growth rates 2010-2014	Avg. Growth rates 2013-2014	2014 share
Total	36 389.4	9.5	-2.2	100.0
0+1	5 160.0	13.3	-0.6	14.2
2+4	920.3	7.5	-2.6	2.5
3	12 332.4	15.1	2.4	33.9
5	4 972.0	7.4	22.8	13.7
6	4 706.8	5.7	-5.4	12.9
7	5 053.5	3.9	-17.9	13.9
8	2 182.4	8.3	-5.6	6.0
9	1 062.0	0.8	-30.5	2.9

Table 3: Merchandise imports by SITC
(Value in million US$, growth and shares in percentage)

SITC	2014	Avg. Growth rates 2010-2014	Avg. Growth rates 2013-2014	2014 share
Total	40 451.4	3.8	-6.0	100.0
0+1	4 436.2	14.9	18.2	11.0
2+4	1 267.3	-3.1	-16.2	3.1
3	11 849.8	-0.4	-5.7	29.3
5	4 598.9	6.3	-0.5	11.4
6	5 697.3	1.9	-13.9	14.1
7	8 346.2	5.5	-18.8	20.6
8	2 374.5	14.3	1.6	5.9
9	1 881.2	0.8	40.3	4.7

SITC Legend

SITC Code	Description
Total	All commodities
0+1	Food, animals + beverages, tobacco
2+4	Crude materials + anim. & veg. oils
3	Mineral fuels, lubricants
5	Chemicals
6	Goods classified chiefly by material
7	Machinery and transport equipment
8	Miscellaneous manufactured articles
9	Not classified elsewhere in the SITC

Graph 4: Merchandise trade balance
(Bln US$ by MDG Regions in 2014)

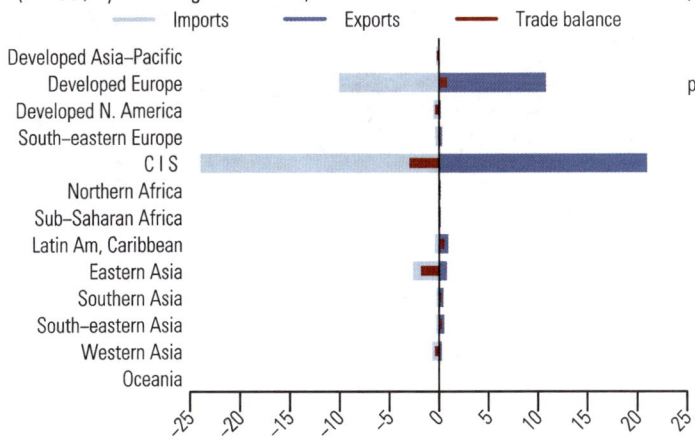

Graph 5: Partner concentration of merchandise trade
(Cumulative share by ranked partners in 2014)

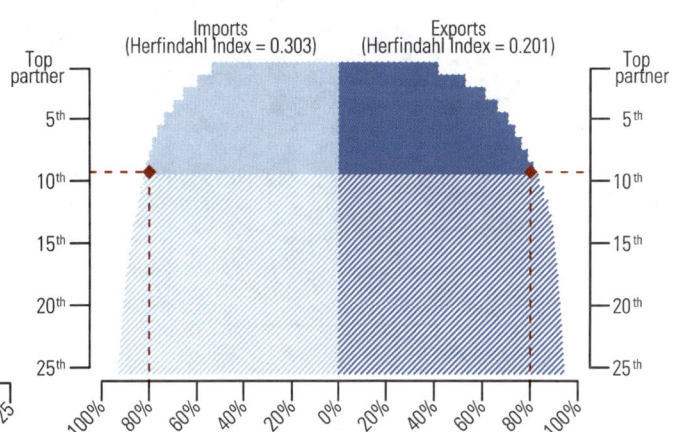

Imports (Herfindahl Index = 0.303)
Exports (Herfindahl Index = 0.201)

Graph 6: Imports of services by EBOPS category
(% share in 2013)

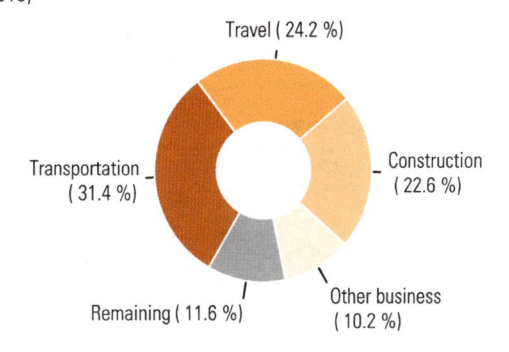

- Travel (24.2 %)
- Transportation (31.4 %)
- Construction (22.6 %)
- Other business (10.2 %)
- Remaining (11.6 %)

Imports Profile:

"Mineral fuels, lubricants" (SITC section 3), "Machinery and transport equipment" (SITC section 7) and "Goods classified chiefly by material" (SITC section 6) were the largest commodity groups for imports in 2014, representing respectively 29.3, 20.6 and 14.1 percent of imported goods (see table 3). From 2012 to 2014, the largest import commodity was "Petroleum oils and oils obtained from bituminous minerals, crude" (HS code 2709) (see table 4). The top three partners for merchandise imports were the Russian Federation, Germany and China, accounting for respectively 55.1, 6.3 and 5.8 percent of total imports. "Transportation" (EBOPS code 205) accounted for the largest share of imports of services in 2013 at 1.4 bln US$, followed by "Travel" (EBOPS code 236) at 1.1 bln US$ and "Construction services" (EBOPS code 249) at 1.0 bln US$ (see graph 6).

Table 4: Top 10 import commodities 2012 to 2014

HS code	4-digit heading of Harmonized System 2012	Value (million US$) 2012	2013	2014	Unit value 2012	2013	2014	Unit	SITC code
	All Commodities	46 404.4	43 022.7	40 451.4					
2709	Petroleum oils and oils obtained from bituminous minerals, crude	8 705.8	8 392.1	7 628.9	0.4	0.4	0.3	US$/kg	333
2711	Petroleum gases and other gaseous hydrocarbons	3 564.4	3 512.2	3 594.6	0.3	0.2	0.3	US$/kg	343
2710	Petroleum oils, other than crude	4 996.0	153.4	282.4	0.6	1.2	0.7	US$/kg	334
9999	Commodities not specified according to kind	1 307.3	1 341.3	1 881.2					931
3004	Medicaments (excluding goods of heading 30.02, 30.05 or 30.06)	438.1	523.6	583.6	65.2	67.4	71.6	US$/kg	542
8703	Motor cars and other motor vehicles principally designed for the transport	413.0	491.6	417.7	18.2	16.9	15.4	thsd US$/unit	781
8708	Parts and accessories of the motor vehicles of headings 87.01 to 87.05	393.3	436.3	377.8	4.6	5.1	5.2	US$/kg	784
7204	Ferrous waste and scrap; remelting scrap ingots of iron or steel	440.2	386.9	374.5	0.3	0.3	0.3	US$/kg	282
8517	Electrical apparatus for line telephony or line telegraphy	289.7	493.3	408.5					764
8408	Compression-ignition internal combustion piston engines	465.4	408.8	272.8	6.9	7.1	5.8	thsd US$/unit	713

2014 International Trade Statistics Yearbook, Vol. I — Source: UN Comtrade and UN ServiceTrade

Belgium

Goods Imports: CIF, by origin/consignment for intra-eu   **Goods Exports:** FOB, by last known destination   **Trade System:** Special

Overview:
In 2014, the value of merchandise exports of Belgium decreased moderately by 7.7 percent to reach 472.2 bln US$, while its merchandise imports decreased moderately by 7.3 percent to reach 452.8 bln US$ (see graph 1, table 2 and table 3). The merchandise trade balance decreased slightly from the record high surplus of 23.1 bln US$ in 2013, and the country recorded a surplus of 19.4 bln US$ in 2014 (see graph 1). The largest merchandise trade balance was with MDG Developed Europe at 35.7 bln US$ (see graph 4). Merchandise exports in Belgium were diversified amongst partners; imports were also diversified. The top 17 partners accounted for 80 percent or more of exports and 16 partners accounted for 80 percent or more of imports (see graph 5). In 2013, the value of exports of services of Belgium increased moderately by 7.3 percent, reaching 109.0 bln US$, while its imports of services increased moderately by 7.3 percent and reached 98.3 bln US$ (see graph 2). There was a relatively small trade in services surplus of 10.7 bln US$.

Graph 1: Total merchandise trade, by value
(Bln US$ by year)

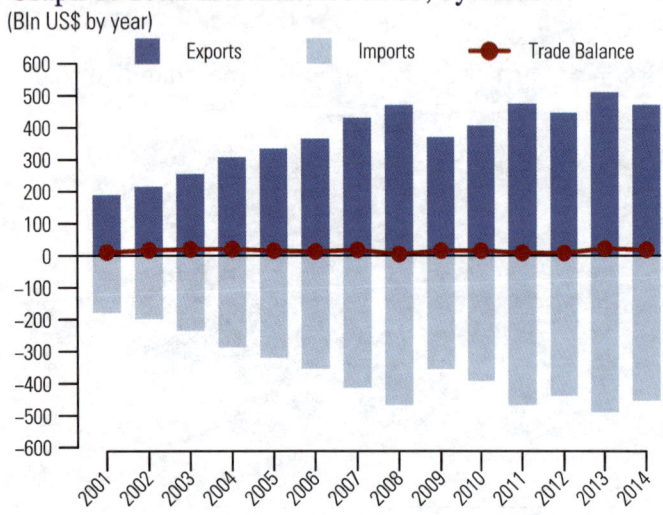

Graph 2: Total services trade, by value
(Bln US$ by year)

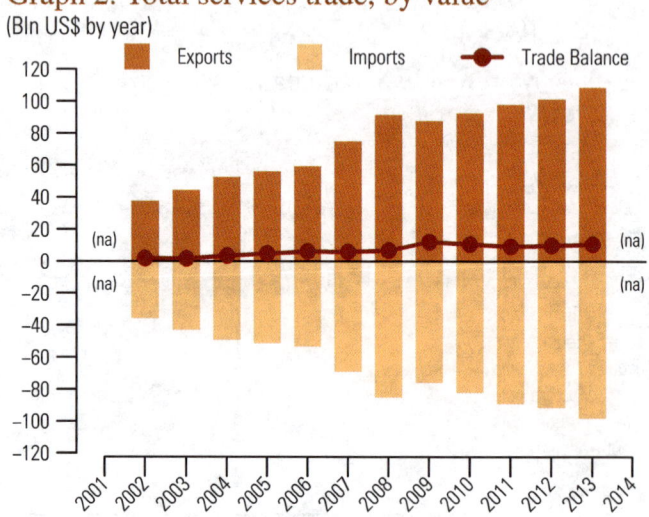

Exports Profile:
"Chemicals" (SITC section 5), "Machinery and transport equipment" (SITC section 7) and "Goods classified chiefly by material" (SITC section 6) were the largest commodity groups for exports in 2014, representing respectively 28.6, 20.3 and 15.5 percent of exported goods. All these commodity groups recorded a negative growth rate in 2014 of respectively 7.7, 7.0 and 7.4 percent (see table 2). From 2012 to 2014, the largest export commodity was "Petroleum oils, other than crude" (HS code 2710) (see table 1). The top three destinations for merchandise exports were Germany, France and the Netherlands, accounting for respectively 17.0, 15.6 and 12.2 percent of total exports. "Other business services" (EBOPS code 268) accounted for the largest share of exports of services in 2012 at 38.5 bln US$, followed by "Transportation" (EBOPS code 205) at 26.1 bln US$ and "Travel" (EBOPS code 236) at 13.0 bln US$ (see graph 3).

Graph 3: Exports of services by EBOPS category
(% share in 2012)

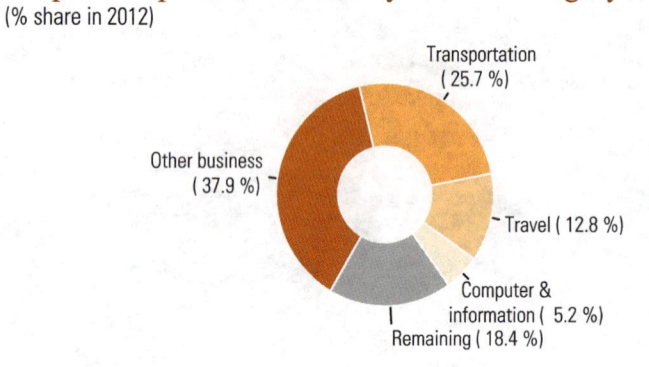

- Transportation (25.7 %)
- Other business (37.9 %)
- Travel (12.8 %)
- Computer & information (5.2 %)
- Remaining (18.4 %)

Table 1: Top 10 export commodities 2012 to 2014

HS code	4-digit heading of Harmonized System 2012	Value (million US$) 2012	2013	2014	Unit value 2012	2013	2014	Unit	SITC code
	All Commodities	446 854.4	511 505.0	472 201.3					
2710	Petroleum oils, other than crude	37 262.9	48 751.7	40 829.2	0.9	0.9	0.8	US$/kg	334
3004	Medicaments (excluding goods of heading 30.02, 30.05 or 30.06)	29 699.1	33 329.6	30 345.9	161.2	164.2	157.0	US$/kg	542
8703	Motor cars and other motor vehicles principally designed for the transport	27 445.1	32 125.5	30 288.7	16.2	16.6	17.7	thsd US$/unit	781
7102	Diamonds, whether or not worked, but not mounted or set	18 076.1	20 866.0	20 562.7					667
3002	Human blood; animal blood prepared for therapeutic uses	12 615.7	14 050.4	16 729.0	1.4	0.9	1.5	thsd US$/kg	541
9999	Commodities not specified according to kind	8 476.0	12 165.8	12 471.3					931
2933	Heterocyclic compounds with nitrogen hetero-atom(s) only	10 794.0	10 982.5	8 101.2	21.4	19.3	16.6	US$/kg	515
2711	Petroleum gases and other gaseous hydrocarbons	8 797.4	11 991.5	8 239.5	0.5	0.5	0.7	US$/kg	343
8708	Parts and accessories of the motor vehicles of headings 87.01 to 87.05	6 169.7	7 307.5	6 306.0	8.3	9.1	8.5	US$/kg	784
3901	Polymers of ethylene, in primary forms	6 259.2	6 770.4	6 218.7	1.8	1.9	1.9	US$/kg	571

Belgium

Services Imports and Exports: EBOPS 2002 categories

Table 2: Merchandise exports by SITC
(Value in million US$, growth and shares in percentage)

SITC	2014	Avg. Growth rates 2010-2014	Avg. Growth rates 2013-2014	2014 share
Total	472 201.3	3.7	-7.7	100.0
0+1	42 256.3	5.2	-3.9	8.9
2+4	13 774.6	2.9	-9.8	2.9
3	53 885.7	10.4	-18.9	11.4
5	134 994.1	2.2	-7.7	28.6
6	73 183.4	0.7	-7.4	15.5
7	95 817.3	3.6	-7.0	20.3
8	44 039.5	5.1	0.7	9.3
9	14 250.3	8.7	3.7	3.0

Table 3: Merchandise imports by SITC
(Value in million US$, growth and shares in percentage)

SITC	2014	Avg. Growth rates 2010-2014	Avg. Growth rates 2013-2014	2014 share
Total	452 772.5	3.7	-7.3	100.0
0+1	36 769.1	6.1	-2.9	8.1
2+4	19 926.4	2.2	-6.2	4.4
3	74 373.6	8.2	-18.9	16.4
5	108 213.1	2.5	-4.7	23.9
6	64 658.1	2.6	-4.9	14.3
7	100 461.6	2.3	-5.9	22.2
8	42 855.3	4.2	-0.8	9.5
9	5 515.3	1.3	-10.7	1.2

SITC Legend

SITC Code	Description
Total	All commodities
0+1	Food, animals + beverages, tobacco
2+4	Crude materials + anim. & veg. oils
3	Mineral fuels, lubricants
5	Chemicals
6	Goods classified chiefly by material
7	Machinery and transport equipment
8	Miscellaneous manufactured articles
9	Not classified elsewhere in the SITC

Graph 4: Merchandise trade balance
(Bln US$ by MDG Regions in 2014)

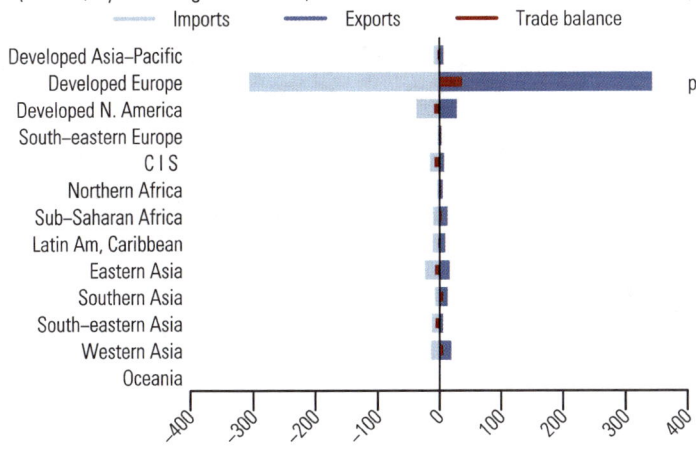

Graph 5: Partner concentration of merchandise trade
(Cumulative share by ranked partners in 2014)

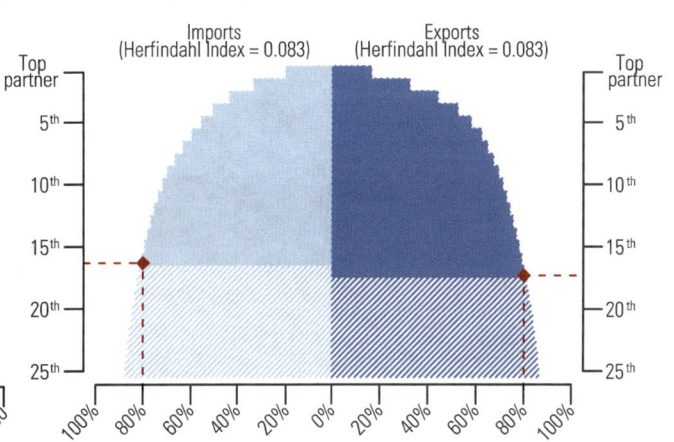

Imports (Herfindahl Index = 0.083) Exports (Herfindahl Index = 0.083)

Graph 6: Imports of services by EBOPS category
(% share in 2012)

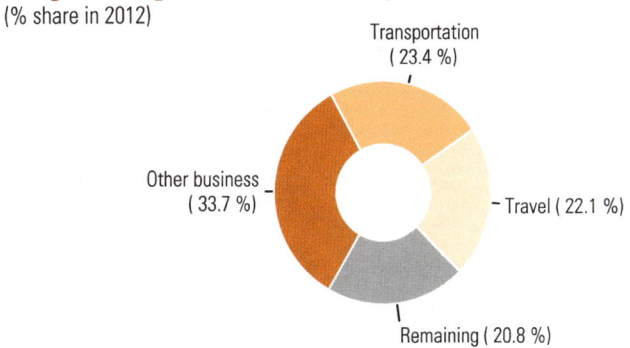

- Transportation (23.4 %)
- Travel (22.1 %)
- Remaining (20.8 %)
- Other business (33.7 %)

Imports Profile:

"Chemicals" (SITC section 5), "Machinery and transport equipment" (SITC section 7) and "Mineral fuels, lubricants" (SITC section 3) were the largest commodity groups for imports in 2014, representing respectively 23.9, 22.2 and 16.4 percent of imported goods (see table 3). From 2012 to 2014, the largest import commodity was "Petroleum oils, other than crude" (HS code 2710) (see table 4). The top three partners for merchandise imports were the Netherlands, Germany and France, accounting for respectively 20.4, 13.6 and 10.4 percent of total imports. "Other business services" (EBOPS code 268) accounted for the largest share of imports of services in 2012 at 30.9 bln US$, followed by "Transportation" (EBOPS code 205) at 21.4 bln US$ and "Travel" (EBOPS code 236) at 20.2 bln US$ (see graph 6).

Table 4: Top 10 import commodities 2012 to 2014

HS code	4-digit heading of Harmonized System 2012	2012	2013	2014	2012	2013	2014	Unit	SITC code
	All Commodities...	437 882.7	488 527.2	452 772.5					
2710	Petroleum oils, other than crude...	27 428.0	36 997.6	29 191.2	0.9	0.8	0.8	US$/kg	334
2709	Petroleum oils and oils obtained from bituminous minerals, crude...	29 045.4	28 489.1	27 379.6	0.8	0.8	0.7	US$/kg	333
8703	Motor cars and other motor vehicles principally designed for the transport...	25 530.2	30 018.4	26 947.4	19.3	19.7	20.4	thsd US$/unit	781
3004	Medicaments (excluding goods of heading 30.02, 30.05 or 30.06)...	21 722.5	25 317.7	23 413.4	121.4	126.5	109.0	US$/kg	542
7102	Diamonds, whether or not worked, but not mounted or set...	18 865.2	20 913.1	19 755.4					667
2711	Petroleum gases and other gaseous hydrocarbons...	16 317.0	20 792.3	13 803.4	0.7	0.6	0.6	US$/kg	343
3002	Human blood; animal blood prepared for therapeutic uses...	11 274.2	12 671.5	13 811.8	1.4	1.3	0.7	thsd US$/kg	541
8708	Parts and accessories of the motor vehicles of headings 87.01 to 87.05...	9 409.1	10 539.9	9 396.8	7.8	8.1	8.1	US$/kg	784
2933	Heterocyclic compounds with nitrogen hetero-atom(s) only...	9 872.5	7 822.7	7 405.7	89.5	62.5	56.8	US$/kg	515
9018	Instruments and appliances used in medical, surgical, dental or veterinary...	4 987.6	5 955.4	5 814.0					872

2014 International Trade Statistics Yearbook, Vol. I Source: UN Comtrade and UN ServiceTrade

Belize

Goods Imports: CIF, by origin **Goods Exports:** FOB, by last known destination **Trade System:** General

Overview:

In 2014, the value of merchandise exports of Belize decreased substantially by 12.7 percent to reach 359.1 mln US$, while its merchandise imports increased moderately by 7.8 percent to reach 1.0 bln US$ (see graph 1, table 2 and table 3). The merchandise trade balance recorded a large deficit of 645.1 mln US$ (see graph 1). The largest merchandise trade balance was with MDG Latin America and the Caribbean at -243.9 mln US$ (see graph 4). Merchandise exports in Belize were moderately concentrated amongst partners; imports were diversified. The top 6 partners accounted for 80 percent or more of exports and 8 partners accounted for 80 percent or more of imports (see graph 5). In 2013, the value of exports of services of Belize increased substantially by 10.3 percent, reaching 447.8 mln US$, while its imports of services increased substantially by 11.6 percent and reached 207.8 mln US$ (see graph 2). There was a large trade in services surplus of 240.1 mln US$.

Graph 1: Total merchandise trade, by value
(Bln US$ by year)

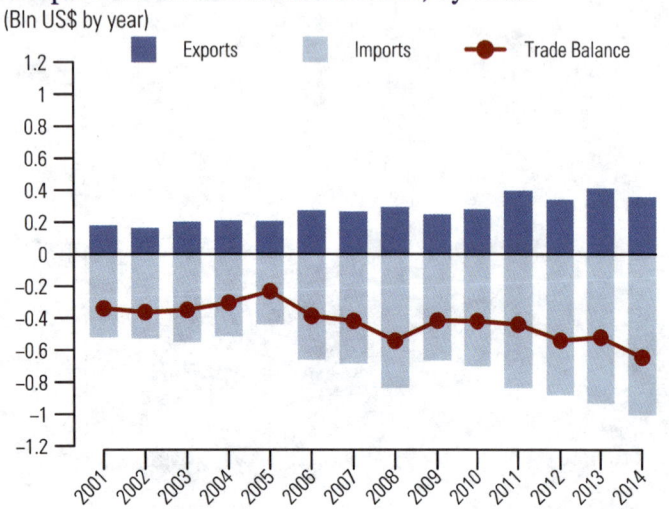

Graph 2: Total services trade, by value
(Mln US$ by year)

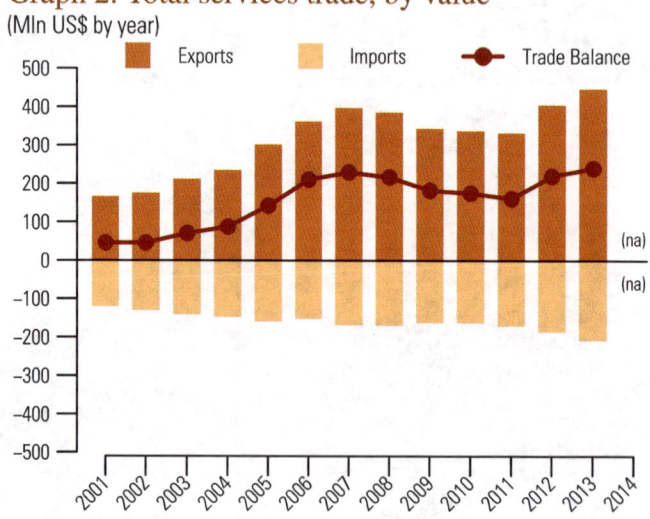

Exports Profile:

"Food, animals + beverages, tobacco" (SITC section 0+1), "Mineral fuels, lubricants" (SITC section 3) and "Not classified elsewhere in the SITC" (SITC section 9) were the largest commodity groups for exports in 2014, representing respectively 55.5, 16.3 and 16.2 percent of exported goods (see table 2). From 2012 to 2014, the largest export commodity was "Petroleum oils and oils obtained from bituminous minerals, crude" (HS code 2709) (see table 1). The top three destinations for merchandise exports were the United States, the United Kingdom and the Netherlands, accounting for respectively 41.1, 22.5 and 5.9 percent of total exports. "Travel" (EBOPS code 236) accounted for the largest share of exports of services in 2013 at 351.0 mln US$, followed by "Other business services" (EBOPS code 268) at 33.7 mln US$ and "Government services, n.i.e." (EBOPS code 291) at 26.6 mln US$ (see graph 3).

Graph 3: Exports of services by EBOPS category
(% share in 2013)

- Travel (78.4 %)
- Other business (7.5 %)
- Gov. services, n.i.e. (5.9 %)
- Transportation (5.2 %)
- Remaining (3.0 %)

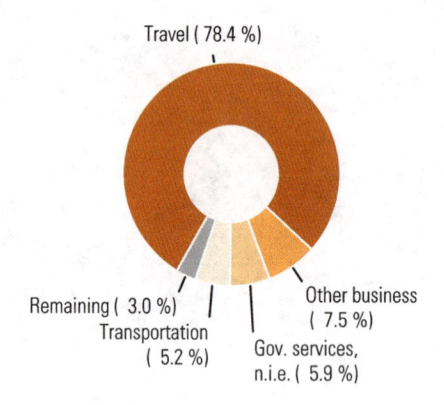

Table 1: Top 10 export commodities 2012 to 2014

HS code	4-digit heading of Harmonized System 2007	Value (million US$) 2012	2013	2014	Unit value 2012	2013	2014	Unit	SITC code
	All Commodities	340.4	411.4	359.1					
2709	Petroleum oils and oils obtained from bituminous minerals, crude	93.2	70.1	51.1	7.1	9.7	1.3	US$/kg	333
2009	Fruit juices (including grape must) and vegetable juices	74.0	54.7	46.2	2.2	1.8	1.9	US$/kg	059
1701	Cane or beet sugar and chemically pure sucrose, in solid form	53.8	53.7	55.1	0.5	0.5	0.5	US$/kg	061
0306	Crustaceans, whether in shell or not	28.0	54.8	50.9	5.1	7.5	7.5	US$/kg	036
9999	Commodities not specified according to kind	0.1	46.7	58.0					931
0803	Bananas, including plantains, fresh or dried	47.4	44.2	...	0.5	0.4		US$/kg	057
2309	Preparations of a kind used in animal feeding	0.4	13.6	12.5	0.2	0.3	0.2	US$/kg	081
0807	Melons (including watermelons) and papaws (papayas), fresh	7.8	10.3	6.6	0.4	0.4	0.4	US$/kg	057
0713	Dried leguminous vegetables, shelled, whether or not skinned or split	5.4	8.0	8.3	1.0	1.3	1.4	US$/kg	054
2710	Petroleum oils, other than crude	...	10.6	7.3		1.0	1.0	US$/kg	334

Source: UN Comtrade and UN ServiceTrade

Belize

Services Imports and Exports: EBOPS 2002 categories

Table 2: Merchandise exports by SITC
(Value in million US$, growth and shares in percentage)

SITC	2014	Avg. Growth rates 2010-2014	Avg. Growth rates 2013-2014	2014 share
Total	359.1	6.2	-12.7	100.0
0+1	199.4	3.8	-22.3	55.5
2+4	4.9	4.8	2.2	1.4
3	58.4	-13.0	-27.6	16.3
5	4.5	19.2	48.7	1.2
6	5.1	37.0	4.1	1.4
7	18.1	372.5	59.2	5.0
8	10.7	171.9	220.1	3.0
9	58.0	235.9	24.1	16.2

Table 3: Merchandise imports by SITC
(Value in million US$, growth and shares in percentage)

SITC	2014	Avg. Growth rates 2010-2014	Avg. Growth rates 2013-2014	2014 share
Total	1 004.3	9.4	7.8	100.0
0+1	218.1	18.0	75.4	21.7
2+4	24.4	22.9	44.4	2.4
3	151.6	7.2	7.3	15.1
5	91.2	8.3	8.9	9.1
6	134.9	7.2	18.5	13.4
7	215.1	15.2	24.9	21.4
8	165.3	4.4	144.0	16.5
9	3.7	-42.0	-98.2	0.4

SITC Legend

SITC Code	Description
Total	All commodities
0+1	Food, animals + beverages, tobacco
2+4	Crude materials + anim. & veg. oils
3	Mineral fuels, lubricants
5	Chemicals
6	Goods classified chiefly by material
7	Machinery and transport equipment
8	Miscellaneous manufactured articles
9	Not classified elsewhere in the SITC

Graph 4: Merchandise trade balance
(Mln US$ by MDG Regions in 2014)

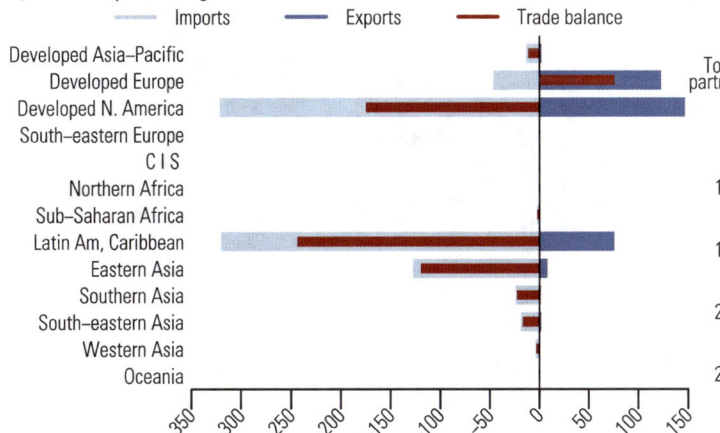

Graph 5: Partner concentration of merchandise trade
(Cumulative share by ranked partners in 2014)

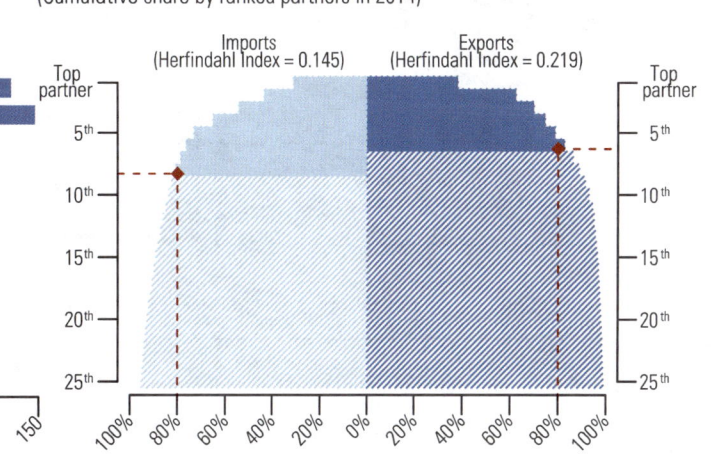

Imports (Herfindahl Index = 0.145)
Exports (Herfindahl Index = 0.219)

Graph 6: Imports of services by EBOPS category
(% share in 2013)

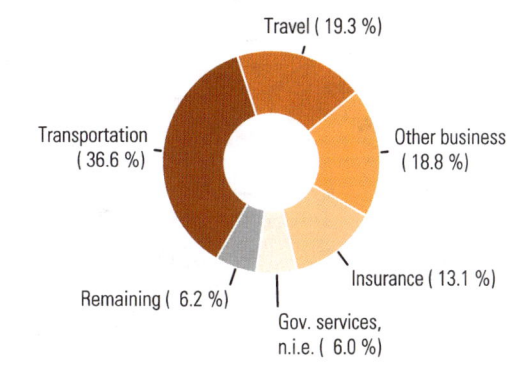

- Travel (19.3 %)
- Transportation (36.6 %)
- Other business (18.8 %)
- Insurance (13.1 %)
- Gov. services, n.i.e. (6.0 %)
- Remaining (6.2 %)

Imports Profile:

"Food, animals + beverages, tobacco" (SITC section 0+1), "Machinery and transport equipment" (SITC section 7) and "Miscellaneous manufactured articles" (SITC section 8) were the largest commodity groups for imports in 2014, representing respectively 21.7, 21.4 and 16.5 percent of imported goods (see table 3). From 2012 to 2014, the largest import commodity was "Commodities not specified according to kind" (HS code 9999) (see table 4). The top three partners for merchandise imports were the United States, Curaçao and China, accounting for respectively 30.9, 13.0 and 11.5 percent of total imports. "Transportation" (EBOPS code 205) accounted for the largest share of imports of services in 2013 at 76.0 mln US$, followed by "Travel" (EBOPS code 236) at 40.1 mln US$ and "Other business services" (EBOPS code 268) at 39.1 mln US$ (see graph 6).

Table 4: Top 10 import commodities 2012 to 2014

HS code	4-digit heading of Harmonized System 2007	Value 2012	Value 2013	Value 2014	Unit value 2012	Unit value 2013	Unit value 2014	Unit	SITC code
	All Commodities	880.3	931.2	1 004.3					
9999	Commodities not specified according to kind	212.1	211.1	3.7					931
2710	Petroleum oils, other than crude	130.0	127.3	134.9	1.1	1.0	1.1	US$/kg	334
2402	Cigars, cheroots, cigarillos and cigarettes	6.9	8.9	59.4	26.1	31.7	5.6	US$/kg	122
8704	Motor vehicles for the transport of goods	14.1	22.3	28.1		9.1		thsd US$/unit	782
8703	Motor cars and other motor vehicles principally designed for the transport	15.5	17.1	20.8	18.9	4.1	22.1	thsd US$/unit	781
2711	Petroleum gases and other gaseous hydrocarbons	13.1	13.9	16.2	0.9	0.9	0.9	US$/kg	343
2523	Portland cement, aluminous cement, slag cement	12.2	14.9	14.2	0.1	0.1	0.1	US$/kg	661
3105	Mineral or chemical fertilisers	15.2	13.1	11.0	0.9	0.5	0.5	US$/kg	562
3808	Insecticides, rodenticides, fungicides, herbicides	11.4	13.5	13.4	4.2	4.6	4.7	US$/kg	591
2309	Preparations of a kind used in animal feeding	6.8	5.8	23.7	0.8	1.0	0.9	US$/kg	081

2014 International Trade Statistics Yearbook, Vol. I Source: UN Comtrade and UN ServiceTrade

Benin

Goods Imports: CIF, by origin **Goods Exports:** FOB, by last known destination **Trade System:** General

Overview:
In 2014, the value of merchandise exports of Benin increased substantially by 58.0 percent to reach 951.0 mln US$, while its merchandise imports increased substantially by 22.3 percent to reach 3.6 bln US$ (see graph 1, table 2 and table 3). The merchandise trade balance recorded a large deficit of 2.6 bln US$ (see graph 1). The largest merchandise trade balance was with MDG Developed Europe at -916.5 mln US$ (see graph 4). Merchandise exports in Benin were diversified amongst partners; imports were also diversified. The top 15 partners accounted for 80 percent or more of exports and 16 partners accounted for 80 percent or more of imports (see graph 5). In 2012, the value of exports of services of Benin decreased slightly by 1.5 percent, reaching 407.1 mln US$, while its imports of services increased substantially by 13.1 percent and reached 569.6 mln US$ (see graph 2). There was a moderate trade in services deficit of 162.4 mln US$.

Graph 1: Total merchandise trade, by value
(Bln US$ by year)

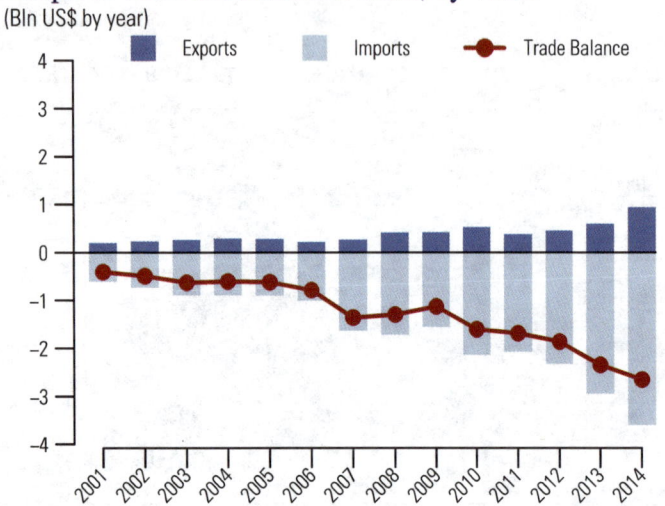

Graph 2: Total services trade, by value
(Mln US$ by year)

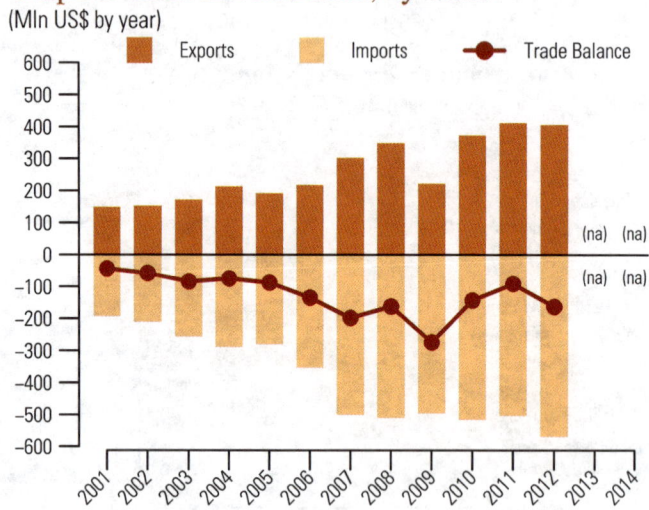

Exports Profile:
"Crude materials + anim. & veg. oils" (SITC section 2+4), "Machinery and transport equipment" (SITC section 7) and "Food, animals + beverages, tobacco" (SITC section 0+1) were the largest commodity groups for exports in 2014, representing respectively 35.0, 23.0 and 13.8 percent of exported goods (see table 2). From 2012 to 2014, the largest export commodity was "Cotton, not carded or combed" (HS code 5201) (see table 1). The top three destinations for merchandise exports were China, India and Nigeria, accounting for respectively 16.4, 10.1 and 7.9 percent of total exports. "Travel" (EBOPS code 236) accounted for the largest share of exports of services in 2012 at 169.4 mln US$, followed by "Transportation" (EBOPS code 205) at 110.6 mln US$ and "Financial services" (EBOPS code 260) at 41.2 mln US$ (see graph 3).

Graph 3: Exports of services by EBOPS category
(% share in 2012)

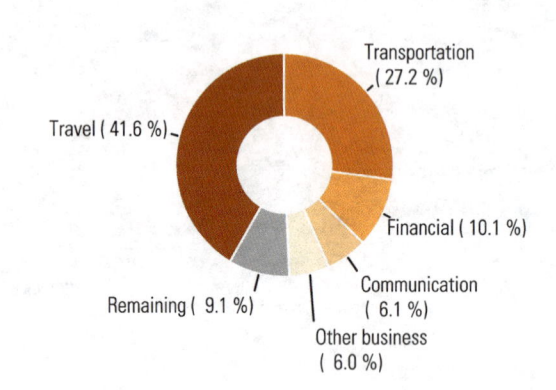

- Transportation (27.2%)
- Travel (41.6%)
- Financial (10.1%)
- Communication (6.1%)
- Other business (6.0%)
- Remaining (9.1%)

Table 1: Top 10 export commodities 2012 to 2014

HS code	4-digit heading of Harmonized System 2002	Value (million US$) 2012	2013	2014	Unit value 2012	2013	2014	Unit	SITC code
	All Commodities	460.3	602.0	951.0					
5201	Cotton, not carded or combed	148.1	235.3	287.9	1.5	1.5	1.6	US$/kg	263
0801	Coconuts, Brazil nuts and cashew nuts, fresh or dried	50.4	62.5	65.1	0.5	0.5	0.6	US$/kg	057
2710	Petroleum oils, other than crude	37.3	34.8	100.2	1.0	1.0	1.0	US$/kg	334
8431	Parts suitable for use principally with the machinery of headings 84.25	0.3	2.8	73.0	3.0	13.3	14.9	US$/kg	723
7213	Bars and rods, hot-rolled, in irregularly wound coils	32.1	25.3	13.0	0.8	0.7	0.6	US$/kg	676
7108	Gold (including gold plated with platinum)	19.5	21.3	21.6	2.0	2.0	2.0	thsd US$/kg	971
2523	Portland cement, aluminous cement, slag cement	2.2	13.0	38.5	0.1	0.1	0.1	US$/kg	661
0802	Other nuts, fresh or dried	8.6	14.8	22.5	0.5	0.6	0.6	US$/kg	057
8802	Other aircraft (for example, helicopters, aeroplanes); spacecraft	...	...	44.7					792
8903	Yachts and other vessels for pleasure or sports; rowing boats and canoes	...	0.1	44.2					793

Benin

Services Imports and Exports: EBOPS 2002 categories

Table 2: Merchandise exports by SITC
(Value in million US$, growth and shares in percentage)

SITC	2014	Avg. Growth rates 2010-2014	Avg. Growth rates 2013-2014	2014 share
Total	951.0	15.5	58.0	100.0
0+1	131.1	-14.6	-4.0	13.8
2+4	332.6	23.3	15.6	35.0
3	104.0	27.1	179.4	10.9
5	9.6	20.7	72.9	1.0
6	116.3	27.7	26.6	12.2
7	219.0	63.1	1073.9	23.0
8	16.7	76.0	532.3	1.8
9	21.6	-1.7	0.2	2.3

Table 3: Merchandise imports by SITC
(Value in million US$, growth and shares in percentage)

SITC	2014	Avg. Growth rates 2010-2014	Avg. Growth rates 2013-2014	2014 share
Total	3596.1	13.9	22.3	100.0
0+1	1622.5	24.7	49.5	45.1
2+4	175.4	-5.4	-4.9	4.9
3	515.0	5.3	24.1	14.3
5	179.4	5.2	10.1	5.0
6	360.7	6.6	-13.2	10.0
7	650.1	21.5	9.9	18.1
8	91.8	-2.5	12.1	2.6
9	1.2	110.2	-71.1	0.0

SITC Legend

SITC Code	Description
Total	All commodities
0+1	Food, animals + beverages, tobacco
2+4	Crude materials + anim. & veg. oils
3	Mineral fuels, lubricants
5	Chemicals
6	Goods classified chiefly by material
7	Machinery and transport equipment
8	Miscellaneous manufactured articles
9	Not classified elsewhere in the SITC

Graph 4: Merchandise trade balance
(Bln US$ by MDG Regions in 2014)

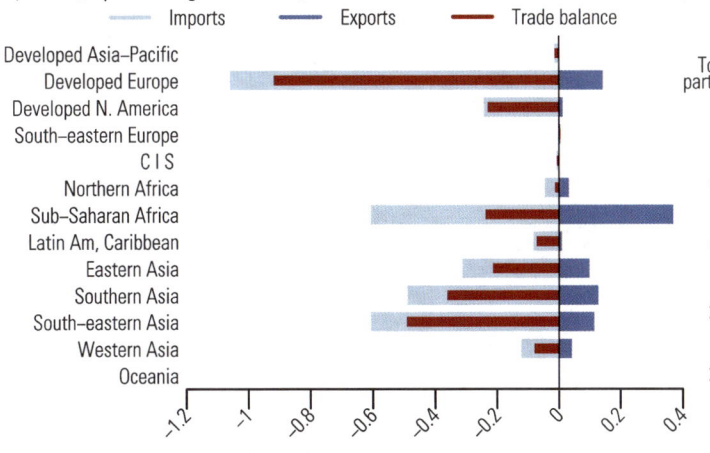

Graph 5: Partner concentration of merchandise trade
(Cumulative share by ranked partners in 2014)

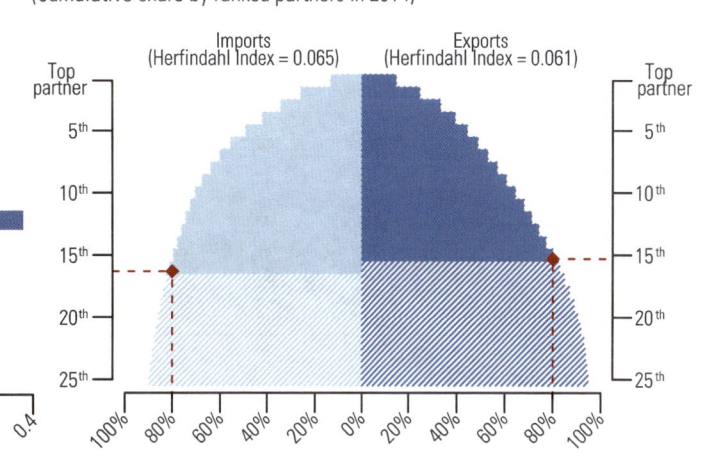

Imports (Herfindahl Index = 0.065)
Exports (Herfindahl Index = 0.061)

Graph 6: Imports of services by EBOPS category
(% share in 2012)

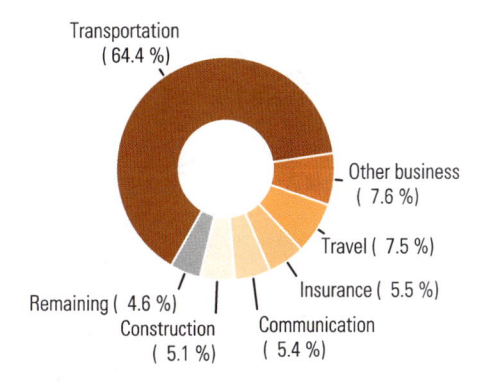

- Transportation (64.4 %)
- Other business (7.6 %)
- Travel (7.5 %)
- Insurance (5.5 %)
- Communication (5.4 %)
- Construction (5.1 %)
- Remaining (4.6 %)

Imports Profile:

"Food, animals + beverages, tobacco" (SITC section 0+1), "Machinery and transport equipment" (SITC section 7) and "Mineral fuels, lubricants" (SITC section 3) were the largest commodity groups for imports in 2014, representing respectively 45.1, 18.1 and 14.3 percent of imported goods (see table 3). From 2012 to 2014, the largest import commodity was "Rice" (HS code 1006) (see table 4). The top three partners for merchandise imports were France, India and Togo, accounting for respectively 10.8, 10.2 and 9.0 percent of total imports. "Transportation" (EBOPS code 205) accounted for the largest share of imports of services in 2012 at 366.8 mln US$, followed by "Other business services" (EBOPS code 268) at 43.4 mln US$ and "Travel" (EBOPS code 236) at 42.5 mln US$ (see graph 6).

Table 4: Top 10 import commodities 2012 to 2014

HS code	4-digit heading of Harmonized System 2002	Value (million US$) 2012	2013	2014	Unit value 2012	2013	2014	Unit	SITC code
	All Commodities	2316.4	2940.7	3596.1					
1006	Rice	315.2	595.4	1023.4	0.6	0.4	0.7	US$/kg	042
2710	Petroleum oils, other than crude	358.0	261.5	348.8	0.7	0.8	0.7	US$/kg	334
0207	Meat and edible offal, of the poultry of heading 01.05	217.9	229.3	244.9	1.2	1.3	1.2	US$/kg	012
2716	Electrical energy	122.0	136.8	136.3	70.2	66.1	60.6	US$/MWh	351
3004	Medicaments (excluding goods of heading 30.02, 30.05 or 30.06)	72.8	77.9	89.8	7.3	15.1	10.8	US$/kg	542
2523	Portland cement, aluminous cement, slag cement	79.5	82.2	46.6	0.1	0.1	0.1	US$/kg	661
8905	Light-vessels, fire-floats, dredgers, floating cranes and other vessels	0.0	50.4	149.3					793
8703	Motor cars and other motor vehicles principally designed for the transport	65.1	63.6	70.1	14.3	18.1	18.3	thsd US$/unit	781
1511	Palm oil and its fractions	62.0	66.2	50.9	0.7	0.7	0.8	US$/kg	422
6309	Worn clothing and other worn articles	55.9	56.3	54.8	1.1	1.1	1.1	US$/kg	269

Source: UN Comtrade and UN ServiceTrade

Bermuda

Goods Imports: CIF, by origin   **Goods Exports:** FOB, by last known destination   **Trade System:** General

Overview:
In 2014, the value of merchandise exports of Bermuda decreased substantially by 44.9 percent to reach 12.0 mln US$, while its merchandise imports decreased slightly by 3.4 percent to reach 961.1 mln US$ (see graph 1, table 2 and table 3). The merchandise trade balance recorded a large deficit of 949.1 mln US$ (see graph 1). The largest merchandise trade balance was with MDG Developed North America at -805.0 mln US$ (see graph 4). Merchandise exports in Bermuda were highly concentrated amongst partners; imports were also highly concentrated. The top 2 partners accounted for 80 percent or more of exports and 2 partners accounted for 80 percent or more of imports (see graph 5). In 2013, the value of exports of services of Bermuda decreased slightly by 0.7 percent, reaching 1.4 bln US$, while its imports of services increased slightly by 0.2 percent and reached 898.3 mln US$ (see graph 2). There was a moderate trade in services surplus of 472.3 mln US$.

Graph 1: Total merchandise trade, by value
(Bln US$ by year)

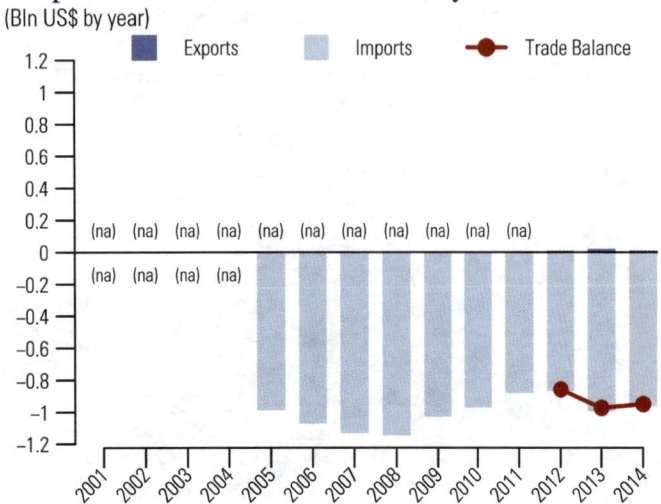

Graph 2: Total services trade, by value
(Bln US$ by year)

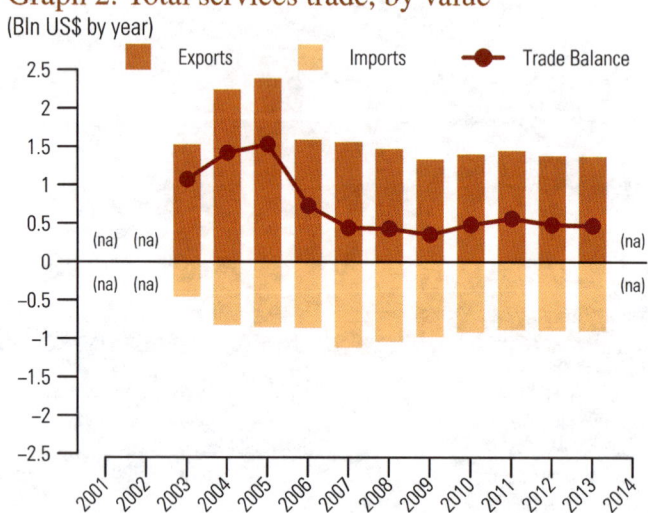

Exports Profile:
"Machinery and transport equipment" (SITC section 7), "Miscellaneous manufactured articles" (SITC section 8) and "Food, animals + beverages, tobacco" (SITC section 0+1) were the largest commodity groups for exports in 2014, representing respectively 31.9, 29.0 and 23.7 percent of exported goods (see table 2). From 2012 to 2014, the largest export commodity was "Other string musical instruments (for example, guitars, violins, harps)" (HS code 9202) (see table 1). The top three destinations for merchandise exports were the United States, the United Kingdom and Areas nes, accounting for respectively 48.6, 37.5 and 10.4 percent of total exports. "Other business services" (EBOPS code 268) accounted for the largest share of exports of services in 2013 at 490.3 mln US$, followed by "Travel" (EBOPS code 236) at 439.1 mln US$ and "Insurance services" (EBOPS code 253) at 77.6 mln US$ (see graph 3).

Graph 3: Exports of services by EBOPS category
(% share in 2013)

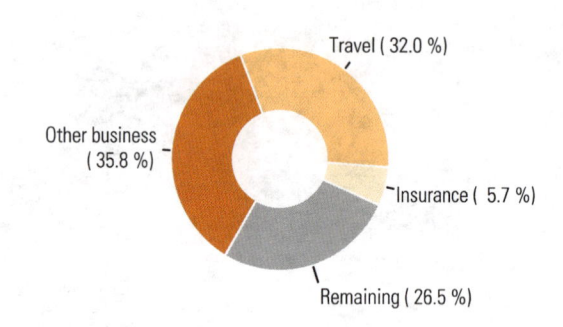

- Travel (32.0 %)
- Other business (35.8 %)
- Insurance (5.7 %)
- Remaining (26.5 %)

Table 1: Top 10 export commodities 2012 to 2014

HS code	4-digit heading of Harmonized System 2012	Value (million US$) 2012	2013	2014	Unit value 2012	2013	2014	Unit	SITC code
	All Commodities	9.6	21.7	12.0					
9202	Other string musical instruments (for example, guitars, violins, harps)	0.0	10.0	0.0			0.7	thsd US$/unit	898
2208	Alcohol of a strength by volume of less than 80 % vol	1.3	...	2.4			3.7	US$/litre	112
8525	Transmission apparatus for radio-telephony, radio-broadcasting	0.1	1.8	0.9	4.5	3.1		thsd US$/unit	764
9209	Parts (for example, mechanisms for musical boxes) and accessories	0.0	2.6	0.0	1.3	0.0		mln US$/kg	898
8803	Parts of goods of heading 88.01 or 88.02	0.5	1.9	0.1	2.2	0.4		thsd US$/kg	792
8501	Electric motors and generators (excluding generating sets)	1.4	0.0	0.0	10.3	6.4		thsd US$/unit	716
9207	Musical instruments	1.3	...	0.0			59.4	US$/unit	898
9705	Collections and collectors'pieces of zoological, botanical, mineralogical	...	...	1.3			1.3	mln US$/kg	896
8511	Electrical ignition or starting equipment	0.0	0.5	0.6					778
8414	Air or vacuum pumps, air or other gas compressors and fans	0.2	0.4	0.4					743

Source: UN Comtrade and UN ServiceTrade

Bermuda

Services Imports and Exports: EBOPS 2002 categories

Table 2: Merchandise exports by SITC
(Value in million US$, growth and shares in percentage)

SITC	2014	Avg. Growth rates 2010-2014	2013-2014	2014 share
Total	12.0	...	-44.9	100.0
0+1	2.8	...	569.8	23.7
2+4	0.0	...	-91.6	0.1
5	0.3	...	270.6	2.9
6	1.3	...	130.1	11.2
7	3.8	...	-39.8	31.9
8	3.5	...	-75.5	29.0
9	0.2	...	934.2	1.3

Table 3: Merchandise imports by SITC
(Value in million US$, growth and shares in percentage)

SITC	2014	Avg. Growth rates 2010-2014	2013-2014	2014 share
Total	961.1	-0.2	-3.4	100.0
0+1	197.5	12.1	4.8	20.6
2+4	11.1	4.3	6.0	1.2
3	152.5	11.8	-3.3	15.9
5	63.2	8.9	-9.6	6.6
6	79.4	-2.7	-16.5	8.3
7	147.3	-2.5	-0.9	15.3
8	198.0	0.3	-6.2	20.6
9	112.1	-17.8	-0.9	11.7

SITC Legend

SITC Code	Description
Total	All commodities
0+1	Food, animals + beverages, tobacco
2+4	Crude materials + anim. & veg. oils
3	Mineral fuels, lubricants
5	Chemicals
6	Goods classified chiefly by material
7	Machinery and transport equipment
8	Miscellaneous manufactured articles
9	Not classified elsewhere in the SITC

Graph 4: Merchandise trade balance
(Mln US$ by MDG Regions in 2014)

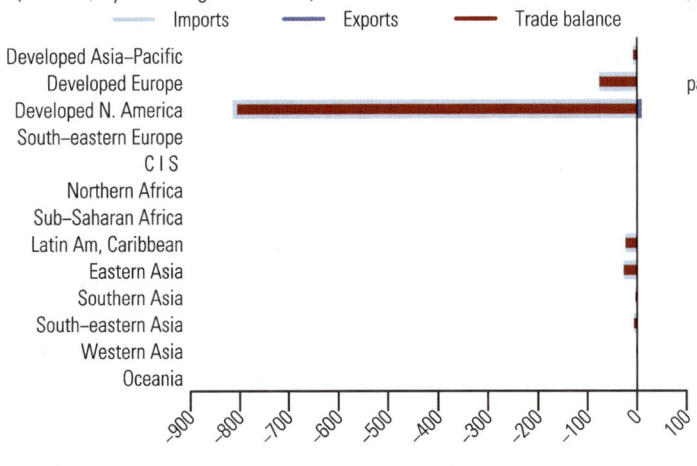

Graph 5: Partner concentration of merchandise trade
(Cumulative share by ranked partners in 2014)

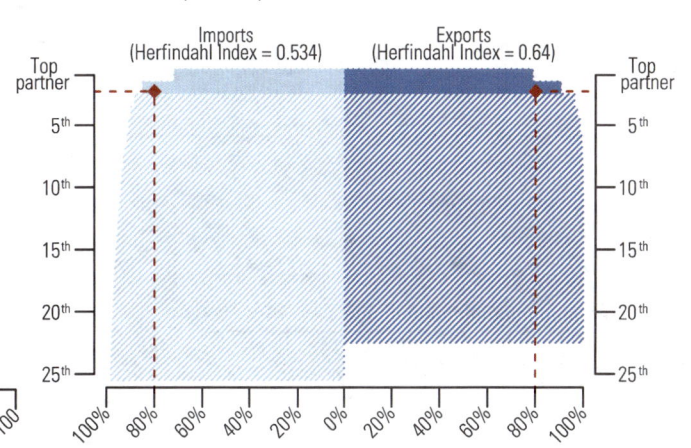

Imports (Herfindahl Index = 0.534) Exports (Herfindahl Index = 0.64)

Graph 6: Imports of services by EBOPS category
(% share in 2013)

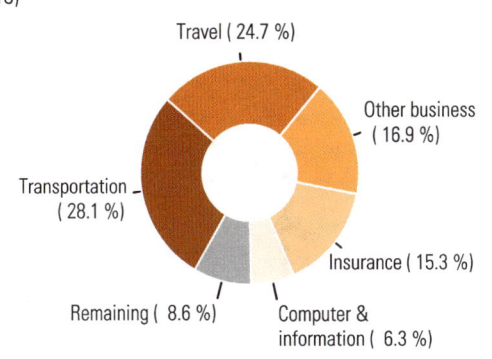

- Travel (24.7 %)
- Other business (16.9 %)
- Insurance (15.3 %)
- Computer & information (6.3 %)
- Remaining (8.6 %)
- Transportation (28.1 %)

Imports Profile:

"Miscellaneous manufactured articles" (SITC section 8), "Food, animals + beverages, tobacco" (SITC section 0+1) and "Mineral fuels, lubricants" (SITC section 3) were the largest commodity groups for imports in 2014, representing respectively 20.6, 20.6 and 15.9 percent of imported goods (see table 3). From 2012 to 2014, the largest import commodity was "Petroleum oils, other than crude" (HS code 2710) (see table 4). The top three partners for merchandise imports were the United States, Canada and the United Kingdom, accounting for respectively 70.0, 12.1 and 3.4 percent of total imports. "Transportation" (EBOPS code 205) accounted for the largest share of imports of services in 2013 at 252.3 mln US$, followed by "Travel" (EBOPS code 236) at 221.8 mln US$ and "Other business services" (EBOPS code 268) at 152.1 mln US$ (see graph 6).

Table 4: Top 10 import commodities 2012 to 2014

HS code	4-digit heading of Harmonized System 2012	Value (million US$) 2012	2013	2014	Unit value 2012	2013	2014	Unit	SITC code
	All Commodities	866.9	994.6	961.1					
2710	Petroleum oils, other than crude	78.7	153.9	149.0		0.9	0.7	US$/kg	334
9999	Commodities not specified according to kind	119.0	111.4	111.9					931
4907	Unused postage, revenue or similar stamps of current or new issue	71.8	82.5	65.3		15.6	0.2	thsd US$/kg	892
3004	Medicaments (excluding goods of heading 30.02, 30.05 or 30.06)	21.7	23.5	20.7		34.6	27.5	US$/kg	542
9403	Other furniture and parts thereof	15.4	18.0	20.6					821
8703	Motor cars and other motor vehicles principally designed for the transport	11.4	13.3	16.8		13.4	12.3	thsd US$/unit	781
1905	Bread, pastry, cakes, biscuits and other bakers'wares	12.4	13.1	12.7		2.2	1.6	US$/kg	048
2204	Wine of fresh grapes, including fortified wines	12.3	10.9	14.3		10.0	9.7	US$/litre	112
8517	Electrical apparatus for line telephony or line telegraphy	15.3	9.7	10.4					764
2202	Waters with added sugar	9.5	8.8	9.4		0.3	0.5	US$/litre	111

2014 International Trade Statistics Yearbook, Vol. I   Source: UN Comtrade and UN ServiceTrade

Bhutan

Goods Imports: CIF, by origin **Goods Exports: FOB, by last known destination** **Trade System: General**

Overview:
In 2012, the value of merchandise exports of Bhutan increased substantially by 17.3 percent to reach 531.2 mln US$, while its merchandise imports decreased moderately by 5.7 percent to reach 991.7 mln US$ (see graph 1, table 2 and table 3). The merchandise trade balance recorded a large deficit of 460.5 mln US$ (see graph 1). The largest merchandise trade balance was with MDG Southern Asia at -273.9 mln US$ (see graph 4). Merchandise exports in Bhutan were highly concentrated amongst partners; imports were also highly concentrated. The top 1 partner accounted for 80 percent or more of exports and 2 partners accounted for 80 percent or more of imports (see graph 5). In 2013, the value of exports of services of Bhutan decreased substantially by 42.4 percent, reaching 73.8 mln US$, while its imports of services decreased substantially by 46.7 percent and reached 100.9 mln US$ (see graph 2). There was a moderate trade in services deficit of 27.2 mln US$.

Graph 1: Total merchandise trade, by value
(Bln US$ by year)

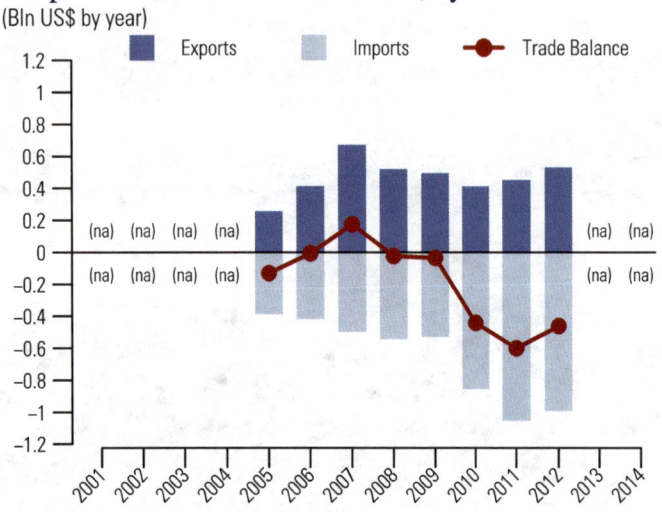

Graph 2: Total services trade, by value
(Mln US$ by year)

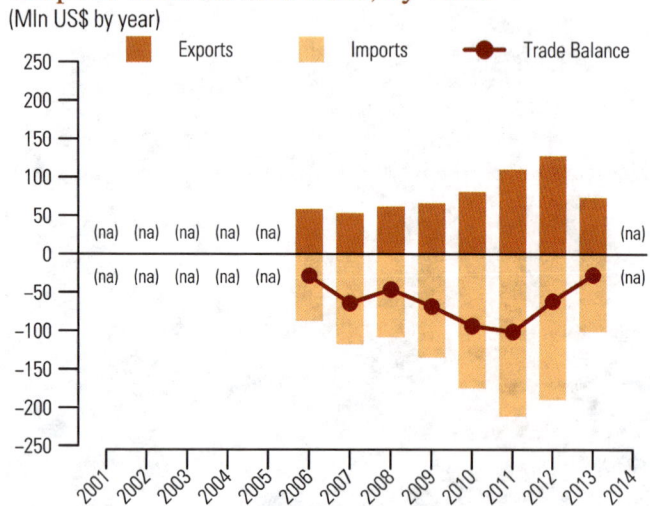

Exports Profile:
"Goods classified chiefly by material" (SITC section 6), "Mineral fuels, lubricants" (SITC section 3) and "Crude materials + anim. & veg. oils" (SITC section 2+4) were the largest commodity groups for exports in 2012, representing respectively 45.5, 32.9 and 7.6 percent of exported goods (see table 2). From 2010 to 2012, the largest export commodity was "Ferro-alloys" (HS code 7202) (see table 1). The top three destinations for merchandise exports were India, China, Hong Kong SAR and Bangladesh, accounting for respectively 84.5, 8.8 and 4.9 percent of total exports. "Travel" (EBOPS code 236) accounted for the largest share of exports of services in 2013 at 48.2 mln US$, followed by "Transportation" (EBOPS code 205) at 22.0 mln US$ (see graph 3).

Graph 3: Exports of services by EBOPS category
(% share in 2013)

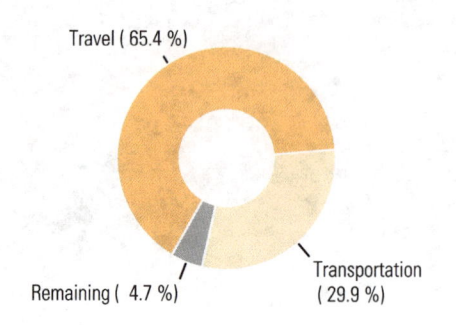

Travel (65.4 %)
Transportation (29.9 %)
Remaining (4.7 %)

Table 1: Top 10 export commodities 2010 to 2012

HS code	4-digit heading of Harmonized System 2007	Value (million US$) 2010	2011	2012	Unit value 2010	2011	2012	Unit	SITC code
	All Commodities	413.5	453.0	531.2					
7202	Ferro-alloys	124.9	132.0	127.5	1.3	1.4	1.2	US$/kg	671
2716	Electrical energy	...	...	170.6			34.9	thsd US$/MWh	351
8523	Prepared unrecorded media for sound recording	46.9	71.9	...	5.1	5.4		thsd US$/unit	898
7408	Copper wire	37.7	42.9	24.2	3.8	5.6	5.7	US$/kg	682
2849	Carbides, whether or not chemically defined	31.0	31.0	29.5	0.8	0.8	0.7	US$/kg	524
2523	Portland cement, aluminous cement, slag cement	30.0	22.9	25.1	0.1	0.1	0.1	US$/kg	661
7214	Other bars and rods of iron or non-alloy steel	16.1	25.1	27.1	0.7	0.8	0.8	US$/kg	676
2518	Dolomite, whether or not calcined or sintered	16.1	16.5	17.6	0.0	0.0	0.0	US$/kg	278
7207	Semi-finished products of iron or non-alloy steel	8.9	3.5	21.6	0.6	0.7	0.4	US$/kg	672
2520	Gypsum; anhydrite; plasters	10.5	12.1	10.3	0.0	0.0	0.0	US$/kg	273

Source: UN Comtrade and UN ServiceTrade

Bhutan

Services Imports and Exports: EBOPS 2002 categories

Table 2: Merchandise exports by SITC
(Value in million US$, growth and shares in percentage)

SITC	2012	Avg. Growth rates 2008-2012	Avg. Growth rates 2011-2012	2012 share
Total	531.2	0.5	17.3	100.0
0+1	36.7	-38.2	-2.8	6.9
2+4	40.4	55.5	-3.3	7.6
3	174.9	-9.0	2811.2	32.9
5	36.8	463.1	-3.9	6.9
6	241.7	144.4	-5.7	45.5
7	0.1	69.0	112.1	0.0
8	0.6	-2.1	-99.1	0.1
9	0.0	-30.9	155.1	0.0

Table 3: Merchandise imports by SITC
(Value in million US$, growth and shares in percentage)

SITC	2012	Avg. Growth rates 2008-2012	Avg. Growth rates 2011-2012	2012 share
Total	991.7	16.2	-5.7	100.0
0+1	116.8	15.6	17.3	11.8
2+4	85.0	6.3	-0.7	8.6
3	182.6	17.8	14.6	18.4
5	56.9	16.9	3.4	5.7
6	277.8	26.3	20.9	28.0
7	225.2	10.5	-40.9	22.7
8	38.3	11.0	-2.9	3.9
9	9.0	72.7	419.2	0.9

SITC Legend

SITC Code	Description
Total	All commodities
0+1	Food, animals + beverages, tobacco
2+4	Crude materials + anim. & veg. oils
3	Mineral fuels, lubricants
5	Chemicals
6	Goods classified chiefly by material
7	Machinery and transport equipment
8	Miscellaneous manufactured articles
9	Not classified elsewhere in the SITC

Graph 4: Merchandise trade balance
(Mln US$ by MDG Regions in 2012)

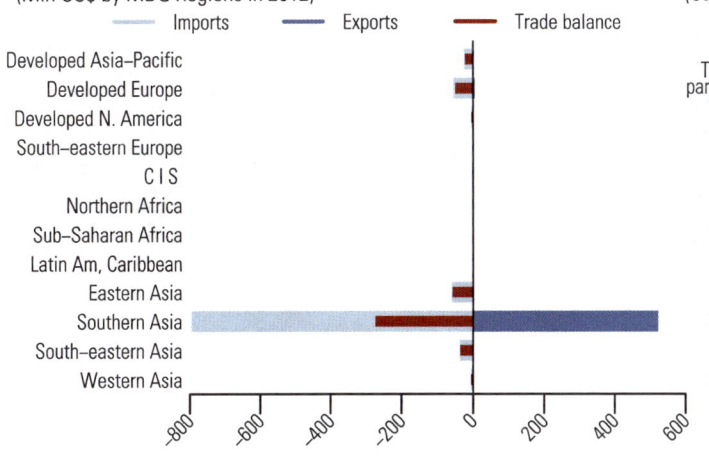

Graph 5: Partner concentration of merchandise trade
(Cumulative share by ranked partners in 2012)

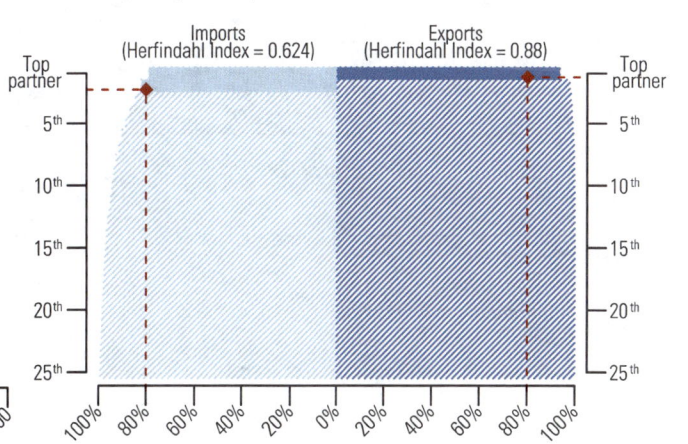

Imports (Herfindahl Index = 0.624)
Exports (Herfindahl Index = 0.88)

Graph 6: Imports of services by EBOPS category
(% share in 2013)

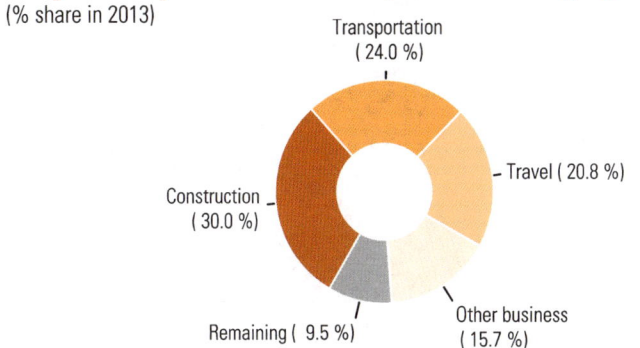

- Transportation (24.0 %)
- Travel (20.8 %)
- Other business (15.7 %)
- Remaining (9.5 %)
- Construction (30.0 %)

Imports Profile:

"Goods classified chiefly by material" (SITC section 6), "Machinery and transport equipment" (SITC section 7) and "Mineral fuels, lubricants" (SITC section 3) were the largest commodity groups for imports in 2012, representing respectively 28.0, 22.7 and 18.4 percent of imported goods (see table 3). From 2010 to 2012, the largest import commodity was "Petroleum oils, other than crude" (HS code 2710) (see table 4). The top three partners for merchandise imports were India, the Republic of Korea and Japan, accounting for respectively 75.3, 4.8 and 2.6 percent of total imports. "Construction services" (EBOPS code 249) accounted for the largest share of imports of services in 2013 at 30.2 mln US$, followed by "Transportation" (EBOPS code 205) at 24.2 mln US$ and "Travel" (EBOPS code 236) at 21.0 mln US$ (see graph 6).

Table 4: Top 10 import commodities 2010 to 2012

HS code	4-digit heading of Harmonized System 2007	Value 2010	Value 2011	Value 2012	Unit value 2010	Unit value 2011	Unit value 2012	Unit	SITC code
	All Commodities	853.8	1051.7	991.7					
2710	Petroleum oils, other than crude	91.9	120.6	130.6					334
8703	Motor cars and other motor vehicles principally designed for the transport	31.2	69.2	21.4	9.0	*10.9*	9.7	thsd US$/unit	781
7408	Copper wire	40.5	42.6	26.5	5.0	5.7	5.9	US$/kg	682
7203	Ferrous products obtained by direct reduction of iron ore	26.9	30.7	40.7	0.4	0.5	0.4	US$/kg	671
8429	Self-propelled bulldozers, angledozers, graders, levellers, scrapers	36.8	38.9	17.5	11.1	32.2	52.7	thsd US$/unit	723
8704	Motor vehicles for the transport of goods	31.6	46.6	13.4	20.5	19.7	18.7	thsd US$/unit	782
7308	Structures (excluding prefabricated buildings of heading 94.06)	19.6	15.6	30.2	1.5	1.7	1.2	US$/kg	691
1006	Rice	18.5	18.4	23.4	0.4	0.3	0.3	US$/kg	042
4402	Wood charcoal (including shell or nut charcoal), whether or not agglomerated	15.5	23.5	18.6	0.2	0.3	0.3	US$/kg	245
7204	Ferrous waste and scrap; remelting scrap ingots of iron or steel	15.4	16.9	21.4	0.4	0.5	0.5	US$/kg	282

Bolivia (Plurinational State of)

Goods Imports: CIF, by origin **Goods Exports:** FOB, by last known destination **Trade System:** General

Overview:
In 2014, the value of merchandise exports of the Plurinational State of Bolivia increased moderately by 5.3 percent to reach 12.9 bln US$, while its merchandise imports increased substantially by 12.2 percent to reach 10.5 bln US$ (see graph 1, table 2 and table 3). The merchandise trade balance recorded a moderate surplus of 2.4 bln US$ (see graph 1). The largest merchandise trade balance was with MDG Latin America and the Caribbean at 3.4 bln US$ (see graph 4). Merchandise exports in the Plurinational State of Bolivia were moderately concentrated amongst partners; imports were diversified. The top 7 partners accounted for 80 percent or more of exports and 12 partners accounted for 80 percent or more of imports (see graph 5). In 2013, the value of exports of services of the Plurinational State of Bolivia increased slightly by 4.0 percent, reaching 1.0 bln US$, while its imports of services increased substantially by 12.5 percent and reached 2.2 bln US$ (see graph 2). There was a large trade in services deficit of 1.1 bln US$.

Graph 1: Total merchandise trade, by value
(Bln US$ by year)

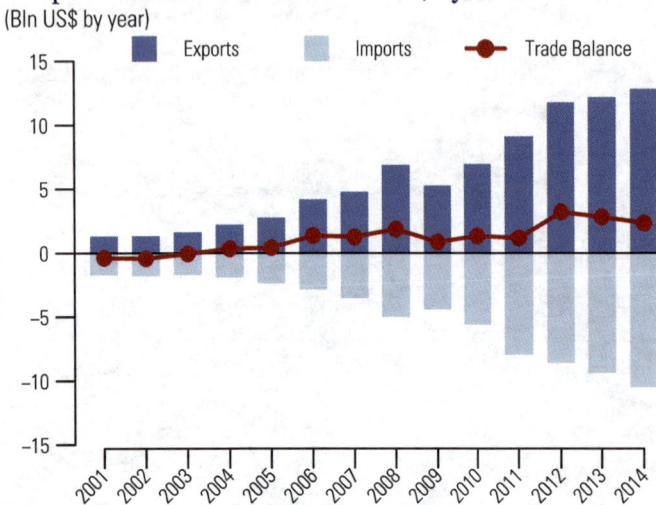

Graph 2: Total services trade, by value
(Bln US$ by year)

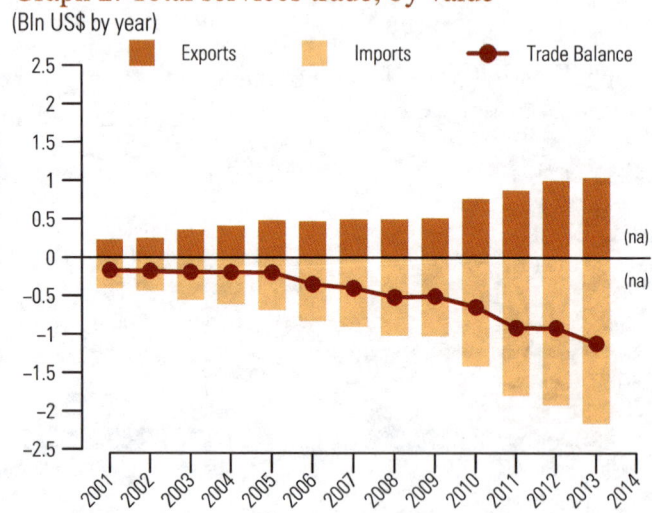

Exports Profile:
"Mineral fuels, lubricants" (SITC section 3), "Crude materials + anim. & veg. oils" (SITC section 2+4) and "Not classified elsewhere in the SITC" (SITC section 9) were the largest commodity groups for exports in 2014, representing respectively 51.7, 20.6 and 10.6 percent of exported goods (see table 2). From 2012 to 2014, the largest export commodity was "Petroleum gases and other gaseous hydrocarbons" (HS code 2711) (see table 1). The top three destinations for merchandise exports were Brazil, Argentina and the United States, accounting for respectively 31.2, 19.4 and 13.5 percent of total exports. "Travel" (EBOPS code 236) accounted for the largest share of exports of services in 2013 at 573.2 mln US$, followed by "Transportation" (EBOPS code 205) at 190.6 mln US$ and "Insurance services" (EBOPS code 253) at 106.7 mln US$ (see graph 3).

Graph 3: Exports of services by EBOPS category
(% share in 2013)

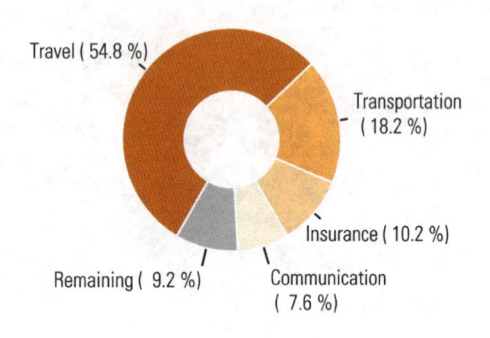

- Travel (54.8 %)
- Transportation (18.2 %)
- Insurance (10.2 %)
- Communication (7.6 %)
- Remaining (9.2 %)

Table 1: Top 10 export commodities 2012 to 2014

HS code	4-digit heading of Harmonized System 2012	Value (million US$) 2012	2013	2014	Unit value 2012	2013	2014	Unit	SITC code
	All Commodities	11 814.3	12 207.5	12 856.1					
2711	Petroleum gases and other gaseous hydrocarbons	5 478.9	6 116.8	6 011.9	0.5	0.5	0.4	US$/kg	343
2616	Precious metal ores and concentrates	1 014.0	866.5	725.9	69.3	54.1	48.1	US$/kg	289
2608	Zinc ores and concentrates	739.4	756.8	980.9	1.0	1.0	1.4	US$/kg	287
2304	Oil-cake and other solid residues	511.6	612.2	662.2	0.4	0.4	0.4	US$/kg	081
7108	Gold (including gold plated with platinum)	90.0	330.8	1 360.9	53.4	40.5	38.0	thsd US$/kg	971
2709	Petroleum oils and oils obtained from bituminous minerals, crude	392.4	511.1	582.5	0.8	0.8	0.8	US$/kg	333
7112	Waste and scrap of precious metal or of metal clad with precious metal	979.2	207.0	0.3	27.0	1.6	8.3	thsd US$/kg	971
8001	Unwrought tin	296.9	335.5	346.8	20.7	22.4	22.0	US$/kg	687
1507	Soya-bean oil and its fractions	292.6	278.1	293.7	1.1	0.9	0.8	US$/kg	421
1201	Soya beans, whether or not broken	157.8	263.8	89.8	0.5	0.5	0.5	US$/kg	222

Source: UN Comtrade and UN ServiceTrade

Bolivia (Plurinational State of)

Services Imports and Exports: EBOPS 2002 categories

Table 2: Merchandise exports by SITC
(Value in million US$, growth and shares in percentage)

SITC	2014	Avg. Growth rates 2010-2014	Avg. Growth rates 2013-2014	2014 share
Total	12 856.1	16.6	5.3	100.0
0+1	1 289.9	17.2	5.5	10.0
2+4	2 650.0	3.4	-4.8	20.6
3	6 646.5	21.9	-0.5	51.7
5	135.0	-5.1	-25.6	1.1
6	619.3	4.3	-0.4	4.8
7	6.7	2.1	-20.0	0.1
8	147.4	-2.1	-13.7	1.1
9	1 361.1	94.8	153.1	10.6

Table 3: Merchandise imports by SITC
(Value in million US$, growth and shares in percentage)

SITC	2014	Avg. Growth rates 2010-2014	Avg. Growth rates 2013-2014	2014 share
Total	10 492.1	17.0	12.2	100.0
0+1	774.7	16.7	16.4	7.4
2+4	92.2	10.9	-0.4	0.9
3	1 239.8	15.9	-4.0	11.8
5	1 418.7	10.4	3.2	13.5
6	1 834.6	13.7	13.8	17.5
7	4 298.8	22.5	18.5	41.0
8	788.5	15.4	24.6	7.5
9	44.8	12.1	-20.7	0.4

SITC Legend

SITC Code	Description
Total	All commodities
0+1	Food, animals + beverages, tobacco
2+4	Crude materials + anim. & veg. oils
3	Mineral fuels, lubricants
5	Chemicals
6	Goods classified chiefly by material
7	Machinery and transport equipment
8	Miscellaneous manufactured articles
9	Not classified elsewhere in the SITC

Graph 4: Merchandise trade balance
(Bln US$ by MDG Regions in 2014)

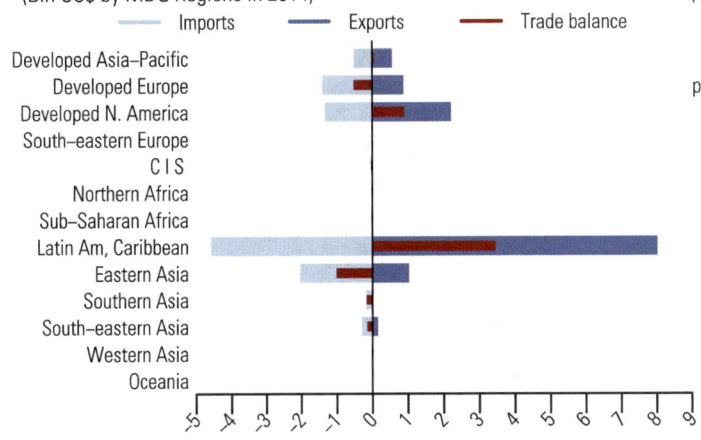

Graph 5: Partner concentration of merchandise trade
(Cumulative share by ranked partners in 2014)

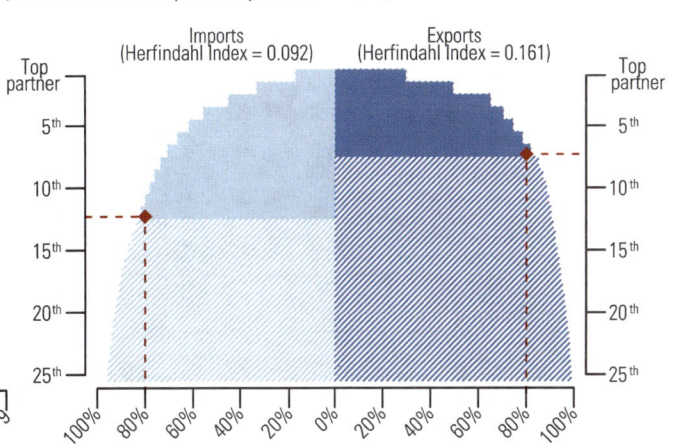

Imports (Herfindahl Index = 0.092)
Exports (Herfindahl Index = 0.161)

Graph 6: Imports of services by EBOPS category
(% share in 2013)

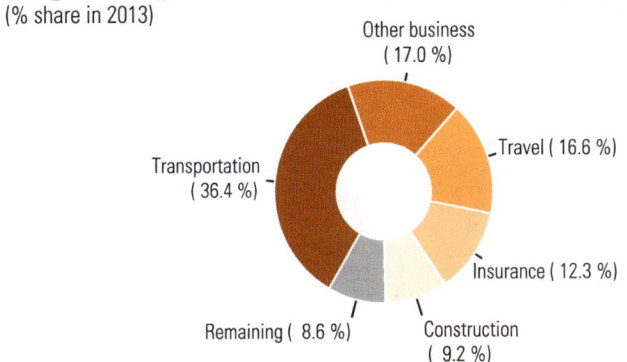

- Transportation (36.4 %)
- Other business (17.0 %)
- Travel (16.6 %)
- Insurance (12.3 %)
- Construction (9.2 %)
- Remaining (8.6 %)

Imports Profile:
"Machinery and transport equipment" (SITC section 7), "Goods classified chiefly by material" (SITC section 6) and "Chemicals" (SITC section 5) were the largest commodity groups for imports in 2014, representing respectively 41.0, 17.5 and 13.5 percent of imported goods (see table 3). From 2012 to 2014, the largest import commodity was "Petroleum oils, other than crude" (HS code 2710) (see table 4). The top three partners for merchandise imports were Brazil, China and the United States, accounting for respectively 16.8, 15.3 and 11.8 percent of total imports. "Transportation" (EBOPS code 205) accounted for the largest share of imports of services in 2013 at 786.6 mln US$, followed by "Other business services" (EBOPS code 268) at 366.8 mln US$ and "Travel" (EBOPS code 236) at 358.9 mln US$ (see graph 6).

Table 4: Top 10 import commodities 2012 to 2014

HS code	4-digit heading of Harmonized System 2012	Value 2012	Value 2013	Value 2014	Unit value 2012	Unit value 2013	Unit value 2014	Unit	SITC code
	All Commodities	8 590.1	9 353.0	10 492.1					
2710	Petroleum oils, other than crude	1 143.1	1 222.7	1 169.6	1.1	1.1	1.1	US$/kg	334
8703	Motor cars and other motor vehicles principally designed for the transport	344.3	456.1	494.1	12.4	12.2	12.0	thsd US$/unit	781
8704	Motor vehicles for the transport of goods	256.1	319.9	319.5	15.5	17.0	17.4	thsd US$/unit	782
3808	Insecticides, rodenticides, fungicides, herbicides	185.2	245.6	248.8	4.7	5.2	5.5	US$/kg	591
7214	Other bars and rods of iron or non-alloy steel	193.6	226.3	257.6	0.9	0.9	0.8	US$/kg	676
8419	Machinery, plant or laboratory equipment	81.7	329.6	249.3					741
8429	Self-propelled bulldozers, angledozers, graders, levellers, scrapers	163.5	215.7	224.5		67.5	72.1	thsd US$/unit	723
8701	Tractors (other than tractors of heading 87.09)	171.8	193.3	165.1	23.8	27.1	9.7	thsd US$/unit	722
8517	Electrical apparatus for line telephony or line telegraphy	89.1	126.5	168.4					764
8411	Turbo-jets, turbo-propellers and other gas turbines	90.9	126.4	141.2					714

2014 International Trade Statistics Yearbook, Vol. I — Source: UN Comtrade and UN ServiceTrade

Bosnia and Herzegovina

Goods Imports: CIF, by origin **Goods Exports:** FOB, by last known destination **Trade System:** Special

Overview:
In 2014, the value of merchandise exports of Bosnia and Herzegovina increased slightly by 3.6 percent to reach 5.9 bln US$, while its merchandise imports increased moderately by 6.8 percent to reach 11.0 bln US$ (see graph 1, table 2 and table 3). The merchandise trade balance recorded a large deficit of 5.1 bln US$ (see graph 1). The largest merchandise trade balance was with MDG Developed Europe at -2.1 bln US$ (see graph 4). Merchandise exports in Bosnia and Herzegovina were diversified amongst partners; imports were also diversified. The top 11 partners accounted for 80 percent or more of exports and 13 partners accounted for 80 percent or more of imports (see graph 5). In 2013, the value of exports of services of Bosnia and Herzegovina increased slightly by 4.9 percent, reaching 2.0 bln US$, while its imports of services decreased slightly by 1.8 percent and reached 483.5 mln US$ (see graph 2). There was a large trade in services surplus of 1.5 bln US$.

Graph 1: Total merchandise trade, by value
(Bln US$ by year)

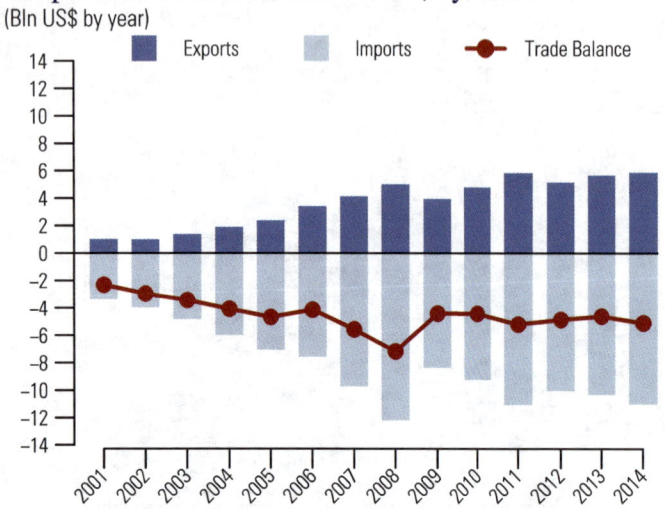

Graph 2: Total services trade, by value
(Bln US$ by year)

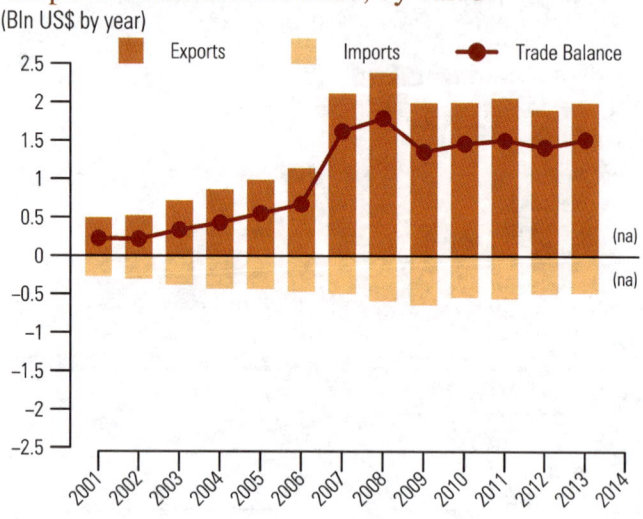

Exports Profile:
"Miscellaneous manufactured articles" (SITC section 8), "Goods classified chiefly by material" (SITC section 6) and "Machinery and transport equipment" (SITC section 7) were the largest commodity groups for exports in 2014, representing respectively 25.5, 23.4 and 14.0 percent of exported goods (see table 2). From 2012 to 2014, the largest export commodity was "Seats (other than those of heading 94.02)" (HS code 9401) (see table 1). The top three destinations for merchandise exports were Germany, Croatia and Italy, accounting for respectively 15.4, 13.3 and 12.6 percent of total exports. "Travel" (EBOPS code 236) accounted for the largest share of exports of services in 2013 at 688.4 mln US$, followed by "Transportation" (EBOPS code 205) at 329.2 mln US$ (see graph 3).

Graph 3: Exports of services by EBOPS category
(% share in 2013)

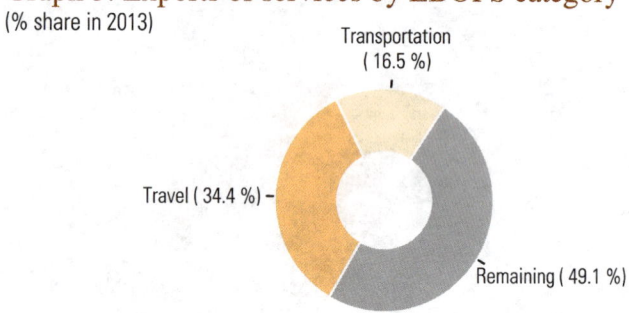

- Transportation (16.5 %)
- Travel (34.4 %)
- Remaining (49.1 %)

Table 1: Top 10 export commodities 2012 to 2014

HS code	4-digit heading of Harmonized System 2012	Value (million US$) 2012	2013	2014	Unit value 2012	2013	2014	Unit	SITC code
	All Commodities	5161.8	5687.5	5892.1					
9401	Seats (other than those of heading 94.02)	342.2	391.5	416.3					821
7601	Unwrought aluminium	300.3	269.5	249.5	2.3	2.2	2.3	US$/kg	684
2716	Electrical energy	98.6	320.3	209.4		65.6	59.5	US$/MWh	351
6403	Footwear with outer soles of rubber, plastics, leather	166.8	204.9	229.0		36.1		US$/pair	851
4407	Wood sawn or chipped lengthwise, sliced or peeled	151.3	164.7	193.6		320.3		US$/m^3	248
2710	Petroleum oils, other than crude	190.1	164.6	153.9	1.0	1.0	0.9	US$/kg	334
9999	Commodities not specified according to kind	169.4	151.2	145.3					931
9403	Other furniture and parts thereof	129.4	148.3	151.4					821
8708	Parts and accessories of the motor vehicles of headings 87.01 to 87.05	104.4	144.3	166.7	3.9	4.2	4.4	US$/kg	784
7213	Bars and rods, hot-rolled, in irregularly wound coils	103.3	99.0	101.9	0.6	0.6	0.6	US$/kg	676

Bosnia and Herzegovina

Services Imports and Exports: EBOPS 2002 categories

Table 2: Merchandise exports by SITC
(Value in million US$, growth and shares in percentage)

SITC	2014	Avg. Growth rates 2010-2014	Avg. Growth rates 2013-2014	2014 share
Total	5 892.1	5.2	3.6	100.0
0+1	350.3	2.7	-3.5	5.9
2+4	745.3	3.9	0.2	12.6
3	565.7	-6.0	-12.6	9.6
5	383.1	12.0	16.7	6.5
6	1 376.4	3.7	2.1	23.4
7	824.1	10.0	10.4	14.0
8	1 500.1	10.7	11.7	25.5
9	147.1	3.9	-12.3	2.5

Table 3: Merchandise imports by SITC
(Value in million US$, growth and shares in percentage)

SITC	2014	Avg. Growth rates 2010-2014	Avg. Growth rates 2013-2014	2014 share
Total	10 990.4	4.5	6.8	100.0
0+1	1 710.4	2.4	0.5	15.6
2+4	394.7	1.1	-1.8	3.6
3	1 831.6	0.7	-8.5	16.7
5	1 386.3	5.7	8.4	12.6
6	2 367.9	7.0	11.8	21.5
7	2 275.9	7.4	20.9	20.7
8	1 013.7	4.0	12.6	9.2
9	9.9	4.6	5.1	0.1

SITC Legend

SITC Code	Description
Total	All commodities
0+1	Food, animals + beverages, tobacco
2+4	Crude materials + anim. & veg. oils
3	Mineral fuels, lubricants
5	Chemicals
6	Goods classified chiefly by material
7	Machinery and transport equipment
8	Miscellaneous manufactured articles
9	Not classified elsewhere in the SITC

Graph 4: Merchandise trade balance
(Bln US$ by MDG Regions in 2014)

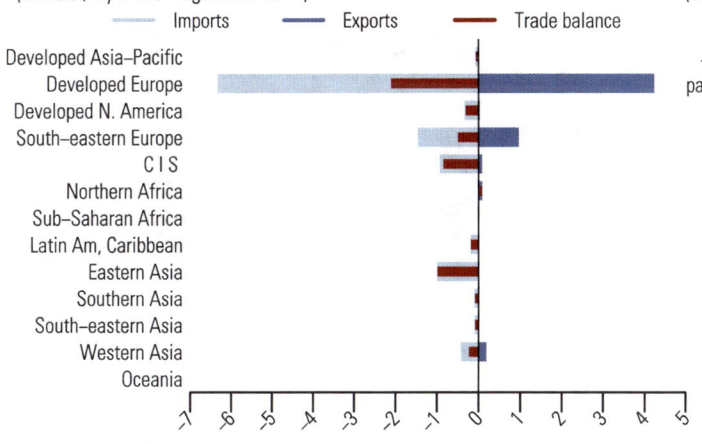

Graph 5: Partner concentration of merchandise trade
(Cumulative share by ranked partners in 2014)

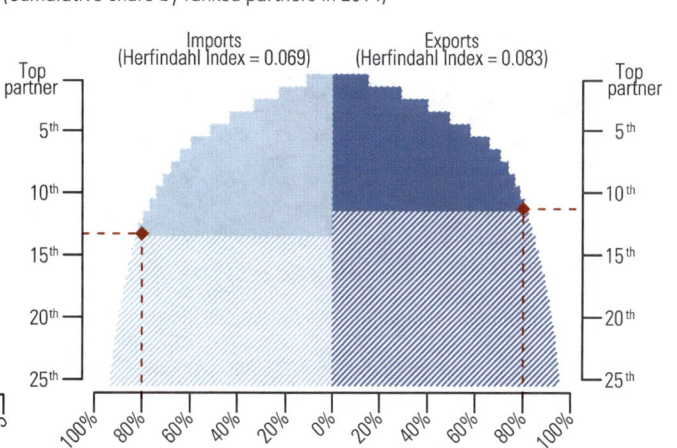

Imports (Herfindahl Index = 0.069)
Exports (Herfindahl Index = 0.083)

Graph 6: Imports of services by EBOPS category
(% share in 2013)

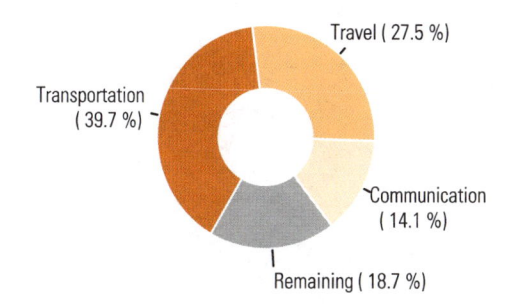

- Travel (27.5 %)
- Transportation (39.7 %)
- Communication (14.1 %)
- Remaining (18.7 %)

Imports Profile:

"Goods classified chiefly by material" (SITC section 6), "Machinery and transport equipment" (SITC section 7) and "Mineral fuels, lubricants" (SITC section 3) were the largest commodity groups for imports in 2014, representing respectively 21.5, 20.7 and 16.7 percent of imported goods (see table 3). From 2012 to 2014, the largest import commodity was "Petroleum oils and oils obtained from bituminous minerals, crude" (HS code 2709) (see table 4). The top three partners for merchandise imports were Croatia, Germany and Italy, accounting for respectively 12.9, 11.4 and 9.8 percent of total imports. "Transportation" (EBOPS code 205) accounted for the largest share of imports of services in 2013 at 191.9 mln US$, followed by "Travel" (EBOPS code 236) at 133.1 mln US$ and "Communications services" (EBOPS code 245) at 68.0 mln US$ (see graph 6).

Table 4: Top 10 import commodities 2012 to 2014

HS code	4-digit heading of Harmonized System 2012	2012	2013	2014	2012	2013	2014	Unit	SITC code
	All Commodities	10 019.1	10 295.2	10 990.4					
2709	Petroleum oils and oils obtained from bituminous minerals, crude	785.8	814.2	701.9	0.8	0.8	0.7	US$/kg	333
2710	Petroleum oils, other than crude	680.3	690.2	664.1	1.0	1.0	0.9	US$/kg	334
8703	Motor cars and other motor vehicles principally designed for the transport	326.2	333.4	356.6		20.6	20.5	thsd US$/unit	781
3004	Medicaments (excluding goods of heading 30.02, 30.05 or 30.06)	270.2	272.7	323.8	42.6	40.6	47.9	US$/kg	542
2701	Coal; briquettes, ovoids and similar solid fuels manufactured from coal	238.9	210.0	215.9	0.2	0.2	0.2	US$/kg	321
2711	Petroleum gases and other gaseous hydrocarbons	202.1	158.1	148.6	0.9	0.8	0.8	US$/kg	343
8517	Electrical apparatus for line telephony or line telegraphy	100.0	115.6	119.4					764
8708	Parts and accessories of the motor vehicles of headings 87.01 to 87.05	90.1	112.2	122.9	2.8	2.6	2.6	US$/kg	784
4107	Leather further prepared after tanning or crusting	76.7	99.4	125.1	31.1	33.5	34.2	US$/kg	611
2203	Beer made from malt	90.5	94.9	97.9		0.7	0.7	US$/litre	112

2014 International Trade Statistics Yearbook, Vol. I Source: UN Comtrade and UN ServiceTrade

Botswana

Goods Imports: CIF, by origin **Goods Exports:** FOB, by last known destination **Trade System:** General

Overview:
In 2013, the value of merchandise exports of Botswana increased substantially by 26.8 percent to reach 7.6 bln US$, while its merchandise imports decreased moderately by 7.4 percent to reach 7.4 bln US$ (see graph 1, table 2 and table 3). The merchandise trade balance recorded a relatively small surplus of 139.8 mln US$ (see graph 1). The largest merchandise trade balance was with MDG Sub-Saharan Africa at -4.3 bln US$ (see graph 4). Merchandise exports in Botswana were highly concentrated amongst partners; imports were also highly concentrated. The top 5 partners accounted for 80 percent or more of exports and 3 partners accounted for 80 percent or more of imports (see graph 5). In 2013, the value of exports of services of Botswana increased substantially by 78.2 percent, reaching 542.4 mln US$, while its imports of services decreased substantially by 21.2 percent and reached 528.3 mln US$ (see graph 2). There was a relatively small trade in services surplus of 14.1 mln US$.

Graph 1: Total merchandise trade, by value
(Bln US$ by year)

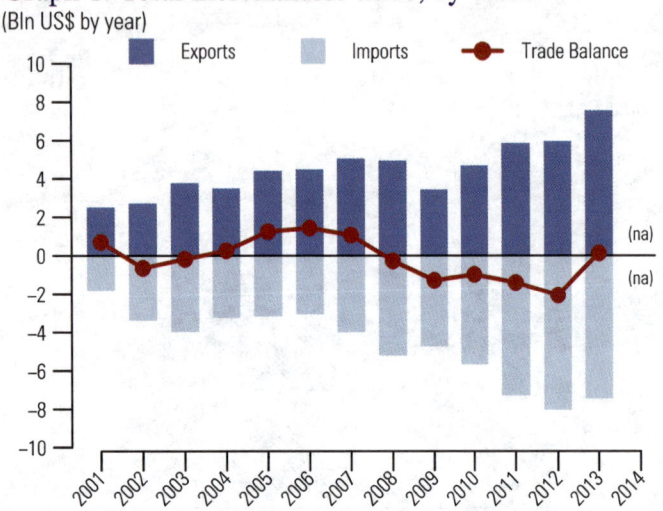

Graph 2: Total services trade, by value
(Mln US$ by year)

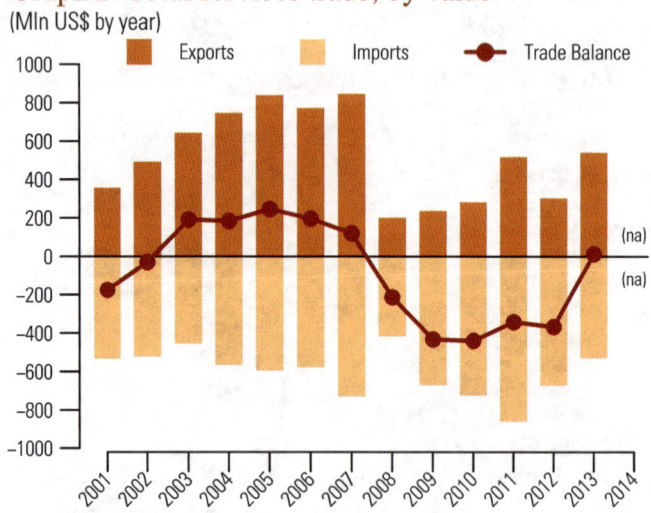

Exports Profile:
"Goods classified chiefly by material" (SITC section 6), "Crude materials + anim. & veg. oils" (SITC section 2+4) and "Machinery and transport equipment" (SITC section 7) were the largest commodity groups for exports in 2013, representing respectively 82.7, 9.3 and 2.7 percent of exported goods (see table 2). From 2011 to 2013, the largest export commodity was "Diamonds, whether or not worked, but not mounted or set" (HS code 7102) (see table 1). The top three destinations for merchandise exports were the United Kingdom, South Africa and Belgium, accounting for respectively 56.7, 12.3 and 7.2 percent of total exports. "Other business services" (EBOPS code 268) accounted for the largest share of exports of services in 2013 at 167.6 mln US$, followed by "Travel" (EBOPS code 236) at 110.1 mln US$ and "Insurance services" (EBOPS code 253) at 82.0 mln US$ (see graph 3).

Graph 3: Exports of services by EBOPS category
(% share in 2013)

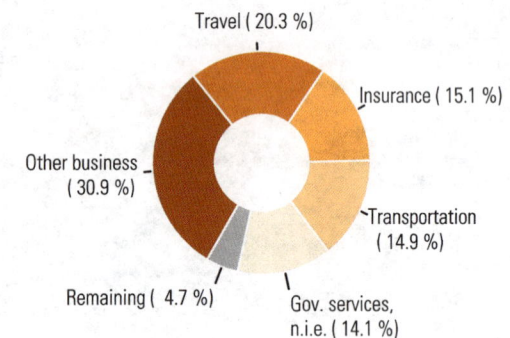

- Travel (20.3 %)
- Insurance (15.1 %)
- Other business (30.9 %)
- Transportation (14.9 %)
- Gov. services, n.i.e. (14.1 %)
- Remaining (4.7 %)

Table 1: Top 10 export commodities 2011 to 2013

HS code	4-digit heading of Harmonized System 2002	Value 2011	Value 2012	Value 2013	UV 2011	UV 2012	UV 2013	Unit	SITC code
	All Commodities	5881.9	5971.2	7573.3					
7102	Diamonds, whether or not worked, but not mounted or set	4448.5	4743.8	6279.2					667
7501	Nickel mattes, nickel oxide sinters and other intermediate products	354.6	333.1	418.6	8.7	7.4	7.5	US$/kg	284
2603	Copper ores and concentrates	74.5	96.4	128.2	2.0	1.6	1.4	US$/kg	283
7108	Gold (including gold plated with platinum)	79.5	84.2	56.1	46.8	54.1	42.2	thsd US$/kg	971
0202	Meat of bovine animals, frozen	27.4	46.6	74.7	4.4	3.7	3.7	US$/kg	011
8544	Insulated (including enamelled or anodised) wire, cable	46.7	48.6	37.4	12.3	15.6		US$/kg	773
2836	Carbonates; peroxocarbonates (percarbonates)	40.8	37.3	36.3	0.2	0.1	0.1	US$/kg	523
8703	Motor cars and other motor vehicles principally designed for the transport	36.6	41.8	25.1		17.3	16.8	thsd US$/unit	781
6203	Men's or boys' suits, ensembles, jackets, blazers, trousers	74.7	13.8	6.7					841
6204	Women's or girls' suits, ensembles, jackets, blazers, dresses, skirts	73.8	15.9	4.6					842

Source: UN Comtrade and UN ServiceTrade

Botswana

Services Imports and Exports: EBOPS 2002 categories

Table 2: Merchandise exports by SITC
(Value in million US$, growth and shares in percentage)

SITC	2013	Avg. Growth rates 2009-2013	2012-2013	2013 share
Total	7 573.3	21.7	26.8	100.0
0+1	174.4	0.3	55.1	2.3
2+4	701.1	6.3	32.7	9.3
3	31.6	30.1	-6.3	0.4
5	76.2	7.1	-4.7	1.0
6	6 263.6	29.6	31.0	82.7
7	204.6	6.2	-21.2	2.7
8	39.8	-32.9	-52.7	0.5
9	82.0	-1.6	-10.3	1.1

Table 3: Merchandise imports by SITC
(Value in million US$, growth and shares in percentage)

SITC	2013	Avg. Growth rates 2009-2013	2012-2013	2013 share
Total	7 433.5	12.0	-7.4	100.0
0+1	710.9	4.9	4.7	9.6
2+4	163.2	2.5	24.1	2.2
3	1 278.5	19.6	-1.3	17.2
5	502.7	5.9	-1.3	6.8
6	2 752.4	26.9	-7.1	37.0
7	1 467.4	1.3	-19.9	19.7
8	465.2	0.5	-5.2	6.3
9	93.1	13.9	-26.2	1.3

SITC Legend

SITC Code	Description
Total	All commodities
0+1	Food, animals + beverages, tobacco
2+4	Crude materials + anim. & veg. oils
3	Mineral fuels, lubricants
5	Chemicals
6	Goods classified chiefly by material
7	Machinery and transport equipment
8	Miscellaneous manufactured articles
9	Not classified elsewhere in the SITC

Graph 4: Merchandise trade balance
(Bln US$ by MDG Regions in 2013)

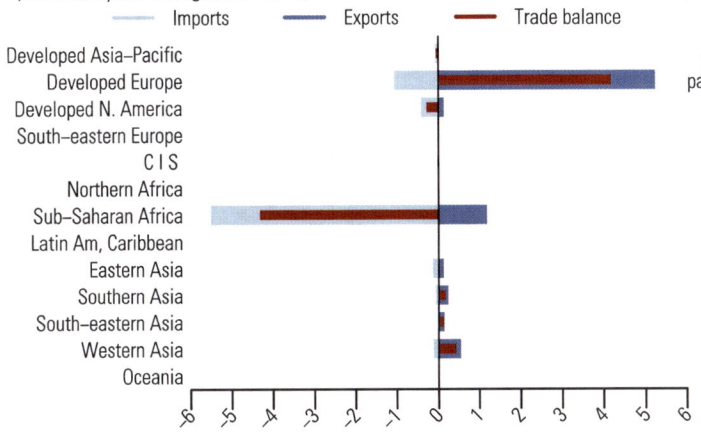

Graph 5: Partner concentration of merchandise trade
(Cumulative share by ranked partners in 2013)

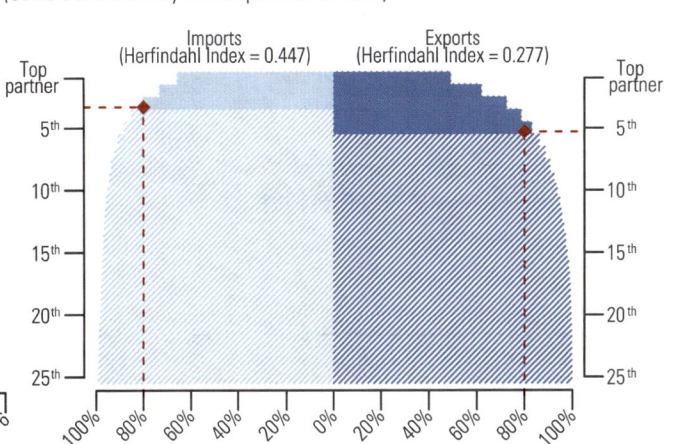

Imports (Herfindahl Index = 0.447)
Exports (Herfindahl Index = 0.277)

Graph 6: Imports of services by EBOPS category
(% share in 2013)

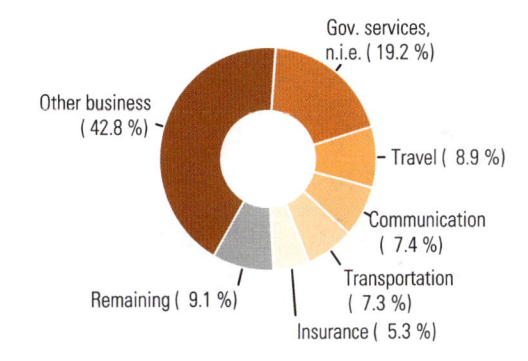

- Gov. services, n.i.e. (19.2 %)
- Other business (42.8 %)
- Travel (8.9 %)
- Communication (7.4 %)
- Transportation (7.3 %)
- Insurance (5.3 %)
- Remaining (9.1 %)

Imports Profile:

"Goods classified chiefly by material" (SITC section 6), "Machinery and transport equipment" (SITC section 7) and "Mineral fuels, lubricants" (SITC section 3) were the largest commodity groups for imports in 2013, representing respectively 37.0, 19.7 and 17.2 percent of imported goods (see table 3). From 2011 to 2013, the largest import commodity was "Diamonds, whether or not worked, but not mounted or set" (HS code 7102) (see table 4). The top three partners for merchandise imports were South Africa, the United Kingdom and China, accounting for respectively 64.7, 11.5 and 4.9 percent of total imports. "Other business services" (EBOPS code 268) accounted for the largest share of imports of services in 2013 at 226.3 mln US$, followed by "Government services, n.i.e." (EBOPS code 291) at 101.4 mln US$ and "Travel" (EBOPS code 236) at 47.1 mln US$ (see graph 6).

Table 4: Top 10 import commodities 2011 to 2013

HS code	4-digit heading of Harmonized System 2002	Value (million US$) 2011	2012	2013	Unit value 2011	2012	2013	Unit	SITC code
	All Commodities	7 272.0	8 025.3	7 433.5					
7102	Diamonds, whether or not worked, but not mounted or set	861.6	2 160.3	2 026.5					667
2710	Petroleum oils, other than crude	930.7	1 031.1	1 017.2	0.3	1.0	1.0	US$/kg	334
2716	Electrical energy	228.9	236.2	240.2		70.2	66.1	US$/MWh	351
8704	Motor vehicles for the transport of goods	233.4	236.1	214.7					782
8703	Motor cars and other motor vehicles principally designed for the transport	188.7	226.1	189.0		19.7	19.4	thsd US$/unit	781
8502	Electric generating sets and rotary converters	238.2	83.9	4.5					716
9999	Commodities not specified according to kind	83.8	125.7	89.6					931
3004	Medicaments (excluding goods of heading 30.02, 30.05 or 30.06)	101.6	100.6	95.0	32.2	40.8	31.9	US$/kg	542
8431	Parts suitable for use principally with the machinery of headings 84.25	94.4	101.6	72.9	11.5	13.6	10.3	US$/kg	723
8708	Parts and accessories of the motor vehicles of headings 87.01 to 87.05	89.6	79.8	70.1	15.6	13.1	10.0	US$/kg	784

Brazil

Goods Imports: FOB, by origin **Goods Exports:** FOB, by last known destination **Trade System:** Special

Overview:
In 2014, the value of merchandise exports of Brazil decreased moderately by 7.1 percent to reach 225.1 bln US$, while its merchandise imports decreased slightly by 4.4 percent to reach 229.1 bln US$ (see graph 1, table 2 and table 3). The merchandise trade balance recorded a relatively small deficit of 4.0 bln US$ (see graph 1). The largest merchandise trade balance was with MDG Developed North America at -8.5 bln US$ (see graph 4). Merchandise exports in Brazil were diversified amongst partners; imports were also diversified. The top 27 partners accounted for 80 percent or more of exports and 22 partners accounted for 80 percent or more of imports (see graph 5). In 2013, the value of exports of services of Brazil decreased slightly by 1.8 percent, reaching 39.1 bln US$, while its imports of services increased moderately by 6.6 percent and reached 86.2 bln US$ (see graph 2). There was a large trade in services deficit of 47.1 bln US$.

Graph 1: Total merchandise trade, by value
(Bln US$ by year)

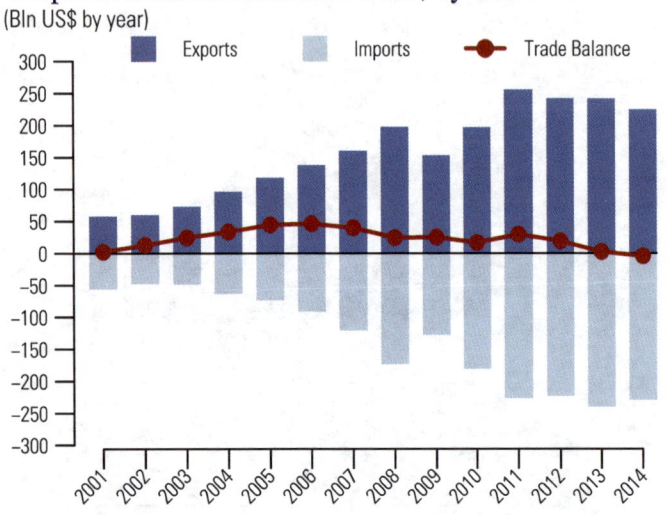

Graph 2: Total services trade, by value
(Bln US$ by year)

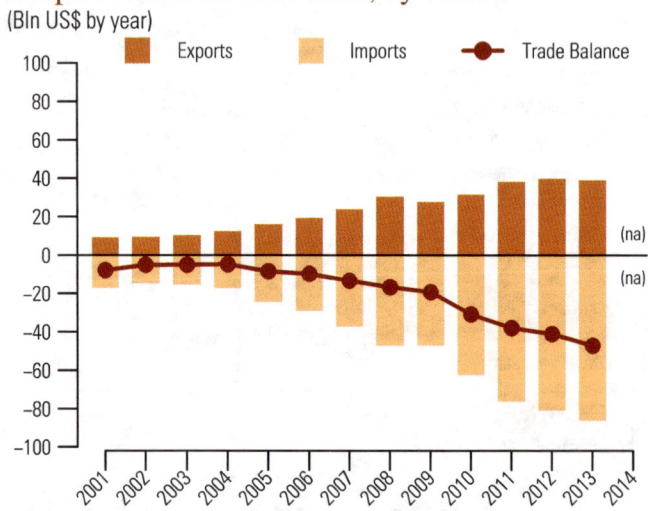

Exports Profile:
"Crude materials + anim. & veg. oils" (SITC section 2+4), "Food, animals + beverages, tobacco" (SITC section 0+1) and "Machinery and transport equipment" (SITC section 7) were the largest commodity groups for exports in 2014, representing respectively 29.3, 24.0 and 14.7 percent of exported goods (see table 2). From 2012 to 2014, the largest export commodity was "Iron ores and concentrates, including roasted iron pyrites" (HS code 2601) (see table 1). The top three destinations for merchandise exports were China, the United States and Argentina, accounting for respectively 18.0, 11.1 and 7.3 percent of total exports. "Other business services" (EBOPS code 268) accounted for the largest share of exports of services in 2013 at 18.9 bln US$, followed by "Travel" (EBOPS code 236) at 6.7 bln US$ and "Transportation" (EBOPS code 205) at 5.4 bln US$ (see graph 3).

Graph 3: Exports of services by EBOPS category
(% share in 2013)

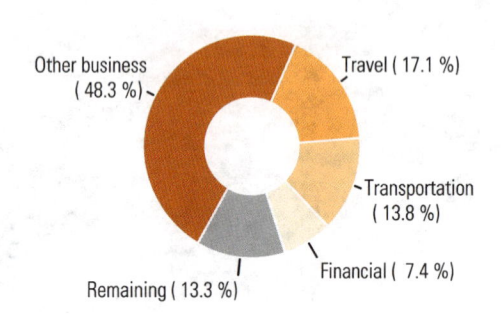

- Other business (48.3 %)
- Travel (17.1 %)
- Transportation (13.8 %)
- Financial (7.4 %)
- Remaining (13.3 %)

Table 1: Top 10 export commodities 2012 to 2014

HS code	4-digit heading of Harmonized System 2012	Value (million US$) 2012	2013	2014	Unit value 2012	2013	2014	Unit	SITC code
	All Commodities	242 579.8	242 178.1	225 098.4					
2601	Iron ores and concentrates, including roasted iron pyrites	30 989.3	32 491.5	25 819.1	0.1	0.1	0.1	US$/kg	281
1201	Soya beans, whether or not broken	17 248.3	22 810.0	23 277.4	0.5	0.5	0.5	US$/kg	222
2709	Petroleum oils and oils obtained from bituminous minerals, crude	20 305.9	12 956.6	16 356.8	0.7	0.7	0.6	US$/kg	333
1701	Cane or beet sugar and chemically pure sucrose, in solid form	12 650.8	11 842.5	9 459.2	0.5	0.4	0.4	US$/kg	061
0207	Meat and edible offal, of the poultry of heading 01.05	6 948.0	7 201.4	7 050.1	1.9	2.0	1.9	US$/kg	012
2304	Oil-cake and other solid residues	6 595.5	6 787.3	7 000.6	0.5	0.5	0.5	US$/kg	081
0901	Coffee, whether or not roasted or decaffeinated	5 740.3	4 598.1	6 052.7	3.8	2.7	3.0	US$/kg	071
1005	Maize (corn)	5 383.3	6 307.6	3 931.9	0.3	0.2	0.2	US$/kg	044
9999	Commodities not specified according to kind	5 637.4	4 837.8	4 800.3					931
4703	Chemical wood pulp, soda or sulphate, other than dissolving grades	4 326.8	4 824.8	4 914.4	0.5	0.5	0.5	US$/kg	251

Source: UN Comtrade and UN ServiceTrade

Brazil

Services Imports and Exports: EBOPS 2002 categories

Table 2: Merchandise exports by SITC
(Value in million US$, growth and shares in percentage)

SITC	2014	Avg. Growth rates 2010-2014	Avg. Growth rates 2013-2014	2014 share
Total	225 098.4	3.3	-7.1	100.0
0+1	53 971.1	2.9	-6.0	24.0
2+4	65 950.6	5.0	-7.8	29.3
3	20 650.1	1.0	15.9	9.2
5	13 221.3	2.0	-7.3	5.9
6	26 579.4	3.3	6.7	11.8
7	33 089.2	0.0	-25.2	14.7
8	4 500.0	-1.0	-0.5	2.0
9	7 136.7	40.7	-5.1	3.2

Table 3: Merchandise imports by SITC
(Value in million US$, growth and shares in percentage)

SITC	2014	Avg. Growth rates 2010-2014	Avg. Growth rates 2013-2014	2014 share
Total	229 060.1	6.1	-4.4	100.0
0+1	9 922.9	7.0	-6.2	4.3
2+4	5 886.1	3.0	-1.6	2.6
3	45 039.5	10.7	-1.4	19.7
5	45 070.7	8.7	-0.4	19.7
6	24 376.7	1.6	-3.0	10.6
7	83 307.3	4.1	-8.5	36.4
8	15 446.7	7.5	-2.8	6.7
9	10.1	44.2	136.8	0.0

SITC Legend

SITC Code	Description
Total	All commodities
0+1	Food, animals + beverages, tobacco
2+4	Crude materials + anim. & veg. oils
3	Mineral fuels, lubricants
5	Chemicals
6	Goods classified chiefly by material
7	Machinery and transport equipment
8	Miscellaneous manufactured articles
9	Not classified elsewhere in the SITC

Graph 4: Merchandise trade balance
(Bln US$ by MDG Regions in 2014)

Graph 5: Partner concentration of merchandise trade
(Cumulative share by ranked partners in 2014)

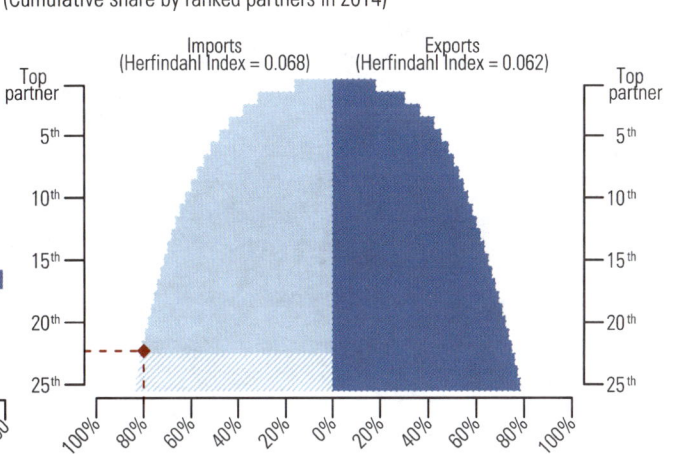

Imports (Herfindahl Index = 0.068)
Exports (Herfindahl Index = 0.062)

Graph 6: Imports of services by EBOPS category
(% share in 2013)

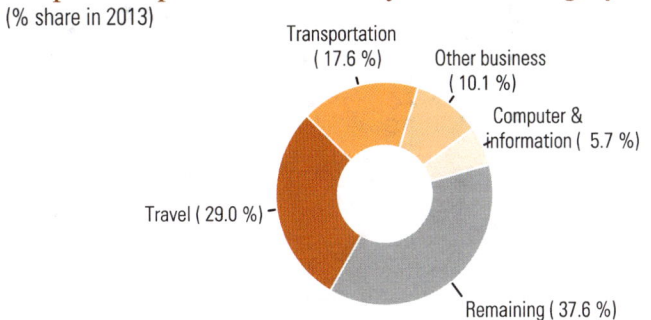

- Transportation (17.6 %)
- Other business (10.1 %)
- Computer & information (5.7 %)
- Travel (29.0 %)
- Remaining (37.6 %)

Imports Profile:

"Machinery and transport equipment" (SITC section 7), "Chemicals" (SITC section 5) and "Mineral fuels, lubricants" (SITC section 3) were the largest commodity groups for imports in 2014, representing respectively 36.4, 19.7 and 19.7 percent of imported goods (see table 3). From 2012 to 2014, the largest import commodity was "Petroleum oils, other than crude" (HS code 2710) (see table 4). The top three partners for merchandise imports were China, the United States and Argentina, accounting for respectively 15.7, 15.1 and 6.8 percent of total imports. "Travel" (EBOPS code 236) accounted for the largest share of imports of services in 2013 at 25.0 bln US$, followed by "Transportation" (EBOPS code 205) at 15.2 bln US$ and "Other business services" (EBOPS code 268) at 8.7 bln US$ (see graph 6).

Table 4: Top 10 import commodities 2012 to 2014

HS code	4-digit heading of Harmonized System 2012	2012	2013	2014	2012	2013	2014	Unit	SITC code
	All Commodities	223 149.1	239 620.9	229 060.1					
2710	Petroleum oils, other than crude	16 365.1	17 757.0	17 630.0	1.0	1.0	0.9	US$/kg	334
2709	Petroleum oils and oils obtained from bituminous minerals, crude	13 405.8	16 320.0	15 533.1	0.9	0.8	0.8	US$/kg	333
8703	Motor cars and other motor vehicles principally designed for the transport	9 566.7	9 081.2	7 675.6	15.0	15.2	16.0	thsd US$/unit	781
2711	Petroleum gases and other gaseous hydrocarbons	5 959.6	7 997.9	8 474.6	0.5	0.6	0.6	US$/kg	343
8708	Parts and accessories of the motor vehicles of headings 87.01 to 87.05	6 771.5	8 296.7	7 143.5	8.3	8.0	8.1	US$/kg	784
8517	Electrical apparatus for line telephony or line telegraphy	3 981.7	5 036.2	5 677.0					764
8542	Electronic integrated circuits	4 139.3	4 748.7	4 444.8					776
3004	Medicaments (excluding goods of heading 30.02, 30.05 or 30.06)	3 591.0	3 734.3	3 682.5	164.9	152.1	140.5	US$/kg	542
8529	Parts suitable for use with the apparatus of headings 85.25 to 85.28	3 502.5	3 565.7	3 184.0	21.3	25.3	21.8	US$/kg	764
3104	Mineral or chemical fertilisers, potassic	3 549.8	3 356.1	2 934.2	0.5	0.4	0.3	US$/kg	562

2014 International Trade Statistics Yearbook, Vol. I — Source: UN Comtrade and UN ServiceTrade

Brunei Darussalam

Goods Imports: CIF, by origin   **Goods Exports:** FOB, by last known destination   **Trade System:** Special

Overview:
In 2014, the value of merchandise exports of Brunei Darussalam decreased moderately by 8.2 percent to reach 10.5 bln US$, while its merchandise imports decreased slightly by 0.4 percent to reach 3.6 bln US$ (see graph 1, table 2 and table 3). The merchandise trade balance recorded a large surplus of 6.9 bln US$ (see graph 1). The largest merchandise trade balance was with MDG Developed Asia-Pacific at 4.9 bln US$ (see graph 4). Merchandise exports in Brunei Darussalam were moderately concentrated amongst partners; imports were diversified. The top 7 partners accounted for 80 percent or more of exports and 8 partners accounted for 80 percent or more of imports (see graph 5). In 2009, the value of exports of services of Brunei Darussalam increased moderately by 5.5 percent, reaching 914.9 mln US$, while its imports of services increased slightly by 2.3 percent and reached 1.4 bln US$ (see graph 2). There was a moderate trade in services deficit of 519.3 mln US$.

Graph 1: Total merchandise trade, by value
(Bln US$ by year)

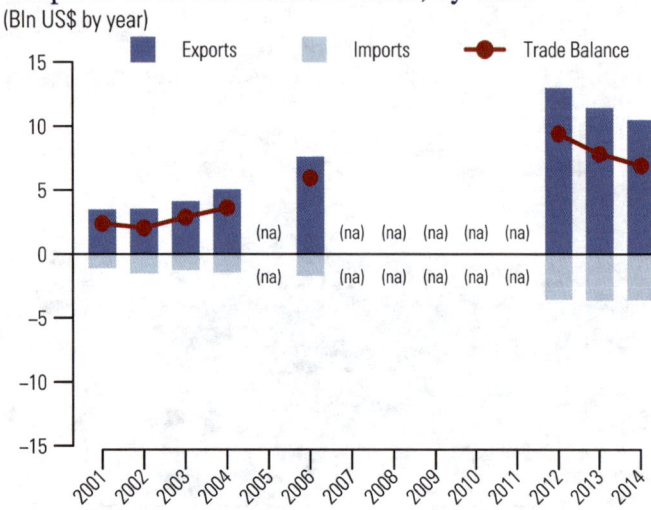

Graph 2: Total services trade, by value
(Bln US$ by year)

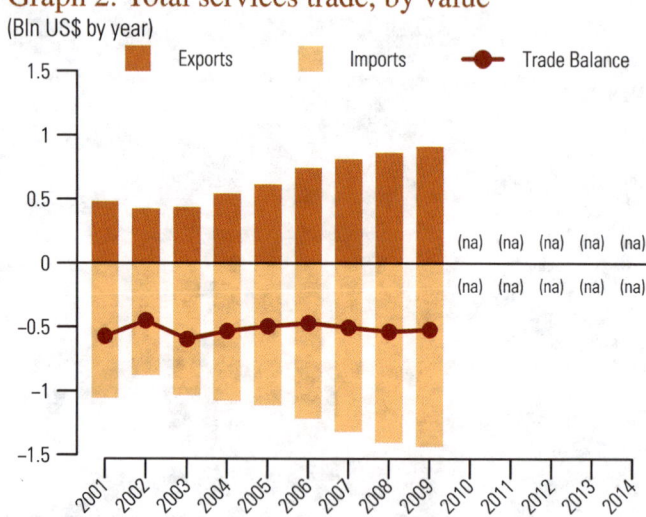

Exports Profile:
"Mineral fuels, lubricants" (SITC section 3), "Chemicals" (SITC section 5) and "Machinery and transport equipment" (SITC section 7) were the largest commodity groups for exports in 2014, representing respectively 92.5, 4.5 and 1.4 percent of exported goods (see table 2). From 2012 to 2014, the largest export commodity was "Petroleum gases and other gaseous hydrocarbons" (HS code 2711) (see table 1). The top three destinations for merchandise exports were Japan, the Republic of Korea and India, accounting for respectively 40.6, 14.5 and 8.5 percent of total exports. "Transportation" (EBOPS code 205) accounted for the largest share of exports of services in 2009 at 451.7 mln US$, followed by "Travel" (EBOPS code 236) at 254.4 mln US$ and "Other business services" (EBOPS code 268) at 174.0 mln US$ (see graph 3).

Graph 3: Exports of services by EBOPS category
(% share in 2009)

- Transportation (49.4 %)
- Travel (27.8 %)
- Other business (19.0 %)
- Remaining (3.8 %)

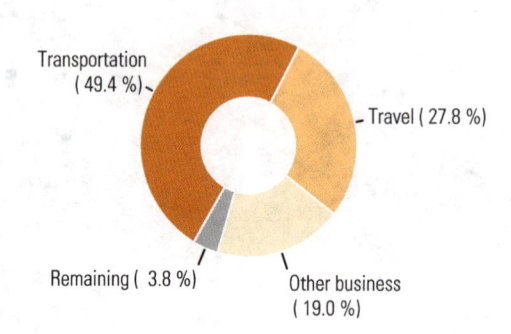

Table 1: Top 10 export commodities 2012 to 2014

HS code	4-digit heading of Harmonized System 2007	Value (million US$) 2012	2013	2014	Unit value 2012	2013	2014	Unit	SITC code
	All Commodities	13 000.8	11 447.2	10 508.8					
2711	Petroleum gases and other gaseous hydrocarbons	6 176.4	5 930.9	5 345.8		0.9	0.9	US$/kg	343
2709	Petroleum oils and oils obtained from bituminous minerals, crude	6 271.3	5 118.0	4 378.6	0.7	0.9	0.8	US$/kg	333
2905	Acyclic alcohols and their derivatives	243.4	82.0	201.4		0.3	0.4	US$/kg	512
2936	Provitamins and vitamins, natural or reproduced by synthesis	0.0	0.0	243.1		0.0	3.9	thsd US$/kg	541
8803	Parts of goods of heading 88.01 or 88.02	24.1	17.3	23.1		379.0	199.3	US$/kg	792
9999	Commodities not specified according to kind	18.5	17.7	14.6					931
8517	Electrical apparatus for line telephony or line telegraphy	21.4	4.9	11.3					764
8431	Parts suitable for use principally with the machinery of headings 84.25	8.3	10.6	14.0	22.9	9.1	12.2	US$/kg	723
7304	Tubes, pipes and hollow profiles, seamless, of iron (other than cast iron)	8.4	19.4	4.9		8.1	2.2	US$/kg	679
8207	Interchangeable tools for hand tools, whether or not power-operated	12.6	11.1	4.4		4.8	11.4	US$/kg	695

Brunei Darussalam

Services Imports and Exports: EBOPS 2002 categories

Table 2: Merchandise exports by SITC
(Value in million US$, growth and shares in percentage)

SITC	2014	Avg. Growth rates 2010-2014	Avg. Growth rates 2013-2014	2014 share
Total	10 508.8	...	-8.2	100.0
0+1	40.9	...	123.3	0.4
2+4	14.0	...	14.9	0.1
3	9 724.9	...	-12.0	92.5
5	471.9	...	411.3	4.5
6	53.2	...	-33.0	0.5
7	143.0	...	10.9	1.4
8	46.4	...	-5.0	0.4
9	14.6	...	-18.0	0.1

Table 3: Merchandise imports by SITC
(Value in million US$, growth and shares in percentage)

SITC	2014	Avg. Growth rates 2010-2014	Avg. Growth rates 2013-2014	2014 share
Total	3 598.7	...	-0.4	100.0
0+1	537.9	...	1.7	14.9
2+4	49.9	...	-4.3	1.4
3	365.4	...	34.8	10.2
5	303.6	...	5.4	8.4
6	540.8	...	-26.4	15.0
7	1 387.4	...	4.7	38.6
8	394.8	...	3.1	11.0
9	19.0	...	-35.7	0.5

SITC Legend

SITC Code	Description
Total	All commodities
0+1	Food, animals + beverages, tobacco
2+4	Crude materials + anim. & veg. oils
3	Mineral fuels, lubricants
5	Chemicals
6	Goods classified chiefly by material
7	Machinery and transport equipment
8	Miscellaneous manufactured articles
9	Not classified elsewhere in the SITC

Graph 4: Merchandise trade balance
(Bln US$ by MDG Regions in 2014)

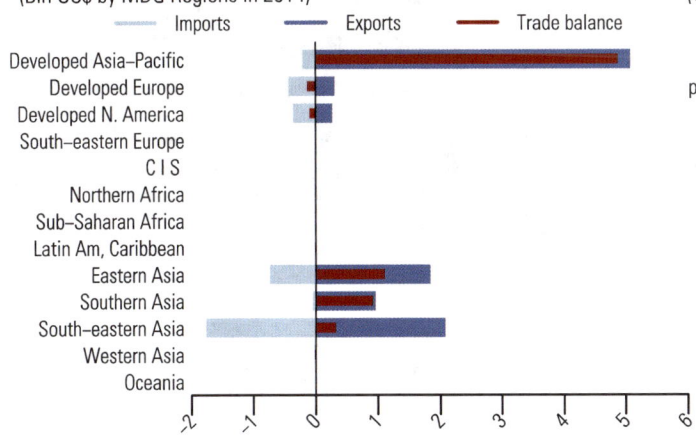

Graph 5: Partner concentration of merchandise trade
(Cumulative share by ranked partners in 2014)

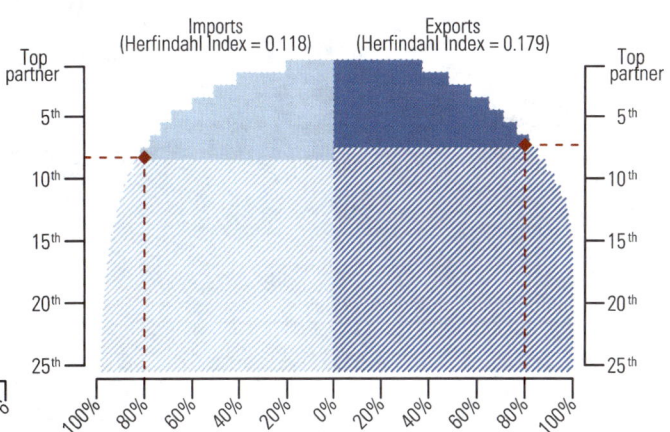

Imports (Herfindahl Index = 0.118)
Exports (Herfindahl Index = 0.179)

Graph 6: Imports of services by EBOPS category
(% share in 2009)

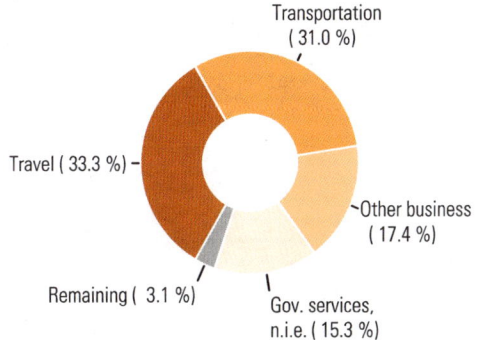

- Transportation (31.0 %)
- Travel (33.3 %)
- Other business (17.4 %)
- Gov. services, n.i.e. (15.3 %)
- Remaining (3.1 %)

Imports Profile:

"Machinery and transport equipment" (SITC section 7), "Goods classified chiefly by material" (SITC section 6) and "Food, animals + beverages, tobacco" (SITC section 0+1) were the largest commodity groups for imports in 2014, representing respectively 38.6, 15.0 and 14.9 percent of imported goods (see table 3). From 2012 to 2014, the largest import commodity was "Petroleum oils, other than crude" (HS code 2710) (see table 4). The top three partners for merchandise imports were Singapore, Malaysia and China, accounting for respectively 21.0, 20.8 and 10.9 percent of total imports. "Travel" (EBOPS code 236) accounted for the largest share of imports of services in 2009 at 477.1 mln US$, followed by "Transportation" (EBOPS code 205) at 444.7 mln US$ and "Other business services" (EBOPS code 268) at 248.8 mln US$ (see graph 6).

Table 4: Top 10 import commodities 2012 to 2014

HS code	4-digit heading of Harmonized System 2007	Value (million US$) 2012	2013	2014	Unit value 2012	2013	2014	Unit	SITC code
	All Commodities	3572.2	3612.4	3598.7					
2710	Petroleum oils, other than crude	342.7	268.3	362.2		1.1	1.0	US$/kg	334
8703	Motor cars and other motor vehicles principally designed for the transport	303.6	319.4	301.7	17.5	17.3	16.0	thsd US$/unit	781
7304	Tubes, pipes and hollow profiles, seamless, of iron (other than cast iron)	89.0	88.7	46.0		0.8	2.1	US$/kg	679
8517	Electrical apparatus for line telephony or line telegraphy	54.8	77.6	79.9					764
8901	Cruise ships, excursion boats, ferry-boats, cargo ships, barges	0.0	0.1	209.7		0.0	69.9	mln US$/unit	793
2309	Preparations of a kind used in animal feeding	54.4	79.1	58.4	1.7	0.8	0.8	US$/kg	081
8481	Taps, cocks, valves and similar appliances for pipes, boiler shells	63.5	66.3	59.1		33.0	30.3	US$/kg	747
7307	Tube or pipe fittings (for example, couplings, elbows, sleeves)	51.3	71.6	41.8		3.5	3.3	US$/kg	679
3004	Medicaments (excluding goods of heading 30.02, 30.05 or 30.06)	51.5	52.4	58.7		34.2	34.4	US$/kg	542
7326	Other articles of iron or steel	75.4	45.7	32.2		1.3	1.5	US$/kg	699

2014 International Trade Statistics Yearbook, Vol. I — Source: UN Comtrade and UN ServiceTrade

Bulgaria

Goods Imports: CIF, by consignment **Goods Exports:** FOB, by last known destination **Trade System:** Special

Overview:
In 2014, the value of merchandise exports of Bulgaria decreased slightly by 0.4 percent to reach 29.4 bln US$, while its merchandise imports increased slightly by 1.3 percent to reach 34.7 bln US$ (see graph 1, table 2 and table 3). The merchandise trade balance recorded a relatively small deficit of 5.4 bln US$ (see graph 1). The largest merchandise trade balance was with MDG CIS at -4.9 bln US$ (see graph 4). Merchandise exports in Bulgaria were diversified amongst partners; imports were also diversified. The top 21 partners accounted for 80 percent or more of exports and 16 partners accounted for 80 percent or more of imports (see graph 5). In 2012, the value of exports of services of Bulgaria decreased slightly by 0.9 percent, reaching 7.4 bln US$, while its imports of services increased slightly by 3.8 percent and reached 4.4 bln US$ (see graph 2). There was a moderate trade in services surplus of 3.0 bln US$.

Graph 1: Total merchandise trade, by value
(Bln US$ by year)

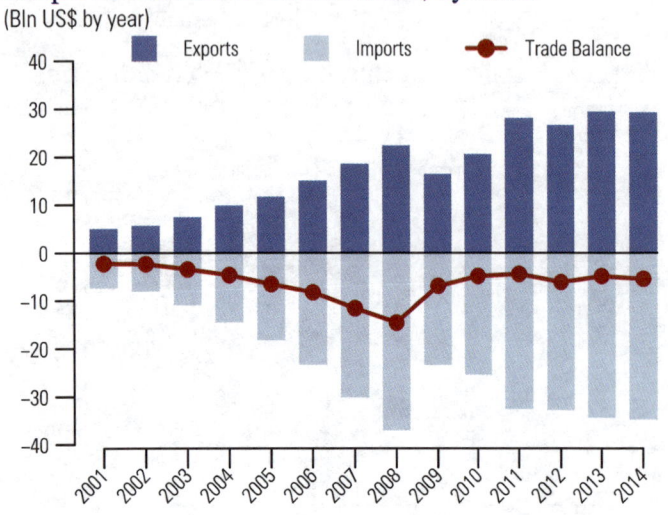

Graph 2: Total services trade, by value
(Bln US$ by year)

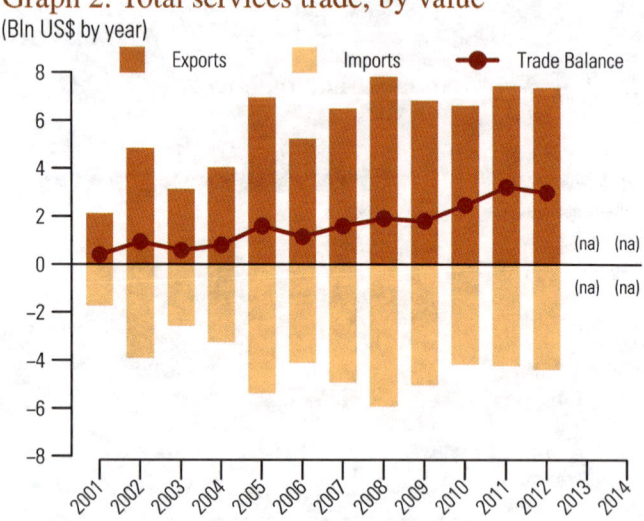

Exports Profile:
"Goods classified chiefly by material" (SITC section 6), "Machinery and transport equipment" (SITC section 7) and "Miscellaneous manufactured articles" (SITC section 8) were the largest commodity groups for exports in 2014, representing respectively 22.1, 18.9 and 13.5 percent of exported goods (see table 2). From 2012 to 2014, the largest export commodity was "Petroleum oils, other than crude" (HS code 2710) (see table 1). The top three destinations for merchandise exports were Germany, Turkey and Italy, accounting for respectively 11.6, 9.3 and 8.7 percent of total exports. "Travel" (EBOPS code 236) accounted for the largest share of exports of services in 2012 at 3.7 bln US$, followed by "Transportation" (EBOPS code 205) at 1.4 bln US$ and "Other business services" (EBOPS code 268) at 933.0 mln US$ (see graph 3).

Graph 3: Exports of services by EBOPS category
(% share in 2012)

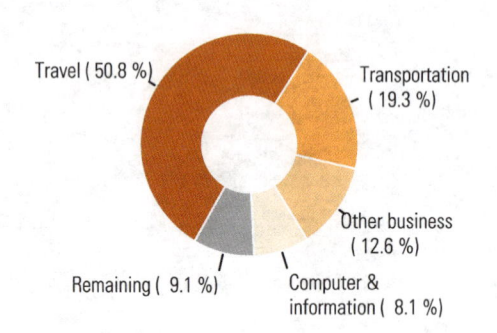

- Travel (50.8 %)
- Transportation (19.3 %)
- Other business (12.6 %)
- Computer & information (8.1 %)
- Remaining (9.1 %)

Table 1: Top 10 export commodities 2012 to 2014

HS code	4-digit heading of Harmonized System 2012	Value (million US$) 2012	2013	2014	Unit value 2012	2013	2014	Unit	SITC code
	All Commodities	26 698.8	29 512.3	29 386.5					
2710	Petroleum oils, other than crude	3 752.2	3 855.2	2 718.7	0.9	0.8	0.8	US$/kg	334
7403	Refined copper and copper alloys, unwrought	1 630.4	1 479.7	1 362.6	8.0	7.4	6.9	US$/kg	682
7402	Unrefined copper; copper anodes for electrolytic refining	658.0	1 028.1	924.8	9.4	8.5	8.0	US$/kg	682
3004	Medicaments (excluding goods of heading 30.02, 30.05 or 30.06)	649.3	780.7	939.8	*41.1*	*52.5*	57.5	US$/kg	542
1001	Wheat and meslin	716.6	950.8	691.3	0.3	0.3	0.2	US$/kg	041
9999	Commodities not specified according to kind	610.5	678.6	915.3					931
1206	Sunflower seeds, whether or not broken	507.3	741.8	496.3	0.7	0.6	0.6	US$/kg	222
2716	Electrical energy	500.9	452.9	526.6	*65.6*	59.0	57.7	US$/MWh	351
8544	Insulated (including enamelled or anodised) wire, cable	355.0	374.2	464.3	*13.2*	*13.8*	*14.8*	US$/kg	773
1005	Maize (corn)	218.8	490.5	386.4	0.3	0.2	0.2	US$/kg	044

Source: UN Comtrade and UN ServiceTrade

Bulgaria

Services Imports and Exports: EBOPS 2002 categories

Table 2: Merchandise exports by SITC
(Value in million US$, growth and shares in percentage)

SITC	2014	Avg. Growth rates 2010-2014	Avg. Growth rates 2013-2014	2014 share
Total	29386.5	9.3	-0.4	100.0
0+1	3699.1	9.2	-6.7	12.6
2+4	2406.5	5.9	-12.4	8.2
3	3703.9	7.8	-14.8	12.6
5	2627.1	13.0	10.6	8.9
6	6492.3	8.2	0.0	22.1
7	5554.3	13.1	6.9	18.9
8	3958.2	7.4	7.8	13.5
9	945.0	9.9	32.3	3.2

Table 3: Merchandise imports by SITC
(Value in million US$, growth and shares in percentage)

SITC	2014	Avg. Growth rates 2010-2014	Avg. Growth rates 2013-2014	2014 share
Total	34740.0	8.2	1.3	100.0
0+1	2851.7	6.3	-0.4	8.2
2+4	3026.2	7.8	-8.2	8.7
3	6941.6	5.4	-12.2	20.0
5	4294.2	10.3	6.3	12.4
6	5886.2	9.0	9.5	16.9
7	8112.4	9.8	5.9	23.4
8	2284.5	6.6	7.3	6.6
9	1343.3	12.7	29.4	3.9

SITC Legend

SITC Code	Description
Total	All commodities
0+1	Food, animals + beverages, tobacco
2+4	Crude materials + anim. & veg. oils
3	Mineral fuels, lubricants
5	Chemicals
6	Goods classified chiefly by material
7	Machinery and transport equipment
8	Miscellaneous manufactured articles
9	Not classified elsewhere in the SITC

Graph 4: Merchandise trade balance
(Bln US$ by MDG Regions in 2014)

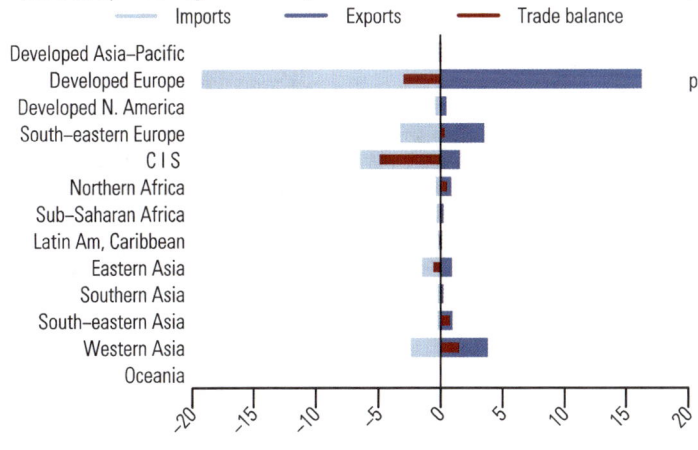

Graph 5: Partner concentration of merchandise trade
(Cumulative share by ranked partners in 2014)

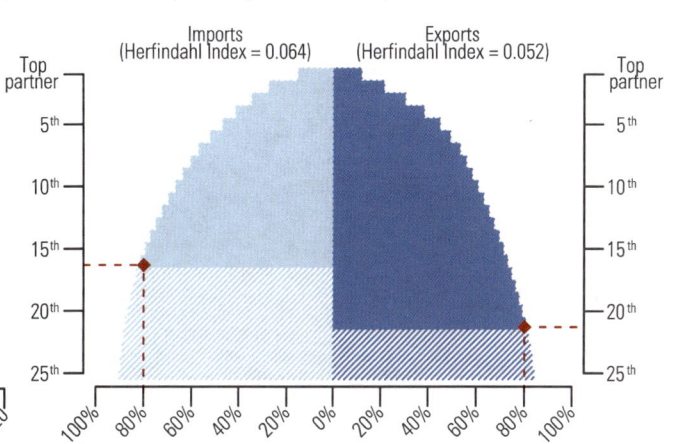

Imports (Herfindahl Index = 0.064)
Exports (Herfindahl Index = 0.052)

Graph 6: Imports of services by EBOPS category
(% share in 2012)

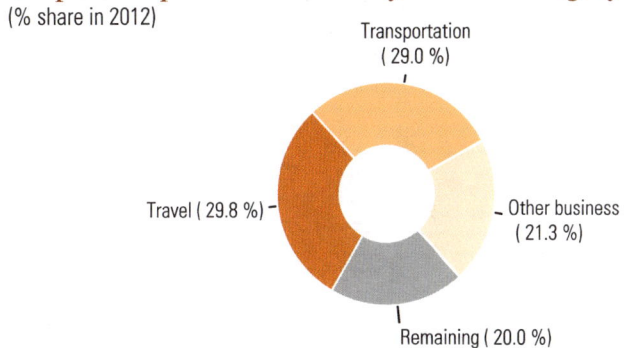

- Transportation (29.0 %)
- Travel (29.8 %)
- Other business (21.3 %)
- Remaining (20.0 %)

Imports Profile:

"Machinery and transport equipment" (SITC section 7), "Mineral fuels, lubricants" (SITC section 3) and "Goods classified chiefly by material" (SITC section 6) were the largest commodity groups for imports in 2014, representing respectively 23.4, 20.0 and 16.9 percent of imported goods (see table 3). From 2012 to 2014, the largest import commodity was "Petroleum oils and oils obtained from bituminous minerals, crude" (HS code 2709) (see table 4). The top three partners for merchandise imports were the Russian Federation, Germany and Italy, accounting for respectively 18.1, 11.4 and 7.0 percent of total imports. "Travel" (EBOPS code 236) accounted for the largest share of imports of services in 2012 at 1.3 bln US$, followed by "Transportation" (EBOPS code 205) at 1.3 bln US$ and "Other business services" (EBOPS code 268) at 932.3 mln US$ (see graph 6).

Table 4: Top 10 import commodities 2012 to 2014

HS code	4-digit heading of Harmonized System 2012	Value (million US$) 2012	2013	2014	Unit value 2012	2013	2014	Unit	SITC code
	All Commodities	32743.1	34306.8	34740.0					
2709	Petroleum oils and oils obtained from bituminous minerals, crude	4753.7	4486.4	3515.4	0.8	0.8	0.7	US$/kg	333
2603	Copper ores and concentrates	1577.3	1950.4	1601.0	2.1	1.9	1.8	US$/kg	283
2710	Petroleum oils, other than crude	1496.5	1709.7	1496.1	0.9	0.9	0.8	US$/kg	334
2711	Petroleum gases and other gaseous hydrocarbons	1402.8	1282.8	1265.9	0.6	0.6	0.6	US$/kg	343
9999	Commodities not specified according to kind	907.4	1028.5	1325.5					931
3004	Medicaments (excluding goods of heading 30.02, 30.05 or 30.06)	885.7	1001.9	1136.1	52.4	62.6	59.0	US$/kg	542
8703	Motor cars and other motor vehicles principally designed for the transport	595.0	761.2	826.9	9.1	10.2	12.4	thsd US$/unit	781
8517	Electrical apparatus for line telephony or line telegraphy	380.6	443.8	540.5					764
7404	Copper waste and scrap	463.8	374.3	384.3	7.2	6.7	6.4	US$/kg	288
8701	Tractors (other than tractors of heading 87.09)	335.0	361.6	369.1	45.5	42.3	40.7	thsd US$/unit	722

Burkina Faso

Goods Imports: CIF, by origin   **Goods Exports: FOB, by last known destination**   **Trade System: General**

Overview:
In 2014, the value of merchandise exports of Burkina Faso increased moderately by 7.4 percent to reach 2.8 bln US$, while its merchandise imports decreased substantially by 18.1 percent to reach 3.6 bln US$ (see graph 1, table 2 and table 3). The merchandise trade balance recorded a moderate deficit of 729.5 mln US$ (see graph 1). The largest merchandise trade balance was with MDG Sub-Saharan Africa at -1.1 bln US$ (see graph 4). Merchandise exports in Burkina Faso were highly concentrated amongst partners; imports were diversified. The top 7 partners accounted for 80 percent or more of exports and 12 partners accounted for 80 percent or more of imports (see graph 5). In 2013, the value of exports of services of Burkina Faso increased substantially by 13.0 percent, reaching 476.6 mln US$, while its imports of services increased substantially by 15.7 percent and reached 1.4 bln US$ (see graph 2). There was a large trade in services deficit of 932.7 mln US$.

Graph 1: Total merchandise trade, by value
(Bln US$ by year)

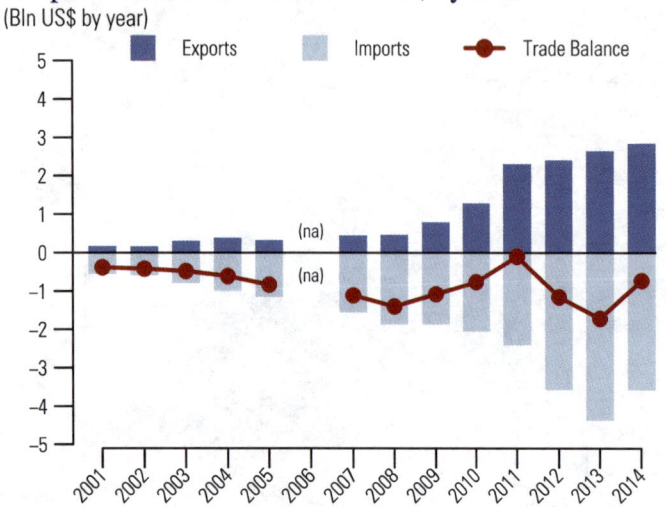

Graph 2: Total services trade, by value
(Bln US$ by year)

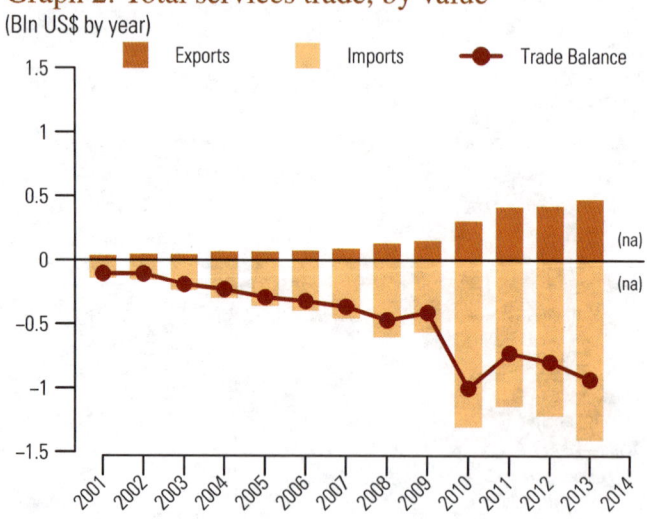

Exports Profile:
"Not classified elsewhere in the SITC" (SITC section 9), "Crude materials + anim. & veg. oils" (SITC section 2+4) and "Mineral fuels, lubricants" (SITC section 3) were the largest commodity groups for exports in 2014, representing respectively 51.4, 25.5 and 9.7 percent of exported goods (see table 2). From 2012 to 2014, the largest export commodity was "Gold (including gold plated with platinum)" (HS code 7108) (see table 1). The top three destinations for merchandise exports were Switzerland, Mali and South Africa, accounting for respectively 53.3, 6.5 and 6.1 percent of total exports. "Communications services" (EBOPS code 245) accounted for the largest share of exports of services in 2013 at 120.7 mln US$, followed by "Travel" (EBOPS code 236) at 97.0 mln US$ and "Construction services" (EBOPS code 249) at 81.8 mln US$ (see graph 3).

Graph 3: Exports of services by EBOPS category
(% share in 2013)

- Travel (20.3 %)
- Construction (17.2 %)
- Transportation (13.4 %)
- Gov. services, n.i.e. (5.9 %)
- Remaining (17.9 %)
- Communication (25.3 %)

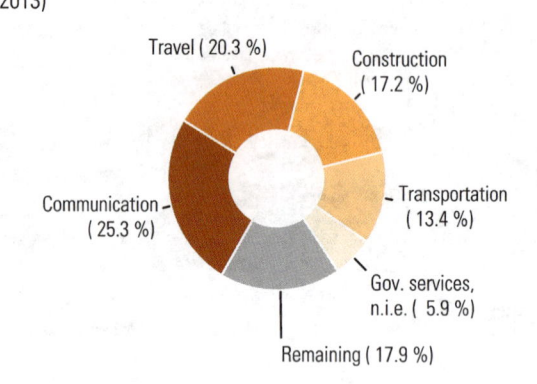

Table 1: Top 10 export commodities 2012 to 2014

HS code	4-digit heading of Harmonized System 2007	Value (million US$) 2012	2013	2014	Unit value 2012	2013	2014	Unit	SITC code
	All Commodities	2 411.0	2 650.5	2 845.6					
7108	Gold (including gold plated with platinum)	1 582.3	1 484.4	1 462.9	44.5	38.1	34.4	thsd US$/kg	971
5201	Cotton, not carded or combed	294.3	439.3	494.9	1.6	1.6	1.6	US$/kg	263
2710	Petroleum oils, other than crude	141.6	231.4	275.3	1.0	1.1	1.1	US$/kg	334
1207	Other oil seeds and oleaginous fruits, whether or not broken	109.1	207.2	194.5	0.6	0.7	0.6	US$/kg	222
0801	Coconuts, Brazil nuts and cashew nuts, fresh or dried	33.2	52.2	43.2	0.7	0.6	0.6	US$/kg	057
7901	Unwrought zinc	...	25.4	87.2		0.4	0.6	US$/kg	686
8502	Electric generating sets and rotary converters	60.5	0.3	1.5					716
8429	Self-propelled bulldozers, angledozers, graders, levellers, scrapers	9.8	13.5	29.5					723
8430	Other moving, grading, levelling, scraping, excavating, tamping, compacting	14.9	15.2	15.9					723
8704	Motor vehicles for the transport of goods	6.4	4.7	21.8					782

Burkina Faso

Services Imports and Exports: EBOPS 2002 categories

Table 2: Merchandise exports by SITC
(Value in million US$, growth and shares in percentage)

SITC	2014	Avg. Growth rates 2010-2014	Avg. Growth rates 2013-2014	2014 share
Total	2845.6	21.9	7.4	100.0
0+1	101.7	14.2	6.4	3.6
2+4	724.4	23.9	9.6	25.5
3	275.3	503.1	19.0	9.7
5	12.0	22.0	1.6	0.4
6	130.8	66.4	98.9	4.6
7	123.1	83.8	46.1	4.3
8	15.4	44.6	-5.2	0.5
9	1462.9	13.4	-1.4	51.4

Table 3: Merchandise imports by SITC
(Value in million US$, growth and shares in percentage)

SITC	2014	Avg. Growth rates 2010-2014	Avg. Growth rates 2013-2014	2014 share
Total	3575.1	14.9	-18.1	100.0
0+1	415.6	9.5	-13.1	11.6
2+4	65.4	7.6	-20.3	1.8
3	1118.3	25.5	-1.6	31.3
5	505.2	15.5	-15.7	14.1
6	576.0	10.8	-23.0	16.1
7	731.4	11.7	-35.7	20.5
8	163.2	6.9	-10.7	4.6
9	0.0	35.4	20.4	0.0

SITC Legend

SITC Code	Description
Total	All commodities
0+1	Food, animals + beverages, tobacco
2+4	Crude materials + anim. & veg. oils
3	Mineral fuels, lubricants
5	Chemicals
6	Goods classified chiefly by material
7	Machinery and transport equipment
8	Miscellaneous manufactured articles
9	Not classified elsewhere in the SITC

Graph 4: Merchandise trade balance
(Bln US$ by MDG Regions in 2014)

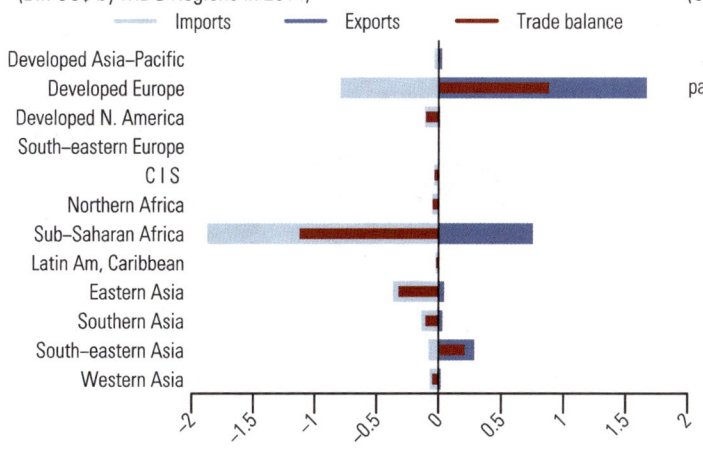

Graph 5: Partner concentration of merchandise trade
(Cumulative share by ranked partners in 2014)

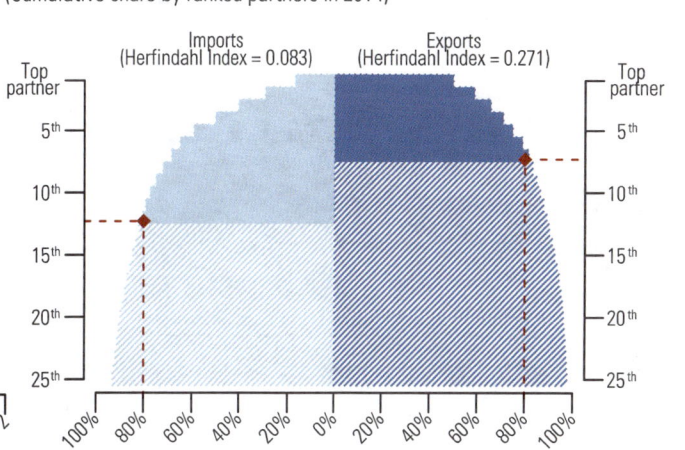

Imports (Herfindahl Index = 0.083)
Exports (Herfindahl Index = 0.271)

Graph 6: Imports of services by EBOPS category
(% share in 2013)

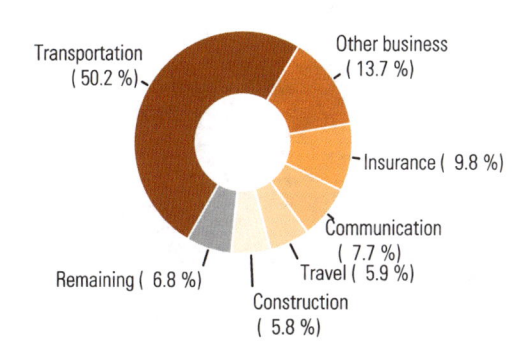

- Transportation (50.2 %)
- Other business (13.7 %)
- Insurance (9.8 %)
- Communication (7.7 %)
- Remaining (6.8 %)
- Travel (5.9 %)
- Construction (5.8 %)

Imports Profile:

"Mineral fuels, lubricants" (SITC section 3), "Machinery and transport equipment" (SITC section 7) and "Goods classified chiefly by material" (SITC section 6) were the largest commodity groups for imports in 2014, representing respectively 31.3, 20.5 and 16.1 percent of imported goods (see table 3). From 2012 to 2014, the largest import commodity was "Petroleum oils, other than crude" (HS code 2710) (see table 4). The top three partners for merchandise imports were Côte d'Ivoire, France and China, accounting for respectively 11.5, 9.3 and 9.2 percent of total imports. "Transportation" (EBOPS code 205) accounted for the largest share of imports of services in 2013 at 708.0 mln US$, followed by "Other business services" (EBOPS code 268) at 193.2 mln US$ and "Insurance services" (EBOPS code 253) at 138.3 mln US$ (see graph 6).

Table 4: Top 10 import commodities 2012 to 2014

HS code	4-digit heading of Harmonized System 2007	Value (million US$) 2012	2013	2014	Unit value 2012	2013	2014	Unit	SITC code
	All Commodities	3568.0	4365.4	3575.1					
2710	Petroleum oils, other than crude	867.8	1071.9	1049.6	1.0	1.1	1.0	US$/kg	334
3004	Medicaments (excluding goods of heading 30.02, 30.05 or 30.06)	100.0	176.9	155.8	16.2	18.4	24.4	US$/kg	542
1006	Rice	115.1	125.4	99.1	0.3	0.3	0.3	US$/kg	042
2523	Portland cement, aluminous cement, slag cement	93.1	108.9	95.0	0.1	0.1	0.1	US$/kg	661
8703	Motor cars and other motor vehicles principally designed for the transport	86.0	93.3	82.7	22.8	21.5	21.2	thsd US$/unit	781
3105	Mineral or chemical fertilisers	86.0	101.7	58.9	0.7	0.7	0.5	US$/kg	562
8704	Motor vehicles for the transport of goods	81.8	93.3	45.9					782
7213	Bars and rods, hot-rolled, in irregularly wound coils	69.4	58.0	72.8	0.7	0.6	0.5	US$/kg	676
8711	Motorcycles (including mopeds) and cycles fitted with an auxiliary motor	71.4	70.8	57.8			2.1	thsd US$/unit	785
8429	Self-propelled bulldozers, angledozers, graders, levellers, scrapers	61.8	89.5	30.8					723

2014 International Trade Statistics Yearbook, Vol. I   Source: UN Comtrade and UN ServiceTrade

Burundi

Goods Imports: CIF, by origin   **Goods Exports:** FOB, by last known destination   **Trade System:** General

Overview:
In 2014, the value of merchandise exports of Burundi decreased substantially by 31.2 percent to reach 141.5 mln US$, while its merchandise imports decreased moderately by 6.8 percent to reach 672.6 mln US$ (see graph 1, table 2 and table 3). The merchandise trade balance recorded a large deficit of 531.1 mln US$ (see graph 1). The largest merchandise trade balance was with MDG Sub-Saharan Africa at -117.0 mln US$ (see graph 4). Merchandise exports in Burundi were diversified amongst partners; imports were also diversified. The top 7 partners accounted for 80 percent or more of exports and 13 partners accounted for 80 percent or more of imports (see graph 5). In 2013, the value of exports of services of Burundi increased substantially by 39.7 percent, reaching 129.9 mln US$, while its imports of services increased moderately by 9.3 percent and reached 231.7 mln US$ (see graph 2). There was a moderate trade in services deficit of 101.8 mln US$.

Graph 1: Total merchandise trade, by value
(Bln US$ by year)

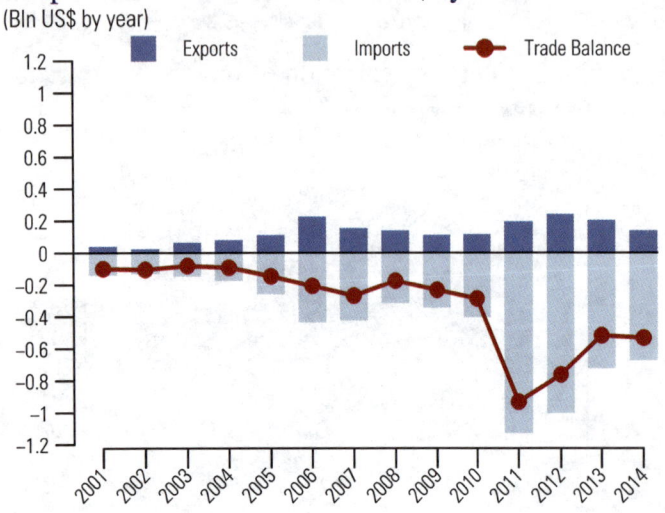

Graph 2: Total services trade, by value
(Mln US$ by year)

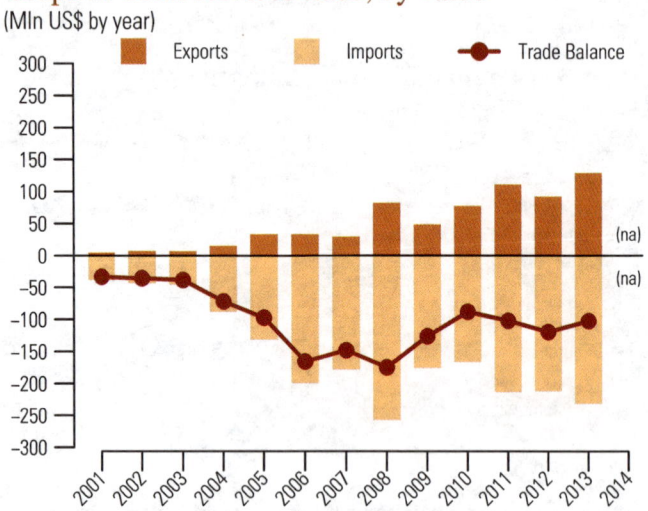

Exports Profile:
"Food, animals + beverages, tobacco" (SITC section 0+1), "Not classified elsewhere in the SITC" (SITC section 9) and "Goods classified chiefly by material" (SITC section 6) were the largest commodity groups for exports in 2014, representing respectively 56.8, 17.2 and 7.4 percent of exported goods (see table 2). From 2012 to 2014, the largest export commodity was "Gold (including gold plated with platinum)" (HS code 7108) (see table 1). The top three destinations for merchandise exports were Areas nes, the United Arab Emirates and Democratic Republic of the Congo, accounting for respectively 94.9, 31.3 and 6.9 percent of total exports. "Government services, n.i.e." (EBOPS code 291) accounted for the largest share of exports of services in 2013 at 97.9 mln US$ (see graph 3).

Graph 3: Exports of services by EBOPS category
(% share in 2013)

Gov. services, n.i.e. (75.4 %)
Remaining (24.6 %)

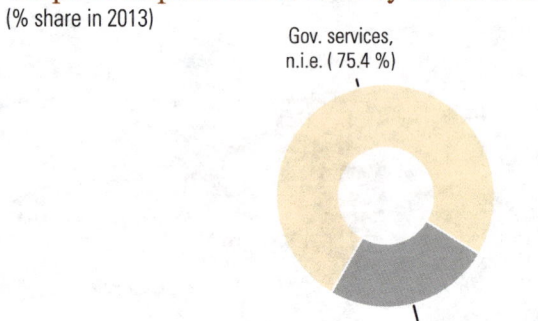

Table 1: Top 10 export commodities 2012 to 2014

HS code	4-digit heading of Harmonized System 2002	Value (million US$) 2012	2013	2014	Unit value 2012	2013	2014	Unit	SITC code
	All Commodities	242.7	205.7	141.5					
7108	Gold (including gold plated with platinum)	105.2	119.8	24.4	49.3	41.1	36.2	thsd US$/kg	971
0901	Coffee, whether or not roasted or decaffeinated	66.1	28.7	51.7	3.0	2.4	3.6	US$/kg	071
0902	Tea, whether or not flavoured	14.4	14.5	13.5	1.5	1.4	1.3	US$/kg	074
3401	Soap; organic surface-active products	5.5	7.9	7.3	1.0	1.0	1.1	US$/kg	554
2617	Other ores and concentrates	16.8	2.0	...	14.9	19.9		US$/kg	287
2203	Beer made from malt	2.7	2.7	5.5	0.5	0.5	0.5	US$/litre	112
2402	Cigars, cheroots, cigarillos and cigarettes	2.8	4.1	3.2	5.9	7.5	7.0	US$/kg	122
3923	Articles for the conveyance or packing of goods, of plastics	2.2	0.0	5.6	4.2	0.9	3.6	US$/kg	893
1101	Wheat or meslin flour	...	2.9	4.6		0.8	0.8	US$/kg	046
7010	Carboys, bottles, flasks, jars, pots, phials, ampoules	2.9	0.1	3.8	1.7	1.0	1.9	US$/kg	665

Burundi

Services Imports and Exports: EBOPS 2002 categories

Table 2: Merchandise exports by SITC
(Value in million US$, growth and shares in percentage)

SITC	2014	Avg. Growth rates 2010-2014	Avg. Growth rates 2013-2014	2014 share
Total	141.5	4.6	-31.2	100.0
0+1	80.3	-1.5	47.6	56.8
2+4	4.1	-21.5	-69.0	2.9
3	0.7	-26.2	>	0.5
5	8.5	53.7	1.0	6.0
6	10.5	82.3	73.6	7.4
7	6.3	23.3	174.2	4.5
8	6.7	57.6	2563.3	4.7
9	24.4	16.5	-79.9	17.2

Table 3: Merchandise imports by SITC
(Value in million US$, growth and shares in percentage)

SITC	2014	Avg. Growth rates 2010-2014	Avg. Growth rates 2013-2014	2014 share
Total	672.6	13.6	-6.8	100.0
0+1	76.2	10.2	-9.9	11.3
2+4	20.5	15.4	-27.4	3.0
3	163.8	109.3	-1.6	24.4
5	96.3	8.6	-17.2	14.3
6	98.7	-1.9	-21.3	14.7
7	178.9	10.2	30.4	26.6
8	36.7	2.5	-31.6	5.5
9	1.5	-2.9	-84.8	0.2

SITC Legend

SITC Code	Description
Total	All commodities
0+1	Food, animals + beverages, tobacco
2+4	Crude materials + anim. & veg. oils
3	Mineral fuels, lubricants
5	Chemicals
6	Goods classified chiefly by material
7	Machinery and transport equipment
8	Miscellaneous manufactured articles
9	Not classified elsewhere in the SITC

Graph 4: Merchandise trade balance
(Mln US$ by MDG Regions in 2014)

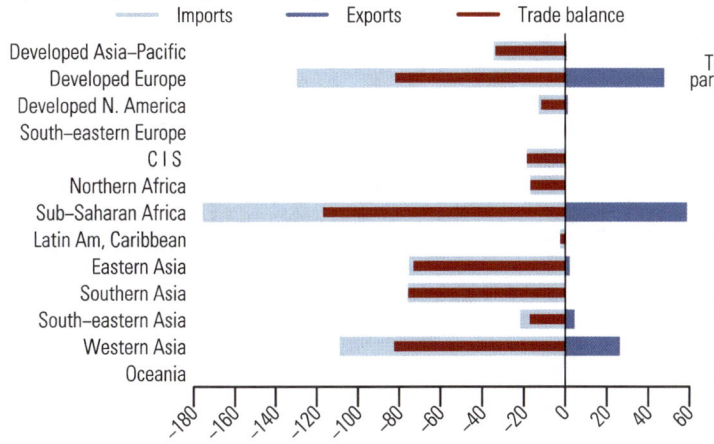

Graph 5: Partner concentration of merchandise trade
(Cumulative share by ranked partners in 2014)

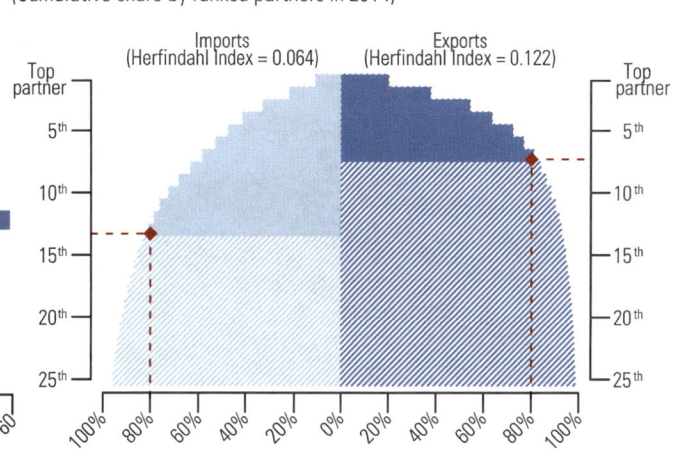

Imports (Herfindahl Index = 0.064)
Exports (Herfindahl Index = 0.122)

Graph 6: Imports of services by EBOPS category
(% share in 2013)

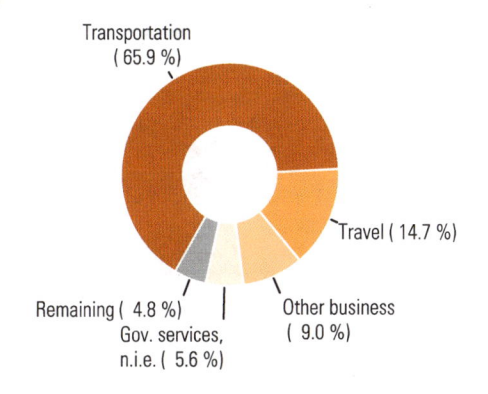

- Transportation (65.9 %)
- Travel (14.7 %)
- Other business (9.0 %)
- Gov. services, n.i.e. (5.6 %)
- Remaining (4.8 %)

Imports Profile:

"Machinery and transport equipment" (SITC section 7), "Mineral fuels, lubricants" (SITC section 3) and "Goods classified chiefly by material" (SITC section 6) were the largest commodity groups for imports in 2014, representing respectively 26.6, 24.4 and 14.7 percent of imported goods (see table 3). From 2012 to 2014, the largest import commodity was "Petroleum oils, other than crude" (HS code 2710) (see table 4). The top three partners for merchandise imports were Saudi Arabia, India and China, accounting for respectively 10.1, 9.6 and 8.9 percent of total imports. "Transportation" (EBOPS code 205) accounted for the largest share of imports of services in 2013 at 152.6 mln US$, followed by "Travel" (EBOPS code 236) at 34.1 mln US$ and "Other business services" (EBOPS code 268) at 20.8 mln US$ (see graph 6).

Table 4: Top 10 import commodities 2012 to 2014

HS code	4-digit heading of Harmonized System 2002	Value 2012	Value 2013	Value 2014	Unit value 2012	Unit value 2013	Unit value 2014	Unit	SITC code
	All Commodities	1 003.1	721.7	672.6					
2710	Petroleum oils, other than crude	161.5	162.8	160.9	1.4	1.3	1.3	US$/kg	334
3004	Medicaments (excluding goods of heading 30.02, 30.05 or 30.06)	41.1	41.8	37.2	11.6	10.6	10.4	US$/kg	542
1201	Soya beans, whether or not broken	109.5	...	0.0			0.1	US$/kg	222
2523	Portland cement, aluminous cement, slag cement	29.7	20.6	19.7	0.2	0.1	0.1	US$/kg	661
8703	Motor cars and other motor vehicles principally designed for the transport	18.5	19.9	28.6	10.3	11.3	17.2	thsd US$/unit	781
8704	Motor vehicles for the transport of goods	15.7	8.1	27.4					782
1001	Wheat and meslin	15.4	14.6	19.0	0.4	0.4	0.3	US$/kg	041
3105	Mineral or chemical fertilisers	10.5	18.7	17.6	0.8	0.8	0.7	US$/kg	562
1208	Flours and meals of oil seeds or oleaginous fruits	37.4	3.0	0.1		1.0	0.7	US$/kg	223
1102	Cereal flours other than of wheat or meslin	30.5	2.5	2.9	2.8	0.4	0.5	US$/kg	047

2014 International Trade Statistics Yearbook, Vol. I   Source: UN Comtrade and UN ServiceTrade

Cabo Verde

Goods Imports: CIF, by origin   **Goods Exports:** FOB, by last known destination   **Trade System:** Special

Overview:
In 2013, the value of merchandise exports of Cabo Verde increased substantially by 24.1 percent to reach 69.2 mln US$, while its merchandise imports decreased slightly by 3.8 percent to reach 726.4 mln US$ (see graph 1, table 2 and table 3). The merchandise trade balance recorded a large deficit of 657.1 mln US$ (see graph 1). The largest merchandise trade balance was with MDG Developed Europe at -513.1 mln US$ (see graph 4). Merchandise exports in Cabo Verde were highly concentrated amongst partners; imports were moderately concentrated. The top 2 partners accounted for 80 percent or more of exports and 7 partners accounted for 80 percent or more of imports (see graph 5). In 2013, the value of exports of services of Cabo Verde increased moderately by 8.8 percent, reaching 650.2 mln US$, while its imports of services decreased moderately by 9.1 percent and reached 268.8 mln US$ (see graph 2). There was a large trade in services surplus of 381.4 mln US$.

Graph 1: Total merchandise trade, by value
(Mln US$ by year)

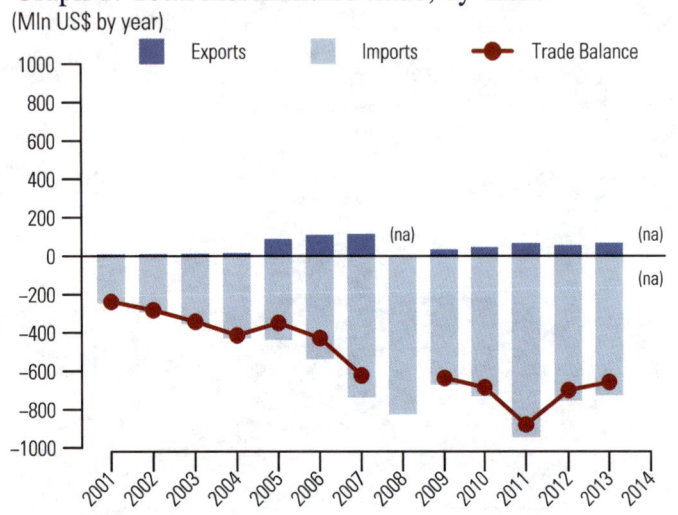

Graph 2: Total services trade, by value
(Mln US$ by year)

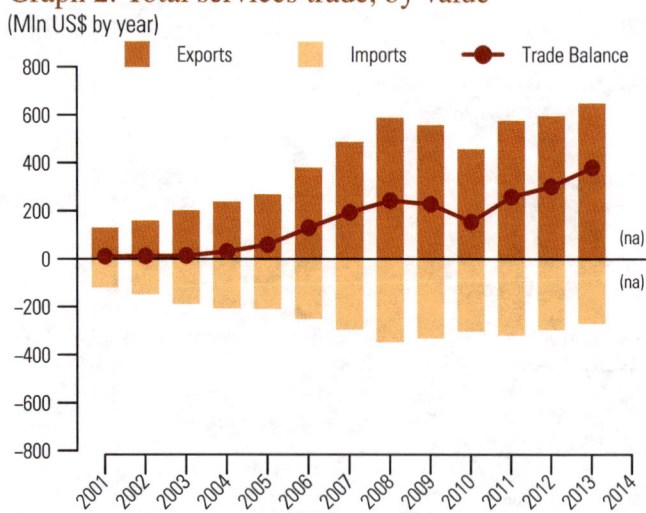

Exports Profile:
"Food, animals + beverages, tobacco" (SITC section 0+1), "Miscellaneous manufactured articles" (SITC section 8) and "Crude materials + anim. & veg. oils" (SITC section 2+4) were the largest commodity groups for exports in 2013, representing respectively 86.1, 13.5 and 0.2 percent of exported goods (see table 2). From 2011 to 2013, the largest export commodity was "Prepared or preserved fish; caviar" (HS code 1604) (see table 1). The top three destinations for merchandise exports were Spain, Portugal and Germany, accounting for respectively 68.1, 15.7 and 4.5 percent of total exports. "Travel" (EBOPS code 236) accounted for the largest share of exports of services in 2013 at 462.5 mln US$, followed by "Transportation" (EBOPS code 205) at 122.2 mln US$ (see graph 3).

Graph 3: Exports of services by EBOPS category
(% share in 2013)

- Travel (71.1 %)
- Transportation (18.8 %)
- Remaining (10.1 %)

Table 1: Top 10 export commodities 2011 to 2013

HS code	4-digit heading of Harmonized System 2007	Value (million US$) 2011	2012	2013	Unit value 2011	2012	2013	Unit	SITC code
	All Commodities	67.9	55.8	69.2					
1604	Prepared or preserved fish; caviar	30.2	22.8	26.9	7.1	6.3	7.6	US$/kg	037
0303	Fish, frozen, excluding fish fillets and other fish meat of heading 03.04	24.5	20.2	29.7	1.8	1.9	2.3	US$/kg	034
6406	Parts of footwear	4.6	4.3	5.1	75.1	69.9	67.1	US$/kg	851
6109	T-shirts, singlets and other vests, knitted or crocheted	1.7	1.1	1.6	5.5	6.2	6.2	US$/unit	845
6203	Men's or boys' suits, ensembles, jackets, blazers, trousers	2.0	0.7	1.4					841
6107	Men's or boys' underpants, briefs, nightshirts, pyjamas, bathrobes	1.5	0.8	1.1		4.1		US$/unit	843
2201	Waters, including natural or artificial mineral waters	0.0	3.2	0.1	0.0	0.6		US$/litre	111
0306	Crustaceans, whether in shell or not	0.9	1.1	1.3	53.6	21.9	46.3	US$/kg	036
2208	Alcohol of a strength by volume of less than 80 % vol	0.7	0.7	0.7	4.1	4.1	3.7	US$/litre	112
3004	Medicaments (excluding goods of heading 30.02, 30.05 or 30.06)	0.4	0.3	0.1	24.0	34.5	22.6	US$/kg	542

Cabo Verde

Services Imports and Exports: EBOPS 2002 categories

Table 2: Merchandise exports by SITC
(Value in million US$, growth and shares in percentage)

SITC	2013	Avg. Growth rates 2009-2013	Avg. Growth rates 2012-2013	2013 share
Total	69.2	18.4	24.1	100.0
0+1	59.6	23.6	22.7	86.1
2+4	0.2	-13.2	731.4	0.2
5	0.1	107.8	-73.0	0.1
6	0.0	17.4	-16.8	0.0
8	9.4	0.0	35.4	13.5
9	0.1	...	...	0.1

Table 3: Merchandise imports by SITC
(Value in million US$, growth and shares in percentage)

SITC	2013	Avg. Growth rates 2009-2013	Avg. Growth rates 2012-2013	2013 share
Total	726.4	2.0	-3.8	100.0
0+1	218.7	4.2	11.2	30.1
2+4	25.1	-0.3	-5.3	3.5
3	154.4	18.5	40.1	21.3
5	49.6	1.6	10.3	6.8
6	107.0	-3.3	-7.3	14.7
7	120.0	-7.3	-41.8	16.5
8	51.6	0.7	-6.4	7.1
9	0.1	...	27507.1	0.0

SITC Legend

SITC Code	Description
Total	All commodities
0+1	Food, animals + beverages, tobacco
2+4	Crude materials + anim. & veg. oils
3	Mineral fuels, lubricants
5	Chemicals
6	Goods classified chiefly by material
7	Machinery and transport equipment
8	Miscellaneous manufactured articles
9	Not classified elsewhere in the SITC

Graph 4: Merchandise trade balance
(Mln US$ by MDG Regions in 2013)

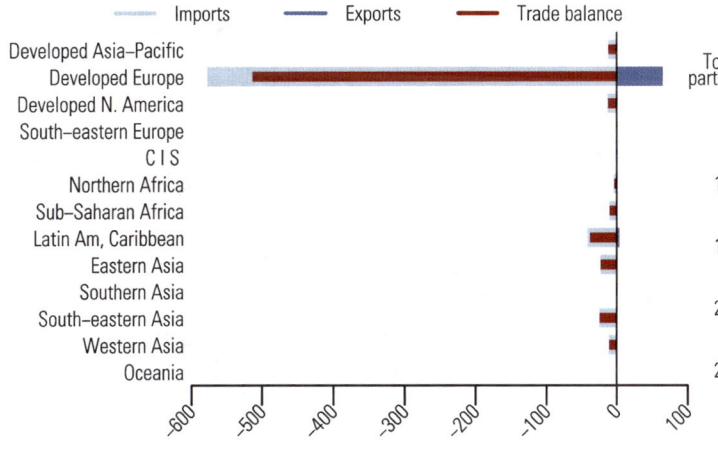

Graph 5: Partner concentration of merchandise trade
(Cumulative share by ranked partners in 2013)

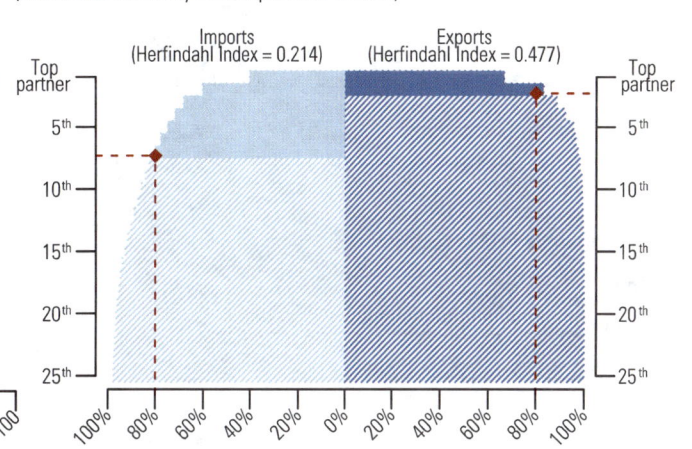

Imports (Herfindahl Index = 0.214)
Exports (Herfindahl Index = 0.477)

Graph 6: Imports of services by EBOPS category
(% share in 2013)

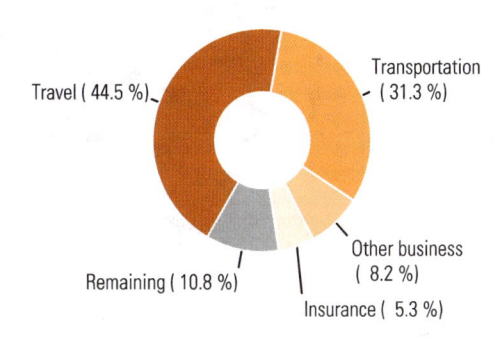

- Travel (44.5 %)
- Transportation (31.3 %)
- Other business (8.2 %)
- Insurance (5.3 %)
- Remaining (10.8 %)

Imports Profile:

"Food, animals + beverages, tobacco" (SITC section 0+1), "Mineral fuels, lubricants" (SITC section 3) and "Machinery and transport equipment" (SITC section 7) were the largest commodity groups for imports in 2013, representing respectively 30.1, 21.3 and 16.5 percent of imported goods (see table 3). From 2011 to 2013, the largest import commodity was "Petroleum oils, other than crude" (HS code 2710) (see table 4). The top three partners for merchandise imports were Portugal, the Netherlands and Spain, accounting for respectively 39.7, 16.0 and 8.7 percent of total imports. "Travel" (EBOPS code 236) accounted for the largest share of imports of services in 2013 at 119.5 mln US$, followed by "Transportation" (EBOPS code 205) at 84.2 mln US$ and "Other business services" (EBOPS code 268) at 21.9 mln US$ (see graph 6).

Table 4: Top 10 import commodities 2011 to 2013

HS code	4-digit heading of Harmonized System 2007	2011	2012	2013	2011	2012	2013	Unit	SITC code
	All Commodities	946.6	754.8	726.4					
2710	Petroleum oils, other than crude	166.6	95.5	141.5	0.8	0.8	0.9	US$/kg	334
2523	Portland cement, aluminous cement, slag cement	29.5	23.6	23.3	0.1	0.1	0.1	US$/kg	661
1006	Rice	24.8	22.3	27.2	0.7	0.7	0.7	US$/kg	042
8802	Other aircraft (for example, helicopters, aeroplanes); spacecraft	...	57.6	...		28.8		mln US$/unit	792
0402	Milk and cream, concentrated or containing added sugar	19.1	16.3	16.5	5.0	4.2	4.7	US$/kg	022
8703	Motor cars and other motor vehicles principally designed for the transport	18.7	15.7	11.2	16.6	18.2	18.2	thsd US$/unit	781
1701	Cane or beet sugar and chemically pure sucrose, in solid form	16.7	11.1	11.9	0.9	0.7	0.7	US$/kg	061
0207	Meat and edible offal, of the poultry of heading 01.05	12.3	12.0	13.3	1.7	1.9	1.8	US$/kg	012
8704	Motor vehicles for the transport of goods	17.5	11.7	8.3					782
7214	Other bars and rods of iron or non-alloy steel	12.9	12.8	9.4	0.8	0.1	0.8	US$/kg	676

Cambodia

Goods Imports: CIF, by origin **Goods Exports:** FOB, by last known destination **Trade System:** General

Overview:
In 2013, the value of merchandise exports of Cambodia increased substantially by 18.0 percent to reach 9.2 bln US$, while its merchandise imports increased substantially by 30.7 percent to reach 9.2 bln US$ (see graph 1, table 2 and table 3). The merchandise trade balance recorded a relatively small surplus of 20.7 mln US$ (see graph 1). The largest merchandise trade balance was with MDG Eastern Asia at -2.6 bln US$ (see graph 4). Merchandise exports in Cambodia were diversified amongst partners; imports were moderately concentrated. The top 10 partners accounted for 80 percent or more of exports and 6 partners accounted for 80 percent or more of imports (see graph 5). In 2013, the value of exports of services of Cambodia increased moderately by 9.5 percent, reaching 2.8 bln US$, while its imports of services increased substantially by 14.4 percent and reached 1.8 bln US$ (see graph 2). There was a moderate trade in services surplus of 1.0 bln US$.

Graph 1: Total merchandise trade, by value
(Bln US$ by year)

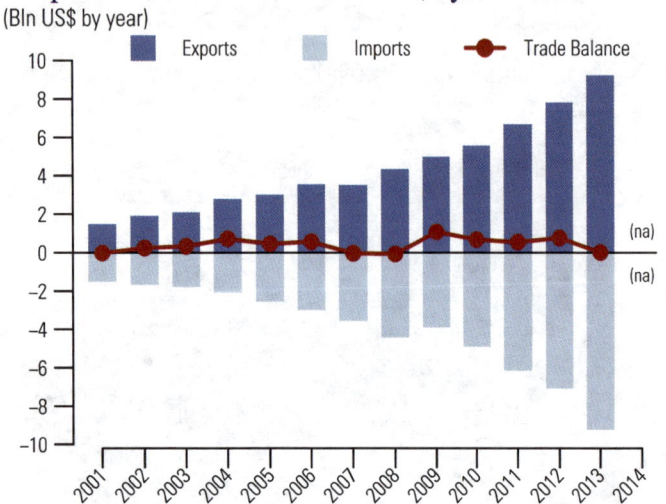

Graph 2: Total services trade, by value
(Bln US$ by year)

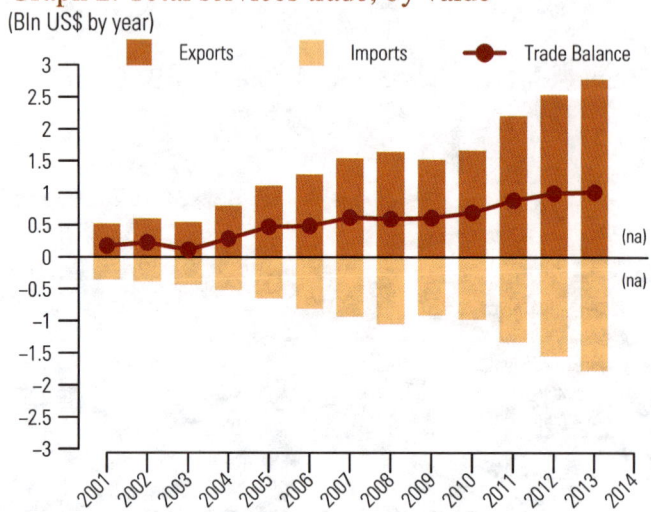

Exports Profile:
"Miscellaneous manufactured articles" (SITC section 8), "Machinery and transport equipment" (SITC section 7) and "Food, animals + beverages, tobacco" (SITC section 0+1) were the largest commodity groups for exports in 2013, representing respectively 83.6, 7.5 and 4.1 percent of exported goods (see table 2). From 2011 to 2013, the largest export commodity was "Unused postage, revenue or similar stamps of current or new issue" (HS code 4907) (see table 1). The top three destinations for merchandise exports were the United States, China, Hong Kong SAR and Singapore, accounting for respectively 26.5, 18.8 and 8.1 percent of total exports. "Travel" (EBOPS code 236) accounted for the largest share of exports of services in 2013 at 1.9 bln US$, followed by "Transportation" (EBOPS code 205) at 343.5 mln US$ and "Other business services" (EBOPS code 268) at 251.1 mln US$ (see graph 3).

Graph 3: Exports of services by EBOPS category
(% share in 2013)

- Travel (69.8 %)
- Transportation (12.3 %)
- Other business (9.0 %)
- Remaining (8.9 %)

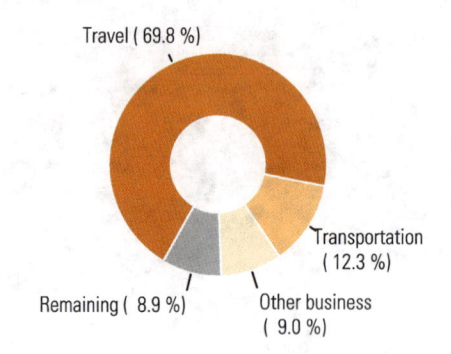

Table 1: Top 10 export commodities 2011 to 2013

HS code	4-digit heading of Harmonized System 2007	Value (million US$) 2011	2012	2013	Unit value 2011	2012	2013	Unit	SITC code
	All Commodities	6704.1	7838.1	9248.1					
4907	Unused postage, revenue or similar stamps of current or new issue	1574.9	2282.1	2260.1	54.0	55.8	56.4	thsd US$/kg	892
6104	Women's or girls' suits, ensembles, jackets, blazers, dresses, skirts	1038.9	1064.8	1199.6					844
6103	Men's, boys' suits, jackets, trousers etc knitted or crocheted	685.4	741.1	865.0					843
6109	T-shirts, singlets and other vests, knitted or crocheted	485.2	586.8	1045.2	6.2	6.1	5.5	US$/unit	845
6110	Jerseys, pullovers, cardigans, waist-coats and similar articles	781.8	754.2	546.4	19.7	18.3	16.9	US$/unit	845
6108	Women's or girls' slips, petticoats, briefs, panties, knitted or crocheted	201.1	250.1	321.3					844
8712	Bicycles and other cycles (including delivery tricycles), not motorised	109.3	253.4	357.6					785
6403	Footwear with outer soles of rubber, plastics, leather	184.4	186.5	207.7	31.5	19.2	21.8	US$/pair	851
4001	Natural rubber, balata, gutta-percha, guayule, chicle	190.8	166.8	176.9	4.3	2.9	2.3	US$/kg	231
1006	Rice	106.4	139.5	258.2	0.6	0.7	0.7	US$/kg	042

Source: UN Comtrade and UN ServiceTrade

Cambodia

Services Imports and Exports: EBOPS 2002 categories

Table 2: Merchandise exports by SITC
(Value in million US$, growth and shares in percentage)

SITC	2013	Avg. Growth rates 2009-2013	Avg. Growth rates 2012-2013	2013 share
Total	9248.1	16.7	18.0	100.0
0+1	380.7	87.4	92.1	4.1
2+4	277.0	28.2	27.4	3.0
3	0.1	...	-91.9	0.0
5	20.4	-2.6	20.5	0.2
6	140.3	50.4	88.9	1.5
7	692.1	57.4	96.3	7.5
8	7734.5	13.8	11.4	83.6
9	3.0	-57.1	-90.6	0.0

Table 3: Merchandise imports by SITC
(Value in million US$, growth and shares in percentage)

SITC	2013	Avg. Growth rates 2009-2013	Avg. Growth rates 2012-2013	2013 share
Total	9227.4	24.0	30.7	100.0
0+1	560.7	16.1	11.7	6.1
2+4	98.1	0.0	-8.8	1.1
3	1004.9	27.3	3.5	10.9
5	511.2	17.2	25.4	5.5
6	3586.4	20.8	13.3	38.9
7	1837.3	23.0	35.9	19.9
8	1544.8	50.0	244.3	16.7
9	84.0	11.4	-22.3	0.9

SITC Legend

SITC Code	Description
Total	All commodities
0+1	Food, animals + beverages, tobacco
2+4	Crude materials + anim. & veg. oils
3	Mineral fuels, lubricants
5	Chemicals
6	Goods classified chiefly by material
7	Machinery and transport equipment
8	Miscellaneous manufactured articles
9	Not classified elsewhere in the SITC

Graph 4: Merchandise trade balance
(Bln US$ by MDG Regions in 2013)

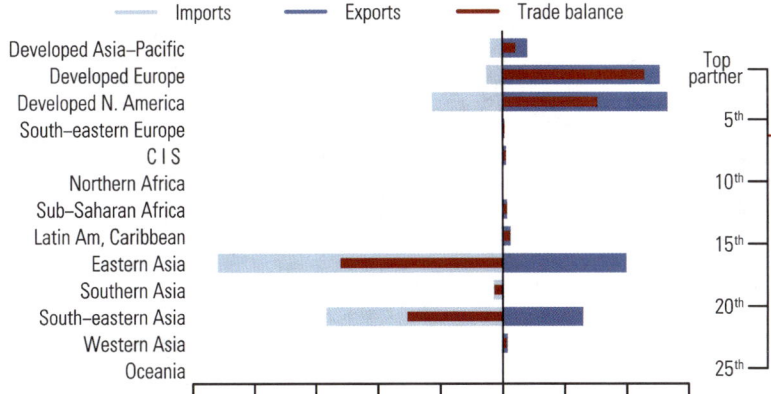

Graph 5: Partner concentration of merchandise trade
(Cumulative share by ranked partners in 2013)

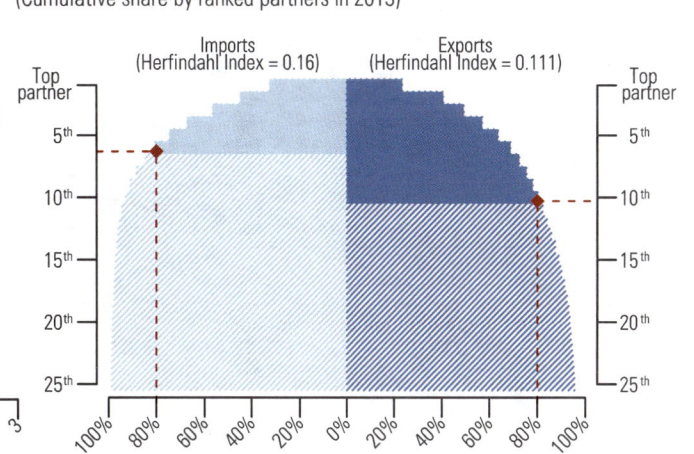

Imports (Herfindahl Index = 0.16)
Exports (Herfindahl Index = 0.111)

Graph 6: Imports of services by EBOPS category
(% share in 2013)

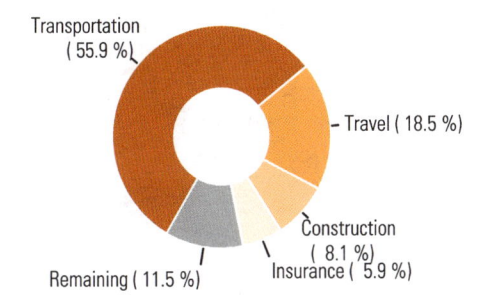

- Transportation (55.9%)
- Travel (18.5%)
- Construction (8.1%)
- Insurance (5.9%)
- Remaining (11.5%)

Imports Profile:

"Goods classified chiefly by material" (SITC section 6), "Machinery and transport equipment" (SITC section 7) and "Miscellaneous manufactured articles" (SITC section 8) were the largest commodity groups for imports in 2013, representing respectively 38.9, 19.9 and 16.7 percent of imported goods (see table 3). From 2011 to 2013, the largest import commodity was "Petroleum oils, other than crude" (HS code 2710) (see table 4). The top three partners for merchandise imports were China, Viet Nam and Thailand, accounting for respectively 30.8, 12.5 and 12.1 percent of total imports. "Transportation" (EBOPS code 205) accounted for the largest share of imports of services in 2013 at 987.9 mln US$, followed by "Travel" (EBOPS code 236) at 327.9 mln US$ and "Construction services" (EBOPS code 249) at 144.0 mln US$ (see graph 6).

Table 4: Top 10 import commodities 2011 to 2013

HS code	4-digit heading of Harmonized System 2007	Value 2011	Value 2012	Value 2013	Unit value 2011	Unit value 2012	Unit value 2013	Unit	SITC code
	All Commodities	6143.3	7062.6	9227.4					
2710	Petroleum oils, other than crude	803.1	910.1	950.3	0.6	0.9	1.0	US$/kg	334
6006	Other knitted or crocheted fabrics	639.0	768.1	815.1	6.0	6.7	6.7	US$/kg	655
6004	Knitted or crocheted fabrics of a width exceeding 30 cm	499.5	593.0	744.0	5.0	5.4	5.8	US$/kg	655
5515	Other woven fabrics of synthetic staple fibres	463.5	554.6	641.6	7.6	7.5	8.0	US$/kg	653
4907	Unused postage, revenue or similar stamps of current or new issue	20.9	0.1	978.5	2.9	0.0	6.6	thsd US$/kg	892
8703	Motor cars and other motor vehicles principally designed for the transport	179.4	207.6	216.6		21.0	22.2	thsd US$/unit	781
2402	Cigars, cheroots, cigarillos and cigarettes	130.0	155.3	184.4	4.7	4.8	5.2	US$/kg	122
5509	Yarn (other than sewing thread) of synthetic staple fibres	144.7	131.5	155.5	5.0	5.1	5.4	US$/kg	651
8704	Motor vehicles for the transport of goods	95.2	149.3	152.5					782
8711	Motorcycles (including mopeds) and cycles fitted with an auxiliary motor	76.9	147.1	126.0					785

Cameroon

Goods Imports: CIF, by origin **Goods Exports:** FOB, by last known destination **Trade System:** Special

Overview:
In 2013, the value of merchandise exports of Cameroon increased moderately by 5.8 percent to reach 4.5 bln US$, while its merchandise imports increased slightly by 2.2 percent to reach 6.7 bln US$ (see graph 1, table 2 and table 3). The merchandise trade balance recorded a moderate deficit of 2.1 bln US$ (see graph 1). The largest merchandise trade balance was with MDG Sub-Saharan Africa at -1.0 bln US$ (see graph 4). Merchandise exports in Cameroon were diversified amongst partners; imports were also diversified. The top 13 partners accounted for 80 percent or more of exports and 19 partners accounted for 80 percent or more of imports (see graph 5). In 2012, the value of exports of services of Cameroon decreased substantially by 12.4 percent, reaching 1.6 bln US$, while its imports of services increased moderately by 7.4 percent and reached 2.1 bln US$ (see graph 2). There was a moderate trade in services deficit of 500.4 mln US$.

Graph 1: Total merchandise trade, by value
(Bln US$ by year)

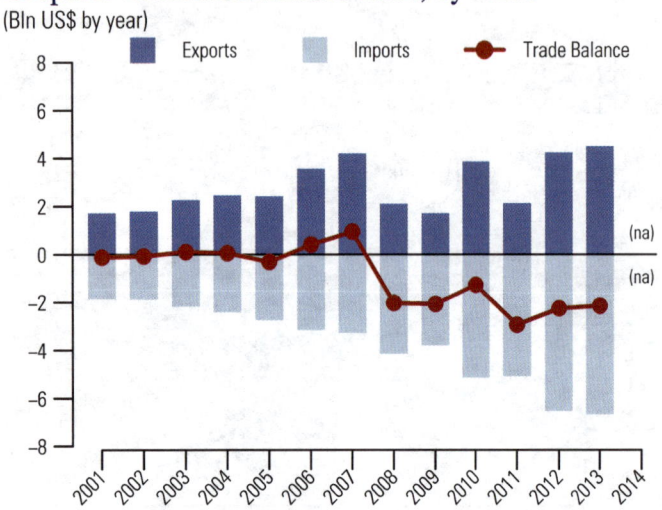

Graph 2: Total services trade, by value
(Bln US$ by year)

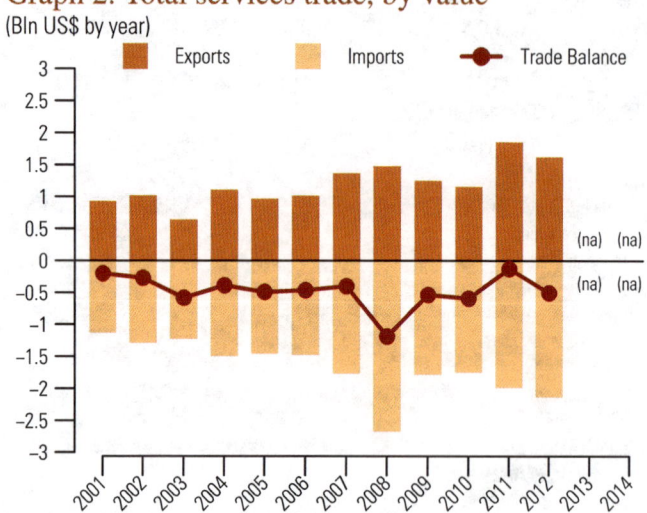

Exports Profile:
"Mineral fuels, lubricants" (SITC section 3), "Food, animals + beverages, tobacco" (SITC section 0+1) and "Crude materials + anim. & veg. oils" (SITC section 2+4) were the largest commodity groups for exports in 2013, representing respectively 55.9, 16.5 and 16.3 percent of exported goods (see table 2). From 2011 to 2013, the largest export commodity was "Petroleum oils, crude" (HS code 2709) (see table 1). The top three destinations for merchandise exports were Portugal, the Netherlands and Spain, accounting for respectively 15.3, 12.5 and 10.4 percent of total exports. "Transportation" (EBOPS code 205) accounted for the largest share of exports of services in 2012 at 536.9 mln US$, followed by "Other business services" (EBOPS code 268) at 391.6 mln US$ and "Travel" (EBOPS code 236) at 349.5 mln US$ (see graph 3).

Graph 3: Exports of services by EBOPS category
(% share in 2012)

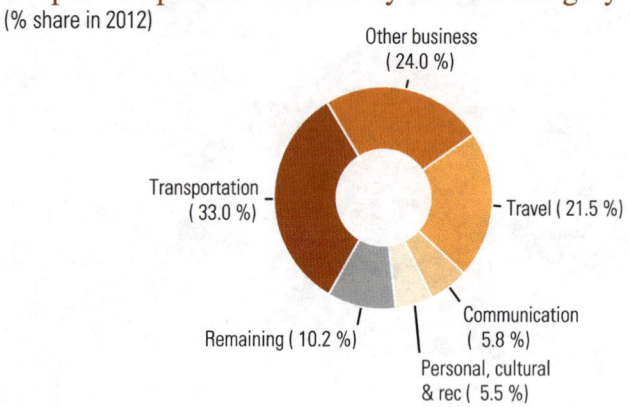

- Other business (24.0 %)
- Travel (21.5 %)
- Communication (5.8 %)
- Personal, cultural & rec (5.5 %)
- Remaining (10.2 %)
- Transportation (33.0 %)

Table 1: Top 10 export commodities 2011 to 2013

HS code	4-digit heading of Harmonized System 2002	Value (million US$) 2011	2012	2013	Unit value 2011	2012	2013	Unit	SITC code
	All Commodities	2147.4	4275.0	4520.9					
2709	Petroleum oils, crude	0.0	1834.1	2204.0	2.1	0.6	0.7	US$/kg	333
1801	Cocoa beans, whole or broken, raw or roasted	512.3	394.8	453.5	2.7	2.3	2.4	US$/kg	072
4407	Wood sawn or chipped lengthwise, sliced or peeled	288.2	279.8	274.7	0.7	0.7	1.2	thsd US$/m³	248
2710	Petroleum oils, other than crude	1.4	527.5	258.2	3.2	0.9	0.8	US$/kg	334
5201	Cotton, not carded or combed	114.0	143.7	173.7	2.0	1.9	1.9	US$/kg	263
4403	Wood in the rough, whether or not stripped of bark or sapwood	141.7	121.8	145.9	863.2			US$/m³	247
4001	Natural rubber, balata, gutta-percha, guayule, chicle	131.3	121.5	122.2	3.6	2.8	2.3	US$/kg	231
0803	Bananas, including plantains	88.7	74.9	83.5	0.4	0.3	0.3	US$/kg	057
7601	Unwrought aluminium	94.4	52.6	64.5	2.3	1.8	1.9	US$/kg	684
0901	Coffee, whether or not roasted or decaffeinated	72.8	87.3	40.2	2.4	2.1	1.9	US$/kg	071

Source: UN Comtrade and UN ServiceTrade

Cameroon

Services Imports and Exports: EBOPS 2002 categories

Table 2: Merchandise exports by SITC
(Value in million US$, growth and shares in percentage)

SITC	2013	Avg. Growth rates 2009-2013	2012-2013	2013 share
Total	4520.9	27.1	5.8	100.0
0+1	744.1	-2.3	2.8	16.5
2+4	738.9	9.4	5.1	16.3
3	2528.7	252.5	6.5	55.9
5	111.6	20.3	-12.1	2.5
6	246.8	5.9	14.2	5.5
7	121.7	8.5	70.5	2.7
8	21.5	1.5	-9.4	0.5
9	7.7	-25.6	-78.2	0.2

Table 3: Merchandise imports by SITC
(Value in million US$, growth and shares in percentage)

SITC	2013	Avg. Growth rates 2009-2013	2012-2013	2013 share
Total	6657.2	15.1	2.2	100.0
0+1	1419.2	10.0	18.6	21.3
2+4	246.5	4.2	2.6	3.7
3	1564.6	84.9	-20.9	23.5
5	725.7	9.1	6.6	10.9
6	918.6	11.1	13.5	13.8
7	1437.4	6.3	9.7	21.6
8	321.1	7.9	8.0	4.8
9	24.2	612.2	924.6	0.4

SITC Legend

SITC Code	Description
Total	All commodities
0+1	Food, animals + beverages, tobacco
2+4	Crude materials + anim. & veg. oils
3	Mineral fuels, lubricants
5	Chemicals
6	Goods classified chiefly by material
7	Machinery and transport equipment
8	Miscellaneous manufactured articles
9	Not classified elsewhere in the SITC

Graph 4: Merchandise trade balance
(Bln US$ by MDG Regions in 2013)

Graph 5: Partner concentration of merchandise trade
(Cumulative share by ranked partners in 2013)

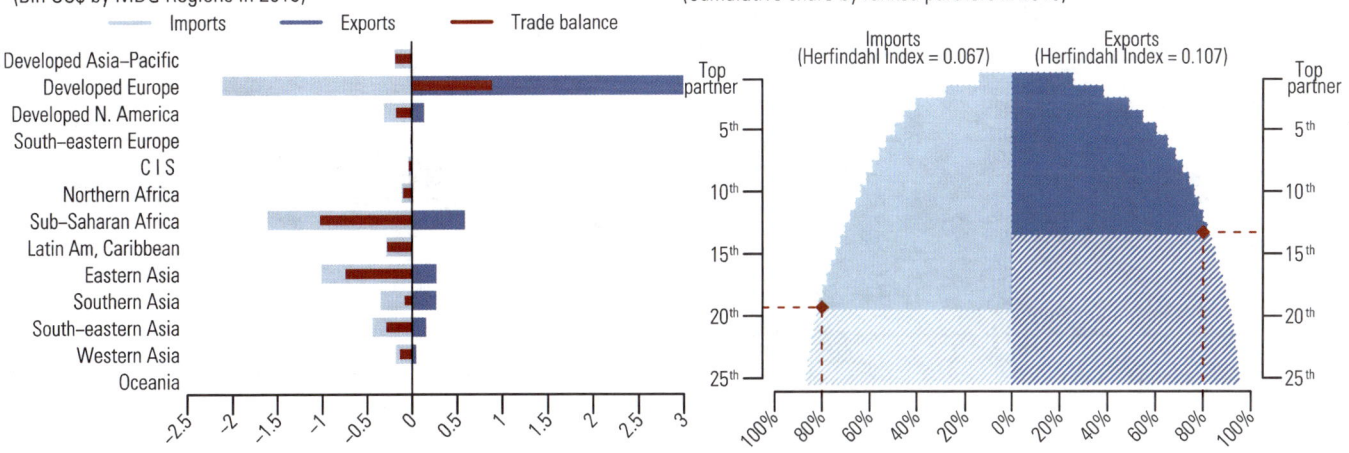

Imports (Herfindahl Index = 0.067)
Exports (Herfindahl Index = 0.107)

Graph 6: Imports of services by EBOPS category
(% share in 2012)

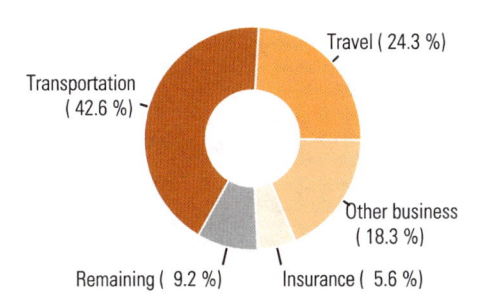

- Transportation (42.6 %)
- Travel (24.3 %)
- Other business (18.3 %)
- Insurance (5.6 %)
- Remaining (9.2 %)

Imports Profile:

"Mineral fuels, lubricants" (SITC section 3), "Machinery and transport equipment" (SITC section 7) and "Food, animals + beverages, tobacco" (SITC section 0+1) were the largest commodity groups for imports in 2013, representing respectively 23.5, 21.6 and 21.3 percent of imported goods (see table 3). From 2011 to 2013, the largest import commodity was "Petroleum oils, crude" (HS code 2709) (see table 4). The top three partners for merchandise imports were France, China and Nigeria, accounting for respectively 13.6, 12.9 and 11.5 percent of total imports. "Transportation" (EBOPS code 205) accounted for the largest share of imports of services in 2012 at 907.2 mln US$, followed by "Travel" (EBOPS code 236) at 517.6 mln US$ and "Other business services" (EBOPS code 268) at 388.9 mln US$ (see graph 6).

Table 4: Top 10 import commodities 2011 to 2013

HS code	4-digit heading of Harmonized System 2002	Value (million US$) 2011	2012	2013	Unit value 2011	2012	2013	Unit	SITC code
	All Commodities	5074.4	6515.1	6657.2					
2709	Petroleum oils, crude	0.1	1300.9	999.4	9.4	0.9	0.9	US$/kg	333
2710	Petroleum oils, other than crude	60.3	565.0	445.4	1.2	1.0	1.0	US$/kg	334
1006	Rice	285.2	306.9	430.7	0.6	0.6	0.5	US$/kg	042
0303	Fish, frozen, excluding fish fillets	315.0	239.4	281.4	1.5	1.3	1.4	US$/kg	034
1001	Wheat and meslin	178.9	196.6	194.2	0.4	0.4	0.4	US$/kg	041
3004	Medicaments (excluding goods of heading 30.02, 30.05 or 30.06)	152.5	165.8	168.3	21.4	21.8	20.5	US$/kg	542
8703	Motor cars and other motor vehicles principally designed for the transport	155.9	147.1	145.0		20.9	20.3	thsd US$/unit	781
2523	Portland cement, aluminous cement, slag cement	127.8	137.8	179.4	0.1	0.1	0.1	US$/kg	661
8704	Motor vehicles for the transport of goods	150.9	100.3	106.4					782
8517	Electrical apparatus for line telephony or line telegraphy	22.0	62.3	154.9					764

Canada

Goods Imports: FOB, by origin **Goods Exports:** FOB, by last known destination **Trade System:** General

Overview:

In 2014, the value of merchandise exports of Canada increased slightly by 3.6 percent to reach 472.9 bln US$, while its merchandise imports increased slightly by 0.1 percent to reach 462.0 bln US$ (see graph 1, table 2 and table 3). The merchandise trade balance recorded a relatively small surplus of 10.9 bln US$ in 2014, following a relatively small deficit of 5.2 bln US$ in 2013 (see graph 1). The largest merchandise trade balance was with MDG Developed North America at 109.0 bln US$ (see graph 4). Merchandise exports in Canada were highly concentrated amongst partners; imports were also highly concentrated. The top 2 partners accounted for 80 percent or more of exports and 7 partners accounted for 80 percent or more of imports (see graph 5). In 2013, the value of exports of services of Canada decreased slightly by 0.3 percent, reaching 85.5 bln US$, while its imports of services decreased slightly by 0.6 percent and reached 110.5 bln US$ (see graph 2). There was a moderate trade in services deficit of 25.0 bln US$.

Graph 1: Total merchandise trade, by value
(Bln US$ by year)

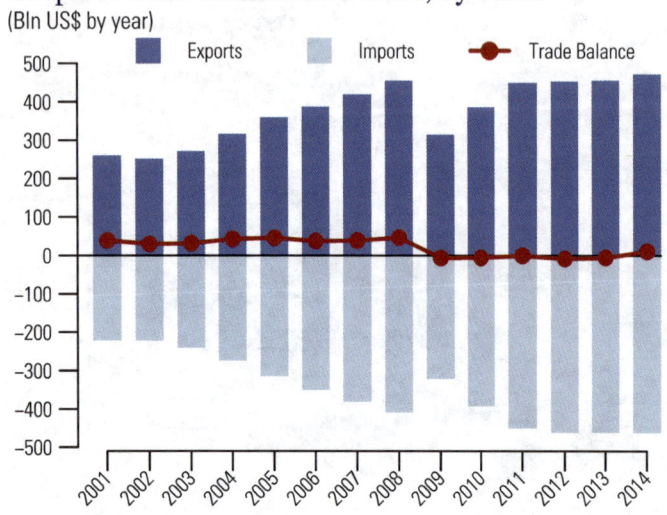

Graph 2: Total services trade, by value
(Bln US$ by year)

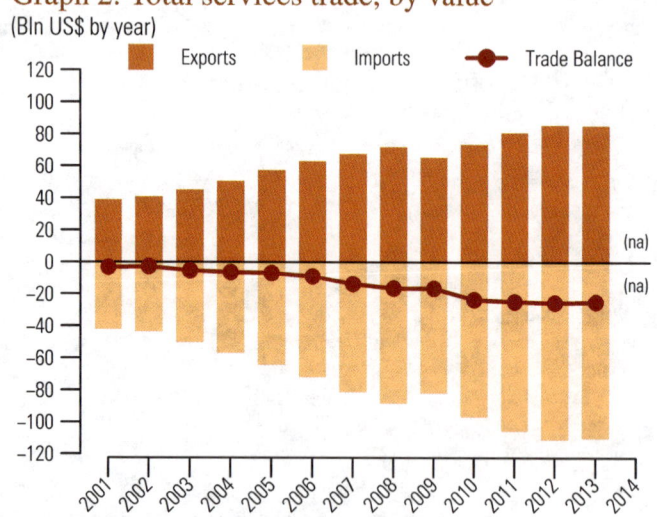

Exports Profile:

"Mineral fuels, lubricants" (SITC section 3), "Machinery and transport equipment" (SITC section 7) and "Goods classified chiefly by material" (SITC section 6) were the largest commodity groups for exports in 2014, representing respectively 27.2, 25.1 and 11.0 percent of exported goods (see table 2). From 2012 to 2014, the largest export commodity was "Petroleum oils and oils obtained from bituminous minerals, crude" (HS code 2709), which increased by 11.0 percent in 2014 (see table 1). The top three destinations for merchandise exports were the United States, China and the United Kingdom, accounting for respectively 75.7, 4.1 and 3.3 percent of total exports. "Other business services" (EBOPS code 268) accounted for the largest share of exports of services in 2013 at 28.4 bln US$, followed by "Travel" (EBOPS code 236) at 17.7 bln US$ and "Transportation" (EBOPS code 205) at 12.7 bln US$ (see graph 3).

Graph 3: Exports of services by EBOPS category
(% share in 2013)

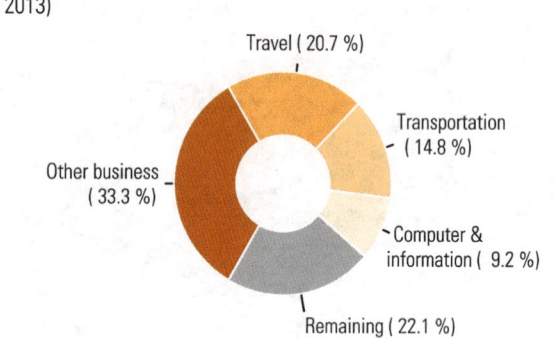

- Travel (20.7 %)
- Transportation (14.8 %)
- Computer & information (9.2 %)
- Remaining (22.1 %)
- Other business (33.3 %)

Table 1: Top 10 export commodities 2012 to 2014

HS code	4-digit heading of Harmonized System 2012	Value (million US$) 2012	2013	2014	Unit value 2012	2013	2014	Unit	SITC code
	All Commodities	454 099.0	456 605.4	472 866.1					
2709	Petroleum oils and oils obtained from bituminous minerals, crude	74 803.8	79 374.0	88 109.4			0.8	US$/kg	333
8703	Motor cars and other motor vehicles principally designed for the transport	46 933.4	45 195.7	44 879.0	21.0	21.0	20.7	thsd US$/unit	781
2710	Petroleum oils, other than crude	19 689.6	18 320.0	15 189.5					334
7108	Gold (including gold plated with platinum)	15 335.1	15 717.8	14 971.4	52.7	44.2	40.2	thsd US$/kg	971
9999	Commodities not specified according to kind	13 582.9	14 619.8	16 019.1					931
2711	Petroleum gases and other gaseous hydrocarbons	11 381.4	12 954.4	16 808.1					343
8708	Parts and accessories of the motor vehicles of headings 87.01 to 87.05	10 128.8	10 394.6	10 756.7	10.4	10.5	10.2	US$/kg	784
4407	Wood sawn or chipped lengthwise, sliced or peeled	5 927.3	7 438.7	7 841.2	169.1	192.0	192.4	US$/m³	248
8802	Other aircraft (for example, helicopters, aeroplanes); spacecraft	6 532.6	6 501.7	8 147.5					792
1001	Wheat and meslin	6 150.7	6 488.7	7 176.6	0.3	0.3	0.3	US$/kg	041

Source: UN Comtrade and UN ServiceTrade

Canada

Services Imports and Exports: EBOPS 2002 categories

Table 2: Merchandise exports by SITC
(Value in million US$, growth and shares in percentage)

SITC	2014	Avg. Growth rates 2010-2014	2013-2014	2014 share
Total	472 866.1	5.2	3.6	100.0
0+1	39 642.8	7.7	7.1	8.4
2+4	43 896.0	5.3	0.0	9.3
3	128 389.0	8.7	6.8	27.2
5	37 993.2	3.5	0.3	8.0
6	52 081.9	0.9	1.3	11.0
7	118 857.5	4.1	2.9	25.1
8	20 300.3	1.7	3.1	4.3
9	31 705.4	5.3	2.2	6.7

Table 3: Merchandise imports by SITC
(Value in million US$, growth and shares in percentage)

SITC	2014	Avg. Growth rates 2010-2014	2013-2014	2014 share
Total	462 000.0	4.2	0.1	100.0
0+1	34 151.1	6.4	3.7	7.4
2+4	13 398.6	3.7	4.7	2.9
3	47 144.1	4.5	-6.1	10.2
5	48 493.9	3.9	1.3	10.5
6	55 887.3	3.8	2.8	12.1
7	190 999.7	4.3	0.4	41.3
8	54 838.7	3.3	0.1	11.9
9	17 086.5	3.0	-7.7	3.7

SITC Legend

SITC Code	Description
Total	All commodities
0+1	Food, animals + beverages, tobacco
2+4	Crude materials + anim. & veg. oils
3	Mineral fuels, lubricants
5	Chemicals
6	Goods classified chiefly by material
7	Machinery and transport equipment
8	Miscellaneous manufactured articles
9	Not classified elsewhere in the SITC

Graph 4: Merchandise trade balance
(Bln US$ by MDG Regions in 2014)

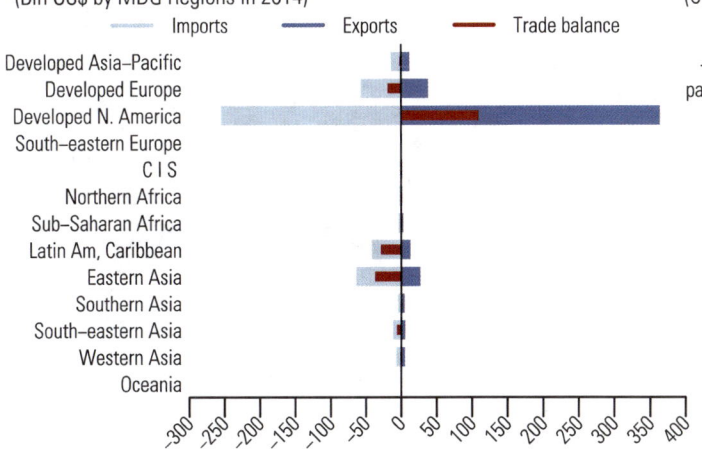

Graph 5: Partner concentration of merchandise trade
(Cumulative share by ranked partners in 2014)

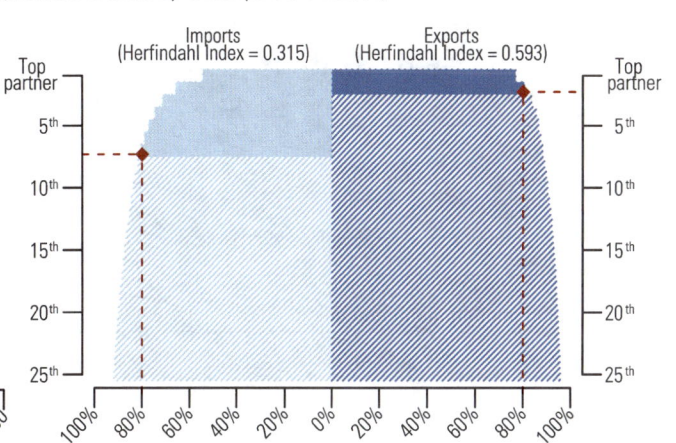

Imports (Herfindahl Index = 0.315)
Exports (Herfindahl Index = 0.593)

Graph 6: Imports of services by EBOPS category
(% share in 2013)

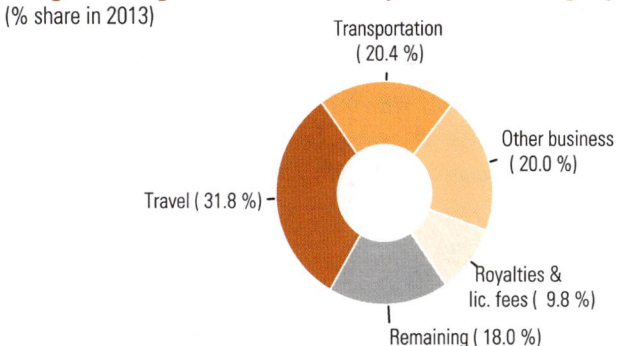

- Transportation (20.4 %)
- Other business (20.0 %)
- Royalties & lic. fees (9.8 %)
- Remaining (18.0 %)
- Travel (31.8 %)

Imports Profile:

"Machinery and transport equipment" (SITC section 7), "Goods classified chiefly by material" (SITC section 6) and "Miscellaneous manufactured articles" (SITC section 8) were the largest commodity groups for imports in 2014, representing respectively 41.3, 12.1 and 11.9 percent of imported goods (see table 3). From 2012 to 2014, the largest import commodity was "Motor cars and other motor vehicles principally designed for the transport" (HS code 8703) (see table 4). The top three partners for merchandise imports were the United States, China and Mexico, accounting for respectively 52.4, 11.2 and 5.6 percent of total imports. "Travel" (EBOPS code 236) accounted for the largest share of imports of services in 2013 at 35.1 bln US$, followed by "Transportation" (EBOPS code 205) at 22.6 bln US$ and "Other business services" (EBOPS code 268) at 22.0 bln US$ (see graph 6).

Table 4: Top 10 import commodities 2012 to 2014

HS code	4-digit heading of Harmonized System 2012	2012	2013	2014	2012	2013	2014	Unit	SITC code
	All Commodities	462 366.2	461 764.1	462 000.0					
8703	Motor cars and other motor vehicles principally designed for the transport	25 927.7	26 336.9	26 995.1	20.4	20.9	20.3	thsd US$/unit	781
2709	Petroleum oils and oils obtained from bituminous minerals, crude	29 788.8	26 233.4	21 699.3			0.8	US$/kg	333
8708	Parts and accessories of the motor vehicles of headings 87.01 to 87.05	21 518.9	21 549.0	20 561.4	12.0	12.1	12.2	US$/kg	784
2710	Petroleum oils, other than crude	15 377.1	17 207.0	17 588.2					334
8704	Motor vehicles for the transport of goods	13 113.3	13 182.6	12 741.0	34.7	33.7	31.4	thsd US$/unit	782
8517	Electrical apparatus for line telephony or line telegraphy	9 386.8	9 411.9	9 105.8					764
7108	Gold (including gold plated with platinum)	9 809.0	9 281.7	8 000.6	28.6	23.2	22.0	thsd US$/kg	971
8471	Automatic data processing machines and units thereof	9 218.1	8 988.7	8 883.8					752
3004	Medicaments (excluding goods of heading 30.02, 30.05 or 30.06)	9 006.0	8 455.4	8 612.5					542
9999	Commodities not specified according to kind	7 312.5	8 464.2	8 385.0					931

2014 International Trade Statistics Yearbook, Vol. I   Source: UN Comtrade and UN ServiceTrade

Central African Republic

Goods Imports: CIF, by origin   **Goods Exports:** FOB, by last known destination   **Trade System:** Special

Overview:

In 2013, the value of merchandise exports of the Central African Republic decreased substantially by 57.5 percent to reach 48.5 mln US$, while its merchandise imports decreased substantially by 40.4 percent to reach 129.7 mln US$ (see graph 1, table 2 and table 3). The merchandise trade balance recorded a large deficit of 81.2 mln US$ (see graph 1). The largest merchandise trade balance was with MDG Developed Europe at -30.2 mln US$ (see graph 4). Merchandise exports in the Central African Republic were moderately concentrated amongst partners; imports were diversified. The top 5 partners accounted for 80 percent or more of exports and 13 partners accounted for 80 percent or more of imports (see graph 5). In 2012, the value of exports of services of the Central African Republic increased moderately by 6.3 percent, reaching 69.1 mln US$, while its imports of services increased substantially by 14.5 percent and reached 179.0 mln US$ (see graph 2). There was a large trade in services deficit of 109.9 mln US$.

Graph 1: Total merchandise trade, by value
(Mln US$ by year)

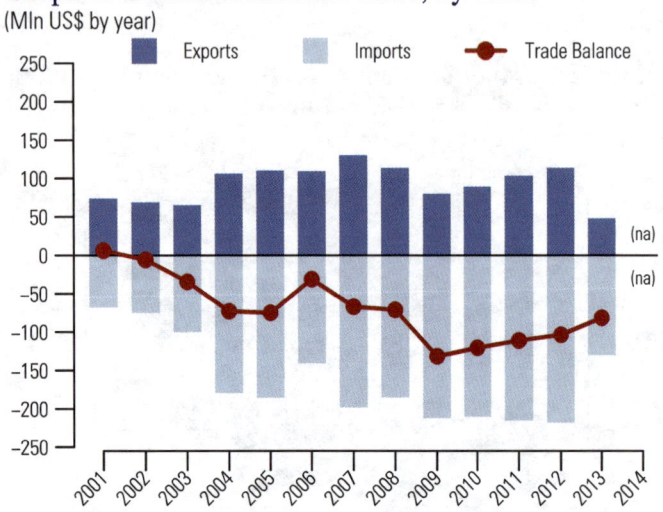

Graph 2: Total services trade, by value
(Mln US$ by year)

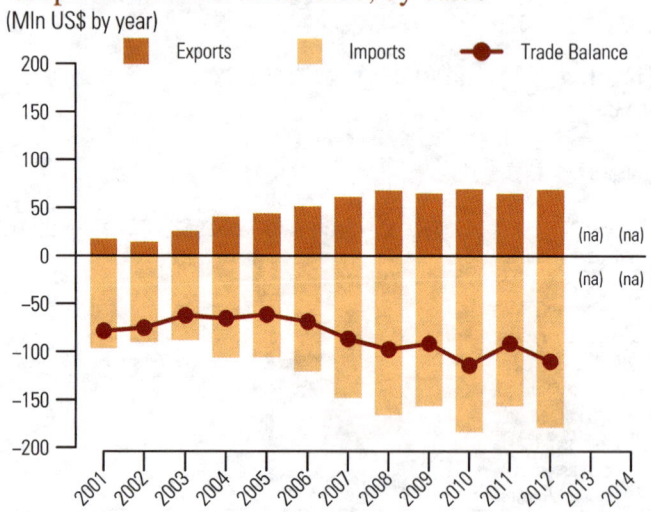

Exports Profile:

"Crude materials + anim. & veg. oils" (SITC section 2+4), "Machinery and transport equipment" (SITC section 7) and "Not classified elsewhere in the SITC" (SITC section 9) were the largest commodity groups for exports in 2013, representing respectively 91.5, 6.4 and 1.2 percent of exported goods (see table 2). From 2011 to 2013, the largest export commodity was "Diamonds, whether or not worked, but not mounted or set" (HS code 7102) (see table 1). The top three destinations for merchandise exports were Belgium, France and China, accounting for respectively 25.9, 16.4 and 12.4 percent of total exports. "Government services, n.i.e." (EBOPS code 291) accounted for the largest share of exports of services in 2012 at 47.1 mln US$, followed by "Travel" (EBOPS code 236) at 11.0 mln US$ and "Transportation" (EBOPS code 205) at 5.5 mln US$ (see graph 3).

Graph 3: Exports of services by EBOPS category
(% share in 2012)

- Gov. services, n.i.e. (68.1 %)
- Travel (15.9 %)
- Transportation (8.0 %)
- Other business (7.9 %)

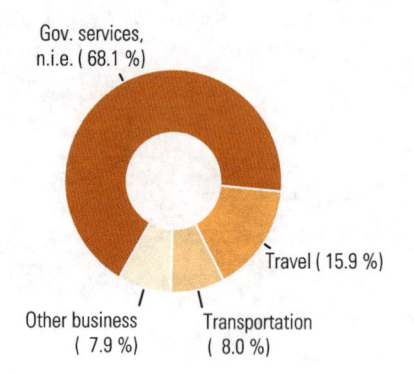

Table 1: Top 10 export commodities 2011 to 2013

HS code	4-digit heading of Harmonized System 2007	Value (million US$) 2011	2012	2013	Unit value 2011	2012	2013	Unit	SITC code
	All Commodities	103.9	114.2	48.5					
7102	Diamonds, whether or not worked, but not mounted or set	63.1	65.2	22.2	140.2			US$/carat	667
4403	Wood in the rough, whether or not stripped of bark or sapwood	17.9	18.6	14.3	0.2			US$/m³	247
4407	Wood sawn or chipped lengthwise, sliced or peeled	8.3	7.2	5.1	0.0	1.2		thsd US$/m³	248
5201	Cotton, not carded or combed	5.7	10.8	2.8	0.0	0.0	1.4	thsd US$/kg	263
8429	Self-propelled bulldozers, angledozers, graders, levellers, scrapers	1.1	2.0	1.0	53.5	45.9	51.3	thsd US$/unit	723
7108	Gold (including gold plated with platinum)	2.5	1.1	0.3	0.1	10.4	0.0	thsd US$/kg	971
8704	Motor vehicles for the transport of goods	0.8	1.8	0.6	30.0		25.7	thsd US$/unit	782
8701	Tractors (other than tractors of heading 87.09)	0.7	1.5	...	35.7			thsd US$/unit	722
0901	Coffee, whether or not roasted or decaffeinated	0.7	0.4	0.0	0.8	0.8	0.8	US$/kg	071
9999	Commodities not specified according to kind	0.3	0.3	0.3					931

Central African Republic

Services Imports and Exports: EBOPS 2002 categories

Table 2: Merchandise exports by SITC
(Value in million US$, growth and shares in percentage)

SITC	2013	Avg. Growth rates 2009-2013	Avg. Growth rates 2012-2013	2013 share
Total	48.5	-11.9	-57.5	100.0
0+1	0.0	-63.4	-89.4	0.1
2+4	44.4	-12.3	-56.8	91.5
3	0.0	...	-14.8	0.1
5	0.0	...	-98.8	0.0
6	0.3	-2.6	-69.2	0.5
7	3.1	46.7	-60.9	6.4
8	0.1	-44.9	-30.4	0.2
9	0.6	-1.3	-62.4	1.2

Table 3: Merchandise imports by SITC
(Value in million US$, growth and shares in percentage)

SITC	2013	Avg. Growth rates 2009-2013	Avg. Growth rates 2012-2013	2013 share
Total	129.7	-11.5	-40.4	100.0
0+1	42.5	-13.5	-28.9	32.8
2+4	6.9	-15.2	-28.8	5.3
3	0.9	-7.8	-71.5	0.7
5	31.7	0.7	17.7	24.4
6	14.3	-16.8	-50.0	11.0
7	24.7	-14.7	-67.3	19.0
8	8.5	-11.1	-39.1	6.6
9	0.3	-3.3	1443.7	0.2

SITC Legend

SITC Code	Description
Total	All commodities
0+1	Food, animals + beverages, tobacco
2+4	Crude materials + anim. & veg. oils
3	Mineral fuels, lubricants
5	Chemicals
6	Goods classified chiefly by material
7	Machinery and transport equipment
8	Miscellaneous manufactured articles
9	Not classified elsewhere in the SITC

Graph 4: Merchandise trade balance
(Mln US$ by MDG Regions in 2013)

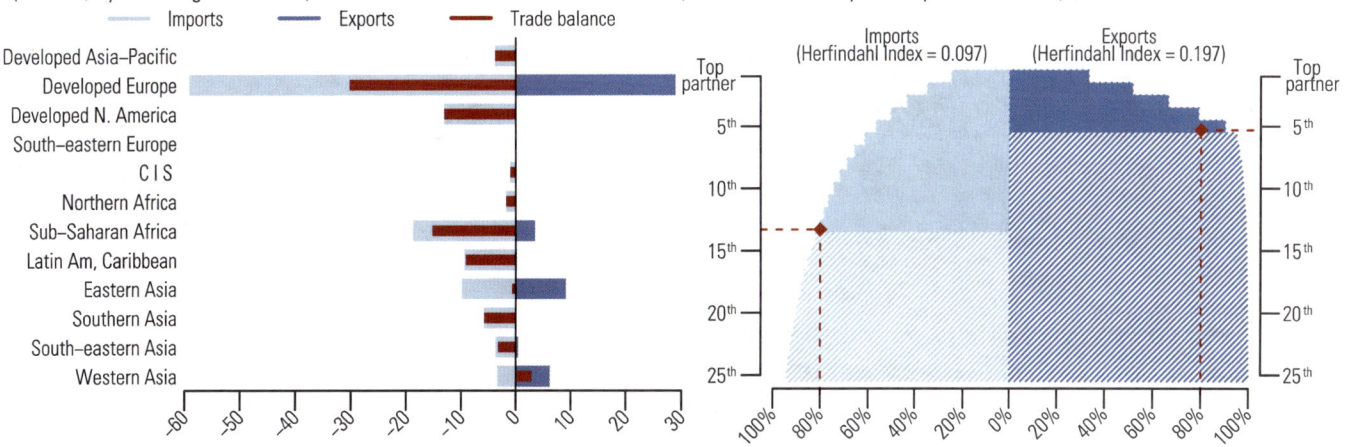

Graph 5: Partner concentration of merchandise trade
(Cumulative share by ranked partners in 2013)

Imports (Herfindahl Index = 0.097)
Exports (Herfindahl Index = 0.197)

Graph 6: Imports of services by EBOPS category
(% share in 2012)

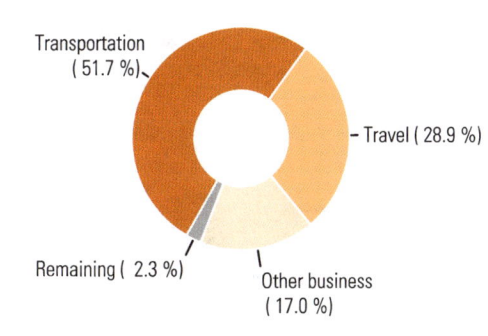

- Transportation (51.7 %)
- Travel (28.9 %)
- Other business (17.0 %)
- Remaining (2.3 %)

Imports Profile:

"Food, animals + beverages, tobacco" (SITC section 0+1), "Chemicals" (SITC section 5) and "Machinery and transport equipment" (SITC section 7) were the largest commodity groups for imports in 2013, representing respectively 32.8, 24.4 and 19.0 percent of imported goods (see table 3). From 2011 to 2013, the largest import commodity was "Medicaments (excluding goods of heading 30.02, 30.05 or 30.06)" (HS code 3004) (see table 4). The top three partners for merchandise imports were France, Japan and China, accounting for respectively 27.5, 8.7 and 8.5 percent of total imports. "Transportation" (EBOPS code 205) accounted for the largest share of imports of services in 2012 at 92.6 mln US$, followed by "Travel" (EBOPS code 236) at 51.8 mln US$ and "Other business services" (EBOPS code 268) at 30.5 mln US$ (see graph 6).

Table 4: Top 10 import commodities 2011 to 2013

HS code	4-digit heading of Harmonized System 2007	Value (million US$) 2011	2012	2013	Unit value 2011	2012	2013	Unit	SITC code
	All Commodities	214.7	217.5	129.7					
3004	Medicaments (excluding goods of heading 30.02, 30.05 or 30.06)	12.1	13.9	20.0	8.5	14.0	26.9	US$/kg	542
1101	Wheat or meslin flour	16.3	17.5	10.3	0.5	0.5	0.5	US$/kg	046
1701	Cane or beet sugar and chemically pure sucrose, in solid form	11.2	10.6	6.6	0.8	0.7	0.6	US$/kg	061
8703	Motor cars and other motor vehicles principally designed for the transport	5.9	12.0	3.7	19.4	27.4	23.7	thsd US$/unit	781
8517	Electrical apparatus for line telephony or line telegraphy	5.8	7.1	3.4					764
2523	Portland cement, aluminous cement, slag cement	6.6	5.5	2.5	0.2	0.1	0.1	US$/kg	661
3002	Human blood; animal blood prepared for therapeutic uses	3.6	4.3	5.5	208.0	241.0	225.7	US$/kg	541
1102	Cereal flours other than of wheat or meslin	7.5	2.0	2.7	0.6	0.5	0.7	US$/kg	047
8704	Motor vehicles for the transport of goods	3.3	7.5	0.9	18.7		23.5	thsd US$/unit	782
2403	Other manufactured tobacco and tobacco substitutes	4.6	4.1	2.9	11.9	11.6	11.5	US$/kg	122

Source: UN Comtrade and UN ServiceTrade

Chile

Goods Imports: CIF, by consignment   **Goods Exports:** FOB, by last known destination   **Trade System:** General

Overview:
In 2014, the value of merchandise exports of Chile decreased slightly by 0.1 percent to reach 76.6 bln US$, while its merchandise imports decreased moderately by 8.6 percent to reach 72.3 bln US$ (see graph 1, table 2 and table 3). The merchandise trade balance recorded a relatively small surplus of 4.3 bln US$ (see graph 1). The largest merchandise trade balance was with MDG Eastern Asia at 7.8 bln US$ (see graph 4). Merchandise exports in Chile were diversified amongst partners; imports were also diversified. The top 15 partners accounted for 80 percent or more of exports and 14 partners accounted for 80 percent or more of imports (see graph 5). In 2013, the value of exports of services of Chile increased slightly by 2.7 percent, reaching 12.8 bln US$, while its imports of services increased moderately by 6.5 percent and reached 15.7 bln US$ (see graph 2). There was a moderate trade in services deficit of 2.9 bln US$.

Graph 1: Total merchandise trade, by value
(Bln US$ by year)

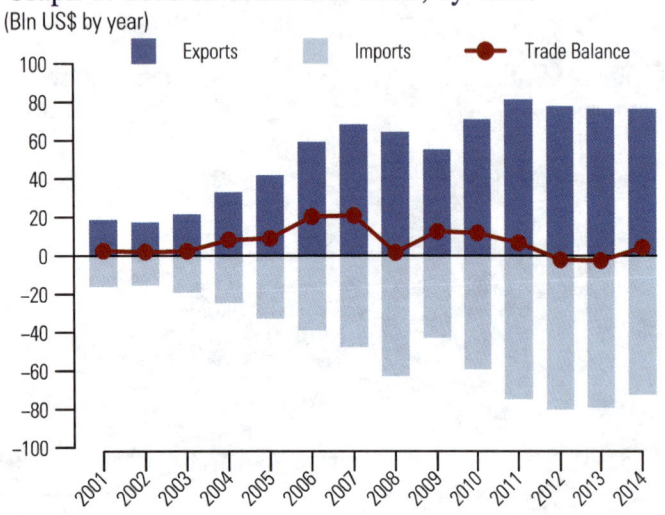

Graph 2: Total services trade, by value
(Bln US$ by year)

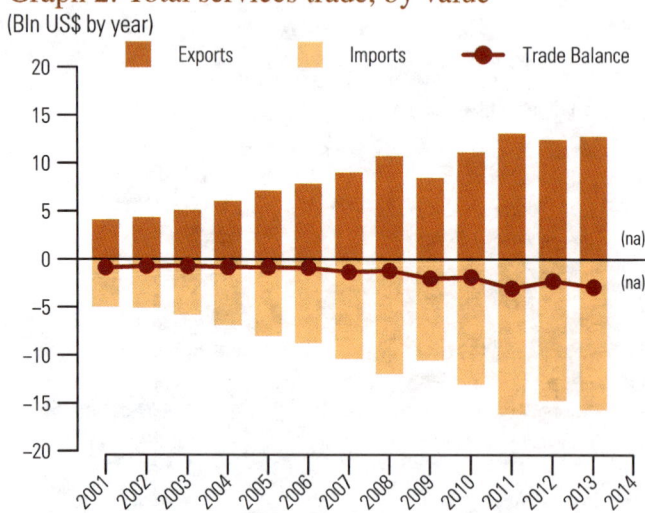

Exports Profile:
"Crude materials + anim. & veg. oils" (SITC section 2+4), "Goods classified chiefly by material" (SITC section 6) and "Food, animals + beverages, tobacco" (SITC section 0+1) were the largest commodity groups for exports in 2014, representing respectively 34.0, 32.8 and 21.7 percent of exported goods (see table 2). From 2012 to 2014, the largest export commodity was "Refined copper and copper alloys, unwrought" (HS code 7403) (see table 1). The top three destinations for merchandise exports were China, the United States and Japan, accounting for respectively 24.2, 12.4 and 10.2 percent of total exports. "Transportation" (EBOPS code 205) accounted for the largest share of exports of services in 2013 at 6.4 bln US$, followed by "Other business services" (EBOPS code 268) at 2.7 bln US$ and "Travel" (EBOPS code 236) at 2.2 bln US$ (see graph 3).

Graph 3: Exports of services by EBOPS category
(% share in 2013)

- Transportation (49.7 %)
- Other business (20.8 %)
- Travel (17.4 %)
- Remaining (12.1 %)

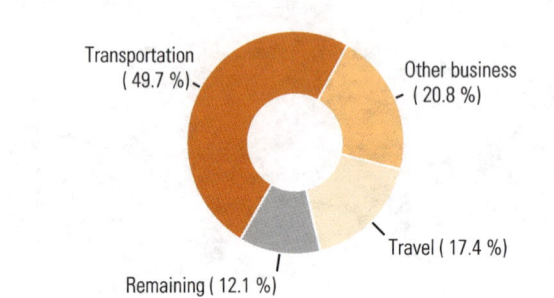

Table 1: Top 10 export commodities 2012 to 2014

HS code	4-digit heading of Harmonized System 2012	Value (million US$) 2012	2013	2014	Unit value 2012	2013	2014	Unit	SITC code
	All Commodities	77 965.4	76 684.1	76 639.2					
7403	Refined copper and copper alloys, unwrought	21 964.4	18 805.1	18 105.6	7.8	7.1	6.8	US$/kg	682
2603	Copper ores and concentrates	15 952.7	16 883.1	16 816.9	7.5	6.8	6.4	US$/kg	283
7402	Unrefined copper; copper anodes for electrolytic refining	3 402.2	3 552.1	3 005.7	8.4	7.5	6.9	US$/kg	682
4703	Chemical wood pulp, soda or sulphate, other than dissolving grades	2 529.1	2 804.9	2 890.1	0.6	0.6	0.6	US$/kg	251
0304	Fish fillets and other fish meat (whether or not minced)	1 548.4	1 988.2	2 332.0	7.2	8.3	9.5	US$/kg	034
2204	Wine of fresh grapes, including fortified wines	1 798.2	1 968.7	1 856.0	2.4	2.2	2.3	US$/litre	112
0806	Grapes, fresh or dried	1 632.4	1 794.0	1 690.2	1.8	1.9	2.1	US$/kg	057
0303	Fish, frozen, excluding fish fillets and other fish meat of heading 03.04	1 303.8	1 367.6	1 707.8	3.9	3.7	4.6	US$/kg	034
7108	Gold (including gold plated with platinum)	1 630.4	1 382.2	1 066.7	51.4	43.8	38.5	thsd US$/kg	971
2601	Iron ores and concentrates, including roasted iron pyrites	1 338.0	1 378.8	1 140.2	0.1	0.1	0.1	US$/kg	281

Chile

Services Imports and Exports: EBOPS 2002 categories

Table 2: Merchandise exports by SITC
(Value in million US$, growth and shares in percentage)

SITC	2014	Avg. Growth rates 2010-2014	Avg. Growth rates 2013-2014	2014 share
Total	76 639.2	1.9	-0.1	100.0
0+1	16 645.1	9.3	6.7	21.7
2+4	26 038.5	4.3	1.1	34.0
3	643.1	1.6	-6.5	0.8
5	3 389.7	4.4	-5.4	4.4
6	25 150.7	-4.4	-4.7	32.8
7	2 642.3	7.4	19.2	3.4
8	1 062.6	4.7	0.0	1.4
9	1 067.2	0.9	-23.0	1.4

Table 3: Merchandise imports by SITC
(Value in million US$, growth and shares in percentage)

SITC	2014	Avg. Growth rates 2010-2014	Avg. Growth rates 2013-2014	2014 share
Total	72 344.3	5.1	-8.6	100.0
0+1	5 528.4	8.5	-1.8	7.6
2+4	1 967.2	7.0	4.6	2.7
3	15 326.7	4.4	-9.3	21.2
5	7 867.4	7.1	-3.8	10.9
6	8 454.8	3.5	-3.2	11.7
7	24 748.6	3.4	-16.0	34.2
8	8 431.5	9.8	0.3	11.7
9	19.7	297.0	22157.1	0.0

SITC Legend

SITC Code	Description
Total	All commodities
0+1	Food, animals + beverages, tobacco
2+4	Crude materials + anim. & veg. oils
3	Mineral fuels, lubricants
5	Chemicals
6	Goods classified chiefly by material
7	Machinery and transport equipment
8	Miscellaneous manufactured articles
9	Not classified elsewhere in the SITC

Graph 4: Merchandise trade balance
(Bln US$ by MDG Regions in 2014)

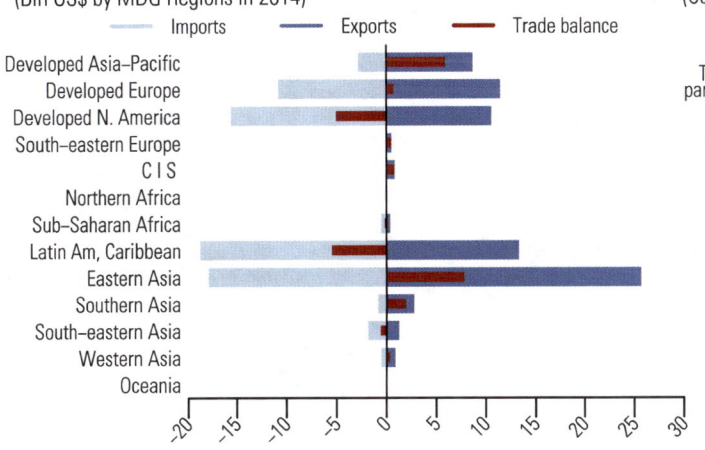

Graph 5: Partner concentration of merchandise trade
(Cumulative share by ranked partners in 2014)

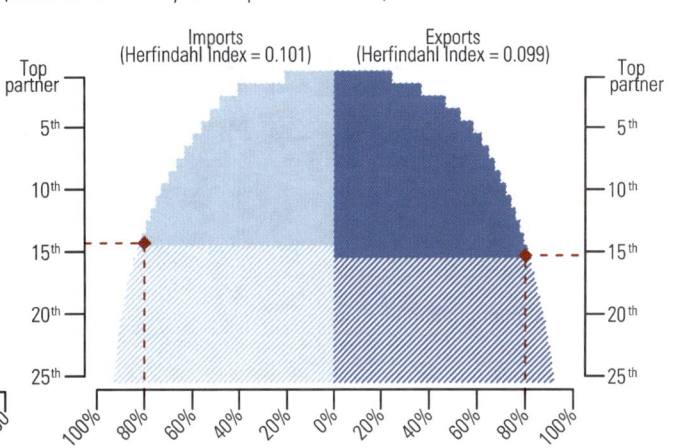

Imports (Herfindahl Index = 0.101)
Exports (Herfindahl Index = 0.099)

Graph 6: Imports of services by EBOPS category
(% share in 2013)

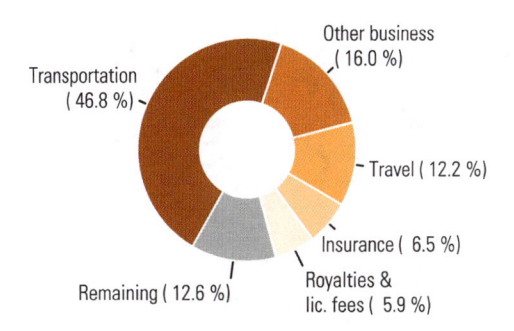

- Transportation (46.8 %)
- Other business (16.0 %)
- Travel (12.2 %)
- Insurance (6.5 %)
- Royalties & lic. fees (5.9 %)
- Remaining (12.6 %)

Imports Profile:

"Machinery and transport equipment" (SITC section 7), "Mineral fuels, lubricants" (SITC section 3) and "Goods classified chiefly by material" (SITC section 6) were the largest commodity groups for imports in 2014, representing respectively 34.2, 21.2 and 11.7 percent of imported goods (see table 3). From 2012 to 2014, the largest import commodity was "Petroleum oils, other than crude" (HS code 2710) (see table 4). The top three partners for merchandise imports were the United States, China and Brazil, accounting for respectively 21.1, 19.5 and 6.9 percent of total imports. "Transportation" (EBOPS code 205) accounted for the largest share of imports of services in 2013 at 7.3 bln US$, followed by "Other business services" (EBOPS code 268) at 2.5 bln US$ and "Travel" (EBOPS code 236) at 1.9 bln US$ (see graph 6).

Table 4: Top 10 import commodities 2012 to 2014

HS code	4-digit heading of Harmonized System 2012	2012	2013	2014	2012	2013	2014	Unit	SITC code
	All Commodities	80 066.8	79 172.8	72 344.3					
2710	Petroleum oils, other than crude	8 160.3	7 088.5	6 272.5	1.1	1.1	1.0	US$/kg	334
2709	Petroleum oils and oils obtained from bituminous minerals, crude	6 107.8	6 633.4	6 040.6	0.8	0.7	0.7	US$/kg	333
8703	Motor cars and other motor vehicles principally designed for the transport	3 758.1	4 476.9	3 744.6	14.8	14.7	15.7	thsd US$/unit	781
8704	Motor vehicles for the transport of goods	3 021.6	2 612.8	1 935.8	32.8			thsd US$/unit	782
8517	Electrical apparatus for line telephony or line telegraphy	2 199.9	2 591.1	2 017.3					764
2711	Petroleum gases and other gaseous hydrocarbons	2 249.7	1 901.1	1 950.7		0.5	0.5	US$/kg	343
8802	Other aircraft (for example, helicopters, aeroplanes); spacecraft	2 514.5	1 279.0	864.5	30.3	14.5	8.5	mln US$/unit	792
8471	Automatic data processing machines and units thereof	1 309.0	1 428.1	1 142.2	152.6	147.0		US$/unit	752
4011	New pneumatic tyres, of rubber	1 244.6	1 216.7	1 095.7	45.5		149.1	US$/unit	625
2701	Coal; briquettes, ovoids and similar solid fuels manufactured from coal	1 114.6	1 076.8	899.7	0.1	0.1	0.1	US$/kg	321

2014 International Trade Statistics Yearbook, Vol. I   Source: UN Comtrade and UN ServiceTrade

China

Goods Imports: CIF, by origin   **Goods Exports:** FOB, by last known destination   **Trade System:** General

Overview:

In 2014, the value of merchandise exports of China increased moderately by 6.0 percent to reach 2342.3 bln US$, while its merchandise imports increased slightly by 0.4 percent to reach 1958.0 bln US$ (see graph 1, table 2 and table 3). The merchandise trade balance recorded a surplus of 384.3 bln US$, the largest surplus recorded (see graph 1). The largest merchandise trade balance was with MDG Developed North America at 242.2 bln US$ (see graph 4). In 2014, China was the world's top exporter of merchandise goods. Merchandise exports in China were diversified amongst partners; imports were also diversified. The top 25 partners accounted for 80 percent or more of exports and 23 partners accounted for 80 percent or more of imports (see graph 5). In 2013, the value of exports of services of China increased moderately by 7.6 percent, reaching 206.0 bln US$, while its imports of services increased substantially by 17.6 percent and reached 330.5 bln US$ (see graph 2). There was a moderate trade in services deficit of 124.5 bln US$.

Graph 1: Total merchandise trade, by value
(Bln US$ by year)

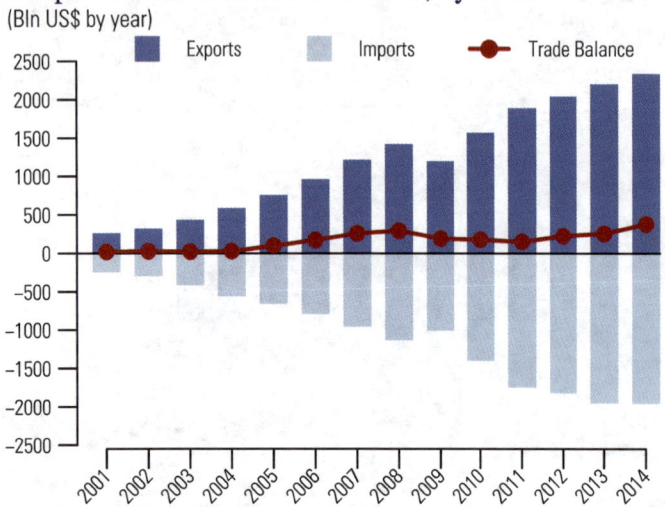

Graph 2: Total services trade, by value
(Bln US$ by year)

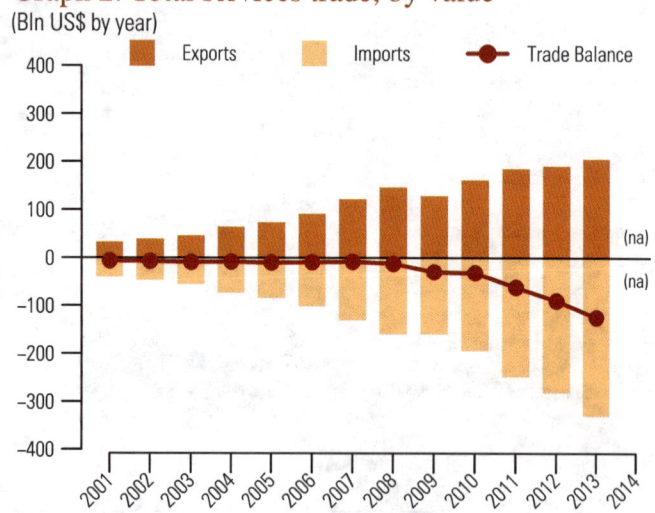

Exports Profile:

"Machinery and transport equipment" (SITC section 7), "Miscellaneous manufactured articles" (SITC section 8) and "Goods classified chiefly by material" (SITC section 6) were the largest commodity groups for exports in 2014, representing respectively 45.8, 26.4 and 17.2 percent of exported goods (see table 2). From 2012 to 2014, the largest export commodity was "Electrical apparatus for line telephony or line telegraphy" (HS code 8517). The export of this commodity recorded a strong growth of 11.7 percent from 2013 to 2014 (see table 1). The top three destinations for merchandise exports were the United States, China, Hong Kong SAR and Japan, accounting for respectively 16.9, 16.2 and 6.8 percent of total exports. "Other business services" (EBOPS code 268) accounted for the largest share of exports of services in 2013 at 79.5 bln US$, followed by "Travel" (EBOPS code 236) at 51.7 bln US$ and "Transportation" (EBOPS code 205) at 37.6 bln US$ (see graph 3).

Graph 3: Exports of services by EBOPS category
(% share in 2013)

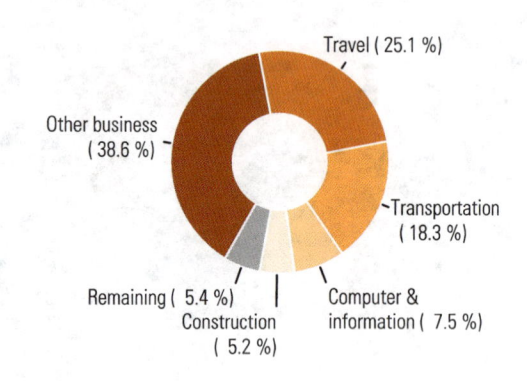

- Travel (25.1 %)
- Other business (38.6 %)
- Transportation (18.3 %)
- Computer & information (7.5 %)
- Construction (5.2 %)
- Remaining (5.4 %)

Table 1: Top 10 export commodities 2012 to 2014

HS code	4-digit heading of Harmonized System 2012	Value (billion US$) 2012	2013	2014	Unit value 2012	2013	2014	Unit	SITC code
	All Commodities	2048.8	2209.0	2342.3					
8517	Electrical apparatus for line telephony or line telegraphy	153.2	174.9	195.3					764
8471	Automatic data processing machines and units thereof	163.4	161.7	163.4	95.9	92.2	90.1	US$/unit	752
8542	Electronic integrated circuits	53.7	87.9	61.2					776
9013	Liquid crystal devices	38.7	38.6	34.7					871
7113	Articles of jewellery and parts thereof, of precious metal	22.9	28.9	48.5	23.8	32.2	50.3	thsd US$/kg	897
8473	Parts and accessories for use with machines of heading 84.69 to 84.72	30.4	29.4	31.2	35.4	37.0	42.9	US$/kg	759
8541	Diodes, transistors and similar semiconductor devices	27.3	27.9	30.6					776
8528	Reception apparatus for television	27.7	26.7	30.3	101.6	98.5	98.7	US$/unit	761
9403	Other furniture and parts thereof	27.0	28.9	28.4					821
4202	Trunks, suit-cases, vanity-cases, executive-cases, brief-cases	25.3	27.6	27.1					831

Source: UN Comtrade and UN ServiceTrade

China

Services Imports and Exports: EBOPS 2002 categories

Table 2: Merchandise exports by SITC
(Value in million US$, growth and shares in percentage)

SITC	2014	Avg. Growth rates 2010-2014	Avg. Growth rates 2013-2014	2014 share
Total	2 342 343.0	10.4	6.0	100.0
0+1	61 796.6	9.5	5.9	2.6
2+4	16 504.4	8.3	8.6	0.7
3	34 445.8	6.6	2.0	1.5
5	134 485.6	11.3	12.5	5.7
6	401 764.8	12.7	11.1	17.2
7	1 071 841.4	8.2	3.1	45.8
8	619 237.3	13.2	6.9	26.4
9	2 267.2	11.5	31.1	0.1

Table 3: Merchandise imports by SITC
(Value in million US$, growth and shares in percentage)

SITC	2014	Avg. Growth rates 2010-2014	Avg. Growth rates 2013-2014	2014 share
Total	1 958 021.3	8.8	0.4	100.0
0+1	51 452.3	21.0	11.3	2.6
2+4	279 130.9	6.0	-6.1	14.3
3	316 804.8	13.8	0.5	16.2
5	191 841.0	6.4	1.2	9.8
6	173 144.0	7.2	16.7	8.8
7	724 889.9	7.2	2.0	37.0
8	137 994.3	5.1	0.1	7.0
9	82 764.1	45.6	-21.0	4.2

SITC Legend

SITC Code	Description
Total	All commodities
0+1	Food, animals + beverages, tobacco
2+4	Crude materials + anim. & veg. oils
3	Mineral fuels, lubricants
5	Chemicals
6	Goods classified chiefly by material
7	Machinery and transport equipment
8	Miscellaneous manufactured articles
9	Not classified elsewhere in the SITC

Graph 4: Merchandise trade balance
(Bln US$ by MDG Regions in 2014)

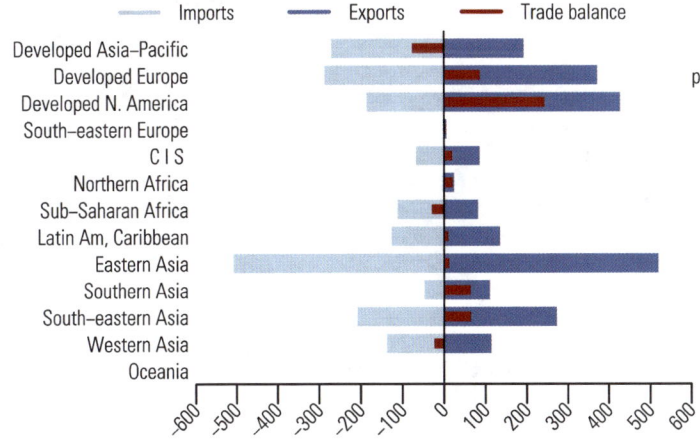

Graph 5: Partner concentration of merchandise trade
(Cumulative share by ranked partners in 2014)

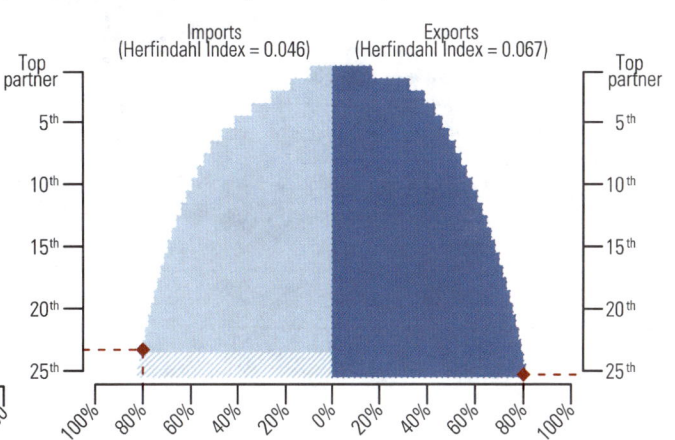

Imports (Herfindahl Index = 0.046)
Exports (Herfindahl Index = 0.067)

Graph 6: Imports of services by EBOPS category
(% share in 2013)

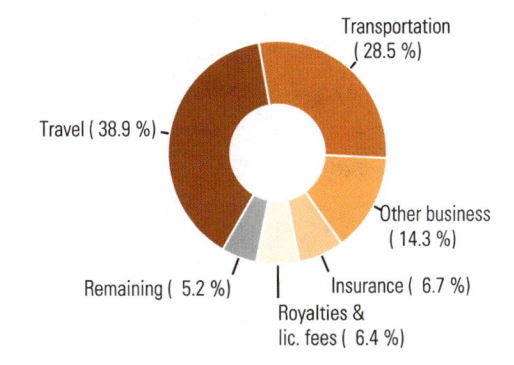

- Transportation (28.5 %)
- Travel (38.9 %)
- Other business (14.3 %)
- Insurance (6.7 %)
- Royalties & lic. fees (6.4 %)
- Remaining (5.2 %)

Imports Profile:

"Machinery and transport equipment" (SITC section 7), "Mineral fuels, lubricants" (SITC section 3) and "Crude materials + anim. & veg. oils" (SITC section 2+4) were the largest commodity groups for imports in 2014, representing respectively 37.0, 16.2 and 14.3 percent of imported goods (see table 3). From 2012 to 2014, the largest import commodity was "Petroleum oils and oils obtained from bituminous minerals, crude" (HS code 2709) (see table 4). The top three partners for merchandise imports were the Republic of Korea, Japan and the United States, accounting for respectively 9.5, 8.8 and 7.8 percent of total imports. "Travel" (EBOPS code 236) accounted for the largest share of imports of services in 2013 at 128.6 bln US$, followed by "Transportation" (EBOPS code 205) at 94.3 bln US$ and "Other business services" (EBOPS code 268) at 47.3 bln US$ (see graph 6).

Table 4: Top 10 import commodities 2012 to 2014

HS code	4-digit heading of Harmonized System 2012	Value (billion US$) 2012	2013	2014	Unit value 2012	2013	2014	Unit	SITC code
	All Commodities	1 818.2	1 950.0	1 958.0					
2709	Petroleum oils and oils obtained from bituminous minerals, crude	220.8	219.7	228.3	0.8	0.8	0.7	US$/kg	333
8542	Electronic integrated circuits	193.0	232.1	218.5					776
2601	Iron ores and concentrates, including roasted iron pyrites	95.6	106.2	93.5	0.1	0.1	0.1	US$/kg	281
9999	Commodities not specified according to kind	68.8	104.7	82.8					931
9013	Liquid crystal devices	55.9	55.4	50.0					871
8703	Motor cars and other motor vehicles principally designed for the transport	45.5	47.5	59.7	40.9	40.1	42.2	thsd US$/unit	781
8517	Electrical apparatus for line telephony or line telegraphy	39.1	46.9	43.9					764
1201	Soya beans, whether or not broken	35.0	38.0	40.3	0.6	0.6	0.6	US$/kg	222
8471	Automatic data processing machines and units thereof	34.9	29.1	28.7	48.4	39.5	38.1	US$/unit	752
2710	Petroleum oils, other than crude	33.0	32.0	23.5	0.8	0.8	0.8	US$/kg	334

China, Hong Kong SAR

Goods Imports: CIF, by consignment **Goods Exports:** FOB, by last known destination **Trade System:** General

Overview:
In 2014, the value of merchandise exports of China, Hong Kong SAR decreased slightly by 2.1 percent to reach 524.1 bln US$, while its merchandise imports decreased slightly by 3.3 percent to reach 600.6 bln US$ (see graph 1, table 2 and table 3). The merchandise trade deficit recorded a deficit of 76.5 bln US$ (see graph 1). The largest merchandise trade balance was with MDG South-eastern Asia at -41.2 bln US$ (see graph 4). Merchandise exports in China, Hong Kong SAR were highly concentrated amongst partners; imports were moderately concentrated. The top 9 partners accounted for 80 percent or more of exports and the same number of partners accounted for 80 percent or more of imports (see graph 5). In 2012, the value of exports of services of China, Hong Kong SAR increased moderately by 7.0 percent, reaching 129.3 bln US$, while its imports of services increased slightly by 4.2 percent and reached 58.7 bln US$ (see graph 2). There was a large trade in services surplus of 70.6 bln US$, up from the trade in services surplus in 2011 of 64.6 bln US$.

Graph 1: Total merchandise trade, by value
(Bln US$ by year)

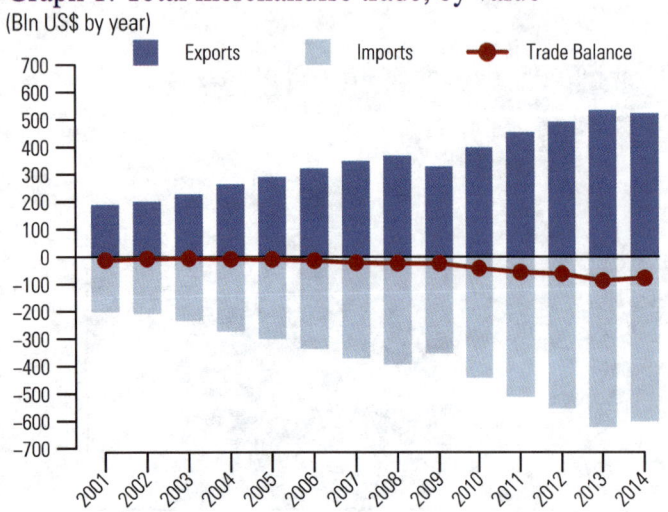

Graph 2: Total services trade, by value
(Bln US$ by year)

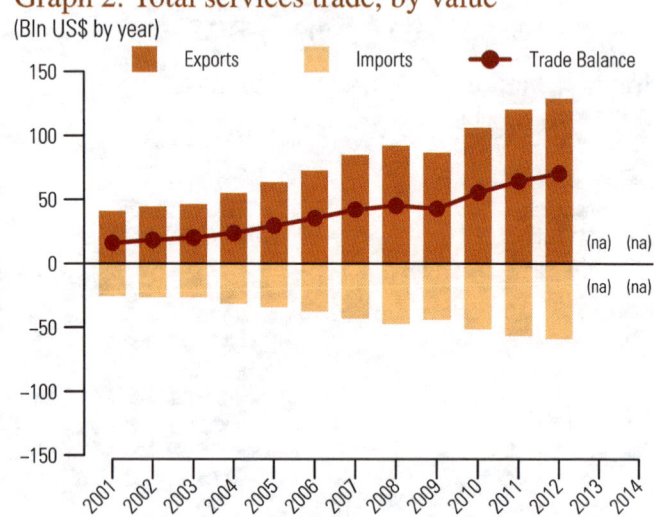

Exports Profile:
"Machinery and transport equipment" (SITC section 7), "Miscellaneous manufactured articles" (SITC section 8) and "Non-monetary gold" (SITC cod 971) were the largest commodity groups for exports in 2014, representing respectively 59.0, 16.4 and 9.7 percent of exported goods (see table 2). From 2012 to 2014, the largest export commodity was "Electronic integrated circuits" (HS code 8542), accounting for 14.8 percent of total merchandise exports by value in 2014 (see table 1). The top three destinations for merchandise exports were China, the United States and Japan, accounting for respectively 58.3, 8.4 and 3.4 percent of total exports. "Other business services" (EBOPS code 268) accounted for the largest share of exports of services in 2012 at 40.2 bln US$, followed by "Travel" (EBOPS code 236) at 33.1 bln US$ and "Transportation" (EBOPS code 205) at 31.7 bln US$ (see graph 3).

Graph 3: Exports of services by EBOPS category
(% share in 2012)

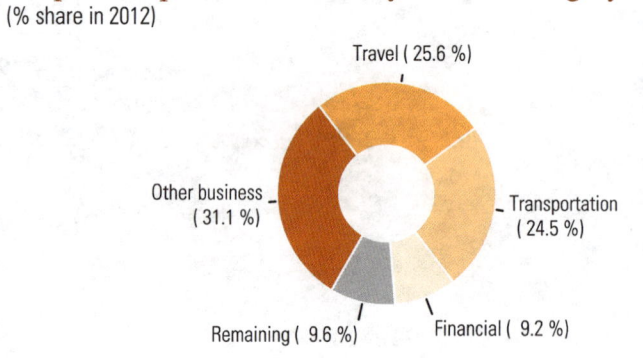

- Travel (25.6 %)
- Transportation (24.5 %)
- Financial (9.2 %)
- Remaining (9.6 %)
- Other business (31.1 %)

Table 1: Top 10 export commodities 2012 to 2014

HS code	4-digit heading of Harmonized System 2012	Value (million US$) 2012	2013	2014	Unit value 2012	2013	2014	Unit	SITC code
	All Commodities	492 907.5	535 186.7	524 064.9					
8542	Electronic integrated circuits	59 672.1	67 365.5	77 458.1					776
8517	Electrical apparatus for line telephony or line telegraphy	52 561.6	64 329.4	69 571.0					764
7108	Gold (including gold plated with platinum)	49 905.2	76 190.6	49 952.6	54.0	*49.3*	41.2	thsd US$/kg	971
8473	Parts and accessories for use with machines of heading 84.69 to 84.72	25 569.2	26 068.8	26 478.7	65.2		84.7	US$/kg	759
8471	Automatic data processing machines and units thereof	18 716.9	16 823.9	17 650.1	50.5		47.9	US$/unit	752
7102	Diamonds, whether or not worked, but not mounted or set	13 485.4	14 786.0	16 105.4					667
8529	Parts suitable for use with the apparatus of headings 85.25 to 85.28	13 961.6	12 926.1	11 607.1	73.8		85.6	US$/kg	764
8504	Electrical transformers, static converters	10 462.7	10 928.1	11 208.8					771
8541	Diodes, transistors and similar semiconductor devices	9 248.8	10 267.3	12 857.6					776
8443	Printing machinery used for printing by means of the printing type, blocks	10 122.1	9 601.8	9 037.6					726

Source: UN Comtrade and UN ServiceTrade

China, Hong Kong SAR

Services Imports and Exports: EBOPS 2002 categories

Table 2: Merchandise exports by SITC
(Value in million US$, growth and shares in percentage)

SITC	2014	Avg. Growth rates 2010-2014	2013-2014	2014 share
Total	524 064.9	6.9	-2.1	100.0
0+1	8 562.3	9.0	10.6	1.6
2+4	3 114.3	-0.2	-10.8	0.6
3	854.2	5.4	-10.9	0.2
5	17 789.0	-0.9	-5.3	3.4
6	48 243.4	4.0	3.6	9.2
7	309 063.6	7.1	6.1	59.0
8	85 750.8	0.2	-4.4	16.4
9	50 687.4	46.5	-34.0	9.7

Table 3: Merchandise imports by SITC
(Value in million US$, growth and shares in percentage)

SITC	2014	Avg. Growth rates 2010-2014	2013-2014	2014 share
Total	600 613.1	8.0	-3.3	100.0
0+1	26 577.0	10.6	10.3	4.4
2+4	3 574.7	-2.0	-21.2	0.6
3	15 762.0	0.7	-11.1	2.6
5	21 907.4	-1.4	-1.6	3.6
6	56 077.1	3.4	0.2	9.3
7	331 857.4	7.6	7.5	55.3
8	88 949.2	4.1	-1.3	14.8
9	55 908.2	60.3	-43.0	9.3

SITC Legend

SITC Code	Description
Total	All commodities
0+1	Food, animals + beverages, tobacco
2+4	Crude materials + anim. & veg. oils
3	Mineral fuels, lubricants
5	Chemicals
6	Goods classified chiefly by material
7	Machinery and transport equipment
8	Miscellaneous manufactured articles
9	Not classified elsewhere in the SITC

Graph 4: Merchandise trade balance
(Bln US$ by MDG Regions in 2014)

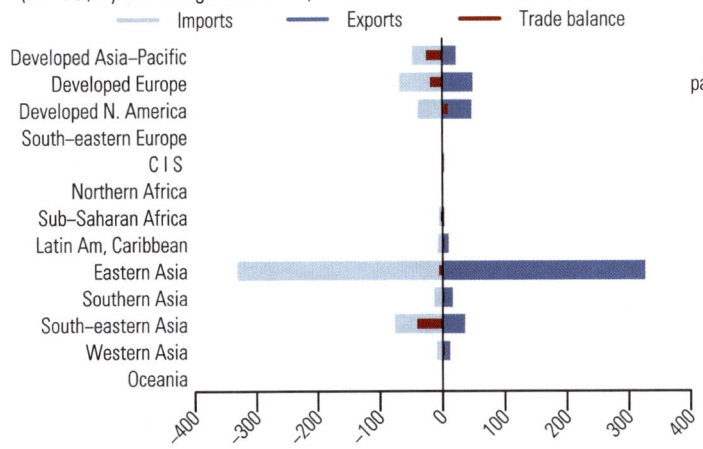

Graph 5: Partner concentration of merchandise trade
(Cumulative share by ranked partners in 2014)

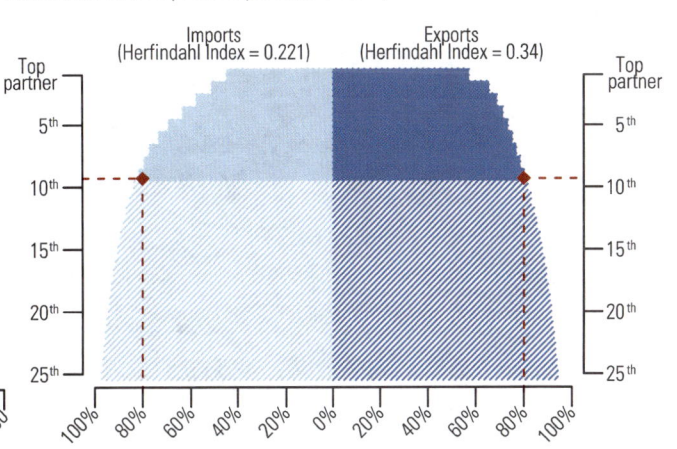

Imports (Herfindahl Index = 0.221)
Exports (Herfindahl Index = 0.34)

Graph 6: Imports of services by EBOPS category
(% share in 2012)

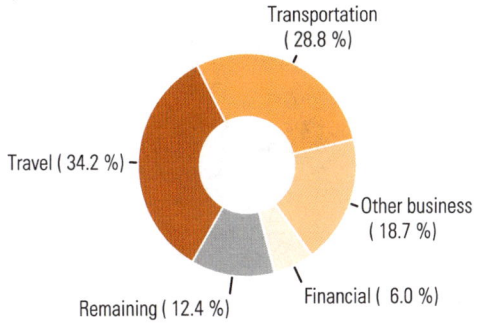

- Transportation (28.8%)
- Travel (34.2%)
- Other business (18.7%)
- Financial (6.0%)
- Remaining (12.4%)

Imports Profile:
"Machinery and transport equipment" (SITC section 7), "Miscellaneous manufactured articles" (SITC section 8) and "Goods classified chiefly by material" (SITC section 6) were the largest commodity groups for imports in 2014, representing respectively 55.3, 14.8 and 9.3 percent of imported goods (see table 3). From 2012 to 2014, the largest import commodity was "Electronic integrated circuits" (HS code 8542), followed by "Gold (including gold plated with platinum)" (HS code 7108) (see table 4). The top three partners for merchandise imports were China, Japan and the United States, accounting for respectively 44.3, 6.8 and 6.0 percent of total imports. "Travel" (EBOPS code 236) accounted for the largest share of imports of services in 2012 at 20.1 bln US$, followed by "Transportation" (EBOPS code 205) at 16.9 bln US$ and "Other business services" (EBOPS code 268) at 11.0 bln US$ (see graph 6).

Table 4: Top 10 import commodities 2012 to 2014

HS code	4-digit heading of Harmonized System 2012	Value (million US$) 2012	2013	2014	Unit value 2012	2013	2014	Unit	SITC code
	All Commodities	553 486.5	621 416.9	600 613.1					
8542	Electronic integrated circuits	71 121.1	81 418.9	98 116.7					776
7108	Gold (including gold plated with platinum)	47 617.2	97 142.9	54 964.5	49.5	43.4	37.9	thsd US$/kg	971
8517	Electrical apparatus for line telephony or line telegraphy	52 821.4	61 337.1	68 951.5					764
8471	Automatic data processing machines and units thereof	22 526.9	22 444.9	22 676.1	53.9		55.2	US$/unit	752
8473	Parts and accessories for use with machines of heading 84.69 to 84.72	22 280.9	21 961.3	19 339.6	61.9		68.0	US$/kg	759
7102	Diamonds, whether or not worked, but not mounted or set	18 357.7	20 068.5	21 926.9					667
2710	Petroleum oils, other than crude	15 388.5	14 717.9	12 726.9		1.6	1.7	US$/kg	334
8541	Diodes, transistors and similar semiconductor devices	11 846.7	12 968.7	15 532.0					776
7113	Articles of jewellery and parts thereof, of precious metal	11 918.3	12 247.2	14 156.3	36.2	36.4	36.6	thsd US$/kg	897
8529	Parts suitable for use with the apparatus of headings 85.25 to 85.28	12 363.2	11 229.7	9 693.5	69.3		71.4	US$/kg	764

2014 International Trade Statistics Yearbook, Vol. I Source: UN Comtrade and UN ServiceTrade

China, Macao SAR

Goods Imports: CIF, by origin   **Goods Exports:** FOB, by last known destination   **Trade System:** General

Overview:

In 2014, the value of merchandise exports of China, Macao SAR was 1.2 bln US$, while its merchandise imports was 11.4 bln US$ (see graph 1, table 2 and table 3). The merchandise trade balance recorded a large deficit of 10.2 bln US$ (see graph 1). The largest merchandise trade balance was with MDG Eastern Asia at -4.4 bln US$ (see graph 4). Merchandise exports in China, Macao SAR were highly concentrated amongst partners; imports were diversified. The top 2 partners accounted for 80 percent or more of exports and 8 partners accounted for 80 percent or more of imports (see graph 5). In 2013, the value of exports of services of China, Macao SAR increased substantially by 18.1 percent, reaching 53.5 bln US$, while its imports of services increased moderately by 7.7 percent and reached 11.7 bln US$ (see graph 2). There was a large trade in services surplus of 41.8 bln US$.

Graph 1: Total merchandise trade, by value
(Bln US$ by year)

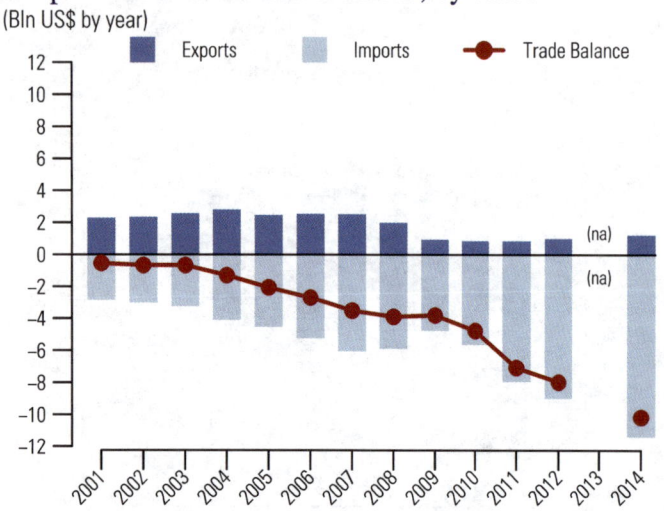

Graph 2: Total services trade, by value
(Bln US$ by year)

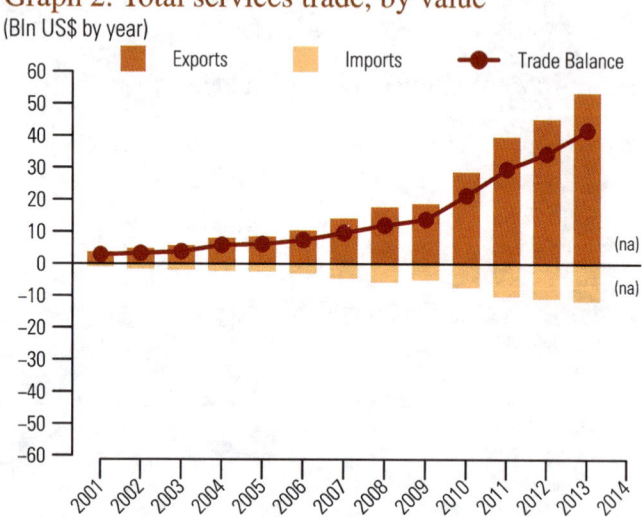

Exports Profile:

"Not classified elsewhere in the SITC" (SITC section 9), "Miscellaneous manufactured articles" (SITC section 8) and "Machinery and transport equipment" (SITC section 7) were the largest commodity groups for exports in 2014, representing respectively 36.0, 27.2 and 23.8 percent of exported goods (see table 2). In 2012 and 2014, the largest export commodity was "Commodities not specified according to kind" (HS code 9999) (see table 1). The top three destinations for merchandise exports were China, Hong Kong SAR, Areas nes and China, accounting for respectively 47.4, 30.9 and 12.5 percent of total exports. "Travel" (EBOPS code 236) accounted for the largest share of exports of services in 2013 at 51.8 bln US$ (see graph 3).

Graph 3: Exports of services by EBOPS category
(% share in 2013)

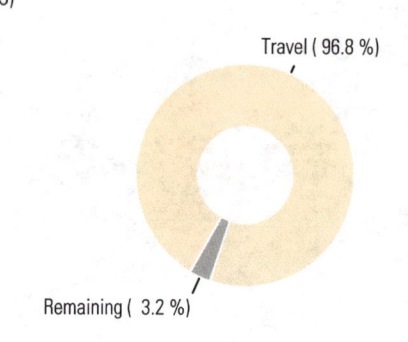

- Travel (96.8 %)
- Remaining (3.2 %)

Table 1: Top 10 export commodities 2012 to 2014

HS code	4-digit heading of Harmonized System 2012	Value (million US$) 2012	2013	2014	Unit value 2012	2013	2014	Unit	SITC code
	All Commodities	1 020.5	...	1 240.0					
9999	Commodities not specified according to kind	642.4	...	447.0					931
8517	Electrical apparatus for line telephony or line telegraphy	125.9	...	116.9					764
9101	Wrist-watches, pocket-watches and other watches, precious metal	...	...	96.6			27.1	thsd US$/unit	885
7113	Articles of jewellery and parts thereof, of precious metal	23.7	...	66.4	188.3		235.6	thsd US$/kg	897
8538	Parts suitable for use with the apparatus of heading 85.35, 85.36 or 85.37	32.0	...	47.9	170.7		380.6	US$/kg	772
2402	Cigars, cheroots, cigarillos and cigarettes	...	...	62.0			42.3	US$/kg	122
8502	Electric generating sets and rotary converters	8.3	...	43.1			141.3	US$/unit	716
6403	Footwear with outer soles of rubber, plastics, leather	11.5	...	23.8			221.3	US$/pair	851
4202	Trunks, suit-cases, vanity-cases, executive-cases, brief-cases	...	...	33.5					831
6204	Women's or girls' suits, ensembles, jackets, blazers, dresses, skirts	20.4	...	12.2			11.9	US$/unit	842

Source: UN Comtrade and UN ServiceTrade

China, Macao SAR

Services Imports and Exports: EBOPS 2002 categories

Table 2: Merchandise exports by SITC
(Value in million US$, growth and shares in percentage)

SITC	2014	Avg. Growth rates 2010-2014	2013-2014	2014 share
Total	1 240.0	9.3	>	100.0
0+1	101.0	52.4	>	8.1
2+4	20.5	104.3	>	1.7
3	0.1	...	>	0.0
5	14.1	71.3	>	1.1
6	24.6	-5.6	>	2.0
7	295.3	47.6	>	23.8
8	337.5	22.4	>	27.2
9	447.0	-7.3	>	36.0

Table 3: Merchandise imports by SITC
(Value in million US$, growth and shares in percentage)

SITC	2014	Avg. Growth rates 2010-2014	2013-2014	2014 share
Total	11 395.9	19.3	>	100.0
0+1	1 650.4	15.3	>	14.5
2+4	69.5	24.6	>	0.6
3	787.2	6.5	>	6.9
5	784.2	21.7	>	6.9
6	729.9	20.3	>	6.4
7	2 616.3	21.0	>	23.0
8	4 148.7	23.6	>	36.4
9	609.7	14.9	>	5.3

SITC Legend

SITC Code	Description
Total	All commodities
0+1	Food, animals + beverages, tobacco
2+4	Crude materials + anim. & veg. oils
3	Mineral fuels, lubricants
5	Chemicals
6	Goods classified chiefly by material
7	Machinery and transport equipment
8	Miscellaneous manufactured articles
9	Not classified elsewhere in the SITC

Graph 4: Merchandise trade balance
(Bln US$ by MDG Regions in 2014)

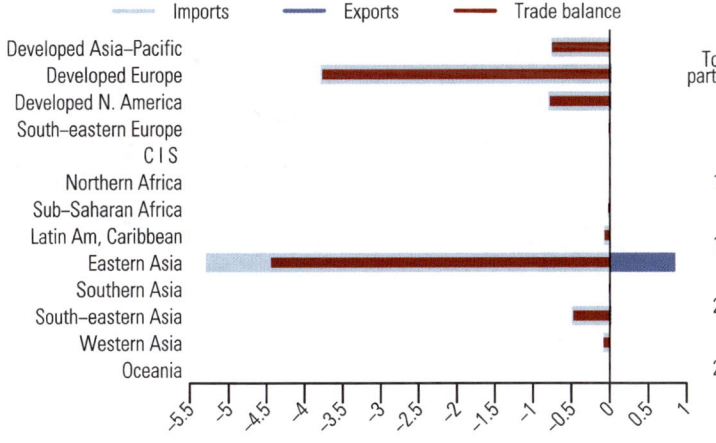

Graph 5: Partner concentration of merchandise trade
(Cumulative share by ranked partners in 2014)

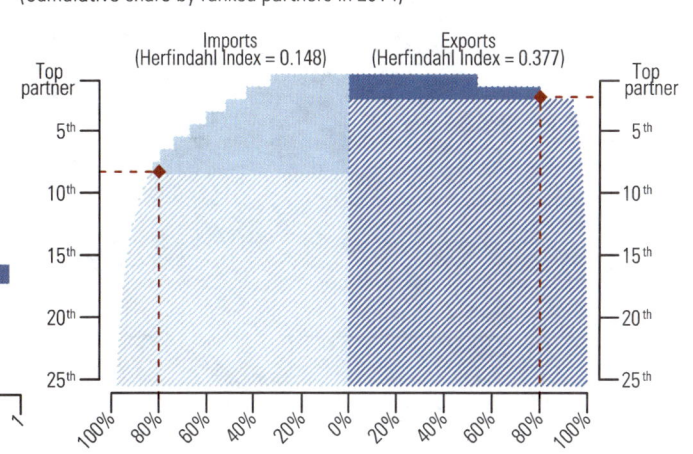

Imports (Herfindahl Index = 0.148)
Exports (Herfindahl Index = 0.377)

Graph 6: Imports of services by EBOPS category
(% share in 2013)

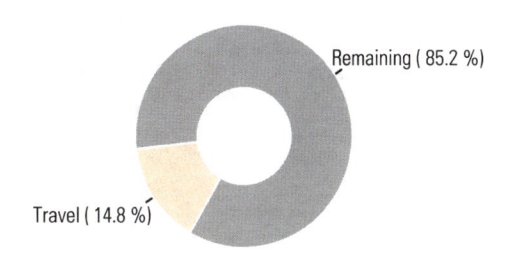

Remaining (85.2 %)
Travel (14.8 %)

Imports Profile:
"Miscellaneous manufactured articles" (SITC section 8), "Machinery and transport equipment" (SITC section 7) and "Food, animals + beverages, tobacco" (SITC section 0+1) were the largest commodity groups for imports in 2014, representing respectively 36.4, 23.0 and 14.5 percent of imported goods (see table 3). In 2012 and 2014, the largest import commodity was "Articles of jewellery and parts thereof, of precious metal" (HS code 7113) (see table 4). The top three partners for merchandise imports were China, China, Hong Kong SAR and France, accounting for respectively 32.6, 10.7 and 8.5 percent of total imports. "Travel" (EBOPS code 236) accounted for the largest share of imports of services in 2013 at 1.7 bln US$ (see graph 6).

Table 4: Top 10 import commodities 2012 to 2014

HS code	4-digit heading of Harmonized System 2012	Value (million US$) 2012	2013	2014	Unit value 2012	2013	2014	Unit	SITC code
	All Commodities	8 982.1	...	11 395.9					
7113	Articles of jewellery and parts thereof, of precious metal	982.6	...	1 361.4	58.1		66.5	thsd US$/kg	897
8517	Electrical apparatus for line telephony or line telegraphy	798.7	...	998.0					764
9101	Wrist-watches, pocket-watches and other watches, precious metal	536.3	...	817.9			12.6	thsd US$/unit	885
4202	Trunks, suit-cases, vanity-cases, executive-cases, brief-cases	518.6	...	475.9					831
8703	Motor cars and other motor vehicles principally designed for the transport	395.9	...	434.3			41.5	thsd US$/unit	781
2716	Electrical energy	394.4	...	432.1			105.4	US$/MWh	351
9999	Commodities not specified according to kind	225.6	...	587.9					931
2710	Petroleum oils, other than crude	507.7	...	298.3	1.1		1.0	US$/kg	334
3304	Beauty or make-up preparations	202.5	...	380.8	51.9		66.4	US$/kg	553
8471	Automatic data processing machines and units thereof	286.7	...	198.2			450.6	US$/unit	752

Colombia

Goods Imports: CIF, by origin **Goods Exports:** FOB, by last known destination **Trade System:** Special

Overview:
In 2014, the value of merchandise exports of Colombia decreased moderately by 6.8 percent to reach 54.8 bln US$, while its merchandise imports increased moderately by 7.8 percent to reach 64.0 bln US$ (see graph 1, table 2 and table 3). The merchandise trade balance recorded a relatively small deficit of 9.2 bln US$ (see graph 1). The largest merchandise trade balance was with MDG Eastern Asia at -7.6 bln US$ (see graph 4). Merchandise exports in Colombia were diversified amongst partners; imports were also diversified. The top 15 partners accounted for 80 percent or more of exports and 14 partners accounted for 80 percent or more of imports (see graph 5). In 2013, the value of exports of services of Colombia increased moderately by 8.0 percent, reaching 6.9 bln US$, while its imports of services increased slightly by 3.6 percent and reached 12.2 bln US$ (see graph 2). There was a moderate trade in services deficit of 5.3 bln US$.

Graph 1: Total merchandise trade, by value
(Bln US$ by year)

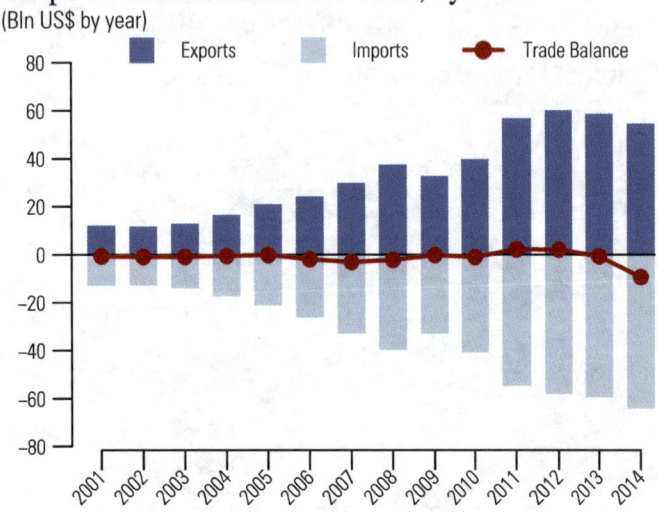

Graph 2: Total services trade, by value
(Bln US$ by year)

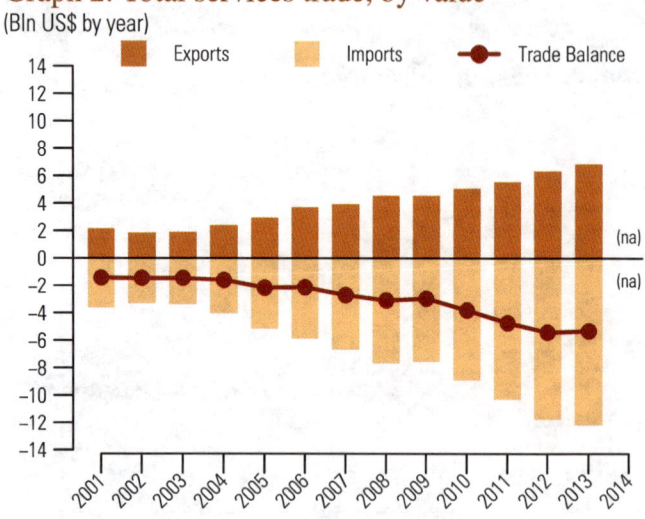

Exports Profile:
"Mineral fuels, lubricants" (SITC section 3), "Food, animals + beverages, tobacco" (SITC section 0+1) and "Chemicals" (SITC section 5) were the largest commodity groups for exports in 2014, representing respectively 65.6, 10.0 and 6.7 percent of exported goods (see table 2). From 2012 to 2014, the largest export commodity was "Petroleum oils and oils obtained from bituminous minerals, crude" (HS code 2709) (see table 1). The top three destinations for merchandise exports were the United States, China and Panama, accounting for respectively 31.8, 8.2 and 5.6 percent of total exports. "Travel" (EBOPS code 236) accounted for the largest share of exports of services in 2013 at 3.6 bln US$, followed by "Transportation" (EBOPS code 205) at 1.7 bln US$ and "Other business services" (EBOPS code 268) at 893.5 mln US$ (see graph 3).

Graph 3: Exports of services by EBOPS category
(% share in 2013)

- Travel (52.5 %)
- Transportation (24.8 %)
- Other business (13.0 %)
- Remaining (9.8 %)

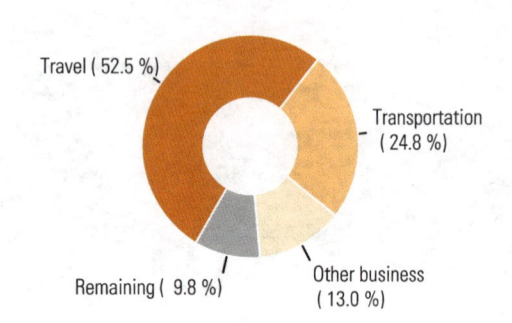

Table 1: Top 10 export commodities 2012 to 2014

HS code	4-digit heading of Harmonized System 2012	Value (million US$) 2012	2013	2014	Unit value 2012	2013	2014	Unit	SITC code
	All Commodities	60 273.6	58 821.9	54 794.8					
2709	Petroleum oils and oils obtained from bituminous minerals, crude	26 556.8	27 644.2	25 760.8	0.7	0.7	0.6	US$/kg	333
2701	Coal; briquettes, ovoids and similar solid fuels manufactured from coal	7 298.8	6 253.8	6 426.7	0.1	0.1	0.1	US$/kg	321
2710	Petroleum oils, other than crude	4 657.3	4 364.6	2 855.1	0.7	0.7	0.6	US$/kg	334
7108	Gold (including gold plated with platinum)	3 385.3	2 226.5	1 581.8	44.2	38.9	33.0	thsd US$/kg	971
0901	Coffee, whether or not roasted or decaffeinated	1 956.1	1 922.5	2 516.7	4.9	3.5	4.0	US$/kg	071
0603	Cut flowers and flower buds of a kind suitable for bouquets	1 270.0	1 334.6	1 374.2	6.3	6.3	6.2	US$/kg	292
0803	Bananas, including plantains, fresh or dried	822.0	763.9	835.5	0.4	0.5	0.5	US$/kg	057
7202	Ferro-alloys	881.7	681.8	642.1	6.0	4.9	4.8	US$/kg	671
3004	Medicaments (excluding goods of heading 30.02, 30.05 or 30.06)	417.1	447.7	480.2	11.8	10.2	9.0	US$/kg	542
2704	Coke and semi-coke of coal, of lignite or of peat	506.3	433.9	383.2	0.3	0.2	0.2	US$/kg	325

Source: UN Comtrade and UN ServiceTrade

Colombia

Services Imports and Exports: EBOPS 2002 categories

Table 2: Merchandise exports by SITC
(Value in million US$, growth and shares in percentage)

SITC	2014	Avg. Growth rates 2010-2014	Avg. Growth rates 2013-2014	2014 share
Total	54 794.8	8.3	-6.8	100.0
0+1	5 481.3	6.2	11.3	10.0
2+4	2 250.4	4.0	0.5	4.1
3	35 930.6	12.3	-8.5	65.6
5	3 684.1	6.7	-1.3	6.7
6	2 962.8	-2.9	-2.8	5.4
7	1 529.0	4.8	-16.7	2.8
8	1 360.4	-1.5	-9.3	2.5
9	1 596.1	-7.0	-29.5	2.9

Table 3: Merchandise imports by SITC
(Value in million US$, growth and shares in percentage)

SITC	2014	Avg. Growth rates 2010-2014	Avg. Growth rates 2013-2014	2014 share
Total	64 027.6	12.0	7.8	100.0
0+1	5 166.3	11.8	1.1	8.1
2+4	1 497.9	3.3	5.9	2.3
3	7 554.4	38.0	18.3	11.8
5	10 785.3	9.7	4.5	16.8
6	9 041.4	9.1	8.7	14.1
7	23 715.2	9.9	7.3	37.0
8	5 604.4	12.3	10.4	8.8
9	662.8	18.4	1.6	1.0

SITC Legend

SITC Code	Description
Total	All commodities
0+1	Food, animals + beverages, tobacco
2+4	Crude materials + anim. & veg. oils
3	Mineral fuels, lubricants
5	Chemicals
6	Goods classified chiefly by material
7	Machinery and transport equipment
8	Miscellaneous manufactured articles
9	Not classified elsewhere in the SITC

Graph 4: Merchandise trade balance
(Bln US$ by MDG Regions in 2014)

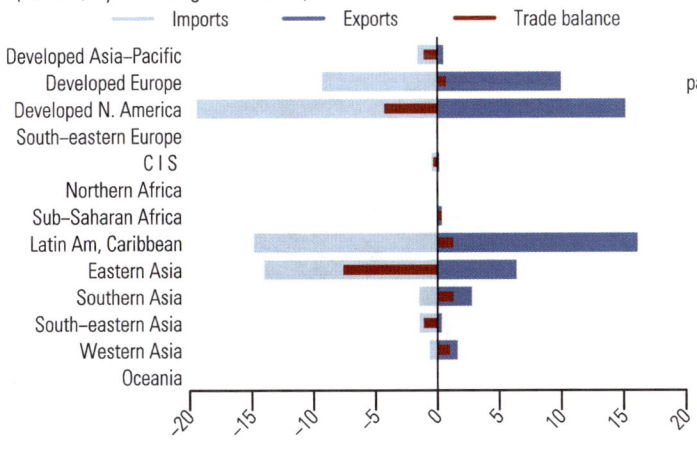

Graph 5: Partner concentration of merchandise trade
(Cumulative share by ranked partners in 2014)

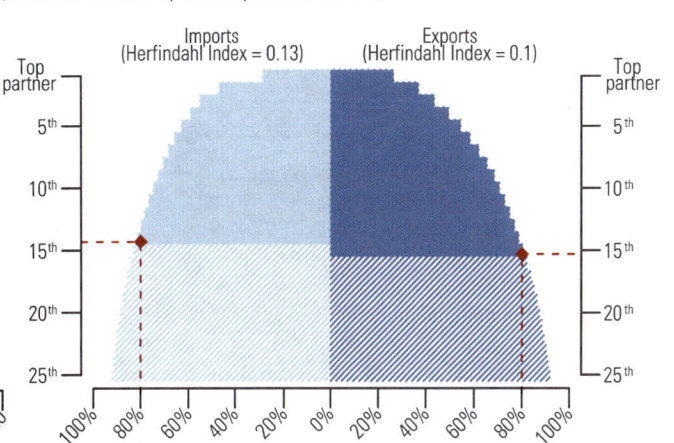

Imports (Herfindahl Index = 0.13)
Exports (Herfindahl Index = 0.1)

Graph 6: Imports of services by EBOPS category
(% share in 2013)

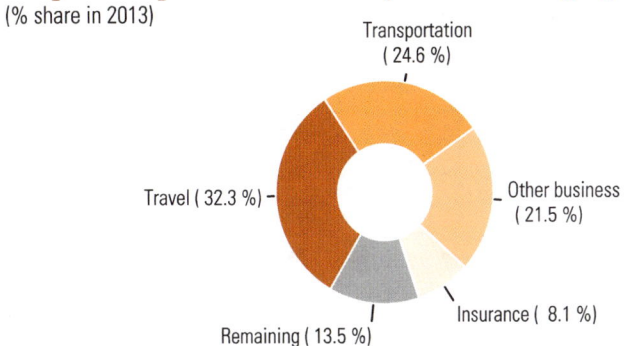

- Transportation (24.6 %)
- Travel (32.3 %)
- Other business (21.5 %)
- Insurance (8.1 %)
- Remaining (13.5 %)

Imports Profile:

"Machinery and transport equipment" (SITC section 7), "Chemicals" (SITC section 5) and "Goods classified chiefly by material" (SITC section 6) were the largest commodity groups for imports in 2014, representing respectively 37.0, 16.8 and 14.1 percent of imported goods (see table 3). From 2012 to 2014, the largest import commodity was "Petroleum oils, other than crude" (HS code 2710) (see table 4). The top three partners for merchandise imports were the United States, China and Mexico, accounting for respectively 26.9, 17.5 and 9.4 percent of total imports. "Travel" (EBOPS code 236) accounted for the largest share of imports of services in 2013 at 3.9 bln US$, followed by "Transportation" (EBOPS code 205) at 3.0 bln US$ and "Other business services" (EBOPS code 268) at 2.6 bln US$ (see graph 6).

Table 4: Top 10 import commodities 2012 to 2014

HS code	4-digit heading of Harmonized System 2012	Value (million US$) 2012	2013	2014	Unit value 2012	2013	2014	Unit	SITC code
	All Commodities..................	58 087.9	59 381.2	64 027.6					
2710	Petroleum oils, other than crude.................	5 600.5	6 332.7	7 492.4	1.0	1.0	0.9	US$/kg	334
8703	Motor cars and other motor vehicles principally designed for the transport...........	2 814.8	2 802.0	3 119.4	11.0	11.5	11.4	thsd US$/unit	781
8517	Electrical apparatus for line telephony or line telegraphy..................	1 899.1	2 318.7	2 613.4					764
8471	Automatic data processing machines and units thereof...............	1 586.3	1 800.1	1 958.7	191.0	163.0	145.4	US$/unit	752
8802	Other aircraft (for example, helicopters, aeroplanes); spacecraft..............	1 031.6	2 033.9	1 963.0	4.8	7.8	7.6	mln US$/unit	792
3004	Medicaments (excluding goods of heading 30.02, 30.05 or 30.06)...............	1 173.4	1 315.3	1 445.9	50.3	39.8	41.8	US$/kg	542
8704	Motor vehicles for the transport of goods................	1 506.0	964.9	1 218.2	27.2	24.1	22.9	thsd US$/unit	782
1005	Maize (corn)................	1 004.2	1 022.4	938.5	0.3	0.3	0.2	US$/kg	044
8528	Reception apparatus for television................	787.3	809.0	917.3	219.8	203.4	233.2	US$/unit	761
4011	New pneumatic tyres, of rubber................	820.9	777.7	755.9	50.1	47.1	44.3	US$/unit	625

Congo

Goods Imports: CIF, by origin **Goods Exports:** FOB, by last known destination **Trade System:** Special

Overview:
In 2013, the value of merchandise exports of the Congo increased substantially by 40.5 percent to reach 10.5 bln US$, while its merchandise imports increased substantially by 13.9 percent to reach 8.4 bln US$ (see graph 1, table 2 and table 3). The merchandise trade balance recorded a moderate surplus of 2.1 bln US$ (see graph 1). The largest merchandise trade balance was with MDG Eastern Asia at 3.9 bln US$ (see graph 4). Merchandise exports in the Congo were moderately concentrated amongst partners; imports were diversified. The top 9 partners accounted for 80 percent or more of exports and 15 partners accounted for 80 percent or more of imports (see graph 5). In 2012, the value of exports of services of the Congo increased slightly by 3.2 percent, reaching 488.5 mln US$, while its imports of services decreased moderately by 5.9 percent and reached 5.1 bln US$ (see graph 2). There was a large trade in services deficit of 4.6 bln US$.

Graph 1: Total merchandise trade, by value
(Bln US$ by year)

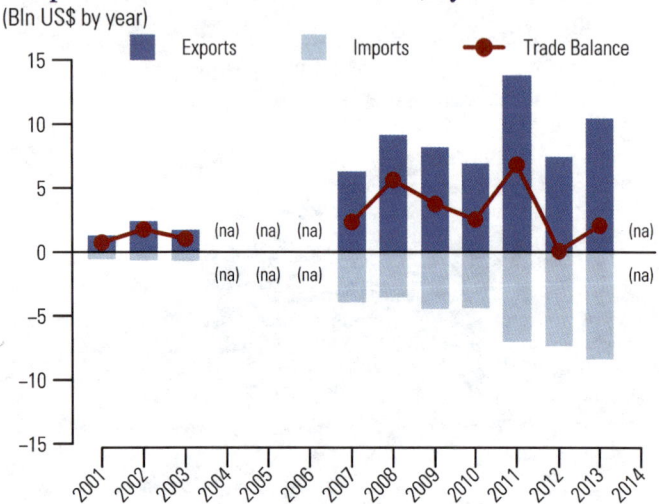

Graph 2: Total services trade, by value
(Bln US$ by year)

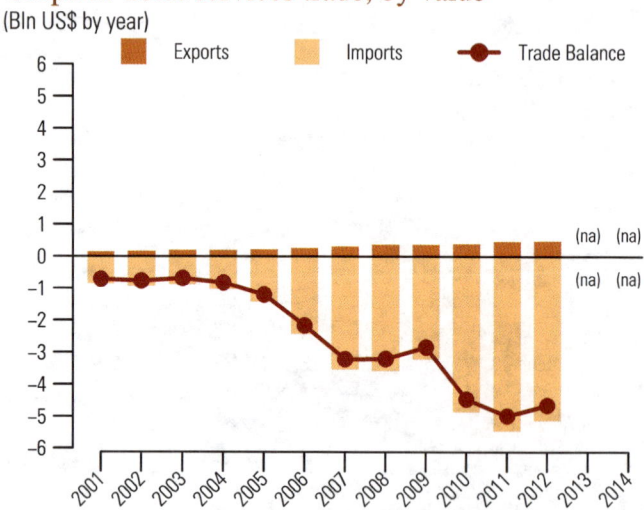

Exports Profile:
"Mineral fuels, lubricants" (SITC section 3), "Machinery and transport equipment" (SITC section 7) and "Crude materials + anim. & veg. oils" (SITC section 2+4) were the largest commodity groups for exports in 2013, representing respectively 75.7, 22.6 and 1.0 percent of exported goods (see table 2). From 2011 to 2013, the largest export commodity was "Petroleum oils, crude" (HS code 2709) (see table 1). The top three destinations for merchandise exports were China, the United States and France, accounting for respectively 30.5, 9.1 and 7.9 percent of total exports. "Other business services" (EBOPS code 268) accounted for the largest share of exports of services in 2007 at 141.0 mln US$, followed by "Insurance services" (EBOPS code 253) at 95.1 mln US$ and "Travel" (EBOPS code 236) at 54.5 mln US$ (see graph 3).

Graph 3: Exports of services by EBOPS category
(% share in 2007)

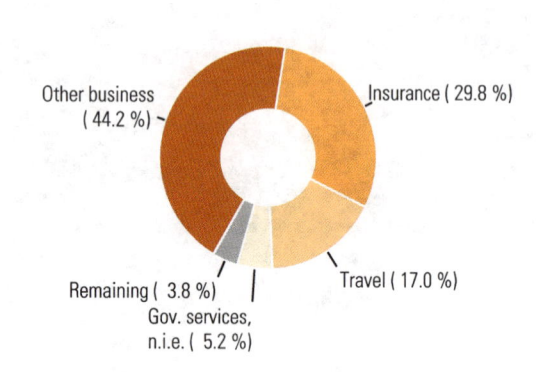

- Other business (44.2 %)
- Insurance (29.8 %)
- Travel (17.0 %)
- Gov. services, n.i.e. (5.2 %)
- Remaining (3.8 %)

Table 1: Top 10 export commodities 2011 to 2013

HS code	4-digit heading of Harmonized System 2002	Value (million US$) 2011	2012	2013	Unit value 2011	2012	2013	Unit	SITC code
	All Commodities	13 823.6	7 437.9	10 453.1					
2709	Petroleum oils, crude	10 496.4	5 779.5	7 666.9	0.5	0.7	0.8	US$/kg	333
8901	Cruise ships, excursion boats, ferry-boats, cargo ships, barges	1 822.5	621.8	1 047.2					793
8905	Light-vessels, fire-floats, dredgers, floating cranes and other vessels	842.6	607.5	1 042.7					793
2711	Petroleum gases and other gaseous hydrocarbons	184.5	73.0	211.5	0.5	0.7	0.6	US$/kg	343
4403	Wood in the rough, whether or not stripped of bark or sapwood	90.6	57.6	64.5	846.8			US$/m³	247
8904	Tugs and pusher craft	4.1	36.7	119.0					793
2710	Petroleum oils, other than crude	55.3	15.8	35.6	1.2		0.8	US$/kg	334
8431	Parts suitable for use principally with the machinery of headings 84.25	38.3	21.6	29.8	28.3	16.3	18.6	US$/kg	723
8802	Other aircraft (for example, helicopters, aeroplanes); spacecraft	48.5	17.9	14.8					792
8906	Other vessels, including warships and lifeboats other than rowing boats	...	9.7	51.6					793

Source: UN Comtrade and UN ServiceTrade

Congo

Services Imports and Exports: EBOPS 2002 categories

Table 2: Merchandise exports by SITC
(Value in million US$, growth and shares in percentage)

SITC	2013	Avg. Growth rates 2009-2013	Avg. Growth rates 2012-2013	2013 share
Total	10453.1	6.3	40.5	100.0
0+1	11.8	-23.5	-0.9	0.1
2+4	102.8	-10.4	64.4	1.0
3	7914.0	8.1	34.9	75.7
5	4.6	-8.7	-52.3	0.0
6	32.6	-21.0	-42.1	0.3
7	2361.5	3.7	70.0	22.6
8	25.9	-25.1	-36.2	0.2

Table 3: Merchandise imports by SITC
(Value in million US$, growth and shares in percentage)

SITC	2013	Avg. Growth rates 2009-2013	Avg. Growth rates 2012-2013	2013 share
Total	8371.6	17.1	13.9	100.0
0+1	528.7	9.3	27.8	6.3
2+4	77.9	13.3	16.7	0.9
3	131.3	4.5	64.6	1.6
5	258.2	18.2	8.2	3.1
6	605.0	17.5	18.5	7.2
7	6528.3	18.2	15.7	78.0
8	242.2	18.8	-38.9	2.9
9	0.0	-7.2	289.1	0.0

SITC Legend

SITC Code	Description
Total	All commodities
0+1	Food, animals + beverages, tobacco
2+4	Crude materials + anim. & veg. oils
3	Mineral fuels, lubricants
5	Chemicals
6	Goods classified chiefly by material
7	Machinery and transport equipment
8	Miscellaneous manufactured articles
9	Not classified elsewhere in the SITC

Graph 4: Merchandise trade balance
(Bln US$ by MDG Regions in 2013)

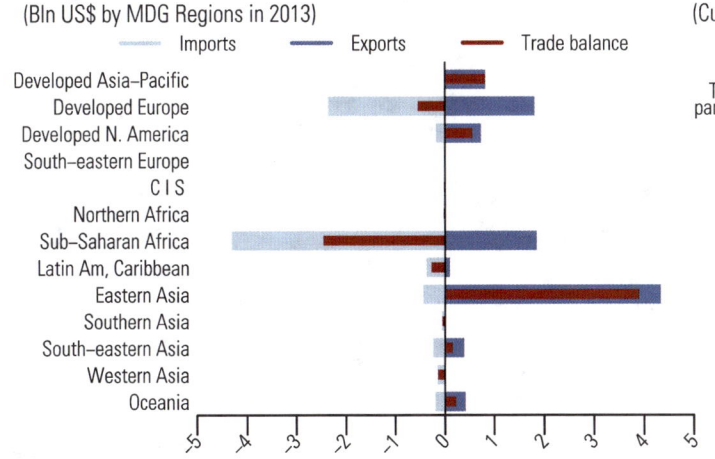

Imports, Exports, Trade balance

- Developed Asia–Pacific
- Developed Europe
- Developed N. America
- South–eastern Europe
- CIS
- Northern Africa
- Sub–Saharan Africa
- Latin Am, Caribbean
- Eastern Asia
- Southern Asia
- South–eastern Asia
- Western Asia
- Oceania

Graph 5: Partner concentration of merchandise trade
(Cumulative share by ranked partners in 2013)

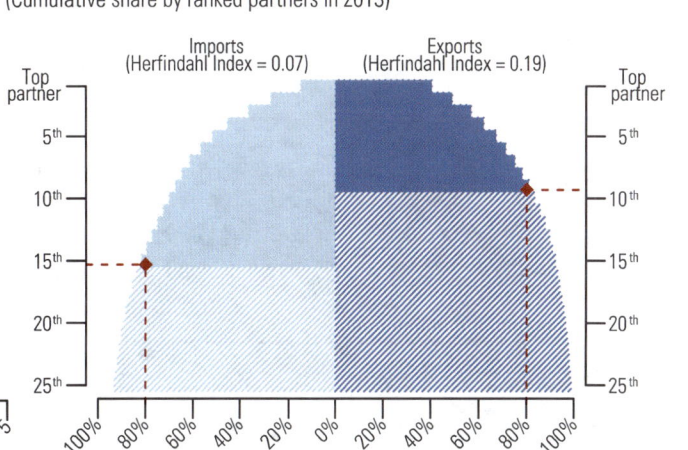

Imports (Herfindahl Index = 0.07)
Exports (Herfindahl Index = 0.19)

Graph 6: Imports of services by EBOPS category
(% share in 2007)

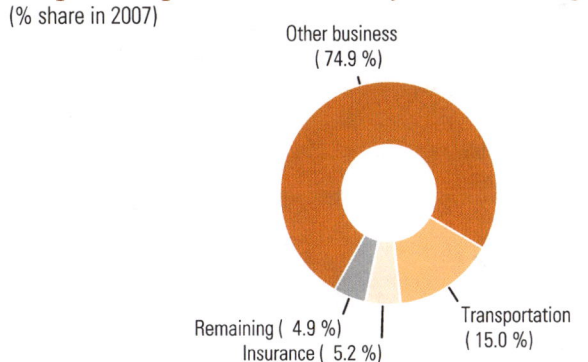

- Other business (74.9 %)
- Transportation (15.0 %)
- Insurance (5.2 %)
- Remaining (4.9 %)

Imports Profile:

"Machinery and transport equipment" (SITC section 7), "Goods classified chiefly by material" (SITC section 6) and "Food, animals + beverages, tobacco" (SITC section 0+1) were the largest commodity groups for imports in 2013, representing respectively 78.0, 7.2 and 6.3 percent of imported goods (see table 3). From 2011 to 2013, the largest import commodity was "Cruise ships, excursion boats, ferry-boats, cargo ships, barges" (HS code 8901) (see table 4). The top three partners for merchandise imports were Angola, Gabon and France, accounting for respectively 17.6, 12.8 and 8.4 percent of total imports. "Other business services" (EBOPS code 268) accounted for the largest share of imports of services in 2007 at 2.6 bln US$, followed by "Transportation" (EBOPS code 205) at 529.1 mln US$ (see graph 6).

Table 4: Top 10 import commodities 2011 to 2013

HS code	4-digit heading of Harmonized System 2002	Value (million US$) 2011	2012	2013	Unit value 2011	2012	2013	Unit	SITC code
	All Commodities	7012.5	7348.6	8371.6					
8901	Cruise ships, excursion boats, ferry-boats, cargo ships, barges	2691.5	2790.4	2407.2					793
8905	Light-vessels, fire-floats, dredgers, floating cranes and other vessels	2107.0	1631.2	2189.2					793
8904	Tugs and pusher craft	83.5	54.8	376.0					793
8906	Other vessels, including warships and lifeboats other than rowing boats	0.4	9.6	441.2					793
2710	Petroleum oils, other than crude	142.1	70.2	105.7	2.0	1.3	0.2	US$/kg	334
2523	Portland cement, aluminous cement, slag cement	80.2	98.2	115.7	0.1	0.1	0.1	US$/kg	661
8703	Motor cars and other motor vehicles principally designed for the transport	62.9	98.1	115.2		19.7	18.8	thsd US$/unit	781
8431	Parts suitable for use principally with the machinery of headings 84.25	77.4	101.8	68.6	23.0	26.6	22.6	US$/kg	723
8481	Taps, cocks, valves and similar appliances for pipes, boiler shells	57.2	67.9	85.8	37.7	30.2	34.4	US$/kg	747
3004	Medicaments (excluding goods of heading 30.02, 30.05 or 30.06)	66.7	70.6	71.7	21.2	21.1	22.6	US$/kg	542

2014 International Trade Statistics Yearbook, Vol. I — Source: UN Comtrade and UN ServiceTrade

Cook Islands

Goods Imports: CIF, by origin   **Goods Exports:** FOB, by last known destination   **Trade System:** General

Overview:
In 2011, the value of merchandise exports of the Cook Islands decreased substantially by 39.5 percent to reach 3.1 mln US$, while its merchandise imports increased substantially by 20.6 percent to reach 109.3 mln US$ (see graph 1, table 2 and table 3). The merchandise trade balance recorded a large deficit of 106.2 mln US$ (see graph 1). The largest merchandise trade balance was with MDG Developed Asia-Pacific at -88.8 mln US$ (see graph 4). Merchandise exports in the Cook Islands were highly concentrated amongst partners; imports were also highly concentrated. The top 4 partners accounted for 80 percent or more of exports and 2 partners accounted for 80 percent or more of imports (see graph 5). No trade in services data is available.

Graph 1: Total merchandise trade, by value
(Mln US$ by year)

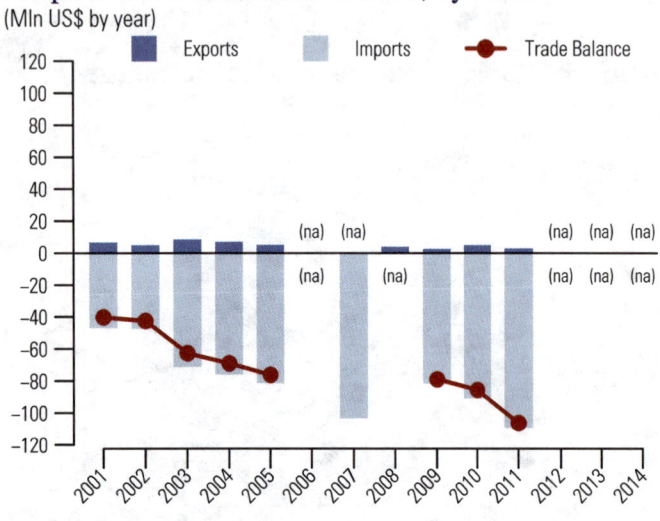

Graph 2: No Data Available

Graph 3: No Data Available

Exports Profile:
"Not classified elsewhere in the SITC" (SITC section 9), "Food, animals + beverages, tobacco" (SITC section 0+1) and "Crude materials + anim. & veg. oils" (SITC section 2+4) were the largest commodity groups for exports in 2011, representing respectively 72.0, 19.7 and 5.3 percent of exported goods (see table 2). From 2009 to 2011, the largest export commodity was "Commodities not specified according to kind" (HS code 9999) (see table 1). The top three destinations for merchandise exports were Japan, China and Indonesia, accounting for respectively 51.4, 16.2 and 8.1 percent of total exports. Services data by detailed EBOPS category is not available for exports.

Table 1: Top 10 export commodities 2009 to 2011

HS code	4-digit heading of Harmonized System 1992	Value (million US$) 2009	2010	2011	Unit value 2009	2010	2011	Unit	SITC code
	All Commodities	2.7	5.2	3.1					
9999	Commodities not specified according to kind	1.5	3.5	2.2					931
2009	Fruit and vegetable juices, not fermented or spirited	0.6	0.7	0.5	3.9	4.7		US$/kg	059
7101	Pearls, natural or cultured, not mounted or set	0.4	0.7	0.1					667
0301	Live fish	0.1	0.2	0.1	20.0		70.9	US$/kg	034
0508	Coral, shell, cuttle bone, etc, unworked, and waste	0.0	0.0	0.2					291
7112	Waste or scrap of precious metal	0.0	0.0	0.0					971
0807	Melons, watermelons and papaws (papayas), fresh	0.0	0.0	...	1.7	1.9		US$/kg	057
8903	Yachts, pleasure, sports vessels, rowing boats, canoes	...	0.0	...		693.0		US$/unit	793
7116	Articles of pearls, precious or semi-precious stones	0.0	0.0	0.0					897
0714	Manioc, arrowroot, salep etc, fresh, dried, sago pith	0.0	0.0	...	4.6	4.9		US$/kg	054

Cook Islands

Services Imports and Exports: EBOPS 2002 categories

Table 2: Merchandise exports by SITC
(Value in million US$, growth and shares in percentage)

SITC	2011	Avg. Growth rates 2007-2011	Avg. Growth rates 2010-2011	2011 share
Total	3.1	...	-39.5	100.0
0+1	0.6	...	-29.7	19.7
2+4	0.2	...	354.5	5.3
6	0.1	...	-88.9	2.5
8	0.0	...	854.1	0.4
9	2.2	...	-36.1	72.0

Table 3: Merchandise imports by SITC
(Value in million US$, growth and shares in percentage)

SITC	2011	Avg. Growth rates 2007-2011	Avg. Growth rates 2010-2011	2011 share
Total	109.3	1.4	20.6	100.0
0+1	23.1	10.6	10.1	21.2
2+4	0.9	-13.1	-27.1	0.9
3	16.0	-4.6	17.9	14.7
5	2.0	4.1	20.2	1.8
6	6.0	-2.3	26.6	5.5
7	7.9	-7.9	14.7	7.3
8	4.1	-7.2	28.3	3.7
9	49.2	4.1	28.7	45.0

SITC Legend

SITC Code	Description
Total	All commodities
0+1	Food, animals + beverages, tobacco
2+4	Crude materials + anim. & veg. oils
3	Mineral fuels, lubricants
5	Chemicals
6	Goods classified chiefly by material
7	Machinery and transport equipment
8	Miscellaneous manufactured articles
9	Not classified elsewhere in the SITC

Graph 4: Merchandise trade balance
(Mln US$ by MDG Regions in 2011)

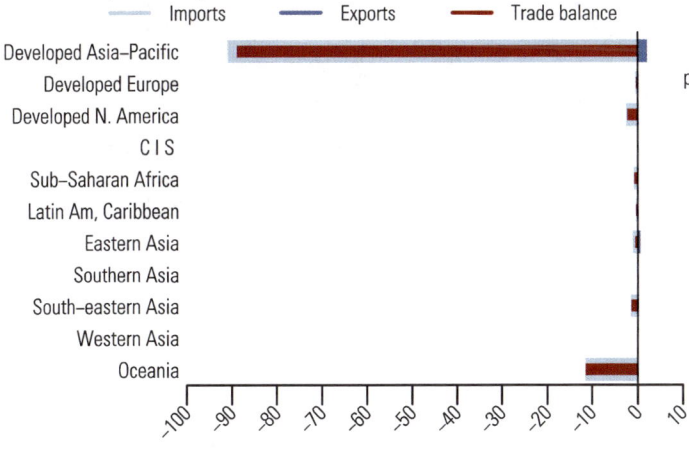

Graph 5: Partner concentration of merchandise trade
(Cumulative share by ranked partners in 2011)

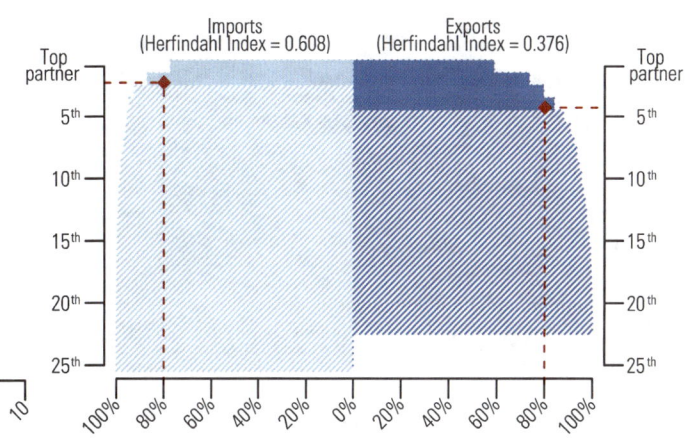

Imports (Herfindahl Index = 0.608)
Exports (Herfindahl Index = 0.376)

Graph 6: No Data Available

Imports Profile:
"Not classified elsewhere in the SITC" (SITC section 9), "Food, animals + beverages, tobacco" (SITC section 0+1) and "Mineral fuels, lubricants" (SITC section 3) were the largest commodity groups for imports in 2011, representing respectively 45.0, 21.2 and 14.7 percent of imported goods (see table 3). From 2009 to 2011, the largest import commodity was "Commodities not specified according to kind" (HS code 9999) (see table 4). The top three partners for merchandise imports were New Zealand, Fiji and Australia, accounting for respectively 76.2, 9.5 and 6.1 percent of total imports. Services data by detailed EBOPS category is not available for imports.

Table 4: Top 10 import commodities 2009 to 2011

HS code	4-digit heading of Harmonized System 1992	Value 2009	Value 2010	Value 2011	Unit value 2009	Unit value 2010	Unit value 2011	Unit	SITC code
	All Commodities	81.6	90.6	109.3					
9999	Commodities not specified according to kind	34.6	38.2	49.1					931
2710	Oils petroleum, bituminous, distillates, except crude	11.9	12.5	14.6	1.3	1.0	1.1	US$/kg	334
1602	Prepared or preserved meat, meat offal and blood, nes	1.6	1.5	1.4	19.1	10.3	17.7	US$/kg	017
0202	Meat of bovine animals, frozen	1.1	1.6	1.7	4.8	3.0	8.3	US$/kg	011
2203	Beer made from malt	1.0	1.2	2.1	1.2	1.2	1.1	US$/litre	112
2202	Waters, non-alcoholic sweetened or flavoured beverages	0.7	1.8	1.8	2.3	0.6	1.3	US$/litre	111
8703	Motor vehicles for transport of persons (except buses)	1.3	1.4	1.6	7.9	6.9	12.2	thsd US$/unit	781
4818	Household, sanitary, hospital paper articles, clothing	0.9	1.1	1.1	3.1	2.8	2.6	US$/kg	642
8525	Radio and TV transmitters, television cameras	0.9	1.0	1.1					764
1905	Baked bread, pastry, wafers, rice paper, biscuits, etc.	0.9	1.1	1.1	3.7	3.4	3.3	US$/kg	048

Source: UN Comtrade and UN ServiceTrade

Costa Rica

| Goods Imports: CIF, by origin | Goods Exports: FOB, by last known destination | Trade System: General |

Overview:
In 2013, the value of merchandise exports of Costa Rica increased slightly by 2.0 percent to reach 11.5 bln US$, while its merchandise imports decreased slightly by 1.3 percent to reach 18.1 bln US$ (see graph 1, table 2 and table 3). The merchandise trade balance recorded a moderate deficit of 6.7 bln US$ (see graph 1). The largest merchandise trade balance was with MDG Developed North America at -4.8 bln US$ (see graph 4). Merchandise exports in Costa Rica were moderately concentrated amongst partners; imports were highly concentrated. The top 12 partners accounted for 80 percent or more of exports and 10 partners accounted for 80 percent or more of imports (see graph 5). In 2013, the value of exports of services of Costa Rica increased moderately by 9.1 percent, reaching 6.0 bln US$, while its imports of services decreased slightly by 2.8 percent and reached 2.0 bln US$ (see graph 2). There was a large trade in services surplus of 4.0 bln US$.

Graph 1: Total merchandise trade, by value
(Bln US$ by year)

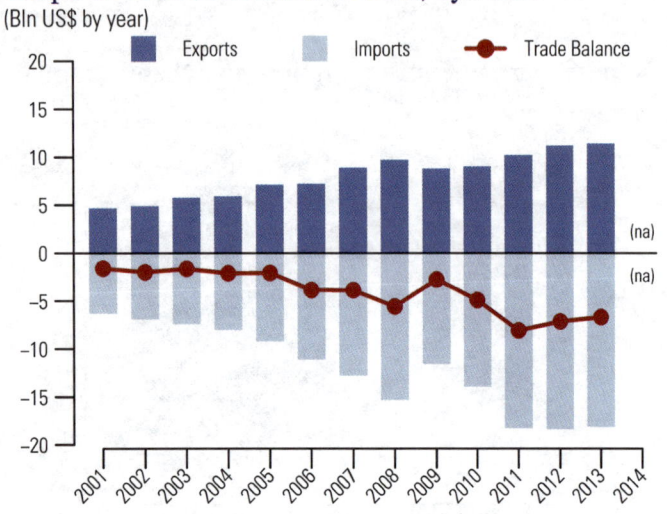

Graph 2: Total services trade, by value
(Bln US$ by year)

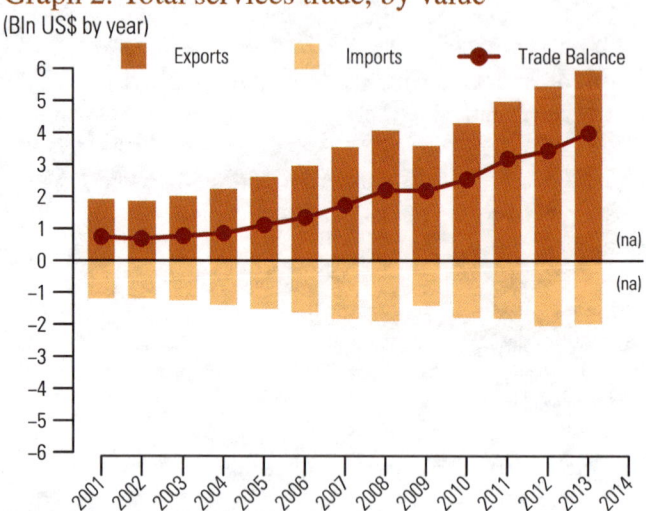

Exports Profile:
"Food, animals + beverages, tobacco" (SITC section 0+1), "Machinery and transport equipment" (SITC section 7) and "Miscellaneous manufactured articles" (SITC section 8) were the largest commodity groups for exports in 2013, representing respectively 32.6, 29.3 and 17.4 percent of exported goods (see table 2). From 2011 to 2013, the largest export commodity was "Electronic integrated circuits" (HS code 8542) (see table 1). The top three destinations for merchandise exports were the United States, the Netherlands and Panama, accounting for respectively 38.3, 7.2 and 5.2 percent of total exports. "Travel" (EBOPS code 236) accounted for the largest share of exports of services in 2013 at 2.6 bln US$, followed by "Computer and information services" (EBOPS code 262) at 2.0 bln US$ and "Other business services" (EBOPS code 268) at 830.9 mln US$ (see graph 3).

Graph 3: Exports of services by EBOPS category
(% share in 2013)

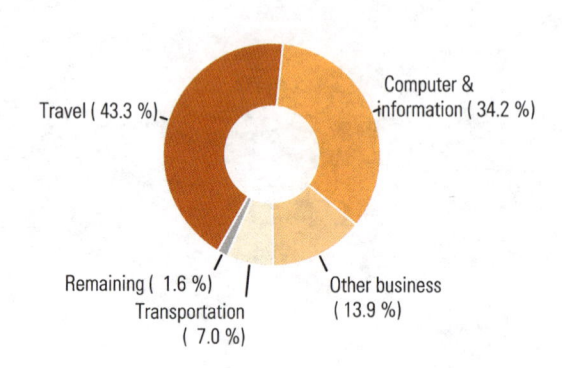

- Travel (43.3 %)
- Computer & information (34.2 %)
- Other business (13.9 %)
- Transportation (7.0 %)
- Remaining (1.6 %)

Table 1: Top 10 export commodities 2011 to 2013

HS code	4-digit heading of Harmonized System 2007	Value (million US$) 2011	2012	2013	Unit value 2011	2012	2013	Unit	SITC code
	All Commodities	10 222.2	11 250.8	11 472.1					
8542	Electronic integrated circuits	1 888.8	2 099.2	2 396.2					776
9018	Instruments and appliances used in medical, surgical, dental or veterinary	837.6	995.9	1 121.5					872
0804	Dates, figs, pineapples, avocados and mangosteens, fresh or dried	727.5	801.9	837.2	0.4	0.4	0.4	US$/kg	057
0803	Bananas, including plantains, fresh or dried	722.1	706.7	780.2	0.4	0.4	0.4	US$/kg	057
0901	Coffee, whether or not roasted or decaffeinated	379.4	423.4	308.1	4.9	4.8	3.7	US$/kg	071
2106	Food preparations not elsewhere specified or included	295.9	301.3	352.2	6.3	8.2	11.2	US$/kg	098
9021	Orthopaedic appliances, including crutches, surgical belts and trusses	289.3	271.5	298.9					899
8544	Insulated (including enamelled or anodised) wire, cable	217.8	320.7	274.1	12.3	8.7	13.4	US$/kg	773
1511	Palm oil and its fractions	201.7	196.3	150.1	1.2	1.1	0.9	US$/kg	422
4011	New pneumatic tyres, of rubber	191.5	158.0	173.3					625

Costa Rica

Services Imports and Exports: EBOPS 2002 categories

Table 2: Merchandise exports by SITC
(Value in million US$, growth and shares in percentage)

SITC	2013	Avg. Growth rates 2009-2013	Avg. Growth rates 2012-2013	2013 share
Total	11 472.1	6.7	2.0	100.0
0+1	3 734.5	15.9	5.1	32.6
2+4	538.2	14.6	-25.5	4.7
3	4.2	-46.3	-12.4	0.0
5	798.6	10.7	4.3	7.0
6	998.3	14.4	-9.4	8.7
7	3 365.1	15.2	8.0	29.3
8	1 998.3	17.0	2.5	17.4
9	34.9	-65.0	0.8	0.3

Table 3: Merchandise imports by SITC
(Value in million US$, growth and shares in percentage)

SITC	2013	Avg. Growth rates 2009-2013	Avg. Growth rates 2012-2013	2013 share
Total	18 124.5	11.9	-1.3	100.0
0+1	1 690.0	23.9	-2.7	9.3
2+4	447.7	17.6	-9.2	2.5
3	2 277.0	23.7	-0.4	12.6
5	2 529.7	15.2	-0.9	14.0
6	2 724.9	20.1	-3.5	15.0
7	6 519.2	18.0	0.5	36.0
8	1 922.5	20.7	-2.1	10.6
9	13.5	-73.2	38.9	0.1

SITC Legend

SITC Code	Description
Total	All commodities
0+1	Food, animals + beverages, tobacco
2+4	Crude materials + anim. & veg. oils
3	Mineral fuels, lubricants
5	Chemicals
6	Goods classified chiefly by material
7	Machinery and transport equipment
8	Miscellaneous manufactured articles
9	Not classified elsewhere in the SITC

Graph 4: Merchandise trade balance
(Bln US$ by MDG Regions in 2013)

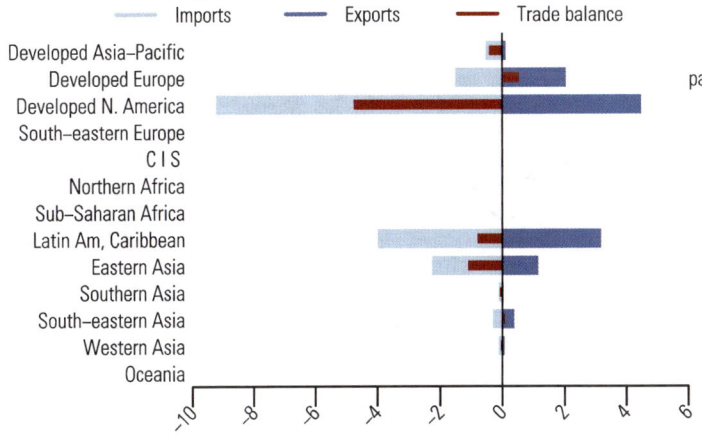

Graph 5: Partner concentration of merchandise trade
(Cumulative share by ranked partners in 2013)

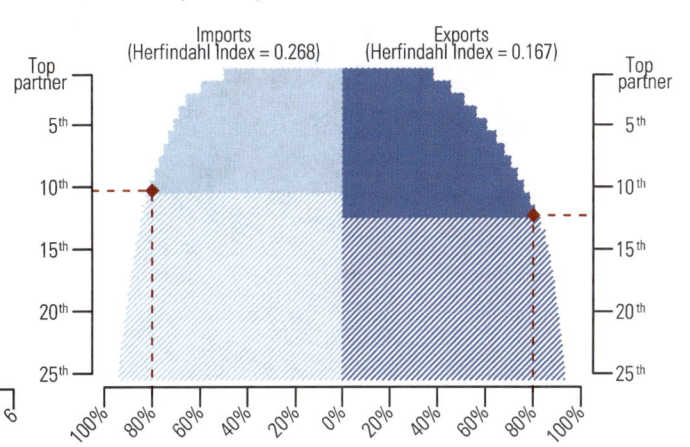

Imports (Herfindahl Index = 0.268)
Exports (Herfindahl Index = 0.167)

Graph 6: Imports of services by EBOPS category
(% share in 2013)

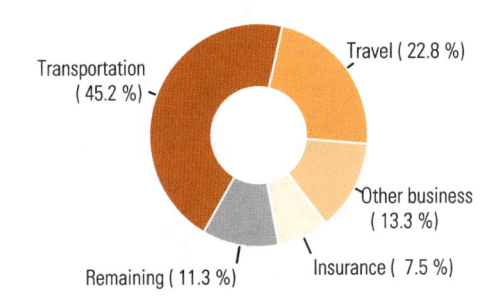

- Transportation (45.2 %)
- Travel (22.8 %)
- Other business (13.3 %)
- Insurance (7.5 %)
- Remaining (11.3 %)

Imports Profile:

"Machinery and transport equipment" (SITC section 7), "Goods classified chiefly by material" (SITC section 6) and "Chemicals" (SITC section 5) were the largest commodity groups for imports in 2013, representing respectively 36.0, 15.0 and 14.0 percent of imported goods (see table 3). From 2011 to 2013, the largest import commodity was "Petroleum oils, other than crude" (HS code 2710) (see table 4). The top three partners for merchandise imports were the United States, China and Mexico, accounting for respectively 49.1, 8.6 and 6.5 percent of total imports. "Transportation" (EBOPS code 205) accounted for the largest share of imports of services in 2013 at 892.1 mln US$, followed by "Travel" (EBOPS code 236) at 449.9 mln US$ and "Other business services" (EBOPS code 268) at 261.9 mln US$ (see graph 6).

Table 4: Top 10 import commodities 2011 to 2013

HS code	4-digit heading of Harmonized System 2007	2011	2012	2013	2011	2012	2013	Unit	SITC code
	All Commodities	18 263.8	18 356.0	18 124.5					
2710	Petroleum oils, other than crude	1 991.2	2 161.6	2 154.6	1.0	1.0	1.0	US$/kg	334
8542	Electronic integrated circuits	1 297.0	1 687.7	1 698.0					776
8703	Motor cars and other motor vehicles principally designed for the transport	739.9	604.7	556.6			18.7	thsd US$/unit	781
8534	Printed circuits	604.5	701.9	517.3	347.2	439.2	438.2	US$/kg	772
8517	Electrical apparatus for line telephony or line telegraphy	472.0	371.7	513.0					764
3004	Medicaments (excluding goods of heading 30.02, 30.05 or 30.06)	432.5	421.1	442.9	56.4	50.1	48.1	US$/kg	542
8471	Automatic data processing machines and units thereof	390.0	219.6	263.7					752
9018	Instruments and appliances used in medical, surgical, dental or veterinary	173.8	280.9	261.8					872
1005	Maize (corn)	193.0	191.1	190.2	0.3	0.3	0.3	US$/kg	044
3926	Other articles of plastics	224.8	149.3	165.6	14.1	10.3	12.0	US$/kg	893

2014 International Trade Statistics Yearbook, Vol. I — Source: UN Comtrade and UN ServiceTrade

Côte d'Ivoire

Goods Imports: CIF, by origin **Goods Exports:** FOB, by last known destination **Trade System:** Special

Overview:

In 2013, the value of merchandise exports of Côte d'Ivoire increased substantially by 11.3 percent to reach 12.1 bln US$, while its merchandise imports increased substantially by 27.8 percent to reach 12.5 bln US$ (see graph 1, table 2 and table 3). The merchandise trade balance recorded a relatively small deficit of 399.2 mln US$ (see graph 1). The largest merchandise trade balance was with MDG Latin America and the Caribbean at -1.7 bln US$ (see graph 4). Merchandise exports in Côte d'Ivoire were diversified amongst partners; imports were also diversified. The top 18 partners accounted for 80 percent or more of exports and 15 partners accounted for 80 percent or more of imports (see graph 5). In 2013, the value of exports of services of Côte d'Ivoire increased slightly by 4.8 percent, reaching 1.0 bln US$, while its imports of services increased substantially by 10.8 percent and reached 3.3 bln US$ (see graph 2). There was a large trade in services deficit of 2.2 bln US$.

Graph 1: Total merchandise trade, by value
(Bln US$ by year)

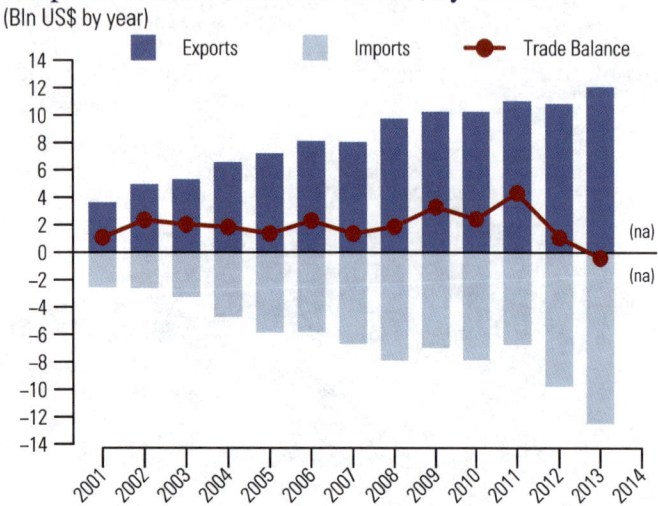

Graph 2: Total services trade, by value
(Bln US$ by year)

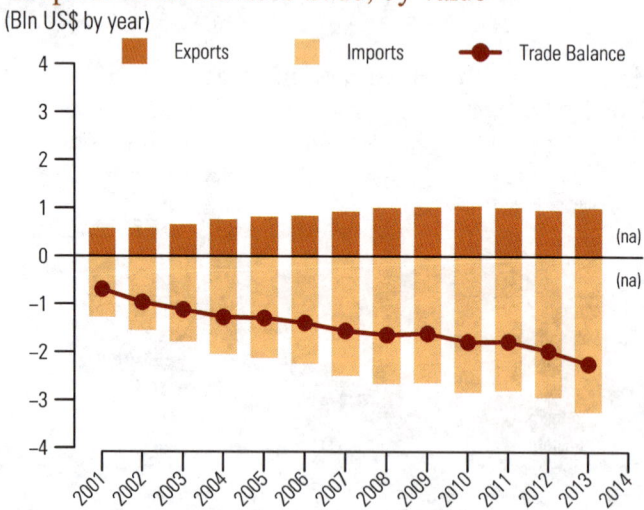

Exports Profile:

"Food, animals + beverages, tobacco" (SITC section 0+1), "Mineral fuels, lubricants" (SITC section 3) and "Machinery and transport equipment" (SITC section 7) were the largest commodity groups for exports in 2013, representing respectively 34.7, 23.8 and 17.0 percent of exported goods (see table 2). From 2011 to 2013, the largest export commodity was "Cocoa beans, whole or broken, raw or roasted" (HS code 1801) (see table 1). The top three destinations for merchandise exports were the Netherlands, the United States and Ghana, accounting for respectively 9.4, 8.6 and 7.6 percent of total exports. "Other business services" (EBOPS code 268) accounted for the largest share of exports of services in 2013 at 285.5 mln US$, followed by "Transportation" (EBOPS code 205) at 194.3 mln US$ and "Travel" (EBOPS code 236) at 182.8 mln US$ (see graph 3).

Graph 3: Exports of services by EBOPS category
(% share in 2013)

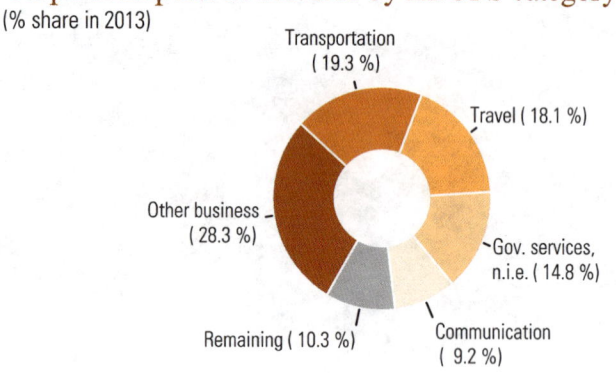

- Transportation (19.3 %)
- Travel (18.1 %)
- Gov. services, n.i.e. (14.8 %)
- Communication (9.2 %)
- Remaining (10.3 %)
- Other business (28.3 %)

Table 1: Top 10 export commodities 2011 to 2013

HS code	4-digit heading of Harmonized System 2007	Value (million US$) 2011	2012	2013	Unit value 2011	2012	2013	Unit	SITC code
	All Commodities	11 049.1	10 861.0	12 083.8					
1801	Cocoa beans, whole or broken, raw or roasted	3 017.4	2 325.0	2 044.5	2.8	2.3	2.5	US$/kg	072
2710	Petroleum oils, other than crude	1 289.2	1 766.0	1 781.8	0.9	1.0	1.0	US$/kg	334
2709	Petroleum oils and oils obtained from bituminous minerals, crude	1 306.0	1 255.6	959.5	0.7	0.8	0.8	US$/kg	333
4001	Natural rubber, balata, gutta-percha, guayule, chicle	1 136.4	808.6	759.6	4.9	3.0	2.9	US$/kg	231
7108	Gold (including gold plated with platinum)	573.3	641.1	575.8	43.7	48.9	40.3	thsd US$/kg	971
8905	Light-vessels, fire-floats, dredgers, floating cranes and other vessels	...	5.5	1 730.8					793
1803	Cocoa paste, whether or not defatted	539.2	437.3	544.1	3.8	3.1	4.1	US$/kg	072
0801	Coconuts, Brazil nuts and cashew nuts, fresh or dried	279.0	351.6	346.0	0.9	0.8	0.8	US$/kg	057
1511	Palm oil and its fractions	264.2	272.2	188.2	1.0	1.0	0.9	US$/kg	422
1804	Cocoa butter, fat and oil	218.9	210.4	265.6	3.9	3.0	4.8	US$/kg	072

Côte d'Ivoire

Services Imports and Exports: EBOPS 2002 categories

Table 2: Merchandise exports by SITC
(Value in million US$, growth and shares in percentage)

SITC	2013	Avg. Growth rates 2009-2013	2012-2013	2013 share
Total	12 083.8	4.1	11.3	100.0
0+1	4 192.9	-2.8	-6.0	34.7
2+4	1 439.9	17.3	-5.0	11.9
3	2 878.9	-1.2	-8.9	23.8
5	330.5	-5.0	-7.3	2.7
6	302.0	-3.4	0.2	2.5
7	2 059.3	34.5	878.9	17.0
8	294.8	10.1	40.0	2.4
9	585.5	27.6	-9.6	4.8

Table 3: Merchandise imports by SITC
(Value in million US$, growth and shares in percentage)

SITC	2013	Avg. Growth rates 2009-2013	2012-2013	2013 share
Total	12 483.0	15.7	27.8	100.0
0+1	1 752.2	2.5	-5.3	14.0
2+4	199.8	10.4	-12.9	1.6
3	3 214.9	16.6	6.3	25.8
5	1 237.3	7.8	9.9	9.9
6	1 089.1	7.5	9.6	8.7
7	4 608.7	33.7	111.8	36.9
8	352.2	6.1	6.1	2.8
9	28.7	-12.0	-22.6	0.2

SITC Legend

SITC Code	Description
Total	All commodities
0+1	Food, animals + beverages, tobacco
2+4	Crude materials + anim. & veg. oils
3	Mineral fuels, lubricants
5	Chemicals
6	Goods classified chiefly by material
7	Machinery and transport equipment
8	Miscellaneous manufactured articles
9	Not classified elsewhere in the SITC

Graph 4: Merchandise trade balance
(Bln US$ by MDG Regions in 2013)

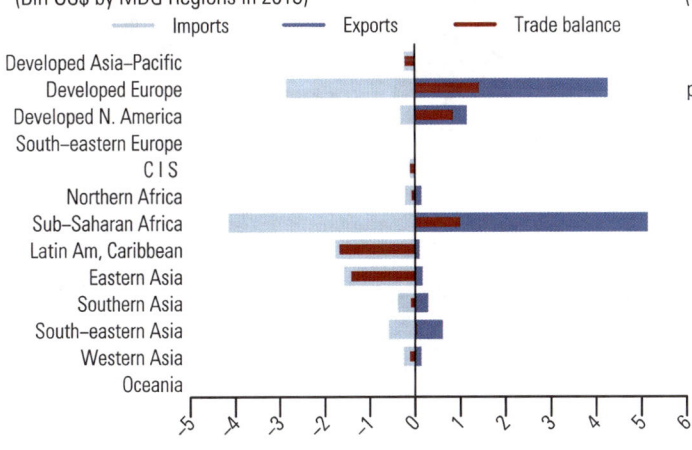

Graph 5: Partner concentration of merchandise trade
(Cumulative share by ranked partners in 2013)

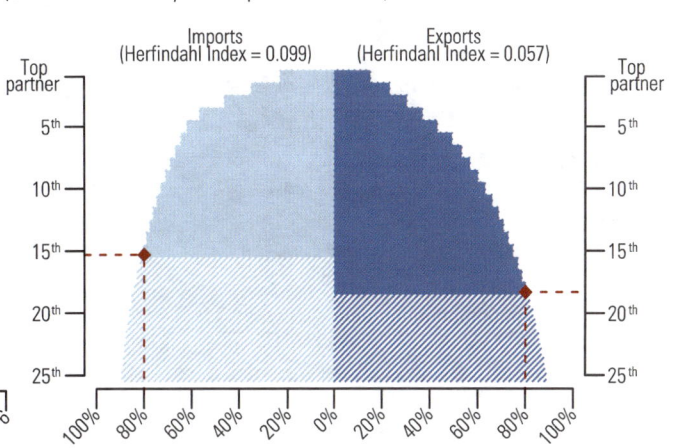

Imports (Herfindahl Index = 0.099)
Exports (Herfindahl Index = 0.057)

Graph 6: Imports of services by EBOPS category
(% share in 2013)

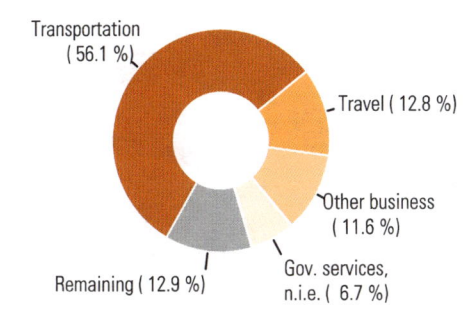

- Transportation (56.1 %)
- Travel (12.8 %)
- Other business (11.6 %)
- Gov. services, n.i.e. (6.7 %)
- Remaining (12.9 %)

Imports Profile:
"Machinery and transport equipment" (SITC section 7), "Mineral fuels, lubricants" (SITC section 3) and "Food, animals + beverages, tobacco" (SITC section 0+1) were the largest commodity groups for imports in 2013, representing respectively 36.9, 25.8 and 14.0 percent of imported goods (see table 3). From 2011 to 2013, the largest import commodity was "Petroleum oils and oils obtained from bituminous minerals, crude" (HS code 2709) (see table 4). The top three partners for merchandise imports were Nigeria, France and China, accounting for respectively 24.0, 11.4 and 9.0 percent of total imports. "Transportation" (EBOPS code 205) accounted for the largest share of imports of services in 2013 at 1.8 bln US$, followed by "Travel" (EBOPS code 236) at 415.6 mln US$ and "Other business services" (EBOPS code 268) at 376.2 mln US$ (see graph 6).

Table 4: Top 10 import commodities 2011 to 2013

HS code	4-digit heading of Harmonized System 2007	Value (million US$) 2011	2012	2013	Unit value 2011	2012	2013	Unit	SITC code
	All Commodities	6 720.0	9 769.7	12 483.0					
2709	Petroleum oils and oils obtained from bituminous minerals, crude	1 749.4	2 752.8	2 928.1	0.8	0.8	0.8	US$/kg	333
8905	Light-vessels, fire-floats, dredgers, floating cranes and other vessels	...	398.2	2 685.7					793
1006	Rice	567.9	684.5	472.5	0.6	0.5	0.6	US$/kg	042
0303	Fish, frozen, excluding fish fillets and other fish meat of heading 03.04	326.2	329.5	358.1	1.1	1.2	1.3	US$/kg	034
3004	Medicaments (excluding goods of heading 30.02, 30.05 or 30.06)	231.3	255.5	247.5	26.7	25.1	26.2	US$/kg	542
8703	Motor cars and other motor vehicles principally designed for the transport	134.3	234.9	258.0		19.9	22.1	thsd US$/unit	781
1001	Wheat and meslin	185.3	218.3	210.9	0.4	0.4	0.4	US$/kg	041
2710	Petroleum oils, other than crude	85.2	149.3	151.9	1.3	1.1	1.1	US$/kg	334
8517	Electrical apparatus for line telephony or line telegraphy	96.0	121.5	123.4					764
2523	Portland cement, aluminous cement, slag cement	87.4	112.6	139.0	0.1	0.1	0.1	US$/kg	661

Croatia

Goods Imports: CIF, by origin **Goods Exports:** FOB, by last known destination **Trade System:** Special

Overview:

In 2014, the value of merchandise exports of Croatia increased moderately by 8.4 percent to reach 13.8 bln US$, while its merchandise imports increased slightly by 4.2 percent to reach 22.9 bln US$ (see graph 1, table 2 and table 3). The merchandise trade balance recorded a moderate deficit of 9.0 bln US$ (see graph 1). The largest merchandise trade balance was with MDG Developed Europe at -8.5 bln US$ (see graph 4). Merchandise exports in Croatia were diversified amongst partners; imports were also diversified. The top 17 partners accounted for 80 percent or more of exports and 14 partners accounted for 80 percent or more of imports (see graph 5). In 2013, the value of exports of services of Croatia increased moderately by 5.8 percent, reaching 12.6 bln US$, while its imports of services decreased slightly by 1.3 percent and reached 3.6 bln US$ (see graph 2). There was a large trade in services surplus of 9.0 bln US$. See footnote*.

Graph 1: Total merchandise trade, by value
(Bln US$ by year)

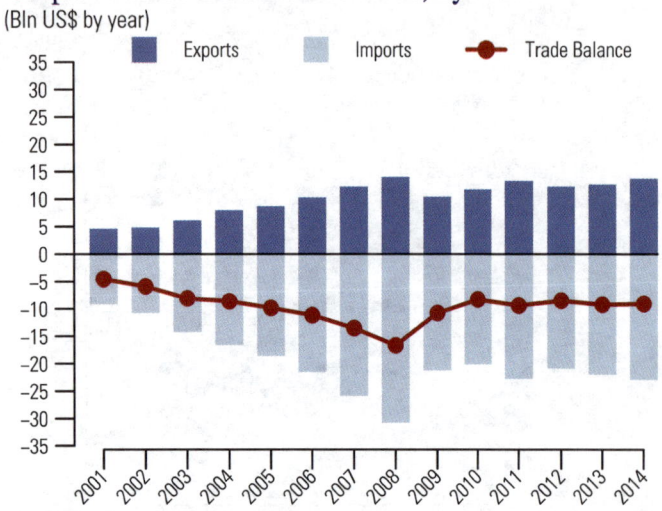

Graph 2: Total services trade, by value
(Bln US$ by year)

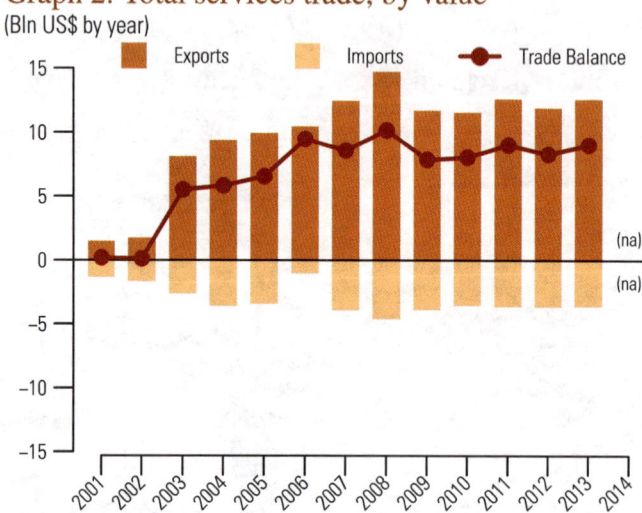

Exports Profile:

"Machinery and transport equipment" (SITC section 7), "Miscellaneous manufactured articles" (SITC section 8) and "Goods classified chiefly by material" (SITC section 6) were the largest commodity groups for exports in 2014, representing respectively 21.9, 16.2 and 16.2 percent of exported goods (see table 2). From 2012 to 2014, the largest export commodity was "Petroleum oils, other than crude" (HS code 2710) (see table 1). The top three destinations for merchandise exports were Italy, Bosnia and Herzegovina and Germany, accounting for respectively 14.5, 12.3 and 11.0 percent of total exports. "Travel" (EBOPS code 236) accounted for the largest share of exports of services in 2013 at 9.5 bln US$, followed by "Transportation" (EBOPS code 205) at 1.2 bln US$ and "Other business services" (EBOPS code 268) at 1.1 bln US$ (see graph 3).

Graph 3: Exports of services by EBOPS category
(% share in 2013)

- Travel (75.6 %)
- Transportation (9.5 %)
- Other business (8.8 %)
- Remaining (6.1 %)

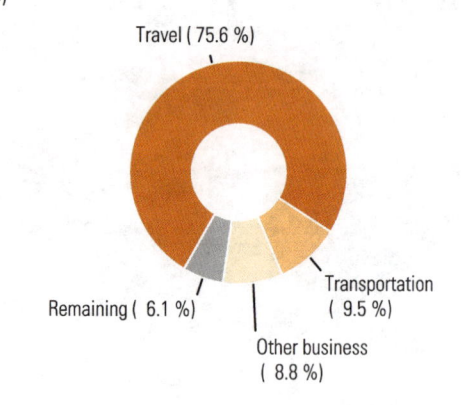

Table 1: Top 10 export commodities 2012 to 2014

HS code	4-digit heading of Harmonized System 2012	Value (million US$) 2012	2013	2014	Unit value 2012	2013	2014	Unit	SITC code
	All Commodities	12 369.0	12 741.6	13 813.8					
2710	Petroleum oils, other than crude	1 310.4	1 207.5	1 140.4	0.9	0.1	0.9	US$/kg	334
3004	Medicaments (excluding goods of heading 30.02, 30.05 or 30.06)	488.8	492.0	489.5	120.0		148.8	US$/kg	542
8504	Electrical transformers, static converters	333.9	315.5	352.0					771
4407	Wood sawn or chipped lengthwise, sliced or peeled	255.7	312.7	418.3	351.4		245.6	US$/m³	248
8901	Cruise ships, excursion boats, ferry-boats, cargo ships, barges	546.6	150.0	150.8		15.0		mln US$/unit	793
2711	Petroleum gases and other gaseous hydrocarbons	251.6	294.2	235.1	0.8		0.6	US$/kg	343
2716	Electrical energy	92.1	237.4	448.8	63.3		54.9	US$/MWh	351
9401	Seats (other than those of heading 94.02)	204.3	246.6	287.7					821
3102	Mineral or chemical fertilisers, nitrogenous	223.3	214.6	223.0		0.1	0.3	US$/kg	562
6115	Panty hose, tights, stockings, socks and other hosiery	140.3	137.7	223.3	33.0		33.8	US$/kg	846

*As of 2003, trade in services data including "travel" category.

Croatia

Services Imports and Exports: EBOPS 2002 categories

Table 2: Merchandise exports by SITC
(Value in million US$, growth and shares in percentage)

SITC	2014	Avg. Growth rates 2010-2014	Avg. Growth rates 2013-2014	2014 share
Total	13 813.8	4.0	8.4	100.0
0+1	1 604.2	6.2	12.3	11.6
2+4	1 139.4	8.4	6.2	8.2
3	1 864.8	6.1	4.6	13.5
5	1 471.1	2.3	4.2	10.6
6	2 239.3	7.6	11.8	16.2
7	3 027.0	-5.2	-1.4	21.9
8	2 240.7	10.8	27.3	16.2
9	227.3	122.8	6.3	1.6

Table 3: Merchandise imports by SITC
(Value in million US$, growth and shares in percentage)

SITC	2014	Avg. Growth rates 2010-2014	Avg. Growth rates 2013-2014	2014 share
Total	22 861.5	3.3	4.2	100.0
0+1	2 812.5	9.1	11.1	12.3
2+4	523.5	5.9	8.4	2.3
3	4 270.0	3.1	-10.4	18.7
5	3 022.9	1.7	2.4	13.2
6	4 052.7	2.9	6.1	17.7
7	5 143.5	0.0	3.2	22.5
8	2 996.6	6.9	25.2	13.1
9	39.7	59.1	868.6	0.2

SITC Legend

SITC Code	Description
Total	All commodities
0+1	Food, animals + beverages, tobacco
2+4	Crude materials + anim. & veg. oils
3	Mineral fuels, lubricants
5	Chemicals
6	Goods classified chiefly by material
7	Machinery and transport equipment
8	Miscellaneous manufactured articles
9	Not classified elsewhere in the SITC

Graph 4: Merchandise trade balance
(Bln US$ by MDG Regions in 2014)

Graph 5: Partner concentration of merchandise trade
(Cumulative share by ranked partners in 2014)
Imports (Herfindahl Index = 0.076)
Exports (Herfindahl Index = 0.071)

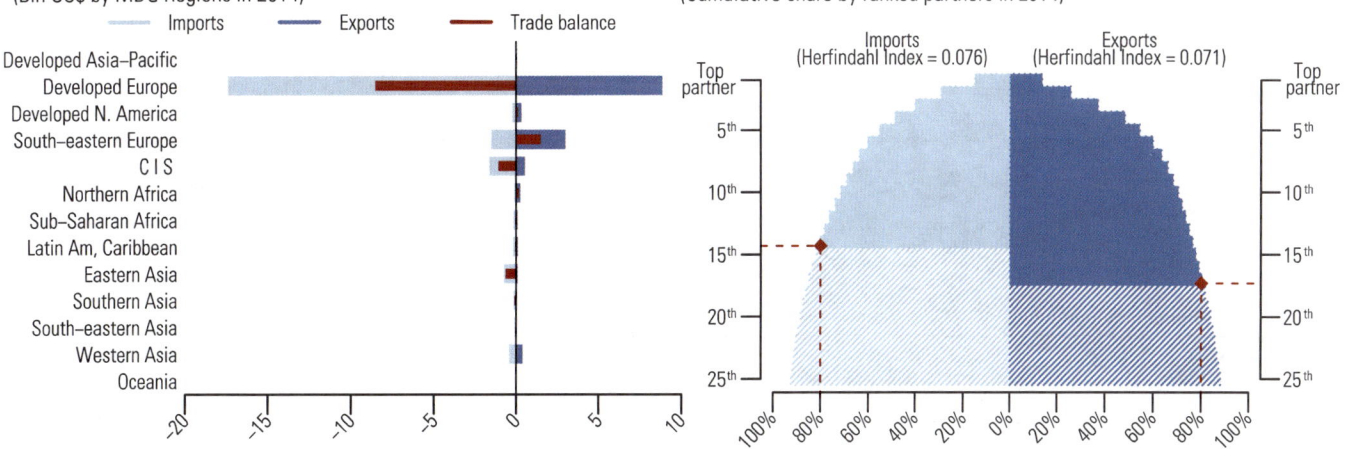

Graph 6: Imports of services by EBOPS category
(% share in 2013)

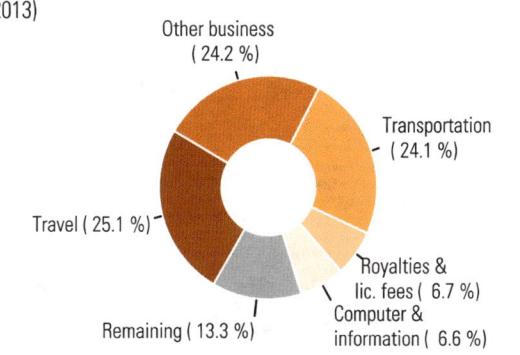

- Other business (24.2 %)
- Transportation (24.1 %)
- Travel (25.1 %)
- Remaining (13.3 %)
- Royalties & lic. fees (6.7 %)
- Computer & information (6.6 %)

Imports Profile:
"Machinery and transport equipment" (SITC section 7), "Mineral fuels, lubricants" (SITC section 3) and "Goods classified chiefly by material" (SITC section 6) were the largest commodity groups for imports in 2014, representing respectively 22.5, 18.7 and 17.7 percent of imported goods (see table 3). From 2012 to 2014, the largest import commodity was "Petroleum oils and oils obtained from bituminous minerals, crude" (HS code 2709) (see table 4). The top three partners for merchandise imports were Italy, Germany and Slovenia, accounting for respectively 14.7, 14.0 and 9.5 percent of total imports. "Travel" (EBOPS code 236) accounted for the largest share of imports of services in 2013 at 901.8 mln US$, followed by "Other business services" (EBOPS code 268) at 869.9 mln US$ and "Transportation" (EBOPS code 205) at 867.2 mln US$ (see graph 6).

Table 4: Top 10 import commodities 2012 to 2014

HS code	4-digit heading of Harmonized System 2012	2012	2013	2014	2012	2013	2014	Unit	SITC code
	All Commodities	20 834.3	21 932.0	22 861.5					
2709	Petroleum oils and oils obtained from bituminous minerals, crude	1 874.8	1 965.5	1 418.8	0.8	0.8	0.8	US$/kg	333
2710	Petroleum oils, other than crude	1 368.6	1 181.1	1 506.2	1.0	0.1	0.9	US$/kg	334
2716	Electrical energy	640.8	624.6	695.5	67.9		54.3	US$/MWh	351
2711	Petroleum gases and other gaseous hydrocarbons	722.9	759.7	438.3	0.7		0.5	US$/kg	343
3004	Medicaments (excluding goods of heading 30.02, 30.05 or 30.06)	606.8	632.6	628.4	78.8		61.2	US$/kg	542
8703	Motor cars and other motor vehicles principally designed for the transport	493.0	566.1	692.7	11.6	12.4	11.1	thsd US$/unit	781
8517	Electrical apparatus for line telephony or line telegraphy	353.6	383.9	401.7					764
8471	Automatic data processing machines and units thereof	212.5	243.1	245.7	107.2	117.7	108.4	US$/unit	752
0203	Meat of swine, fresh, chilled or frozen	142.8	184.7	211.6	3.0		2.8	US$/kg	012
7601	Unwrought aluminium	193.2	178.1	162.1	2.3		2.3	US$/kg	684

2014 International Trade Statistics Yearbook, Vol. I — Source: UN Comtrade and UN ServiceTrade

Cyprus

Goods Imports: CIF, by origin/consignment for intra-eu **Goods Exports:** FOB, by last known destination **Trade System:** General

Overview:
In 2014, the value of merchandise exports of Cyprus decreased moderately by 10.0 percent to reach 1.9 bln US$, while its merchandise imports increased moderately by 6.1 percent to reach 6.8 bln US$ (see graph 1, table 2 and table 3). The merchandise trade balance recorded a large deficit of 4.9 bln US$ (see graph 1). The largest merchandise trade balance was with MDG Developed Europe at -3.9 bln US$ (see graph 4). Merchandise exports in Cyprus were diversified amongst partners; imports were also diversified. The top 25 partners accounted for 80 percent or more of exports and 11 partners accounted for 80 percent or more of imports (see graph 5). In 2013, the value of exports of services of Cyprus increased substantially by 33.3 percent, reaching 10.6 bln US$, while its imports of services increased substantially by 78.4 percent and reached 6.6 bln US$ (see graph 2). There was a moderate trade in services surplus of 4.0 bln US$.

Graph 1: Total merchandise trade, by value
(Bln US$ by year)

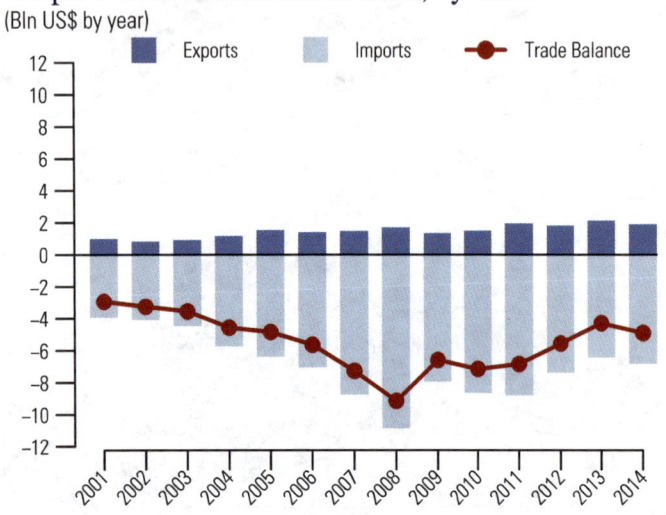

Graph 2: Total services trade, by value
(Bln US$ by year)

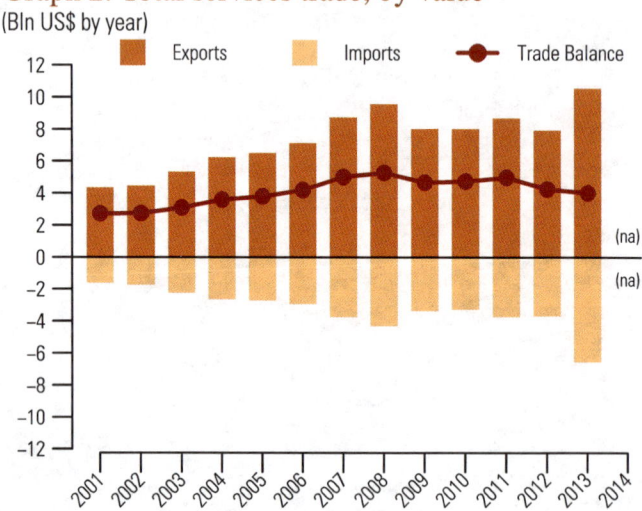

Exports Profile:
"Food, animals + beverages, tobacco" (SITC section 0+1), "Chemicals" (SITC section 5) and "Machinery and transport equipment" (SITC section 7) were the largest commodity groups for exports in 2014, representing respectively 21.8, 21.8 and 17.9 percent of exported goods (see table 2). From 2012 to 2014, the largest export commodity was "Medicaments (excluding goods of heading 30.02, 30.05 or 30.06)" (HS code 3004) (see table 1). The top three destinations for merchandise exports were Greece, Bunkers, ship stores and the United Kingdom, accounting for respectively 17.3, 17.0 and 10.6 percent of total exports. "Travel" (EBOPS code 236) accounted for the largest share of exports of services in 2012 at 2.6 bln US$, followed by "Other business services" (EBOPS code 268) at 2.4 bln US$ and "Transportation" (EBOPS code 205) at 1.8 bln US$ (see graph 3).

Graph 3: Exports of services by EBOPS category
(% share in 2012)

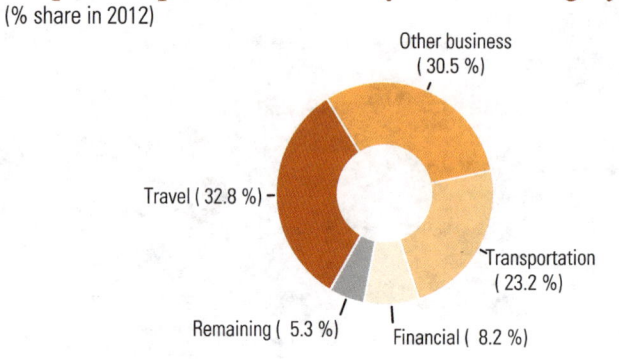

- Other business (30.5 %)
- Travel (32.8 %)
- Transportation (23.2 %)
- Financial (8.2 %)
- Remaining (5.3 %)

Table 1: Top 10 export commodities 2012 to 2014

HS code	4-digit heading of Harmonized System 2012	Value (million US$) 2012	2013	2014	Unit value 2012	2013	2014	Unit	SITC code
	All Commodities	1 826.0	2 134.4	1 921.2					
3004	Medicaments (excluding goods of heading 30.02, 30.05 or 30.06)	240.6	286.3	292.6	55.3	51.9	55.3	US$/kg	542
9999	Commodities not specified according to kind	255.1	240.4	6.2					931
2710	Petroleum oils, other than crude	83.4	91.0	312.4	0.9	0.9	0.9	US$/kg	334
0406	Cheese and curd	79.2	102.0	120.6	8.0	8.8	8.9	US$/kg	024
8802	Other aircraft (for example, helicopters, aeroplanes); spacecraft	28.4	208.5	0.1	9.5	29.8	0.1	mln US$/unit	792
8517	Electrical apparatus for line telephony or line telegraphy	28.5	70.0	84.9					764
2402	Cigars, cheroots, cigarillos and cigarettes	58.7	63.2	53.0	33.7	31.2	45.8	US$/kg	122
7108	Gold (including gold plated with platinum)	55.6	53.4	64.5	36.8	36.3	29.8	thsd US$/kg	971
0701	Potatoes, fresh or chilled	42.8	71.5	55.0	0.6	0.7	0.5	US$/kg	054
2523	Portland cement, aluminous cement, slag cement	12.8	51.9	62.6	0.1	0.0	0.1	US$/kg	661

Cyprus

Services Imports and Exports: EBOPS 2002 categories

Table 2: Merchandise exports by SITC
(Value in million US$, growth and shares in percentage)

SITC	2014	Avg. Growth rates 2010-2014	2013-2014	2014 share
Total	1 921.2	6.3	-10.0	100.0
0+1	419.6	5.4	-2.4	21.8
2+4	89.5	-2.0	-19.6	4.7
3	312.4	9.8	243.0	16.3
5	419.6	4.2	-9.5	21.8
6	120.6	15.9	9.7	6.3
7	343.4	7.9	-30.8	17.9
8	144.9	-3.0	5.8	7.5
9	71.3	52.0	-75.8	3.7

Table 3: Merchandise imports by SITC
(Value in million US$, growth and shares in percentage)

SITC	2014	Avg. Growth rates 2010-2014	2013-2014	2014 share
Total	6 812.8	-5.8	6.1	100.0
0+1	1 308.6	1.3	4.5	19.2
2+4	94.4	-6.4	2.7	1.4
3	1 681.8	-0.9	-9.4	24.7
5	789.6	-1.5	-1.5	11.6
6	622.5	-13.2	-2.2	9.1
7	1 337.9	-12.1	44.5	19.6
8	972.9	-5.3	14.7	14.3
9	5.1	-57.5	-18.2	0.1

SITC Legend

SITC Code	Description
Total	All commodities
0+1	Food, animals + beverages, tobacco
2+4	Crude materials + anim. & veg. oils
3	Mineral fuels, lubricants
5	Chemicals
6	Goods classified chiefly by material
7	Machinery and transport equipment
8	Miscellaneous manufactured articles
9	Not classified elsewhere in the SITC

Graph 4: Merchandise trade balance
(Bln US$ by MDG Regions in 2014)

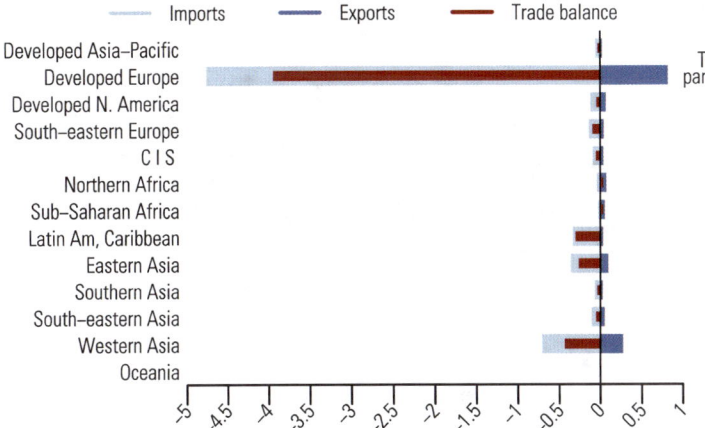

Graph 5: Partner concentration of merchandise trade
(Cumulative share by ranked partners in 2014)

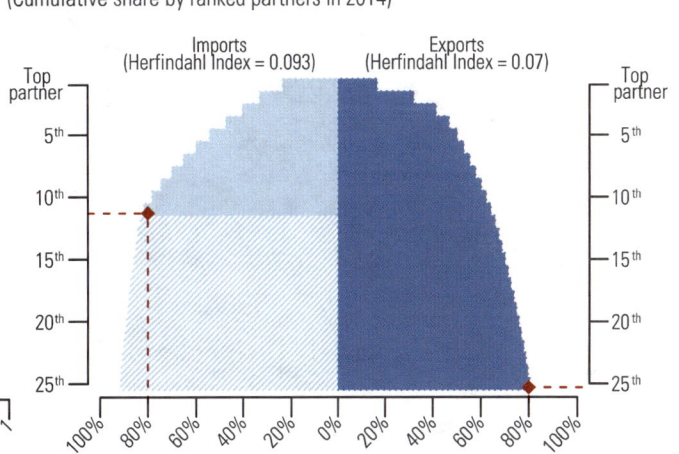

Imports (Herfindahl Index = 0.093)
Exports (Herfindahl Index = 0.07)

Graph 6: Imports of services by EBOPS category
(% share in 2012)

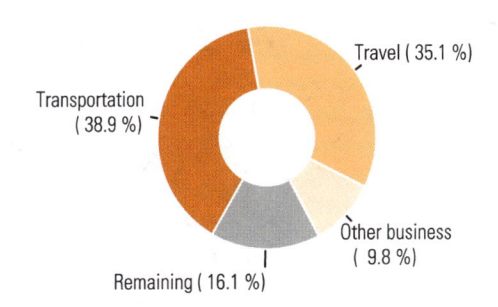

- Travel (35.1 %)
- Transportation (38.9 %)
- Other business (9.8 %)
- Remaining (16.1 %)

Imports Profile:

"Mineral fuels, lubricants" (SITC section 3), "Machinery and transport equipment" (SITC section 7) and "Food, animals + beverages, tobacco" (SITC section 0+1) were the largest commodity groups for imports in 2014, representing respectively 24.7, 19.6 and 19.2 percent of imported goods (see table 3). From 2012 to 2014, the largest import commodity was "Petroleum oils, other than crude" (HS code 2710) (see table 4). The top three partners for merchandise imports were Greece, Israel and Italy, accounting for respectively 22.6, 11.6 and 7.4 percent of total imports. "Transportation" (EBOPS code 205) accounted for the largest share of imports of services in 2012 at 1.4 bln US$, followed by "Travel" (EBOPS code 236) at 1.3 bln US$ and "Other business services" (EBOPS code 268) at 359.9 mln US$ (see graph 6).

Table 4: Top 10 import commodities 2012 to 2014

HS code	4-digit heading of Harmonized System 2012	Value (million US$) 2012	2013	2014	Unit value 2012	2013	2014	Unit	SITC code
	All Commodities	7 376.9	6 418.2	6 812.8					
2710	Petroleum oils, other than crude	2 141.7	1 767.8	1 606.9	0.9	0.9	0.8	US$/kg	334
8703	Motor cars and other motor vehicles principally designed for the transport	281.8	167.6	245.5	15.8	16.0	16.5	thsd US$/unit	781
3004	Medicaments (excluding goods of heading 30.02, 30.05 or 30.06)	219.2	212.8	205.8	61.7	59.3	48.7	US$/kg	542
8517	Electrical apparatus for line telephony or line telegraphy	109.5	132.1	119.7					764
2402	Cigars, cheroots, cigarillos and cigarettes	105.9	98.5	95.5	38.6	39.9	35.7	US$/kg	122
8903	Yachts and other vessels for pleasure or sports; rowing boats and canoes	16.5	9.6	246.6	54.0	57.6	197.4	thsd US$/unit	793
2208	Alcohol of a strength by volume of less than 80 % vol	57.8	67.3	66.3	17.8	21.3	21.0	US$/litre	112
8471	Automatic data processing machines and units thereof	68.7	59.3	58.5	108.5	163.3	151.9	US$/unit	752
6204	Women's or girls' suits, ensembles, jackets, blazers, dresses, skirts	63.1	56.4	65.7	19.7	16.1	16.7	US$/unit	842
9403	Other furniture and parts thereof	75.5	55.4	53.7					821

2014 International Trade Statistics Yearbook, Vol. I   Source: UN Comtrade and UN ServiceTrade

Czech Republic

Goods Imports: CIF, by origin   **Goods Exports:** FOB, by last known destination   **Trade System:** Special

Overview:
In 2014, the value of merchandise exports of the Czech Republic increased moderately by 7.6 percent to reach 173.7 bln US$, while its merchandise imports increased moderately by 6.7 percent to reach 152.0 bln US$ (see graph 1, table 2 and table 3). The merchandise trade balance recorded a relatively small surplus of 21.7 bln US$ (see graph 1). The largest merchandise trade balance was with MDG Developed Europe at 41.8 bln US$ (see graph 4). Merchandise exports in the Czech Republic were diversified amongst partners; imports were also diversified. The top 13 partners accounted for 80 percent or more of exports and 15 partners accounted for 80 percent or more of imports (see graph 5). In 2013, the value of exports of services of the Czech Republic increased moderately by 8.8 percent, reaching 24.0 bln US$, while its imports of services increased slightly by 4.2 percent and reached 20.3 bln US$ (see graph 2). There was a relatively small trade in services surplus of 3.7 bln US$.

Graph 1: Total merchandise trade, by value
(Bln US$ by year)

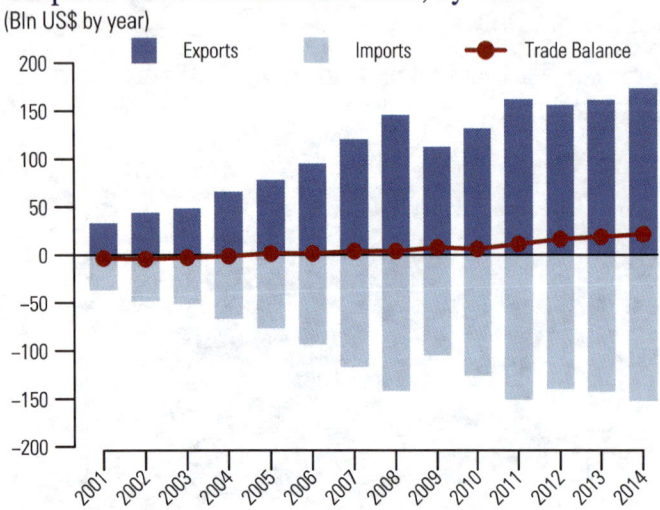

Graph 2: Total services trade, by value
(Bln US$ by year)

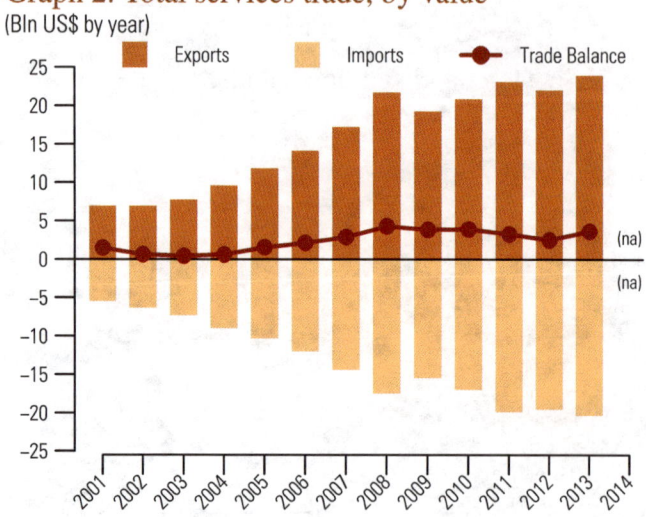

Exports Profile:
"Machinery and transport equipment" (SITC section 7), "Goods classified chiefly by material" (SITC section 6) and "Miscellaneous manufactured articles" (SITC section 8) were the largest commodity groups for exports in 2014, representing respectively 55.2, 16.6 and 11.7 percent of exported goods (see table 2). From 2012 to 2014, the largest export commodity was "Motor cars and other motor vehicles principally designed for the transport" (HS code 8703) (see table 1). The top three destinations for merchandise exports were Germany, Slovakia and Poland, accounting for respectively 31.6, 8.7 and 6.0 percent of total exports. "Travel" (EBOPS code 236) accounted for the largest share of exports of services in 2013 at 7.4 bln US$, followed by "Transportation" (EBOPS code 205) at 5.3 bln US$ and "Other business services" (EBOPS code 268) at 5.3 bln US$ (see graph 3).

Graph 3: Exports of services by EBOPS category
(% share in 2013)

- Transportation (22.3 %)
- Other business (22.2 %)
- Travel (30.7 %)
- Remaining (24.8 %)

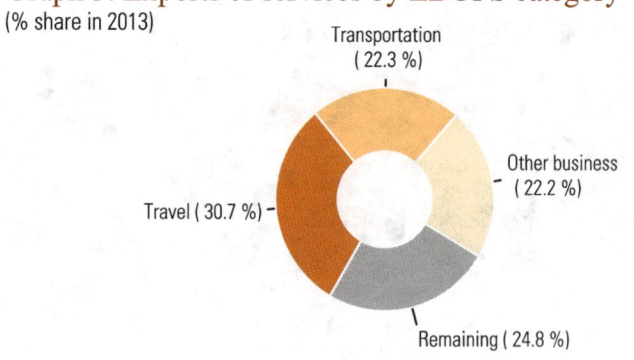

Table 1: Top 10 export commodities 2012 to 2014

HS code	4-digit heading of Harmonized System 2012	Value (million US$) 2012	2013	2014	Unit value 2012	2013	2014	Unit	SITC code
	All Commodities	156 422.7	161 524.2	173 726.7					
8703	Motor cars and other motor vehicles principally designed for the transport	15 197.2	15 345.2	17 767.2	14.5	15.0	15.7	thsd US$/unit	781
8708	Parts and accessories of the motor vehicles of headings 87.01 to 87.05	10 147.8	11 564.3	13 159.4	7.8	8.1	8.5	US$/kg	784
8471	Automatic data processing machines and units thereof	10 283.8	9 212.7	9 804.3	215.2	211.2	234.2	US$/unit	752
8517	Electrical apparatus for line telephony or line telegraphy	3 594.8	4 168.6	4 932.7					764
8544	Insulated (including enamelled or anodised) wire, cable	2 659.6	2 796.5	2 956.9	11.2	9.0	9.7	US$/kg	773
9503	Tricycles, scooters, wheeled toys; dolls' carriages; dolls; other toys	2 006.3	2 369.1	2 645.1	23.8	21.9	24.9	US$/kg	894
4011	New pneumatic tyres, of rubber	2 352.6	2 330.1	2 331.1	79.5	77.5	74.5	US$/unit	625
8536	Electrical apparatus for switching or protecting electrical circuits	1 982.8	2 296.3	2 665.7	19.0	18.8	29.7	US$/kg	772
8528	Reception apparatus for television	2 570.8	1 958.2	2 223.5	248.8	302.2	241.8	US$/unit	761
9401	Seats (other than those of heading 94.02)	1 790.7	2 230.7	2 632.0					821

Source: UN Comtrade and UN ServiceTrade

Czech Republic

Services Imports and Exports: EBOPS 2002 categories

Table 2: Merchandise exports by SITC
(Value in million US$, growth and shares in percentage)

SITC	2014	Avg. Growth rates 2010-2014	Avg. Growth rates 2013-2014	2014 share
Total	173 726.7	7.1	7.6	100.0
0+1	7 568.4	12.6	6.8	4.4
2+4	4 784.8	4.2	-0.8	2.8
3	4 626.1	-1.2	-3.2	2.7
5	11 187.8	8.0	12.2	6.4
6	28 832.0	6.7	2.6	16.6
7	95 904.4	8.0	9.6	55.2
8	20 402.8	9.6	8.1	11.7
9	420.3	-40.3	0.4	0.2

Table 3: Merchandise imports by SITC
(Value in million US$, growth and shares in percentage)

SITC	2014	Avg. Growth rates 2010-2014	Avg. Growth rates 2013-2014	2014 share
Total	152 004.1	4.9	6.7	100.0
0+1	8 512.9	7.2	0.6	5.6
2+4	4 175.0	5.0	-3.7	2.7
3	12 335.0	0.7	-8.6	8.1
5	17 636.3	8.5	8.1	11.6
6	26 944.7	5.9	4.4	17.7
7	66 206.0	5.6	12.0	43.6
8	15 812.3	6.5	9.1	10.4
9	381.8	-44.9	-18.2	0.3

SITC Legend

SITC Code	Description
Total	All commodities
0+1	Food, animals + beverages, tobacco
2+4	Crude materials + anim. & veg. oils
3	Mineral fuels, lubricants
5	Chemicals
6	Goods classified chiefly by material
7	Machinery and transport equipment
8	Miscellaneous manufactured articles
9	Not classified elsewhere in the SITC

Graph 4: Merchandise trade balance
(Bln US$ by MDG Regions in 2014)

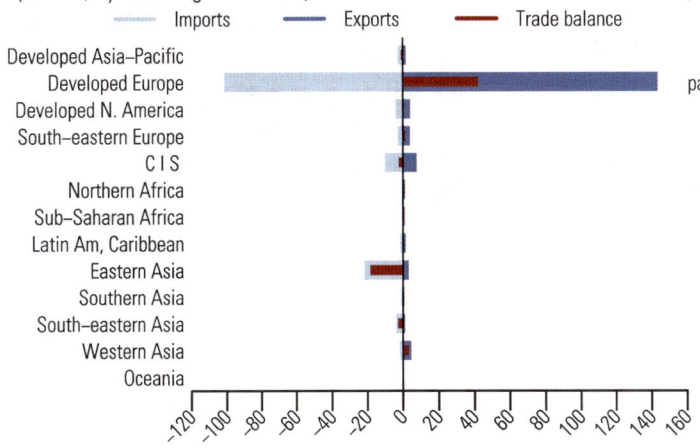

Graph 5: Partner concentration of merchandise trade
(Cumulative share by ranked partners in 2014)

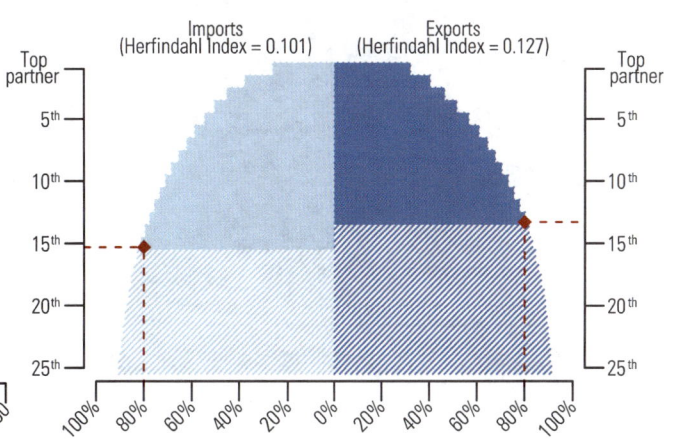

Imports (Herfindahl Index = 0.101)
Exports (Herfindahl Index = 0.127)

Graph 6: Imports of services by EBOPS category
(% share in 2013)

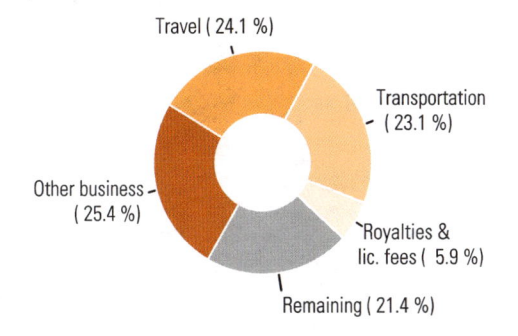

- Travel (24.1 %)
- Transportation (23.1 %)
- Royalties & lic. fees (5.9 %)
- Remaining (21.4 %)
- Other business (25.4 %)

Imports Profile:

"Machinery and transport equipment" (SITC section 7), "Goods classified chiefly by material" (SITC section 6) and "Chemicals" (SITC section 5) were the largest commodity groups for imports in 2014, representing respectively 43.6, 17.7 and 11.6 percent of imported goods (see table 3). From 2012 to 2014, the largest import commodity was "Parts and accessories of the motor vehicles of headings 87.01 to 87.05" (HS code 8708) (see table 4). The top three partners for merchandise imports were Germany, China and Poland, accounting for respectively 25.9, 11.1 and 7.5 percent of total imports. "Other business services" (EBOPS code 268) accounted for the largest share of imports of services in 2013 at 5.2 bln US$, followed by "Travel" (EBOPS code 236) at 4.9 bln US$ and "Transportation" (EBOPS code 205) at 4.7 bln US$ (see graph 6).

Table 4: Top 10 import commodities 2012 to 2014

HS code	4-digit heading of Harmonized System 2012	2012	2013	2014	2012	2013	2014	Unit	SITC code
	All Commodities	139 726.8	142 525.8	152 004.1					
8708	Parts and accessories of the motor vehicles of headings 87.01 to 87.05	7 300.9	7 479.0	8 542.2	6.6	6.9	7.0	US$/kg	784
8471	Automatic data processing machines and units thereof	6 482.5	5 614.2	5 678.7	96.5	88.3	90.4	US$/unit	752
2709	Petroleum oils and oils obtained from bituminous minerals, crude	5 876.1	5 414.2	5 656.8	0.8	0.8	0.8	US$/kg	333
8517	Electrical apparatus for line telephony or line telegraphy	3 150.9	4 062.0	4 667.3					764
2711	Petroleum gases and other gaseous hydrocarbons	3 982.3	4 054.9	2 601.2	0.7	0.6	0.5	US$/kg	343
3004	Medicaments (excluding goods of heading 30.02, 30.05 or 30.06)	2 980.1	3 041.2	3 661.7	72.5	85.6	105.8	US$/kg	542
8473	Parts and accessories for use with machines of heading 84.69 to 84.72	2 860.4	2 599.9	3 077.0	44.0	45.1	44.3	US$/kg	759
8542	Electronic integrated circuits	2 753.5	2 617.7	3 020.8					776
8703	Motor cars and other motor vehicles principally designed for the transport	2 460.9	2 519.2	2 933.4	16.6	17.6	17.1	thsd US$/unit	781
2710	Petroleum oils, other than crude	2 195.4	2 502.4	2 576.9	1.1	1.0	0.9	US$/kg	334

Denmark

Goods Imports: CIF, by origin/consignment for intra-eu   **Goods Exports:** FOB, by last known destination   **Trade System:** General

Overview:
In 2014, the value of merchandise exports of Denmark decreased slightly by 0.6 percent to reach 109.8 bln US$, while its merchandise imports increased slightly by 1.5 percent to reach 99.0 bln US$ (see graph 1, table 2 and table 3). The merchandise trade balance recorded a relatively small surplus of 10.7 bln US$ (see graph 1). The largest merchandise trade balance was with MDG Eastern Asia at -4.3 bln US$ (see graph 4). Merchandise exports in Denmark were diversified amongst partners; imports were also diversified. The top 17 partners accounted for 80 percent or more of exports and 15 partners accounted for 80 percent or more of imports (see graph 5). In 2013, the value of exports of services of Denmark increased moderately by 9.1 percent, reaching 72.1 bln US$, while its imports of services increased substantially by 10.8 percent and reached 64.5 bln US$ (see graph 2). There was a relatively small trade in services surplus of 7.6 bln US$.

Graph 1: Total merchandise trade, by value
(Bln US$ by year)

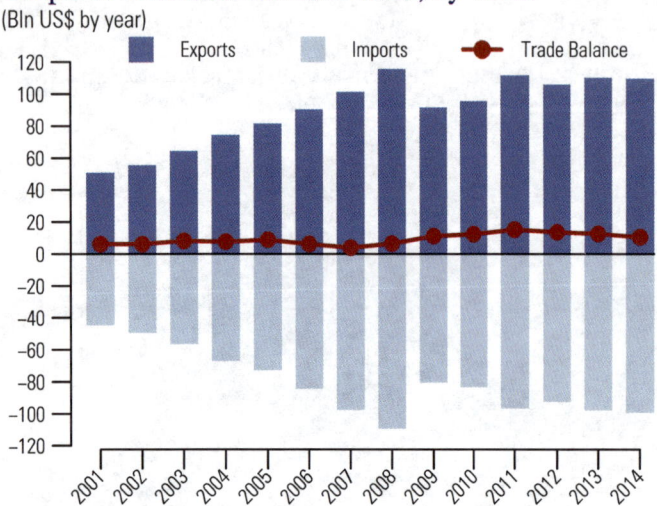

Graph 2: Total services trade, by value
(Bln US$ by year)

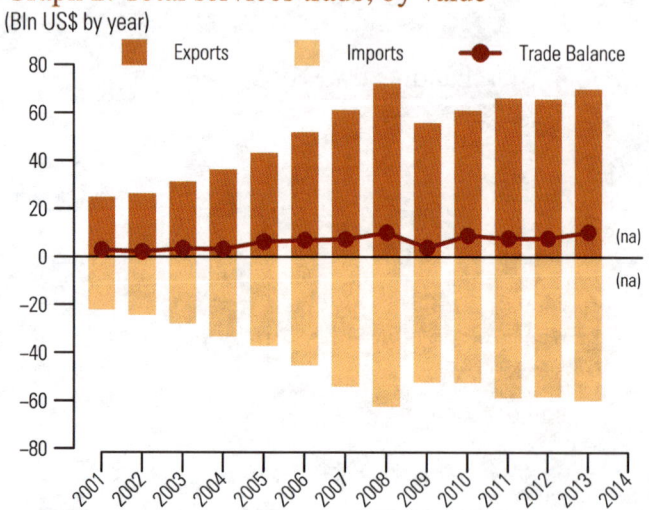

Exports Profile:
"Machinery and transport equipment" (SITC section 7), "Food, animals + beverages, tobacco" (SITC section 0+1) and "Miscellaneous manufactured articles" (SITC section 8) were the largest commodity groups for exports in 2014, representing respectively 26.4, 17.9 and 14.6 percent of exported goods (see table 2). From 2012 to 2014, the largest export commodity was "Commodities not specified according to kind" (HS code 9999) (see table 1). The top three destinations for merchandise exports were Germany, Sweden and Special Categories, accounting for respectively 15.4, 12.0 and 9.4 percent of total exports. "Transportation" (EBOPS code 205) accounted for the largest share of exports of services in 2013 at 44.5 bln US$, followed by "Travel" (EBOPS code 236) at 42.8 bln US$ and "Royalties and license fees" (EBOPS code 266) at 13.4 bln US$ (see graph 3).

Graph 3: Exports of services by EBOPS category
(% share in 2013)

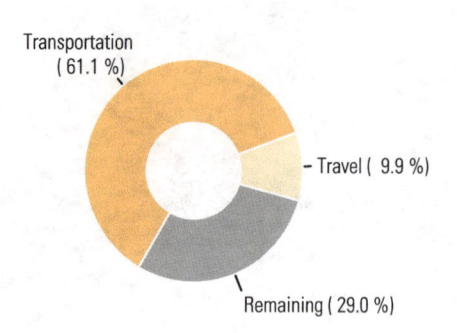

- Transportation (61.1 %)
- Travel (9.9 %)
- Remaining (29.0 %)

Table 1: Top 10 export commodities 2012 to 2014

HS code	4-digit heading of Harmonized System 2012	Value (million US$) 2012	2013	2014	Unit value 2012	2013	2014	Unit	SITC code
	All Commodities	106 126.0	110 413.9	109 758.0					
9999	Commodities not specified according to kind	9 096.7	9 595.6	9 715.9					931
2710	Petroleum oils, other than crude	5 291.9	5 023.6	3 772.2	0.9	0.8	*0.8*	US$/kg	334
2709	Petroleum oils and oils obtained from bituminous minerals, crude	4 853.1	4 915.1	3 039.6	0.8	0.8	0.7	US$/kg	333
0203	Meat of swine, fresh, chilled or frozen	3 326.6	3 392.5	3 221.2	3.0	3.1	3.0	US$/kg	012
3004	Medicaments (excluding goods of heading 30.02, 30.05 or 30.06)	2 999.0	3 206.2	3 228.0	198.1	223.9	*230.5*	US$/kg	542
8502	Electric generating sets and rotary converters	1 704.7	2 889.5	3 671.3	191.7	358.5	504.2	thsd US$/unit	716
3002	Human blood; animal blood prepared for therapeutic uses	1 866.6	2 318.8	2 381.0	416.0	523.8	*454.9*	US$/kg	541
4301	Raw furskins (including heads, tails, paws and other pieces or cuttings	1 881.0	2 303.6	1 398.7	536.8	653.5	337.8	US$/kg	212
0406	Cheese and curd	1 429.3	1 575.8	1 696.9	5.2	5.4	*5.4*	US$/kg	024
2106	Food preparations not elsewhere specified or included	1 312.3	1 568.8	1 382.5	4.8	5.2	*5.0*	US$/kg	098

Denmark

Services Imports and Exports: EBOPS 2002 categories

Table 2: Merchandise exports by SITC
(Value in million US$, growth and shares in percentage)

SITC	2014	Avg. Growth rates 2010-2014	Avg. Growth rates 2013-2014	2014 share
Total	109 758.0	3.5	-0.6	100.0
0+1	19 660.2	3.6	-0.8	17.9
2+4	5 020.1	3.2	-9.0	4.6
3	7 222.7	-2.3	-30.7	6.6
5	13 476.4	5.7	2.0	12.3
6	9 641.0	2.9	-4.5	8.8
7	28 968.9	4.9	7.8	26.4
8	16 023.8	1.5	8.0	14.6
9	9 744.9	5.5	1.1	8.9

Table 3: Merchandise imports by SITC
(Value in million US$, growth and shares in percentage)

SITC	2014	Avg. Growth rates 2010-2014	Avg. Growth rates 2013-2014	2014 share
Total	99 027.6	4.5	1.5	100.0
0+1	12 690.9	5.4	2.2	12.8
2+4	3 956.6	6.2	5.4	4.0
3	8 201.3	6.2	-25.8	8.3
5	11 791.4	6.2	4.1	11.9
6	13 287.8	2.9	2.4	13.4
7	31 162.8	4.4	7.0	31.5
8	15 558.4	2.1	7.6	15.7
9	2 378.3	8.7	-4.4	2.4

SITC Legend

SITC Code	Description
Total	All commodities
0+1	Food, animals + beverages, tobacco
2+4	Crude materials + anim. & veg. oils
3	Mineral fuels, lubricants
5	Chemicals
6	Goods classified chiefly by material
7	Machinery and transport equipment
8	Miscellaneous manufactured articles
9	Not classified elsewhere in the SITC

Graph 4: Merchandise trade balance
(Bln US$ by MDG Regions in 2014)

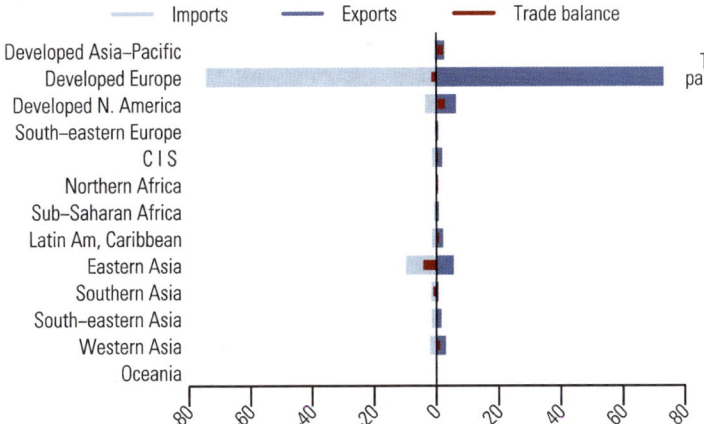

Graph 5: Partner concentration of merchandise trade
(Cumulative share by ranked partners in 2014)

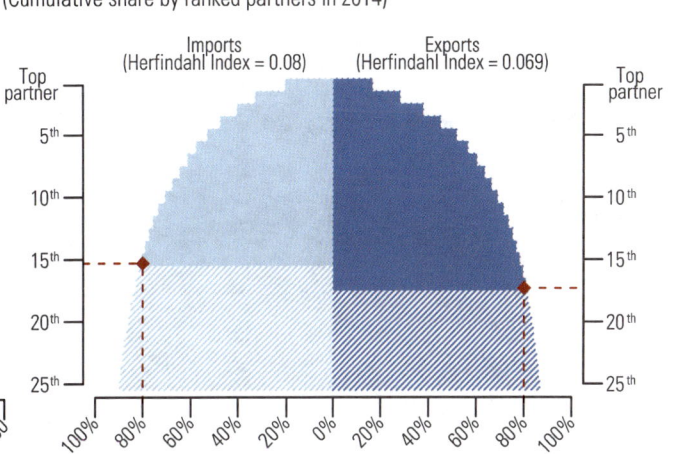

Imports (Herfindahl Index = 0.08)
Exports (Herfindahl Index = 0.069)

Graph 6: Imports of services by EBOPS category
(% share in 2013)

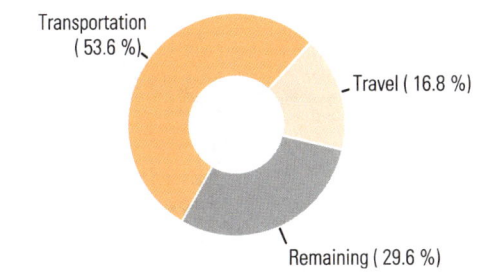

- Transportation (53.6 %)
- Travel (16.8 %)
- Remaining (29.6 %)

Imports Profile:

"Machinery and transport equipment" (SITC section 7), "Miscellaneous manufactured articles" (SITC section 8) and "Goods classified chiefly by material" (SITC section 6) were the largest commodity groups for imports in 2014, representing respectively 31.5, 15.7 and 13.4 percent of imported goods (see table 3). From 2012 to 2014, the largest import commodity was "Petroleum oils, other than crude" (HS code 2710) (see table 4). The top three partners for merchandise imports were Germany, Sweden and the Netherlands, accounting for respectively 20.5, 12.6 and 7.4 percent of total imports. "Travel" (EBOPS code 236) accounted for the largest share of imports of services in 2013 at 94.9 bln US$, followed by "Transportation" (EBOPS code 205) at 33.4 bln US$ and "Other business services" (EBOPS code 268) at 10.3 bln US$ (see graph 6).

Table 4: Top 10 import commodities 2012 to 2014

HS code	4-digit heading of Harmonized System 2012	2012	2013	2014	2012	2013	2014	Unit	SITC code
	All Commodities	92 296.8	97 589.7	99 027.6					
2710	Petroleum oils, other than crude	5 578.1	6 696.0	4 926.8	0.9	0.9	0.8	US$/kg	334
8703	Motor cars and other motor vehicles principally designed for the transport	2 747.0	3 088.6	3 493.9	13.4	14.0	15.1	thsd US$/unit	781
2709	Petroleum oils and oils obtained from bituminous minerals, crude	2 727.1	3 580.5	2 587.2	0.9	0.8	0.8	US$/kg	333
3004	Medicaments (excluding goods of heading 30.02, 30.05 or 30.06)	2 544.9	2 798.9	3 054.8	123.0	135.4	143.2	US$/kg	542
9999	Commodities not specified according to kind	2 249.6	2 469.0	2 360.2					931
8471	Automatic data processing machines and units thereof	2 299.6	2 073.9	2 013.9	242.8	109.7	226.5	US$/unit	752
8517	Electrical apparatus for line telephony or line telegraphy	1 879.7	1 852.9	2 087.2					764
8901	Cruise ships, excursion boats, ferry-boats, cargo ships, barges	424.1	1 514.4	2 506.1	14.1	45.9	57.0	mln US$/unit	793
8708	Parts and accessories of the motor vehicles of headings 87.01 to 87.05	874.1	1 008.4	961.7	9.4	10.2	10.5	US$/kg	784
9018	Instruments and appliances used in medical, surgical, dental or veterinary	906.5	870.5	801.5					872

2014 International Trade Statistics Yearbook, Vol. I — Source: UN Comtrade and UN ServiceTrade

Dominica

Goods Imports: CIF, by origin | **Goods Exports:** FOB, by last known destination | **Trade System:** Special

Overview:
In 2012, the value of merchandise exports of Dominica was at 37.0 mln US$ while its merchandise imports reached 211.9 mln US$ (see graph 1, table 2 and table 3). The merchandise trade balance recorded a large deficit of 174.9 mln US$ (see graph 1). The largest merchandise trade balance was with MDG Developed North America at -81.2 mln US$ (see graph 4). Merchandise exports in Dominica were diversified amongst partners; imports were moderately concentrated. The top 8 partners accounted for 80 percent or more of exports and 11 partners accounted for 80 percent or more of imports (see graph 5). In 2012, the value of exports of services of Dominica decreased substantially by 19.8 percent, reaching 124.1 mln US$, while its imports of services increased slightly by 2.6 percent and reached 67.6 mln US$ (see graph 2). There was a moderate trade in services surplus of 56.5 mln US$.

Graph 1: Total merchandise trade, by value
(Mln US$ by year)

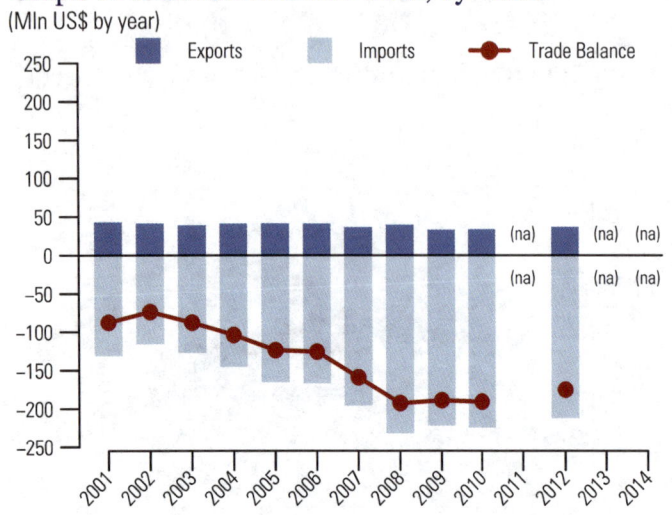

Graph 2: Total services trade, by value
(Mln US$ by year)

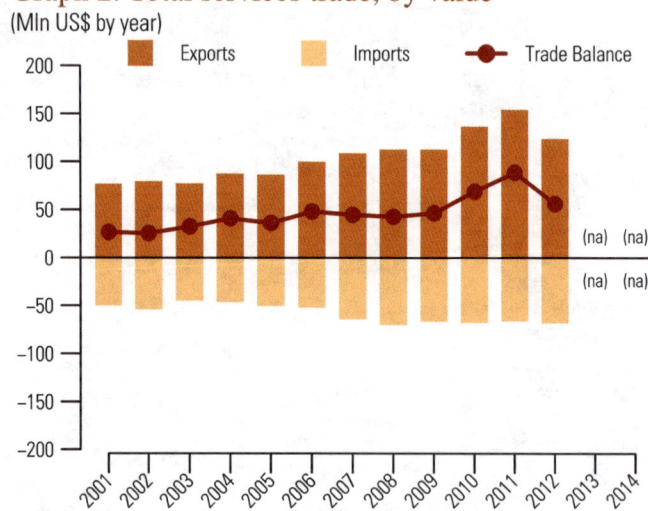

Exports Profile:
"Chemicals" (SITC section 5), "Miscellaneous manufactured articles" (SITC section 8) and "Machinery and transport equipment" (SITC section 7) were the largest commodity groups for exports in 2012, representing respectively 50.9, 14.6 and 11.6 percent of exported goods (see table 2). From 2010 to 2012, the largest export commodity was "Soap; organic surface-active products" (HS code 3401) (see table 1). The top three destinations for merchandise exports were Jamaica, Trinidad and Tobago and Saint Kitts and Nevis, accounting for respectively 16.9, 16.3 and 16.0 percent of total exports. "Travel" (EBOPS code 236) accounted for the largest share of exports of services in 2012 at 78.6 mln US$, followed by "Other business services" (EBOPS code 268) at 26.2 mln US$ and "Government services, n.i.e." (EBOPS code 291) at 13.5 mln US$ (see graph 3).

Graph 3: Exports of services by EBOPS category
(% share in 2012)

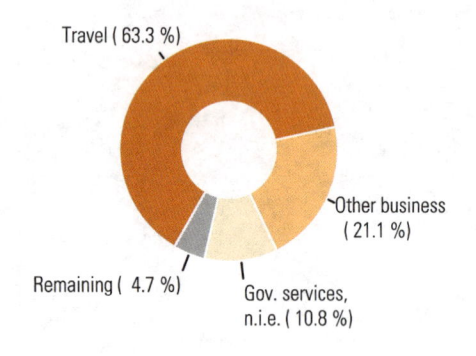

- Travel (63.3 %)
- Other business (21.1 %)
- Gov. services, n.i.e. (10.8 %)
- Remaining (4.7 %)

Table 1: Top 10 export commodities 2010 to 2012

HS code	4-digit heading of Harmonized System 2007	Value (million US$) 2010	2011	2012	Unit value 2010	2011	2012	Unit	SITC code
	All Commodities	34.1	...	37.0					
3401	Soap; organic surface-active products	13.8	...	16.5	3.9			US$/kg	554
4907	Unused postage, revenue or similar stamps of current or new issue	4.5	...	4.5			55.7	thsd US$/kg	892
0803	Bananas, including plantains, fresh or dried	3.1	...	1.1	0.8			US$/kg	057
3210	Other paints and varnishes	1.8	...	1.5	4.3		27.2	US$/kg	533
2517	Pebbles, gravel, broken or crushed stone	0.9	...	2.4	0.0			US$/kg	273
0714	Manioc, arrowroot, sweet potatoes and similar roots	1.7	...	1.2	3.2		3.2	US$/kg	054
8518	Microphones and stands therefor; loudspeakers	0.6	...	1.5					764
2505	Natural sands of all kinds	0.9	...	1.1	0.0		6.2	US$/kg	273
8525	Transmission apparatus for radio-telephony, radio-broadcasting	0.0	...	1.1					764
3301	Essential oils (terpeneless or not), including concretes	0.6	...	0.4					551

Source: UN Comtrade and UN ServiceTrade

Dominica

Services Imports and Exports: EBOPS 2002 categories

Table 2: Merchandise exports by SITC
(Value in million US$, growth and shares in percentage)

SITC	2012	Avg. Growth rates 2008-2012	2011-2012	2012 share
Total	37.0	-1.9	...	100.0
0+1	4.2	-28.1	...	11.3
2+4	3.6	-9.9	...	9.7
3	0.0	-2.6	...	0.0
5	18.8	1.5	...	50.9
6	0.7	35.1	...	1.9
7	4.3	62.7	...	11.6
8	5.4	92.8	...	14.6
9	0.0	...	...	0.0

Table 3: Merchandise imports by SITC
(Value in million US$, growth and shares in percentage)

SITC	2012	Avg. Growth rates 2008-2012	2011-2012	2012 share
Total	211.9	-2.3	...	100.0
0+1	47.7	2.3	...	22.5
2+4	10.3	-4.3	...	4.8
3	46.9	6.6	...	22.1
5	17.0	-4.4	...	8.0
6	31.1	-5.5	...	14.7
7	36.1	-10.5	...	17.0
8	22.7	-0.6	...	10.7
9	0.3	-34.5	...	0.1

SITC Legend

SITC Code	Description
Total	All commodities
0+1	Food, animals + beverages, tobacco
2+4	Crude materials + anim. & veg. oils
3	Mineral fuels, lubricants
5	Chemicals
6	Goods classified chiefly by material
7	Machinery and transport equipment
8	Miscellaneous manufactured articles
9	Not classified elsewhere in the SITC

Graph 4: Merchandise trade balance
(Mln US$ by MDG Regions in 2012)

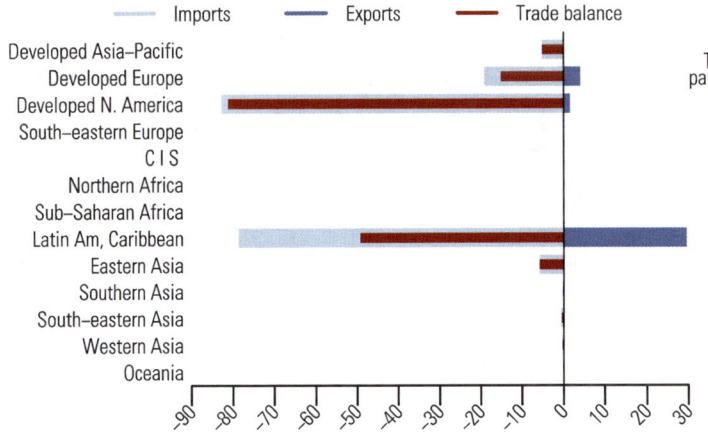

Graph 5: Partner concentration of merchandise trade
(Cumulative share by ranked partners in 2012)

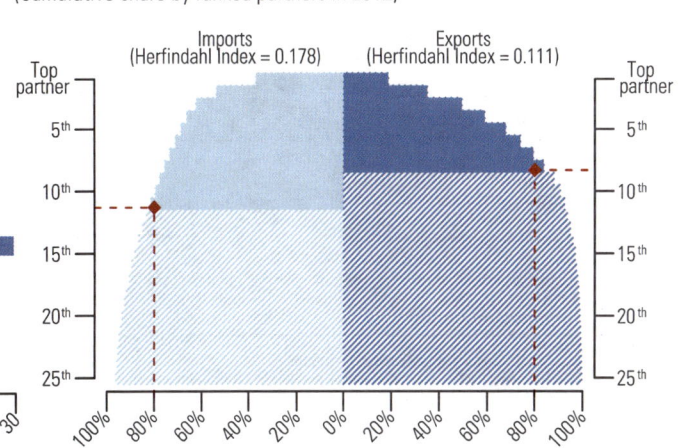

Imports (Herfindahl Index = 0.178)
Exports (Herfindahl Index = 0.111)

Graph 6: Imports of services by EBOPS category
(% share in 2012)

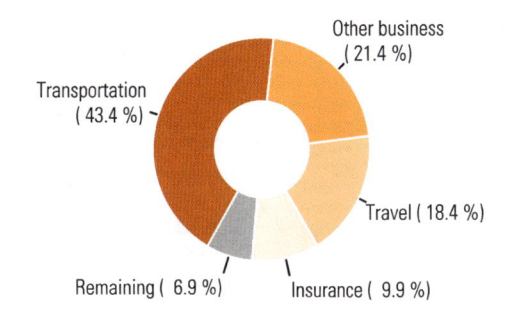

- Transportation (43.4%)
- Other business (21.4%)
- Travel (18.4%)
- Insurance (9.9%)
- Remaining (6.9%)

Imports Profile:

"Food, animals + beverages, tobacco" (SITC section 0+1), "Mineral fuels, lubricants" (SITC section 3) and "Machinery and transport equipment" (SITC section 7) were the largest commodity groups for imports in 2012, representing respectively 22.5, 22.1 and 17.0 percent of imported goods (see table 3). From 2010 to 2012, the largest import commodity was "Petroleum oils, other than crude" (HS code 2710) (see table 4). The top three partners for merchandise imports were the United States, Trinidad and Tobago and Areas nes, accounting for respectively 39.4, 16.1 and 4.6 percent of total imports. "Transportation" (EBOPS code 205) accounted for the largest share of imports of services in 2012 at 29.4 mln US$, followed by "Other business services" (EBOPS code 268) at 14.4 mln US$ and "Travel" (EBOPS code 236) at 12.4 mln US$ (see graph 6).

Table 4: Top 10 import commodities 2010 to 2012

HS code	4-digit heading of Harmonized System 2007	Value (million US$) 2010	2011	2012	Unit value 2010	2011	2012	Unit	SITC code
	All Commodities	224.6	...	211.9					
2710	Petroleum oils, other than crude	35.3	...	43.2	1.2		4.1	US$/kg	334
0207	Meat and edible offal, of the poultry of heading 01.05	5.5	...	5.4	3.9			US$/kg	012
8703	Motor cars and other motor vehicles principally designed for the transport	5.5	...	3.5	16.3		18.2	thsd US$/unit	781
1502	Fats of bovine animals, sheep or goats, other than those of heading 15.03	5.2	...	3.4					411
0402	Milk and cream, concentrated or containing added sugar	3.7	...	3.3	4.2			US$/kg	022
2523	Portland cement, aluminous cement, slag cement	3.1	...	3.5					661
1101	Wheat or meslin flour	3.1	...	3.4	1.6			US$/kg	046
2202	Waters with added sugar	2.9	...	3.6	2.2		5.2	US$/litre	111
8517	Electrical apparatus for line telephony or line telegraphy	3.4	...	2.4					764
8704	Motor vehicles for the transport of goods	3.7	...	1.8					782

2014 International Trade Statistics Yearbook, Vol. I   Source: UN Comtrade and UN ServiceTrade

Dominican Republic

Goods Imports: FOB, by origin **Goods Exports:** FOB, by last known destination **Trade System:** General

Overview:
In 2014, the value of merchandise exports of Dominican Republic increased substantially by 24.7 percent to reach 9.9 bln US$, while its merchandise imports decreased slightly by 0.5 percent to reach 17.8 bln US$ (see graph 1, table 2 and table 3). The merchandise trade balance recorded a moderate deficit of 7.8 bln US$ (see graph 1). The largest merchandise trade balance was with MDG Latin America and the Caribbean at -2.8 bln US$ (see graph 4). Merchandise exports in Dominican Republic were highly concentrated amongst partners; imports were moderately concentrated. The top 5 partners accounted for 80 percent or more of exports and 12 partners accounted for 80 percent or more of imports (see graph 5). In 2013, the value of exports of services of Dominican Republic increased moderately by 6.5 percent, reaching 6.4 bln US$, while its imports of services decreased slightly by 0.1 percent and reached 2.8 bln US$ (see graph 2). There was a large trade in services surplus of 3.5 bln US$.

Graph 1: Total merchandise trade, by value
(Bln US$ by year)

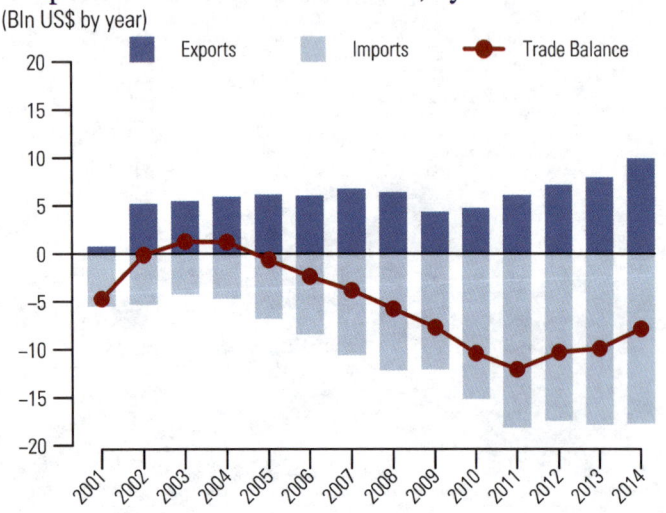

Graph 2: Total services trade, by value
(Bln US$ by year)

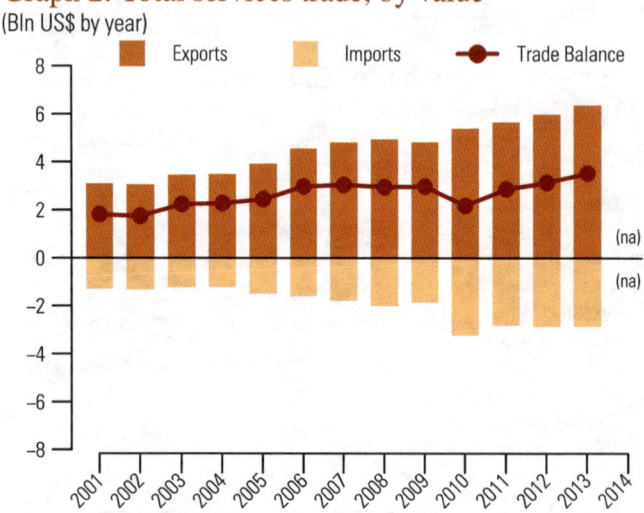

Exports Profile:
"Miscellaneous manufactured articles" (SITC section 8), "Food, animals + beverages, tobacco" (SITC section 0+1) and "Not classified elsewhere in the SITC" (SITC section 9) were the largest commodity groups for exports in 2014, representing respectively 28.8, 21.9 and 16.0 percent of exported goods (see table 2). From 2012 to 2014, the largest export commodity was "Gold (including gold plated with platinum)" (HS code 7108) (see table 1). The top three destinations for merchandise exports were the United States, Haiti and Canada, accounting for respectively 51.4, 14.0 and 7.8 percent of total exports. "Travel" (EBOPS code 236) accounted for the largest share of exports of services in 2013 at 5.1 bln US$, followed by "Transportation" (EBOPS code 205) at 497.6 mln US$ and "Government services, n.i.e." (EBOPS code 291) at 354.7 mln US$ (see graph 3).

Graph 3: Exports of services by EBOPS category
(% share in 2013)

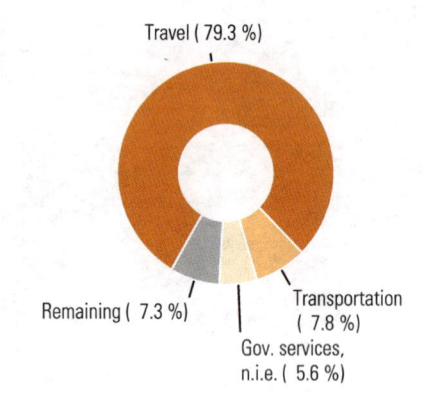

- Travel (79.3 %)
- Transportation (7.8 %)
- Gov. services, n.i.e. (5.6 %)
- Remaining (7.3 %)

Table 1: Top 10 export commodities 2012 to 2014

HS code	4-digit heading of Harmonized System 2012	Value (million US$) 2012	2013	2014	Unit value 2012	2013	2014	Unit	SITC code
	All Commodities...	7168.5	7961.0	9927.8					
7108	Gold (including gold plated with platinum).......................	169.5	1198.4	1582.0	7.5	11.9	0.7	thsd US$/kg	971
9018	Instruments and appliances used in medical, surgical, dental or veterinary............	688.5	752.7	874.4					872
2402	Cigars, cheroots, cigarillos and cigarettes......................	408.8	510.5	526.5	16.5	22.6		US$/kg	122
8536	Electrical apparatus for switching or protecting electrical circuits............	368.2	367.0	484.4					772
2710	Petroleum oils, other than crude.....................................	447.1	153.0	558.7					334
6109	T-shirts, singlets and other vests, knitted or crocheted...	352.1	204.6	313.4	5.2	5.2	4.8	US$/unit	845
3006	Pharmaceutical goods specified in Note 4 to this Chapter......	329.6	278.2	227.0					541
0803	Bananas, including plantains, fresh or dried...................	138.2	167.9	331.6	0.5	0.5	0.6	US$/kg	057
7113	Articles of jewellery and parts thereof, of precious metal....	133.6	194.8	250.5					897
6403	Footwear with outer soles of rubber, plastics, leather.....	183.9	218.4	158.3	31.3	31.8		US$/pair	851

Dominican Republic

Services Imports and Exports: EBOPS 2002 categories

Table 2: Merchandise exports by SITC
(Value in million US$, growth and shares in percentage)

SITC	2014	Avg. Growth rates 2010-2014	Avg. Growth rates 2013-2014	2014 share
Total	9927.8	20.1	24.7	100.0
0+1	2177.6	14.1	26.7	21.9
2+4	333.2	18.7	-1.6	3.4
3	565.8	230.3	261.8	5.7
5	570.5	15.6	14.7	5.7
6	1022.9	8.6	-8.6	10.3
7	812.8	15.4	33.1	8.2
8	2857.8	12.4	25.4	28.8
9	1587.2	473.2	28.0	16.0

Table 3: Merchandise imports by SITC
(Value in million US$, growth and shares in percentage)

SITC	2014	Avg. Growth rates 2010-2014	Avg. Growth rates 2013-2014	2014 share
Total	17751.7	4.1	-0.5	100.0
0+1	2230.5	7.7	6.9	12.6
2+4	674.2	3.3	18.9	3.8
3	4026.9	2.1	-20.2	22.7
5	2137.6	7.5	2.1	12.0
6	3160.4	4.9	9.6	17.8
7	3482.9	-0.4	3.4	19.6
8	1948.7	9.4	13.8	11.0
9	90.4	8.3	5.8	0.5

SITC Legend

SITC Code	Description
Total	All commodities
0+1	Food, animals + beverages, tobacco
2+4	Crude materials + anim. & veg. oils
3	Mineral fuels, lubricants
5	Chemicals
6	Goods classified chiefly by material
7	Machinery and transport equipment
8	Miscellaneous manufactured articles
9	Not classified elsewhere in the SITC

Graph 4: Merchandise trade balance
(Bln US$ by MDG Regions in 2014)

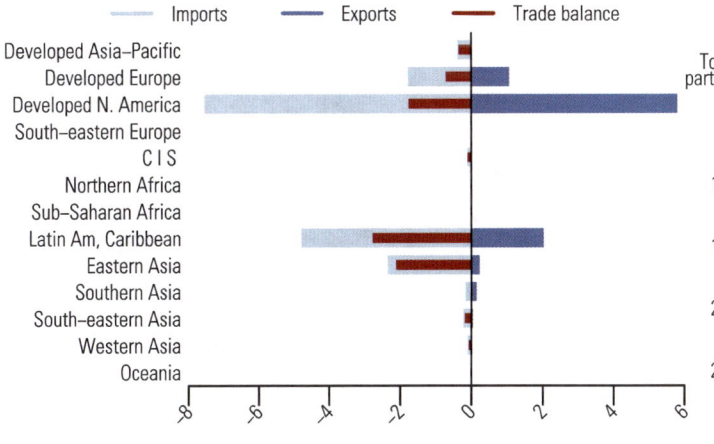

Graph 5: Partner concentration of merchandise trade
(Cumulative share by ranked partners in 2014)

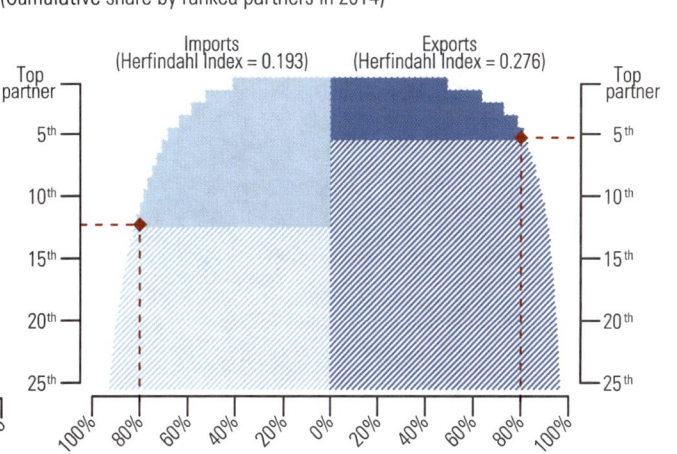

Imports (Herfindahl Index = 0.193)
Exports (Herfindahl Index = 0.276)

Graph 6: Imports of services by EBOPS category
(% share in 2013)

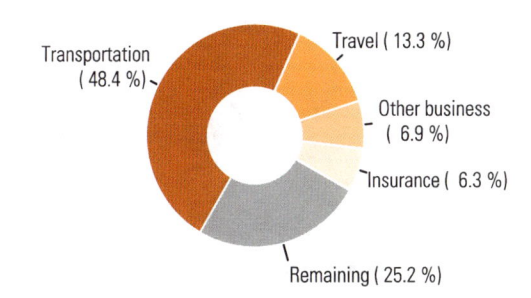

- Transportation (48.4%)
- Travel (13.3%)
- Other business (6.9%)
- Insurance (6.3%)
- Remaining (25.2%)

Imports Profile:

"Mineral fuels, lubricants" (SITC section 3), "Machinery and transport equipment" (SITC section 7) and "Goods classified chiefly by material" (SITC section 6) were the largest commodity groups for imports in 2014, representing respectively 22.7, 19.6 and 17.8 percent of imported goods (see table 3). From 2012 to 2014, the largest import commodity was "Petroleum oils, other than crude" (HS code 2710) (see table 4). The top three partners for merchandise imports were the United States, China and the Bolivarian Republic of Venezuela, accounting for respectively 39.3, 10.7 and 6.4 percent of total imports. "Transportation" (EBOPS code 205) accounted for the largest share of imports of services in 2013 at 1.4 bln US$, followed by "Travel" (EBOPS code 236) at 377.9 mln US$ and "Other business services" (EBOPS code 268) at 196.5 mln US$ (see graph 6).

Table 4: Top 10 import commodities 2012 to 2014

HS code	4-digit heading of Harmonized System 2012	Value (million US$) 2012	2013	2014	Unit value 2012	2013	2014	Unit	SITC code
	All Commodities	17430.2	17845.0	17751.7					
2710	Petroleum oils, other than crude	2498.3	2869.2	2210.0					334
2709	Petroleum oils and oils obtained from bituminous minerals, crude	1021.9	1226.4	941.3	0.8	0.8	0.8	US$/kg	333
2711	Petroleum gases and other gaseous hydrocarbons	721.0	706.3	756.7					343
8703	Motor cars and other motor vehicles principally designed for the transport	478.0	518.1	617.5	22.9	22.3	20.9	thsd US$/unit	781
3004	Medicaments (excluding goods of heading 30.02, 30.05 or 30.06)	386.8	426.9	418.4					542
3926	Other articles of plastics	302.2	329.0	359.7	12.2	12.2	12.7	US$/kg	893
8517	Electrical apparatus for line telephony or line telegraphy	275.9	323.2	303.5					764
1005	Maize (corn)	288.1	278.7	227.9			0.4	US$/kg	044
8536	Electrical apparatus for switching or protecting electrical circuits	274.2	272.5	79.0					772
1001	Wheat and meslin	188.7	157.4	163.5	0.4	0.4		US$/kg	041

Ecuador

Goods Imports: CIF, by origin | **Goods Exports: FOB, by last known destination** | **Trade System: Special**

Overview:
In 2014, the value of merchandise exports of Ecuador increased slightly by 3.1 percent to reach 25.7 bln US$, while its merchandise imports increased slightly by 1.7 percent to reach 27.5 bln US$ (see graph 1, table 2 and table 3). The merchandise trade balance recorded a relatively small deficit of 1.8 bln US$ (see graph 1). The largest merchandise trade balance was with MDG Eastern Asia at -5.2 bln US$ (see graph 4). Merchandise exports in Ecuador were moderately concentrated amongst partners; imports were diversified. The top 11 partners accounted for 80 percent or more of exports and 13 partners accounted for 80 percent or more of imports (see graph 5). In 2012, the value of exports of services of Ecuador increased substantially by 14.0 percent, reaching 1.8 bln US$, while its imports of services increased slightly by 2.1 percent and reached 3.2 bln US$ (see graph 2). There was a moderate trade in services deficit of 1.4 bln US$.

Graph 1: Total merchandise trade, by value
(Bln US$ by year)

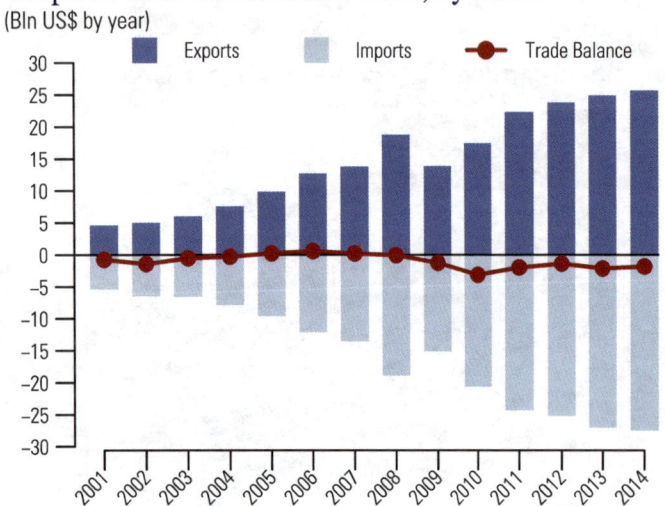

Graph 2: Total services trade, by value
(Bln US$ by year)

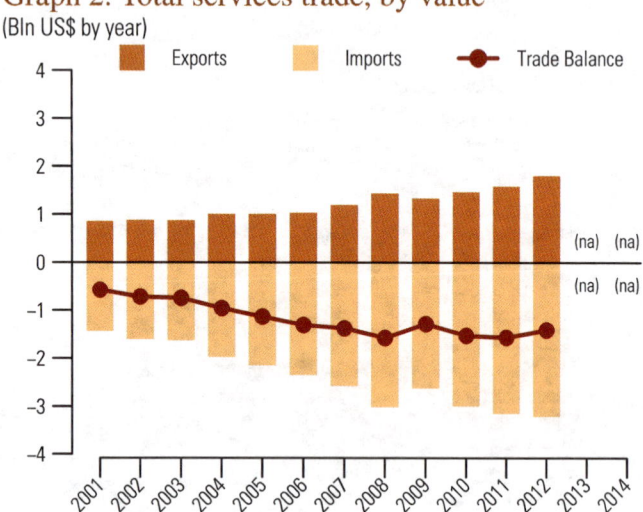

Exports Profile:
"Mineral fuels, lubricants" (SITC section 3), "Food, animals + beverages, tobacco" (SITC section 0+1) and "Crude materials + anim. & veg. oils" (SITC section 2+4) were the largest commodity groups for exports in 2014, representing respectively 51.7, 33.0 and 6.2 percent of exported goods (see table 2). From 2012 to 2014, the largest export commodity was "Petroleum oils and oils obtained from bituminous minerals, crude" (HS code 2709) (see table 1). The top three destinations for merchandise exports were the United States, Chile and Peru, accounting for respectively 44.4, 9.1 and 7.3 percent of total exports. "Travel" (EBOPS code 236) accounted for the largest share of exports of services in 2012 at 1.0 bln US$, followed by "Transportation" (EBOPS code 205) at 413.4 mln US$ and "Communications services" (EBOPS code 245) at 143.9 mln US$ (see graph 3).

Graph 3: Exports of services by EBOPS category
(% share in 2012)

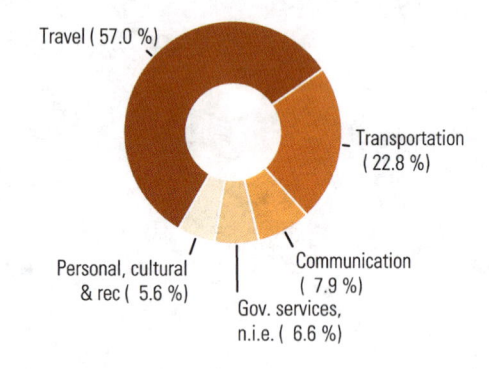

- Travel (57.0 %)
- Transportation (22.8 %)
- Communication (7.9 %)
- Gov. services, n.i.e. (6.6 %)
- Personal, cultural & rec (5.6 %)

Table 1: Top 10 export commodities 2012 to 2014

HS code	4-digit heading of Harmonized System 2007	Value (million US$) 2012	2013	2014	Unit value 2012	2013	2014	Unit	SITC code
	All Commodities	23852.0	24957.6	25730.1					
2709	Petroleum oils and oils obtained from bituminous minerals, crude	12711.2	13411.8	13016.0	0.7	0.7	0.6	US$/kg	333
0803	Bananas, including plantains, fresh or dried	2082.0	2332.2	2620.7	0.4	0.4	0.4	US$/kg	057
0306	Crustaceans, whether in shell or not	1279.8	1795.0	2580.6	6.1	8.1	8.6	US$/kg	036
1604	Prepared or preserved fish; caviar	1112.8	1337.9	1241.5	4.8	5.1	4.5	US$/kg	037
0603	Cut flowers and flower buds of a kind suitable for bouquets	771.3	837.3	798.4	6.1	5.3	5.7	US$/kg	292
7108	Gold (including gold plated with platinum)	387.2	467.8	854.0			34.4	thsd US$/kg	971
2710	Petroleum oils, other than crude	863.7	551.9	192.4	0.7	0.6	0.5	US$/kg	334
1801	Cocoa beans, whole or broken, raw or roasted	346.2	433.3	587.8	2.3	2.4	3.0	US$/kg	072
1511	Palm oil and its fractions	300.9	208.4	225.0	1.1	1.0	1.0	US$/kg	422
2101	Extracts, essences and concentrates, of coffee, tea or mate	184.8	190.1	152.9	7.9	7.8	6.8	US$/kg	071

Ecuador

Services Imports and Exports: EBOPS 2002 categories

Table 2: Merchandise exports by SITC
(Value in million US$, growth and shares in percentage)

SITC	2014	Avg. Growth rates 2010-2014	Avg. Growth rates 2013-2014	2014 share
Total	25730.1	10.1	3.1	100.0
0+1	8482.7	14.0	16.0	33.0
2+4	1588.6	11.5	9.0	6.2
3	13300.7	8.3	-5.7	51.7
5	287.4	0.8	-7.8	1.1
6	661.3	3.3	-2.4	2.6
7	337.7	-11.9	-9.9	1.3
8	213.9	-6.3	14.3	0.8
9	857.8	86.2	62.1	3.3

Table 3: Merchandise imports by SITC
(Value in million US$, growth and shares in percentage)

SITC	2014	Avg. Growth rates 2010-2014	Avg. Growth rates 2013-2014	2014 share
Total	27515.4	7.5	1.7	100.0
0+1	1958.8	6.0	10.6	7.1
2+4	615.2	7.9	5.0	2.2
3	6647.2	11.0	5.6	24.2
5	4241.3	7.6	4.8	15.4
6	3748.3	6.9	-2.3	13.6
7	8260.8	4.8	-2.2	30.0
8	1930.1	11.7	-0.9	7.0
9	113.9	6.3	-14.9	0.4

SITC Legend

SITC Code	Description
Total	All commodities
0+1	Food, animals + beverages, tobacco
2+4	Crude materials + anim. & veg. oils
3	Mineral fuels, lubricants
5	Chemicals
6	Goods classified chiefly by material
7	Machinery and transport equipment
8	Miscellaneous manufactured articles
9	Not classified elsewhere in the SITC

Graph 4: Merchandise trade balance
(Bln US$ by MDG Regions in 2014)

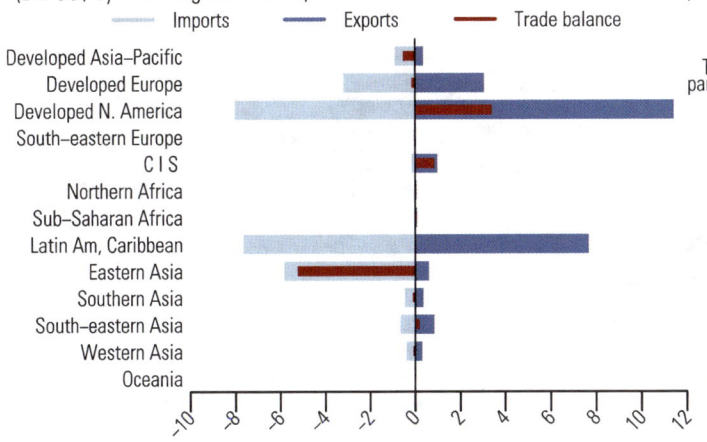

Graph 5: Partner concentration of merchandise trade
(Cumulative share by ranked partners in 2014)

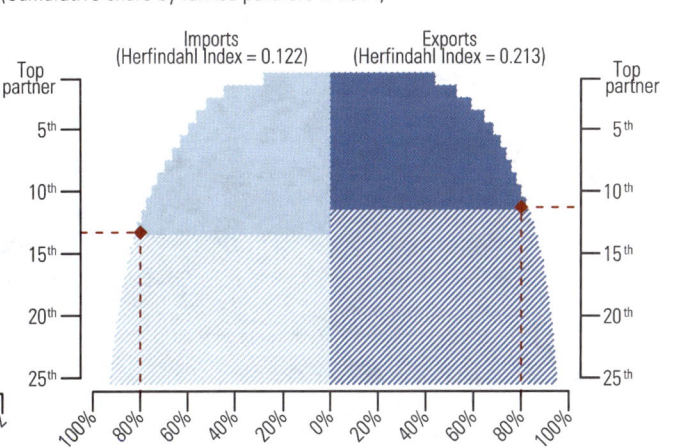

Imports (Herfindahl Index = 0.122)
Exports (Herfindahl Index = 0.213)

Graph 6: Imports of services by EBOPS category
(% share in 2012)

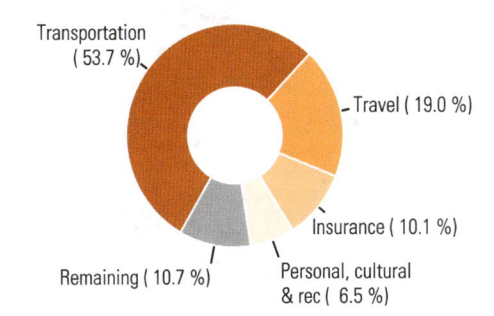

- Transportation (53.7 %)
- Travel (19.0 %)
- Insurance (10.1 %)
- Personal, cultural & rec (6.5 %)
- Remaining (10.7 %)

Imports Profile:

"Machinery and transport equipment" (SITC section 7), "Mineral fuels, lubricants" (SITC section 3) and "Chemicals" (SITC section 5) were the largest commodity groups for imports in 2014, representing respectively 30.0, 24.2 and 15.4 percent of imported goods (see table 3). From 2012 to 2014, the largest import commodity was "Petroleum oils, other than crude" (HS code 2710) (see table 4). The top three partners for merchandise imports were the United States, China and Colombia, accounting for respectively 26.7, 14.9 and 8.0 percent of total imports. "Transportation" (EBOPS code 205) accounted for the largest share of imports of services in 2012 at 1.7 bln US$, followed by "Travel" (EBOPS code 236) at 610.6 mln US$ and "Insurance services" (EBOPS code 253) at 324.9 mln US$ (see graph 6).

Table 4: Top 10 import commodities 2012 to 2014

HS code	4-digit heading of Harmonized System 2007	2012	2013	2014	2012	2013	2014	Unit	SITC code
	All Commodities	25196.5	27064.5	27515.4					
2710	Petroleum oils, other than crude	2887.1	3403.9	3362.7	1.0	1.0	0.9	US$/kg	334
2707	Oils and other products of high temperature coal tar	2052.8	2113.4	2430.4	1.2	1.1	1.0	US$/kg	335
3004	Medicaments (excluding goods of heading 30.02, 30.05 or 30.06)	788.8	803.1	858.7	32.0	34.7	34.9	US$/kg	542
8703	Motor cars and other motor vehicles principally designed for the transport	764.5	784.5	778.6	15.8	15.8	16.4	thsd US$/unit	781
2711	Petroleum gases and other gaseous hydrocarbons	644.5	657.8	698.2	0.8	0.8	0.8	US$/kg	343
8704	Motor vehicles for the transport of goods	691.8	564.8	598.9					782
8517	Electrical apparatus for line telephony or line telegraphy	440.9	513.0	508.4					764
8471	Automatic data processing machines and units thereof	402.9	482.2	489.4					752
7304	Tubes, pipes and hollow profiles, seamless, of iron (other than cast iron)	347.1	358.9	406.2	2.2	2.1	2.0	US$/kg	679
2304	Oil-cake and other solid residues	251.7	336.0	406.7	0.5	0.5	0.5	US$/kg	081

2014 International Trade Statistics Yearbook, Vol. I — Source: UN Comtrade and UN ServiceTrade

Egypt

Goods Imports: CIF, by consignment **Goods Exports:** FOB, by last known destination **Trade System:** General

Overview:

In 2014, the value of merchandise exports of Egypt decreased moderately by 6.8 percent to reach 26.8 bln US$, while its merchandise imports increased moderately by 7.0 percent to reach 71.3 bln US$ (see graph 1, table 2 and table 3). The merchandise trade balance recorded a large deficit of 44.5 bln US$ (see graph 1). The largest merchandise trade balance was with MDG Developed Europe at -14.7 bln US$ (see graph 4). Merchandise exports in Egypt were diversified amongst partners; imports were also diversified. The top 26 partners accounted for 80 percent or more of exports and 22 partners accounted for 80 percent or more of imports (see graph 5). In 2013, the value of exports of services of Egypt decreased substantially by 16.1 percent, reaching 18.3 bln US$, while its imports of services decreased slightly by 0.7 percent and reached 16.3 bln US$ (see graph 2). There was a relatively small trade in services surplus of 1.9 bln US$. See footnote*.

Graph 1: Total merchandise trade, by value
(Bln US$ by year)

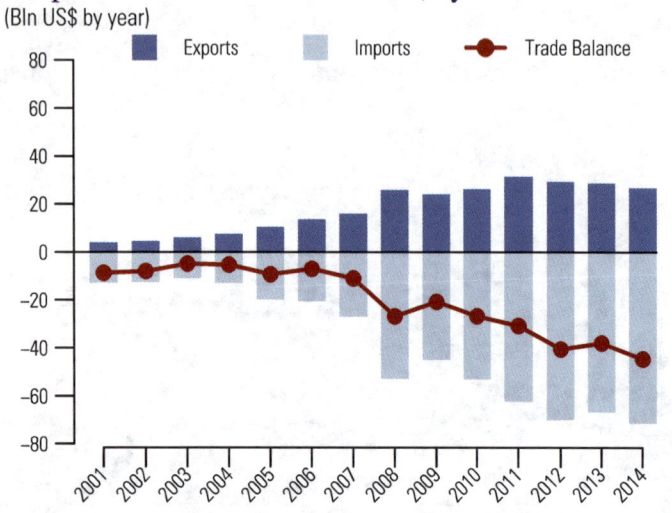

Graph 2: Total services trade, by value
(Bln US$ by year)

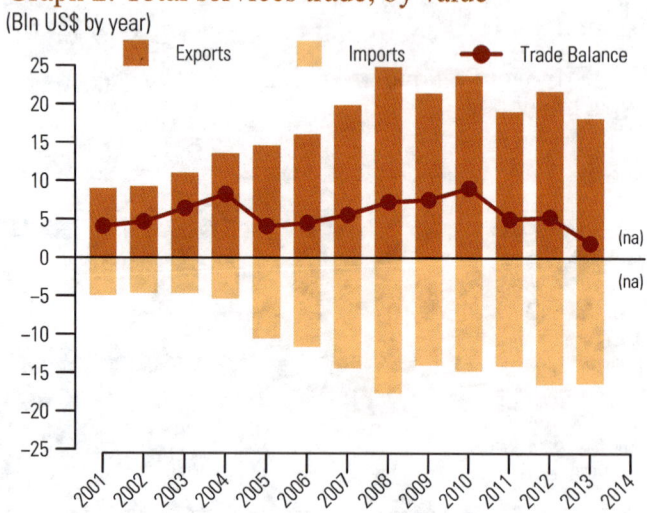

Exports Profile:

"Mineral fuels, lubricants" (SITC section 3), "Goods classified chiefly by material" (SITC section 6) and "Chemicals" (SITC section 5) were the largest commodity groups for exports in 2014, representing respectively 23.4, 19.5 and 16.5 percent of exported goods (see table 2). From 2012 to 2014, the largest export commodity was "Petroleum oils and oils obtained from bituminous minerals, crude" (HS code 2709) (see table 1). The top three destinations for merchandise exports were Italy, India and Saudi Arabia, accounting for respectively 8.8, 7.2 and 6.8 percent of total exports. "Transportation" (EBOPS code 205) accounted for the largest share of exports of services in 2013 at 9.4 bln US$, followed by "Travel" (EBOPS code 236) at 6.0 bln US$ (see graph 3).

Graph 3: Exports of services by EBOPS category
(% share in 2013)

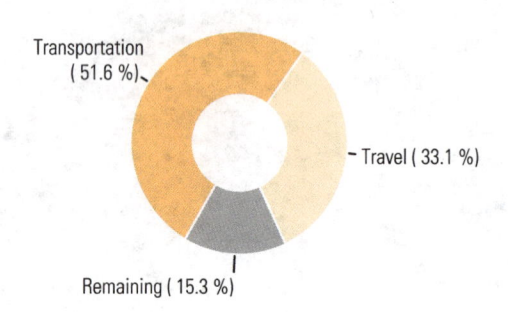

- Transportation (51.6 %)
- Travel (33.1 %)
- Remaining (15.3 %)

Table 1: Top 10 export commodities 2012 to 2014

HS code	4-digit heading of Harmonized System 2007	Value (million US$) 2012	2013	2014	Unit value 2012	2013	2014	Unit	SITC code
	All Commodities	29 417.0	28 779.4	26 812.0					
2709	Petroleum oils and oils obtained from bituminous minerals, crude	3 022.6	3 059.5	3 050.5	0.7	0.7	0.6	US$/kg	333
2710	Petroleum oils, other than crude	3 150.4	2 548.9	2 437.2	1.3	0.9	0.8	US$/kg	334
2711	Petroleum gases and other gaseous hydrocarbons	2 179.9	1 559.7	379.8		0.4	0.5	US$/kg	343
3102	Mineral or chemical fertilisers, nitrogenous	1 184.9	1 077.1	644.7		0.4	0.3	US$/kg	562
7108	Gold (including gold plated with platinum)	1 318.7	901.1	659.3	45.2	43.5	38.5	thsd US$/kg	971
8544	Insulated (including enamelled or anodised) wire, cable	880.2	895.9	1 001.8		8.6	7.7	US$/kg	773
0805	Citrus fruit, fresh or dried	489.9	533.3	475.3	0.8	0.4	0.4	US$/kg	057
5701	Carpets and other textile floor coverings, knotted, whether or not made up	373.7	376.8	377.5			6.3	US$/m²	659
0406	Cheese and curd	361.5	374.9	378.9	4.8	3.8	3.3	US$/kg	024
6203	Men's or boys' suits, ensembles, jackets, blazers, trousers	301.4	372.1	321.0			9.1	US$/unit	841

*Special trade system up to 2007.

Source: UN Comtrade and UN ServiceTrade

Egypt

Services Imports and Exports: EBOPS 2002 categories

Table 2: Merchandise exports by SITC
(Value in million US$, growth and shares in percentage)

SITC	2014	Avg. Growth rates 2010-2014	Avg. Growth rates 2013-2014	2014 share
Total	26812.2	0.5	-6.8	100.0
0+1	4226.5	0.7	-0.4	15.8
2+4	1170.0	-5.3	-22.4	4.4
3	6262.0	-4.6	-16.6	23.4
5	4415.5	5.8	-6.5	16.5
6	5231.6	-0.9	-10.0	19.5
7	2325.7	19.7	48.0	8.7
8	2239.2	2.6	-3.4	8.4
9	941.6	-3.9	-14.3	3.5

Table 3: Merchandise imports by SITC
(Value in million US$, growth and shares in percentage)

SITC	2014	Avg. Growth rates 2010-2014	Avg. Growth rates 2013-2014	2014 share
Total	71337.7	7.7	7.0	100.0
0+1	12592.9	10.9	41.7	17.7
2+4	6477.0	7.1	-2.9	9.1
3	9808.6	8.3	5.6	13.7
5	9164.8	9.8	1.9	12.8
6	13274.2	5.1	3.9	18.6
7	15933.1	5.3	14.3	22.3
8	2948.9	4.9	19.4	4.1
9	1138.4	115.5	-68.7	1.6

SITC Legend

SITC Code	Description
Total	All commodities
0+1	Food, animals + beverages, tobacco
2+4	Crude materials + anim. & veg. oils
3	Mineral fuels, lubricants
5	Chemicals
6	Goods classified chiefly by material
7	Machinery and transport equipment
8	Miscellaneous manufactured articles
9	Not classified elsewhere in the SITC

Graph 4: Merchandise trade balance
(Bln US$ by MDG Regions in 2014)

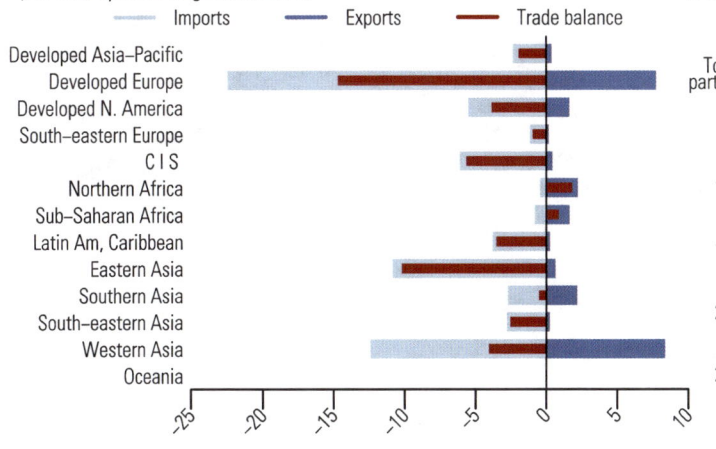

Graph 5: Partner concentration of merchandise trade
(Cumulative share by ranked partners in 2014)

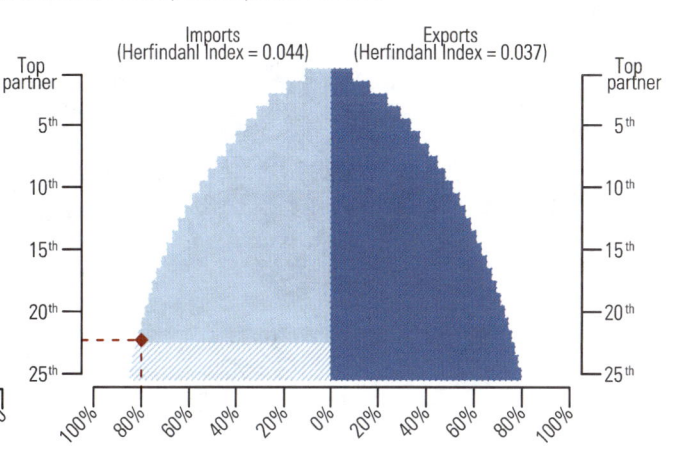

Graph 6: Imports of services by EBOPS category
(% share in 2013)

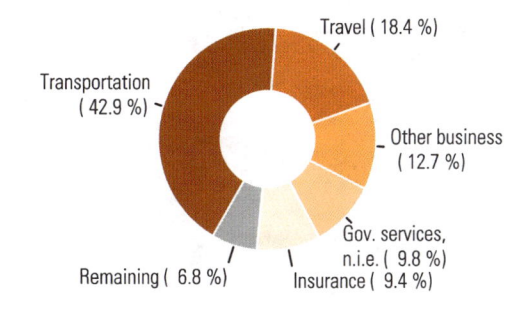

- Transportation (42.9 %)
- Travel (18.4 %)
- Other business (12.7 %)
- Gov. services, n.i.e. (9.8 %)
- Insurance (9.4 %)
- Remaining (6.8 %)

Imports Profile:
"Machinery and transport equipment" (SITC section 7), "Goods classified chiefly by material" (SITC section 6) and "Food, animals + beverages, tobacco" (SITC section 0+1) were the largest commodity groups for imports in 2014, representing respectively 22.3, 18.6 and 17.7 percent of imported goods (see table 3). From 2012 to 2014, the largest import commodity was "Petroleum oils, other than crude" (HS code 2710) (see table 4). The top three partners for merchandise imports were China, the United States and Germany, accounting for respectively 10.4, 7.5 and 7.4 percent of total imports. "Transportation" (EBOPS code 205) accounted for the largest share of imports of services in 2013 at 7.0 bln US$, followed by "Travel" (EBOPS code 236) at 3.0 bln US$ and "Other business services" (EBOPS code 268) at 2.1 bln US$ (see graph 6).

Table 4: Top 10 import commodities 2012 to 2014

HS code	4-digit heading of Harmonized System 2007	2012	2013	2014	2012	2013	2014	Unit	SITC code
	All Commodities	69865.6	66666.4	71337.7					
2710	Petroleum oils, other than crude	7718.7	5527.0	5548.4	1.1	0.9	0.8	US$/kg	334
2709	Petroleum oils and oils obtained from bituminous minerals, crude	2933.3	2028.6	3044.0	0.8	0.8	0.7	US$/kg	333
1001	Wheat and meslin	3196.9	721.7	3066.2	0.4	5.9	2.4	US$/kg	041
1005	Maize (corn)	1958.5	1985.0	1951.6					044
8703	Motor cars and other motor vehicles principally designed for the transport	1427.8	1266.2	2556.6	17.6	16.0	1.3	thsd US$/unit	781
2711	Petroleum gases and other gaseous hydrocarbons	2230.9	1573.5	1022.3		0.9	0.8	US$/kg	343
3004	Medicaments (excluding goods of heading 30.02, 30.05 or 30.06)	1483.5	1599.5	1662.3		39.1	127.6	US$/kg	542
7207	Semi-finished products of iron or non-alloy steel	1625.0	1527.6	1513.2		0.0	0.5	US$/kg	672
8517	Electrical apparatus for line telephony or line telegraphy	1286.1	1278.9	1653.2					764
4407	Wood sawn or chipped lengthwise, sliced or peeled	1207.7	1015.6	1390.7		305.9	189.9	US$/m³	248

Source: UN Comtrade and UN ServiceTrade

El Salvador

Goods Imports: CIF, by origin **Goods Exports:** FOB, by last known destination **Trade System:** General

Overview:

In 2014, the value of merchandise exports of El Salvador decreased slightly by 4.0 percent to reach 5.3 bln US$, while its merchandise imports decreased slightly by 2.4 percent to reach 10.5 bln US$ (see graph 1, table 2 and table 3). The merchandise trade balance recorded a large deficit of 5.2 bln US$ (see graph 1). The largest merchandise trade balance was with MDG Developed North America at -1.9 bln US$ (see graph 4). Merchandise exports in El Salvador were highly concentrated amongst partners; imports were moderately concentrated. The top 4 partners accounted for 80 percent or more of exports and 11 partners accounted for 80 percent or more of imports (see graph 5). In 2013, the value of exports of services of El Salvador increased substantially by 13.3 percent, reaching 1.5 bln US$, while its imports of services increased substantially by 11.1 percent and reached 1.3 bln US$ (see graph 2). There was a relatively small trade in services surplus of 184.1 mln US$.

Graph 1: Total merchandise trade, by value
(Bln US$ by year)

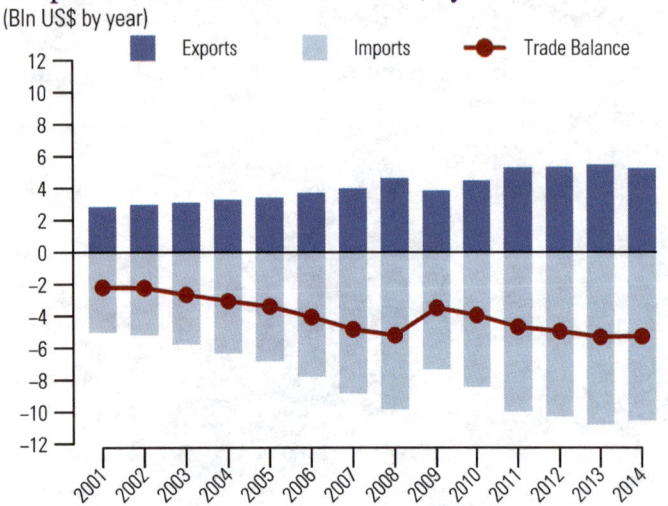

Graph 2: Total services trade, by value
(Bln US$ by year)

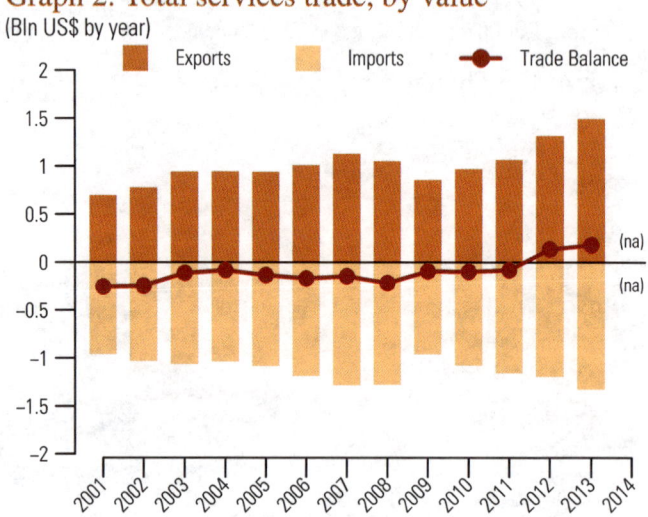

Exports Profile:

"Miscellaneous manufactured articles" (SITC section 8), "Food, animals + beverages, tobacco" (SITC section 0+1) and "Goods classified chiefly by material" (SITC section 6) were the largest commodity groups for exports in 2014, representing respectively 48.1, 18.8 and 16.0 percent of exported goods (see table 2). From 2012 to 2014, the largest export commodity was "T-shirts, singlets and other vests, knitted or crocheted" (HS code 6109) (see table 1). The top three destinations for merchandise exports were the United States, Honduras and Guatemala, accounting for respectively 46.3, 14.3 and 13.3 percent of total exports. "Travel" (EBOPS code 236) accounted for the largest share of exports of services in 2013 at 621.2 mln US$, followed by "Transportation" (EBOPS code 205) at 509.4 mln US$ and "Communications services" (EBOPS code 245) at 90.3 mln US$ (see graph 3).

Graph 3: Exports of services by EBOPS category
(% share in 2013)

- Travel (41.3 %)
- Transportation (33.9 %)
- Communication (6.0 %)
- Remaining (18.8 %)

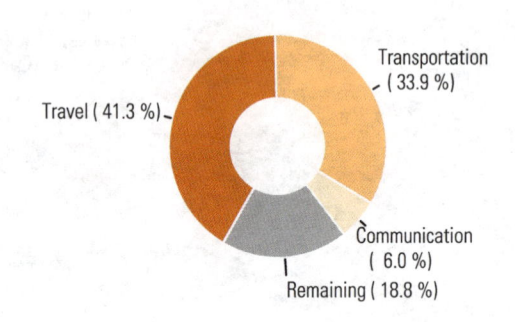

Table 1: Top 10 export commodities 2012 to 2014

HS code	4-digit heading of Harmonized System 2012	Value (million US$) 2012	2013	2014	Unit value 2012	2013	2014	Unit	SITC code
	All Commodities	5339.1	5491.1	5272.7					
6109	T-shirts, singlets and other vests, knitted or crocheted	791.0	810.7	753.3		5.3	5.0	US$/unit	845
6115	Panty hose, tights, stockings, socks and other hosiery	234.2	228.4	253.7	10.9	11.5	11.9	US$/kg	846
6110	Jerseys, pullovers, cardigans, waist-coats and similar articles	188.2	240.8	286.3		13.6	12.6	US$/unit	845
0901	Coffee, whether or not roasted or decaffeinated	300.1	233.9	110.5	4.6	3.5	3.9	US$/kg	071
1701	Cane or beet sugar and chemically pure sucrose, in solid form	198.5	209.2	192.0	0.5	0.5	0.4	US$/kg	061
8532	Electrical capacitors, fixed, variable or adjustable (pre-set)	178.1	171.0	171.2	204.1	206.8	209.5	US$/kg	778
3923	Articles for the conveyance or packing of goods, of plastics	167.4	172.0	178.0	2.3	2.3	2.3	US$/kg	893
4818	Toilet paper and similar paper	113.9	129.4	128.8	1.7	1.6	1.7	US$/kg	642
2710	Petroleum oils, other than crude	151.9	106.3	101.1	1.2	1.5	1.3	US$/kg	334
6107	Men's or boys' underpants, briefs, nightshirts, pyjamas, bathrobes	101.8	109.9	122.7					843

El Salvador

Services Imports and Exports: EBOPS 2002 categories

Table 2: Merchandise exports by SITC
(Value in million US$, growth and shares in percentage)

SITC	2014	Avg. Growth rates 2010-2014	Avg. Growth rates 2013-2014	2014 share
Total	5272.7	4.0	-4.0	100.0
0+1	993.3	6.4	-16.4	18.8
2+4	103.7	3.8	5.5	2.0
3	135.3	0.7	5.2	2.6
5	336.4	4.0	-11.2	6.4
6	845.1	6.6	-5.6	16.0
7	301.0	2.4	7.5	5.7
8	2534.8	5.8	1.8	48.1
9	23.1	-45.6	-32.0	0.4

Table 3: Merchandise imports by SITC
(Value in million US$, growth and shares in percentage)

SITC	2014	Avg. Growth rates 2010-2014	Avg. Growth rates 2013-2014	2014 share
Total	10512.9	5.7	-2.4	100.0
0+1	1583.6	7.7	6.7	15.1
2+4	345.6	1.5	-4.5	3.3
3	1830.7	7.4	-9.9	17.4
5	1633.0	5.4	-2.4	15.5
6	2271.6	5.4	-2.4	21.6
7	1728.7	6.1	-1.4	16.4
8	1104.9	7.0	-1.9	10.5
9	14.7	-45.3	3.8	0.1

SITC Legend

SITC Code	Description
Total	All commodities
0+1	Food, animals + beverages, tobacco
2+4	Crude materials + anim. & veg. oils
3	Mineral fuels, lubricants
5	Chemicals
6	Goods classified chiefly by material
7	Machinery and transport equipment
8	Miscellaneous manufactured articles
9	Not classified elsewhere in the SITC

Graph 4: Merchandise trade balance
(Bln US$ by MDG Regions in 2014)

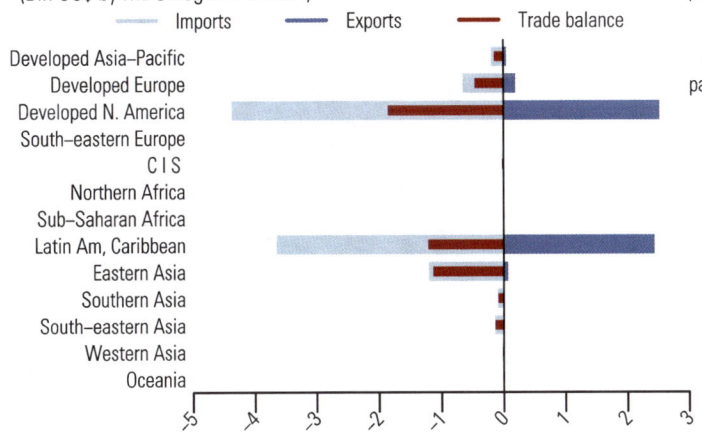

Graph 5: Partner concentration of merchandise trade
(Cumulative share by ranked partners in 2014)

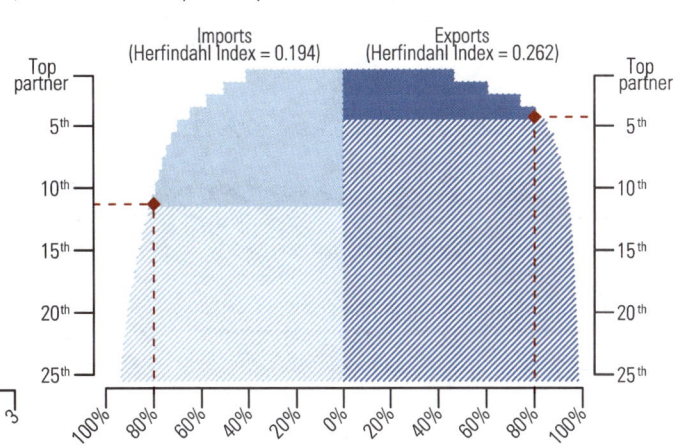

Imports (Herfindahl index = 0.194)
Exports (Herfindahl index = 0.262)

Graph 6: Imports of services by EBOPS category
(% share in 2013)

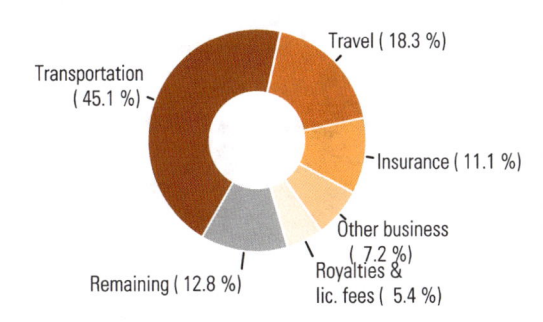

- Transportation (45.1 %)
- Travel (18.3 %)
- Insurance (11.1 %)
- Other business (7.2 %)
- Royalties & lic. fees (5.4 %)
- Remaining (12.8 %)

Imports Profile:

"Goods classified chiefly by material" (SITC section 6), "Mineral fuels, lubricants" (SITC section 3) and "Machinery and transport equipment" (SITC section 7) were the largest commodity groups for imports in 2014, representing respectively 21.6, 17.4 and 16.4 percent of imported goods (see table 3). From 2012 to 2014, the largest import commodity was "Petroleum oils, other than crude" (HS code 2710) (see table 4). The top three partners for merchandise imports were the United States, Guatemala and Mexico, accounting for respectively 39.3, 9.3 and 6.9 percent of total imports. "Transportation" (EBOPS code 205) accounted for the largest share of imports of services in 2013 at 595.7 mln US$, followed by "Travel" (EBOPS code 236) at 242.1 mln US$ and "Insurance services" (EBOPS code 253) at 146.0 mln US$ (see graph 6).

Table 4: Top 10 import commodities 2012 to 2014

HS code	4-digit heading of Harmonized System 2012	Value 2012	Value 2013	Value 2014	Unit value 2012	Unit value 2013	Unit value 2014	Unit	SITC code
	All Commodities	10269.6	10772.0	10512.9					
2710	Petroleum oils, other than crude	1333.3	1790.7	1521.5	1.0	0.9	0.9	US$/kg	334
6006	Other knitted or crocheted fabrics	328.4	349.6	325.1	5.5	5.2	5.0	US$/kg	655
3004	Medicaments (excluding goods of heading 30.02, 30.05 or 30.06)	304.5	266.1	267.0	31.8	27.9	21.8	US$/kg	542
8517	Electrical apparatus for line telephony or line telegraphy	208.4	227.3	253.1					764
2711	Petroleum gases and other gaseous hydrocarbons	149.8	171.7	216.9	0.8	0.8	0.9	US$/kg	343
5205	Cotton yarn (other than sewing thread), containing 85 % or more	135.3	155.2	155.8	3.5	3.3	3.4	US$/kg	651
2709	Petroleum oils and oils obtained from bituminous minerals, crude	409.5	0.0	0.0	0.8	11.0	6.5	US$/kg	333
8703	Motor cars and other motor vehicles principally designed for the transport	120.6	147.0	136.6		17.3	17.7	thsd US$/unit	781
5402	Synthetic filament yarn (other than sewing thread)	106.8	140.1	156.6	3.7	3.9	3.9	US$/kg	651
3907	Polyacetals, other polyethers and epoxide resins, in primary forms	127.0	120.7	120.7	1.7	1.7	1.6	US$/kg	574

2014 International Trade Statistics Yearbook, Vol. I — Source: UN Comtrade and UN ServiceTrade

Estonia

Goods Imports: CIF, by consignment **Goods Exports:** FOB, by last known destination **Trade System:** General

Overview:
In 2014, the value of merchandise exports of Estonia decreased slightly by 3.9 percent to reach 17.6 bln US$, while its merchandise imports decreased slightly by 0.3 percent to reach 20.1 bln US$ (see graph 1, table 2 and table 3). The merchandise trade balance recorded a relatively small deficit of 2.5 bln US$ (see graph 1). The largest merchandise trade balance was with MDG Developed Europe at -1.7 bln US$ (see graph 4). Merchandise exports in Estonia were diversified amongst partners; imports were also diversified. The top 12 partners accounted for 80 percent or more of exports and 15 partners accounted for 80 percent or more of imports (see graph 5). In 2013, the value of exports of services of Estonia increased substantially by 16.5 percent, reaching 6.4 bln US$, while its imports of services increased substantially by 21.0 percent and reached 4.7 bln US$ (see graph 2). There was a moderate trade in services surplus of 1.6 bln US$.

Graph 1: Total merchandise trade, by value
(Bln US$ by year)

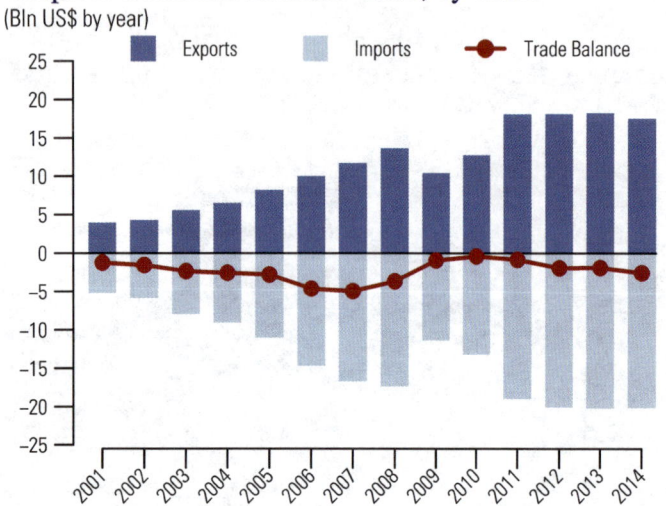

Graph 2: Total services trade, by value
(Bln US$ by year)

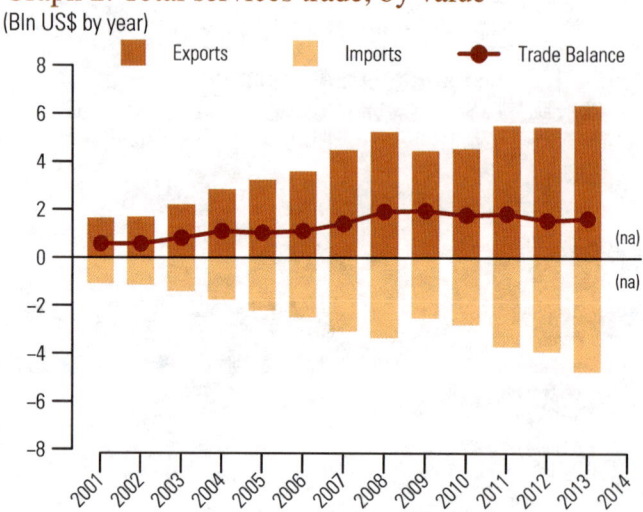

Exports Profile:
"Machinery and transport equipment" (SITC section 7), "Miscellaneous manufactured articles" (SITC section 8) and "Goods classified chiefly by material" (SITC section 6) were the largest commodity groups for exports in 2014, representing respectively 32.1, 14.3 and 13.6 percent of exported goods (see table 2). From 2012 to 2014, the largest export commodity was "Electrical apparatus for line telephony or line telegraphy" (HS code 8517) (see table 1). The top three destinations for merchandise exports were the Russian Federation, Sweden and Finland, accounting for respectively 16.5, 15.1 and 13.7 percent of total exports. "Transportation" (EBOPS code 205) accounted for the largest share of exports of services in 2013 at 2.3 bln US$, followed by "Travel" (EBOPS code 236) at 1.5 bln US$ and "Other business services" (EBOPS code 268) at 1.1 bln US$ (see graph 3).

Graph 3: Exports of services by EBOPS category
(% share in 2013)

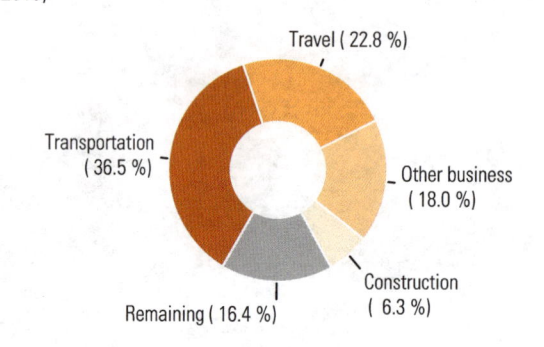

- Travel (22.8 %)
- Transportation (36.5 %)
- Other business (18.0 %)
- Construction (6.3 %)
- Remaining (16.4 %)

Table 1: Top 10 export commodities 2012 to 2014

HS code	4-digit heading of Harmonized System 2012	Value (million US$) 2012	2013	2014	Unit value 2012	2013	2014	Unit	SITC code
	All Commodities	18 161.2	18 296.3	17 574.0					
8517	Electrical apparatus for line telephony or line telegraphy	1 701.7	1 875.2	1 961.8					764
2710	Petroleum oils, other than crude	2 480.0	1 330.0	1 419.7	0.8	0.7	0.6	US$/kg	334
9999	Commodities not specified according to kind	718.2	825.2	999.2					931
8544	Insulated (including enamelled or anodised) wire, cable	342.0	366.8	360.0	14.4	14.9	14.0	US$/kg	773
2716	Electrical energy	263.4	365.7	326.8	53.2	58.1	50.4	US$/MWh	351
8703	Motor cars and other motor vehicles principally designed for the transport	240.2	318.8	363.9	22.6	24.3	25.3	thsd US$/unit	781
9406	Prefabricated buildings	258.1	290.3	322.2	2.0	2.1	2.1	US$/kg	811
4011	New pneumatic tyres, of rubber	332.3	309.1	225.1	84.7	75.0	56.1	US$/unit	625
4418	Builders' joinery and carpentry of wood	263.9	288.7	307.1	2.1	2.2	2.3	US$/kg	635
4407	Wood sawn or chipped lengthwise, sliced or peeled	237.7	264.8	284.5	314.5	327.7	336.3	US$/m³	248

Source: UN Comtrade and UN ServiceTrade

Estonia

Services Imports and Exports: EBOPS 2002 categories

Table 2: Merchandise exports by SITC
(Value in million US$, growth and shares in percentage)

SITC	2014	Avg. Growth rates 2010-2014	Avg. Growth rates 2013-2014	2014 share
Total	17 574.0	8.2	-3.9	100.0
0+1	1 709.8	9.9	-2.1	9.7
2+4	1 295.0	4.6	-0.5	7.4
3	2 006.9	-0.1	7.3	11.4
5	929.6	7.7	-17.2	5.3
6	2 387.1	5.3	-14.7	13.6
7	5 638.0	12.3	-3.5	32.1
8	2 521.4	7.8	-4.9	14.3
9	1 086.1	21.4	12.9	6.2

Table 3: Merchandise imports by SITC
(Value in million US$, growth and shares in percentage)

SITC	2014	Avg. Growth rates 2010-2014	Avg. Growth rates 2013-2014	2014 share
Total	20 116.1	11.1	-0.3	100.0
0+1	1 945.6	7.5	-2.4	9.7
2+4	628.7	11.8	-3.1	3.1
3	3 141.8	9.4	12.3	15.6
5	1 854.6	8.0	-1.6	9.2
6	2 700.6	5.9	-3.3	13.4
7	6 375.2	14.2	-6.5	31.7
8	1 766.2	8.4	6.0	8.8
9	1 703.5	29.5	8.5	8.5

SITC Legend

SITC Code	Description
Total	All commodities
0+1	Food, animals + beverages, tobacco
2+4	Crude materials + anim. & veg. oils
3	Mineral fuels, lubricants
5	Chemicals
6	Goods classified chiefly by material
7	Machinery and transport equipment
8	Miscellaneous manufactured articles
9	Not classified elsewhere in the SITC

Graph 4: Merchandise trade balance
(Bln US$ by MDG Regions in 2014)

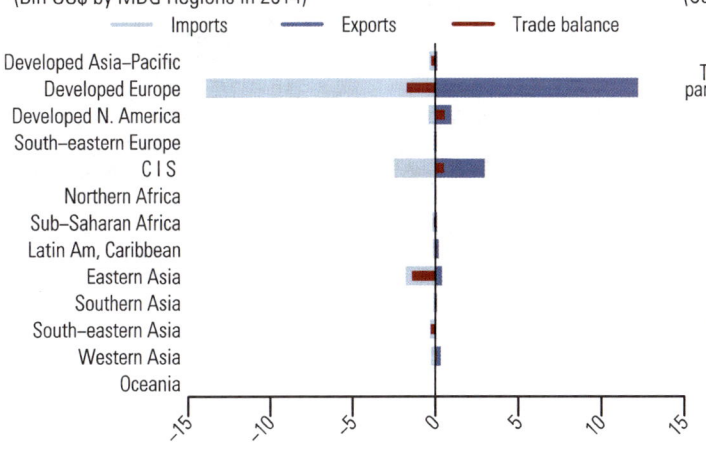

Graph 5: Partner concentration of merchandise trade
(Cumulative share by ranked partners in 2014)

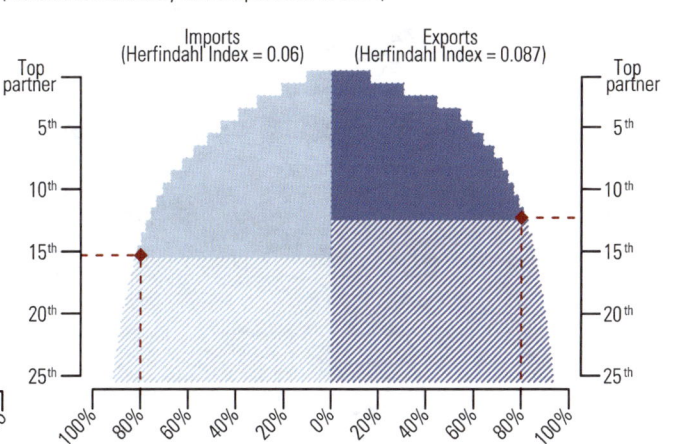

Imports (Herfindahl Index = 0.06)
Exports (Herfindahl Index = 0.087)

Graph 6: Imports of services by EBOPS category
(% share in 2013)

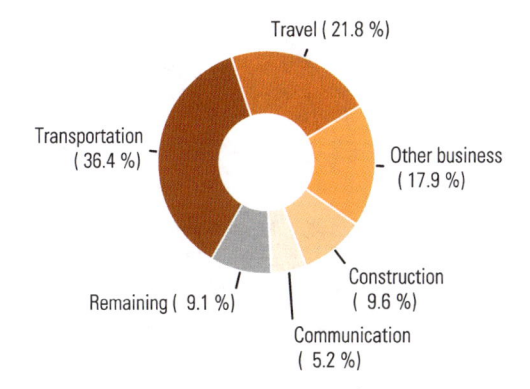

- Transportation (36.4 %)
- Travel (21.8 %)
- Other business (17.9 %)
- Construction (9.6 %)
- Communication (5.2 %)
- Remaining (9.1 %)

Imports Profile:

"Machinery and transport equipment" (SITC section 7), "Mineral fuels, lubricants" (SITC section 3) and "Goods classified chiefly by material" (SITC section 6) were the largest commodity groups for imports in 2014, representing respectively 31.7, 15.6 and 13.4 percent of imported goods (see table 3). From 2012 to 2014, the largest import commodity was "Petroleum oils, other than crude" (HS code 2710) (see table 4). The top three partners for merchandise imports were the Russian Federation, Finland and Germany, accounting for respectively 10.5, 10.2 and 9.5 percent of total imports. "Transportation" (EBOPS code 205) accounted for the largest share of imports of services in 2013 at 1.7 bln US$, followed by "Travel" (EBOPS code 236) at 1.0 bln US$ and "Other business services" (EBOPS code 268) at 848.0 mln US$ (see graph 6).

Table 4: Top 10 import commodities 2012 to 2014

HS code	4-digit heading of Harmonized System 2012	Value (million US$) 2012	2013	2014	Unit value 2012	2013	2014	Unit	SITC code
	All Commodities	20 070.4	20 170.2	20 116.1					
2710	Petroleum oils, other than crude	2 963.2	2 143.5	2 397.7	0.8	0.8	0.7	US$/kg	334
9999	Commodities not specified according to kind	1 278.5	1 455.4	1 630.5					931
8517	Electrical apparatus for line telephony or line telegraphy	1 013.5	1 077.9	1 209.0					764
8703	Motor cars and other motor vehicles principally designed for the transport	635.3	755.0	820.2	21.1	22.6	23.1	thsd US$/unit	781
8542	Electronic integrated circuits	438.8	429.1	432.5					776
4011	New pneumatic tyres, of rubber	365.7	342.1	275.2	78.8	72.8	57.0	US$/unit	625
3004	Medicaments (excluding goods of heading 30.02, 30.05 or 30.06)	298.8	322.0	343.2	92.4	101.7	110.9	US$/kg	542
2711	Petroleum gases and other gaseous hydrocarbons	278.5	326.6	237.6	0.6	0.6	0.6	US$/kg	343
8429	Self-propelled bulldozers, angledozers, graders, levellers, scrapers	329.1	316.7	167.5	79.3	83.1	88.3	thsd US$/unit	723
8544	Insulated (including enamelled or anodised) wire, cable	296.4	226.6	216.3	10.9	9.2	11.0	US$/kg	773

Source: UN Comtrade and UN ServiceTrade

Ethiopia

Goods Imports: CIF, by origin   **Goods Exports:** FOB, by last known destination   **Trade System:** General

Overview:
In 2013, the value of merchandise exports of Ethiopia increased substantially by 41.0 percent to reach 4.1 bln US$, while its merchandise imports increased substantially by 25.1 percent to reach 14.9 bln US$ (see graph 1, table 2 and table 3). The merchandise trade balance recorded a large deficit of 10.8 bln US$ (see graph 1). The largest merchandise trade balance was with MDG Eastern Asia at -3.1 bln US$ (see graph 4). Merchandise exports in Ethiopia were diversified amongst partners; imports were also diversified. The top 15 partners accounted for 80 percent or more of exports and 12 partners accounted for 80 percent or more of imports (see graph 5). In 2013, the value of exports of services of Ethiopia increased substantially by 19.6 percent, reaching 3.3 bln US$, while its imports of services increased substantially by 22.7 percent and reached 4.3 bln US$ (see graph 2). There was a moderate trade in services deficit of 1.1 bln US$.

Graph 1: Total merchandise trade, by value
(Bln US$ by year)

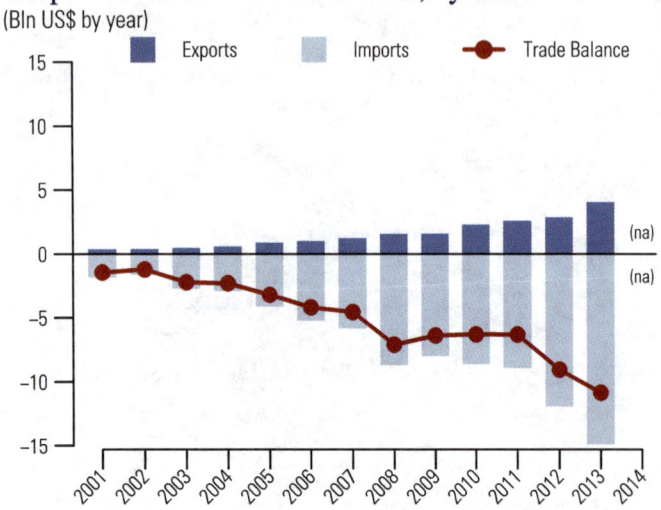

Graph 2: Total services trade, by value
(Bln US$ by year)

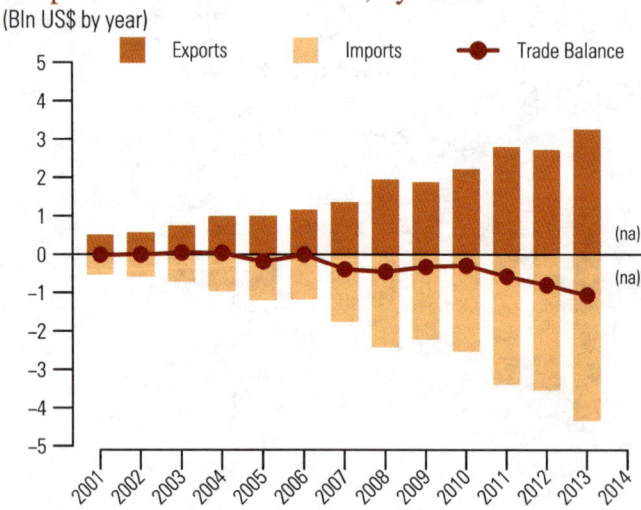

Exports Profile:
"Food, animals + beverages, tobacco" (SITC section 0+1), "Crude materials + anim. & veg. oils" (SITC section 2+4) and "Mineral fuels, lubricants" (SITC section 3) were the largest commodity groups for exports in 2013, representing respectively 52.3, 29.2 and 6.4 percent of exported goods (see table 2). From 2011 to 2013, the largest export commodity was "Coffee, whether or not roasted or decaffeinated" (HS code 0901) (see table 1). The top three destinations for merchandise exports were Somalia, China and Germany, accounting for respectively 12.0, 9.7 and 9.3 percent of total exports. "Transportation" (EBOPS code 205) accounted for the largest share of exports of services in 2013 at 2.0 bln US$, followed by "Travel" (EBOPS code 236) at 765.2 mln US$ and "Government services, n.i.e." (EBOPS code 291) at 190.7 mln US$ (see graph 3).

Graph 3: Exports of services by EBOPS category
(% share in 2013)

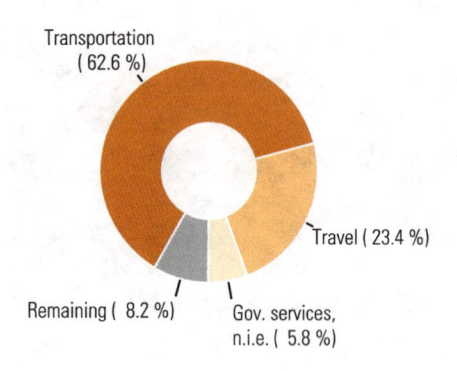

- Transportation (62.6 %)
- Travel (23.4 %)
- Gov. services, n.i.e. (5.8 %)
- Remaining (8.2 %)

Table 1: Top 10 export commodities 2011 to 2013

HS code	4-digit heading of Harmonized System 2007	Value (million US$) 2011	2012	2013	Unit value 2011	2012	2013	Unit	SITC code
	All Commodities	2614.9	2891.3	4076.9					
0901	Coffee, whether or not roasted or decaffeinated	846.9	891.1	770.8	5.3	4.4	3.5	US$/kg	071
1207	Other oil seeds and oleaginous fruits, whether or not broken	363.8	459.2	527.1	1.3	1.3	1.9	US$/kg	222
0709	Other vegetables, fresh or chilled	238.1	247.8	558.8	5.6	5.5	5.5	US$/kg	054
0603	Cut flowers and flower buds of a kind suitable for bouquets	168.9	165.6	527.1	3.9	4.0	4.0	US$/kg	292
0713	Dried leguminous vegetables, shelled, whether or not skinned or split	139.3	199.3	239.4	0.7	0.7	0.7	US$/kg	054
7108	Gold (including gold plated with platinum)	124.6	174.8	157.4	40.0	42.1	34.3	thsd US$/kg	971
0102	Live bovine animals	137.8	96.0	215.2	*811.0*	*468.2*	*512.7*	US$/unit	001
2710	Petroleum oils, other than crude	0.0	0.0	260.5	3.0	13.0	1.1	US$/kg	334
0204	Meat of sheep or goats, fresh, chilled or frozen	67.6	69.7	70.5	4.6	5.1	5.3	US$/kg	012
0106	Other live animals	36.6	59.8	73.6		392.9		US$/unit	001

Source: UN Comtrade and UN ServiceTrade

Ethiopia

Services Imports and Exports: EBOPS 2002 categories

Table 2: Merchandise exports by SITC
(Value in million US$, growth and shares in percentage)

SITC	2013	Avg. Growth rates 2009-2013	2012-2013	2013 share
Total	4076.9	26.0	41.0	100.0
0+1	2132.6	28.1	22.9	52.3
2+4	1188.5	20.0	63.7	29.2
3	260.5	1072.3	>	6.4
5	4.2	-5.8	-26.2	0.1
6	176.0	31.0	34.6	4.3
7	73.3	-1.6	39.2	1.8
8	84.4	45.2	28.4	2.1
9	157.4	14.2	-10.6	3.9

Table 3: Merchandise imports by SITC
(Value in million US$, growth and shares in percentage)

SITC	2013	Avg. Growth rates 2009-2013	2012-2013	2013 share
Total	14899.1	16.9	25.1	100.0
0+1	1332.0	21.7	67.6	8.9
2+4	723.2	19.8	31.5	4.9
3	1805.7	9.4	-25.9	12.1
5	2198.5	18.7	51.1	14.8
6	2820.1	17.2	37.2	18.9
7	4922.6	16.2	28.2	33.0
8	1084.5	24.9	40.4	7.3
9	12.5	69.9	59.8	0.1

SITC Legend

SITC Code	Description
Total	All commodities
0+1	Food, animals + beverages, tobacco
2+4	Crude materials + anim. & veg. oils
3	Mineral fuels, lubricants
5	Chemicals
6	Goods classified chiefly by material
7	Machinery and transport equipment
8	Miscellaneous manufactured articles
9	Not classified elsewhere in the SITC

Graph 4: Merchandise trade balance
(Bln US$ by MDG Regions in 2013)

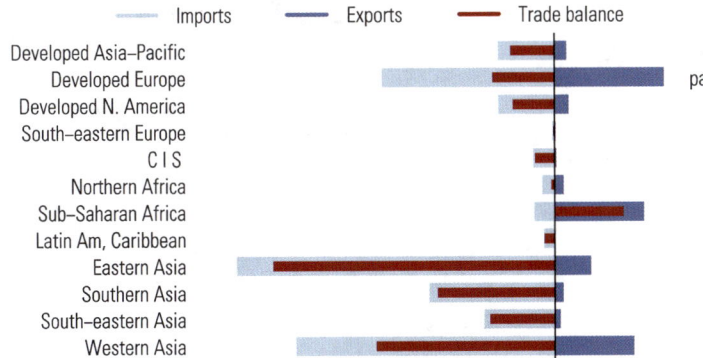

Graph 5: Partner concentration of merchandise trade
(Cumulative share by ranked partners in 2013)

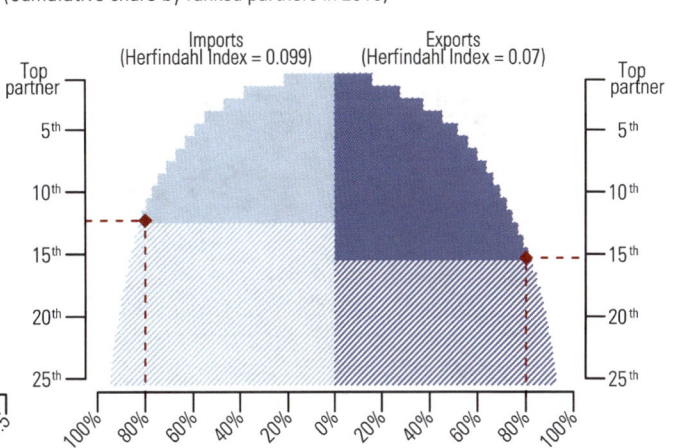

Imports (Herfindahl Index = 0.099)
Exports (Herfindahl Index = 0.07)

Graph 6: Imports of services by EBOPS category
(% share in 2013)

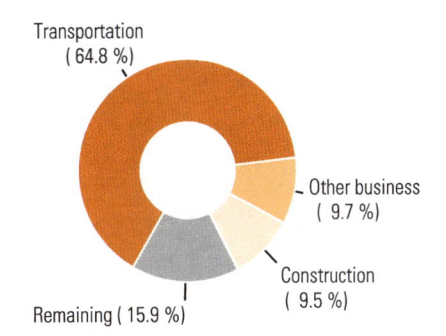

- Transportation (64.8 %)
- Other business (9.7 %)
- Construction (9.5 %)
- Remaining (15.9 %)

Imports Profile:

"Machinery and transport equipment" (SITC section 7), "Goods classified chiefly by material" (SITC section 6) and "Chemicals" (SITC section 5) were the largest commodity groups for imports in 2013, representing respectively 33.0, 18.9 and 14.8 percent of imported goods (see table 3). From 2011 to 2013, the largest import commodity was "Petroleum oils, other than crude" (HS code 2710) (see table 4). The top three partners for merchandise imports were China, Saudi Arabia and Areas nes, accounting for respectively 21.1, 10.5 and 10.3 percent of total imports. "Transportation" (EBOPS code 205) accounted for the largest share of imports of services in 2013 at 2.8 bln US$, followed by "Other business services" (EBOPS code 268) at 420.5 mln US$ and "Construction services" (EBOPS code 249) at 412.0 mln US$ (see graph 6).

Table 4: Top 10 import commodities 2011 to 2013

HS code	4-digit heading of Harmonized System 2007	Value (million US$) 2011	2012	2013	Unit value 2011	2012	2013	Unit	SITC code
	All Commodities	8896.3	11912.9	14899.1					
2710	Petroleum oils, other than crude	1484.3	2361.5	1687.1	0.9	1.0	1.0	US$/kg	334
8704	Motor vehicles for the transport of goods	357.6	530.1	762.3		7.7		thsd US$/unit	782
1001	Wheat and meslin	402.6	333.0	527.6	0.4	0.3	0.4	US$/kg	041
1511	Palm oil and its fractions	330.9	372.9	375.0	1.4	1.3	1.1	US$/kg	422
8429	Self-propelled bulldozers, angledozers, graders, levellers, scrapers	195.4	432.6	449.0	69.5			thsd US$/unit	723
3105	Mineral or chemical fertilisers	250.2	438.0	199.7	0.6	0.7	0.6	US$/kg	562
8703	Motor cars and other motor vehicles principally designed for the transport	192.9	261.3	313.0		12.2	*15.3*	thsd US$/unit	781
3004	Medicaments (excluding goods of heading 30.02, 30.05 or 30.06)	110.5	153.3	410.5	16.4	12.9	33.2	US$/kg	542
7214	Other bars and rods of iron or non-alloy steel	156.6	298.6	212.8	0.4	0.8	0.7	US$/kg	676
1701	Cane or beet sugar and chemically pure sucrose, in solid form	175.9	137.5	213.3	0.7	0.7	0.6	US$/kg	061

Fiji

Goods Imports: CIF, by purchase **Goods Exports:** FOB, by sale **Trade System:** General

Overview:
In 2014, the value of merchandise exports of Fiji increased substantially by 23.9 percent to reach 1.4 bln US$, while its merchandise imports increased substantially by 15.0 percent to reach 3.3 bln US$ (see graph 1, table 2 and table 3). The merchandise trade balance recorded a large deficit of 1.9 bln US$ (see graph 1). The largest merchandise trade balance was with MDG South-eastern Asia at -1.0 bln US$ (see graph 4). Merchandise exports in Fiji were diversified amongst partners; imports were also diversified. The top 14 partners accounted for 80 percent or more of exports and 8 partners accounted for 80 percent or more of imports (see graph 5). In 2012, the value of exports of services of Fiji increased slightly by 4.4 percent, reaching 1.2 bln US$, while its imports of services increased moderately by 6.4 percent and reached 570.8 mln US$ (see graph 2). There was a large trade in services surplus of 637.5 mln US$.

Graph 1: Total merchandise trade, by value
(Bln US$ by year)

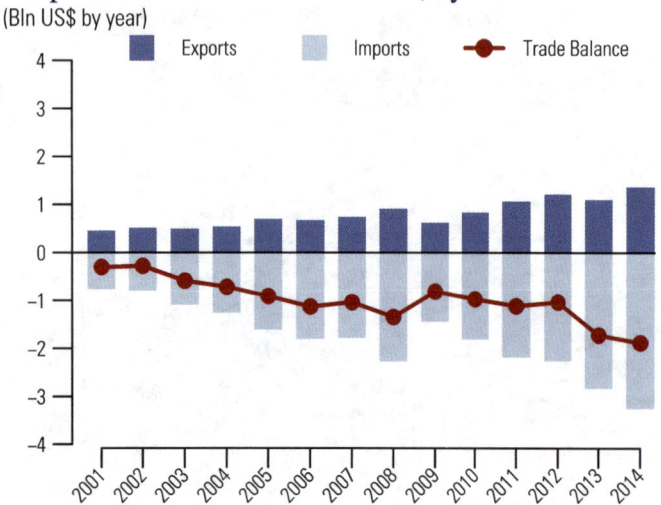

Graph 2: Total services trade, by value
(Bln US$ by year)

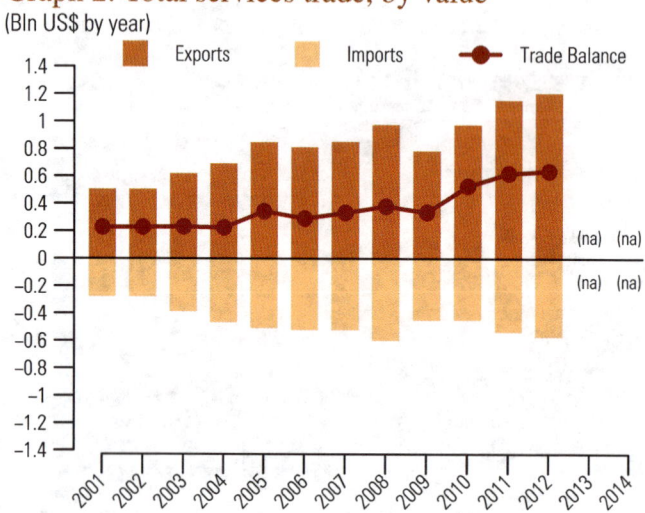

Exports Profile:
"Food, animals + beverages, tobacco" (SITC section 0+1), "Mineral fuels, lubricants" (SITC section 3) and "Machinery and transport equipment" (SITC section 7) were the largest commodity groups for exports in 2014, representing respectively 40.1, 25.1 and 9.6 percent of exported goods (see table 2). From 2012 to 2014, the largest export commodity was "Petroleum oils, other than crude" (HS code 2710) (see table 1). The top three destinations for merchandise exports were Bunkers, ship stores, Australia and the United States, accounting for respectively 17.0, 13.2 and 12.7 percent of total exports. "Travel" (EBOPS code 236) accounted for the largest share of exports of services in 2012 at 729.6 mln US$, followed by "Transportation" (EBOPS code 205) at 309.9 mln US$ and "Government services, n.i.e." (EBOPS code 291) at 108.8 mln US$ (see graph 3).

Graph 3: Exports of services by EBOPS category
(% share in 2012)

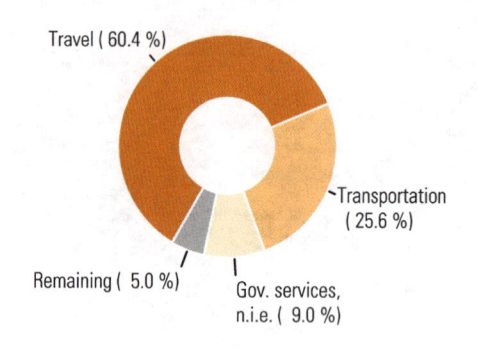

- Travel (60.4 %)
- Transportation (25.6 %)
- Gov. services, n.i.e. (9.0 %)
- Remaining (5.0 %)

Table 1: Top 10 export commodities 2012 to 2014

HS code	4-digit heading of Harmonized System 2012	Value (million US$) 2012	2013	2014	Unit value 2012	2013	2014	Unit	SITC code
	All Commodities..	1 220.6	1 108.0	1 373.3					
2710	Petroleum oils, other than crude...................................	327.3	316.9	343.6			1.1	US$/kg	334
0303	Fish, frozen, excluding fish fillets and other fish meat of heading 03.04...............	120.4	89.7	126.8	2.7		2.2	US$/kg	034
2201	Waters, including natural or artificial mineral waters.................	89.7	85.4	113.1		0.5		US$/litre	111
1701	Cane or beet sugar and chemically pure sucrose, in solid form...............	97.6	64.3	111.1	0.7	2.1	0.5	US$/kg	061
7108	Gold (including gold plated with platinum)........................	77.0	45.2	48.7	48.6	41.1	39.1	thsd US$/kg	971
1905	Bread, pastry, cakes, biscuits and other bakers' wares................	30.6	27.6	28.4		2.1	1.9	US$/kg	048
0302	Fish, fresh or chilled, excluding fish fillets..........................	35.9	16.8	20.4	2.3		3.6	US$/kg	034
4407	Wood sawn or chipped lengthwise, sliced or peeled................	19.0	21.7	22.4		403.6	249.4	US$/m³	248
6203	Men's or boys' suits, ensembles, jackets, blazers, trousers............	16.6	19.5	20.4		18.5		US$/unit	841
8802	Other aircraft (for example, helicopters, aeroplanes); spacecraft......	27.2	20.3	5.2					792

Source: UN Comtrade and UN ServiceTrade

Fiji

Services Imports and Exports: EBOPS 2002 categories

Table 2: Merchandise exports by SITC
(Value in million US$, growth and shares in percentage)

SITC	2014	Avg. Growth rates 2010-2014	Avg. Growth rates 2013-2014	2014 share
Total	1373.3	13.0	23.9	100.0
0+1	550.9	13.3	28.4	40.1
2+4	87.2	13.0	43.9	6.3
3	344.6	12.8	8.3	25.1
5	37.1	10.2	11.8	2.7
6	78.0	14.6	38.3	5.7
7	132.2	54.4	85.3	9.6
8	82.7	5.4	3.5	6.0
9	60.5	-6.8	2.3	4.4

Table 3: Merchandise imports by SITC
(Value in million US$, growth and shares in percentage)

SITC	2014	Avg. Growth rates 2010-2014	Avg. Growth rates 2013-2014	2014 share
Total	3250.5	15.8	15.0	100.0
0+1	548.3	14.7	28.8	16.9
2+4	55.3	16.3	9.7	1.7
3	787.7	8.2	19.2	24.2
5	213.8	9.3	19.0	6.6
6	388.8	12.1	26.7	12.0
7	992.9	31.9	0.3	30.5
8	239.5	11.6	22.9	7.4
9	24.3	29.3	35.7	0.7

SITC Legend

SITC Code	Description
Total	All commodities
0+1	Food, animals + beverages, tobacco
2+4	Crude materials + anim. & veg. oils
3	Mineral fuels, lubricants
5	Chemicals
6	Goods classified chiefly by material
7	Machinery and transport equipment
8	Miscellaneous manufactured articles
9	Not classified elsewhere in the SITC

Graph 4: Merchandise trade balance
(Bln US$ by MDG Regions in 2014)

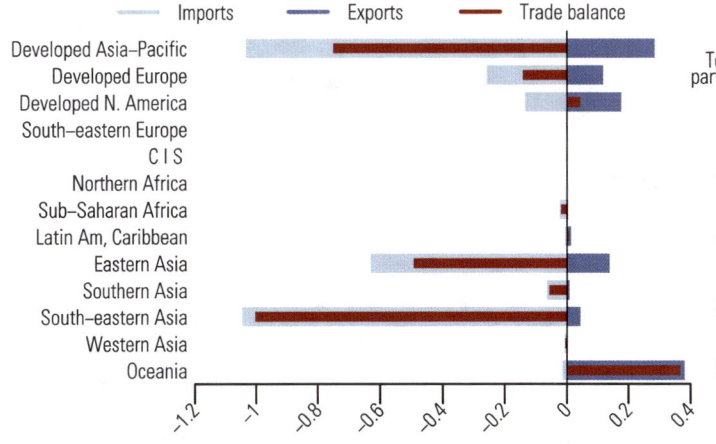

Graph 5: Partner concentration of merchandise trade
(Cumulative share by ranked partners in 2014)

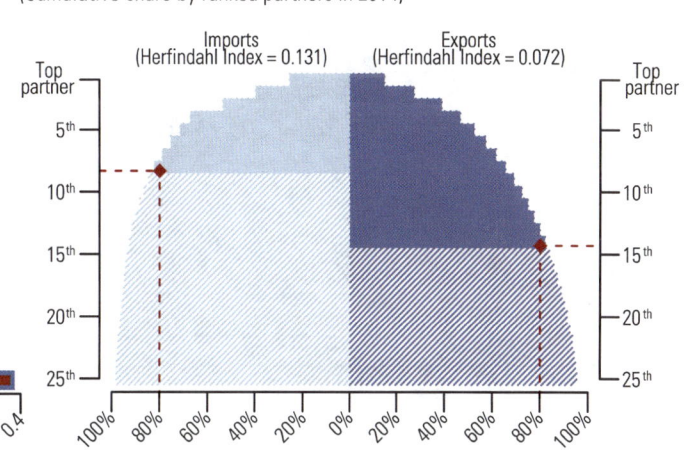

Imports (Herfindahl Index = 0.131)
Exports (Herfindahl Index = 0.072)

Graph 6: Imports of services by EBOPS category
(% share in 2012)

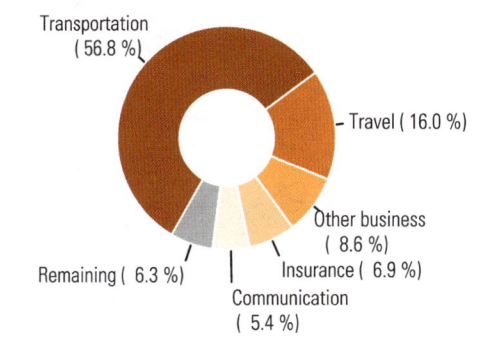

- Transportation (56.8%)
- Travel (16.0%)
- Other business (8.6%)
- Insurance (6.9%)
- Communication (5.4%)
- Remaining (6.3%)

Imports Profile:

"Machinery and transport equipment" (SITC section 7), "Mineral fuels, lubricants" (SITC section 3) and "Food, animals + beverages, tobacco" (SITC section 0+1) were the largest commodity groups for imports in 2014, representing respectively 30.5, 24.2 and 16.9 percent of imported goods (see table 3). From 2012 to 2014, the largest import commodity was "Petroleum oils, other than crude" (HS code 2710) (see table 4). The top three partners for merchandise imports were Singapore, Australia and New Zealand, accounting for respectively 25.8, 15.0 and 13.3 percent of total imports. "Transportation" (EBOPS code 205) accounted for the largest share of imports of services in 2012 at 324.0 mln US$, followed by "Travel" (EBOPS code 236) at 91.5 mln US$ and "Other business services" (EBOPS code 268) at 49.2 mln US$ (see graph 6).

Table 4: Top 10 import commodities 2012 to 2014

HS code	4-digit heading of Harmonized System 2012	Value 2012	Value 2013	Value 2014	Unit value 2012	Unit value 2013	Unit value 2014	Unit	SITC code
	All Commodities	2252.6	2825.7	3250.5					
2710	Petroleum oils, other than crude	651.6	634.3	754.9			*1.1*	US$/kg	334
8802	Other aircraft (for example, helicopters, aeroplanes); spacecraft	8.1	443.8	175.8					792
0303	Fish, frozen, excluding fish fillets and other fish meat of heading 03.04	124.2	92.8	177.1	1.9		1.6	US$/kg	034
1001	Wheat and meslin	60.6	68.9	61.4	0.4	0.4	0.7	US$/kg	041
8703	Motor cars and other motor vehicles principally designed for the transport	31.4	50.6	72.4		*12.2*	*10.9*	thsd US$/unit	781
8704	Motor vehicles for the transport of goods	27.1	52.5	60.2					782
8517	Electrical apparatus for line telephony or line telegraphy	34.7	40.7	62.5					764
8803	Parts of goods of heading 88.01 or 88.02	21.7	34.5	28.5	47.5	46.8	131.9	US$/kg	792
2711	Petroleum gases and other gaseous hydrocarbons	25.0	26.0	32.2	1.3	1.2	1.2	US$/kg	343
0402	Milk and cream, concentrated or containing added sugar	20.5	20.8	38.0	4.2	5.0	5.2	US$/kg	022

Source: UN Comtrade and UN ServiceTrade

Finland

Goods Imports: CIF, by origin **Goods Exports:** FOB, by last known destination **Trade System:** Special

Overview:
In 2014, the value of merchandise exports of Finland decreased slightly by 0.4 percent to reach 74.2 bln US$, while its merchandise imports decreased slightly by 1.3 percent to reach 76.6 bln US$ (see graph 1, table 2 and table 3). The merchandise trade balance recorded a relatively small deficit of 2.4 bln US$ (see graph 1). The largest merchandise trade balance was with MDG CIS at -5.4 bln US$ (see graph 4). Merchandise exports in Finland were diversified amongst partners; imports were also diversified. The top 19 partners accounted for 80 percent or more of exports and 16 partners accounted for 80 percent or more of imports (see graph 5). In 2013, the value of exports of services of Finland increased slightly by 1.1 percent, reaching 28.5 bln US$, while its imports of services increased slightly by 1.9 percent and reached 30.7 bln US$ (see graph 2). There was a relatively small trade in services deficit of 2.2 bln US$.

Graph 1: Total merchandise trade, by value
(Bln US$ by year)

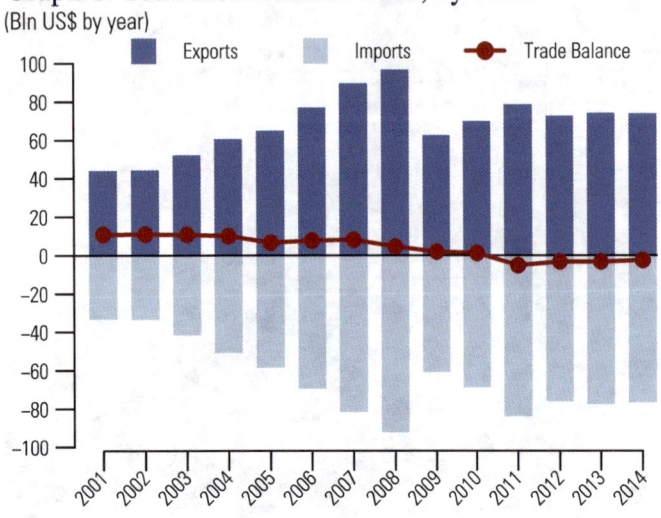

Graph 2: Total services trade, by value
(Bln US$ by year)

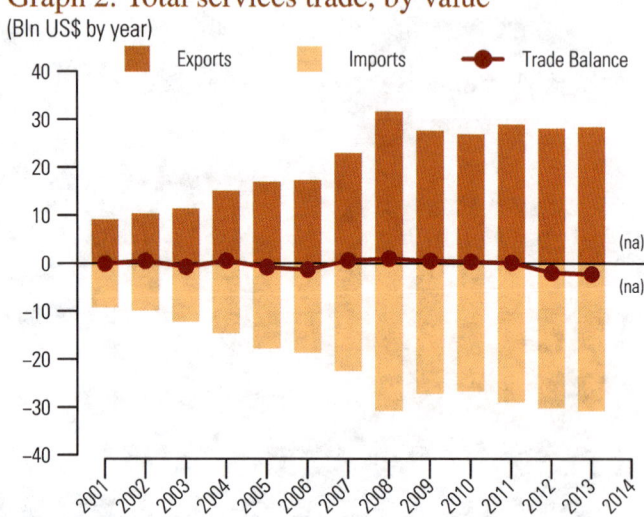

Exports Profile:
"Goods classified chiefly by material" (SITC section 6), "Machinery and transport equipment" (SITC section 7) and "Chemicals" (SITC section 5) were the largest commodity groups for exports in 2014, representing respectively 29.3, 28.7 and 11.0 percent of exported goods (see table 2). From 2012 to 2014, the largest export commodity was "Petroleum oils, other than crude" (HS code 2710) (see table 1). The top three destinations for merchandise exports were Sweden, Germany and the Russian Federation, accounting for respectively 11.1, 9.9 and 9.2 percent of total exports. "Other business services" (EBOPS code 268) accounted for the largest share of exports of services in 2013 at 4.5 bln US$, followed by "Travel" (EBOPS code 236) at 4.2 bln US$ and "Transportation" (EBOPS code 205) at 3.7 bln US$ (see graph 3).

Graph 3: Exports of services by EBOPS category
(% share in 2013)

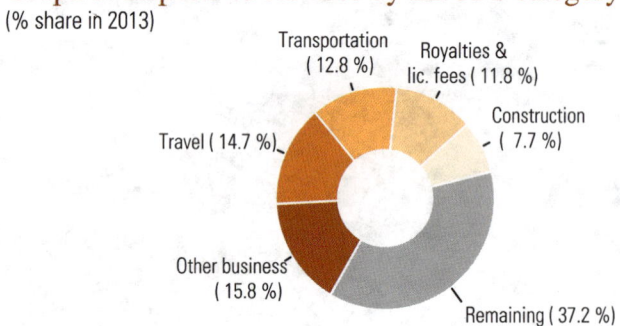

- Transportation (12.8 %)
- Royalties & lic. fees (11.8 %)
- Construction (7.7 %)
- Remaining (37.2 %)
- Other business (15.8 %)
- Travel (14.7 %)

Table 1: Top 10 export commodities 2012 to 2014

HS code	4-digit heading of Harmonized System 2012	Value (million US$) 2012	2013	2014	Unit value 2012	2013	2014	Unit	SITC code
	All Commodities	72 974.5	74 445.4	74 150.3					
2710	Petroleum oils, other than crude	7 791.2	8 880.3	7 725.7	2.9	1.0	0.9	US$/kg	334
4810	Paper and paperboard, coated on one or both sides with kaolin	5 206.5	5 201.3	5 093.9	0.9	0.9	0.9	US$/kg	641
7219	Flat-rolled products of stainless steel, of a width of 600 mm or more	2 735.6	2 699.2	2 794.4	3.2	3.1	2.8	US$/kg	675
4407	Wood sawn or chipped lengthwise, sliced or peeled	1 596.2	1 892.8	2 045.2		264.6	273.5	US$/m³	248
4703	Chemical wood pulp, soda or sulphate, other than dissolving grades	1 517.3	1 824.5	1 909.3		0.7	0.7	US$/kg	251
4802	Uncoated paper and paperboard, of a kind used for writing	1 777.4	1 725.9	1 619.3		0.8	0.8	US$/kg	641
9999	Commodities not specified according to kind	1 515.6	1 508.6	1 478.4					931
8504	Electrical transformers, static converters	1 345.0	1 369.4	1 366.9					771
9018	Instruments and appliances used in medical, surgical, dental or veterinary	1 065.1	1 099.4	1 295.6					872
8517	Electrical apparatus for line telephony or line telegraphy	1 888.3	679.9	780.5					764

Source: UN Comtrade and UN ServiceTrade   2014 International Trade Statistics Yearbook, Vol. I

Finland

Services Imports and Exports: EBOPS 2002 categories

Table 2: Merchandise exports by SITC
(Value in million US$, growth and shares in percentage)

SITC	2014	Avg. Growth rates 2010-2014	Avg. Growth rates 2013-2014	2014 share
Total	74 150.3	1.4	-0.4	100.0
0+1	2 011.9	4.4	-2.1	2.7
2+4	6 154.3	6.1	-5.8	8.3
3	8 007.8	9.3	-11.9	10.8
5	8 164.1	1.3	-0.6	11.0
6	21 702.0	-0.6	-0.3	29.3
7	21 317.1	-1.6	5.8	28.7
8	4 886.5	5.7	6.0	6.6
9	1 906.6	11.0	-5.7	2.6

Table 3: Merchandise imports by SITC
(Value in million US$, growth and shares in percentage)

SITC	2014	Avg. Growth rates 2010-2014	Avg. Growth rates 2013-2014	2014 share
Total	76 566.9	2.7	-1.3	100.0
0+1	5 485.0	5.5	-1.3	7.2
2+4	6 426.7	-0.5	2.0	8.4
3	15 879.9	6.0	-10.4	20.7
5	8 993.7	3.4	-1.0	11.7
6	8 437.0	-0.3	0.9	11.0
7	20 814.7	1.3	1.5	27.2
8	7 281.8	2.0	-1.0	9.5
9	3 248.1	9.4	21.1	4.2

SITC Legend

SITC Code	Description
Total	All commodities
0+1	Food, animals + beverages, tobacco
2+4	Crude materials + anim. & veg. oils
3	Mineral fuels, lubricants
5	Chemicals
6	Goods classified chiefly by material
7	Machinery and transport equipment
8	Miscellaneous manufactured articles
9	Not classified elsewhere in the SITC

Graph 4: Merchandise trade balance
(Bln US$ by MDG Regions in 2014)

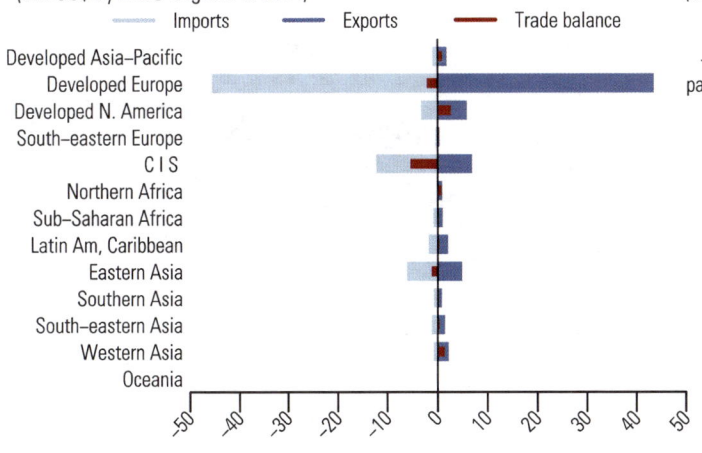

Graph 5: Partner concentration of merchandise trade
(Cumulative share by ranked partners in 2014)

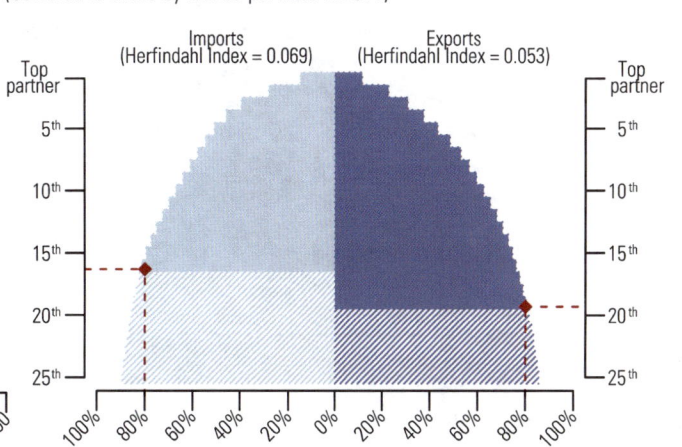

Imports (Herfindahl Index = 0.069)
Exports (Herfindahl Index = 0.053)

Graph 6: Imports of services by EBOPS category
(% share in 2013)

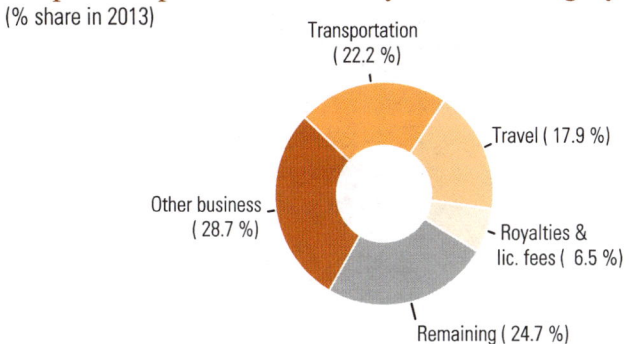

- Transportation (22.2 %)
- Travel (17.9 %)
- Royalties & lic. fees (6.5 %)
- Remaining (24.7 %)
- Other business (28.7 %)

Imports Profile:

"Machinery and transport equipment" (SITC section 7), "Mineral fuels, lubricants" (SITC section 3) and "Chemicals" (SITC section 5) were the largest commodity groups for imports in 2014, representing respectively 27.2, 20.7 and 11.7 percent of imported goods (see table 3). From 2012 to 2014, the largest import commodity was "Petroleum oils and oils obtained from bituminous minerals, crude" (HS code 2709) (see table 4). The top three partners for merchandise imports were the Russian Federation, Germany and Sweden, accounting for respectively 16.8, 12.5 and 11.0 percent of total imports. "Other business services" (EBOPS code 268) accounted for the largest share of imports of services in 2013 at 8.8 bln US$, followed by "Transportation" (EBOPS code 205) at 6.8 bln US$ and "Travel" (EBOPS code 236) at 5.5 bln US$ (see graph 6).

Table 4: Top 10 import commodities 2012 to 2014

HS code	4-digit heading of Harmonized System 2012	Value 2012	Value 2013	Value 2014	Unit value 2012	Unit value 2013	Unit value 2014	Unit	SITC code
	All Commodities	76 089.0	77 587.0	76 566.9					
2709	Petroleum oils and oils obtained from bituminous minerals, crude	9 207.6	9 342.2	8 466.3		0.8	0.7	US$/kg	333
2710	Petroleum oils, other than crude	3 982.7	5 131.1	4 322.9	12.6	1.0	0.9	US$/kg	334
9999	Commodities not specified according to kind	2 426.4	2 648.6	3 216.4					931
8703	Motor cars and other motor vehicles principally designed for the transport	2 392.5	2 581.3	2 650.7	19.2	20.3	21.1	thsd US$/unit	781
3004	Medicaments (excluding goods of heading 30.02, 30.05 or 30.06)	1 859.1	1 884.7	1 889.9		139.4	135.0	US$/kg	542
8517	Electrical apparatus for line telephony or line telegraphy	2 036.9	1 322.2	1 435.8					764
2711	Petroleum gases and other gaseous hydrocarbons	1 708.1	1 542.7	1 319.0		0.6	0.6	US$/kg	343
8471	Automatic data processing machines and units thereof	1 312.3	1 310.0	1 314.7	257.6	269.6	278.4	US$/unit	752
7204	Ferrous waste and scrap; remelting scrap ingots of iron or steel	1 243.7	1 028.9	1 193.6		1.9	1.5	US$/kg	282
2716	Electrical energy	976.7	940.9	1 025.4		53.5	47.1	US$/MWh	351

France including Monaco

Goods Imports: CIF, by origin | **Goods Exports: FOB, by last known destination** | **Trade System: Special**

Overview:

In 2014, the value of merchandise exports of France decreased slightly by 0.2 percent to reach 566.7 bln US$, and its merchandise imports also decreased slightly by 1.7 percent to reach 659.9 bln US$ (see graph 1, table 2 and table 3). The merchandise trade balance recorded a relatively small deficit of 93.2 bln US$, a slight reduction from the deficit of 101.8 bln US$ in 2013 (see graph 1). The largest merchandise trade balance was with MDG Developed Europe at -49.9 bln US$ (see graph 4). Merchandise exports in France were diversified amongst partners; imports were also diversified. The top 24 partners accounted for 80 percent or more of exports and 22 partners accounted for 80 percent or more of imports (see graph 5). In 2013, the value of exports of services of France increased substantially by 16.5 percent, reaching 252.1 bln US$, while its imports of services increased substantially by 33.7 percent and reached 233.2 bln US$ (see graph 2). There was a relatively small trade in services surplus of 18.9 bln US$.

Graph 1: Total merchandise trade, by value
(Bln US$ by year)

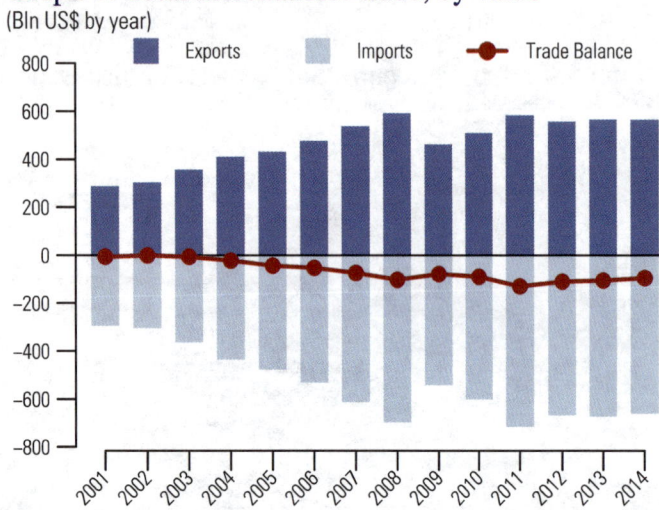

Graph 2: Total services trade, by value
(Bln US$ by year)

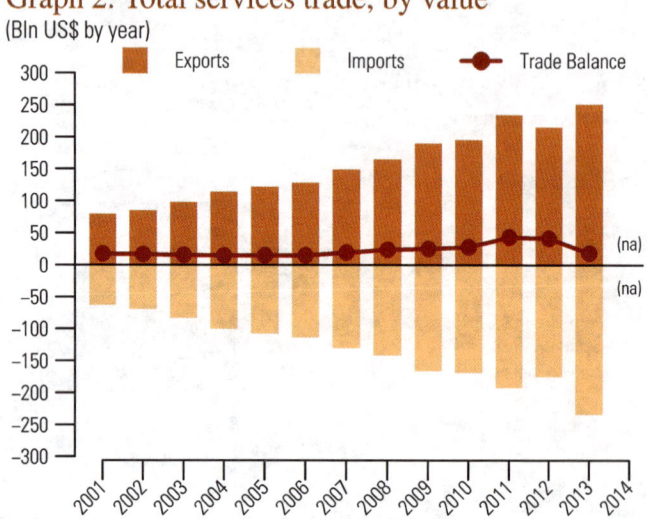

Exports Profile:

"Machinery and transport equipment" (SITC section 7), "Chemicals" (SITC section 5) and "Food, animals + beverages, tobacco" (SITC section 0+1) were the largest commodity groups for exports in 2014, representing respectively 38.4, 17.8 and 12.2 percent of exported goods (see table 2). From 2012 to 2014, the largest export commodity was "Other aircraft (for example, helicopters, aeroplanes); spacecraft" (HS code 8802) (see table 1). In this time period, France has been the world's largest exporter of this commodity. The top three destinations for merchandise exports were Germany, Belgium and Italy, accounting for respectively 16.5, 7.4 and 7.2 percent of total exports. "Other business services" (EBOPS code 268) accounted for the largest share of exports of services in 2013 at 77.3 bln US$, followed by "Travel" (EBOPS code 236) at 58.9 bln US$ and "Transportation" (EBOPS code 205) at 50.9 bln US$ (see graph 3).

Graph 3: Exports of services by EBOPS category
(% share in 2013)

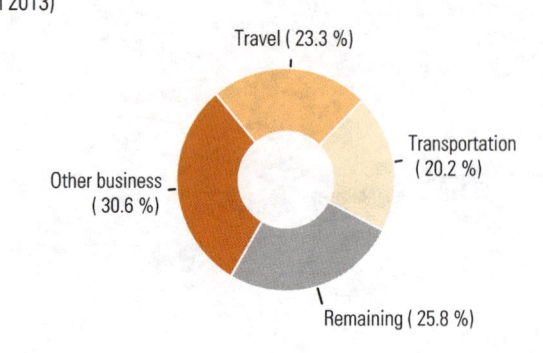

- Travel (23.3 %)
- Transportation (20.2 %)
- Remaining (25.8 %)
- Other business (30.6 %)

Table 1: Top 10 export commodities 2012 to 2014

HS code	4-digit heading of Harmonized System 2012	Value (million US$) 2012	2013	2014	Unit value 2012	2013	2014	Unit	SITC code
	All Commodities	558 460.5	567 987.7	566 656.2					
8802	Other aircraft (for example, helicopters, aeroplanes); spacecraft	47 363.6	48 756.2	49 798.6	32.9	41.7	43.4	mln US$/unit	792
3004	Medicaments (excluding goods of heading 30.02, 30.05 or 30.06)	27 465.2	27 848.9	25 725.4	86.8	87.7	79.6	US$/kg	542
8703	Motor cars and other motor vehicles principally designed for the transport	20 315.5	18 664.3	19 192.7	13.8	14.2	14.4	thsd US$/unit	781
8708	Parts and accessories of the motor vehicles of headings 87.01 to 87.05	16 600.4	17 364.5	16 771.9	8.5	8.8	9.0	US$/kg	784
2710	Petroleum oils, other than crude	16 009.9	14 396.1	13 627.2	0.9	0.9	0.8	US$/kg	334
9999	Commodities not specified according to kind	14 045.9	13 872.7	14 160.6					931
8411	Turbo-jets, turbo-propellers and other gas turbines	11 322.9	11 632.8	12 404.1					714
2204	Wine of fresh grapes, including fortified wines	10 100.0	10 396.1	10 262.3	6.7	7.1	7.1	US$/litre	112
8803	Parts of goods of heading 88.01 or 88.02	7 176.9	7 772.6	7 820.7	431.5	443.2	396.3	US$/kg	792
8542	Electronic integrated circuits	7 531.4	7 682.1	7 296.0					776

Source: UN Comtrade and UN ServiceTrade

France including Monaco

Services Imports and Exports: EBOPS 2002 categories

Table 2: Merchandise exports by SITC
(Value in million US$, growth and shares in percentage)

SITC	2014	Avg. Growth rates 2010-2014	2013-2014	2014 share
Total	566 656.2	2.6	-0.2	100.0
0+1	69 130.5	4.1	-3.6	12.2
2+4	14 339.3	1.6	-1.9	2.5
3	21 983.8	4.1	-1.1	3.9
5	100 776.2	2.5	-0.6	17.8
6	62 089.6	0.3	0.2	11.0
7	217 571.5	2.2	0.4	38.4
8	65 520.0	4.7	2.6	11.6
9	15 245.2	2.3	-2.3	2.7

Table 3: Merchandise imports by SITC
(Value in million US$, growth and shares in percentage)

SITC	2014	Avg. Growth rates 2010-2014	2013-2014	2014 share
Total	659 872.1	2.4	-1.7	100.0
0+1	57 401.5	4.6	0.6	8.7
2+4	16 689.6	-0.7	-6.6	2.5
3	96 175.0	3.8	-13.0	14.6
5	93 272.8	2.5	0.1	14.1
6	79 583.6	0.8	-0.5	12.1
7	218 737.4	1.7	0.0	33.1
8	96 898.4	3.5	4.3	14.7
9	1 113.8	11.7	3.6	0.2

SITC Legend

SITC Code	Description
Total	All commodities
0+1	Food, animals + beverages, tobacco
2+4	Crude materials + anim. & veg. oils
3	Mineral fuels, lubricants
5	Chemicals
6	Goods classified chiefly by material
7	Machinery and transport equipment
8	Miscellaneous manufactured articles
9	Not classified elsewhere in the SITC

Graph 4: Merchandise trade balance
(Bln US$ by MDG Regions in 2014)

Graph 5: Partner concentration of merchandise trade
(Cumulative share by ranked partners in 2014)

Imports (Herfindahl Index = 0.063)
Exports (Herfindahl Index = 0.059)

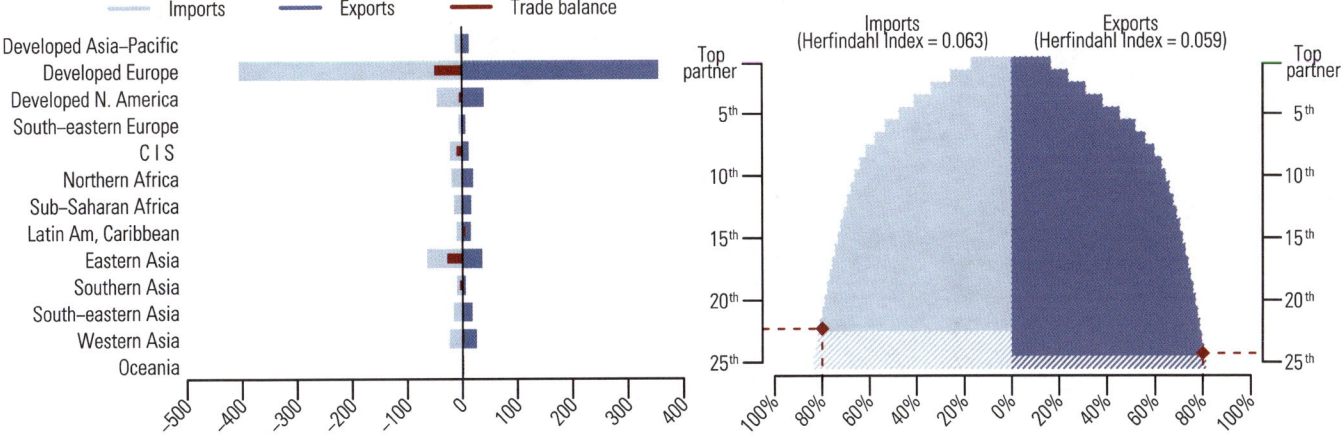

Graph 6: Imports of services by EBOPS category
(% share in 2013)

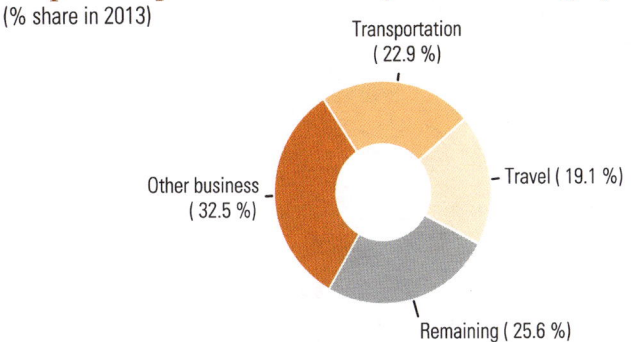

- Transportation (22.9 %)
- Travel (19.1 %)
- Remaining (25.6 %)
- Other business (32.5 %)

Imports Profile:

"Machinery and transport equipment" (SITC section 7), "Miscellaneous manufactured articles" (SITC section 8) and "Mineral fuels, lubricants" (SITC section 3) were the largest commodity groups for imports in 2014, representing respectively 33.1, 14.7 and 14.6 percent of imported goods (see table 3). From 2012 to 2014, the largest import commodity was "Petroleum oils and oils obtained from bituminous minerals, crude" (HS code 2709) (see table 4). The top three partners for merchandise imports were Germany, China and Belgium, accounting for respectively 17.2, 8.2 and 7.8 percent of total imports. "Other business services" (EBOPS code 268) accounted for the largest share of imports of services in 2013 at 75.7 bln US$, followed by "Transportation" (EBOPS code 205) at 53.3 bln US$ and "Travel" (EBOPS code 236) at 44.6 bln US$ (see graph 6).

Table 4: Top 10 import commodities 2012 to 2014

HS code	4-digit heading of Harmonized System 2012	Value (million US$) 2012	2013	2014	Unit value 2012	2013	2014	Unit	SITC code
	All Commodities	666 675.2	671 253.6	659 872.1					
2709	Petroleum oils and oils obtained from bituminous minerals, crude	47 631.0	45 645.0	38 874.2	0.8	0.8	0.8	US$/kg	333
2710	Petroleum oils, other than crude	37 365.3	35 165.8	32 474.2	1.0	0.9	0.9	US$/kg	334
8703	Motor cars and other motor vehicles principally designed for the transport	29 929.2	29 712.2	30 969.1	17.8	17.8	18.8	thsd US$/unit	781
2711	Petroleum gases and other gaseous hydrocarbons	24 260.5	24 777.4	20 835.0	0.6	0.6	0.6	US$/kg	343
3004	Medicaments (excluding goods of heading 30.02, 30.05 or 30.06)	19 380.7	18 298.2	18 290.5	90.8	84.3	73.3	US$/kg	542
8803	Parts of goods of heading 88.01 or 88.02	14 665.0	15 774.5	16 581.1	286.7	277.0	299.5	US$/kg	792
8802	Other aircraft (for example, helicopters, aeroplanes); spacecraft	16 438.6	14 034.0	12 987.9	34.5	35.8	16.6	mln US$/unit	792
8708	Parts and accessories of the motor vehicles of headings 87.01 to 87.05	12 431.3	12 778.1	13 195.6	7.1	7.7	8.3	US$/kg	784
8517	Electrical apparatus for line telephony or line telegraphy	10 756.8	11 594.5	11 645.7					764
8471	Automatic data processing machines and units thereof	10 010.9	10 318.0	9 736.8	173.0	179.5	167.8	US$/unit	752

Source: UN Comtrade and UN ServiceTrade

French Polynesia

Goods Imports: CIF, by origin **Goods Exports: FOB, by last known destination** **Trade System: Special**

Overview:
In 2013, the value of merchandise exports of French Polynesia increased moderately by 9.0 percent to reach 151.5 mln US$, while its merchandise imports increased moderately by 6.4 percent to reach 1.8 bln US$ (see graph 1, table 2 and table 3). The merchandise trade balance recorded a large deficit of 1.7 bln US$ (see graph 1). The largest merchandise trade balance was with MDG Developed Europe at -673.8 mln US$ (see graph 4). Merchandise exports in French Polynesia were moderately concentrated amongst partners; imports were diversified. The top 4 partners accounted for 80 percent or more of exports and 10 partners accounted for 80 percent or more of imports (see graph 5). In 2012, the value of exports of services of French Polynesia increased substantially by 31.6 percent, reaching 1.1 bln US$, while its imports of services increased slightly by 2.5 percent and reached 517.2 mln US$ (see graph 2). There was a large trade in services surplus of 615.7 mln US$.

Graph 1: Total merchandise trade, by value
(Bln US$ by year)

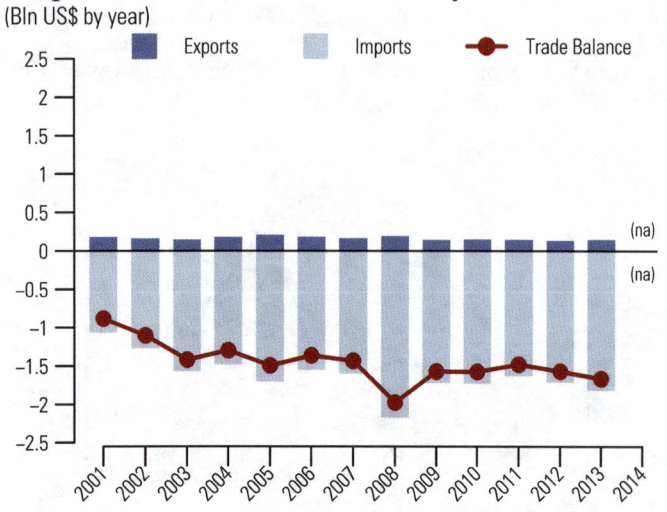

Graph 2: Total services trade, by value
(Bln US$ by year)

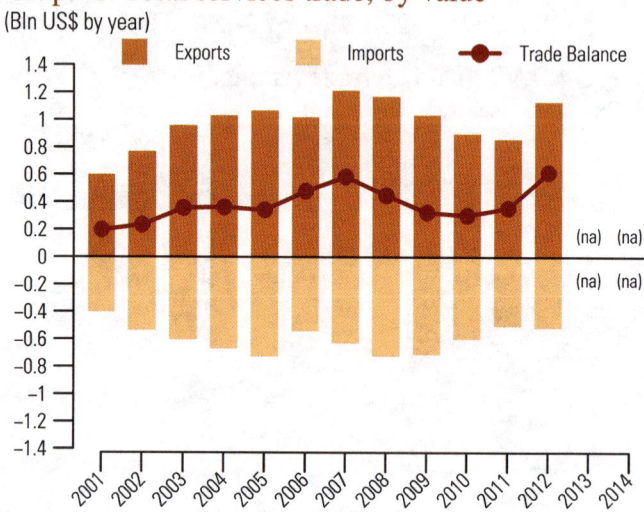

Exports Profile:
"Goods classified chiefly by material" (SITC section 6), "Food, animals + beverages, tobacco" (SITC section 0+1) and "Machinery and transport equipment" (SITC section 7) were the largest commodity groups for exports in 2013, representing respectively 58.6, 15.7 and 9.2 percent of exported goods (see table 2). From 2011 to 2013, the largest export commodity was "Pearls, natural or cultured" (HS code 7101) (see table 1). The top three destinations for merchandise exports were China, Hong Kong SAR, Japan and France, accounting for respectively 27.2, 26.0 and 16.6 percent of total exports. "Travel" (EBOPS code 236) accounted for the largest share of exports of services in 2012 at 437.8 mln US$, followed by "Transportation" (EBOPS code 205) at 305.1 mln US$ and "Government services, n.i.e." (EBOPS code 291) at 254.8 mln US$ (see graph 3).

Graph 3: Exports of services by EBOPS category
(% share in 2012)

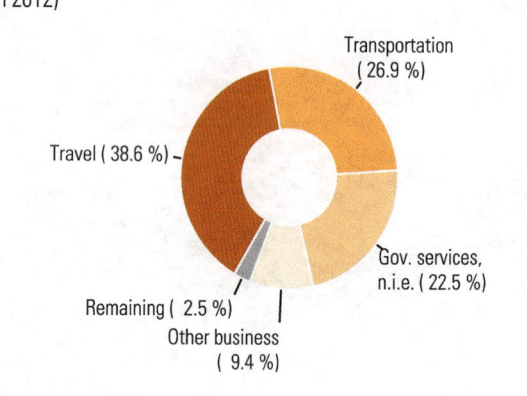

- Travel (38.6 %)
- Transportation (26.9 %)
- Gov. services, n.i.e. (22.5 %)
- Other business (9.4 %)
- Remaining (2.5 %)

Table 1: Top 10 export commodities 2011 to 2013

HS code	4-digit heading of Harmonized System 2007	Value (million US$) 2011	2012	2013	Unit value 2011	2012	2013	Unit	SITC code
	All Commodities	149.8	139.0	151.5					
7101	Pearls, natural or cultured	76.2	76.2	86.6	5.1	5.3		thsd US$/kg	667
0302	Fish, fresh or chilled, excluding fish fillets	3.7	9.6	7.9	7.0	9.0	8.7	US$/kg	034
1513	Coconut (copra), palm kernel or babassu oil	7.7	7.7	4.7	1.3	1.1	0.8	US$/kg	422
8802	Other aircraft (for example, helicopters, aeroplanes); spacecraft	9.6	0.6	6.7					792
2007	Jams, fruit jellies, marmalades, fruit or nut pastes	6.9	5.4	4.1	2.9	3.0	3.1	US$/kg	058
0508	Coral and similar materials, unworked or simply prepared	3.1	2.9	4.3	1.1	1.1	1.4	US$/kg	291
0304	Fish fillets and other fish meat (whether or not minced)	2.9	3.9	3.5	10.1	12.6	13.6	US$/kg	034
0905	Vanilla	2.3	3.2	3.5	180.9	188.1	201.2	US$/kg	075
7112	Waste and scrap of precious metal or of metal clad with precious metal	0.6	3.7	4.2		31.0	25.4	thsd US$/kg	289
3304	Beauty or make-up preparations	2.8	2.6	2.4	8.3	9.3	9.9	US$/kg	553

French Polynesia

Services Imports and Exports: EBOPS 2002 categories

Table 2: Merchandise exports by SITC
(Value in million US$, growth and shares in percentage)

SITC	2013	Avg. Growth rates 2009-2013	2012-2013	2013 share
Total	151.5	0.5	9.0	100.0
0+1	23.8	5.3	-16.4	15.7
2+4	10.5	12.9	-16.6	6.9
3	0.0	-24.7	85.5	0.0
5	3.0	8.2	-4.6	2.0
6	88.8	-0.8	14.4	58.6
7	14.0	-5.9	94.1	9.2
8	5.3	-15.7	18.6	3.5
9	6.1	1072.2	9.7	4.0

Table 3: Merchandise imports by SITC
(Value in million US$, growth and shares in percentage)

SITC	2013	Avg. Growth rates 2009-2013	2012-2013	2013 share
Total	1814.8	1.4	6.4	100.0
0+1	428.0	2.0	1.0	23.6
2+4	32.7	2.4	13.2	1.8
3	310.4	12.1	5.1	17.1
5	177.4	-0.9	5.1	9.8
6	199.0	-0.5	0.5	11.0
7	466.7	-0.4	16.8	25.7
8	200.7	-3.7	4.6	11.1
9	0.1	-31.8	-22.5	0.0

SITC Legend

SITC Code	Description
Total	All commodities
0+1	Food, animals + beverages, tobacco
2+4	Crude materials + anim. & veg. oils
3	Mineral fuels, lubricants
5	Chemicals
6	Goods classified chiefly by material
7	Machinery and transport equipment
8	Miscellaneous manufactured articles
9	Not classified elsewhere in the SITC

Graph 4: Merchandise trade balance
(Mln US$ by MDG Regions in 2013)

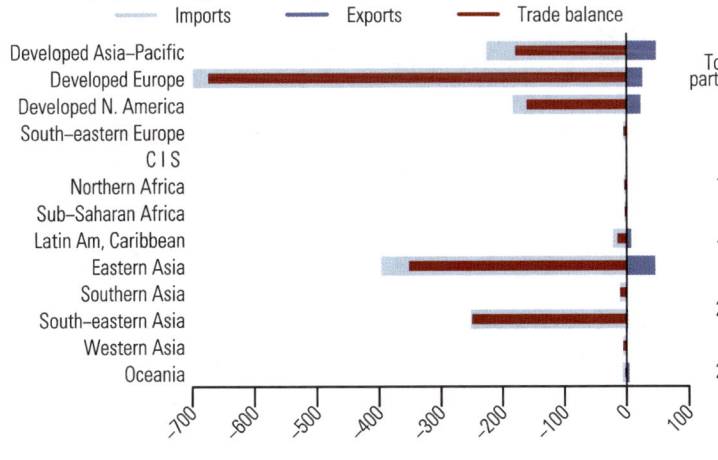

Graph 5: Partner concentration of merchandise trade
(Cumulative share by ranked partners in 2013)

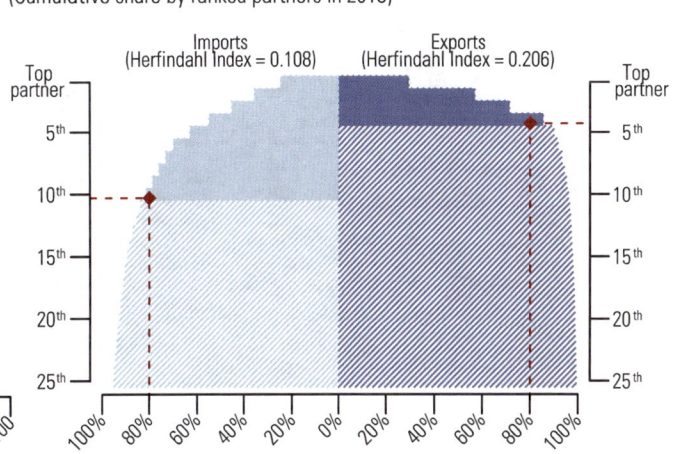

Imports (Herfindahl Index = 0.108)
Exports (Herfindahl Index = 0.206)

Graph 6: Imports of services by EBOPS category
(% share in 2012)

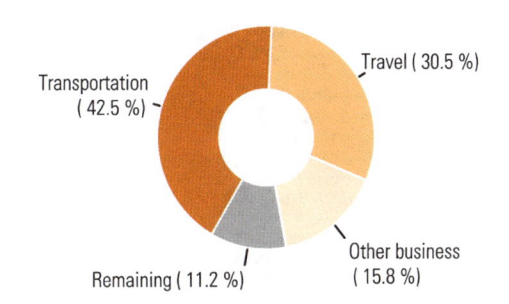

- Transportation (42.5 %)
- Travel (30.5 %)
- Other business (15.8 %)
- Remaining (11.2 %)

Imports Profile:

"Machinery and transport equipment" (SITC section 7), "Food, animals + beverages, tobacco" (SITC section 0+1) and "Mineral fuels, lubricants" (SITC section 3) were the largest commodity groups for imports in 2013, representing respectively 25.7, 23.6 and 17.1 percent of imported goods (see table 3). From 2011 to 2013, the largest import commodity was "Petroleum oils, other than crude" (HS code 2710) (see table 4). The top three partners for merchandise imports were France, Singapore and the United States, accounting for respectively 25.0, 10.1 and 9.8 percent of total imports. "Transportation" (EBOPS code 205) accounted for the largest share of imports of services in 2012 at 219.5 mln US$, followed by "Travel" (EBOPS code 236) at 158.0 mln US$ and "Other business services" (EBOPS code 268) at 81.5 mln US$ (see graph 6).

Table 4: Top 10 import commodities 2011 to 2013

HS code	4-digit heading of Harmonized System 2007	2011	2012	2013	2011	2012	2013	Unit	SITC code
	All Commodities	1627.7	1706.3	1814.8					
2710	Petroleum oils, other than crude	245.8	279.0	292.1	0.9	1.0	1.0	US$/kg	334
3004	Medicaments (excluding goods of heading 30.02, 30.05 or 30.06)	67.9	64.9	70.9	63.3	58.8	63.5	US$/kg	542
8703	Motor cars and other motor vehicles principally designed for the transport	65.6	63.9	69.0			18.9	thsd US$/unit	781
0207	Meat and edible offal, of the poultry of heading 01.05	29.3	32.0	32.9	2.0	2.3	2.2	US$/kg	012
1905	Bread, pastry, cakes, biscuits and other bakers' wares	25.1	27.5	26.4	5.1	5.6	5.7	US$/kg	048
8471	Automatic data processing machines and units thereof	25.1	25.0	28.6					752
8517	Electrical apparatus for line telephony or line telegraphy	18.7	27.8	29.6					764
8901	Cruise ships, excursion boats, ferry-boats, cargo ships, barges	0.8	21.0	46.2					793
0202	Meat of bovine animals, frozen	22.2	22.8	22.8	4.8	5.2	5.4	US$/kg	011
0201	Meat of bovine animals, fresh or chilled	20.7	23.1	22.8	8.6	9.6	9.7	US$/kg	011

Gambia

Goods Imports: CIF, by origin **Goods Exports:** FOB, by last known destination **Trade System:** General

Overview:
In 2013, the value of merchandise exports of the Gambia decreased substantially by 10.6 percent to reach 106.2 mln US$, while its merchandise imports decreased moderately by 7.8 percent to reach 350.2 mln US$ (see graph 1, table 2 and table 3). The merchandise trade balance recorded a large deficit of 244.0 mln US$ (see graph 1). The largest merchandise trade balance was with MDG Developed Europe at -80.3 mln US$ (see graph 4). Merchandise exports in the Gambia were highly concentrated amongst partners; imports were diversified. The top 3 partners accounted for 80 percent or more of exports and 13 partners accounted for 80 percent or more of imports (see graph 5). In 2012, the value of exports of services of the Gambia increased moderately by 5.4 percent, reaching 151.5 mln US$, while its imports of services increased substantially by 17.3 percent and reached 80.3 mln US$ (see graph 2). There was a large trade in services surplus of 71.2 mln US$. See footnote*.

Graph 1: Total merchandise trade, by value
(Mln US$ by year)

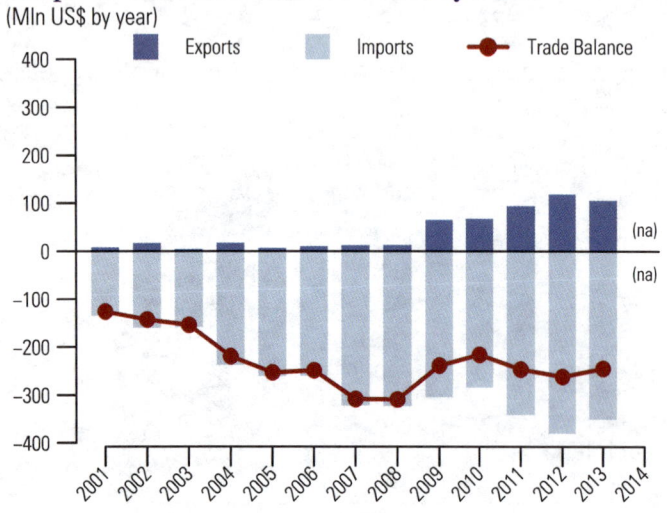

Graph 2: Total services trade, by value
(Mln US$ by year)

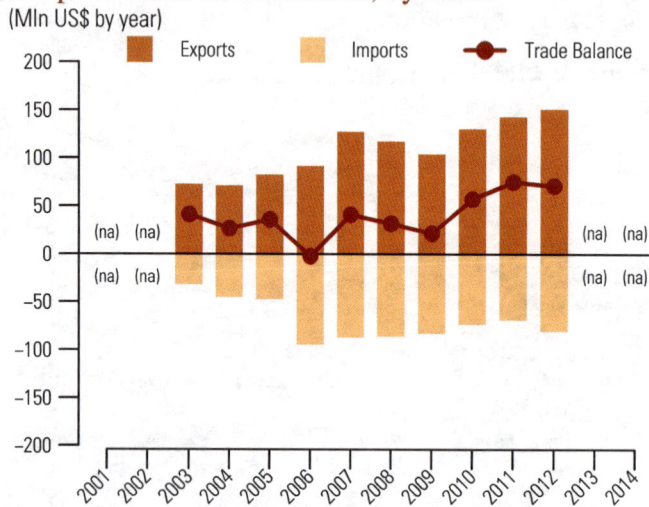

Exports Profile:
"Goods classified chiefly by material" (SITC section 6), "Food, animals + beverages, tobacco" (SITC section 0+1) and "Machinery and transport equipment" (SITC section 7) were the largest commodity groups for exports in 2013, representing respectively 64.9, 18.5 and 6.5 percent of exported goods (see table 2). From 2011 to 2013, the largest export commodity was "Woven fabrics of artificial filament yarn" (HS code 5408) (see table 1). The top three destinations for merchandise exports were Mali, Guinea and Senegal, accounting for respectively 28.6, 28.2 and 21.6 percent of total exports. "Travel" (EBOPS code 236) accounted for the largest share of exports of services in 2012 at 87.6 mln US$, followed by "Transportation" (EBOPS code 205) at 50.4 mln US$ and "Insurance services" (EBOPS code 253) at 9.1 mln US$ (see graph 3).

Graph 3: Exports of services by EBOPS category
(% share in 2012)

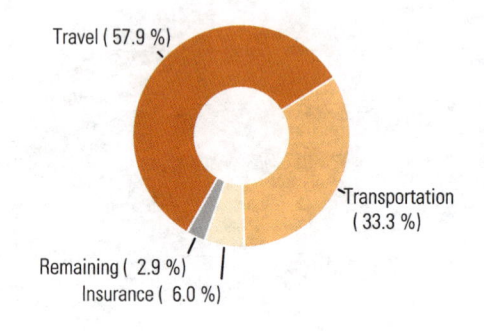

- Travel (57.9 %)
- Transportation (33.3 %)
- Insurance (6.0 %)
- Remaining (2.9 %)

Table 1: Top 10 export commodities 2011 to 2013

HS code	4-digit heading of Harmonized System 2007	Value (million US$) 2011	2012	2013	Unit value 2011	2012	2013	Unit	SITC code
	All Commodities	94.9	118.8	106.2					
5408	Woven fabrics of artificial filament yarn	41.3	58.3	67.3	4.5	0.9	1.8	US$/kg	653
6309	Worn clothing and other worn articles	5.2	5.1	1.3	3.3	4.3	2.7	US$/kg	269
0801	Coconuts, Brazil nuts and cashew nuts, fresh or dried	2.1	3.0	5.3	0.1	0.1	0.1	US$/kg	057
2710	Petroleum oils, other than crude	0.7	6.3	2.3	0.8	0.4	0.4	US$/kg	334
0402	Milk and cream, concentrated or containing added sugar	1.6	5.1	2.5	0.1	3.0	2.6	US$/kg	022
1701	Cane or beet sugar and chemically pure sucrose, in solid form	3.0	1.8	3.3	1.7	0.8	1.2	US$/kg	061
4408	Sheets for veneering	0.5	5.7	0.4	0.1	0.1	0.1	US$/kg	634
1202	Ground-nuts, not roasted or otherwise cooked, whether or not shelled or broken	1.9	1.6	2.6	0.8	1.1	0.6	US$/kg	222
1604	Prepared or preserved fish; caviar	2.5	3.0	0.5	1.9	1.8	1.7	US$/kg	037
1515	Other fixed vegetable fats and oils	2.0	1.8	2.0	0.4	1.6	1.8	US$/kg	42

*As of 2009, merchandise trade includes re-exports.

Gambia

Services Imports and Exports: EBOPS 2002 categories

Table 2: Merchandise exports by SITC
(Value in million US$, growth and shares in percentage)

SITC	2013	Avg. Growth rates 2009-2013	Avg. Growth rates 2012-2013	2013 share
Total	106.2	12.7	-10.6	100.0
0+1	19.7	-5.3	-22.9	18.5
2+4	6.4	-20.1	-51.8	6.0
3	2.3	422.5	-62.7	2.2
5	0.8	9.4	-43.3	0.7
6	68.9	41.6	3.7	64.9
7	6.9	7.9	88.2	6.5
8	1.3	-20.5	-48.0	1.2

Table 3: Merchandise imports by SITC
(Value in million US$, growth and shares in percentage)

SITC	2013	Avg. Growth rates 2009-2013	Avg. Growth rates 2012-2013	2013 share
Total	350.2	3.6	-7.8	100.0
0+1	113.2	8.4	5.7	32.3
2+4	23.0	-3.1	-10.0	6.6
3	82.6	15.0	-19.5	23.6
5	14.1	-11.3	-35.6	4.0
6	38.7	-2.6	-5.1	11.0
7	58.9	-1.1	-5.2	16.8
8	19.7	-1.4	-0.7	5.6
9	0.0	-30.7	5.5	0.0

SITC Legend

SITC Code	Description
Total	All commodities
0+1	Food, animals + beverages, tobacco
2+4	Crude materials + anim. & veg. oils
3	Mineral fuels, lubricants
5	Chemicals
6	Goods classified chiefly by material
7	Machinery and transport equipment
8	Miscellaneous manufactured articles
9	Not classified elsewhere in the SITC

Graph 4: Merchandise trade balance
(Mln US$ by MDG Regions in 2013)

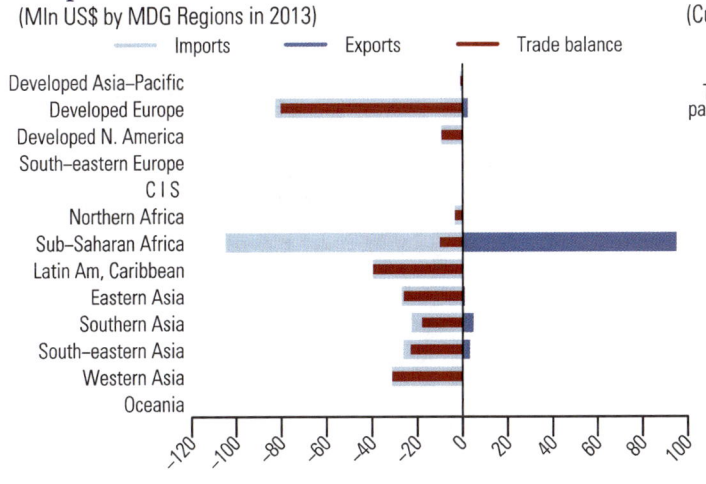

Graph 5: Partner concentration of merchandise trade
(Cumulative share by ranked partners in 2013)

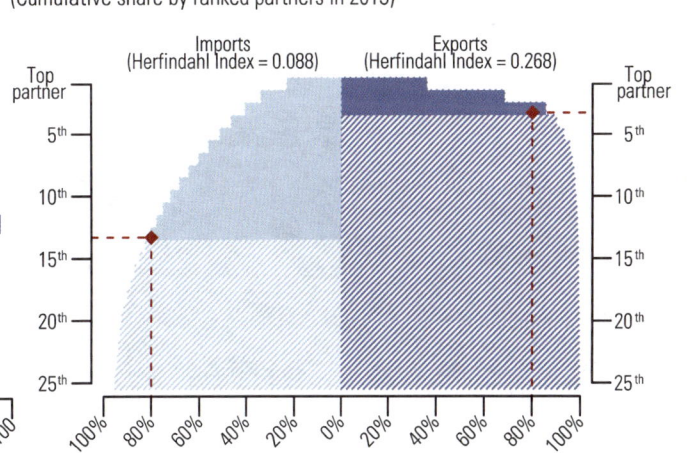

Imports (Herfindahl Index = 0.088)
Exports (Herfindahl Index = 0.268)

Graph 6: Imports of services by EBOPS category
(% share in 2012)

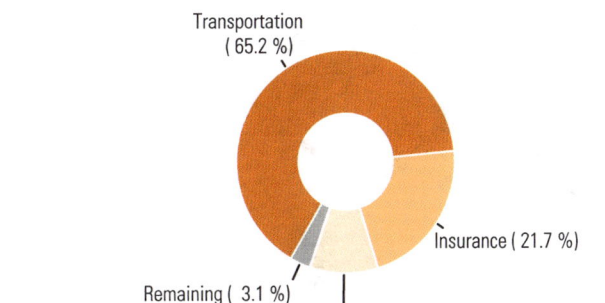

- Transportation (65.2 %)
- Insurance (21.7 %)
- Travel (10.1 %)
- Remaining (3.1 %)

Imports Profile:

"Food, animals + beverages, tobacco" (SITC section 0+1), "Mineral fuels, lubricants" (SITC section 3) and "Machinery and transport equipment" (SITC section 7) were the largest commodity groups for imports in 2013, representing respectively 32.3, 23.6 and 16.8 percent of imported goods (see table 3). From 2011 to 2013, the largest import commodity was "Petroleum oils, other than crude" (HS code 2710) (see table 4). The top three partners for merchandise imports were Côte d'Ivoire, Brazil and China, accounting for respectively 23.7, 9.7 and 8.0 percent of total imports. "Transportation" (EBOPS code 205) accounted for the largest share of imports of services in 2012 at 52.3 mln US$, followed by "Insurance services" (EBOPS code 253) at 17.4 mln US$ and "Travel" (EBOPS code 236) at 8.1 mln US$ (see graph 6).

Table 4: Top 10 import commodities 2011 to 2013

HS code	4-digit heading of Harmonized System 2007	Value 2011	Value 2012	Value 2013	Unit value 2011	Unit value 2012	Unit value 2013	Unit	SITC code
	All Commodities	340.7	380.0	350.2					
2710	Petroleum oils, other than crude	75.6	102.5	82.4	1.0	1.1	1.0	US$/kg	334
1006	Rice	35.9	44.2	31.7	0.2	0.5	0.4	US$/kg	042
8703	Motor cars and other motor vehicles principally designed for the transport	16.8	20.5	22.2		18.4	18.1	thsd US$/unit	781
1701	Cane or beet sugar and chemically pure sucrose, in solid form	14.7	16.6	27.2	0.2	0.3	0.4	US$/kg	061
1515	Other fixed vegetable fats and oils	16.7	18.0	16.6	0.5	0.4	0.4	US$/kg	42
1101	Wheat or meslin flour	11.2	14.1	18.7	0.2	0.2	0.4	US$/kg	046
2523	Portland cement, aluminous cement, slag cement	11.0	12.9	10.3	0.1	0.1	0.1	US$/kg	661
5408	Woven fabrics of artificial filament yarn	8.9	7.5	7.4	0.5	0.5	0.5	US$/kg	653
3004	Medicaments (excluding goods of heading 30.02, 30.05 or 30.06)	5.5	5.0	3.4	6.5	7.4	4.5	US$/kg	542
2402	Cigars, cheroots, cigarillos and cigarettes	3.9	3.7	3.7	7.4	7.8	7.9	US$/kg	122

Georgia

Goods Imports: CIF, by consignment **Goods Exports:** FOB, by last known destination **Trade System:** General

Overview:
In 2014, the value of merchandise exports of Georgia decreased slightly by 1.6 percent to reach 2.9 bln US$, while its merchandise imports increased moderately by 7.1 percent to reach 8.6 bln US$ (see graph 1, table 2 and table 3). The merchandise trade balance recorded a large deficit of 5.7 bln US$ (see graph 1). The largest merchandise trade balance was with MDG Western Asia at -1.7 bln US$ (see graph 4). Merchandise exports in Georgia were diversified amongst partners; imports were also diversified. The top 13 partners accounted for 80 percent or more of exports and 16 partners accounted for 80 percent or more of imports (see graph 5). In 2013, the value of exports of services of Georgia increased substantially by 16.5 percent, reaching 3.0 bln US$, while its imports of services increased moderately by 8.0 percent and reached 1.6 bln US$ (see graph 2). There was a large trade in services surplus of 1.4 bln US$.

Graph 1: Total merchandise trade, by value
(Bln US$ by year)

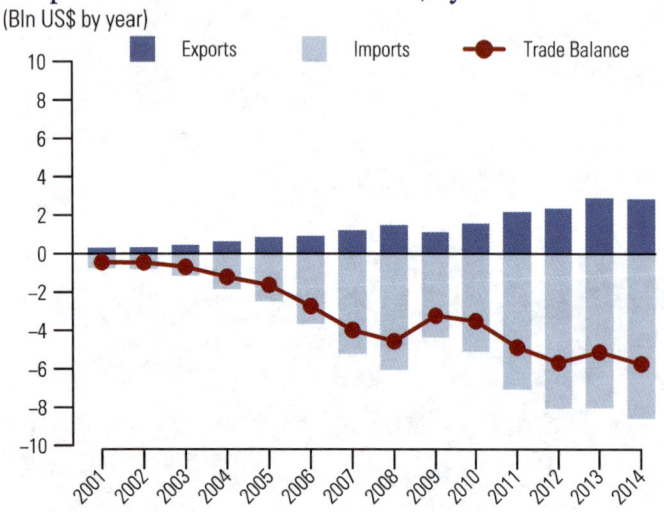

Graph 2: Total services trade, by value
(Bln US$ by year)

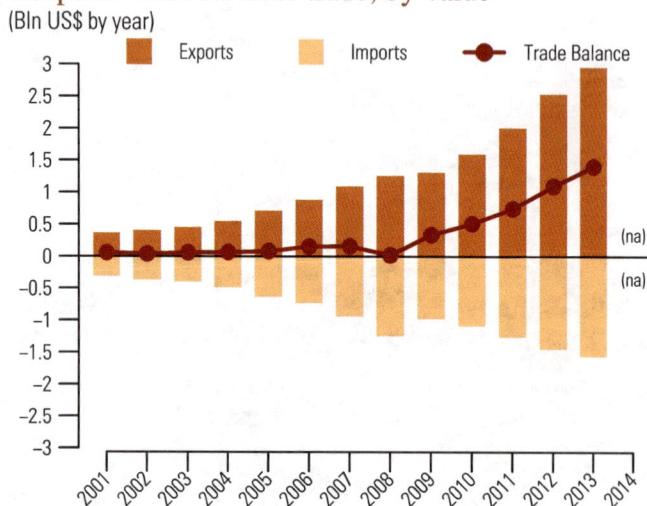

Exports Profile:
"Food, animals + beverages, tobacco" (SITC section 0+1), "Machinery and transport equipment" (SITC section 7) and "Goods classified chiefly by material" (SITC section 6) were the largest commodity groups for exports in 2014, representing respectively 28.4, 23.1 and 17.8 percent of exported goods (see table 2). From 2012 to 2014, the largest export commodity was "Motor cars and other motor vehicles principally designed for the transport" (HS code 8703) (see table 1). The top three destinations for merchandise exports were Azerbaijan, Armenia and the United States, accounting for respectively 23.1, 10.6 and 7.0 percent of total exports. "Travel" (EBOPS code 236) accounted for the largest share of exports of services in 2013 at 1.7 bln US$, followed by "Transportation" (EBOPS code 205) at 960.8 mln US$ (see graph 3).

Graph 3: Exports of services by EBOPS category
(% share in 2013)

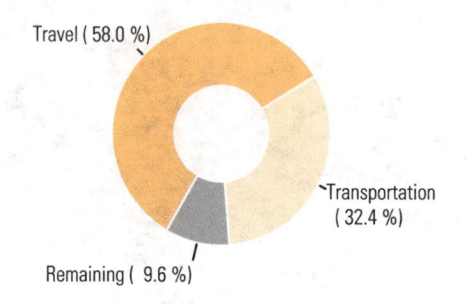

- Travel (58.0 %)
- Transportation (32.4 %)
- Remaining (9.6 %)

Table 1: Top 10 export commodities 2012 to 2014

HS code	4-digit heading of Harmonized System 2012	2012	2013	2014	2012	2013	2014	Unit	SITC code
	All Commodities	2375.4	2908.4	2861.2					
8703	Motor cars and other motor vehicles principally designed for the transport	587.3	703.9	517.8	10.1	9.6	11.4	thsd US$/unit	781
7202	Ferro-alloys	260.5	229.9	285.8	1.1	1.0	1.1	US$/kg	671
2603	Copper ores and concentrates	53.5	161.6	248.1	1.6	1.3	1.3	US$/kg	283
0802	Other nuts, fresh or dried, whether or not shelled or peeled	83.6	166.7	183.4	5.3	5.5	9.2	US$/kg	057
3102	Mineral or chemical fertilisers, nitrogenous	137.2	130.6	137.6	0.3	0.3	0.3	US$/kg	562
2204	Wine of fresh grapes, including fortified wines	64.9	127.9	180.7	3.2	3.6	3.9	US$/litre	112
2201	Waters, including natural or artificial mineral waters	59.3	106.9	137.1	0.7	0.8	0.9	US$/litre	111
2208	Alcohol of a strength by volume of less than 80 % vol	80.0	99.9	95.2	6.1	8.9	10.1	US$/litre	112
7108	Gold (including gold plated with platinum)	88.0	73.3	39.3	22.8	17.1	17.3	thsd US$/kg	971
3004	Medicaments (excluding goods of heading 30.02, 30.05 or 30.06)	51.9	52.1	92.1	31.5	23.6	33.3	US$/kg	542

Georgia

Services Imports and Exports: EBOPS 2002 categories

Table 2: Merchandise exports by SITC
(Value in million US$, growth and shares in percentage)

SITC	2014	Avg. Growth rates 2010-2014	Avg. Growth rates 2013-2014	2014 share
Total	2861.2	15.9	-1.6	100.0
0+1	812.1	27.6	17.4	28.4
2+4	328.1	5.3	25.8	11.5
3	77.2	2.6	8.8	2.7
5	298.5	23.8	12.6	10.4
6	508.9	10.4	4.6	17.8
7	660.6	18.6	-25.4	23.1
8	128.5	28.6	25.1	4.5
9	47.3	-14.7	-67.4	1.7

Table 3: Merchandise imports by SITC
(Value in million US$, growth and shares in percentage)

SITC	2014	Avg. Growth rates 2010-2014	Avg. Growth rates 2013-2014	2014 share
Total	8596.3	14.0	7.1	100.0
0+1	1217.8	8.8	13.5	14.2
2+4	384.4	19.9	16.4	4.5
3	1432.6	11.4	2.9	16.7
5	914.9	14.5	10.0	10.6
6	1338.3	13.5	13.8	15.6
7	2441.5	18.6	8.0	28.4
8	820.4	12.1	14.7	9.5
9	46.2	26.5	-81.3	0.5

SITC Legend

SITC Code	Description
Total	All commodities
0+1	Food, animals + beverages, tobacco
2+4	Crude materials + anim. & veg. oils
3	Mineral fuels, lubricants
5	Chemicals
6	Goods classified chiefly by material
7	Machinery and transport equipment
8	Miscellaneous manufactured articles
9	Not classified elsewhere in the SITC

Graph 4: Merchandise trade balance
(Bln US$ by MDG Regions in 2014)

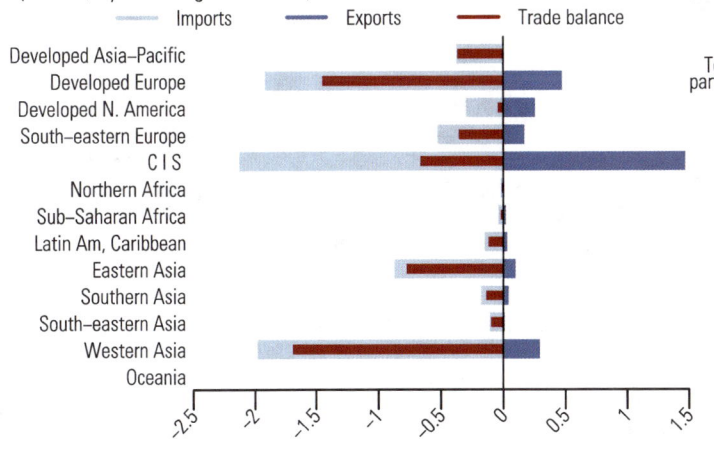

Graph 5: Partner concentration of merchandise trade
(Cumulative share by ranked partners in 2014)

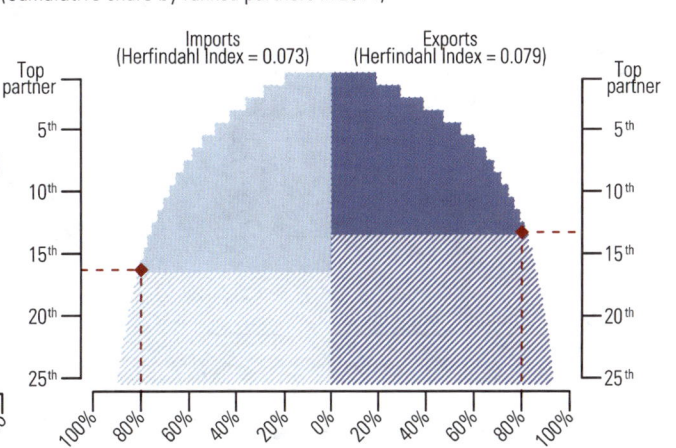

Imports (Herfindahl Index = 0.073)
Exports (Herfindahl Index = 0.079)

Graph 6: Imports of services by EBOPS category
(% share in 2013)

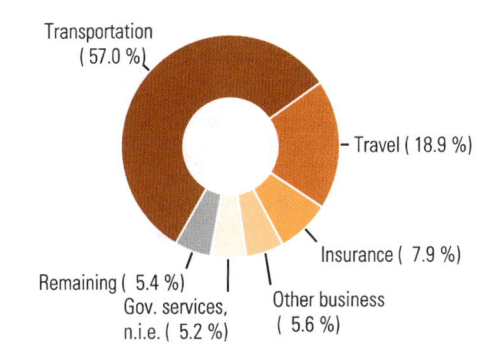

- Transportation (57.0 %)
- Travel (18.9 %)
- Insurance (7.9 %)
- Other business (5.6 %)
- Gov. services, n.i.e. (5.2 %)
- Remaining (5.4 %)

Imports Profile:

"Machinery and transport equipment" (SITC section 7), "Mineral fuels, lubricants" (SITC section 3) and "Goods classified chiefly by material" (SITC section 6) were the largest commodity groups for imports in 2014, representing respectively 28.4, 16.7 and 15.6 percent of imported goods (see table 3). From 2012 to 2014, the largest import commodity was "Petroleum oils, other than crude" (HS code 2710) (see table 4). The top three partners for merchandise imports were Turkey, Azerbaijan and China, accounting for respectively 18.7, 8.0 and 7.9 percent of total imports. "Transportation" (EBOPS code 205) accounted for the largest share of imports of services in 2013 at 888.2 mln US$, followed by "Travel" (EBOPS code 236) at 294.1 mln US$ and "Insurance services" (EBOPS code 253) at 122.9 mln US$ (see graph 6).

Table 4: Top 10 import commodities 2012 to 2014

HS code	4-digit heading of Harmonized System 2012	Value (million US$) 2012	2013	2014	Unit value 2012	2013	2014	Unit	SITC code
	All Commodities	8047.0	8025.2	8596.3					
2710	Petroleum oils, other than crude	951.0	954.4	918.3	1.0	1.0	0.9	US$/kg	334
8703	Motor cars and other motor vehicles principally designed for the transport	662.8	710.5	715.1	9.9	8.7	7.4	thsd US$/unit	781
2711	Petroleum gases and other gaseous hydrocarbons	318.0	316.7	368.9	0.2	0.2	0.2	US$/kg	343
3004	Medicaments (excluding goods of heading 30.02, 30.05 or 30.06)	232.6	280.7	314.6	34.4	34.6	33.6	US$/kg	542
9999	Commodities not specified according to kind	284.7	246.6	46.2					931
1001	Wheat and meslin	170.8	182.9	151.7	0.3	0.3	0.3	US$/kg	041
8517	Electrical apparatus for line telephony or line telegraphy	119.3	152.6	195.6					764
2402	Cigars, cheroots, cigarillos and cigarettes	90.6	95.7	115.5	13.7	12.5	12.8	US$/kg	122
8471	Automatic data processing machines and units thereof	105.0	90.6	104.1	80.3	98.6	111.1	US$/unit	752
2603	Copper ores and concentrates	0.0	113.1	165.3	0.1	1.5	0.8	US$/kg	283

2014 International Trade Statistics Yearbook, Vol. I   Source: UN Comtrade and UN ServiceTrade

Germany

Goods Imports: CIF, by origin **Goods Exports:** FOB, by last known destination **Trade System:** Special

Overview:
In 2014, the value of merchandise exports of Germany increased slightly by 3.6 percent to reach 1511.1 bln US$, while its merchandise imports increased slightly by 2.5 percent to reach 1223.8 bln US$ (see graph 1, table 2 and table 3). The merchandise trade balance recorded a surplus of 287.3 bln US$, the largest surplus the country has ever recorded (see graph 1). The largest merchandise trade balance was with MDG Developed Europe at 157.2 bln US$ (see graph 4). Merchandise exports in Germany were diversified amongst partners; imports were also diversified. The top 22 partners accounted for 80 percent or more of exports and 20 partners accounted for 80 percent or more of imports (see graph 5). In 2013, the value of exports of services of Germany decreased slightly by 4.6 percent, reaching 258.1 bln US$, while its imports of services increased moderately by 8.0 percent and reached 319.6 bln US$ (see graph 2). There was a moderate trade in services deficit of 61.5 bln US$.

Graph 1: Total merchandise trade, by value
(Bln US$ by year)

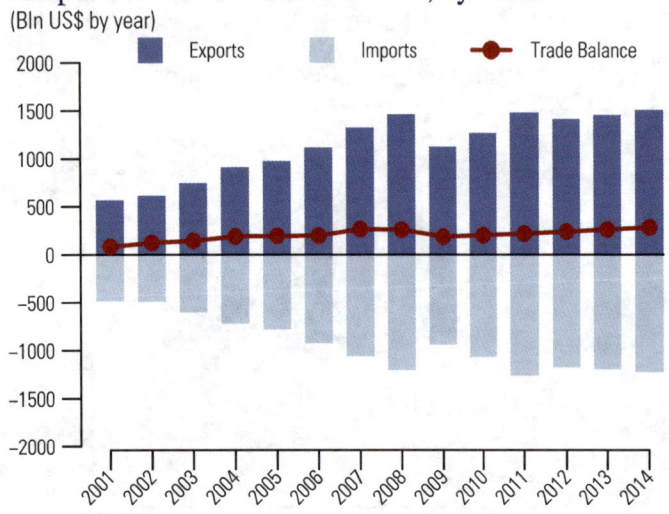

Graph 2: Total services trade, by value
(Bln US$ by year)

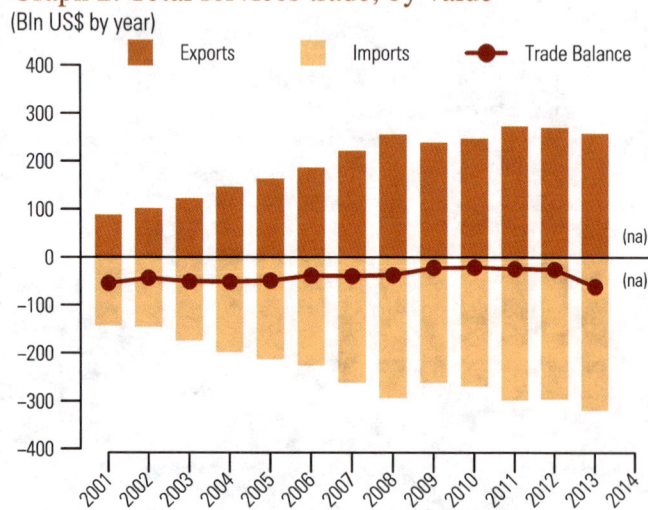

Exports Profile:
"Machinery and transport equipment" (SITC section 7), "Chemicals" (SITC section 5) and "Goods classified chiefly by material" (SITC section 6) were the largest commodity groups for exports in 2014, representing respectively 47.2, 14.9 and 12.2 percent of exported goods (see table 2). From 2012 to 2014, the largest export commodity was "Motor cars and other motor vehicles principally designed for the transport" (HS code 8703) (see table 1). Germany is the world's largest exporter of this commodity. The top three destinations for merchandise exports were France, the United States and the United Kingdom, accounting for respectively 9.2, 8.2 and 6.7 percent of total exports. "Other business services" (EBOPS code 268) accounted for the largest share of exports of services in 2013 at 75.5 bln US$, followed by "Transportation" (EBOPS code 205) at 60.0 bln US$ and "Travel" (EBOPS code 236) at 42.8 bln US$ (see graph 3).

Graph 3: Exports of services by EBOPS category
(% share in 2013)

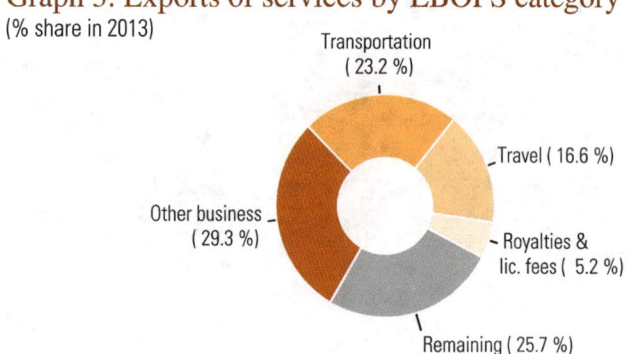

- Transportation (23.2 %)
- Travel (16.6 %)
- Royalties & lic. fees (5.2 %)
- Remaining (25.7 %)
- Other business (29.3 %)

Table 1: Top 10 export commodities 2012 to 2014

HS code	4-digit heading of Harmonized System 2012	Value (billion US$) 2012	2013	2014	Unit value 2012	2013	2014	Unit	SITC code
	All Commodities	1416.2	1458.6	1511.1					
8703	Motor cars and other motor vehicles principally designed for the transport	146.3	148.7	160.1		19.7	19.1	thsd US$/unit	781
9999	Commodities not specified according to kind	76.0	72.3	79.0					931
8708	Parts and accessories of the motor vehicles of headings 87.01 to 87.05	51.6	56.0	60.2	10.0	10.7	10.9	US$/kg	784
3004	Medicaments (excluding goods of heading 30.02, 30.05 or 30.06)	45.3	48.5	51.6	78.9	81.0	86.6	US$/kg	542
8802	Other aircraft (for example, helicopters, aeroplanes); spacecraft	33.9	34.7	33.7					792
3002	Human blood; animal blood prepared for therapeutic uses	17.1	20.6	22.3	0.9	1.0	1.0	thsd US$/kg	541
2710	Petroleum oils, other than crude	18.0	18.3	17.9	1.1	1.0	1.0	US$/kg	334
8409	Parts suitable for use with the engines of heading 84	14.1	14.8	15.4	13.6	14.5	15.0	US$/kg	713
2711	Petroleum gases and other gaseous hydrocarbons	12.1	14.5	14.6	0.5	0.5	0.4	US$/kg	343
8479	Machines and mechanical appliances having individual functions	13.3	13.5	14.3					728

Source: UN Comtrade and UN ServiceTrade

Germany

Services Imports and Exports: EBOPS 2002 categories

Table 2: Merchandise exports by SITC
(Value in million US$, growth and shares in percentage)

SITC	2014	Avg. Growth rates 2010-2014	Avg. Growth rates 2013-2014	2014 share
Total	1 511 136.5	4.4	3.6	100.0
0+1	81 132.1	6.6	2.4	5.4
2+4	28 412.3	2.3	-0.9	1.9
3	40 509.6	14.1	-1.8	2.7
5	224 613.8	4.6	3.7	14.9
6	184 583.4	2.8	1.8	12.2
7	712 646.9	5.1	4.3	47.2
8	154 688.5	4.6	4.2	10.2
9	84 549.9	-2.1	5.9	5.6

Table 3: Merchandise imports by SITC
(Value in million US$, growth and shares in percentage)

SITC	2014	Avg. Growth rates 2010-2014	Avg. Growth rates 2013-2014	2014 share
Total	1 223 836.6	3.5	2.5	100.0
0+1	84 687.3	5.5	3.4	6.9
2+4	48 699.3	2.2	-2.3	4.0
3	155 808.4	6.3	-10.4	12.7
5	154 366.1	3.5	4.4	12.6
6	154 855.5	3.6	4.3	12.7
7	408 288.1	3.0	5.9	33.4
8	147 974.3	6.0	8.1	12.1
9	69 157.4	-4.6	-1.1	5.7

SITC Legend

SITC Code	Description
Total	All commodities
0+1	Food, animals + beverages, tobacco
2+4	Crude materials + anim. & veg. oils
3	Mineral fuels, lubricants
5	Chemicals
6	Goods classified chiefly by material
7	Machinery and transport equipment
8	Miscellaneous manufactured articles
9	Not classified elsewhere in the SITC

Graph 4: Merchandise trade balance
(Bln US$ by MDG Regions in 2014)

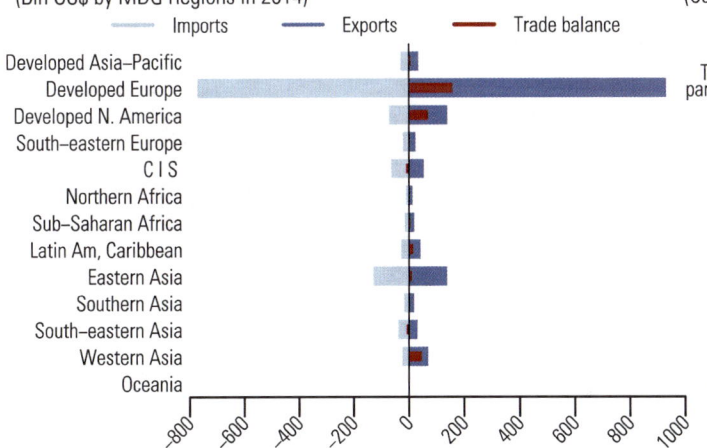

Graph 5: Partner concentration of merchandise trade
(Cumulative share by ranked partners in 2014)

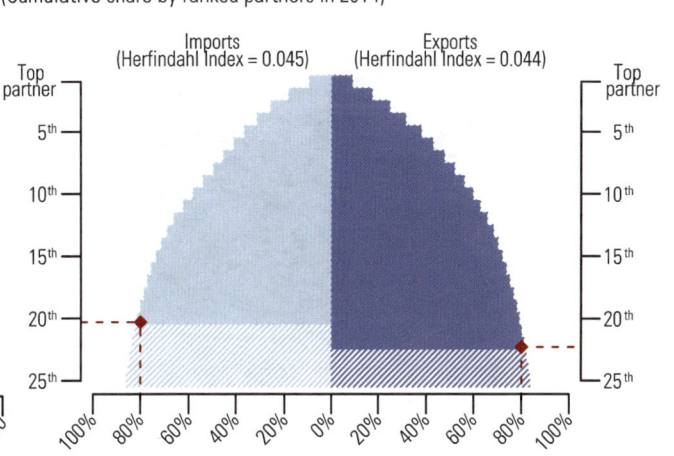

Imports (Herfindahl Index = 0.045)
Exports (Herfindahl Index = 0.044)

Graph 6: Imports of services by EBOPS category
(% share in 2013)

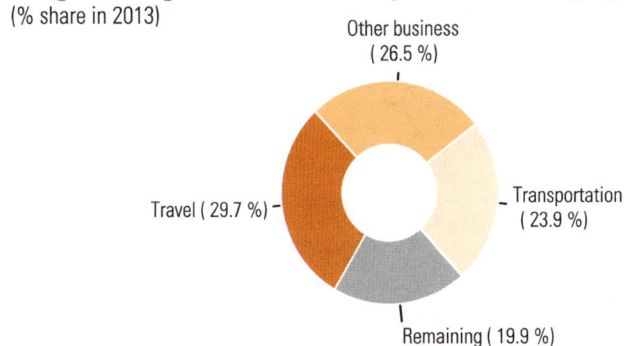

- Other business (26.5 %)
- Transportation (23.9 %)
- Remaining (19.9 %)
- Travel (29.7 %)

Imports Profile:

"Machinery and transport equipment" (SITC section 7), "Mineral fuels, lubricants" (SITC section 3) and "Goods classified chiefly by material" (SITC section 6) were the largest commodity groups for imports in 2014, representing respectively 33.4, 12.7 and 12.7 percent of imported goods (see table 3). From 2012 to 2014, the largest import commodity was "Petroleum oils and oils obtained from bituminous minerals, crude" (HS code 2709) (see table 4). The top three partners for merchandise imports were the Netherlands, China and France, accounting for respectively 9.3, 8.5 and 7.2 percent of total imports. "Travel" (EBOPS code 236) accounted for the largest share of imports of services in 2013 at 94.9 bln US$, followed by "Other business services" (EBOPS code 268) at 84.8 bln US$ and "Transportation" (EBOPS code 205) at 76.3 bln US$ (see graph 6).

Table 4: Top 10 import commodities 2012 to 2014

HS code	4-digit heading of Harmonized System 2012	2012	2013	2014	2012	2013	2014	Unit	SITC code
	All Commodities	1 173.3	1 194.5	1 223.8					
2709	Petroleum oils and oils obtained from bituminous minerals, crude	76.3	74.3	65.7	0.8	0.8	0.8	US$/kg	333
9999	Commodities not specified according to kind	69.9	62.0	63.6					931
2711	Petroleum gases and other gaseous hydrocarbons	51.0	52.4	45.9	0.5	0.5	0.4	US$/kg	343
8703	Motor cars and other motor vehicles principally designed for the transport	40.2	40.9	46.1		17.9	17.7	thsd US$/unit	781
8708	Parts and accessories of the motor vehicles of headings 87.01 to 87.05	31.9	35.1	37.7	7.9	8.4	8.4	US$/kg	784
2710	Petroleum oils, other than crude	34.0	36.6	32.7	1.0	1.0	0.9	US$/kg	334
3004	Medicaments (excluding goods of heading 30.02, 30.05 or 30.06)	24.5	24.0	26.2	91.5	90.6	99.5	US$/kg	542
8471	Automatic data processing machines and units thereof	18.7	18.0	21.4					752
8517	Electrical apparatus for line telephony or line telegraphy	17.1	18.5	19.7					764
8802	Other aircraft (for example, helicopters, aeroplanes); spacecraft	14.9	18.3	19.8					792

Ghana

Goods Imports: CIF, by origin | **Goods Exports: FOB, by last known destination** | **Trade System: General**

Overview:
In 2013, the value of merchandise exports of Ghana decreased substantially by 19.8 percent to reach 12.6 bln US$, while its merchandise imports decreased moderately by 5.8 percent to reach 12.8 bln US$ (see graph 1, table 2 and table 3). The merchandise trade balance recorded a relatively small deficit of 143.3 mln US$ (see graph 1). The largest merchandise trade balance was with MDG Sub-Saharan Africa at 2.8 bln US$ (see graph 4). Merchandise exports in Ghana were diversified amongst partners; imports were also diversified. The top 10 partners accounted for 80 percent or more of exports and 21 partners accounted for 80 percent or more of imports (see graph 5). In 2012, the value of exports of services of Ghana increased substantially by 74.2 percent, reaching 3.3 bln US$, while its imports of services increased substantially by 15.5 percent and reached 4.2 bln US$ (see graph 2). There was a moderate trade in services deficit of 977.0 mln US$. See footnote*.

Graph 1: Total merchandise trade, by value
(Bln US$ by year)

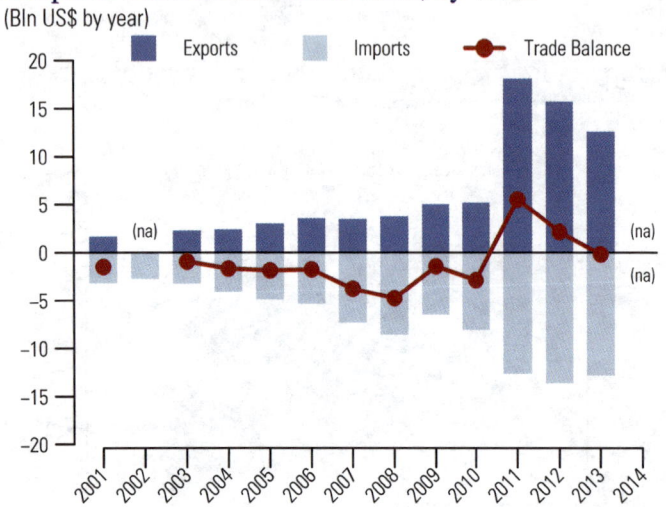

Graph 2: Total services trade, by value
(Bln US$ by year)

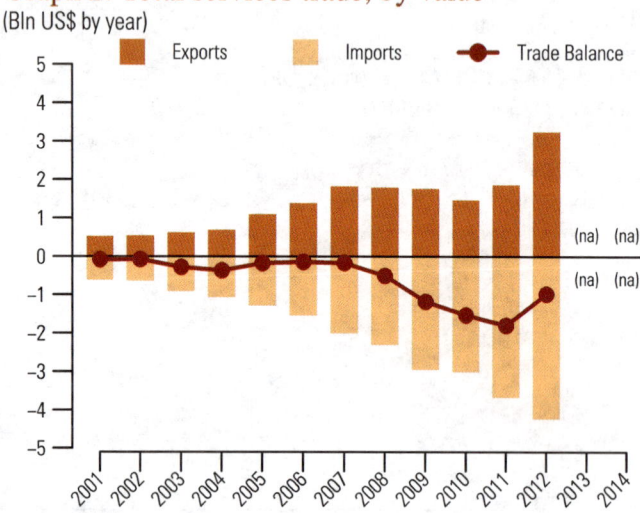

Exports Profile:
"Not classified elsewhere in the SITC" (SITC section 9), "Mineral fuels, lubricants" (SITC section 3) and "Food, animals + beverages, tobacco" (SITC section 0+1) were the largest commodity groups for exports in 2013, representing respectively 42.6, 24.7 and 16.3 percent of exported goods (see table 2). From 2011 to 2013, the largest export commodity was "Gold (including gold plated with platinum)" (HS code 7108) (see table 1). The top three destinations for merchandise exports were South Africa, Togo and the United Arab Emirates, accounting for respectively 22.6, 11.9 and 9.2 percent of total exports. "Other business services" (EBOPS code 268) accounted for the largest share of exports of services in 2012 at 1.3 bln US$, followed by "Transportation" (EBOPS code 205) at 929.9 mln US$ and "Travel" (EBOPS code 236) at 914.4 mln US$ (see graph 3).

Graph 3: Exports of services by EBOPS category
(% share in 2012)

- Transportation (28.5 %)
- Other business (40.4 %)
- Remaining (3.0 %)
- Travel (28.1 %)

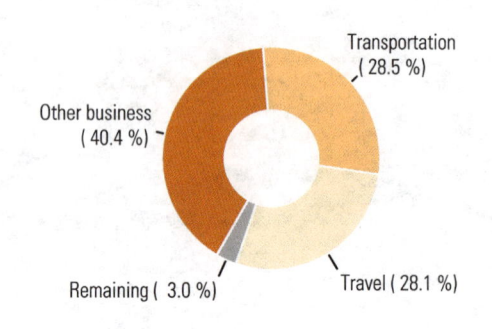

Table 1: Top 10 export commodities 2011 to 2013

HS code	4-digit heading of Harmonized System 2007	Value (million US$) 2011	2012	2013	Unit value 2011	2012	2013	Unit	SITC code
	All Commodities	18 146.7	15 761.2	12 643.9					
7108	Gold (including gold plated with platinum)	4 836.6	7 093.2	5 364.6	41.7	31.7	38.4	thsd US$/kg	971
2709	Petroleum oils and oils obtained from bituminous minerals, crude	2 862.0	3 683.9	3 015.4	0.7	0.6	0.5	US$/kg	333
1801	Cocoa beans, whole or broken, raw or roasted	2 071.6	1 967.8	1 380.5	3.3	3.4	2.6	US$/kg	072
2711	Petroleum gases and other gaseous hydrocarbons	4 330.8	620.2	10.6			2.2	US$/kg	343
0801	Coconuts, Brazil nuts and cashew nuts, fresh or dried	512.4	160.8	417.8	3.2	1.4	2.2	US$/kg	057
0714	Manioc, arrowroot, sweet potatoes and similar roots	422.0	11.2	19.7	19.6	0.5	0.8	US$/kg	054
3304	Beauty or make-up preparations	78.2	124.8	238.5	6.0	59.0	151.0	US$/kg	553
4407	Wood sawn or chipped lengthwise, sliced or peeled	127.8	79.7	231.2					248
2710	Petroleum oils, other than crude	76.1	214.8	101.6	1.0	1.4	0.1	US$/kg	334
2602	Manganese ores and concentrates	107.4	104.3	134.6	62.1	67.6	68.8	US$/kg	287

*In 2011, Ghana exported crude petroleum & natural gas in large quantities.

Ghana

Services Imports and Exports: EBOPS 2002 categories

Table 2: Merchandise exports by SITC
(Value in million US$, growth and shares in percentage)

SITC	2013	Avg. Growth rates 2009-2013	Avg. Growth rates 2012-2013	2013 share
Total	12643.9	25.7	-19.8	100.0
0+1	2059.1	13.0	-15.9	16.3
2+4	771.3	37.1	29.1	6.1
3	3128.7	143.6	-31.5	24.7
5	417.7	53.1	66.8	3.3
6	532.7	17.8	5.3	4.2
7	220.7	28.6	16.1	1.7
8	121.8	1.2	9.9	1.0
9	5391.9	16.3	-24.0	42.6

Table 3: Merchandise imports by SITC
(Value in million US$, growth and shares in percentage)

SITC	2013	Avg. Growth rates 2009-2013	Avg. Growth rates 2012-2013	2013 share
Total	12787.2	18.6	-5.8	100.0
0+1	1986.5	19.0	12.9	15.5
2+4	308.8	14.4	-4.5	2.4
3	471.9	24.5	-14.3	3.7
5	1650.6	17.3	-5.8	12.9
6	2398.0	17.4	-10.2	18.8
7	5057.1	20.6	-11.8	39.5
8	795.1	20.8	2.1	6.2
9	119.4	-11.7	1379.7	0.9

SITC Legend

SITC Code	Description
Total	All commodities
0+1	Food, animals + beverages, tobacco
2+4	Crude materials + anim. & veg. oils
3	Mineral fuels, lubricants
5	Chemicals
6	Goods classified chiefly by material
7	Machinery and transport equipment
8	Miscellaneous manufactured articles
9	Not classified elsewhere in the SITC

Graph 4: Merchandise trade balance
(Bln US$ by MDG Regions in 2013)

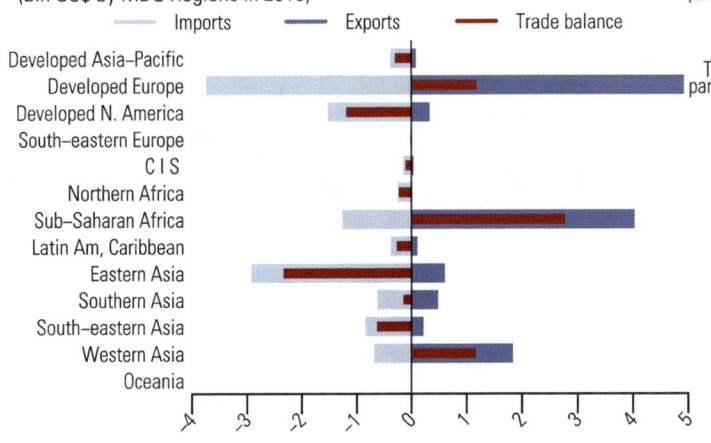

Graph 5: Partner concentration of merchandise trade
(Cumulative share by ranked partners in 2013)
Imports (Herfindahl Index = 0.062)
Exports (Herfindahl Index = 0.099)

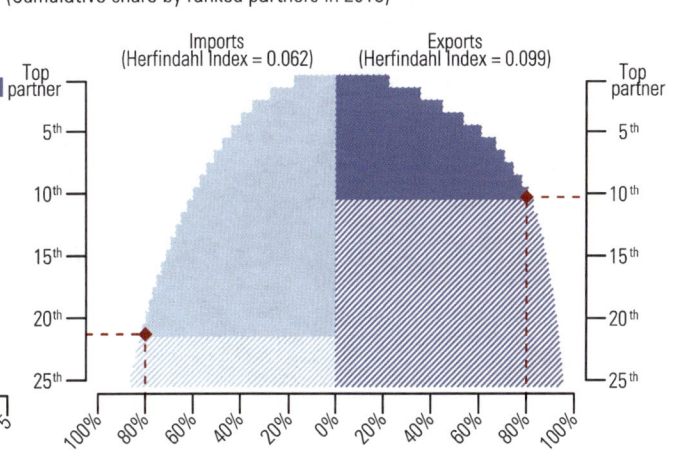

Graph 6: Imports of services by EBOPS category
(% share in 2012)

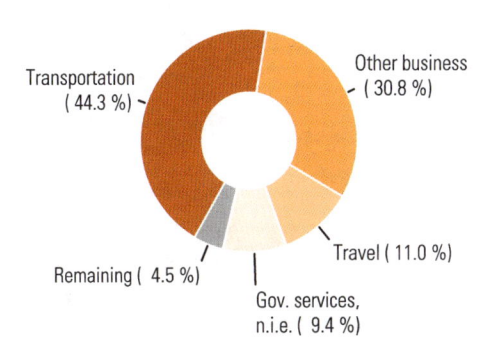

- Transportation (44.3 %)
- Other business (30.8 %)
- Travel (11.0 %)
- Gov. services, n.i.e. (9.4 %)
- Remaining (4.5 %)

Imports Profile:

"Machinery and transport equipment" (SITC section 7), "Goods classified chiefly by material" (SITC section 6) and "Food, animals + beverages, tobacco" (SITC section 0+1) were the largest commodity groups for imports in 2013, representing respectively 39.5, 18.8 and 15.5 percent of imported goods (see table 3). From 2011 to 2013, the largest import commodity was "Motor cars and other motor vehicles principally designed for the transport" (HS code 8703) (see table 4). The top three partners for merchandise imports were China, the United States and Belgium, accounting for respectively 17.3, 10.6 and 6.8 percent of total imports. "Transportation" (EBOPS code 205) accounted for the largest share of imports of services in 2012 at 1.9 bln US$, followed by "Other business services" (EBOPS code 268) at 1.3 bln US$ and "Travel" (EBOPS code 236) at 467.4 mln US$ (see graph 6).

Table 4: Top 10 import commodities 2011 to 2013

HS code	4-digit heading of Harmonized System 2007	Value 2011	Value 2012	Value 2013	Unit value 2011	Unit value 2012	Unit value 2013	Unit	SITC code
	All Commodities	12602.7	13578.1	12787.2					
8703	Motor cars and other motor vehicles principally designed for the transport	860.4	1070.9	1093.0		19.7	19.2	thsd US$/unit	781
8704	Motor vehicles for the transport of goods	628.0	802.7	612.2					782
2709	Petroleum oils and oils obtained from bituminous minerals, crude	787.7	430.7	308.7	117.8	111.5	109.2	US$/kg	333
1006	Rice	390.6	356.3	421.3	0.7	0.7	0.7	US$/kg	042
2523	Portland cement, aluminous cement, slag cement	308.0	353.6	303.5	0.0	0.1	0.1	US$/kg	661
3808	Insecticides, rodenticides, fungicides, herbicides	370.9	336.6	241.2	5.0	4.3	4.0	US$/kg	591
8517	Electrical apparatus for line telephony or line telegraphy	400.3	291.0	193.5					764
8429	Self-propelled bulldozers, angledozers, graders, levellers, scrapers	219.4	358.7	286.0	62.1			thsd US$/unit	723
0303	Fish, frozen, excluding fish fillets and other fish meat of heading 03.04	237.1	216.2	257.8	0.8	1.0	1.1	US$/kg	034
0207	Meat and edible offal, of the poultry of heading 01.05	178.1	188.0	200.4	1.1	1.2	1.2	US$/kg	012

2014 International Trade Statistics Yearbook, Vol. I   Source: UN Comtrade and UN ServiceTrade

Greece

Goods Imports: CIF, by origin/consignment for intra-eu **Goods Exports:** FOB, by last known destination **Trade System:** Special

Overview:
In 2014, the value of merchandise exports of Greece decreased slightly by 1.4 percent to reach 35.8 bln US$, while its merchandise imports increased slightly by 1.7 percent to reach 62.2 bln US$ (see graph 1, table 2 and table 3). The merchandise trade balance recorded a moderate deficit of 26.4 bln US$ (see graph 1). The largest merchandise trade balance was with MDG Developed Europe at -14.1 bln US$ (see graph 4). Merchandise exports in Greece were diversified amongst partners; imports were also diversified. The top 24 partners accounted for 80 percent or more of exports and 18 partners accounted for 80 percent or more of imports (see graph 5). In 2013, the value of exports of services of Greece increased moderately by 9.0 percent, reaching 38.6 bln US$, while its imports of services decreased moderately by 5.1 percent and reached 15.1 bln US$ (see graph 2). There was a large trade in services surplus of 23.5 bln US$.

Graph 1: Total merchandise trade, by value
(Bln US$ by year)

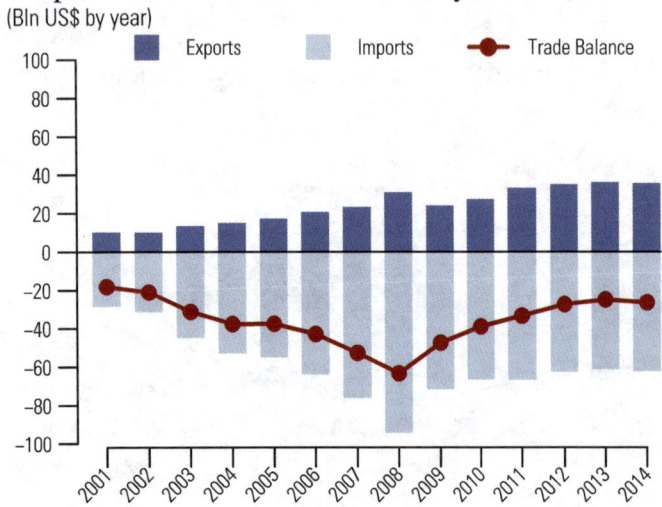

Graph 2: Total services trade, by value
(Bln US$ by year)

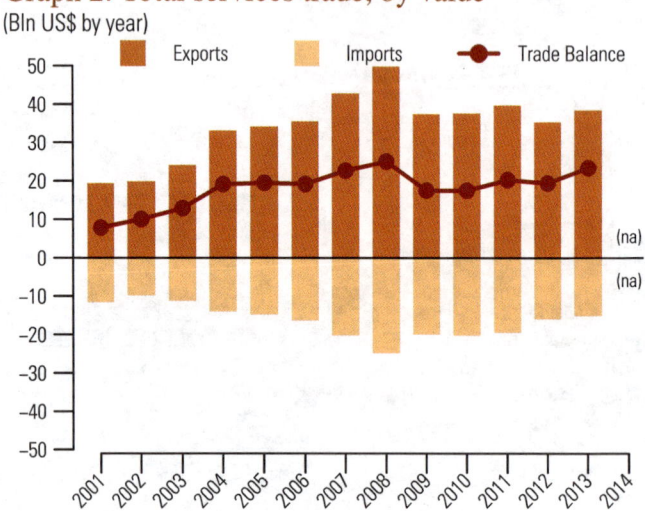

Exports Profile:
"Mineral fuels, lubricants" (SITC section 3), "Food, animals + beverages, tobacco" (SITC section 0+1) and "Goods classified chiefly by material" (SITC section 6) were the largest commodity groups for exports in 2014, representing respectively 38.4, 15.9 and 13.8 percent of exported goods (see table 2). From 2012 to 2014, the largest export commodity was "Petroleum oils, other than crude" (HS code 2710) (see table 1). The top three destinations for merchandise exports were Turkey, Italy and Germany, accounting for respectively 11.6, 8.6 and 6.5 percent of total exports. "Travel" (EBOPS code 236) accounted for the largest share of exports of services in 2013 at 16.8 bln US$, followed by "Transportation" (EBOPS code 205) at 16.7 bln US$ and "Other business services" (EBOPS code 268) at 2.1 bln US$ (see graph 3).

Graph 3: Exports of services by EBOPS category
(% share in 2013)

- Travel (43.5 %)
- Transportation (43.2 %)
- Other business (5.3 %)
- Remaining (8.0 %)

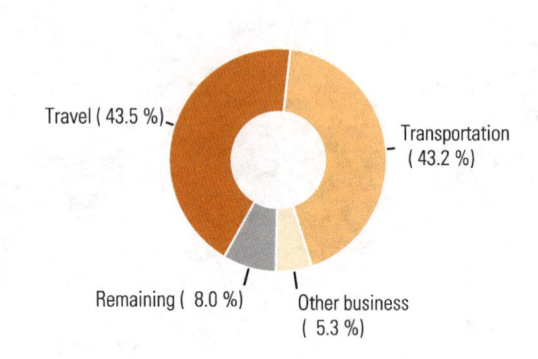

Table 1: Top 10 export commodities 2012 to 2014

HS code	4-digit heading of Harmonized System 2012	Value (million US$) 2012	2013	2014	Unit value 2012	2013	2014	Unit	SITC code
	All Commodities	35 151.1	36 261.6	35 755.4					
2710	Petroleum oils, other than crude	12 985.1	13 639.5	13 212.3	0.9	0.9	0.8	US$/kg	334
3004	Medicaments (excluding goods of heading 30.02, 30.05 or 30.06)	1 120.2	1 284.3	1 263.6	68.8	58.5	49.1	US$/kg	542
9999	Commodities not specified according to kind	713.9	699.4	724.0					931
7606	Aluminium plates, sheets and strip, of a thickness exceeding 0.2 mm	717.3	661.0	723.7	3.8	3.7	3.5	US$/kg	684
0302	Fish, fresh or chilled, excluding fish fillets	594.1	582.6	578.3	6.3	6.0	6.7	US$/kg	034
5201	Cotton, not carded or combed	550.8	492.1	410.0	1.8	1.9	1.7	US$/kg	263
1509	Olive oil and its fractions	417.7	656.5	345.9	3.3	3.9	4.7	US$/kg	421
2005	Other vegetables prepared or preserved	399.8	449.0	467.1	3.1	3.0	3.5	US$/kg	056
2008	Fruit, nuts and other edible parts of plants	432.1	450.0	406.8	1.3	1.4	1.5	US$/kg	058
7411	Copper tubes and pipes	433.4	429.5	419.8	8.7	8.3	7.6	US$/kg	682

Greece

Services Imports and Exports: EBOPS 2002 categories

Table 2: Merchandise exports by SITC
(Value in million US$, growth and shares in percentage)

SITC	2014	Avg. Growth rates 2010-2014	Avg. Growth rates 2013-2014	2014 share
Total	35 755.4	6.7	-1.4	100.0
0+1	5 689.8	3.1	2.2	15.9
2+4	1 793.6	-0.2	-21.1	5.0
3	13 747.9	17.6	-4.9	38.4
5	3 519.6	1.5	3.3	9.8
6	4 948.7	2.1	0.9	13.8
7	2 997.0	2.0	12.5	8.4
8	2 292.7	1.0	3.4	6.4
9	766.1	2.1	-0.8	2.1

Table 3: Merchandise imports by SITC
(Value in million US$, growth and shares in percentage)

SITC	2014	Avg. Growth rates 2010-2014	Avg. Growth rates 2013-2014	2014 share
Total	62 180.6	-1.6	1.7	100.0
0+1	7 305.1	-1.0	-0.8	11.7
2+4	1 908.2	-0.3	-0.9	3.1
3	21 355.8	7.0	-6.4	34.3
5	8 609.4	-3.3	1.0	13.8
6	6 193.4	-3.7	3.4	10.0
7	10 995.4	-8.7	19.1	17.7
8	5 784.9	-7.0	9.6	9.3
9	28.4	-10.9	61.3	0.0

SITC Legend

SITC Code	Description
Total	All commodities
0+1	Food, animals + beverages, tobacco
2+4	Crude materials + anim. & veg. oils
3	Mineral fuels, lubricants
5	Chemicals
6	Goods classified chiefly by material
7	Machinery and transport equipment
8	Miscellaneous manufactured articles
9	Not classified elsewhere in the SITC

Graph 4: Merchandise trade balance
(Bln US$ by MDG Regions in 2014)

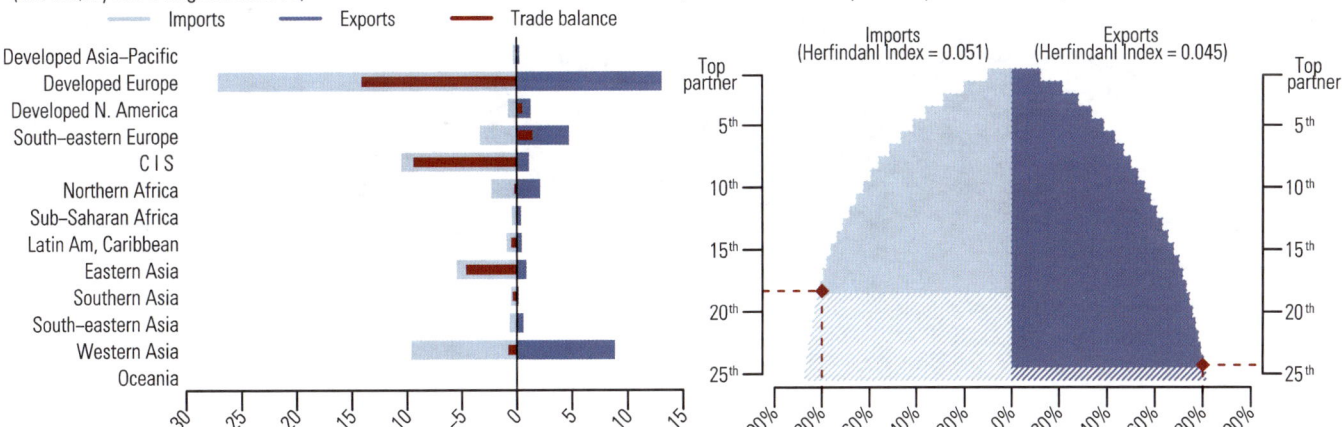

Graph 5: Partner concentration of merchandise trade
(Cumulative share by ranked partners in 2014)

Imports (Herfindahl Index = 0.051)
Exports (Herfindahl Index = 0.045)

Graph 6: Imports of services by EBOPS category
(% share in 2013)

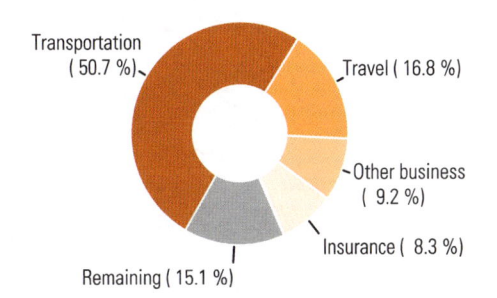

- Transportation (50.7 %)
- Travel (16.8 %)
- Other business (9.2 %)
- Insurance (8.3 %)
- Remaining (15.1 %)

Imports Profile:

"Mineral fuels, lubricants" (SITC section 3), "Machinery and transport equipment" (SITC section 7) and "Chemicals" (SITC section 5) were the largest commodity groups for imports in 2014, representing respectively 34.3, 17.7 and 13.8 percent of imported goods (see table 3). From 2012 to 2014, the largest import commodity was "Petroleum oils and oils obtained from bituminous minerals, crude" (HS code 2709) (see table 4). The top three partners for merchandise imports were the Russian Federation, Germany and Italy, accounting for respectively 12.3, 9.6 and 7.7 percent of total imports. "Transportation" (EBOPS code 205) accounted for the largest share of imports of services in 2013 at 7.7 bln US$, followed by "Travel" (EBOPS code 236) at 2.5 bln US$ and "Other business services" (EBOPS code 268) at 1.4 bln US$ (see graph 6).

Table 4: Top 10 import commodities 2012 to 2014

HS code	4-digit heading of Harmonized System 2012	2012	2013	2014	2012	2013	2014	Unit	SITC code
	All Commodities	62 504.4	61 148.1	62 180.6					
2709	Petroleum oils and oils obtained from bituminous minerals, crude	16 522.3	16 052.2	14 928.0	0.8	0.8	0.7	US$/kg	333
2710	Petroleum oils, other than crude	4 285.6	4 371.4	4 473.2	0.9	0.8	0.7	US$/kg	334
3004	Medicaments (excluding goods of heading 30.02, 30.05 or 30.06)	3 110.4	2 953.5	2 865.4	114.1	116.1	98.0	US$/kg	542
8901	Cruise ships, excursion boats, ferry-boats, cargo ships, barges	2 475.6	1 579.0	2 390.2	2.4	1.0	2.1	mln US$/unit	793
2711	Petroleum gases and other gaseous hydrocarbons	2 105.9	1 894.3	1 263.2	0.5	0.7	0.6	US$/kg	343
8703	Motor cars and other motor vehicles principally designed for the transport	667.9	787.1	1 117.3	7.5	7.6	6.5	thsd US$/unit	781
8517	Electrical apparatus for line telephony or line telegraphy	707.8	691.6	690.0					764
0203	Meat of swine, fresh, chilled or frozen	552.7	576.8	566.4	2.9	2.9	2.9	US$/kg	012
0406	Cheese and curd	503.7	568.9	578.7	4.6	5.0	4.9	US$/kg	024
8541	Diodes, transistors and similar semiconductor devices	1 174.2	373.9	46.5					776

Source: UN Comtrade and UN ServiceTrade

Greenland

Goods Imports: CIF, by origin **Goods Exports:** FOB, by last known destination **Trade System:** General

Overview:

In 2014, the value of merchandise exports of Greenland increased moderately by 10.3 percent to reach 540.5 mln US$, while its merchandise imports decreased moderately by 6.5 percent to reach 768.3 mln US$ (see graph 1, table 2 and table 3). The merchandise trade balance recorded a moderate deficit of 227.8 mln US$ (see graph 1). The largest merchandise trade balance was with MDG Developed Europe at -200.8 mln US$ (see graph 4). Merchandise exports in Greenland were highly concentrated amongst partners; imports were also highly concentrated. The top 2 partners accounted for 80 percent or more of exports and 2 partners accounted for 80 percent or more of imports (see graph 5). In 2006, the value of exports of services of Greenland decreased moderately by 9.8 percent, reaching 203.0 mln US$, while its imports of services increased moderately by 6.4 percent and reached 315.1 mln US$ (see graph 2). There was a moderate trade in services deficit of 112.1 mln US$.

Graph 1: Total merchandise trade, by value
(Mln US$ by year)

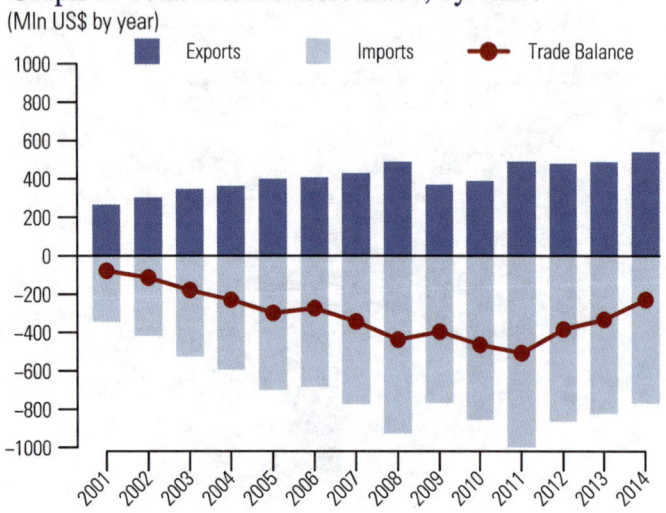

Graph 2: Total services trade, by value
(Mln US$ by year)

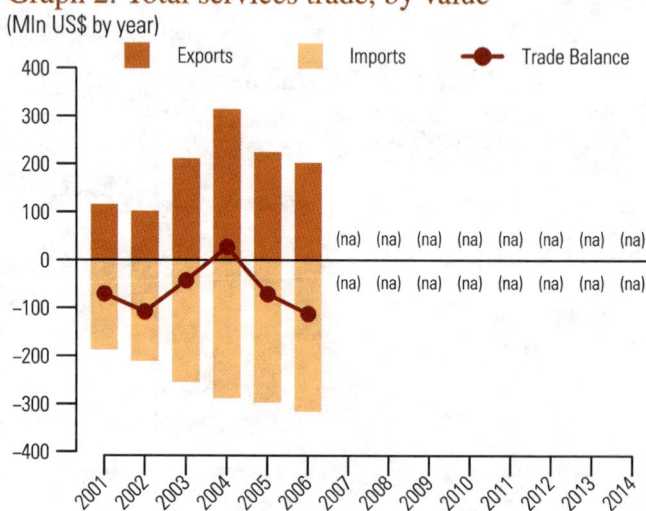

Exports Profile:

"Food, animals + beverages, tobacco" (SITC section 0+1) was the largest commodity group for exports in 2014, representing 91.4 percent of exported goods, followed distantly by "Not classified elsewhere in the SITC" (SITC section 9) and "Crude materials + anim. & veg. oils" (SITC section 2+4), representing respectively 7.3 percent and 0.5 percent (see table 2). From 2012 to 2014, the largest export commodity was "Fish, frozen, excluding fish fillets and other fish meat of heading 03.04" (HS code 0303) (see table 1). The top three destinations for merchandise exports were Denmark, Portugal and Iceland, accounting for respectively 85.0, 4.4 and 4.1 percent of total exports. "Transportation" (EBOPS code 205) accounted for the largest share of exports of services in 2006 at 169.0 mln US$, followed by "Travel" (EBOPS code 236) at 13.5 mln US$ and "Communications services" (EBOPS code 245) at 11.7 mln US$ (see graph 3).

Graph 3: Exports of services by EBOPS category
(% share in 2006)

- Transportation (83.3 %)
- Travel (6.7 %)
- Communication (5.8 %)
- Remaining (4.3 %)

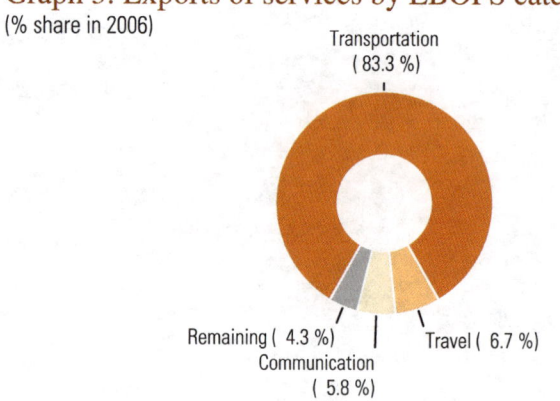

Table 1: Top 10 export commodities 2012 to 2014

HS code	4-digit heading of Harmonized System 2012	Value (million US$) 2012	2013	2014	Unit value 2012	2013	2014	Unit	SITC code
	All Commodities	480.6	490.1	540.5					
0303	Fish, frozen, excluding fish fillets and other fish meat of heading 03.04	126.1	128.9	203.2	2.1	1.8	1.8	US$/kg	034
0306	Crustaceans, whether in shell or not	120.6	120.2	133.5	2.9	3.2	3.4	US$/kg	036
1605	Crustaceans, molluscs and other aquatic invertebrates, prepared or preserved	131.6	120.4	114.0	6.1	6.4	7.0	US$/kg	037
9999	Commodities not specified according to kind	43.8	50.6	39.3					931
0304	Fish fillets and other fish meat (whether or not minced)	21.8	28.2	28.7	4.7	5.6	5.1	US$/kg	034
0305	Fish, dried, salted or in brine	13.3	14.1	9.8	8.0	7.5	5.3	US$/kg	035
7108	Gold (including gold plated with platinum)	12.8	12.2	0.0	45.1	38.9	15.0	thsd US$/kg	971
8902	Fishing vessels; factory ships and other vessels for processing	...	5.3	...					793
0302	Fish, fresh or chilled, excluding fish fillets	1.1	1.9	2.2	0.5	0.8	0.3	US$/kg	034
4302	Tanned or dressed furskins (including heads, tails, paws)	1.0	2.1	1.0	37.5	63.7	41.8	US$/kg	613

Source: UN Comtrade and UN ServiceTrade

Greenland

Services Imports and Exports: EBOPS 2002 categories

Table 2: Merchandise exports by SITC
(Value in million US$, growth and shares in percentage)

SITC	2014	Avg. Growth rates 2010-2014	Avg. Growth rates 2013-2014	2014 share
Total	540.5	8.4	10.3	100.0
0+1	493.8	11.0	18.8	91.4
2+4	2.8	-5.0	342.7	0.5
3	0.0	-43.9	-46.3	0.0
5	0.0	-10.1	-79.1	0.0
6	1.3	5.0	-49.5	0.2
7	1.4	-50.5	-78.4	0.3
8	1.8	-16.0	-6.2	0.3
9	39.3	3.8	-37.3	7.3

Table 3: Merchandise imports by SITC
(Value in million US$, growth and shares in percentage)

SITC	2014	Avg. Growth rates 2010-2014	Avg. Growth rates 2013-2014	2014 share
Total	768.3	-2.6	-6.5	100.0
0+1	173.7	1.8	1.0	22.6
2+4	10.6	-1.5	-3.1	1.4
3	160.2	-2.2	-18.5	20.8
5	54.8	3.2	2.4	7.1
6	97.6	-1.5	-14.2	12.7
7	156.3	-9.9	5.5	20.3
8	87.5	-2.3	-12.1	11.4
9	27.7	6.3	-0.4	3.6

SITC Legend

SITC Code	Description
Total	All commodities
0+1	Food, animals + beverages, tobacco
2+4	Crude materials + anim. & veg. oils
3	Mineral fuels, lubricants
5	Chemicals
6	Goods classified chiefly by material
7	Machinery and transport equipment
8	Miscellaneous manufactured articles
9	Not classified elsewhere in the SITC

Graph 4: Merchandise trade balance
(Mln US$ by MDG Regions in 2014)

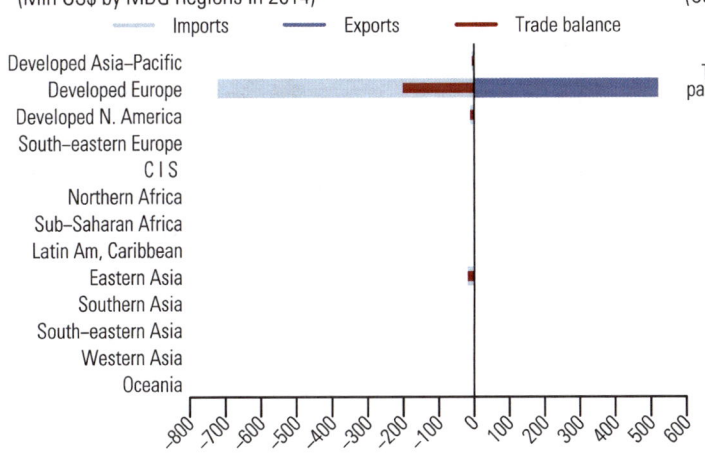

Graph 5: Partner concentration of merchandise trade
(Cumulative share by ranked partners in 2014)

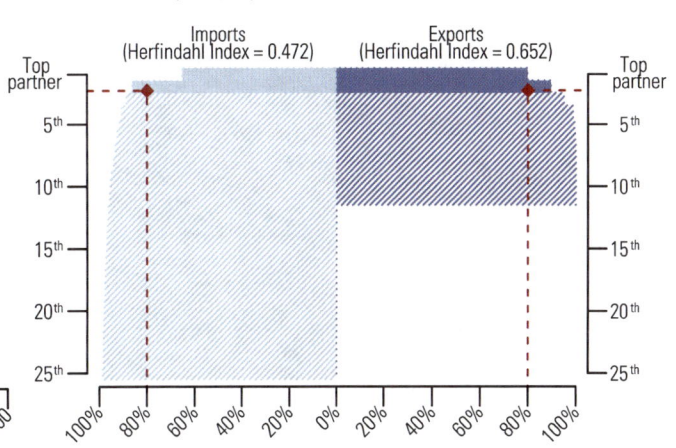

Imports (Herfindahl Index = 0.472)
Exports (Herfindahl Index = 0.652)

Graph 6: Imports of services by EBOPS category
(% share in 2006)

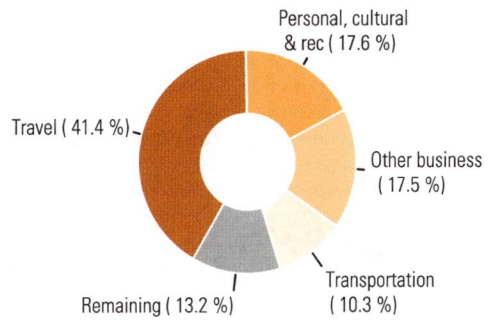

- Travel (41.4 %)
- Personal, cultural & rec (17.6 %)
- Other business (17.5 %)
- Transportation (10.3 %)
- Remaining (13.2 %)

Imports Profile:

"Food, animals + beverages, tobacco" (SITC section 0+1), "Mineral fuels, lubricants" (SITC section 3) and "Machinery and transport equipment" (SITC section 7) were the largest commodity groups for imports in 2014, representing respectively 22.6, 20.8 and 20.3 percent of imported goods (see table 3). From 2012 to 2014, the largest import commodity was "Petroleum oils, other than crude" (HS code 2710) (see table 4). The top three partners for merchandise imports were Denmark, Sweden and China, accounting for respectively 62.2, 21.9 and 2.6 percent of total imports. "Travel" (EBOPS code 236) accounted for the largest share of imports of services in 2006 at 130.4 mln US$, followed by "Personal, cultural, and recreational services" (EBOPS code 287) at 55.5 mln US$ and "Other business services" (EBOPS code 268) at 55.1 mln US$ (see graph 6).

Table 4: Top 10 import commodities 2012 to 2014

HS code	4-digit heading of Harmonized System 2012	Value 2012	Value 2013	Value 2014	Unit value 2012	Unit value 2013	Unit value 2014	Unit	SITC code
	All Commodities..	862.9	822.1	768.3					
2710	Petroleum oils, other than crude.......................................	216.4	195.5	159.4	1.2	1.1	1.0	US$/kg	334
9999	Commodities not specified according to kind......................	22.1	27.8	27.7					931
3004	Medicaments (excluding goods of heading 30.02, 30.05 or 30.06)........	14.5	17.7	17.8	88.4	63.8	63.6	US$/kg	542
8803	Parts of goods of heading 88.01 or 88.02...........................	21.0	13.0	14.5	639.0	438.4	486.3	US$/kg	792
9403	Other furniture and parts thereof......................................	15.9	13.6	11.8					821
8517	Electrical apparatus for line telephony or line telegraphy........	12.4	14.6	12.0					764
1905	Bread, pastry, cakes, biscuits and other bakers' wares............	12.3	12.8	12.9	5.5	5.8	5.8	US$/kg	048
8207	Interchangeable tools for hand tools, whether or not power-operated......	12.5	10.9	6.1	67.1	60.3	28.4	US$/kg	695
8708	Parts and accessories of the motor vehicles of headings 87.01 to 87.05........	10.6	8.7	7.4	20.1	24.0	23.3	US$/kg	784
0203	Meat of swine, fresh, chilled or frozen..............................	8.8	8.8	9.2	5.9	6.3	6.5	US$/kg	012

2014 International Trade Statistics Yearbook, Vol. I — Source: UN Comtrade and UN ServiceTrade

Guatemala

Goods Imports: CIF, by origin **Goods Exports:** FOB, by last known destination **Trade System:** General

Overview:

In 2014, the value of merchandise exports of Guatemala increased moderately by 8.2 percent to reach 10.9 bln US$, while its merchandise imports increased slightly by 4.3 percent to reach 18.3 bln US$ (see graph 1, table 2 and table 3). The merchandise trade balance recorded a moderate deficit of 7.4 bln US$ (see graph 1). The largest merchandise trade balance was with MDG Developed North America at -3.3 bln US$ (see graph 4). Merchandise exports in Guatemala were moderately concentrated amongst partners; imports were also moderately concentrated. The top 12 partners accounted for 80 percent or more of exports and 10 partners accounted for 80 percent or more of imports (see graph 5). In 2012, the value of exports of services of Guatemala increased slightly by 3.3 percent, reaching 2.3 bln US$, while its imports of services increased slightly by 0.3 percent and reached 2.4 bln US$ (see graph 2). There was a relatively small trade in services deficit of 52.0 mln US$.

Graph 1: Total merchandise trade, by value
(Bln US$ by year)

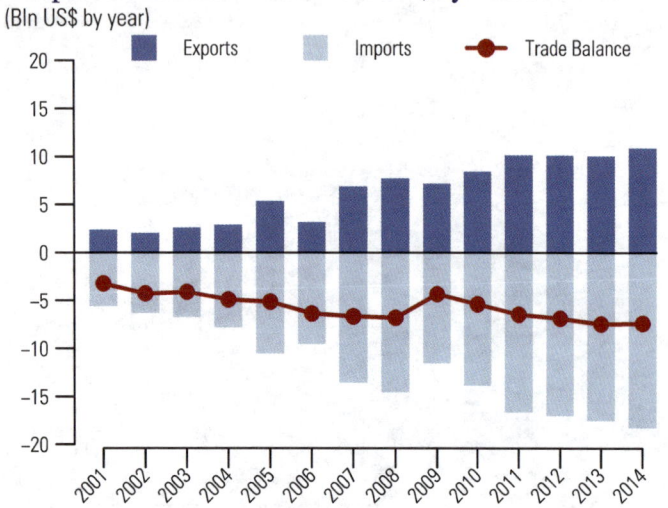

Graph 2: Total services trade, by value
(Bln US$ by year)

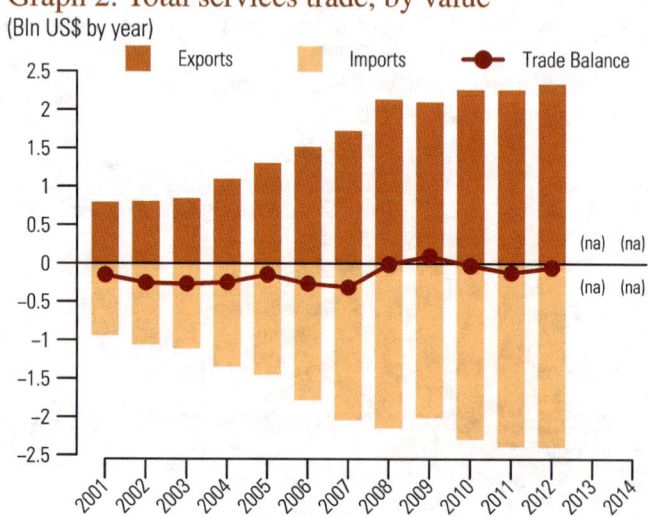

Exports Profile:

"Food, animals + beverages, tobacco" (SITC section 0+1), "Miscellaneous manufactured articles" (SITC section 8) and "Crude materials + anim. & veg. oils" (SITC section 2+4) were the largest commodity groups for exports in 2014, representing respectively 38.7, 16.1 and 14.9 percent of exported goods (see table 2). From 2012 to 2014, the largest export commodity was "Cane or beet sugar and chemically pure sucrose, in solid form" (HS code 1701) (see table 1). The top three destinations for merchandise exports were the United States, El Salvador and Honduras, accounting for respectively 38.5, 11.2 and 8.0 percent of total exports. "Travel" (EBOPS code 236) accounted for the largest share of exports of services in 2012 at 1.4 bln US$, followed by "Transportation" (EBOPS code 205) at 334.0 mln US$ and "Communications services" (EBOPS code 245) at 301.0 mln US$ (see graph 3).

Graph 3: Exports of services by EBOPS category
(% share in 2012)

- Travel (60.6 %)
- Transportation (14.3 %)
- Communication (12.9 %)
- Remaining (12.3 %)

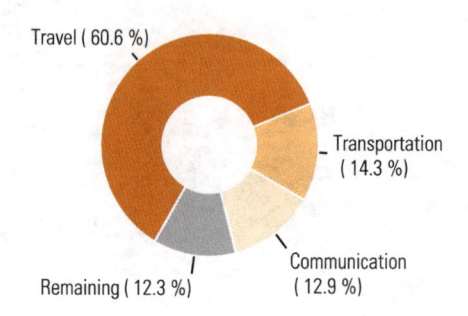

Table 1: Top 10 export commodities 2012 to 2014

HS code	4-digit heading of Harmonized System 2012	Value (million US$) 2012	2013	2014	Unit value 2012	2013	2014	Unit	SITC code
	All Commodities	10124.6	10065.3	10890.7					
1701	Cane or beet sugar and chemically pure sucrose, in solid form	793.3	941.9	952.2	0.5	0.5	0.4	US$/kg	061
0901	Coffee, whether or not roasted or decaffeinated	958.7	716.0	668.0	4.2	3.3	3.6	US$/kg	071
0803	Bananas, including plantains, fresh or dried	618.3	652.0	721.4	0.3	0.3	0.3	US$/kg	057
2616	Precious metal ores and concentrates	567.3	448.5	359.3	2.4	1.8	1.3	thsd US$/kg	289
6106	Women's or girls' blouses, shirts and shirt-blouses, knitted or crocheted	420.8	457.8	419.9		8.2	7.4	US$/unit	844
2709	Petroleum oils and oils obtained from bituminous minerals, crude	291.7	277.4	277.0	0.6	0.6	0.6	US$/kg	333
1511	Palm oil and its fractions	252.4	269.8	288.2	0.9	0.7	0.7	US$/kg	422
6105	Men's or boys' shirts, knitted or crocheted	256.6	264.2	263.7		10.3		US$/unit	843
4001	Natural rubber, balata, gutta-percha, guayule, chicle	294.2	238.8	182.3	2.9	2.3	1.7	US$/kg	231
0908	Nutmeg, mace and cardamoms	248.5	217.5	240.6	7.0	5.6	6.2	US$/kg	075

Source: UN Comtrade and UN ServiceTrade

Guatemala

Services Imports and Exports: EBOPS 2002 categories

Table 2: Merchandise exports by SITC
(Value in million US$, growth and shares in percentage)

SITC	2014	Avg. Growth rates 2010-2014	Avg. Growth rates 2013-2014	2014 share
Total	10890.7	6.5	8.2	100.0
0+1	4215.6	6.1	5.0	38.7
2+4	1626.8	9.6	19.7	14.9
3	712.5	16.8	53.7	6.5
5	1232.7	6.3	1.8	11.3
6	1059.0	5.6	10.2	9.7
7	232.9	-4.7	-8.8	2.1
8	1748.7	3.6	0.8	16.1
9	62.5	80.7	-5.3	0.6

Table 3: Merchandise imports by SITC
(Value in million US$, growth and shares in percentage)

SITC	2014	Avg. Growth rates 2010-2014	Avg. Growth rates 2013-2014	2014 share
Total	18263.2	7.2	4.3	100.0
0+1	2265.4	8.7	8.3	12.4
2+4	496.1	2.5	-2.8	2.7
3	3561.8	9.2	6.7	19.5
5	3128.6	6.8	2.9	17.1
6	3199.6	4.3	-0.2	17.5
7	4093.6	7.9	4.7	22.4
8	1476.5	7.3	8.9	8.1
9	41.5	31.3	-26.0	0.2

SITC Legend

SITC Code	Description
Total	All commodities
0+1	Food, animals + beverages, tobacco
2+4	Crude materials + anim. & veg. oils
3	Mineral fuels, lubricants
5	Chemicals
6	Goods classified chiefly by material
7	Machinery and transport equipment
8	Miscellaneous manufactured articles
9	Not classified elsewhere in the SITC

Graph 4: Merchandise trade balance
(Bln US$ by MDG Regions in 2014)

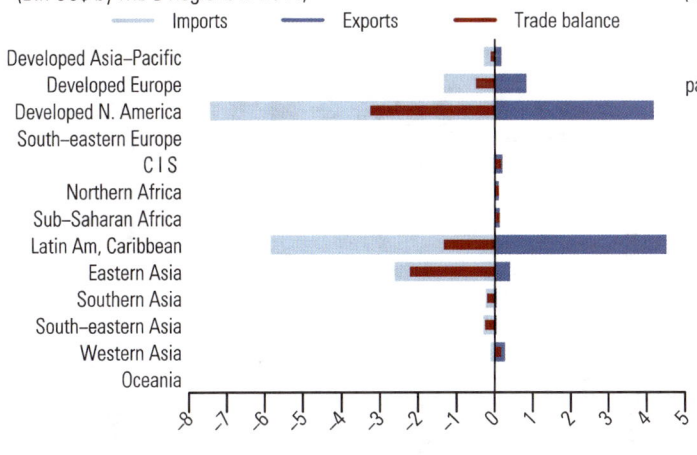

Graph 5: Partner concentration of merchandise trade
(Cumulative share by ranked partners in 2014)

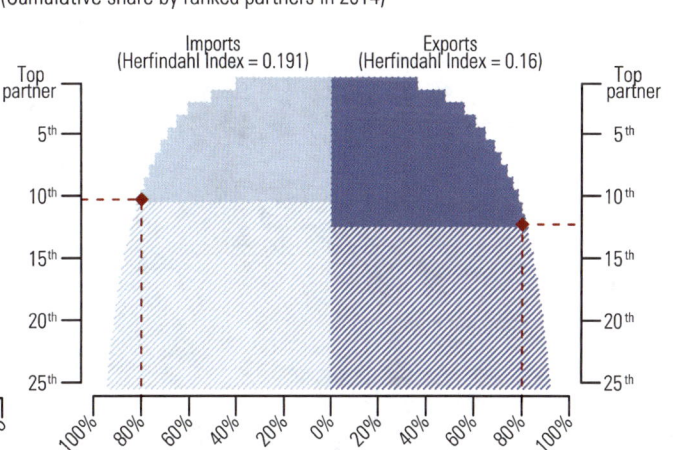

Imports (Herfindahl Index = 0.191)
Exports (Herfindahl Index = 0.16)

Graph 6: Imports of services by EBOPS category
(% share in 2012)

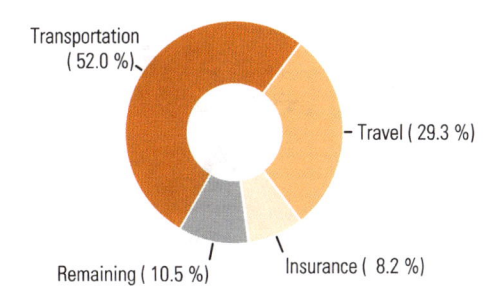

- Transportation (52.0 %)
- Travel (29.3 %)
- Insurance (8.2 %)
- Remaining (10.5 %)

Imports Profile:

"Machinery and transport equipment" (SITC section 7), "Mineral fuels, lubricants" (SITC section 3) and "Goods classified chiefly by material" (SITC section 6) were the largest commodity groups for imports in 2014, representing respectively 22.4, 19.5 and 17.5 percent of imported goods (see table 3). From 2012 to 2014, the largest import commodity was "Petroleum oils, other than crude" (HS code 2710) (see table 4). The top three partners for merchandise imports were the United States, Mexico and China, accounting for respectively 38.5, 10.9 and 8.5 percent of total imports. "Transportation" (EBOPS code 205) accounted for the largest share of imports of services in 2012 at 1.2 bln US$, followed by "Travel" (EBOPS code 236) at 702.0 mln US$ and "Insurance services" (EBOPS code 253) at 197.0 mln US$ (see graph 6).

Table 4: Top 10 import commodities 2012 to 2014

HS code	4-digit heading of Harmonized System 2012	Value 2012	Value 2013	Value 2014	Unit value 2012	Unit value 2013	Unit value 2014	Unit	SITC code
	All Commodities	16978.7	17504.0	18263.2					
2710	Petroleum oils, other than crude	2897.3	2868.1	2970.8	1.0	0.9	0.9	US$/kg	334
3004	Medicaments (excluding goods of heading 30.02, 30.05 or 30.06)	415.8	470.8	501.5	17.9	19.8	19.8	US$/kg	542
8517	Electrical apparatus for line telephony or line telegraphy	418.2	472.9	484.6					764
8703	Motor cars and other motor vehicles principally designed for the transport	414.8	392.7	458.2		18.3	17.9	thsd US$/unit	781
2711	Petroleum gases and other gaseous hydrocarbons	250.9	297.4	334.7	0.7	0.7	0.8	US$/kg	343
8704	Motor vehicles for the transport of goods	306.5	247.4	265.5					782
1005	Maize (corn)	223.7	205.8	212.6	0.3	0.3	0.2	US$/kg	044
3901	Polymers of ethylene, in primary forms	161.6	193.6	226.6	1.5	1.6	1.8	US$/kg	571
8471	Automatic data processing machines and units thereof	180.0	197.7	193.3					752
4804	Uncoated kraft paper and paperboard, in rolls or sheets	160.4	173.7	188.5	0.6	0.7	0.7	US$/kg	641

Source: UN Comtrade and UN ServiceTrade

Guyana

Goods Imports: CIF, by origin   **Goods Exports:** FOB, by last known destination   **Trade System:** Special

Overview:

In 2014, the value of merchandise exports of Guyana decreased substantially by 16.6 percent to reach 1.1 bln US$, while its merchandise imports decreased moderately by 6.5 percent to reach 1.7 bln US$ (see graph 1, table 2 and table 3). The merchandise trade balance recorded a moderate deficit of 597.4 mln US$ (see graph 1). The largest merchandise trade balance was with MDG Latin America and the Caribbean at -392.1 mln US$ (see graph 4). Merchandise exports in Guyana were diversified amongst partners; imports were also diversified. The top 11 partners accounted for 80 percent or more of exports and 11 partners accounted for 80 percent or more of imports (see graph 5). In 2013, the value of exports of services of Guyana decreased substantially by 44.7 percent, reaching 164.7 mln US$, while its imports of services decreased slightly by 4.9 percent and reached 500.3 mln US$ (see graph 2). There was a large trade in services deficit of 335.7 mln US$.

Graph 1: Total merchandise trade, by value
(Bln US$ by year)

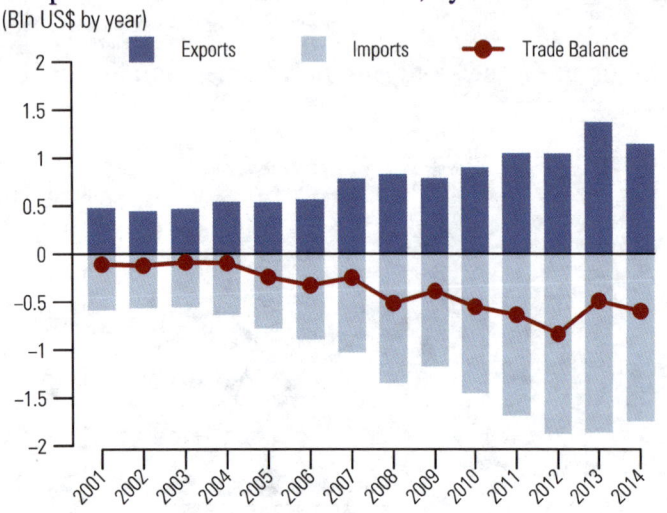

Graph 2: Total services trade, by value
(Mln US$ by year)

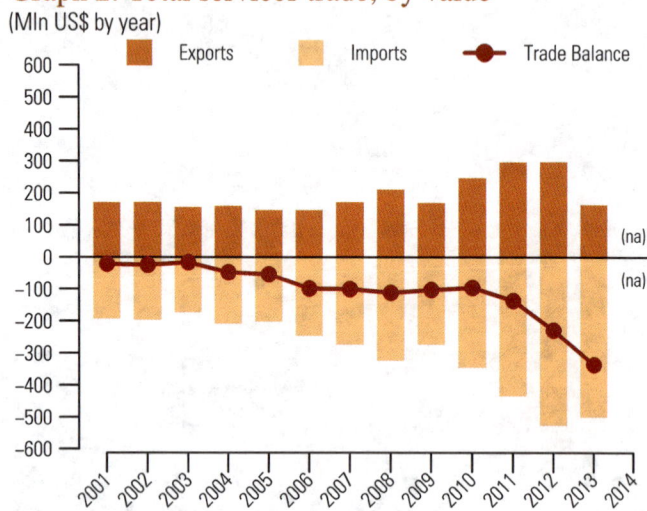

Exports Profile:

"Food, animals + beverages, tobacco" (SITC section 0+1), "Not classified elsewhere in the SITC" (SITC section 9) and "Crude materials + anim. & veg. oils" (SITC section 2+4) were the largest commodity groups for exports in 2014, representing respectively 49.3, 24.2 and 16.0 percent of exported goods (see table 2). From 2012 to 2014, the largest export commodity was "Gold (including gold plated with platinum)" (HS code 7108) (see table 1). The top three destinations for merchandise exports were the United States, Canada and the Bolivarian Republic of Venezuela, accounting for respectively 27.3, 16.7 and 11.8 percent of total exports. "Travel" (EBOPS code 236) accounted for the largest share of exports of services in 2013 at 76.8 mln US$, followed by "Other business services" (EBOPS code 268) at 34.7 mln US$ and "Transportation" (EBOPS code 205) at 23.1 mln US$ (see graph 3).

Graph 3: Exports of services by EBOPS category
(% share in 2013)

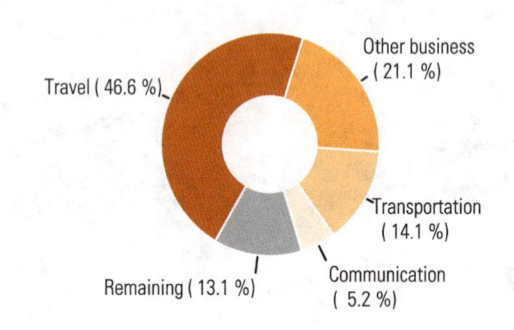

- Travel (46.6 %)
- Other business (21.1 %)
- Transportation (14.1 %)
- Communication (5.2 %)
- Remaining (13.1 %)

Table 1: Top 10 export commodities 2012 to 2014

HS code	4-digit heading of Harmonized System 2007	Value (million US$) 2012	2013	2014	Unit value 2012	2013	2014	Unit	SITC code
	All Commodities	1 045.3	1 375.9	1 147.5					
7108	Gold (including gold plated with platinum)	239.3	644.2	277.8	19.6	42.9	22.0	thsd US$/kg	971
1006	Rice	196.0	239.0	240.5	2.0	0.6	2.1	US$/kg	042
1701	Cane or beet sugar and chemically pure sucrose, in solid form	165.5	114.2	157.4	0.6	0.7	0.7	US$/kg	061
2606	Aluminium ores and concentrates	154.4	133.4	141.9	0.2	0.1	0.3	US$/kg	285
0306	Crustaceans, whether in shell or not	48.6	53.3	33.2	2.7	3.7	3.9	US$/kg	036
2208	Alcohol of a strength by volume of less than 80 % vol	41.3	42.9	48.8	*2.0*	2.1	*3.4*	US$/litre	112
8609	Containers (including containers for the transport of fluids)	44.0	...	41.5	*1.1*		*1.1*	thsd US$/unit	786
4407	Wood sawn or chipped lengthwise, sliced or peeled	15.5	14.0	15.0	*0.4*	0.0		US$/m³	248
0304	Fish fillets and other fish meat (whether or not minced)	16.2	16.4	10.9	3.4	3.5	2.1	US$/kg	034
4404	Hoopwood; split poles; piles, pickets and stakes of wood	12.5	8.7	17.4	0.0	0.2	0.0	US$/kg	634

Source: UN Comtrade and UN ServiceTrade

Guyana

Services Imports and Exports: EBOPS 2002 categories

Table 2: Merchandise exports by SITC
(Value in million US$, growth and shares in percentage)

SITC	2014	Avg. Growth rates 2010-2014	Avg. Growth rates 2013-2014	2014 share
Total	1 147.5	6.2	-16.6	100.0
0+1	566.3	12.4	10.4	49.3
2+4	183.5	4.9	9.2	16.0
3	0.0	3.8	-73.9	0.0
5	6.5	7.9	18.7	0.6
6	41.3	7.6	43.9	3.6
7	48.2	86.8	664.4	4.2
8	23.9	23.3	139.4	2.1
9	277.8	-5.2	-56.9	24.2

Table 3: Merchandise imports by SITC
(Value in million US$, growth and shares in percentage)

SITC	2014	Avg. Growth rates 2010-2014	Avg. Growth rates 2013-2014	2014 share
Total	1 744.9	4.7	-6.5	100.0
0+1	243.1	4.6	-4.8	13.9
2+4	30.7	7.8	11.1	1.8
3	537.3	5.5	-9.9	30.8
5	146.9	-2.1	-18.1	8.4
6	221.0	6.4	-1.5	12.7
7	432.1	5.3	-7.1	24.8
8	133.8	5.6	13.9	7.7
9	0.0	169.3	138.8	0.0

SITC Legend

SITC Code	Description
Total	All commodities
0+1	Food, animals + beverages, tobacco
2+4	Crude materials + anim. & veg. oils
3	Mineral fuels, lubricants
5	Chemicals
6	Goods classified chiefly by material
7	Machinery and transport equipment
8	Miscellaneous manufactured articles
9	Not classified elsewhere in the SITC

Graph 4: Merchandise trade balance
(Mln US$ by MDG Regions in 2014)

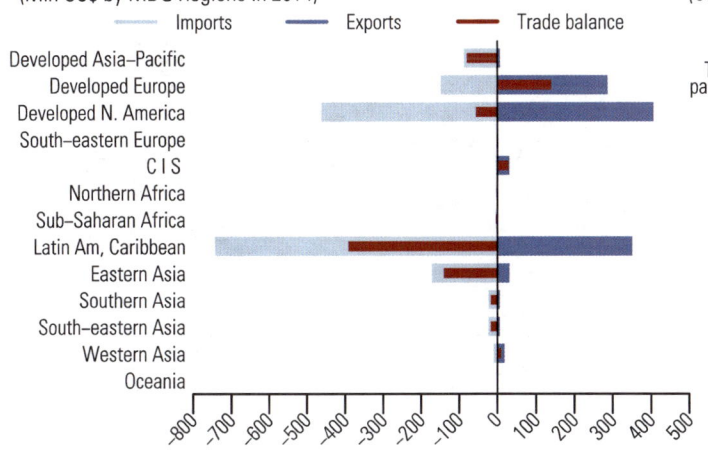

Graph 5: Partner concentration of merchandise trade
(Cumulative share by ranked partners in 2014)

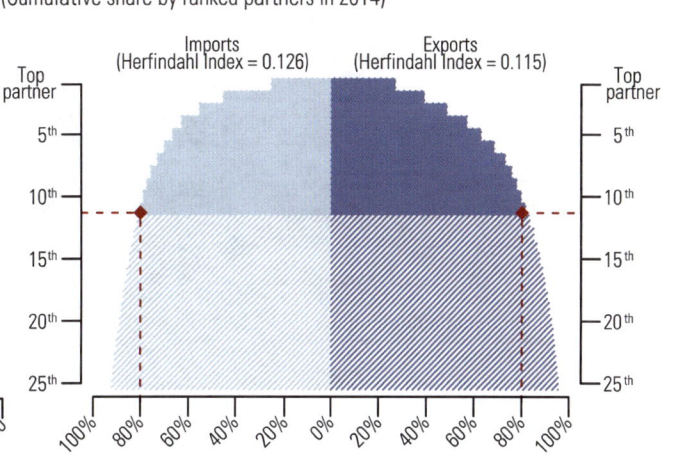

Imports (Herfindahl Index = 0.126)
Exports (Herfindahl Index = 0.115)

Graph 6: Imports of services by EBOPS category
(% share in 2013)

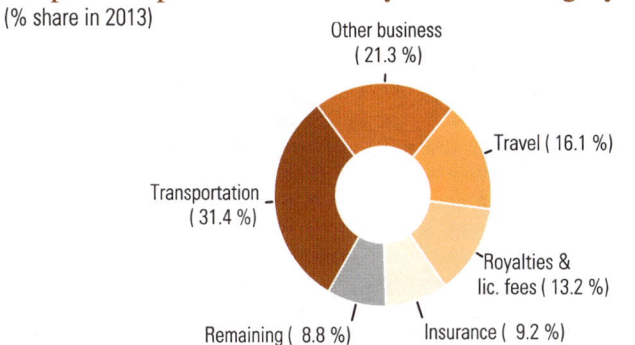

- Transportation (31.4 %)
- Other business (21.3 %)
- Travel (16.1 %)
- Royalties & lic. fees (13.2 %)
- Insurance (9.2 %)
- Remaining (8.8 %)

Imports Profile:

"Mineral fuels, lubricants" (SITC section 3), "Machinery and transport equipment" (SITC section 7) and "Food, animals + beverages, tobacco" (SITC section 0+1) were the largest commodity groups for imports in 2014, representing respectively 30.8, 24.8 and 13.9 percent of imported goods (see table 3). From 2012 to 2014, the largest import commodity was "Petroleum oils, other than crude" (HS code 2710) (see table 4). The top three partners for merchandise imports were the United States, Trinidad and Tobago and China, accounting for respectively 24.4, 18.0 and 9.0 percent of total imports. "Transportation" (EBOPS code 205) accounted for the largest share of imports of services in 2013 at 157.0 mln US$, followed by "Other business services" (EBOPS code 268) at 106.4 mln US$ and "Travel" (EBOPS code 236) at 80.5 mln US$ (see graph 6).

Table 4: Top 10 import commodities 2012 to 2014

HS code	4-digit heading of Harmonized System 2007	2012	2013	2014	2012	2013	2014	Unit	SITC code
	All Commodities	1 878.4	1 866.3	1 744.9					
2710	Petroleum oils, other than crude	473.2	561.1	516.2	2.4	0.7	2.4	US$/kg	334
8429	Self-propelled bulldozers, angledozers, graders, levellers, scrapers	78.2	51.9	42.1	81.9	74.0	42.5	thsd US$/unit	723
8703	Motor cars and other motor vehicles principally designed for the transport	48.4	43.6	41.6	5.1	4.6	6.0	thsd US$/unit	781
8704	Motor vehicles for the transport of goods	40.8	39.5	36.6	16.6	17.3	19.8	thsd US$/unit	782
0402	Milk and cream, concentrated or containing added sugar	34.4	33.8	24.4	3.1	5.9	3.5	US$/kg	022
2523	Portland cement, aluminous cement, slag cement	25.1	32.7	30.6	0.1	0.1	0.1	US$/kg	661
3102	Mineral or chemical fertilisers, nitrogenous	22.2	40.7	23.4	0.7	0.9	0.6	US$/kg	562
3004	Medicaments (excluding goods of heading 30.02, 30.05 or 30.06)	31.1	27.7	18.2	51.4	29.4	14.9	US$/kg	542
3923	Articles for the conveyance or packing of goods, of plastics	26.3	24.8	25.7	2.9	3.1	0.9	US$/kg	893
8471	Automatic data processing machines and units thereof	54.8	9.1	11.8	840.3	119.4	174.6	US$/unit	752

Source: UN Comtrade and UN ServiceTrade

Honduras

Goods Imports: CIF, by origin   **Goods Exports:** FOB, by last known destination   **Trade System:** Special

Overview:
In 2013, the value of merchandise exports of Honduras decreased substantially by 22.3 percent to reach 3.6 bln US$, while its merchandise imports decreased slightly by 0.9 percent to reach 8.6 bln US$ (see graph 1, table 2 and table 3). The merchandise trade balance recorded a large deficit of 4.9 bln US$ (see graph 1). The largest merchandise trade balance was with MDG Developed North America at -2.1 bln US$ (see graph 4). Merchandise exports in Honduras were moderately concentrated amongst partners; imports were also moderately concentrated. The top 10 partners accounted for 80 percent or more of exports and 10 partners accounted for 80 percent or more of imports (see graph 5). In 2013, the value of exports of services of Honduras increased moderately by 6.5 percent, reaching 1.1 bln US$, while its imports of services increased moderately by 8.4 percent and reached 1.6 bln US$ (see graph 2). There was a moderate trade in services deficit of 504.0 mln US$.

Graph 1: Total merchandise trade, by value
(Bln US$ by year)

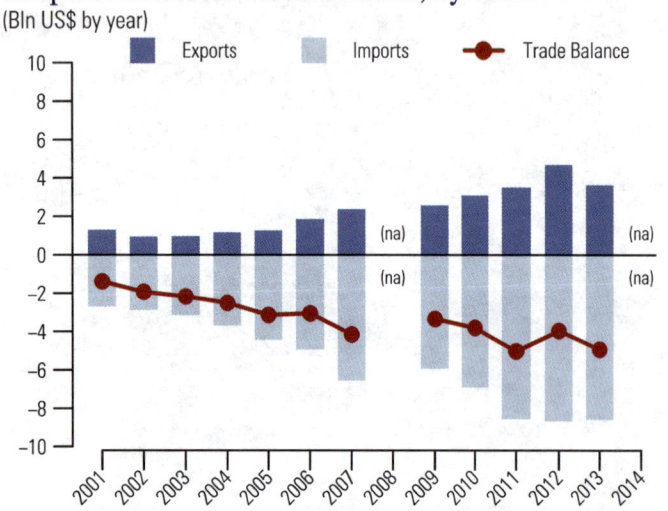

Graph 2: Total services trade, by value
(Bln US$ by year)

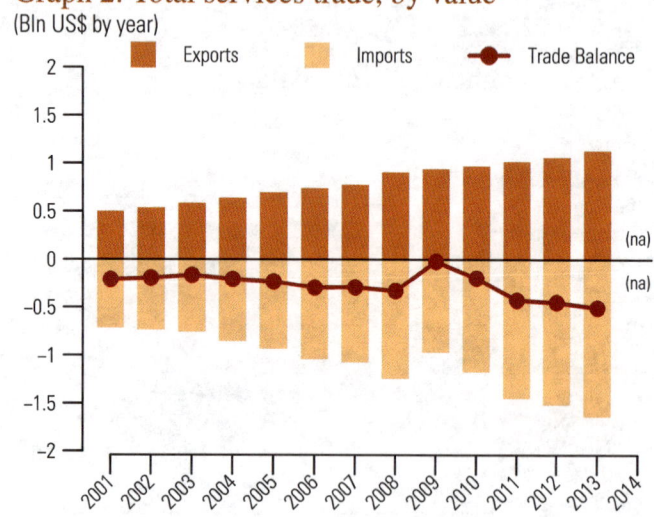

Exports Profile:
"Food, animals + beverages, tobacco" (SITC section 0+1), "Crude materials + anim. & veg. oils" (SITC section 2+4) and "Goods classified chiefly by material" (SITC section 6) were the largest commodity groups for exports in 2013, representing respectively 55.0, 12.2 and 11.5 percent of exported goods (see table 2). From 2011 to 2013, the largest export commodity was "Coffee, whether or not roasted or decaffeinated" (HS code 0901) (see table 1). The top three destinations for merchandise exports were the United States, Germany and El Salvador, accounting for respectively 39.8, 9.7 and 6.9 percent of total exports. "Travel" (EBOPS code 236) accounted for the largest share of exports of services in 2013 at 697.6 mln US$, followed by "Communications services" (EBOPS code 245) at 240.7 mln US$ and "Transportation" (EBOPS code 205) at 89.5 mln US$ (see graph 3).

Graph 3: Exports of services by EBOPS category
(% share in 2013)

- Travel (61.4 %)
- Communication (21.2 %)
- Transportation (7.9 %)
- Remaining (9.5 %)

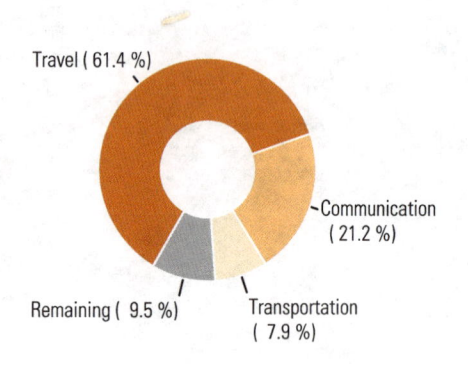

Table 1: Top 10 export commodities 2011 to 2013

HS code	4-digit heading of Harmonized System 2007	Value (million US$) 2011	2012	2013	Unit value 2011	2012	2013	Unit	SITC code
	All Commodities	3533.6	4696.2	3648.8					
0901	Coffee, whether or not roasted or decaffeinated	1266.8	1339.1	796.8	5.4	4.2		US$/kg	071
1511	Palm oil and its fractions	162.8	279.6	253.9	1.2	1.0	*1.1*	US$/kg	422
8544	Insulated (including enamelled or anodised) wire, cable	169.4	497.8	14.5	12.4	17.9		US$/kg	773
0306	Crustaceans, whether in shell or not	111.9	197.6	281.1	6.9	6.4	*9.4*	US$/kg	036
0803	Bananas, including plantains, fresh or dried	194.0	75.4	269.9	0.4	0.3	*0.6*	US$/kg	057
2711	Petroleum gases and other gaseous hydrocarbons	142.1	179.8	138.1	0.9	0.8		US$/kg	343
7108	Gold (including gold plated with platinum)	124.2	102.2	99.3	24.4	30.3	*49.6*	thsd US$/kg	971
7112	Waste and scrap of precious metal or of metal clad with precious metal	85.2	99.7	98.9	20.4	24.4		thsd US$/kg	289
3401	Soap; organic surface-active products	78.1	50.8	96.0	1.3	1.2	*2.0*	US$/kg	554
2402	Cigars, cheroots, cigarillos and cigarettes	62.6	99.5	51.7	11.0	11.2	*21.2*	US$/kg	122

Source: UN Comtrade and UN ServiceTrade

Honduras

Services Imports and Exports: EBOPS 2002 categories

Table 2: Merchandise exports by SITC
(Value in million US$, growth and shares in percentage)

SITC	2013	Avg. Growth rates 2009-2013	Avg. Growth rates 2012-2013	2013 share
Total	3 648.8	8.9	-22.3	100.0
0+1	2 007.8	12.4	-10.1	55.0
2+4	443.6	9.0	-15.6	12.2
3	140.5	-3.2	-23.5	3.8
5	274.8	17.4	22.7	7.5
6	420.8	34.5	50.3	11.5
7	33.6	-39.8	-95.3	0.9
8	77.8	-14.1	-61.6	2.1
9	250.0	7.1	-25.2	6.9

Table 3: Merchandise imports by SITC
(Value in million US$, growth and shares in percentage)

SITC	2013	Avg. Growth rates 2009-2013	Avg. Growth rates 2012-2013	2013 share
Total	8 566.1	9.7	-0.9	100.0
0+1	1 425.6	8.3	7.1	16.6
2+4	168.8	3.5	-19.5	2.0
3	2 216.2	17.9	1.6	25.9
5	1 376.3	7.6	-1.8	16.1
6	1 119.4	8.9	-2.5	13.1
7	1 591.8	5.8	-7.1	18.6
8	665.3	7.6	2.3	7.8
9	2.6	160.3	-75.3	0.0

SITC Legend

SITC Code	Description
Total	All commodities
0+1	Food, animals + beverages, tobacco
2+4	Crude materials + anim. & veg. oils
3	Mineral fuels, lubricants
5	Chemicals
6	Goods classified chiefly by material
7	Machinery and transport equipment
8	Miscellaneous manufactured articles
9	Not classified elsewhere in the SITC

Graph 4: Merchandise trade balance
(Bln US$ by MDG Regions in 2013)

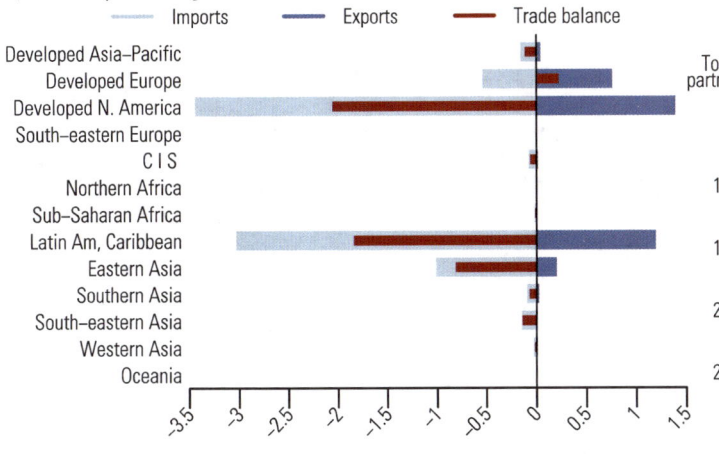

Graph 5: Partner concentration of merchandise trade
(Cumulative share by ranked partners in 2013)

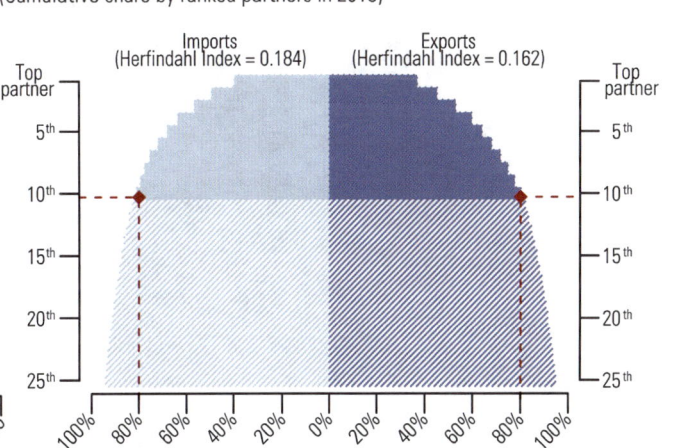

Imports (Herfindahl Index = 0.184) Exports (Herfindahl Index = 0.162)

Graph 6: Imports of services by EBOPS category
(% share in 2013)

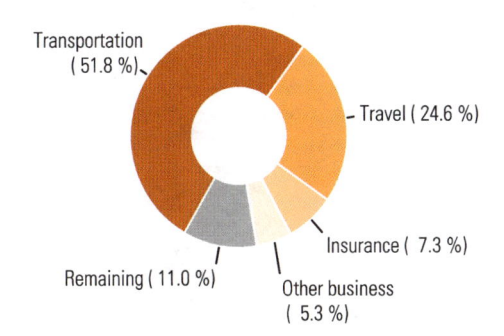

- Transportation (51.8 %)
- Travel (24.6 %)
- Insurance (7.3 %)
- Other business (5.3 %)
- Remaining (11.0 %)

Imports Profile:

"Mineral fuels, lubricants" (SITC section 3), "Machinery and transport equipment" (SITC section 7) and "Food, animals + beverages, tobacco" (SITC section 0+1) were the largest commodity groups for imports in 2013, representing respectively 25.9, 18.6 and 16.6 percent of imported goods (see table 3). From 2011 to 2013, the largest import commodity was "Petroleum oils, other than crude" (HS code 2710) (see table 4). The top three partners for merchandise imports were the United States, China and Mexico, accounting for respectively 41.2, 8.8 and 7.2 percent of total imports. "Transportation" (EBOPS code 205) accounted for the largest share of imports of services in 2013 at 850.2 mln US$, followed by "Travel" (EBOPS code 236) at 403.0 mln US$ and "Insurance services" (EBOPS code 253) at 120.0 mln US$ (see graph 6).

Table 4: Top 10 import commodities 2011 to 2013

HS code	4-digit heading of Harmonized System 2007	2011	2012	2013	2011	2012	2013	Unit	SITC code
	All Commodities	8541.8	8646.8	8566.1					
2710	Petroleum oils, other than crude	1987.4	2096.6	2156.5	1.2	1.3		US$/kg	334
3004	Medicaments (excluding goods of heading 30.02, 30.05 or 30.06)	407.4	392.4	341.8	38.4	40.6		US$/kg	542
8704	Motor vehicles for the transport of goods	165.5	195.0	158.4					782
8517	Electrical apparatus for line telephony or line telegraphy	152.0	157.9	173.1					764
8703	Motor cars and other motor vehicles principally designed for the transport	127.8	148.2	142.1		19.2	18.5	thsd US$/unit	781
1005	Maize (corn)	150.4	121.6	113.7	0.3	0.3		US$/kg	044
2106	Food preparations not elsewhere specified or included	106.5	132.0	145.2	3.5	4.3		US$/kg	098
8471	Automatic data processing machines and units thereof	101.7	108.9	116.9					752
4818	Toilet paper and similar paper	89.0	96.2	101.5	2.2	2.3	2.7	US$/kg	642
2304	Oil-cake and other solid residues	72.9	95.5	105.9	0.4	0.5	0.6	US$/kg	081

2014 International Trade Statistics Yearbook, Vol. I   Source: UN Comtrade and UN ServiceTrade

Hungary

Goods Imports: CIF, by consignment   **Goods Exports:** FOB, by last known destination   **Trade System:** Special

Overview:
In 2013, the value of merchandise exports of Hungary increased slightly by 4.6 percent to reach 107.7 bln US$, while its merchandise imports increased slightly by 4.7 percent to reach 98.7 bln US$ (see graph 1, table 2 and table 3). The merchandise trade balance recorded a relatively small surplus of 9.1 bln US$ (see graph 1). The largest merchandise trade balance was with MDG Developed Europe at 9.0 bln US$ (see graph 4). Merchandise exports in Hungary were diversified amongst partners; imports were also diversified. The top 16 partners accounted for 80 percent or more of exports and 14 partners accounted for 80 percent or more of imports (see graph 5). In 2013, the value of exports of services of Hungary increased substantially by 10.8 percent, reaching 22.6 bln US$, while its imports of services increased moderately by 7.4 percent and reached 17.2 bln US$ (see graph 2). There was a moderate trade in services surplus of 5.4 bln US$.

Graph 1: Total merchandise trade, by value
(Bln US$ by year)

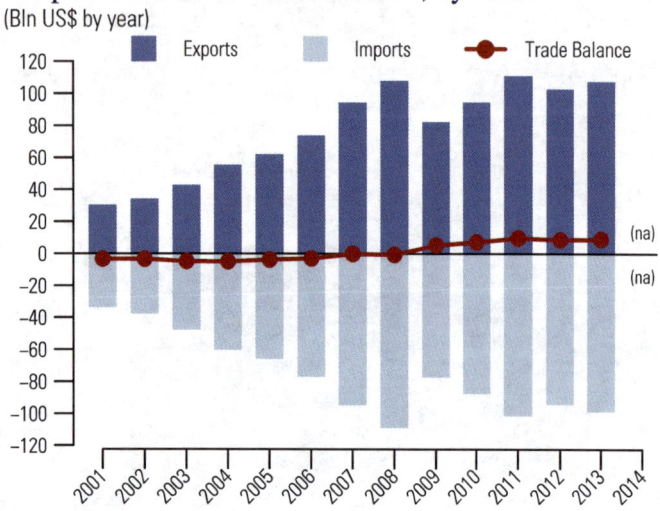

Graph 2: Total services trade, by value
(Bln US$ by year)

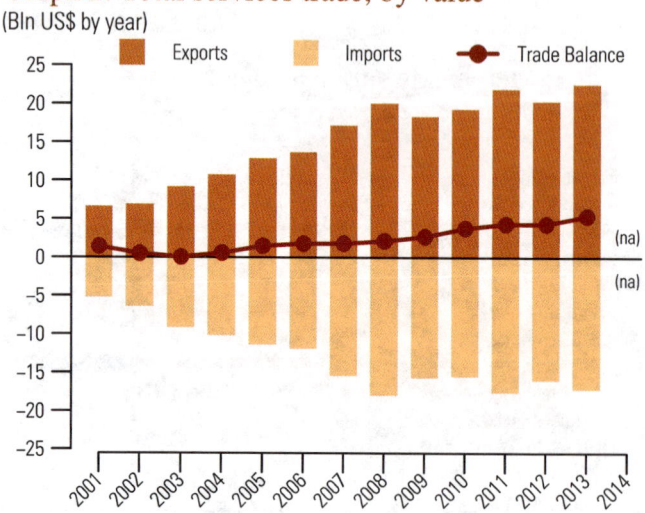

Exports Profile:
"Machinery and transport equipment" (SITC section 7), "Goods classified chiefly by material" (SITC section 6) and "Chemicals" (SITC section 5) were the largest commodity groups for exports in 2013, representing respectively 52.6, 10.7 and 10.5 percent of exported goods (see table 2). From 2011 to 2013, the largest export commodity was "Electrical apparatus for line telephony or line telegraphy" (HS code 8517) (see table 1). The top three destinations for merchandise exports were Germany, Romania and Slovakia, accounting for respectively 25.2, 5.9 and 5.7 percent of total exports. "Transportation" (EBOPS code 205) accounted for the largest share of exports of services in 2013 at 5.5 bln US$, followed by "Travel" (EBOPS code 236) at 5.5 bln US$ and "Other business services" (EBOPS code 268) at 4.4 bln US$ (see graph 3).

Graph 3: Exports of services by EBOPS category
(% share in 2013)

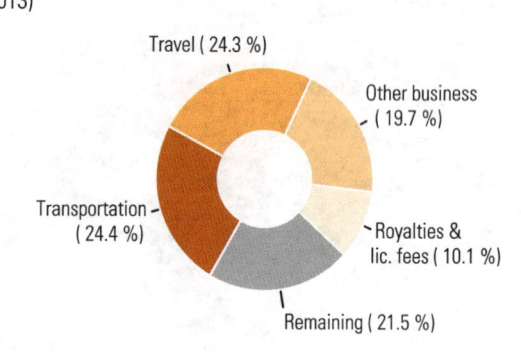

- Travel (24.3 %)
- Other business (19.7 %)
- Royalties & lic. fees (10.1 %)
- Remaining (21.5 %)
- Transportation (24.4 %)

Table 1: Top 10 export commodities 2011 to 2013

HS code	4-digit heading of Harmonized System 2007	Value (million US$) 2011	2012	2013	Unit value 2011	2012	2013	Unit	SITC code
	All Commodities	111 216.8	103 006.0	107 730.0					
8517	Electrical apparatus for line telephony or line telegraphy	12 116.3	7 029.6	5 938.0					764
8703	Motor cars and other motor vehicles principally designed for the transport	4 898.4	5 093.6	7 399.1			19.0	thsd US$/unit	781
8708	Parts and accessories of the motor vehicles of headings 87.01 to 87.05	4 217.5	3 855.3	4 576.0	10.2	8.9	9.6	US$/kg	784
9999	Commodities not specified according to kind	4 542.4	4 783.4	2 920.9					931
8528	Reception apparatus for television	4 219.8	3 830.3	3 149.2			265.9	US$/unit	761
3004	Medicaments (excluding goods of heading 30.02, 30.05 or 30.06)	3 687.4	3 648.3	3 852.1	109.5	121.1	124.7	US$/kg	542
8407	Spark-ignition reciprocating or rotary internal combustion piston engines	3 346.7	3 659.1	4 070.0			2.7	thsd US$/unit	713
8471	Automatic data processing machines and units thereof	2 987.8	2 928.8	3 014.7			464.9	US$/unit	752
8408	Compression-ignition internal combustion piston engines	2 700.5	2 244.0	2 444.5			3.3	thsd US$/unit	713
8544	Insulated (including enamelled or anodised) wire, cable	2 455.8	1 930.3	2 125.0	16.5	14.0	15.1	US$/kg	773

Hungary

Services Imports and Exports: EBOPS 2002 categories

Table 2: Merchandise exports by SITC
(Value in million US$, growth and shares in percentage)

SITC	2013	Avg. Growth rates 2010-2013	2012-2013	2013 share
Total	107730.0	4.4	4.6	100.0
0+1	8235.4	9.3	6.3	7.6
2+4	3139.8	12.5	-1.8	2.9
3	3894.5	15.7	-3.9	3.6
5	11365.1	11.8	11.0	10.5
6	11538.5	9.3	8.2	10.7
7	56625.6	1.3	6.6	52.6
8	9869.2	9.3	9.7	9.2
9	3061.7	-13.5	-38.4	2.8

Table 3: Merchandise imports by SITC
(Value in million US$, growth and shares in percentage)

SITC	2013	Avg. Growth rates 2010-2013	2012-2013	2013 share
Total	98661.8	4.1	4.7	100.0
0+1	4577.1	5.2	6.6	4.6
2+4	2194.4	8.0	6.2	2.2
3	12475.8	10.3	4.4	12.6
5	10850.8	8.0	6.0	11.0
6	13516.6	7.6	12.1	13.7
7	43120.7	2.4	10.0	43.7
8	6474.7	6.8	16.6	6.6
9	5451.7	-10.1	-38.9	5.5

SITC Legend

SITC Code	Description
Total	All commodities
0+1	Food, animals + beverages, tobacco
2+4	Crude materials + anim. & veg. oils
3	Mineral fuels, lubricants
5	Chemicals
6	Goods classified chiefly by material
7	Machinery and transport equipment
8	Miscellaneous manufactured articles
9	Not classified elsewhere in the SITC

Graph 4: Merchandise trade balance
(Bln US$ by MDG Regions in 2013)

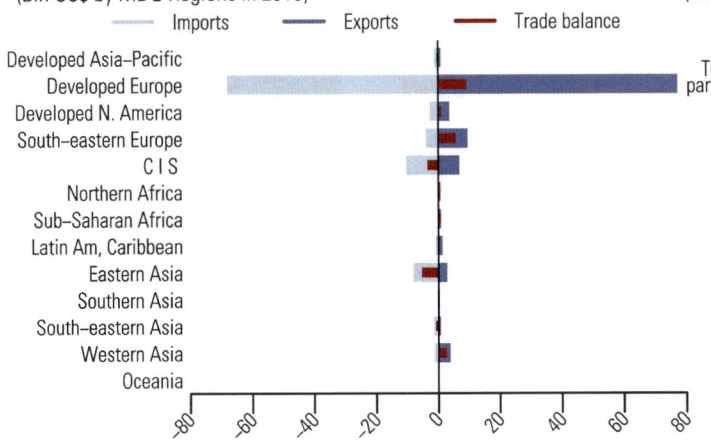

Graph 5: Partner concentration of merchandise trade
(Cumulative share by ranked partners in 2013)

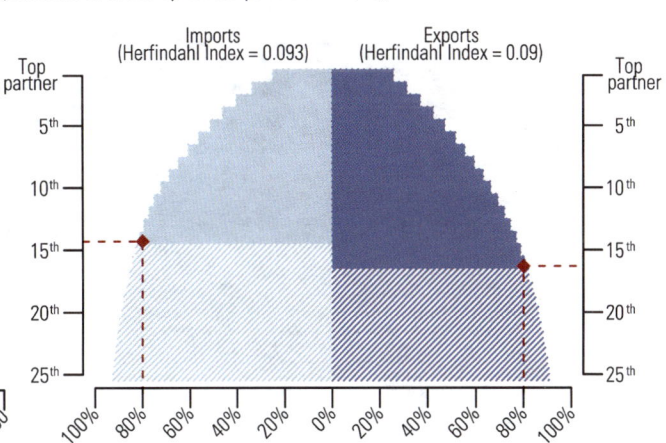

Imports (Herfindahl Index = 0.093)
Exports (Herfindahl Index = 0.09)

Graph 6: Imports of services by EBOPS category
(% share in 2013)

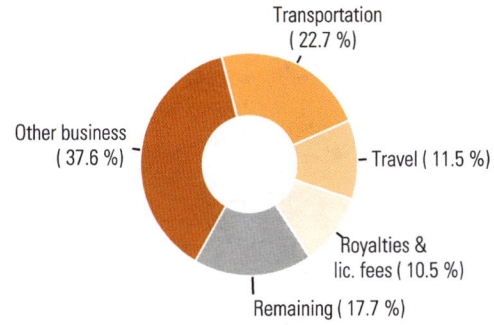

- Transportation (22.7%)
- Travel (11.5%)
- Royalties & lic. fees (10.5%)
- Remaining (17.7%)
- Other business (37.6%)

Imports Profile:

"Machinery and transport equipment" (SITC section 7), "Goods classified chiefly by material" (SITC section 6) and "Mineral fuels, lubricants" (SITC section 3) were the largest commodity groups for imports in 2013, representing respectively 43.7, 13.7 and 12.6 percent of imported goods (see table 3). From 2011 to 2013, the largest import commodity was "Commodities not specified according to kind" (HS code 9999) (see table 4). The top three partners for merchandise imports were Germany, the Russian Federation and Austria, accounting for respectively 24.5, 8.7 and 6.7 percent of total imports. "Other business services" (EBOPS code 268) accounted for the largest share of imports of services in 2013 at 6.4 bln US$, followed by "Transportation" (EBOPS code 205) at 3.9 bln US$ and "Travel" (EBOPS code 236) at 2.0 bln US$ (see graph 6).

Table 4: Top 10 import commodities 2011 to 2013

HS code	4-digit heading of Harmonized System 2007	Value (million US$) 2011	2012	2013	Unit value 2011	2012	2013	Unit	SITC code
	All Commodities	101370.0	94266.2	98661.8					
9999	Commodities not specified according to kind	7120.8	8827.2	5367.6					931
8517	Electrical apparatus for line telephony or line telegraphy	5841.5	5062.2	4908.0					764
2709	Petroleum oils and oils obtained from bituminous minerals, crude	4649.3	4395.2	4488.6	0.8	0.8	0.8	US$/kg	333
2711	Petroleum gases and other gaseous hydrocarbons	3478.5	3526.4	3884.7	0.6		0.6	US$/kg	343
8708	Parts and accessories of the motor vehicles of headings 87.01 to 87.05	2893.6	2587.3	3862.6	9.0	8.2	10.4	US$/kg	784
3004	Medicaments (excluding goods of heading 30.02, 30.05 or 30.06)	3054.0	2750.0	2672.7	86.0	81.7	74.4	US$/kg	542
8542	Electronic integrated circuits	3083.4	2178.8	2141.6					776
8529	Parts suitable for use with the apparatus of headings 85.25 to 85.28	2500.2	2506.2	2076.9	32.6	38.9	44.5	US$/kg	764
8409	Parts suitable for use with the engines of heading 84	2297.7	2149.6	2342.6		9.2	9.3	US$/kg	713
2710	Petroleum oils, other than crude	2207.6	2042.5	2263.4	1.0	1.0	1.0	US$/kg	334

2014 International Trade Statistics Yearbook, Vol. I   Source: UN Comtrade and UN ServiceTrade

Iceland

Goods Imports: CIF, by origin | **Goods Exports: FOB, by last known destination** | **Trade System: Special**

Overview:
In 2014, the value of merchandise exports of Iceland increased slightly by 0.5 percent to reach 5.0 bln US$, while its merchandise imports increased moderately by 6.7 percent to reach 5.4 bln US$ (see graph 1, table 2 and table 3). The merchandise trade balance recorded a relatively small deficit of 334.8 mln US$ (see graph 1). The largest merchandise trade balance was with MDG Developed Europe at 521.1 mln US$ (see graph 4). Merchandise exports in Iceland were diversified amongst partners; imports were also diversified. The top 12 partners accounted for 80 percent or more of exports and 15 partners accounted for 80 percent or more of imports (see graph 5). In 2012, the value of exports of services of Iceland increased slightly by 1.3 percent, reaching 3.0 bln US$, while its imports of services increased moderately by 7.1 percent and reached 2.8 bln US$ (see graph 2). There was a relatively small trade in services surplus of 210.4 mln US$.

Graph 1: Total merchandise trade, by value
(Bln US$ by year)

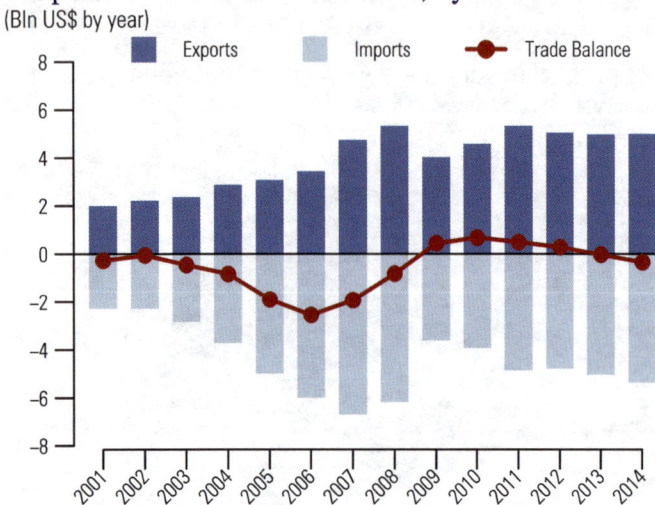

Graph 2: Total services trade, by value
(Bln US$ by year)

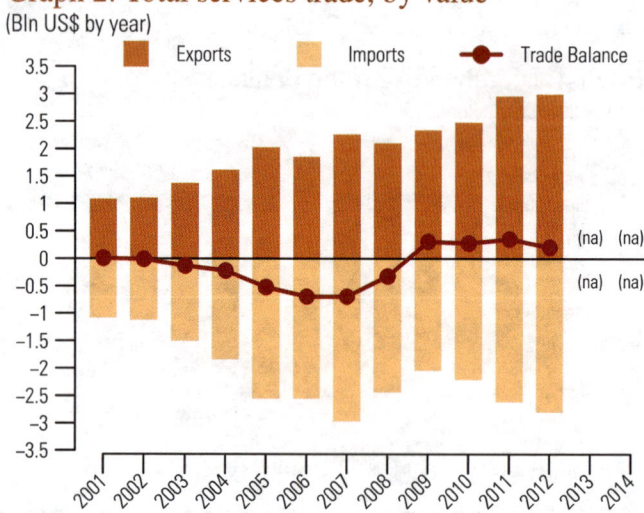

Exports Profile:
"Goods classified chiefly by material" (SITC section 6), "Food, animals + beverages, tobacco" (SITC section 0+1) and "Machinery and transport equipment" (SITC section 7) were the largest commodity groups for exports in 2014, representing respectively 42.2, 41.7 and 5.8 percent of exported goods (see table 2). From 2012 to 2014, the largest export commodity was "Unwrought aluminium" (HS code 7601) (see table 1). The top three destinations for merchandise exports were the Netherlands, Germany and the United Kingdom, accounting for respectively 29.8, 10.4 and 10.2 percent of total exports. "Transportation" (EBOPS code 205) accounted for the largest share of exports of services in 2012 at 1.4 bln US$, followed by "Travel" (EBOPS code 236) at 854.5 mln US$ (see graph 3).

Graph 3: Exports of services by EBOPS category
(% share in 2012)

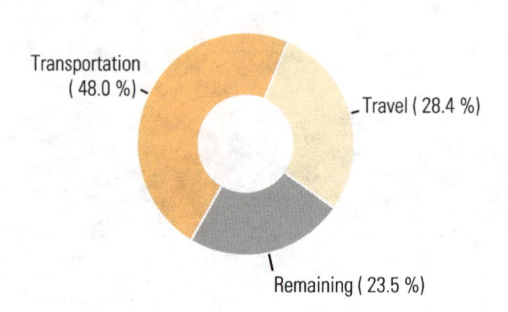

- Transportation (48.0 %)
- Travel (28.4 %)
- Remaining (23.5 %)

Table 1: Top 10 export commodities 2012 to 2014

HS code	4-digit heading of Harmonized System 2012	Value (million US$) 2012	2013	2014	Unit value 2012	2013	2014	Unit	SITC code
	All Commodities	5063.4	4997.7	5020.5					
7601	Unwrought aluminium	1746.0	1665.1	1502.5	2.2	2.1	2.1	US$/kg	684
0304	Fish fillets and other fish meat (whether or not minced)	814.8	847.2	834.0	5.0	5.1	5.5	US$/kg	034
0303	Fish, frozen, excluding fish fillets and other fish meat of heading 03.04	475.4	524.1	448.2	1.8	1.8	1.9	US$/kg	034
0305	Fish, dried, salted or in brine	364.7	334.7	354.6	5.8	5.0	5.3	US$/kg	035
2301	Flours, meals and pellets, of meat or meat offal	178.3	217.9	136.1	1.5	1.8	1.7	US$/kg	081
7202	Ferro-alloys	173.4	163.8	156.5	1.3	1.3	1.4	US$/kg	671
1504	Fats and oils and their fractions, of fish or marine mammals	117.1	135.5	90.9	2.0	2.3	2.5	US$/kg	411
7605	Aluminium wire	54.9	96.0	173.4	2.2	2.2	2.3	US$/kg	684
2710	Petroleum oils, other than crude	101.9	79.9	99.5	0.9	0.9	0.9	US$/kg	334
3004	Medicaments (excluding goods of heading 30.02, 30.05 or 30.06)	113.6	87.6	78.1	108.1	92.7	98.8	US$/kg	542

Source: UN Comtrade and UN ServiceTrade

Iceland

Services Imports and Exports: EBOPS 2002 categories

Table 2: Merchandise exports by SITC
(Value in million US$, growth and shares in percentage)

SITC	2014	Avg. Growth rates 2010-2014	Avg. Growth rates 2013-2014	2014 share
Total	5 020.5	2.2	0.5	100.0
0+1	2 095.6	3.4	-5.2	41.7
2+4	164.3	6.3	-23.9	3.3
3	99.7	20.5	24.7	2.0
5	108.4	-9.6	-8.8	2.2
6	2 119.3	0.3	3.1	42.2
7	289.3	6.4	48.2	5.8
8	112.9	3.3	12.2	2.2
9	31.0	13.1	38.0	0.6

Table 3: Merchandise imports by SITC
(Value in million US$, growth and shares in percentage)

SITC	2014	Avg. Growth rates 2010-2014	Avg. Growth rates 2013-2014	2014 share
Total	5 355.3	8.2	6.7	100.0
0+1	534.9	7.0	12.9	10.0
2+4	621.0	0.1	-4.3	11.6
3	913.1	15.6	-4.5	17.1
5	489.2	5.4	7.8	9.1
6	576.6	5.7	7.2	10.8
7	1 667.9	11.8	16.0	31.1
8	546.2	5.1	8.3	10.2
9	6.4	14.3	-0.1	0.1

SITC Legend

SITC Code	Description
Total	All commodities
0+1	Food, animals + beverages, tobacco
2+4	Crude materials + anim. & veg. oils
3	Mineral fuels, lubricants
5	Chemicals
6	Goods classified chiefly by material
7	Machinery and transport equipment
8	Miscellaneous manufactured articles
9	Not classified elsewhere in the SITC

Graph 4: Merchandise trade balance
(Bln US$ by MDG Regions in 2014)

Graph 5: Partner concentration of merchandise trade
(Cumulative share by ranked partners in 2014)

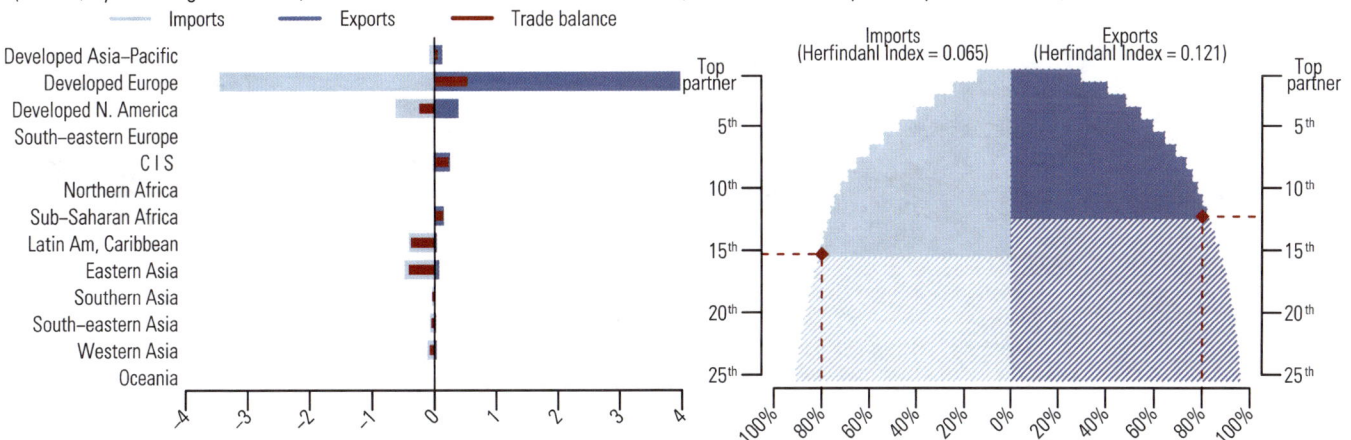

Imports (Herfindahl Index = 0.065)
Exports (Herfindahl Index = 0.121)

Graph 6: Imports of services by EBOPS category
(% share in 2012)

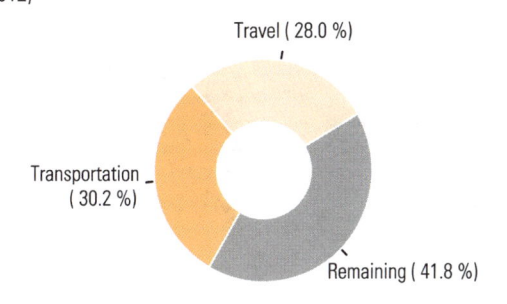

- Travel (28.0 %)
- Transportation (30.2 %)
- Remaining (41.8 %)

Imports Profile:
"Machinery and transport equipment" (SITC section 7), "Mineral fuels, lubricants" (SITC section 3) and "Crude materials + anim. & veg. oils" (SITC section 2+4) were the largest commodity groups for imports in 2014, representing respectively 31.1, 17.1 and 11.6 percent of imported goods (see table 3). From 2012 to 2014, the largest import commodity was "Petroleum oils, other than crude" (HS code 2710) (see table 4). The top three partners for merchandise imports were Norway, the United States and Germany, accounting for respectively 15.4, 10.0 and 8.2 percent of total imports. "Transportation" (EBOPS code 205) accounted for the largest share of imports of services in 2012 at 845.5 mln US$, followed by "Travel" (EBOPS code 236) at 782.6 mln US$ (see graph 6).

Table 4: Top 10 import commodities 2012 to 2014

HS code	4-digit heading of Harmonized System 2012	Value 2012	Value 2013	Value 2014	Unit value 2012	Unit value 2013	Unit value 2014	Unit	SITC code
	All Commodities	4 771.9	5 019.2	5 355.3					
2710	Petroleum oils, other than crude	663.4	896.0	873.3	1.0	1.0	0.9	US$/kg	334
2818	Artificial corundum, whether or not chemically defined	508.3	502.6	494.1	0.3	0.3	0.3	US$/kg	522
8545	Carbon electrodes, carbon brushes, lamp carbons, battery carbons	361.8	365.9	369.8	0.9	0.8	0.8	US$/kg	778
8703	Motor cars and other motor vehicles principally designed for the transport	177.7	156.2	216.2	198.2	190.5	195.4	US$/unit	781
3004	Medicaments (excluding goods of heading 30.02, 30.05 or 30.06)	118.8	124.3	129.3	126.2	134.1	138.9	US$/kg	542
8471	Automatic data processing machines and units thereof	70.6	88.4	105.6					752
8802	Other aircraft (for example, helicopters, aeroplanes); spacecraft	147.7	39.4	46.4	77.7	35.8		thsd US$/unit	792
8517	Electrical apparatus for line telephony or line telegraphy	55.0	76.3	92.0					764
8902	Fishing vessels; factory ships and other vessels for processing	80.3	26.9	73.4	66.9	29.8	91.8	thsd US$/unit	793
7607	Aluminium foil (whether or not printed or backed with paper, paperboard	49.6	62.6	59.5	26.7	28.1	27.1	US$/kg	684

India

Goods Imports: CIF, by origin **Goods Exports:** FOB, by last known destination **Trade System:** General

Overview:

In 2014, the value of merchandise exports of India decreased moderately by 5.7 percent to reach 317.5 bln US$, while its merchandise imports decreased slightly by 1.4 percent to reach 459.4 bln US$ (see graph 1, table 2 and table 3). After a reduction in the merchandise trade deficit in 2013, the deficit increased to 141.8 bln US$ in 2014, mainly as a result of decreasing exports (see graph 1). The largest merchandise trade balance was with MDG Western Asia at -50.1 bln US$ (see graph 4). Merchandise exports in India were diversified amongst partners; imports were also diversified. The top 31 partners accounted for 80 percent or more of exports and 24 partners accounted for 80 percent or more of imports (see graph 5). In 2013, the value of exports of services of India increased slightly by 2.1 percent, reaching 148.6 bln US$, while its imports of services decreased slightly by 2.0 percent and reached 78.3 bln US$ (see graph 2). The trade in services surplus increased for the fourth consecutive year, resulting in a large surplus of 70.3 bln US$.

Graph 1: Total merchandise trade, by value
(Bln US$ by year)

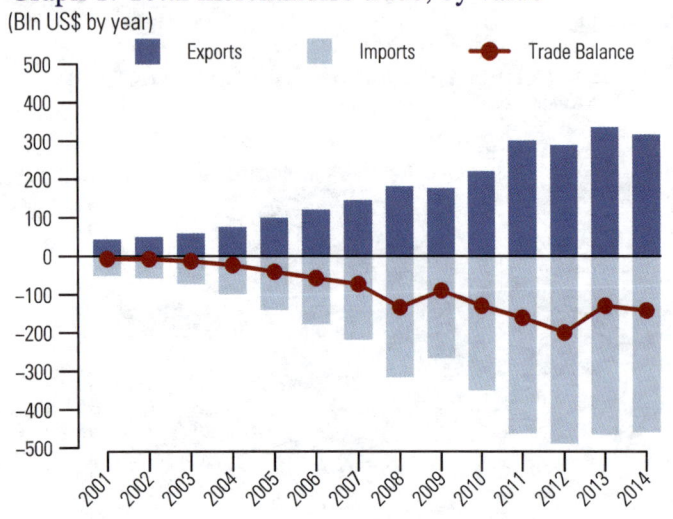

Graph 2: Total services trade, by value
(Bln US$ by year)

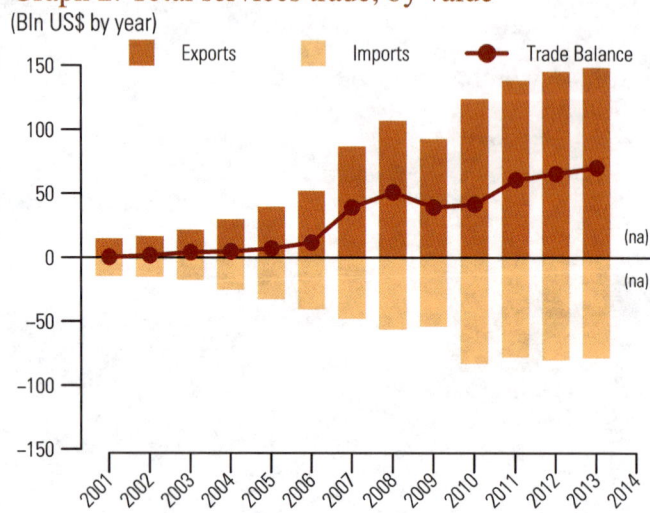

Exports Profile:

"Goods classified chiefly by material" (SITC section 6), "Mineral fuels, lubricants" (SITC section 3) and "Machinery and transport equipment" (SITC section 7) were the largest commodity groups for exports in 2014, representing respectively 24.2, 19.6 and 15.3 percent of exported goods (see table 2). From 2012 to 2014, the largest export commodity was "Petroleum oils, other than crude" (HS code 2710) (see table 1). The top three destinations for merchandise exports were the United States, the United Arab Emirates and China, accounting for respectively 12.9, 10.9 and 4.7 percent of total exports. "Computer and information services" (EBOPS code 262) accounted for the largest share of exports of services in 2013 at 68.8 bln US$, followed by "Other business services" (EBOPS code 268) at 28.5 bln US$ and "Travel" (EBOPS code 236) at 18.4 bln US$ (see graph 3). India was the world's largest exporter of "computer and information services" in 2013.

Graph 3: Exports of services by EBOPS category
(% share in 2013)

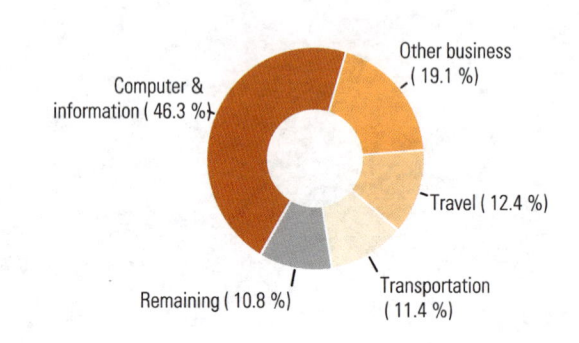

- Computer & information (46.3 %)
- Other business (19.1 %)
- Travel (12.4 %)
- Transportation (11.4 %)
- Remaining (10.8 %)

Table 1: Top 10 export commodities 2012 to 2014

HS code	4-digit heading of Harmonized System 2007	Value (million US$) 2012	2013	2014	Unit value 2012	2013	2014	Unit	SITC code
	All Commodities	289 564.8	336 611.4	317 544.6					
2710	Petroleum oils, other than crude	52 763.9	67 075.2	60 838.6	0.9		0.9	US$/kg	334
7102	Diamonds, whether or not worked, but not mounted or set	22 353.5	28 952.1	24 064.5	367.2			US$/carat	667
7113	Articles of jewellery and parts thereof, of precious metal	18 201.6	10 603.3	13 087.6	25.3			thsd US$/kg	897
3004	Medicaments (excluding goods of heading 30.02, 30.05 or 30.06)	8 404.5	10 314.0	10 302.7	26.1	26.4	26.7	US$/kg	542
1006	Rice	6 128.0	8 169.5	7 905.7	0.6	0.7	0.7	US$/kg	042
8703	Motor cars and other motor vehicles principally designed for the transport	4 238.2	5 556.5	5 769.0	2.1	5.5	5.5	thsd US$/unit	781
0202	Meat of bovine animals, frozen	2 962.6	4 411.0	4 719.1	2.9	2.9	3.2	US$/kg	011
5205	Cotton yarn (other than sewing thread), containing 85 % or more	3 155.2	4 773.1	4 095.4	3.4	3.5	3.3	US$/kg	651
1302	Vegetable saps and extracts; pectic substances	6 414.7	2 915.8	2 216.2	9.9	4.2	2.7	US$/kg	292
8708	Parts and accessories of the motor vehicles of headings 87.01 to 87.05	3 515.1	3 912.8	4 001.3	5.5	5.9	5.7	US$/kg	784

Source: UN Comtrade and UN ServiceTrade

India

Services Imports and Exports: EBOPS 2002 categories

Table 2: Merchandise exports by SITC
(Value in million US$, growth and shares in percentage)

SITC	2014	Avg. Growth rates 2010-2014	Avg. Growth rates 2013-2014	2014 share
Total	317 544.6	9.6	-5.7	100.0
0+1	33 158.2	19.1	-5.0	10.4
2+4	13 781.0	-4.0	-19.8	4.3
3	62 347.0	13.2	-10.4	19.6
5	37 117.7	12.0	-5.9	11.7
6	76 837.5	5.3	-7.5	24.2
7	48 578.9	11.1	5.4	15.3
8	42 297.3	11.7	8.6	13.3
9	3 427.2	-7.0	-54.2	1.1

Table 3: Merchandise imports by SITC
(Value in million US$, growth and shares in percentage)

SITC	2014	Avg. Growth rates 2010-2014	Avg. Growth rates 2013-2014	2014 share
Total	459 369.5	7.0	-1.4	100.0
0+1	8 036.6	9.4	22.9	1.7
2+4	35 644.4	10.9	2.3	7.8
3	176 925.4	12.4	-3.9	38.5
5	48 052.0	8.7	7.8	10.5
6	59 539.2	2.3	4.3	13.0
7	74 776.5	4.1	-1.5	16.3
8	14 756.2	9.3	7.8	3.2
9	41 639.3	-3.1	-15.4	9.1

SITC Legend

SITC Code	Description
Total	All commodities
0+1	Food, animals + beverages, tobacco
2+4	Crude materials + anim. & veg. oils
3	Mineral fuels, lubricants
5	Chemicals
6	Goods classified chiefly by material
7	Machinery and transport equipment
8	Miscellaneous manufactured articles
9	Not classified elsewhere in the SITC

Graph 4: Merchandise trade balance
(Bln US$ by MDG Regions in 2014)

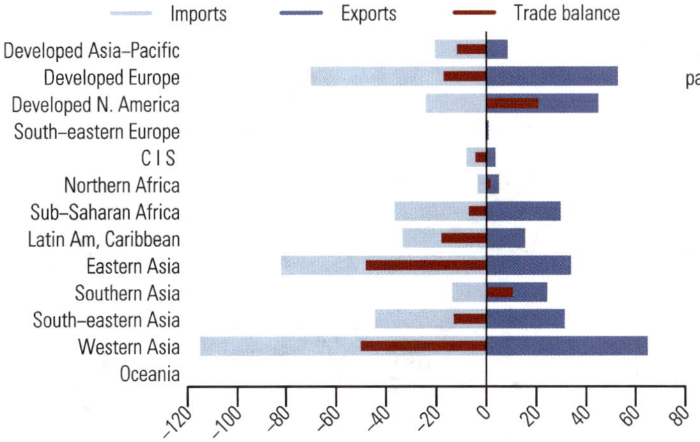

Graph 5: Partner concentration of merchandise trade
(Cumulative share by ranked partners in 2014)

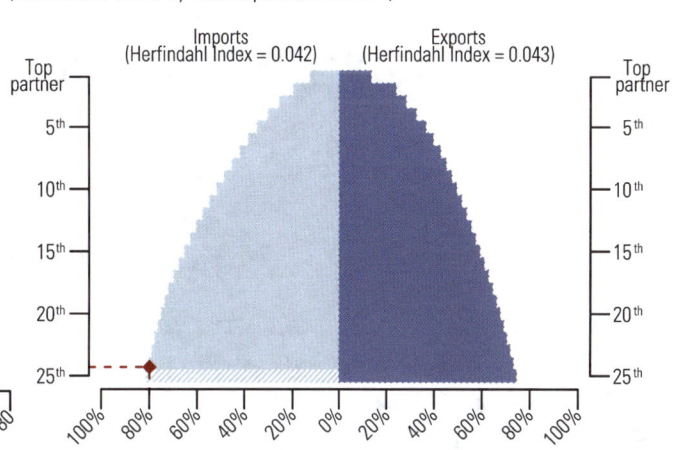

Imports (Herfindahl Index = 0.042)
Exports (Herfindahl Index = 0.043)

Graph 6: Imports of services by EBOPS category
(% share in 2013)

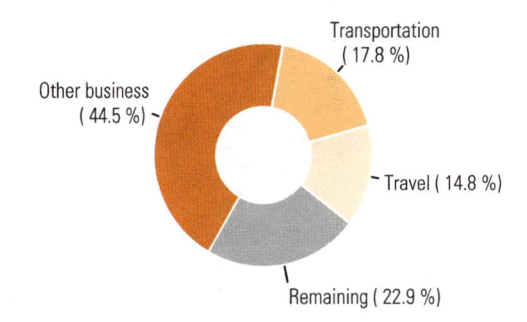

- Transportation (17.8 %)
- Other business (44.5 %)
- Travel (14.8 %)
- Remaining (22.9 %)

Imports Profile:

"Mineral fuels, lubricants" (SITC section 3), "Machinery and transport equipment" (SITC section 7) and "Goods classified chiefly by material" (SITC section 6) were the largest commodity groups for imports in 2014, representing respectively 38.5, 16.3 and 13.0 percent of imported goods (see table 3). From 2012 to 2014, the largest import commodity was "Petroleum oils and oils obtained from bituminous minerals, crude" (HS code 2709) (see table 4). The top three partners for merchandise imports were China, Saudi Arabia and the United Arab Emirates, accounting for respectively 11.6, 7.2 and 6.9 percent of total imports. "Other business services" (EBOPS code 268) accounted for the largest share of imports of services in 2013 at 34.9 bln US$, followed by "Transportation" (EBOPS code 205) at 14.0 bln US$ and "Travel" (EBOPS code 236) at 11.6 bln US$ (see graph 6).

Table 4: Top 10 import commodities 2012 to 2014

HS code	4-digit heading of Harmonized System 2007	Value (million US$) 2012	2013	2014	Unit value 2012	2013	2014	Unit	SITC code
	All Commodities	488 976.4	466 045.6	459 369.5					
2709	Petroleum oils and oils obtained from bituminous minerals, crude	148 757.0	148 046.7	135 826.2	0.8	0.8	0.7	US$/kg	333
7108	Gold (including gold plated with platinum)	52 606.8	37 711.8	31 039.7	53.5	45.1		thsd US$/kg	971
7102	Diamonds, whether or not worked, but not mounted or set	20 882.5	22 649.6	21 609.7	146.5			US$/carat	667
2701	Coal; briquettes, ovoids and similar solid fuels manufactured from coal	15 148.0	14 931.2	16 395.3	0.1	0.1	0.1	US$/kg	321
2711	Petroleum gases and other gaseous hydrocarbons	14 006.9	14 272.7	17 627.2	0.7	0.7	0.8	US$/kg	343
9999	Commodities not specified according to kind	12 031.3	11 504.7	10 599.3					931
8517	Electrical apparatus for line telephony or line telegraphy	9 586.9	10 916.4	13 432.3					764
1511	Palm oil and its fractions	7 896.4	6 966.8	6 551.4	1.0	0.8	0.8	US$/kg	422
2603	Copper ores and concentrates	4 884.5	7 443.4	5 320.2	2.5	2.5	2.7	US$/kg	283
2710	Petroleum oils, other than crude	5 172.4	4 419.4	4 203.1	1.0		0.9	US$/kg	334

Indonesia

Goods Imports: CIF, by origin   **Goods Exports:** FOB, by last known destination   **Trade System:** General

Overview:
In 2013, the value of merchandise exports of Indonesia decreased slightly by 3.9 percent to reach 182.6 bln US$, while its merchandise imports decreased slightly by 2.6 percent to reach 186.6 bln US$ (see graph 1, table 2 and table 3). The merchandise trade balance recorded a relatively small deficit of 4.1 bln US$ (see graph 1). The largest merchandise trade balance was with MDG South-eastern Asia at -13.2 bln US$ (see graph 4). Merchandise exports in Indonesia were diversified amongst partners; imports were also diversified. The top 14 partners accounted for 80 percent or more of exports and 14 partners accounted for 80 percent or more of imports (see graph 5). In 2013, the value of exports of services of Indonesia decreased slightly by 3.3 percent, reaching 22.3 bln US$, while its imports of services increased slightly by 2.9 percent and reached 34.4 bln US$ (see graph 2). There was a moderate trade in services deficit of 12.1 bln US$. See footnote*.

Graph 1: Total merchandise trade, by value
(Bln US$ by year)

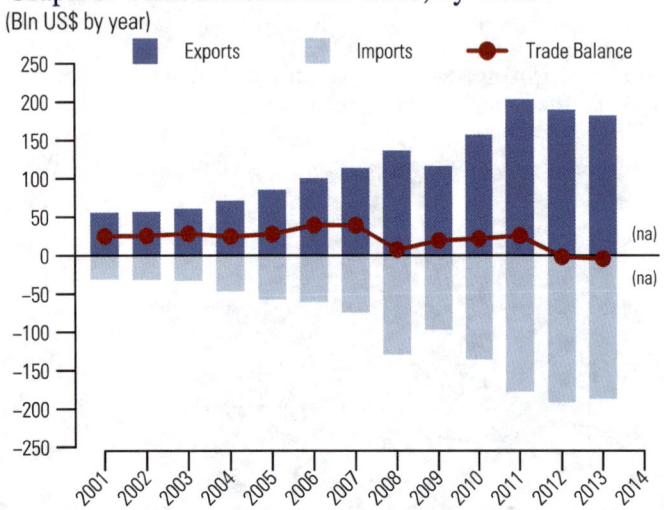

Graph 2: Total services trade, by value
(Bln US$ by year)

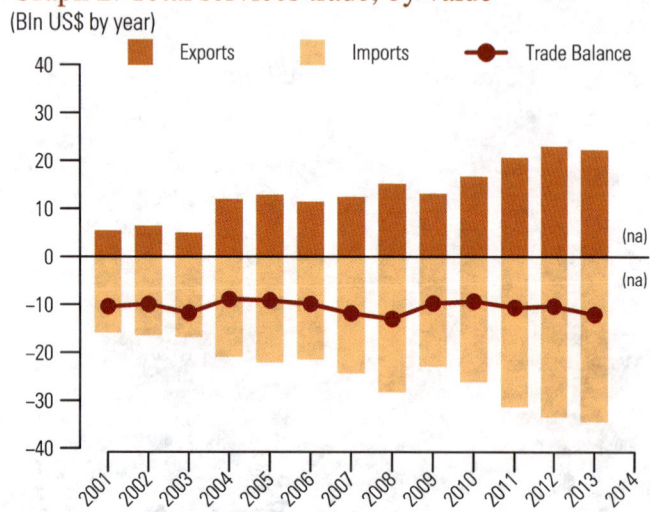

Exports Profile:
"Mineral fuels, lubricants" (SITC section 3), "Crude materials + anim. & veg. oils" (SITC section 2+4) and "Machinery and transport equipment" (SITC section 7) were the largest commodity groups for exports in 2013, representing respectively 31.4, 21.5 and 12.1 percent of exported goods (see table 2). From 2011 to 2013, the largest export commodity was "Coal; briquettes, ovoids and similar solid fuels manufactured from coal" (HS code 2701) (see table 1). The top three destinations for merchandise exports were Japan, China and Singapore, accounting for respectively 15.8, 11.7 and 9.1 percent of total exports. "Travel" (EBOPS code 236) accounted for the largest share of exports of services in 2013 at 9.1 bln US$, followed by "Other business services" (EBOPS code 268) at 6.6 bln US$ and "Transportation" (EBOPS code 205) at 3.6 bln US$ (see graph 3).

Graph 3: Exports of services by EBOPS category
(% share in 2013)

- Travel (40.8 %)
- Other business (29.7 %)
- Transportation (16.2 %)
- Remaining (13.3 %)

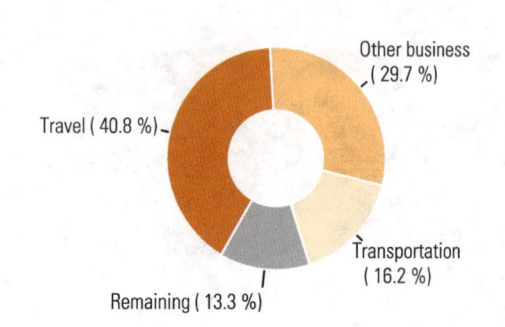

Table 1: Top 10 export commodities 2011 to 2013

HS code	4-digit heading of Harmonized System 2007	Value (million US$) 2011	2012	2013	Unit value 2011	2012	2013	Unit	SITC code
	All Commodities	203 496.6	190 031.8	182 551.8					
2701	Coal; briquettes, ovoids and similar solid fuels manufactured from coal	25 523.2	24 293.2	22 773.2	0.1	0.1	0.1	US$/kg	321
2711	Petroleum gases and other gaseous hydrocarbons	22 871.5	20 520.5	18 129.2	0.7	0.7	0.7	US$/kg	343
1511	Palm oil and its fractions	17 261.2	17 602.2	15 838.9	1.1	0.9	0.8	US$/kg	422
2709	Petroleum oils and oils obtained from bituminous minerals, crude	13 828.7	12 293.4	10 204.7	0.8	0.8	0.8	US$/kg	333
4001	Natural rubber, balata, gutta-percha, guayule, chicle	11 766.2	7 864.5	6 910.7	4.6	3.2	2.6	US$/kg	231
2603	Copper ores and concentrates	4 700.4	2 594.7	3 006.8	3.2	2.3	2.1	US$/kg	283
1513	Coconut (copra), palm kernel or babassu oil	3 051.6	2 458.2	1 829.5	1.5	1.1	0.8	US$/kg	422
2713	Petroleum coke and other residues	1 858.4	2 379.2	2 674.3	0.6	0.7	0.7	US$/kg	335
6403	Footwear with outer soles of rubber, plastics, leather	2 198.6	2 195.9	2 272.1	*30.1*		*29.5*	US$/pair	851
8001	Unwrought tin	2 403.9	2 051.3	1 959.8	24.7	20.3	22.2	US$/kg	687

*Merchandise imports data follows special trade system up to 2007.

Indonesia

Services Imports and Exports: EBOPS 2002 categories

Table 2: Merchandise exports by SITC
(Value in million US$, growth and shares in percentage)

SITC	2013	Avg. Growth rates 2009-2013	2012-2013	2013 share
Total	182 551.8	11.9	-3.9	100.0
0+1	11 978.5	11.9	3.1	6.6
2+4	39 199.7	12.8	-3.2	21.5
3	57 395.8	14.9	-9.4	31.4
5	10 978.6	17.3	3.6	6.0
6	22 002.1	6.5	-3.0	12.1
7	22 138.3	8.3	-2.8	12.1
8	17 039.6	9.7	3.5	9.3
9	1 819.2	18.2	-9.4	1.0

Table 3: Merchandise imports by SITC
(Value in million US$, growth and shares in percentage)

SITC	2013	Avg. Growth rates 2009-2013	2012-2013	2013 share
Total	186 628.6	17.8	-2.6	100.0
0+1	14 693.3	17.6	3.5	7.9
2+4	9 474.3	16.6	2.8	5.1
3	45 510.1	24.3	6.5	24.4
5	23 556.3	18.9	-0.4	12.6
6	28 593.8	19.3	-4.4	15.3
7	56 460.7	12.1	-11.1	30.3
8	6 893.9	20.8	10.2	3.7
9	1 446.2	176.3	-35.3	0.8

SITC Legend

SITC Code	Description
Total	All commodities
0+1	Food, animals + beverages, tobacco
2+4	Crude materials + anim. & veg. oils
3	Mineral fuels, lubricants
5	Chemicals
6	Goods classified chiefly by material
7	Machinery and transport equipment
8	Miscellaneous manufactured articles
9	Not classified elsewhere in the SITC

Graph 4: Merchandise trade balance
(Bln US$ by MDG Regions in 2013)

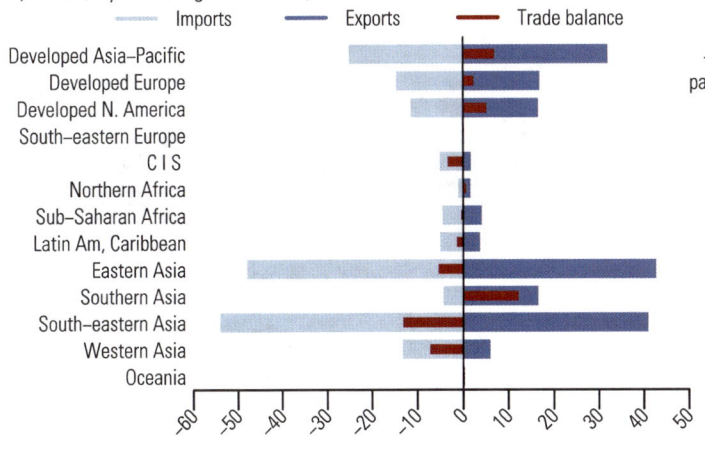

Graph 5: Partner concentration of merchandise trade
(Cumulative share by ranked partners in 2013)

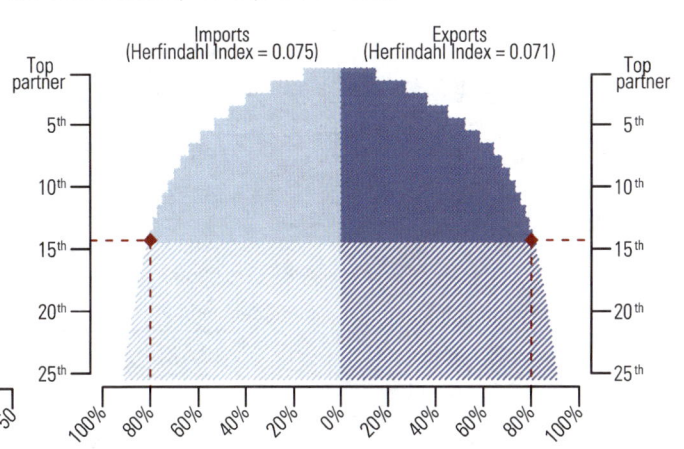

Imports (Herfindahl Index = 0.075)
Exports (Herfindahl Index = 0.071)

Graph 6: Imports of services by EBOPS category
(% share in 2013)

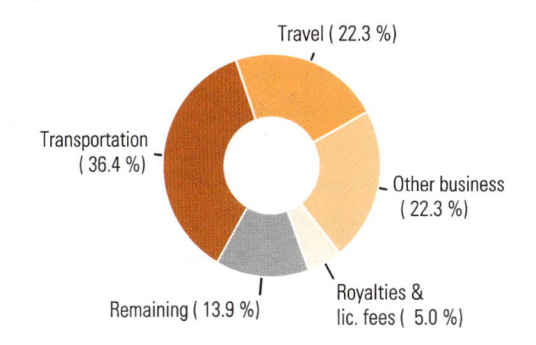

- Travel (22.3 %)
- Transportation (36.4 %)
- Other business (22.3 %)
- Royalties & lic. fees (5.0 %)
- Remaining (13.9 %)

Imports Profile:

"Machinery and transport equipment" (SITC section 7), "Mineral fuels, lubricants" (SITC section 3) and "Goods classified chiefly by material" (SITC section 6) were the largest commodity groups for imports in 2013, representing respectively 30.3, 24.4 and 15.3 percent of imported goods (see table 3). From 2011 to 2013, the largest import commodity was "Petroleum oils, other than crude" (HS code 2710) (see table 4). The top three partners for merchandise imports were China, Singapore and Japan, accounting for respectively 15.4, 14.0 and 11.1 percent of total imports. "Transportation" (EBOPS code 205) accounted for the largest share of imports of services in 2013 at 12.5 bln US$, followed by "Travel" (EBOPS code 236) at 7.7 bln US$ and "Other business services" (EBOPS code 268) at 7.7 bln US$ (see graph 6).

Table 4: Top 10 import commodities 2011 to 2013

HS code	4-digit heading of Harmonized System 2007	Value (million US$) 2011	2012	2013	Unit value 2011	2012	2013	Unit	SITC code
	All Commodities	177 435.6	191 690.9	186 628.6					
2710	Petroleum oils, other than crude	27 721.8	28 038.2	27 850.9	1.0	1.0	1.0	US$/kg	334
2709	Petroleum oils and oils obtained from bituminous minerals, crude	11 154.5	10 803.2	13 585.8	0.8	0.9	0.8	US$/kg	333
8517	Electrical apparatus for line telephony or line telegraphy	4 570.0	5 113.4	5 291.2					764
8708	Parts and accessories of the motor vehicles of headings 87.01 to 87.05	2 276.7	2 982.3	3 218.3	8.8	10.1	9.5	US$/kg	784
2711	Petroleum gases and other gaseous hydrocarbons	1 412.5	3 081.6	3 113.0	0.9	1.0	0.9	US$/kg	343
8802	Other aircraft (for example, helicopters, aeroplanes); spacecraft	2 880.7	3 960.4	589.9					792
8471	Automatic data processing machines and units thereof	2 193.6	2 299.4	2 443.8					752
1001	Wheat and meslin	2 194.0	2 253.9	2 440.0	0.4	0.4	0.4	US$/kg	041
8703	Motor cars and other motor vehicles principally designed for the transport	1 763.9	2 728.2	2 231.2			15.8	thsd US$/unit	781
8704	Motor vehicles for the transport of goods	2 326.0	2 640.2	892.2					782

2014 International Trade Statistics Yearbook, Vol. I — Source: UN Comtrade and UN ServiceTrade

Iran (Islamic Republic of)

Goods Imports: CIF, by origin   **Goods Exports: FOB, by last known destination**   **Trade System: Special**

Overview:

In 2011, the value of merchandise exports of the Islamic Republic of Iran increased substantially by 55.8 percent to reach 130.5 bln US$, while its merchandise imports increased substantially by 24.9 percent to reach 68.3 bln US$ (see graph 1, table 2 and table 3). The merchandise trade balance recorded a large surplus of 62.2 bln US$ (see graph 1). The largest merchandise trade balance was with MDG Eastern Asia at 55.8 bln US$ (see graph 4). Merchandise exports in the Islamic Republic of Iran were highly concentrated amongst partners; imports were diversified. The top 5 partners accounted for 80 percent or more of exports and 11 partners accounted for 80 percent or more of imports (see graph 5). In 2012, the value of exports of services of the Islamic Republic of Iran decreased substantially by 22.4 percent, reaching 6.7 bln US$, while its imports of services decreased substantially by 23.9 percent and reached 13.0 bln US$ (see graph 2). There was a large trade in services deficit of 6.3 bln US$.

Graph 1: Total merchandise trade, by value
(Bln US$ by year)

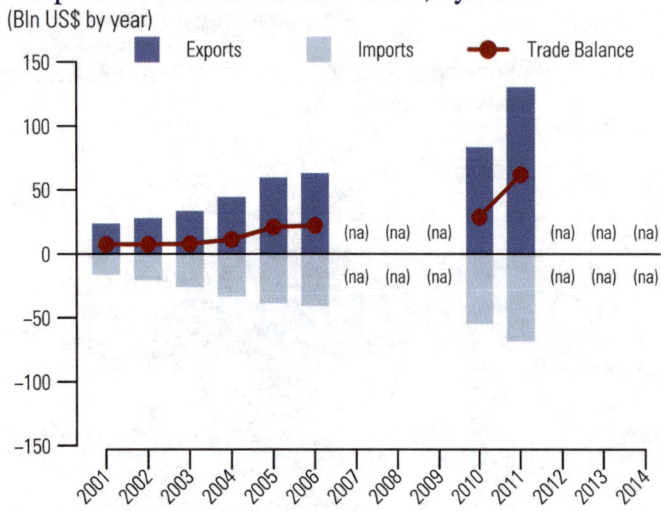

Graph 2: Total services trade, by value
(Bln US$ by year)

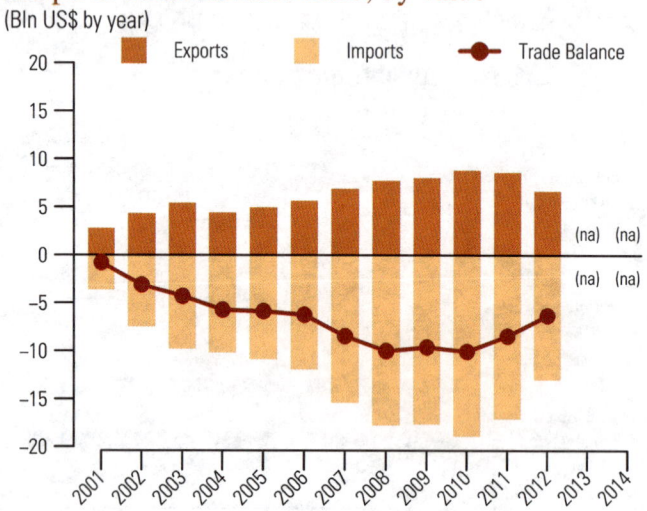

Exports Profile:

"Mineral fuels, lubricants" (SITC section 3), "Not classified elsewhere in the SITC" (SITC section 9) and "Chemicals" (SITC section 5) were the largest commodity groups for exports in 2011, representing respectively 70.5, 11.3 and 7.0 percent of exported goods (see table 2). From 2010 to 2011, the largest export commodity was "Petroleum oils, crude" (HS code 2709) (see table 1). The top three destinations for merchandise exports were Other Asia nes, Rest of Europe nes and Areas nes, accounting for respectively 45.6, 18.9 and 5.9 percent of total exports. "Transportation" (EBOPS code 205) accounted for the largest share of exports of services in 2006 at 2.9 bln US$, followed by "Travel" (EBOPS code 236) at 1.2 bln US$ and "Construction services" (EBOPS code 249) at 996.0 mln US$ (see graph 3).

Graph 3: Exports of services by EBOPS category
(% share in 2006)

- Transportation (51.9 %)
- Travel (21.4 %)
- Construction (17.6 %)
- Remaining (9.1 %)

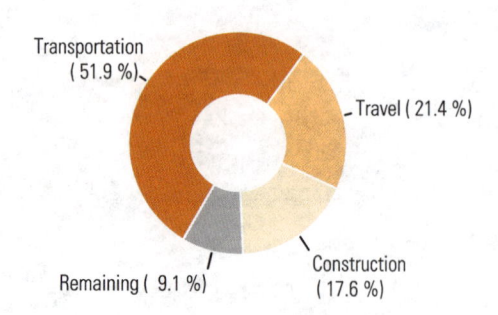

Table 1: Top 10 export commodities 2009 to 2011

HS code	4-digit heading of Harmonized System 2002	Value (million US$) 2009	2010	2011	Unit value 2009	2010	2011	Unit	SITC code
	All Commodities	...	83 785.0	130 544.0					
2709	Petroleum oils, crude	...	46 709.4	84 381.6		0.4	0.7	US$/kg	333
9999	Commodities not specified according to kind	...	3 326.2	14 755.6					931
2710	Petroleum oils, other than crude	...	8 482.5	1 075.7	0.7	0.9		US$/kg	334
2711	Petroleum gases and other gaseous hydrocarbons	...	3 167.2	5 544.8		0.7	0.9	US$/kg	343
3901	Polymers of ethylene, in primary forms	...	1 814.4	2 074.8		1.1	1.3	US$/kg	571
2905	Acyclic alcohols and their derivatives	...	1 220.1	1 672.7		0.3	0.4	US$/kg	512
0802	Other nuts, fresh or dried	...	1 175.3	1 034.8		7.6	7.8	US$/kg	057
2902	Cyclic hydrocarbons	...	831.6	1 130.0		1.0	1.1	US$/kg	511
2601	Iron ores and concentrates	...	1 124.3	789.9		0.1	0.0	US$/kg	281
2713	Petroleum coke and other residues	...	668.1	713.8		0.5	0.5	US$/kg	335

Iran (Islamic Republic of)

Services Imports and Exports: EBOPS 2002 categories

Table 2: Merchandise exports by SITC
(Value in million US$, growth and shares in percentage)

SITC	2011	Avg. Growth rates 2007-2011	Avg. Growth rates 2010-2011	2011 share
Total	130 544.0	...	55.8	100.0
0+1	4 694.5	...	-7.8	3.6
2+4	1 620.2	...	-13.9	1.2
3	92 038.9	...	55.2	70.5
5	9 113.4	...	26.4	7.0
6	5 555.6	...	21.2	4.3
7	1 425.0	...	-6.1	1.1
8	1 329.7	...	58.0	1.0
9	14 766.7	...	342.7	11.3

Table 3: Merchandise imports by SITC
(Value in million US$, growth and shares in percentage)

SITC	2011	Avg. Growth rates 2007-2011	Avg. Growth rates 2010-2011	2011 share
Total	68 319.0	...	24.9	100.0
0+1	7 391.3	...	9.8	10.8
2+4	4 192.3	...	32.6	6.1
3	973.9	...	-33.9	1.4
5	7 449.4	...	12.0	10.9
6	14 125.5	...	5.3	20.7
7	19 334.6	...	14.9	28.3
8	2 078.9	...	3.6	3.0
9	12 773.2	...	188.4	18.7

SITC Legend

SITC Code	Description
Total	All commodities
0+1	Food, animals + beverages, tobacco
2+4	Crude materials + anim. & veg. oils
3	Mineral fuels, lubricants
5	Chemicals
6	Goods classified chiefly by material
7	Machinery and transport equipment
8	Miscellaneous manufactured articles
9	Not classified elsewhere in the SITC

Graph 4: Merchandise trade balance
(Bln US$ by MDG Regions in 2011)

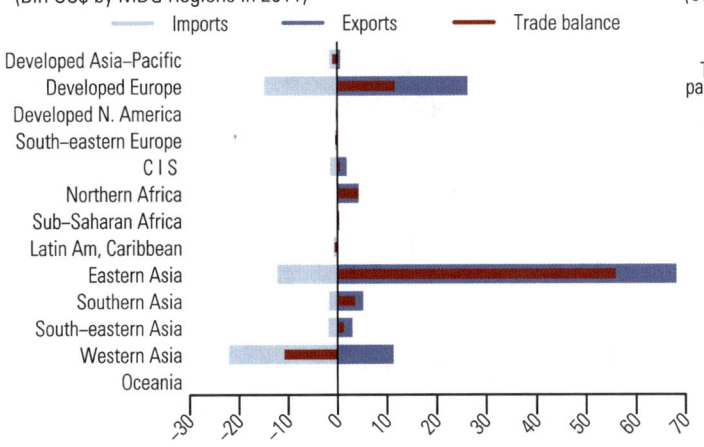

Graph 5: Partner concentration of merchandise trade
(Cumulative share by ranked partners in 2011)

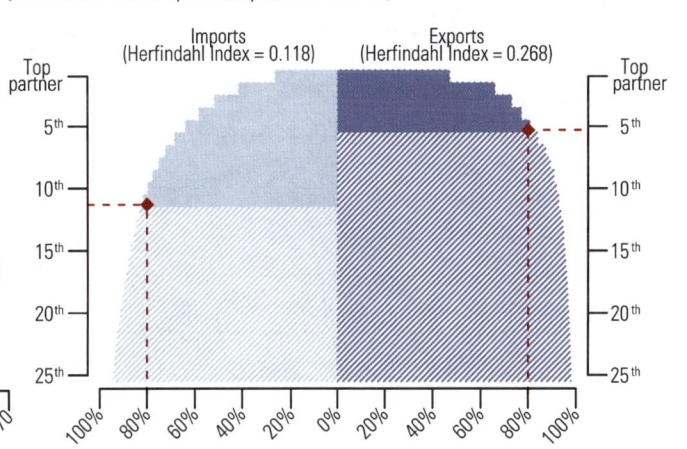

Imports (Herfindahl Index = 0.118)
Exports (Herfindahl Index = 0.268)

Graph 6: Imports of services by EBOPS category
(% share in 2006)

- Transportation (24.8 %)
- Travel (39.4 %)
- Construction (19.1 %)
- Remaining (16.7 %)

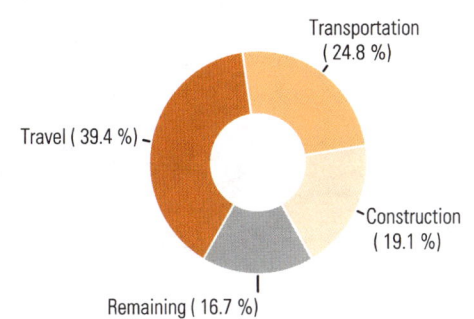

Imports Profile:
"Machinery and transport equipment" (SITC section 7), "Goods classified chiefly by material" (SITC section 6) and "Not classified elsewhere in the SITC" (SITC section 9) were the largest commodity groups for imports in 2011, representing respectively 28.3, 20.7 and 18.7 percent of imported goods (see table 3). From 2010 to 2011, the largest import commodity was "Commodities not specified according to kind" (HS code 9999) (see table 4). The top three partners for merchandise imports were the United Arab Emirates, China and Areas nes, accounting for respectively 27.5, 10.4 and 8.2 percent of total imports. "Travel" (EBOPS code 236) accounted for the largest share of imports of services in 2006 at 4.7 bln US$, followed by "Transportation" (EBOPS code 205) at 3.0 bln US$ and "Construction services" (EBOPS code 249) at 2.3 bln US$ (see graph 6).

Table 4: Top 10 import commodities 2009 to 2011

HS code	4-digit heading of Harmonized System 2002	Value 2009	Value 2010	Value 2011	Unit value 2009	Unit value 2010	Unit value 2011	Unit	SITC code
	All Commodities	...	54 697.2	68 319.0					
9999	Commodities not specified according to kind	...	3 977.2	12 773.2					931
7206	Iron and non-alloy steel in ingots or other primary forms	...	2 479.3	2 867.7		0.6	0.7	US$/kg	672
7208	Flat-rolled products of iron or non-alloy steel	...	1 977.8	1 613.8		0.7	0.8	US$/kg	673
1005	Maize (corn)	...	919.6	1 294.0		0.3	0.4	US$/kg	044
3004	Medicaments (excluding goods of heading 30.02, 30.05 or 30.06)	...	943.4	1 120.0		130.5	130.2	US$/kg	542
1006	Rice	...	942.0	975.4		0.8	0.9	US$/kg	042
8471	Automatic data processing machines and units thereof	...	873.0	1 013.9					752
8411	Turbo-jets, turbo-propellers and other gas turbines	...	1 192.2	629.7					714
2304	Oil-cake and other solid residues	...	735.5	844.8		0.4	0.5	US$/kg	081
0202	Meat of bovine animals, frozen	...	777.4	769.3		4.1	5.3	US$/kg	011

Ireland

Goods Imports: CIF, by origin **Goods Exports:** FOB, by last known destination **Trade System:** General

Overview:
In 2014, the value of merchandise exports of Ireland increased slightly by 2.6 percent to reach 118.3 bln US$, while its merchandise imports increased moderately by 7.7 percent to reach 71.0 bln US$ (see graph 1, table 2 and table 3). The merchandise trade balance recorded a moderate surplus of 47.2 bln US$ (see graph 1). The largest merchandise trade balance was with MDG Developed Europe at 24.6 bln US$ (see graph 4). Merchandise exports in Ireland were diversified amongst partners; imports were also diversified. The top 11 partners accounted for 80 percent or more of exports and 12 partners accounted for 80 percent or more of imports (see graph 5). In 2013, the value of exports of services of Ireland increased moderately by 9.7 percent, reaching 127.3 bln US$, while its imports of services increased substantially by 13.4 percent and reached 127.0 bln US$ (see graph 2). There was a relatively small trade in services surplus of 322.7 mln US$.

Graph 1: Total merchandise trade, by value
(Bln US$ by year)

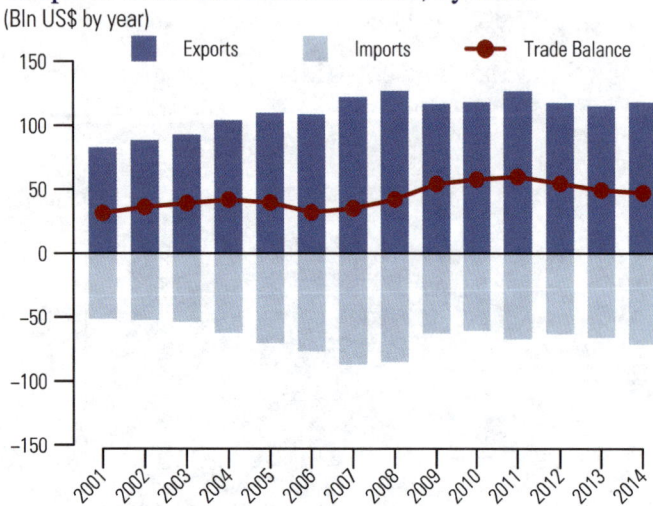

Graph 2: Total services trade, by value
(Bln US$ by year)

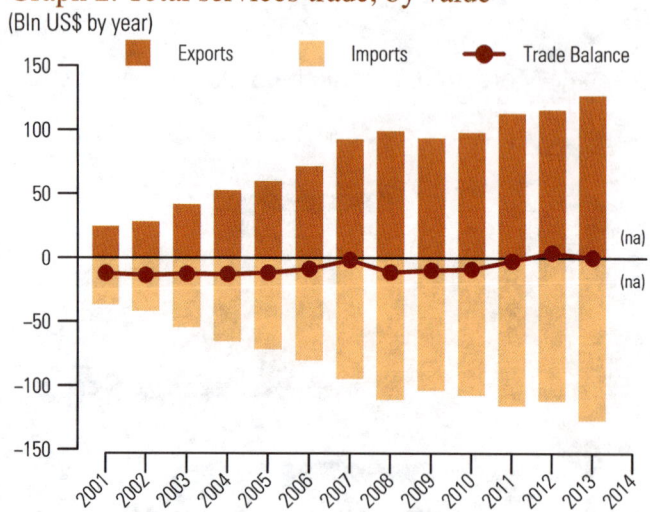

Exports Profile:
"Chemicals" (SITC section 5), "Miscellaneous manufactured articles" (SITC section 8) and "Food, animals + beverages, tobacco" (SITC section 0+1) were the largest commodity groups for exports in 2014, representing respectively 57.8, 12.8 and 11.7 percent of exported goods (see table 2). From 2012 to 2014, the largest export commodity was "Medicaments (excluding goods of heading 30.02, 30.05 or 30.06)" (HS code 3004) (see table 1). The top three destinations for merchandise exports were the United States, the United Kingdom and Belgium, accounting for respectively 21.1, 15.9 and 13.7 percent of total exports. "Other business services" (EBOPS code 268) accounted for the largest share of exports of services in 2013 at 28.4 bln US$, followed by "Insurance services" (EBOPS code 253) at 12.4 bln US$ (see graph 3).

Graph 3: Exports of services by EBOPS category
(% share in 2013)

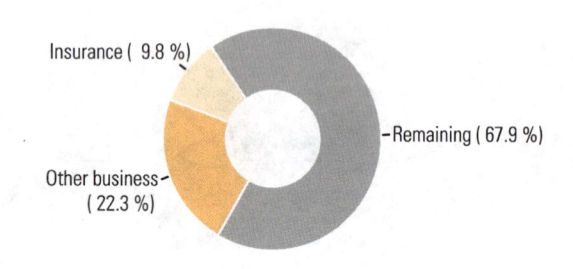

- Insurance (9.8 %)
- Other business (22.3 %)
- Remaining (67.9 %)

Table 1: Top 10 export commodities 2012 to 2014

HS code	4-digit heading of Harmonized System 2012	Value (million US$) 2012	2013	2014	Unit value 2012	2013	2014	Unit	SITC code
	All Commodities	117 769.7	115 323.5	118 287.4					
3004	Medicaments (excluding goods of heading 30.02, 30.05 or 30.06)	19 132.3	18 152.6	19 662.2	120.9	115.6	121.1	US$/kg	542
2933	Heterocyclic compounds with nitrogen hetero-atom(s) only	15 559.1	15 128.0	13 926.1					515
3302	Mixtures of odoriferous substances and mixtures	7 272.3	7 388.0	8 306.9	53.5	56.0	62.3	US$/kg	551
3002	Human blood; animal blood prepared for therapeutic uses	8 468.0	6 216.4	5 961.0	8.1	5.1	4.8	thsd US$/kg	541
9021	Orthopaedic appliances, including crutches, surgical belts and trusses	4 693.1	4 881.2	4 865.2					899
2934	Nucleic acids and their salts	5 032.3	4 233.0	4 478.7	22.9		18.9	thsd US$/kg	515
9018	Instruments and appliances used in medical, surgical, dental or veterinary	3 786.7	3 990.8	4 386.3					872
8471	Automatic data processing machines and units thereof	2 816.7	3 396.8	3 738.9	0.5	1.0	1.3	thsd US$/unit	752
2935	Sulphonamides	2 623.5	2 277.9	3 357.2	18.8	21.2	19.1	thsd US$/kg	515
3824	Prepared binders for foundry moulds or cores	2 739.0	2 760.6	2 688.4	22.0	24.6	24.1	US$/kg	598

Ireland

Services Imports and Exports: EBOPS 2002 categories

Table 2: Merchandise exports by SITC
(Value in million US$, growth and shares in percentage)

SITC	2014	Avg. Growth rates 2010-2014	Avg. Growth rates 2013-2014	2014 share
Total	118 287.4	0.0	2.6	100.0
0+1	13 897.9	6.4	5.5	11.7
2+4	2 424.0	5.9	8.8	2.0
3	1 096.5	-5.3	0.3	0.9
5	68 375.0	-0.3	2.4	57.8
6	2 459.0	6.3	8.6	2.1
7	13 268.2	-2.3	-4.3	11.2
8	15 086.4	1.8	5.3	12.8
9	1 680.5	-21.8	4.1	1.4

Table 3: Merchandise imports by SITC
(Value in million US$, growth and shares in percentage)

SITC	2014	Avg. Growth rates 2010-2014	Avg. Growth rates 2013-2014	2014 share
Total	71 049.0	4.1	7.7	100.0
0+1	9 262.7	6.7	1.5	13.0
2+4	1 266.4	3.4	3.2	1.8
3	8 583.7	3.8	-6.2	12.1
5	15 082.4	6.8	4.7	21.2
6	5 579.7	4.7	9.1	7.9
7	19 218.6	4.2	19.8	27.0
8	9 050.0	2.6	13.1	12.7
9	3 005.6	-7.9	3.8	4.2

SITC Legend

SITC Code	Description
Total	All commodities
0+1	Food, animals + beverages, tobacco
2+4	Crude materials + anim. & veg. oils
3	Mineral fuels, lubricants
5	Chemicals
6	Goods classified chiefly by material
7	Machinery and transport equipment
8	Miscellaneous manufactured articles
9	Not classified elsewhere in the SITC

Graph 4: Merchandise trade balance
(Bln US$ by MDG Regions in 2014)

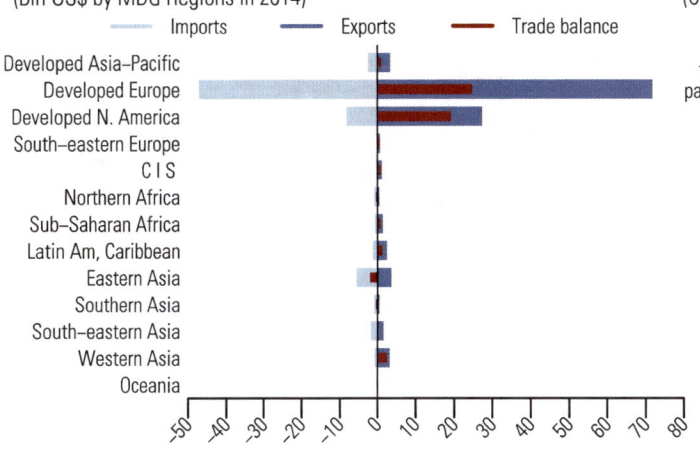

Graph 5: Partner concentration of merchandise trade
(Cumulative share by ranked partners in 2014)

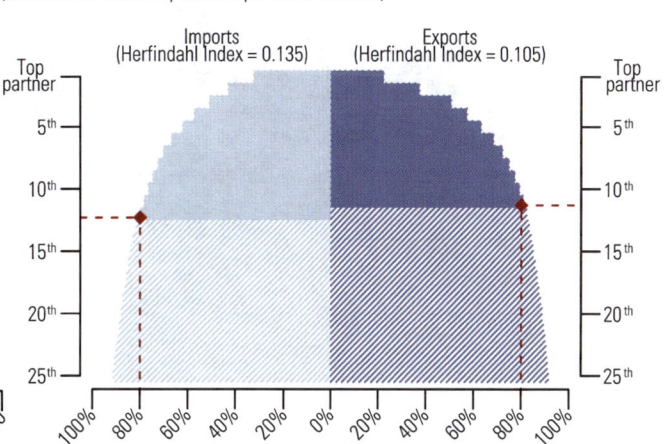

Imports (Herfindahl Index = 0.135)
Exports (Herfindahl Index = 0.105)

Graph 6: Imports of services by EBOPS category
(% share in 2013)

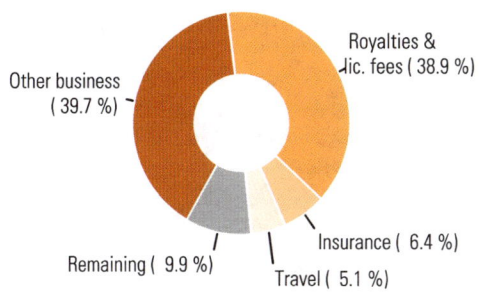

- Royalties & lic. fees (38.9 %)
- Other business (39.7 %)
- Remaining (9.9 %)
- Insurance (6.4 %)
- Travel (5.1 %)

Imports Profile:

"Machinery and transport equipment" (SITC section 7), "Chemicals" (SITC section 5) and "Food, animals + beverages, tobacco" (SITC section 0+1) were the largest commodity groups for imports in 2014, representing respectively 27.0, 21.2 and 13.0 percent of imported goods (see table 3). From 2012 to 2014, the largest import commodity was "Petroleum oils, other than crude" (HS code 2710) (see table 4). The top three partners for merchandise imports were the United Kingdom, the United States and Germany, accounting for respectively 33.1, 11.5 and 7.7 percent of total imports. "Other business services" (EBOPS code 268) accounted for the largest share of imports of services in 2013 at 50.4 bln US$, followed by "Royalties and license fees" (EBOPS code 266) at 49.4 bln US$ and "Insurance services" (EBOPS code 253) at 8.2 bln US$ (see graph 6).

Table 4: Top 10 import commodities 2012 to 2014

HS code	4-digit heading of Harmonized System 2012	Value 2012	Value 2013	Value 2014	Unit value 2012	Unit value 2013	Unit value 2014	Unit	SITC code
	All Commodities	63 222.9	65 950.7	71 049.0					
2710	Petroleum oils, other than crude	4 487.1	4 016.0	4 318.6	1.0	1.0	1.0	US$/kg	334
3004	Medicaments (excluding goods of heading 30.02, 30.05 or 30.06)	3 283.9	3 478.6	3 216.1	115.5	122.3	64.3	US$/kg	542
9999	Commodities not specified according to kind	2 559.1	2 875.8	2 991.9					931
2709	Petroleum oils and oils obtained from bituminous minerals, crude	2 404.4	2 492.1	2 114.3	0.8	0.8	0.8	US$/kg	333
8471	Automatic data processing machines and units thereof	2 122.4	1 973.1	2 345.1	207.1	113.6	272.6	US$/unit	752
2711	Petroleum gases and other gaseous hydrocarbons	1 865.1	2 093.7	1 698.3	0.4	0.5	0.4	US$/kg	343
8703	Motor cars and other motor vehicles principally designed for the transport	1 290.5	1 528.2	2 220.1	8.8	5.5	9.4	thsd US$/unit	781
8802	Other aircraft (for example, helicopters, aeroplanes); spacecraft	2 927.5	1 037.4	950.7					792
8473	Parts and accessories for use with machines of heading 84.69 to 84.72	1 077.5	1 567.7	1 517.6	110.4	136.5	149.4	US$/kg	759
2933	Heterocyclic compounds with nitrogen hetero-atom(s) only	899.3	1 182.2	1 627.0					515

Israel

Goods Imports: CIF, by origin | **Goods Exports: FOB, by sale** | **Trade System: Special**

Overview:

In 2014, the value of merchandise exports of Israel increased slightly by 3.3 percent to reach 69.0 bln US$, while its merchandise imports increased slightly by 0.5 percent to reach 72.3 bln US$ (see graph 1, table 2 and table 3). The merchandise trade balance recorded a relatively small deficit of 3.4 bln US$ (see graph 1). The largest merchandise trade balance was with MDG Developed North America at 10.3 bln US$ (see graph 4). Merchandise exports in Israel were diversified amongst partners; imports were also diversified. The top 17 partners accounted for 80 percent or more of exports and 14 partners accounted for 80 percent or more of imports (see graph 5). In 2012, the value of exports of services of Israel increased substantially by 12.7 percent, reaching 30.9 bln US$, while its imports of services increased slightly by 2.5 percent and reached 21.0 bln US$ (see graph 2). There was a moderate trade in services surplus of 9.8 bln US$.

Graph 1: Total merchandise trade, by value
(Bln US$ by year)

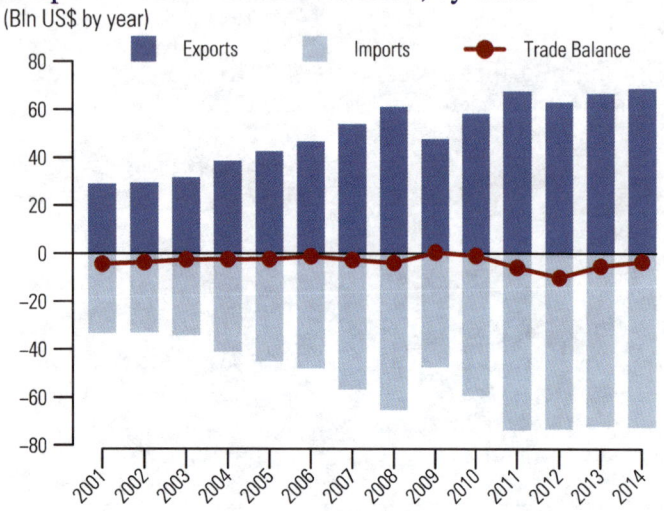

Graph 2: Total services trade, by value
(Bln US$ by year)

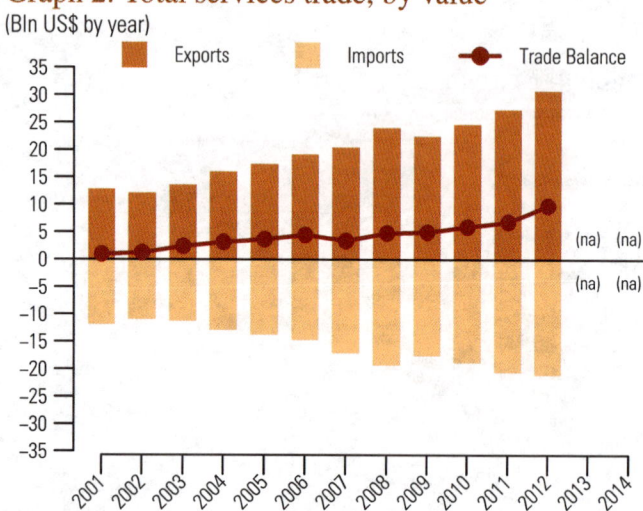

Exports Profile:

"Goods classified chiefly by material" (SITC section 6), "Chemicals" (SITC section 5) and "Machinery and transport equipment" (SITC section 7) were the largest commodity groups for exports in 2014, representing respectively 34.9, 26.2 and 24.0 percent of exported goods (see table 2). From 2012 to 2014, the largest export commodity was "Diamonds, whether or not worked, but not mounted or set" (HS code 7102) (see table 1). The top three destinations for merchandise exports were the United States, China, Hong Kong SAR and the United Kingdom, accounting for respectively 27.0, 8.2 and 5.7 percent of total exports. "Travel" (EBOPS code 236) accounted for the largest share of exports of services in 2012 at 5.5 bln US$, followed by "Transportation" (EBOPS code 205) at 4.5 bln US$ and "Computer and information services" (EBOPS code 262) at 4.3 bln US$ (see graph 3).

Graph 3: Exports of services by EBOPS category
(% share in 2012)

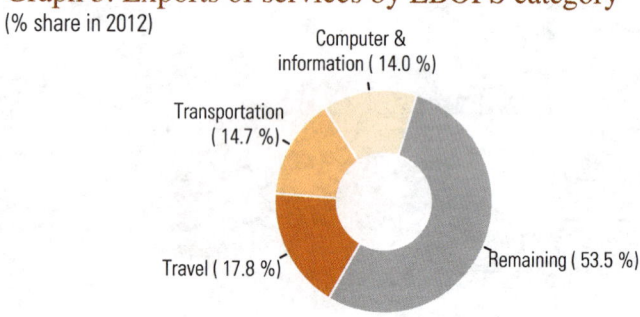

- Computer & information (14.0 %)
- Transportation (14.7 %)
- Travel (17.8 %)
- Remaining (53.5 %)

Table 1: Top 10 export commodities 2012 to 2014

HS code	4-digit heading of Harmonized System 2012	Value (million US$) 2012	2013	2014	Unit value 2012	2013	2014	Unit	SITC code
	All Commodities	63 140.6	66 781.2	68 965.0					
7102	Diamonds, whether or not worked, but not mounted or set	17 470.2	19 016.2	20 546.6					667
3004	Medicaments (excluding goods of heading 30.02, 30.05 or 30.06)	4 415.3	3 284.1	3 846.1					542
8542	Electronic integrated circuits	2 828.9	4 075.4	3 910.2					776
3824	Prepared binders for foundry moulds or cores	2 203.1	4 039.9	4 167.8					598
3003	Medicaments (excluding goods of heading 30.02, 30.05 or 30.06)	1 954.4	2 592.1	2 160.0					542
8517	Electrical apparatus for line telephony or line telegraphy	2 053.8	1 788.2	1 790.5					764
8803	Parts of goods of heading 88.01 or 88.02	1 576.8	1 865.3	1 534.1					792
3105	Mineral or chemical fertilisers	1 562.5	1 439.9	1 260.6	0.5	0.5	1.5	US$/kg	562
9018	Instruments and appliances used in medical, surgical, dental or veterinary	1 204.9	1 320.9	1 506.5					872
9031	Measuring or checking instruments, appliances and machines	1 046.9	1 186.2	939.8					874

Israel

Services Imports and Exports: EBOPS 2002 categories

Table 2: Merchandise exports by SITC
(Value in million US$, growth and shares in percentage)

SITC	2014	Avg. Growth rates 2010-2014	Avg. Growth rates 2013-2014	2014 share
Total	68 965.0	4.2	3.3	100.0
0+1	2 035.9	3.7	-2.7	3.0
2+4	1 034.1	-1.6	1.8	1.5
3	788.3	11.8	-25.3	1.1
5	18 092.1	3.6	-0.1	26.2
6	24 057.9	5.0	7.9	34.9
7	16 524.0	3.0	2.4	24.0
8	5 509.6	4.0	1.5	8.0
9	923.2	60.5	41.5	1.3

Table 3: Merchandise imports by SITC
(Value in million US$, growth and shares in percentage)

SITC	2014	Avg. Growth rates 2010-2014	Avg. Growth rates 2013-2014	2014 share
Total	72 331.8	5.1	0.5	100.0
0+1	5 000.1	7.0	4.6	6.9
2+4	1 597.4	2.2	0.8	2.2
3	12 758.1	5.1	-12.3	17.6
5	8 178.7	4.9	2.3	11.3
6	16 518.0	3.4	2.8	22.8
7	21 106.4	5.9	4.2	29.2
8	6 716.6	6.9	6.0	9.3
9	456.4	7.7	8.2	0.6

SITC Legend

SITC Code	Description
Total	All commodities
0+1	Food, animals + beverages, tobacco
2+4	Crude materials + anim. & veg. oils
3	Mineral fuels, lubricants
5	Chemicals
6	Goods classified chiefly by material
7	Machinery and transport equipment
8	Miscellaneous manufactured articles
9	Not classified elsewhere in the SITC

Graph 4: Merchandise trade balance
(Bln US$ by MDG Regions in 2014)

Graph 5: Partner concentration of merchandise trade
(Cumulative share by ranked partners in 2014)

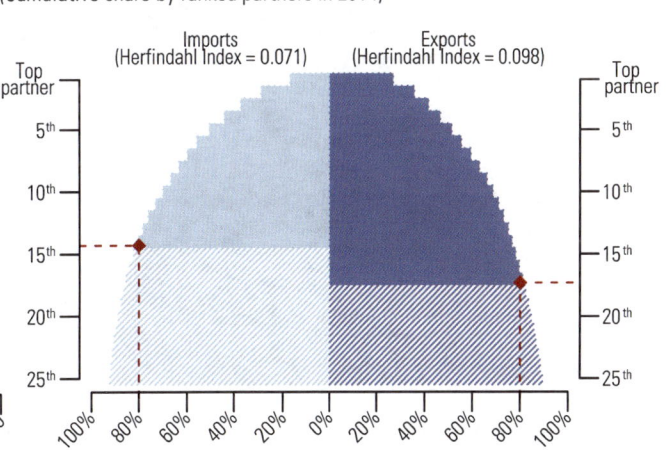

Imports (Herfindahl Index = 0.071)
Exports (Herfindahl Index = 0.098)

Graph 6: Imports of services by EBOPS category
(% share in 2012)

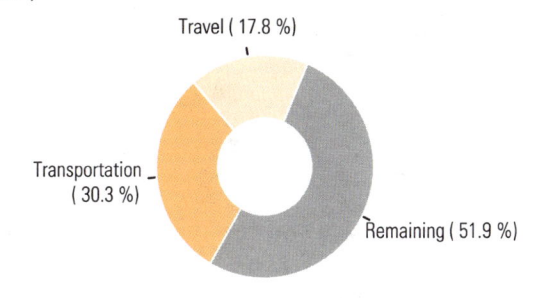

- Travel (17.8%)
- Transportation (30.3%)
- Remaining (51.9%)

Imports Profile:
"Machinery and transport equipment" (SITC section 7), "Goods classified chiefly by material" (SITC section 6) and "Mineral fuels, lubricants" (SITC section 3) were the largest commodity groups for imports in 2014, representing respectively 29.2, 22.8 and 17.6 percent of imported goods (see table 3). From 2012 to 2014, the largest import commodity was "Petroleum oils and oils obtained from bituminous minerals, crude" (HS code 2709) (see table 4). The top three partners for merchandise imports were Areas nes, the United States and China, accounting for respectively 18.8, 12.0 and 7.8 percent of total imports. "Transportation" (EBOPS code 205) accounted for the largest share of imports of services in 2012 at 6.4 bln US$, followed by "Travel" (EBOPS code 236) at 3.8 bln US$ (see graph 6).

Table 4: Top 10 import commodities 2012 to 2014

HS code	4-digit heading of Harmonized System 2012	Value 2012	Value 2013	Value 2014	Unit value 2012	Unit value 2013	Unit value 2014	Unit	SITC code
	All Commodities	73 112.1	71 995.0	72 331.8					
2709	Petroleum oils and oils obtained from bituminous minerals, crude	9 472.0	9 062.5	8 459.6	0.1	0.1	0.8	US$/kg	333
7102	Diamonds, whether or not worked, but not mounted or set	8 225.9	9 014.2	9 301.2					667
2710	Petroleum oils, other than crude	4 764.2	3 698.8	3 031.8					334
8703	Motor cars and other motor vehicles principally designed for the transport	2 896.3	3 220.1	4 062.9	14.0	14.1	14.6	thsd US$/unit	781
8542	Electronic integrated circuits	2 080.2	1 846.6	1 735.4					776
8517	Electrical apparatus for line telephony or line telegraphy	1 464.0	1 450.9	1 642.9					764
3004	Medicaments (excluding goods of heading 30.02, 30.05 or 30.06)	1 321.8	1 471.4	1 363.9					542
8471	Automatic data processing machines and units thereof	1 293.5	1 298.3	1 345.9					752
2701	Coal; briquettes, ovoids and similar solid fuels manufactured from coal	1 463.4	1 157.1	929.1	0.1	0.1	0.1	US$/kg	321
8704	Motor vehicles for the transport of goods	637.1	773.1	613.5			40.2	thsd US$/unit	782

2014 International Trade Statistics Yearbook, Vol. I   Source: UN Comtrade and UN ServiceTrade

Italy

Goods Imports: CIF, by origin/consignment for intra-eu   **Goods Exports:** FOB, by last known destination   **Trade System:** General

Overview:
In 2014, the value of merchandise exports of Italy increased slightly by 2.0 percent to reach 528.4 bln US$, while its merchandise imports decreased slightly by 1.6 percent to reach 471.7 bln US$ (see graph 1, table 2 and table 3). Despite growth since 2009, the value of exports was still less than its peak in 2008 at 541.8 bln US$. The merchandise trade balance recorded a relatively small surplus of 56.7 bln US$ (see graph 1). The largest merchandise trade balance was with MDG Developed Europe at 31.6 bln US$ (see graph 4). Merchandise exports in Italy were diversified amongst partners; imports were also diversified. The top 29 partners accounted for 80 percent or more of exports and 26 partners accounted for 80 percent or more of imports (see graph 5). In 2013, the value of exports of services of Italy increased substantially by 10.1 percent, reaching 115.8 bln US$, while its imports of services increased moderately by 6.3 percent and reached 112.8 bln US$ (see graph 2). There was a relatively small trade in services surplus of 3.0 bln US$, the first trade in services surplus since 2004.

Graph 1: Total merchandise trade, by value
(Bln US$ by year)

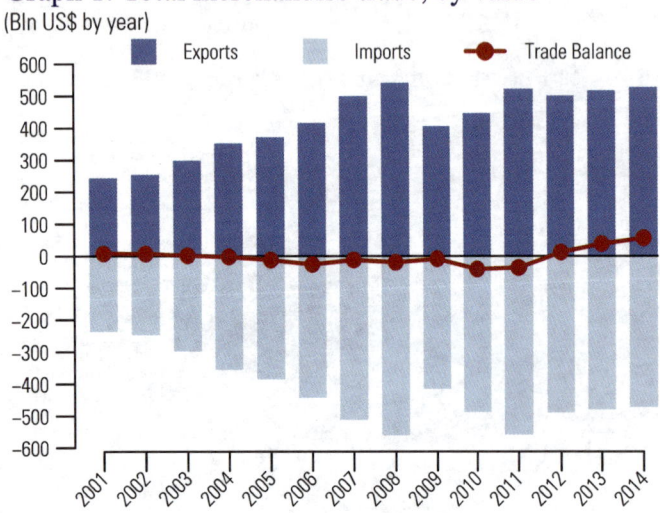

Graph 2: Total services trade, by value
(Bln US$ by year)

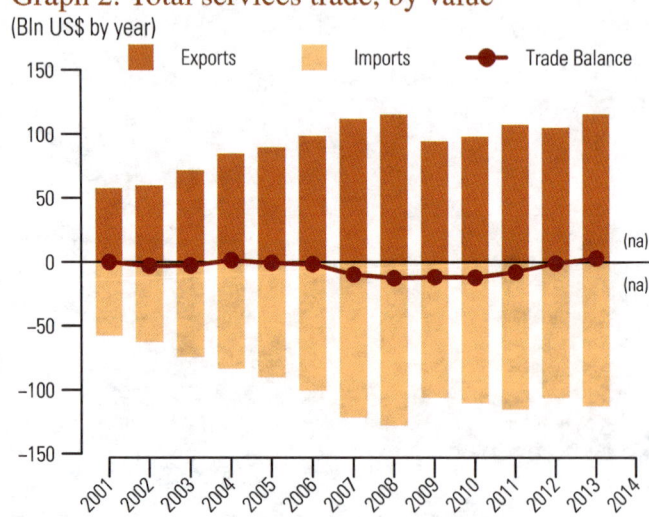

Exports Profile:
"Machinery and transport equipment" (SITC section 7), "Goods classified chiefly by material" (SITC section 6) and "Miscellaneous manufactured articles" (SITC section 8) were the largest commodity groups for exports in 2014, representing respectively 35.3, 18.5 and 17.9 percent of exported goods (see table 2). From 2012 to 2014, the largest export commodity was "Petroleum oils, other than crude" (HS code 2710), although in 2013 and 2014, "Medicaments (excluding goods of heading 30.02, 30.05 or 30.06)" (HS code 3004) exceeded the former as the largest export commodity (see table 1). The top three destinations for merchandise exports were Germany, France and the United States, accounting for respectively 12.5, 10.8 and 7.1 percent of total exports. "Travel" (EBOPS code 236) accounted for the largest share of exports of services in 2013 at 45.6 bln US$, followed by "Other business services" (EBOPS code 268) at 29.1 bln US$ and "Transportation" (EBOPS code 205) at 15.4 bln US$ (see graph 3).

Graph 3: Exports of services by EBOPS category
(% share in 2013)

- Travel (39.4 %)
- Other business (25.1 %)
- Transportation (13.3 %)
- Remaining (22.2 %)

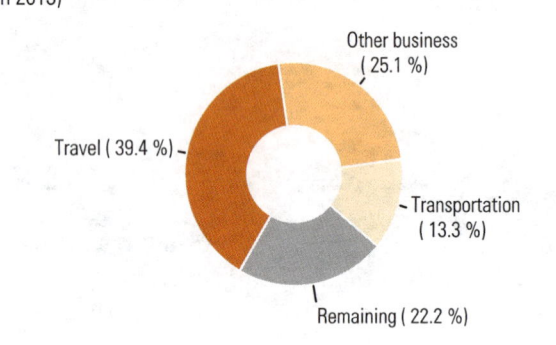

Table 1: Top 10 export commodities 2012 to 2014

HS code	4-digit heading of Harmonized System 2012	Value (million US$) 2012	2013	2014	Unit value 2012	2013	2014	Unit	SITC code
	All Commodities...	501 528.9	518 095.1	528 368.4					
2710	Petroleum oils, other than crude............................	24 979.1	20 432.5	17 474.9	0.9	0.9	0.9	US$/kg	334
3004	Medicaments (excluding goods of heading 30.02, 30.05 or 30.06)........	17 661.4	20 898.5	22 069.8	*90.1*	*112.4*	113.1	US$/kg	542
8708	Parts and accessories of the motor vehicles of headings 87.01 to 87.05....	13 771.2	15 000.2	14 557.7	7.5	*8.0*	8.0	US$/kg	784
9999	Commodities not specified according to kind...............	10 951.0	11 430.0	11 107.9					931
8703	Motor cars and other motor vehicles principally designed for the transport....	9 220.2	10 021.0	11 613.7	19.5	23.1	26.8	thsd US$/unit	781
6403	Footwear with outer soles of rubber, plastics, leather........	8 135.2	8 839.2	9 129.1	60.7	*66.3*	69.1	US$/pair	851
8481	Taps, cocks, valves and similar appliances for pipes, boiler shells........	8 233.9	8 814.9	9 025.2	*21.1*	*22.7*	23.0	US$/kg	747
9403	Other furniture and parts thereof............................	7 293.5	7 726.3	7 905.5					821
8422	Dish washing machines; machinery for cleaning or drying bottles..........	6 363.8	6 951.0	7 030.3					745
7113	Articles of jewellery and parts thereof, of precious metal.............	6 224.8	6 982.6	6 940.7	*7.9*	*8.3*	7.4	thsd US$/kg	897

Italy

Services Imports and Exports: EBOPS 2002 categories

Table 2: Merchandise exports by SITC
(Value in million US$, growth and shares in percentage)

SITC	2014	Avg. Growth rates 2010-2014	Avg. Growth rates 2013-2014	2014 share
Total	528 368.4	4.3	2.0	100.0
0+1	40 842.6	5.7	3.6	7.7
2+4	8 743.1	2.6	0.0	1.7
3	19 605.3	-1.4	-14.9	3.7
5	65 716.9	6.4	4.0	12.4
6	97 695.7	3.5	2.3	18.5
7	186 354.9	4.0	4.1	35.3
8	94 360.5	5.4	3.3	17.9
9	15 049.3	3.4	-15.4	2.8

Table 3: Merchandise imports by SITC
(Value in million US$, growth and shares in percentage)

SITC	2014	Avg. Growth rates 2010-2014	Avg. Growth rates 2013-2014	2014 share
Total	471 659.5	-0.8	-1.6	100.0
0+1	45 009.7	3.3	2.0	9.5
2+4	25 214.7	1.3	1.4	5.3
3	76 837.6	-3.8	-19.5	16.3
5	72 493.1	2.5	-2.0	15.4
6	71 722.1	0.8	5.1	15.2
7	113 579.6	-4.1	4.4	24.1
8	55 694.3	1.4	6.8	11.8
9	11 108.4	0.0	-5.8	2.4

SITC Legend

SITC Code	Description
Total	All commodities
0+1	Food, animals + beverages, tobacco
2+4	Crude materials + anim. & veg. oils
3	Mineral fuels, lubricants
5	Chemicals
6	Goods classified chiefly by material
7	Machinery and transport equipment
8	Miscellaneous manufactured articles
9	Not classified elsewhere in the SITC

Graph 4: Merchandise trade balance
(Bln US$ by MDG Regions in 2014)

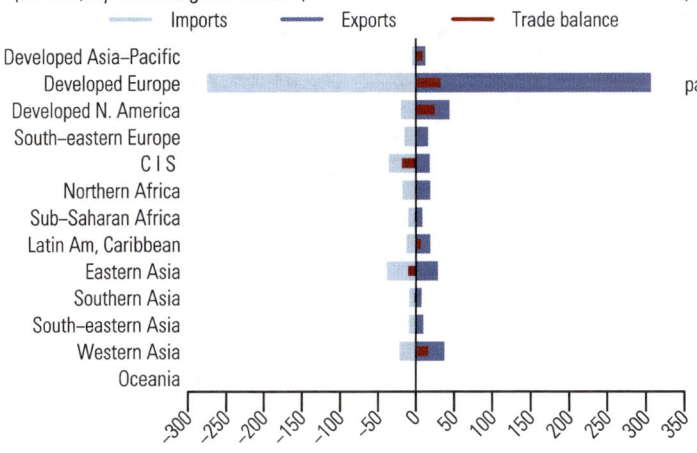

Graph 5: Partner concentration of merchandise trade
(Cumulative share by ranked partners in 2014)

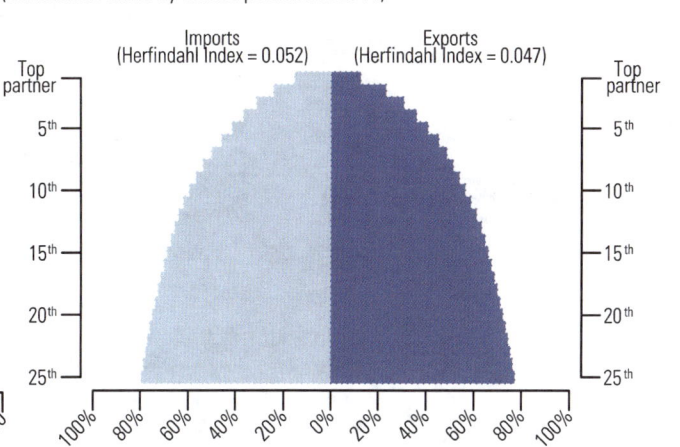

Imports (Herfindahl Index = 0.052)
Exports (Herfindahl Index = 0.047)

Graph 6: Imports of services by EBOPS category
(% share in 2013)

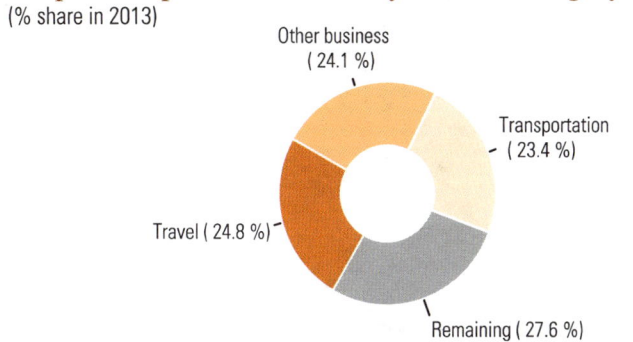

- Other business (24.1 %)
- Transportation (23.4 %)
- Travel (24.8 %)
- Remaining (27.6 %)

Imports Profile:

"Machinery and transport equipment" (SITC section 7), "Mineral fuels, lubricants" (SITC section 3) and "Chemicals" (SITC section 5) were the largest commodity groups for imports in 2014, representing respectively 24.1, 16.3 and 15.4 percent of imported goods (see table 3). From 2012 to 2014, the largest import commodity was "Petroleum oils and oils obtained from bituminous minerals, crude" (HS code 2709) (see table 4), originating mostly from Azerbaijan, Russian Federation, Iraq, Saudi Arabia and Kazakhstan. The top three partners for merchandise imports were Germany, France and China, accounting for respectively 14.9, 8.5 and 6.7 percent of total imports. "Travel" (EBOPS code 236) accounted for the largest share of imports of services in 2013 at 28.0 bln US$, followed by "Other business services" (EBOPS code 268) at 27.2 bln US$ and "Transportation" (EBOPS code 205) at 26.4 bln US$ (see graph 6).

Table 4: Top 10 import commodities 2012 to 2014

HS code	4-digit heading of Harmonized System 2012	Value (million US$) 2012	2013	2014	Unit value 2012	2013	2014	Unit	SITC code
	All Commodities	489 104.1	479 336.4	471 659.5					
2709	Petroleum oils and oils obtained from bituminous minerals, crude	56 916.3	46 459.8	38 589.0	0.8	0.8	0.7	US$/kg	333
2711	Petroleum gases and other gaseous hydrocarbons	33 125.0	29 068.4	21 684.8	0.7	0.6	0.5	US$/kg	343
8703	Motor cars and other motor vehicles principally designed for the transport	20 280.1	20 206.4	22 755.9	16.5	17.0	17.4	thsd US$/unit	781
3004	Medicaments (excluding goods of heading 30.02, 30.05 or 30.06)	14 976.4	15 528.0	14 864.9	112.1	108.3	107.2	US$/kg	542
2710	Petroleum oils, other than crude	11 296.0	13 821.5	11 551.4	0.9	0.8	0.8	US$/kg	334
8517	Electrical apparatus for line telephony or line telegraphy	7 015.3	7 723.7	7 324.6					764
8708	Parts and accessories of the motor vehicles of headings 87.01 to 87.05	6 014.9	6 584.8	6 934.3	8.3	8.4	8.4	US$/kg	784
9999	Commodities not specified according to kind	5 813.5	5 991.6	6 191.5					931
7108	Gold (including gold plated with platinum)	7 532.0	5 611.4	4 790.4	38.6	32.0	32.9	thsd US$/kg	971
8471	Automatic data processing machines and units thereof	5 874.3	5 717.5	5 503.8	177.7			US$/unit	752

Jamaica

Goods Imports: CIF, by origin **Goods Exports:** FOB, by last known destination **Trade System:** Special

Overview:
In 2014, the value of merchandise exports of Jamaica decreased moderately by 7.5 percent to reach 1.5 bln US$, while its merchandise imports decreased moderately by 6.1 percent to reach 5.8 bln US$ (see graph 1, table 2 and table 3). The merchandise trade balance recorded a large deficit of 4.4 bln US$ (see graph 1). The largest merchandise trade balance was with MDG Latin America and the Caribbean at -1.8 bln US$ (see graph 4). Merchandise exports in Jamaica were moderately concentrated amongst partners; imports were also moderately concentrated. The top 8 partners accounted for 80 percent or more of exports and 11 partners accounted for 80 percent or more of imports (see graph 5). In 2013, the value of exports of services of Jamaica decreased slightly by 1.1 percent, reaching 2.7 bln US$, while its imports of services decreased moderately by 5.0 percent and reached 2.1 bln US$ (see graph 2). There was a moderate trade in services surplus of 598.4 mln US$.

Graph 1: Total merchandise trade, by value
(Bln US$ by year)

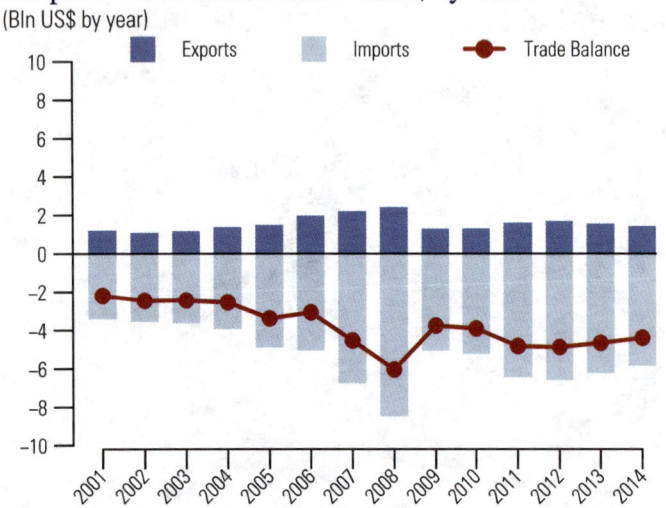

Graph 2: Total services trade, by value
(Bln US$ by year)

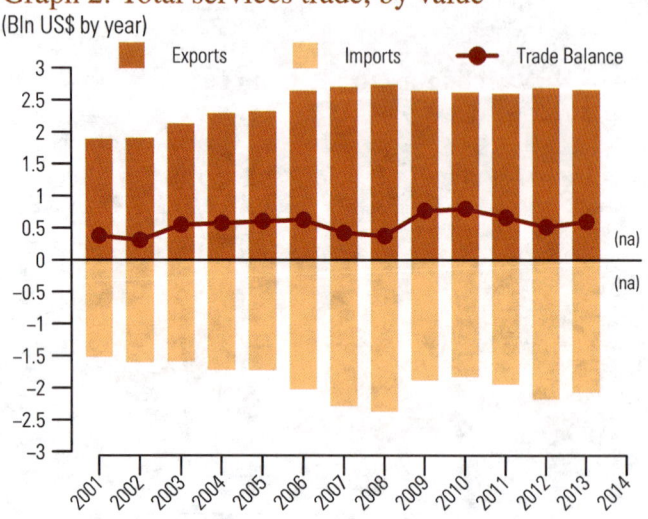

Exports Profile:
"Crude materials + anim. & veg. oils" (SITC section 2+4), "Mineral fuels, lubricants" (SITC section 3) and "Food, animals + beverages, tobacco" (SITC section 0+1) were the largest commodity groups for exports in 2014, representing respectively 47.6, 21.2 and 18.1 percent of exported goods (see table 2). From 2012 to 2014, the largest export commodity was "Artificial corundum, whether or not chemically defined" (HS code 2818) (see table 1). The top three destinations for merchandise exports were the United States, Canada and the Netherlands, accounting for respectively 45.8, 12.0 and 5.5 percent of total exports. "Travel" (EBOPS code 236) accounted for the largest share of exports of services in 2013 at 2.1 bln US$, followed by "Transportation" (EBOPS code 205) at 225.9 mln US$ (see graph 3).

Graph 3: Exports of services by EBOPS category
(% share in 2013)

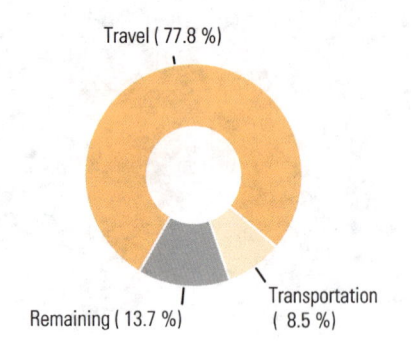

Travel (77.8 %)
Remaining (13.7 %)
Transportation (8.5 %)

Table 1: Top 10 export commodities 2012 to 2014

HS code	4-digit heading of Harmonized System 2007	Value (million US$) 2012	2013	2014	Unit value 2012	2013	2014	Unit	SITC code
	All Commodities	1711.8	1569.1	1452.0					
2818	Artificial corundum, whether or not chemically defined	515.6	535.8	537.3	0.3	0.3	0.3	US$/kg	285
2710	Petroleum oils, other than crude	365.6	333.7	298.6	0.9	0.8	0.8	US$/kg	334
2606	Aluminium ores and concentrates	130.4	129.4	131.2	0.0	0.0	0.0	US$/kg	285
2207	Alcohol of a strength by volume of 80 % vol or higher	179.2	85.2	0.1	*0.9*	*0.9*	*0.9*	US$/litre	512
2208	Alcohol of a strength by volume of less than 80 % vol	59.5	52.4	50.7	*2.7*	*2.5*	*2.9*	US$/litre	112
1701	Cane or beet sugar and chemically pure sucrose, in solid form	92.6	52.7	0.1	0.9	0.9	1.5	US$/kg	061
0714	Manioc, arrowroot, sweet potatoes and similar roots	24.6	28.0	26.8	2.0	2.3	2.1	US$/kg	054
9999	Commodities not specified according to kind	5.8	6.1	64.0					931
0901	Coffee, whether or not roasted or decaffeinated	17.0	19.0	15.8	21.0	22.9	28.8	US$/kg	071
2103	Sauces and preparations therefor	15.4	16.3	17.6	4.2	4.1	3.7	US$/kg	098

Jamaica

Services Imports and Exports: EBOPS 2002 categories

Table 2: Merchandise exports by SITC
(Value in million US$, growth and shares in percentage)

SITC	2014	Avg. Growth rates 2010-2014	Avg. Growth rates 2013-2014	2014 share
Total	1452.0	2.3	-7.5	100.0
0+1	263.0	-4.2	-19.6	18.1
2+4	691.1	5.6	1.4	47.6
3	307.4	2.2	-13.3	21.2
5	28.2	-23.7	-74.4	1.9
6	50.5	32.7	283.1	3.5
7	21.8	-11.2	-44.3	1.5
8	16.3	-8.4	-32.4	1.1
9	73.5	40.0	292.2	5.1

Table 3: Merchandise imports by SITC
(Value in million US$, growth and shares in percentage)

SITC	2014	Avg. Growth rates 2010-2014	Avg. Growth rates 2013-2014	2014 share
Total	5835.5	2.8	-6.1	100.0
0+1	932.0	1.2	-10.1	16.0
2+4	104.5	2.5	4.6	1.8
3	1936.3	5.1	-14.3	33.2
5	615.6	-3.1	-19.1	10.5
6	614.3	1.1	2.1	10.5
7	967.6	5.0	7.6	16.6
8	493.4	0.6	11.0	8.5
9	171.9	16.5	51.3	2.9

SITC Legend

SITC Code	Description
Total	All commodities
0+1	Food, animals + beverages, tobacco
2+4	Crude materials + anim. & veg. oils
3	Mineral fuels, lubricants
5	Chemicals
6	Goods classified chiefly by material
7	Machinery and transport equipment
8	Miscellaneous manufactured articles
9	Not classified elsewhere in the SITC

Graph 4: Merchandise trade balance
(Bln US$ by MDG Regions in 2014)

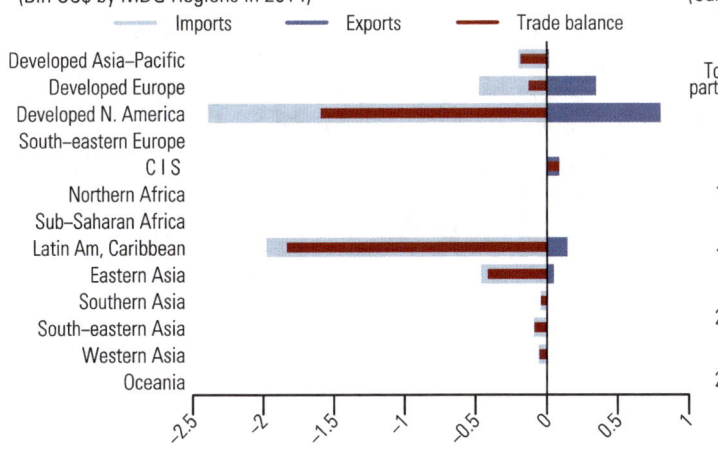

Graph 5: Partner concentration of merchandise trade
(Cumulative share by ranked partners in 2014)

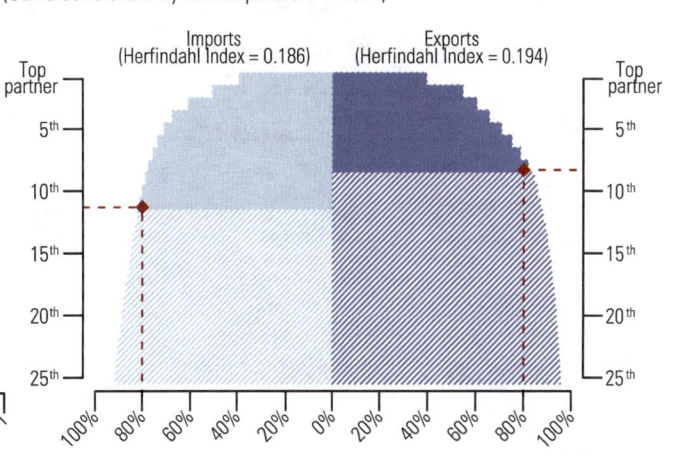

Imports (Herfindahl Index = 0.186)
Exports (Herfindahl Index = 0.194)

Graph 6: Imports of services by EBOPS category
(% share in 2013)

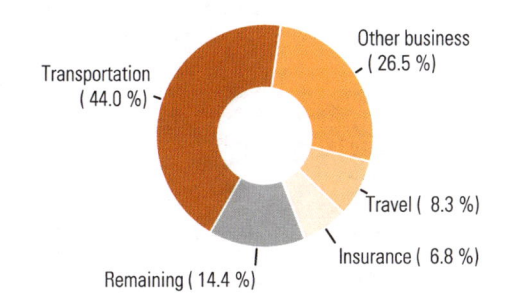

- Transportation (44.0 %)
- Other business (26.5 %)
- Remaining (14.4 %)
- Travel (8.3 %)
- Insurance (6.8 %)

Imports Profile:

"Mineral fuels, lubricants" (SITC section 3), "Machinery and transport equipment" (SITC section 7) and "Food, animals + beverages, tobacco" (SITC section 0+1) were the largest commodity groups for imports in 2014, representing respectively 33.2, 16.6 and 16.0 percent of imported goods (see table 3). From 2012 to 2014, the largest import commodity was "Petroleum oils, other than crude" (HS code 2710) (see table 4). The top three partners for merchandise imports were the United States, the Bolivarian Republic of Venezuela and Trinidad and Tobago, accounting for respectively 36.3, 14.0 and 11.1 percent of total imports. "Transportation" (EBOPS code 205) accounted for the largest share of imports of services in 2013 at 909.7 mln US$, followed by "Other business services" (EBOPS code 268) at 547.5 mln US$ and "Travel" (EBOPS code 236) at 171.2 mln US$ (see graph 6).

Table 4: Top 10 import commodities 2012 to 2014

HS code	4-digit heading of Harmonized System 2007	2012	2013	2014	2012	2013	2014	Unit	SITC code
	All Commodities	6580.4	6216.2	5835.5					
2710	Petroleum oils, other than crude	1362.0	1265.7	1218.1	0.9	0.8	0.8	US$/kg	334
2709	Petroleum oils and oils obtained from bituminous minerals, crude	939.3	921.2	642.6	0.7	0.8	0.7	US$/kg	333
2207	Alcohol of a strength by volume of 80 % vol or higher	384.3	231.8	82.7	1.0	1.0	0.9	US$/litre	512
8703	Motor cars and other motor vehicles principally designed for the transport	224.4	210.0	173.4	17.5	16.8	17.0	thsd US$/unit	781
9999	Commodities not specified according to kind	116.3	113.6	171.9					931
3004	Medicaments (excluding goods of heading 30.02, 30.05 or 30.06)	132.6	122.5	137.6	43.7	49.2	22.5	US$/kg	542
8517	Electrical apparatus for line telephony or line telegraphy	59.7	66.2	103.4					764
2815	Sodium hydroxide (caustic soda)	85.5	79.7	63.7	0.3	0.8	0.2	US$/kg	522
1005	Maize (corn)	77.6	81.3	69.4	0.5	0.5	0.3	US$/kg	044
2106	Food preparations not elsewhere specified or included	64.5	71.1	71.6	9.0	6.1	5.5	US$/kg	098

Japan

Goods Imports: CIF, by origin   **Goods Exports: FOB, by last known destination**   **Trade System: General**

Overview:

In 2014, the value of merchandise exports of Japan decreased slightly by 4.4 percent to reach 683.8 bln US$, while its merchandise imports decreased slightly by 1.3 percent to reach 822.3 bln US$ (see graph 1, table 2 and table 3). In spite of yen depreciation in 2014, Japan's trade deficit continued to increase and reached 138.4 bln US$ in 2014, mainly due lower exports in manufactured goods (see graph 1). The largest merchandise trade balance was with MDG Western Asia at -114.0 bln US$ (see graph 4). Merchandise exports in Japan were diversified amongst partners; imports were also diversified. The top 16 partners accounted for 80 percent or more of exports and 17 partners accounted for 80 percent or more of imports (see graph 5). In 2013, the value of exports of services of Japan increased slightly by 0.8 percent, reaching 146.7 bln US$, while its imports of services decreased moderately by 8.2 percent and reached 162.3 bln US$ (see graph 2). There was a relatively small trade in services deficit of 15.6 bln US$.

Graph 1: Total merchandise trade, by value
(Bln US$ by year)

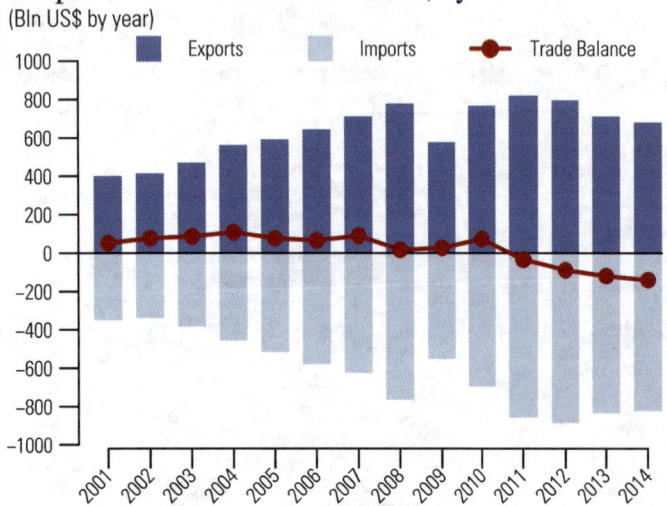

Graph 2: Total services trade, by value
(Bln US$ by year)

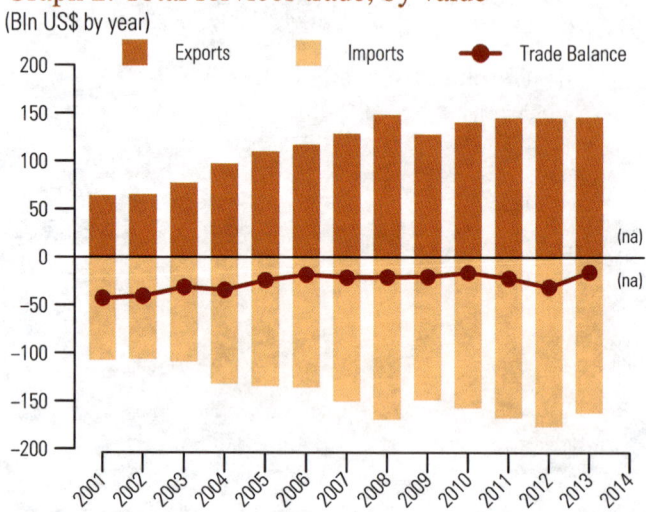

Exports Profile:

"Machinery and transport equipment" (SITC section 7), "Goods classified chiefly by material" (SITC section 6) and "Chemicals" (SITC section 5) were the largest commodity groups for exports in 2014, representing respectively 58.6, 12.1 and 10.6 percent of exported goods (see table 2). From 2012 to 2014, the largest export commodity was "Motor cars and other motor vehicles principally designed for the transport" (HS code 8703) (see table 1), but exports of this commodity dropped by 3.3 percent from 2013 to 2014. The top three destinations for merchandise exports were the United States, China and the Republic of Korea, accounting for respectively 18.5, 18.1 and 7.7 percent of total exports. "Other business services" (EBOPS code 268) accounted for the largest share of exports of services in 2013 at 40.6 bln US$, followed by "Transportation" (EBOPS code 205) at 39.6 bln US$ and "Royalties and license fees" (EBOPS code 266) at 31.6 bln US$ (see graph 3).

Graph 3: Exports of services by EBOPS category
(% share in 2013)

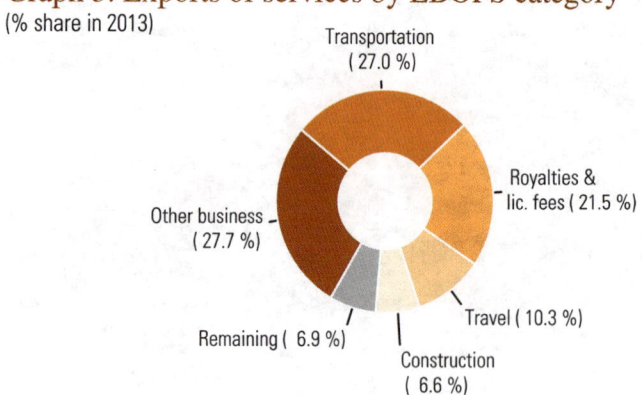

- Transportation (27.0 %)
- Royalties & lic. fees (21.5 %)
- Travel (10.3 %)
- Construction (6.6 %)
- Remaining (6.9 %)
- Other business (27.7 %)

Table 1: Top 10 export commodities 2012 to 2014

HS code	4-digit heading of Harmonized System 2012	Value (million US$) 2012	2013	2014	Unit value 2012	2013	2014	Unit	SITC code
	All Commodities	798 620.0	715 097.2	683 845.6					
8703	Motor cars and other motor vehicles principally designed for the transport	97 460.1	91 688.8	88 666.3	*19.4*	*18.5*	*18.3*	thsd US$/unit	781
8708	Parts and accessories of the motor vehicles of headings 87.01 to 87.05	39 781.8	35 301.2	32 538.6	13.7	12.7	12.1	US$/kg	784
9999	Commodities not specified according to kind	35 510.1	35 791.4	35 894.9					931
8542	Electronic integrated circuits	30 586.2	26 994.8	25 513.3					776
8901	Cruise ships, excursion boats, ferry-boats, cargo ships, barges	21 473.8	14 867.8	12 262.5					793
8486	Machines and apparatus used for the manufacture of semiconductor devices	14 645.6	12 691.2	13 042.4					728
2710	Petroleum oils, other than crude	11 630.9	14 665.6	13 433.0	0.9	*0.9*	0.9	US$/kg	334
8443	Printing machinery used for printing by means of the printing type, blocks	13 748.3	12 512.5	11 527.5					726
8704	Motor vehicles for the transport of goods	12 512.2	10 105.1	10 507.2	*24.4*	*18.5*	*17.4*	thsd US$/unit	782
8541	Diodes, transistors and similar semiconductor devices	10 848.2	9 062.4	9 058.7					776

Source: UN Comtrade and UN ServiceTrade

Japan

Services Imports and Exports: EBOPS 2002 categories

Table 2: Merchandise exports by SITC
(Value in million US$, growth and shares in percentage)

SITC	2014	Avg. Growth rates 2010-2014	2013-2014	2014 share
Total	683 845.6	-2.9	-4.4	100.0
0+1	4 536.2	-0.4	2.0	0.7
2+4	11 467.9	1.1	-8.5	1.7
3	15 886.2	5.0	-4.8	2.3
5	72 246.0	-2.0	-4.7	10.6
6	82 448.4	-4.7	-12.6	12.1
7	400 680.6	-3.3	-3.3	58.6
8	56 029.1	-1.0	0.2	8.2
9	40 551.3	-3.3	-1.2	5.9

Table 3: Merchandise imports by SITC
(Value in million US$, growth and shares in percentage)

SITC	2014	Avg. Growth rates 2010-2014	2013-2014	2014 share
Total	822 251.1	4.3	-1.3	100.0
0+1	63 571.8	1.7	-4.0	7.7
2+4	56 625.1	-0.2	-2.1	6.9
3	262 063.8	7.1	-6.9	31.9
5	64 271.9	1.4	-2.1	7.8
6	69 606.2	4.3	12.8	8.5
7	194 566.0	4.8	3.1	23.7
8	99 554.1	4.2	0.0	12.1
9	11 992.2	-2.0	0.7	1.5

SITC Legend

SITC Code	Description
Total	All commodities
0+1	Food, animals + beverages, tobacco
2+4	Crude materials + anim. & veg. oils
3	Mineral fuels, lubricants
5	Chemicals
6	Goods classified chiefly by material
7	Machinery and transport equipment
8	Miscellaneous manufactured articles
9	Not classified elsewhere in the SITC

Graph 4: Merchandise trade balance
(Bln US$ by MDG Regions in 2014)

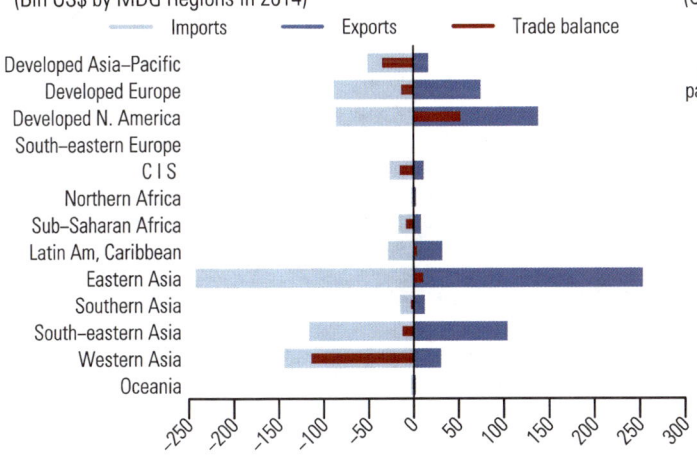

Graph 5: Partner concentration of merchandise trade
(Cumulative share by ranked partners in 2014)

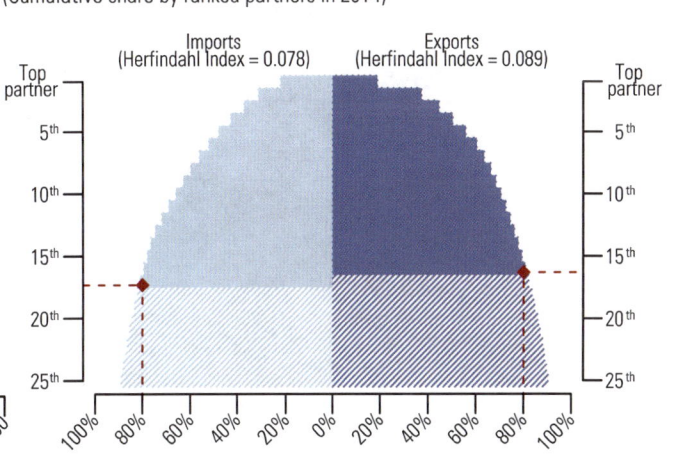

Imports (Herfindahl Index = 0.078)
Exports (Herfindahl Index = 0.089)

Graph 6: Imports of services by EBOPS category
(% share in 2013)

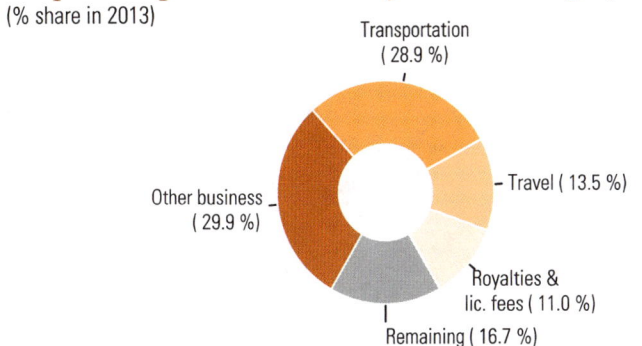

- Transportation (28.9 %)
- Travel (13.5 %)
- Royalties & lic. fees (11.0 %)
- Remaining (16.7 %)
- Other business (29.9 %)

Imports Profile:

"Mineral fuels, lubricants" (SITC section 3), "Machinery and transport equipment" (SITC section 7) and "Miscellaneous manufactured articles" (SITC section 8) were the largest commodity groups for imports in 2014, representing respectively 31.9, 23.7 and 12.1 percent of imported goods (see table 3). From 2012 to 2014, the largest import commodity was "Petroleum oils and oils obtained from bituminous minerals, crude" (HS code 2709) (see table 4). The top three partners for merchandise imports were China, the United States and Australia, accounting for respectively 21.7, 8.8 and 6.1 percent of total imports. "Other business services" (EBOPS code 268) accounted for the largest share of imports of services in 2013 at 48.6 bln US$, followed by "Transportation" (EBOPS code 205) at 46.9 bln US$ and "Travel" (EBOPS code 236) at 21.8 bln US$ (see graph 6).

Table 4: Top 10 import commodities 2012 to 2014

HS code	4-digit heading of Harmonized System 2012	2012	2013	2014	2012	2013	2014	Unit	SITC code
	All Commodities	886 031.1	833 166.1	822 251.1					
2709	Petroleum oils and oils obtained from bituminous minerals, crude	153 107.4	145 720.8	130 690.3	0.9	0.8	0.8	US$/kg	333
2711	Petroleum gases and other gaseous hydrocarbons	88 058.1	83 330.4	84 493.3					343
2710	Petroleum oils, other than crude	30 034.3	26 882.1	24 946.8	1.0	0.9	0.9	US$/kg	334
8517	Electrical apparatus for line telephony or line telegraphy	25 524.7	25 991.0	25 501.4					764
2701	Coal; briquettes, ovoids and similar solid fuels manufactured from coal	29 117.8	23 608.1	19 692.4	0.2	0.1	0.1	US$/kg	321
2601	Iron ores and concentrates, including roasted iron pyrites	19 130.5	17 391.5	15 935.6	0.1	0.1	0.1	US$/kg	281
8542	Electronic integrated circuits	17 425.5	16 501.6	16 790.1					776
8471	Automatic data processing machines and units thereof	17 012.5	16 473.9	16 806.0	185.2	179.8	189.0	US$/unit	752
3004	Medicaments (excluding goods of heading 30.02, 30.05 or 30.06)	16 703.2	14 790.8	13 719.3	325.9	278.6	267.1	US$/kg	542
9999	Commodities not specified according to kind	12 201.0	10 484.6	10 434.4					931

2014 International Trade Statistics Yearbook, Vol. I Source: UN Comtrade and UN ServiceTrade

Jordan

Goods Imports: CIF, by origin **Goods Exports:** FOB, by last known destination **Trade System:** Special

Overview:
In 2014, the value of merchandise exports of Jordan increased moderately by 5.9 percent to reach 8.4 bln US$, while its merchandise imports increased moderately by 5.5 percent to reach 22.7 bln US$ (see graph 1, table 2 and table 3). The merchandise trade balance recorded a large deficit of 14.4 bln US$ (see graph 1). The largest merchandise trade balance was with MDG Developed Europe at -4.3 bln US$ (see graph 4). Merchandise exports in Jordan were diversified amongst partners; imports were also diversified. The top 14 partners accounted for 80 percent or more of exports and 19 partners accounted for 80 percent or more of imports (see graph 5). In 2013, the value of exports of services of Jordan decreased slightly by 1.0 percent, reaching 6.4 bln US$, while its imports of services increased slightly by 0.7 percent and reached 4.6 bln US$ (see graph 2). There was a moderate trade in services surplus of 1.8 bln US$.

Graph 1: Total merchandise trade, by value
(Bln US$ by year)

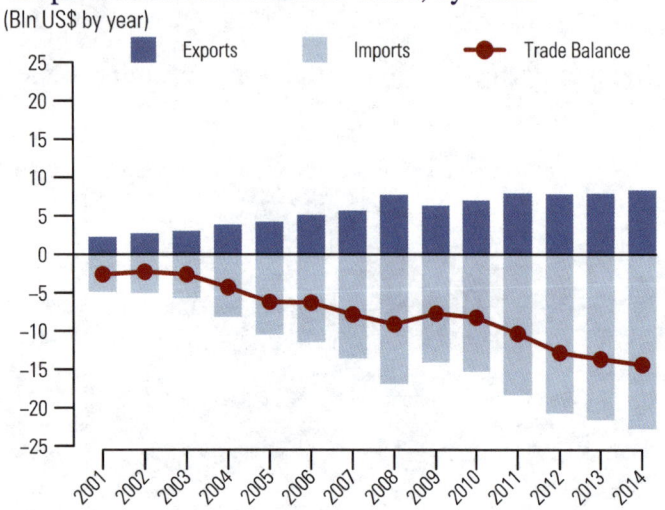

Graph 2: Total services trade, by value
(Bln US$ by year)

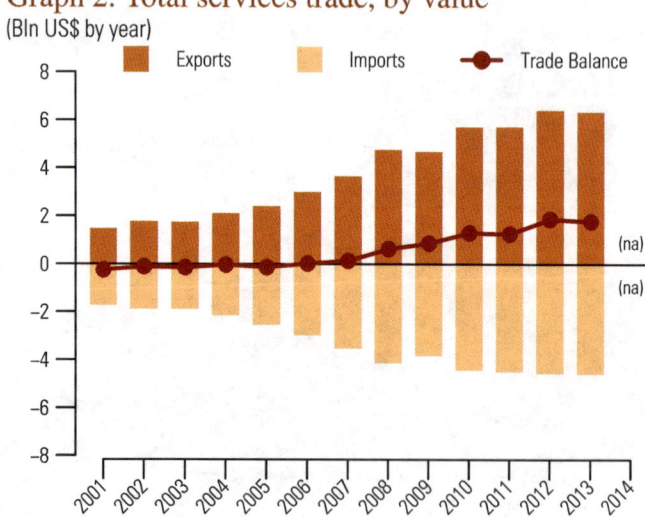

Exports Profile:
"Chemicals" (SITC section 5), "Miscellaneous manufactured articles" (SITC section 8) and "Food, animals + beverages, tobacco" (SITC section 0+1) were the largest commodity groups for exports in 2014, representing respectively 31.8, 21.6 and 19.4 percent of exported goods (see table 2). From 2012 to 2014, the largest export commodity was "Other garments, knitted or crocheted" (HS code 6114) (see table 1). The top three destinations for merchandise exports were Iraq, the United States and Saudi Arabia, accounting for respectively 16.1, 15.1 and 11.5 percent of total exports. "Travel" (EBOPS code 236) accounted for the largest share of exports of services in 2013 at 4.1 bln US$, followed by "Transportation" (EBOPS code 205) at 1.4 bln US$ and "Government services, n.i.e." (EBOPS code 291) at 331.4 mln US$ (see graph 3).

Graph 3: Exports of services by EBOPS category
(% share in 2013)

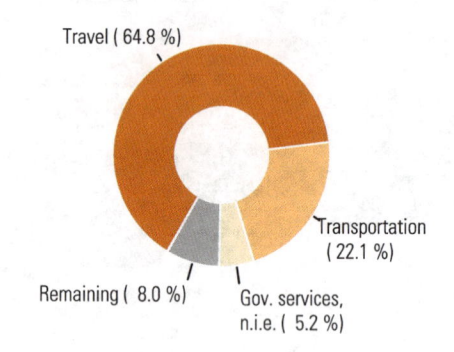

- Travel (64.8 %)
- Transportation (22.1 %)
- Gov. services, n.i.e. (5.2 %)
- Remaining (8.0 %)

Table 1: Top 10 export commodities 2012 to 2014

HS code	4-digit heading of Harmonized System 2012	Value (million US$) 2012	2013	2014	Unit value 2012	2013	2014	Unit	SITC code
	All Commodities	7877.1	7919.6	8385.3					
6114	Other garments, knitted or crocheted	816.7	905.6	1021.2	21.3	23.1	23.5	US$/kg	845
3104	Mineral or chemical fertilisers, potassic	673.4	604.7	602.5			0.9	US$/kg	562
2510	Natural calcium phosphates	601.3	376.7	469.7	0.1	0.1	0.1	US$/kg	272
3004	Medicaments (excluding goods of heading 30.02, 30.05 or 30.06)	431.7	451.8	386.9	48.7	56.4	50.1	US$/kg	542
0702	Tomatoes, fresh or chilled	250.2	316.3	399.0	0.6	0.5	0.8	US$/kg	054
3102	Mineral or chemical fertilisers, nitrogenous	287.4	220.9	297.1	0.6	0.5	0.5	US$/kg	562
3003	Medicaments (excluding goods of heading 30.02, 30.05 or 30.06)	186.1	256.8	256.2	16.8	21.3	20.8	US$/kg	542
0104	Live sheep and goats	137.0	218.0	206.0					001
8544	Insulated (including enamelled or anodised) wire, cable	161.7	185.3	205.2	5.5	5.4	5.5	US$/kg	773
7113	Articles of jewellery and parts thereof, of precious metal	106.8	107.8	137.3	10.1	10.4	13.3	thsd US$/kg	897

Jordan

Services Imports and Exports: EBOPS 2002 categories

Table 2: Merchandise exports by SITC
(Value in million US$, growth and shares in percentage)

SITC	2014	Avg. Growth rates 2010-2014	Avg. Growth rates 2013-2014	2014 share
Total	8 385.3	4.5	5.9	100.0
0+1	1 625.7	10.3	7.1	19.4
2+4	609.6	4.8	10.8	7.3
3	16.2	-29.7	-32.6	0.2
5	2 666.8	3.0	2.4	31.8
6	793.3	0.7	-1.7	9.5
7	839.0	3.4	8.4	10.0
8	1 811.9	9.4	12.8	21.6
9	22.7	-42.7	-37.4	0.3

Table 3: Merchandise imports by SITC
(Value in million US$, growth and shares in percentage)

SITC	2014	Avg. Growth rates 2010-2014	Avg. Growth rates 2013-2014	2014 share
Total	22 740.3	10.5	5.5	100.0
0+1	3 773.7	13.0	9.6	16.6
2+4	589.5	9.9	9.7	2.6
3	6 196.1	16.5	11.9	27.2
5	2 302.5	7.5	2.7	10.1
6	3 299.2	6.0	-6.8	14.5
7	4 173.2	4.4	6.2	18.4
8	1 485.6	8.5	1.1	6.5
9	920.5	37.5	8.0	4.0

SITC Legend

SITC Code	Description
Total	All commodities
0+1	Food, animals + beverages, tobacco
2+4	Crude materials + anim. & veg. oils
3	Mineral fuels, lubricants
5	Chemicals
6	Goods classified chiefly by material
7	Machinery and transport equipment
8	Miscellaneous manufactured articles
9	Not classified elsewhere in the SITC

Graph 4: Merchandise trade balance
(Bln US$ by MDG Regions in 2014)

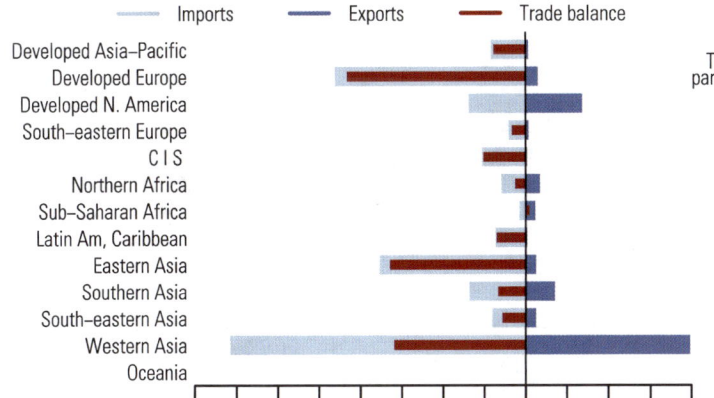

Graph 5: Partner concentration of merchandise trade
(Cumulative share by ranked partners in 2014)

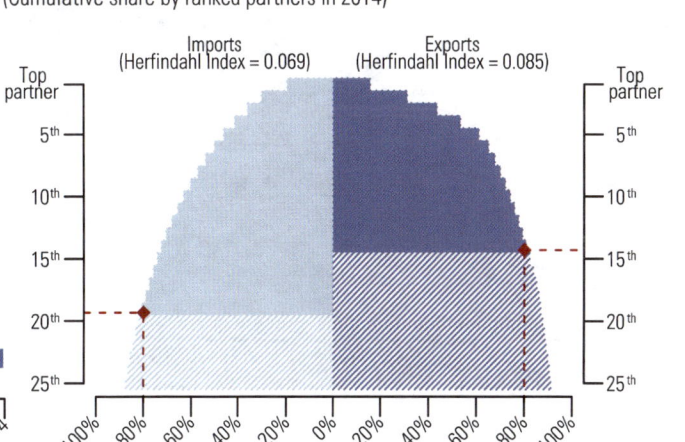

Imports (Herfindahl Index = 0.069)
Exports (Herfindahl Index = 0.085)

Graph 6: Imports of services by EBOPS category
(% share in 2013)

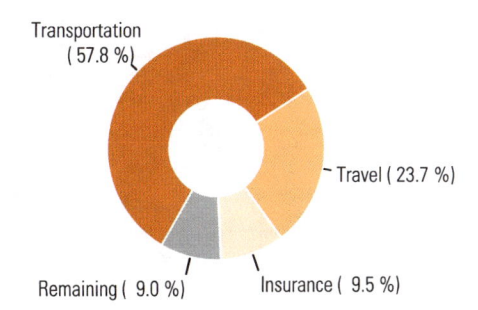

- Transportation (57.8%)
- Travel (23.7%)
- Insurance (9.5%)
- Remaining (9.0%)

Imports Profile:

"Mineral fuels, lubricants" (SITC section 3), "Machinery and transport equipment" (SITC section 7) and "Food, animals + beverages, tobacco" (SITC section 0+1) were the largest commodity groups for imports in 2014, representing respectively 27.2, 18.4 and 16.6 percent of imported goods (see table 3). From 2012 to 2014, the largest import commodity was "Petroleum oils, other than crude" (HS code 2710) (see table 4). The top three partners for merchandise imports were Saudi Arabia, China and the United States, accounting for respectively 20.5, 10.1 and 6.3 percent of total imports. "Transportation" (EBOPS code 205) accounted for the largest share of imports of services in 2013 at 2.6 bln US$, followed by "Travel" (EBOPS code 236) at 1.1 bln US$ and "Insurance services" (EBOPS code 253) at 435.7 mln US$ (see graph 6).

Table 4: Top 10 import commodities 2012 to 2014

HS code	4-digit heading of Harmonized System 2012	Value (million US$) 2012	2013	2014	Unit value 2012	2013	2014	Unit	SITC code
	All Commodities	20 691.4	21 549.0	22 740.3					
2710	Petroleum oils, other than crude	3 430.0	2 634.8	3 421.1	0.9	0.9	0.8	US$/kg	334
2709	Petroleum oils and oils obtained from bituminous minerals, crude	2 637.6	2 284.7	2 313.6	0.8	0.8	0.7	US$/kg	333
8703	Motor cars and other motor vehicles principally designed for the transport	650.8	733.6	975.3		18.9	18.5	thsd US$/unit	781
2711	Petroleum gases and other gaseous hydrocarbons	426.8	464.3	295.0	0.5	0.4	0.6	US$/kg	343
3004	Medicaments (excluding goods of heading 30.02, 30.05 or 30.06)	372.6	390.9	405.2	44.0	43.8	41.3	US$/kg	542
7108	Gold (including gold plated with platinum)	44.4	522.3	543.9	50.6	44.3	39.5	thsd US$/kg	971
8517	Electrical apparatus for line telephony or line telegraphy	343.3	388.7	374.1					764
9999	Commodities not specified according to kind	313.9	329.9	376.6					931
6006	Other knitted or crocheted fabrics	257.9	245.0	321.1	8.5	8.4	8.4	US$/kg	655
1001	Wheat and meslin	291.7	216.2	281.2	0.3	0.3	0.3	US$/kg	041

2014 International Trade Statistics Yearbook, Vol. I Source: UN Comtrade and UN ServiceTrade

Kazakhstan

Goods Imports: CIF, by origin **Goods Exports:** FOB, by last known destination **Trade System:** General

Overview:
In 2014, the value of merchandise exports of Kazakhstan decreased moderately by 5.2 percent to reach 78.2 bln US$, while its merchandise imports decreased substantially by 15.7 percent to reach 41.2 bln US$ (see graph 1, table 2 and table 3). The merchandise trade balance recorded a large surplus of 37.0 bln US$ (see graph 1). The largest merchandise trade balance was with MDG Developed Europe at 37.4 bln US$ (see graph 4). Merchandise exports in Kazakhstan were diversified amongst partners; imports were moderately concentrated. The top 12 partners accounted for 80 percent or more of exports and 12 partners accounted for 80 percent or more of imports (see graph 5). In 2013, the value of exports of services of Kazakhstan increased moderately by 9.2 percent, reaching 5.3 bln US$, while its imports of services decreased moderately by 5.0 percent and reached 12.1 bln US$ (see graph 2). There was a large trade in services deficit of 6.8 bln US$.

Graph 1: Total merchandise trade, by value
(Bln US$ by year)

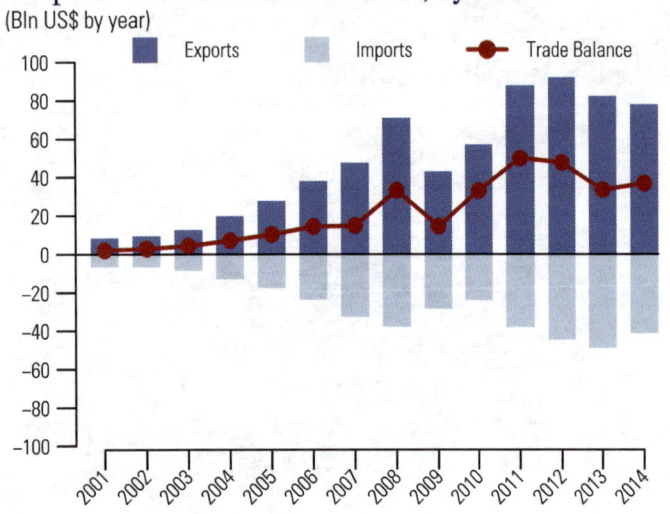

Graph 2: Total services trade, by value
(Bln US$ by year)

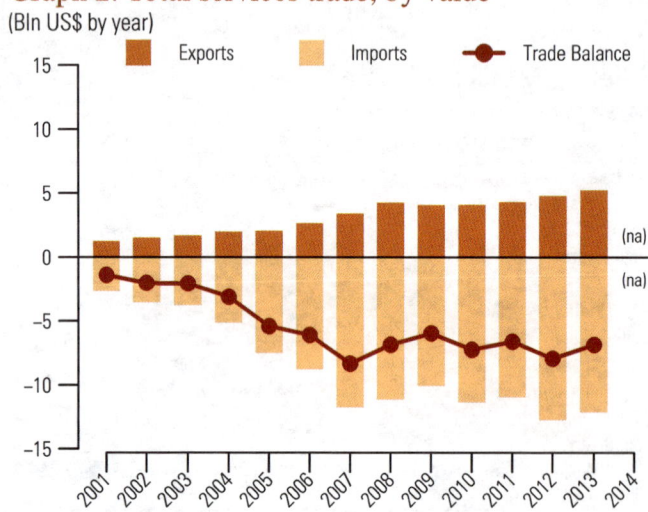

Exports Profile:
"Mineral fuels, lubricants" (SITC section 3), "Goods classified chiefly by material" (SITC section 6) and "Crude materials + anim. & veg. oils" (SITC section 2+4) were the largest commodity groups for exports in 2014, representing respectively 77.6, 8.9 and 5.0 percent of exported goods (see table 2). From 2012 to 2014, the largest export commodity was "Petroleum oils and oils obtained from bituminous minerals, crude" (HS code 2709) (see table 1). The top three destinations for merchandise exports were Italy, China and the Netherlands, accounting for respectively 18.5, 16.1 and 10.2 percent of total exports. "Transportation" (EBOPS code 205) accounted for the largest share of exports of services in 2013 at 2.9 bln US$, followed by "Travel" (EBOPS code 236) at 1.5 bln US$ and "Other business services" (EBOPS code 268) at 484.0 mln US$ (see graph 3).

Graph 3: Exports of services by EBOPS category
(% share in 2013)

- Transportation (54.2 %)
- Travel (27.7 %)
- Other business (9.2 %)
- Remaining (8.9 %)

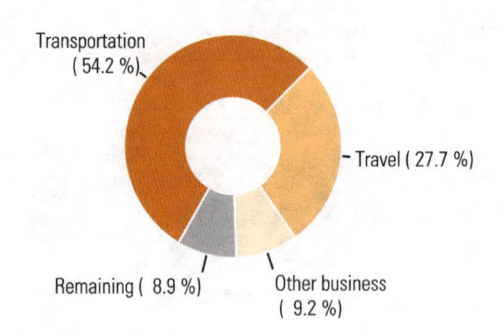

Table 1: Top 10 export commodities 2012 to 2014

HS code	4-digit heading of Harmonized System 2012	Value (million US$) 2012	2013	2014	Unit value 2012	2013	2014	Unit	SITC code
	All Commodities	92281.5	82510.0	78236.7					
2709	Petroleum oils and oils obtained from bituminous minerals, crude	56442.4	55221.4	53630.0	0.8	0.8	0.8	US$/kg	333
2711	Petroleum gases and other gaseous hydrocarbons	3620.0	3385.3	3296.6	0.2	0.2	0.2	US$/kg	343
2710	Petroleum oils, other than crude	3226.8	3144.3	2969.9	0.6	0.6	0.6	US$/kg	334
7403	Refined copper and copper alloys, unwrought	3427.9	2678.0	1711.6	7.6	7.1	6.6	US$/kg	682
7202	Ferro-alloys	3893.0	1715.7	1557.1	1.4	1.3	1.3	US$/kg	671
2844	Radioactive chemical elements and radioactive isotopes	2752.9	2338.5	1912.2		82.1	70.0	US$/kg	525
2601	Iron ores and concentrates, including roasted iron pyrites	2416.2	1561.5	1105.8	0.1	0.1	0.1	US$/kg	281
1001	Wheat and meslin	1599.1	1235.0	960.0	0.2	0.2	0.2	US$/kg	041
2603	Copper ores and concentrates	818.1	590.2	840.0		1.1	1.3	US$/kg	283
2701	Coal; briquettes, ovoids and similar solid fuels manufactured from coal	967.1	571.1	558.7	0.0	0.0	0.0	US$/kg	321

Source: UN Comtrade and UN ServiceTrade

Kazakhstan

Services Imports and Exports: EBOPS 2002 categories

Table 2: Merchandise exports by SITC
(Value in million US$, growth and shares in percentage)

SITC	2014	Avg. Growth rates 2010-2014	Avg. Growth rates 2013-2014	2014 share
Total	78 236.7	8.1	-5.2	100.0
0+1	2 290.5	5.3	-5.7	2.9
2+4	3 916.5	5.8	-7.2	5.0
3	60 696.1	10.3	-3.0	77.6
5	2 673.0	1.6	-13.7	3.4
6	6 986.8	-1.5	-15.4	8.9
7	1 197.2	36.4	-2.0	1.5
8	223.1	41.2	-10.4	0.3
9	253.5	-26.6	-45.2	0.3

Table 3: Merchandise imports by SITC
(Value in million US$, growth and shares in percentage)

SITC	2014	Avg. Growth rates 2010-2014	Avg. Growth rates 2013-2014	2014 share
Total	41 212.8	14.4	-15.7	100.0
0+1	4 045.7	17.0	-5.2	9.8
2+4	968.6	22.8	8.4	2.4
3	2 300.4	-0.8	-57.7	5.6
5	4 650.9	12.9	-9.0	11.3
6	7 430.2	14.4	-22.5	18.0
7	16 895.0	15.0	-4.6	41.0
8	4 861.1	22.4	-15.8	11.8
9	61.0	39.0	-34.4	0.1

SITC Legend

SITC Code	Description
Total	All commodities
0+1	Food, animals + beverages, tobacco
2+4	Crude materials + anim. & veg. oils
3	Mineral fuels, lubricants
5	Chemicals
6	Goods classified chiefly by material
7	Machinery and transport equipment
8	Miscellaneous manufactured articles
9	Not classified elsewhere in the SITC

Graph 4: Merchandise trade balance
(Bln US$ by MDG Regions in 2014)

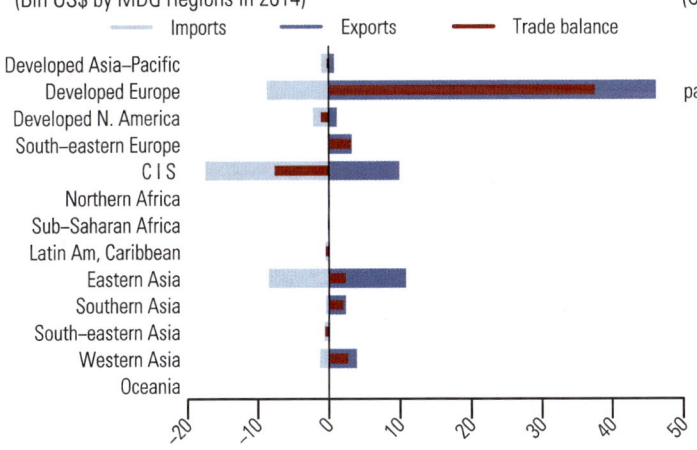

Graph 5: Partner concentration of merchandise trade
(Cumulative share by ranked partners in 2014)

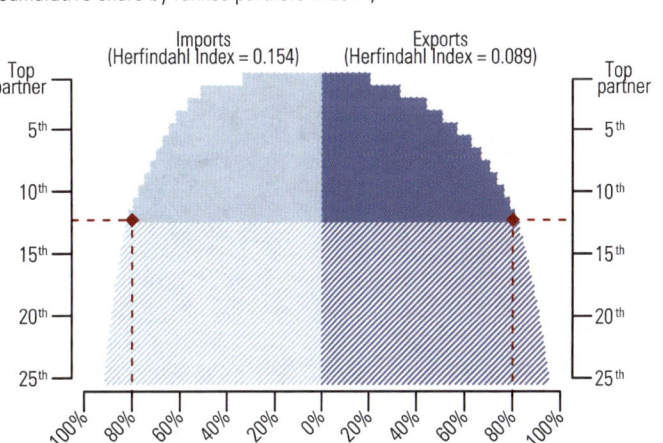

Imports (Herfindahl Index = 0.154)
Exports (Herfindahl Index = 0.089)

Graph 6: Imports of services by EBOPS category
(% share in 2013)

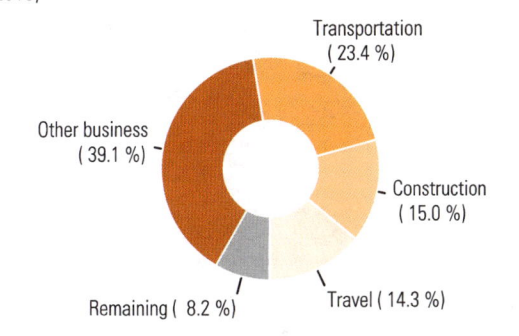

- Transportation (23.4 %)
- Other business (39.1 %)
- Construction (15.0 %)
- Travel (14.3 %)
- Remaining (8.2 %)

Imports Profile:

"Machinery and transport equipment" (SITC section 7), "Goods classified chiefly by material" (SITC section 6) and "Miscellaneous manufactured articles" (SITC section 8) were the largest commodity groups for imports in 2014, representing respectively 41.0, 18.0 and 11.8 percent of imported goods (see table 3). From 2012 to 2014, the largest import commodity was "Motor cars and other motor vehicles principally designed for the transport" (HS code 8703) (see table 4). The top three partners for merchandise imports were the Russian Federation, China and Germany, accounting for respectively 36.0, 17.1 and 5.5 percent of total imports. "Other business services" (EBOPS code 268) accounted for the largest share of imports of services in 2013 at 4.7 bln US$, followed by "Transportation" (EBOPS code 205) at 2.8 bln US$ and "Construction services" (EBOPS code 249) at 1.8 bln US$ (see graph 6).

Table 4: Top 10 import commodities 2012 to 2014

HS code	4-digit heading of Harmonized System 2012	Value (million US$) 2012	2013	2014	Unit value 2012	2013	2014	Unit	SITC code
	All Commodities	44 538.1	48 871.9	41 212.8					
8703	Motor cars and other motor vehicles principally designed for the transport	1 384.1	2 137.5	2 320.4	11.4	12.6	13.7	thsd US$/unit	781
2709	Petroleum oils and oils obtained from bituminous minerals, crude	2 198.9	2 839.9	188.2	0.4	0.4	0.4	US$/kg	333
2710	Petroleum oils, other than crude	1 455.0	1 573.0	1 397.1	0.7	0.6	0.7	US$/kg	334
3004	Medicaments (excluding goods of heading 30.02, 30.05 or 30.06)	1 018.1	1 275.4	1 108.2	32.6	34.9	34.5	US$/kg	542
7305	Other tubes and pipes (for example, welded, riveted or similarly closed)	997.6	1 719.8	269.2	2.3	1.1	1.6	US$/kg	679
8517	Electrical apparatus for line telephony or line telegraphy	779.6	1 013.0	1 064.2					764
8471	Automatic data processing machines and units thereof	906.9	1 027.9	630.4	78.5	70.6	87.0	US$/unit	752
8606	Railway or tramway goods vans and wagons, not self-propelled	1 642.2	318.6	266.1	75.9	35.0	30.3	thsd US$/unit	791
7304	Tubes, pipes and hollow profiles, seamless, of iron (other than cast iron)	565.8	741.1	682.1		2.1	1.8	US$/kg	679
8704	Motor vehicles for the transport of goods	588.3	696.7	533.3	28.3	21.6	26.4	thsd US$/unit	782

2014 International Trade Statistics Yearbook, Vol. I   Source: UN Comtrade and UN ServiceTrade

Kenya

Goods Imports: CIF, by origin　　**Goods Exports:** FOB, by last known destination　　**Trade System:** General

Overview:
In 2013, the value of merchandise exports of Kenya was 5.5 bln US$, while its merchandise imports were 16.4 bln US$ (see graph 1, table 2 and table 3). The merchandise trade balance recorded a large deficit of 10.9 bln US$ (see graph 1). The largest merchandise trade balance was with MDG Southern Asia at -2.6 bln US$ (see graph 4). Merchandise exports in Kenya were diversified amongst partners; imports were also diversified. The top 21 partners accounted for 80 percent or more of exports and 18 partners accounted for 80 percent or more of imports (see graph 5). In 2013, the value of exports of services of Kenya increased slightly by 1.4 percent, reaching 4.8 bln US$, while its imports of services decreased moderately by 5.5 percent and reached 2.2 bln US$ (see graph 2). There was a large trade in services surplus of 2.6 bln US$.

Graph 1: Total merchandise trade, by value
(Bln US$ by year)

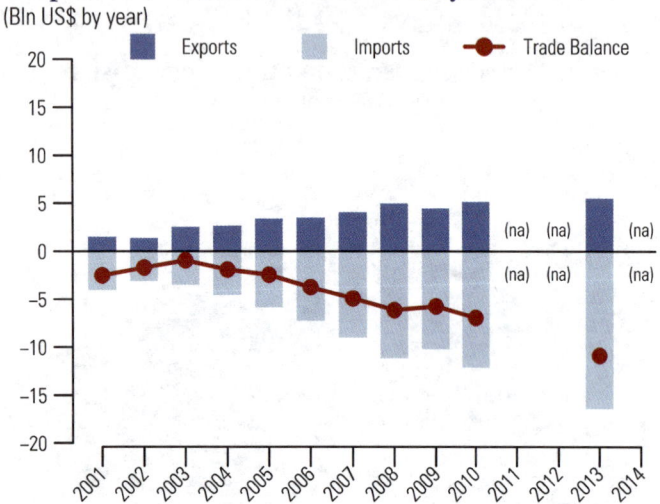

Graph 2: Total services trade, by value
(Bln US$ by year)

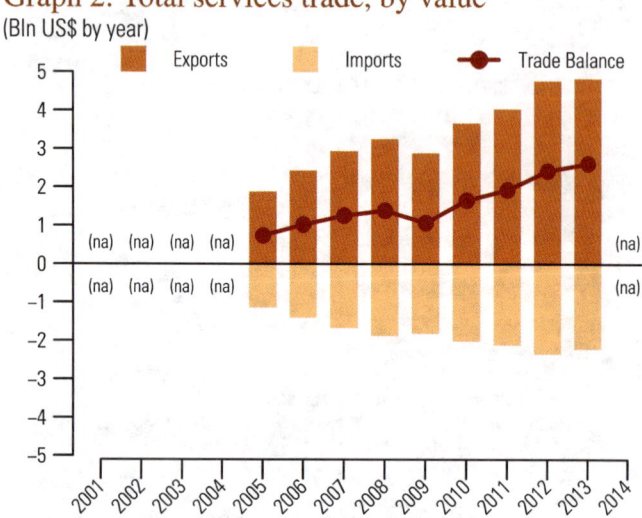

Exports Profile:
"Food, animals + beverages, tobacco" (SITC section 0+1), "Crude materials + anim. & veg. oils" (SITC section 2+4) and "Goods classified chiefly by material" (SITC section 6) were the largest commodity groups for exports in 2013, representing respectively 42.0, 15.0 and 12.8 percent of exported goods (see table 2). In 2013, the largest export commodity was "Tea, whether or not flavoured" (HS code 0902) (see table 1). The top three destinations for merchandise exports were Uganda, the United Kingdom and the United Republic of Tanzania, accounting for respectively 11.9, 7.9 and 7.7 percent of total exports. "Transportation" (EBOPS code 205) accounted for the largest share of exports of services in 2013 at 2.2 bln US$, followed by "Government services, n.i.e." (EBOPS code 291) at 917.8 mln US$ and "Travel" (EBOPS code 236) at 867.2 mln US$ (see graph 3).

Graph 3: Exports of services by EBOPS category
(% share in 2013)

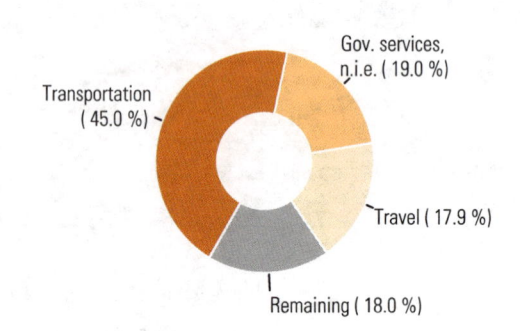

- Transportation (45.0 %)
- Gov. services, n.i.e. (19.0 %)
- Travel (17.9 %)
- Remaining (18.0 %)

Table 1: Top 10 export commodities 2011 to 2013

HS code	4-digit heading of Harmonized System 2007	Value (million US$) 2011	2012	2013	Unit value 2011	2012	2013	Unit	SITC code
	All Commodities	...	...	5 537.0					
0902	Tea, whether or not flavoured	...	...	1 218.2			2.7	US$/kg	074
0603	Cut flowers and flower buds of a kind suitable for bouquets	...	...	480.0			4.0	US$/kg	292
2710	Petroleum oils, other than crude	...	...	203.7					334
0901	Coffee, whether or not roasted or decaffeinated	...	...	190.8			3.8	US$/kg	071
0708	Leguminous vegetables, shelled or unshelled, fresh or chilled	...	...	126.7			3.0	US$/kg	054
2836	Carbonates; peroxocarbonates (percarbonates)	...	...	107.8			0.2	US$/kg	523
2523	Portland cement, aluminous cement, slag cement	...	...	103.6			0.1	US$/kg	661
2402	Cigars, cheroots, cigarillos and cigarettes	...	...	103.4					122
3923	Articles for the conveyance or packing of goods, of plastics	...	...	90.6			2.6	US$/kg	893
7108	Gold (including gold plated with platinum)	...	...	88.9			3.1	thsd US$/kg	971

Source: UN Comtrade and UN ServiceTrade

Kenya

Services Imports and Exports: EBOPS 2002 categories

Table 2: Merchandise exports by SITC
(Value in million US$, growth and shares in percentage)

SITC	2013	Avg. Growth rates 2009-2013	2012-2013	2013 share
Total	5537.0	5.5	>	100.0
0+1	2327.2	5.6	>	42.0
2+4	830.1	3.8	>	15.0
3	218.3	3.9	>	3.9
5	485.8	1.5	>	8.8
6	710.0	6.7	>	12.8
7	213.8	-1.8	>	3.9
8	586.2	8.1	>	10.6
9	165.5	56.9	>	3.0

Table 3: Merchandise imports by SITC
(Value in million US$, growth and shares in percentage)

SITC	2013	Avg. Growth rates 2009-2013	2012-2013	2013 share
Total	16394.5	12.6	>	100.0
0+1	1170.7	-0.3	>	7.1
2+4	859.1	10.3	>	5.2
3	3870.3	15.3	>	23.6
5	2282.5	14.5	>	13.9
6	2627.4	16.9	>	16.0
7	4623.7	10.5	>	28.2
8	794.6	17.5	>	4.8
9	166.0	276.9	>	1.0

SITC Legend

SITC Code	Description
Total	All commodities
0+1	Food, animals + beverages, tobacco
2+4	Crude materials + anim. & veg. oils
3	Mineral fuels, lubricants
5	Chemicals
6	Goods classified chiefly by material
7	Machinery and transport equipment
8	Miscellaneous manufactured articles
9	Not classified elsewhere in the SITC

Graph 4: Merchandise trade balance
(Bln US$ by MDG Regions in 2013)

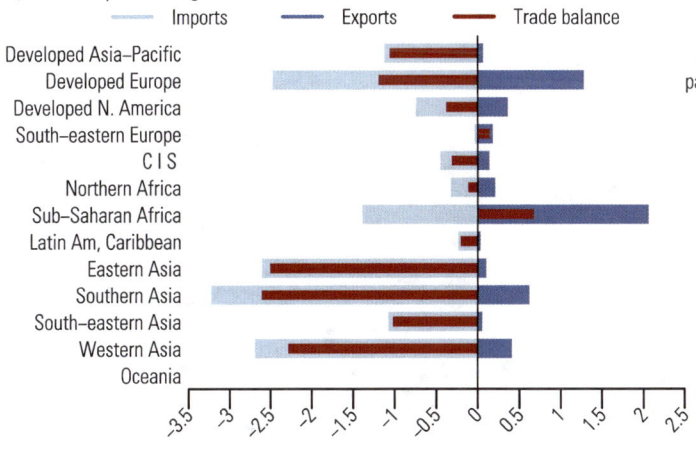

Graph 5: Partner concentration of merchandise trade
(Cumulative share by ranked partners in 2013)

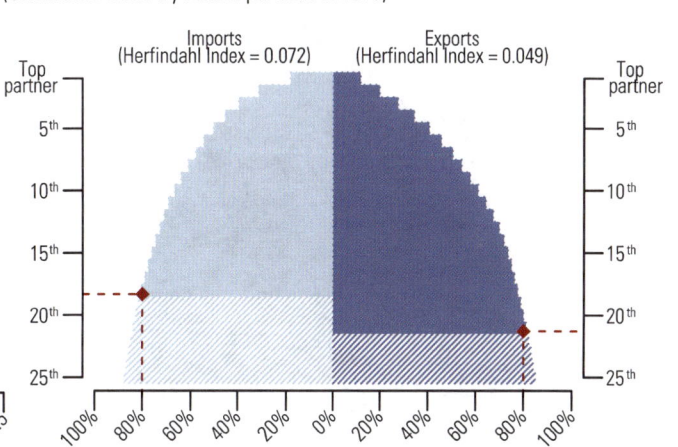

Imports (Herfindahl Index = 0.072)
Exports (Herfindahl Index = 0.049)

Graph 6: Imports of services by EBOPS category
(% share in 2013)

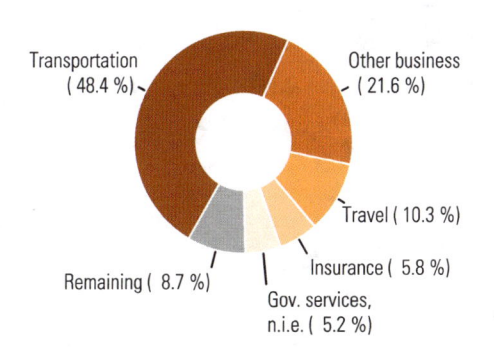

- Transportation (48.4 %)
- Other business (21.6 %)
- Travel (10.3 %)
- Insurance (5.8 %)
- Gov. services, n.i.e. (5.2 %)
- Remaining (8.7 %)

Imports Profile:

"Machinery and transport equipment" (SITC section 7), "Mineral fuels, lubricants" (SITC section 3) and "Goods classified chiefly by material" (SITC section 6) were the largest commodity groups for imports in 2013, representing respectively 28.2, 23.6 and 16.0 percent of imported goods (see table 3). In 2013, the largest import commodity was "Petroleum oils, other than crude" (HS code 2710) (see table 4). The top three partners for merchandise imports were India, China and the United Arab Emirates, accounting for respectively 18.3, 12.9 and 8.3 percent of total imports. "Transportation" (EBOPS code 205) accounted for the largest share of imports of services in 2013 at 1.1 bln US$, followed by "Other business services" (EBOPS code 268) at 478.7 mln US$ and "Travel" (EBOPS code 236) at 229.6 mln US$ (see graph 6).

Table 4: Top 10 import commodities 2011 to 2013

HS code	4-digit heading of Harmonized System 2007	2011	2012	2013	2011	2012	2013	Unit	SITC code
	All Commodities	...	...	16394.5					
2710	Petroleum oils, other than crude	...	...	3231.6					334
1511	Palm oil and its fractions	...	...	518.9			0.9	US$/kg	422
8703	Motor cars and other motor vehicles principally designed for the transport	...	...	496.4			6.7	thsd US$/unit	781
2709	Petroleum oils and oils obtained from bituminous minerals, crude	...	...	476.5			0.8	US$/kg	333
8517	Electrical apparatus for line telephony or line telegraphy	...	...	407.2					764
7208	Flat-rolled products of iron or non-alloy steel	...	...	381.3			0.7	US$/kg	673
3004	Medicaments (excluding goods of heading 30.02, 30.05 or 30.06)	...	...	355.0			24.8	US$/kg	542
1001	Wheat and meslin	...	...	256.3			0.4	US$/kg	041
8701	Tractors (other than tractors of heading 87.09)	...	...	231.4			36.2	thsd US$/unit	722
3105	Mineral or chemical fertilisers	...	...	230.7			0.5	US$/kg	562

Kiribati

Goods Imports: CIF, by origin **Goods Exports:** FOB, by last known destination **Trade System:** Special

Overview:
In 2013, the value of merchandise exports of Kiribati increased substantially by 14.8 percent to reach 6.7 mln US$, while its merchandise imports decreased substantially by 10.5 percent to reach 97.1 mln US$ (see graph 1, table 2 and table 3). The merchandise trade balance recorded a large deficit of 90.4 mln US$ (see graph 1). The largest merchandise trade balance was with MDG Developed Asia-Pacific at -41.9 mln US$ (see graph 4). Merchandise exports in Kiribati were diversified amongst partners; imports were moderately concentrated. The top 7 partners accounted for 80 percent or more of exports and 5 partners accounted for 80 percent or more of imports (see graph 5). In 2009, the value of exports of services of Kiribati decreased moderately by 7.0 percent, reaching 4.8 mln US$, while its imports of services decreased substantially by 14.2 percent and reached 50.0 mln US$ (see graph 2). There was a large trade in services deficit of 45.2 mln US$.

Graph 1: Total merchandise trade, by value
(Mln US$ by year)

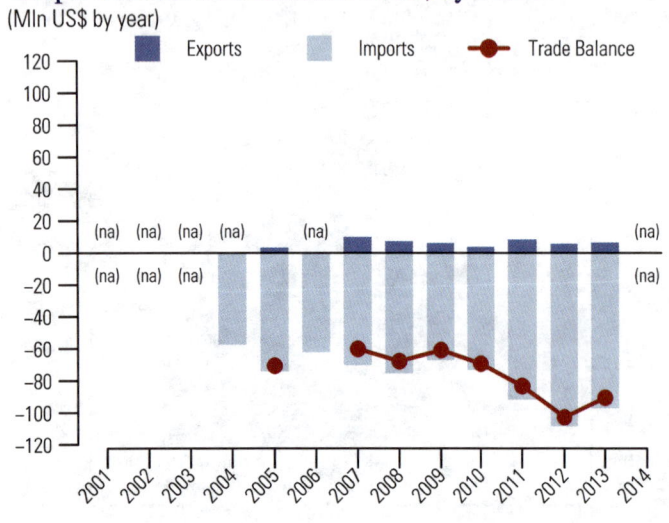

Graph 2: Total services trade, by value
(Mln US$ by year)

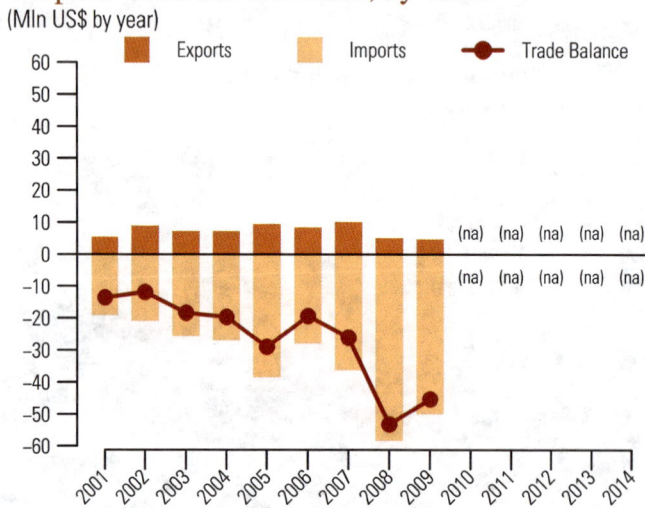

Exports Profile:
"Crude materials + anim. & veg. oils" (SITC section 2+4), "Mineral fuels, lubricants" (SITC section 3) and "Food, animals + beverages, tobacco" (SITC section 0+1) were the largest commodity groups for exports in 2013, representing respectively 49.4, 32.5 and 11.6 percent of exported goods (see table 2). From 2011 to 2013, the largest export commodity was "Coconut (copra), palm kernel or babassu oil" (HS code 1513) (see table 1). The top three destinations for merchandise exports were Other Asia nes, Morocco and Marshall Islands, accounting for respectively 30.0, 27.1 and 12.9 percent of total exports. "Travel" (EBOPS code 236) accounted for the largest share of exports of services in 2009 at 2.7 mln US$, followed by "Transportation" (EBOPS code 205) at 0.6 mln US$ (see graph 3).

Graph 3: Exports of services by EBOPS category
(% share in 2009)

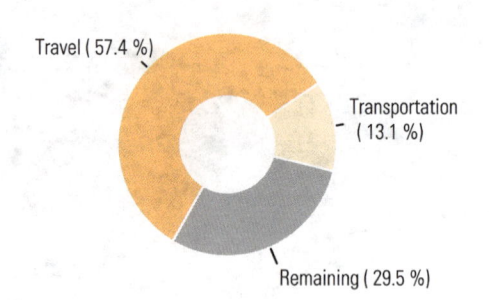

- Travel (57.4 %)
- Transportation (13.1 %)
- Remaining (29.5 %)

Table 1: Top 10 export commodities 2011 to 2013

HS code	4-digit heading of Harmonized System 2002	Value (million US$) 2011	2012	2013	Unit value 2011	2012	2013	Unit	SITC code
	All Commodities	8.6	5.8	6.7					
1513	Coconut (copra), palm kernel or babassu oil	5.8	3.8	2.3	1.1	2.1		US$/kg	422
2710	Petroleum oils, other than crude	0.0	0.0	2.2					334
0305	Fish, dried, salted or in brine	0.8	0.9	0.3	7.9	7.6	18.0	US$/kg	035
1203	Copra	...	...	0.8			2.0	US$/kg	223
2306	Oil-cake and other solid residues	0.3	0.2	0.1	0.6	0.6	1.7	US$/kg	081
1212	Locust beans, seaweeds and other algae	0.4	...	0.2	8.3		0.9	US$/kg	292
8903	Yachts and other vessels for pleasure or sports; rowing boats and canoes	0.6	...	...	624.4			thsd US$/unit	793
9999	Commodities not specified according to kind	0.3	0.1	0.1					931
0302	Fish, fresh or chilled, excluding fish fillets	...	0.0	0.3					034
7616	Other articles of aluminium	0.0	0.1	0.1	0.5	0.5	0.5	US$/kg	699

Kiribati

Services Imports and Exports: EBOPS 2002 categories

Table 2: Merchandise exports by SITC
(Value in million US$, growth and shares in percentage)

SITC	2013	Avg. Growth rates 2009-2013	Avg. Growth rates 2012-2013	2013 share
Total	6.7	1.6	14.8	100.0
0+1	0.8	-25.3	-41.2	11.6
2+4	3.3	11.2	-13.2	49.4
3	2.2	...	>	32.5
6	0.1	-4.4	-49.4	1.0
7	0.3	-32.3	38.2	4.1
8	0.0	-3.9	-84.5	0.6
9	0.1	-24.4	-32.1	0.8

Table 3: Merchandise imports by SITC
(Value in million US$, growth and shares in percentage)

SITC	2013	Avg. Growth rates 2009-2013	Avg. Growth rates 2012-2013	2013 share
Total	97.1	9.7	-10.5	100.0
0+1	34.5	5.4	-3.9	35.6
2+4	2.3	20.2	8.2	2.4
3	18.8	14.6	5.3	19.4
5	3.4	2.6	-21.8	3.5
6	9.7	10.8	-50.5	9.9
7	22.0	11.9	-1.1	22.6
8	5.2	12.7	0.6	5.3
9	1.3	40.0	-11.8	1.3

SITC Legend

SITC Code	Description
Total	All commodities
0+1	Food, animals + beverages, tobacco
2+4	Crude materials + anim. & veg. oils
3	Mineral fuels, lubricants
5	Chemicals
6	Goods classified chiefly by material
7	Machinery and transport equipment
8	Miscellaneous manufactured articles
9	Not classified elsewhere in the SITC

Graph 4: Merchandise trade balance (Mln US$ by MDG Regions in 2013)

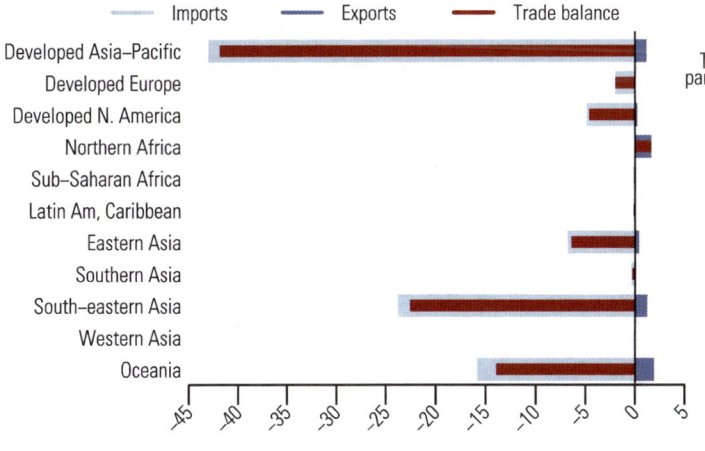

Graph 5: Partner concentration of merchandise trade (Cumulative share by ranked partners in 2013)

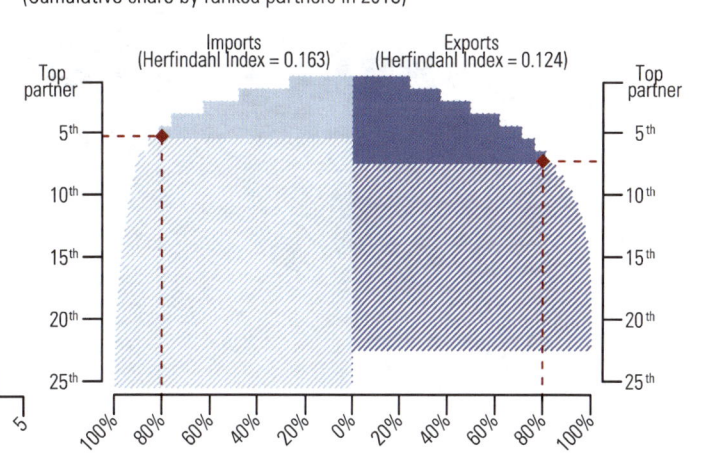

Imports (Herfindahl Index = 0.163); Exports (Herfindahl Index = 0.124)

Graph 6: Imports of services by EBOPS category (% share in 2009)

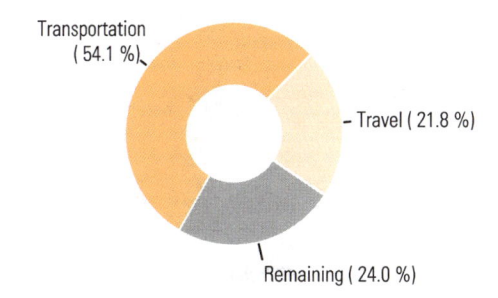

- Transportation (54.1 %)
- Travel (21.8 %)
- Remaining (24.0 %)

Imports Profile:
"Food, animals + beverages, tobacco" (SITC section 0+1), "Machinery and transport equipment" (SITC section 7) and "Mineral fuels, lubricants" (SITC section 3) were the largest commodity groups for imports in 2013, representing respectively 35.6, 22.6 and 19.4 percent of imported goods (see table 3). From 2011 to 2013, the largest import commodity was "Petroleum oils, other than crude" (HS code 2710) (see table 4). The top three partners for merchandise imports were Australia, Singapore and Fiji, accounting for respectively 28.8, 18.0 and 14.1 percent of total imports. "Transportation" (EBOPS code 205) accounted for the largest share of imports of services in 2009 at 27.1 mln US$, followed by "Travel" (EBOPS code 236) at 10.9 mln US$ (see graph 6).

Table 4: Top 10 import commodities 2011 to 2013

HS code	4-digit heading of Harmonized System 2002	2011	2012	2013	2011	2012	2013	Unit	SITC code
	All Commodities	91.7	108.6	97.1					
2710	Petroleum oils, other than crude	17.3	17.6	18.5					334
1006	Rice	10.3	8.4	8.5	1.0	0.9	0.8	US$/kg	042
2403	Other manufactured tobacco and tobacco substitutes	3.8	5.0	3.7	43.4	48.0	45.4	US$/kg	122
1701	Cane or beet sugar and pure sucrose, in solid form	5.5	2.7	3.0	0.9	0.8	0.7	US$/kg	061
1602	Other prepared or preserved meat, meat offal or blood	3.2	2.1	2.2	6.5	15.7	6.1	US$/kg	017
1101	Wheat or meslin flour	2.7	2.3	2.1	0.8	0.7	0.7	US$/kg	046
8903	Yachts and other vessels for pleasure or sports; rowing boats and canoes	0.1	6.9	0.2	6.8	7.0	8.2	thsd US$/unit	793
1212	Locust beans, seaweeds and other algae	2.0	2.2	2.0	20.8	17.6	20.5	US$/kg	292
8901	Cruise ships, excursion boats, ferry-boats, cargo ships, barges	0.6	1.1	3.4	304.5	90.0	427.6	thsd US$/unit	793
0207	Meat and edible offal, of the poultry of heading 01.05	1.7	1.5	1.5	2.3	2.3	2.2	US$/kg	012

Source: UN Comtrade and UN ServiceTrade

Korea, Republic of

Goods Imports: CIF, by origin **Goods Exports:** FOB, by last known destination **Trade System:** General

Overview:
In 2013, the value of merchandise exports of the Republic of Korea increased slightly by 2.1 percent to reach 559.6 bln US$, while its merchandise imports decreased slightly by 0.8 percent to reach 515.6 bln US$ (see graph 1, table 2 and table 3). The merchandise trade balance recorded a relatively small surplus of 44.0 bln US$ (see graph 1). The largest merchandise trade balance was with MDG Western Asia at -90.3 bln US$ (see graph 4). Merchandise exports in the Republic of Korea were diversified amongst partners; imports were also diversified. The top 20 partners accounted for 80 percent or more of exports and 18 partners accounted for 80 percent or more of imports (see graph 5). In 2012, the value of exports of services of the Republic of Korea increased substantially by 16.4 percent, reaching 110.9 bln US$, while its imports of services increased moderately by 7.0 percent and reached 108.2 bln US$ (see graph 2). There was a relatively small trade in services surplus of 2.7 bln US$.

Graph 1: Total merchandise trade, by value
(Bln US$ by year)

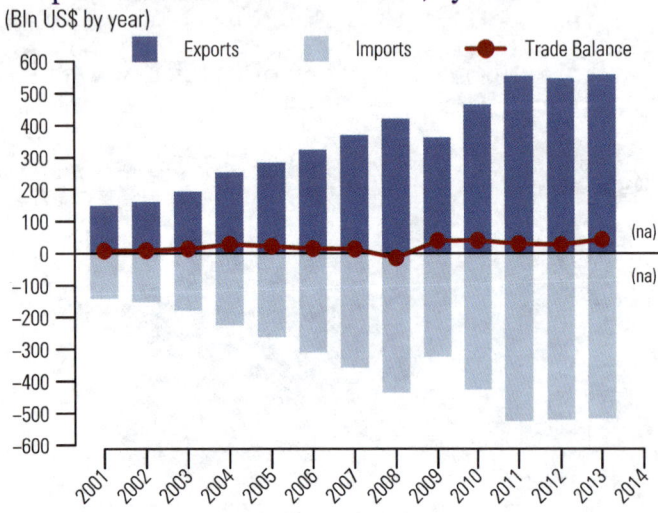

Graph 2: Total services trade, by value
(Bln US$ by year)

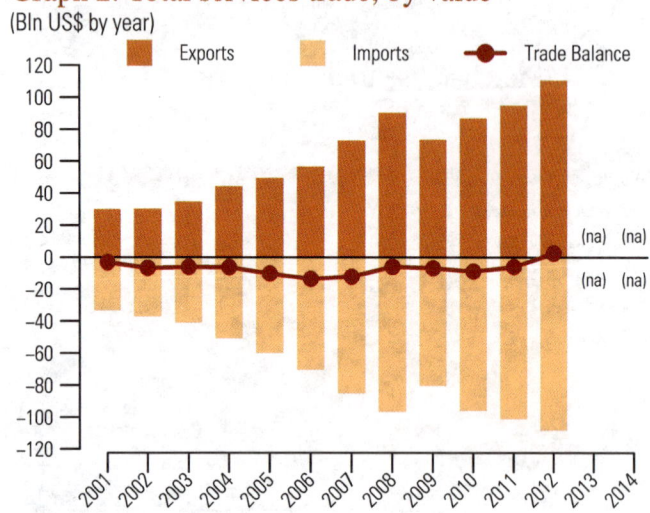

Exports Profile:
"Machinery and transport equipment" (SITC section 7), "Goods classified chiefly by material" (SITC section 6) and "Chemicals" (SITC section 5) were the largest commodity groups for exports in 2013, representing respectively 54.6, 12.8 and 11.8 percent of exported goods (see table 2). From 2011 to 2013, the largest export commodity was "Petroleum oils, other than crude" (HS code 2710) (see table 1). The top three destinations for merchandise exports were China, the United States and Japan, accounting for respectively 24.9, 10.7 and 6.8 percent of total exports. "Transportation" (EBOPS code 205) accounted for the largest share of exports of services in 2012 at 40.7 bln US$, followed by "Other business services" (EBOPS code 268) at 22.9 bln US$ and "Construction services" (EBOPS code 249) at 21.9 bln US$ (see graph 3).

Graph 3: Exports of services by EBOPS category
(% share in 2012)

- Other business (20.6 %)
- Construction (19.8 %)
- Travel (12.8 %)
- Remaining (10.0 %)
- Transportation (36.7 %)

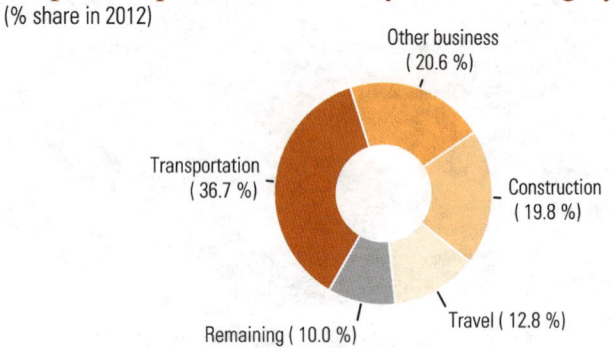

Table 1: Top 10 export commodities 2011 to 2013

HS code	4-digit heading of Harmonized System 2007	Value (million US$) 2011	2012	2013	Unit value 2011	2012	2013	Unit	SITC code
	All Commodities	555 208.9	547 854.4	559 618.6					
2710	Petroleum oils, other than crude	50 371.1	54 726.3	51 003.4	1.0	1.0	0.9	US$/kg	334
8542	Electronic integrated circuits	39 664.8	41 346.6	47 118.0					776
8703	Motor cars and other motor vehicles principally designed for the transport	40 909.9	42 387.5	44 283.4			15.9	thsd US$/unit	781
8901	Cruise ships, excursion boats, ferry-boats, cargo ships, barges	37 969.8	30 566.1	24 365.5					793
9013	Liquid crystal devices	27 656.2	27 525.0	25 308.8					871
8517	Electrical apparatus for line telephony or line telegraphy	25 802.4	20 962.1	25 604.6					764
8708	Parts and accessories of the motor vehicles of headings 87.01 to 87.05	21 583.4	22 632.1	23 840.0	8.1	8.1	8.3	US$/kg	784
8905	Light-vessels, fire-floats, dredgers, floating cranes and other vessels	16 043.7	7 216.0	11 328.8					793
2902	Cyclic hydrocarbons	7 987.3	9 065.8	10 408.3	1.3	1.3	1.4	US$/kg	511
8529	Parts suitable for use with the apparatus of headings 85.25 to 85.28	8 444.3	7 091.8	7 951.8	24.3	23.2	29.1	US$/kg	764

Source: UN Comtrade and UN ServiceTrade

Korea, Republic of

Services Imports and Exports: EBOPS 2002 categories

Table 2: Merchandise exports by SITC
(Value in million US$, growth and shares in percentage)

SITC	2013	Avg. Growth rates 2009-2013	2012-2013	2013 share
Total	559 618.6	11.4	2.1	100.0
0+1	6 124.6	10.7	-2.7	1.1
2+4	6 780.0	14.0	-10.1	1.2
3	54 112.6	22.8	-5.9	9.7
5	66 160.9	15.3	8.0	11.8
6	71 686.6	10.5	-5.4	12.8
7	305 646.4	10.3	6.2	54.6
8	47 682.4	6.6	-1.6	8.5
9	1 425.0	-16.1	-54.9	0.3

Table 3: Merchandise imports by SITC
(Value in million US$, growth and shares in percentage)

SITC	2013	Avg. Growth rates 2009-2013	2012-2013	2013 share
Total	515 573.0	12.4	-0.8	100.0
0+1	22 900.2	12.7	2.7	4.4
2+4	35 822.7	13.9	-10.1	6.9
3	180 431.3	18.4	-3.1	35.0
5	46 665.0	10.4	-0.9	9.1
6	55 141.3	6.3	-3.0	10.7
7	134 750.0	8.6	5.4	26.1
8	38 455.5	13.4	1.5	7.5
9	1 406.9	5.8	-8.4	0.3

SITC Legend

SITC Code	Description
Total	All commodities
0+1	Food, animals + beverages, tobacco
2+4	Crude materials + anim. & veg. oils
3	Mineral fuels, lubricants
5	Chemicals
6	Goods classified chiefly by material
7	Machinery and transport equipment
8	Miscellaneous manufactured articles
9	Not classified elsewhere in the SITC

Graph 4: Merchandise trade balance
(Bln US$ by MDG Regions in 2013)

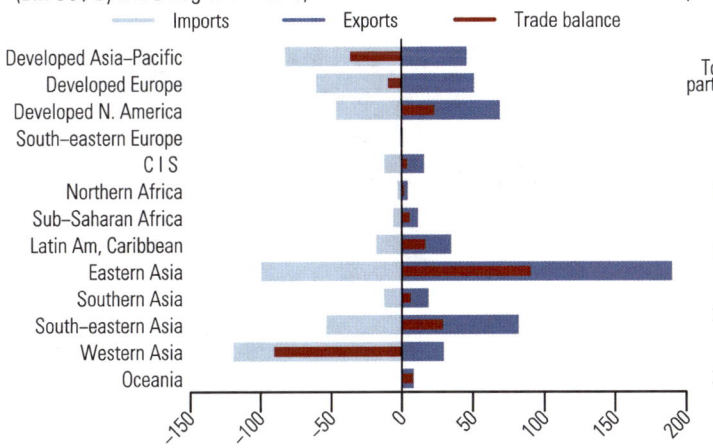

Graph 5: Partner concentration of merchandise trade
(Cumulative share by ranked partners in 2013)

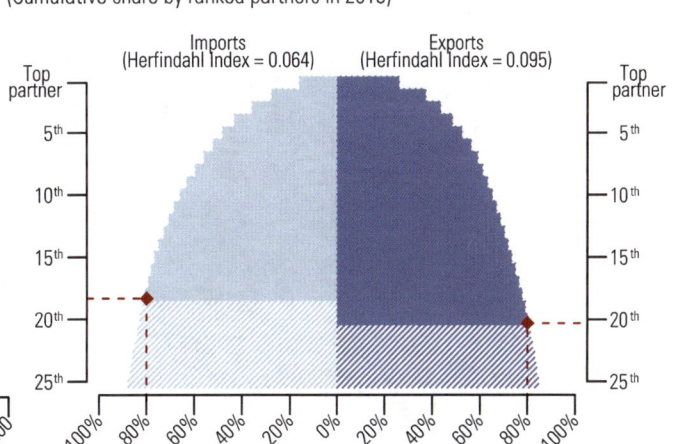

Imports (Herfindahl Index = 0.064)
Exports (Herfindahl Index = 0.095)

Graph 6: Imports of services by EBOPS category
(% share in 2012)

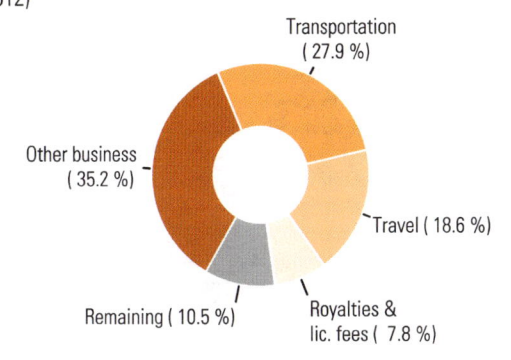

- Transportation (27.9 %)
- Travel (18.6 %)
- Royalties & lic. fees (7.8 %)
- Remaining (10.5 %)
- Other business (35.2 %)

Imports Profile:

"Mineral fuels, lubricants" (SITC section 3), "Machinery and transport equipment" (SITC section 7) and "Goods classified chiefly by material" (SITC section 6) were the largest commodity groups for imports in 2013, representing respectively 35.0, 26.1 and 10.7 percent of imported goods (see table 3). From 2011 to 2013, the largest import commodity was "Petroleum oils and oils obtained from bituminous minerals, crude" (HS code 2709) (see table 4). The top three partners for merchandise imports were China, Japan and the United States, accounting for respectively 16.0, 12.4 and 8.4 percent of total imports. "Other business services" (EBOPS code 268) accounted for the largest share of imports of services in 2012 at 38.1 bln US$, followed by "Transportation" (EBOPS code 205) at 30.1 bln US$ and "Travel" (EBOPS code 236) at 20.1 bln US$ (see graph 6).

Table 4: Top 10 import commodities 2011 to 2013

HS code	4-digit heading of Harmonized System 2007	Value (million US$) 2011	2012	2013	Unit value 2011	2012	2013	Unit	SITC code
	All Commodities	524 405.2	519 575.6	515 573.0					
2709	Petroleum oils and oils obtained from bituminous minerals, crude	100 805.6	108 298.2	99 333.2	0.8	0.8	0.8	US$/kg	333
2711	Petroleum gases and other gaseous hydrocarbons	30 182.7	33 834.1	36 320.7	0.7	0.8	0.8	US$/kg	343
8542	Electronic integrated circuits	25 369.8	25 421.6	27 808.5					776
2710	Petroleum oils, other than crude	22 029.9	25 700.6	28 842.4	0.9	0.9	0.9	US$/kg	334
2701	Coal; briquettes, ovoids and similar solid fuels manufactured from coal	18 283.7	15 908.0	12 951.0	0.1	0.1	0.1	US$/kg	321
2601	Iron ores and concentrates, including roasted iron pyrites	11 380.8	9 531.7	8 354.2	0.2	0.1	0.1	US$/kg	281
8486	Machines and apparatus used for the manufacture of semiconductor devices	10 336.2	8 219.3	6 436.7					728
8517	Electrical apparatus for line telephony or line telegraphy	8 492.5	5 373.1	5 857.8					764
7208	Flat-rolled products of iron or non-alloy steel	7 775.2	5 994.8	4 233.6	0.8	0.7	0.6	US$/kg	673
8541	Diodes, transistors and similar semiconductor devices	4 713.9	4 820.2	5 032.6					776

2014 International Trade Statistics Yearbook, Vol. I   Source: UN Comtrade and UN ServiceTrade

Kuwait

Goods Imports: CIF, by origin   **Goods Exports: FOB, by last known destination**   **Trade System: Special**

Overview:
In 2013, the value of merchandise exports of Kuwait reached 114.4 bln US$, while its merchandise imports reached 29.6 bln US$ (see graph 1, table 2 and table 3). The merchandise trade balance recorded a large surplus of 84.8 bln US$ (see graph 1). The largest merchandise trade balance was with MDG Developed Europe at -7.4 bln US$ (see graph 4). Merchandise exports in Kuwait were highly concentrated amongst partners; imports were diversified. One partner accounted for 80 percent or more of exports and 18 partners accounted for 80 percent or more of imports (see graph 5). In 2012, the value of exports of services of Kuwait increased slightly by 1.6 percent, reaching 10.0 bln US$, while its imports of services increased moderately by 9.8 percent and reached 19.6 bln US$ (see graph 2). There was a large trade in services deficit of 9.6 bln US$.

Graph 1: Total merchandise trade, by value
(Bln US$ by year)

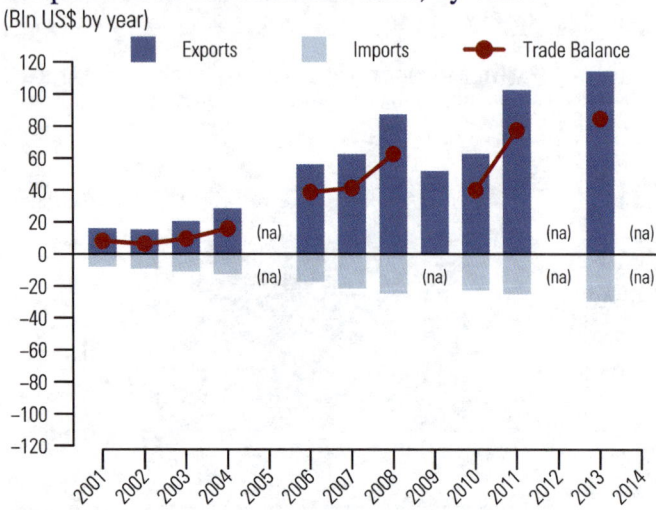

Graph 2: Total services trade, by value
(Bln US$ by year)

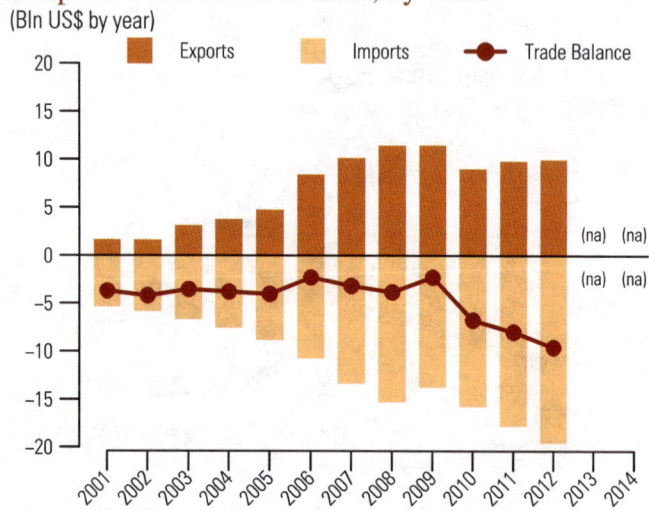

Exports Profile:
"Mineral fuels, lubricants" (SITC section 3), "Chemicals" (SITC section 5) and "Machinery and transport equipment" (SITC section 7) were the largest commodity groups for exports in 2013, representing respectively 94.2, 3.2 and 1.1 percent of exported goods (see table 2). In 2011 and 2013, the largest export commodity was "Petroleum oils and oils obtained from bituminous minerals, crude" (HS code 2709) (see table 1). The top three destinations for merchandise exports were Areas nes, China and the United Arab Emirates, accounting for respectively 94.5, 0.9 and 0.7 percent of total exports. "Transportation" (EBOPS code 205) accounted for the largest share of exports of services in 2012 at 5.0 bln US$, followed by "Communications services" (EBOPS code 245) at 3.4 bln US$ and "Government services, n.i.e." (EBOPS code 291) at 585.5 mln US$ (see graph 3).

Graph 3: Exports of services by EBOPS category
(% share in 2012)

- Transportation (50.5 %)
- Communication (34.5 %)
- Gov. services, n.i.e. (5.9 %)
- Remaining (9.2 %)

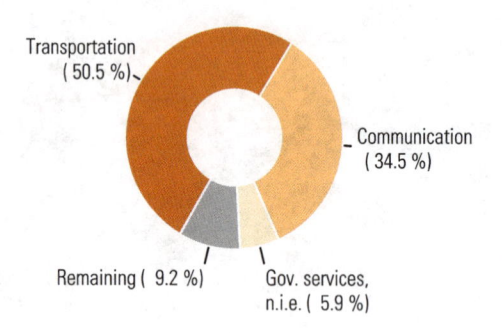

Table 1: Top 10 export commodities 2011 to 2013

HS code	4-digit heading of Harmonized System 2007	2011	2012	2013	2011	2012	2013	Unit	SITC code
	All Commodities	102 695.8	...	114 404.1					
2709	Petroleum oils and oils obtained from bituminous minerals, crude	68 810.9	...	79 041.0			0.8	US$/kg	333
2710	Petroleum oils, other than crude	25 273.8	...	24 980.5			0.9	US$/kg	334
2711	Petroleum gases and other gaseous hydrocarbons	3 308.8	...	3 764.8					343
3901	Polymers of ethylene, in primary forms	619.9	...	1 419.2	1.0		1.1	US$/kg	571
2905	Acyclic alcohols and their derivatives	866.9	...	1 149.9	1.1		1.1	US$/kg	512
3921	Other plates, sheets, film, foil and strip, of plastics	886.8	...	15.6	1.6		2.8	US$/kg	582
3102	Mineral or chemical fertilisers, nitrogenous	444.0	...	402.7	0.4		0.4	US$/kg	562
8703	Motor cars and other motor vehicles principally designed for the transport	199.2	...	506.6	17.8		19.5	thsd US$/unit	781
7113	Articles of jewellery and parts thereof, of precious metal	138.7	...	290.0			45.6	thsd US$/kg	897
8704	Motor vehicles for the transport of goods	98.6	...	236.8	14.8		14.9	thsd US$/unit	782

Kuwait

Services Imports and Exports: EBOPS 2002 categories

Table 2: Merchandise exports by SITC
(Value in million US$, growth and shares in percentage)

SITC	2013	Avg. Growth rates 2009-2013	2012-2013	2013 share
Total	114 404.1	21.8	...	100.0
0+1	476.6	27.8	...	0.4
2+4	222.3	8.7	...	0.2
3	107 788.3	23.1	...	94.2
5	3 603.8	7.8	...	3.2
6	542.9	14.0	...	0.5
7	1 267.4	-4.3	...	1.1
8	502.8	25.5	...	0.4
9	0.0	-62.1	...	0.0

Table 3: Merchandise imports by SITC
(Value in million US$, growth and shares in percentage)

SITC	2013	Avg. Growth rates 2009-2013	2012-2013	2013 share
Total	29 645.6	...	...	100.0
0+1	4 262.2	...	...	14.4
2+4	584.4	...	...	2.0
3	205.2	...	...	0.7
5	2 940.2	...	...	9.9
6	4 883.3	...	...	16.5
7	11 688.5	...	...	39.4
8	4 285.9	...	...	14.5
9	796.1	...	...	2.7

SITC Legend

SITC Code	Description
Total	All commodities
0+1	Food, animals + beverages, tobacco
2+4	Crude materials + anim. & veg. oils
3	Mineral fuels, lubricants
5	Chemicals
6	Goods classified chiefly by material
7	Machinery and transport equipment
8	Miscellaneous manufactured articles
9	Not classified elsewhere in the SITC

Graph 4: Merchandise trade balance
(Bln US$ by MDG Regions in 2013)

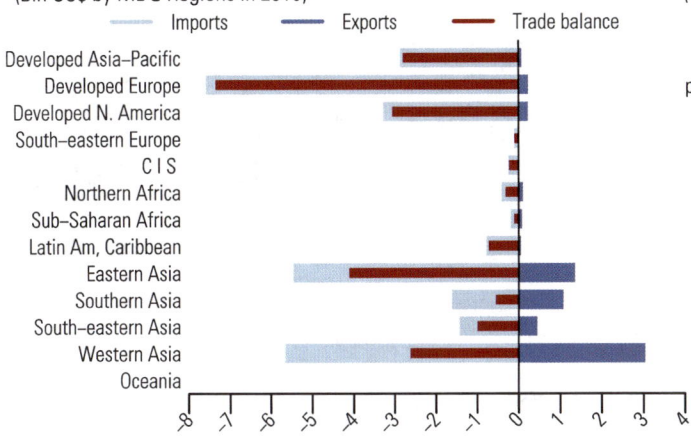

Graph 5: Partner concentration of merchandise trade
(Cumulative share by ranked partners in 2013)

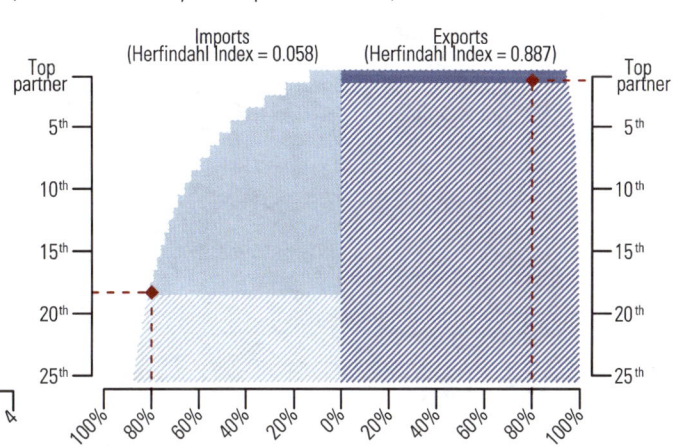

Imports (Herfindahl Index = 0.058)
Exports (Herfindahl Index = 0.887)

Graph 6: Imports of services by EBOPS category
(% share in 2012)

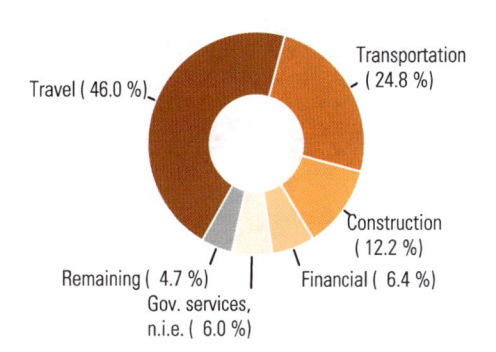

- Travel (46.0 %)
- Transportation (24.8 %)
- Construction (12.2 %)
- Financial (6.4 %)
- Gov. services, n.i.e. (6.0 %)
- Remaining (4.7 %)

Imports Profile:

"Machinery and transport equipment" (SITC section 7), "Goods classified chiefly by material" (SITC section 6) and "Miscellaneous manufactured articles" (SITC section 8) were the largest commodity groups for imports in 2013, representing respectively 39.4, 16.5 and 14.5 percent of imported goods (see table 3). In 2011 and 2013, the largest import commodity was "Motor cars and other motor vehicles principally designed for the transport" (HS code 8703) (see table 4). The top three partners for merchandise imports were China, the United States and the United Arab Emirates, accounting for respectively 14.1, 10.3 and 7.7 percent of total imports. "Travel" (EBOPS code 236) accounted for the largest share of imports of services in 2012 at 9.0 bln US$, followed by "Transportation" (EBOPS code 205) at 4.8 bln US$ and "Construction services" (EBOPS code 249) at 2.4 bln US$ (see graph 6).

Table 4: Top 10 import commodities 2011 to 2013

HS code	4-digit heading of Harmonized System 2007	Value 2011	Value 2012	Value 2013	Unit 2011	Unit 2012	Unit 2013	Unit	SITC code
	All Commodities	25 142.0	...	29 645.6					
8703	Motor cars and other motor vehicles principally designed for the transport	2 767.3	...	4 055.9	23.4		27.6	thsd US$/unit	781
8517	Electrical apparatus for line telephony or line telegraphy	1 107.0	...	1 164.0					764
3004	Medicaments (excluding goods of heading 30.02, 30.05 or 30.06)	634.4	...	771.3	106.2		113.0	US$/kg	542
7108	Gold (including gold plated with platinum)	362.2	...	795.9			54.7	thsd US$/kg	971
7113	Articles of jewellery and parts thereof, of precious metal	360.3	...	554.9			49.2	thsd US$/kg	897
8544	Insulated (including enamelled or anodised) wire, cable	352.3	...	506.5	6.5		6.1	US$/kg	773
7304	Tubes, pipes and hollow profiles, seamless, of iron (other than cast iron)	462.6	...	383.0	1.4		1.5	US$/kg	679
8471	Automatic data processing machines and units thereof	363.8	...	428.9	255.8		293.2	US$/unit	752
8704	Motor vehicles for the transport of goods	293.7	...	479.1	21.5		11.2	thsd US$/unit	782
0207	Meat and edible offal, of the poultry of heading 01.05	275.9	...	339.7	2.4		2.6	US$/kg	012

Kyrgyzstan

Goods Imports: CIF, by origin   **Goods Exports:** FOB, by last known destination   **Trade System:** General

Overview:

In 2013, the value of merchandise exports of Kyrgyzstan increased moderately by 5.3 percent to reach 1.8 bln US$, while its merchandise imports increased substantially by 11.3 percent to reach 6.0 bln US$ (see graph 1, table 2 and table 3). The merchandise trade balance recorded a large deficit of 4.2 bln US$ (see graph 1). The largest merchandise trade balance was with MDG CIS at -2.2 bln US$ (see graph 4). Merchandise exports in Kyrgyzstan were moderately concentrated amongst partners; imports were also moderately concentrated. The top 5 partners accounted for 80 percent or more of exports and 7 partners accounted for 80 percent or more of imports (see graph 5). In 2013, the value of exports of services of Kyrgyzstan increased substantially by 10.9 percent, reaching 1.4 bln US$, while its imports of services decreased substantially by 13.9 percent and reached 1.3 bln US$ (see graph 2). There was a relatively small trade in services surplus of 45.3 mln US$.

Graph 1: Total merchandise trade, by value
(Bln US$ by year)

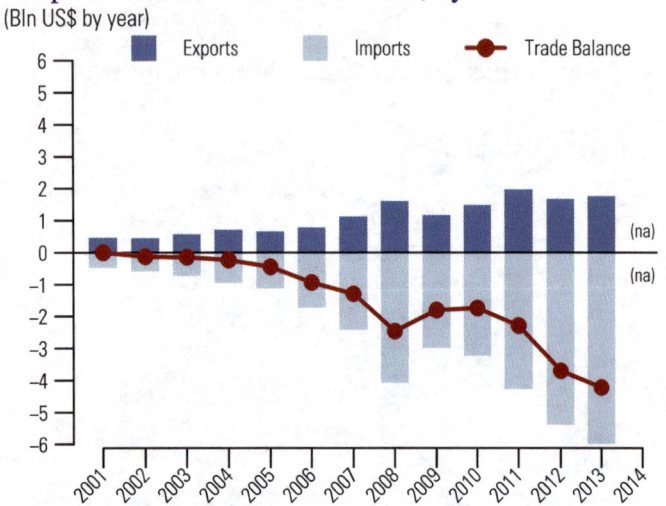

Graph 2: Total services trade, by value
(Bln US$ by year)

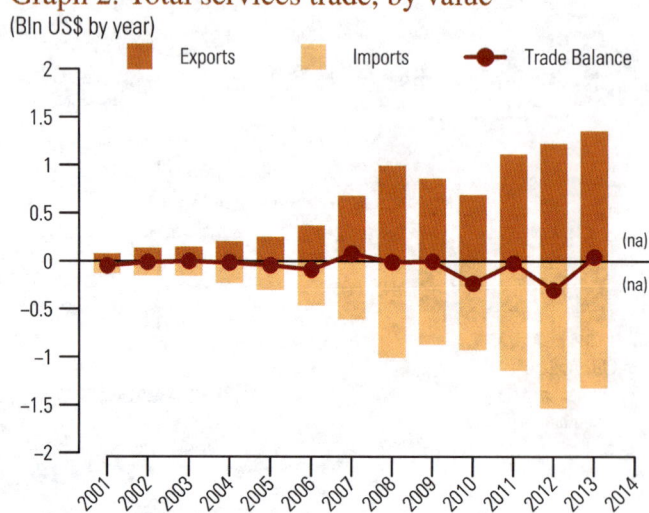

Exports Profile:

"Not classified elsewhere in the SITC" (SITC section 9), "Food, animals + beverages, tobacco" (SITC section 0+1) and "Machinery and transport equipment" (SITC section 7) were the largest commodity groups for exports in 2013, representing respectively 44.2, 13.4 and 10.0 percent of exported goods (see table 2). From 2011 to 2013, the largest export commodity was "Gold (including gold plated with platinum)" (HS code 7108) (see table 1). The top three destinations for merchandise exports were Switzerland, Kazakhstan and the Russian Federation, accounting for respectively 35.6, 19.8 and 12.1 percent of total exports. "Travel" (EBOPS code 236) accounted for the largest share of exports of services in 2013 at 850.5 mln US$, followed by "Transportation" (EBOPS code 205) at 184.2 mln US$ and "Other business services" (EBOPS code 268) at 145.5 mln US$ (see graph 3).

Graph 3: Exports of services by EBOPS category
(% share in 2013)

- Travel (62.4 %)
- Transportation (13.5 %)
- Other business (10.7 %)
- Remaining (13.4 %)

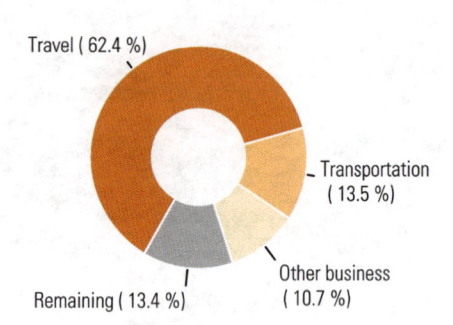

Table 1: Top 10 export commodities 2011 to 2013

HS code	4-digit heading of Harmonized System 2007	Value (million US$) 2011	2012	2013	Unit value 2011	2012	2013	Unit	SITC code
	All Commodities	1 978.9	1 683.2	1 773.2					
7108	Gold (including gold plated with platinum)	1 006.2	562.3	736.8	49.7	54.0	43.5	thsd US$/kg	971
2710	Petroleum oils, other than crude	101.0	115.4	140.0	0.9	1.1	1.0	US$/kg	334
0713	Dried leguminous vegetables, shelled, whether or not skinned or split	51.8	48.3	73.7	0.7	0.8	1.2	US$/kg	054
9999	Commodities not specified according to kind	60.1	51.4	46.3					931
2716	Electrical energy	80.4	56.4	20.3	28.8	28.9	31.5	US$/MWh	351
6204	Women's or girls' suits, ensembles, jackets, blazers, dresses, skirts	49.0	57.6	41.0	1.9	1.6	9.8	US$/unit	842
8704	Motor vehicles for the transport of goods	22.4	77.8	26.0	226.5	342.8	155.8	thsd US$/unit	782
2616	Precious metal ores and concentrates	17.2	55.5	18.3	0.4	0.6	0.3	US$/kg	289
5201	Cotton, not carded or combed	31.0	33.9	19.9	1.5	*1.3*	1.3	US$/kg	263
8708	Parts and accessories of the motor vehicles of headings 87.01 to 87.05	23.1	27.4	33.4	4.3	4.9	6.6	US$/kg	784

Kyrgyzstan

Services Imports and Exports: EBOPS 2002 categories

Table 2: Merchandise exports by SITC
(Value in million US$, growth and shares in percentage)

SITC	2013	Avg. Growth rates 2009-2013	Avg. Growth rates 2012-2013	2013 share
Total	1773.2	10.8	5.3	100.0
0+1	237.1	11.3	7.0	13.4
2+4	72.8	13.9	-42.9	4.1
3	166.7	42.8	-5.7	9.4
5	24.7	37.4	17.5	1.4
6	163.4	39.1	28.6	9.2
7	177.0	21.7	-16.2	10.0
8	148.4	12.6	-19.5	8.4
9	783.0	2.2	27.6	44.2

Table 3: Merchandise imports by SITC
(Value in million US$, growth and shares in percentage)

SITC	2013	Avg. Growth rates 2009-2013	Avg. Growth rates 2012-2013	2013 share
Total	5983.0	19.1	11.3	100.0
0+1	771.8	13.6	7.6	12.9
2+4	203.3	21.1	16.3	3.4
3	1282.0	83.9	9.9	21.4
5	620.5	23.0	14.3	10.4
6	1039.1	22.5	19.4	17.4
7	1498.6	32.2	10.7	25.0
8	527.4	18.1	5.4	8.8
9	40.2	-52.8	-13.7	0.7

SITC Legend

SITC Code	Description
Total	All commodities
0+1	Food, animals + beverages, tobacco
2+4	Crude materials + anim. & veg. oils
3	Mineral fuels, lubricants
5	Chemicals
6	Goods classified chiefly by material
7	Machinery and transport equipment
8	Miscellaneous manufactured articles
9	Not classified elsewhere in the SITC

Graph 4: Merchandise trade balance
(Bln US$ by MDG Regions in 2013)

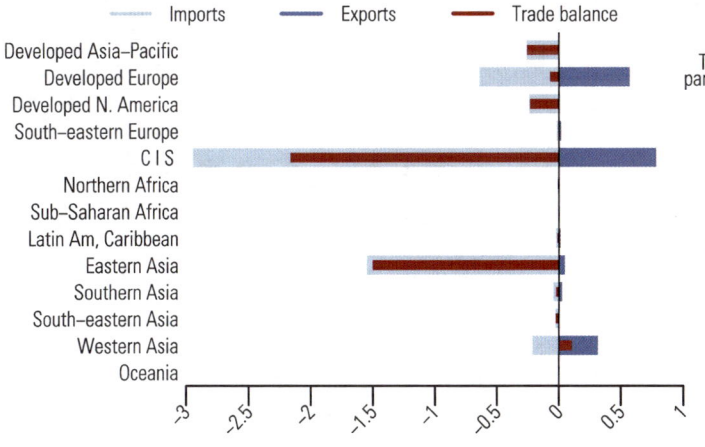

Graph 5: Partner concentration of merchandise trade
(Cumulative share by ranked partners in 2013)

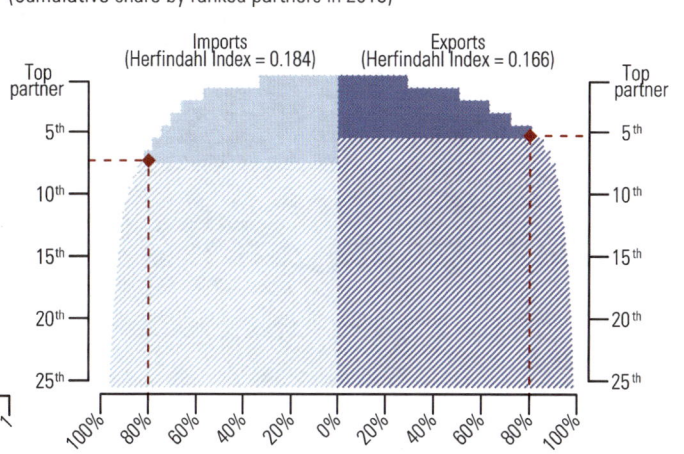

Imports (Herfindahl Index = 0.184)
Exports (Herfindahl Index = 0.166)

Graph 6: Imports of services by EBOPS category
(% share in 2013)

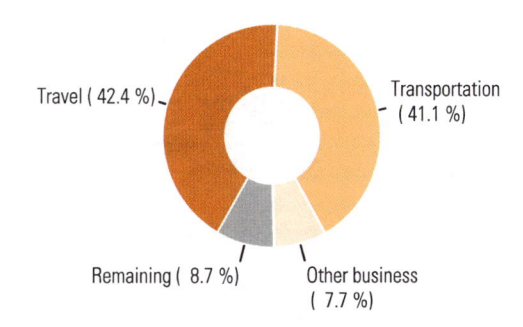

- Travel (42.4%)
- Transportation (41.1%)
- Other business (7.7%)
- Remaining (8.7%)

Imports Profile:

"Machinery and transport equipment" (SITC section 7), "Mineral fuels, lubricants" (SITC section 3) and "Goods classified chiefly by material" (SITC section 6) were the largest commodity groups for imports in 2013, representing respectively 25.0, 21.4 and 17.4 percent of imported goods (see table 3). From 2011 to 2013, the largest import commodity was "Petroleum oils, other than crude" (HS code 2710) (see table 4). The top three partners for merchandise imports were the Russian Federation, China and Kazakhstan, accounting for respectively 33.3, 22.8 and 9.5 percent of total imports. "Travel" (EBOPS code 236) accounted for the largest share of imports of services in 2013 at 559.3 mln US$, followed by "Transportation" (EBOPS code 205) at 542.2 mln US$ and "Other business services" (EBOPS code 268) at 102.2 mln US$ (see graph 6).

Table 4: Top 10 import commodities 2011 to 2013

HS code	4-digit heading of Harmonized System 2007	2011	2012	2013	2011	2012	2013	Unit	SITC code
	All Commodities	4260.7	5373.2	5983.0					
2710	Petroleum oils, other than crude	833.6	1013.4	1139.7	0.7	0.8	0.7	US$/kg	334
8703	Motor cars and other motor vehicles principally designed for the transport	236.9	300.7	372.4	4.3	4.2	5.2	thsd US$/unit	781
8704	Motor vehicles for the transport of goods	113.5	228.7	156.3	15.2	18.2	15.3	thsd US$/unit	782
3004	Medicaments (excluding goods of heading 30.02, 30.05 or 30.06)	148.7	172.3	169.6	26.5	26.4	19.9	US$/kg	542
8517	Electrical apparatus for line telephony or line telegraphy	110.0	75.1	73.1					764
1001	Wheat and meslin	67.0	88.1	89.8	0.2	0.2	0.2	US$/kg	041
2711	Petroleum gases and other gaseous hydrocarbons	74.7	85.0	69.7	0.4	0.5	0.6	US$/kg	343
1806	Chocolate and other food preparations containing cocoa	67.2	83.4	70.2	3.5	4.2	3.5	US$/kg	073
1701	Cane or beet sugar and chemically pure sucrose, in solid form	77.9	64.8	57.0	0.9	0.8	0.7	US$/kg	061
0207	Meat and edible offal, of the poultry of heading 01.05	57.3	58.0	75.5	0.8	0.9	1.4	US$/kg	012

Source: UN Comtrade and UN ServiceTrade

Latvia

Goods Imports: CIF, by origin/consignment for intra-eu   **Goods Exports:** FOB, by last known destination   **Trade System:** Special

Overview:
In 2014, the value of merchandise exports of Latvia increased slightly by 1.9 percent to reach 13.6 bln US$, while its merchandise imports decreased slightly by 0.4 percent to reach 16.7 bln US$ (see graph 1, table 2 and table 3). The merchandise trade balance recorded a moderate deficit of 3.1 bln US$ (see graph 1). The largest merchandise trade balance was with MDG Developed Europe at -3.4 bln US$ (see graph 4). Merchandise exports in Latvia were diversified amongst partners; imports were also diversified. The top 15 partners accounted for 80 percent or more of exports and 12 partners accounted for 80 percent or more of imports (see graph 5). In 2013, the value of exports of services of Latvia increased substantially by 14.2 percent, reaching 5.2 bln US$, while its imports of services increased moderately by 8.0 percent and reached 2.8 bln US$ (see graph 2). There was a moderate trade in services surplus of 2.4 bln US$.

Graph 1: Total merchandise trade, by value
(Bln US$ by year)

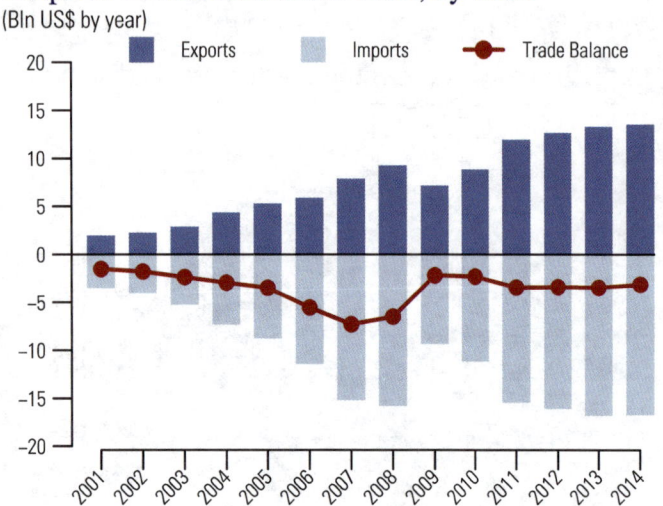

Graph 2: Total services trade, by value
(Bln US$ by year)

Exports Profile:
"Machinery and transport equipment" (SITC section 7), "Goods classified chiefly by material" (SITC section 6) and "Food, animals + beverages, tobacco" (SITC section 0+1) were the largest commodity groups for exports in 2014, representing respectively 19.5, 17.4 and 17.1 percent of exported goods (see table 2). From 2012 to 2014, the largest export commodity was "Commodities not specified according to kind" (HS code 9999) (see table 1). The top three destinations for merchandise exports were Lithuania, Estonia and the Russian Federation, accounting for respectively 17.3, 12.5 and 11.3 percent of total exports. "Transportation" (EBOPS code 205) accounted for the largest share of exports of services in 2013 at 2.3 bln US$, followed by "Travel" (EBOPS code 236) at 897.8 mln US$ and "Other business services" (EBOPS code 268) at 795.7 mln US$ (see graph 3).

Graph 3: Exports of services by EBOPS category
(% share in 2013)

- Transportation (44.5 %)
- Travel (17.4 %)
- Other business (15.4 %)
- Remaining (22.7 %)

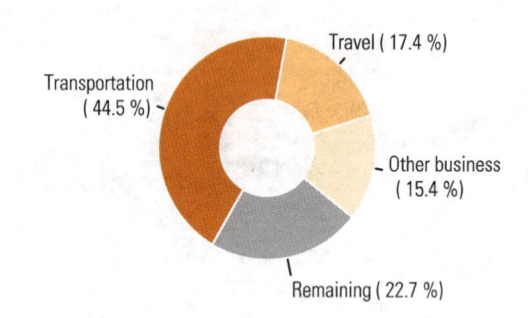

Table 1: Top 10 export commodities 2012 to 2014

HS code	4-digit heading of Harmonized System 2012	Value (million US$) 2012	2013	2014	Unit value 2012	2013	2014	Unit	SITC code
	All Commodities	12 685.5	13 324.7	13 576.3					
9999	Commodities not specified according to kind	749.3	931.5	1 098.5					931
2710	Petroleum oils, other than crude	663.2	708.5	690.8	1.0	1.0	0.9	US$/kg	334
4407	Wood sawn or chipped lengthwise, sliced or peeled	557.2	640.0	737.1	238.8	253.6	267.1	US$/m³	248
8517	Electrical apparatus for line telephony or line telegraphy	297.9	552.2	768.4					764
2208	Alcohol of a strength by volume of less than 80 % vol	452.5	513.4	523.8	17.3	18.4	16.8	US$/litre	112
1001	Wheat and meslin	460.0	340.2	345.9	0.3	0.3	0.3	US$/kg	041
3004	Medicaments (excluding goods of heading 30.02, 30.05 or 30.06)	305.0	343.0	354.8	141.7	151.5	156.8	US$/kg	542
4401	Fuel wood, in logs, in billets, in twigs, in faggots or in similar forms	275.2	317.3	321.1	0.1	0.1	0.1	US$/kg	246
7214	Other bars and rods of iron or non-alloy steel	544.0	186.8	25.6	0.7	0.7	0.7	US$/kg	676
4403	Wood in the rough, whether or not stripped of bark or sapwood	244.9	247.8	258.7	59.6	66.3	68.2	US$/m³	247

Latvia

Services Imports and Exports: EBOPS 2002 categories

Table 2: Merchandise exports by SITC
(Value in million US$, growth and shares in percentage)

SITC	2014	Avg. Growth rates 2010-2014	2013-2014	2014 share
Total	13 576.3	11.3	1.9	100.0
0+1	2 321.6	13.9	-1.2	17.1
2+4	1 836.7	5.0	2.6	13.5
3	1 005.5	21.0	-2.0	7.4
5	993.1	7.9	4.2	7.3
6	2 365.5	4.6	-5.6	17.4
7	2 650.6	13.0	7.1	19.5
8	1 259.2	10.3	1.3	9.3
9	1 144.1	39.6	16.8	8.4

Table 3: Merchandise imports by SITC
(Value in million US$, growth and shares in percentage)

SITC	2014	Avg. Growth rates 2010-2014	2013-2014	2014 share
Total	16 716.5	10.7	-0.4	100.0
0+1	2 165.6	9.0	1.3	13.0
2+4	693.0	9.5	1.4	4.1
3	2 331.7	9.1	-11.9	13.9
5	1 817.6	5.5	1.9	10.9
6	2 379.3	8.2	2.0	14.2
7	4 002.9	13.3	3.6	23.9
8	1 592.0	12.3	2.0	9.5
9	1 734.4	19.3	-1.8	10.4

SITC Legend

SITC Code	Description
Total	All commodities
0+1	Food, animals + beverages, tobacco
2+4	Crude materials + anim. & veg. oils
3	Mineral fuels, lubricants
5	Chemicals
6	Goods classified chiefly by material
7	Machinery and transport equipment
8	Miscellaneous manufactured articles
9	Not classified elsewhere in the SITC

Graph 4: Merchandise trade balance
(Bln US$ by MDG Regions in 2014)

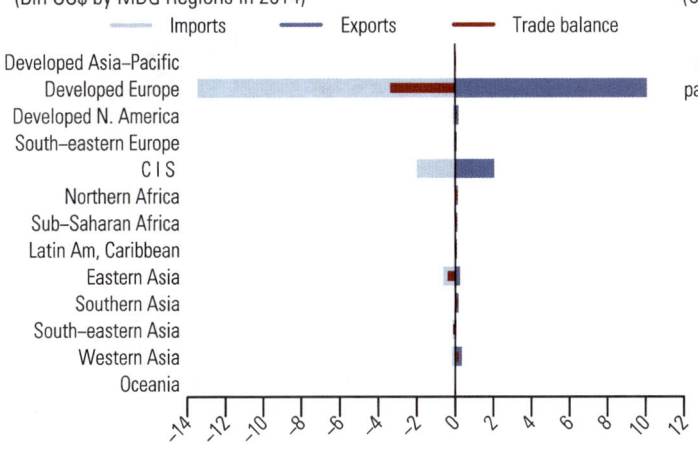

Graph 5: Partner concentration of merchandise trade
(Cumulative share by ranked partners in 2014)

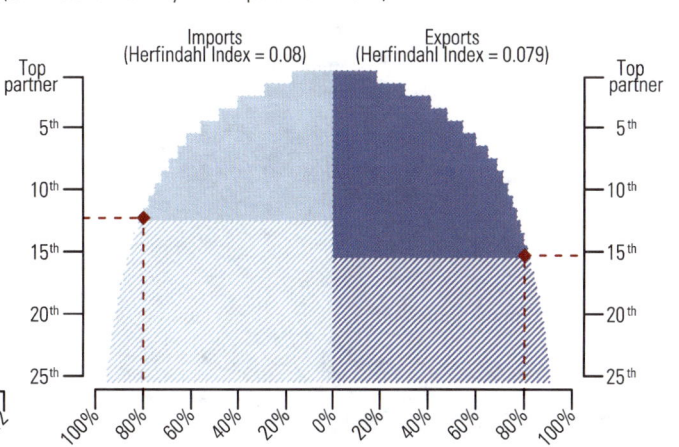

Imports (Herfindahl Index = 0.08)
Exports (Herfindahl Index = 0.079)

Graph 6: Imports of services by EBOPS category
(% share in 2013)

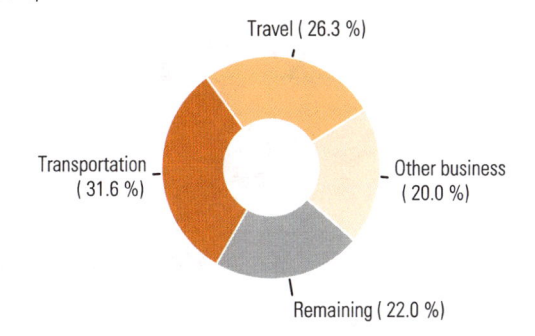

- Travel (26.3 %)
- Transportation (31.6 %)
- Other business (20.0 %)
- Remaining (22.0 %)

Imports Profile:

"Machinery and transport equipment" (SITC section 7), "Goods classified chiefly by material" (SITC section 6) and "Mineral fuels, lubricants" (SITC section 3) were the largest commodity groups for imports in 2014, representing respectively 23.9, 14.2 and 13.9 percent of imported goods (see table 3). From 2012 to 2014, the largest import commodity was "Petroleum oils, other than crude" (HS code 2710) (see table 4). The top three partners for merchandise imports were Lithuania, Germany and Poland, accounting for respectively 19.3, 11.5 and 9.9 percent of total imports. "Transportation" (EBOPS code 205) accounted for the largest share of imports of services in 2013 at 892.3 mln US$, followed by "Travel" (EBOPS code 236) at 742.0 mln US$ and "Other business services" (EBOPS code 268) at 565.4 mln US$ (see graph 6).

Table 4: Top 10 import commodities 2012 to 2014

HS code	4-digit heading of Harmonized System 2012	2012	2013	2014	2012	2013	2014	Unit	SITC code
	All Commodities	16 082.4	16 778.9	16 716.5					
2710	Petroleum oils, other than crude	1 735.2	1 713.3	1 567.5	1.0	1.0	0.9	US$/kg	334
9999	Commodities not specified according to kind	1 366.4	1 733.6	1 703.2					931
2711	Petroleum gases and other gaseous hydrocarbons	717.1	755.2	628.8	0.6	0.6	0.6	US$/kg	343
8517	Electrical apparatus for line telephony or line telegraphy	331.5	543.3	771.4					764
8703	Motor cars and other motor vehicles principally designed for the transport	461.4	468.7	536.3	22.0	23.8	22.9	thsd US$/unit	781
3004	Medicaments (excluding goods of heading 30.02, 30.05 or 30.06)	417.0	483.9	502.8	70.4	77.8	91.5	US$/kg	542
8528	Reception apparatus for television	251.9	217.9	237.6	262.2	299.0	324.4	US$/unit	761
8471	Automatic data processing machines and units thereof	204.7	201.4	202.8	156.7	105.0	151.5	US$/unit	752
7204	Ferrous waste and scrap; remelting scrap ingots of iron or steel	360.5	111.5	70.7	0.4	0.4	0.3	US$/kg	282
8708	Parts and accessories of the motor vehicles of headings 87.01 to 87.05	165.4	186.9	178.9	10.3	10.1	9.3	US$/kg	784

2014 International Trade Statistics Yearbook, Vol. I — Source: UN Comtrade and UN ServiceTrade

Lebanon

Goods Imports: CIF, by origin **Goods Exports: FOB, by last known destination** **Trade System: Special**

Overview:
In 2013, the value of merchandise exports of Lebanon decreased substantially by 11.5 percent to reach 3.9 bln US$, while its merchandise imports increased slightly by 0.4 percent to reach 21.2 bln US$ (see graph 1, table 2 and table 3). The merchandise trade balance recorded a large deficit of 17.3 bln US$ (see graph 1). The largest merchandise trade balance was with MDG Developed Europe at -8.0 bln US$ (see graph 4). Merchandise exports in Lebanon were diversified amongst partners; imports were also diversified. The top 21 partners accounted for 80 percent or more of exports and 22 partners accounted for 80 percent or more of imports (see graph 5). In 2013, the value of exports of services of Lebanon decreased substantially by 10.4 percent, reaching 14.7 bln US$, while its imports of services increased substantially by 10.6 percent and reached 13.1 bln US$ (see graph 2). There was a relatively small trade in services surplus of 1.6 bln US$.

Graph 1: Total merchandise trade, by value
(Bln US$ by year)

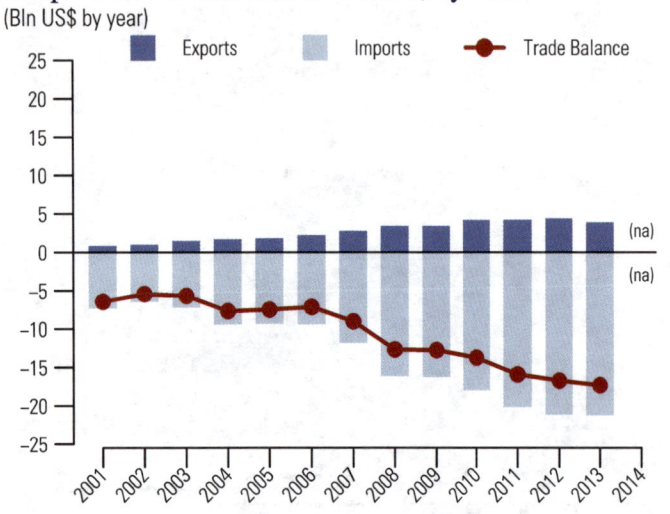

Graph 2: Total services trade, by value
(Bln US$ by year)

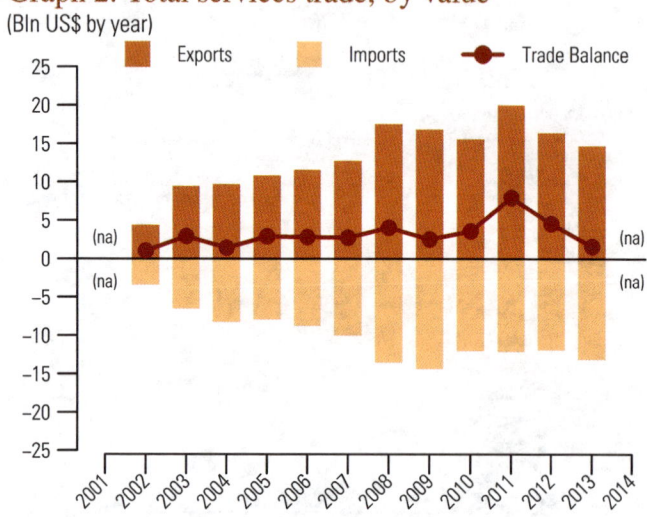

Exports Profile:
"Food, animals + beverages, tobacco" (SITC section 0+1), "Not classified elsewhere in the SITC" (SITC section 9) and "Machinery and transport equipment" (SITC section 7) were the largest commodity groups for exports in 2013, representing respectively 17.4, 14.3 and 13.7 percent of exported goods (see table 2). From 2011 to 2013, the largest export commodity was "Gold (including gold plated with platinum)" (HS code 7108) (see table 1). The top three destinations for merchandise exports were South Africa, Switzerland and the Syrian Arab Republic, accounting for respectively 15.3, 9.8 and 8.2 percent of total exports. "Travel" (EBOPS code 236) accounted for the largest share of exports of services in 2013 at 5.9 bln US$, followed by "Other business services" (EBOPS code 268) at 4.5 bln US$ and "Transportation" (EBOPS code 205) at 1.1 bln US$ (see graph 3).

Graph 3: Exports of services by EBOPS category
(% share in 2013)

- Travel (39.8 %)
- Other business (30.3 %)
- Transportation (7.3 %)
- Remaining (22.5 %)

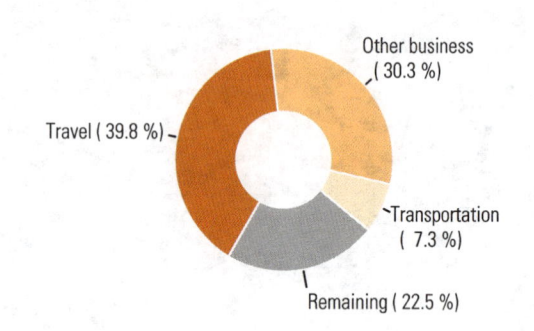

Table 1: Top 10 export commodities 2011 to 2013

HS code	4-digit heading of Harmonized System 2007	Value (million US$) 2011	2012	2013	Unit value 2011	2012	2013	Unit	SITC code
	All Commodities	4266.9	4446.2	3937.1					
7108	Gold (including gold plated with platinum)	1169.1	1396.1	558.7	42.3	46.5	41.4	thsd US$/kg	971
7102	Diamonds, whether or not worked, but not mounted or set	248.8	197.5	110.2					667
7204	Ferrous waste and scrap; remelting scrap ingots of iron or steel	232.1	133.8	147.0	0.4	0.4	0.3	US$/kg	282
8502	Electric generating sets and rotary converters	175.3	144.0	136.4					716
7404	Copper waste and scrap	103.1	157.2	187.9	7.0	6.4	5.9	US$/kg	288
2710	Petroleum oils, other than crude	3.8	72.4	298.6	1.3	1.0	1.0	US$/kg	334
3103	Mineral or chemical fertilisers, phosphatic	118.6	85.2	72.9	0.5	0.4	0.3	US$/kg	562
7113	Articles of jewellery and parts thereof, of precious metal	54.4	105.9	81.8	37.5	43.5	44.3	thsd US$/kg	897
4901	Printed books, brochures, leaflets and similar printed matter	51.0	74.7	73.8	1.0	1.5	1.5	US$/kg	892
9403	Other furniture and parts thereof	60.6	53.8	53.4					821

Source: UN Comtrade and UN ServiceTrade

Lebanon

Services Imports and Exports: EBOPS 2002 categories

Table 2: Merchandise exports by SITC
(Value in million US$, growth and shares in percentage)

SITC	2013	Avg. Growth rates 2009-2013	Avg. Growth rates 2012-2013	2013 share
Total	3 937.1	3.1	-11.5	100.0
0+1	685.2	13.5	18.8	17.4
2+4	432.9	20.8	15.3	11.0
3	336.9	131.2	275.5	8.6
5	417.6	7.3	-4.2	10.6
6	511.6	-5.8	-18.5	13.0
7	540.1	-0.6	12.9	13.7
8	450.2	-2.0	-2.7	11.4
9	562.7	-9.8	-59.8	14.3

Table 3: Merchandise imports by SITC
(Value in million US$, growth and shares in percentage)

SITC	2013	Avg. Growth rates 2009-2013	Avg. Growth rates 2012-2013	2013 share
Total	21 234.2	6.9	0.4	100.0
0+1	3 093.9	8.3	3.9	14.6
2+4	584.4	5.6	-3.3	2.8
3	5 001.2	11.5	-15.2	23.6
5	2 444.0	10.1	12.2	11.5
6	3 121.2	7.1	1.0	14.7
7	4 359.4	0.2	25.2	20.5
8	1 767.9	4.9	2.6	8.3
9	862.1	17.0	-28.0	4.1

SITC Legend

SITC Code	Description
Total	All commodities
0+1	Food, animals + beverages, tobacco
2+4	Crude materials + anim. & veg. oils
3	Mineral fuels, lubricants
5	Chemicals
6	Goods classified chiefly by material
7	Machinery and transport equipment
8	Miscellaneous manufactured articles
9	Not classified elsewhere in the SITC

Graph 4: Merchandise trade balance
(Bln US$ by MDG Regions in 2013)

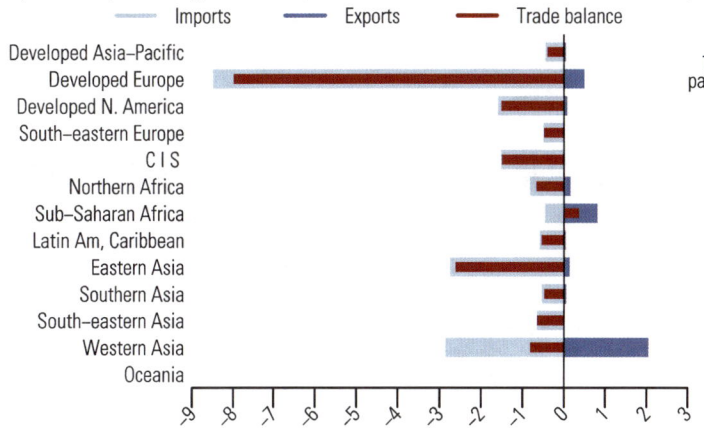

Graph 5: Partner concentration of merchandise trade
(Cumulative share by ranked partners in 2013)

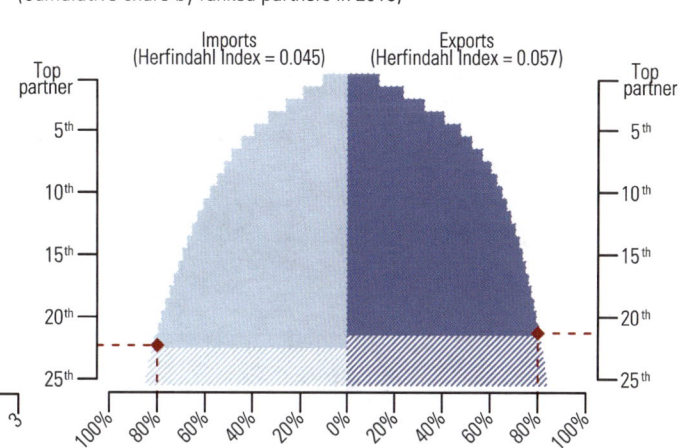

Imports (Herfindahl Index = 0.045)
Exports (Herfindahl Index = 0.057)

Graph 6: Imports of services by EBOPS category
(% share in 2013)

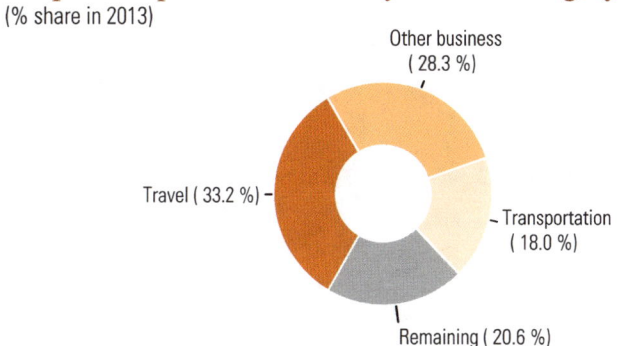

- Other business (28.3 %)
- Travel (33.2 %)
- Transportation (18.0 %)
- Remaining (20.6 %)

Imports Profile:

"Mineral fuels, lubricants" (SITC section 3), "Machinery and transport equipment" (SITC section 7) and "Goods classified chiefly by material" (SITC section 6) were the largest commodity groups for imports in 2013, representing respectively 23.6, 20.5 and 14.7 percent of imported goods (see table 3). From 2011 to 2013, the largest import commodity was "Petroleum oils, other than crude" (HS code 2710) (see table 4). The top three partners for merchandise imports were the United States, China and Italy, accounting for respectively 9.4, 9.0 and 8.7 percent of total imports. "Travel" (EBOPS code 236) accounted for the largest share of imports of services in 2013 at 4.4 bln US$, followed by "Other business services" (EBOPS code 268) at 3.7 bln US$ and "Transportation" (EBOPS code 205) at 2.4 bln US$ (see graph 6).

Table 4: Top 10 import commodities 2011 to 2013

HS code	4-digit heading of Harmonized System 2007	Value (million US$) 2011	2012	2013	Unit value 2011	2012	2013	Unit	SITC code
	All Commodities	20 162.6	21 146.5	21 234.2					
2710	Petroleum oils, other than crude	4 157.3	5 517.5	4 664.7	0.9	1.0	1.0	US$/kg	334
7108	Gold (including gold plated with platinum)	1 686.0	1 186.4	852.1	45.8	47.6	43.6	thsd US$/kg	971
8703	Motor cars and other motor vehicles principally designed for the transport	1 092.1	1 101.5	1 168.2			21.4	thsd US$/unit	781
3004	Medicaments (excluding goods of heading 30.02, 30.05 or 30.06)	845.0	831.4	935.7	112.5	115.7	116.7	US$/kg	542
7102	Diamonds, whether or not worked, but not mounted or set	378.3	279.7	198.8					667
7228	Other bars and rods of other alloy steel	91.5	280.9	478.2	0.7	0.6	0.6	US$/kg	676
0102	Live bovine animals	281.5	270.3	277.3	932.4		950.8	US$/unit	001
2402	Cigars, cheroots, cigarillos and cigarettes	244.5	309.2	242.1	21.5	21.5	21.9	US$/kg	122
7214	Other bars and rods of iron or non-alloy steel	455.2	268.4	65.9	0.7	0.7	0.6	US$/kg	676
2711	Petroleum gases and other gaseous hydrocarbons	175.5	224.0	226.1	1.0	1.1	1.0	US$/kg	343

Lesotho

Goods Imports: CIF, by consignment **Goods Exports:** FOB, by last known destination **Trade System:** General

Overview:
In 2012, the value of merchandise exports of Lesotho decreased substantially by 11.9 percent to reach 678.2 mln US$, while its merchandise imports increased moderately by 9.2 percent to reach 1.6 bln US$ (see graph 1, table 2 and table 3). The merchandise trade balance recorded a large deficit of 916.1 mln US$ (see graph 1). The largest merchandise trade balance was with MDG Sub-Saharan Africa at -1.1 bln US$ (see graph 4). Merchandise exports in Lesotho were highly concentrated amongst partners; imports were also highly concentrated. The top 2 partners accounted for 80 percent or more of exports and 1 partner accounted for 80 percent or more of imports (see graph 5). In 2012, the value of exports of services of Lesotho increased substantially by 41.3 percent, reaching 63.5 mln US$, while its imports of services decreased moderately by 6.1 percent and reached 174.9 mln US$ (see graph 2). There was a large trade in services deficit of 111.4 mln US$.

Graph 1: Total merchandise trade, by value
(Bln US$ by year)

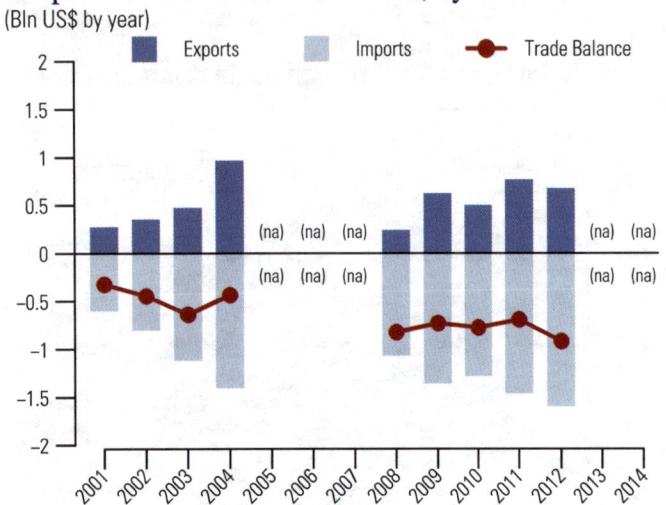

Graph 2: Total services trade, by value
(Mln US$ by year)

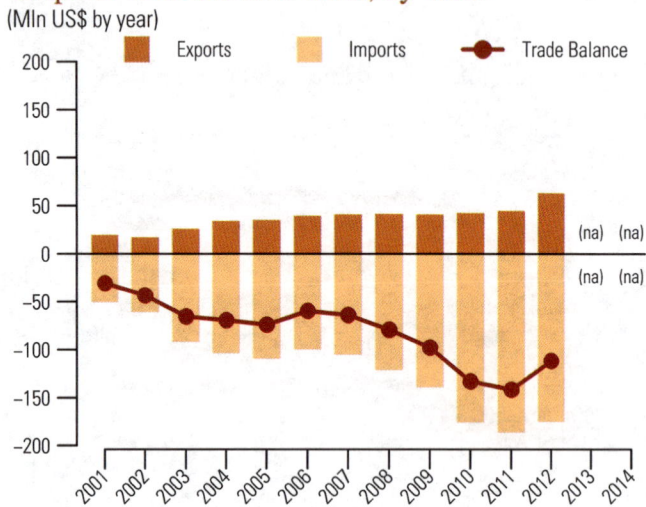

Exports Profile:
"Miscellaneous manufactured articles" (SITC section 8), "Food, animals + beverages, tobacco" (SITC section 0+1) and "Machinery and transport equipment" (SITC section 7) were the largest commodity groups for exports in 2012, representing respectively 60.1, 14.3 and 11.4 percent of exported goods (see table 2). From 2010 to 2012, the largest export commodity was "Men's or boys' suits, jackets, trousers etc" (HS code 6203) (see table 1). The top three destinations for merchandise exports were South Africa, the United States and Belgium, accounting for respectively 53.5, 36.8 and 3.4 percent of total exports. "Travel" (EBOPS code 236) accounted for the largest share of exports of services in 2012 at 46.2 mln US$, followed by "Communications services" (EBOPS code 245) at 6.2 mln US$ and "Other business services" (EBOPS code 268) at 5.6 mln US$ (see graph 3).

Graph 3: Exports of services by EBOPS category
(% share in 2012)

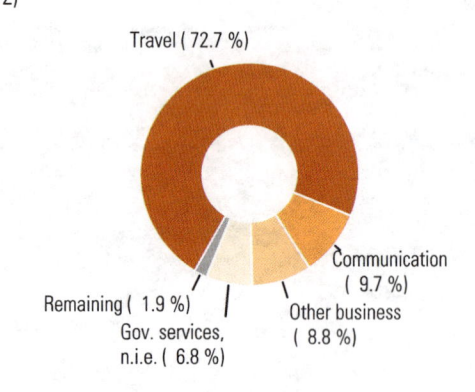

- Travel (72.7 %)
- Communication (9.7 %)
- Other business (8.8 %)
- Gov. services, n.i.e. (6.8 %)
- Remaining (1.9 %)

Table 1: Top 10 export commodities 2010 to 2012

HS code	4-digit heading of Harmonized System 1996	Value (million US$) 2010	2011	2012	Unit value 2010	2011	2012	Unit	SITC code
	All Commodities	503.3	770.1	678.2					
6203	Men's or boys' suits, jackets, trousers etc	52.0	139.5	110.4					841
2201	Unsweetened beverage waters, ice and snow	60.1	67.5	64.5					111
6104	Womens, girls suit, dress, skirt, etc, knit or crocheted	29.8	64.9	77.7					844
6110	Jerseys, pullovers, cardigans, etc, knitted or crocheted	26.1	56.2	33.1	11.7	12.1	12.6	US$/unit	845
9999	Commodities not elsewhere specified	78.2	34.5	2.1					931
8538	Parts for electrical switches, protectors, connectors	39.7	40.2	34.7					772
6204	Women's or girls' suits, jacket, dress, skirt, etc	24.9	53.2	33.0					842
6105	Men's or boys' shirts, knitted or crocheted	13.0	36.0	43.7					843
5101	Wool, not carded or combed	16.5	17.3	36.1	1.8			US$/kg	268
6109	T-shirts, singlets and other vests, knitted or crocheted	11.4	21.4	33.3	5.2	5.4	6.5	US$/unit	845

Lesotho

Services Imports and Exports: EBOPS 2002 categories

Table 2: Merchandise exports by SITC
(Value in million US$, growth and shares in percentage)

SITC	2012	Avg. Growth rates 2008-2012	2011-2012	2012 share
Total	678.2	29.0	-11.9	100.0
0+1	97.3	31.1	-10.8	14.3
2+4	41.4	10.2	46.6	6.1
3	0.8	-2.9	-27.1	0.1
5	0.6	-18.5	-30.3	0.1
6	50.9	33.0	-21.3	7.5
7	77.6	-6.2	22.3	11.4
8	407.7	58.4	-12.9	60.1
9	2.1	59.3	-94.1	0.3

Table 3: Merchandise imports by SITC
(Value in million US$, growth and shares in percentage)

SITC	2012	Avg. Growth rates 2008-2012	2011-2012	2012 share
Total	1 594.2	10.6	9.2	100.0
0+1	314.3	10.7	-4.3	19.7
2+4	69.9	22.4	2.6	4.4
3	193.5	14.2	-4.0	12.1
5	161.6	15.8	7.9	10.1
6	316.0	27.3	26.3	19.8
7	290.1	8.6	18.1	18.2
8	187.8	5.4	22.1	11.8
9	61.1	-18.9	-1.9	3.8

SITC Legend

SITC Code	Description
Total	All commodities
0+1	Food, animals + beverages, tobacco
2+4	Crude materials + anim. & veg. oils
3	Mineral fuels, lubricants
5	Chemicals
6	Goods classified chiefly by material
7	Machinery and transport equipment
8	Miscellaneous manufactured articles
9	Not classified elsewhere in the SITC

Graph 4: Merchandise trade balance
(Bln US$ by MDG Regions in 2012)

Graph 5: Partner concentration of merchandise trade
(Cumulative share by ranked partners in 2012)

Imports (Herfindahl Index = 0.794)
Exports (Herfindahl Index = 0.418)

Graph 6: Imports of services by EBOPS category
(% share in 2012)

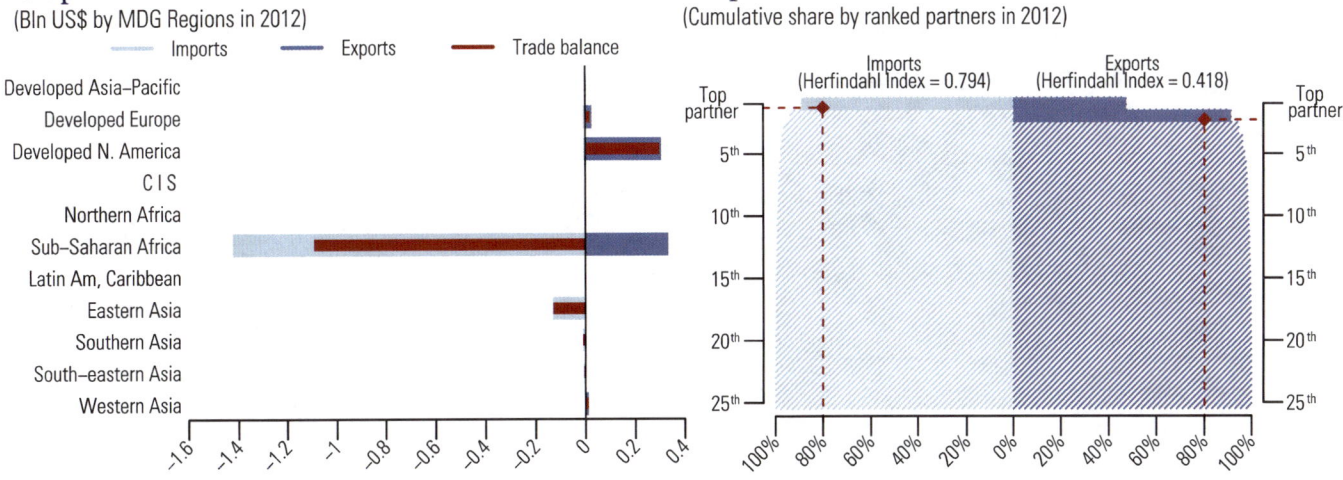

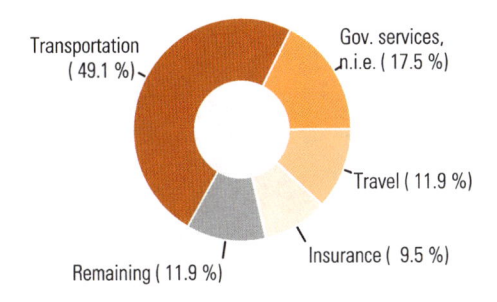

- Transportation (49.1 %)
- Gov. services, n.i.e. (17.5 %)
- Travel (11.9 %)
- Insurance (9.5 %)
- Remaining (11.9 %)

Imports Profile:

"Goods classified chiefly by material" (SITC section 6), "Food, animals + beverages, tobacco" (SITC section 0+1) and "Machinery and transport equipment" (SITC section 7) were the largest commodity groups for imports in 2012, representing respectively 19.8, 19.7 and 18.2 percent of imported goods (see table 3). From 2010 to 2012, the largest import commodity was "Oils petroleum, bituminous, distillates, except crude" (HS code 2710) (see table 4). The top three partners for merchandise imports were South Africa, Other Asia nes and China, accounting for respectively 88.5, 3.4 and 1.9 percent of total imports. "Transportation" (EBOPS code 205) accounted for the largest share of imports of services in 2012 at 85.9 mln US$, followed by "Government services, n.i.e." (EBOPS code 291) at 30.6 mln US$ and "Travel" (EBOPS code 236) at 20.8 mln US$ (see graph 6).

Table 4: Top 10 import commodities 2010 to 2012

HS code	4-digit heading of Harmonized System 1996	2010	2011	2012	2010	2011	2012	Unit	SITC code
	All Commodities..	1 276.6	1 459.7	1 594.2					
2710	Oils petroleum, bituminous, distillates, except crude..................	61.4	156.0	150.9	1.0	0.8	1.2	US$/kg	334
9999	Commodities not elsewhere specified..................	31.0	62.3	61.1					931
8703	Motor vehicles for transport of persons (except buses)..................	20.3	30.9	44.1	12.0		12.4	thsd US$/unit	781
8708	Parts and accessories for motor vehicles..................	26.7	25.4	26.2	12.2		13.5	US$/kg	784
5201	Cotton, not carded or combed..................	16.0	32.1	29.1	1.4	1.9	3.3	US$/kg	263
2711	Petroleum gases and other gaseous hydrocarbons..................	31.2	29.9	14.0					343
0207	Meat, edible offal of domestic poultry..................	21.7	26.2	24.5		1.8	1.7	US$/kg	012
8704	Motor vehicles for the transport of goods..................	17.2	24.7	29.5					782
5209	Woven cotton nes, >85% cotton, >200g/m2..................	31.4	10.4	29.6	6.5	6.6	8.5	US$/kg	652
3923	Containers, bobbins and packages, of plastics..................	15.9	14.1	38.8	4.0	4.4	3.9	US$/kg	893

Libya

Goods Imports: CIF, by origin   **Goods Exports: FOB, by last known destination**   **Trade System: General**

Overview:
In 2010, the value of merchandise exports of Libya increased substantially by 33.7 percent to reach 36.4 bln US$, while its merchandise imports increased substantially by 37.4 percent to reach 17.7 bln US$ (see graph 1, table 2 and table 3). The merchandise trade balance recorded a large surplus of 18.8 bln US$ (see graph 1). The largest merchandise trade balance was with MDG Developed Europe at 22.5 bln US$ (see graph 4). Merchandise exports in Libya were moderately concentrated amongst partners; imports were diversified. The top 5 partners accounted for 80 percent or more of exports and 13 partners accounted for 80 percent or more of imports (see graph 5). In 2013, the value of exports of services of Libya remained at 410.1 mln US$, while its imports of services remained at 6.1 bln US$ (see graph 2). There was a large trade in services deficit of 5.7 bln US$.

Graph 1: Total merchandise trade, by value
(Bln US$ by year)

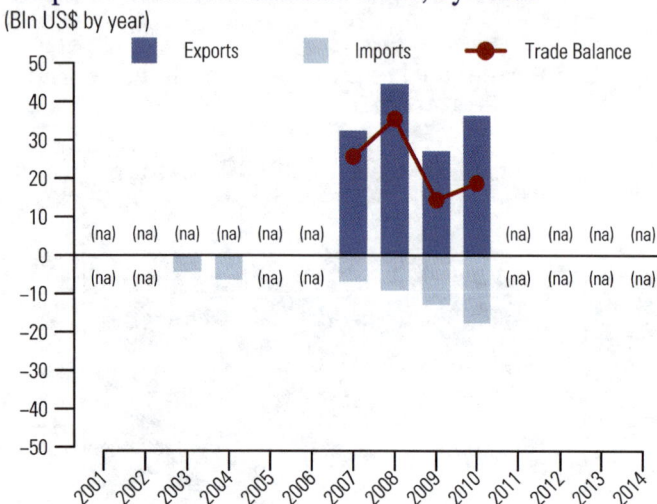

Graph 2: Total services trade, by value
(Bln US$ by year)

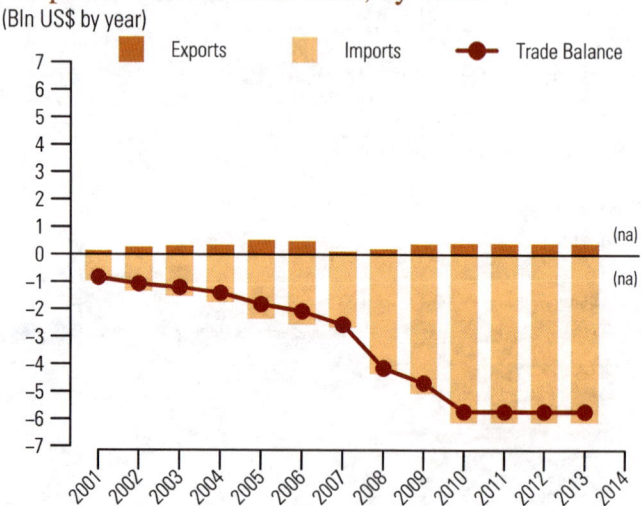

Exports Profile:
"Mineral fuels, lubricants" (SITC section 3), "Chemicals" (SITC section 5) and "Goods classified chiefly by material" (SITC section 6) were the largest commodity groups for exports in 2010, representing respectively 97.7, 1.5 and 0.8 percent of exported goods (see table 2). From 2008 to 2010, the largest export commodity was "Petroleum oils, crude" (HS code 2709) (see table 1). The top three destinations for merchandise exports were Italy, France and China, accounting for respectively 41.2, 12.3 and 7.7 percent of total exports. "Transportation" (EBOPS code 205) accounted for the largest share of exports of services in 2013 at 262.5 mln US$, followed by "Insurance services" (EBOPS code 253) at 75.6 mln US$ and "Travel" (EBOPS code 236) at 60.0 mln US$ (see graph 3).

Graph 3: Exports of services by EBOPS category
(% share in 2013)

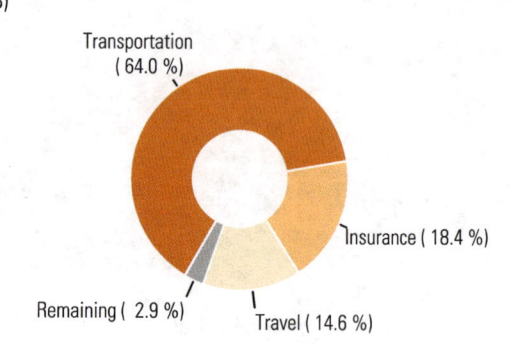

- Transportation (64.0 %)
- Insurance (18.4 %)
- Travel (14.6 %)
- Remaining (2.9 %)

Table 1: Top 10 export commodities 2008 to 2010

HS code	4-digit heading of Harmonized System 2002	Value (million US$) 2008	2009	2010	Unit value 2008	2009	2010	Unit	SITC code
	All Commodities	44 696.4	27 255.5	36 440.4					
2709	Petroleum oils, crude	35 641.5	21 979.4	30 544.9	0.7	0.4	0.6	US$/kg	333
2710	Petroleum oils, other than crude	6 291.0	4 116.7	473.6	0.7	0.5	0.6	US$/kg	334
2711	Petroleum gases and other gaseous hydrocarbons	1 305.8	585.4	4 590.4	0.5	0.4	0.5	US$/kg	343
2901	Acyclic hydrocarbons	397.2	202.0	280.2	1.2	0.7	1.0	US$/kg	511
2905	Acyclic alcohols and their derivatives	278.0	120.0	164.8	0.4	0.2	0.3	US$/kg	512
7208	Flat-rolled products of iron or non-alloy steel	213.3	68.3	146.7	0.8	0.4	0.6	US$/kg	673
3102	Mineral or chemical fertilisers, nitrogenous	266.0	38.4	...	0.4	0.2		US$/kg	562
3901	Polymers of ethylene, in primary forms	110.2	86.0	91.5	1.5	0.9	1.1	US$/kg	571
7301	Sheet piling of iron or steel	105.2	19.9	37.0	0.8	0.4	0.4	US$/kg	676
7201	Pig iron and spiegeleisen in pigs, blocks or other primary forms	...	13.1	80.5		0.4	0.4	US$/kg	671

Source: UN Comtrade and UN ServiceTrade

Libya

Services Imports and Exports: EBOPS 2002 categories

Table 2: Merchandise exports by SITC
(Value in million US$, growth and shares in percentage)

SITC	2010	Avg. Growth rates 2006-2010	Avg. Growth rates 2009-2010	2010 share
Total	36 440.4	...	33.7	100.0
0+1	0.7	...	-55.3	0.0
2+4	0.6	...	-35.9	0.0
3	35 608.9	...	33.5	97.7
5	552.9	...	22.9	1.5
6	277.2	...	128.2	0.8
8	0.1	...	96.7	0.0

Table 3: Merchandise imports by SITC
(Value in million US$, growth and shares in percentage)

SITC	2010	Avg. Growth rates 2006-2010	Avg. Growth rates 2009-2010	2010 share
Total	17 674.4	...	37.4	100.0
0+1	1 911.6	...	37.0	10.8
2+4	542.7	...	82.9	3.1
3	186.5	...	53.8	1.1
5	1 015.2	...	20.2	5.7
6	3 782.7	...	47.0	21.4
7	8 705.5	...	36.5	49.3
8	1 493.9	...	21.1	8.5
9	36.3	...	94.9	0.2

SITC Legend

SITC Code	Description
Total	All commodities
0+1	Food, animals + beverages, tobacco
2+4	Crude materials + anim. & veg. oils
3	Mineral fuels, lubricants
5	Chemicals
6	Goods classified chiefly by material
7	Machinery and transport equipment
8	Miscellaneous manufactured articles
9	Not classified elsewhere in the SITC

Graph 4: Merchandise trade balance
(Bln US$ by MDG Regions in 2010)

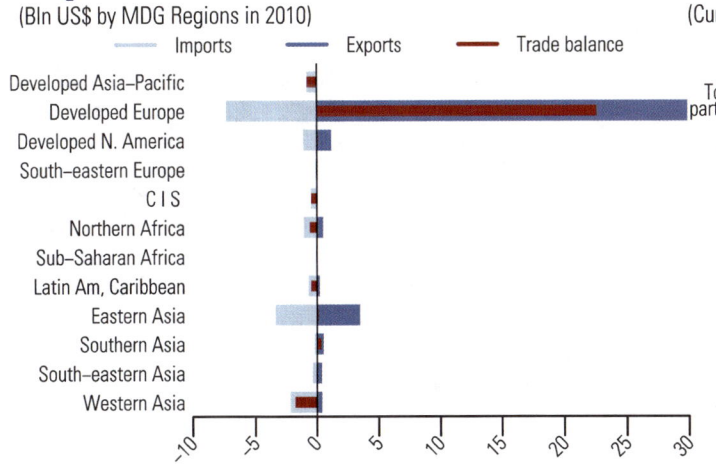

Graph 5: Partner concentration of merchandise trade
(Cumulative share by ranked partners in 2010)

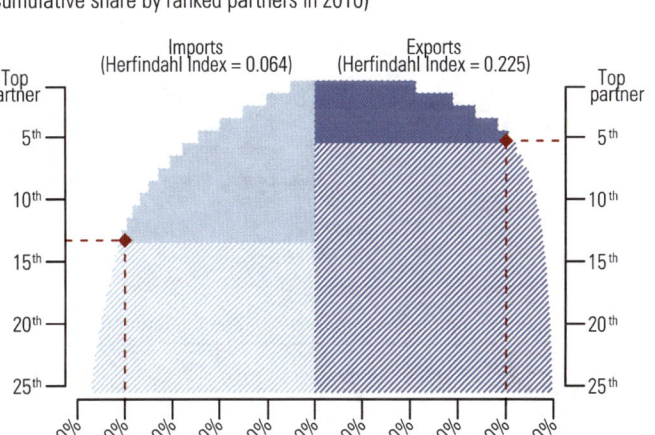

Imports (Herfindahl Index = 0.064)
Exports (Herfindahl Index = 0.225)

Graph 6: Imports of services by EBOPS category
(% share in 2013)

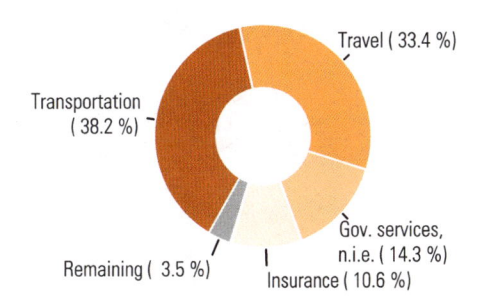

- Transportation (38.2 %)
- Travel (33.4 %)
- Gov. services, n.i.e. (14.3 %)
- Insurance (10.6 %)
- Remaining (3.5 %)

Imports Profile:

"Machinery and transport equipment" (SITC section 7), "Goods classified chiefly by material" (SITC section 6) and "Food, animals + beverages, tobacco" (SITC section 0+1) were the largest commodity groups for imports in 2010, representing respectively 49.3, 21.4 and 10.8 percent of imported goods (see table 3). From 2008 to 2010, the largest import commodity was "Motor cars and other motor vehicles principally designed for the transport" (HS code 8703) (see table 4). The top three partners for merchandise imports were Rest of Europe nes, China and Turkey, accounting for respectively 14.7, 10.8 and 8.9 percent of total imports. "Transportation" (EBOPS code 205) accounted for the largest share of imports of services in 2013 at 2.3 bln US$, followed by "Travel" (EBOPS code 236) at 2.0 bln US$ and "Government services, n.i.e." (EBOPS code 291) at 876.0 mln US$ (see graph 6).

Table 4: Top 10 import commodities 2008 to 2010

HS code	4-digit heading of Harmonized System 2002	Value 2008	Value 2009	Value 2010	Unit value 2008	Unit value 2009	Unit value 2010	Unit	SITC code
	All Commodities	9 116.5	12 859.4	17 674.4					
8703	Motor cars and other motor vehicles principally designed for the transport	840.3	1 074.0	1 341.1	11.8	11.5	11.5	thsd US$/unit	781
8544	Insulated (including enamelled or anodised) wire, cable	211.1	335.6	640.4	3.2	2.7	3.2	US$/kg	773
7304	Tubes, pipes and hollow profiles, seamless, of iron (other than cast iron)	205.4	367.8	471.0	2.2	2.3	2.0	US$/kg	679
8411	Turbo-jets, turbo-propellers and other gas turbines	441.2	225.7	356.7	12.9			US$/kg	714
1001	Wheat and meslin	173.8	312.2	519.5	0.7	0.4	0.5	US$/kg	041
8704	Motor vehicles for the transport of goods	130.0	268.2	460.3	21.9	17.2	22.2	thsd US$/unit	782
8517	Electrical apparatus for line telephony or line telegraphy	177.1	350.1	330.1					764
7308	Structures (excluding prefabricated buildings of heading 94.06)	128.1	234.1	305.8	2.5	2.9	2.6	US$/kg	691
8504	Electrical transformers, static converters (for example, rectifiers)	60.6	240.9	298.7					771
8415	Air conditioning machines, comprising a motor-driven fan	289.8	119.9	172.0					741

Source: UN Comtrade and UN ServiceTrade

Lithuania

Goods Imports: CIF, by origin **Goods Exports:** FOB, by last known destination **Trade System:** Special

Overview:

In 2014, the value of merchandise exports of Lithuania decreased slightly by 0.6 percent to reach 32.4 bln US$, while its merchandise imports increased slightly by 1.2 percent to reach 35.2 bln US$ (see graph 1, table 2 and table 3). The merchandise trade balance recorded a relatively small deficit of 2.8 bln US$ (see graph 1). The largest merchandise trade balance was with MDG Developed Europe at -4.1 bln US$ (see graph 4). Merchandise exports in Lithuania were diversified amongst partners; imports were also diversified. The top 14 partners accounted for 80 percent or more of exports and 14 partners accounted for 80 percent or more of imports (see graph 5). In 2013, the value of exports of services of Lithuania increased substantially by 25.8 percent, reaching 7.4 bln US$, while its imports of services increased substantially by 27.0 percent and reached 5.5 bln US$ (see graph 2). There was a moderate trade in services surplus of 1.9 bln US$.

Graph 1: Total merchandise trade, by value
(Bln US$ by year)

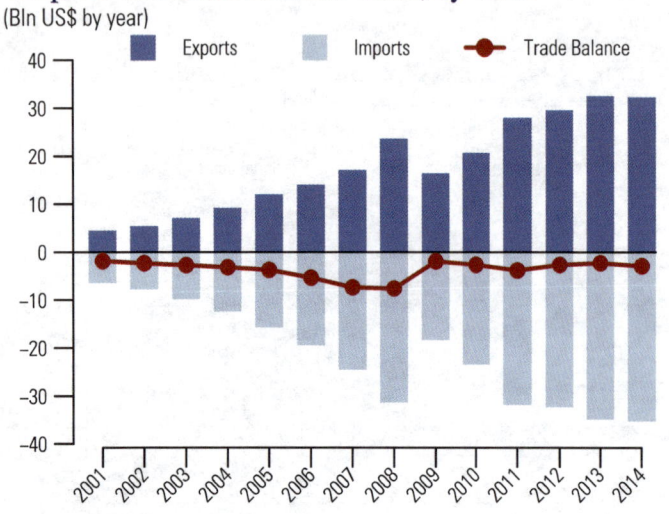

Graph 2: Total services trade, by value
(Bln US$ by year)

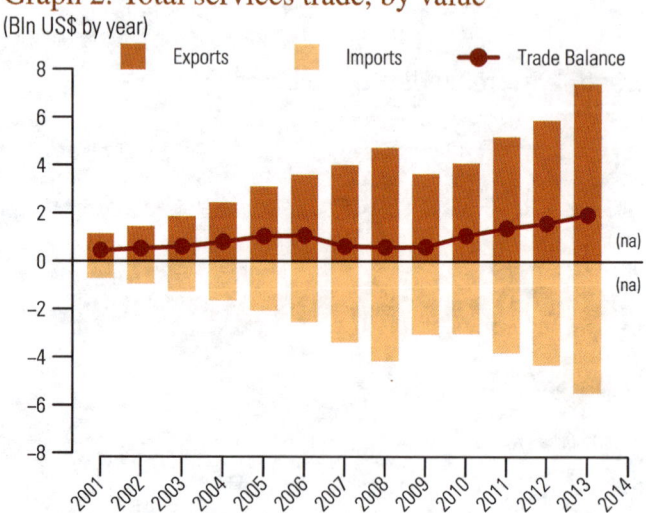

Exports Profile:

"Machinery and transport equipment" (SITC section 7), "Mineral fuels, lubricants" (SITC section 3) and "Food, animals + beverages, tobacco" (SITC section 0+1) were the largest commodity groups for exports in 2014, representing respectively 19.7, 17.5 and 17.2 percent of exported goods (see table 2). From 2012 to 2014, the largest export commodity was "Petroleum oils, other than crude" (HS code 2710) (see table 1). The top three destinations for merchandise exports were the Russian Federation, Latvia and Germany, accounting for respectively 19.9, 10.0 and 7.4 percent of total exports. "Transportation" (EBOPS code 205) accounted for the largest share of exports of services in 2013 at 4.5 bln US$, followed by "Travel" (EBOPS code 236) at 1.4 bln US$ and "Other business services" (EBOPS code 268) at 605.8 mln US$ (see graph 3).

Graph 3: Exports of services by EBOPS category
(% share in 2013)

- Transportation (61.0 %)
- Travel (19.2 %)
- Other business (8.2 %)
- Remaining (11.6 %)

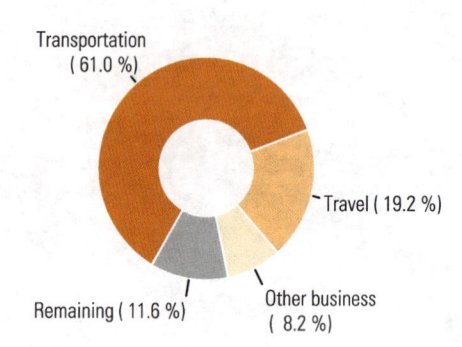

Table 1: Top 10 export commodities 2012 to 2014

HS code	4-digit heading of Harmonized System 2012	Value (million US$) 2012	2013	2014	Unit value 2012	2013	2014	Unit	SITC code
	All Commodities	29 652.7	32 599.7	32 394.3					
2710	Petroleum oils, other than crude	6 815.8	7 104.8	5 372.1	0.9	0.9	0.8	US$/kg	334
9403	Other furniture and parts thereof	926.9	1 044.0	1 206.4					821
3907	Polyacetals, other polyethers and epoxide resins, in primary forms	701.3	706.7	646.3	1.7	1.6	1.5	US$/kg	574
3102	Mineral or chemical fertilisers, nitrogenous	770.6	593.8	656.1	0.3	0.3	0.3	US$/kg	562
8703	Motor cars and other motor vehicles principally designed for the transport	671.2	738.0	553.5	5.1	5.0	5.5	thsd US$/unit	781
9999	Commodities not specified according to kind	559.6	583.5	799.4					931
1001	Wheat and meslin	562.4	594.0	646.0	0.3	0.3	0.3	US$/kg	041
3105	Mineral or chemical fertilisers	494.2	459.6	458.1	0.5	0.5	0.5	US$/kg	562
3004	Medicaments (excluding goods of heading 30.02, 30.05 or 30.06)	361.2	452.0	570.7	144.7	153.4	147.6	US$/kg	542
9401	Seats (other than those of heading 94.02)	341.6	382.5	416.2					821

Lithuania

Services Imports and Exports: EBOPS 2002 categories

Table 2: Merchandise exports by SITC
(Value in million US$, growth and shares in percentage)

SITC	2014	Avg. Growth rates 2010-2014	Avg. Growth rates 2013-2014	2014 share
Total	32 394.3	11.7	-0.6	100.0
0+1	5 575.6	13.1	-1.6	17.2
2+4	1 490.1	11.9	1.4	4.6
3	5 684.9	4.0	-24.3	17.5
5	4 240.4	12.2	7.5	13.1
6	3 329.5	12.5	3.9	10.3
7	6 371.4	14.7	11.3	19.7
8	4 899.5	14.7	9.1	15.1
9	802.9	25.4	36.8	2.5

Table 3: Merchandise imports by SITC
(Value in million US$, growth and shares in percentage)

SITC	2014	Avg. Growth rates 2010-2014	Avg. Growth rates 2013-2014	2014 share
Total	35 217.4	10.8	1.2	100.0
0+1	4 323.7	12.2	-1.7	12.3
2+4	1 355.5	11.4	1.4	3.8
3	8 579.0	3.4	-17.7	24.4
5	4 639.3	10.3	7.2	13.2
6	4 301.1	13.2	11.0	12.2
7	8 294.5	16.2	13.2	23.6
8	2 622.8	16.2	20.3	7.4
9	1 101.5	19.5	16.1	3.1

SITC Legend

SITC Code	Description
Total	All commodities
0+1	Food, animals + beverages, tobacco
2+4	Crude materials + anim. & veg. oils
3	Mineral fuels, lubricants
5	Chemicals
6	Goods classified chiefly by material
7	Machinery and transport equipment
8	Miscellaneous manufactured articles
9	Not classified elsewhere in the SITC

Graph 4: Merchandise trade balance
(Bln US$ by MDG Regions in 2014)

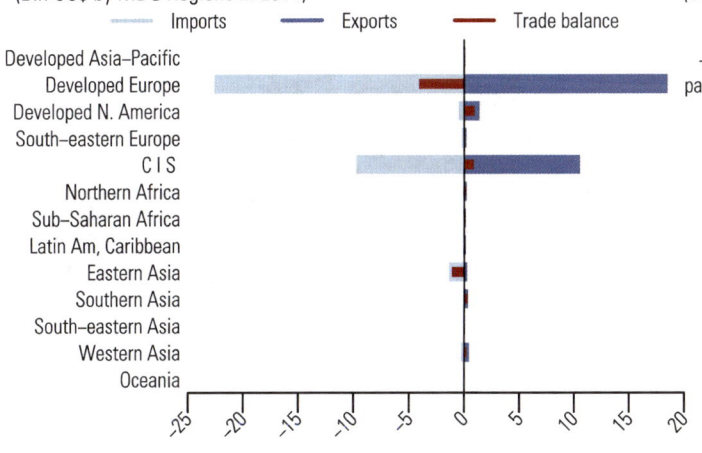

Graph 5: Partner concentration of merchandise trade
(Cumulative share by ranked partners in 2014)

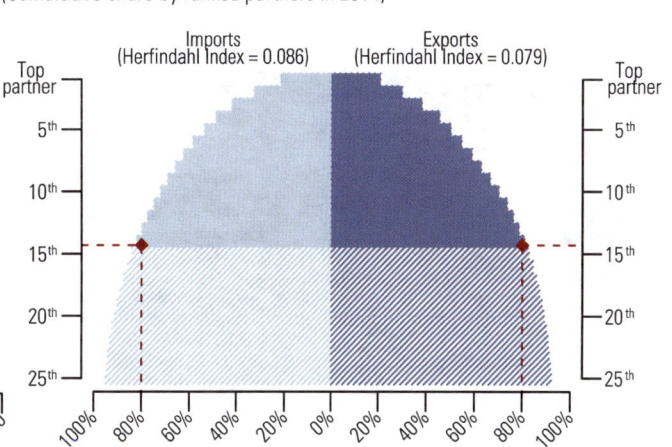

Imports (Herfindahl Index = 0.086)
Exports (Herfindahl Index = 0.079)

Graph 6: Imports of services by EBOPS category
(% share in 2013)

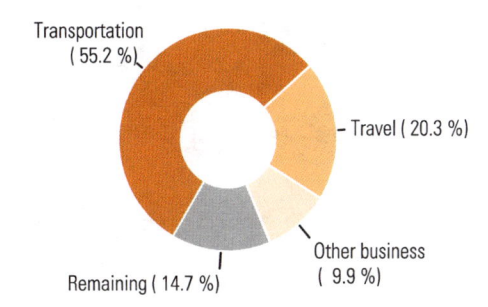

- Transportation (55.2 %)
- Travel (20.3 %)
- Other business (9.9 %)
- Remaining (14.7 %)

Imports Profile:

"Mineral fuels, lubricants" (SITC section 3), "Machinery and transport equipment" (SITC section 7) and "Chemicals" (SITC section 5) were the largest commodity groups for imports in 2014, representing respectively 24.4, 23.6 and 13.2 percent of imported goods (see table 3). From 2012 to 2014, the largest import commodity was "Petroleum oils and oils obtained from bituminous minerals, crude" (HS code 2709) (see table 4). The top three partners for merchandise imports were the Russian Federation, Germany and Poland, accounting for respectively 27.2, 10.4 and 9.6 percent of total imports. "Transportation" (EBOPS code 205) accounted for the largest share of imports of services in 2013 at 3.0 bln US$, followed by "Travel" (EBOPS code 236) at 1.1 bln US$ and "Other business services" (EBOPS code 268) at 541.0 mln US$ (see graph 6).

Table 4: Top 10 import commodities 2012 to 2014

HS code	4-digit heading of Harmonized System 2012	Value (million US$) 2012	2013	2014	Unit value 2012	2013	2014	Unit	SITC code
	All Commodities	32 237.6	34 813.2	35 217.4					
2709	Petroleum oils and oils obtained from bituminous minerals, crude	7 463.8	7 170.5	5 643.5	0.9	0.8	0.8	US$/kg	333
2711	Petroleum gases and other gaseous hydrocarbons	1 627.6	1 392.4	1 203.6	0.7	0.7	0.6	US$/kg	343
2710	Petroleum oils, other than crude	1 271.3	1 407.6	1 415.3	1.0	1.0	0.9	US$/kg	334
9999	Commodities not specified according to kind	931.4	940.0	1 093.8					931
8703	Motor cars and other motor vehicles principally designed for the transport	958.6	1 026.6	969.2	7.5	7.8	8.6	thsd US$/unit	781
3004	Medicaments (excluding goods of heading 30.02, 30.05 or 30.06)	711.7	790.1	866.4	84.3	78.3	80.5	US$/kg	542
2917	Polycarboxylic acids, their anhydrides	533.4	496.9	468.6	1.2	1.2	1.0	US$/kg	513
8701	Tractors (other than tractors of heading 87.09)	494.3	510.9	284.8	46.0	46.6	38.9	thsd US$/unit	722
8517	Electrical apparatus for line telephony or line telegraphy	291.3	374.3	416.4					764
8471	Automatic data processing machines and units thereof	323.9	331.6	342.8	109.0	136.1	139.7	US$/unit	752

Source: UN Comtrade and UN ServiceTrade

Luxembourg

Goods Imports: CIF, by origin/consignment for intra-eu **Goods Exports:** FOB, by last known destination **Trade System:** Special

Overview:
In 2014, the value of merchandise exports of Luxembourg increased moderately by 6.8 percent to reach 14.7 bln US$, while its merchandise imports decreased slightly by 0.5 percent to reach 23.8 bln US$ (see graph 1, table 2 and table 3). The merchandise trade balance recorded a moderate deficit of 9.1 bln US$ (see graph 1). The largest merchandise trade balance was with MDG Developed Europe at -7.3 bln US$ (see graph 4). Merchandise exports in Luxembourg were diversified amongst partners; imports were also diversified. The top 12 partners accounted for 80 percent or more of exports and 7 partners accounted for 80 percent or more of imports (see graph 5). In 2013, the value of exports of services of Luxembourg increased substantially by 22.8 percent, reaching 88.7 bln US$, while its imports of services increased substantially by 44.0 percent and reached 60.8 bln US$ (see graph 2). There was a moderate trade in services surplus of 27.9 bln US$.

Graph 1: Total merchandise trade, by value
(Bln US$ by year)

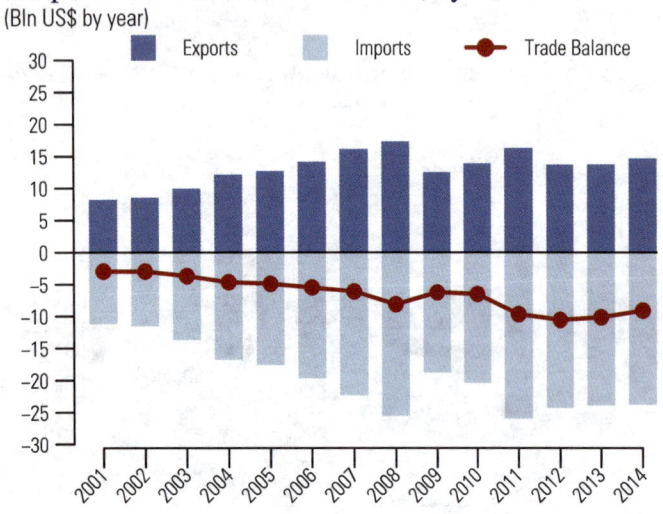

Graph 2: Total services trade, by value
(Bln US$ by year)

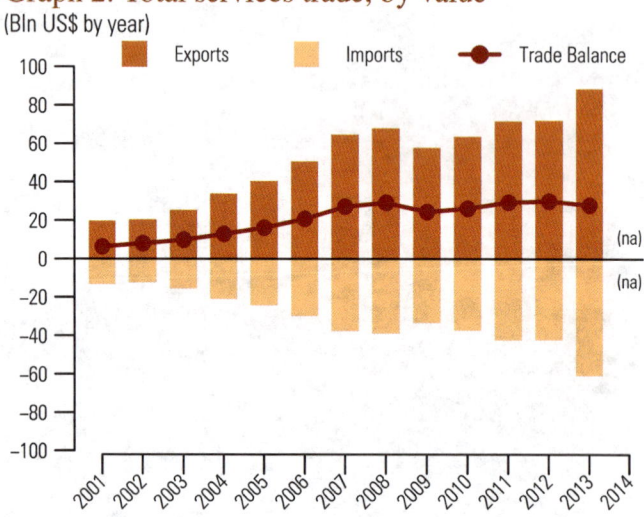

Exports Profile:
"Goods classified chiefly by material" (SITC section 6), "Machinery and transport equipment" (SITC section 7) and "Food, animals + beverages, tobacco" (SITC section 0+1) were the largest commodity groups for exports in 2014, representing respectively 41.3, 21.8 and 10.5 percent of exported goods (see table 2). From 2012 to 2014, the largest export commodity was "Angles, shapes and sections of iron or non-alloy steel" (HS code 7216) (see table 1). The top three destinations for merchandise exports were Germany, France and Belgium, accounting for respectively 27.5, 14.4 and 13.2 percent of total exports. "Other business services" (EBOPS code 268) accounted for the largest share of exports of services in 2013 at 14.5 bln US$, followed by "Travel" (EBOPS code 236) at 5.0 bln US$ and "Personal, cultural, and recreational services" (EBOPS code 287) at 4.8 bln US$ (see graph 3).

Graph 3: Exports of services by EBOPS category
(% share in 2013)

- Transportation (5.3 %)
- Personal, cultural & rec (5.4 %)
- Travel (5.7 %)
- Other business (16.3 %)
- Remaining (67.3 %)

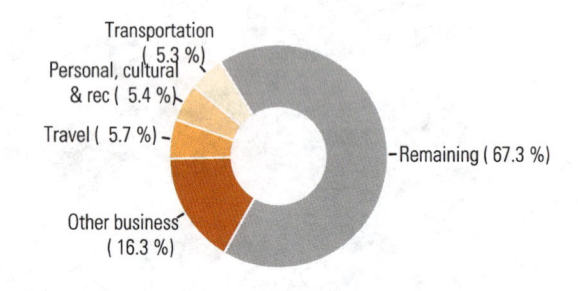

Table 1: Top 10 export commodities 2012 to 2014

HS code	4-digit heading of Harmonized System 2012	Value (million US$) 2012	2013	2014	Unit value 2012	2013	2014	Unit	SITC code
	All Commodities	13726.9	13753.5	14689.8					
7216	Angles, shapes and sections of iron or non-alloy steel	1124.6	983.1	1065.0	0.8	0.8	0.7	US$/kg	676
4011	New pneumatic tyres, of rubber	659.1	674.8	634.8	332.6	320.9	305.3	US$/unit	625
7301	Sheet piling of iron or steel	600.5	597.6	564.2	1.0	1.0	1.0	US$/kg	676
7210	Flat-rolled products of iron or non-alloy steel	435.6	504.3	587.6	0.9	0.9	0.9	US$/kg	674
8703	Motor cars and other motor vehicles principally designed for the transport	425.3	460.0	514.0	15.7	13.9	7.0	thsd US$/unit	781
9999	Commodities not specified according to kind	387.2	380.8	448.6					931
4811	Paper, paperboard, cellulose wadding and webs of cellulose fibres	375.6	363.4	364.6	2.6	2.8	2.8	US$/kg	641
7601	Unwrought aluminium	347.5	340.4	357.4	2.4	2.3	2.3	US$/kg	684
0406	Cheese and curd	265.2	326.8	440.2	5.8	6.7	8.6	US$/kg	024
5902	Tyre cord fabric of high tenacity yarn of nylon or other polyamides	282.5	272.4	230.2	4.5	4.5	4.5	US$/kg	657

Luxembourg

Services Imports and Exports: EBOPS 2002 categories

Table 2: Merchandise exports by SITC
(Value in million US$, growth and shares in percentage)

SITC	2014	Avg. Growth rates 2010-2014	Avg. Growth rates 2013-2014	2014 share
Total	14689.8	1.4	6.8	100.0
0+1	1541.5	8.0	18.8	10.5
2+4	378.5	-7.3	-13.0	2.6
3	116.7	-2.9	-6.9	0.8
5	1344.0	6.3	12.2	9.1
6	6068.8	-1.0	2.6	41.3
7	3208.2	0.6	4.5	21.8
8	1332.9	1.9	3.4	9.1
9	699.2	14.8	64.9	4.8

Table 3: Merchandise imports by SITC
(Value in million US$, growth and shares in percentage)

SITC	2014	Avg. Growth rates 2010-2014	Avg. Growth rates 2013-2014	2014 share
Total	23783.8	3.9	-0.5	100.0
0+1	2744.6	5.1	6.4	11.5
2+4	1717.0	2.1	-13.1	7.2
3	2314.0	3.6	-11.5	9.7
5	2377.8	4.5	3.1	10.0
6	3709.4	2.3	4.6	15.6
7	7481.9	6.2	3.4	31.5
8	2196.4	2.5	3.0	9.2
9	1242.8	-1.4	-17.2	5.2

SITC Legend

SITC Code	Description
Total	All commodities
0+1	Food, animals + beverages, tobacco
2+4	Crude materials + anim. & veg. oils
3	Mineral fuels, lubricants
5	Chemicals
6	Goods classified chiefly by material
7	Machinery and transport equipment
8	Miscellaneous manufactured articles
9	Not classified elsewhere in the SITC

Graph 4: Merchandise trade balance
(Bln US$ by MDG Regions in 2014)

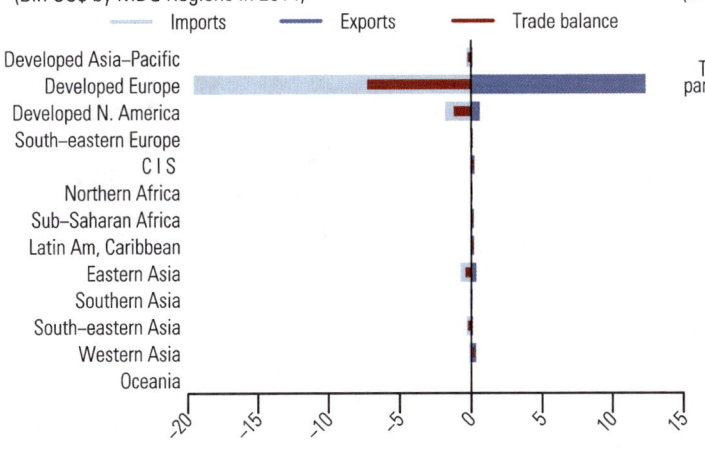

Graph 5: Partner concentration of merchandise trade
(Cumulative share by ranked partners in 2014)

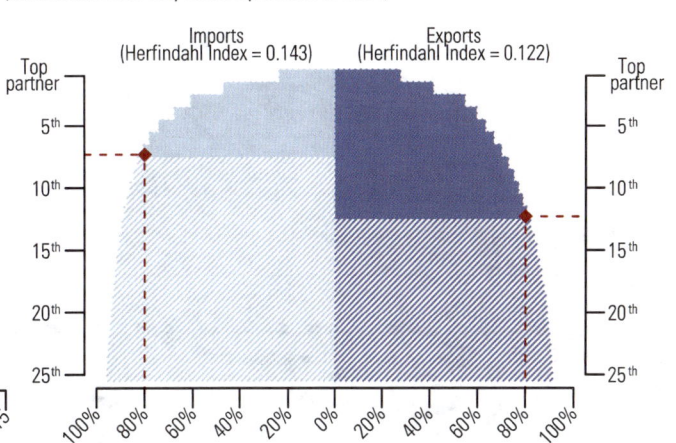

Imports (Herfindahl Index = 0.143)
Exports (Herfindahl Index = 0.122)

Graph 6: Imports of services by EBOPS category
(% share in 2013)

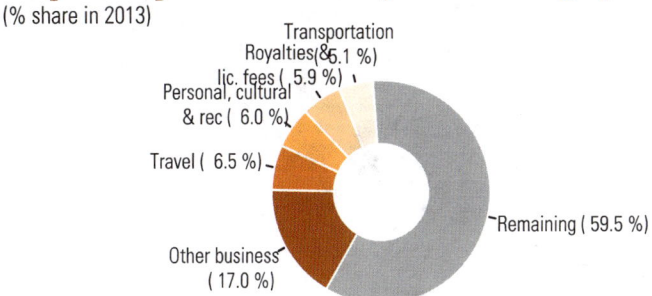

- Transportation (5.1 %)
- Royalties & lic. fees (5.9 %)
- Personal, cultural & rec (6.0 %)
- Travel (6.5 %)
- Other business (17.0 %)
- Remaining (59.5 %)

Imports Profile:

"Machinery and transport equipment" (SITC section 7), "Goods classified chiefly by material" (SITC section 6) and "Food, animals + beverages, tobacco" (SITC section 0+1) were the largest commodity groups for imports in 2014, representing respectively 31.5, 15.6 and 11.5 percent of imported goods (see table 3). From 2012 to 2014, the largest import commodity was "Petroleum oils, other than crude" (HS code 2710) (see table 4). The top three partners for merchandise imports were Belgium, Germany and France, accounting for respectively 24.3, 23.1 and 13.3 percent of total imports. "Other business services" (EBOPS code 268) accounted for the largest share of imports of services in 2013 at 10.4 bln US$, followed by "Travel" (EBOPS code 236) at 3.9 bln US$ and "Personal, cultural, and recreational services" (EBOPS code 287) at 3.6 bln US$ (see graph 6).

Table 4: Top 10 import commodities 2012 to 2014

HS code	4-digit heading of Harmonized System 2012	Value (million US$) 2012	2013	2014	Unit value 2012	2013	2014	Unit	SITC code
	All Commodities	24284.9	23895.9	23783.8					
2710	Petroleum oils, other than crude	2778.2	2559.7	2265.9	0.9	1.0	0.9	US$/kg	334
8703	Motor cars and other motor vehicles principally designed for the transport	1872.2	1837.7	2053.6	28.6	29.6	27.0	thsd US$/unit	781
8802	Other aircraft (for example, helicopters, aeroplanes); spacecraft	1819.2	1647.0	1412.0	55.1	68.6	58.8	mln US$/unit	792
9999	Commodities not specified according to kind	1342.0	1363.4	1177.4					931
7204	Ferrous waste and scrap; remelting scrap ingots of iron or steel	927.1	897.5	766.6	0.4	0.4	0.3	US$/kg	282
3004	Medicaments (excluding goods of heading 30.02, 30.05 or 30.06)	364.2	359.0	390.9	18.8	15.8	14.0	US$/kg	542
0406	Cheese and curd	338.5	374.3	399.0	6.1	6.5	6.8	US$/kg	024
8517	Electrical apparatus for line telephony or line telegraphy	283.1	315.3	369.0					764
7602	Aluminium waste and scrap	298.5	303.8	274.9	1.8	1.8	2.0	US$/kg	288
7209	Flat-rolled products of iron or non-alloy steel	208.5	285.9	243.4	0.7	0.6	0.6	US$/kg	673

Madagascar

| Goods Imports: CIF, by origin | Goods Exports: FOB, by consumption | Trade System: General |

Overview:
In 2013, the value of merchandise exports of Madagascar increased substantially by 50.1 percent to reach 1.8 bln US$, while its merchandise imports increased by 16.0 percent to reach 3.1 bln US$ (see graph 1, table 2 and table 3). The merchandise trade balance recorded a moderate deficit of 1.2 bln US$ (see graph 1). The largest merchandise trade balance was with MDG Western Asia at -841.6 mln US$ (see graph 4). Merchandise exports in Madagascar were diversified amongst partners; imports were also diversified. The top 13 partners accounted for 80 percent or more of exports and 15 partners accounted for 80 percent or more of imports (see graph 5). In 2013, the value of exports of services of Madagascar increased substantially by 58.2 percent, reaching 2.1 bln US$, while its imports of services increased moderately by 8.9 percent and reached 1.5 bln US$ (see graph 2). There was a moderate trade in services surplus of 648.6 mln US$.

Graph 1: Total merchandise trade, by value
(Bln US$ by year)

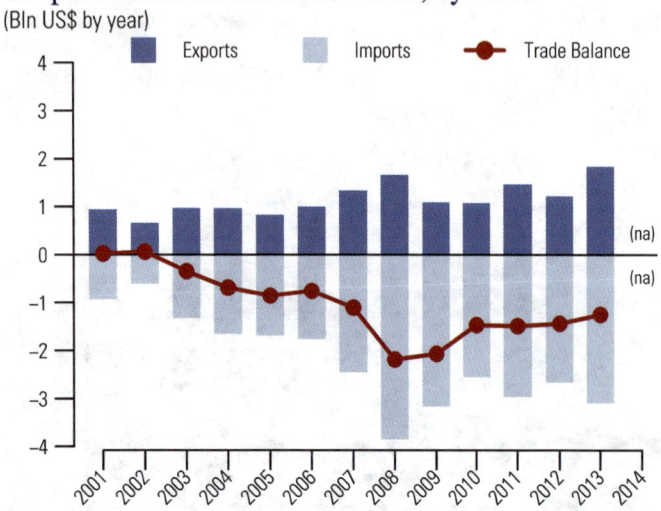

Graph 2: Total services trade, by value
(Bln US$ by year)

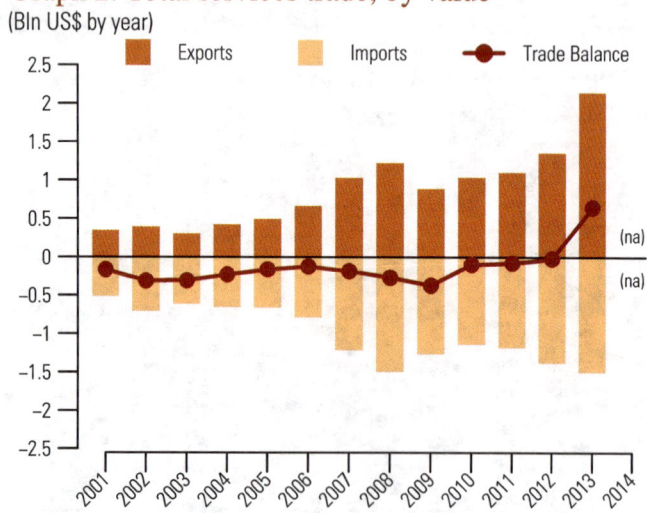

Exports Profile:
"Goods classified chiefly by material" (SITC section 6), "Food, animals + beverages, tobacco" (SITC section 0+1) and "Miscellaneous manufactured articles" (SITC section 8) were the largest commodity groups for exports in 2013, representing respectively 28.7, 25.6 and 24.1 percent of exported goods (see table 2). From 2011 to 2013, the largest export commodity was "Cloves (whole fruit, cloves and stems)" (HS code 0907) (see table 1). The top three destinations for merchandise exports were France, China and Germany, accounting for respectively 29.7, 7.2 and 5.9 percent of total exports. "Travel" (EBOPS code 236) accounted for the largest share of exports of services in 2013 at 717.2 mln US$, followed by "Financial services" (EBOPS code 260) at 547.4 mln US$ and "Transportation" (EBOPS code 205) at 503.6 mln US$ (see graph 3).

Graph 3: Exports of services by EBOPS category
(% share in 2013)

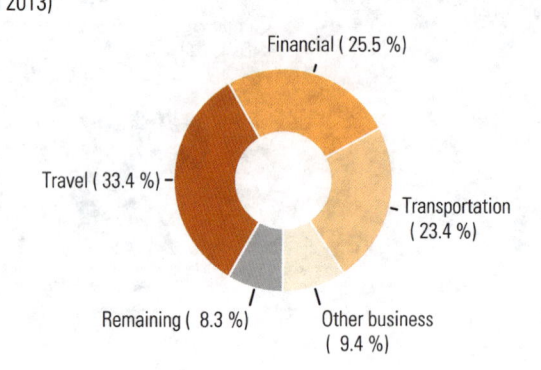

- Financial (25.5 %)
- Transportation (23.4 %)
- Other business (9.4 %)
- Remaining (8.3 %)
- Travel (33.4 %)

Table 1: Top 10 export commodities 2011 to 2013

HS code	4-digit heading of Harmonized System 2007	Value 2011	Value 2012	Value 2013	Unit value 2011	Unit value 2012	Unit value 2013	Unit	SITC code
	All Commodities	1 471.5	1 224.5	1 838.0					
0907	Cloves (whole fruit, cloves and stems)	172.8	167.7	102.8	7.8	8.8	8.8	US$/kg	075
7502	Unwrought nickel	...	59.4	373.9		17.3	14.6	US$/kg	683
6110	Jerseys, pullovers, cardigans, waist-coats and similar articles	135.9	116.4	133.2	24.0		33.0	US$/unit	845
0306	Crustaceans, whether in shell or not	101.3	65.6	93.9	9.6	8.9	9.9	US$/kg	036
2710	Petroleum oils, other than crude	93.4	81.0	81.7	1.3	1.3	1.3	US$/kg	334
2614	Titanium ores and concentrates	74.2	72.2	76.2	0.1	0.1	0.1	US$/kg	287
6214	Shawls, scarves, mufflers, mantillas, veils and the like	45.5	38.2	56.2					846
1604	Prepared or preserved fish; caviar	43.6	37.7	50.0	3.9	5.0	5.8	US$/kg	037
6203	Men's or boys' suits, ensembles, jackets, blazers, trousers	31.9	32.6	52.7					841
8802	Other aircraft (for example, helicopters, aeroplanes); spacecraft	56.1	0.4	39.3					792

Madagascar

Services Imports and Exports: EBOPS 2002 categories

Table 2: Merchandise exports by SITC
(Value in million US$, growth and shares in percentage)

SITC	2013	Avg. Growth rates 2009-2013	2012-2013	2013 share
Total	1838.0	13.8	50.1	100.0
0+1	471.0	13.1	20.7	25.6
2+4	182.5	22.0	-7.0	9.9
3	83.4	14.2	1.0	4.5
5	55.1	26.4	165.2	3.0
6	526.9	53.0	222.3	28.7
7	68.0	0.1	196.1	3.7
8	443.7	-1.7	29.7	24.1
9	7.5	-18.7	20.7	0.4

Table 3: Merchandise imports by SITC
(Value in million US$, growth and shares in percentage)

SITC	2013	Avg. Growth rates 2009-2013	2012-2013	2013 share
Total	3085.4	-0.6	16.0	100.0
0+1	502.5	18.7	43.0	16.3
2+4	233.9	21.4	47.9	7.6
3	757.4	23.3	23.0	24.5
5	283.2	10.1	6.1	9.2
6	648.9	-13.1	14.5	21.0
7	492.0	-13.6	-8.1	15.9
8	161.6	-10.3	5.8	5.2
9	6.0	-7.4	-51.7	0.2

SITC Legend

SITC Code	Description
Total	All commodities
0+1	Food, animals + beverages, tobacco
2+4	Crude materials + anim. & veg. oils
3	Mineral fuels, lubricants
5	Chemicals
6	Goods classified chiefly by material
7	Machinery and transport equipment
8	Miscellaneous manufactured articles
9	Not classified elsewhere in the SITC

Graph 4: Merchandise trade balance
(Mln US$ by MDG Regions in 2013)

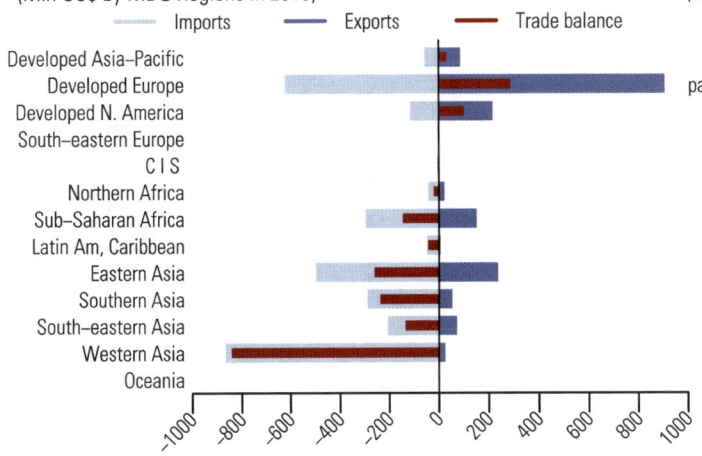

Graph 5: Partner concentration of merchandise trade
(Cumulative share by ranked partners in 2013)

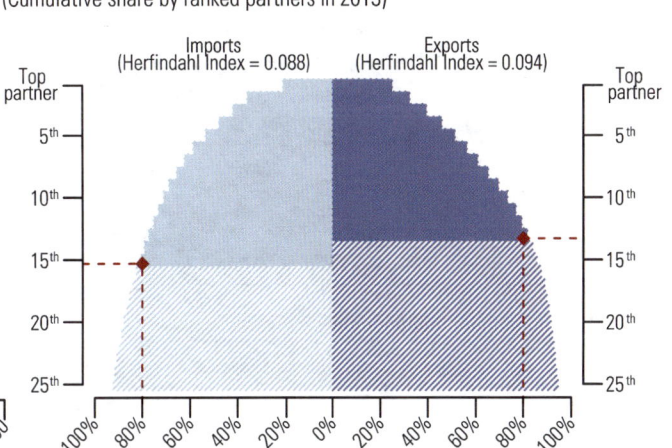

Imports (Herfindahl Index = 0.088)
Exports (Herfindahl Index = 0.094)

Graph 6: Imports of services by EBOPS category
(% share in 2013)

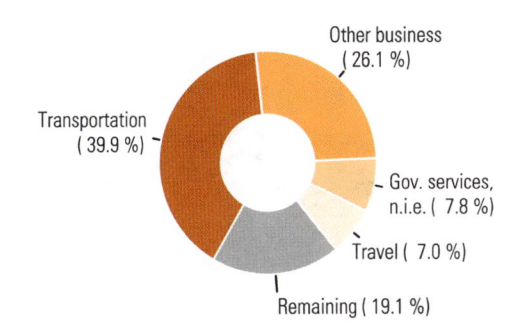

- Transportation (39.9 %)
- Other business (26.1 %)
- Gov. services, n.i.e. (7.8 %)
- Travel (7.0 %)
- Remaining (19.1 %)

Imports Profile:

"Mineral fuels, lubricants" (SITC section 3), "Goods classified chiefly by material" (SITC section 6) and "Food, animals + beverages, tobacco" (SITC section 0+1) were the largest commodity groups for imports in 2013, representing respectively 24.5, 21.0 and 16.3 percent of imported goods (see table 3). From 2011 to 2013, the largest import commodity was "Petroleum oils, other than crude" (HS code 2710) (see table 4). The top three partners for merchandise imports were the United Arab Emirates, China and Rest of Europe nes, accounting for respectively 17.8, 14.2 and 6.5 percent of total imports. "Transportation" (EBOPS code 205) accounted for the largest share of imports of services in 2013 at 599.3 mln US$, followed by "Other business services" (EBOPS code 268) at 391.2 mln US$ and "Government services, n.i.e." (EBOPS code 291) at 117.3 mln US$ (see graph 6).

Table 4: Top 10 import commodities 2011 to 2013

HS code	4-digit heading of Harmonized System 2007	Value (million US$) 2011	2012	2013	Unit value 2011	2012	2013	Unit	SITC code
	All Commodities	2957.1	2659.0	3085.4					
2710	Petroleum oils, other than crude	628.7	569.3	693.1	0.5	1.0	1.0	US$/kg	334
1006	Rice	92.9	85.9	175.6	0.5	0.5	0.5	US$/kg	042
1701	Cane or beet sugar and chemically pure sucrose, in solid form	85.7	57.5	66.8	0.8	0.7	0.6	US$/kg	061
8703	Motor cars and other motor vehicles principally designed for the transport	56.3	81.6	62.0			19.1	thsd US$/unit	781
8704	Motor vehicles for the transport of goods	39.7	68.6	59.3					782
3004	Medicaments (excluding goods of heading 30.02, 30.05 or 30.06)	58.1	49.3	55.8	11.4	12.0	11.3	US$/kg	542
1101	Wheat or meslin flour	50.3	48.6	55.1	0.5	0.5	0.5	US$/kg	046
0303	Fish, frozen, excluding fish fillets and other fish meat of heading 03.04	37.7	31.1	54.8	1.9	2.3	2.3	US$/kg	034
5208	Woven fabrics of cotton, containing 85 % or more by weight of cotton	46.0	29.2	46.7	15.8	15.6	15.2	US$/kg	652
1511	Palm oil and its fractions	47.7	23.3	34.5	1.3	1.1	1.0	US$/kg	422

Malawi

Goods Imports: CIF, by origin **Goods Exports:** FOB, by last known destination **Trade System:** General

Overview:
In 2013, the value of merchandise exports of Malawi was 1.2 bln US$, while its merchandise imports were 2.8 bln US$ (see graph 1 and tables 2 & 3). The merchandise trade balance recorded a relatively large deficit of 1.6 bln US$ (see graph 1). The merchandise trade balance recorded a large deficit of 1.6 bln US$ (see graph 1). The largest merchandise trade balance was with MDG Sub-Saharan Africa at -954.1 mln US$ (see graph 4). Merchandise exports in Malawi were diversified amongst partners; imports were also diversified. The top 17 partners accounted for 80 percent or more of exports and 14 partners accounted for 80 percent or more of imports (see graph 5). In 2013, the value of exports of services of Malawi increased by 19.3 percent, reaching 136.6 mln US$, while its imports of services increased substantially by 71.0 percent and reached 396.6 mln US$ (see graph 2). There was a relatively large trade in services deficit of 260.0 mln US$.

Graph 1: Total merchandise trade, by value
(Bln US$ by year)

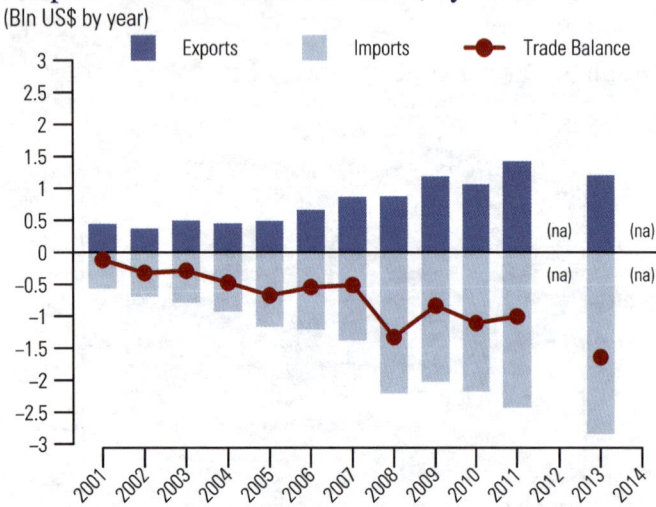

Graph 2: Total services trade, by value
(Mln US$ by year)

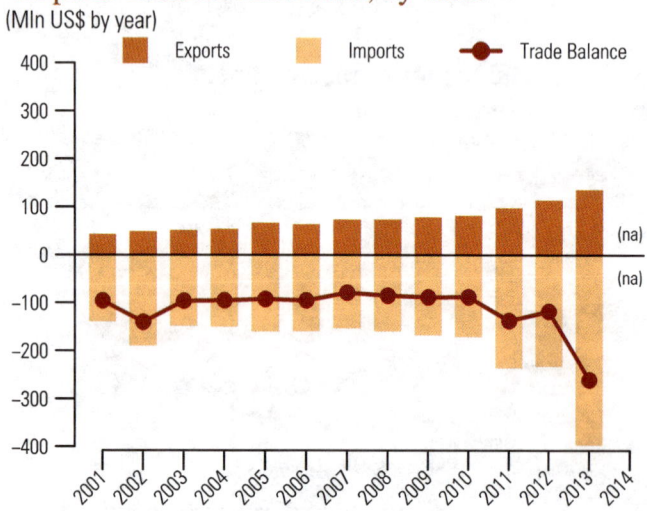

Exports Profile:
"Food, animals + beverages, tobacco" (SITC section 0+1) and "Crude materials + anim. & veg. oils" (SITC section 2+4) were the largest commodity groups for exports in 2013, representing respectively 69.4 and 22.4 percent of exported goods (see table 2). In 2011 and 2013, the largest export commodity was "Unmanufactured tobacco; tobacco refuse" (HS code 2401) (see table 1). The top three destinations for merchandise exports were Canada, South Africa and Belgium, accounting for respectively 10.1, 8.0 and 7.3 percent of total exports. "Travel" (EBOPS code 236) accounted for the largest share of exports of services in 2013 at 34.6 mln US$, followed by "Transportation" (EBOPS code 205) at 23.5 mln US$ and "Financial services" (EBOPS code 260) at 16.7 mln US$ (see graph 3).

Graph 3: Exports of services by EBOPS category
(% share in 2013)

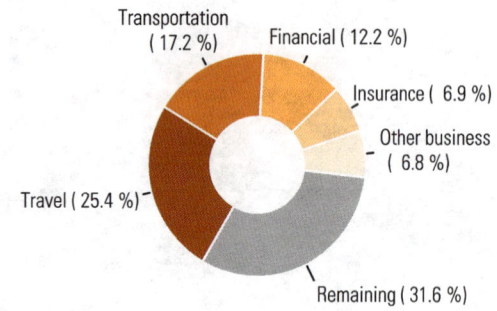

- Transportation (17.2 %)
- Financial (12.2 %)
- Insurance (6.9 %)
- Other business (6.8 %)
- Remaining (31.6 %)
- Travel (25.4 %)

Table 1: Top 10 export commodities 2011 to 2013

HS code	4-digit heading of Harmonized System 2007	Value (million US$) 2011	2012	2013	Unit value 2011	2012	2013	Unit	SITC code
	All Commodities	1 425.3	...	1 208.0					
2401	Unmanufactured tobacco; tobacco refuse	569.7	...	562.6	3.6		4.1	US$/kg	121
1701	Cane or beet sugar and chemically pure sucrose, in solid form	213.9	...	114.2	0.8		0.6	US$/kg	061
2612	Uranium or thorium ores and concentrates	120.3	...	136.6	89.6		81.0	US$/kg	286
0902	Tea, whether or not flavoured	86.3	...	86.0	1.9		2.0	US$/kg	074
1202	Ground-nuts, not roasted or otherwise cooked, whether or not shelled or broken	29.3	...	60.3	0.9		1.3	US$/kg	222
1005	Maize (corn)	84.9	...	1.7	0.2		0.9	US$/kg	044
0713	Dried leguminous vegetables, shelled, whether or not skinned or split	26.4	...	29.0	0.4		0.7	US$/kg	054
5201	Cotton, not carded or combed	31.1	...	19.4	3.3		1.7	US$/kg	263
3923	Articles for the conveyance or packing of goods, of plastics	13.9	...	11.9	6.6		3.5	US$/kg	893
0802	Other nuts, fresh or dried, whether or not shelled or peeled	11.9	...	13.7	4.1		9.0	US$/kg	057

Malawi

Services Imports and Exports: EBOPS 2002 categories

Table 2: Merchandise exports by SITC
(Value in million US$, growth and shares in percentage)

SITC	2013	Avg. Growth rates 2009-2013	2012-2013	2013 share
Total	1 208.0	0.4	...	100.0
0+1	838.3	-3.7	...	69.4
2+4	270.7	25.2	...	22.4
3	0.4	-24.4	...	0.0
5	13.2	12.4	...	1.1
6	18.6	11.4	...	1.5
7	27.6	-0.4	...	2.3
8	38.7	-7.6	...	3.2
9	0.3	-8.1	...	0.0

Table 3: Merchandise imports by SITC
(Value in million US$, growth and shares in percentage)

SITC	2013	Avg. Growth rates 2009-2013	2012-2013	2013 share
Total	2 844.6	8.9	...	100.0
0+1	270.8	5.2	...	9.5
2+4	121.8	12.6	...	4.3
3	411.3	18.2	...	14.5
5	845.3	16.2	...	29.7
6	429.9	6.9	...	15.1
7	565.8	1.7	...	19.9
8	196.0	0.6	...	6.9
9	3.7	72.8	...	0.1

SITC Legend

SITC Code	Description
Total	All commodities
0+1	Food, animals + beverages, tobacco
2+4	Crude materials + anim. & veg. oils
3	Mineral fuels, lubricants
5	Chemicals
6	Goods classified chiefly by material
7	Machinery and transport equipment
8	Miscellaneous manufactured articles
9	Not classified elsewhere in the SITC

Graph 4: Merchandise trade balance
(Bln US$ by MDG Regions in 2013)

Graph 5: Partner concentration of merchandise trade
(Cumulative share by ranked partners in 2013)

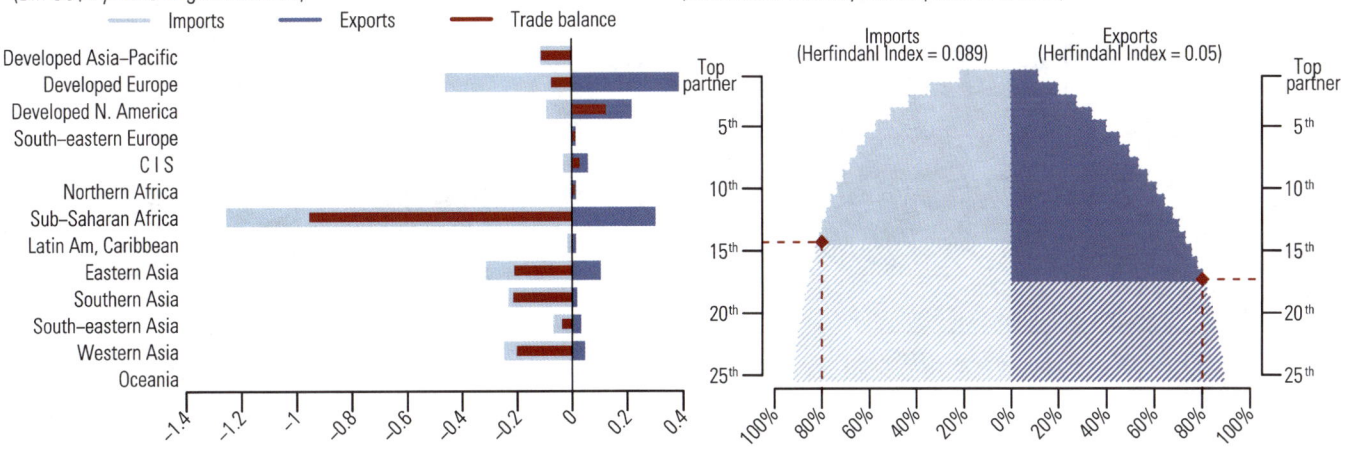

Imports (Herfindahl Index = 0.089)
Exports (Herfindahl Index = 0.05)

Graph 6: Imports of services by EBOPS category
(% share in 2013)

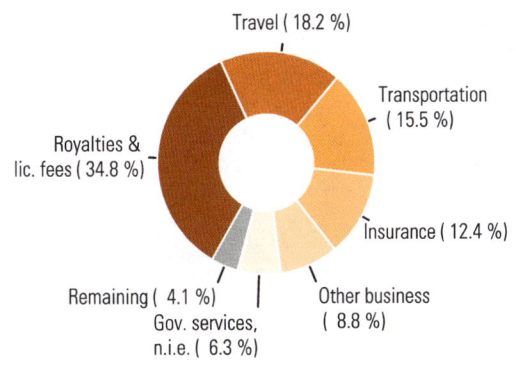

- Travel (18.2 %)
- Transportation (15.5 %)
- Royalties & lic. fees (34.8 %)
- Insurance (12.4 %)
- Other business (8.8 %)
- Gov. services, n.i.e. (6.3 %)
- Remaining (4.1 %)

Imports Profile:

"Chemicals" (SITC section 5), "Machinery and transport equipment" (SITC section 7) and "Goods classified chiefly by material" (SITC section 6) were the largest commodity groups for imports in 2013, representing respectively 29.7, 19.9 and 15.1 percent of imported goods (see table 3). In 2011 and 2013, the largest import commodity was "Petroleum oils, other than crude" (HS code 2710) (see table 4). The top three partners for merchandise imports were South Africa, India and China, accounting for respectively 23.2, 9.5 and 9.3 percent of total imports. "Royalties and license fees" (EBOPS code 266) accounted for the largest share of imports of services in 2013 at 138.1 mln US$, followed by "Travel" (EBOPS code 236) at 72.0 mln US$ and "Transportation" (EBOPS code 205) at 61.6 mln US$ (see graph 6).

Table 4: Top 10 import commodities 2011 to 2013

HS code	4-digit heading of Harmonized System 2007	Value (million US$) 2011	2012	2013	Unit value 2011	2012	2013	Unit	SITC code
	All Commodities	2 427.7	...	2 844.6					
2710	Petroleum oils, other than crude	199.1	...	389.2	0.8		1.4	US$/kg	334
3102	Mineral or chemical fertilisers, nitrogenous	137.1	...	211.8	0.7		0.7	US$/kg	562
3004	Medicaments (excluding goods of heading 30.02, 30.05 or 30.06)	129.7	...	161.7	33.6		38.0	US$/kg	542
1001	Wheat and meslin	82.1	...	87.4	0.6		0.5	US$/kg	041
2401	Unmanufactured tobacco; tobacco refuse	83.0	...	86.0	3.0		3.5	US$/kg	121
3105	Mineral or chemical fertilisers	45.7	...	119.8	0.7		0.8	US$/kg	562
2523	Portland cement, aluminous cement, slag cement	69.5	...	63.7	0.2		0.2	US$/kg	661
9018	Instruments and appliances used in medical, surgical, dental or veterinary	112.4	...	16.0					872
4907	Unused postage, revenue or similar stamps of current or new issue	61.0	...	55.6	280.3		117.7	US$/kg	892
8703	Motor cars and other motor vehicles principally designed for the transport	47.7	...	58.9	*7.9*		7.0	thsd US$/unit	781

Malaysia

Goods Imports: CIF, by origin   **Goods Exports:** FOB, by last known destination   **Trade System:** General

Overview:
In 2013, the value of merchandise exports of Malaysia increased slightly by 0.4 percent to reach 228.3 bln US$, while its merchandise imports increased slightly by 4.9 percent to reach 205.8 bln US$ (see graph 1, table 2 and table 3). The merchandise trade balance recorded a relatively small surplus of 22.5 bln US$ (see graph 1). The largest merchandise trade balance was with MDG Developed Asia-Pacific at 11.8 bln US$ (see graph 4). Merchandise exports in Malaysia were diversified amongst partners; imports were also diversified. The top 13 partners accounted for 80 percent or more of exports and 14 partners accounted for 80 percent or more of imports (see graph 5). In 2012, the value of exports of services of Malaysia increased moderately by 5.4 percent, reaching 37.9 bln US$, while its imports of services increased moderately by 9.4 percent and reached 42.2 bln US$ (see graph 2). There was a relatively small trade in services deficit of 4.3 bln US$.

Graph 1: Total merchandise trade, by value
(Bln US$ by year)

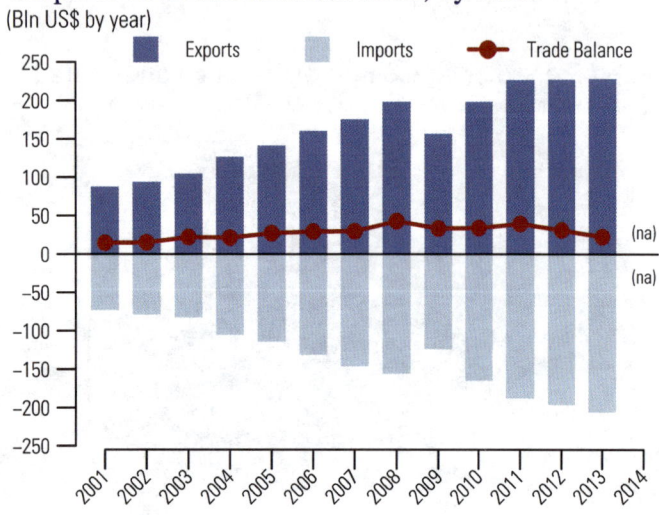

Graph 2: Total services trade, by value
(Bln US$ by year)

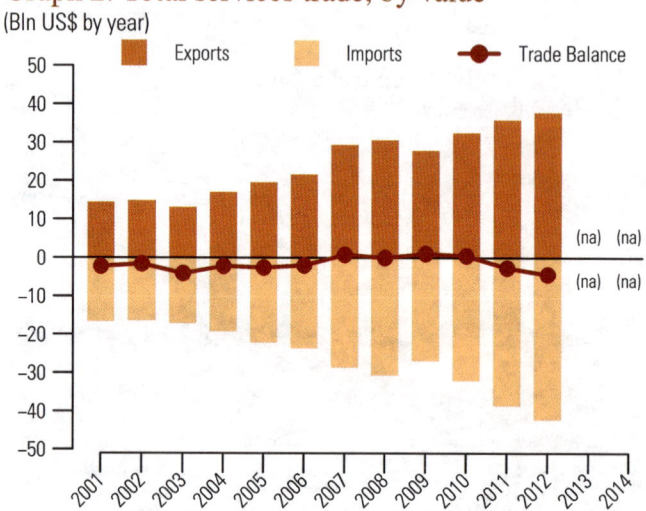

Exports Profile:
"Machinery and transport equipment" (SITC section 7), "Mineral fuels, lubricants" (SITC section 3) and "Crude materials + anim. & veg. oils" (SITC section 2+4) were the largest commodity groups for exports in 2013, representing respectively 38.1, 22.3 and 10.1 percent of exported goods (see table 2). From 2011 to 2013, the largest export commodity was "Electronic integrated circuits" (HS code 8542) (see table 1). The top three destinations for merchandise exports were Singapore, China and Japan, accounting for respectively 13.4, 13.1 and 11.5 percent of total exports. "Travel" (EBOPS code 236) accounted for the largest share of exports of services in 2012 at 19.7 bln US$, followed by "Other business services" (EBOPS code 268) at 8.1 bln US$ and "Transportation" (EBOPS code 205) at 4.3 bln US$ (see graph 3).

Graph 3: Exports of services by EBOPS category
(% share in 2012)

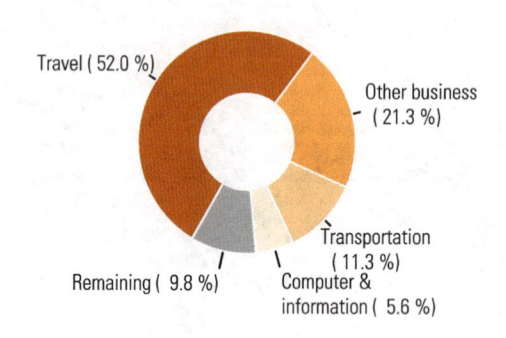

- Travel (52.0 %)
- Other business (21.3 %)
- Transportation (11.3 %)
- Computer & information (5.6 %)
- Remaining (9.8 %)

Table 1: Top 10 export commodities 2011 to 2013

HS code	4-digit heading of Harmonized System 2007	Value (million US$) 2011	2012	2013	Unit value 2011	2012	2013	Unit	SITC code
	All Commodities	226 992.7	227 449.5	228 316.1					
8542	Electronic integrated circuits	27 239.5	26 082.0	27 791.6					776
2711	Petroleum gases and other gaseous hydrocarbons	18 210.2	19 790.4	20 467.7	0.7	0.8	0.8	US$/kg	343
2710	Petroleum oils, other than crude	10 797.4	15 419.3	19 433.7	0.9	0.9	0.9	US$/kg	334
1511	Palm oil and its fractions	17 446.9	15 410.9	12 288.9	1.1	1.0	0.8	US$/kg	422
2709	Petroleum oils and oils obtained from bituminous minerals, crude	10 760.3	10 440.1	10 220.8	0.8	0.9	0.8	US$/kg	333
8471	Automatic data processing machines and units thereof	9 691.2	9 733.7	8 867.2	76.2	84.7	82.8	US$/unit	752
8541	Diodes, transistors and similar semiconductor devices	7 480.6	6 727.3	7 523.3					776
8473	Parts and accessories for use with machines of heading 84.69 to 84.72	6 318.7	5 490.3	5 424.7	35.3	41.8	49.3	US$/kg	759
8528	Reception apparatus for television	4 832.9	3 968.4	3 994.8	289.7	290.1	265.3	US$/unit	761
4015	Articles of apparel and clothing accessories	3 253.3	3 435.9	3 390.7	6.6	6.0	5.6	US$/kg	848

Source: UN Comtrade and UN ServiceTrade

Malaysia

Services Imports and Exports: EBOPS 2002 categories

Table 2: Merchandise exports by SITC
(Value in million US$, growth and shares in percentage)

SITC	2013	Avg. Growth rates 2009-2013	Avg. Growth rates 2012-2013	2013 share
Total	228316.1	9.8	0.4	100.0
0+1	8240.5	12.2	4.3	3.6
2+4	23014.0	9.3	-15.4	10.1
3	50851.4	21.7	9.6	22.3
5	15127.5	12.4	1.4	6.6
6	21470.0	11.2	4.2	9.4
7	86916.9	4.4	0.6	38.1
8	21224.2	9.6	-4.1	9.3
9	1471.5	3.0	-20.4	0.6

Table 3: Merchandise imports by SITC
(Value in million US$, growth and shares in percentage)

SITC	2013	Avg. Growth rates 2009-2013	Avg. Growth rates 2012-2013	2013 share
Total	205813.5	13.6	4.9	100.0
0+1	13625.0	13.5	5.6	6.6
2+4	9121.0	12.7	-18.6	4.4
3	33334.2	34.6	19.7	16.2
5	18623.2	13.5	5.5	9.0
6	27097.8	15.9	11.4	13.2
7	87750.2	8.5	1.7	42.6
8	11715.1	12.6	-2.8	5.7
9	4547.0	13.9	15.2	2.2

SITC Legend

SITC Code	Description
Total	All commodities
0+1	Food, animals + beverages, tobacco
2+4	Crude materials + anim. & veg. oils
3	Mineral fuels, lubricants
5	Chemicals
6	Goods classified chiefly by material
7	Machinery and transport equipment
8	Miscellaneous manufactured articles
9	Not classified elsewhere in the SITC

Graph 4: Merchandise trade balance
(Bln US$ by MDG Regions in 2013)

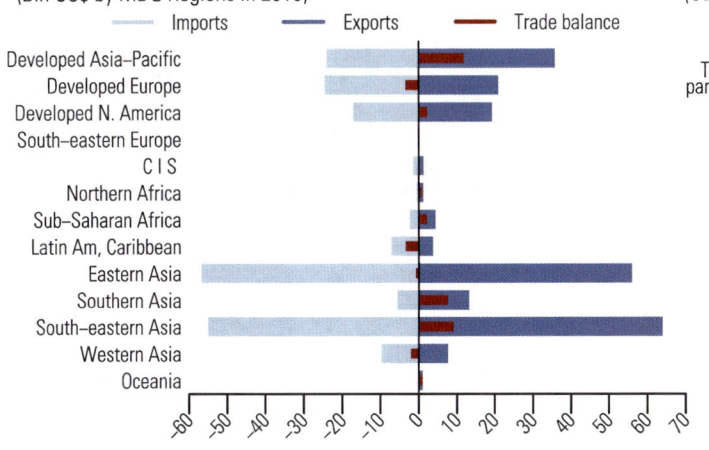

Graph 5: Partner concentration of merchandise trade
(Cumulative share by ranked partners in 2013)

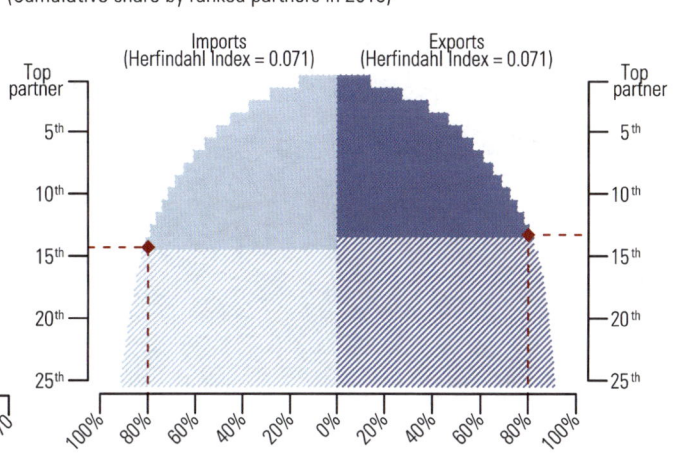

Imports (Herfindahl index = 0.071)
Exports (Herfindahl index = 0.071)

Graph 6: Imports of services by EBOPS category
(% share in 2012)

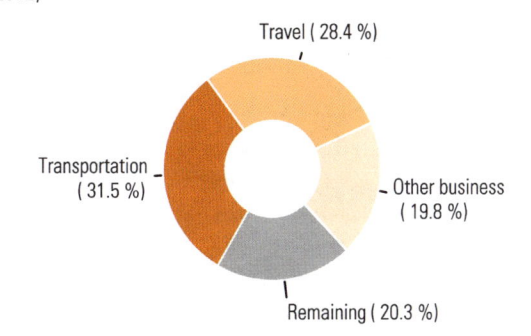

- Travel (28.4%)
- Transportation (31.5%)
- Other business (19.8%)
- Remaining (20.3%)

Imports Profile:

"Machinery and transport equipment" (SITC section 7), "Mineral fuels, lubricants" (SITC section 3) and "Goods classified chiefly by material" (SITC section 6) were the largest commodity groups for imports in 2013, representing respectively 42.6, 16.2 and 13.2 percent of imported goods (see table 3). From 2011 to 2013, the largest import commodity was "Electronic integrated circuits" (HS code 8542) (see table 4). The top three partners for merchandise imports were China, Singapore and Japan, accounting for respectively 15.0, 12.8 and 10.1 percent of total imports. "Transportation" (EBOPS code 205) accounted for the largest share of imports of services in 2012 at 13.3 bln US$, followed by "Travel" (EBOPS code 236) at 12.0 bln US$ and "Other business services" (EBOPS code 268) at 8.4 bln US$ (see graph 6).

Table 4: Top 10 import commodities 2011 to 2013

HS code	4-digit heading of Harmonized System 2007	Value 2011	Value 2012	Value 2013	Unit value 2011	Unit value 2012	Unit value 2013	Unit	SITC code
	All Commodities	187573.0	196196.6	205813.5					
8542	Electronic integrated circuits	26631.6	25896.9	26553.8					776
2710	Petroleum oils, other than crude	10632.4	15596.2	22082.0	0.8	0.9	0.9	US$/kg	334
2709	Petroleum oils and oils obtained from bituminous minerals, crude	7846.4	8963.3	7152.9	0.8	0.8	0.8	US$/kg	333
8473	Parts and accessories for use with machines of heading 84.69 to 84.72	4693.2	3908.5	3647.7	56.2	4.0	49.9	US$/kg	759
8541	Diodes, transistors and similar semiconductor devices	3539.5	3070.9	3885.1					776
8802	Other aircraft (for example, helicopters, aeroplanes); spacecraft	2792.7	3392.3	4177.0	25.9	28.7	49.7	mln US$/unit	792
8517	Electrical apparatus for line telephony or line telegraphy	2806.3	3333.9	3883.5					764
8471	Automatic data processing machines and units thereof	3170.1	3260.1	2955.7	91.4	86.6	61.9	US$/unit	752
7108	Gold (including gold plated with platinum)	2545.7	2652.1	3427.1	38.9	50.8	43.9	thsd US$/kg	971
8703	Motor cars and other motor vehicles principally designed for the transport	2526.5	2818.5	2741.7	6.3	8.0	9.2	thsd US$/unit	781

2014 International Trade Statistics Yearbook, Vol. I   Source: UN Comtrade and UN ServiceTrade

Maldives

Goods Imports: CIF, by consignment   **Goods Exports: FOB, by last known destination**   **Trade System: General**

Overview:
In 2014, the value of merchandise exports of Maldives decreased substantially by 13.0 percent to reach 144.8 mln US$, while its merchandise imports increased substantially by 15.0 percent to reach 2.0 bln US$ (see graph 1, table 2 and table 3). The merchandise trade balance recorded a large deficit of 1.8 bln US$ (see graph 1). The largest merchandise trade balance was with MDG Western Asia at -578.2 mln US$ (see graph 4). Merchandise exports in Maldives were moderately concentrated amongst partners; imports were diversified. The top 8 partners accounted for 80 percent or more of exports and 10 partners accounted for 80 percent or more of imports (see graph 5). In 2013, the value of exports of services of Maldives increased substantially by 18.9 percent, reaching 2.5 bln US$, while its imports of services increased substantially by 13.4 percent and reached 652.5 mln US$ (see graph 2). There was a large trade in services surplus of 1.9 bln US$. See footnote*.

Graph 1: Total merchandise trade, by value
(Bln US$ by year)

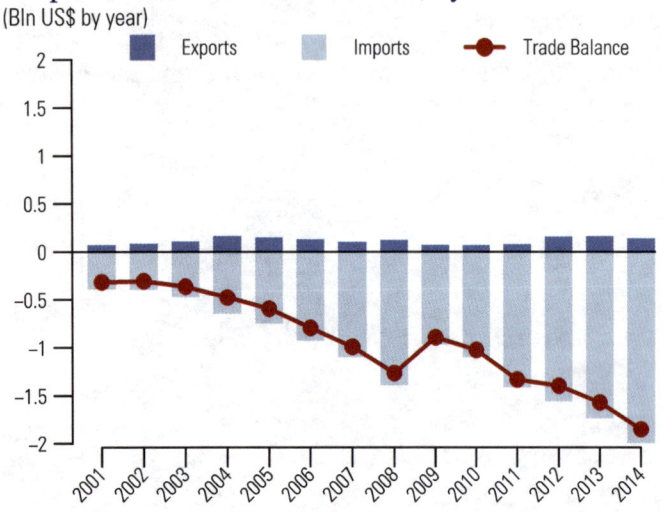

Graph 2: Total services trade, by value
(Bln US$ by year)

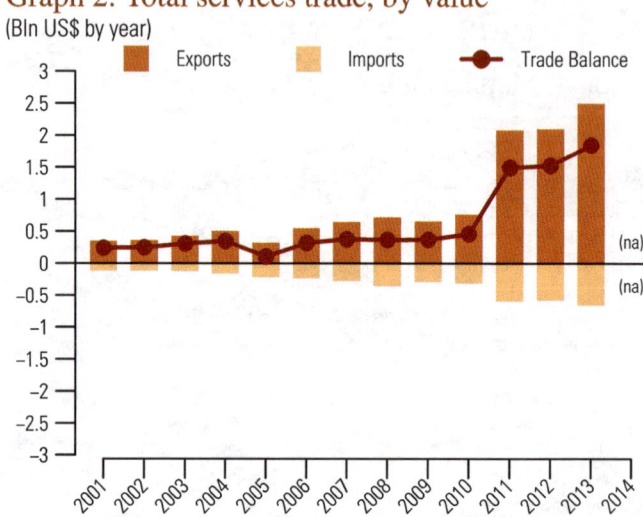

Exports Profile:
"Food, animals + beverages, tobacco" (SITC section 0+1), "Crude materials + anim. & veg. oils" (SITC section 2+4) and "Machinery and transport equipment" (SITC section 7) were the largest commodity groups for exports in 2014, representing respectively 97.7, 2.0 and 0.1 percent of exported goods (see table 2). From 2012 to 2014, the largest export commodity was "Fish, frozen, excluding fish fillets and other fish meat of heading 03.04" (HS code 0303) (see table 1). The top three destinations for merchandise exports were Thailand, France and Sri Lanka, accounting for respectively 32.3, 14.8 and 6.3 percent of total exports. "Travel" (EBOPS code 236) accounted for the largest share of exports of services in 2013 at 2.3 bln US$ (see graph 3).

Graph 3: Exports of services by EBOPS category
(% share in 2013)

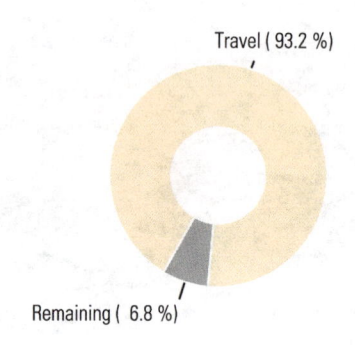

Travel (93.2 %)
Remaining (6.8 %)

Table 1: Top 10 export commodities 2012 to 2014

HS code	4-digit heading of Harmonized System 2012	Value (million US$) 2012	2013	2014	Unit value 2012	2013	2014	Unit	SITC code
	All Commodities	161.6	166.5	144.8					
0303	Fish, frozen, excluding fish fillets and other fish meat of heading 03.04	51.7	72.0	49.7	2.2	2.0	1.5	US$/kg	034
0304	Fish fillets and other fish meat (whether or not minced)	42.8	33.0	30.8	7.3	7.6	7.5	US$/kg	034
0302	Fish, fresh or chilled, excluding fish fillets	38.1	31.4	35.9	5.3	5.6	5.2	US$/kg	034
1604	Prepared or preserved fish; caviar	13.8	16.5	15.8	6.7	7.0	6.1	US$/kg	037
0305	Fish, dried, salted or in brine	9.6	8.5	7.4	4.4	3.7	2.8	US$/kg	035
7204	Ferrous waste and scrap; remelting scrap ingots of iron or steel	2.0	1.7	1.6	0.2	0.3	0.3	US$/kg	282
0301	Live fish	1.2	1.0	1.1					034
7404	Copper waste and scrap	0.7	0.7	1.0	3.4	4.9	4.8	US$/kg	288
2301	Flours, meals and pellets, of meat or meat offal	0.7	0.7	0.5	0.8	0.9	1.0	US$/kg	081
0308	Aquatic invertebrates other than crustaceans and molluscs	0.7	0.6	0.3	2.8	4.9		US$/kg	036

*Merchandise trade data does not include re-exports. As of 2011, trade in services data reflect the improvement of the coverage of balance of payments statistics that was implemented in September 2012.

Maldives

Services Imports and Exports: EBOPS 2002 categories

Table 2: Merchandise exports by SITC
(Value in million US$, growth and shares in percentage)

SITC	2014	Avg. Growth rates 2010-2014	Avg. Growth rates 2013-2014	2014 share
Total	144.8	18.2	-13.0	100.0
0+1	141.6	18.7	-13.6	97.7
2+4	2.9	1.2	15.8	2.0
3	0.1	40.7	-12.3	0.0
5	0.1	107.6	46.3	0.1
6	0.0	-22.0	216.2	0.0
7	0.1	...	...	0.1
8	0.0	27.8	...	0.0

Table 3: Merchandise imports by SITC
(Value in million US$, growth and shares in percentage)

SITC	2014	Avg. Growth rates 2010-2014	Avg. Growth rates 2013-2014	2014 share
Total	1 992.7	16.1	15.0	100.0
0+1	406.8	14.2	6.9	20.4
2+4	88.6	14.5	29.7	4.4
3	571.5	22.7	13.4	28.7
5	119.4	16.2	32.6	6.0
6	218.2	12.1	17.3	11.0
7	427.0	14.6	22.0	21.4
8	161.2	12.6	4.4	8.1
9	0.0	28.4	-76.8	0.0

SITC Legend

SITC Code	Description
Total	All commodities
0+1	Food, animals + beverages, tobacco
2+4	Crude materials + anim. & veg. oils
3	Mineral fuels, lubricants
5	Chemicals
6	Goods classified chiefly by material
7	Machinery and transport equipment
8	Miscellaneous manufactured articles
9	Not classified elsewhere in the SITC

Graph 4: Merchandise trade balance
(Mln US$ by MDG Regions in 2014)

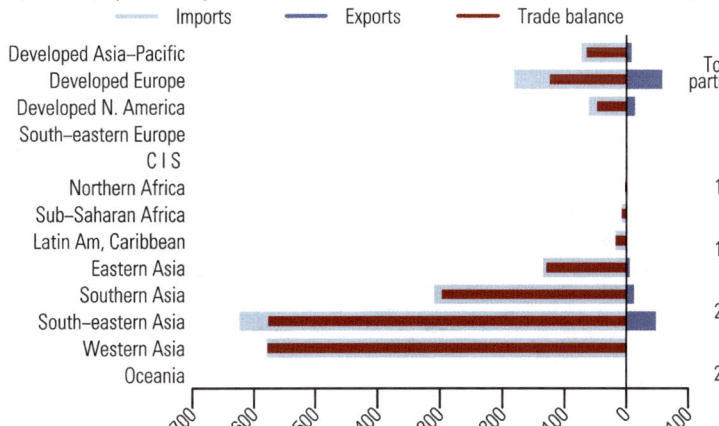

Graph 5: Partner concentration of merchandise trade
(Cumulative share by ranked partners in 2014)

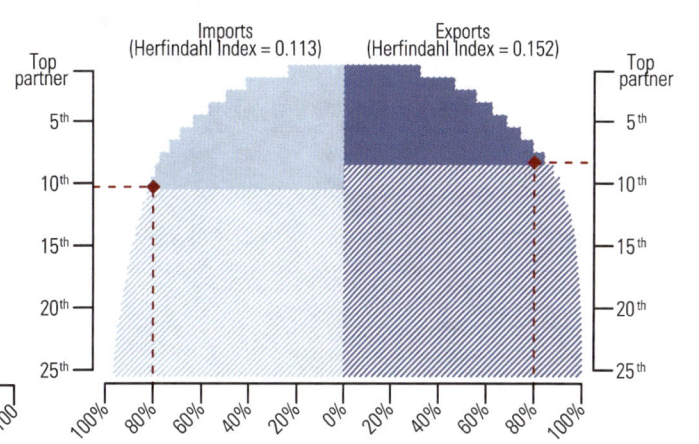

Imports (Herfindahl Index = 0.113)
Exports (Herfindahl Index = 0.152)

Graph 6: Imports of services by EBOPS category
(% share in 2013)

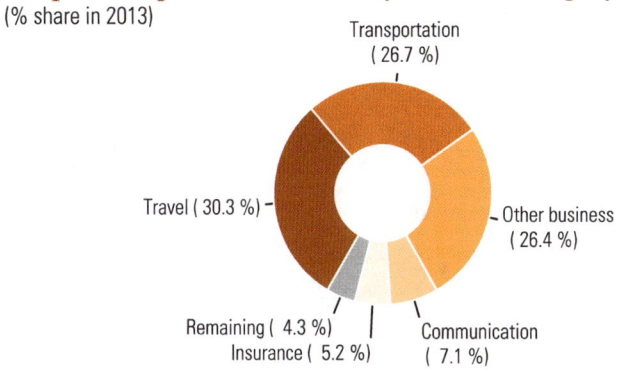

- Transportation (26.7 %)
- Travel (30.3 %)
- Other business (26.4 %)
- Communication (7.1 %)
- Insurance (5.2 %)
- Remaining (4.3 %)

Imports Profile:

"Mineral fuels, lubricants" (SITC section 3), "Machinery and transport equipment" (SITC section 7) and "Food, animals + beverages, tobacco" (SITC section 0+1) were the largest commodity groups for imports in 2014, representing respectively 28.7, 21.4 and 20.4 percent of imported goods (see table 3). From 2012 to 2014, the largest import commodity was "Petroleum oils, other than crude" (HS code 2710) (see table 4). The top three partners for merchandise imports were the United Arab Emirates, Singapore and India, accounting for respectively 27.1, 17.3 and 8.9 percent of total imports. "Travel" (EBOPS code 236) accounted for the largest share of imports of services in 2013 at 197.9 mln US$, followed by "Transportation" (EBOPS code 205) at 173.9 mln US$ and "Other business services" (EBOPS code 268) at 172.1 mln US$ (see graph 6).

Table 4: Top 10 import commodities 2012 to 2014

HS code	4-digit heading of Harmonized System 2012	2012	2013	2014	2012	2013	2014	Unit	SITC code
	All Commodities	1 554.5	1 733.3	1 992.7					
2710	Petroleum oils, other than crude	436.3	445.2	500.2	1.0	1.0	0.8	US$/kg	334
2711	Petroleum gases and other gaseous hydrocarbons	49.7	57.8	70.5	1.0	1.0	1.2	US$/kg	343
8517	Electrical apparatus for line telephony or line telegraphy	24.1	36.8	34.7					764
8802	Other aircraft (for example, helicopters, aeroplanes); spacecraft	9.1	40.2	39.8	4.5	20.1	4.0	mln US$/unit	792
9403	Other furniture and parts thereof	16.9	22.7	25.1					821
0402	Milk and cream, concentrated or containing added sugar	17.3	20.9	22.5	3.0	3.2	3.3	US$/kg	022
0207	Meat and edible offal, of the poultry of heading 01.05	13.6	23.5	21.9	2.0	2.3	2.4	US$/kg	012
2202	Waters with added sugar	15.3	17.5	22.6	1.4	1.6	1.7	US$/litre	111
4407	Wood sawn or chipped lengthwise, sliced or peeled	17.7	19.4	17.8	752.2	747.0	733.8	US$/m^3	248
8471	Automatic data processing machines and units thereof	19.1	17.5	17.7	198.8	159.6	113.4	US$/unit	752

Source: UN Comtrade and UN ServiceTrade

Mali

Goods Imports: CIF, by origin   **Goods Exports:** FOB, by last known destination   **Trade System:** General

Overview:
In 2012, the value of merchandise exports of Mali increased moderately by 9.9 percent to reach 2.6 bln US$, while its merchandise imports increased slightly by 3.3 percent to reach 3.5 bln US$ (see graph 1, table 2 and table 3). The merchandise trade balance recorded a moderate deficit of 852.3 mln US$ (see graph 1). The largest merchandise trade balance was with MDG Developed Europe at -264.8 mln US$ (see graph 4). Merchandise exports in Mali were highly concentrated amongst partners; imports were diversified. The top 5 partners accounted for 80 percent or more of exports and 14 partners accounted for 80 percent or more of imports (see graph 5). In 2012, the value of exports of services of Mali decreased moderately by 9.2 percent, reaching 352.2 mln US$, while its imports of services increased slightly by 2.0 percent and reached 1.1 bln US$ (see graph 2). There was a large trade in services deficit of 734.4 mln US$.

Graph 1: Total merchandise trade, by value
(Bln US$ by year)

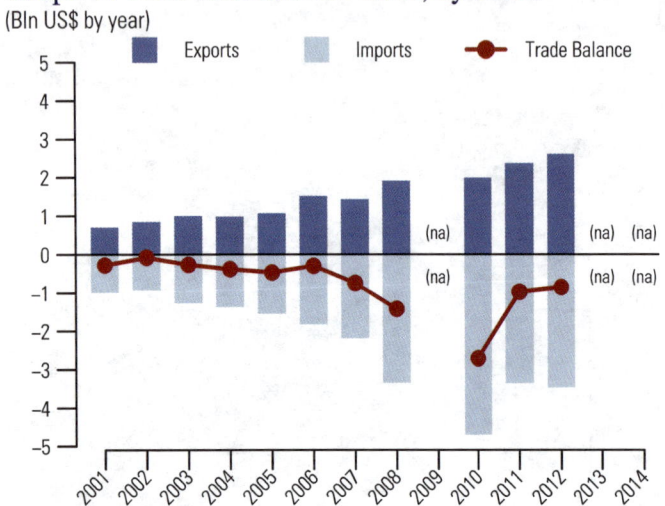

Graph 2: Total services trade, by value
(Bln US$ by year)

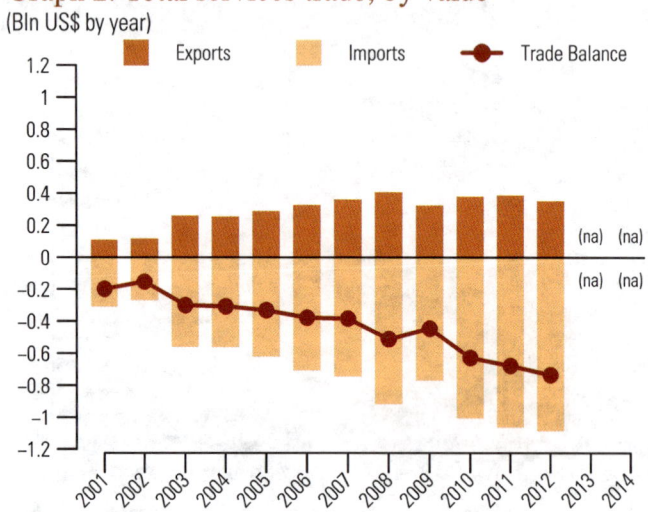

Exports Profile:
"Not classified elsewhere in the SITC" (SITC section 9), "Crude materials + anim. & veg. oils" (SITC section 2+4) and "Chemicals" (SITC section 5) were the largest commodity groups for exports in 2012, representing respectively 65.6, 16.1 and 6.7 percent of exported goods (see table 2). From 2010 to 2012, the largest export commodity was "Gold (including gold plated with platinum)" (HS code 7108) (see table 1). The top three destinations for merchandise exports were South Africa, Switzerland and China, accounting for respectively 55.0, 11.8 and 4.7 percent of total exports. "Travel" (EBOPS code 236) accounted for the largest share of exports of services in 2012 at 144.7 mln US$, followed by "Communications services" (EBOPS code 245) at 141.6 mln US$ and "Government services, n.i.e." (EBOPS code 291) at 34.2 mln US$ (see graph 3).

Graph 3: Exports of services by EBOPS category
(% share in 2012)

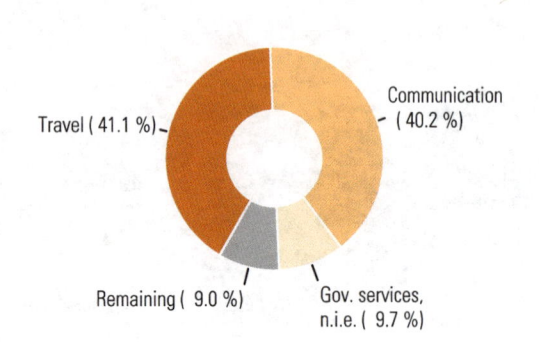

- Travel (41.1 %)
- Communication (40.2 %)
- Gov. services, n.i.e. (9.7 %)
- Remaining (9.0 %)

Table 1: Top 10 export commodities 2010 to 2012

HS code	4-digit heading of Harmonized System 2007	Value (million US$) 2010	2011	2012	Unit value 2010	2011	2012	Unit	SITC code
	All Commodities	1996.3	2374.5	2610.4					
7108	Gold (including gold plated with platinum)	1578.7	1691.1	1709.3	32.5	39.9	38.0	thsd US$/kg	971
5203	Cotton, carded or combed	139.4	55.6	372.2	1.5	1.7	2.6	US$/kg	263
3105	Mineral or chemical fertilisers	30.0	113.7	119.0	0.6	0.7	0.6	US$/kg	562
5201	Cotton, not carded or combed	27.9	149.3	13.2	1.1	1.6	1.1	US$/kg	263
0102	Live bovine animals	48.6	54.7	84.2	0.8	1.1	2.3	thsd US$/unit	001
2710	Petroleum oils, other than crude	28.4	55.5	14.1	0.8	1.1	1.0	US$/kg	334
0104	Live sheep and goats	20.5	15.9	27.9					001
0804	Dates, figs, pineapples, avocados and mangosteens, fresh or dried	14.9	17.8	13.2	1.1	0.9	0.6	US$/kg	057
3102	Mineral or chemical fertilisers, nitrogenous	0.1	17.6	25.1	0.7	0.4	0.5	US$/kg	562
3104	Mineral or chemical fertilisers, potassic	...	23.8	16.0		0.6	0.6	US$/kg	562

Mali

Services Imports and Exports: EBOPS 2002 categories

Table 2: Merchandise exports by SITC
(Value in million US$, growth and shares in percentage)

SITC	2012	Avg. Growth rates 2008-2012	Avg. Growth rates 2011-2012	2012 share
Total	2610.4	8.0	9.9	100.0
0+1	147.9	3.4	24.0	5.7
2+4	420.0	18.5	76.6	16.1
3	16.0	-13.5	-71.1	0.6
5	174.3	57.2	1.4	6.7
6	44.5	40.6	64.4	1.7
7	87.6	10.6	51.1	3.4
8	8.2	3.8	-17.2	0.3
9	1711.8	4.4	1.0	65.6

Table 3: Merchandise imports by SITC
(Value in million US$, growth and shares in percentage)

SITC	2012	Avg. Growth rates 2008-2012	Avg. Growth rates 2011-2012	2012 share
Total	3462.7	0.9	3.3	100.0
0+1	440.3	5.2	4.7	12.7
2+4	62.1	-7.3	-12.0	1.8
3	993.6	8.6	1.2	28.7
5	508.3	1.9	19.7	14.7
6	560.0	-4.8	-7.2	16.2
7	765.4	-2.9	3.3	22.1
8	130.4	-5.4	21.7	3.8
9	2.6	-10.6	1.9	0.1

SITC Legend

SITC Code	Description
Total	All commodities
0+1	Food, animals + beverages, tobacco
2+4	Crude materials + anim. & veg. oils
3	Mineral fuels, lubricants
5	Chemicals
6	Goods classified chiefly by material
7	Machinery and transport equipment
8	Miscellaneous manufactured articles
9	Not classified elsewhere in the SITC

Graph 4: Merchandise trade balance
(Bln US$ by MDG Regions in 2012)

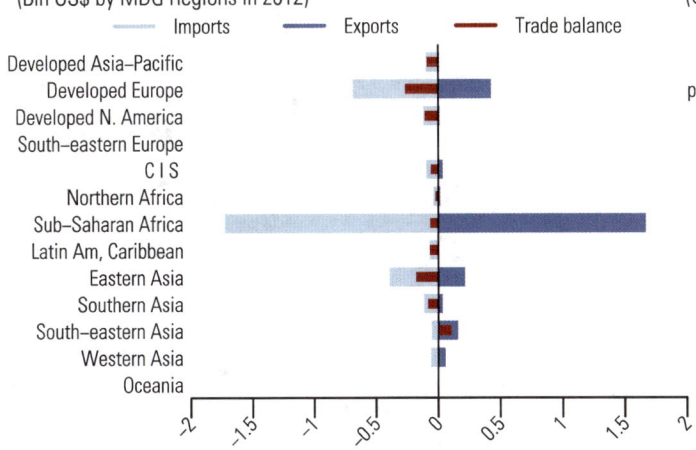

Graph 5: Partner concentration of merchandise trade
(Cumulative share by ranked partners in 2012)

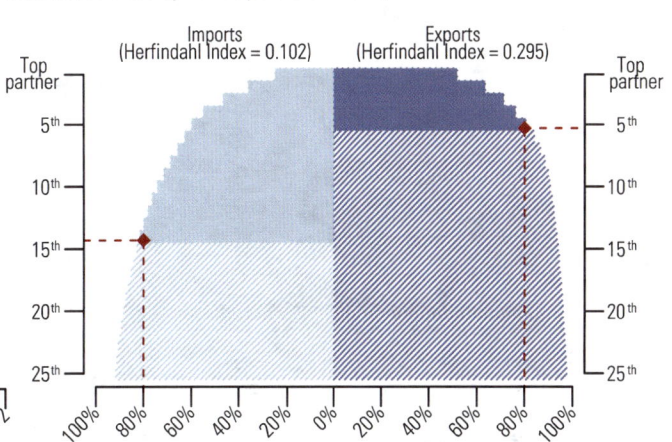

Imports (Herfindahl Index = 0.102)
Exports (Herfindahl Index = 0.295)

Graph 6: Imports of services by EBOPS category
(% share in 2012)

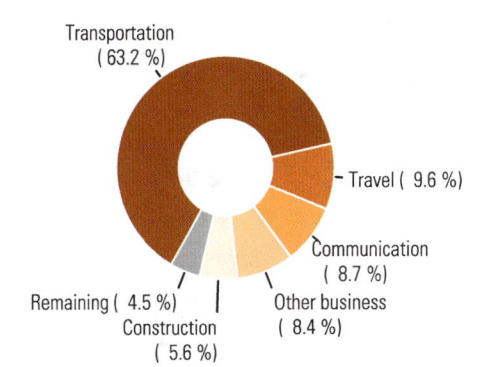

- Transportation (63.2 %)
- Travel (9.6 %)
- Communication (8.7 %)
- Other business (8.4 %)
- Construction (5.6 %)
- Remaining (4.5 %)

Imports Profile:

"Mineral fuels, lubricants" (SITC section 3), "Machinery and transport equipment" (SITC section 7) and "Goods classified chiefly by material" (SITC section 6) were the largest commodity groups for imports in 2012, representing respectively 28.7, 22.1 and 16.2 percent of imported goods (see table 3). From 2010 to 2012, the largest import commodity was "Petroleum oils, other than crude" (HS code 2710) (see table 4). The top three partners for merchandise imports were Senegal, France and China, accounting for respectively 19.3, 11.7 and 10.4 percent of total imports. "Transportation" (EBOPS code 205) accounted for the largest share of imports of services in 2012 at 686.8 mln US$, followed by "Travel" (EBOPS code 236) at 104.1 mln US$ and "Communications services" (EBOPS code 245) at 94.0 mln US$ (see graph 6).

Table 4: Top 10 import commodities 2010 to 2012

HS code	4-digit heading of Harmonized System 2007	Value 2010	Value 2011	Value 2012	Unit value 2010	Unit value 2011	Unit value 2012	Unit	SITC code
	All Commodities	4703.5	3351.5	3462.7					
2710	Petroleum oils, other than crude	1201.2	961.1	963.3	0.8	1.1	1.1	US$/kg	334
2523	Portland cement, aluminous cement, slag cement	185.3	201.2	176.2	0.1	0.1	0.1	US$/kg	661
3004	Medicaments (excluding goods of heading 30.02, 30.05 or 30.06)	309.5	97.2	141.5	43.0	13.1	20.9	US$/kg	542
8431	Parts suitable for use principally with the machinery of headings 84.25	100.5	73.8	69.1	26.6	18.1	18.7	US$/kg	723
3102	Mineral or chemical fertilisers, nitrogenous	56.2	92.8	93.1	0.3	0.4	0.4	US$/kg	562
8703	Motor cars and other motor vehicles principally designed for the transport	101.1	66.4	51.7	15.9		14.0	thsd US$/unit	781
8704	Motor vehicles for the transport of goods	81.5	67.2	47.2					782
8517	Electrical apparatus for line telephony or line telegraphy	56.8	52.1	76.2					764
1001	Wheat and meslin	63.5	60.5	60.0	0.3	0.5	0.4	US$/kg	041
1006	Rice	50.0	44.9	87.8	0.2	0.2	0.2	US$/kg	042

Source: UN Comtrade and UN ServiceTrade

Malta

Goods Imports: CIF, by origin/consignment for intra-eu **Goods Exports:** FOB, by last known destination **Trade System:** General

Overview:
In 2014, the value of merchandise exports of Malta decreased slightly by 4.5 percent to reach 5.0 bln US$, while its merchandise imports increased substantially by 12.2 percent to reach 8.4 bln US$ (see graph 1, table 2 and table 3). The merchandise trade balance recorded a moderate deficit of 3.5 bln US$ (see graph 1). The largest merchandise trade balance was with MDG Developed Europe at -3.0 bln US$ (see graph 4). Merchandise exports in Malta were diversified amongst partners; imports were also diversified. The top 17 partners accounted for 80 percent or more of exports and 19 partners accounted for 80 percent or more of imports (see graph 5). In 2013, the value of exports of services of Malta increased slightly by 3.3 percent, reaching 5.0 bln US$, while its imports of services increased slightly by 2.8 percent and reached 3.1 bln US$ (see graph 2). There was a moderate trade in services surplus of 1.9 bln US$.

Graph 1: Total merchandise trade, by value
(Bln US$ by year)

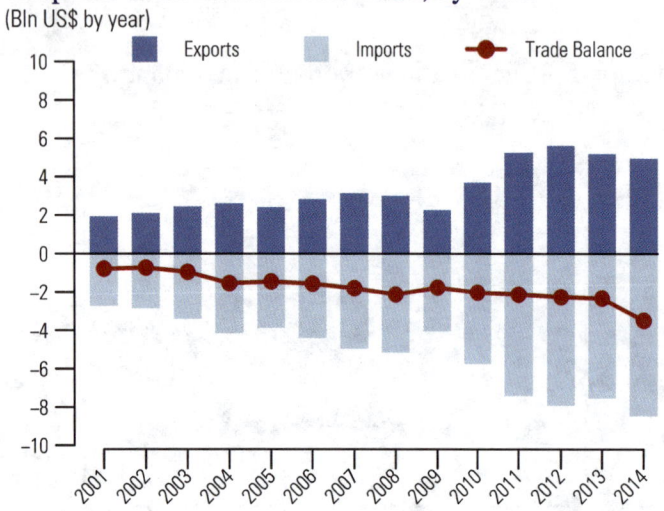

Graph 2: Total services trade, by value
(Bln US$ by year)

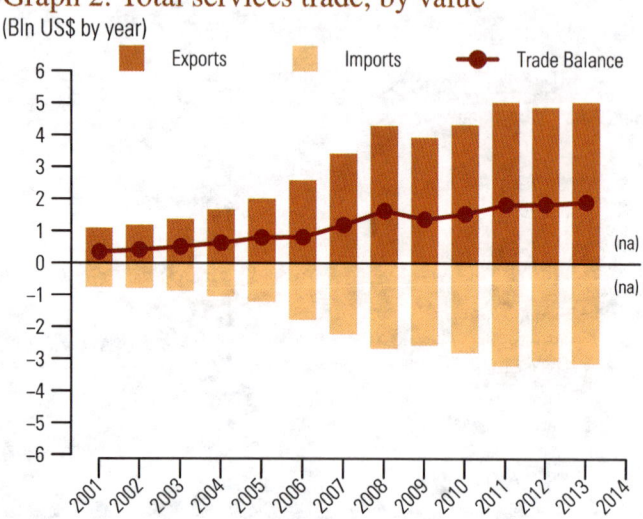

Exports Profile:
"Mineral fuels, lubricants" (SITC section 3), "Machinery and transport equipment" (SITC section 7) and "Chemicals" (SITC section 5) were the largest commodity groups for exports in 2014, representing respectively 43.0, 26.8 and 10.1 percent of exported goods (see table 2). From 2012 to 2014, the largest export commodity was "Petroleum oils, other than crude" (HS code 2710) (see table 1). The top three destinations for merchandise exports were Bunkers, ship stores, Germany and Egypt, accounting for respectively 14.6, 8.4 and 7.6 percent of total exports. "Personal, cultural, and recreational services" (EBOPS code 287) accounted for the largest share of exports of services in 2013 at 2.2 bln US$, followed by "Travel" (EBOPS code 236) at 1.4 bln US$ and "Other business services" (EBOPS code 268) at 464.8 mln US$ (see graph 3).

Graph 3: Exports of services by EBOPS category
(% share in 2013)

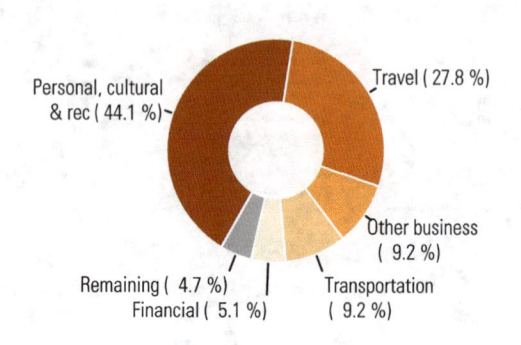

- Personal, cultural & rec (44.1 %)
- Travel (27.8 %)
- Other business (9.2 %)
- Transportation (9.2 %)
- Financial (5.1 %)
- Remaining (4.7 %)

Table 1: Top 10 export commodities 2012 to 2014

HS code	4-digit heading of Harmonized System 2012	Value (million US$) 2012	2013	2014	Unit value 2012	2013	2014	Unit	SITC code
	All Commodities	5646.3	5206.2	4970.8					
2710	Petroleum oils, other than crude	2545.1	2209.6	2139.4	0.8	0.7	0.6	US$/kg	334
8542	Electronic integrated circuits	1064.6	720.4	396.3					776
3004	Medicaments (excluding goods of heading 30.02, 30.05 or 30.06)	327.2	341.6	328.7	34.4	104.7	103.7	US$/kg	542
8541	Diodes, transistors and similar semiconductor devices	31.3	217.8	316.5					776
8536	Electrical apparatus for switching or protecting electrical circuits	146.0	194.3	185.3	56.3	54.0	59.1	US$/kg	772
9503	Tricycles, scooters, wheeled toys; dolls'carriages; dolls; other toys	129.9	143.1	131.7	26.1	30.2	36.6	US$/kg	894
8803	Parts of goods of heading 88.01 or 88.02	148.1	106.0	94.0	648.1	657.0	656.4	US$/kg	792
4907	Unused postage, revenue or similar stamps of current or new issue	87.2	113.6	98.9	39.8	54.2	61.1	US$/kg	892
0303	Fish, frozen, excluding fish fillets and other fish meat of heading 03.04	51.8	119.4	110.5	23.9	21.5	18.5	US$/kg	034
2106	Food preparations not elsewhere specified or included	61.1	69.3	73.3	3.1	3.2	3.3	US$/kg	098

Source: UN Comtrade and UN ServiceTrade

Malta

Services Imports and Exports: EBOPS 2002 categories

Table 2: Merchandise exports by SITC
(Value in million US$, growth and shares in percentage)

SITC	2014	Avg. Growth rates 2010-2014	Avg. Growth rates 2013-2014	2014 share
Total	4970.8	7.5	-4.5	100.0
0+1	301.7	11.8	-2.6	6.1
2+4	21.5	4.3	5.5	0.4
3	2139.5	22.5	-3.2	43.0
5	501.0	8.4	6.5	10.1
6	152.0	-1.8	-2.7	3.1
7	1330.7	-3.9	-9.9	26.8
8	485.9	3.1	-7.2	9.8
9	38.3	-0.6	-3.1	0.8

Table 3: Merchandise imports by SITC
(Value in million US$, growth and shares in percentage)

SITC	2014	Avg. Growth rates 2010-2014	Avg. Growth rates 2013-2014	2014 share
Total	8445.2	10.2	12.2	100.0
0+1	783.9	6.7	2.6	9.3
2+4	43.5	-3.8	-5.6	0.5
3	3399.3	24.8	14.7	40.3
5	665.7	7.6	14.9	7.9
6	449.7	1.0	9.6	5.3
7	2535.7	3.9	14.7	30.0
8	547.1	1.5	6.5	6.5
9	20.3	-23.1	-43.6	0.2

SITC Legend

SITC Code	Description
Total	All commodities
0+1	Food, animals + beverages, tobacco
2+4	Crude materials + anim. & veg. oils
3	Mineral fuels, lubricants
5	Chemicals
6	Goods classified chiefly by material
7	Machinery and transport equipment
8	Miscellaneous manufactured articles
9	Not classified elsewhere in the SITC

Graph 4: Merchandise trade balance
(Bln US$ by MDG Regions in 2014)

Graph 5: Partner concentration of merchandise trade
(Cumulative share by ranked partners in 2014)

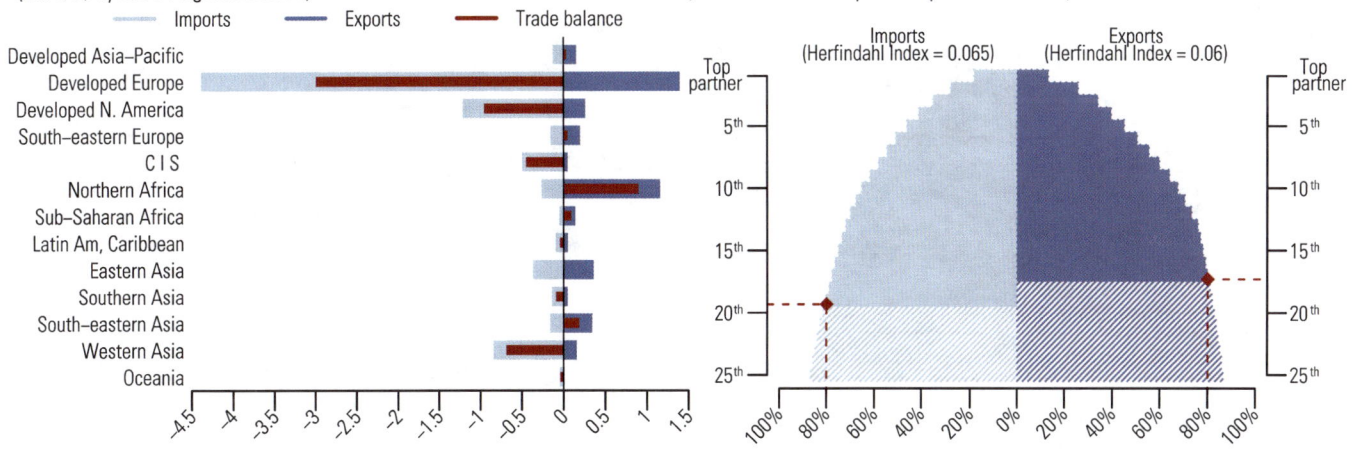

Imports (Herfindahl Index = 0.065)
Exports (Herfindahl Index = 0.06)

Graph 6: Imports of services by EBOPS category
(% share in 2013)

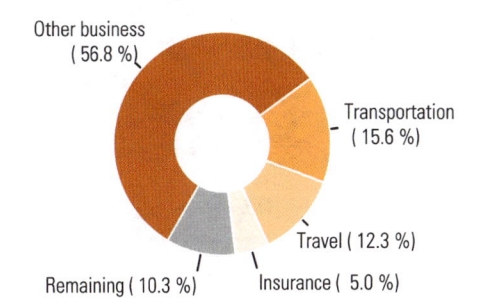

- Other business (56.8 %)
- Transportation (15.6 %)
- Travel (12.3 %)
- Insurance (5.0 %)
- Remaining (10.3 %)

Imports Profile:

"Mineral fuels, lubricants" (SITC section 3), "Machinery and transport equipment" (SITC section 7) and "Food, animals + beverages, tobacco" (SITC section 0+1) were the largest commodity groups for imports in 2014, representing respectively 40.3, 30.0 and 9.3 percent of imported goods (see table 3). From 2012 to 2014, the largest import commodity was "Petroleum oils, other than crude" (HS code 2710) (see table 4). The top three partners for merchandise imports were Italy, the United Kingdom and Turkey, accounting for respectively 24.9, 5.8 and 5.6 percent of total imports. "Other business services" (EBOPS code 268) accounted for the largest share of imports of services in 2013 at 1.8 bln US$, followed by "Transportation" (EBOPS code 205) at 488.7 mln US$ and "Travel" (EBOPS code 236) at 383.8 mln US$ (see graph 6).

Table 4: Top 10 import commodities 2012 to 2014

HS code	4-digit heading of Harmonized System 2012	2012	2013	2014	2012	2013	2014	Unit	SITC code
	All Commodities	7896.2	7525.4	8445.2					
2710	Petroleum oils, other than crude	3539.7	2930.4	3375.8	0.8	0.7	0.7	US$/kg	334
8542	Electronic integrated circuits	670.5	655.9	351.8					776
8903	Yachts and other vessels for pleasure or sports; rowing boats and canoes	353.2	461.6	647.8	280.8	202.5	191.4	thsd US$/unit	793
8802	Other aircraft (for example, helicopters, aeroplanes); spacecraft	145.5	140.1	444.7	0.6	17.5	29.6	mln US$/unit	792
3004	Medicaments (excluding goods of heading 30.02, 30.05 or 30.06)	125.2	138.4	141.8	57.1	56.2	51.4	US$/kg	542
8803	Parts of goods of heading 88.01 or 88.02	133.3	135.6	119.3	415.8	459.3	553.5	US$/kg	792
8703	Motor cars and other motor vehicles principally designed for the transport	84.1	89.8	119.9	10.1	11.4	4.4	thsd US$/unit	781
2933	Heterocyclic compounds with nitrogen hetero-atom(s) only	69.6	61.5	54.0	235.5	275.7	250.3	US$/kg	515
8534	Printed circuits	54.5	58.3	49.2	315.2	300.6	282.5	US$/kg	772
4802	Uncoated paper and paperboard, of a kind used for writing	52.4	54.8	52.2	6.2	6.4	6.7	US$/kg	641

Source: UN Comtrade and UN ServiceTrade

Mauritania

Goods Imports: CIF, by origin **Goods Exports:** FOB, by last known destination **Trade System:** General

Overview:
In 2014, the value of merchandise exports of Mauritania decreased substantially by 13.1 percent to reach 2.1 bln US$, while its merchandise imports decreased moderately by 8.5 percent to reach 3.6 bln US$ (see graph 1, table 2 and table 3). The merchandise trade balance recorded a moderate deficit of 1.5 bln US$ (see graph 1). The largest merchandise trade balance was with MDG Developed North America at -870.7 mln US$ (see graph 4). Merchandise exports in Mauritania were moderately concentrated amongst partners; imports were diversified. The top 8 partners accounted for 80 percent or more of exports and 11 partners accounted for 80 percent or more of imports (see graph 5). In 2013, the value of exports of services of Mauritania increased substantially by 15.8 percent, reaching 186.3 mln US$, while its imports of services decreased slightly by 2.3 percent and reached 1.0 bln US$ (see graph 2). There was a large trade in services deficit of 815.0 mln US$.

Graph 1: Total merchandise trade, by value
(Bln US$ by year)

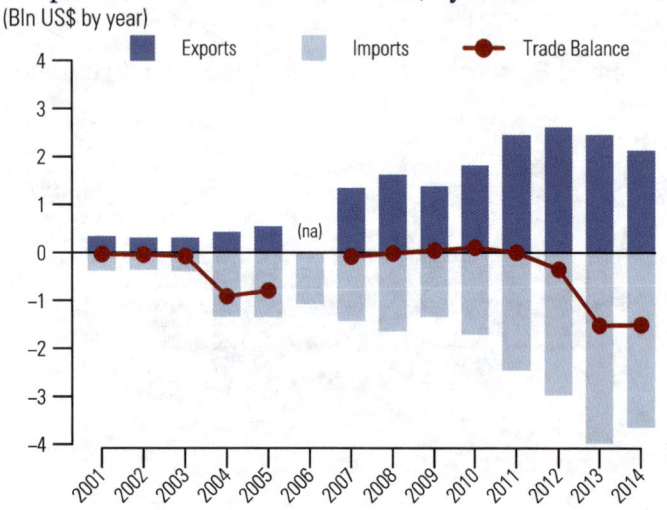

Graph 2: Total services trade, by value
(Bln US$ by year)

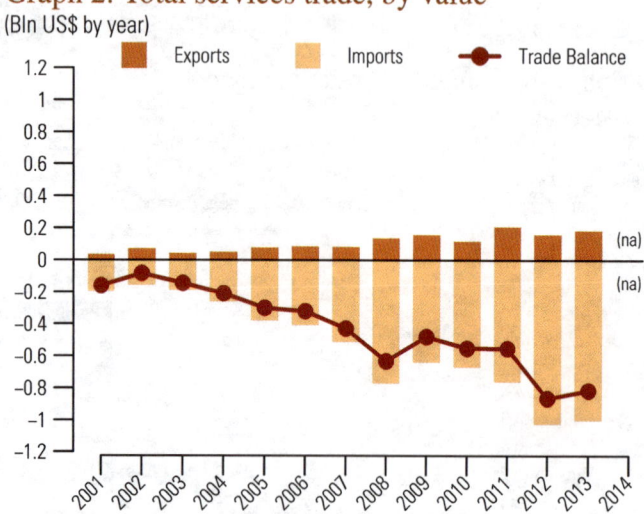

Exports Profile:
"Crude materials + anim. & veg. oils" (SITC section 2+4), "Food, animals + beverages, tobacco" (SITC section 0+1) and "Not classified elsewhere in the SITC" (SITC section 9) were the largest commodity groups for exports in 2014, representing respectively 51.4, 30.7 and 15.1 percent of exported goods (see table 2). From 2012 to 2014, the largest export commodity was "Iron ores and concentrates, including roasted iron pyrites" (HS code 2601) (see table 1). The top three destinations for merchandise exports were China, Switzerland and Italy, accounting for respectively 42.9, 13.6 and 6.1 percent of total exports. "Travel" (EBOPS code 236) accounted for the largest share of exports of services in 2001 at 6.3 mln US$ (see graph 3).

Graph 3: Exports of services by EBOPS category
(% share in 2001)

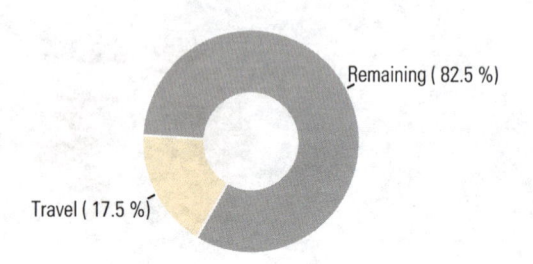

Remaining (82.5 %)
Travel (17.5 %)

Table 1: Top 10 export commodities 2012 to 2014

HS code	4-digit heading of Harmonized System 2007	Value (million US$) 2012	2013	2014	Unit value 2012	2013	2014	Unit	SITC code
	All Commodities	2 623.8	2 462.5	2 139.8					
2601	Iron ores and concentrates, including roasted iron pyrites	1 011.1	1 269.2	854.2	0.1	0.1	0.1	US$/kg	281
7108	Gold (including gold plated with platinum)	317.4	352.9	322.2	50.2	42.6	37.3	thsd US$/kg	971
2603	Copper ores and concentrates	312.2	303.5	216.5	1.6	1.6	1.4	US$/kg	283
0307	Molluscs, whether in shell or not	380.4	199.4	227.1	6.7	4.9	7.0	US$/kg	036
0303	Fish, frozen, excluding fish fillets and other fish meat of heading 03.04	144.1	167.5	288.3	0.4	0.6	0.5	US$/kg	034
2709	Petroleum oils and oils obtained from bituminous minerals, crude	271.3	...	...	0.8			US$/kg	333
2710	Petroleum oils, other than crude	73.8	62.6	59.3	1.0	0.8	0.3	US$/kg	334
2301	Flours, meals and pellets, of meat or meat offal	36.1	43.1	76.1	1.0	1.1	1.1	US$/kg	081
0302	Fish, fresh or chilled, excluding fish fillets	28.5	25.0	25.9	0.7	1.5	1.4	US$/kg	034
0306	Crustaceans, whether in shell or not	12.8	6.4	24.3	5.8	6.0	7.7	US$/kg	036

Mauritania

Services Imports and Exports: EBOPS 2002 categories

Table 2: Merchandise exports by SITC
(Value in million US$, growth and shares in percentage)

SITC	2014	Avg. Growth rates 2010-2014	2013-2014	2014 share
Total	2139.8	4.1	-13.1	100.0
0+1	657.8	25.7	46.4	30.7
2+4	1099.9	14.3	-31.1	51.4
3	59.7	-31.0	-4.7	2.8
6	0.3	53.4	4.2	0.0
9	322.2	-16.1	-8.7	15.1

Table 3: Merchandise imports by SITC
(Value in million US$, growth and shares in percentage)

SITC	2014	Avg. Growth rates 2010-2014	2013-2014	2014 share
Total	3641.8	20.8	-8.5	100.0
0+1	392.3	7.1	1.4	10.8
2+4	63.6	9.4	-6.2	1.7
3	750.3	13.4	-6.3	20.6
5	149.8	18.7	-4.8	4.1
6	450.7	24.4	25.9	12.4
7	1766.3	31.0	-17.1	48.5
8	68.7	15.2	-11.0	1.9
9	0.0	-86.5	...	0.0

SITC Legend

SITC Code	Description
Total	All commodities
0+1	Food, animals + beverages, tobacco
2+4	Crude materials + anim. & veg. oils
3	Mineral fuels, lubricants
5	Chemicals
6	Goods classified chiefly by material
7	Machinery and transport equipment
8	Miscellaneous manufactured articles
9	Not classified elsewhere in the SITC

Graph 4: Merchandise trade balance
(Bln US$ by MDG Regions in 2014)

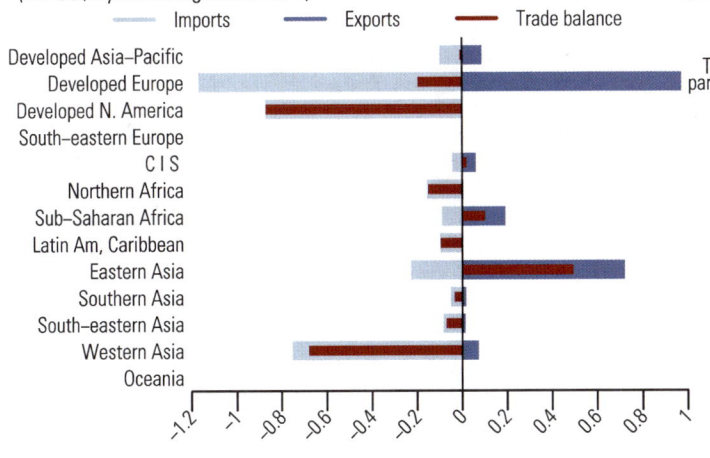

Imports, Exports, Trade balance by region: Developed Asia–Pacific, Developed Europe, Developed N. America, South–eastern Europe, CIS, Northern Africa, Sub–Saharan Africa, Latin Am, Caribbean, Eastern Asia, Southern Asia, South–eastern Asia, Western Asia, Oceania

Graph 5: Partner concentration of merchandise trade
(Cumulative share by ranked partners in 2014)

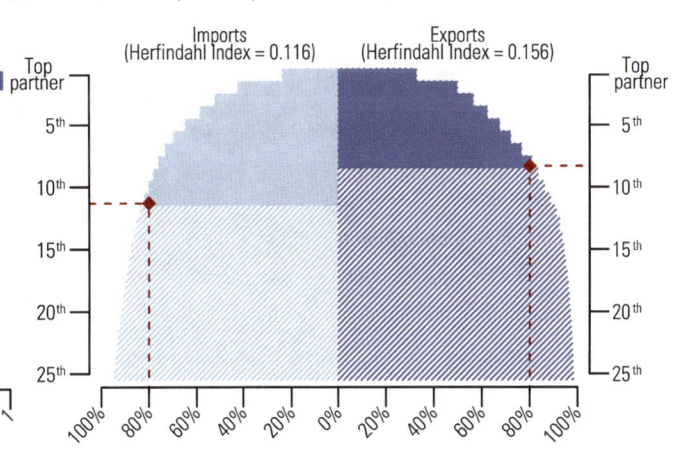

Imports (Herfindahl Index = 0.116)
Exports (Herfindahl Index = 0.156)

Graph 6: Imports of services by EBOPS category
(% share in 2001)

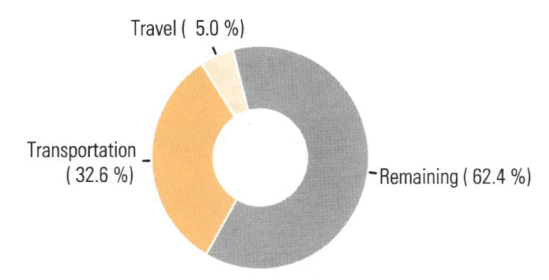

- Travel (5.0 %)
- Transportation (32.6 %)
- Remaining (62.4 %)

Imports Profile:
"Machinery and transport equipment" (SITC section 7), "Mineral fuels, lubricants" (SITC section 3) and "Goods classified chiefly by material" (SITC section 6) were the largest commodity groups for imports in 2014, representing respectively 48.5, 20.6 and 12.4 percent of imported goods (see table 3). From 2012 to 2014, the largest import commodity was "Petroleum oils, other than crude" (HS code 2710) (see table 4). The top three partners for merchandise imports were the United Arab Emirates, the United States and France, accounting for respectively 20.1, 11.7 and 10.2 percent of total imports. "Transportation" (EBOPS code 205) accounted for the largest share of imports of services in 2001 at 63.2 mln US$ (see graph 6).

Table 4: Top 10 import commodities 2012 to 2014

HS code	4-digit heading of Harmonized System 2007	Value (million US$) 2012	2013	2014	Unit value 2012	2013	2014	Unit	SITC code
	All Commodities	2970.6	3978.5	3641.8					
2710	Petroleum oils, other than crude	730.3	733.6	686.2	0.9	1.0	0.9	US$/kg	334
8905	Light-vessels, fire-floats, dredgers, floating cranes and other vessels	19.4	926.9	687.3					793
8431	Parts suitable for use principally with the machinery of headings 84.25	195.1	247.0	204.2	14.0	12.2	17.5	US$/kg	723
1001	Wheat and meslin	139.0	107.2	110.4	0.3	0.3	0.2	US$/kg	041
8703	Motor cars and other motor vehicles principally designed for the transport	108.3	103.8	105.4	22.2	21.7	22.6	thsd US$/unit	781
8474	Machinery for sorting, screening, separating, washing, crushing, grinding	87.5	62.9	41.7					728
8429	Self-propelled bulldozers, angledozers, graders, levellers, scrapers	85.8	81.8	24.4					723
1006	Rice	54.0	59.8	60.1	0.3	0.3	0.4	US$/kg	042
8904	Tugs and pusher craft	...	76.0	92.5					793
8428	Other lifting, handling, loading or unloading machinery	36.2	91.9	22.2					744

2014 International Trade Statistics Yearbook, Vol. I — Source: UN Comtrade and UN ServiceTrade

Mauritius

Goods Imports: CIF, by origin **Goods Exports: FOB, by last known destination** **Trade System: General**

Overview:
In 2014, the value of merchandise exports of Mauritius increased substantially by 13.6 percent to reach 2.7 bln US$, while its merchandise imports increased slightly by 3.9 percent to reach 5.6 bln US$ (see graph 1, table 2 and table 3). The merchandise trade balance recorded a large deficit of 2.9 bln US$ (see graph 1). The largest merchandise trade balance was with MDG Southern Asia at -1.2 bln US$ (see graph 4). Merchandise exports in Mauritius were diversified amongst partners; imports were also diversified. The top 10 partners accounted for 80 percent or more of exports and 17 partners accounted for 80 percent or more of imports (see graph 5). In 2013, the value of exports of services of Mauritius increased slightly by 0.4 percent, reaching 3.3 bln US$, while its imports of services increased substantially by 11.2 percent and reached 2.6 bln US$ (see graph 2). There was a moderate trade in services surplus of 674.2 mln US$.

Graph 1: Total merchandise trade, by value
(Bln US$ by year)

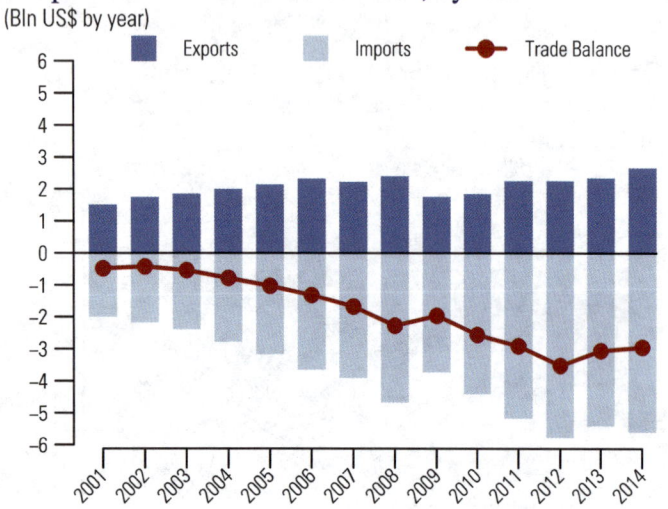

Graph 2: Total services trade, by value
(Bln US$ by year)

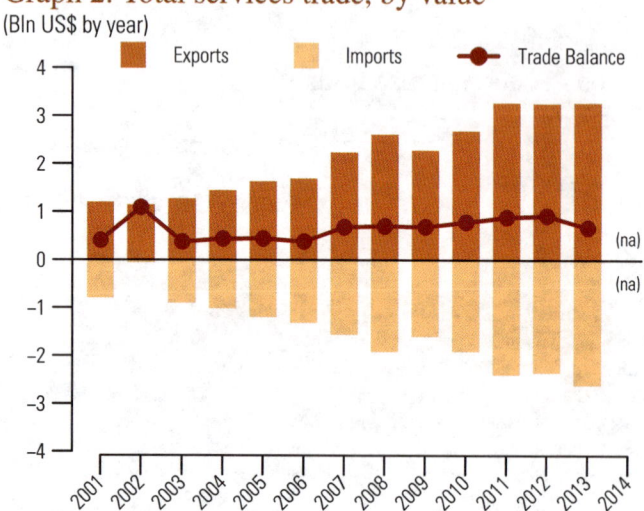

Exports Profile:
"Miscellaneous manufactured articles" (SITC section 8), "Food, animals + beverages, tobacco" (SITC section 0+1) and "Machinery and transport equipment" (SITC section 7) were the largest commodity groups for exports in 2014, representing respectively 37.8, 31.7 and 14.3 percent of exported goods (see table 2). From 2012 to 2014, the largest export commodity was "Prepared or preserved fish; caviar" (HS code 1604) (see table 1). The top three destinations for merchandise exports were the United Kingdom, France and the United States, accounting for respectively 16.2, 15.0 and 10.2 percent of total exports. "Other business services" (EBOPS code 268) accounted for the largest share of exports of services in 2013 at 1.7 bln US$, followed by "Travel" (EBOPS code 236) at 1.3 bln US$ and "Transportation" (EBOPS code 205) at 345.6 mln US$ (see graph 3).

Graph 3: Exports of services by EBOPS category
(% share in 2013)

- Other business (50.7 %)
- Travel (38.8 %)
- Transportation (10.5 %)

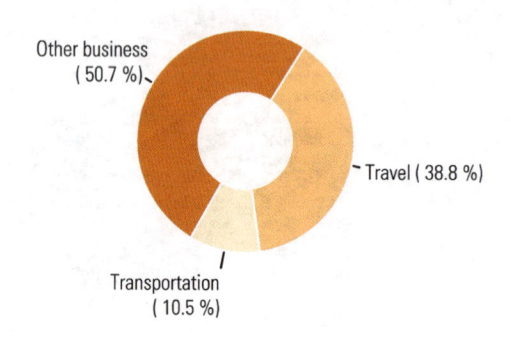

Table 1: Top 10 export commodities 2012 to 2014

HS code	4-digit heading of Harmonized System 2012	Value (million US$) 2012	2013	2014	Unit value 2012	2013	2014	Unit	SITC code
	All Commodities	2 257.7	2 344.6	2 663.0					
1604	Prepared or preserved fish; caviar	344.6	375.6	320.3	5.4	5.6	4.7	US$/kg	037
1701	Cane or beet sugar and chemically pure sucrose, in solid form	261.6	308.9	254.0		0.7	0.6	US$/kg	061
6109	T-shirts, singlets and other vests, knitted or crocheted	256.5	209.1	232.6	4.1	4.3	4.3	US$/unit	845
6205	Men's or boys'shirts	150.4	168.1	167.6	10.0	10.1	10.2	US$/unit	841
8517	Electrical apparatus for line telephony or line telegraphy	11.1	55.3	299.8					764
6203	Men's or boys'suits, ensembles, jackets, blazers, trousers	114.6	106.5	117.1	13.3	13.6	13.3	US$/unit	841
7102	Diamonds, whether or not worked, but not mounted or set	62.0	83.4	112.8					667
0303	Fish, frozen, excluding fish fillets and other fish meat of heading 03.04	65.9	83.1	89.0		2.3	1.7	US$/kg	034
6110	Jerseys, pullovers, cardigans, waist-coats and similar articles	83.3	69.3	65.3	11.2	11.0	10.6	US$/unit	845
6104	Women's or girls'suits, ensembles, jackets, blazers, dresses, skirts	55.2	59.4	59.3	6.3	6.7	6.7	US$/unit	844

Source: UN Comtrade and UN ServiceTrade

Mauritius

Services Imports and Exports: EBOPS 2002 categories

Table 2: Merchandise exports by SITC
(Value in million US$, growth and shares in percentage)

SITC	2014	Avg. Growth rates 2010-2014	Avg. Growth rates 2013-2014	2014 share
Total	2663.0	9.5	13.6	100.0
0+1	843.5	5.4	-7.1	31.7
2+4	41.6	4.2	4.2	1.6
3	1.6	-31.0	65.7	0.1
5	99.9	10.8	26.2	3.8
6	278.8	11.5	15.8	10.5
7	380.5	62.8	232.3	14.3
8	1005.3	5.2	5.6	37.8
9	11.7	38.0	33.2	0.4

Table 3: Merchandise imports by SITC
(Value in million US$, growth and shares in percentage)

SITC	2014	Avg. Growth rates 2010-2014	Avg. Growth rates 2013-2014	2014 share
Total	5607.2	6.2	3.9	100.0
0+1	1131.4	6.4	-0.4	20.2
2+4	189.7	6.9	2.3	3.4
3	1073.8	6.2	-8.2	19.1
5	438.8	2.0	4.5	7.8
6	905.0	2.6	-3.5	16.1
7	1373.5	11.5	29.0	24.5
8	471.5	4.5	2.0	8.4
9	23.6	0.3	6.4	0.4

SITC Legend

SITC Code	Description
Total	All commodities
0+1	Food, animals + beverages, tobacco
2+4	Crude materials + anim. & veg. oils
3	Mineral fuels, lubricants
5	Chemicals
6	Goods classified chiefly by material
7	Machinery and transport equipment
8	Miscellaneous manufactured articles
9	Not classified elsewhere in the SITC

Graph 4: Merchandise trade balance
(Bln US$ by MDG Regions in 2014)

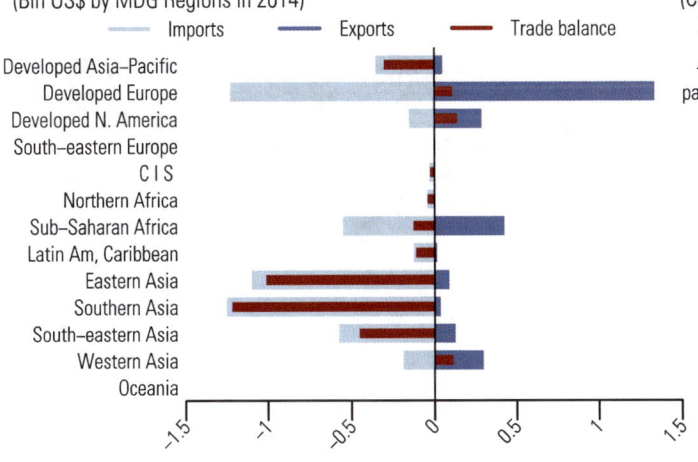

Graph 5: Partner concentration of merchandise trade
(Cumulative share by ranked partners in 2014)

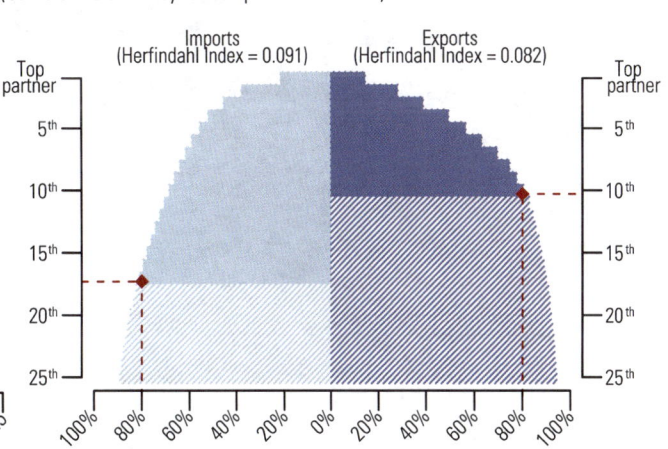

Imports (Herfindahl Index = 0.091)
Exports (Herfindahl Index = 0.082)

Graph 6: Imports of services by EBOPS category
(% share in 2013)

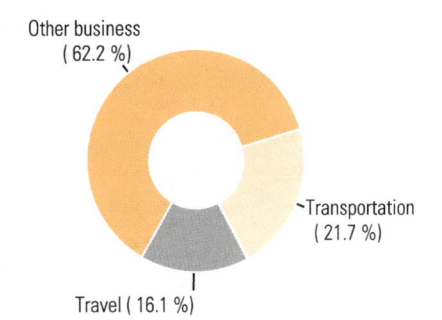

- Other business (62.2 %)
- Transportation (21.7 %)
- Travel (16.1 %)

Imports Profile:

"Machinery and transport equipment" (SITC section 7), "Food, animals + beverages, tobacco" (SITC section 0+1) and "Mineral fuels, lubricants" (SITC section 3) were the largest commodity groups for imports in 2014, representing respectively 24.5, 20.2 and 19.1 percent of imported goods (see table 3). From 2012 to 2014, the largest import commodity was "Petroleum oils, other than crude" (HS code 2710) (see table 4). The top three partners for merchandise imports were India, China and France, accounting for respectively 22.8, 15.7 and 8.1 percent of total imports. "Other business services" (EBOPS code 268) accounted for the largest share of imports of services in 2013 at 1.6 bln US$, followed by "Transportation" (EBOPS code 205) at 566.9 mln US$ and "Travel" (EBOPS code 236) at 420.0 mln US$ (see graph 6).

Table 4: Top 10 import commodities 2012 to 2014

HS code	4-digit heading of Harmonized System 2012	Value (million US$) 2012	2013	2014	Unit value 2012	2013	2014	Unit	SITC code
	All Commodities	5772.0	5397.6	5607.2					
2710	Petroleum oils, other than crude	1019.0	1018.6	890.0		1.6	1.8	US$/kg	334
0303	Fish, frozen, excluding fish fillets and other fish meat of heading 03.04	334.3	336.8	283.7		2.1	1.7	US$/kg	034
8517	Electrical apparatus for line telephony or line telegraphy	103.4	129.0	374.0					764
8703	Motor cars and other motor vehicles principally designed for the transport	183.0	166.0	182.6	10.8	11.0	11.6	thsd US$/unit	781
3004	Medicaments (excluding goods of heading 30.02, 30.05 or 30.06)	102.5	93.3	106.0	21.2	23.2	19.8	US$/kg	542
7102	Diamonds, whether or not worked, but not mounted or set	72.4	91.0	116.0					667
2711	Petroleum gases and other gaseous hydrocarbons	74.8	68.1	105.3	1.0	1.0	0.9	US$/kg	343
5208	Woven fabrics of cotton, containing 85 % or more by weight of cotton	75.2	79.7	78.6		13.6	14.3	US$/kg	652
2701	Coal; briquettes, ovoids and similar solid fuels manufactured from coal	90.3	69.1	69.5		0.1	0.1	US$/kg	321
8471	Automatic data processing machines and units thereof	78.7	73.2	75.5	314.4	230.7	187.5	US$/unit	752

Mexico

Goods Imports: CIF, by origin **Goods Exports:** FOB, by last known destination **Trade System:** General

Overview:
In 2014, the value of merchandise exports of Mexico increased slightly by 4.6 percent to reach 397.5 bln US$, while its merchandise imports increased slightly by 4.9 percent to reach 400.0 bln US$ (see graph 1, table 2 and table 3). Mexico's trade with its largest partner, the United States, increased for both exports and imports, increasing by 6.5 and 4.3 percent respectively in 2014. The overall merchandise trade balance recorded a relatively small deficit of 2.5 bln US$ (see graph 1). Mexico recorded a merchandise trade surplus of 123.3 bln US$ with the United States, a 10.0 percent increase compared to the surplus with the United States in 2013. The largest merchandise trade balance was with MDG Developed North America at 124.0 bln US$ (see graph 4). Merchandise exports in Mexico were highly concentrated amongst partners; imports were also highly concentrated. The top 1 partner accounted for 80 percent or more of exports and 7 partners accounted for 80 percent or more of imports (see graph 5). In 2013, the value of exports of services of Mexico increased substantially by 24.6 percent, reaching 20.1 bln US$, while its imports of services increased slightly by 4.8 percent and reached 31.9 bln US$ (see graph 2). There was a moderate trade in services deficit of 11.8 bln US$ in 2013, which was a 17.5 percent decrease compared to the deficit recorded in 2012.

Graph 1: Total merchandise trade, by value
(Bln US$ by year)

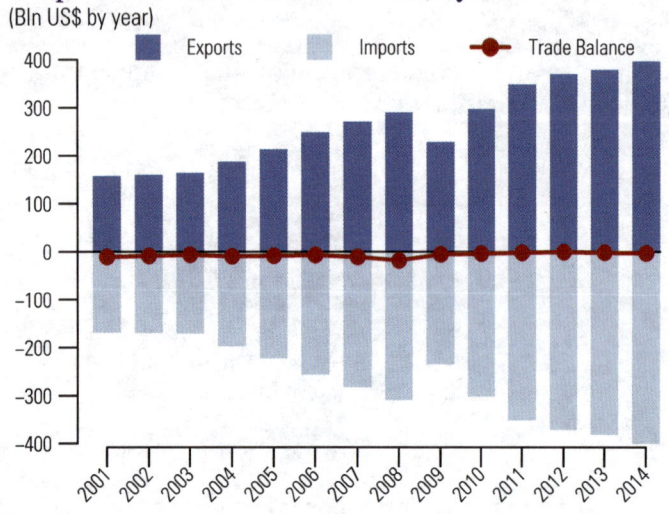

Graph 2: Total services trade, by value
(Bln US$ by year)

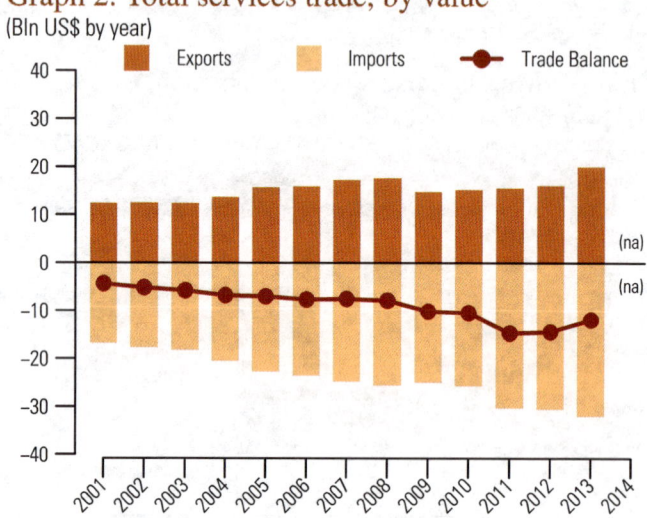

Exports Profile:
"Machinery and transport equipment" (SITC section 7), "Mineral fuels, lubricants" (SITC section 3) and "Miscellaneous manufactured articles" (SITC section 8) were the largest commodity groups for exports in 2014, representing respectively 58.3, 10.6 and 9.5 percent of exported goods (see table 2). Despite falling by 15.2 percent in 2014, "Petroleum oils and oils obtained from bituminous minerals, crude" (HS code 2709) remained the largest export commodity (see table 1). The top three destinations for merchandise exports were the United States, Canada and Spain, accounting for respectively 79.0, 2.8 and 1.8 percent of total exports. "Travel" (EBOPS code 236) accounted for the largest share of exports of services in 2013 at 13.9 bln US$, followed by "Insurance services" (EBOPS code 253) at 2.8 bln US$ and "Royalties and license fees" (EBOPS code 266) at 2.3 bln US$ (see graph 3).

Graph 3: Exports of services by EBOPS category
(% share in 2013)

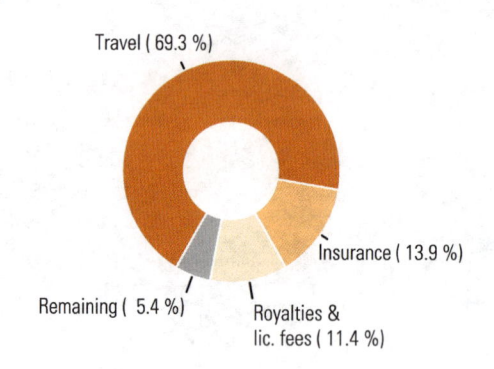

- Travel (69.3 %)
- Insurance (13.9 %)
- Royalties & lic. fees (11.4 %)
- Remaining (5.4 %)

Table 1: Top 10 export commodities 2012 to 2014

HS code	4-digit heading of Harmonized System 2012	Value (million US$) 2012	2013	2014	Unit value 2012	2013	2014	Unit	SITC code
	All Commodities.........	370 706.7	379 960.8	397 505.6					
2709	Petroleum oils and oils obtained from bituminous minerals, crude.............	46 852.4	42 723.2	36 248.0	0.7	0.7	0.8	US$/kg	333
8703	Motor cars and other motor vehicles principally designed for the transport...............	29 169.3	32 389.4	32 391.3	15.4	16.8	16.1	thsd US$/unit	781
8708	Parts and accessories of the motor vehicles of headings 87.01 to 87.05................	19 046.0	20 521.9	22 820.3	10.7	10.7	10.7	US$/kg	784
8471	Automatic data processing machines and units thereof....................	18 438.7	17 401.3	20 737.9	328.8	458.0	630.0	US$/unit	752
8704	Motor vehicles for the transport of goods....................	14 800.0	17 560.5	21 503.5	21.1	24.9	25.2	thsd US$/unit	782
8528	Reception apparatus for television.......................	17 767.6	16 688.9	16 869.5	290.0	273.2	263.2	US$/unit	761
8517	Electrical apparatus for line telephony or line telegraphy................	17 186.3	17 975.6	15 750.8					764
8544	Insulated (including enamelled or anodised) wire, cable.................	8 851.7	10 161.1	11 110.6	15.6	13.7	5.8	US$/kg	773
8701	Tractors (other than tractors of heading 87.09).................	6 035.9	5 565.7	7 777.2	60.9	24.4	83.3	thsd US$/unit	722
7108	Gold (including gold plated with platinum).................	7 974.1	5 816.3	4 691.4	19.0	11.8	8.6	thsd US$/kg	971

Mexico

Services Imports and Exports: EBOPS 2002 categories

Table 2: Merchandise exports by SITC
(Value in million US$, growth and shares in percentage)

SITC	2014	Avg. Growth rates 2010-2014	Avg. Growth rates 2013-2014	2014 share
Total	397 505.6	7.4	4.6	100.0
0+1	24 857.7	9.0	5.7	6.3
2+4	7 846.8	11.5	0.1	2.0
3	42 182.5	0.7	-13.4	10.6
5	15 726.0	7.3	0.9	4.0
6	28 715.0	6.4	1.5	7.2
7	231 621.9	8.7	9.0	58.3
8	37 847.4	8.7	10.8	9.5
9	8 708.3	4.3	-6.5	2.2

Table 3: Merchandise imports by SITC
(Value in million US$, growth and shares in percentage)

SITC	2014	Avg. Growth rates 2010-2014	Avg. Growth rates 2013-2014	2014 share
Total	399 976.9	7.3	4.9	100.0
0+1	21 253.6	8.2	4.6	5.3
2+4	10 723.0	1.4	-1.4	2.7
3	33 220.3	8.4	1.0	8.3
5	45 544.2	7.5	5.6	11.4
6	54 837.8	7.5	6.9	13.7
7	188 244.1	7.2	4.1	47.1
8	35 376.9	5.6	6.9	8.8
9	10 777.1	16.0	23.5	2.7

SITC Legend

SITC Code	Description
Total	All commodities
0+1	Food, animals + beverages, tobacco
2+4	Crude materials + anim. & veg. oils
3	Mineral fuels, lubricants
5	Chemicals
6	Goods classified chiefly by material
7	Machinery and transport equipment
8	Miscellaneous manufactured articles
9	Not classified elsewhere in the SITC

Graph 4: Merchandise trade balance
(Bln US$ by MDG Regions in 2014)

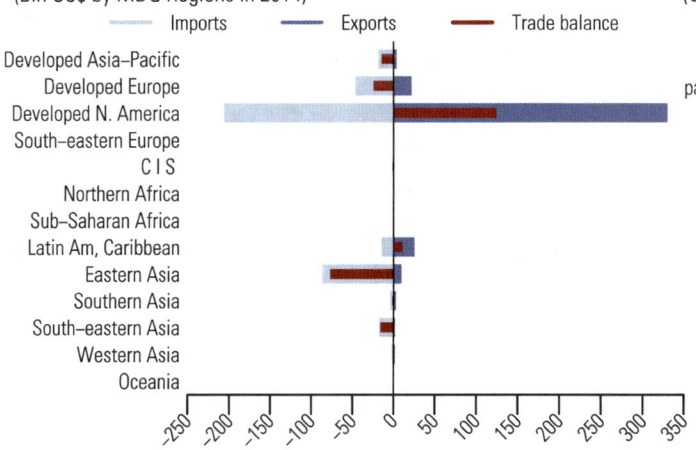

Graph 5: Partner concentration of merchandise trade
(Cumulative share by ranked partners in 2014)

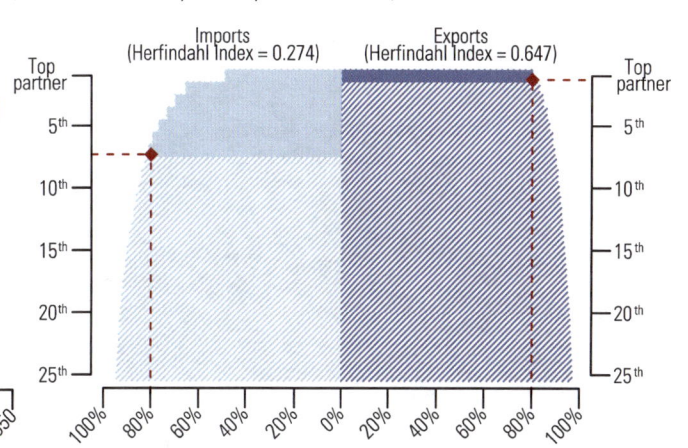

Imports (Herfindahl Index = 0.274)
Exports (Herfindahl Index = 0.647)

Graph 6: Imports of services by EBOPS category
(% share in 2013)

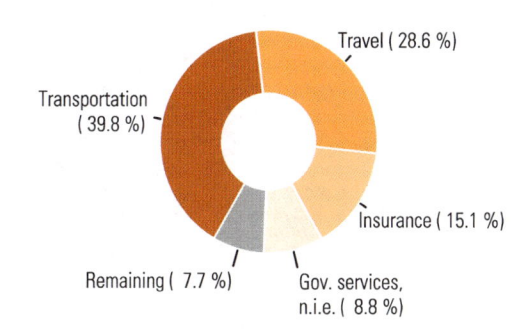

- Transportation (39.8 %)
- Travel (28.6 %)
- Insurance (15.1 %)
- Gov. services, n.i.e. (8.8 %)
- Remaining (7.7 %)

Imports Profile:

"Machinery and transport equipment" (SITC section 7), "Goods classified chiefly by material" (SITC section 6) and "Chemicals" (SITC section 5) were the largest commodity groups for imports in 2014, representing respectively 47.1, 13.7 and 11.4 percent of imported goods (see table 3). From 2012 to 2014, the largest import commodity was "Petroleum oils, other than crude" (HS code 2710) (see table 4). The top three partners for merchandise imports were the United States, China and Japan, accounting for respectively 49.4, 16.0 and 4.5 percent of total imports. "Transportation" (EBOPS code 205) accounted for the largest share of imports of services in 2013 at 12.7 bln US$, followed by "Travel" (EBOPS code 236) at 9.1 bln US$ and "Insurance services" (EBOPS code 253) at 4.8 bln US$ (see graph 6).

Table 4: Top 10 import commodities 2012 to 2014

HS code	4-digit heading of Harmonized System 2012	Value 2012	Value 2013	Value 2014	Unit value 2012	Unit value 2013	Unit value 2014	Unit	SITC code
	All Commodities	370 751.4	381 210.1	399 976.9					
2710	Petroleum oils, other than crude	27 229.5	25 329.9	24 352.5					334
8708	Parts and accessories of the motor vehicles of headings 87.01 to 87.05	20 598.7	20 611.1	22 921.5	12.2	12.2	12.5	US$/kg	784
8517	Electrical apparatus for line telephony or line telegraphy	13 379.0	15 060.0	13 436.2					764
8542	Electronic integrated circuits	11 662.6	13 359.8	13 933.6					776
9999	Commodities not specified according to kind	10 440.0	8 583.1	10 672.9					931
8529	Parts suitable for use with the apparatus of headings 85.25 to 85.28	9 910.3	9 555.5	9 535.1	26.6	25.7		US$/kg	764
8471	Automatic data processing machines and units thereof	8 338.8	8 832.6	8 973.9	70.1	74.9	77.2	US$/unit	752
8703	Motor cars and other motor vehicles principally designed for the transport	7 643.2	8 452.6	8 574.9	9.4	8.7	10.3	thsd US$/unit	781
8473	Parts and accessories for use with machines of heading 84.69 to 84.72	5 695.1	5 555.8	5 583.9	26.9	32.6		US$/kg	759
8536	Electrical apparatus for switching or protecting electrical circuits	5 086.2	5 608.3	5 949.6	10.2	17.2	11.1	US$/kg	772

Micronesia (Federated states of)

Goods Imports: CIF, by origin **Goods Exports:** FOB, by last known destination **Trade System:** General

Overview:
In 2013, the value of merchandise exports of Micronesia (Federated states of) decreased substantially by 38.7 percent to reach 27.6 mln US$, while its merchandise imports decreased slightly by 3.1 percent to reach 187.7 mln US$ (see graph 1, table 2 and table 3). The merchandise trade balance recorded a large deficit of 160.1 mln US$ (see graph 1). The largest merchandise trade balance was with MDG Developed North America at -68.6 mln US$ (see graph 4). Merchandise exports in Micronesia (Federated states of) were highly concentrated amongst partners; imports were moderately concentrated. The top 2 partners accounted for 80 percent or more of exports and 6 partners accounted for 80 percent or more of imports (see graph 5). In 2008, the value of exports of services of Micronesia (Federated states of) increased moderately by 7.3 percent, reaching 26.3 mln US$, while its imports of services increased moderately by 7.9 percent and reached 64.1 mln US$ (see graph 2). There was a large trade in services deficit of 37.8 mln US$.

Graph 1: Total merchandise trade, by value
(Mln US$ by year)

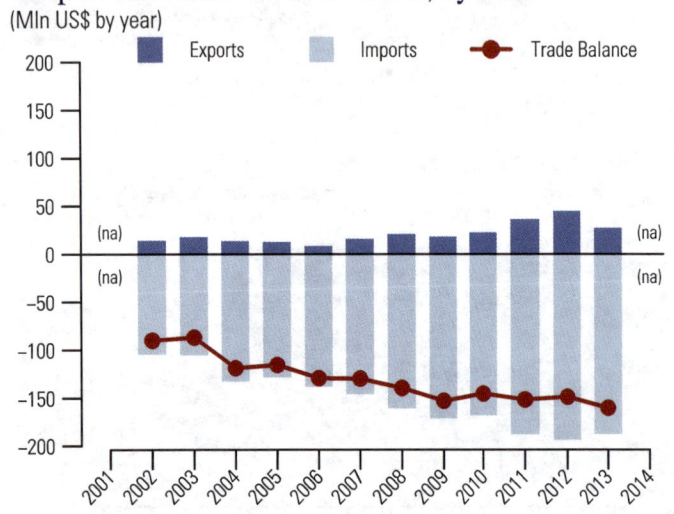

Graph 2: Total services trade, by value
(Mln US$ by year)

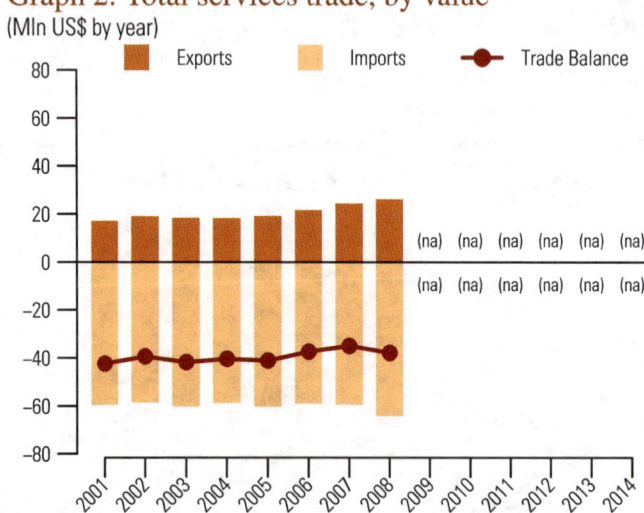

Exports Profile:
"Food, animals + beverages, tobacco" (SITC section 0+1), "Crude materials + anim. & veg. oils" (SITC section 2+4) and "Goods classified chiefly by material" (SITC section 6) were the largest commodity groups for exports in 2013, representing respectively 99.1, 0.5 and 0.4 percent of exported goods (see table 2). From 2011 to 2013, the largest export commodity was "Fish, frozen, excluding fish fillets" (HS code 0303) (see table 1). The top three destinations for merchandise exports were Areas nes, Guam and Northern Mariana Islands, accounting for respectively 83.6, 11.0 and 3.0 percent of total exports. "Travel" (EBOPS code 236) accounted for the largest share of exports of services in 2008 at 19.7 mln US$, followed by "Transportation" (EBOPS code 205) at 4.9 mln US$ and "Communications services" (EBOPS code 245) at 1.8 mln US$ (see graph 3).

Graph 3: Exports of services by EBOPS category
(% share in 2008)

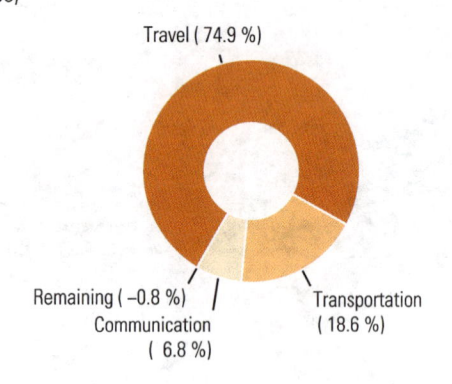

- Travel (74.9 %)
- Transportation (18.6 %)
- Communication (6.8 %)
- Remaining (–0.8 %)

Table 1: Top 10 export commodities 2011 to 2013

HS code	4-digit heading of Harmonized System 2002	Value (million US$) 2011	2012	2013	Unit value 2011	2012	2013	Unit	SITC code
	All Commodities	36.7	45.1	27.6					
0303	Fish, frozen, excluding fish fillets	30.6	39.9	22.8	1.5	1.9		US$/kg	034
0802	Other nuts, fresh or dried	4.5	3.5	3.4	13.7	13.8		US$/kg	057
1212	Locust beans, seaweeds and other algae	0.2	0.5	0.5					292
2106	Food preparations not elsewhere specified or included	0.4	0.3	0.4	5.2			US$/kg	098
0307	Molluscs, whether in shell or not	0.4	0.2	0.2			43.4	US$/kg	036
0604	Foliage, branches and other parts of plants	0.2	0.2	0.1	6.4	6.3		US$/kg	292
0301	Live fish	0.1	0.1	0.1	12.1			US$/kg	034
1203	Copra	0.1	0.2	0.0		0.5	0.1	US$/kg	223
4421	Other articles of wood	0.1	0.1	0.1	10.2	9.3	10.8	US$/kg	635
0306	Crustaceans, whether in shell or not	0.1	0.0	0.0	6.1	3.9	5.7	US$/kg	036

Micronesia (Federated states of)

Services Imports and Exports: EBOPS 2002 categories

Table 2: Merchandise exports by SITC
(Value in million US$, growth and shares in percentage)

SITC	2013	Avg. Growth rates 2009-2013	Avg. Growth rates 2012-2013	2013 share
Total	27.6	10.8	-38.7	100.0
0+1	27.4	10.9	-38.7	99.1
2+4	0.1	7.1	-62.0	0.5
6	0.1	0.6	17.2	0.4
8	0.0	195.8	200.2	0.1

Table 3: Merchandise imports by SITC
(Value in million US$, growth and shares in percentage)

SITC	2013	Avg. Growth rates 2009-2013	Avg. Growth rates 2012-2013	2013 share
Total	187.7	2.4	-3.1	100.0
0+1	51.1	-0.1	-9.6	27.2
2+4	4.7	-6.7	-42.0	2.5
3	56.4	9.2	-0.9	30.1
5	8.8	-3.8	-14.6	4.7
6	18.4	-0.5	-17.1	9.8
7	27.7	0.9	19.2	14.7
8	14.1	-1.7	-10.6	7.5
9	6.5	20.5	955.9	3.5

SITC Legend

SITC Code	Description
Total	All commodities
0+1	Food, animals + beverages, tobacco
2+4	Crude materials + anim. & veg. oils
3	Mineral fuels, lubricants
5	Chemicals
6	Goods classified chiefly by material
7	Machinery and transport equipment
8	Miscellaneous manufactured articles
9	Not classified elsewhere in the SITC

Graph 4: Merchandise trade balance
(Mln US$ by MDG Regions in 2013)

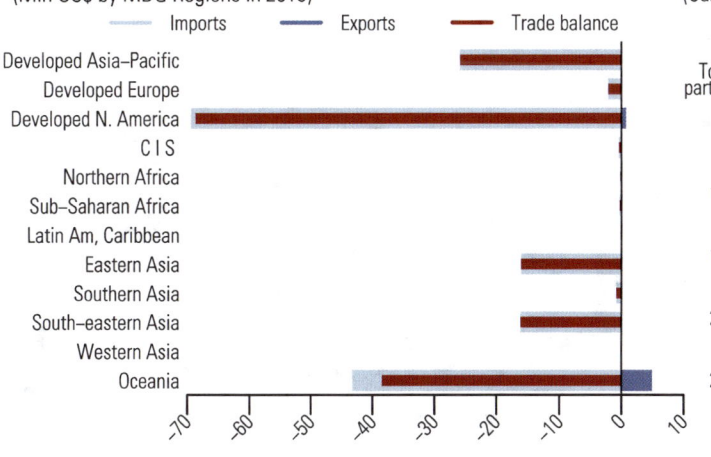

Graph 5: Partner concentration of merchandise trade
(Cumulative share by ranked partners in 2013)

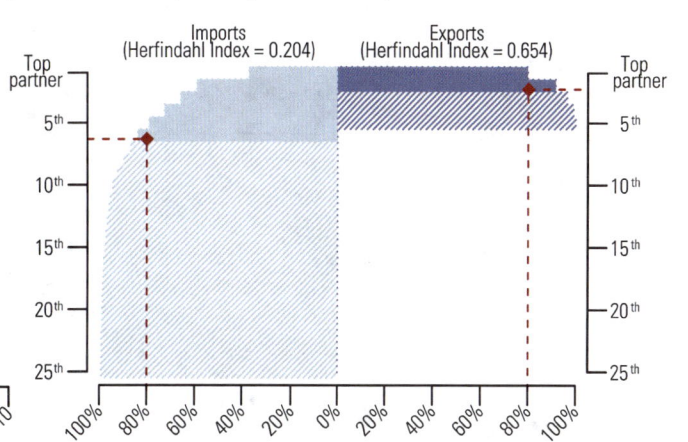

Imports (Herfindahl Index = 0.204)
Exports (Herfindahl Index = 0.654)

Graph 6: Imports of services by EBOPS category
(% share in 2008)

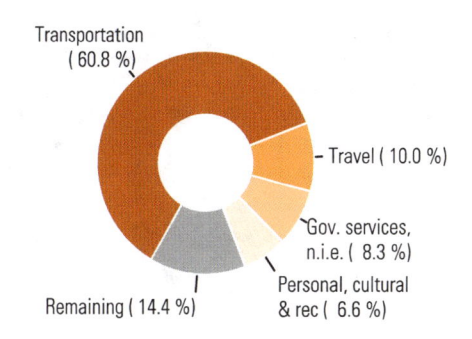

- Transportation (60.8 %)
- Travel (10.0 %)
- Gov. services, n.i.e. (8.3 %)
- Personal, cultural & rec (6.6 %)
- Remaining (14.4 %)

Imports Profile:

"Mineral fuels, lubricants" (SITC section 3), "Food, animals + beverages, tobacco" (SITC section 0+1) and "Machinery and transport equipment" (SITC section 7) were the largest commodity groups for imports in 2013, representing respectively 30.1, 27.2 and 14.7 percent of imported goods (see table 3). From 2011 to 2013, the largest import commodity was "Petroleum oils, other than crude" (HS code 2710) (see table 4). The top three partners for merchandise imports were the United States, Guam and Japan, accounting for respectively 37.3, 24.2 and 7.1 percent of total imports. "Transportation" (EBOPS code 205) accounted for the largest share of imports of services in 2008 at 39.0 mln US$, followed by "Travel" (EBOPS code 236) at 6.4 mln US$ and "Government services, n.i.e." (EBOPS code 291) at 5.3 mln US$ (see graph 6).

Table 4: Top 10 import commodities 2011 to 2013

HS code	4-digit heading of Harmonized System 2002	2011	2012	2013	2011	2012	2013	Unit	SITC code
	All Commodities	188.1	193.6	187.7					
2710	Petroleum oils, other than crude	44.1	54.8	54.8					334
1006	Rice	8.2	10.3	9.4	0.4	0.5	0.5	US$/kg	042
8703	Motor cars and other motor vehicles principally designed for the transport	6.6	6.2	6.1		7.5	8.5	thsd US$/unit	781
0207	Meat and edible offal, of the poultry of heading 01.05	5.5	6.7	6.0	1.6	1.8		US$/kg	012
9999	Commodities not specified according to kind	10.0	0.6	6.5					931
1604	Prepared or preserved fish; caviar	3.3	3.8	3.0	3.2		3.8	US$/kg	037
1602	Other prepared or preserved meat, meat offal or blood	2.6	2.7	2.5	5.1	5.7	5.7	US$/kg	017
1902	Pasta, whether or not cooked or stuffed	2.6	2.5	2.4	1.5		1.6	US$/kg	048
1905	Bread, pastry, cakes, biscuits and other bakers' wares	2.5	2.5	2.3	3.2	3.5	3.4	US$/kg	048
2202	Waters with added sugar	2.3	2.5	2.1	1.0	1.0	1.0	US$/litre	111

Source: UN Comtrade and UN ServiceTrade

Mongolia

Goods Imports: CIF, by origin   **Goods Exports: FOB, by last known destination**   **Trade System: General**

Overview:

In 2014, the value of merchandise exports of Mongolia increased substantially by 35.3 percent to reach 5.8 bln US$, while its merchandise imports decreased substantially by 19.3 percent to reach 5.1 bln US$ (see graph 1, table 2 and table 3). The merchandise trade balance recorded a relatively small surplus of 642.9 mln US$ (see graph 1). The largest merchandise trade balance was with MDG Eastern Asia at 3.0 bln US$ (see graph 4). Merchandise exports in Mongolia were highly concentrated amongst partners; imports were moderately concentrated. The top 1 partner accounted for 80 percent or more of exports and 5 partners accounted for 80 percent or more of imports (see graph 5). In 2013, the value of exports of services of Mongolia decreased substantially by 26.1 percent, reaching 710.0 mln US$, while its imports of services decreased slightly by 1.8 percent and reached 2.0 bln US$ (see graph 2). There was a large trade in services deficit of 1.3 bln US$.

Graph 1: Total merchandise trade, by value
(Bln US$ by year)

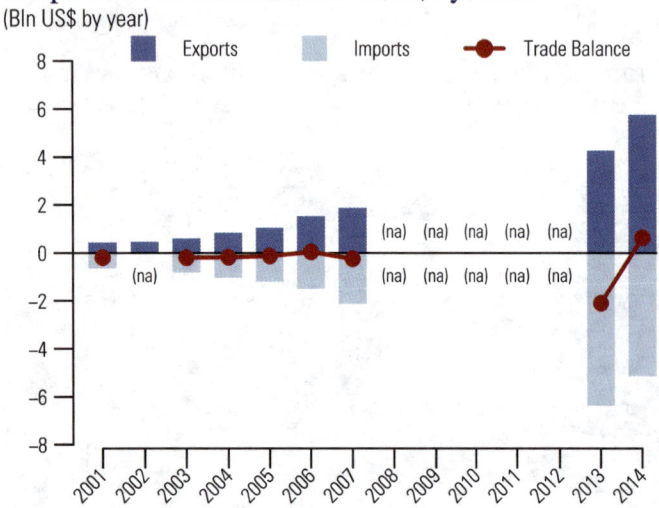

Graph 2: Total services trade, by value
(Bln US$ by year)

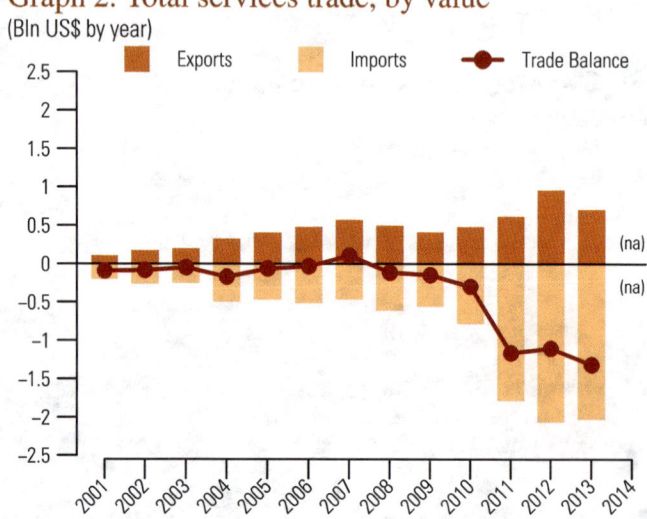

Exports Profile:

"Crude materials + anim. & veg. oils" (SITC section 2+4), "Mineral fuels, lubricants" (SITC section 3) and "Not classified elsewhere in the SITC" (SITC section 9) were the largest commodity groups for exports in 2014, representing respectively 63.0, 25.9 and 7.0 percent of exported goods (see table 2). From 2012 to 2014, the largest export commodity was "Copper ores and concentrates" (HS code 2603) (see table 1). The top three destinations for merchandise exports were China, the United Kingdom and Canada, accounting for respectively 87.3, 6.0 and 1.4 percent of total exports. "Other business services" (EBOPS code 268) accounted for the largest share of exports of services in 2013 at 241.6 mln US$, followed by "Transportation" (EBOPS code 205) at 228.6 mln US$ and "Travel" (EBOPS code 236) at 189.3 mln US$ (see graph 3).

Graph 3: Exports of services by EBOPS category
(% share in 2013)

- Transportation (32.2 %)
- Other business (34.0 %)
- Travel (26.7 %)
- Remaining (7.1 %)

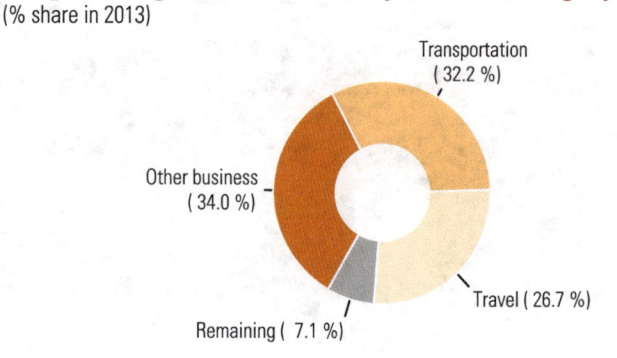

Table 1: Top 10 export commodities 2012 to 2014

HS code	4-digit heading of Harmonized System 2007	Value (million US$) 2012	2013	2014	Unit value 2012	2013	2014	Unit	SITC code
	All Commodities	...	4 269.1	5 774.3					
2603	Copper ores and concentrates	...	949.0	2 574.7		1.5	1.9	US$/kg	283
2701	Coal; briquettes, ovoids and similar solid fuels manufactured from coal	...	1 116.2	848.6		0.1	0.0	US$/kg	321
2709	Petroleum oils and oils obtained from bituminous minerals, crude	...	515.5	634.6		0.7	0.7	US$/kg	333
2601	Iron ores and concentrates, including roasted iron pyrites	...	654.3	446.4		0.1	0.1	US$/kg	281
7108	Gold (including gold plated with platinum)	...	309.8	405.2		41.0	40.4	thsd US$/kg	971
5102	Fine or coarse animal hair, not carded or combed	...	193.9	235.7		30.0	32.6	US$/kg	268
2608	Zinc ores and concentrates	...	119.1	113.2		0.9	1.1	US$/kg	287
2529	Feldspar; leucite, nepheline and nepheline syenite; fluorspar	...	83.3	71.5		0.2	0.2	US$/kg	278
5105	Wool and fine or coarse animal hair, carded or combed	...	58.0	63.4		74.9	81.9	US$/kg	268
2613	Molybdenum ores and concentrates	...	29.5	35.1		7.4	8.8	US$/kg	287

Mongolia

Services Imports and Exports: EBOPS 2002 categories

Table 2: Merchandise exports by SITC
(Value in million US$, growth and shares in percentage)

SITC	2014	Avg. Growth rates 2010-2014	Avg. Growth rates 2013-2014	2014 share
Total	5774.3	...	35.3	100.0
0+1	20.4	...	-32.2	0.4
2+4	3638.1	...	71.3	63.0
3	1496.1	...	-9.3	25.9
5	2.2	...	11.4	0.0
6	86.7	...	49.7	1.5
7	93.6	...	40.5	1.6
8	31.9	...	11.0	0.6
9	405.2	...	30.8	7.0

Table 3: Merchandise imports by SITC
(Value in million US$, growth and shares in percentage)

SITC	2014	Avg. Growth rates 2010-2014	Avg. Growth rates 2013-2014	2014 share
Total	5131.5	...	-19.3	100.0
0+1	433.9	...	-20.4	8.5
2+4	56.4	...	-3.1	1.1
3	1356.8	...	-16.6	26.4
5	368.0	...	1.0	7.2
6	1001.3	...	-3.4	19.5
7	1604.9	...	-32.9	31.3
8	309.7	...	-7.1	6.0
9	0.4	...	-28.2	0.0

SITC Legend

SITC Code	Description
Total	All commodities
0+1	Food, animals + beverages, tobacco
2+4	Crude materials + anim. & veg. oils
3	Mineral fuels, lubricants
5	Chemicals
6	Goods classified chiefly by material
7	Machinery and transport equipment
8	Miscellaneous manufactured articles
9	Not classified elsewhere in the SITC

Graph 4: Merchandise trade balance
(Bln US$ by MDG Regions in 2014)

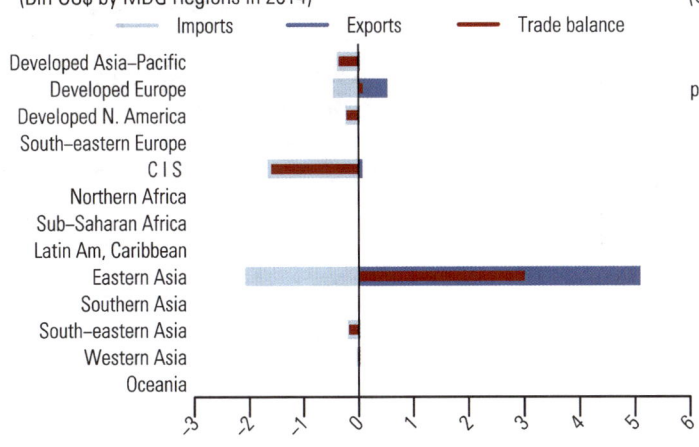

Graph 5: Partner concentration of merchandise trade
(Cumulative share by ranked partners in 2014)

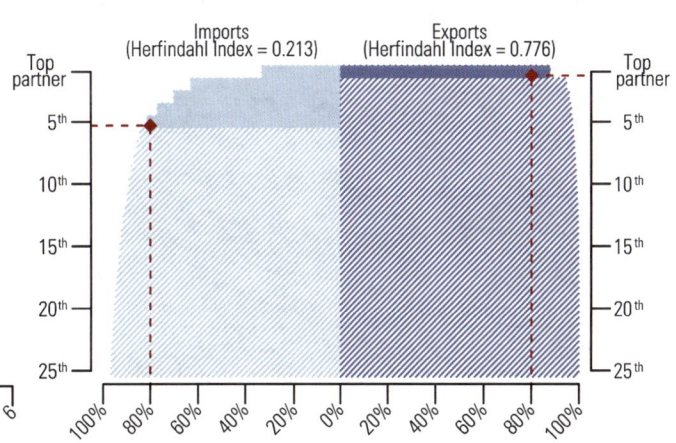

Imports (Herfindahl Index = 0.213)
Exports (Herfindahl Index = 0.776)

Graph 6: Imports of services by EBOPS category
(% share in 2013)

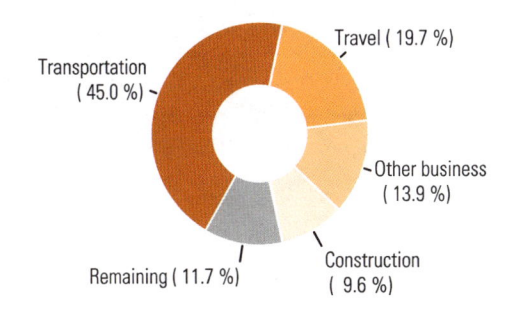

- Transportation (45.0 %)
- Travel (19.7 %)
- Other business (13.9 %)
- Construction (9.6 %)
- Remaining (11.7 %)

Imports Profile:

"Machinery and transport equipment" (SITC section 7), "Mineral fuels, lubricants" (SITC section 3) and "Goods classified chiefly by material" (SITC section 6) were the largest commodity groups for imports in 2014, representing respectively 31.3, 26.4 and 19.5 percent of imported goods (see table 3). From 2012 to 2014, the largest import commodity was "Petroleum oils, other than crude" (HS code 2710) (see table 4). The top three partners for merchandise imports were China, the Russian Federation and the Republic of Korea, accounting for respectively 30.3, 27.0 and 7.5 percent of total imports. "Transportation" (EBOPS code 205) accounted for the largest share of imports of services in 2013 at 911.7 mln US$, followed by "Travel" (EBOPS code 236) at 399.3 mln US$ and "Other business services" (EBOPS code 268) at 280.7 mln US$ (see graph 6).

Table 4: Top 10 import commodities 2012 to 2014

HS code	4-digit heading of Harmonized System 2007	Value 2012	Value 2013	Value 2014	Unit value 2012	Unit value 2013	Unit value 2014	Unit	SITC code
	All Commodities	...	6357.8	5131.5					
2710	Petroleum oils, other than crude	...	1409.8	1154.6		1.2	1.0	US$/kg	334
8703	Motor cars and other motor vehicles principally designed for the transport	...	373.0	289.2		8.3	7.0	thsd US$/unit	781
8704	Motor vehicles for the transport of goods	...	307.0	107.8		17.1	8.6	thsd US$/unit	782
2716	Electrical energy	...	112.8	130.0		94.4	96.4	US$/MWh	351
8474	Machinery for sorting, screening, separating, washing, crushing, grinding	...	117.5	113.7					728
8429	Self-propelled bulldozers, angledozers, graders, levellers, scrapers	...	168.8	51.4		124.3	72.1	thsd US$/unit	723
2523	Portland cement, aluminous cement, slag cement	...	97.8	91.6		0.1	0.1	US$/kg	661
8802	Other aircraft (for example, helicopters, aeroplanes); spacecraft	...	132.0	51.4		14.7	5.1	mln US$/unit	792
7308	Structures (excluding prefabricated buildings of heading 94.06)	...	95.5	82.6		*1.5*	*1.5*	US$/kg	691
7214	Other bars and rods of iron or non-alloy steel	...	90.2	81.7		0.6	0.6	US$/kg	676

Source: UN Comtrade and UN ServiceTrade

Montenegro

Goods Imports: CIF, by origin **Goods Exports:** FOB, by last known destination **Trade System:** Special

Overview:
In 2014, the value of merchandise exports of Montenegro decreased moderately by 9.7 percent to reach 446.5 mln US$, while its merchandise imports increased slightly by 0.5 percent to reach 2.4 bln US$ (see graph 1, table 2 and table 3). The merchandise trade balance recorded a large deficit of 1.9 bln US$ (see graph 1). The largest merchandise trade balance was with MDG Developed Europe at -898.7 mln US$ (see graph 4). Merchandise exports in Montenegro were diversified amongst partners; imports were also diversified. The top 9 partners accounted for 80 percent or more of exports and 12 partners accounted for 80 percent or more of imports (see graph 5). In 2013, the value of exports of services of Montenegro increased moderately by 9.6 percent, reaching 1.4 bln US$, while its imports of services increased substantially by 10.2 percent and reached 545.6 mln US$ (see graph 2). There was a large trade in services surplus of 858.8 mln US$.

Graph 1: Total merchandise trade, by value
(Bln US$ by year)

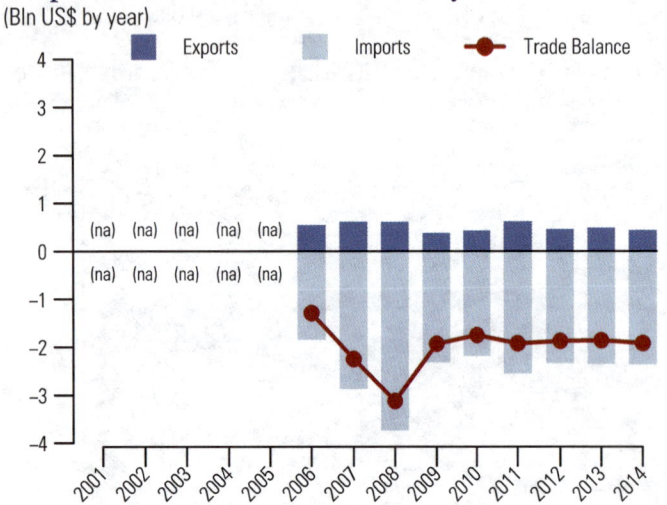

Graph 2: Total services trade, by value
(Bln US$ by year)

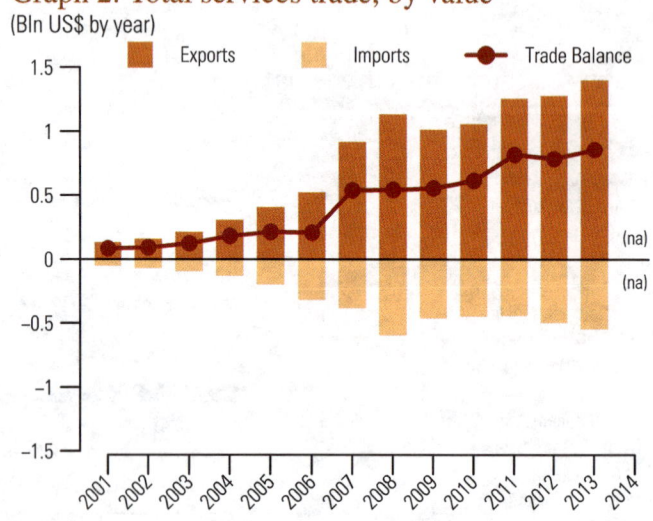

Exports Profile:
"Food, animals + beverages, tobacco" (SITC section 0+1), "Goods classified chiefly by material" (SITC section 6) and "Crude materials + anim. & veg. oils" (SITC section 2+4) were the largest commodity groups for exports in 2014, representing respectively 25.8, 24.4 and 20.6 percent of exported goods (see table 2). From 2012 to 2014, the largest export commodity was "Unwrought aluminium" (HS code 7601) (see table 1). The top three destinations for merchandise exports were Serbia, Croatia and Slovenia, accounting for respectively 27.7, 16.3 and 7.3 percent of total exports. "Travel" (EBOPS code 236) accounted for the largest share of exports of services in 2013 at 883.8 mln US$, followed by "Transportation" (EBOPS code 205) at 228.9 mln US$ and "Other business services" (EBOPS code 268) at 156.3 mln US$ (see graph 3).

Graph 3: Exports of services by EBOPS category
(% share in 2013)

- Travel (62.9 %)
- Transportation (16.3 %)
- Other business (11.1 %)
- Remaining (9.6 %)

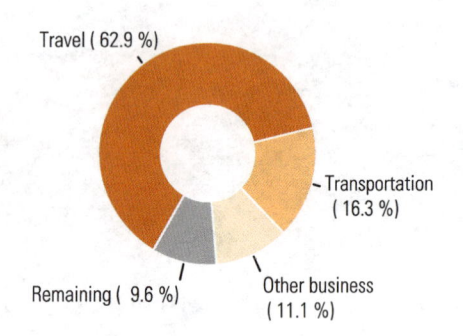

Table 1: Top 10 export commodities 2012 to 2014

HS code	4-digit heading of Harmonized System 2012	Value (million US$) 2012	2013	2014	Unit value 2012	2013	2014	Unit	SITC code
	All Commodities	468.8	494.4	446.5					
7601	Unwrought aluminium	164.6	105.9	94.3	2.2	2.2	2.2	US$/kg	684
2716	Electrical energy	49.2	126.8	49.9	59.6	64.1	74.1	US$/MWh	351
2204	Wine of fresh grapes, including fortified wines	23.2	17.5	18.6	*3.7*	*2.5*	3.0	US$/litre	112
7204	Ferrous waste and scrap; remelting scrap ingots of iron or steel	16.0	19.1	16.9	0.4	0.3	0.3	US$/kg	282
4407	Wood sawn or chipped lengthwise, sliced or peeled	14.1	14.5	18.5		*29.2*		US$/m³	248
0203	Meat of swine, fresh, chilled or frozen	0.4	0.1	43.3	2.7	3.4	3.8	US$/kg	012
2710	Petroleum oils, other than crude	12.2	14.9	15.8	1.1	1.1	1.0	US$/kg	334
8483	Transmission shafts (including cam shafts and crank shafts) and cranks	13.3	12.7	13.5					748
7404	Copper waste and scrap	10.4	9.0	8.3	6.3	5.3	5.2	US$/kg	288
3004	Medicaments (excluding goods of heading 30.02, 30.05 or 30.06)	12.1	8.3	7.3	7.9	7.8	7.5	US$/kg	542

Source: UN Comtrade and UN ServiceTrade

Montenegro

Services Imports and Exports: EBOPS 2002 categories

Table 2: Merchandise exports by SITC
(Value in million US$, growth and shares in percentage)

SITC	2014	Avg. Growth rates 2010-2014	Avg. Growth rates 2013-2014	2014 share
Total	446.5	0.6	-9.7	100.0
0+1	115.3	18.0	62.5	25.8
2+4	92.1	11.0	12.1	20.6
3	67.8	11.4	-52.7	15.2
5	16.8	-0.4	37.3	3.8
6	109.1	-14.9	-19.3	24.4
7	30.2	-4.1	-12.1	6.8
8	14.5	5.3	20.5	3.3
9	0.6	...	-84.3	0.1

Table 3: Merchandise imports by SITC
(Value in million US$, growth and shares in percentage)

SITC	2014	Avg. Growth rates 2010-2014	Avg. Growth rates 2013-2014	2014 share
Total	2 359.7	2.0	0.5	100.0
0+1	609.5	4.5	6.0	25.8
2+4	74.7	-9.1	-10.7	3.2
3	313.5	3.2	-8.5	13.3
5	238.5	2.6	0.3	10.1
6	359.4	0.6	2.6	15.2
7	448.8	0.0	-2.3	19.0
8	315.2	3.8	5.0	13.4
9	0.0	...	-94.9	0.0

SITC Legend

SITC Code	Description
Total	All commodities
0+1	Food, animals + beverages, tobacco
2+4	Crude materials + anim. & veg. oils
3	Mineral fuels, lubricants
5	Chemicals
6	Goods classified chiefly by material
7	Machinery and transport equipment
8	Miscellaneous manufactured articles
9	Not classified elsewhere in the SITC

Graph 4: Merchandise trade balance
(Bln US$ by MDG Regions in 2014)

Graph 5: Partner concentration of merchandise trade
(Cumulative share by ranked partners in 2014)

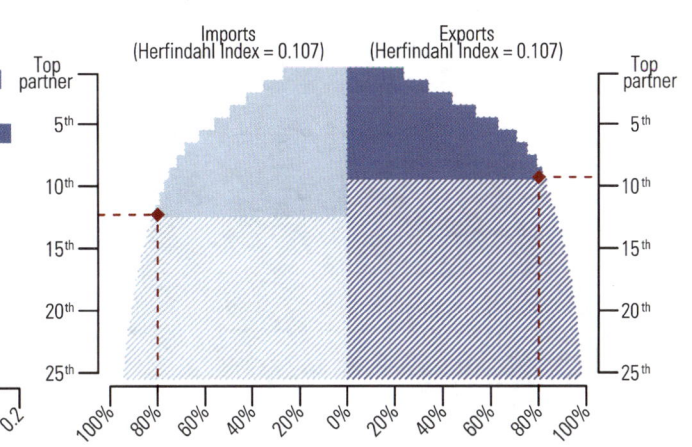

Imports (Herfindahl Index = 0.107)
Exports (Herfindahl Index = 0.107)

Graph 6: Imports of services by EBOPS category
(% share in 2013)

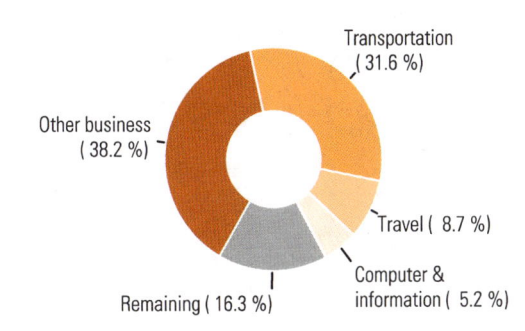

- Transportation (31.6%)
- Other business (38.2%)
- Travel (8.7%)
- Computer & information (5.2%)
- Remaining (16.3%)

Imports Profile:

"Food, animals + beverages, tobacco" (SITC section 0+1), "Machinery and transport equipment" (SITC section 7) and "Goods classified chiefly by material" (SITC section 6) were the largest commodity groups for imports in 2014, representing respectively 25.8, 19.0 and 15.2 percent of imported goods (see table 3). From 2012 to 2014, the largest import commodity was "Petroleum oils, other than crude" (HS code 2710) (see table 4). The top three partners for merchandise imports were Serbia, Greece and China, accounting for respectively 28.3, 8.4 and 7.6 percent of total imports. "Other business services" (EBOPS code 268) accounted for the largest share of imports of services in 2013 at 208.4 mln US$, followed by "Transportation" (EBOPS code 205) at 172.5 mln US$ and "Travel" (EBOPS code 236) at 47.7 mln US$ (see graph 6).

Table 4: Top 10 import commodities 2012 to 2014

HS code	4-digit heading of Harmonized System 2012	Value 2012	Value 2013	Value 2014	Unit value 2012	Unit value 2013	Unit value 2014	Unit	SITC code
	All Commodities	2 336.4	2 348.9	2 359.7					
2710	Petroleum oils, other than crude	248.9	239.6	231.3	1.0	1.0	0.9	US$/kg	334
2716	Electrical energy	136.7	72.3	51.2	58.6	49.7	48.3	US$/MWh	351
8703	Motor cars and other motor vehicles principally designed for the transport	82.1	83.3	83.2	5.0	4.6	4.5	thsd US$/unit	781
0203	Meat of swine, fresh, chilled or frozen	57.3	64.1	100.5	3.0	3.2	3.1	US$/kg	012
3004	Medicaments (excluding goods of heading 30.02, 30.05 or 30.06)	56.3	60.7	59.1	55.2	61.5	68.3	US$/kg	542
2818	Artificial corundum, whether or not chemically defined	52.2	35.8	32.3	0.4	0.4	0.4	US$/kg	522
2202	Waters with added sugar	38.8	37.7	34.6		0.6	0.6	US$/litre	111
9403	Other furniture and parts thereof	31.2	32.7	37.7					821
8517	Electrical apparatus for line telephony or line telegraphy	22.7	32.9	43.2					764
2523	Portland cement, aluminous cement, slag cement	27.9	29.9	30.1	0.1	0.1	0.1	US$/kg	661

Source: UN Comtrade and UN ServiceTrade

Montserrat

Goods Imports: CIF, by origin | **Goods Exports: FOB, by last known destination** | **Trade System: Special**

Overview:

In 2013, the value of merchandise exports of Montserrat increased substantially by 232.9 percent to reach 6.0 mln US$, while its merchandise imports increased substantially by 13.9 percent to reach 42.1 mln US$ (see graph 1, table 2 and table 3). The merchandise trade balance recorded a large deficit of 36.1 mln US$ (see graph 1). The largest merchandise trade balance was with MDG Developed North America at -28.7 mln US$ (see graph 4). Merchandise exports in Montserrat were highly concentrated amongst partners; imports were also highly concentrated. The top 3 partners accounted for 80 percent or more of exports and 3 partners accounted for 80 percent or more of imports (see graph 5). In 2012, the value of exports of services of Montserrat increased substantially by 11.2 percent, reaching 13.3 mln US$, while its imports of services increased slightly by 1.4 percent and reached 18.2 mln US$ (see graph 2). There was a moderate trade in services deficit of 4.9 mln US$.

Graph 1: Total merchandise trade, by value
(Mln US$ by year)

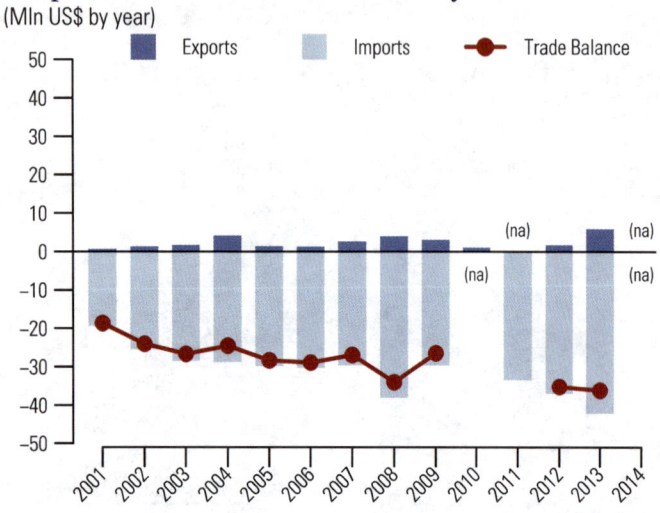

Graph 2: Total services trade, by value
(Mln US$ by year)

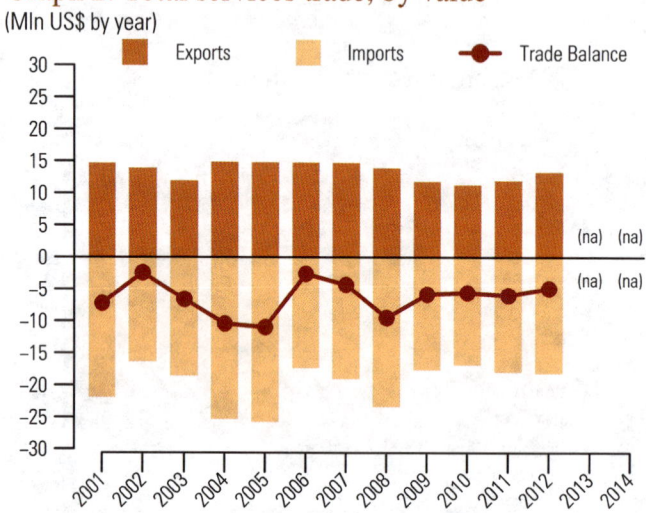

Exports Profile:

"Machinery and transport equipment" (SITC section 7), "Goods classified chiefly by material" (SITC section 6) and "Crude materials + anim. & veg. oils" (SITC section 2+4) were the largest commodity groups for exports in 2013, representing respectively 47.6, 28.4 and 18.8 percent of exported goods (see table 2). From 2012 to 2013, the largest export commodity was "Natural sands of all kinds" (HS code 2505) (see table 1). The top three destinations for merchandise exports were Dominica, the United States and Anguilla, accounting for respectively 41.0, 17.9 and 7.7 percent of total exports. "Travel" (EBOPS code 236) accounted for the largest share of exports of services in 2012 at 7.0 mln US$, followed by "Other business services" (EBOPS code 268) at 4.0 mln US$ and "Transportation" (EBOPS code 205) at 1.9 mln US$ (see graph 3).

Graph 3: Exports of services by EBOPS category
(% share in 2012)

- Travel (52.9 %)
- Other business (30.2 %)
- Transportation (14.1 %)
- Remaining (2.9 %)

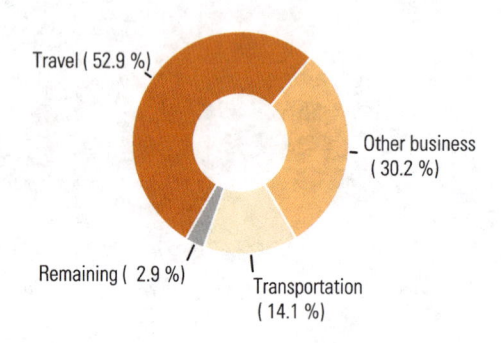

Table 1: Top 10 export commodities 2011 to 2013

HS code	4-digit heading of Harmonized System 2007	Value (million US$) 2011	2012	2013	Unit value 2011	2012	2013	Unit	SITC code
	All Commodities..	...	1.8	6.0					
2505	Natural sands of all kinds...	...	1.1	0.9		0.0	0.0	US$/kg	273
8716	Trailers and semi-trailers...	...	...	1.1					786
8431	Parts suitable for use principally with the machinery of headings 84.25......	...	0.0	0.6		20.9	2.3	US$/kg	723
8307	Flexible tubing of base metal, with or without fittings........................	...	...	0.6			9.6	US$/kg	699
9031	Measuring or checking instruments, appliances and machines......................	...	0.2	0.2					874
8207	Interchangeable tools for hand tools, whether or not power-operated.............	...	0.0	0.4		25.1	9.1	US$/kg	695
7304	Tubes, pipes and hollow profiles, seamless, of iron (other than cast iron).....	...	...	0.4			4.8	US$/kg	679
8414	Air or vacuum pumps, air or other gas compressors and fans......................	...	0.0	0.2					743
8426	Ships' derricks; cranes, including cable cranes; mobile lifting frames.........	...	...	0.2					744
8705	Special purpose motor vehicles..	...	...	0.2					782

Source: UN Comtrade and UN ServiceTrade

Montserrat

Services Imports and Exports: EBOPS 2002 categories

Table 2: Merchandise exports by SITC
(Value in million US$, growth and shares in percentage)

SITC	2013	Avg. Growth rates 2009-2013	Avg. Growth rates 2012-2013	2013 share
Total	6.0	17.3	232.9	100.0
0+1	0.0	18.6	147.7	0.1
2+4	1.1	0.8	-3.7	18.8
3	0.0	...	34.2	0.0
5	0.0	183.1	774.5	0.1
6	1.7	102.9	1842.9	28.4
7	2.8	22.5	1375.0	47.6
8	0.3	-3.4	-2.1	4.6
9	0.0	-50.6	-63.4	0.4

Table 3: Merchandise imports by SITC
(Value in million US$, growth and shares in percentage)

SITC	2013	Avg. Growth rates 2009-2013	Avg. Growth rates 2012-2013	2013 share
Total	42.1	9.2	13.9	100.0
0+1	6.8	3.9	-0.2	16.2
2+4	0.9	11.7	16.9	2.2
3	14.2	15.8	16.7	33.8
5	2.3	6.6	-11.0	5.5
6	5.9	3.1	17.9	14.0
7	8.8	10.2	33.5	21.0
8	2.7	5.1	-5.9	6.3
9	0.4	49.9	409.3	0.9

SITC Legend

SITC Code	Description
Total	All commodities
0+1	Food, animals + beverages, tobacco
2+4	Crude materials + anim. & veg. oils
3	Mineral fuels, lubricants
5	Chemicals
6	Goods classified chiefly by material
7	Machinery and transport equipment
8	Miscellaneous manufactured articles
9	Not classified elsewhere in the SITC

Graph 4: Merchandise trade balance
(Mln US$ by MDG Regions in 2013)

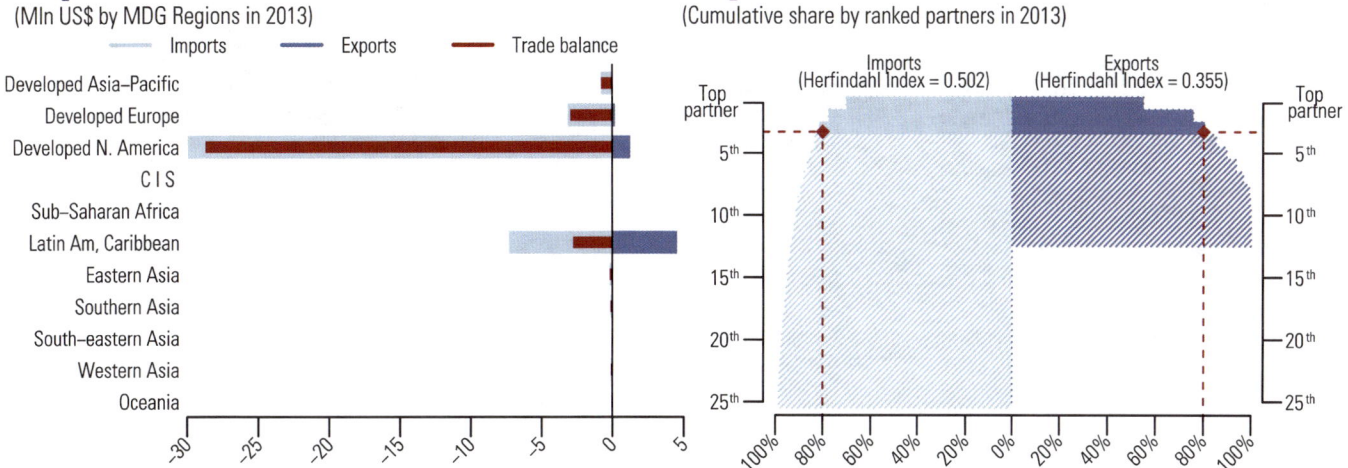

Graph 5: Partner concentration of merchandise trade
(Cumulative share by ranked partners in 2013)

Imports (Herfindahl Index = 0.502)
Exports (Herfindahl Index = 0.355)

Graph 6: Imports of services by EBOPS category
(% share in 2012)

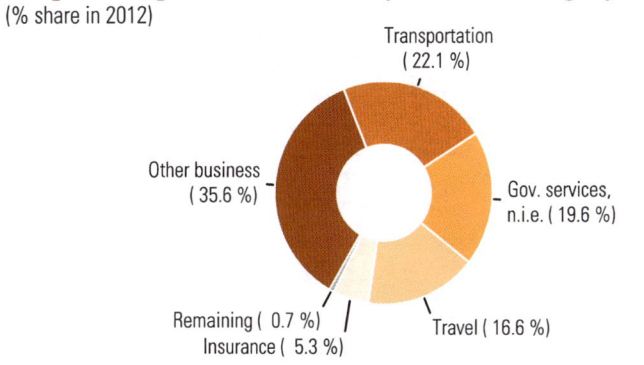

- Transportation (22.1 %)
- Gov. services, n.i.e. (19.6 %)
- Travel (16.6 %)
- Insurance (5.3 %)
- Remaining (0.7 %)
- Other business (35.6 %)

Imports Profile:

"Mineral fuels, lubricants" (SITC section 3), "Machinery and transport equipment" (SITC section 7) and "Food, animals + beverages, tobacco" (SITC section 0+1) were the largest commodity groups for imports in 2013, representing respectively 33.8, 21.0 and 16.2 percent of imported goods (see table 3). From 2011 to 2013, the largest import commodity was "Petroleum oils, other than crude" (HS code 2710) (see table 4). The top three partners for merchandise imports were the United States, Trinidad and Tobago and the United Kingdom, accounting for respectively 71.2, 6.9 and 4.3 percent of total imports. "Other business services" (EBOPS code 268) accounted for the largest share of imports of services in 2012 at 6.5 mln US$, followed by "Transportation" (EBOPS code 205) at 4.0 mln US$ and "Government services, n.i.e." (EBOPS code 291) at 3.6 mln US$ (see graph 6).

Table 4: Top 10 import commodities 2011 to 2013

HS code	4-digit heading of Harmonized System 2007	2011	2012	2013	2011	2012	2013	Unit	SITC code
	All Commodities	33.4	36.9	42.1					
2710	Petroleum oils, other than crude	10.5	11.5	13.5	0.9	0.9	0.8	US$/kg	334
8703	Motor cars and other motor vehicles principally designed for the transport	1.1	1.0	1.2		19.0	18.8	thsd US$/unit	781
2711	Petroleum gases and other gaseous hydrocarbons	1.0	0.7	0.7	0.8	1.0	1.0	US$/kg	343
0207	Meat and edible offal, of the poultry of heading 01.05	0.6	0.7	0.7	3.1	2.3	2.1	US$/kg	012
2202	Waters with added sugar	0.5	0.6	0.5	1.7	1.4	1.2	US$/litre	111
8471	Automatic data processing machines and units thereof	0.4	0.6	0.5					752
2523	Portland cement, aluminous cement, slag cement	0.4	0.5	0.5	0.1	0.1	0.2	US$/kg	661
2203	Beer made from malt	0.5	0.5	0.5	1.3	1.2	1.2	US$/litre	112
2106	Food preparations not elsewhere specified or included	0.3	0.6	0.5	2.7	1.7	2.1	US$/kg	098
7610	Aluminium structures (excluding prefabricated buildings of heading 94.06)	0.4	0.4	0.4	7.5	8.5	8.7	US$/kg	691

Source: UN Comtrade and UN ServiceTrade

Morocco

Goods Imports: CIF, by origin   **Goods Exports: FOB, by last known destination**   **Trade System: Special**

Overview:
In 2013, the value of merchandise exports of Morocco increased slightly by 2.6 percent to reach 22.0 bln US$, while its merchandise imports increased slightly by 0.9 percent to reach 45.2 bln US$ (see graph 1, table 2 and table 3). The merchandise trade balance recorded a large deficit of 23.2 bln US$ (see graph 1). The largest merchandise trade balance was with MDG Developed Europe at -8.9 bln US$ (see graph 4). Merchandise exports in Morocco were diversified amongst partners; imports were also diversified. The top 18 partners accounted for 80 percent or more of exports and 17 partners accounted for 80 percent or more of imports (see graph 5). In 2012, the value of exports of services of Morocco increased moderately by 6.2 percent, reaching 13.8 bln US$, while its imports of services increased slightly by 3.9 percent and reached 8.4 bln US$ (see graph 2). There was a moderate trade in services surplus of 5.5 bln US$.

Graph 1: Total merchandise trade, by value
(Bln US$ by year)

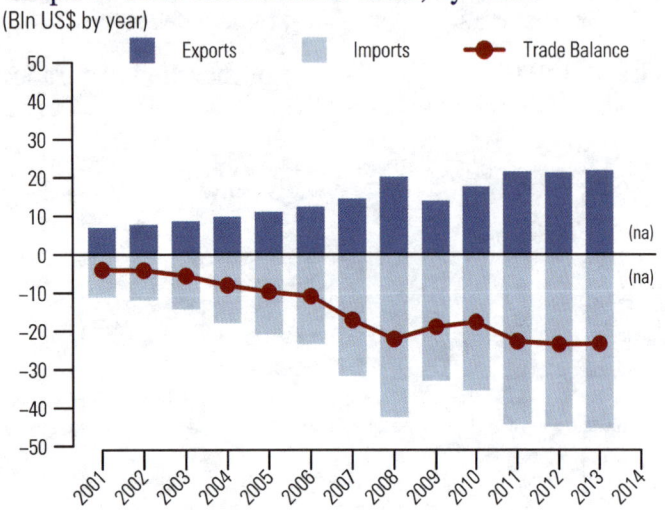

Graph 2: Total services trade, by value
(Bln US$ by year)

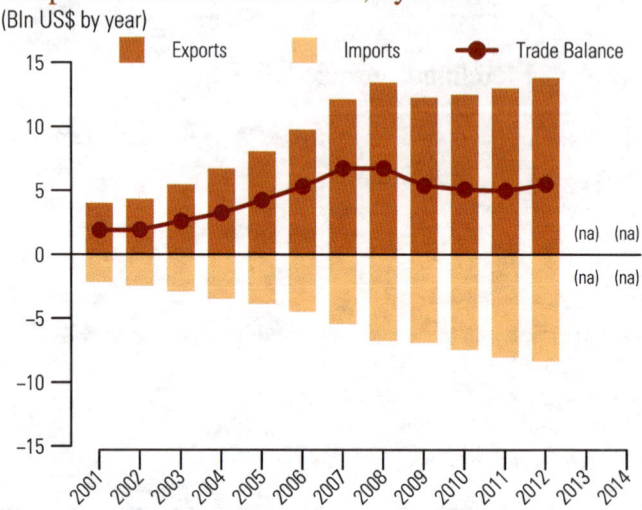

Exports Profile:
"Machinery and transport equipment" (SITC section 7), "Food, animals + beverages, tobacco" (SITC section 0+1) and "Miscellaneous manufactured articles" (SITC section 8) were the largest commodity groups for exports in 2013, representing respectively 25.4, 18.3 and 17.3 percent of exported goods (see table 2). From 2011 to 2013, the largest export commodity was "Insulated (including enamelled or anodised) wire, cable" (HS code 8544) (see table 1). The top three destinations for merchandise exports were France, Spain and Brazil, accounting for respectively 21.4, 17.9 and 5.7 percent of total exports. "Travel" (EBOPS code 236) accounted for the largest share of exports of services in 2012 at 6.9 bln US$, followed by "Other business services" (EBOPS code 268) at 2.9 bln US$ and "Transportation" (EBOPS code 205) at 2.8 bln US$ (see graph 3).

Graph 3: Exports of services by EBOPS category
(% share in 2012)

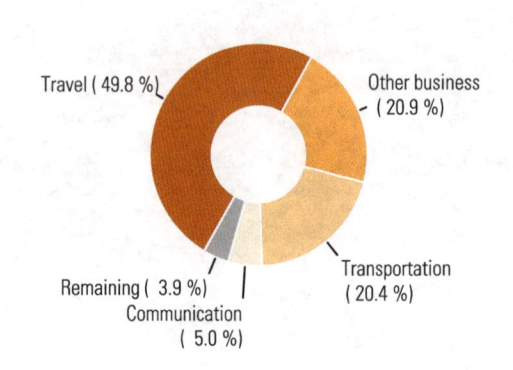

- Travel (49.8 %)
- Other business (20.9 %)
- Transportation (20.4 %)
- Communication (5.0 %)
- Remaining (3.9 %)

Table 1: Top 10 export commodities 2011 to 2013

HS code	4-digit heading of Harmonized System 2002	Value (million US$) 2011	2012	2013	Unit value 2011	2012	2013	Unit	SITC code
	All Commodities	21 649.9	21 417.2	21 965.4					
8544	Insulated (including enamelled or anodised) wire, cable	2 103.2	1 761.4	2 084.8	*20.9*	*17.8*	*19.4*	US$/kg	773
3105	Mineral or chemical fertilisers	1 924.4	2 036.5	1 504.0	0.6	0.6	0.5	US$/kg	562
2809	Diphosphorus pentaoxide; phosphoric acid	2 117.4	1 649.8	1 433.5	1.0	0.9	0.7	US$/kg	522
2510	Natural calcium phosphates	1 560.1	1 543.5	1 082.0	0.2	0.2	0.1	US$/kg	272
6204	Women's or girls' suits, ensembles, jackets, blazers, dresses, skirts	991.5	987.3	1 046.5					842
8703	Motor cars and other motor vehicles principally designed for the transport	264.7	836.6	1 500.9		*15.7*	*14.8*	thsd US$/unit	781
2710	Petroleum oils, other than crude	547.4	792.3	1 068.0	*1.0*	1.0	0.9	US$/kg	334
1604	Prepared or preserved fish; caviar	518.8	643.7	679.4	4.6	4.6	4.7	US$/kg	037
8541	Diodes, transistors and similar semiconductor devices	607.7	517.6	496.8					776
0307	Molluscs, whether in shell or not	476.7	491.0	537.5	7.5	6.5	5.0	US$/kg	036

Source: UN Comtrade and UN ServiceTrade   2014 International Trade Statistics Yearbook, Vol. I

Morocco

Services Imports and Exports: EBOPS 2002 categories

Table 2: Merchandise exports by SITC
(Value in million US$, growth and shares in percentage)

SITC	2013	Avg. Growth rates 2009-2013	Avg. Growth rates 2012-2013	2013 share
Total	21 965.4	11.8	2.6	100.0
0+1	4 023.6	6.2	12.8	18.3
2+4	2 079.6	14.6	-20.2	9.5
3	1 585.4	33.2	28.4	7.2
5	3 665.1	17.0	-15.8	16.7
6	1 218.6	7.4	-9.7	5.5
7	5 571.1	21.2	26.1	25.4
8	3 793.8	0.6	-1.2	17.3
9	28.2	-9.1	-44.3	0.1

Table 3: Merchandise imports by SITC
(Value in million US$, growth and shares in percentage)

SITC	2013	Avg. Growth rates 2009-2013	Avg. Growth rates 2012-2013	2013 share
Total	45 186.4	8.3	0.9	100.0
0+1	4 251.5	8.8	-12.5	9.4
2+4	2 153.5	5.7	-20.8	4.8
3	12 143.5	15.8	-1.7	26.9
5	4 516.2	9.7	6.6	10.0
6	7 969.0	7.2	6.4	17.6
7	11 853.9	4.0	9.1	26.2
8	2 252.3	3.3	0.4	5.0
9	46.6	-22.8	138.6	0.1

SITC Legend

SITC Code	Description
Total	All commodities
0+1	Food, animals + beverages, tobacco
2+4	Crude materials + anim. & veg. oils
3	Mineral fuels, lubricants
5	Chemicals
6	Goods classified chiefly by material
7	Machinery and transport equipment
8	Miscellaneous manufactured articles
9	Not classified elsewhere in the SITC

Graph 4: Merchandise trade balance
(Bln US$ by MDG Regions in 2013)

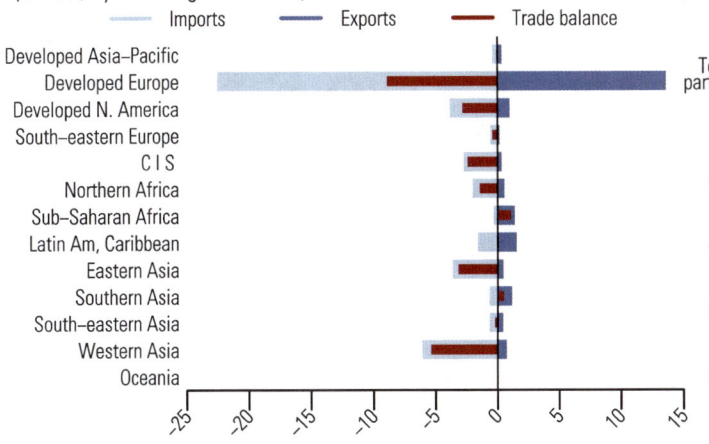

Graph 5: Partner concentration of merchandise trade
(Cumulative share by ranked partners in 2013)

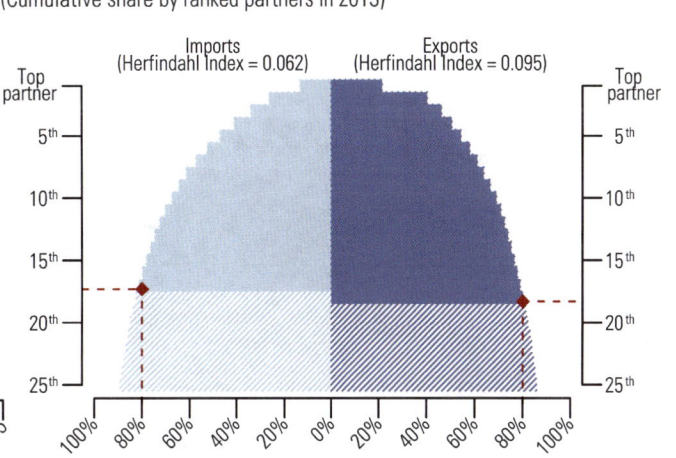

Graph 6: Imports of services by EBOPS category
(% share in 2012)

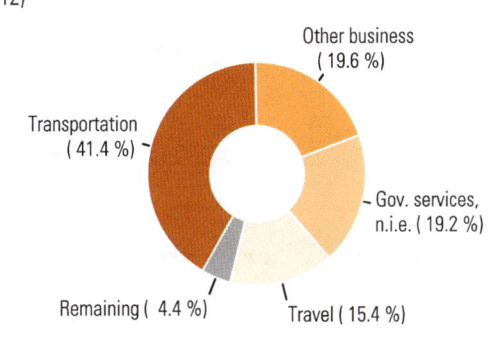

- Transportation (41.4 %)
- Other business (19.6 %)
- Gov. services, n.i.e. (19.2 %)
- Travel (15.4 %)
- Remaining (4.4 %)

Imports Profile:

"Mineral fuels, lubricants" (SITC section 3), "Machinery and transport equipment" (SITC section 7) and "Goods classified chiefly by material" (SITC section 6) were the largest commodity groups for imports in 2013, representing respectively 26.9, 26.2 and 17.6 percent of imported goods (see table 3). From 2011 to 2013, the largest import commodity was "Petroleum oils, other than crude" (HS code 2710) (see table 4). The top three partners for merchandise imports were France, Spain and the United States, accounting for respectively 13.2, 12.6 and 7.3 percent of total imports. "Transportation" (EBOPS code 205) accounted for the largest share of imports of services in 2012 at 3.5 bln US$, followed by "Other business services" (EBOPS code 268) at 1.6 bln US$ and "Government services, n.i.e." (EBOPS code 291) at 1.6 bln US$ (see graph 6).

Table 4: Top 10 import commodities 2011 to 2013

HS code	4-digit heading of Harmonized System 2002	2011	2012	2013	2011	2012	2013	Unit	SITC code
	All Commodities	44 262.9	44 789.8	45 186.4					
2710	Petroleum oils, other than crude	4 197.1	4 607.9	4 533.4	0.8	0.9	0.9	US$/kg	334
2709	Petroleum oils, crude	3 888.0	4 352.0	4 320.7	0.8	0.8	0.7	US$/kg	333
2711	Petroleum gases and other gaseous hydrocarbons	1 995.4	2 338.8	2 274.8	0.8	0.8	0.7	US$/kg	343
8703	Motor cars and other motor vehicles principally designed for the transport	1 375.4	1 609.0	1 502.5		18.2	18.4	thsd US$/unit	781
1001	Wheat and meslin	1 440.1	1 399.8	977.9	0.4	0.3	0.4	US$/kg	041
2503	Sulphur of all kinds	821.8	827.4	522.4	0.2	0.2	0.1	US$/kg	274
8544	Insulated (including enamelled or anodised) wire, cable	744.0	609.6	788.6	15.5	14.7	16.7	US$/kg	773
8708	Parts and accessories of the motor vehicles of headings 87.01 to 87.05	628.2	604.9	600.4	6.9	6.7	7.8	US$/kg	784
1005	Maize (corn)	591.4	636.2	484.2	0.3	0.3	0.3	US$/kg	044
1701	Cane or beet sugar and pure sucrose, in solid form	596.4	591.7	441.6	0.7	0.6	0.5	US$/kg	061

2014 International Trade Statistics Yearbook, Vol. I — Source: UN Comtrade and UN ServiceTrade

Mozambique

Goods Imports: CIF, by origin **Goods Exports:** FOB, by last known destination **Trade System:** General

Overview:
In 2014, the value of merchandise exports of Mozambique increased substantially by 17.4 percent to reach 4.7 bln US$, while its merchandise imports decreased substantially by 13.4 percent to reach 8.7 bln US$ (see graph 1, table 2 and table 3). The merchandise trade balance recorded a moderate deficit of 4.0 bln US$ (see graph 1). The largest merchandise trade balance was with MDG Sub-Saharan Africa at -1.9 bln US$ (see graph 4). Merchandise exports in Mozambique were diversified amongst partners; imports were also diversified. The top 11 partners accounted for 80 percent or more of exports and 12 partners accounted for 80 percent or more of imports (see graph 5). In 2012, the value of exports of services of Mozambique increased substantially by 50.9 percent, reaching 1.1 bln US$, while its imports of services increased substantially by 92.7 percent and reached 4.2 bln US$ (see graph 2). There was a large trade in services deficit of 3.1 bln US$.

Graph 1: Total merchandise trade, by value
(Bln US$ by year)

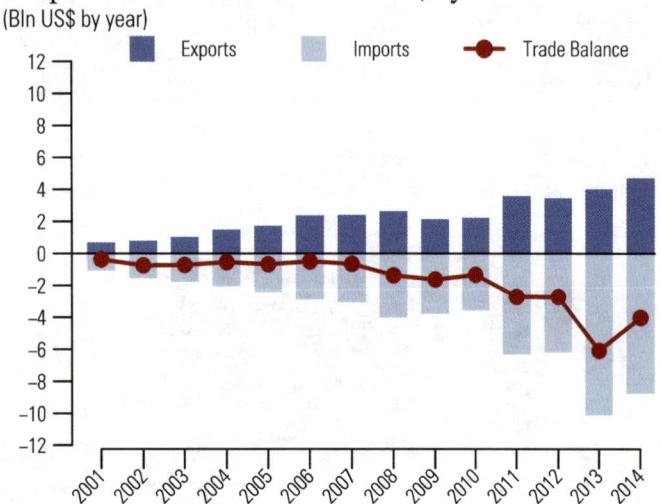

Graph 2: Total services trade, by value
(Bln US$ by year)

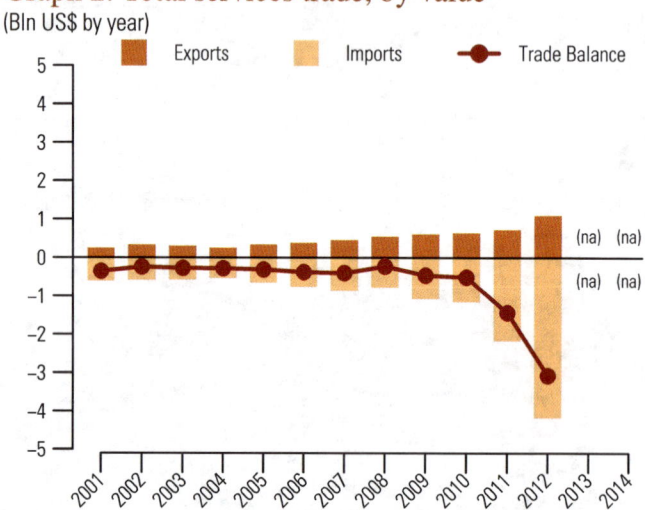

Exports Profile:
"Goods classified chiefly by material" (SITC section 6), "Mineral fuels, lubricants" (SITC section 3) and "Food, animals + beverages, tobacco" (SITC section 0+1) were the largest commodity groups for exports in 2014, representing respectively 32.9, 30.0 and 13.1 percent of exported goods (see table 2). From 2012 to 2014, the largest export commodity was "Aluminium bars, rods and profiles" (HS code 7604) (see table 1). The top three destinations for merchandise exports were the Netherlands, South Africa and India, accounting for respectively 26.1, 20.6 and 10.0 percent of total exports. "Other business services" (EBOPS code 268) accounted for the largest share of exports of services in 2012 at 305.3 mln US$, followed by "Travel" (EBOPS code 236) at 249.9 mln US$ and "Transportation" (EBOPS code 205) at 161.8 mln US$ (see graph 3).

Graph 3: Exports of services by EBOPS category
(% share in 2012)

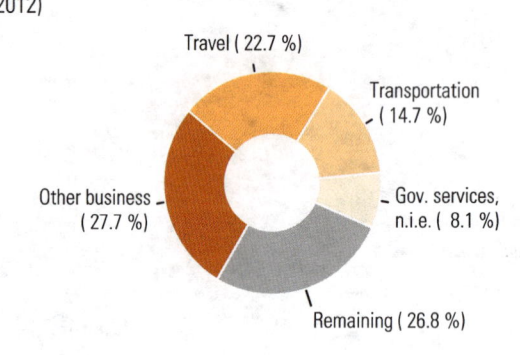

- Travel (22.7 %)
- Transportation (14.7 %)
- Gov. services, n.i.e. (8.1 %)
- Remaining (26.8 %)
- Other business (27.7 %)

Table 1: Top 10 export commodities 2012 to 2014

HS code	4-digit heading of Harmonized System 2007	Value (million US$) 2012	2013	2014	Unit value 2012	2013	2014	Unit	SITC code
	All Commodities	3 469.9	4 023.7	4 725.3					
7604	Aluminium bars, rods and profiles	1 088.6	1 063.2	1 045.7	8.6	13.3		US$/kg	684
2704	Coke and semi-coke of coal, of lignite or of peat	435.2	526.6	484.1	0.2	0.3	0.2	US$/kg	325
2711	Petroleum gases and other gaseous hydrocarbons	248.2	445.4	568.7	0.5	0.0	0.1	US$/kg	343
2716	Electrical energy	233.4	275.5	301.2	24.4	27.7	36.8	US$/MWh	351
2401	Unmanufactured tobacco; tobacco refuse	227.9	257.3	258.0	4.1	4.4	4.4	US$/kg	121
3802	Activated carbon; activated natural mineral products	111.1	52.5	442.4	0.3	0.1	0.1	US$/kg	598
2614	Titanium ores and concentrates	211.5	126.6	134.3	0.2	0.1	0.0	US$/kg	287
1701	Cane or beet sugar and chemically pure sucrose, in solid form	146.1	185.7	81.7	0.6	0.6	0.6	US$/kg	061
7601	Unwrought aluminium	...	...	366.6			1.8	US$/kg	684
2710	Petroleum oils, other than crude	47.5	97.3	64.0	0.9	1.5	0.3	US$/kg	334

Source: UN Comtrade and UN ServiceTrade

Mozambique

Services Imports and Exports: EBOPS 2002 categories

Table 2: Merchandise exports by SITC
(Value in million US$, growth and shares in percentage)

SITC	2014	Avg. Growth rates 2010-2014	Avg. Growth rates 2013-2014	2014 share
Total	4725.3	20.5	17.4	100.0
0+1	620.8	18.7	3.1	13.1
2+4	495.9	31.9	22.9	10.5
3	1419.4	33.5	5.4	30.0
5	477.5	316.0	612.0	10.1
6	1556.0	7.3	37.7	32.9
7	104.3	28.3	-72.9	2.2
8	51.3	25.7	-41.6	1.1
9	0.1	-82.2	-92.6	0.0

Table 3: Merchandise imports by SITC
(Value in million US$, growth and shares in percentage)

SITC	2014	Avg. Growth rates 2010-2014	Avg. Growth rates 2013-2014	2014 share
Total	8743.1	25.1	-13.4	100.0
0+1	936.4	29.2	5.0	10.7
2+4	305.0	24.7	-1.7	3.5
3	1702.4	24.4	-42.6	19.5
5	718.0	31.4	16.9	8.2
6	1788.9	41.3	16.5	20.5
7	2809.7	31.9	19.4	32.1
8	482.5	32.3	-66.2	5.5
9	0.0	-91.7	-69.8	0.0

SITC Legend

SITC Code	Description
Total	All commodities
0+1	Food, animals + beverages, tobacco
2+4	Crude materials + anim. & veg. oils
3	Mineral fuels, lubricants
5	Chemicals
6	Goods classified chiefly by material
7	Machinery and transport equipment
8	Miscellaneous manufactured articles
9	Not classified elsewhere in the SITC

Graph 4: Merchandise trade balance
(Bln US$ by MDG Regions in 2014)

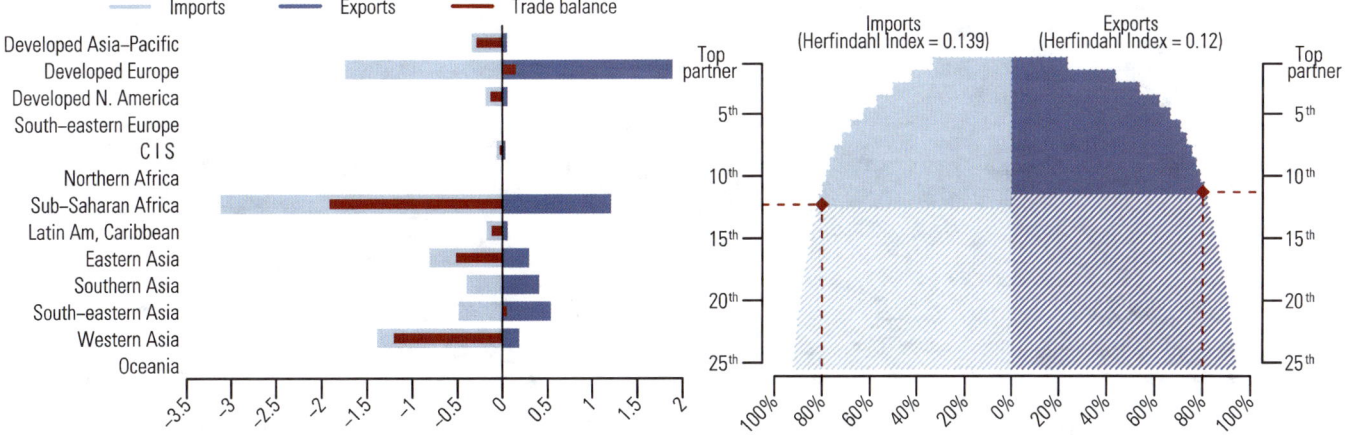

Graph 5: Partner concentration of merchandise trade
(Cumulative share by ranked partners in 2014)
Imports (Herfindahl Index = 0.139); Exports (Herfindahl Index = 0.12)

Graph 6: Imports of services by EBOPS category
(% share in 2012)

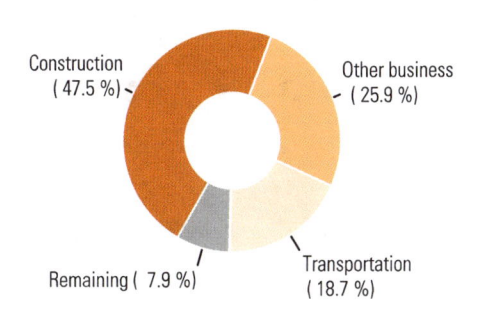

- Construction (47.5%)
- Other business (25.9%)
- Transportation (18.7%)
- Remaining (7.9%)

Imports Profile:
"Machinery and transport equipment" (SITC section 7), "Goods classified chiefly by material" (SITC section 6) and "Mineral fuels, lubricants" (SITC section 3) were the largest commodity groups for imports in 2014, representing respectively 32.1, 20.5 and 19.5 percent of imported goods (see table 3). From 2012 to 2014, the largest import commodity was "Petroleum oils, other than crude" (HS code 2710) (see table 4). The top three partners for merchandise imports were South Africa, the United Arab Emirates and Bahrain, accounting for respectively 32.5, 7.2 and 7.0 percent of total imports. "Construction services" (EBOPS code 249) accounted for the largest share of imports of services in 2012 at 2.0 bln US$, followed by "Other business services" (EBOPS code 268) at 1.1 bln US$ and "Transportation" (EBOPS code 205) at 781.8 mln US$ (see graph 6).

Table 4: Top 10 import commodities 2012 to 2014

HS code	4-digit heading of Harmonized System 2007	Value 2012	Value 2013	Value 2014	Unit value 2012	Unit value 2013	Unit value 2014	Unit	SITC code
	All Commodities	6177.2	10099.1	8743.1					
2710	Petroleum oils, other than crude	1135.1	2063.1	1350.2	0.1	1.1	1.0	US$/kg	334
7601	Unwrought aluminium	295.3	488.2	529.0	6.3	5.5	0.2	thsd US$/kg	684
9027	Instruments and apparatus for physical or chemical analysis	2.1	973.5	6.2					874
8704	Motor vehicles for the transport of goods	241.3	331.7	348.3	517.9	304.9	519.7	US$/unit	782
2716	Electrical energy	306.3	292.4	269.7	60.0	37.8		US$/MWh	351
2711	Petroleum gases and other gaseous hydrocarbons	19.2	570.3	39.4	2.0	11.9	2.0	US$/kg	343
1006	Rice	94.5	248.7	187.4	0.3	0.0	0.1	US$/kg	042
8703	Motor cars and other motor vehicles principally designed for the transport	86.1	178.0	184.9	548.0	319.1	323.7	US$/unit	781
8429	Self-propelled bulldozers, angledozers, graders, levellers, scrapers	99.5	137.5	162.3	416.7	99.6	18.7	US$/unit	723
8517	Electrical apparatus for line telephony or line telegraphy	45.7	166.3	179.3					764

Myanmar

Goods Imports: CIF, by origin | **Goods Exports:** FOB, by last known destination | **Trade System:** General

Overview:
In 2010, the value of merchandise exports of Myanmar was 7.6 bln US$, while its merchandise imports were 4.2 bln US$ (see graph 1, table 2 and table 3). The merchandise trade balance recorded a moderate surplus of 3.5 bln US$ (see graph 1). The largest merchandise trade balance was with MDG South-eastern Asia at 1.7 bln US$ (see graph 4). Merchandise exports in Myanmar were moderately concentrated amongst partners; imports were also moderately concentrated. The top 4 partners accounted for 80 percent or more of exports and 6 partners accounted for 80 percent or more of imports (see graph 5). In 2011, the value of exports of services of Myanmar increased substantially by 68.6 percent, reaching 612.0 mln US$, while its imports of services increased substantially by 38.2 percent and reached 1.1 bln US$ (see graph 2). There was a moderate trade in services deficit of 478.2 mln US$.

Graph 1: Total merchandise trade, by value
(Bln US$ by year)

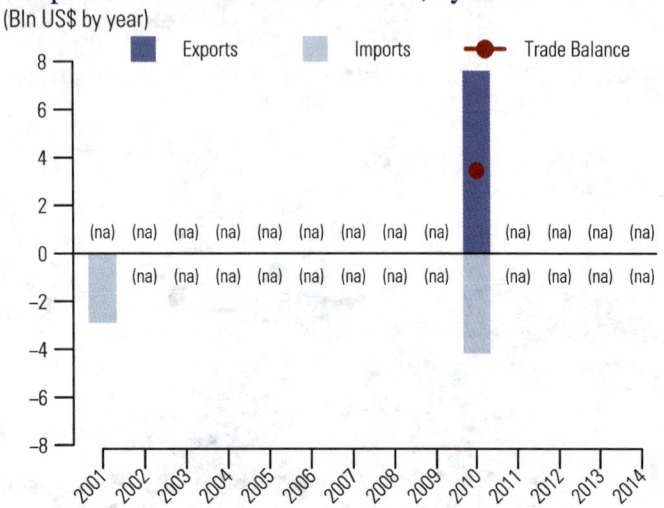

Graph 2: Total services trade, by value
(Bln US$ by year)

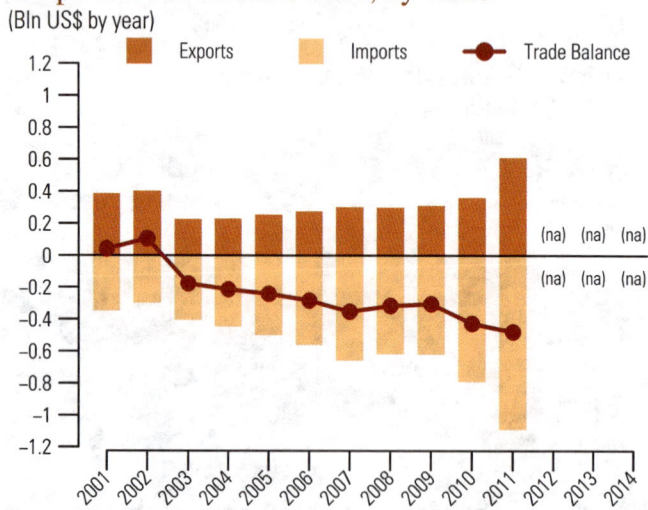

Exports Profile:
"Mineral fuels, lubricants" (SITC section 3), "Goods classified chiefly by material" (SITC section 6) and "Food, animals + beverages, tobacco" (SITC section 0+1) were the largest commodity groups for exports in 2010, representing respectively 38.5, 25.3 and 18.7 percent of exported goods (see table 2). In 2010, the largest export commodity was "Petroleum gases and other gaseous hydrocarbons" (HS code 2711) (see table 1). The top three destinations for merchandise exports were Thailand, China, Hong Kong SAR and India, accounting for respectively 41.7, 21.1 and 12.6 percent of total exports. "Travel" (EBOPS code 236) accounted for the largest share of exports of services in 2011 at 280.6 mln US$, followed by "Transportation" (EBOPS code 205) at 173.8 mln US$ and "Other business services" (EBOPS code 268) at 111.1 mln US$ (see graph 3).

Graph 3: Exports of services by EBOPS category
(% share in 2011)

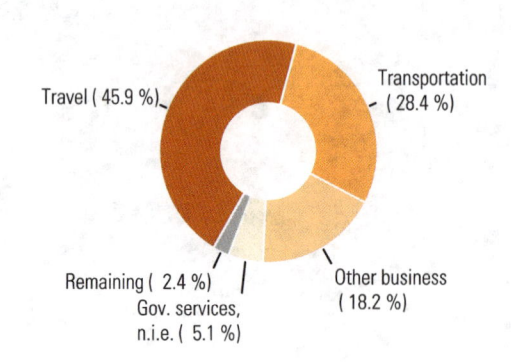

- Travel (45.9 %)
- Transportation (28.4 %)
- Other business (18.2 %)
- Gov. services, n.i.e. (5.1 %)
- Remaining (2.4 %)

Table 1: Top 10 export commodities 2008 to 2010

HS code	4-digit heading of Harmonized System 2007	Value (million US$) 2008	2009	2010	Unit value 2008	2009	2010	Unit	SITC code
	All Commodities	...	...	7 625.2					
2711	Petroleum gases and other gaseous hydrocarbons	...	...	2 936.0			0.5	US$/kg	343
7103	Precious stones (other than diamonds) and semi-precious stones	...	...	1 864.0					667
0713	Dried leguminous vegetables, shelled, whether or not skinned or split	...	...	889.9			1.0	US$/kg	054
4403	Wood in the rough, whether or not stripped of bark or sapwood	...	...	553.9			544.4	US$/m³	247
0302	Fish, fresh or chilled, excluding fish fillets	...	...	204.5			1.3	US$/kg	034
4001	Natural rubber, balata, gutta-percha, guayule, chicle	...	...	194.9			2.8	US$/kg	231
1006	Rice	...	...	156.3			0.3	US$/kg	042
6203	Men's or boys' suits, ensembles, jackets, blazers, trousers	...	...	85.2			7.1	US$/unit	841
0306	Crustaceans, whether in shell or not	...	...	79.7			3.5	US$/kg	036
6205	Men's or boys' shirts	...	...	70.5			4.1	US$/unit	841

Source: UN Comtrade and UN ServiceTrade

Myanmar

Services Imports and Exports: EBOPS 2002 categories

Table 2: Merchandise exports by SITC
(Value in million US$, growth and shares in percentage)

SITC	2010	Avg. Growth rates 2006-2010	Avg. Growth rates 2009-2010	2010 share
Total	7625.2	...	...	100.0
0+1	1427.3	...	...	18.7
2+4	894.4	...	...	11.7
3	2936.0	...	...	38.5
5	1.8	...	...	0.0
6	1930.0	...	...	25.3
7	4.0	...	...	0.1
8	406.5	...	...	5.3
9	25.2	...	...	0.3

Table 3: Merchandise imports by SITC
(Value in million US$, growth and shares in percentage)

SITC	2010	Avg. Growth rates 2006-2010	Avg. Growth rates 2009-2010	2010 share
Total	4164.3	...	...	100.0
0+1	174.4	...	...	4.2
2+4	207.0	...	...	5.0
3	934.2	...	...	22.4
5	476.4	...	...	11.4
6	1122.0	...	...	26.9
7	1142.8	...	...	27.4
8	107.7	...	...	2.6

SITC Legend

SITC Code	Description
Total	All commodities
0+1	Food, animals + beverages, tobacco
2+4	Crude materials + anim. & veg. oils
3	Mineral fuels, lubricants
5	Chemicals
6	Goods classified chiefly by material
7	Machinery and transport equipment
8	Miscellaneous manufactured articles
9	Not classified elsewhere in the SITC

Graph 4: Merchandise trade balance
(Bln US$ by MDG Regions in 2010)

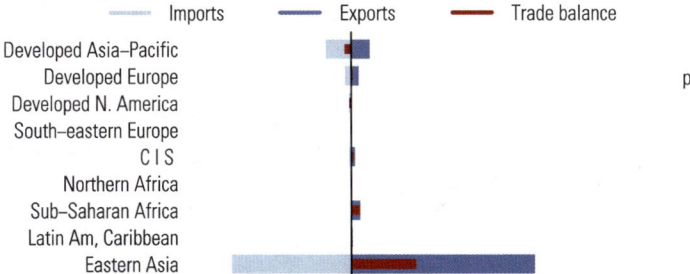

Graph 5: Partner concentration of merchandise trade
(Cumulative share by ranked partners in 2010)

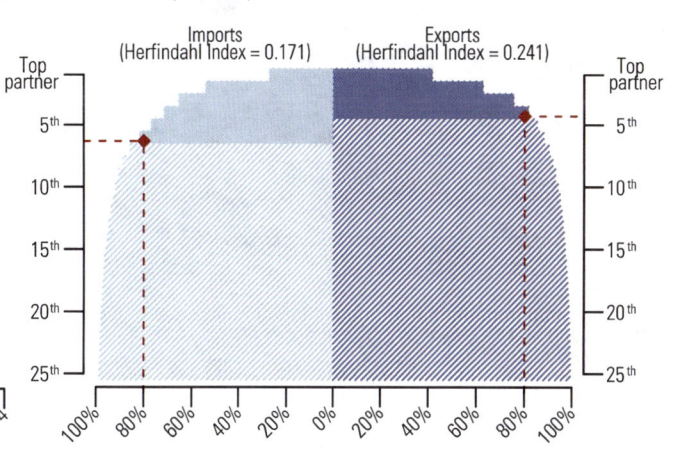

Imports (Herfindahl Index = 0.171)
Exports (Herfindahl Index = 0.241)

Graph 6: Imports of services by EBOPS category
(% share in 2011)

- Transportation (68.9 %)
- Other business (17.6 %)
- Travel (11.3 %)
- Remaining (2.2 %)

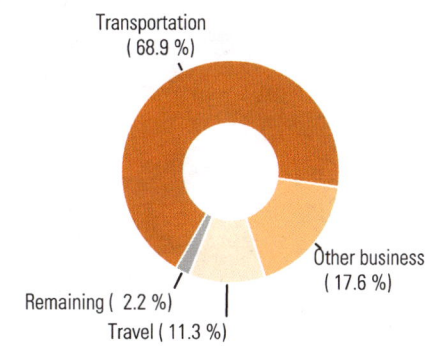

Imports Profile:

"Machinery and transport equipment" (SITC section 7), "Goods classified chiefly by material" (SITC section 6) and "Mineral fuels, lubricants" (SITC section 3) were the largest commodity groups for imports in 2010, representing respectively 27.4, 26.9 and 22.4 percent of imported goods (see table 3). In 2010, the largest import commodity was "Petroleum oils, other than crude" (HS code 2710) (see table 4). The top three partners for merchandise imports were China, Singapore and Thailand, accounting for respectively 27.1, 27.0 and 11.4 percent of total imports. "Transportation" (EBOPS code 205) accounted for the largest share of imports of services in 2011 at 750.7 mln US$, followed by "Other business services" (EBOPS code 268) at 192.4 mln US$ and "Travel" (EBOPS code 236) at 123.4 mln US$ (see graph 6).

Table 4: Top 10 import commodities 2008 to 2010

HS code	4-digit heading of Harmonized System 2007	Value 2008	Value 2009	Value 2010	Unit value 2008	Unit value 2009	Unit value 2010	Unit	SITC code
	All Commodities	...	...	4164.3					
2710	Petroleum oils, other than crude	...	...	913.6			0.7	US$/kg	334
8429	Self-propelled bulldozers, angledozers, graders, levellers, scrapers	...	...	196.8			3.2	thsd US$/unit	723
8905	Light-vessels, fire-floats, dredgers, floating cranes and other vessels	...	...	168.9			337.7	thsd US$/unit	793
1511	Palm oil and its fractions	...	...	167.7			0.8	US$/kg	422
3004	Medicaments (excluding goods of heading 30.02, 30.05 or 30.06)	...	...	160.1			6.3	US$/kg	542
5514	Woven fabrics of synthetic staple fibres	...	...	129.3			4.8	US$/kg	653
3902	Polymers of propylene or of other olefins, in primary forms	...	...	106.4			1.2	US$/kg	575
7304	Tubes, pipes and hollow profiles, seamless, of iron (other than cast iron)	...	...	95.8			1.1	US$/kg	679
2523	Portland cement, aluminous cement, slag cement	...	...	91.4			0.1	US$/kg	661
7308	Structures (excluding prefabricated buildings of heading 94.06)	...	...	74.1			2.1	US$/kg	691

2014 International Trade Statistics Yearbook, Vol. I   Source: UN Comtrade and UN ServiceTrade

Namibia

Goods Imports: CIF, by origin **Goods Exports:** FOB, by last known destination **Trade System:** General

Overview:
In 2013, the value of merchandise exports of Namibia increased substantially by 17.9 percent to reach 6.3 bln US$, while its merchandise imports increased moderately by 6.2 percent to reach 7.6 bln US$ (see graph 1, table 2 and table 3). The merchandise trade balance recorded a relatively small deficit of 1.2 bln US$ (see graph 1). The largest merchandise trade balance was with MDG Sub-Saharan Africa at -1.7 bln US$ (see graph 4). Merchandise exports in Namibia were diversified amongst partners; imports were highly concentrated. The top 12 partners accounted for 80 percent or more of exports and 6 partners accounted for 80 percent or more of imports (see graph 5). In 2013, the value of exports of services of Namibia decreased substantially by 15.8 percent, reaching 570.3 mln US$, while its imports of services increased substantially by 15.4 percent and reached 804.8 mln US$ (see graph 2). There was a moderate trade in services deficit of 234.5 mln US$.

Graph 1: Total merchandise trade, by value
(Bln US$ by year)

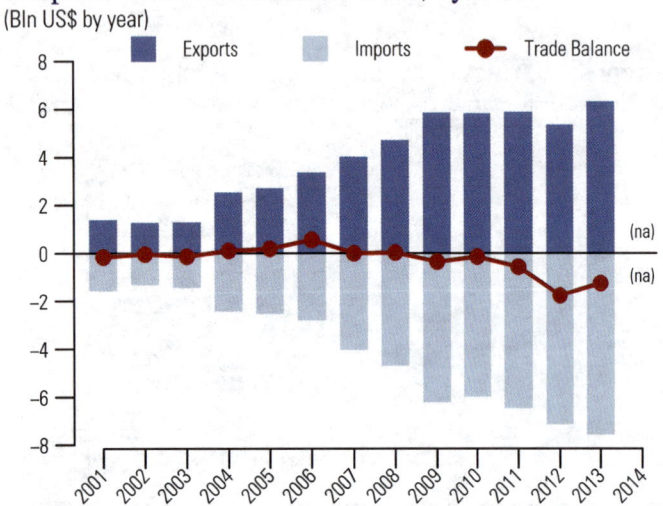

Graph 2: Total services trade, by value
(Mln US$ by year)

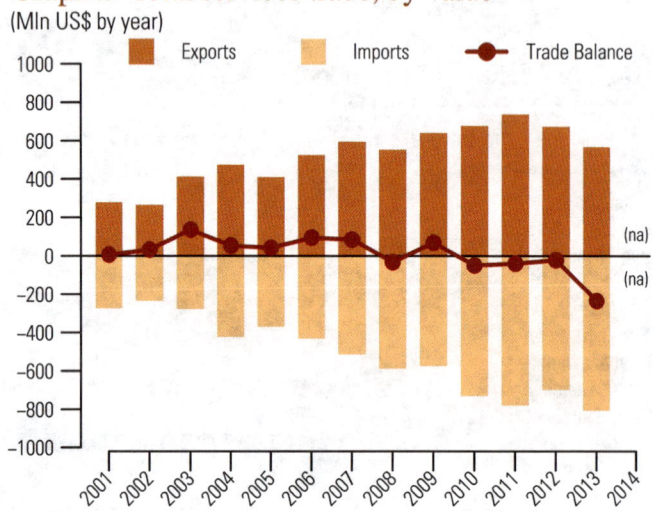

Exports Profile:
"Goods classified chiefly by material" (SITC section 6), "Machinery and transport equipment" (SITC section 7) and "Food, animals + beverages, tobacco" (SITC section 0+1) were the largest commodity groups for exports in 2013, representing respectively 30.9, 24.0 and 21.3 percent of exported goods (see table 2). From 2011 to 2013, the largest export commodity was "Diamonds, whether or not worked, but not mounted or set" (HS code 7102) (see table 1). The top three destinations for merchandise exports were South Africa, the United Kingdom and Angola, accounting for respectively 24.7, 9.2 and 8.3 percent of total exports. "Travel" (EBOPS code 236) accounted for the largest share of exports of services in 2013 at 409.8 mln US$, followed by "Transportation" (EBOPS code 205) at 112.3 mln US$ (see graph 3).

Graph 3: Exports of services by EBOPS category
(% share in 2013)

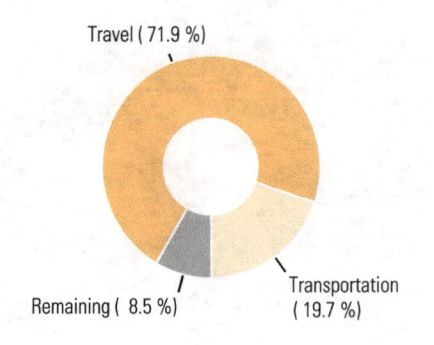

Travel (71.9 %)
Transportation (19.7 %)
Remaining (8.5 %)

Table 1: Top 10 export commodities 2011 to 2013

HS code	4-digit heading of Harmonized System 2007	Value (million US$) 2011	2012	2013	Unit value 2011	2012	2013	Unit	SITC code
	All Commodities....................	5 900.9	5 377.0	6 337.2					
7102	Diamonds, whether or not worked, but not mounted or set...............	1 300.2	1 344.2	1 338.6	102.3			US$/carat	667
2612	Uranium or thorium ores and concentrates..................	616.0	613.0	639.1	125.0	100.9	88.1	US$/kg	286
0303	Fish, frozen, excluding fish fillets and other fish meat of heading 03.04............	396.1	444.0	498.5	1.6	1.7	1.6	US$/kg	034
7901	Unwrought zinc..................	327.4	272.0	274.1	2.2	2.0	2.2	US$/kg	686
0304	Fish fillets and other fish meat (whether or not minced).............	255.8	197.4	168.4	4.5	4.2	4.0	US$/kg	034
8905	Light-vessels, fire-floats, dredgers, floating cranes and other vessels..........	0.0	7.9	612.3		17.1		thsd US$/unit	793
4907	Unused postage, revenue or similar stamps of current or new issue............	570.8	0.1	...	31.4	2.5		thsd US$/kg	892
2203	Beer made from malt................	172.0	159.1	148.9	1.1	1.3	1.0	US$/litre	112
7402	Unrefined copper; copper anodes for electrolytic refining............	341.5	86.4	2.0	8.4	7.2	1.6	US$/kg	682
2603	Copper ores and concentrates................	30.0	176.6	215.0	2.4	4.3	4.3	US$/kg	283

Source: UN Comtrade and UN ServiceTrade 2014 International Trade Statistics Yearbook, Vol. I

Namibia

Services Imports and Exports: EBOPS 2002 categories

Table 2: Merchandise exports by SITC
(Value in million US$, growth and shares in percentage)

SITC	2013	Avg. Growth rates 2009-2013	Avg. Growth rates 2012-2013	2013 share
Total	6337.2	1.9	17.9	100.0
0+1	1350.9	-0.6	-0.9	21.3
2+4	1132.3	2.0	8.8	17.9
3	70.6	10.1	46.4	1.1
5	39.0	-12.0	-72.5	0.6
6	1956.8	5.1	0.6	30.9
7	1524.0	36.4	157.2	24.0
8	165.9	-38.6	43.8	2.6
9	97.8	-5.0	-25.5	1.5

Table 3: Merchandise imports by SITC
(Value in million US$, growth and shares in percentage)

SITC	2013	Avg. Growth rates 2009-2013	Avg. Growth rates 2012-2013	2013 share
Total	7574.5	5.1	6.2	100.0
0+1	952.6	1.8	7.0	12.6
2+4	588.7	52.4	22.8	7.8
3	749.2	11.8	-12.3	9.9
5	630.4	1.0	-3.5	8.3
6	1449.2	5.7	4.9	19.1
7	2499.2	3.5	14.6	33.0
8	698.5	-1.7	1.8	9.2
9	6.7	-35.8	-14.4	0.1

SITC Legend

SITC Code	Description
Total	All commodities
0+1	Food, animals + beverages, tobacco
2+4	Crude materials + anim. & veg. oils
3	Mineral fuels, lubricants
5	Chemicals
6	Goods classified chiefly by material
7	Machinery and transport equipment
8	Miscellaneous manufactured articles
9	Not classified elsewhere in the SITC

Graph 4: Merchandise trade balance
(Bln US$ by MDG Regions in 2013)

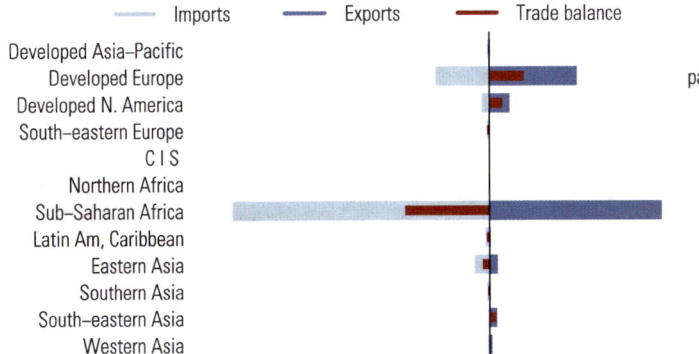

Graph 5: Partner concentration of merchandise trade
(Cumulative share by ranked partners in 2013)

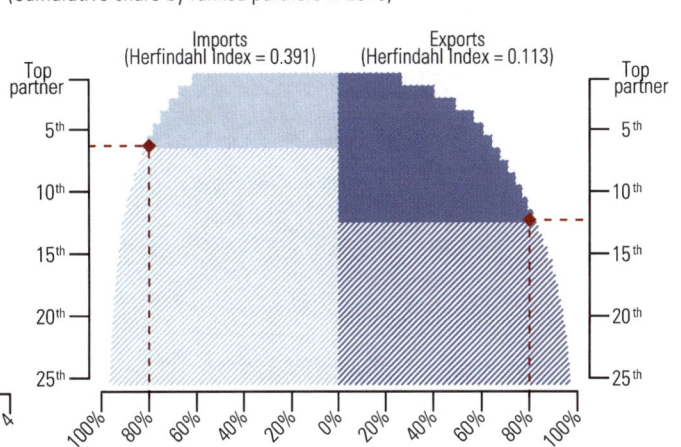

Imports (Herfindahl Index = 0.391)
Exports (Herfindahl Index = 0.113)

Graph 6: Imports of services by EBOPS category
(% share in 2013)

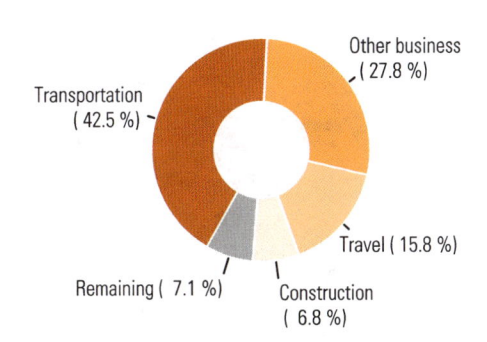

- Transportation (42.5 %)
- Other business (27.8 %)
- Travel (15.8 %)
- Construction (6.8 %)
- Remaining (7.1 %)

Imports Profile:

"Machinery and transport equipment" (SITC section 7), "Goods classified chiefly by material" (SITC section 6) and "Food, animals + beverages, tobacco" (SITC section 0+1) were the largest commodity groups for imports in 2013, representing respectively 33.0, 19.1 and 12.6 percent of imported goods (see table 3). From 2011 to 2013, the largest import commodity was "Petroleum oils, other than crude" (HS code 2710) (see table 4). The top three partners for merchandise imports were South Africa, Switzerland and China, accounting for respectively 68.7, 4.3 and 3.7 percent of total imports. "Transportation" (EBOPS code 205) accounted for the largest share of imports of services in 2013 at 342.3 mln US$, followed by "Other business services" (EBOPS code 268) at 223.6 mln US$ and "Travel" (EBOPS code 236) at 127.3 mln US$ (see graph 6).

Table 4: Top 10 import commodities 2011 to 2013

HS code	4-digit heading of Harmonized System 2007	2011	2012	2013	2011	2012	2013	Unit	SITC code
	All Commodities	6457.3	7132.0	7574.5					
2710	Petroleum oils, other than crude	558.0	816.2	715.9	0.7	1.0	0.9	US$/kg	334
8703	Motor cars and other motor vehicles principally designed for the transport	420.2	423.6	379.9			18.7	thsd US$/unit	781
7102	Diamonds, whether or not worked, but not mounted or set	172.1	368.8	407.3	162.6			US$/carat	667
2603	Copper ores and concentrates	0.0	348.4	478.7	11.7	2.5	2.3	US$/kg	283
8704	Motor vehicles for the transport of goods	187.8	172.8	259.2					782
3004	Medicaments (excluding goods of heading 30.02, 30.05 or 30.06)	141.6	128.3	115.9	35.8	24.6	31.1	US$/kg	542
8905	Light-vessels, fire-floats, dredgers, floating cranes and other vessels	0.2	16.2	334.0		267.0		US$/unit	793
7403	Refined copper and copper alloys, unwrought	62.4	92.3	156.3	7.8	8.3	10.0	US$/kg	682
8708	Parts and accessories of the motor vehicles of headings 87.01 to 87.05	109.6	96.7	98.6	1.2	9.6	10.3	US$/kg	784
8517	Electrical apparatus for line telephony or line telegraphy	80.9	77.5	119.0					764

Nepal

Goods Imports: CIF, by origin **Goods Exports: FOB, by last known destination** **Trade System: Special**

Overview:

In 2013, the value of merchandise exports of Nepal decreased slightly by 0.9 percent to reach 863.3 mln US$, while its merchandise imports increased moderately by 7.2 percent to reach 6.5 bln US$ (see graph 1, table 2 and table 3). The merchandise trade balance recorded a large deficit of 5.6 bln US$ (see graph 1). The largest merchandise trade balance was with MDG Southern Asia at -3.5 bln US$ (see graph 4). Merchandise exports in Nepal were highly concentrated amongst partners; imports were also highly concentrated. The top 4 partners accounted for 80 percent or more of exports and 4 partners accounted for 80 percent or more of imports (see graph 5). In 2013, the value of exports of services of Nepal increased substantially by 27.8 percent, reaching 1.2 bln US$, while its imports of services increased moderately by 9.1 percent and reached 978.0 mln US$ (see graph 2). There was a relatively small trade in services surplus of 204.2 mln US$. See footnote*.

Graph 1: Total merchandise trade, by value
(Bln US$ by year)

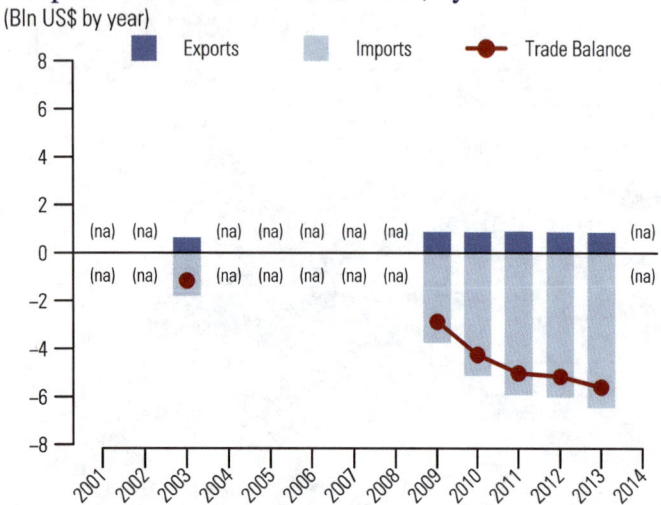

Graph 2: Total services trade, by value
(Bln US$ by year)

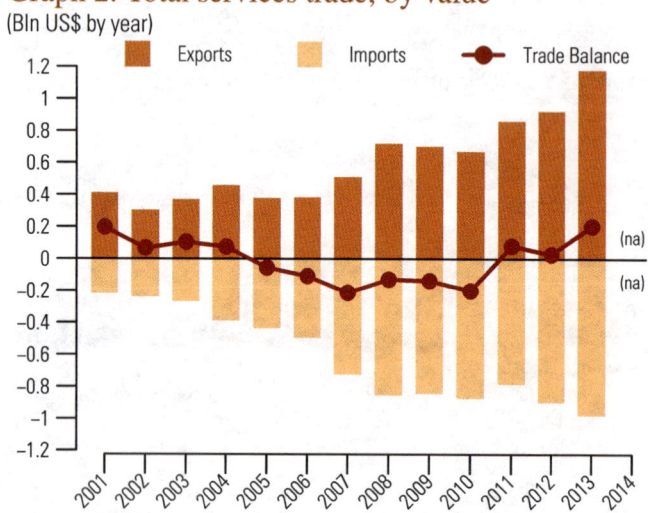

Exports Profile:

"Goods classified chiefly by material" (SITC section 6), "Food, animals + beverages, tobacco" (SITC section 0+1) and "Miscellaneous manufactured articles" (SITC section 8) were the largest commodity groups for exports in 2013, representing respectively 50.4, 20.2 and 14.6 percent of exported goods (see table 2). From 2011 to 2013, the largest export commodity was "Carpets and other textile floor coverings, knotted, whether or not made up" (HS code 5701) (see table 1). The top three destinations for merchandise exports were India, the United States and Germany, accounting for respectively 67.9, 7.4 and 3.9 percent of total exports. "Travel" (EBOPS code 236) accounted for the largest share of exports of services in 2013 at 433.3 mln US$, followed by "Communications services" (EBOPS code 245) at 355.1 mln US$ and "Government services, n.i.e." (EBOPS code 291) at 220.4 mln US$ (see graph 3).

Graph 3: Exports of services by EBOPS category
(% share in 2013)

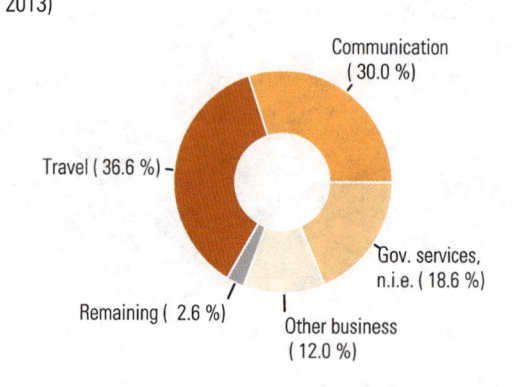

- Communication (30.0 %)
- Travel (36.6 %)
- Gov. services, n.i.e. (18.6 %)
- Other business (12.0 %)
- Remaining (2.6 %)

Table 1: Top 10 export commodities 2011 to 2013

HS code	4-digit heading of Harmonized System 2007	Value (million US$) 2011	2012	2013	Unit value 2011	2012	2013	Unit	SITC code
	All Commodities	907.6	870.7	863.3					
5701	Carpets and other textile floor coverings, knotted, whether or not made up	76.5	63.9	71.8	96.9	101.2	73.7	US$/m²	659
7210	Flat-rolled products of iron or non-alloy steel	87.7	56.2	66.7	1.3	1.1	0.9	US$/kg	674
5509	Yarn (other than sewing thread) of synthetic staple fibres	66.0	66.2	60.7	2.6	2.2	2.3	US$/kg	651
5407	Woven fabrics of synthetic filament yarn	53.9	63.5	59.2		3.5		US$/kg	653
2009	Fruit juices (including grape must) and vegetable juices	33.9	39.3	44.8	0.7	0.8	0.8	US$/kg	059
6305	Sacks and bags, of a kind used for the packing of goods	40.3	36.1	32.9					658
0908	Nutmeg, mace and cardamoms	30.7	45.8	19.2	7.5	7.7	8.8	US$/kg	075
7306	Other tubes, pipes and hollow profiles	23.2	37.4	31.8	0.8	0.8	0.7	US$/kg	679
7217	Wire of iron or non-alloy steel	28.5	33.4	25.3	1.0	1.0	0.9	US$/kg	678
0713	Dried leguminous vegetables, shelled, whether or not skinned or split	24.7	39.7	16.9	1.1	1.2	1.4	US$/kg	054

*Merchandise trade data up to 2009 reported by fiscal year and beginning 2010 reported by calendar year.

Nepal

Services Imports and Exports: EBOPS 2002 categories

Table 2: Merchandise exports by SITC
(Value in million US$, growth and shares in percentage)

SITC	2013	Avg. Growth rates 2009-2013	Avg. Growth rates 2012-2013	2013 share
Total	863.3	-0.6	-0.9	100.0
0+1	174.6	-5.2	-15.4	20.2
2+4	37.9	-11.5	-13.5	4.4
3	0.0	16.3	-75.3	0.0
5	45.6	-5.4	3.6	5.3
6	435.1	1.3	-5.5	50.4
7	5.2	-7.2	-31.3	0.6
8	125.8	-0.9	16.3	14.6
9	39.0	450.5	>	4.5

Table 3: Merchandise imports by SITC
(Value in million US$, growth and shares in percentage)

SITC	2013	Avg. Growth rates 2009-2013	Avg. Growth rates 2012-2013	2013 share
Total	6451.7	14.5	7.2	100.0
0+1	692.6	20.1	5.8	10.7
2+4	707.3	20.0	34.8	11.0
3	1212.3	18.4	-10.4	18.8
5	754.6	15.7	24.0	11.7
6	1408.9	16.0	19.6	21.8
7	1010.7	4.4	-5.2	15.7
8	321.6	7.1	-4.7	5.0
9	343.7	19.8	16.2	5.3

SITC Legend

SITC Code	Description
Total	All commodities
0+1	Food, animals + beverages, tobacco
2+4	Crude materials + anim. & veg. oils
3	Mineral fuels, lubricants
5	Chemicals
6	Goods classified chiefly by material
7	Machinery and transport equipment
8	Miscellaneous manufactured articles
9	Not classified elsewhere in the SITC

Graph 4: Merchandise trade balance
(Bln US$ by MDG Regions in 2013)

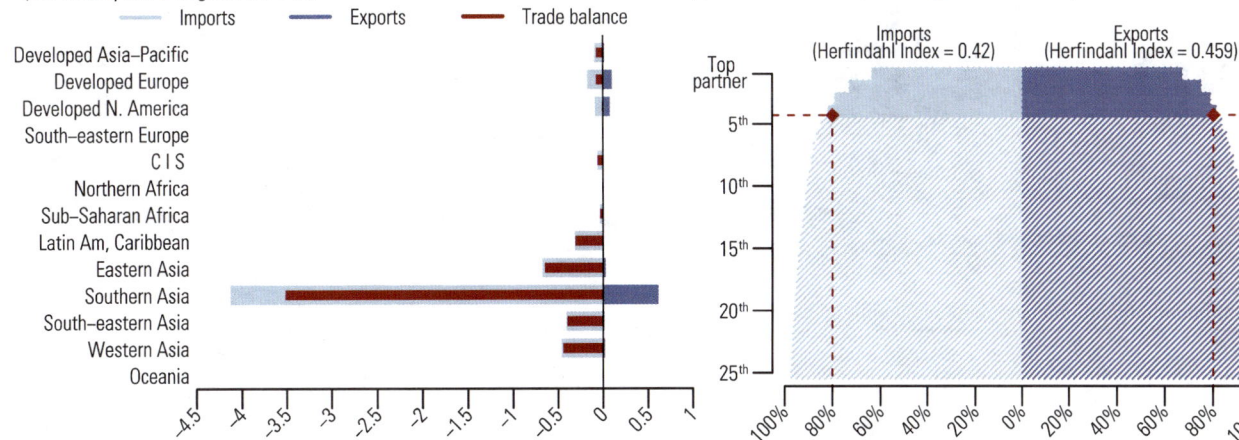

Graph 5: Partner concentration of merchandise trade
(Cumulative share by ranked partners in 2013)

Imports (Herfindahl Index = 0.42), Exports (Herfindahl Index = 0.459)

Graph 6: Imports of services by EBOPS category
(% share in 2013)

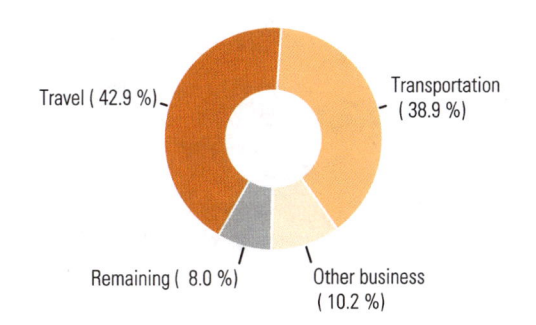

- Travel (42.9%)
- Transportation (38.9%)
- Other business (10.2%)
- Remaining (8.0%)

Imports Profile:
"Goods classified chiefly by material" (SITC section 6), "Mineral fuels, lubricants" (SITC section 3) and "Machinery and transport equipment" (SITC section 7) were the largest commodity groups for imports in 2013, representing respectively 21.8, 18.8 and 15.7 percent of imported goods (see table 3). From 2011 to 2013, the largest import commodity was "Petroleum oils, other than crude" (HS code 2710) (see table 4). The top three partners for merchandise imports were India, China and the United Arab Emirates, accounting for respectively 64.1, 10.8 and 6.0 percent of total imports. "Travel" (EBOPS code 236) accounted for the largest share of imports of services in 2013 at 419.2 mln US$, followed by "Transportation" (EBOPS code 205) at 380.1 mln US$ and "Other business services" (EBOPS code 268) at 100.1 mln US$ (see graph 6).

Table 4: Top 10 import commodities 2011 to 2013

HS code	4-digit heading of Harmonized System 2007	Value (million US$) 2011	2012	2013	Unit value 2011	2012	2013	Unit	SITC code
	All Commodities	5915.9	6017.5	6451.7					
2710	Petroleum oils, other than crude	956.5	994.6	866.0	0.8	1.1	1.7	US$/kg	334
7108	Gold (including gold plated with platinum)	267.7	295.7	275.9	52.4	53.3	47.5	thsd US$/kg	971
7207	Semi-finished products of iron or non-alloy steel	200.9	220.8	297.2	0.7	0.6	0.5	US$/kg	672
2711	Petroleum gases and other gaseous hydrocarbons	202.3	242.3	221.8	2.0	1.3	1.2	US$/kg	343
1507	Soya-bean oil and its fractions	128.8	140.3	302.8	1.3	1.3	1.0	US$/kg	421
2523	Portland cement, aluminous cement, slag cement	149.2	127.8	113.9	0.1	0.1	0.1	US$/kg	661
8517	Electrical apparatus for line telephony or line telegraphy	155.5	129.9	97.9					764
7208	Flat-rolled products of iron or non-alloy steel	84.7	118.5	163.4	0.7	0.7	0.5	US$/kg	673
3003	Medicaments (excluding goods of heading 30.02, 30.05 or 30.06)	121.2	117.6	100.1	5.1	6.7	7.9	US$/kg	542
1006	Rice	49.4	136.4	124.4	0.3	0.3	0.3	US$/kg	042

Source: UN Comtrade and UN ServiceTrade

Netherlands

Goods Imports: CIF, by origin/consignment for intra-eu   **Goods Exports:** FOB, by last known destination   **Trade System:** Special

Overview:
In 2014, the value of merchandise exports of the Netherlands increased slightly by 0.6 percent to reach 574.5 bln US$, while its merchandise imports increased slightly by 0.4 percent to reach 508.4 bln US$ (see graph 1, table 2 and table 3). In 2014, both merchandise exports and imports were higher than the level before the financial crisis in 2008. The merchandise trade balance recorded a surplus of 66.0 bln US$, the largest surplus the country has ever recorded (see graph 1). The largest merchandise trade balance was with MDG Developed Europe at 142.4 bln US$ (see graph 4). Merchandise exports in the Netherlands were diversified amongst partners; imports were also diversified. The top 20 partners accounted for 80 percent or more of exports and 20 partners accounted for 80 percent or more of imports (see graph 5). In 2013, the value of exports of services of the Netherlands increased substantially by 39.3 percent, reaching 185.9 bln US$, while its imports of services increased substantially by 30.9 percent and reached 157.4 bln US$ (see graph 2). There was a relatively small trade in services surplus of 28.5 bln US$.

Graph 1: Total merchandise trade, by value
(Bln US$ by year)

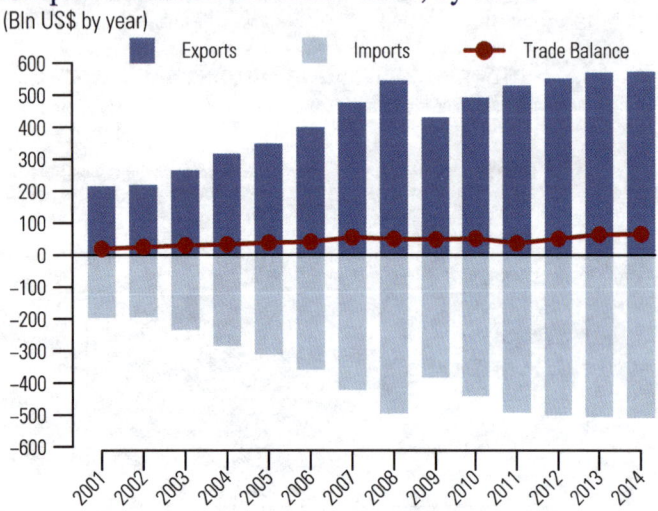

Graph 2: Total services trade, by value
(Bln US$ by year)

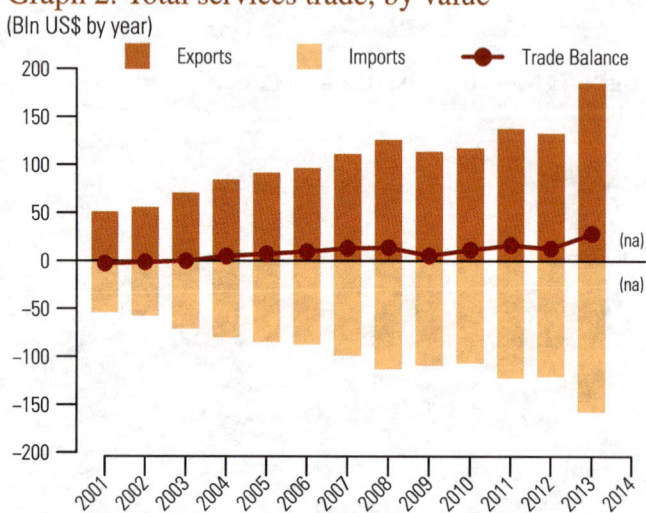

Exports Profile:
"Machinery and transport equipment" (SITC section 7), "Chemicals" (SITC section 5) and "Mineral fuels, lubricants" (SITC section 3) were the largest commodity groups for exports in 2014, representing respectively 26.5, 17.0 and 16.7 percent of exported goods (see table 2). From 2012 to 2014, the largest export commodity was "Petroleum oils, other than crude" (HS code 2710) (see table 1). The top three destinations for merchandise exports were Germany, Belgium and the United Kingdom, accounting for respectively 24.5, 11.1 and 8.3 percent of total exports. "Other business services" (EBOPS code 268) accounted for the largest share of exports of services in 2012 at 39.6 bln US$, followed by "Royalties and license fees" (EBOPS code 266) at 30.9 bln US$ and "Transportation" (EBOPS code 205) at 29.4 bln US$ (see graph 3).

Graph 3: Exports of services by EBOPS category
(% share in 2012)

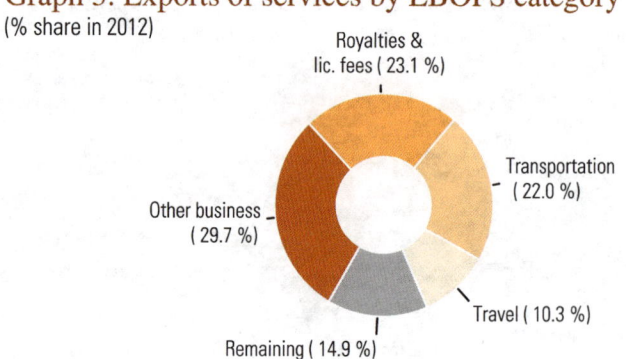

- Royalties & lic. fees (23.1 %)
- Transportation (22.0 %)
- Travel (10.3 %)
- Remaining (14.9 %)
- Other business (29.7 %)

Table 1: Top 10 export commodities 2012 to 2014

HS code	4-digit heading of Harmonized System 2012	Value (million US$) 2012	2013	2014	Unit value 2012	2013	2014	Unit	SITC code
	All Commodities	552 461.8	571 246.9	574 475.7					
2710	Petroleum oils, other than crude	71 431.1	75 502.3	64 782.2	0.9	*0.9*	0.8	US$/kg	334
9999	Commodities not specified according to kind	41 279.3	1 642.5	6 122.1					931
8471	Automatic data processing machines and units thereof	15 543.4	15 591.5	15 475.9	186.9	191.3	178.7	US$/unit	752
2711	Petroleum gases and other gaseous hydrocarbons	1 619.9	24 755.7	19 585.3	*1.0*	0.6	0.6	US$/kg	343
8517	Electrical apparatus for line telephony or line telegraphy	13 362.3	14 425.7	16 402.0					764
3004	Medicaments (excluding goods of heading 30.02, 30.05 or 30.06)	13 123.6	13 480.7	15 865.4	*225.9*	*228.5*	*251.7*	US$/kg	542
8443	Printing machinery used for printing by means of the printing type, blocks	10 153.5	9 958.8	9 953.3					726
8473	Parts and accessories for use with machines of heading 84.69 to 84.72	9 399.0	9 347.0	9 292.0	142.5	185.2	191.1	US$/kg	759
9018	Instruments and appliances used in medical, surgical, dental or veterinary	8 213.9	8 107.2	8 609.3					872
8486	Machines and apparatus used for the manufacture of semiconductor devices	5 985.1	6 861.2	7 920.4					728

Source: UN Comtrade and UN ServiceTrade

Netherlands

Services Imports and Exports: EBOPS 2002 categories

Table 2: Merchandise exports by SITC
(Value in million US$, growth and shares in percentage)

SITC	2014	Avg. Growth rates 2010-2014	2013-2014	2014 share
Total	574 475.7	3.9	0.6	100.0
0+1	82 819.1	7.8	2.4	14.4
2+4	31 843.3	5.8	-1.5	5.5
3	96 097.9	17.7	-15.1	16.7
5	97 941.7	8.2	1.7	17.0
6	49 395.9	6.7	6.5	8.6
7	152 414.1	3.5	5.2	26.5
8	56 899.3	8.7	5.6	9.9
9	7 064.3	-44.2	114.4	1.2

Table 3: Merchandise imports by SITC
(Value in million US$, growth and shares in percentage)

SITC	2014	Avg. Growth rates 2010-2014	2013-2014	2014 share
Total	508 438.2	3.7	0.4	100.0
0+1	52 380.0	8.8	1.1	10.3
2+4	23 689.4	4.5	-3.1	4.7
3	107 647.7	10.7	-14.3	21.2
5	62 190.4	7.7	-5.5	12.2
6	48 393.1	6.6	7.5	9.5
7	144 814.6	3.7	4.9	28.5
8	57 564.6	6.3	7.3	11.3
9	11 758.4	-32.6	543.0	2.3

SITC Legend

SITC Code	Description
Total	All commodities
0+1	Food, animals + beverages, tobacco
2+4	Crude materials + anim. & veg. oils
3	Mineral fuels, lubricants
5	Chemicals
6	Goods classified chiefly by material
7	Machinery and transport equipment
8	Miscellaneous manufactured articles
9	Not classified elsewhere in the SITC

Graph 4: Merchandise trade balance
(Bln US$ by MDG Regions in 2014)

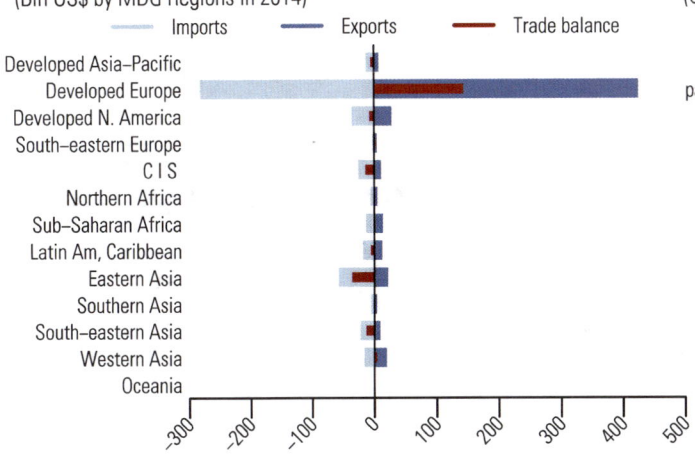

Graph 5: Partner concentration of merchandise trade
(Cumulative share by ranked partners in 2014)

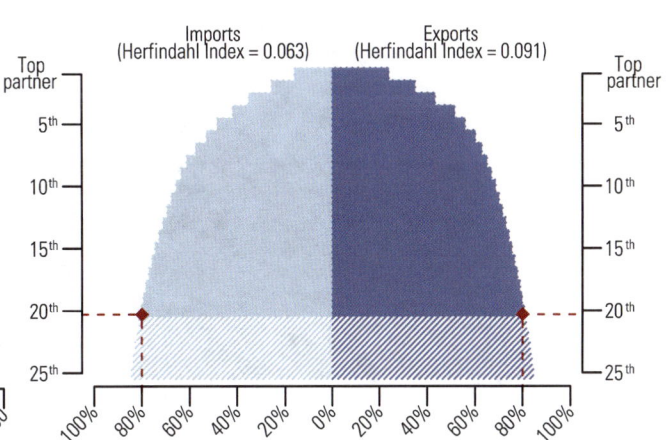

Imports (Herfindahl Index = 0.063)
Exports (Herfindahl Index = 0.091)

Graph 6: Imports of services by EBOPS category
(% share in 2012)

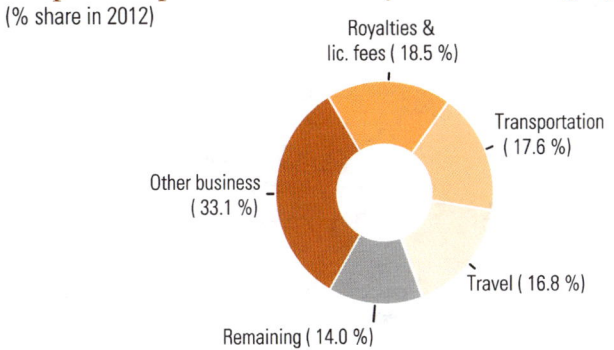

- Royalties & lic. fees (18.5 %)
- Transportation (17.6 %)
- Travel (16.8 %)
- Remaining (14.0 %)
- Other business (33.1 %)

Imports Profile:

"Machinery and transport equipment" (SITC section 7), "Mineral fuels, lubricants" (SITC section 3) and "Chemicals" (SITC section 5) were the largest commodity groups for imports in 2014, representing respectively 28.5, 21.2 and 12.2 percent of imported goods (see table 3). From 2012 to 2014, the largest import commodity was "Petroleum oils and oils obtained from bituminous minerals, crude" (HS code 2709) (see table 4). The top three partners for merchandise imports were Germany, Belgium and China, accounting for respectively 16.2, 9.7 and 8.6 percent of total imports. "Other business services" (EBOPS code 268) accounted for the largest share of imports of services in 2012 at 39.8 bln US$, followed by "Royalties and license fees" (EBOPS code 266) at 22.2 bln US$ and "Transportation" (EBOPS code 205) at 21.2 bln US$ (see graph 6).

Table 4: Top 10 import commodities 2012 to 2014

HS code	4-digit heading of Harmonized System 2012	2012	2013	2014	2012	2013	2014	Unit	SITC code
	All Commodities	500 605.3	506 162.3	508 438.2					
2709	Petroleum oils and oils obtained from bituminous minerals, crude	53 293.7	52 164.0	46 634.8	0.8	0.8	0.8	US$/kg	333
2710	Petroleum oils, other than crude	49 620.3	50 573.8	40 576.2	0.9	0.9	0.8	US$/kg	334
8471	Automatic data processing machines and units thereof	17 519.0	17 645.4	18 326.9	167.7	172.1	162.4	US$/unit	752
8517	Electrical apparatus for line telephony or line telegraphy	15 556.6	17 873.7	18 836.2					764
3004	Medicaments (excluding goods of heading 30.02, 30.05 or 30.06)	12 046.5	12 142.0	11 132.2	160.7	163.1	142.0	US$/kg	542
8703	Motor cars and other motor vehicles principally designed for the transport	11 195.0	11 015.3	11 420.0	16.8	18.7	18.1	thsd US$/unit	781
9999	Commodities not specified according to kind	19 843.8	263.2	10 947.2					931
2711	Petroleum gases and other gaseous hydrocarbons	2 152.8	12 897.9	12 407.6	0.9	1.9	1.1	US$/kg	343
8443	Printing machinery used for printing by means of the printing type, blocks	8 812.3	8 740.8	8 378.1					726
8473	Parts and accessories for use with machines of heading 84.69 to 84.72	9 066.1	8 477.1	8 352.3	184.8	190.5	181.7	US$/kg	759

2014 International Trade Statistics Yearbook, Vol. I — Source: UN Comtrade and UN ServiceTrade

New Caledonia

Goods Imports: CIF, by consignment **Goods Exports:** FOB, by last known destination **Trade System:** General

Overview:

In 2014, the value of merchandise exports of New Caledonia increased substantially by 30.8 percent to reach 1.6 bln US$, while its merchandise imports increased slightly by 2.4 percent to reach 3.3 bln US$ (see graph 1, table 2 and table 3). The merchandise trade balance recorded a large deficit of 1.7 bln US$ (see graph 1). The largest merchandise trade balance was with MDG Developed Europe at -899.5 mln US$ (see graph 4). Merchandise exports in New Caledonia were diversified amongst partners; imports were also diversified. The top 7 partners accounted for 80 percent or more of exports and 11 partners accounted for 80 percent or more of imports (see graph 5). In 2011, the value of exports of services of New Caledonia increased slightly by 2.3 percent, reaching 497.7 mln US$, while its imports of services decreased slightly by 1.2 percent and reached 1.4 bln US$ (see graph 2). There was a large trade in services deficit of 876.0 mln US$.

Graph 1: Total merchandise trade, by value
(Bln US$ by year)

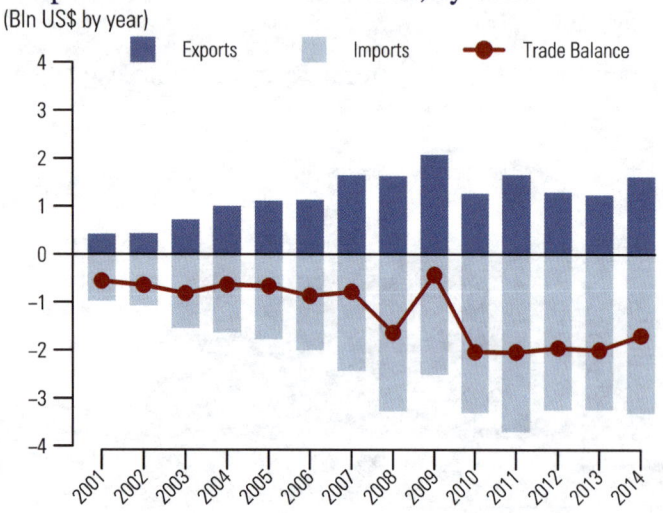

Graph 2: Total services trade, by value
(Bln US$ by year)

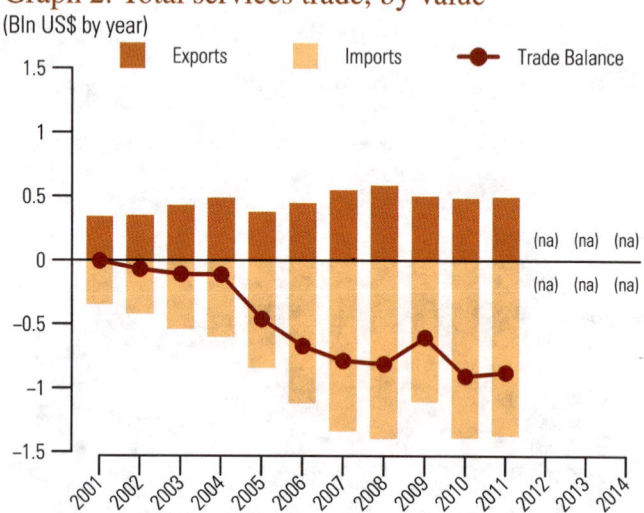

Exports Profile:

"Goods classified chiefly by material" (SITC section 6), "Crude materials + anim. & veg. oils" (SITC section 2+4) and "Chemicals" (SITC section 5) were the largest commodity groups for exports in 2014, representing respectively 53.3, 32.2 and 9.1 percent of exported goods (see table 2). From 2012 to 2014, the largest export commodity was "Ferro-alloys" (HS code 7202) (see table 1). The top three destinations for merchandise exports were Japan, France and China, accounting for respectively 15.2, 14.7 and 14.0 percent of total exports. "Travel" (EBOPS code 236) accounted for the largest share of exports of services in 2011 at 146.8 mln US$, followed by "Transportation" (EBOPS code 205) at 132.7 mln US$ and "Government services, n.i.e." (EBOPS code 291) at 106.9 mln US$ (see graph 3).

Graph 3: Exports of services by EBOPS category
(% share in 2011)

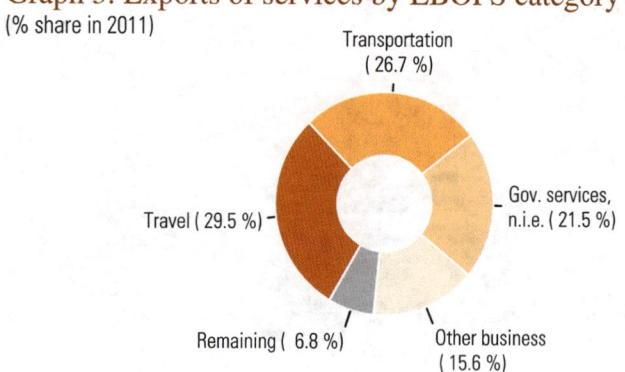

- Transportation (26.7 %)
- Gov. services, n.i.e. (21.5 %)
- Other business (15.6 %)
- Remaining (6.8 %)
- Travel (29.5 %)

Table 1: Top 10 export commodities 2012 to 2014

HS code	4-digit heading of Harmonized System 2007	Value (million US$) 2012	2013	2014	Unit value 2012	2013	2014	Unit	SITC code
	All Commodities	1 292.9	1 237.4	1 619.0					
7202	Ferro-alloys	674.4	546.0	853.2	3.6	3.2	3.8	US$/kg	671
7501	Nickel mattes, nickel oxide sinters and other intermediate products	202.8	259.1	246.1	10.4	9.1	11.4	US$/kg	284
2604	Nickel ores and concentrates	243.4	195.3	264.8	0.1	0.0	0.0	US$/kg	284
2825	Hydrazine and hydroxylamine and their inorganic salts	79.3	88.0	130.4	3.8	2.0	1.9	US$/kg	522
9999	Commodities not specified according to kind	18.0	18.5	23.4					931
0306	Crustaceans, whether in shell or not	12.3	14.5	15.9	15.1	16.7	16.6	US$/kg	036
7204	Ferrous waste and scrap; remelting scrap ingots of iron or steel	3.3	14.3	6.7	0.6	0.6	1.8	US$/kg	282
2836	Carbonates; peroxocarbonates (percarbonates)	1.2	13.2	9.1	9.3	8.8	9.1	US$/kg	523
8609	Containers (including containers for the transport of fluids)	3.0	6.3	3.4					786
3301	Essential oils (terpeneless or not), including concretes	3.2	4.2	5.0	453.2	637.2	620.7	US$/kg	551

New Caledonia

Services Imports and Exports: EBOPS 2002 categories

Table 2: Merchandise exports by SITC
(Value in million US$, growth and shares in percentage)

SITC	2014	Avg. Growth rates 2010-2014	Avg. Growth rates 2013-2014	2014 share
Total	1 619.0	6.3	30.8	100.0
0+1	26.4	4.8	3.9	1.6
2+4	521.9	0.3	7.7	32.2
3	0.0	-56.9	-80.9	0.0
5	147.8	117.8	36.2	9.1
6	863.4	5.8	56.5	53.3
7	28.8	15.1	-28.1	1.8
8	6.9	-13.9	-7.3	0.4
9	23.7	51.1	21.5	1.5

Table 3: Merchandise imports by SITC
(Value in million US$, growth and shares in percentage)

SITC	2014	Avg. Growth rates 2010-2014	Avg. Growth rates 2013-2014	2014 share
Total	3 315.2	0.1	2.4	100.0
0+1	436.7	5.1	1.8	13.2
2+4	76.9	11.3	8.4	2.3
3	869.9	13.4	2.3	26.2
5	261.5	0.6	-6.2	7.9
6	376.6	-2.1	9.0	11.4
7	930.6	0.2	9.1	28.1
8	320.9	1.6	1.5	9.7
9	42.1	-45.6	-54.7	1.3

SITC Legend

SITC Code	Description
Total	All commodities
0+1	Food, animals + beverages, tobacco
2+4	Crude materials + anim. & veg. oils
3	Mineral fuels, lubricants
5	Chemicals
6	Goods classified chiefly by material
7	Machinery and transport equipment
8	Miscellaneous manufactured articles
9	Not classified elsewhere in the SITC

Graph 4: Merchandise trade balance
(Bln US$ by MDG Regions in 2014)

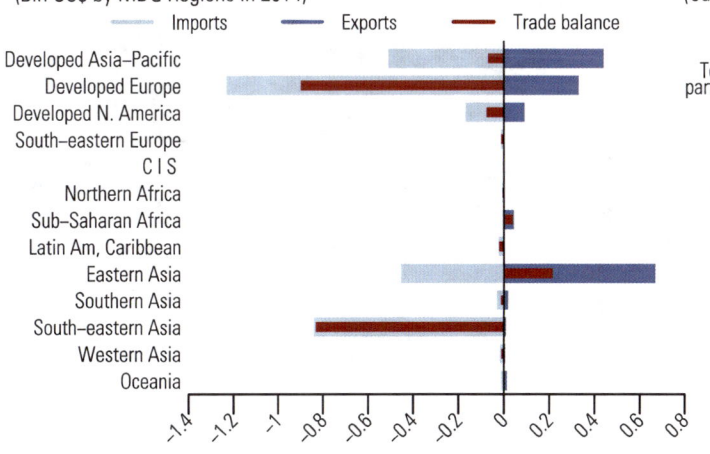

Graph 5: Partner concentration of merchandise trade
(Cumulative share by ranked partners in 2014)

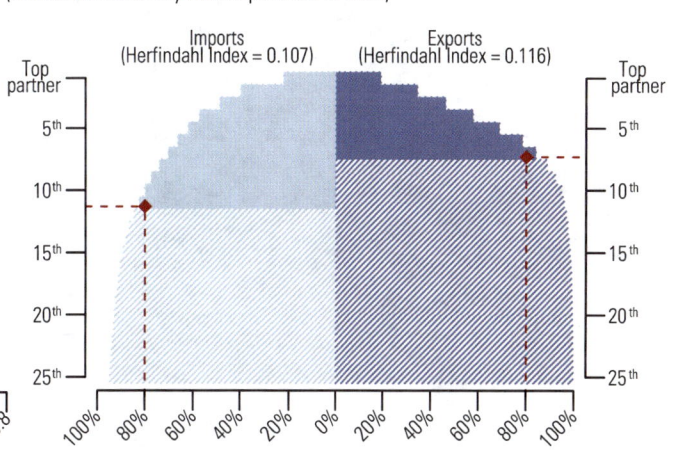

Imports (Herfindahl Index = 0.107)
Exports (Herfindahl Index = 0.116)

Graph 6: Imports of services by EBOPS category
(% share in 2011)

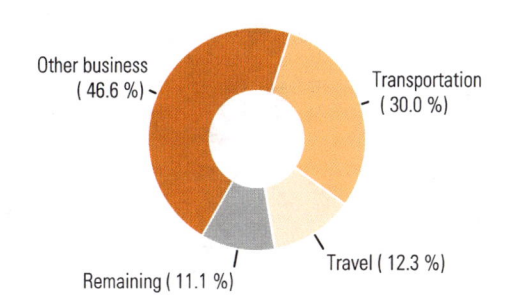

- Other business (46.6 %)
- Transportation (30.0 %)
- Travel (12.3 %)
- Remaining (11.1 %)

Imports Profile:

"Machinery and transport equipment" (SITC section 7), "Mineral fuels, lubricants" (SITC section 3) and "Food, animals + beverages, tobacco" (SITC section 0+1) were the largest commodity groups for imports in 2014, representing respectively 28.1, 26.2 and 13.2 percent of imported goods (see table 3). From 2012 to 2014, the largest import commodity was "Petroleum oils, other than crude" (HS code 2710) (see table 4). The top three partners for merchandise imports were France, Singapore and Australia, accounting for respectively 22.6, 18.5 and 9.6 percent of total imports. "Other business services" (EBOPS code 268) accounted for the largest share of imports of services in 2011 at 640.6 mln US$, followed by "Transportation" (EBOPS code 205) at 412.4 mln US$ and "Travel" (EBOPS code 236) at 168.5 mln US$ (see graph 6).

Table 4: Top 10 import commodities 2012 to 2014

HS code	4-digit heading of Harmonized System 2007	Value 2012	Value 2013	Value 2014	Unit value 2012	Unit value 2013	Unit value 2014	Unit	SITC code
	All Commodities	3 245.0	3 237.0	3 315.2					
2710	Petroleum oils, other than crude	641.3	742.9	762.7	0.9	0.8	0.8	US$/kg	334
8703	Motor cars and other motor vehicles principally designed for the transport	185.1	166.1	169.5	19.4	18.9	19.4	thsd US$/unit	781
9999	Commodities not specified according to kind	188.1	92.8	41.9					931
3004	Medicaments (excluding goods of heading 30.02, 30.05 or 30.06)	76.5	74.8	75.0	63.1	60.9	54.2	US$/kg	542
2701	Coal; briquettes, ovoids and similar solid fuels manufactured from coal	79.3	70.3	63.4	0.2	0.1	0.1	US$/kg	321
8704	Motor vehicles for the transport of goods	64.6	43.5	83.8					782
8429	Self-propelled bulldozers, angledozers, graders, levellers, scrapers	36.3	22.7	51.0			77.9	thsd US$/unit	723
8471	Automatic data processing machines and units thereof	34.1	35.4	35.6					752
4011	New pneumatic tyres, of rubber	32.9	36.0	34.7					625
8708	Parts and accessories of the motor vehicles of headings 87.01 to 87.05	31.1	32.2	34.9	21.1	22.2	20.6	US$/kg	784

Source: UN Comtrade and UN ServiceTrade

New Zealand

Goods Imports: CIF, by origin **Goods Exports:** FOB, by last known destination **Trade System:** General

Overview:
In 2014, the value of merchandise exports of New Zealand increased moderately by 5.6 percent to reach 41.6 bln US$, while its merchandise imports increased moderately by 7.3 percent to reach 42.5 bln US$ (see graph 1, table 2 and table 3). The merchandise trade balance recorded a relatively small deficit of 862.1 mln US$ (see graph 1). The largest merchandise trade balance was with MDG Developed Europe at -3.4 bln US$ (see graph 4). Merchandise exports in New Zealand were diversified amongst partners; imports were also diversified. The top 19 partners accounted for 80 percent or more of exports and 15 partners accounted for 80 percent or more of imports (see graph 5). In 2012, the value of exports of services of New Zealand increased slightly by 0.9 percent, reaching 13.1 bln US$, while its imports of services increased slightly by 2.6 percent and reached 12.1 bln US$ (see graph 2). There was a relatively small trade in services surplus of 999.0 mln US$.

Graph 1: Total merchandise trade, by value (Bln US$ by year)

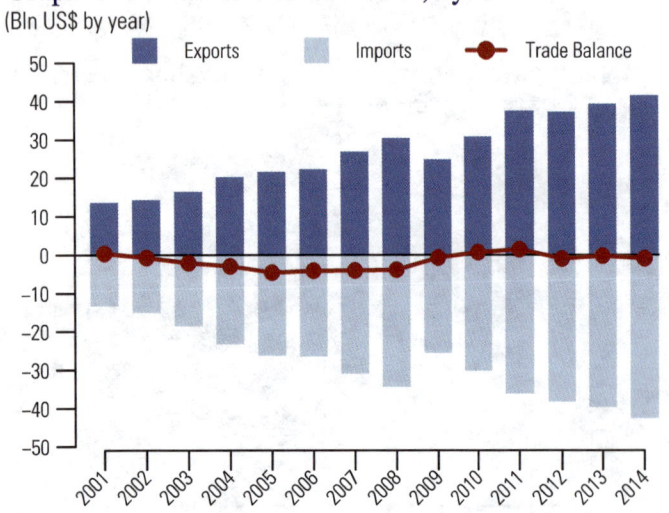

Graph 2: Total services trade, by value (Bln US$ by year)

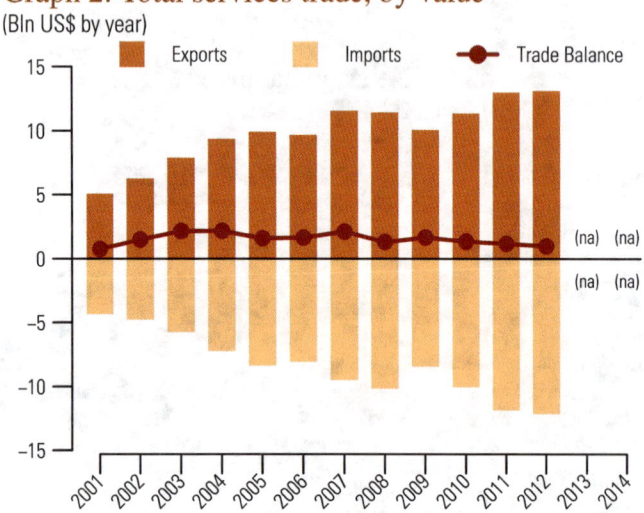

Exports Profile:
"Food, animals + beverages, tobacco" (SITC section 0+1), "Crude materials + anim. & veg. oils" (SITC section 2+4) and "Goods classified chiefly by material" (SITC section 6) were the largest commodity groups for exports in 2014, representing respectively 58.1, 12.2 and 7.3 percent of exported goods (see table 2). From 2012 to 2014, the largest export commodity was "Milk and cream, concentrated or containing added sugar" (HS code 0402) (see table 1). The top three destinations for merchandise exports were Australia, China and the United States, accounting for respectively 19.3, 18.6 and 9.0 percent of total exports. "Travel" (EBOPS code 236) accounted for the largest share of exports of services in 2012 at 7.1 bln US$, followed by "Transportation" (EBOPS code 205) at 2.0 bln US$ and "Other business services" (EBOPS code 268) at 1.8 bln US$ (see graph 3).

Graph 3: Exports of services by EBOPS category (% share in 2012)

- Travel (54.2 %)
- Transportation (15.4 %)
- Other business (13.9 %)
- Remaining (16.5 %)

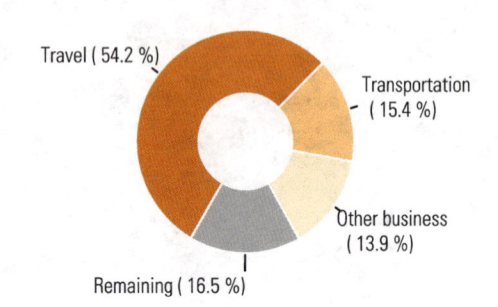

Table 1: Top 10 export commodities 2012 to 2014

HS code	4-digit heading of Harmonized System 2012	Value (million US$) 2012	2013	2014	Unit value 2012	2013	2014	Unit	SITC code
	All Commodities	37 304.7	39 443.6	41 635.6					
0402	Milk and cream, concentrated or containing added sugar	5 554.8	7 142.5	7 647.9	3.3	4.2	4.2	US$/kg	022
0204	Meat of sheep or goats, fresh, chilled or frozen	2 135.5	2 240.1	2 494.4	4.9	5.4	6.0	US$/kg	012
0405	Butter and other fats and oils derived from milk; dairy spreads	1 613.3	1 824.7	2 149.8	3.3	3.8	4.0	US$/kg	023
4403	Wood in the rough, whether or not stripped of bark or sapwood	1 276.2	1 931.3	1 890.5	92.7	116.3	113.9	US$/m³	247
0202	Meat of bovine animals, frozen	1 466.8	1 508.7	1 825.1	4.3	4.3	4.7	US$/kg	011
9999	Commodities not specified according to kind	1 359.4	1 325.8	1 482.1					931
2709	Petroleum oils and oils obtained from bituminous minerals, crude	1 487.4	1 176.4	1 128.6	0.8	0.8	0.8	US$/kg	333
0406	Cheese and curd	1 176.4	1 156.1	1 280.8	3.7	4.0	4.4	US$/kg	024
2204	Wine of fresh grapes, including fortified wines	985.0	1 030.3	1 123.5	5.6	5.9	5.8	US$/litre	112
0810	Other fruit, fresh	870.2	692.2	869.4	2.1	1.9	2.2	US$/kg	057

New Zealand

Services Imports and Exports: EBOPS 2002 categories

Table 2: Merchandise exports by SITC
(Value in million US$, growth and shares in percentage)

SITC	2014	Avg. Growth rates 2010-2014	Avg. Growth rates 2013-2014	2014 share
Total	41 635.6	7.7	5.6	100.0
0+1	24 209.7	10.5	9.9	58.1
2+4	5 062.9	8.9	-3.0	12.2
3	1 316.9	-2.6	-7.1	3.2
5	2 090.9	11.3	8.8	5.0
6	3 034.7	0.9	-0.5	7.3
7	2 562.0	0.7	1.1	6.2
8	1 525.4	4.7	1.8	3.7
9	1 833.1	4.0	3.3	4.4

Table 3: Merchandise imports by SITC
(Value in million US$, growth and shares in percentage)

SITC	2014	Avg. Growth rates 2010-2014	Avg. Growth rates 2013-2014	2014 share
Total	42 497.7	9.0	7.3	100.0
0+1	4 422.8	10.0	10.3	10.4
2+4	960.4	4.8	-2.2	2.3
3	6 374.2	8.4	-4.6	15.0
5	4 419.2	5.7	3.0	10.4
6	4 484.1	5.7	5.1	10.6
7	16 121.0	12.5	16.1	37.9
8	5 418.1	6.1	4.3	12.7
9	298.0	2.8	-5.5	0.7

SITC Legend

SITC Code	Description
Total	All commodities
0+1	Food, animals + beverages, tobacco
2+4	Crude materials + anim. & veg. oils
3	Mineral fuels, lubricants
5	Chemicals
6	Goods classified chiefly by material
7	Machinery and transport equipment
8	Miscellaneous manufactured articles
9	Not classified elsewhere in the SITC

Graph 4: Merchandise trade balance
(Bln US$ by MDG Regions in 2014)

Graph 5: Partner concentration of merchandise trade
(Cumulative share by ranked partners in 2014)

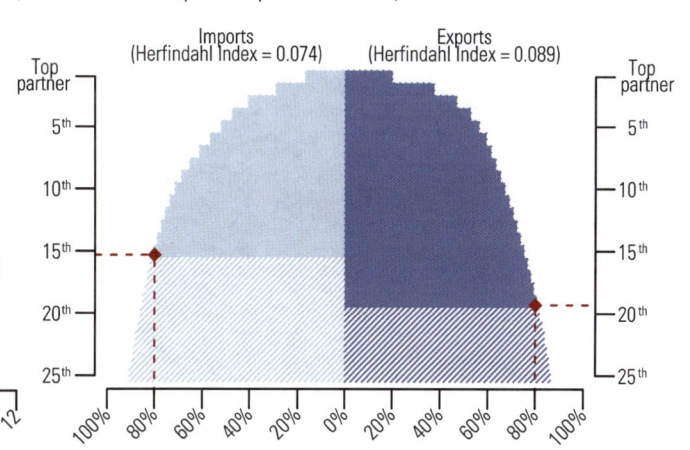

Imports (Herfindahl Index = 0.074)
Exports (Herfindahl Index = 0.089)

Graph 6: Imports of services by EBOPS category
(% share in 2012)

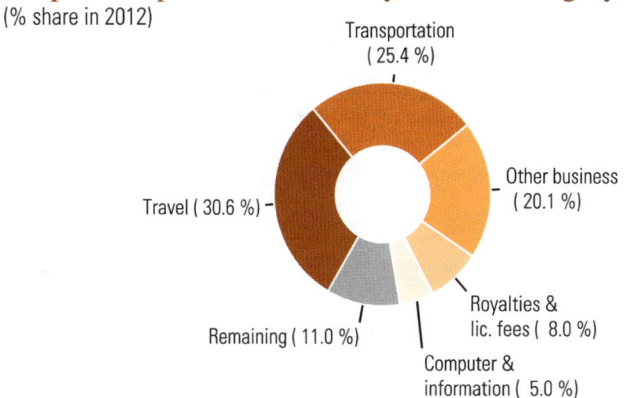

- Transportation (25.4 %)
- Travel (30.6 %)
- Other business (20.1 %)
- Royalties & lic. fees (8.0 %)
- Computer & information (5.0 %)
- Remaining (11.0 %)

Imports Profile:

"Machinery and transport equipment" (SITC section 7), "Mineral fuels, lubricants" (SITC section 3) and "Miscellaneous manufactured articles" (SITC section 8) were the largest commodity groups for imports in 2014, representing respectively 37.9, 15.0 and 12.7 percent of imported goods (see table 3). From 2012 to 2014, the largest import commodity was "Petroleum oils and oils obtained from bituminous minerals, crude" (HS code 2709) (see table 4). The top three partners for merchandise imports were China, Australia and the United States, accounting for respectively 16.8, 13.5 and 10.2 percent of total imports. "Travel" (EBOPS code 236) accounted for the largest share of imports of services in 2012 at 3.7 bln US$, followed by "Transportation" (EBOPS code 205) at 3.1 bln US$ and "Other business services" (EBOPS code 268) at 2.4 bln US$ (see graph 6).

Table 4: Top 10 import commodities 2012 to 2014

HS code	4-digit heading of Harmonized System 2012	Value 2012	Value 2013	Value 2014	Unit value 2012	Unit value 2013	Unit value 2014	Unit	SITC code
	All Commodities	38 242.7	39 619.2	42 497.7					
2709	Petroleum oils and oils obtained from bituminous minerals, crude	4 608.7	4 399.5	3 966.8	0.9	0.9	0.8	US$/kg	333
8703	Motor cars and other motor vehicles principally designed for the transport	2 685.0	3 067.5	3 387.7	15.6	14.5	12.9	thsd US$/unit	781
2710	Petroleum oils, other than crude	2 045.2	2 169.2	2 303.6	1.2	1.1	1.1	US$/kg	334
8471	Automatic data processing machines and units thereof	972.1	989.7	970.3					752
8704	Motor vehicles for the transport of goods	686.4	837.5	1 185.8	33.2	28.8	32.4	thsd US$/unit	782
8517	Electrical apparatus for line telephony or line telegraphy	814.6	922.8	926.5					764
8802	Other aircraft (for example, helicopters, aeroplanes); spacecraft	357.1	446.2	1 331.5	2.4	2.6	2.0	mln US$/unit	792
3004	Medicaments (excluding goods of heading 30.02, 30.05 or 30.06)	688.3	646.7	653.3	40.1	38.7	36.8	US$/kg	542
8411	Turbo-jets, turbo-propellers and other gas turbines	355.9	379.0	451.8					714
9018	Instruments and appliances used in medical, surgical, dental or veterinary	329.1	355.1	360.6					872

Source: UN Comtrade and UN ServiceTrade

Nicaragua

Goods Imports: CIF, by origin | **Goods Exports:** FOB, by last known destination | **Trade System:** General

Overview:
In 2014, the value of merchandise exports of Nicaragua increased moderately by 8.3 percent to reach 5.0 bln US$, while its merchandise imports increased slightly by 4.5 percent to reach 5.7 bln US$ (see graph 1, table 2 and table 3). The merchandise trade balance recorded a relatively small deficit of 772.9 mln US$ (see graph 1). The largest merchandise trade balance was with MDG Developed North America at 1.7 bln US$ (see graph 4). Merchandise exports in Nicaragua were highly concentrated amongst partners; imports were diversified. The top 6 partners accounted for 80 percent or more of exports and 11 partners accounted for 80 percent or more of imports (see graph 5). In 2013, the value of exports of services of Nicaragua increased slightly by 0.7 percent, reaching 731.4 mln US$, while its imports of services increased slightly by 1.3 percent and reached 933.8 mln US$ (see graph 2). There was a moderate trade in services deficit of 202.4 mln US$.

Graph 1: Total merchandise trade, by value
(Bln US$ by year)

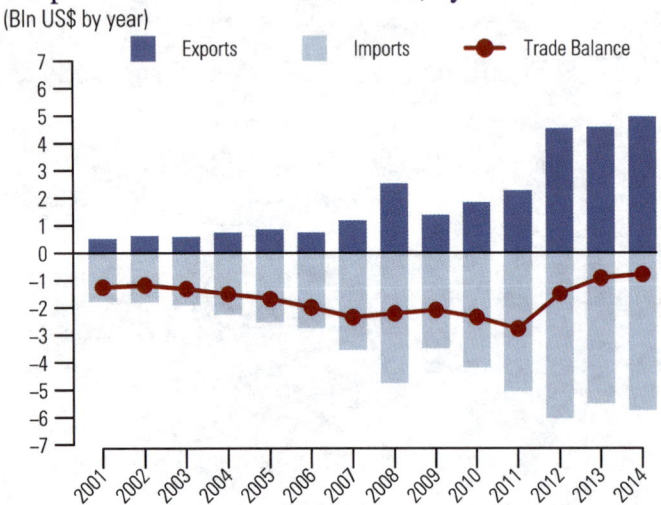

Graph 2: Total services trade, by value
(Mln US$ by year)

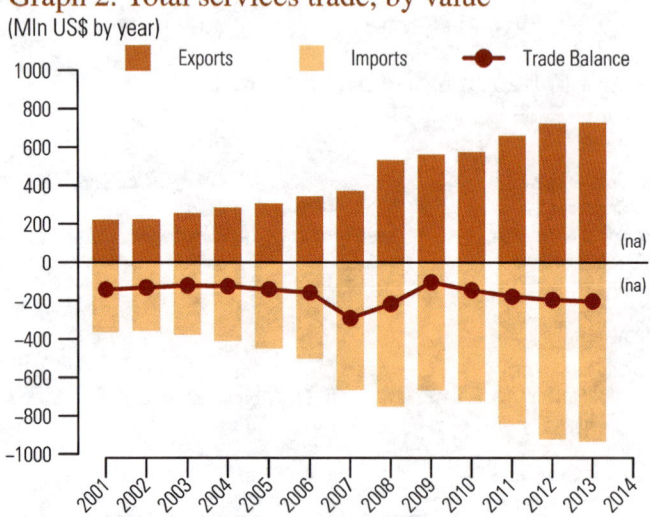

Exports Profile:
"Food, animals + beverages, tobacco" (SITC section 0+1), "Miscellaneous manufactured articles" (SITC section 8) and "Machinery and transport equipment" (SITC section 7) were the largest commodity groups for exports in 2014, representing respectively 42.7, 28.6 and 11.7 percent of exported goods (see table 2). From 2012 to 2014, the largest export commodity was "Insulated (including enamelled or anodised) wire, cable" (HS code 8544) (see table 1). The top three destinations for merchandise exports were the United States, Mexico and the Bolivarian Republic of Venezuela, accounting for respectively 46.6, 12.1 and 8.6 percent of total exports. "Travel" (EBOPS code 236) accounted for the largest share of exports of services in 2013 at 417.2 mln US$, followed by "Communications services" (EBOPS code 245) at 155.7 mln US$ and "Government services, n.i.e." (EBOPS code 291) at 89.0 mln US$ (see graph 3).

Graph 3: Exports of services by EBOPS category
(% share in 2013)

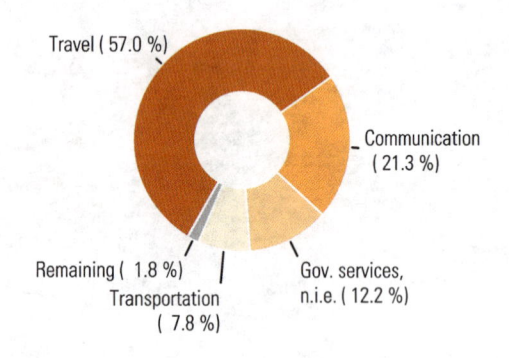

- Travel (57.0 %)
- Communication (21.3 %)
- Gov. services, n.i.e. (12.2 %)
- Transportation (7.8 %)
- Remaining (1.8 %)

Table 1: Top 10 export commodities 2012 to 2014

HS code	4-digit heading of Harmonized System 2012	Value (million US$) 2012	2013	2014	Unit value 2012	2013	2014	Unit	SITC code
	All Commodities	4550.6	4594.1	4973.5					
8544	Insulated (including enamelled or anodised) wire, cable	451.0	572.8	562.1	14.2	15.2	15.7	US$/kg	773
0901	Coffee, whether or not roasted or decaffeinated	525.5	352.9	399.5	4.2	3.6	3.5	US$/kg	071
7108	Gold (including gold plated with platinum)	432.0	436.6	387.0	31.9	29.6	27.0	thsd US$/kg	971
0202	Meat of bovine animals, frozen	368.0	288.9	330.3	4.2	4.2	4.7	US$/kg	011
6206	Women's or girls' blouses, shirts and shirt-blouses	300.2	309.6	277.1					842
6104	Women's or girls' suits, ensembles, jackets, blazers, dresses, skirts	291.5	398.2	64.0					844
0306	Crustaceans, whether in shell or not	175.4	225.5	261.5	6.2	7.2	7.7	US$/kg	036
6109	T-shirts, singlets and other vests, knitted or crocheted	127.4	142.3	373.9	7.3	7.3	5.5	US$/unit	845
1701	Cane or beet sugar and chemically pure sucrose, in solid form	195.0	186.8	207.5	0.6	0.5	0.5	US$/kg	061
6203	Men's or boys' suits, ensembles, jackets, blazers, trousers	146.8	149.0	127.9					841

Nicaragua

Services Imports and Exports: EBOPS 2002 categories

Table 2: Merchandise exports by SITC
(Value in million US$, growth and shares in percentage)

SITC	2014	Avg. Growth rates 2010-2014	Avg. Growth rates 2013-2014	2014 share
Total	4 973.5	28.1	8.3	100.0
0+1	2 123.6	12.4	15.3	42.7
2+4	312.1	20.3	18.6	6.3
3	15.6	-8.9	-21.2	0.3
5	35.3	7.4	-3.3	0.7
6	91.1	30.0	-7.9	1.8
7	584.0	153.6	-2.0	11.7
8	1 423.6	132.4	9.5	28.6
9	388.2	14.9	-11.3	7.8

Table 3: Merchandise imports by SITC
(Value in million US$, growth and shares in percentage)

SITC	2014	Avg. Growth rates 2010-2014	Avg. Growth rates 2013-2014	2014 share
Total	5 746.4	8.2	4.5	100.0
0+1	840.5	9.6	0.4	14.6
2+4	176.9	6.3	2.9	3.1
3	1 008.9	2.6	-2.5	17.6
5	947.4	5.8	1.7	16.5
6	832.7	11.8	1.5	14.5
7	1 378.5	10.8	14.0	24.0
8	556.4	12.3	13.7	9.7
9	5.2	-2.3	-1.4	0.1

SITC Legend

SITC Code	Description
Total	All commodities
0+1	Food, animals + beverages, tobacco
2+4	Crude materials + anim. & veg. oils
3	Mineral fuels, lubricants
5	Chemicals
6	Goods classified chiefly by material
7	Machinery and transport equipment
8	Miscellaneous manufactured articles
9	Not classified elsewhere in the SITC

Graph 4: Merchandise trade balance
(Bln US$ by MDG Regions in 2014)

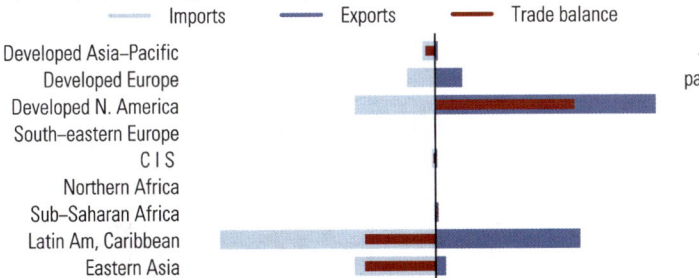

Graph 5: Partner concentration of merchandise trade
(Cumulative share by ranked partners in 2014)

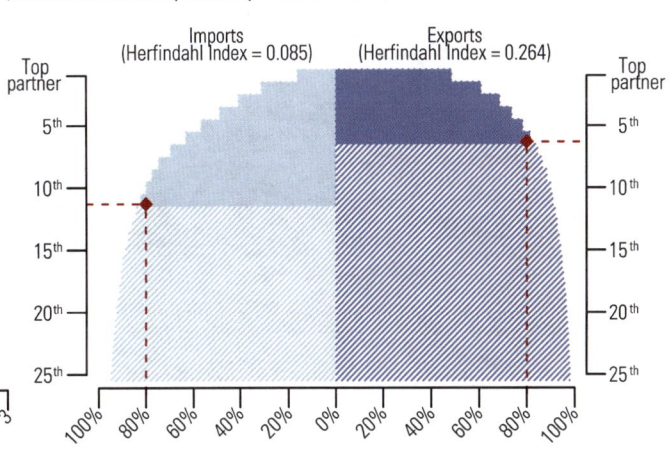

Imports (Herfindahl Index = 0.085)
Exports (Herfindahl Index = 0.264)

Graph 6: Imports of services by EBOPS category
(% share in 2013)

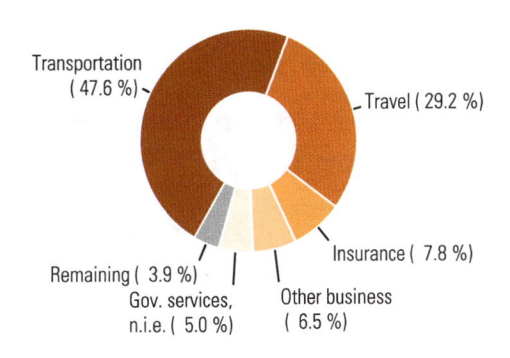

- Transportation (47.6%)
- Travel (29.2%)
- Insurance (7.8%)
- Other business (6.5%)
- Gov. services, n.i.e. (5.0%)
- Remaining (3.9%)

Imports Profile:

"Machinery and transport equipment" (SITC section 7), "Mineral fuels, lubricants" (SITC section 3) and "Chemicals" (SITC section 5) were the largest commodity groups for imports in 2014, representing respectively 24.0, 17.6 and 16.5 percent of imported goods (see table 3). From 2012 to 2014, the largest import commodity was "Petroleum oils, other than crude" (HS code 2710) (see table 4). The top three partners for merchandise imports were the United States, China and Curaçao, accounting for respectively 17.0, 12.0 and 10.0 percent of total imports. "Transportation" (EBOPS code 205) accounted for the largest share of imports of services in 2013 at 444.5 mln US$, followed by "Travel" (EBOPS code 236) at 272.8 mln US$ and "Insurance services" (EBOPS code 253) at 72.6 mln US$ (see graph 6).

Table 4: Top 10 import commodities 2012 to 2014

HS code	4-digit heading of Harmonized System 2012	2012	2013	2014	2012	2013	2014	Unit	SITC code
	All Commodities	6 029.7	5 498.8	5 746.4					
2710	Petroleum oils, other than crude	960.4	457.0	429.8	0.9	1.0	1.0	US$/kg	334
2709	Petroleum oils and oils obtained from bituminous minerals, crude	440.5	505.5	508.1	0.8	0.8	0.7	US$/kg	333
3004	Medicaments (excluding goods of heading 30.02, 30.05 or 30.06)	299.4	298.8	311.3	28.9	27.2	23.5	US$/kg	542
8704	Motor vehicles for the transport of goods	131.1	150.2	157.0					782
8517	Electrical apparatus for line telephony or line telegraphy	118.2	99.1	158.5					764
8703	Motor cars and other motor vehicles principally designed for the transport	124.4	118.2	116.2	16.1	15.0	14.7	thsd US$/unit	781
3808	Insecticides, rodenticides, fungicides, herbicides	87.6	94.2	93.1	4.9	5.1	4.9	US$/kg	591
3923	Articles for the conveyance or packing of goods, of plastics	78.8	78.0	84.4	2.5	2.3	2.3	US$/kg	893
2106	Food preparations not elsewhere specified or included	60.1	65.2	70.0	6.1	6.6	6.2	US$/kg	098
2711	Petroleum gases and other gaseous hydrocarbons	55.9	62.0	66.4	0.8	0.8	0.9	US$/kg	343

2014 International Trade Statistics Yearbook, Vol. I — Source: UN Comtrade and UN ServiceTrade

Niger

Goods Imports: CIF, by origin **Goods Exports: FOB, by last known destination** **Trade System: General**

Overview:
In 2014, the value of merchandise exports of the Niger decreased substantially by 21.5 percent to reach 1.0 bln US$, while its merchandise imports increased substantially by 25.5 percent to reach 2.2 bln US$ (see graph 1, table 2 and table 3). The merchandise trade balance recorded a large deficit of 1.1 bln US$ (see graph 1). The largest merchandise trade balance was with MDG Eastern Asia at -440.1 mln US$ (see graph 4). Merchandise exports in the Niger were moderately concentrated amongst partners; imports were diversified. The top 6 partners accounted for 80 percent or more of exports and 14 partners accounted for 80 percent or more of imports (see graph 5). In 2012, the value of exports of services of the Niger increased moderately by 8.4 percent, reaching 75.1 mln US$, while its imports of services decreased moderately by 5.1 percent and reached 826.1 mln US$ (see graph 2). There was a large trade in services deficit of 751.0 mln US$.

Graph 1: Total merchandise trade, by value
(Bln US$ by year)

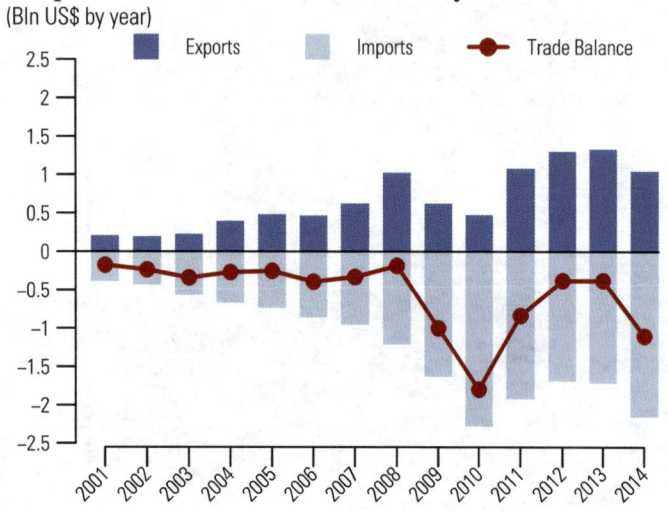

Graph 2: Total services trade, by value
(Mln US$ by year)

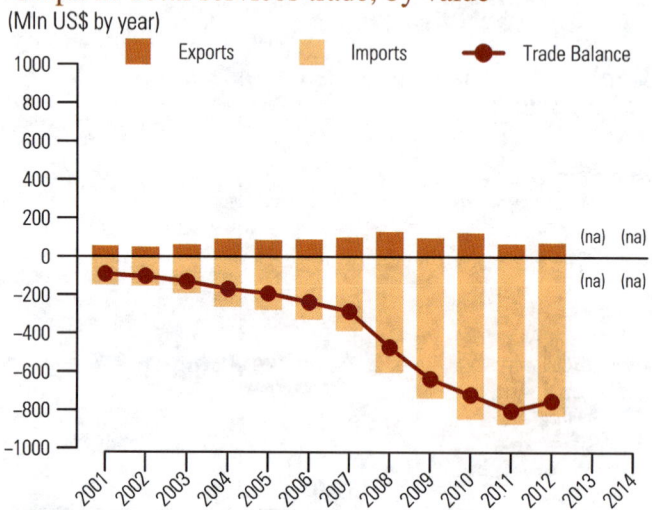

Exports Profile:
"Crude materials + anim. & veg. oils" (SITC section 2+4), "Mineral fuels, lubricants" (SITC section 3) and "Food, animals + beverages, tobacco" (SITC section 0+1) were the largest commodity groups for exports in 2014, representing respectively 49.3, 27.0 and 9.5 percent of exported goods (see table 2). From 2012 to 2014, the largest export commodity was "Uranium or thorium ores and concentrates" (HS code 2612) (see table 1). The top three destinations for merchandise exports were France, Nigeria and Burkina Faso, accounting for respectively 38.6, 12.4 and 11.3 percent of total exports. "Travel" (EBOPS code 236) accounted for the largest share of exports of services in 2012 at 49.7 mln US$, followed by "Other business services" (EBOPS code 268) at 8.9 mln US$ and "Government services, n.i.e." (EBOPS code 291) at 6.7 mln US$ (see graph 3).

Graph 3: Exports of services by EBOPS category
(% share in 2012)

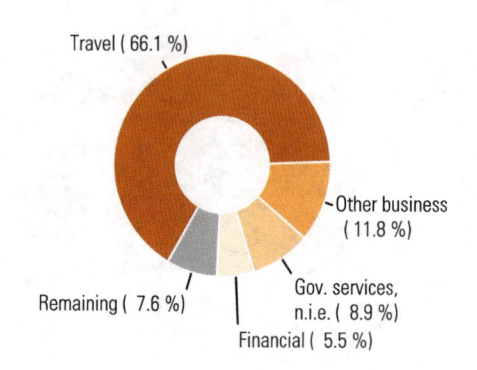

- Travel (66.1 %)
- Other business (11.8 %)
- Gov. services, n.i.e. (8.9 %)
- Financial (5.5 %)
- Remaining (7.6 %)

Table 1: Top 10 export commodities 2012 to 2014

HS code	4-digit heading of Harmonized System 2007	Value (million US$) 2012	2013	2014	Unit value 2012	2013	2014	Unit	SITC code
	All Commodities	1 306.7	1 337.2	1 049.7					
2612	Uranium or thorium ores and concentrates	662.6	659.4	478.2	143.3	140.8	116.7	US$/kg	286
2710	Petroleum oils, other than crude	229.7	383.9	271.8	1.1	1.0	1.0	US$/kg	334
9999	Commodities not specified according to kind	88.8	...	27.1					931
6309	Worn clothing and other worn articles	71.7	20.3	14.9	1.8	1.2	0.8	US$/kg	269
9015	Surveying (including photogrammetrical surveying), hydrographic	0.7	21.1	68.4					874
1006	Rice	30.7	22.7	23.4	0.7	0.6	0.6	US$/kg	042
5208	Woven fabrics of cotton, containing 85 % or more by weight of cotton	29.9	16.9	15.0	25.6	34.9	26.7	US$/kg	652
1701	Cane or beet sugar and chemically pure sucrose, in solid form	36.5	8.6	10.3	0.8	0.6	0.6	US$/kg	061
7108	Gold (including gold plated with platinum)	...	54.9	...		48.5		thsd US$/kg	971
0703	Onions, shallots, garlic, leeks and other alliaceous vegetables	16.6	16.0	13.4	0.2	0.2	0.2	US$/kg	054

Source: UN Comtrade and UN ServiceTrade

Niger

Services Imports and Exports: EBOPS 2002 categories

Table 2: Merchandise exports by SITC
(Value in million US$, growth and shares in percentage)

SITC	2014	Avg. Growth rates 2010-2014	Avg. Growth rates 2013-2014	2014 share
Total	1 049.7	21.7	-21.5	100.0
0+1	99.9	4.4	13.1	9.5
2+4	518.0	19.3	-25.7	49.3
3	283.7	148.1	-29.7	27.0
5	1.5	10.3	-93.6	0.1
6	16.8	5.1	-11.4	1.6
7	31.7	-4.4	23.5	3.0
8	71.0	101.3	194.3	6.8
9	27.1	-22.3	-50.7	2.6

Table 3: Merchandise imports by SITC
(Value in million US$, growth and shares in percentage)

SITC	2014	Avg. Growth rates 2010-2014	Avg. Growth rates 2013-2014	2014 share
Total	2 151.1	-1.4	25.5	100.0
0+1	459.5	10.1	-9.0	21.4
2+4	128.4	7.0	0.4	6.0
3	78.1	-27.6	2.9	3.6
5	194.3	8.2	15.3	9.0
6	306.8	-14.2	8.3	14.3
7	800.7	1.6	74.4	37.2
8	183.3	11.8	94.1	8.5

SITC Legend

SITC Code	Description
Total	All commodities
0+1	Food, animals + beverages, tobacco
2+4	Crude materials + anim. & veg. oils
3	Mineral fuels, lubricants
5	Chemicals
6	Goods classified chiefly by material
7	Machinery and transport equipment
8	Miscellaneous manufactured articles
9	Not classified elsewhere in the SITC

Graph 4: Merchandise trade balance
(Mln US$ by MDG Regions in 2014)

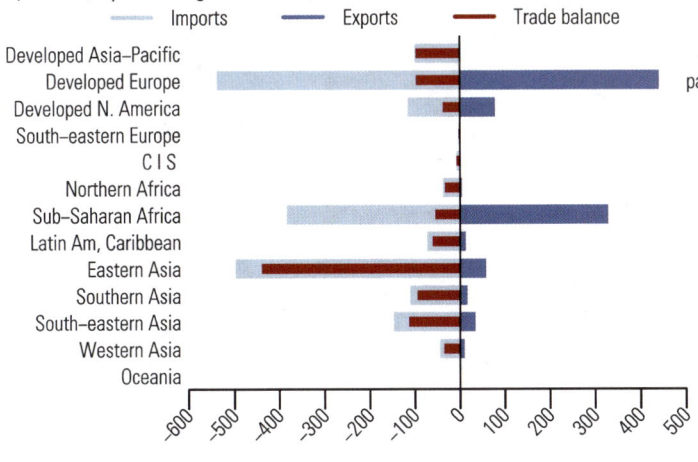

Graph 5: Partner concentration of merchandise trade
(Cumulative share by ranked partners in 2014)

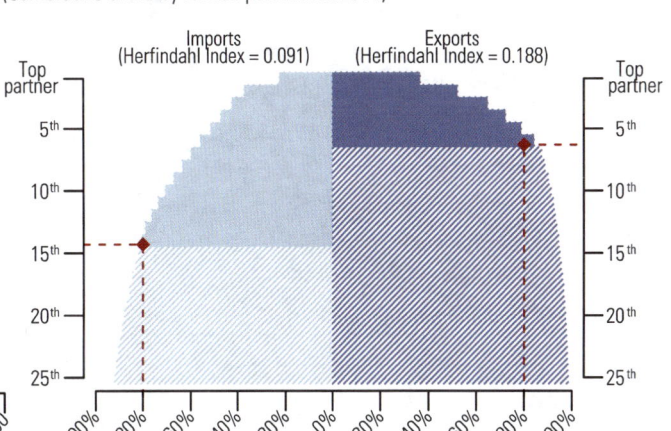

Imports (Herfindahl Index = 0.091)
Exports (Herfindahl Index = 0.188)

Graph 6: Imports of services by EBOPS category
(% share in 2012)

- Transportation (69.6 %)
- Construction (11.8 %)
- Other business (11.5 %)
- Remaining (7.1 %)

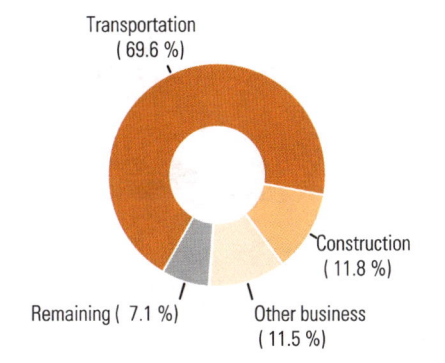

Imports Profile:

"Machinery and transport equipment" (SITC section 7), "Food, animals + beverages, tobacco" (SITC section 0+1) and "Goods classified chiefly by material" (SITC section 6) were the largest commodity groups for imports in 2014, representing respectively 37.2, 21.4 and 14.3 percent of imported goods (see table 3). From 2012 to 2014, the largest import commodity was "Rice" (HS code 1006) (see table 4). The top three partners for merchandise imports were China, France and the United States, accounting for respectively 22.5, 12.3 and 5.9 percent of total imports. "Transportation" (EBOPS code 205) accounted for the largest share of imports of services in 2012 at 574.7 mln US$, followed by "Construction services" (EBOPS code 249) at 97.7 mln US$ and "Other business services" (EBOPS code 268) at 94.9 mln US$ (see graph 6).

Table 4: Top 10 import commodities 2012 to 2014

HS code	4-digit heading of Harmonized System 2007	Value 2012	Value 2013	Value 2014	Unit value 2012	Unit value 2013	Unit value 2014	Unit	SITC code
	All Commodities	1 684.8	1 714.1	2 151.1					
1006	Rice	168.8	195.6	160.5	0.5	0.5	0.4	US$/kg	042
2523	Portland cement, aluminous cement, slag cement	66.1	81.5	106.2	0.2	0.2	0.2	US$/kg	661
8431	Parts suitable for use principally with the machinery of headings 84.25	71.6	64.6	89.9	29.8	37.7	27.3	US$/kg	723
8704	Motor vehicles for the transport of goods	88.8	42.3	47.8					782
8703	Motor cars and other motor vehicles principally designed for the transport	42.5	53.2	66.9	*16.8*	*14.8*	*16.6*	thsd US$/unit	781
8803	Parts of goods of heading 88.01 or 88.02	5.7	20.5	131.7	891.8	557.2	18.7	US$/kg	792
3004	Medicaments (excluding goods of heading 30.02, 30.05 or 30.06)	44.4	53.5	57.4	7.9	14.9	14.1	US$/kg	542
1511	Palm oil and its fractions	42.2	44.5	57.4	0.8	0.9	0.9	US$/kg	422
2402	Cigars, cheroots, cigarillos and cigarettes	41.2	51.1	48.4	9.6	10.5	8.0	US$/kg	122
2710	Petroleum oils, other than crude	36.8	52.4	45.4	1.2	1.4	1.2	US$/kg	334

2014 International Trade Statistics Yearbook, Vol. I — Source: UN Comtrade and UN ServiceTrade

Nigeria

Goods Imports: CIF, by origin **Goods Exports:** FOB, by last known destination **Trade System:** General

Overview:
In 2013, the value of merchandise exports of Nigeria decreased substantially by 36.7 percent to reach 90.6 bln US$, while its merchandise imports increased substantially by 24.3 percent to reach 44.6 bln US$ (see graph 1, table 2 and table 3). The merchandise trade balance recorded a large surplus of 46.0 bln US$ (see graph 1). The largest merchandise trade balance was with MDG Developed Europe at 24.1 bln US$ (see graph 4). Merchandise exports in Nigeria were diversified amongst partners; imports were also diversified. The top 13 partners accounted for 80 percent or more of exports and 17 partners accounted for 80 percent or more of imports (see graph 5). In 2012, the value of exports of services of Nigeria decreased substantially by 29.1 percent, reaching 2.4 bln US$, while its imports of services decreased slightly by 2.6 percent and reached 24.1 bln US$ (see graph 2). There was a large trade in services deficit of 21.7 bln US$.

Graph 1: Total merchandise trade, by value
(Bln US$ by year)

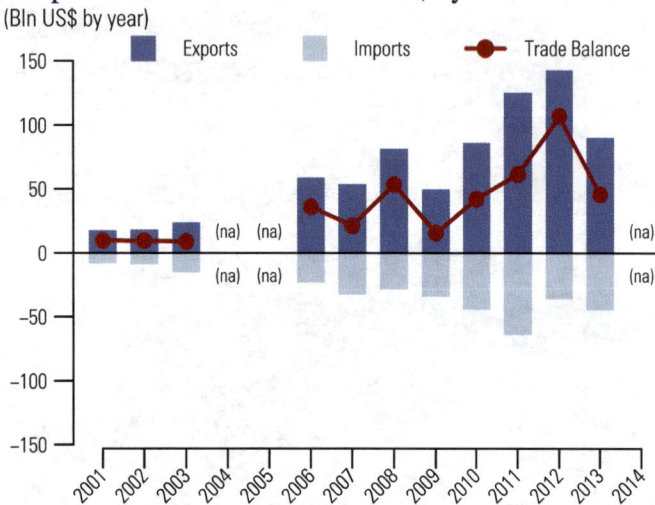

Graph 2: Total services trade, by value
(Bln US$ by year)

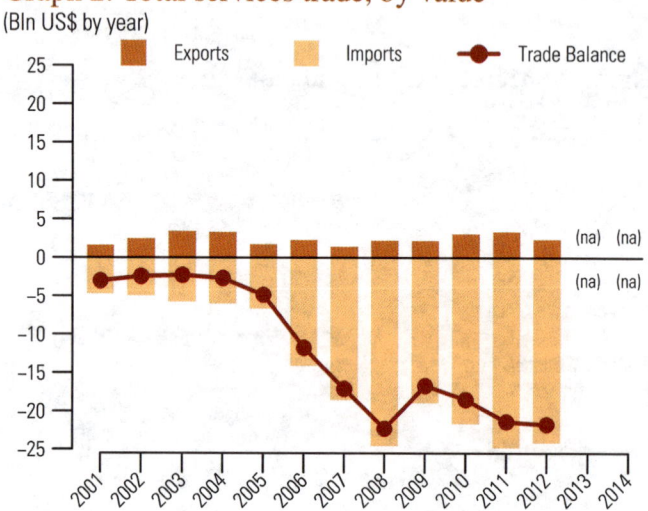

Exports Profile:
"Mineral fuels, lubricants" (SITC section 3), "Crude materials + anim. & veg. oils" (SITC section 2+4) and "Food, animals + beverages, tobacco" (SITC section 0+1) were the largest commodity groups for exports in 2013, representing respectively 87.6, 4.3 and 4.0 percent of exported goods (see table 2). From 2011 to 2013, the largest export commodity was "Petroleum oils and oils obtained from bituminous minerals, crude" (HS code 2709) (see table 1). The top three destinations for merchandise exports were the United States, India and Brazil, accounting for respectively 16.7, 11.2 and 8.3 percent of total exports. "Transportation" (EBOPS code 205) accounted for the largest share of exports of services in 2012 at 1.4 bln US$, followed by "Travel" (EBOPS code 236) at 559.0 mln US$ and "Government services, n.i.e." (EBOPS code 291) at 335.7 mln US$ (see graph 3).

Graph 3: Exports of services by EBOPS category
(% share in 2012)

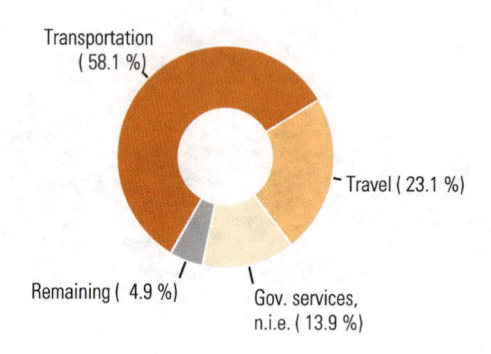

- Transportation (58.1 %)
- Travel (23.1 %)
- Gov. services, n.i.e. (13.9 %)
- Remaining (4.9 %)

Table 1: Top 10 export commodities 2011 to 2013

HS code	4-digit heading of Harmonized System 2007	Value (million US$) 2011	2012	2013	Unit value 2011	2012	2013	Unit	SITC code
	All Commodities..	125 641.0	143 151.2	90 554.5					
2709	Petroleum oils and oils obtained from bituminous minerals, crude............	90 118.9	99 054.5	74 953.8					333
2710	Petroleum oils, other than crude..	15 176.2	12 279.1	2 426.1	2.7			US$/kg	334
4001	Natural rubber, balata, gutta-percha, guayule, chicle.............................	7 445.5	10 067.7	2 427.3					231
2711	Petroleum gases and other gaseous hydrocarbons.................................	6 677.8	8 968.5	1 963.7					343
1801	Cocoa beans, whole or broken, raw or roasted.....................................	958.8	3 033.0	1 542.7	3.9	14.4	8.4	US$/kg	072
8905	Light-vessels, fire-floats, dredgers, floating cranes and other vessels........	774.5	603.7	403.2					793
1207	Other oil seeds and oleaginous fruits, whether or not broken..................	390.2	497.6	867.4	2.3	2.1	4.8	US$/kg	222
4113	Leather further prepared after tanning or crusting................................	431.0	686.1	413.1	10.0	20.7	10.2	US$/kg	611
4106	Tanned or crust hides and skins of other animals, without wool or hair on...	329.0	378.0	431.4	16.2	46.8	14.3	US$/kg	611
0801	Coconuts, Brazil nuts and cashew nuts, fresh or dried...........................	204.6	634.4	285.3	4.2	7.8	4.4	US$/kg	057

Nigeria

Services Imports and Exports: EBOPS 2002 categories

Table 2: Merchandise exports by SITC
(Value in million US$, growth and shares in percentage)

SITC	2013	Avg. Growth rates 2009-2013	2012-2013	2013 share
Total	90 554.5	16.0	-36.7	100.0
0+1	3 662.0	15.4	-48.8	4.0
2+4	3 898.2	49.9	-64.5	4.3
3	79 346.9	15.2	-34.0	87.6
5	346.7	3.6	7.1	0.4
6	1 769.6	20.9	-17.4	2.0
7	842.9	11.1	-55.7	0.9
8	594.2	31.5	105.0	0.7
9	94.0	0.9	97.1	0.1

Table 3: Merchandise imports by SITC
(Value in million US$, growth and shares in percentage)

SITC	2013	Avg. Growth rates 2009-2013	2012-2013	2013 share
Total	44 598.2	7.1	24.3	100.0
0+1	7 588.4	17.9	-4.0	17.0
2+4	1 795.5	34.3	170.1	4.0
3	8 989.8	127.7	959.1	20.2
5	5 445.1	4.6	26.3	12.2
6	6 030.4	-1.2	6.9	13.5
7	13 279.1	-4.9	-12.8	29.8
8	1 459.1	-3.6	15.9	3.3
9	10.8	-55.2	7.9	0.0

SITC Legend

SITC Code	Description
Total	All commodities
0+1	Food, animals + beverages, tobacco
2+4	Crude materials + anim. & veg. oils
3	Mineral fuels, lubricants
5	Chemicals
6	Goods classified chiefly by material
7	Machinery and transport equipment
8	Miscellaneous manufactured articles
9	Not classified elsewhere in the SITC

Graph 4: Merchandise trade balance
(Bln US$ by MDG Regions in 2013)

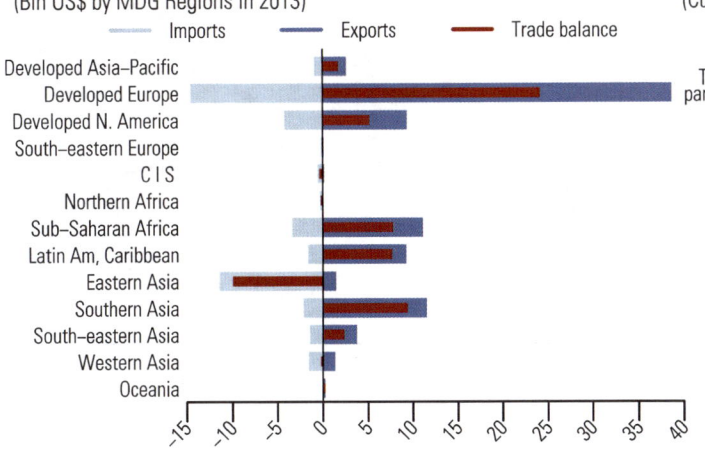

Graph 5: Partner concentration of merchandise trade
(Cumulative share by ranked partners in 2013)

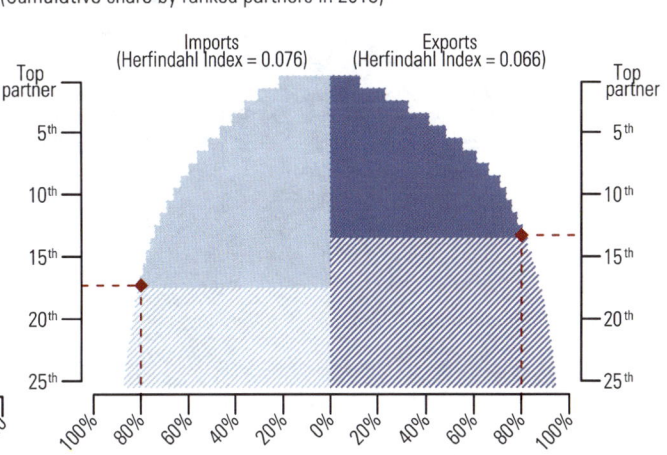

Imports (Herfindahl Index = 0.076)
Exports (Herfindahl Index = 0.066)

Graph 6: Imports of services by EBOPS category
(% share in 2012)

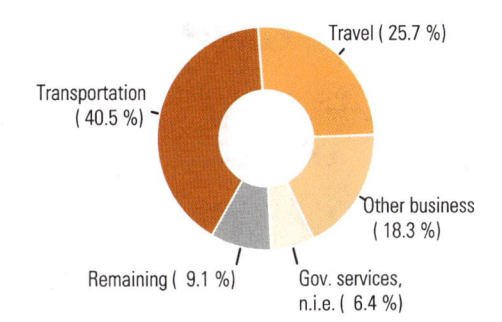

- Transportation (40.5 %)
- Travel (25.7 %)
- Other business (18.3 %)
- Gov. services, n.i.e. (6.4 %)
- Remaining (9.1 %)

Imports Profile:

"Machinery and transport equipment" (SITC section 7), "Mineral fuels, lubricants" (SITC section 3) and "Food, animals + beverages, tobacco" (SITC section 0+1) were the largest commodity groups for imports in 2013, representing respectively 29.8, 20.2 and 17.0 percent of imported goods (see table 3). From 2011 to 2013, the largest import commodity was "Petroleum oils, other than crude" (HS code 2710) (see table 4). The top three partners for merchandise imports were China, the United States and Brazil, accounting for respectively 18.6, 14.1 and 5.3 percent of total imports. "Transportation" (EBOPS code 205) accounted for the largest share of imports of services in 2012 at 9.8 bln US$, followed by "Travel" (EBOPS code 236) at 6.2 bln US$ and "Other business services" (EBOPS code 268) at 4.4 bln US$ (see graph 6).

Table 4: Top 10 import commodities 2011 to 2013

HS code	4-digit heading of Harmonized System 2007	2011	2012	2013	2011	2012	2013	Unit	SITC code
	All Commodities	63 971.5	35 872.5	44 598.2					
2710	Petroleum oils, other than crude	5 815.2	534.0	8 598.6	5.0	3.5	10.6	US$/kg	334
8703	Motor cars and other motor vehicles principally designed for the transport	3 014.1	3 607.0	1 071.6		20.2	18.7	thsd US$/unit	781
1001	Wheat and meslin	3 476.0	1 491.3	1 294.9	2.0	0.8	0.7	US$/kg	041
0303	Fish, frozen, excluding fish fillets and other fish meat of heading 03.04	1 786.9	1 231.0	970.3	4.4	2.9	2.9	US$/kg	034
1902	Pasta, whether or not cooked or stuffed	3 745.2	1.7	4.0	4.4	0.0	0.0	thsd US$/kg	048
1006	Rice	1 652.9	1 920.2	38.0	3.7	4.0	1.9	US$/kg	042
1701	Cane or beet sugar and chemically pure sucrose, in solid form	1 478.7	948.4	873.3	1.0	0.8	0.6	US$/kg	061
8704	Motor vehicles for the transport of goods	1 089.0	1 078.9	598.3					782
8517	Electrical apparatus for line telephony or line telegraphy	830.6	947.5	633.5					764
0402	Milk and cream, concentrated or containing added sugar	1 582.3	426.6	387.3	10.5	3.2	3.5	US$/kg	022

Norway, including Svalbard and Jan Mayen Islands

Goods Imports: CIF, by origin   **Goods Exports:** FOB, by last known destination   **Trade System:** General

Overview:

In 2014, the value of merchandise exports of Norway decreased moderately by 7.5 percent to reach 142.8 bln US$, while its merchandise imports decreased slightly by 0.7 percent to reach 89.2 bln US$ (see graph 1, table 2 and table 3). The merchandise trade balance recorded a moderate surplus of 53.7 bln US$ (see graph 1). The largest merchandise trade balance was with MDG Developed Europe at 60.3 bln US$ (see graph 4). Merchandise exports in Norway were diversified amongst partners; imports were also diversified. The top 10 partners accounted for 80 percent or more of exports and 17 partners accounted for 80 percent or more of imports (see graph 5). In 2012, the value of exports of services of Norway increased slightly by 1.5 percent, reaching 42.9 bln US$, while its imports of services increased slightly by 2.9 percent and reached 48.5 bln US$ (see graph 2). There was a relatively small trade in services deficit of 5.6 bln US$.

Graph 1: Total merchandise trade, by value
(Bln US$ by year)

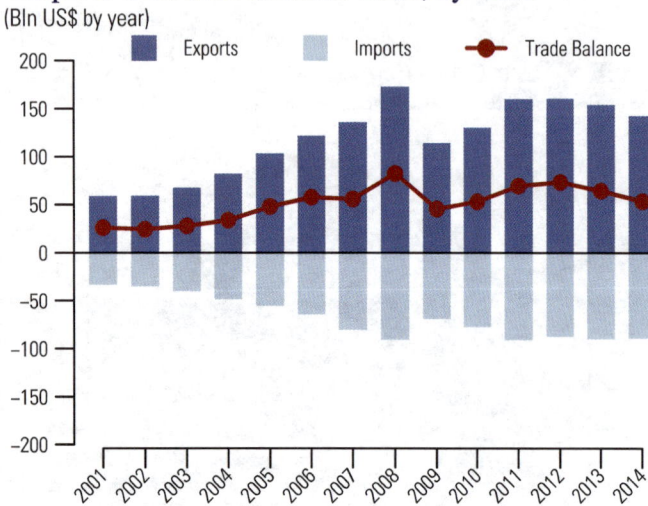

Graph 2: Total services trade, by value
(Bln US$ by year)

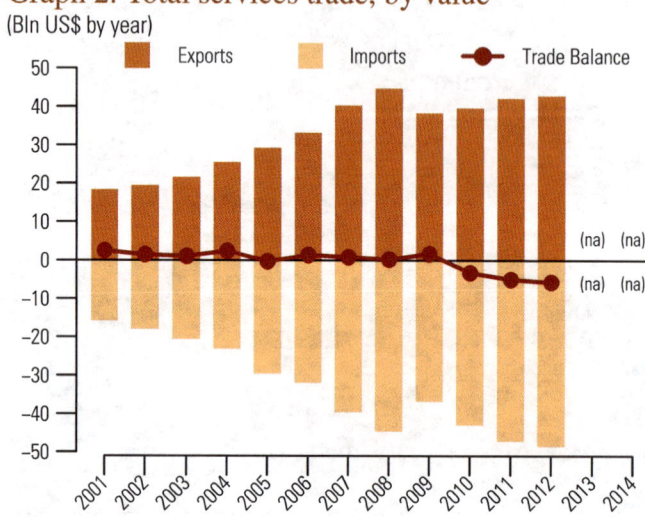

Exports Profile:

"Mineral fuels, lubricants" (SITC section 3), "Machinery and transport equipment" (SITC section 7) and "Food, animals + beverages, tobacco" (SITC section 0+1) were the largest commodity groups for exports in 2014, representing respectively 64.4, 9.5 and 8.1 percent of exported goods (see table 2). From 2012 to 2014, the largest export commodity was "Petroleum oils and oils obtained from bituminous minerals, crude" (HS code 2709) (see table 1). The top three destinations for merchandise exports were the United Kingdom, Germany and the Netherlands, accounting for respectively 24.6, 15.3 and 11.9 percent of total exports. "Transportation" (EBOPS code 205) accounted for the largest share of exports of services in 2012 at 17.2 bln US$, followed by "Other business services" (EBOPS code 268) at 13.8 bln US$ and "Travel" (EBOPS code 236) at 5.4 bln US$ (see graph 3).

Graph 3: Exports of services by EBOPS category
(% share in 2012)

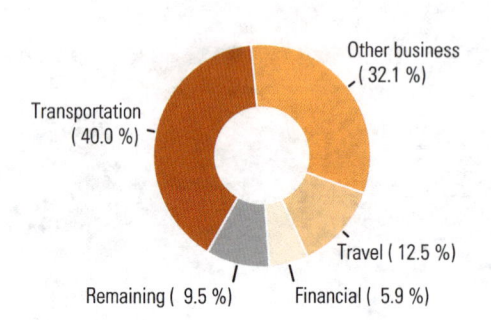

- Transportation (40.0 %)
- Other business (32.1 %)
- Travel (12.5 %)
- Financial (5.9 %)
- Remaining (9.5 %)

Table 1: Top 10 export commodities 2012 to 2014

HS code	4-digit heading of Harmonized System 2012	Value (million US$) 2012	2013	2014	Unit value 2012	2013	2014	Unit	SITC code
	All Commodities	160 952.2	154 391.1	142 825.1					
2709	Petroleum oils and oils obtained from bituminous minerals, crude	54 655.9	48 748.6	44 162.4	0.8	0.8	0.7	US$/kg	333
2711	Petroleum gases and other gaseous hydrocarbons	47 840.3	46 067.3	39 324.0	0.5	0.5	0.5	US$/kg	343
2710	Petroleum oils, other than crude	8 949.6	8 392.0	7 591.4	0.9	0.9	0.8	US$/kg	334
0302	Fish, fresh or chilled, excluding fish fillets	4 473.9	5 993.3	6 007.4	4.0	5.6	5.0	US$/kg	034
9999	Commodities not specified according to kind	4 897.9	4 996.4	4 705.6					931
7601	Unwrought aluminium	3 346.0	2 973.0	3 185.5	2.5	2.4	2.4	US$/kg	684
0303	Fish, frozen, excluding fish fillets and other fish meat of heading 03.04	1 574.5	1 658.5	1 765.8	1.9	2.1	2.1	US$/kg	034
0304	Fish fillets and other fish meat (whether or not minced)	1 502.7	1 527.1	1 728.6	5.2	6.0	6.4	US$/kg	034
7502	Unwrought nickel	1 626.9	1 378.3	1 450.2	17.8	15.4	16.8	US$/kg	683
8431	Parts suitable for use principally with the machinery of headings 84.25	1 379.4	1 369.1	1 244.4	32.8	38.0	38.6	US$/kg	723

Norway, including Svalbard and Jan Mayen Islands

Services Imports and Exports: EBOPS 2002 categories

Table 2: Merchandise exports by SITC
(Value in million US$, growth and shares in percentage)

SITC	2014	Avg. Growth rates 2010-2014	Avg. Growth rates 2013-2014	2014 share
Total	142 825.1	2.3	-7.5	100.0
0+1	11 497.6	5.6	4.8	8.1
2+4	2 521.5	8.0	1.7	1.8
3	92 014.9	2.5	-11.5	64.4
5	3 848.2	-4.1	5.6	2.7
6	10 546.8	-1.9	-0.6	7.4
7	13 631.6	2.6	0.8	9.5
8	3 907.3	4.1	-0.4	2.7
9	4 857.2	0.4	-7.0	3.4

Table 3: Merchandise imports by SITC
(Value in million US$, growth and shares in percentage)

SITC	2014	Avg. Growth rates 2010-2014	Avg. Growth rates 2013-2014	2014 share
Total	89 164.0	3.6	-0.7	100.0
0+1	7 275.1	8.0	2.1	8.2
2+4	5 819.6	-0.1	-0.8	6.5
3	4 714.4	-1.7	-25.9	5.3
5	8 149.9	2.3	1.5	9.1
6	13 636.5	4.7	4.9	15.3
7	34 959.5	4.0	0.5	39.2
8	13 552.1	4.3	0.6	15.2
9	1 056.9	1.2	-10.2	1.2

SITC Legend

SITC Code	Description
Total	All commodities
0+1	Food, animals + beverages, tobacco
2+4	Crude materials + anim. & veg. oils
3	Mineral fuels, lubricants
5	Chemicals
6	Goods classified chiefly by material
7	Machinery and transport equipment
8	Miscellaneous manufactured articles
9	Not classified elsewhere in the SITC

Graph 4: Merchandise trade balance
(Bln US$ by MDG Regions in 2014)

Graph 5: Partner concentration of merchandise trade
(Cumulative share by ranked partners in 2014)

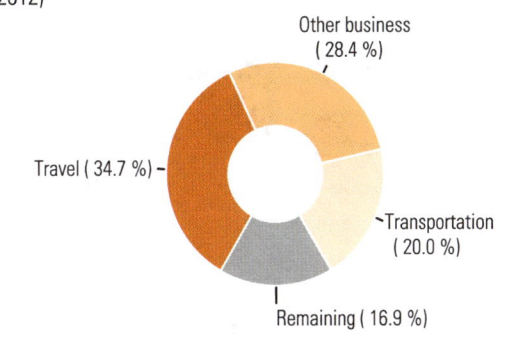

Imports (Herfindahl Index = 0.059)
Exports (Herfindahl Index = 0.112)

Graph 6: Imports of services by EBOPS category
(% share in 2012)

- Other business (28.4 %)
- Travel (34.7 %)
- Transportation (20.0 %)
- Remaining (16.9 %)

Imports Profile:

"Machinery and transport equipment" (SITC section 7), "Goods classified chiefly by material" (SITC section 6) and "Miscellaneous manufactured articles" (SITC section 8) were the largest commodity groups for imports in 2014, representing respectively 39.2, 15.3 and 15.2 percent of imported goods (see table 3). From 2012 to 2014, the largest import commodity was "Motor cars and other motor vehicles principally designed for the transport" (HS code 8703) (see table 4). The top three partners for merchandise imports were Sweden, Germany and China, accounting for respectively 13.0, 12.2 and 9.3 percent of total imports. "Travel" (EBOPS code 236) accounted for the largest share of imports of services in 2012 at 16.9 bln US$, followed by "Other business services" (EBOPS code 268) at 13.8 bln US$ and "Transportation" (EBOPS code 205) at 9.7 bln US$ (see graph 6).

Table 4: Top 10 import commodities 2012 to 2014

HS code	4-digit heading of Harmonized System 2012	Value 2012	Value 2013	Value 2014	Unit value 2012	Unit value 2013	Unit value 2014	Unit	SITC code
	All Commodities	87 307.8	89 815.6	89 164.0					
8703	Motor cars and other motor vehicles principally designed for the transport	5 271.4	5 693.2	5 550.6	27.2	28.4	28.6	thsd US$/unit	781
2710	Petroleum oils, other than crude	3 332.8	3 680.5	2 860.3	1.0	0.9	0.9	US$/kg	334
7501	Nickel mattes, nickel oxide sinters and other intermediate products	2 280.2	1 846.3	1 859.8	12.0	10.3	11.5	US$/kg	284
8517	Electrical apparatus for line telephony or line telegraphy	1 757.2	1 925.2	1 885.8					764
8471	Automatic data processing machines and units thereof	1 804.2	1 786.9	1 740.7	291.2	249.5	302.8	US$/unit	752
3004	Medicaments (excluding goods of heading 30.02, 30.05 or 30.06)	1 438.1	1 403.9	1 529.2	130.9	136.2	136.3	US$/kg	542
8704	Motor vehicles for the transport of goods	1 458.6	1 422.9	1 301.4	46.0	52.0	49.9	thsd US$/unit	782
9403	Other furniture and parts thereof	1 292.9	1 255.1	1 297.0					821
8901	Cruise ships, excursion boats, ferry-boats, cargo ships, barges	1 365.7	1 502.9	812.7	35.9	48.5	29.0	mln US$/unit	793
7308	Structures (excluding prefabricated buildings of heading 94.06)	1 212.3	1 120.0	1 255.8	4.1	3.8	4.4	US$/kg	691

2014 International Trade Statistics Yearbook, Vol. I — Source: UN Comtrade and UN ServiceTrade

Oman

Goods Imports: CIF, by origin   **Goods Exports: FOB, by last known destination**   **Trade System: General**

Overview:
In 2013, the value of merchandise exports of Oman increased moderately by 6.4 percent to reach 55.5 bln US$, while its merchandise imports increased substantially by 22.1 percent to reach 34.3 bln US$ (see graph 1, table 2 and table 3). The merchandise trade balance recorded a moderate surplus of 21.2 bln US$ (see graph 1). The largest merchandise trade balance was with MDG Western Asia at -5.7 bln US$ (see graph 4). Merchandise exports in Oman were highly concentrated amongst partners; imports were diversified. The top 6 partners accounted for 80 percent or more of exports and 14 partners accounted for 80 percent or more of imports (see graph 5). In 2012, the value of exports of services of Oman increased substantially by 33.8 percent, reaching 2.9 bln US$, while its imports of services increased substantially by 22.9 percent and reached 8.7 bln US$ (see graph 2). There was a large trade in services deficit of 5.8 bln US$.

Graph 1: Total merchandise trade, by value
(Bln US$ by year)

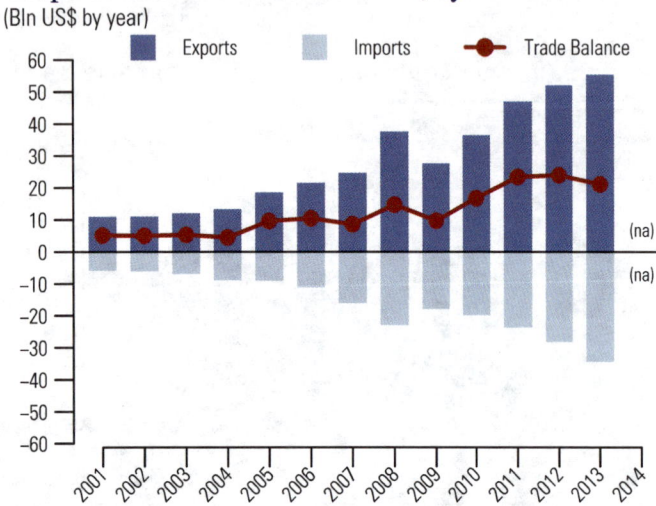

Graph 2: Total services trade, by value
(Bln US$ by year)

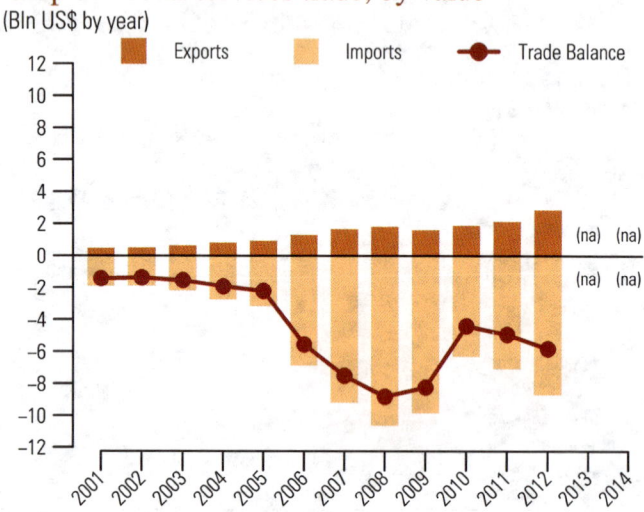

Exports Profile:
"Mineral fuels, lubricants" (SITC section 3), "Not classified elsewhere in the SITC" (SITC section 9) and "Chemicals" (SITC section 5) were the largest commodity groups for exports in 2013, representing respectively 74.8, 8.2 and 5.6 percent of exported goods (see table 2). From 2011 to 2013, the largest export commodity was "Petroleum oils, crude" (HS code 2709) (see table 1). The top three destinations for merchandise exports were Areas nes, China and the United Arab Emirates, accounting for respectively 50.5, 10.9 and 6.7 percent of total exports. "Travel" (EBOPS code 236) accounted for the largest share of exports of services in 2012 at 1.1 bln US$, followed by "Transportation" (EBOPS code 205) at 1.0 bln US$ and "Other business services" (EBOPS code 268) at 616.4 mln US$ (see graph 3).

Graph 3: Exports of services by EBOPS category
(% share in 2012)

- Transportation (36.4 %)
- Travel (38.1 %)
- Other business (21.4 %)
- Remaining (4.1 %)

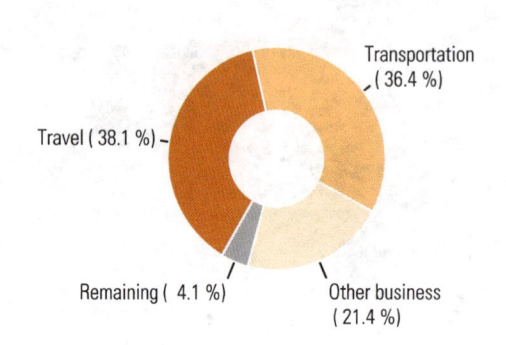

Table 1: Top 10 export commodities 2011 to 2013

HS code	4-digit heading of Harmonized System 2002	Value (million US$) 2011	2012	2013	Unit value 2011	2012	2013	Unit	SITC code
	All Commodities	47091.9	52138.2	55497.1					
2709	Petroleum oils, crude	27723.4	30676.6	32087.1	0.8			US$/kg	333
9999	Commodities not specified according to kind	6920.5	4011.1	4543.6					931
2710	Petroleum oils, other than crude	1924.1	4411.2	4959.8	1.0	1.0	1.1	US$/kg	334
2711	Petroleum gases and other gaseous hydrocarbons	2313.0	4215.5	4369.1	1.1		0.5	US$/kg	343
3102	Mineral or chemical fertilisers, nitrogenous	961.5	990.6	905.9	0.4	0.3	0.2	US$/kg	562
2902	Cyclic hydrocarbons	1264.1	948.2	380.2	2.0	1.1	0.5	US$/kg	511
2601	Iron ores and concentrates	149.8	816.7	1259.6	0.1	0.5	0.2	US$/kg	281
7601	Unwrought aluminium	499.1	733.2	691.2	0.2	1.5	1.0	US$/kg	684
2905	Acyclic alcohols and their derivatives	664.2	620.3	609.4	0.5	0.4	0.4	US$/kg	512
7203	Ferrous products obtained by direct reduction of iron ore	442.5	438.0	619.1	0.7	0.7	0.3	US$/kg	671

Oman

Services Imports and Exports: EBOPS 2002 categories

Table 2: Merchandise exports by SITC
(Value in million US$, growth and shares in percentage)

SITC	2013	Avg. Growth rates 2009-2013	Avg. Growth rates 2012-2013	2013 share
Total	55497.1	19.0	6.4	100.0
0+1	1236.4	17.7	23.5	2.2
2+4	1740.3	49.2	43.6	3.1
3	41484.5	23.6	5.5	74.8
5	3132.4	21.3	-9.9	5.6
6	2336.2	17.2	11.3	4.2
7	813.1	-6.3	-1.2	1.5
8	204.1	-12.7	-0.2	0.4
9	4550.2	-1.2	13.2	8.2

Table 3: Merchandise imports by SITC
(Value in million US$, growth and shares in percentage)

SITC	2013	Avg. Growth rates 2009-2013	Avg. Growth rates 2012-2013	2013 share
Total	34331.2	17.8	22.1	100.0
0+1	2922.7	12.6	8.6	8.5
2+4	2081.5	38.6	15.0	6.1
3	7640.4	65.9	216.3	22.3
5	2973.9	18.6	17.9	8.7
6	5120.2	13.3	0.1	14.9
7	11512.4	8.4	115.2	33.5
8	1835.8	17.6	14.1	5.3
9	244.3	-18.6	-96.3	0.7

SITC Legend

SITC Code	Description
Total	All commodities
0+1	Food, animals + beverages, tobacco
2+4	Crude materials + anim. & veg. oils
3	Mineral fuels, lubricants
5	Chemicals
6	Goods classified chiefly by material
7	Machinery and transport equipment
8	Miscellaneous manufactured articles
9	Not classified elsewhere in the SITC

Graph 4: Merchandise trade balance
(Bln US$ by MDG Regions in 2013)

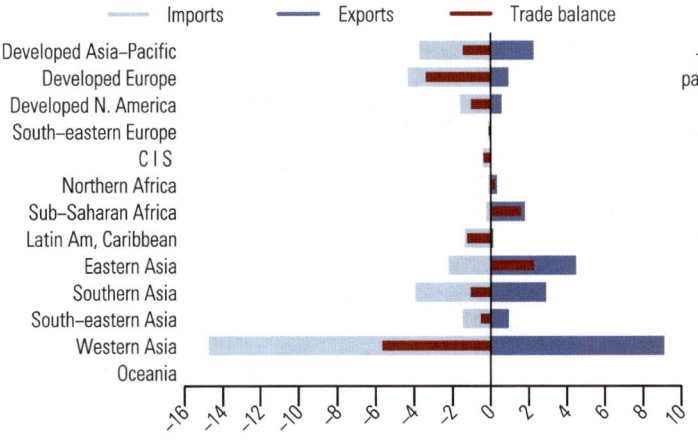

Graph 5: Partner concentration of merchandise trade
(Cumulative share by ranked partners in 2013)

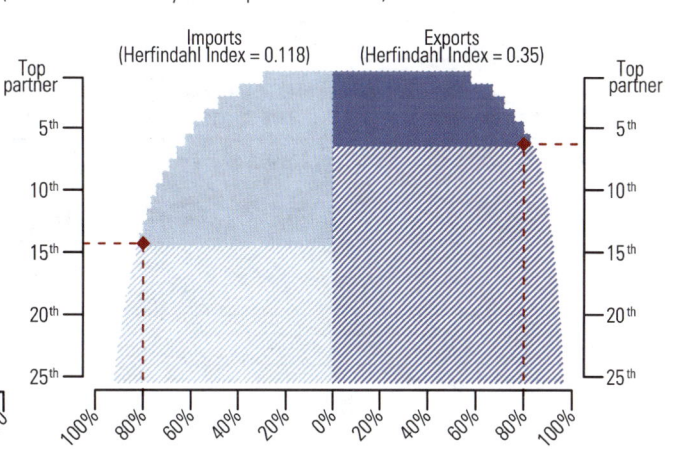

Imports (Herfindahl Index = 0.118)
Exports (Herfindahl Index = 0.35)

Graph 6: Imports of services by EBOPS category
(% share in 2012)

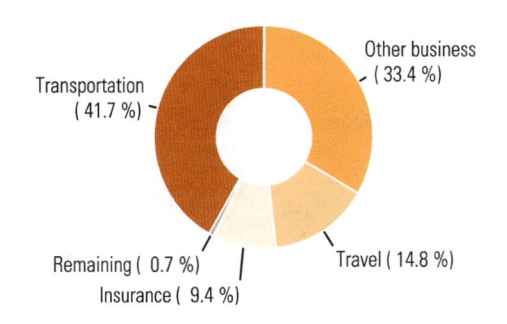

- Transportation (41.7 %)
- Other business (33.4 %)
- Travel (14.8 %)
- Insurance (9.4 %)
- Remaining (0.7 %)

Imports Profile:

"Machinery and transport equipment" (SITC section 7), "Mineral fuels, lubricants" (SITC section 3) and "Goods classified chiefly by material" (SITC section 6) were the largest commodity groups for imports in 2013, representing respectively 33.5, 22.3 and 14.9 percent of imported goods (see table 3). From 2011 to 2013, the largest import commodity was "Petroleum oils, other than crude" (HS code 2710) (see table 4). The top three partners for merchandise imports were the United Arab Emirates, Areas nes and Japan, accounting for respectively 26.9, 11.3 and 8.0 percent of total imports. "Transportation" (EBOPS code 205) accounted for the largest share of imports of services in 2012 at 3.6 bln US$, followed by "Other business services" (EBOPS code 268) at 2.9 bln US$ and "Travel" (EBOPS code 236) at 1.3 bln US$ (see graph 6).

Table 4: Top 10 import commodities 2011 to 2013

HS code	4-digit heading of Harmonized System 2002	2011	2012	2013	2011	2012	2013	Unit	SITC code
	All Commodities	23619.4	28117.6	34331.2					
2710	Petroleum oils, other than crude	2315.9	2027.9	7184.3	0.9	1.5	1.0	US$/kg	334
8703	Motor cars and other motor vehicles principally designed for the transport	3126.8	...	3885.0			28.5	thsd US$/unit	781
9999	Commodities not specified according to kind	338.2	6496.6	17.3					931
2601	Iron ores and concentrates	537.2	1034.9	1235.9	0.3	0.5	0.2	US$/kg	281
7304	Tubes, pipes and hollow profiles, seamless, of iron (other than cast iron)	377.3	701.3	527.6	1.7	1.8	2.0	US$/kg	679
8431	Parts suitable for use principally with the machinery of headings 84.25	524.3	463.6	441.6	1.8	10.0	10.4	US$/kg	723
8708	Parts and accessories of the motor vehicles of headings 87.01 to 87.05	687.3	...	653.3	18.0		15.2	US$/kg	784
8704	Motor vehicles for the transport of goods	461.1	...	781.5					782
2917	Polycarboxylic acids, their anhydrides	298.6	374.2	467.9	1.3	1.2	1.2	US$/kg	513
7407	Copper bars, rods and profiles	333.5	282.5	406.0	8.8	7.6	7.9	US$/kg	682

2014 International Trade Statistics Yearbook, Vol. I   Source: UN Comtrade and UN ServiceTrade

Pakistan

Goods Imports: CIF, by origin | **Goods Exports: FOB, by last known destination** | **Trade System: General**

Overview:
In 2014, the value of merchandise exports of Pakistan decreased slightly by 1.6 percent to reach 24.7 bln US$, while its merchandise imports increased moderately by 8.6 percent to reach 47.5 bln US$ (see graph 1, table 2 and table 3). The merchandise trade balance recorded a large deficit of 22.8 bln US$ (see graph 1). The largest merchandise trade balance was with MDG Western Asia at -13.2 bln US$ (see graph 4). Merchandise exports in Pakistan were diversified amongst partners; imports were also diversified. The top 24 partners accounted for 80 percent or more of exports and 15 partners accounted for 80 percent or more of imports (see graph 5). In 2013, the value of exports of services of Pakistan decreased substantially by 25.8 percent, reaching 4.9 bln US$, while its imports of services decreased moderately by 7.0 percent and reached 7.8 bln US$ (see graph 2). There was a moderate trade in services deficit of 2.9 bln US$.

Graph 1: Total merchandise trade, by value
(Bln US$ by year)

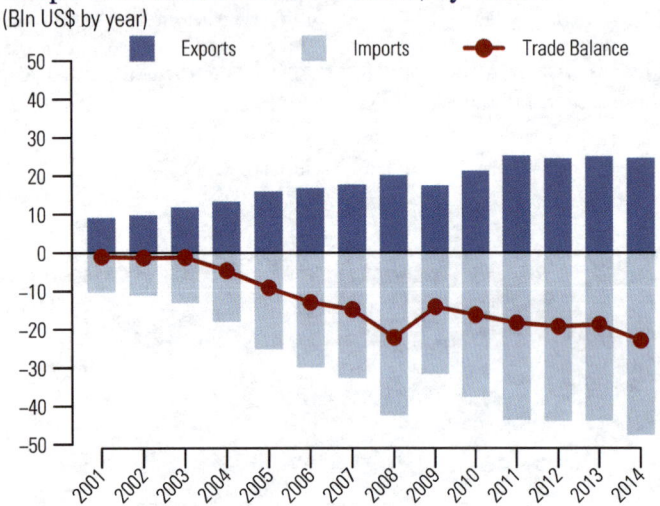

Graph 2: Total services trade, by value
(Bln US$ by year)

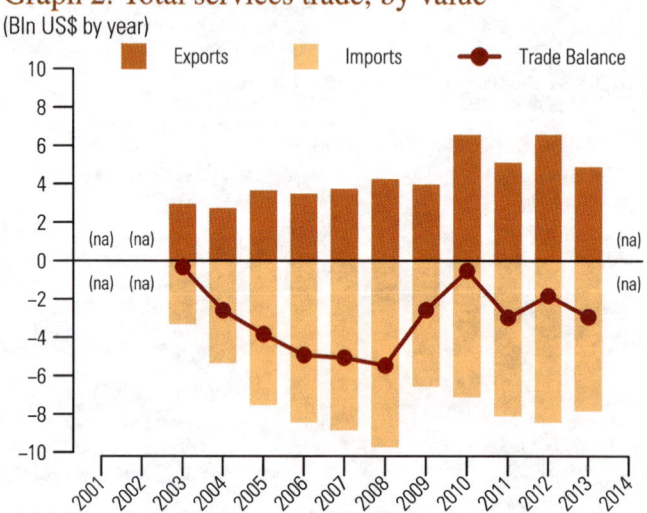

Exports Profile:
"Goods classified chiefly by material" (SITC section 6), "Miscellaneous manufactured articles" (SITC section 8) and "Food, animals + beverages, tobacco" (SITC section 0+1) were the largest commodity groups for exports in 2014, representing respectively 43.6, 25.2 and 18.1 percent of exported goods (see table 2). From 2012 to 2014, the largest export commodity was "Bed linen, table linen, toilet linen and kitchen linen" (HS code 6302) (see table 1). The top three destinations for merchandise exports were the United States, China and Afghanistan, accounting for respectively 14.9, 10.1 and 8.0 percent of total exports. "Government services, n.i.e." (EBOPS code 291) accounted for the largest share of exports of services in 2013 at 1.6 bln US$, followed by "Transportation" (EBOPS code 205) at 1.2 bln US$ and "Other business services" (EBOPS code 268) at 759.0 mln US$ (see graph 3).

Graph 3: Exports of services by EBOPS category
(% share in 2013)

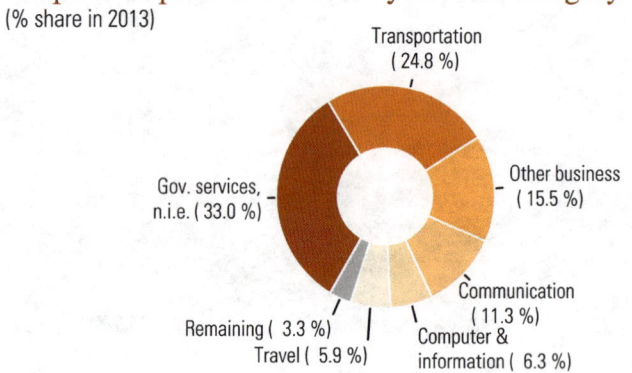

- Transportation (24.8 %)
- Other business (15.5 %)
- Communication (11.3 %)
- Computer & information (6.3 %)
- Travel (5.9 %)
- Remaining (3.3 %)
- Gov. services, n.i.e. (33.0 %)

Table 1: Top 10 export commodities 2012 to 2014

HS code	4-digit heading of Harmonized System 2012	Value (million US$) 2012	2013	2014	Unit value 2012	2013	2014	Unit	SITC code
	All Commodities	24 613.7	25 120.9	24 722.2					
6302	Bed linen, table linen, toilet linen and kitchen linen	2 516.7	2 852.5	3 026.7	5.9	5.9	5.9	US$/kg	658
1006	Rice	1 882.1	2 111.0	2 199.6		0.5	0.6	US$/kg	042
5205	Cotton yarn (other than sewing thread), containing 85 % or more	2 102.7	2 205.4	1 871.6	3.0	3.1	2.9	US$/kg	651
5209	Woven fabrics of cotton, containing 85 % or more by weight of cotton	1 087.6	1 210.2	1 059.3		8.6	8.9	US$/kg	652
6203	Men's or boys'suits, ensembles, jackets, blazers, trousers	921.2	969.6	1 084.5	6.4	6.6	6.0	US$/unit	841
5208	Woven fabrics of cotton, containing 85 % or more by weight of cotton	728.1	746.7	730.7					652
7113	Articles of jewellery and parts thereof, of precious metal	1 610.9	425.9	105.5					897
4203	Articles of apparel and clothing accessories, of leather	633.2	696.6	703.5					848
6204	Women's or girls'suits, ensembles, jackets, blazers, dresses, skirts	590.9	691.2	698.8	6.7	6.7	6.7	US$/unit	842
2523	Portland cement, aluminous cement, slag cement	570.3	529.7	516.9	0.1	0.1	0.1	US$/kg	661

Pakistan

Services Imports and Exports: EBOPS 2002 categories

Table 2: Merchandise exports by SITC
(Value in million US$, growth and shares in percentage)

SITC	2014	Avg. Growth rates 2010-2014	Avg. Growth rates 2013-2014	2014 share
Total	24722.2	3.7	-1.6	100.0
0+1	4483.0	6.9	-6.0	18.1
2+4	1077.8	8.0	-15.1	4.4
3	647.6	-14.3	22.9	2.6
5	1067.2	7.6	-4.2	4.3
6	10786.5	4.1	-2.0	43.6
7	436.5	-6.3	13.2	1.8
8	6222.2	3.4	2.8	25.2
9	1.4	7.0	518.3	0.0

Table 3: Merchandise imports by SITC
(Value in million US$, growth and shares in percentage)

SITC	2014	Avg. Growth rates 2010-2014	Avg. Growth rates 2013-2014	2014 share
Total	47544.9	6.1	8.6	100.0
0+1	2708.9	2.5	32.3	5.7
2+4	5824.3	3.9	13.5	12.3
3	14821.7	6.8	-2.8	31.2
5	7295.1	6.0	14.2	15.3
6	5525.4	8.6	20.5	11.6
7	9508.6	5.4	17.6	20.0
8	1826.5	13.0	-3.4	3.8
9	34.4	-28.0	-91.3	0.1

SITC Legend

SITC Code	Description
Total	All commodities
0+1	Food, animals + beverages, tobacco
2+4	Crude materials + anim. & veg. oils
3	Mineral fuels, lubricants
5	Chemicals
6	Goods classified chiefly by material
7	Machinery and transport equipment
8	Miscellaneous manufactured articles
9	Not classified elsewhere in the SITC

Graph 4: Merchandise trade balance
(Bln US$ by MDG Regions in 2014)

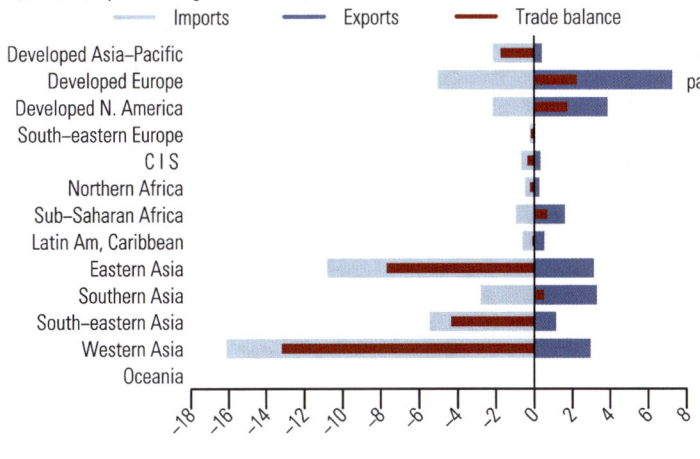

Graph 5: Partner concentration of merchandise trade
(Cumulative share by ranked partners in 2014)

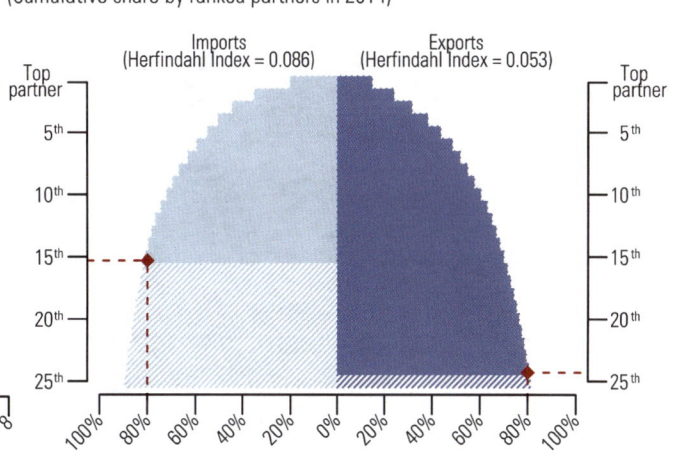

Imports (Herfindahl Index = 0.086) Exports (Herfindahl Index = 0.053)

Graph 6: Imports of services by EBOPS category
(% share in 2013)

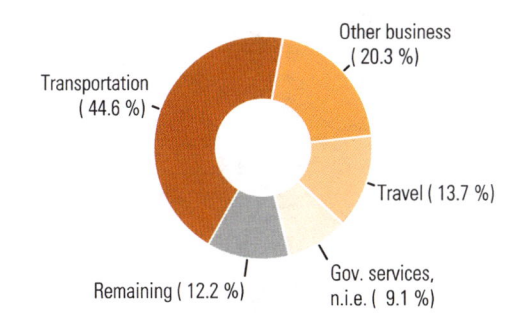

- Transportation (44.6 %)
- Other business (20.3 %)
- Travel (13.7 %)
- Gov. services, n.i.e. (9.1 %)
- Remaining (12.2 %)

Imports Profile:

"Mineral fuels, lubricants" (SITC section 3), "Machinery and transport equipment" (SITC section 7) and "Chemicals" (SITC section 5) were the largest commodity groups for imports in 2014, representing respectively 31.2, 20.0 and 15.3 percent of imported goods (see table 3). From 2012 to 2014, the largest import commodity was "Petroleum oils, other than crude" (HS code 2710) (see table 4). The top three partners for merchandise imports were China, the United Arab Emirates and Saudi Arabia, accounting for respectively 16.9, 16.3 and 9.3 percent of total imports. "Transportation" (EBOPS code 205) accounted for the largest share of imports of services in 2013 at 3.5 bln US$, followed by "Other business services" (EBOPS code 268) at 1.6 bln US$ and "Travel" (EBOPS code 236) at 1.1 bln US$ (see graph 6).

Table 4: Top 10 import commodities 2012 to 2014

HS code	4-digit heading of Harmonized System 2012	Value 2012	Value 2013	Value 2014	Unit 2012	Unit 2013	Unit 2014	Unit	SITC code
	All Commodities	43813.3	43775.2	47544.9					
2710	Petroleum oils, other than crude	9966.1	9258.0	8558.1	0.8	0.8	0.7	US$/kg	334
2709	Petroleum oils and oils obtained from bituminous minerals, crude	5270.3	5473.3	5609.1	0.8	0.8	0.8	US$/kg	333
1511	Palm oil and its fractions	2131.6	1842.9	1943.6	1.0	0.8	0.8	US$/kg	422
8517	Electrical apparatus for line telephony or line telegraphy	1394.7	1161.2	1353.8					764
8703	Motor cars and other motor vehicles principally designed for the transport	900.6	689.4	703.3			538.8	US$/unit	781
7204	Ferrous waste and scrap; remelting scrap ingots of iron or steel	617.4	662.2	908.4	0.3	0.4	0.4	US$/kg	282
8908	Vessels and other floating structures for breaking up	525.3	962.8	581.1	6.3	6.6	0.1	mln US$/unit	793
5201	Cotton, not carded or combed	565.0	757.3	521.6	2.3	2.0	2.2	US$/kg	263
2902	Cyclic hydrocarbons	611.4	613.7	474.1	1.5	1.6	1.4	US$/kg	511
3902	Polymers of propylene or of other olefins, in primary forms	451.7	476.1	586.3	1.5	1.6	1.6	US$/kg	575

Panama

Goods Imports: CIF, by origin **Goods Exports:** FOB, by last known destination **Trade System:** Special

Overview:
In 2014, the value of merchandise exports of Panama decreased slightly by 3.0 percent to reach 818.2 mln US$, while its merchandise imports increased moderately by 5.2 percent to reach 13.7 bln US$ (see graph 1, table 2 and table 3). The merchandise trade balance recorded a large deficit of 12.9 bln US$ (see graph 1). The largest merchandise trade balance was with MDG Developed North America at -3.4 bln US$ (see graph 4). Merchandise exports in Panama were diversified amongst partners; imports were also diversified. The top 17 partners accounted for 80 percent or more of exports and 11 partners accounted for 80 percent or more of imports (see graph 5). In 2013, the value of exports of services of Panama increased slightly by 4.5 percent, reaching 9.8 bln US$, while its imports of services increased substantially by 12.7 percent and reached 4.7 bln US$ (see graph 2). There was a large trade in services surplus of 5.1 bln US$. See footnote*.

Graph 1: Total merchandise trade, by value
(Bln US$ by year)

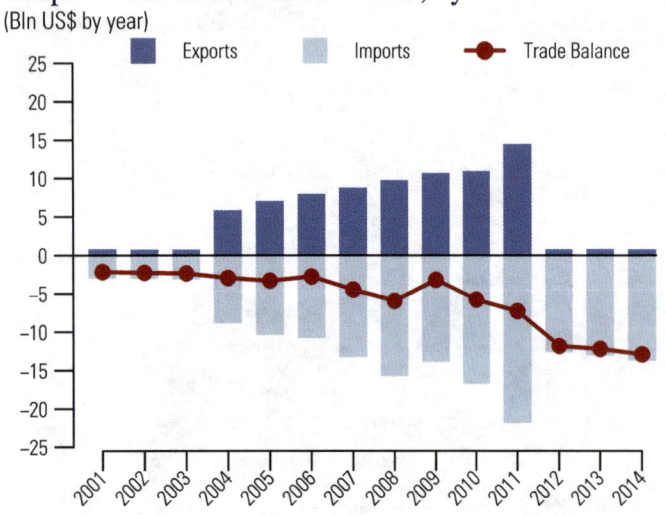

Graph 2: Total services trade, by value
(Bln US$ by year)

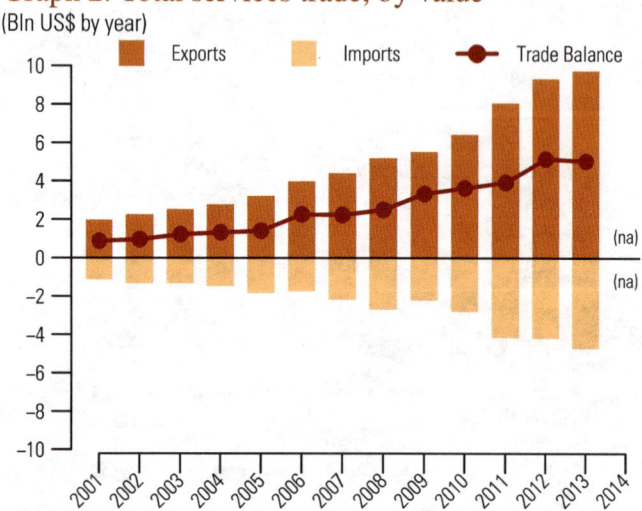

Exports Profile:
"Food, animals + beverages, tobacco" (SITC section 0+1), "Crude materials + anim. & veg. oils" (SITC section 2+4) and "Goods classified chiefly by material" (SITC section 6) were the largest commodity groups for exports in 2014, representing respectively 63.5, 20.6 and 9.3 percent of exported goods (see table 2). From 2012 to 2014, the largest export commodity was "Bananas, including plantains, fresh or dried" (HS code 0803) (see table 1). The top three destinations for merchandise exports were the United States, Canada and Costa Rica, accounting for respectively 19.6, 7.5 and 6.4 percent of total exports. "Transportation" (EBOPS code 205) accounted for the largest share of exports of services in 2013 at 4.8 bln US$, followed by "Travel" (EBOPS code 236) at 3.3 bln US$ (see graph 3).

Graph 3: Exports of services by EBOPS category
(% share in 2013)

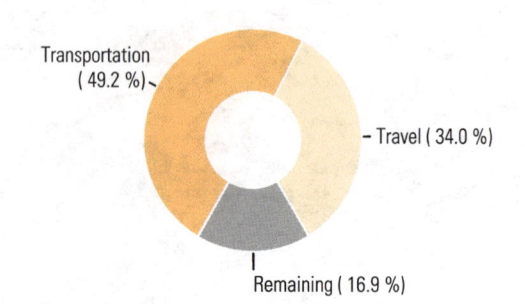

- Transportation (49.2 %)
- Travel (34.0 %)
- Remaining (16.9 %)

Table 1: Top 10 export commodities 2012 to 2014

HS code	4-digit heading of Harmonized System 2012	Value (million US$) 2012	2013	2014	Unit value 2012	2013	2014	Unit	SITC code
	All Commodities	821.9	843.9	818.2					
0803	Bananas, including plantains, fresh or dried	89.3	95.6	97.9	0.4	0.4	0.4	US$/kg	057
0306	Crustaceans, whether in shell or not	42.6	75.3	80.9	6.1	8.1	6.9	US$/kg	036
7108	Gold (including gold plated with platinum)	115.8	66.5	1.1	38.7	33.3	23.7	thsd US$/kg	971
7204	Ferrous waste and scrap; remelting scrap ingots of iron or steel	56.9	45.9	45.7	0.2	0.1	0.2	US$/kg	282
0302	Fish, fresh or chilled, excluding fish fillets	37.7	47.2	54.2	3.1	2.8	2.8	US$/kg	034
0804	Dates, figs, pineapples, avocados and mangosteens, fresh or dried	37.1	44.1	31.9	0.5	0.5	0.5	US$/kg	057
1701	Cane or beet sugar and chemically pure sucrose, in solid form	34.5	24.0	27.7	0.7	0.5	0.5	US$/kg	061
2301	Flours, meals and pellets, of meat or meat offal	16.4	28.4	41.0	0.8	1.0	1.0	US$/kg	081
4403	Wood in the rough, whether or not stripped of bark or sapwood	21.0	28.7	28.2					247
7404	Copper waste and scrap	19.8	25.7	22.7	3.2	4.0	3.6	US$/kg	288

*From 2004 to 2011 merchandise data including Zona Libre de Colon.

Panama

Services Imports and Exports: EBOPS 2002 categories

Table 2: Merchandise exports by SITC
(Value in million US$, growth and shares in percentage)

SITC	2014	Avg. Growth rates 2010-2014	Avg. Growth rates 2013-2014	2014 share
Total	818.2	-47.8	-3.0	100.0
0+1	519.8	-9.8	7.0	63.5
2+4	168.7	11.7	3.1	20.6
3	1.3	-22.8	-63.0	0.2
5	30.9	-69.4	6.3	3.8
6	76.1	-44.3	6.0	9.3
8	16.1	-74.5	3.7	2.0
9	5.3	-49.3	-92.9	0.6

Table 3: Merchandise imports by SITC
(Value in million US$, growth and shares in percentage)

SITC	2014	Avg. Growth rates 2010-2014	Avg. Growth rates 2013-2014	2014 share
Total	13 705.3	-4.9	5.2	100.0
0+1	1 551.8	4.8	9.5	11.3
2+4	132.1	6.0	2.1	1.0
3	2 803.0	83.9	4.7	20.5
5	1 246.6	-24.5	-0.1	9.1
6	2 152.7	1.5	17.1	15.7
7	3 945.5	-3.4	1.0	28.8
8	1 853.8	-20.7	3.3	13.5
9	19.8	2.2	29.2	0.1

SITC Legend

SITC Code	Description
Total	All commodities
0+1	Food, animals + beverages, tobacco
2+4	Crude materials + anim. & veg. oils
3	Mineral fuels, lubricants
5	Chemicals
6	Goods classified chiefly by material
7	Machinery and transport equipment
8	Miscellaneous manufactured articles
9	Not classified elsewhere in the SITC

Graph 4: Merchandise trade balance
(Bln US$ by MDG Regions in 2014)

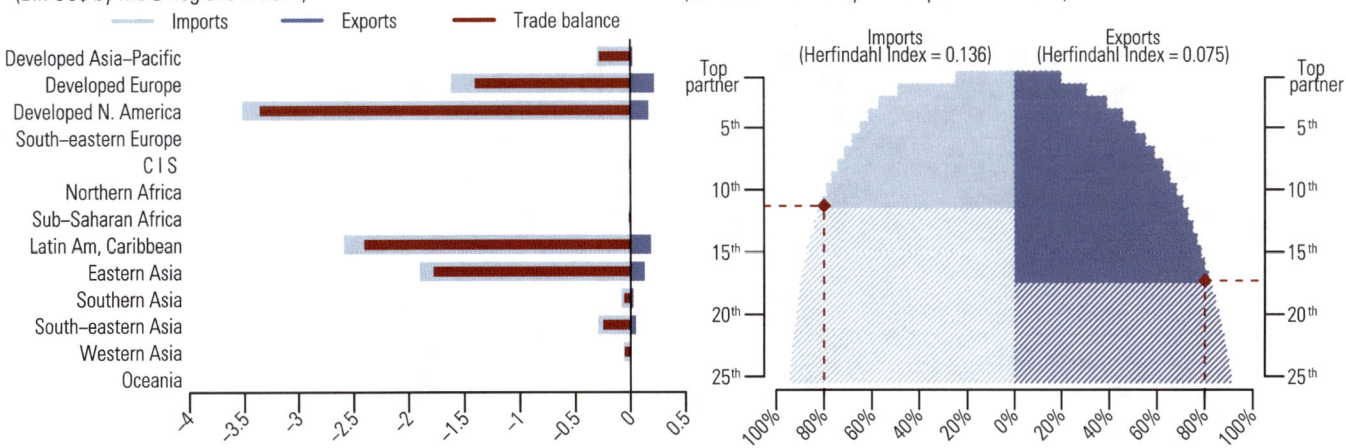

Graph 5: Partner concentration of merchandise trade
(Cumulative share by ranked partners in 2014)

Imports (Herfindahl Index = 0.136)
Exports (Herfindahl Index = 0.075)

Graph 6: Imports of services by EBOPS category
(% share in 2013)

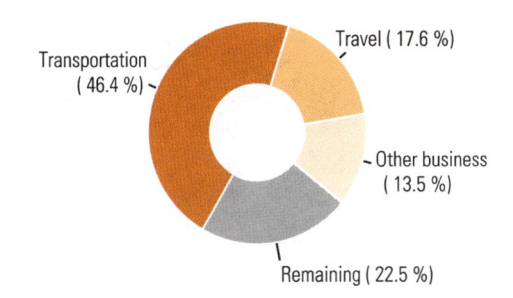

- Transportation (46.4 %)
- Travel (17.6 %)
- Other business (13.5 %)
- Remaining (22.5 %)

Imports Profile:

"Machinery and transport equipment" (SITC section 7), "Mineral fuels, lubricants" (SITC section 3) and "Goods classified chiefly by material" (SITC section 6) were the largest commodity groups for imports in 2014, representing respectively 28.8, 20.5 and 15.7 percent of imported goods (see table 3). From 2012 to 2014, the largest import commodity was "Petroleum oils, other than crude" (HS code 2710) (see table 4). The top three partners for merchandise imports were the United States, Free zones and Panama, accounting for respectively 24.3, 15.1 and 13.0 percent of total imports. "Transportation" (EBOPS code 205) accounted for the largest share of imports of services in 2013 at 2.2 bln US$, followed by "Travel" (EBOPS code 236) at 829.6 mln US$ and "Other business services" (EBOPS code 268) at 638.6 mln US$ (see graph 6).

Table 4: Top 10 import commodities 2012 to 2014

HS code	4-digit heading of Harmonized System 2012	Value 2012	Value 2013	Value 2014	Unit 2012	Unit 2013	Unit 2014	Unit	SITC code
	All Commodities	12 623.4	13 024.0	13 705.3					
2710	Petroleum oils, other than crude	2 661.8	2 530.7	2 639.2	1.0	1.0	1.0	US$/kg	334
8703	Motor cars and other motor vehicles principally designed for the transport	754.1	794.2	840.2	19.1	18.4	18.0	thsd US$/unit	781
3004	Medicaments (excluding goods of heading 30.02, 30.05 or 30.06)	338.9	336.1	289.6	40.5	39.1	30.5	US$/kg	542
7308	Structures (excluding prefabricated buildings of heading 94.06)	94.1	179.7	454.3	2.6	3.6	4.6	US$/kg	691
8517	Electrical apparatus for line telephony or line telegraphy	197.6	206.3	206.9					764
7214	Other bars and rods of iron or non-alloy steel	185.3	192.3	186.4	0.7	0.7	0.6	US$/kg	676
8471	Automatic data processing machines and units thereof	204.7	180.4	169.2					752
8704	Motor vehicles for the transport of goods	125.2	185.5	121.6					782
9403	Other furniture and parts thereof	143.9	138.5	149.4					821
6402	Other footwear with outer soles and uppers of rubber or plastics	118.6	120.4	120.0	10.0	9.9	10.4	US$/pair	851

2014 International Trade Statistics Yearbook, Vol. I — Source: UN Comtrade and UN ServiceTrade

Papua New Guinea

Goods Imports: CIF, by origin **Goods Exports:** FOB, by consignment **Trade System:** General

Overview:
In 2012, the value of merchandise exports of Papua New Guinea decreased substantially by 17.9 percent to reach 4.5 bln US$, while its merchandise imports increased substantially by 36.6 percent to reach 8.3 bln US$ (see graph 1, table 2 and table 3). The merchandise trade balance recorded a moderate deficit of 3.8 bln US$ (see graph 1). The largest merchandise trade balance was with MDG South-eastern Asia at -1.8 bln US$ (see graph 4). Merchandise exports in Papua New Guinea were moderately concentrated amongst partners; imports were also moderately concentrated. The top 9 partners accounted for 80 percent or more of exports and 8 partners accounted for 80 percent or more of imports (see graph 5). In 2012, the value of exports of services of Papua New Guinea increased substantially by 12.4 percent, reaching 476.9 mln US$, while its imports of services increased substantially by 25.9 percent and reached 3.7 bln US$ (see graph 2). There was a large trade in services deficit of 3.3 bln US$.

Graph 1: Total merchandise trade, by value
(Bln US$ by year)

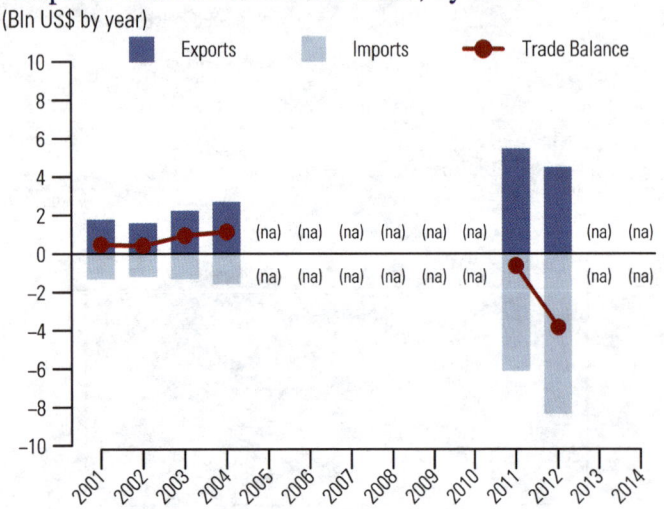

Graph 2: Total services trade, by value
(Bln US$ by year)

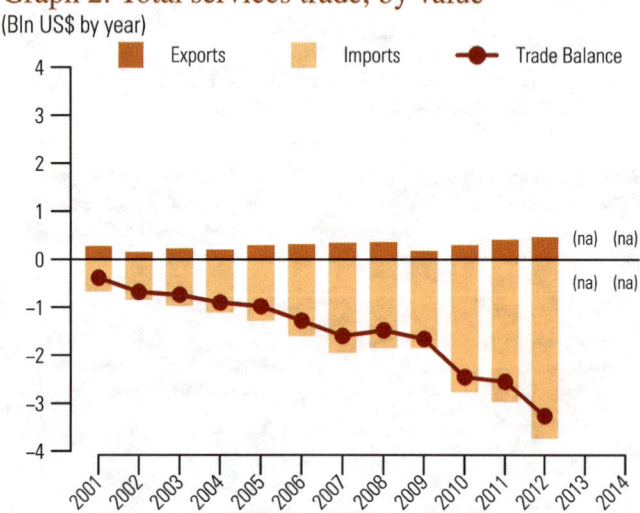

Exports Profile:
"Crude materials + anim. & veg. oils" (SITC section 2+4), "Goods classified chiefly by material" (SITC section 6) and "Food, animals + beverages, tobacco" (SITC section 0+1) were the largest commodity groups for exports in 2012, representing respectively 41.3, 33.6 and 13.5 percent of exported goods (see table 2). From 2010 to 2012, the largest export commodity was "Base metals, silver or gold, clad with platinum" (HS code 7111) (see table 1). The top three destinations for merchandise exports were Australia, Japan and Germany, accounting for respectively 39.7, 9.1 and 6.6 percent of total exports. "Other business services" (EBOPS code 268) accounted for the largest share of exports of services in 2012 at 304.4 mln US$, followed by "Transportation" (EBOPS code 205) at 70.4 mln US$ and "Government services, n.i.e." (EBOPS code 291) at 46.2 mln US$ (see graph 3).

Graph 3: Exports of services by EBOPS category
(% share in 2012)

- Other business (63.8 %)
- Transportation (14.8 %)
- Gov. services, n.i.e. (9.7 %)
- Construction (8.2 %)
- Remaining (3.6 %)

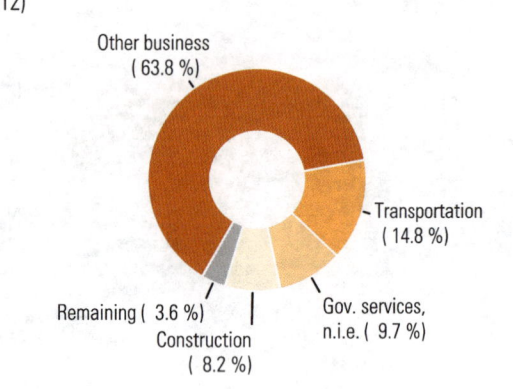

Table 1: Top 10 export commodities 2010 to 2012

HS code	4-digit heading of Harmonized System 2007	Value (million US$) 2010	2011	2012	Unit value 2010	2011	2012	Unit	SITC code
	All Commodities................................	...	5499.3	4517.7					
7111	Base metals, silver or gold, clad with platinum.............	...	2291.9	1493.4		301.8	302.4	thsd US$/kg	681
1511	Palm oil and its fractions................................	...	629.0	506.7		0.9		US$/kg	422
2603	Copper ores and concentrates.........................	...	444.6	406.2		0.0	34.2	US$/kg	283
0901	Coffee, whether or not roasted or decaffeinated.............	...	404.2	254.1		31.4	31.6	US$/kg	071
2616	Precious metal ores and concentrates....................	...	298.2	320.5		1.3	17.4	thsd US$/kg	289
4403	Wood in the rough, whether or not stripped of bark or sapwood....	...	209.5	240.5		84.4	90.7	US$/m^3	247
1513	Coconut (copra), palm kernel or babassu oil.............	...	165.5	81.3		1.1		US$/kg	422
2707	Oils and other products of high temperature coal tar..........	...	175.9	57.2		1.3		US$/kg	335
1801	Cocoa beans, whole or broken, raw or roasted.............	...	147.8	83.9		0.1	0.1	US$/kg	072
1604	Prepared or preserved fish; caviar.......................	...	80.0	102.9		5.1	5.3	US$/kg	037

Papua New Guinea

Services Imports and Exports: EBOPS 2002 categories

Table 2: Merchandise exports by SITC
(Value in million US$, growth and shares in percentage)

SITC	2012	Avg. Growth rates 2008-2012	Avg. Growth rates 2011-2012	2012 share
Total	4517.7	...	-17.9	100.0
0+1	607.9	...	-19.6	13.5
2+4	1866.4	...	-2.1	41.3
3	132.1	...	-36.8	2.9
5	219.6	...	476.2	4.9
6	1519.4	...	-34.6	33.6
7	135.6	...	-32.4	3.0
8	13.2	...	-11.6	0.3
9	23.4	...	-53.6	0.5

Table 3: Merchandise imports by SITC
(Value in million US$, growth and shares in percentage)

SITC	2012	Avg. Growth rates 2008-2012	Avg. Growth rates 2011-2012	2012 share
Total	8340.7	...	36.6	100.0
0+1	860.4	...	27.4	10.3
2+4	114.8	...	54.5	1.4
3	1445.9	...	165.1	17.3
5	484.4	...	23.6	5.8
6	1229.7	...	6.5	14.7
7	3538.3	...	34.7	42.4
8	551.0	...	15.1	6.6
9	116.1	...	-26.7	1.4

SITC Legend

SITC Code	Description
Total	All commodities
0+1	Food, animals + beverages, tobacco
2+4	Crude materials + anim. & veg. oils
3	Mineral fuels, lubricants
5	Chemicals
6	Goods classified chiefly by material
7	Machinery and transport equipment
8	Miscellaneous manufactured articles
9	Not classified elsewhere in the SITC

Graph 4: Merchandise trade balance
(Bln US$ by MDG Regions in 2012)

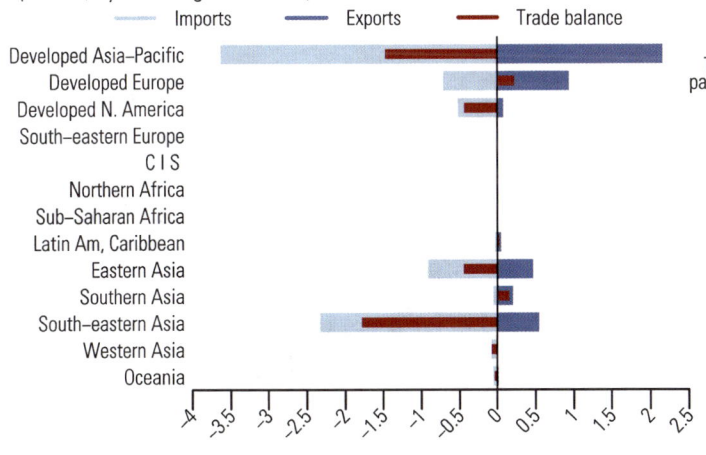

Graph 5: Partner concentration of merchandise trade
(Cumulative share by ranked partners in 2012)

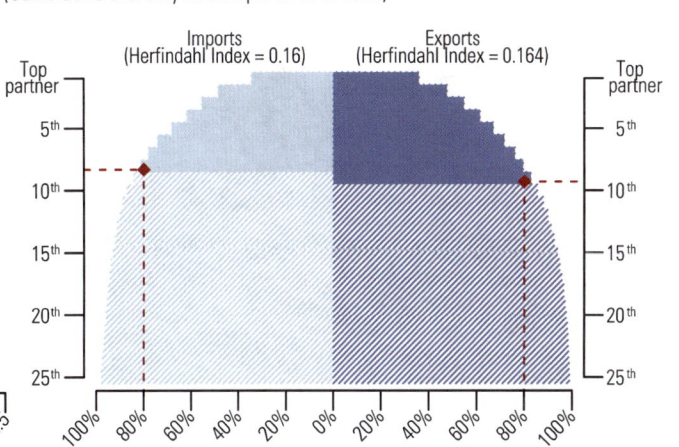

Imports (Herfindahl Index = 0.16)
Exports (Herfindahl Index = 0.164)

Graph 6: Imports of services by EBOPS category
(% share in 2012)

- Construction (33.3%)
- Other business (33.6%)
- Transportation (20.8%)
- Remaining (12.3%)

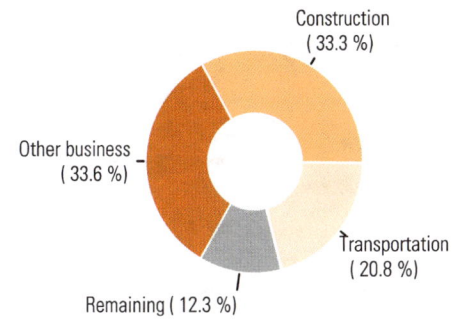

Imports Profile:

"Machinery and transport equipment" (SITC section 7), "Mineral fuels, lubricants" (SITC section 3) and "Goods classified chiefly by material" (SITC section 6) were the largest commodity groups for imports in 2012, representing respectively 42.4, 17.3 and 14.7 percent of imported goods (see table 3). From 2010 to 2012, the largest import commodity was "Petroleum oils, other than crude" (HS code 2710) (see table 4). The top three partners for merchandise imports were Australia, Singapore and China, accounting for respectively 36.5, 12.9 and 7.0 percent of total imports. "Other business services" (EBOPS code 268) accounted for the largest share of imports of services in 2012 at 1.3 bln US$, followed by "Construction services" (EBOPS code 249) at 1.2 bln US$ and "Transportation" (EBOPS code 205) at 777.4 mln US$ (see graph 6).

Table 4: Top 10 import commodities 2010 to 2012

HS code	4-digit heading of Harmonized System 2007	2010	2011	2012	2010	2011	2012	Unit	SITC code
	All Commodities	...	6105.5	8340.7					
2710	Petroleum oils, other than crude	...	465.0	561.1					334
2709	Petroleum oils and oils obtained from bituminous minerals, crude	...	65.7	846.0		0.8		US$/kg	333
8704	Motor vehicles for the transport of goods	...	211.3	288.5		1.5	33.9	thsd US$/unit	782
8431	Parts suitable for use principally with the machinery of headings 84.25	...	214.1	240.0		12.9		US$/kg	723
1006	Rice	...	126.1	218.0		7.1	25.8	US$/kg	042
7308	Structures (excluding prefabricated buildings of heading 94.06)	...	106.1	193.5					691
9999	Commodities not specified according to kind	...	158.3	116.1					931
8481	Taps, cocks, valves and similar appliances for pipes, boiler shells	...	59.9	186.5					747
8702	Motor vehicles for the transport of ten or more persons, including the driver	...	96.8	149.5			30.4	thsd US$/unit	783
8414	Air or vacuum pumps, air or other gas compressors and fans	...	18.5	219.5					743

2014 International Trade Statistics Yearbook, Vol. I Source: UN Comtrade and UN ServiceTrade

Paraguay

Goods Imports: CIF, by origin **Goods Exports: FOB, by last known destination** **Trade System: General**

Overview:
In 2014, the value of merchandise exports of Paraguay increased slightly by 2.4 percent to reach 9.7 bln US$, while its merchandise imports increased slightly by 0.2 percent to reach 12.2 bln US$ (see graph 1, table 2 and table 3). The merchandise trade balance recorded a moderate deficit of 2.5 bln US$ (see graph 1). The largest merchandise trade balance was with MDG Eastern Asia at -3.2 bln US$ (see graph 4). Merchandise exports in Paraguay were diversified amongst partners; imports were moderately concentrated. The top 15 partners accounted for 80 percent or more of exports and 6 partners accounted for 80 percent or more of imports (see graph 5). In 2013, the value of exports of services of Paraguay increased substantially by 11.4 percent, reaching 842.2 mln US$, while its imports of services increased substantially by 15.4 percent and reached 1.1 bln US$ (see graph 2). There was a moderate trade in services deficit of 227.4 mln US$.

Graph 1: Total merchandise trade, by value
(Bln US$ by year)

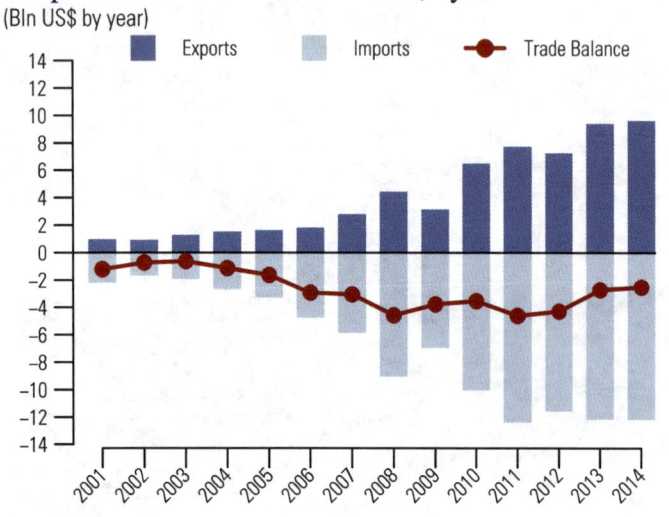

Graph 2: Total services trade, by value
(Bln US$ by year)

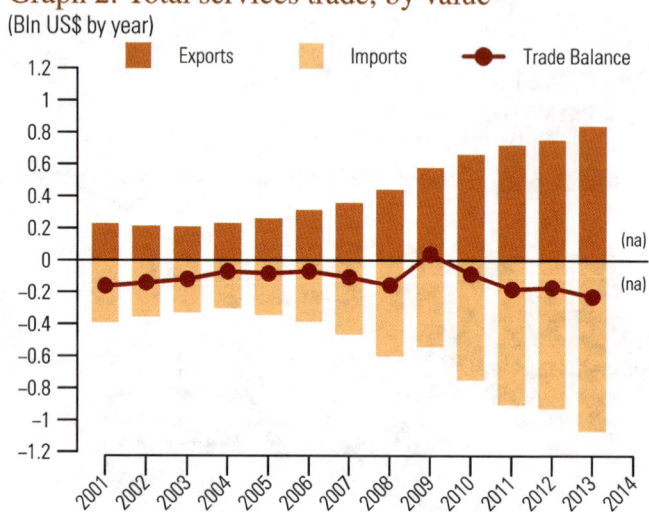

Exports Profile:
"Food, animals + beverages, tobacco" (SITC section 0+1), "Crude materials + anim. & veg. oils" (SITC section 2+4) and "Mineral fuels, lubricants" (SITC section 3) were the largest commodity groups for exports in 2014, representing respectively 34.1, 33.2 and 23.0 percent of exported goods (see table 2). From 2012 to 2014, the largest export commodity was "Electrical energy" (HS code 2716) (see table 1). The top three destinations for merchandise exports were Brazil, the Russian Federation and Argentina, accounting for respectively 32.8, 10.2 and 7.7 percent of total exports. "Transportation" (EBOPS code 205) accounted for the largest share of exports of services in 2013 at 374.0 mln US$, followed by "Travel" (EBOPS code 236) at 272.7 mln US$ and "Government services, n.i.e." (EBOPS code 291) at 156.3 mln US$ (see graph 3).

Graph 3: Exports of services by EBOPS category
(% share in 2013)

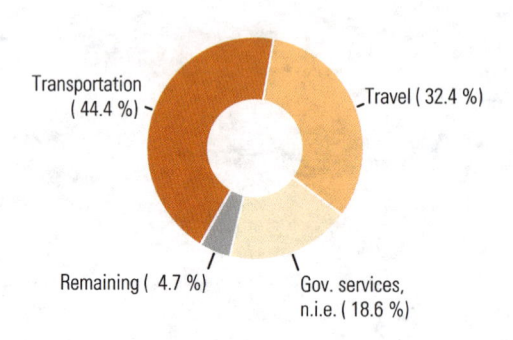

- Transportation (44.4 %)
- Travel (32.4 %)
- Gov. services, n.i.e. (18.6 %)
- Remaining (4.7 %)

Table 1: Top 10 export commodities 2012 to 2014

HS code	4-digit heading of Harmonized System 2012	Value (million US$) 2012	2013	2014	Unit value 2012	2013	2014	Unit	SITC code
	All Commodities	7 271.3	9 432.3	9 655.4					
2716	Electrical energy	2 232.2	2 236.6	2 179.6		65.6	59.5	US$/MWh	351
1201	Soya beans, whether or not broken	1 576.6	2 509.1	2 305.1	0.5	0.5	0.5	US$/kg	222
0202	Meat of bovine animals, frozen	654.4	771.5	831.1	4.1	4.1	4.3	US$/kg	011
2304	Oil-cake and other solid residues	192.5	923.0	1 107.4	0.4	0.5	0.5	US$/kg	081
1005	Maize (corn)	548.9	463.7	356.9	0.2	0.2	0.2	US$/kg	044
1507	Soya-bean oil and its fractions	137.1	467.5	481.1	1.1	0.9	0.8	US$/kg	421
0201	Meat of bovine animals, fresh or chilled	100.8	233.2	453.8	4.7	5.3	5.5	US$/kg	011
1001	Wheat and meslin	358.8	146.1	79.4	0.3	0.3	0.2	US$/kg	041
1006	Rice	117.8	165.4	177.6	0.4	0.4	0.4	US$/kg	042
4104	Tanned or crust hides and skins of bovine (including buffalo)	105.4	153.2	195.3	2.8	3.1	3.7	US$/kg	611

Paraguay

Services Imports and Exports: EBOPS 2002 categories

Table 2: Merchandise exports by SITC
(Value in million US$, growth and shares in percentage)

SITC	2014	Avg. Growth rates 2010-2014	2013-2014	2014 share
Total	9 655.4	10.4	2.4	100.0
0+1	3 294.5	14.4	9.6	34.1
2+4	3 201.4	11.1	-5.1	33.2
3	2 222.1	2.8	-1.6	23.0
5	188.4	12.8	-7.8	2.0
6	362.9	14.2	21.7	3.8
7	158.1	48.4	92.7	1.6
8	201.9	12.9	12.9	2.1
9	26.1	109.8	-24.1	0.3

Table 3: Merchandise imports by SITC
(Value in million US$, growth and shares in percentage)

SITC	2014	Avg. Growth rates 2010-2014	2013-2014	2014 share
Total	12 168.6	4.9	0.2	100.0
0+1	966.7	7.5	4.5	7.9
2+4	164.9	12.0	9.3	1.4
3	1 875.4	11.9	8.3	15.4
5	2 007.3	10.9	3.2	16.5
6	1 614.0	9.4	6.8	13.3
7	4 375.7	0.4	-7.1	36.0
8	1 164.1	-1.7	-0.3	9.6
9	0.4	132.6	-71.5	0.0

SITC Legend

SITC Code	Description
Total	All commodities
0+1	Food, animals + beverages, tobacco
2+4	Crude materials + anim. & veg. oils
3	Mineral fuels, lubricants
5	Chemicals
6	Goods classified chiefly by material
7	Machinery and transport equipment
8	Miscellaneous manufactured articles
9	Not classified elsewhere in the SITC

Graph 4: Merchandise trade balance
(Bln US$ by MDG Regions in 2014)

Graph 5: Partner concentration of merchandise trade
(Cumulative share by ranked partners in 2014)

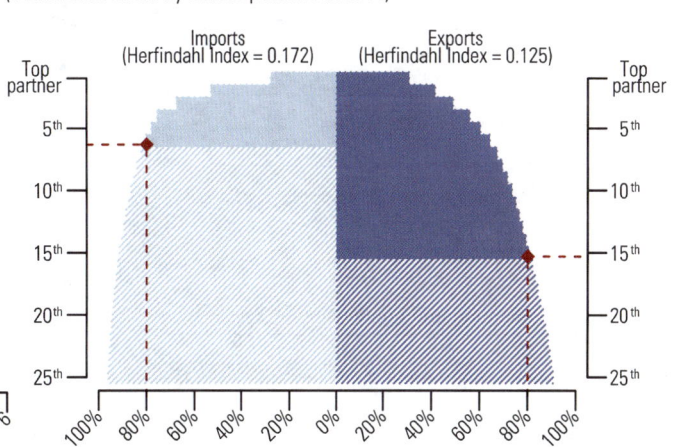

Imports (Herfindahl Index = 0.172)
Exports (Herfindahl Index = 0.125)

Graph 6: Imports of services by EBOPS category
(% share in 2013)

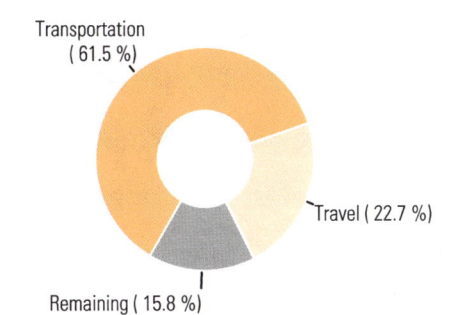

- Transportation (61.5 %)
- Travel (22.7 %)
- Remaining (15.8 %)

Imports Profile:

"Machinery and transport equipment" (SITC section 7), "Chemicals" (SITC section 5) and "Mineral fuels, lubricants" (SITC section 3) were the largest commodity groups for imports in 2014, representing respectively 36.0, 16.5 and 15.4 percent of imported goods (see table 3). From 2012 to 2014, the largest import commodity was "Petroleum oils, other than crude" (HS code 2710) (see table 4). The top three partners for merchandise imports were China, Brazil and Argentina, accounting for respectively 27.0, 25.9 and 15.0 percent of total imports. "Transportation" (EBOPS code 205) accounted for the largest share of imports of services in 2013 at 657.9 mln US$, followed by "Travel" (EBOPS code 236) at 243.0 mln US$ (see graph 6).

Table 4: Top 10 import commodities 2012 to 2014

HS code	4-digit heading of Harmonized System 2012	2012	2013	2014	2012	2013	2014	Unit	SITC code
	All Commodities	11 555.1	12 142.0	12 168.6					
2710	Petroleum oils, other than crude	1 734.4	1 639.1	1 793.5	1.1	1.1	1.1	US$/kg	334
8517	Electrical apparatus for line telephony or line telegraphy	630.7	783.3	644.6					764
8703	Motor cars and other motor vehicles principally designed for the transport	468.3	489.6	538.9		16.1	16.6	thsd US$/unit	781
3105	Mineral or chemical fertilisers	366.1	421.7	414.9	0.6	0.6	0.5	US$/kg	562
8471	Automatic data processing machines and units thereof	424.5	361.9	284.1					752
3808	Insecticides, rodenticides, fungicides, herbicides	248.5	310.5	323.5	8.0	8.4	9.3	US$/kg	591
9504	Articles for funfair, table or parlour games, including pintables	327.4	253.1	240.6					894
8704	Motor vehicles for the transport of goods	271.0	252.3	257.3					782
4011	New pneumatic tyres, of rubber	186.1	211.5	196.8					625
8528	Reception apparatus for television	187.3	210.3	196.6					761

2014 International Trade Statistics Yearbook, Vol. I — Source: UN Comtrade and UN ServiceTrade

Peru

Goods Imports: CIF, by origin   **Goods Exports:** FOB, by last known destination   **Trade System:** Special

Overview:

In 2013, the value of merchandise exports of Peru decreased moderately by 8.9 percent to reach 41.9 bln US$, while its merchandise imports increased slightly by 2.6 percent to reach 43.4 bln US$ (see graph 1, table 2 and table 3). The merchandise trade balance recorded a relatively small deficit of 1.5 bln US$ (see graph 1). The largest merchandise trade balance was with MDG Developed Europe at 4.3 bln US$ (see graph 4). Merchandise exports in Peru were diversified amongst partners; imports were also diversified. The top 14 partners accounted for 80 percent or more of exports and 14 partners accounted for 80 percent or more of imports (see graph 5). In 2012, the value of exports of services of Peru increased substantially by 17.5 percent, reaching 5.1 bln US$, while its imports of services increased substantially by 13.7 percent and reached 7.4 bln US$ (see graph 2). There was a moderate trade in services deficit of 2.3 bln US$.

Graph 1: Total merchandise trade, by value
(Bln US$ by year)

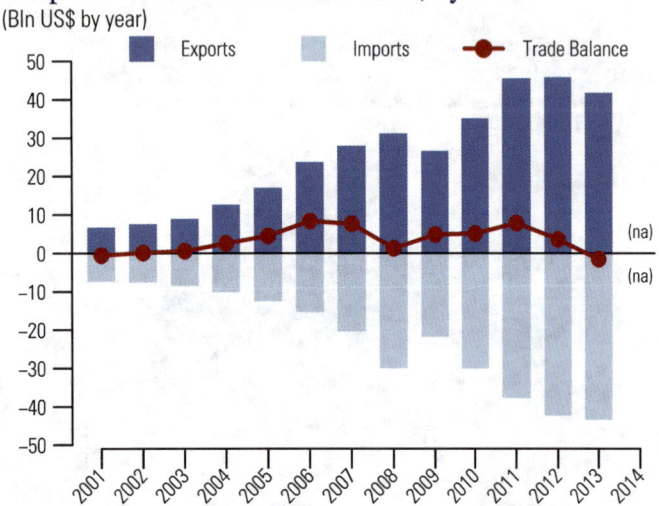

Graph 2: Total services trade, by value
(Bln US$ by year)

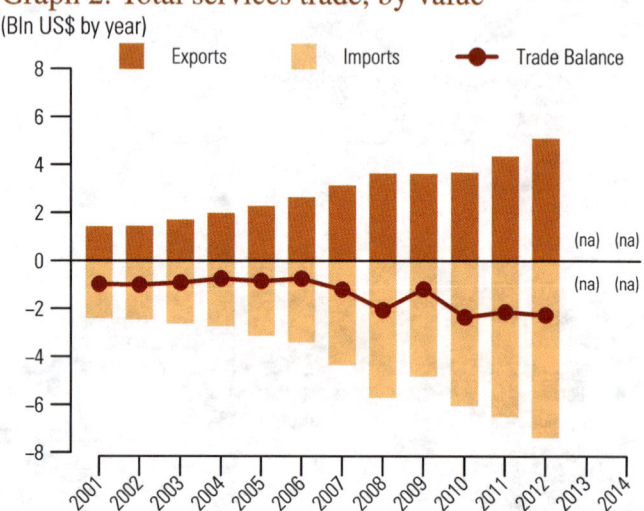

Exports Profile:

"Crude materials + anim. & veg. oils" (SITC section 2+4), "Not classified elsewhere in the SITC" (SITC section 9) and "Food, animals + beverages, tobacco" (SITC section 0+1) were the largest commodity groups for exports in 2013, representing respectively 30.8, 19.2 and 15.1 percent of exported goods (see table 2). From 2011 to 2013, the largest export commodity was "Gold (including gold plated with platinum)" (HS code 7108) (see table 1). The top three destinations for merchandise exports were China, the United States and Switzerland, accounting for respectively 16.6, 15.0 and 10.5 percent of total exports. "Travel" (EBOPS code 236) accounted for the largest share of exports of services in 2012 at 2.7 bln US$, followed by "Transportation" (EBOPS code 205) at 1.2 bln US$ and "Other business services" (EBOPS code 268) at 469.1 mln US$ (see graph 3).

Graph 3: Exports of services by EBOPS category
(% share in 2012)

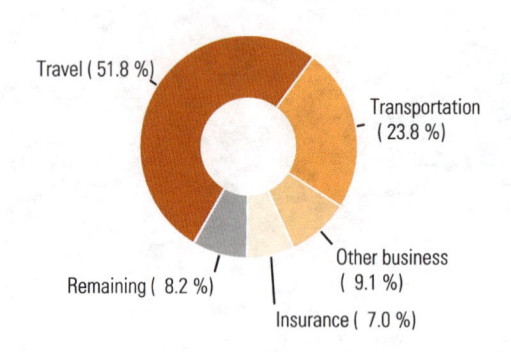

- Travel (51.8 %)
- Transportation (23.8 %)
- Other business (9.1 %)
- Insurance (7.0 %)
- Remaining (8.2 %)

Table 1: Top 10 export commodities 2011 to 2013

HS code	4-digit heading of Harmonized System 2007	Value (million US$) 2011	2012	2013	Unit value 2011	2012	2013	Unit	SITC code
	All Commodities	45 636.1	45 946.2	41 871.7					
7108	Gold (including gold plated with platinum)	9 930.8	9 673.5	8 028.4	28.3	31.4	27.6	thsd US$/kg	971
2603	Copper ores and concentrates	7 796.7	8 426.4	7 601.5	2.5	2.2	2.0	US$/kg	283
2710	Petroleum oils, other than crude	2 933.9	3 305.2	3 301.2	0.8	0.8	0.8	US$/kg	334
7403	Refined copper and copper alloys, unwrought	2 745.3	1 967.3	2 110.9	8.9	7.9	7.4	US$/kg	682
2301	Flours, meals and pellets, of meat or meat offal	1 781.7	1 797.8	1 382.6	1.4	1.3	1.6	US$/kg	081
2607	Lead ores and concentrates	1 783.1	1 996.1	1 145.0	4.4	3.6	3.0	US$/kg	287
2711	Petroleum gases and other gaseous hydrocarbons	1 486.9	1 436.6	1 584.9	0.3	0.4	0.4	US$/kg	343
0901	Coffee, whether or not roasted or decaffeinated	1 580.8	1 020.7	695.6	5.4	3.8	2.9	US$/kg	071
2608	Zinc ores and concentrates	1 182.9	1 041.1	1 038.3	0.7	0.7	0.6	US$/kg	287
2601	Iron ores and concentrates, including roasted iron pyrites	1 023.1	856.4	856.8	0.1	0.1	0.1	US$/kg	281

Source: UN Comtrade and UN ServiceTrade

Peru

Services Imports and Exports: EBOPS 2002 categories

Table 2: Merchandise exports by SITC
(Value in million US$, growth and shares in percentage)

SITC	2013	Avg. Growth rates 2009-2013	Avg. Growth rates 2012-2013	2013 share
Total	41871.7	11.9	-8.9	100.0
0+1	6317.7	10.1	-5.7	15.1
2+4	12894.4	14.9	-13.7	30.8
3	5453.2	27.4	1.7	13.0
5	1185.1	14.8	-10.8	2.8
6	5629.3	10.9	5.6	13.4
7	446.4	9.9	-0.6	1.1
8	1917.1	6.1	-10.7	4.6
9	8028.6	4.4	-17.1	19.2

Table 3: Merchandise imports by SITC
(Value in million US$, growth and shares in percentage)

SITC	2013	Avg. Growth rates 2009-2013	Avg. Growth rates 2012-2013	2013 share
Total	43357.3	18.7	2.6	100.0
0+1	3634.8	15.9	0.9	8.4
2+4	1462.1	15.0	2.1	3.4
3	6687.5	21.3	9.9	15.4
5	6104.7	16.8	4.1	14.1
6	6370.7	16.4	-4.0	14.7
7	15642.2	19.8	0.5	36.1
8	3446.4	22.7	14.4	7.9
9	8.9	105.9	-89.2	0.0

SITC Legend

SITC Code	Description
Total	All commodities
0+1	Food, animals + beverages, tobacco
2+4	Crude materials + anim. & veg. oils
3	Mineral fuels, lubricants
5	Chemicals
6	Goods classified chiefly by material
7	Machinery and transport equipment
8	Miscellaneous manufactured articles
9	Not classified elsewhere in the SITC

Graph 4: Merchandise trade balance
(Bln US$ by MDG Regions in 2013)

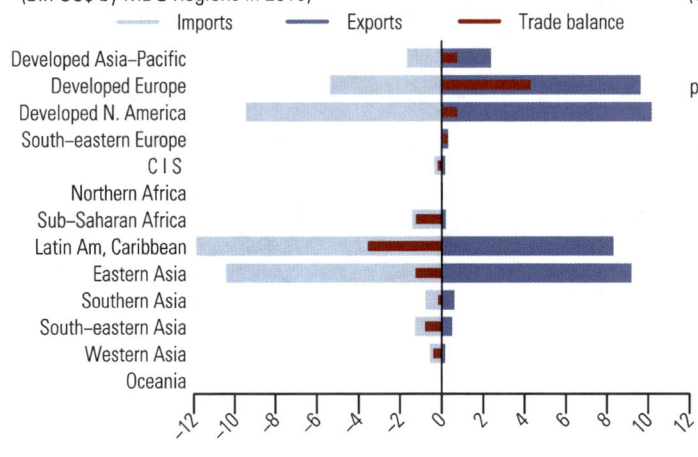

Graph 5: Partner concentration of merchandise trade
(Cumulative share by ranked partners in 2013)

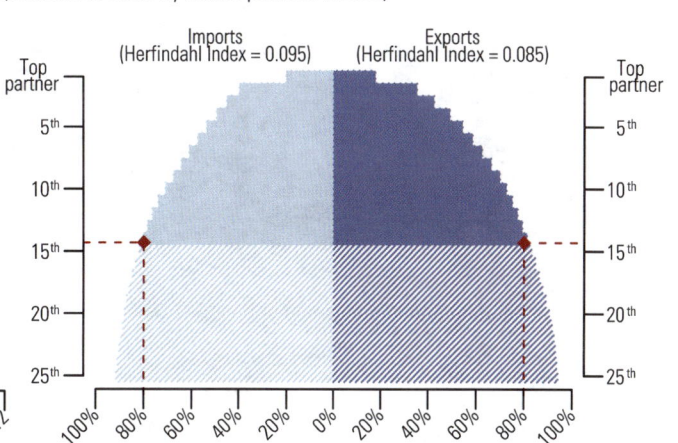

Imports (Herfindahl Index = 0.095)
Exports (Herfindahl Index = 0.085)

Graph 6: Imports of services by EBOPS category
(% share in 2012)

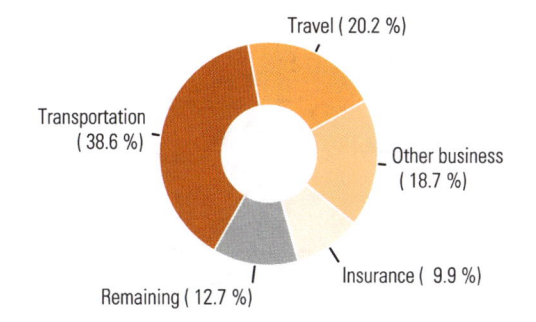

- Transportation (38.6%)
- Travel (20.2%)
- Other business (18.7%)
- Insurance (9.9%)
- Remaining (12.7%)

Imports Profile:

"Machinery and transport equipment" (SITC section 7), "Mineral fuels, lubricants" (SITC section 3) and "Goods classified chiefly by material" (SITC section 6) were the largest commodity groups for imports in 2013, representing respectively 36.1, 15.4 and 14.7 percent of imported goods (see table 3). From 2011 to 2013, the largest import commodity was "Petroleum oils and oils obtained from bituminous minerals, crude" (HS code 2709) (see table 4). The top three partners for merchandise imports were the United States, China and Brazil, accounting for respectively 19.7, 18.3 and 5.9 percent of total imports. "Transportation" (EBOPS code 205) accounted for the largest share of imports of services in 2012 at 2.9 bln US$, followed by "Travel" (EBOPS code 236) at 1.5 bln US$ and "Other business services" (EBOPS code 268) at 1.4 bln US$ (see graph 6).

Table 4: Top 10 import commodities 2011 to 2013

HS code	4-digit heading of Harmonized System 2007	Value 2011	Value 2012	Value 2013	Unit value 2011	Unit value 2012	Unit value 2013	Unit	SITC code
	All Commodities	37747.1	42274.3	43357.3					
2709	Petroleum oils and oils obtained from bituminous minerals, crude	3642.4	3675.7	3355.5	0.8	0.8	0.8	US$/kg	333
2710	Petroleum oils, other than crude	2172.0	2291.4	3176.4	1.0	1.1	1.0	US$/kg	334
8703	Motor cars and other motor vehicles principally designed for the transport	1229.0	1771.2	1777.4	11.0	11.5	10.9	thsd US$/unit	781
8704	Motor vehicles for the transport of goods	1156.8	1548.0	1564.4	13.9	33.8	31.6	thsd US$/unit	782
8517	Electrical apparatus for line telephony or line telegraphy	900.4	1036.9	1239.5					764
8429	Self-propelled bulldozers, angledozers, graders, levellers, scrapers	742.6	957.8	795.6	99.7	132.6	102.1	thsd US$/unit	723
8471	Automatic data processing machines and units thereof	655.3	760.7	800.6	88.8	97.1	89.2	US$/unit	752
1001	Wheat and meslin	592.0	570.9	625.9	0.4	0.3	0.3	US$/kg	041
1005	Maize (corn)	627.7	569.1	581.1	0.3	0.3	0.3	US$/kg	044
8528	Reception apparatus for television	493.4	563.5	586.8	180.2	186.6	185.7	US$/unit	761

Source: UN Comtrade and UN ServiceTrade

Philippines

Goods Imports: CIF, by origin **Goods Exports:** FOB, by last known destination **Trade System:** General

Overview:
In 2014, the value of merchandise exports of the Philippines increased moderately by 9.0 percent to reach 61.8 bln US$, while its merchandise imports increased slightly by 3.1 percent to reach 67.7 bln US$ (see graph 1, table 2 and table 3). The merchandise trade balance recorded a relatively small deficit of 5.9 bln US$ (see graph 1). The largest merchandise trade balance was with MDG Developed Asia-Pacific at 8.0 bln US$ (see graph 4). Merchandise exports in the Philippines were diversified amongst partners; imports were also diversified. The top 9 partners accounted for 80 percent or more of exports and 12 partners accounted for 80 percent or more of imports (see graph 5). In 2013, the value of exports of services of the Philippines increased substantially by 19.9 percent, reaching 21.7 bln US$, while its imports of services increased slightly by 1.6 percent and reached 14.6 bln US$ (see graph 2). There was a moderate trade in services surplus of 7.1 bln US$.

Graph 1: Total merchandise trade, by value
(Bln US$ by year)

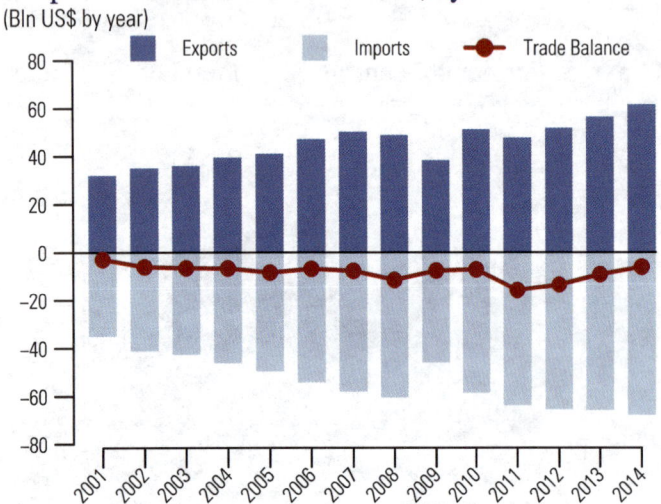

Graph 2: Total services trade, by value
(Bln US$ by year)

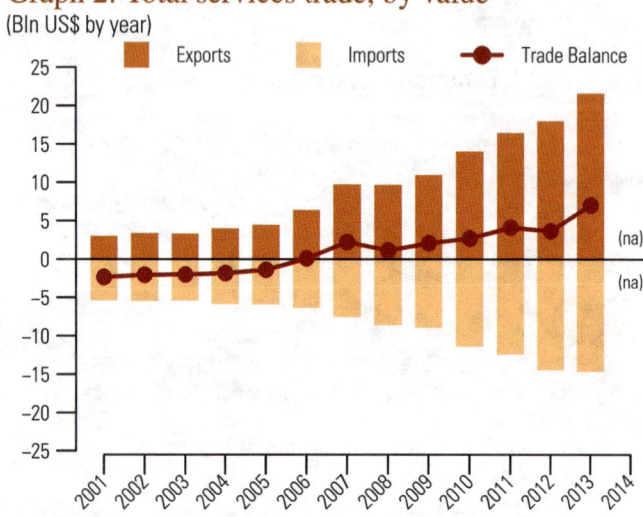

Exports Profile:
"Machinery and transport equipment" (SITC section 7), "Miscellaneous manufactured articles" (SITC section 8) and "Goods classified chiefly by material" (SITC section 6) were the largest commodity groups for exports in 2014, representing respectively 57.6, 9.8 and 9.0 percent of exported goods (see table 2). From 2012 to 2014, the largest export commodity was "Electronic integrated circuits and microassemblies" (HS code 8542) (see table 1). The top three destinations for merchandise exports were Japan, the United States and China, accounting for respectively 21.0, 14.4 and 12.4 percent of total exports. "Other business services" (EBOPS code 268) accounted for the largest share of exports of services in 2013 at 11.8 bln US$, followed by "Travel" (EBOPS code 236) at 4.7 bln US$ and "Computer and information services" (EBOPS code 262) at 2.8 bln US$ (see graph 3).

Graph 3: Exports of services by EBOPS category
(% share in 2013)

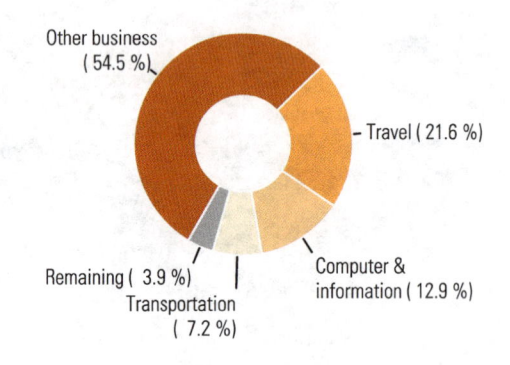

- Other business (54.5 %)
- Travel (21.6 %)
- Computer & information (12.9 %)
- Transportation (7.2 %)
- Remaining (3.9 %)

Table 1: Top 10 export commodities 2012 to 2014

HS code	4-digit heading of Harmonized System 2002	Value (million US$) 2012	2013	2014	Unit value 2012	2013	2014	Unit	SITC code
	All Commodities	51 995.2	56 697.8	61 809.8					
8542	Electronic integrated circuits and microassemblies	9 615.3	11 099.4	12 157.7					776
8471	Automatic data processing machines and units thereof	3 944.7	3 890.2	4 793.0		135.1		US$/unit	752
8541	Diodes, transistors and similar semiconductor devices	2 674.4	2 535.6	2 954.6					776
4418	Builders' joinery and carpentry of wood	2 134.6	3 032.3	2 925.3	3.6	3.3	3.0	US$/kg	635
8473	Parts and accessories for use with machines of heading 84.69 to 84.72	1 573.5	2 001.4	2 199.4	2.1	2.3	7.6	US$/kg	759
8544	Insulated (including enamelled or anodised) wire, cable	1 534.5	1 825.4	2 174.5	16.1	*14.3*	*2.1*	US$/kg	773
8504	Electrical transformers, static converters (for example, rectifiers)	1 858.0	1 904.6	1 557.4					771
8708	Parts and accessories of the motor vehicles of headings 87.01 to 87.05	1 387.4	1 489.6	1 472.3	13.5	15.2	*12.3*	US$/kg	784
2604	Nickel ores and concentrates	661.1	1 018.1	1 717.4	0.0	0.0	0.0	US$/kg	284
1513	Coconut (copra), palm kernel or babassu oil	1 026.0	1 006.0	1 345.9	1.2	0.9	1.5	US$/kg	422

Source: UN Comtrade and UN ServiceTrade

Philippines

Services Imports and Exports: EBOPS 2002 categories

Table 2: Merchandise exports by SITC
(Value in million US$, growth and shares in percentage)

SITC	2014	Avg. Growth rates 2010-2014	Avg. Growth rates 2013-2014	2014 share
Total	61 809.8	4.7	9.0	100.0
0+1	4 799.4	18.0	5.3	7.8
2+4	5 520.9	20.4	24.3	8.9
3	1 837.5	14.8	-14.0	3.0
5	2 212.0	9.2	-4.7	3.6
6	5 542.4	13.4	-9.0	9.0
7	35 579.0	11.8	12.7	57.6
8	6 026.8	27.0	15.2	9.8
9	291.7	-62.8	-15.5	0.5

Table 3: Merchandise imports by SITC
(Value in million US$, growth and shares in percentage)

SITC	2014	Avg. Growth rates 2010-2014	Avg. Growth rates 2013-2014	2014 share
Total	67 718.9	3.7	3.1	100.0
0+1	7 511.2	5.1	17.7	11.1
2+4	1 549.5	-8.7	-30.6	2.3
3	13 589.6	8.2	0.4	20.1
5	7 453.4	7.5	14.5	11.0
6	6 761.4	9.6	11.4	10.0
7	27 597.5	0.1	-2.2	40.8
8	2 909.7	10.8	14.3	4.3
9	346.5	-7.3	58.2	0.5

SITC Legend

SITC Code	Description
Total	All commodities
0+1	Food, animals + beverages, tobacco
2+4	Crude materials + anim. & veg. oils
3	Mineral fuels, lubricants
5	Chemicals
6	Goods classified chiefly by material
7	Machinery and transport equipment
8	Miscellaneous manufactured articles
9	Not classified elsewhere in the SITC

Graph 4: Merchandise trade balance
(Bln US$ by MDG Regions in 2014)

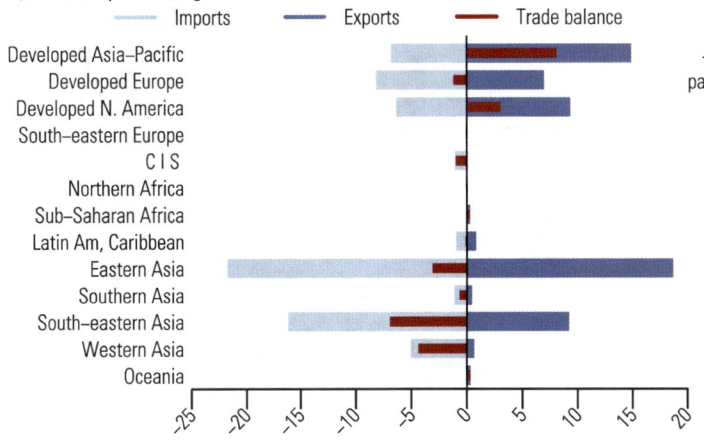

Graph 5: Partner concentration of merchandise trade
(Cumulative share by ranked partners in 2014)

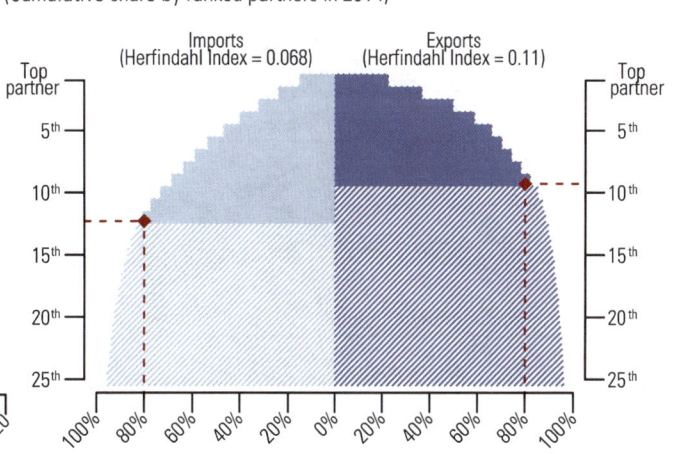

Imports (Herfindahl Index = 0.068)
Exports (Herfindahl Index = 0.11)

Graph 6: Imports of services by EBOPS category
(% share in 2013)

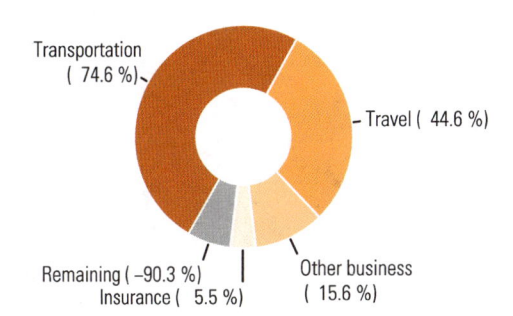

- Transportation (74.6 %)
- Travel (44.6 %)
- Other business (15.6 %)
- Insurance (5.5 %)
- Remaining (-90.3 %)

Imports Profile:

"Machinery and transport equipment" (SITC section 7), "Mineral fuels, lubricants" (SITC section 3) and "Food, animals + beverages, tobacco" (SITC section 0+1) were the largest commodity groups for imports in 2014, representing respectively 40.8, 20.1 and 11.1 percent of imported goods (see table 3). From 2012 to 2014, the largest import commodity was "Electronic integrated circuits and microassemblies" (HS code 8542) (see table 4). The top three partners for merchandise imports were China, the United States and Japan, accounting for respectively 13.1, 10.6 and 9.1 percent of total imports. "Transportation" (EBOPS code 205) accounted for the largest share of imports of services in 2013 at 10.9 bln US$, followed by "Travel" (EBOPS code 236) at 6.5 bln US$ and "Other business services" (EBOPS code 268) at 2.3 bln US$ (see graph 6).

Table 4: Top 10 import commodities 2012 to 2014

HS code	4-digit heading of Harmonized System 2002	2012	2013	2014	2012	2013	2014	Unit	SITC code
	All Commodities	65 349.8	65 705.4	67 718.9					
8542	Electronic integrated circuits and microassemblies	10 738.4	10 585.5	9 915.8					776
2709	Petroleum oils, crude	7 618.8	6 611.6	6 340.0	0.9	0.8	0.8	US$/kg	333
2710	Petroleum oils, other than crude	4 977.5	5 285.1	5 857.4	1.0	1.0	0.9	US$/kg	334
8473	Parts and accessories for use with machines of heading 84.69 to 84.72	3 152.6	2 181.9	1 803.1	33.6	25.1	22.3	US$/kg	759
8802	Other aircraft (for example, helicopters, aeroplanes); spacecraft	1 115.7	2 316.3	2 128.5	19.9	46.3	34.3	mln US$/unit	792
8703	Motor cars and other motor vehicles principally designed for the transport	1 686.8	1 714.9	1 720.6	5.7	8.8	3.3	thsd US$/unit	781
1001	Wheat and meslin	974.3	868.9	922.5	0.3	0.4	0.3	US$/kg	041
3004	Medicaments (excluding goods of heading 30.02, 30.05 or 30.06)	784.1	833.2	799.6	27.7	26.5	22.1	US$/kg	542
2304	Oil-cake and other solid residues	686.8	758.9	969.5	0.5	0.5	0.5	US$/kg	081
2701	Coal; briquettes, ovoids and similar solid fuels manufactured from coal	780.4	821.6	762.0	0.1	0.1	0.1	US$/kg	321

Poland

Goods Imports: CIF, by origin　　**Goods Exports:** FOB, by last known destination　　**Trade System:** Special

Overview:
In 2014, the value of merchandise exports of Poland increased moderately by 5.2 percent to reach 214.5 bln US$, while its merchandise imports increased moderately by 5.4 percent to reach 216.7 bln US$ (see graph 1, table 2 and table 3). The merchandise trade balance recorded a relatively small deficit of 2.2 bln US$ (see graph 1). The largest merchandise trade balance was with MDG Developed Europe at 37.9 bln US$ (see graph 4). Merchandise exports in Poland were diversified amongst partners; imports were also diversified. The top 18 partners accounted for 80 percent or more of exports and 18 partners accounted for 80 percent or more of imports (see graph 5). In 2013, the value of exports of services of Poland increased substantially by 19.5 percent, reaching 45.3 bln US$, while its imports of services increased moderately by 7.0 percent and reached 34.2 bln US$ (see graph 2). There was a moderate trade in services surplus of 11.1 bln US$.

Graph 1: Total merchandise trade, by value
(Bln US$ by year)

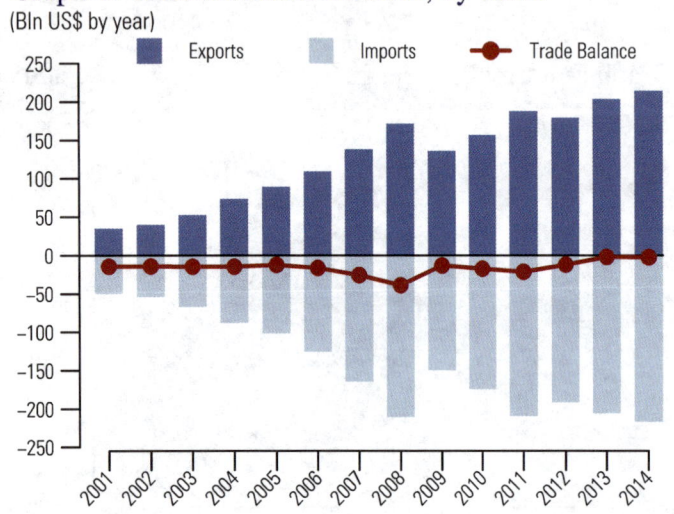

Graph 2: Total services trade, by value
(Bln US$ by year)

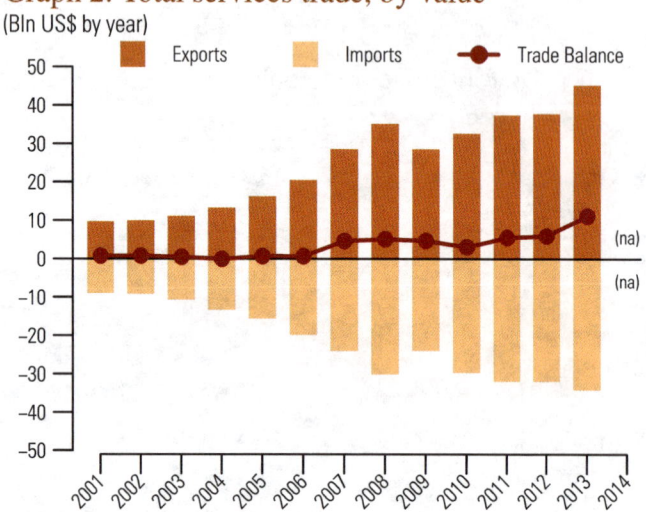

Exports Profile:
"Machinery and transport equipment" (SITC section 7), "Goods classified chiefly by material" (SITC section 6) and "Miscellaneous manufactured articles" (SITC section 8) were the largest commodity groups for exports in 2014, representing respectively 38.3, 19.8 and 13.6 percent of exported goods (see table 2). From 2012 to 2014, the largest export commodity was "Parts and accessories of the motor vehicles of headings 87.01 to 87.05" (HS code 8708) (see table 1). The top three destinations for merchandise exports were Germany, the United Kingdom and the Czech Republic, accounting for respectively 25.3, 6.5 and 6.2 percent of total exports. "Transportation" (EBOPS code 205) accounted for the largest share of exports of services in 2013 at 12.9 bln US$, followed by "Travel" (EBOPS code 236) at 11.8 bln US$ and "Other business services" (EBOPS code 268) at 10.2 bln US$ (see graph 3).

Graph 3: Exports of services by EBOPS category
(% share in 2013)

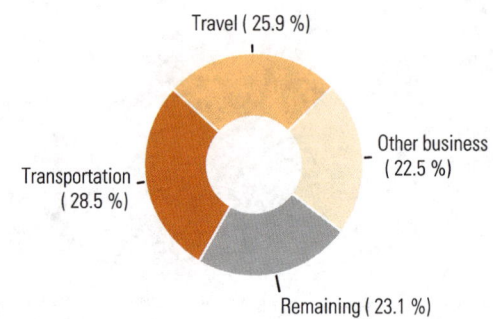

- Travel (25.9 %)
- Other business (22.5 %)
- Remaining (23.1 %)
- Transportation (28.5 %)

Table 1: Top 10 export commodities 2012 to 2014

HS code	4-digit heading of Harmonized System 2012	Value (million US$) 2012	2013	2014	Unit value 2012	2013	2014	Unit	SITC code
	All Commodities..	179 603.6	203 847.9	214 476.8					
8708	Parts and accessories of the motor vehicles of headings 87.01 to 87.05..............	8 363.4	9 613.4	10 537.7	7.1	7.4	7.6	US$/kg	784
8703	Motor cars and other motor vehicles principally designed for the transport............	6 786.6	6 900.9	6 554.7	11.9	12.5	12.6	thsd US$/unit	781
9401	Seats (other than those of heading 94.02)...	4 525.0	4 982.3	5 519.6					821
8528	Reception apparatus for television..	4 891.6	4 744.7	5 068.0	261.6	282.7	289.5	US$/unit	761
2710	Petroleum oils, other than crude...	4 390.3	4 622.4	4 607.2	0.9	0.8	0.8	US$/kg	334
9403	Other furniture and parts thereof...	3 154.3	3 693.9	4 234.3					821
8901	Cruise ships, excursion boats, ferry-boats, cargo ships, barges......................	3 003.4	3 720.2	4 061.9	14.7	14.2	13.5	mln US$/unit	793
8517	Electrical apparatus for line telephony or line telegraphy............................	1 650.0	3 483.8	4 804.0					764
8471	Automatic data processing machines and units thereof.............................	2 963.5	2 794.6	3 423.6	260.2	209.1	202.2	US$/unit	752
8408	Compression-ignition internal combustion piston engines...........................	2 708.3	2 893.4	2 914.5	2.4	2.6	2.6	thsd US$/unit	713

Source: UN Comtrade and UN ServiceTrade

Poland

Services Imports and Exports: EBOPS 2002 categories

Table 2: Merchandise exports by SITC
(Value in million US$, growth and shares in percentage)

SITC	2014	Avg. Growth rates 2010-2014	Avg. Growth rates 2013-2014	2014 share
Total	214 476.8	8.1	5.2	100.0
0+1	26 350.3	12.5	5.1	12.3
2+4	5 714.7	10.2	1.8	2.7
3	8 874.9	8.0	-7.3	4.1
5	19 578.5	9.9	4.7	9.1
6	42 424.0	7.7	3.7	19.8
7	82 150.7	5.9	6.3	38.3
8	29 086.6	10.1	11.4	13.6
9	297.1	29.5	-46.7	0.1

Table 3: Merchandise imports by SITC
(Value in million US$, growth and shares in percentage)

SITC	2014	Avg. Growth rates 2010-2014	Avg. Growth rates 2013-2014	2014 share
Total	216 687.3	5.6	5.4	100.0
0+1	16 936.2	8.0	3.0	7.8
2+4	7 885.0	7.8	2.4	3.6
3	23 397.8	5.4	-2.2	10.8
5	31 182.5	6.0	6.4	14.4
6	37 628.5	5.2	6.4	17.4
7	73 205.6	5.1	5.8	33.8
8	22 315.4	6.1	20.4	10.3
9	4 136.4	1.9	-19.8	1.9

SITC Legend

SITC Code	Description
Total	All commodities
0+1	Food, animals + beverages, tobacco
2+4	Crude materials + anim. & veg. oils
3	Mineral fuels, lubricants
5	Chemicals
6	Goods classified chiefly by material
7	Machinery and transport equipment
8	Miscellaneous manufactured articles
9	Not classified elsewhere in the SITC

Graph 4: Merchandise trade balance
(Bln US$ by MDG Regions in 2014)

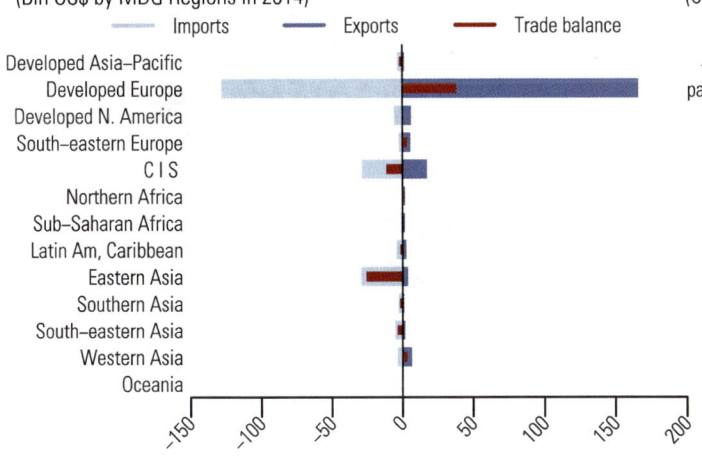

Graph 5: Partner concentration of merchandise trade
(Cumulative share by ranked partners in 2014)

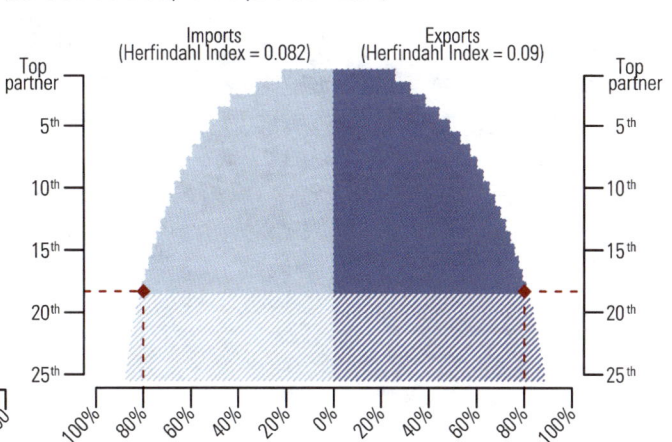

Imports (Herfindahl Index = 0.082)
Exports (Herfindahl Index = 0.09)

Graph 6: Imports of services by EBOPS category
(% share in 2013)

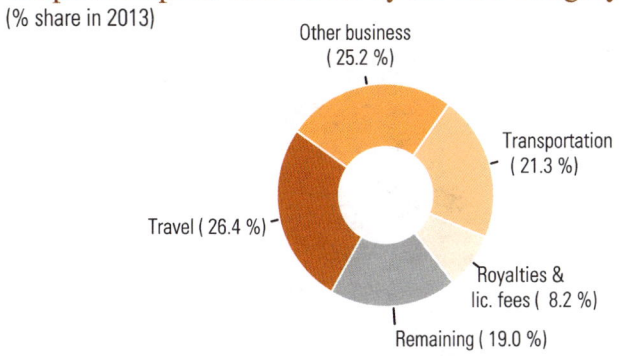

- Other business (25.2 %)
- Transportation (21.3 %)
- Royalties & lic. fees (8.2 %)
- Remaining (19.0 %)
- Travel (26.4 %)

Imports Profile:

"Machinery and transport equipment" (SITC section 7), "Goods classified chiefly by material" (SITC section 6) and "Chemicals" (SITC section 5) were the largest commodity groups for imports in 2014, representing respectively 33.8, 17.4 and 14.4 percent of imported goods (see table 3). From 2012 to 2014, the largest import commodity was "Petroleum oils and oils obtained from bituminous minerals, crude" (HS code 2709)(see table 4). The top three partners for merchandise imports were Germany, the Russian Federation and China, accounting for respectively 21.4, 12.5 and 9.7 percent of total imports. "Travel" (EBOPS code 236) accounted for the largest share of imports of services in 2013 at 9.0 bln US$, followed by "Other business services" (EBOPS code 268) at 8.6 bln US$ and "Transportation" (EBOPS code 205) at 7.3 bln US$ (see graph 6).

Table 4: Top 10 import commodities 2012 to 2014

HS code	4-digit heading of Harmonized System 2012	Value (million US$) 2012	2013	2014	Unit value 2012	2013	2014	Unit	SITC code
	All Commodities	191 430.1	205 613.8	216 687.3					
2709	Petroleum oils and oils obtained from bituminous minerals, crude	19 620.1	18 048.9	17 195.1	0.8	0.8	0.7	US$/kg	333
8708	Parts and accessories of the motor vehicles of headings 87.01 to 87.05	5 326.1	5 995.1	6 357.7	7.3	7.7	7.5	US$/kg	784
8703	Motor cars and other motor vehicles principally designed for the transport	4 906.6	5 208.3	5 986.9	15.4	15.9	16.6	thsd US$/unit	781
9999	Commodities not specified according to kind	5 575.9	5 036.9	4 055.3					931
3004	Medicaments (excluding goods of heading 30.02, 30.05 or 30.06)	4 101.3	4 456.7	4 517.0	67.3	64.8	65.2	US$/kg	542
8471	Automatic data processing machines and units thereof	3 267.2	3 437.4	3 529.7	79.5	68.0	70.8	US$/unit	752
8517	Electrical apparatus for line telephony or line telegraphy	2 591.9	3 504.2	3 719.7					764
8901	Cruise ships, excursion boats, ferry-boats, cargo ships, barges	2 582.4	3 351.1	3 549.2	13.7	13.5	12.9	mln US$/unit	793
8529	Parts suitable for use with the apparatus of headings 85.25 to 85.28	2 876.2	2 934.3	2 934.5	39.3	39.3	34.6	US$/kg	764
2710	Petroleum oils, other than crude	2 433.8	1 997.2	2 108.2	1.1	1.1	1.0	US$/kg	334

Source: UN Comtrade and UN ServiceTrade

Portugal

Goods Imports: CIF, by origin/consignment for intra-eu   **Goods Exports:** FOB, by last known destination   **Trade System:** Special

Overview:
In 2014, the value of merchandise exports of Portugal increased slightly by 2.0 percent to reach 64.0 bln US$, while its merchandise imports increased slightly by 3.2 percent to reach 78.0 bln US$ (see graph 1, table 2 and table 3). The merchandise trade balance recorded a relatively small deficit of 14.0 bln US$ (see graph 1). The largest merchandise trade balance was with MDG Developed Europe at -13.0 bln US$ (see graph 4). Merchandise exports in Portugal were diversified amongst partners; imports were also diversified. The top 13 partners accounted for 80 percent or more of exports and 14 partners accounted for 80 percent or more of imports (see graph 5). In 2013, the value of exports of services of Portugal increased substantially by 20.0 percent, reaching 29.5 bln US$, while its imports of services increased moderately by 6.3 percent and reached 14.2 bln US$ (see graph 2). There was a large trade in services surplus of 15.2 bln US$.

Graph 1: Total merchandise trade, by value
(Bln US$ by year)

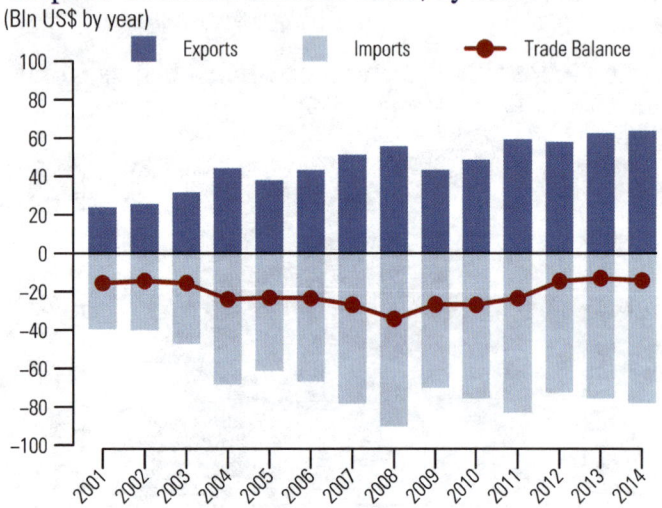

Graph 2: Total services trade, by value
(Bln US$ by year)

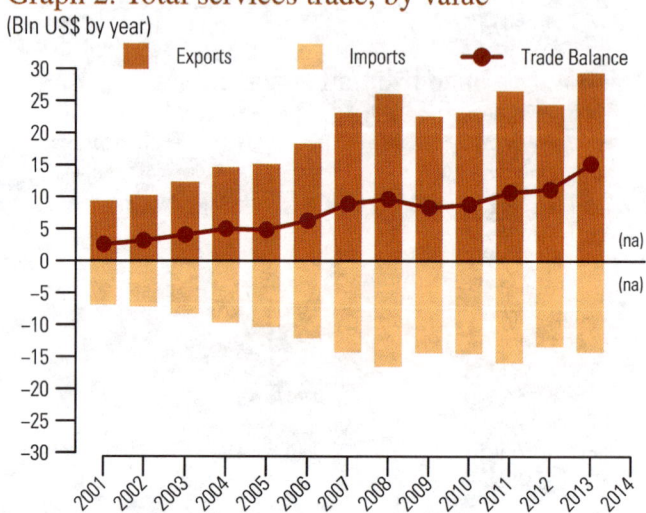

Exports Profile:
"Machinery and transport equipment" (SITC section 7), "Goods classified chiefly by material" (SITC section 6) and "Miscellaneous manufactured articles" (SITC section 8) were the largest commodity groups for exports in 2014, representing respectively 25.3, 23.1 and 17.5 percent of exported goods (see table 2). From 2012 to 2014, the largest export commodity was "Petroleum oils, other than crude" (HS code 2710) (see table 1). The top three destinations for merchandise exports were Spain, Germany and France, accounting for respectively 23.2, 11.9 and 11.7 percent of total exports. "Travel" (EBOPS code 236) accounted for the largest share of exports of services in 2013 at 12.8 bln US$, followed by "Transportation" (EBOPS code 205) at 7.5 bln US$ and "Other business services" (EBOPS code 268) at 5.1 bln US$ (see graph 3).

Graph 3: Exports of services by EBOPS category
(% share in 2013)

- Transportation (25.6 %)
- Travel (43.3 %)
- Other business (17.3 %)
- Remaining (13.8 %)

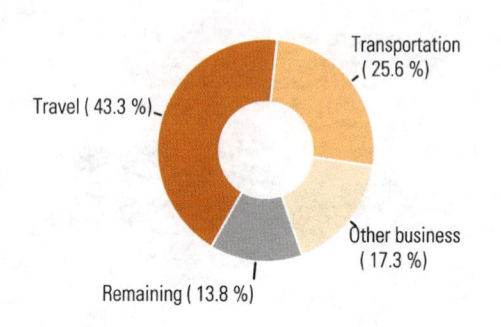

Table 1: Top 10 export commodities 2012 to 2014

HS code	4-digit heading of Harmonized System 2012	Value (million US$) 2012	2013	2014	Unit value 2012	2013	2014	Unit	SITC code
	All Commodities	58 140.5	62 745.8	63 986.5					
2710	Petroleum oils, other than crude	4 388.9	5 831.5	4 760.3		0.9	0.8	US$/kg	334
8703	Motor cars and other motor vehicles principally designed for the transport	2 680.2	2 453.6	2 629.1	18.3	18.1	21.3	thsd US$/unit	781
8708	Parts and accessories of the motor vehicles of headings 87.01 to 87.05	2 194.8	2 363.9	2 660.2	7.8	7.8	7.9	US$/kg	784
6403	Footwear with outer soles of rubber, plastics, leather	1 822.0	2 032.6	2 171.4	38.6	38.9	36.6	US$/pair	851
4802	Uncoated paper and paperboard, of a kind used for writing	1 414.0	1 535.7	1 565.9	1.0	1.1	1.0	US$/kg	641
4011	New pneumatic tyres, of rubber	1 080.8	1 130.8	1 106.4			62.9	US$/unit	625
2204	Wine of fresh grapes, including fortified wines	904.7	955.7	967.9	2.7	3.2	3.4	US$/litre	112
6109	T-shirts, singlets and other vests, knitted or crocheted	844.9	936.2	1 022.7	5.6	5.7	6.5	US$/unit	845
3004	Medicaments (excluding goods of heading 30.02, 30.05 or 30.06)	790.5	839.3	999.4	39.1	39.8	44.5	US$/kg	542
8544	Insulated (including enamelled or anodised) wire, cable	804.3	894.9	872.9	8.7	9.0	8.9	US$/kg	773

Portugal

Services Imports and Exports: EBOPS 2002 categories

Table 2: Merchandise exports by SITC
(Value in million US$, growth and shares in percentage)

SITC	2014	Avg. Growth rates 2010-2014	Avg. Growth rates 2013-2014	2014 share
Total	63 986.5	7.0	2.0	100.0
0+1	7 082.1	8.5	9.2	11.1
2+4	3 317.1	4.0	-4.3	5.2
3	5 437.8	13.7	-16.8	8.5
5	5 667.8	8.9	1.4	8.9
6	14 800.5	8.0	4.7	23.1
7	16 157.7	5.1	2.6	25.3
8	11 177.5	8.6	9.2	17.5
9	346.0	-29.0	-38.0	0.5

Table 3: Merchandise imports by SITC
(Value in million US$, growth and shares in percentage)

SITC	2014	Avg. Growth rates 2010-2014	Avg. Growth rates 2013-2014	2014 share
Total	77 989.2	0.8	3.2	100.0
0+1	10 136.2	2.9	-0.4	13.0
2+4	3 531.8	4.2	-6.2	4.5
3	13 539.2	5.3	-8.6	17.4
5	10 670.2	3.0	4.8	13.7
6	11 655.1	0.8	4.6	14.9
7	19 962.9	-3.3	13.0	25.6
8	8 435.5	0.1	9.2	10.8
9	58.2	-42.6	-36.5	0.1

SITC Legend

SITC Code	Description
Total	All commodities
0+1	Food, animals + beverages, tobacco
2+4	Crude materials + anim. & veg. oils
3	Mineral fuels, lubricants
5	Chemicals
6	Goods classified chiefly by material
7	Machinery and transport equipment
8	Miscellaneous manufactured articles
9	Not classified elsewhere in the SITC

Graph 4: Merchandise trade balance
(Bln US$ by MDG Regions in 2014)

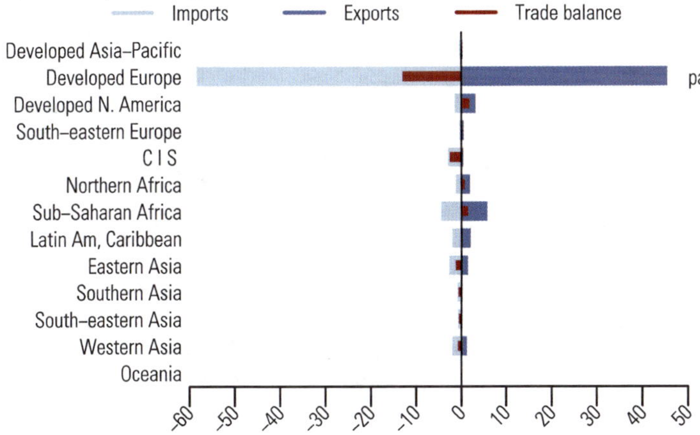

Graph 5: Partner concentration of merchandise trade
(Cumulative share by ranked partners in 2014)

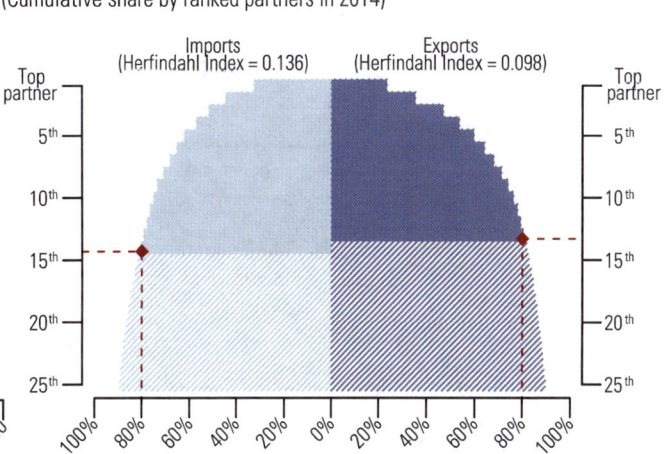

Imports (Herfindahl Index = 0.136)
Exports (Herfindahl Index = 0.098)

Graph 6: Imports of services by EBOPS category
(% share in 2013)

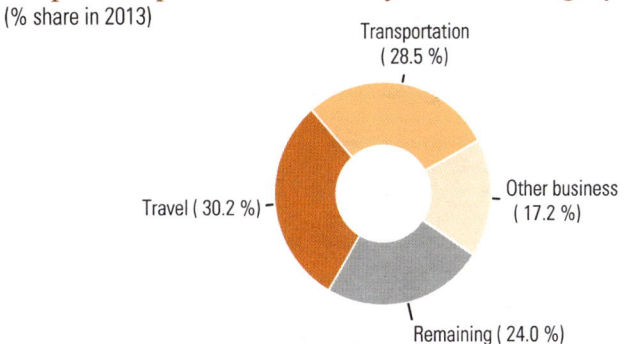

- Transportation (28.5 %)
- Travel (30.2 %)
- Other business (17.2 %)
- Remaining (24.0 %)

Imports Profile:

"Machinery and transport equipment" (SITC section 7), "Mineral fuels, lubricants" (SITC section 3) and "Goods classified chiefly by material" (SITC section 6) were the largest commodity groups for imports in 2014, representing respectively 25.6, 17.4 and 14.9 percent of imported goods (see table 3). From 2012 to 2014, the largest import commodity was "Petroleum oils and oils obtained from bituminous minerals, crude" (HS code 2709) (see table 4). The top three partners for merchandise imports were Spain, Germany and France, accounting for respectively 28.8, 11.1 and 6.4 percent of total imports. "Travel" (EBOPS code 236) accounted for the largest share of imports of services in 2013 at 4.3 bln US$, followed by "Transportation" (EBOPS code 205) at 4.1 bln US$ and "Other business services" (EBOPS code 268) at 2.4 bln US$ (see graph 6).

Table 4: Top 10 import commodities 2012 to 2014

HS code	4-digit heading of Harmonized System 2012	2012	2013	2014	2012	2013	2014	Unit	SITC code
	All Commodities	72 506.5	75 572.1	77 989.2					
2709	Petroleum oils and oils obtained from bituminous minerals, crude	9 555.2	9 355.1	8 159.1	0.8	0.8	0.7	US$/kg	333
8708	Parts and accessories of the motor vehicles of headings 87.01 to 87.05	2 652.1	2 682.4	2 747.2	10.0	10.0	10.2	US$/kg	784
8703	Motor cars and other motor vehicles principally designed for the transport	2 136.6	2 437.7	3 447.8	17.4	17.2	18.6	thsd US$/unit	781
2711	Petroleum gases and other gaseous hydrocarbons	2 182.2	2 470.2	2 404.1	0.6	0.6	0.6	US$/kg	343
3004	Medicaments (excluding goods of heading 30.02, 30.05 or 30.06)	2 213.9	2 174.9	2 212.4	69.2	64.1	65.0	US$/kg	542
2710	Petroleum oils, other than crude	1 856.1	1 972.5	2 107.8		0.9	0.8	US$/kg	334
8517	Electrical apparatus for line telephony or line telegraphy	837.4	920.6	1 034.9					764
8471	Automatic data processing machines and units thereof	713.5	771.7	795.9			154.2	US$/unit	752
7208	Flat-rolled products of iron or non-alloy steel	467.3	556.8	531.6	0.7	0.7	0.6	US$/kg	673
7204	Ferrous waste and scrap; remelting scrap ingots of iron or steel	469.3	515.3	532.5	0.4	0.4	0.3	US$/kg	282

Qatar

Goods Imports: CIF, by origin | Goods Exports: FOB, by last known destination | Trade System: General

Overview:
In 2013, the value of merchandise exports of Qatar increased slightly by 2.3 percent to reach 136.9 bln US$, while its merchandise imports decreased substantially by 12.2 percent to reach 27.0 bln US$ (see graph 1, table 2 and table 3). The merchandise trade balance recorded a large surplus of 109.8 bln US$ (see graph 1). The largest merchandise trade balance was with MDG Developed Asia-Pacific at 38.6 bln US$ (see graph 4). Merchandise exports in Qatar were diversified amongst partners; imports were also diversified. The top 8 partners accounted for 80 percent or more of exports and 18 partners accounted for 80 percent or more of imports (see graph 5). In 2013, the value of exports of services of Qatar increased substantially by 12.6 percent, reaching 11.2 bln US$, while its imports of services increased substantially by 14.9 percent and reached 27.5 bln US$ (see graph 2). There was a large trade in services deficit of 16.3 bln US$.

Graph 1: Total merchandise trade, by value
(Bln US$ by year)

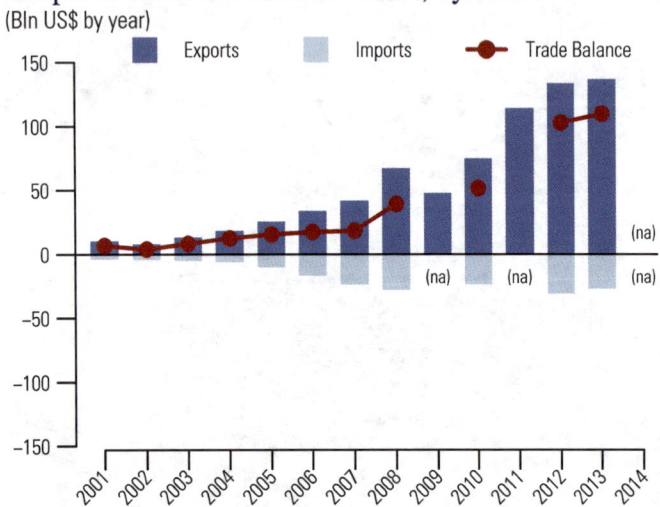

Graph 2: Total services trade, by value
(Bln US$ by year)

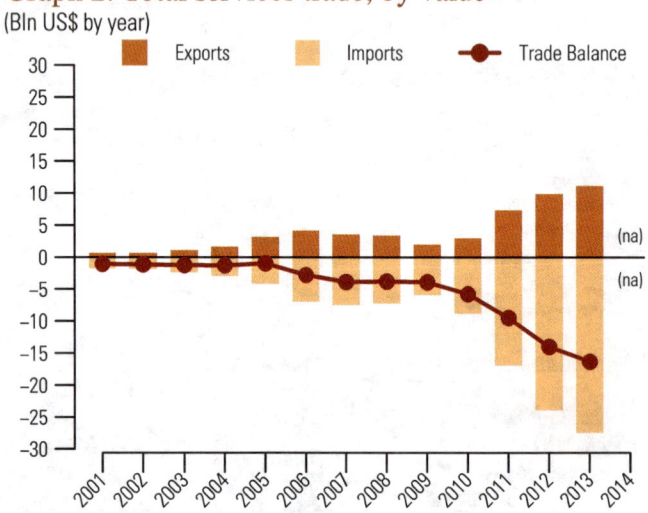

Exports Profile:
"Mineral fuels, lubricants" (SITC section 3), "Not classified elsewhere in the SITC" (SITC section 9) and "Chemicals" (SITC section 5) were the largest commodity groups for exports in 2013, representing respectively 87.7, 8.5 and 3.5 percent of exported goods (see table 2). From 2011 to 2013, the largest export commodity was "Petroleum gases and other gaseous hydrocarbons" (HS code 2711) (see table 1). The top three destinations for merchandise exports were Japan, the Republic of Korea and India, accounting for respectively 27.7, 18.0 and 10.3 percent of total exports. "Transportation" (EBOPS code 205) accounted for the largest share of exports of services in 2013 at 5.6 bln US$, followed by "Travel" (EBOPS code 236) at 3.5 bln US$ and "Government services, n.i.e." (EBOPS code 291) at 880.2 mln US$ (see graph 3).

Graph 3: Exports of services by EBOPS category
(% share in 2013)

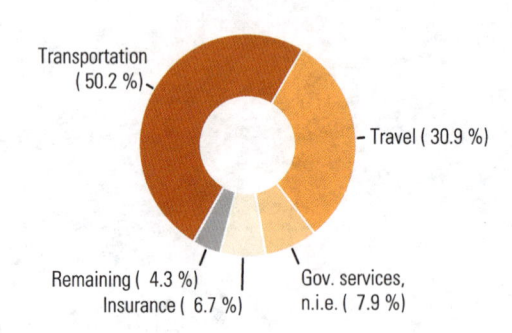

- Transportation (50.2 %)
- Travel (30.9 %)
- Gov. services, n.i.e. (7.9 %)
- Insurance (6.7 %)
- Remaining (4.3 %)

Table 1: Top 10 export commodities 2011 to 2013

HS code	4-digit heading of Harmonized System 2002	Value (million US$) 2011	Value 2012	Value 2013	Unit value 2011	2012	2013	Unit	SITC code
	All Commodities	114 448.1	133 717.0	136 855.1					
2711	Petroleum gases and other gaseous hydrocarbons	71 245.5	82 640.5	87 538.4	0.7		0.8	US$/kg	343
2709	Petroleum oils, crude	26 404.3	26 115.2	24 877.7	0.8		0.8	US$/kg	333
2710	Petroleum oils, other than crude	7 355.1	8 240.3	7 544.1	0.9		0.9	US$/kg	334
9999	Commodities not specified according to kind	6 891.0	732.8	11 656.7					931
3901	Polymers of ethylene, in primary forms	2 014.7	3 581.5	4 632.0	1.5		1.5	US$/kg	571
7601	Unwrought aluminium	...	2 600.5	...					684
3102	Mineral or chemical fertilisers, nitrogenous	...	2 080.1	...					562
2503	Sulphur of all kinds	381.2	387.9	270.2	0.2		0.1	US$/kg	274
2909	Ethers, ether-alcohols, ether-phenols, ether-alcohol-phenols	...	919.6	...					516
7208	Flat-rolled products of iron or non-alloy steel	...	551.4	...					673

Source: UN Comtrade and UN ServiceTrade

Qatar

Services Imports and Exports: EBOPS 2002 categories

Table 2: Merchandise exports by SITC
(Value in million US$, growth and shares in percentage)

SITC	2013	Avg. Growth rates 2009-2013	Avg. Growth rates 2012-2013	2013 share
Total	136 855.1	29.9	2.3	100.0
0+1	8.5	-34.1	-87.4	0.0
2+4	298.2	45.1	-41.0	0.2
3	119 960.5	36.4	2.5	87.7
5	4 806.7	11.0	-49.7	3.5
6	16.7	-57.6	-99.6	0.0
7	10.0	-67.3	-99.1	0.0
8	97.7	5.2	-34.5	0.1
9	11 656.7	7.8	1484.3	8.5

Table 3: Merchandise imports by SITC
(Value in million US$, growth and shares in percentage)

SITC	2013	Avg. Growth rates 2009-2013	Avg. Growth rates 2012-2013	2013 share
Total	27 034.1	...	-12.2	100.0
0+1	2 487.2	...	0.3	9.2
2+4	1 635.6	...	2.1	6.1
3	262.6	...	-6.2	1.0
5	2 150.7	...	14.5	8.0
6	4 244.7	...	-2.7	15.7
7	12 639.9	...	12.2	46.8
8	3 271.6	...	11.0	12.1
9	341.8	...	-94.3	1.3

SITC Legend

SITC Code	Description
Total	All commodities
0+1	Food, animals + beverages, tobacco
2+4	Crude materials + anim. & veg. oils
3	Mineral fuels, lubricants
5	Chemicals
6	Goods classified chiefly by material
7	Machinery and transport equipment
8	Miscellaneous manufactured articles
9	Not classified elsewhere in the SITC

Graph 4: Merchandise trade balance
(Bln US$ by MDG Regions in 2013)

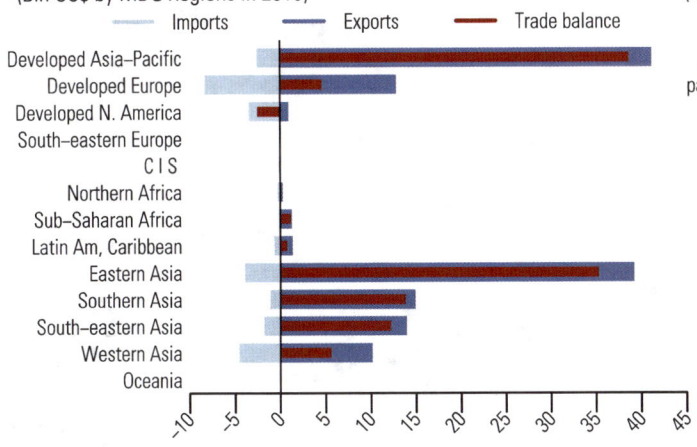

Graph 5: Partner concentration of merchandise trade
(Cumulative share by ranked partners in 2013)

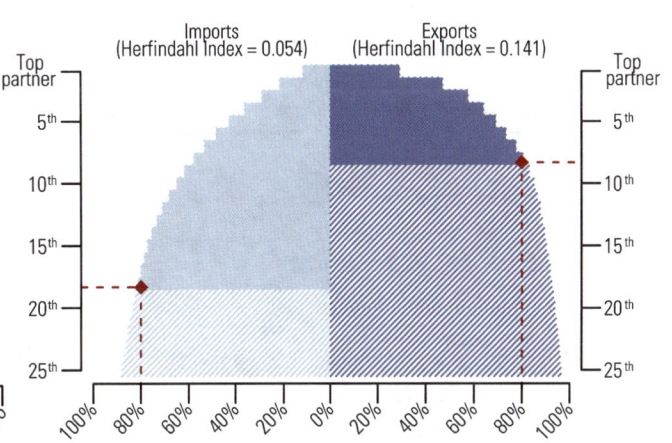

Imports (Herfindahl Index = 0.054)
Exports (Herfindahl Index = 0.141)

Graph 6: Imports of services by EBOPS category
(% share in 2013)

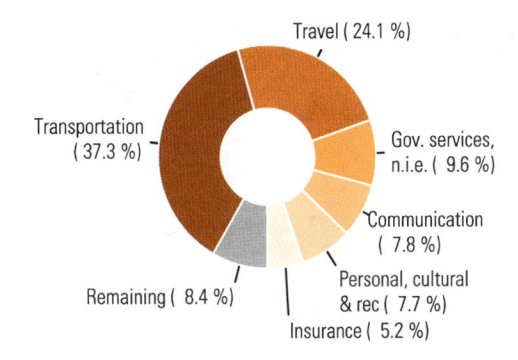

- Transportation (37.3 %)
- Travel (24.1 %)
- Gov. services, n.i.e. (9.6 %)
- Communication (7.8 %)
- Personal, cultural & rec (7.7 %)
- Insurance (5.2 %)
- Remaining (8.4 %)

Imports Profile:

"Machinery and transport equipment" (SITC section 7), "Goods classified chiefly by material" (SITC section 6) and "Miscellaneous manufactured articles" (SITC section 8) were the largest commodity groups for imports in 2013, representing respectively 46.8, 15.7 and 12.1 percent of imported goods (see table 3). From 2011 to 2013, the largest import commodity was "Commodities not specified according to kind" (HS code 9999) (see table 4). The top three partners for merchandise imports were the United States, Areas nes and China, accounting for respectively 10.3, 9.7 and 8.9 percent of total imports. "Transportation" (EBOPS code 205) accounted for the largest share of imports of services in 2013 at 10.2 bln US$, followed by "Travel" (EBOPS code 236) at 6.6 bln US$ and "Government services, n.i.e." (EBOPS code 291) at 2.6 bln US$ (see graph 6).

Table 4: Top 10 import commodities 2011 to 2013

HS code	4-digit heading of Harmonized System 2002	Value 2011	Value 2012	Value 2013	Unit value 2011	Unit value 2012	Unit value 2013	Unit	SITC code
	All Commodities	...	30 787.0	27 034.1					
9999	Commodities not specified according to kind	...	5 616.1	68.6					931
8703	Motor cars and other motor vehicles principally designed for the transport	...	2 712.3	2 534.7			12.7	thsd US$/unit	781
8803	Parts of goods of heading 88.01 or 88.02	...	1 021.6	1 435.6			465.1	US$/kg	792
2601	Iron ores and concentrates	...	496.0	593.9			0.2	US$/kg	281
8544	Insulated (including enamelled or anodised) wire, cable	...	565.8	449.9			7.3	US$/kg	773
8471	Automatic data processing machines and units thereof	...	409.6	465.2					752
8481	Taps, cocks, valves and similar appliances for pipes, boiler shells	...	383.6	468.0			23.2	US$/kg	747
8704	Motor vehicles for the transport of goods	...	396.9	443.0					782
7113	Articles of jewellery and parts thereof, of precious metal	...	398.2	389.2			172.0	US$/kg	897
2818	Artificial corundum, whether or not chemically defined	...	419.8	357.6			0.4	US$/kg	285

Source: UN Comtrade and UN ServiceTrade

Republic of Moldova

Goods Imports: CIF, by origin **Goods Exports:** FOB, by last known destination **Trade System:** General

Overview:
In 2014, the value of merchandise exports of the Republic of Moldova decreased slightly by 3.7 percent to reach 2.3 bln US$, while its merchandise imports decreased slightly by 3.2 percent to reach 5.3 bln US$ (see graph 1, table 2 and table 3). The merchandise trade balance recorded a large deficit of 3.0 bln US$ (see graph 1). The largest merchandise trade balance was with MDG Developed Europe at -926.2 mln US$ (see graph 4). Merchandise exports in the Republic of Moldova were diversified amongst partners; imports were also diversified. The top 12 partners accounted for 80 percent or more of exports and 13 partners accounted for 80 percent or more of imports (see graph 5). In 2012, the value of exports of services of the Republic of Moldova increased moderately by 6.2 percent, reaching 936.3 mln US$, while its imports of services increased moderately by 8.3 percent and reached 957.4 mln US$ (see graph 2). There was a relatively small trade in services deficit of 21.1 mln US$.

Graph 1: Total merchandise trade, by value
(Bln US$ by year)

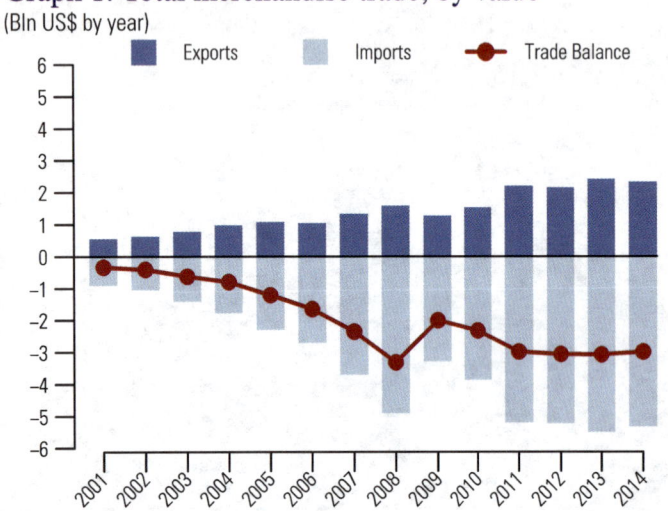

Graph 2: Total services trade, by value
(Mln US$ by year)

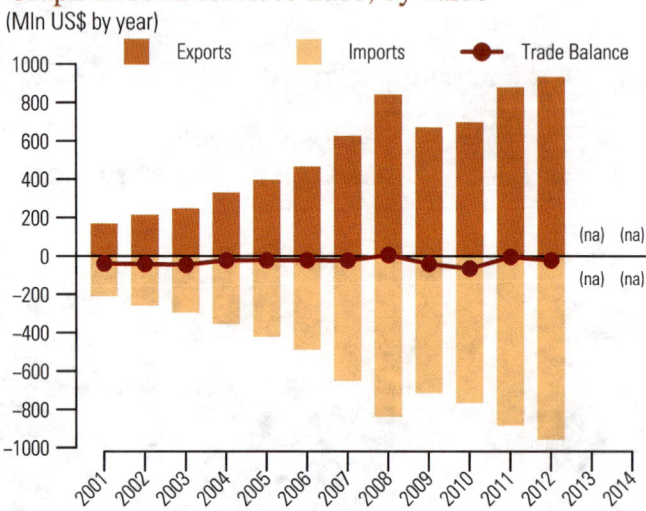

Exports Profile:
"Food, animals + beverages, tobacco" (SITC section 0+1), "Miscellaneous manufactured articles" (SITC section 8) and "Machinery and transport equipment" (SITC section 7) were the largest commodity groups for exports in 2014, representing respectively 35.4, 22.1 and 14.4 percent of exported goods (see table 2). From 2012 to 2014, the largest export commodity was "Insulated (including enamelled or anodised) wire, cable" (HS code 8544) (see table 1). The top three destinations for merchandise exports were the Russian Federation, Romania and Italy, accounting for respectively 24.7, 17.3 and 9.1 percent of total exports. "Transportation" (EBOPS code 205) accounted for the largest share of exports of services in 2012 at 363.1 mln US$, followed by "Travel" (EBOPS code 236) at 212.5 mln US$ and "Communications services" (EBOPS code 245) at 140.0 mln US$ (see graph 3).

Graph 3: Exports of services by EBOPS category
(% share in 2012)

- Travel (22.7 %)
- Transportation (38.8 %)
- Communication (15.0 %)
- Other business (9.8 %)
- Computer & information (6.0 %)
- Remaining (7.8 %)

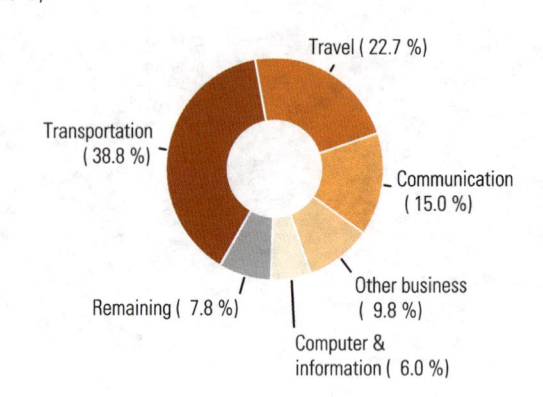

Table 1: Top 10 export commodities 2012 to 2014

HS code	4-digit heading of Harmonized System 2007	Value (million US$) 2012	2013	2014	Unit value 2012	2013	2014	Unit	SITC code
	All Commodities	2 161.9	2 428.3	2 339.5					
8544	Insulated (including enamelled or anodised) wire, cable	167.0	213.1	216.8	16.6		13.7	US$/kg	773
2204	Wine of fresh grapes, including fortified wines	142.1	149.6	111.8	1.2	1.2	1.1	US$/litre	112
3004	Medicaments (excluding goods of heading 30.02, 30.05 or 30.06)	93.4	112.4	124.5	68.9	66.9	74.7	US$/kg	542
1206	Sunflower seeds, whether or not broken	72.6	136.2	105.6	0.6	0.5	0.4	US$/kg	222
0802	Other nuts, fresh or dried, whether or not shelled or peeled	102.0	97.5	110.8	6.4	7.3	7.7	US$/kg	057
2208	Alcohol of a strength by volume of less than 80 % vol	64.9	92.2	68.9	6.6	6.6	6.5	US$/litre	112
9401	Seats (other than those of heading 94.02)	61.1	75.7	86.7					821
1512	Sunflower-seed, safflower or cotton-seed oil	80.7	41.6	74.1	1.2	1.0	0.8	US$/kg	421
1001	Wheat and meslin	16.0	65.9	81.3	0.3	0.2	0.2	US$/kg	041
6204	Women's or girls' suits, ensembles, jackets, blazers, dresses, skirts	50.2	46.7	49.8	11.4	11.0	10.9	US$/unit	842

Republic of Moldova

Services Imports and Exports: EBOPS 2002 categories

Table 2: Merchandise exports by SITC
(Value in million US$, growth and shares in percentage)

SITC	2014	Avg. Growth rates 2010-2014	2013-2014	2014 share
Total	2339.5	11.0	-3.7	100.0
0+1	828.3	8.7	3.2	35.4
2+4	290.6	10.8	-2.1	12.4
3	16.1	20.1	-40.2	0.7
5	176.0	22.0	-2.9	7.5
6	173.8	10.3	-29.6	7.4
7	337.0	15.0	-6.6	14.4
8	516.9	9.6	0.9	22.1
9	0.9	38.4	60.0	0.0

Table 3: Merchandise imports by SITC
(Value in million US$, growth and shares in percentage)

SITC	2014	Avg. Growth rates 2010-2014	2013-2014	2014 share
Total	5317.0	8.4	-3.2	100.0
0+1	660.7	4.9	-8.3	12.4
2+4	125.4	7.1	-5.5	2.4
3	689.1	-3.4	-7.4	13.0
5	796.8	11.2	1.9	15.0
6	992.3	7.7	-0.5	18.7
7	1125.8	8.7	-0.4	21.2
8	475.9	7.6	-3.2	9.0
9	451.0	322.9	-8.7	8.5

SITC Legend

SITC Code	Description
Total	All commodities
0+1	Food, animals + beverages, tobacco
2+4	Crude materials + anim. & veg. oils
3	Mineral fuels, lubricants
5	Chemicals
6	Goods classified chiefly by material
7	Machinery and transport equipment
8	Miscellaneous manufactured articles
9	Not classified elsewhere in the SITC

Graph 4: Merchandise trade balance
(Bln US$ by MDG Regions in 2014)

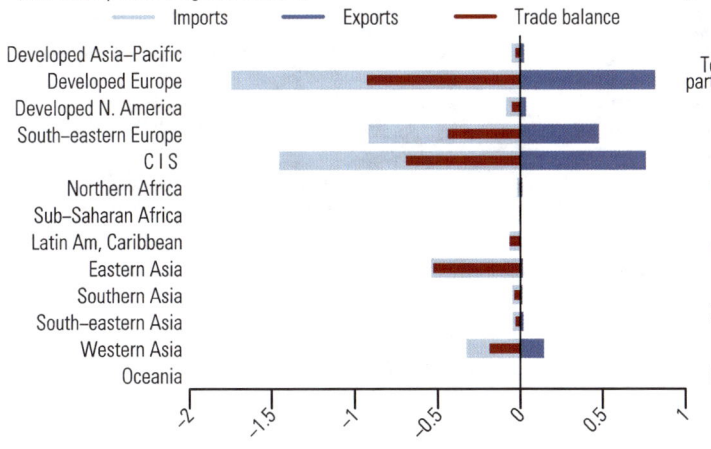

Graph 5: Partner concentration of merchandise trade
(Cumulative share by ranked partners in 2014)

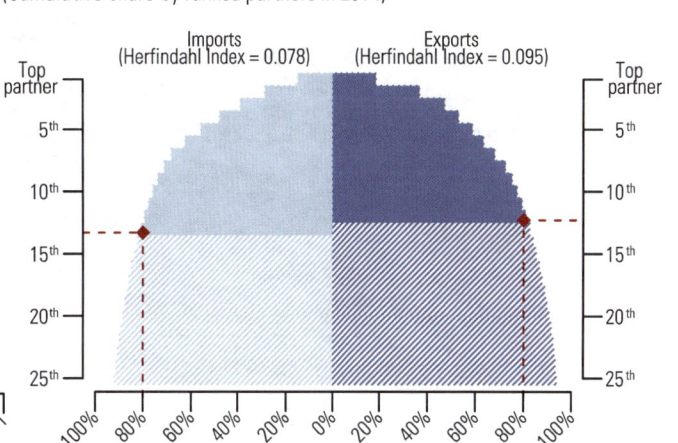

Imports (Herfindahl Index = 0.078)
Exports (Herfindahl Index = 0.095)

Graph 6: Imports of services by EBOPS category
(% share in 2012)

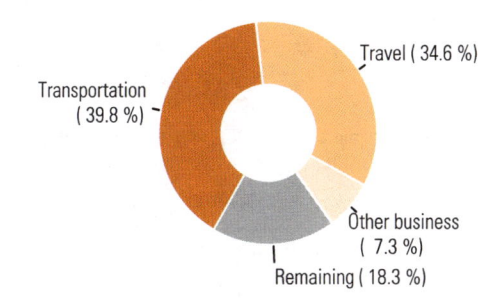

- Travel (34.6 %)
- Transportation (39.8 %)
- Other business (7.3 %)
- Remaining (18.3 %)

Imports Profile:

"Machinery and transport equipment" (SITC section 7), "Goods classified chiefly by material" (SITC section 6) and "Chemicals" (SITC section 5) were the largest commodity groups for imports in 2014, representing respectively 21.2, 18.7 and 15.0 percent of imported goods (see table 3). From 2012 to 2014, the largest import commodity was "Petroleum oils, other than crude" (HS code 2710) (see table 4). The top three partners for merchandise imports were the Russian Federation, Romania and Ukraine, accounting for respectively 14.5, 13.4 and 11.2 percent of total imports. "Transportation" (EBOPS code 205) accounted for the largest share of imports of services in 2012 at 381.5 mln US$, followed by "Travel" (EBOPS code 236) at 331.5 mln US$ and "Other business services" (EBOPS code 268) at 69.5 mln US$ (see graph 6).

Table 4: Top 10 import commodities 2012 to 2014

HS code	4-digit heading of Harmonized System 2007	2012	2013	2014	2012	2013	2014	Unit	SITC code
	All Commodities	5212.9	5492.4	5317.0					
2710	Petroleum oils, other than crude	584.8	620.7	581.2	1.1	1.0	0.9	US$/kg	334
9999	Commodities not specified according to kind	490.7	493.7	450.9					931
3004	Medicaments (excluding goods of heading 30.02, 30.05 or 30.06)	201.4	225.4	249.1	33.2	35.8	37.9	US$/kg	542
8703	Motor cars and other motor vehicles principally designed for the transport	110.9	131.8	132.2	18.3	18.7	20.2	thsd US$/unit	781
8544	Insulated (including enamelled or anodised) wire, cable	115.3	125.3	91.4	8.5		8.2	US$/kg	773
8517	Electrical apparatus for line telephony or line telegraphy	74.9	76.2	62.8					764
2711	Petroleum gases and other gaseous hydrocarbons	64.9	66.4	61.3	0.8	0.7	0.8	US$/kg	343
2402	Cigars, cheroots, cigarillos and cigarettes	67.0	65.6	51.6	14.4	14.0	13.6	US$/kg	122
3808	Insecticides, rodenticides, fungicides, herbicides	53.8	61.4	58.1	11.1	12.4	12.5	US$/kg	591
8701	Tractors (other than tractors of heading 87.09)	54.4	48.9	60.7	7.4	6.8	4.3	thsd US$/unit	722

Source: UN Comtrade and UN ServiceTrade

Romania

Goods Imports: CIF, by origin | **Goods Exports:** FOB, by last known destination | **Trade System:** Special

Overview:

In 2014, the value of merchandise exports of Romania increased moderately by 6.1 percent to reach 69.9 bln US$, while its merchandise imports increased moderately by 6.0 percent to reach 77.9 bln US$ (see graph 1, table 2 and table 3). The merchandise trade balance recorded a relatively small deficit of 8.0 bln US$ (see graph 1). The largest merchandise trade balance was with MDG Developed Europe at -8.7 bln US$ (see graph 4). Merchandise exports in Romania were diversified amongst partners; imports were also diversified. The top 20 partners accounted for 80 percent or more of exports and 15 partners accounted for 80 percent or more of imports (see graph 5). In 2013, the value of exports of services of Romania increased substantially by 67.7 percent, reaching 18.1 bln US$, while its imports of services increased substantially by 21.7 percent and reached 11.4 bln US$ (see graph 2). There was a moderate trade in services surplus of 6.8 bln US$.

Graph 1: Total merchandise trade, by value
(Bln US$ by year)

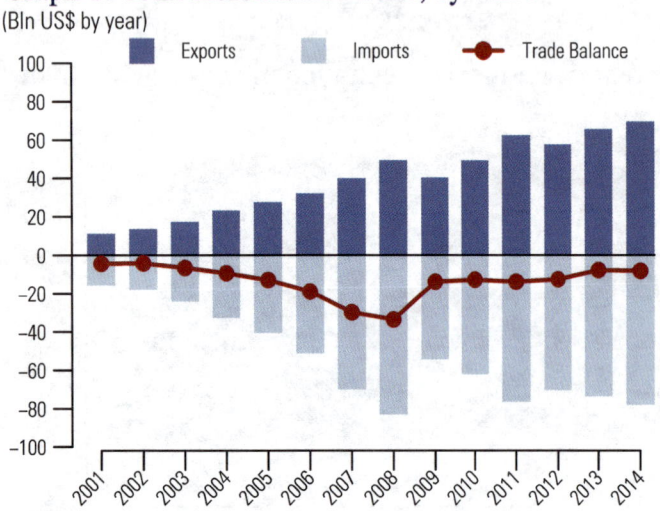

Graph 2: Total services trade, by value
(Bln US$ by year)

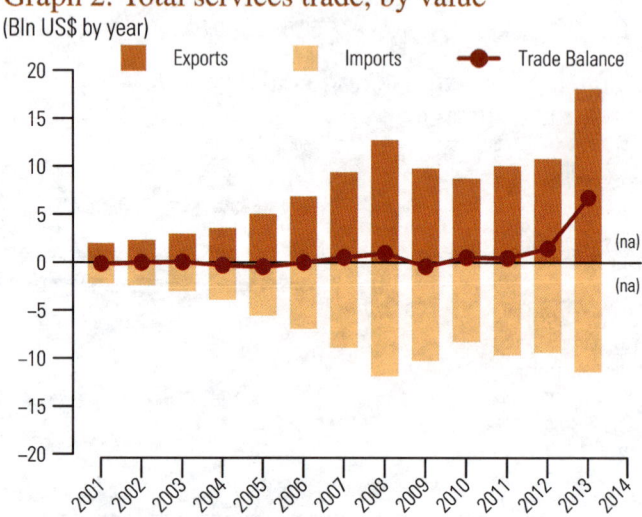

Exports Profile:

"Machinery and transport equipment" (SITC section 7), "Goods classified chiefly by material" (SITC section 6) and "Miscellaneous manufactured articles" (SITC section 8) were the largest commodity groups for exports in 2014, representing respectively 41.7, 16.0 and 14.7 percent of exported goods (see table 2). From 2012 to 2014, the largest export commodity was "Parts and accessories of the motor vehicles of headings 87.01 to 87.05" (HS code 8708) (see table 1). The top three destinations for merchandise exports were Germany, Italy and France, accounting for respectively 18.8, 11.8 and 6.8 percent of total exports. "Transportation" (EBOPS code 205) accounted for the largest share of exports of services in 2013 at 5.2 bln US$, followed by "Other business services" (EBOPS code 268) at 4.1 bln US$ and "Travel" (EBOPS code 236) at 1.7 bln US$ (see graph 3).

Graph 3: Exports of services by EBOPS category
(% share in 2013)

- Other business (22.4 %)
- Travel (9.1 %)
- Transportation (28.7 %)
- Remaining (39.7 %)

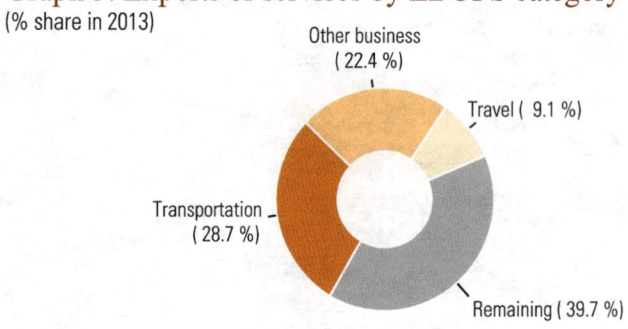

Table 1: Top 10 export commodities 2012 to 2014

HS code	4-digit heading of Harmonized System 2012	Value 2012	Value 2013	Value 2014	UV 2012	UV 2013	UV 2014	Unit	SITC code
	All Commodities	57 904.3	65 881.4	69 877.9					
8708	Parts and accessories of the motor vehicles of headings 87.01 to 87.05	3 608.3	4 530.0	5 267.3	9.0	9.6	10.4	US$/kg	784
8703	Motor cars and other motor vehicles principally designed for the transport	3 254.5	4 208.3	3 974.0	10.2	10.3	10.3	thsd US$/unit	781
8544	Insulated (including enamelled or anodised) wire, cable	3 181.9	3 576.5	3 841.8	14.8	16.3	14.9	US$/kg	773
2710	Petroleum oils, other than crude	2 491.6	2 675.1	3 242.6	1.0	1.0	0.9	US$/kg	334
9999	Commodities not specified according to kind	1 637.5	2 413.7	2 136.9					931
4011	New pneumatic tyres, of rubber	1 326.5	1 510.5	1 606.8	55.4	57.1	58.1	US$/unit	625
9401	Seats (other than those of heading 94.02)	1 018.1	1 339.9	1 702.4					821
8517	Electrical apparatus for line telephony or line telegraphy	1 223.1	1 149.6	1 264.0					764
3004	Medicaments (excluding goods of heading 30.02, 30.05 or 30.06)	1 103.4	1 172.5	1 068.5	47.7	49.9	45.1	US$/kg	542
1001	Wheat and meslin	693.5	1 303.0	1 280.7	0.3	0.3	0.3	US$/kg	041

Source: UN Comtrade and UN ServiceTrade

Romania

Services Imports and Exports: EBOPS 2002 categories

Table 2: Merchandise exports by SITC
(Value in million US$, growth and shares in percentage)

SITC	2014	Avg. Growth rates 2010-2014	Avg. Growth rates 2013-2014	2014 share
Total	69877.9	9.0	6.1	100.0
0+1	5776.4	17.3	7.3	8.3
2+4	3633.7	2.1	-7.8	5.2
3	4188.6	12.5	22.0	6.0
5	3510.3	5.5	-2.1	5.0
6	11206.1	7.7	5.1	16.0
7	29122.8	8.9	7.5	41.7
8	10303.2	8.0	10.0	14.7
9	2136.9	22.8	-11.5	3.1

Table 3: Merchandise imports by SITC
(Value in million US$, growth and shares in percentage)

SITC	2014	Avg. Growth rates 2010-2014	Avg. Growth rates 2013-2014	2014 share
Total	77889.1	5.9	6.0	100.0
0+1	5752.7	8.0	3.9	7.4
2+4	2339.0	2.4	-4.1	3.0
3	7245.3	3.9	0.6	9.3
5	10249.3	6.4	2.5	13.2
6	15856.7	4.8	7.1	20.4
7	26625.7	5.7	7.2	34.2
8	6809.6	6.6	12.3	8.7
9	3010.8	15.2	17.8	3.9

SITC Legend

SITC Code	Description
Total	All commodities
0+1	Food, animals + beverages, tobacco
2+4	Crude materials + anim. & veg. oils
3	Mineral fuels, lubricants
5	Chemicals
6	Goods classified chiefly by material
7	Machinery and transport equipment
8	Miscellaneous manufactured articles
9	Not classified elsewhere in the SITC

Graph 4: Merchandise trade balance
(Bln US$ by MDG Regions in 2014)

Graph 5: Partner concentration of merchandise trade
(Cumulative share by ranked partners in 2014)

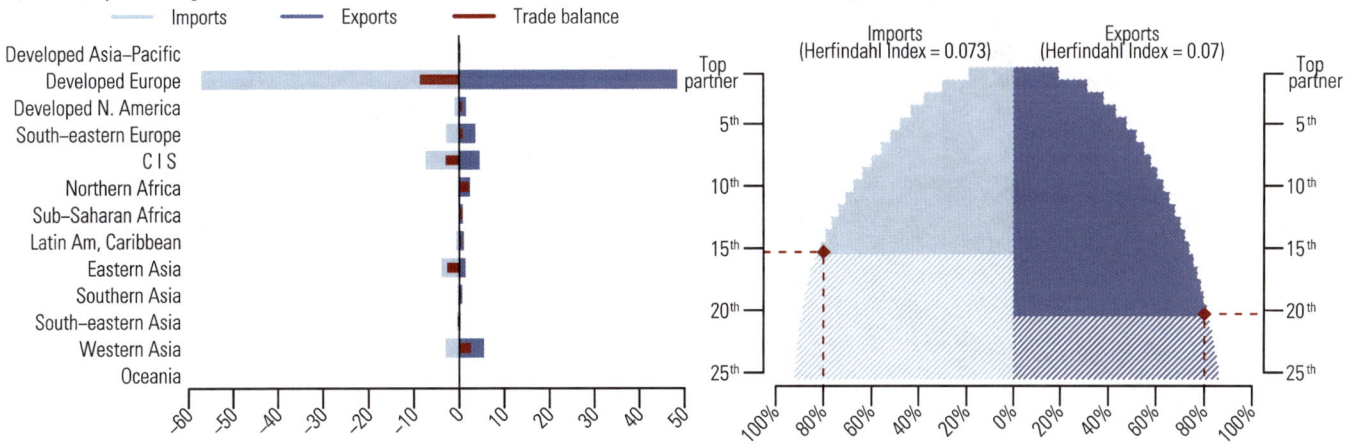

Imports (Herfindahl Index = 0.073)
Exports (Herfindahl Index = 0.07)

Graph 6: Imports of services by EBOPS category
(% share in 2013)

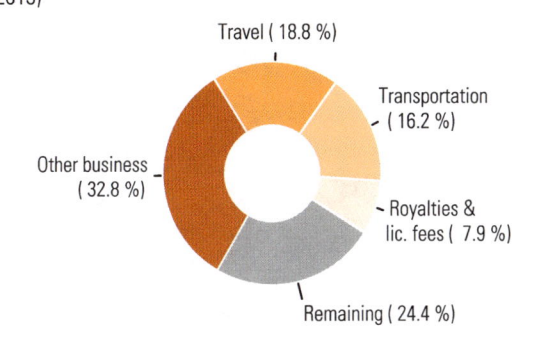

- Travel (18.8 %)
- Transportation (16.2 %)
- Royalties & lic. fees (7.9 %)
- Remaining (24.4 %)
- Other business (32.8 %)

Imports Profile:

"Machinery and transport equipment" (SITC section 7), "Goods classified chiefly by material" (SITC section 6) and "Chemicals" (SITC section 5) were the largest commodity groups for imports in 2014, representing respectively 34.2, 20.4 and 13.2 percent of imported goods (see table 3). From 2012 to 2014, the largest import commodity was "Petroleum oils and oils obtained from bituminous minerals, crude" (HS code 2709) (see table 4). The top three partners for merchandise imports were Germany, Italy and Hungary, accounting for respectively 18.4, 10.9 and 8.3 percent of total imports. "Other business services" (EBOPS code 268) accounted for the largest share of imports of services in 2013 at 3.7 bln US$, followed by "Travel" (EBOPS code 236) at 2.1 bln US$ and "Transportation" (EBOPS code 205) at 1.8 bln US$ (see graph 6).

Table 4: Top 10 import commodities 2012 to 2014

HS code	4-digit heading of Harmonized System 2012	2012	2013	2014	2012	2013	2014	Unit	SITC code
	All Commodities	70259.7	73452.2	77889.1					
2709	Petroleum oils and oils obtained from bituminous minerals, crude	4167.6	4190.1	4795.5	0.8	0.8	0.7	US$/kg	333
3004	Medicaments (excluding goods of heading 30.02, 30.05 or 30.06)	2592.2	2886.3	2872.9	63.2	75.7	71.1	US$/kg	542
8708	Parts and accessories of the motor vehicles of headings 87.01 to 87.05	2224.5	2637.5	3028.5	6.8	7.2	8.1	US$/kg	784
9999	Commodities not specified according to kind	1886.0	2555.9	3010.8					931
2710	Petroleum oils, other than crude	1987.3	1644.8	1539.8	1.1	1.1	1.0	US$/kg	334
8544	Insulated (including enamelled or anodised) wire, cable	1366.5	1566.8	1577.0	10.8	11.1	11.5	US$/kg	773
8517	Electrical apparatus for line telephony or line telegraphy	1366.5	1402.4	1704.3					764
8703	Motor cars and other motor vehicles principally designed for the transport	1222.3	1188.1	1433.1	17.9	19.1	19.1	thsd US$/unit	781
8536	Electrical apparatus for switching or protecting electrical circuits	833.8	994.3	1091.7	26.9	27.7	29.4	US$/kg	772
2711	Petroleum gases and other gaseous hydrocarbons	1438.8	714.1	324.8			0.6	US$/kg	343

Source: UN Comtrade and UN ServiceTrade

Russian Federation

Goods Imports: CIF, by origin | **Goods Exports: FOB, by last known destination** | **Trade System: General**

Overview:
In 2013, the value of merchandise exports of the Russian Federation increased slightly by 0.5 percent to reach 527.3 bln US$, while its merchandise imports decreased slightly by 0.4 percent to reach 314.9 bln US$ (see graph 1, table 2 and table 3). The merchandise trade balance recorded a moderate surplus of 212.3 bln US$ (see graph 1). The largest merchandise trade balance was with MDG Developed Europe at 109.4 bln US$ (see graph 4). Merchandise exports in the Russian Federation were diversified amongst partners; imports were also diversified. The top 21 partners accounted for 80 percent or more of exports and 21 partners accounted for 80 percent or more of imports (see graph 5). In 2013, the value of exports of services of the Russian Federation increased substantially by 13.0 percent, reaching 66.0 bln US$, while its imports of services increased substantially by 17.9 percent and reached 126.4 bln US$ (see graph 2). There was a large trade in services deficit of 60.4 bln US$.

Graph 1: Total merchandise trade, by value
(Bln US$ by year)

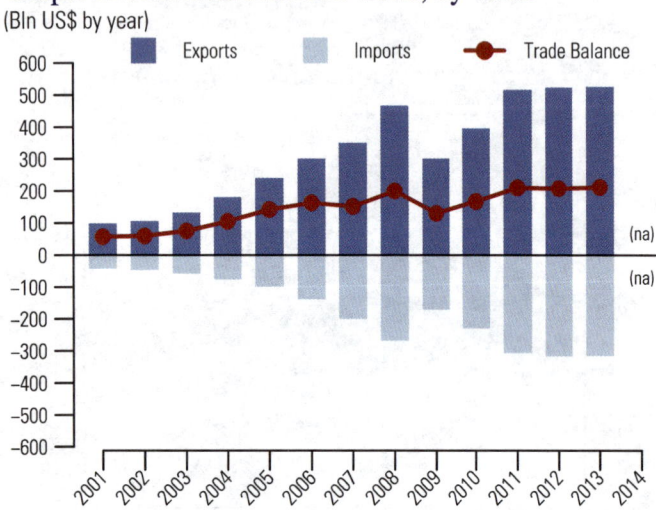

Graph 2: Total services trade, by value
(Bln US$ by year)

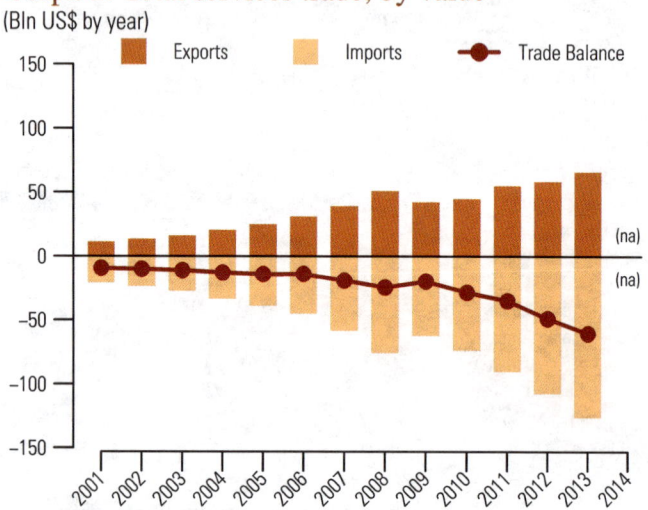

Exports Profile:
"Mineral fuels, lubricants" (SITC section 3) was the largest commodity group for exports in 2013, representing 70.6 percent of exported goods, followed distantly by "Goods classified chiefly by material" (SITC section 6) and "Chemicals" (SITC section 5), representing 10.2 and 4.5 percent, respectively (see table 2). From 2011 to 2013, the largest export commodity was "Petroleum oils and oils obtained from bituminous minerals, crude" (HS code 2709) (see table 1). The top three destinations for merchandise exports were the Netherlands, Areas nes and China, accounting for respectively 13.2, 12.9 and 6.8 percent of total exports. "Transportation" (EBOPS code 205) accounted for the largest share of exports of services in 2013 at 20.6 bln US$, followed by "Other business services" (EBOPS code 268) at 18.4 bln US$ and "Travel" (EBOPS code 236) at 12.0 bln US$ (see graph 3).

Graph 3: Exports of services by EBOPS category
(% share in 2013)

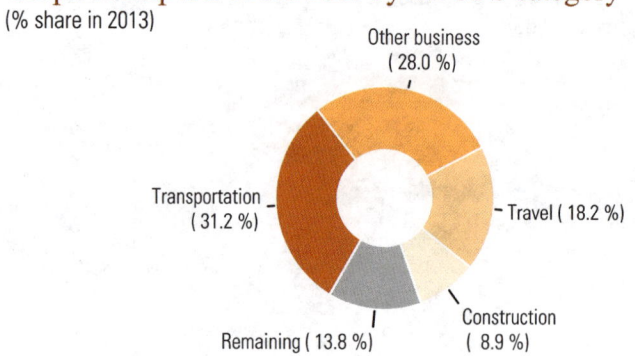

- Other business (28.0 %)
- Travel (18.2 %)
- Construction (8.9 %)
- Remaining (13.8 %)
- Transportation (31.2 %)

Table 1: Top 10 export commodities 2011 to 2013

HS code	4-digit heading of Harmonized System 2007	Value (million US$) 2011	2012	2013	Unit value 2011	2012	2013	Unit	SITC code
	All Commodities	516 992.6	524 766.4	527 265.9					
2709	Petroleum oils and oils obtained from bituminous minerals, crude	171 686.2	180 929.7	173 669.6	0.8	0.8	0.7	US$/kg	333
2710	Petroleum oils, other than crude	91 480.4	103 624.2	109 415.4	0.7	0.7	0.7	US$/kg	334
2711	Petroleum gases and other gaseous hydrocarbons	69 673.3	68 834.6	74 639.1	0.4		0.5	US$/kg	343
9999	Commodities not specified according to kind	56 023.8	12 711.3	13 208.2					931
2701	Coal; briquettes, ovoids and similar solid fuels manufactured from coal	11 372.3	13 014.7	11 821.2	0.1	0.1	0.1	US$/kg	321
7207	Semi-finished products of iron or non-alloy steel	7 720.4	7 868.2	6 471.4	0.6	0.5	0.5	US$/kg	672
7601	Unwrought aluminium	6 755.1	6 334.0	6 132.8	2.0	1.8	1.8	US$/kg	684
7102	Diamonds, whether or not worked, but not mounted or set	3 724.7	4 655.3	4 969.3	115.5			US$/carat	667
7502	Unwrought nickel	4 486.6	3 721.1	3 626.4	23.0	17.0	15.2	US$/kg	683
1001	Wheat and meslin	3 671.2	4 524.0	3 482.7	0.2	0.3	0.3	US$/kg	041

Russian Federation

Services Imports and Exports: EBOPS 2002 categories

Table 2: Merchandise exports by SITC
(Value in million US$, growth and shares in percentage)

SITC	2013	Avg. Growth rates 2009-2013	Avg. Growth rates 2012-2013	2013 share
Total	527 265.9	15.0	0.5	100.0
0+1	13 708.8	13.2	-3.0	2.6
2+4	18 171.9	16.1	-3.3	3.4
3	372 036.1	18.3	0.9	70.6
5	23 532.6	17.2	-4.4	4.5
6	53 831.1	9.7	-5.9	10.2
7	21 364.8	18.4	15.6	4.1
8	5 830.4	26.3	20.1	1.1
9	18 790.3	-11.4	5.3	3.6

Table 3: Merchandise imports by SITC
(Value in million US$, growth and shares in percentage)

SITC	2013	Avg. Growth rates 2009-2013	Avg. Growth rates 2012-2013	2013 share
Total	314 945.1	16.5	-0.4	100.0
0+1	39 119.8	11.4	7.1	12.4
2+4	10 363.5	12.8	-2.4	3.3
3	3 641.5	11.2	-10.1	1.2
5	40 165.6	15.7	4.9	12.8
6	40 183.0	19.5	-1.3	12.8
7	141 440.8	22.2	-4.1	44.9
8	38 324.3	21.7	3.4	12.2
9	1 706.6	-40.6	20.1	0.5

SITC Legend

SITC Code	Description
Total	All commodities
0+1	Food, animals + beverages, tobacco
2+4	Crude materials + anim. & veg. oils
3	Mineral fuels, lubricants
5	Chemicals
6	Goods classified chiefly by material
7	Machinery and transport equipment
8	Miscellaneous manufactured articles
9	Not classified elsewhere in the SITC

Graph 4: Merchandise trade balance
(Bln US$ by MDG Regions in 2013)

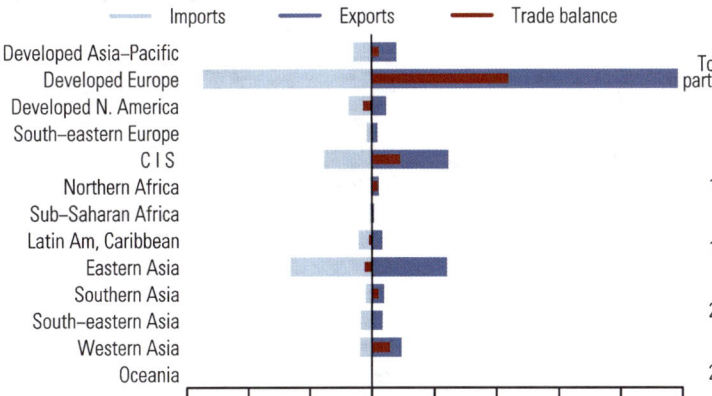

Graph 5: Partner concentration of merchandise trade
(Cumulative share by ranked partners in 2013)

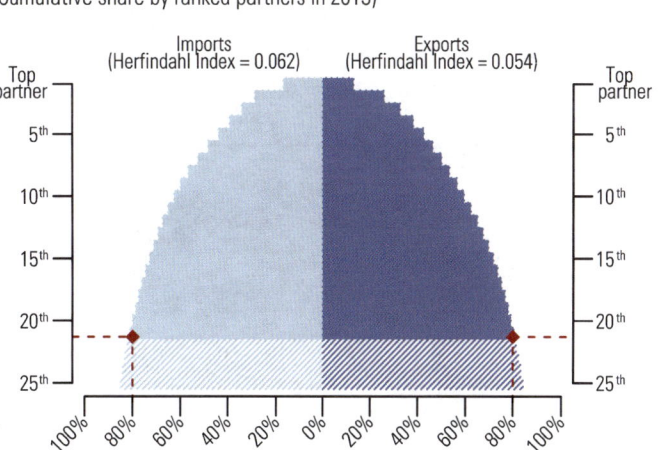

Imports (Herfindahl Index = 0.062)
Exports (Herfindahl Index = 0.054)

Graph 6: Imports of services by EBOPS category
(% share in 2013)

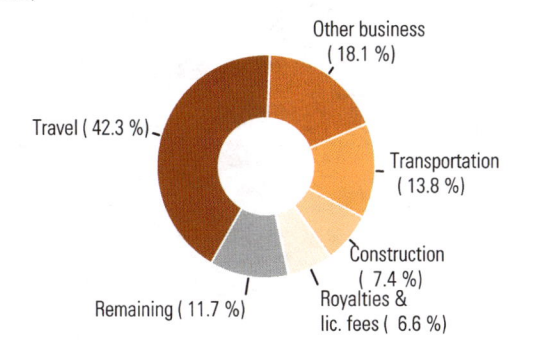

- Travel (42.3%)
- Other business (18.1%)
- Transportation (13.8%)
- Construction (7.4%)
- Royalties & lic. fees (6.6%)
- Remaining (11.7%)

Imports Profile:

"Machinery and transport equipment" (SITC section 7), "Goods classified chiefly by material" (SITC section 6) and "Chemicals" (SITC section 5) were the largest commodity groups for imports in 2013, representing respectively 44.9, 12.8 and 12.8 percent of imported goods (see table 3). From 2011 to 2013, the largest import commodity was "Motor cars and other motor vehicles principally designed for the transport" (HS code 8703) (see table 4). The top three partners for merchandise imports were China, Germany and Ukraine, accounting for respectively 16.3, 12.1 and 5.7 percent of total imports. "Travel" (EBOPS code 236) accounted for the largest share of imports of services in 2013 at 53.5 bln US$, followed by "Other business services" (EBOPS code 268) at 22.9 bln US$ and "Transportation" (EBOPS code 205) at 17.5 bln US$ (see graph 6).

Table 4: Top 10 import commodities 2011 to 2013

HS code	4-digit heading of Harmonized System 2007	Value 2011	Value 2012	Value 2013	Unit value 2011	Unit value 2012	Unit value 2013	Unit	SITC code
	All Commodities	306 091.5	316 192.9	314 945.1					
8703	Motor cars and other motor vehicles principally designed for the transport	18 590.2	20 241.5	16 996.9	18.9	18.8	19.0	thsd US$/unit	781
3004	Medicaments (excluding goods of heading 30.02, 30.05 or 30.06)	10 836.7	10 630.5	11 629.5	87.3	75.2	77.1	US$/kg	542
8708	Parts and accessories of the motor vehicles of headings 87.01 to 87.05	8 787.2	10 827.5	11 488.9	7.6	7.5	7.6	US$/kg	784
9999	Commodities not specified according to kind	27 902.9	1 417.9	1 700.5					931
8517	Electrical apparatus for line telephony or line telegraphy	7 738.8	7 335.1	7 685.1					764
8471	Automatic data processing machines and units thereof	5 260.4	5 827.8	4 864.6	76.6	85.6	78.8	US$/unit	752
8707	Bodies (including cabs), for the motor vehicles of headings 87.01 to 87.05	2 927.6	3 829.2	4 060.5	8.7	9.4	10.6	thsd US$/unit	784
8429	Self-propelled bulldozers, angledozers, graders, levellers, scrapers	3 176.0	3 718.7	3 072.2	59.7	88.5	73.6	thsd US$/unit	723
8704	Motor vehicles for the transport of goods	2 511.3	3 808.4	2 950.2	25.2	31.6	33.1	thsd US$/unit	782
8529	Parts suitable for use with the apparatus of headings 85.25 to 85.28	2 369.5	3 041.2	2 551.3	29.2	31.7	33.5	US$/kg	764

Rwanda

Goods Imports: CIF, by origin | **Goods Exports:** FOB, by last known destination | **Trade System:** General

Overview:
In 2013, the value of merchandise exports of Rwanda increased substantially by 22.7 percent to reach 620.5 mln US$, while its merchandise imports increased slightly by 4.8 percent to reach 1.7 bln US$ (see graph 1, table 2 and table 3). The merchandise trade balance recorded a large deficit of 1.1 bln US$ (see graph 1). The largest merchandise trade balance was with MDG Eastern Asia at -315.7 mln US$ (see graph 4). Merchandise exports in Rwanda were highly concentrated amongst partners; imports were diversified. The top 4 partners accounted for 80 percent or more of exports and 14 partners accounted for 80 percent or more of imports (see graph 5). In 2013, the value of exports of services of Rwanda increased substantially by 18.1 percent, reaching 502.2 mln US$, while its imports of services increased substantially by 22.1 percent and reached 633.3 mln US$ (see graph 2). There was a moderate trade in services deficit of 131.1 mln US$.

Graph 1: Total merchandise trade, by value
(Bln US$ by year)

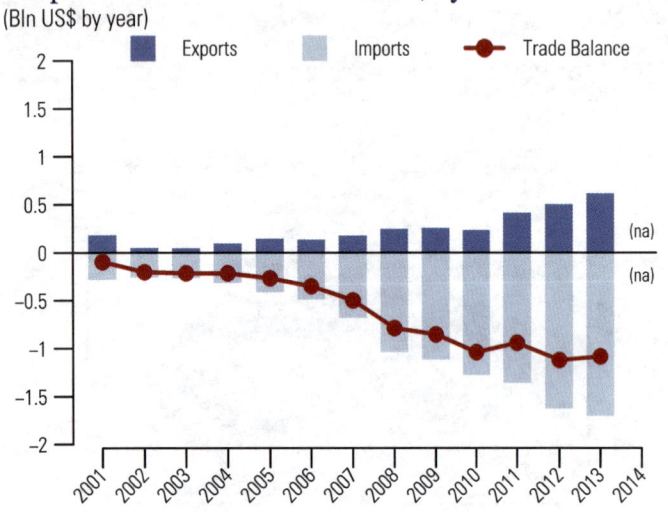

Graph 2: Total services trade, by value
(Mln US$ by year)

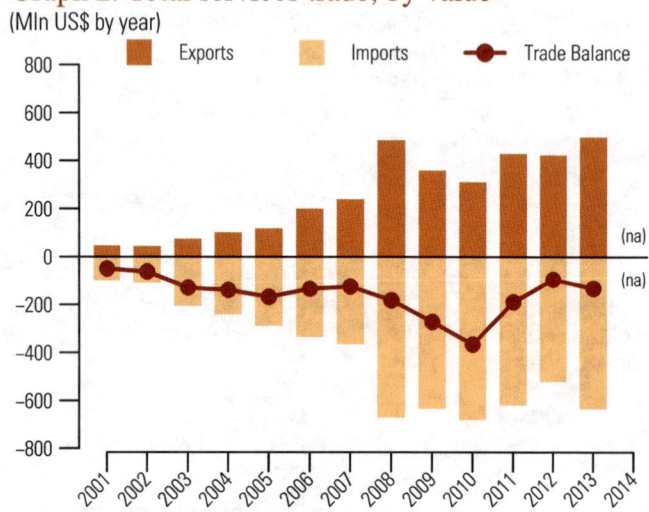

Exports Profile:
"Crude materials + anim. & veg. oils" (SITC section 2+4), "Food, animals + beverages, tobacco" (SITC section 0+1) and "Mineral fuels, lubricants" (SITC section 3) were the largest commodity groups for exports in 2013, representing respectively 41.7, 37.7 and 8.1 percent of exported goods (see table 2). From 2011 to 2013, the largest export commodity was "Niobium, tantalum, vanadium or zirconium ores and concentrates" (HS code 2615) (see table 1). The top three destinations for merchandise exports were the United Republic of Tanzania, Democratic Republic of the Congo and Kenya, accounting for respectively 27.3, 19.6 and 15.3 percent of total exports. "Travel" (EBOPS code 236) accounted for the largest share of exports of services in 2013 at 293.6 mln US$, followed by "Government services, n.i.e." (EBOPS code 291) at 81.5 mln US$ and "Transportation" (EBOPS code 205) at 72.5 mln US$ (see graph 3).

Graph 3: Exports of services by EBOPS category
(% share in 2013)

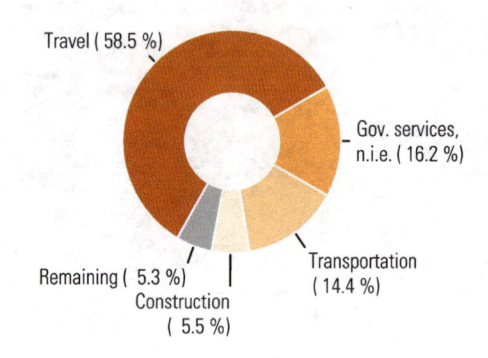

- Travel (58.5 %)
- Gov. services, n.i.e. (16.2 %)
- Transportation (14.4 %)
- Construction (5.5 %)
- Remaining (5.3 %)

Table 1: Top 10 export commodities 2011 to 2013

HS code	4-digit heading of Harmonized System 2007	Value 2011	Value 2012	Value 2013	Unit value 2011	Unit value 2012	Unit value 2013	Unit	SITC code
	All Commodities	417.3	505.7	620.5					
2615	Niobium, tantalum, vanadium or zirconium ores and concentrates	39.0	56.7	134.6	42.6	49.8	54.6	US$/kg	287
2609	Tin ores and concentrates	101.9	52.9	58.0	13.9	11.4	12.0	US$/kg	287
0902	Tea, whether or not flavoured	52.8	86.6	61.5	2.3	3.8	2.8	US$/kg	074
0901	Coffee, whether or not roasted or decaffeinated	76.3	71.2	51.6	4.8	3.6	2.7	US$/kg	071
2710	Petroleum oils, other than crude	20.1	44.7	49.7	1.2	1.2	1.4	US$/kg	334
2611	Tungsten ores and concentrates	11.7	21.4	28.9	14.9	15.6	13.6	US$/kg	287
8703	Motor cars and other motor vehicles principally designed for the transport	15.3	24.7	8.1	33.4	*30.6*	*23.9*	thsd US$/unit	781
1101	Wheat or meslin flour	7.0	17.0	13.2	0.8	0.8	0.8	US$/kg	046
2203	Beer made from malt	3.4	8.9	17.8	9.2	*1.1*	*1.0*	US$/litre	112
4101	Raw hides and skins of bovine (including buffalo) or equine animals	7.0	7.1	11.7	1.2	1.3	1.4	US$/kg	211

Source: UN Comtrade and UN ServiceTrade

Rwanda

Services Imports and Exports: EBOPS 2002 categories

Table 2: Merchandise exports by SITC
(Value in million US$, growth and shares in percentage)

SITC	2013	Avg. Growth rates 2009-2013	Avg. Growth rates 2012-2013	2013 share
Total	620.5	24.2	22.7	100.0
0+1	233.9	18.7	6.4	37.7
2+4	258.5	37.8	58.6	41.7
3	50.0	212.3	-2.5	8.1
5	4.5	22.2	26.2	0.7
6	34.9	34.1	105.5	5.6
7	25.6	-4.5	-30.1	4.1
8	13.1	-7.9	-10.0	2.1
9	0.0	-90.3	...	0.0

Table 3: Merchandise imports by SITC
(Value in million US$, growth and shares in percentage)

SITC	2013	Avg. Growth rates 2009-2013	Avg. Growth rates 2012-2013	2013 share
Total	1701.4	11.2	4.8	100.0
0+1	165.1	12.1	-18.2	9.7
2+4	107.6	11.2	-13.4	6.3
3	98.8	2.4	-13.0	5.8
5	234.7	5.8	6.0	13.8
6	345.4	11.4	-3.2	20.3
7	595.3	15.0	26.6	35.0
8	154.7	13.6	13.5	9.1
9	0.0	-86.2	-62.4	0.0

SITC Legend

SITC Code	Description
Total	All commodities
0+1	Food, animals + beverages, tobacco
2+4	Crude materials + anim. & veg. oils
3	Mineral fuels, lubricants
5	Chemicals
6	Goods classified chiefly by material
7	Machinery and transport equipment
8	Miscellaneous manufactured articles
9	Not classified elsewhere in the SITC

Graph 4: Merchandise trade balance
(Mln US$ by MDG Regions in 2013)

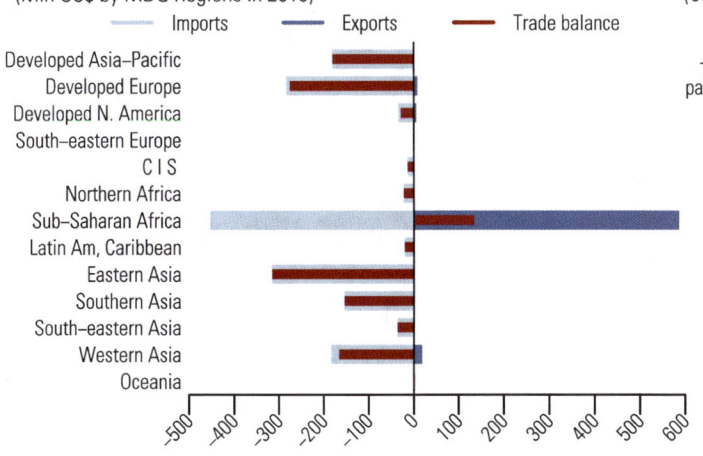

Graph 5: Partner concentration of merchandise trade
(Cumulative share by ranked partners in 2013)

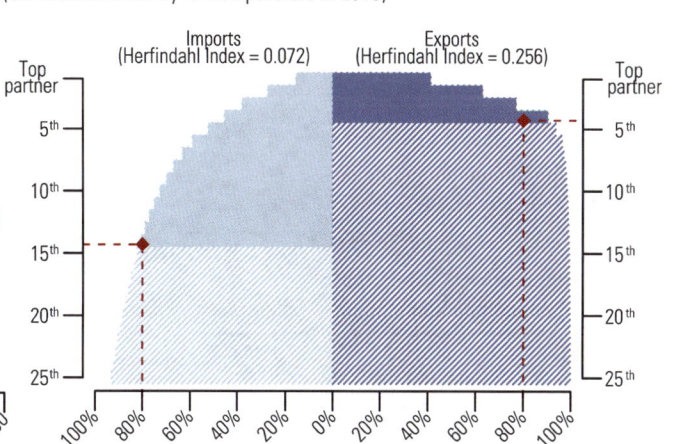

Imports (Herfindahl Index = 0.072)
Exports (Herfindahl Index = 0.256)

Graph 6: Imports of services by EBOPS category
(% share in 2013)

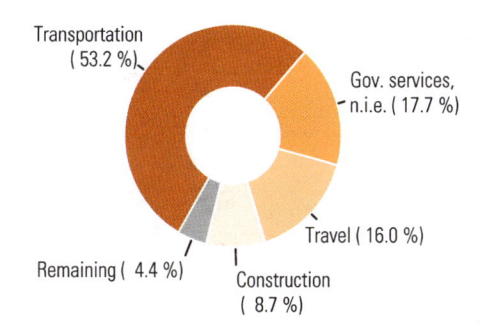

- Transportation (53.2 %)
- Gov. services, n.i.e. (17.7 %)
- Travel (16.0 %)
- Construction (8.7 %)
- Remaining (4.4 %)

Imports Profile:

"Machinery and transport equipment" (SITC section 7), "Goods classified chiefly by material" (SITC section 6) and "Chemicals" (SITC section 5) were the largest commodity groups for imports in 2013, representing respectively 35.0, 20.3 and 13.8 percent of imported goods (see table 3). From 2011 to 2013, the largest import commodity was "Petroleum oils, other than crude" (HS code 2710) (see table 4). The top three partners for merchandise imports were China, Uganda and Kenya, accounting for respectively 13.7, 13.3 and 7.9 percent of total imports. "Transportation" (EBOPS code 205) accounted for the largest share of imports of services in 2013 at 337.1 mln US$, followed by "Government services, n.i.e." (EBOPS code 291) at 112.1 mln US$ and "Travel" (EBOPS code 236) at 101.2 mln US$ (see graph 6).

Table 4: Top 10 import commodities 2011 to 2013

HS code	4-digit heading of Harmonized System 2007	Value (million US$) 2011	2012	2013	Unit value 2011	2012	2013	Unit	SITC code
	All Commodities	1356.6	1624.2	1701.4					
2710	Petroleum oils, other than crude	105.6	107.3	91.7	1.2	1.2	1.0	US$/kg	334
8703	Motor cars and other motor vehicles principally designed for the transport	51.8	57.9	165.8	5.4	*21.7*	*34.6*	thsd US$/unit	781
2523	Portland cement, aluminous cement, slag cement	51.8	66.7	67.2	0.2	0.2	0.2	US$/kg	661
8517	Electrical apparatus for line telephony or line telegraphy	30.3	47.0	60.1					764
3004	Medicaments (excluding goods of heading 30.02, 30.05 or 30.06)	32.9	51.1	49.5	8.8	9.2	16.3	US$/kg	542
1701	Cane or beet sugar and chemically pure sucrose, in solid form	37.3	45.0	34.5	0.8	0.7	0.6	US$/kg	061
8471	Automatic data processing machines and units thereof	31.7	35.1	26.2	509.8			US$/unit	752
1511	Palm oil and its fractions	30.4	34.6	27.0	1.0	1.3	1.2	US$/kg	422
3002	Human blood; animal blood prepared for therapeutic uses	33.6	14.5	43.3	100.4	60.7	149.6	US$/kg	541
1516	Animal or vegetable fats and oils	17.5	30.0	34.2	1.5	1.6	1.4	US$/kg	431

Saint Kitts and Nevis

Goods Imports: CIF, by origin **Goods Exports:** FOB, by last known destination **Trade System:** Special

Overview:
In 2011, the value of merchandise exports of Saint Kitts and Nevis increased substantially by 40.2 percent to reach 44.9 mln US$, while its merchandise imports decreased moderately by 8.6 percent to reach 246.7 mln US$ (see graph 1, table 2 and table 3). The merchandise trade balance recorded a large deficit of 201.8 mln US$ (see graph 1). The largest merchandise trade balance was with MDG Developed North America at -134.8 mln US$ (see graph 4). Merchandise exports in Saint Kitts and Nevis were highly concentrated amongst partners; imports were also highly concentrated. One partner accounted for 80 percent or more of exports and 4 partners accounted for 80 percent or more of imports (see graph 5). In 2012, the value of exports of services of Saint Kitts and Nevis increased substantially by 12.2 percent, reaching 194.3 mln US$, while its imports of services increased slightly by 3.7 percent and reached 119.6 mln US$ (see graph 2). There was a moderate trade in services surplus of 74.7 mln US$.

Graph 1: Total merchandise trade, by value
(Mln US$ by year)

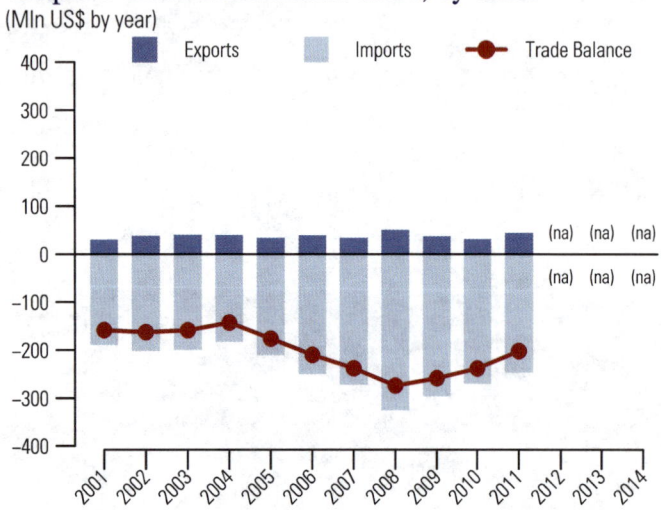

Graph 2: Total services trade, by value
(Mln US$ by year)

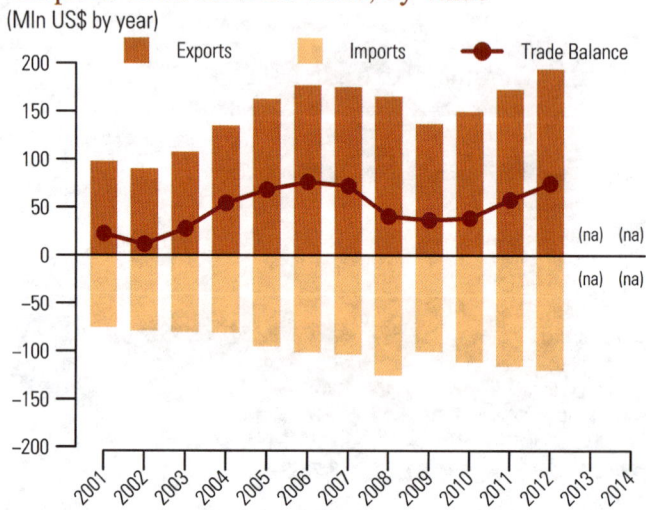

Exports Profile:
"Machinery and transport equipment" (SITC section 7), "Miscellaneous manufactured articles" (SITC section 8) and "Food, animals + beverages, tobacco" (SITC section 0+1) were the largest commodity groups for exports in 2011, representing respectively 67.6, 20.4 and 10.4 percent of exported goods (see table 2). From 2009 to 2011, the largest export commodity was "Electrical apparatus for switching or protecting electrical circuits" (HS code 8536) (see table 1). The top three destinations for merchandise exports were the United States, Antigua and Barbuda and Saint Lucia, accounting for respectively 79.3, 3.4 and 2.6 percent of total exports. "Travel" (EBOPS code 236) accounted for the largest share of exports of services in 2012 at 95.0 mln US$, followed by "Government services, n.i.e." (EBOPS code 291) at 57.6 mln US$ and "Other business services" (EBOPS code 268) at 24.7 mln US$ (see graph 3).

Graph 3: Exports of services by EBOPS category
(% share in 2012)

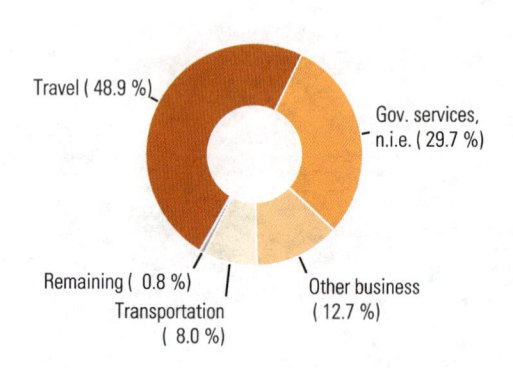

- Travel (48.9 %)
- Gov. services, n.i.e. (29.7 %)
- Other business (12.7 %)
- Transportation (8.0 %)
- Remaining (0.8 %)

Table 1: Top 10 export commodities 2009 to 2011

HS code	4-digit heading of Harmonized System 2007	2009	2010	2011	2009	2010	2011	Unit	SITC code
	All Commodities	37.7	32.0	44.9					
8536	Electrical apparatus for switching or protecting electrical circuits	14.2	13.4	15.2	29.7	15.8	7.8	US$/kg	772
8529	Parts suitable for use with the apparatus of headings 85.25 to 85.28	12.5	6.1	10.1	67.8	71.9	76.4	US$/kg	764
4907	Unused postage, revenue or similar stamps of current or new issue	2.6	3.0	7.6	132.2	108.4	298.0	US$/kg	892
8707	Bodies (including cabs), for the motor vehicles of headings 87.01 to 87.05	0.1	0.6	3.0					784
2203	Beer made from malt	1.5	0.9	1.2	0.7	0.6	0.6	US$/litre	112
2202	Waters with added sugar	0.6	0.8	1.4	0.9	0.8	0.5	US$/litre	111
3925	Builders' ware of plastics, not elsewhere specified or included	0.7	0.9	0.8	11.2	17.3	15.5	US$/kg	893
0306	Crustaceans, whether in shell or not	0.4	0.4	0.7	5.8	3.3	0.3	US$/kg	036
2208	Alcohol of a strength by volume of less than 80 % vol	0.1	0.5	0.6	1.9	2.8	4.3	US$/litre	112
8311	Wire, rods, tubes, plates, electrodes and similar products, of base metal	0.0	1.1	...	5.5	41.7		US$/kg	699

Saint Kitts and Nevis

Services Imports and Exports: EBOPS 2002 categories

Table 2: Merchandise exports by SITC
(Value in million US$, growth and shares in percentage)

SITC	2011	Avg. Growth rates 2007-2011	Avg. Growth rates 2010-2011	2011 share
Total	44.9	7.1	40.2	100.0
0+1	4.7	8.3	32.9	10.4
2+4	0.0	37.6	2.5	0.1
3	0.0	-13.7	-77.6	0.0
5	0.3	26.3	9.1	0.6
6	0.4	-15.9	-74.6	0.8
7	30.4	1.6	39.6	67.6
8	9.2	63.0	85.0	20.4

Table 3: Merchandise imports by SITC
(Value in million US$, growth and shares in percentage)

SITC	2011	Avg. Growth rates 2007-2011	Avg. Growth rates 2010-2011	2011 share
Total	246.7	-2.4	-8.6	100.0
0+1	57.6	3.5	9.7	23.3
2+4	6.7	1.6	-14.2	2.7
3	6.9	-22.1	-30.3	2.8
5	20.4	1.7	3.0	8.3
6	46.3	-1.5	-7.8	18.8
7	66.5	-5.8	-8.5	27.0
8	42.3	-0.7	-25.7	17.2
9	0.0	56.3	258.2	0.0

SITC Legend

SITC Code	Description
Total	All commodities
0+1	Food, animals + beverages, tobacco
2+4	Crude materials + anim. & veg. oils
3	Mineral fuels, lubricants
5	Chemicals
6	Goods classified chiefly by material
7	Machinery and transport equipment
8	Miscellaneous manufactured articles
9	Not classified elsewhere in the SITC

Graph 4: Merchandise trade balance
(Mln US$ by MDG Regions in 2011)

Graph 5: Partner concentration of merchandise trade
(Cumulative share by ranked partners in 2011)

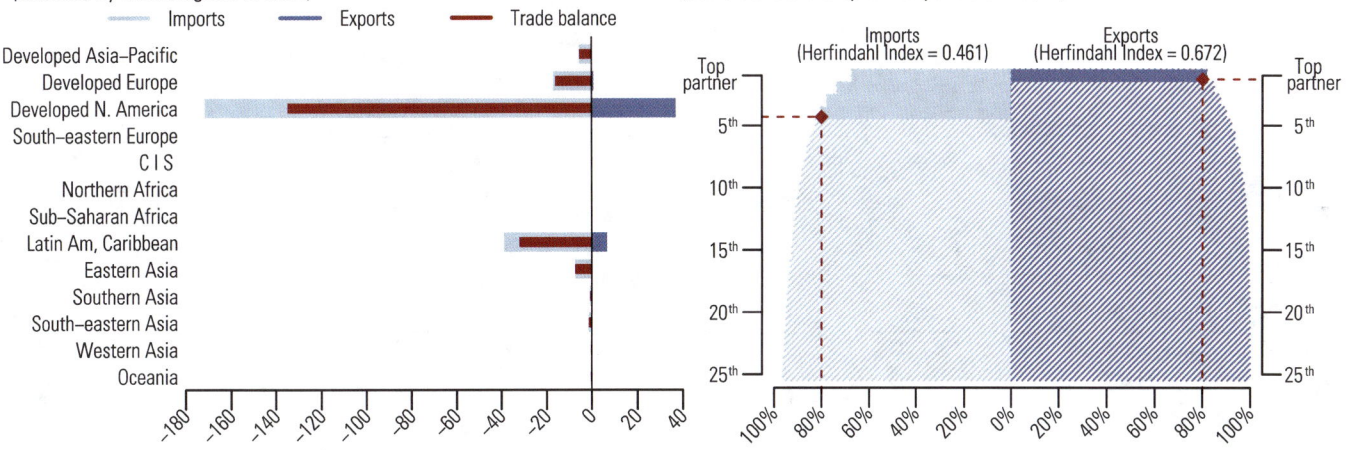

Imports (Herfindahl Index = 0.461)
Exports (Herfindahl Index = 0.672)

Graph 6: Imports of services by EBOPS category
(% share in 2012)

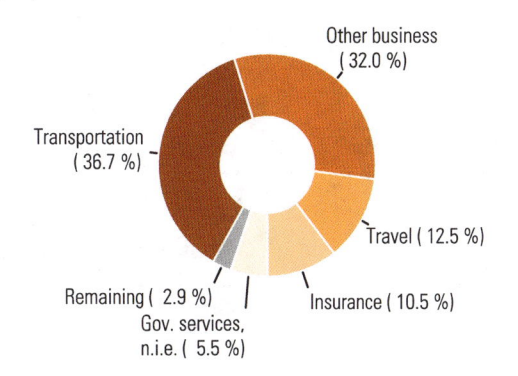

- Transportation (36.7 %)
- Other business (32.0 %)
- Travel (12.5 %)
- Insurance (10.5 %)
- Gov. services, n.i.e. (5.5 %)
- Remaining (2.9 %)

Imports Profile:

"Machinery and transport equipment" (SITC section 7), "Food, animals + beverages, tobacco" (SITC section 0+1) and "Goods classified chiefly by material" (SITC section 6) were the largest commodity groups for imports in 2011, representing respectively 27.0, 23.3 and 18.8 percent of imported goods (see table 3). From 2009 to 2011, the largest import commodity was "Articles of jewellery and parts thereof, of precious metal" (HS code 7113) (see table 4). The top three partners for merchandise imports were the United States, Trinidad and Tobago and the United Kingdom, accounting for respectively 67.1, 6.8 and 3.7 percent of total imports. "Transportation" (EBOPS code 205) accounted for the largest share of imports of services in 2012 at 43.9 mln US$, followed by "Other business services" (EBOPS code 268) at 38.2 mln US$ and "Travel" (EBOPS code 236) at 14.9 mln US$ (see graph 6).

Table 4: Top 10 import commodities 2009 to 2011

HS code	4-digit heading of Harmonized System 2007	Value (million US$) 2009	2010	2011	Unit value 2009	2010	2011	Unit	SITC code
	All Commodities	295.8	269.8	246.7					
7113	Articles of jewellery and parts thereof, of precious metal	23.7	17.3	5.3	13.5	11.3	5.6	thsd US$/kg	897
8703	Motor cars and other motor vehicles principally designed for the transport	10.0	9.2	7.1	15.7	17.0		thsd US$/unit	781
2710	Petroleum oils, other than crude	10.7	9.0	6.3	0.6	0.7	1.1	US$/kg	334
9403	Other furniture and parts thereof	7.7	6.9	5.9					821
7326	Other articles of iron or steel	6.2	5.7	6.1	17.6	12.9	16.4	US$/kg	699
2106	Food preparations not elsewhere specified or included	6.2	3.8	7.4	2.3	3.3	5.0	US$/kg	098
0207	Meat and edible offal, of the poultry of heading 01.05	5.5	5.4	5.8	1.5	1.3	1.5	US$/kg	012
8538	Parts suitable for use with the apparatus of heading 85.35, 85.36 or 85.37	1.5	3.9	7.5	21.2	21.4	17.7	US$/kg	772
8502	Electric generating sets and rotary converters	3.9	8.2	0.7					716
2523	Portland cement, aluminous cement, slag cement	5.9	3.5	2.9	0.1	0.1	0.1	US$/kg	661

Saint Vincent and the Grenadines

Goods Imports: CIF, by origin **Goods Exports:** FOB, by last known destination **Trade System:** Special

Overview:
In 2012, the value of merchandise exports of Saint Vincent and the Grenadines increased substantially by 12.0 percent to reach 43.0 mln US$, while its merchandise imports increased moderately by 5.2 percent to reach 403.2 mln US$ (see graph 1, table 2 and table 3). The merchandise trade balance recorded a large deficit of 360.2 mln US$ (see graph 1). The largest merchandise trade balance was with MDG Latin America and the Caribbean at -148.3 mln US$ (see graph 4). Merchandise exports in Saint Vincent and the Grenadines were moderately diversified amongst partners; imports were moderately concentrated. The top 6 partners accounted for 80 percent or more of exports and 7 partners accounted for 80 percent or more of imports (see graph 5). In 2012, the value of exports of services of Saint Vincent and the Grenadines increased slightly by 0.9 percent, reaching 140.6 mln US$, while its imports of services increased slightly by 3.3 percent and reached 87.1 mln US$ (see graph 2). There was a moderate trade in services surplus of 53.5 mln US$.

Graph 1: Total merchandise trade, by value
(Mln US$ by year)

Graph 2: Total services trade, by value
(Mln US$ by year)

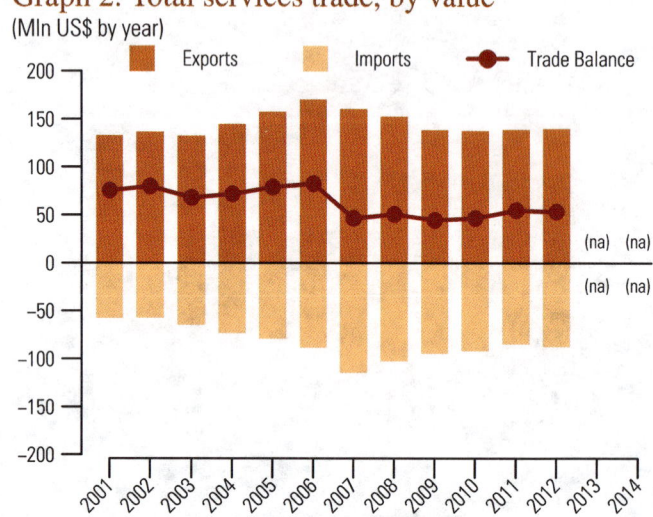

Exports Profile:
"Food, animals + beverages, tobacco" (SITC section 0+1), "Goods classified chiefly by material" (SITC section 6) and "Machinery and transport equipment" (SITC section 7) were the largest commodity groups for exports in 2012, representing respectively 74.7, 11.6 and 5.8 percent of exported goods (see table 2). From 2010 to 2012, the largest export commodity was "Wheat or meslin flour" (HS code 1101) (see table 1). The top three destinations for merchandise exports were Saint Lucia, Trinidad and Tobago and Barbados, accounting for respectively 22.9, 15.6 and 12.7 percent of total exports. "Travel" (EBOPS code 236) accounted for the largest share of exports of services in 2012 at 94.2 mln US$, followed by "Other business services" (EBOPS code 268) at 34.5 mln US$ and "Transportation" (EBOPS code 205) at 7.1 mln US$ (see graph 3).

Graph 3: Exports of services by EBOPS category
(% share in 2012)

- Travel (67.0 %)
- Other business (24.5 %)
- Transportation (5.1 %)
- Remaining (3.4 %)

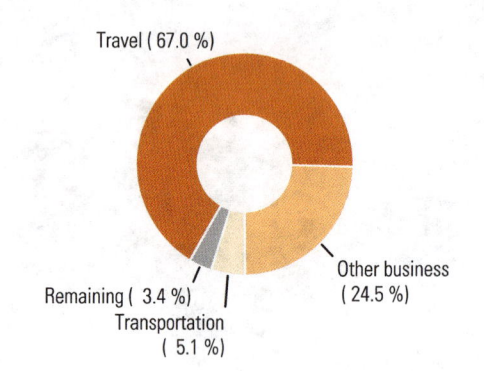

Table 1: Top 10 export commodities 2010 to 2012

HS code	4-digit heading of Harmonized System 2007	Value (million US$) 2010	2011	2012	Unit value 2010	2011	2012	Unit	SITC code
	All Commodities	41.5	38.4	43.0					
1101	Wheat or meslin flour	8.6	10.3	11.6	0.7	0.8	0.8	US$/kg	046
0714	Manioc, arrowroot, sweet potatoes and similar roots	3.9	4.3	5.0	0.6	0.6	0.6	US$/kg	054
1006	Rice	3.8	4.1	4.4	1.1	0.9	1.1	US$/kg	042
0803	Bananas, including plantains, fresh or dried	5.9	1.2	1.5	0.5	0.4	0.5	US$/kg	057
2309	Preparations of a kind used in animal feeding	1.8	2.8	3.6	0.4	0.4	0.4	US$/kg	081
2202	Waters with added sugar	2.2	1.7	2.0	*1.3*	*1.5*	*1.1*	US$/litre	111
4819	Cartons, boxes, cases, bags and other packing containers, of paper	1.8	2.0	1.7	1.7	1.8	1.8	US$/kg	642
7210	Flat-rolled products of iron or non-alloy steel	1.8	1.7	1.6	2.1	2.1	2.2	US$/kg	674
2203	Beer made from malt	0.0	1.1	2.3	*1.0*	*1.0*	*0.8*	US$/litre	112
7610	Aluminium structures (excluding prefabricated buildings of heading 94.06)	0.8	0.7	0.6	5.7	6.7	5.5	US$/kg	691

Source: UN Comtrade and UN ServiceTrade

Saint Vincent and the Grenadines

Services Imports and Exports: EBOPS 2002 categories

Table 2: Merchandise exports by SITC
(Value in million US$, growth and shares in percentage)

SITC	2012	Avg. Growth rates 2008-2012	Avg. Growth rates 2011-2012	2012 share
Total	43.0	-4.7	12.0	100.0
0+1	32.2	0.0	17.6	74.7
2+4	1.1	22.9	-16.2	2.5
3	0.5	-10.5	699.7	1.1
5	0.2	4.3	-15.5	0.5
6	5.0	1.8	-1.5	11.6
7	2.5	-32.4	-13.8	5.8
8	1.6	-3.1	7.0	3.7

Table 3: Merchandise imports by SITC
(Value in million US$, growth and shares in percentage)

SITC	2012	Avg. Growth rates 2008-2012	Avg. Growth rates 2011-2012	2012 share
Total	403.2	2.0	5.2	100.0
0+1	96.6	3.4	7.1	24.0
2+4	9.7	-4.4	6.6	2.4
3	114.9	20.1	8.7	28.5
5	27.3	-1.3	6.1	6.8
6	59.3	-3.1	4.2	14.7
7	61.2	-8.2	-0.4	15.2
8	34.4	-3.6	-0.2	8.5

SITC Legend

SITC Code	Description
Total	All commodities
0+1	Food, animals + beverages, tobacco
2+4	Crude materials + anim. & veg. oils
3	Mineral fuels, lubricants
5	Chemicals
6	Goods classified chiefly by material
7	Machinery and transport equipment
8	Miscellaneous manufactured articles
9	Not classified elsewhere in the SITC

Graph 4: Merchandise trade balance
(Mln US$ by MDG Regions in 2012)

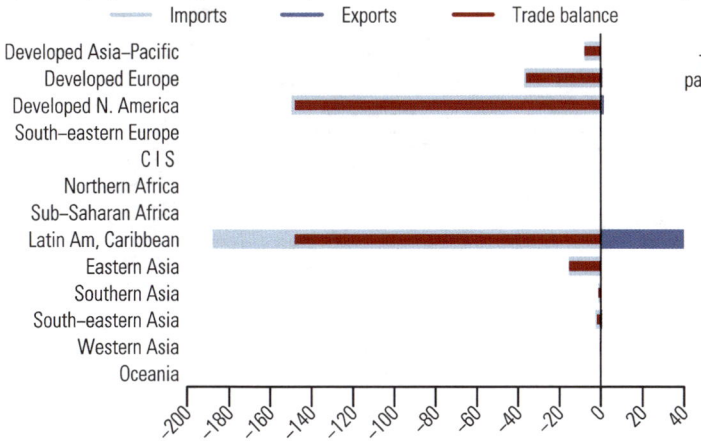

Graph 5: Partner concentration of merchandise trade
(Cumulative share by ranked partners in 2012)

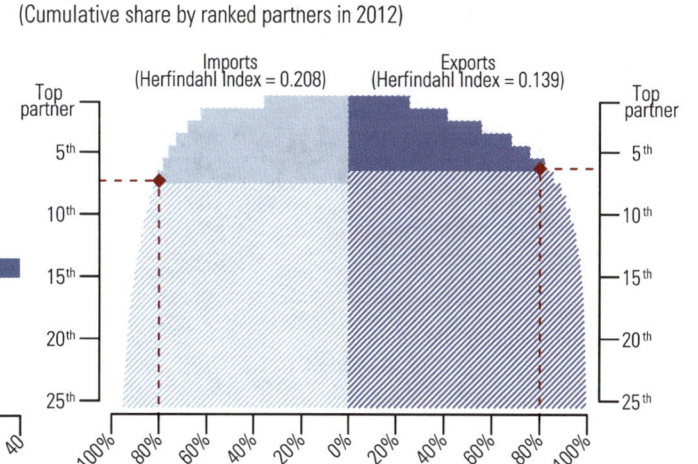

Imports (Herfindahl Index = 0.208)
Exports (Herfindahl Index = 0.139)

Graph 6: Imports of services by EBOPS category
(% share in 2012)

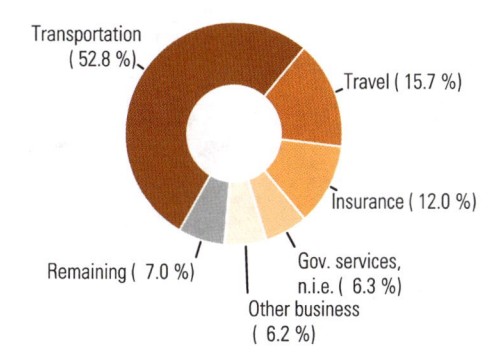

- Transportation (52.8 %)
- Travel (15.7 %)
- Insurance (12.0 %)
- Gov. services, n.i.e. (6.3 %)
- Other business (6.2 %)
- Remaining (7.0 %)

Imports Profile:

"Mineral fuels, lubricants" (SITC section 3), "Food, animals + beverages, tobacco" (SITC section 0+1) and "Machinery and transport equipment" (SITC section 7) were the largest commodity groups for imports in 2012, representing respectively 28.5, 24.0 and 15.2 percent of imported goods (see table 3). From 2010 to 2012, the largest import commodity was "Petroleum oils, other than crude" (HS code 2710) (see table 4). The top three partners for merchandise imports were the United States, Trinidad and Tobago and the United Kingdom, accounting for respectively 34.2, 28.3 and 5.2 percent of total imports. "Transportation" (EBOPS code 205) accounted for the largest share of imports of services in 2012 at 45.9 mln US$, followed by "Travel" (EBOPS code 236) at 13.7 mln US$ and "Insurance services" (EBOPS code 253) at 10.4 mln US$ (see graph 6).

Table 4: Top 10 import commodities 2010 to 2012

HS code	4-digit heading of Harmonized System 2007	Value 2010	Value 2011	Value 2012	Unit value 2010	Unit value 2011	Unit value 2012	Unit	SITC code
	All Commodities	379.5	383.5	403.2					
2710	Petroleum oils, other than crude	78.1	98.0	109.0	0.6	0.8	0.8	US$/kg	334
0207	Meat and edible offal, of the poultry of heading 01.05	10.0	10.9	11.6	1.5	1.5	1.8	US$/kg	012
1001	Wheat and meslin	8.4	10.3	13.0	0.4	0.5	0.5	US$/kg	041
2523	Portland cement, aluminous cement, slag cement	7.2	7.7	7.1	0.1	0.1	0.4	US$/kg	661
8703	Motor cars and other motor vehicles principally designed for the transport	7.5	5.9	5.0	14.0		17.4	thsd US$/unit	781
2711	Petroleum gases and other gaseous hydrocarbons	4.9	7.6	5.8	1.2	2.0	0.8	US$/kg	343
2106	Food preparations not elsewhere specified or included	5.0	6.6	6.4	1.3	1.5	1.8	US$/kg	098
9403	Other furniture and parts thereof	8.0	4.6	4.4					821
1006	Rice	4.3	4.7	6.0	0.8	0.7	0.8	US$/kg	042
2202	Waters with added sugar	3.8	4.8	4.8	1.9	0.9	1.4	US$/litre	111

Source: UN Comtrade and UN ServiceTrade

Samoa

Goods Imports: CIF, by origin   **Goods Exports: FOB, by last known destination**   **Trade System: General**

Overview:
In 2014, the value of merchandise exports of Samoa decreased substantially by 18.0 percent to reach 50.9 mln US$, while its merchandise imports increased moderately by 5.8 percent to reach 388.0 mln US$ (see graph 1, table 2 and table 3). The merchandise trade balance recorded a large deficit of 337.1 mln US$ (see graph 1). The largest merchandise trade balance was with MDG South-eastern Asia at -119.2 mln US$ (see graph 4). Merchandise exports in Samoa were highly concentrated amongst partners; imports were moderately concentrated. The top 3 partners accounted for 80 percent or more of exports and 5 partners accounted for 80 percent or more of imports (see graph 5). In 2012, the value of exports of services of Samoa increased substantially by 12.8 percent, reaching 193.0 mln US$, while its imports of services increased substantially by 28.8 percent and reached 100.2 mln US$ (see graph 2). There was a large trade in services surplus of 92.8 mln US$.

Graph 1: Total merchandise trade, by value
(Mln US$ by year)

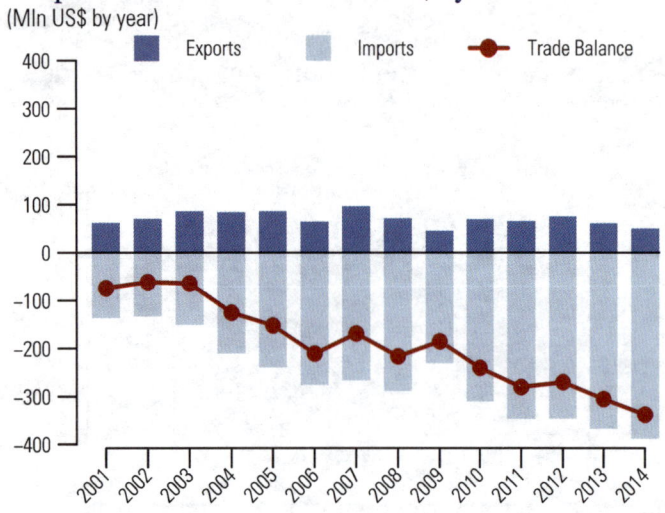

Graph 2: Total services trade, by value
(Mln US$ by year)

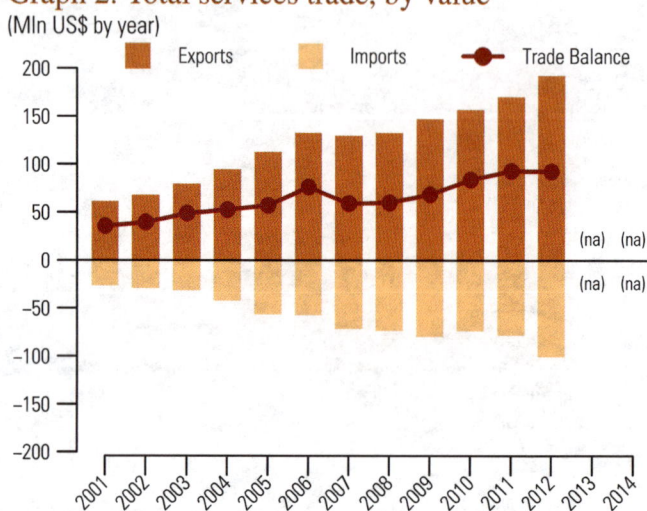

Exports Profile:
"Machinery and transport equipment" (SITC section 7), "Not classified elsewhere in the SITC" (SITC section 9) and "Food, animals + beverages, tobacco" (SITC section 0+1) were the largest commodity groups for exports in 2014, representing respectively 40.9, 33.7 and 19.3 percent of exported goods (see table 2). From 2012 to 2014, the largest export commodity was "Insulated (including enamelled or anodised) wire, cable" (HS code 8544) (see table 1). The top three destinations for merchandise exports were Australia, Areas nes and New Zealand, accounting for respectively 51.0, 17.1 and 11.9 percent of total exports. "Travel" (EBOPS code 236) accounted for the largest share of exports of services in 2012 at 147.6 mln US$, followed by "Construction services" (EBOPS code 249) at 10.5 mln US$ and "Other business services" (EBOPS code 268) at 10.4 mln US$ (see graph 3).

Graph 3: Exports of services by EBOPS category
(% share in 2012)

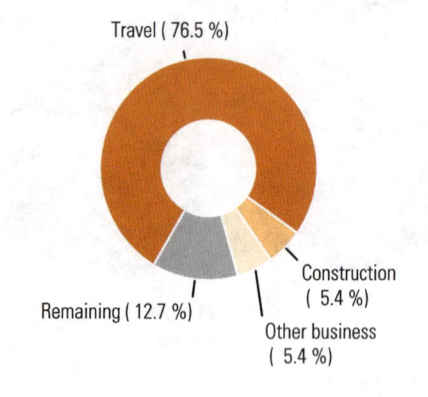

Travel (76.5 %)
Remaining (12.7 %)
Construction (5.4 %)
Other business (5.4 %)

Table 1: Top 10 export commodities 2012 to 2014

HS code	4-digit heading of Harmonized System 2012	Value (million US$) 2012	2013	2014	Unit value 2012	2013	2014	Unit	SITC code
	All Commodities	76.1	62.1	50.9					
8544	Insulated (including enamelled or anodised) wire, cable	35.8	27.8	19.4					773
2710	Petroleum oils, other than crude	17.6	15.0	0.0	1.1	0.0		US$/kg	334
9999	Commodities not specified according to kind	2.0	1.0	17.1					931
2203	Beer made from malt	2.6	4.9	2.5	2.4	2.5	1.7	US$/litre	112
0303	Fish, frozen, excluding fish fillets and other fish meat of heading 03.04	3.6	4.3	1.8	3.0	1.6	1.8	US$/kg	034
1513	Coconut (copra), palm kernel or babassu oil	3.4	0.6	1.5					422
0302	Fish, fresh or chilled, excluding fish fillets	4.1	0.2	0.6	4.0	0.5	2.1	US$/kg	034
2009	Fruit juices (including grape must) and vegetable juices	0.3	1.4	1.5					059
2402	Cigars, cheroots, cigarillos and cigarettes	1.7	0.5	0.2	10.5	31.7	72.9	US$/kg	122
0801	Coconuts, Brazil nuts and cashew nuts, fresh or dried	0.7	0.8	0.8	0.4	0.3	0.6	US$/kg	057

Samoa

Services Imports and Exports: EBOPS 2002 categories

Table 2: Merchandise exports by SITC
(Value in million US$, growth and shares in percentage)

SITC	2014	Avg. Growth rates 2010-2014	Avg. Growth rates 2013-2014	2014 share
Total	50.9	-7.7	-18.0	100.0
0+1	9.8	-0.9	-31.9	19.3
2+4	2.2	-5.9	68.6	4.3
3	0.0	-84.5	-100.0	0.0
5	0.1	13.6	-83.5	0.1
6	0.2	-14.9	-73.2	0.3
7	20.8	-17.7	-27.1	40.9
8	0.7	0.6	-0.2	1.5
9	17.1	573.1	1634.5	33.7

Table 3: Merchandise imports by SITC
(Value in million US$, growth and shares in percentage)

SITC	2014	Avg. Growth rates 2010-2014	Avg. Growth rates 2013-2014	2014 share
Total	388.0	5.8	5.8	100.0
0+1	92.1	5.6	-6.4	23.7
2+4	13.0	5.5	-7.8	3.3
3	93.9	14.6	16.4	24.2
5	26.4	10.7	23.2	6.8
6	59.8	4.4	1.1	15.4
7	65.2	-3.2	11.8	16.8
8	36.5	9.0	18.0	9.4
9	1.2	-16.6	-66.4	0.3

SITC Legend

SITC Code	Description
Total	All commodities
0+1	Food, animals + beverages, tobacco
2+4	Crude materials + anim. & veg. oils
3	Mineral fuels, lubricants
5	Chemicals
6	Goods classified chiefly by material
7	Machinery and transport equipment
8	Miscellaneous manufactured articles
9	Not classified elsewhere in the SITC

Graph 4: Merchandise trade balance
(Mln US$ by MDG Regions in 2014)

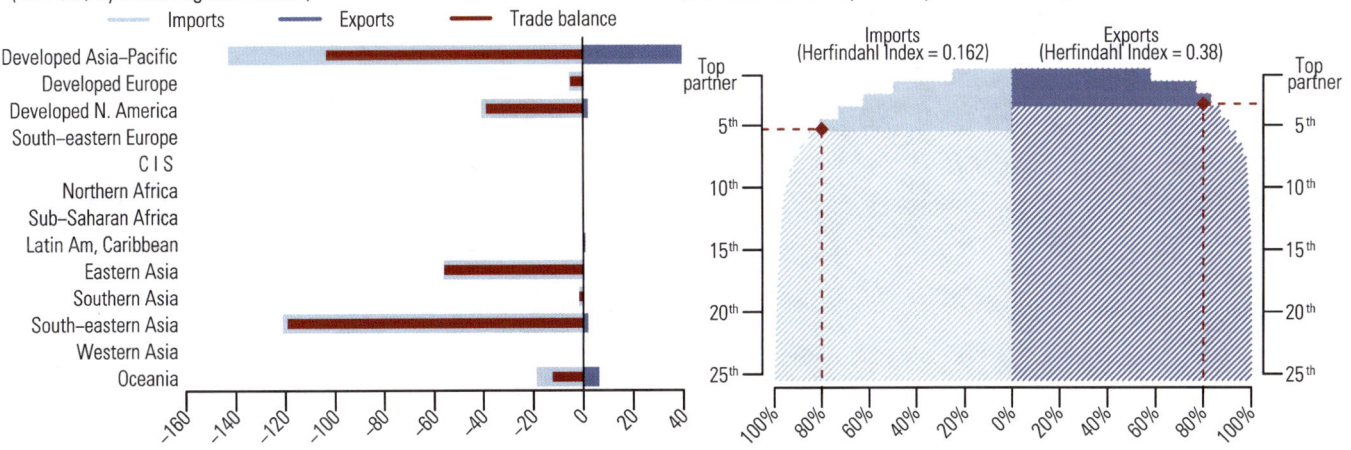

Graph 5: Partner concentration of merchandise trade
(Cumulative share by ranked partners in 2014)

Imports (Herfindahl Index = 0.162)
Exports (Herfindahl Index = 0.38)

Graph 6: Imports of services by EBOPS category
(% share in 2012)

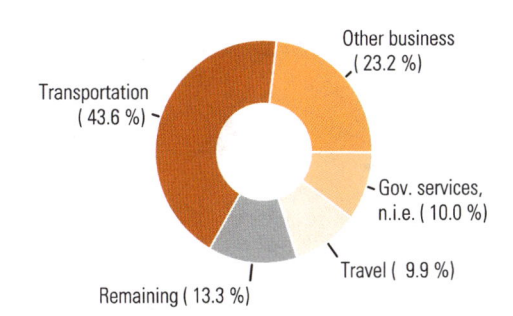

- Transportation (43.6 %)
- Other business (23.2 %)
- Gov. services, n.i.e. (10.0 %)
- Travel (9.9 %)
- Remaining (13.3 %)

Imports Profile:

"Mineral fuels, lubricants" (SITC section 3), "Food, animals + beverages, tobacco" (SITC section 0+1) and "Machinery and transport equipment" (SITC section 7) were the largest commodity groups for imports in 2014, representing respectively 24.2, 23.7 and 16.8 percent of imported goods (see table 3). From 2012 to 2014, the largest import commodity was "Petroleum oils, other than crude" (HS code 2710) (see table 4). The top three partners for merchandise imports were New Zealand, Singapore and the United States, accounting for respectively 26.4, 23.6 and 11.8 percent of total imports. "Transportation" (EBOPS code 205) accounted for the largest share of imports of services in 2012 at 43.7 mln US$, followed by "Other business services" (EBOPS code 268) at 23.3 mln US$ and "Government services, n.i.e." (EBOPS code 291) at 10.0 mln US$ (see graph 6).

Table 4: Top 10 import commodities 2012 to 2014

HS code	4-digit heading of Harmonized System 2012	2012	2013	2014	2012	2013	2014	Unit	SITC code
	All Commodities	345.5	366.6	388.0					
2710	Petroleum oils, other than crude	76.4	78.4	90.6		1.2	1.1	US$/kg	334
0207	Meat and edible offal, of the poultry of heading 01.05	20.1	19.8	19.9	1.4	1.5	1.2	US$/kg	012
8703	Motor cars and other motor vehicles principally designed for the transport	4.5	6.3	8.2	13.3	52.8	2.7	thsd US$/unit	781
1604	Prepared or preserved fish; caviar	5.8	6.3	5.6	1.8	2.8	1.8	US$/kg	037
4407	Wood sawn or chipped lengthwise, sliced or peeled	4.4	6.4	6.4	223.7	97.8	9.1	US$/m³	248
2523	Portland cement, aluminous cement, slag cement	5.0	5.7	5.9	0.1	0.7	0.2	US$/kg	661
1006	Rice	5.8	6.4	4.4	0.0	0.5	0.5	US$/kg	042
8704	Motor vehicles for the transport of goods	4.9	5.7	5.6	24.5	2.4	19.7	thsd US$/unit	782
3926	Other articles of plastics	4.1	5.2	6.4		11.6	12.6	US$/kg	893
1701	Cane or beet sugar and chemically pure sucrose, in solid form	4.3	5.8	5.4		0.1	0.2	US$/kg	061

2014 International Trade Statistics Yearbook, Vol. I — Source: UN Comtrade and UN ServiceTrade

Sao Tome and Principe

Goods Imports: CIF, by origin | **Goods Exports: FOB, by last known destination** | **Trade System: Special**

Overview:

In 2014, the value of merchandise exports of Sao Tome and Principe increased substantially by 51.3 percent to reach 10.5 mln US$, while its merchandise imports increased substantially by 11.6 percent to reach 169.7 mln US$ (see graph 1, table 2 and table 3). The merchandise trade balance recorded a large deficit of 159.2 mln US$ (see graph 1). The largest merchandise trade balance was with MDG Developed Europe at -103.7 mln US$ (see graph 4). Merchandise exports in Sao Tome and Principe were moderately concentrated amongst partners; imports were highly concentrated. The top 5 partners accounted for 80 percent or more of exports and 2 partners accounted for 80 percent or more of imports (see graph 5). In 2012, the value of exports of services of Sao Tome and Principe decreased slightly by 4.4 percent, reaching 17.6 mln US$, while its imports of services decreased substantially by 19.5 percent and reached 25.3 mln US$ (see graph 2). There was a moderate trade in services deficit of 7.7 mln US$.

Graph 1: Total merchandise trade, by value
(Mln US$ by year)

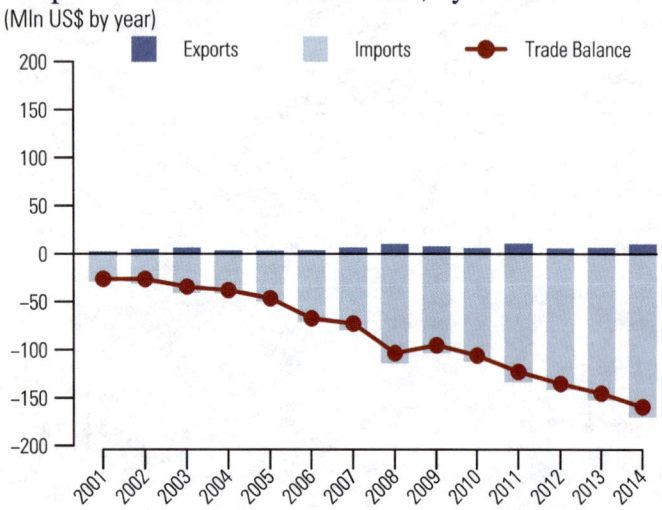

Graph 2: Total services trade, by value
(Mln US$ by year)

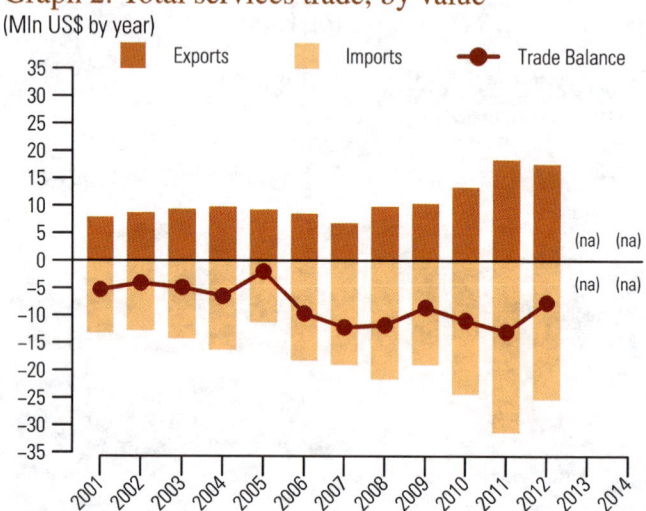

Exports Profile:

"Food, animals + beverages, tobacco" (SITC section 0+1), "Machinery and transport equipment" (SITC section 7) and "Miscellaneous manufactured articles" (SITC section 8) were the largest commodity groups for exports in 2014, representing respectively 96.9, 1.4 and 0.9 percent of exported goods (see table 2). From 2012 to 2014, the largest export commodity was "Cocoa beans, whole or broken, raw or roasted" (HS code 1801) (see table 1). The top three destinations for merchandise exports were the Netherlands, Belgium and Spain, accounting for respectively 29.5, 17.9 and 15.4 percent of total exports. "Travel" (EBOPS code 236) accounted for the largest share of exports of services in 2012 at 15.0 mln US$, followed by "Communications services" (EBOPS code 245) at 1.3 mln US$ (see graph 3).

Graph 3: Exports of services by EBOPS category
(% share in 2012)

- Travel (85.2 %)
- Remaining (7.7 %)
- Communication (7.1 %)

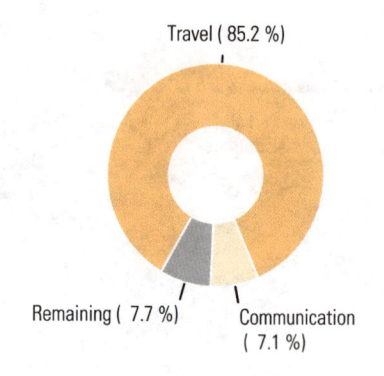

Table 1: Top 10 export commodities 2012 to 2014

HS code	4-digit heading of Harmonized System 2007	Value (million US$) 2012	2013	2014	Unit value 2012	2013	2014	Unit	SITC code
	All Commodities..........	6.0	6.9	10.5					
1801	Cocoa beans, whole or broken, raw or roasted..........	4.8	5.4	9.3	2.2	2.1	2.9	US$/kg	072
1806	Chocolate and other food preparations containing cocoa..........	0.2	0.2	0.3	33.6	31.1	40.9	US$/kg	073
0801	Coconuts, Brazil nuts and cashew nuts, fresh or dried..........	0.1	0.1	0.2	0.3	0.3	0.2	US$/kg	057
8422	Dish washing machines; machinery for cleaning or drying bottles..........	...	0.3	0.0					745
8703	Motor cars and other motor vehicles principally designed for the transport..........	0.1	0.0	0.1	*24.0*	*48.2*	*14.7*	thsd US$/unit	781
0904	Pepper of the genus Piper..........	0.1	0.0	0.1	8.3	13.2	14.5	US$/kg	075
7326	Other articles of iron or steel..........	0.2	0.0	0.0	0.2	30.7	0.0	US$/kg	699
1006	Rice..........	...	...	0.2		0.6		US$/kg	042
6309	Worn clothing and other worn articles..........	0.0	0.1	0.0	5.6	129.7	7.2	US$/kg	269
0901	Coffee, whether or not roasted or decaffeinated..........	0.0	0.0	0.0	4.4	9.5	3.8	US$/kg	071

Sao Tome and Principe

Services Imports and Exports: EBOPS 2002 categories

Table 2: Merchandise exports by SITC
(Value in million US$, growth and shares in percentage)

SITC	2014	Avg. Growth rates 2010-2014	Avg. Growth rates 2013-2014	2014 share
Total	10.5	13.3	51.3	100.0
0+1	10.2	15.1	73.7	96.9
2+4	0.0	-45.1	-89.3	0.2
5	0.0	...	-96.3	0.0
6	0.1	14.1	-64.9	0.5
7	0.1	-8.4	-74.9	1.4
8	0.1	13.0	10.3	0.9
9	0.0	-48.1	...	0.0

Table 3: Merchandise imports by SITC
(Value in million US$, growth and shares in percentage)

SITC	2014	Avg. Growth rates 2010-2014	Avg. Growth rates 2013-2014	2014 share
Total	169.7	10.9	11.6	100.0
0+1	51.2	13.5	20.1	30.2
2+4	5.7	8.4	-8.1	3.4
3	38.7	21.0	-2.9	22.8
5	8.7	10.8	3.9	5.1
6	22.7	14.2	25.8	13.4
7	31.1	0.5	12.2	18.3
8	11.5	5.5	25.3	6.8
9	0.0	-36.1	130.8	0.0

SITC Legend

SITC Code	Description
Total	All commodities
0+1	Food, animals + beverages, tobacco
2+4	Crude materials + anim. & veg. oils
3	Mineral fuels, lubricants
5	Chemicals
6	Goods classified chiefly by material
7	Machinery and transport equipment
8	Miscellaneous manufactured articles
9	Not classified elsewhere in the SITC

Graph 4: Merchandise trade balance
(Mln US$ by MDG Regions in 2014)

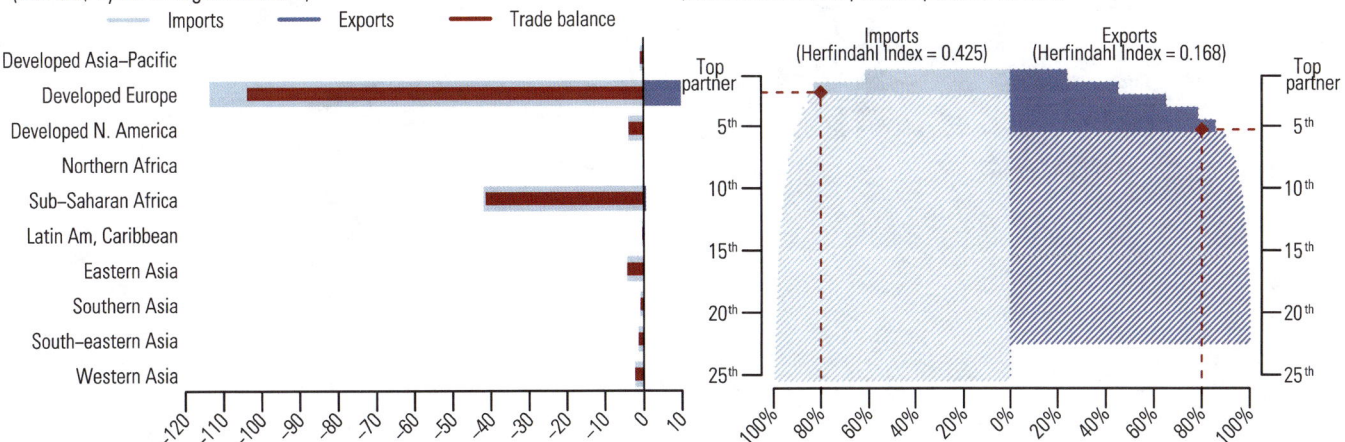

Graph 5: Partner concentration of merchandise trade
(Cumulative share by ranked partners in 2014)

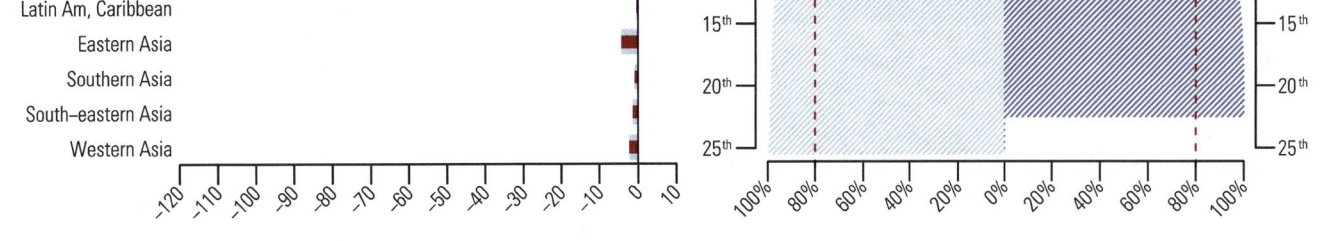

Imports (Herfindahl Index = 0.425)
Exports (Herfindahl Index = 0.168)

Graph 6: Imports of services by EBOPS category
(% share in 2012)

- Transportation (79.6 %)
- Gov. services, n.i.e. (8.0 %)
- Remaining (12.5 %)

Imports Profile:

"Food, animals + beverages, tobacco" (SITC section 0+1), "Mineral fuels, lubricants" (SITC section 3) and "Machinery and transport equipment" (SITC section 7) were the largest commodity groups for imports in 2014, representing respectively 30.2, 22.8 and 18.3 percent of imported goods (see table 3). From 2012 to 2014, the largest import commodity was "Petroleum oils, other than crude" (HS code 2710) (see table 4). The top three partners for merchandise imports were Portugal, Angola and Belgium, accounting for respectively 57.8, 22.9 and 2.3 percent of total imports. "Transportation" (EBOPS code 205) accounted for the largest share of imports of services in 2012 at 20.1 mln US$, followed by "Government services, n.i.e." (EBOPS code 291) at 2.0 mln US$ (see graph 6).

Table 4: Top 10 import commodities 2012 to 2014

HS code	4-digit heading of Harmonized System 2007	Value 2012	Value 2013	Value 2014	Unit value 2012	Unit value 2013	Unit value 2014	Unit	SITC code
	All Commodities	141.3	152.1	169.7					
2710	Petroleum oils, other than crude	35.2	39.5	37.9	1.1	1.5	1.0	US$/kg	334
8703	Motor cars and other motor vehicles principally designed for the transport	6.5	4.7	7.0	21.8	17.7	20.7	thsd US$/unit	781
2204	Wine of fresh grapes, including fortified wines	5.2	5.4	6.1	1.3	1.3	1.5	US$/litre	112
1006	Rice	5.2	4.9	6.5	0.8	0.7	0.8	US$/kg	042
2523	Portland cement, aluminous cement, slag cement	3.3	3.8	5.7	0.2	0.1	0.2	US$/kg	661
1101	Wheat or meslin flour	4.2	4.3	4.0	0.6	0.6	0.6	US$/kg	046
1507	Soya-bean oil and its fractions	3.9	3.6	3.1	1.5	1.4	1.4	US$/kg	421
0207	Meat and edible offal, of the poultry of heading 01.05	2.3	2.7	4.6	1.9	2.0	2.1	US$/kg	012
2202	Waters with added sugar	2.4	3.1	3.4	0.9	0.1	1.0	US$/litre	111
8517	Electrical apparatus for line telephony or line telegraphy	1.0	3.3	3.6					764

2014 International Trade Statistics Yearbook, Vol. I — Source: UN Comtrade and UN ServiceTrade

Saudi Arabia

Goods Imports: CIF, by origin Goods Exports: FOB, by last known destination Trade System: General

Overview:
In 2013, the value of merchandise exports of Saudi Arabia decreased slightly by 3.3 percent to reach 375.4 bln US$, while its merchandise imports increased moderately by 5.2 percent to reach 163.7 bln US$ (see graph 1, table 2 and table 3). The merchandise trade balance recorded a large surplus of 211.7 bln US$ (see graph 1). The largest merchandise trade balance was with MDG Eastern Asia at 176.8 bln US$ (see graph 4). Merchandise exports in Saudi Arabia were highly concentrated amongst partners; imports were diversified. The top 4 partners accounted for 80 percent or more of exports and 22 partners accounted for 80 percent or more of imports (see graph 5). In 2013, the value of exports of services of Saudi Arabia increased moderately by 5.7 percent, reaching 11.7 bln US$, while its imports of services increased slightly by 4.4 percent and reached 76.7 bln US$ (see graph 2). There was a large trade in services deficit of 65.0 bln US$. See footnote*.

Graph 1: Total merchandise trade, by value
(Bln US$ by year)

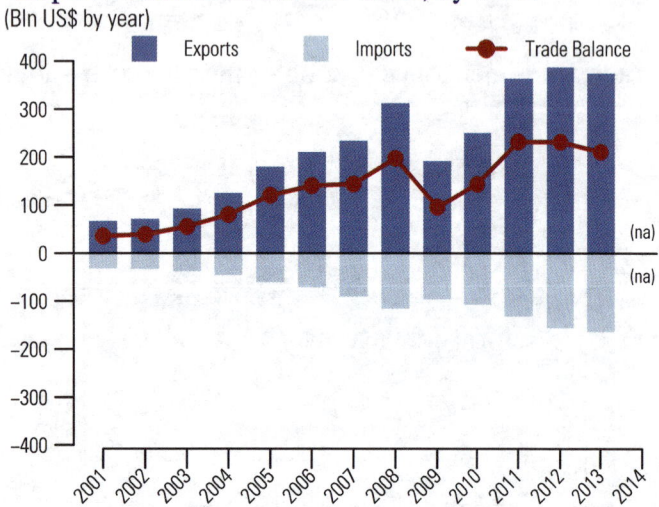

Graph 2: Total services trade, by value
(Bln US$ by year)

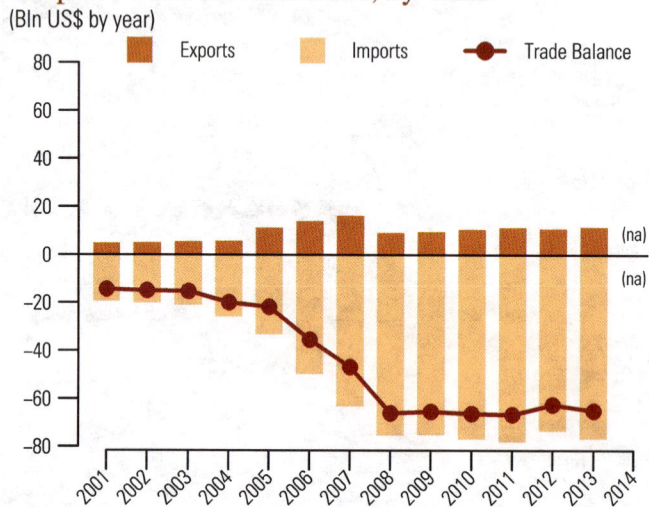

Exports Profile:
"Mineral fuels, lubricants" (SITC section 3), "Chemicals" (SITC section 5) and "Machinery and transport equipment" (SITC section 7) were the largest commodity groups for exports in 2013, representing respectively 85.8, 9.3 and 1.9 percent of exported goods (see table 2). From 2011 to 2013, the largest export commodity was "Petroleum oils and oils obtained from bituminous minerals, crude" (HS code 2709) (see table 1). The top three destinations for merchandise exports were Other Asia nes, North and Central America, Caribbean nes and Rest of Europe nes, accounting for respectively 56.0, 14.6 and 11.4 percent of total exports. "Travel" (EBOPS code 236) accounted for the largest share of exports of services in 2013 at 7.7 bln US$, followed by "Transportation" (EBOPS code 205) at 2.5 bln US$ (see graph 3).

Graph 3: Exports of services by EBOPS category
(% share in 2013)

- Travel (65.5 %)
- Transportation (21.4 %)
- Remaining (13.1 %)

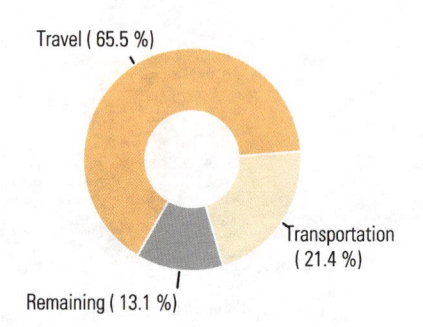

Table 1: Top 10 export commodities 2011 to 2013

HS code	4-digit heading of Harmonized System 2007	Value (million US$) 2011	2012	2013	Unit value 2011	2012	2013	Unit	SITC code
	All Commodities	364 697.7	388 401.1	375 396.6					
2709	Petroleum oils and oils obtained from bituminous minerals, crude	284 976.0	305 237.2	293 994.6	0.8	0.8	0.8	US$/kg	333
2710	Petroleum oils, other than crude	22 972.6	22 731.1	19 060.0	0.8	0.8	0.8	US$/kg	334
3901	Polymers of ethylene, in primary forms	8 033.2	8 262.0	9 299.1	1.2	1.2	1.3	US$/kg	571
2711	Petroleum gases and other gaseous hydrocarbons	8 176.5	8 155.7	7 849.0	0.9	0.9	0.9	US$/kg	343
3902	Polymers of propylene or of other olefins, in primary forms	4 571.3	5 181.6	5 713.3	1.5	1.3	1.4	US$/kg	575
2905	Acyclic alcohols and their derivatives	6 125.2	4 968.9	3 404.2	0.5		0.5	US$/kg	512
2909	Ethers, ether-alcohols, ether-phenols, ether-alcohol-phenols	1 676.9	3 527.7	5 602.7	0.8		0.9	US$/kg	516
2902	Cyclic hydrocarbons	2 011.0	2 079.2	2 148.6	1.1	1.1	1.5	US$/kg	511
3102	Mineral or chemical fertilisers, nitrogenous	1 559.3	1 609.3	1 027.9	0.4	0.4	0.3	US$/kg	562
2901	Acyclic hydrocarbons	1 337.5	1 223.0	859.5	0.9	0.9	1.2	US$/kg	511

*Major export partners were defined as regions only and resulted in high partner concentration for exports in graph 5.

Saudi Arabia

Services Imports and Exports: EBOPS 2002 categories

Table 2: Merchandise exports by SITC
(Value in million US$, growth and shares in percentage)

SITC	2013	Avg. Growth rates 2009-2013	Avg. Growth rates 2012-2013	2013 share
Total	375 396.6	18.2	-3.3	100.0
0+1	3 235.7	4.9	-1.7	0.9
2+4	1 395.7	30.3	56.4	0.4
3	321 929.0	18.5	-4.6	85.8
5	35 073.5	25.8	5.4	9.3
6	4 883.4	4.8	2.3	1.3
7	7 111.5	3.2	17.6	1.9
8	1 501.0	7.0	-6.4	0.4
9	266.7	-18.2	-73.8	0.1

Table 3: Merchandise imports by SITC
(Value in million US$, growth and shares in percentage)

SITC	2013	Avg. Growth rates 2009-2013	Avg. Growth rates 2012-2013	2013 share
Total	163 712.8	14.4	5.2	100.0
0+1	22 364.7	14.0	12.2	13.7
2+4	4 387.5	15.7	-8.0	2.7
3	2 193.7	79.5	233.5	1.3
5	15 466.5	13.0	3.4	9.4
6	29 901.7	16.4	-1.4	18.3
7	71 100.2	13.0	5.7	43.4
8	13 807.2	10.0	7.7	8.4
9	4 491.2	52.7	-8.4	2.7

SITC Legend

SITC Code	Description
Total	All commodities
0+1	Food, animals + beverages, tobacco
2+4	Crude materials + anim. & veg. oils
3	Mineral fuels, lubricants
5	Chemicals
6	Goods classified chiefly by material
7	Machinery and transport equipment
8	Miscellaneous manufactured articles
9	Not classified elsewhere in the SITC

Graph 4: Merchandise trade balance
(Bln US$ by MDG Regions in 2013)

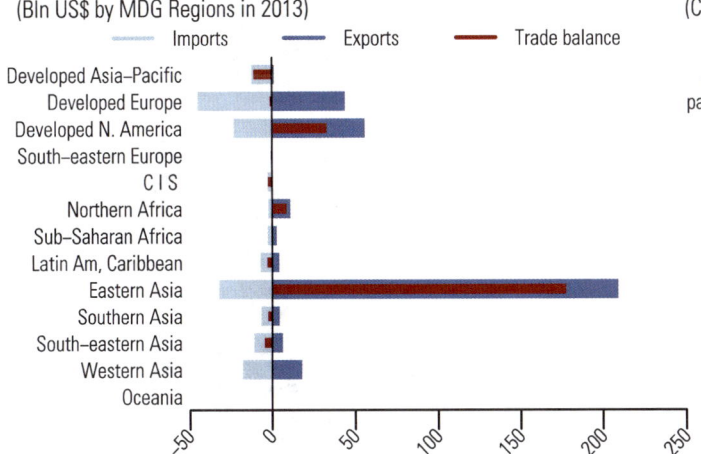

Graph 5: Partner concentration of merchandise trade
(Cumulative share by ranked partners in 2013)

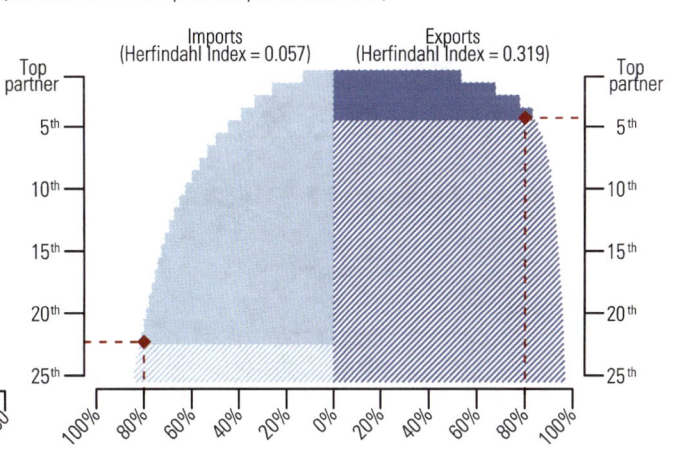

Imports (Herfindahl Index = 0.057)
Exports (Herfindahl Index = 0.319)

Graph 6: Imports of services by EBOPS category
(% share in 2013)

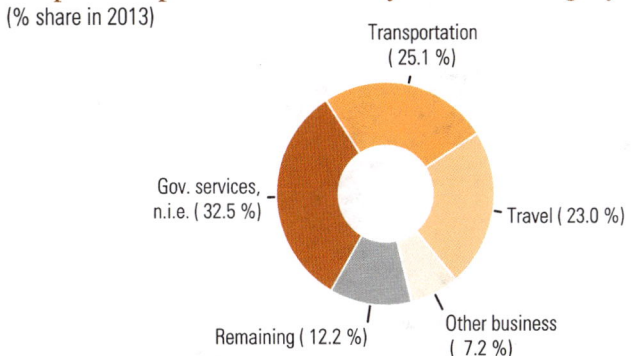

- Transportation (25.1 %)
- Travel (23.0 %)
- Other business (7.2 %)
- Remaining (12.2 %)
- Gov. services, n.i.e. (32.5 %)

Imports Profile:

"Machinery and transport equipment" (SITC section 7), "Goods classified chiefly by material" (SITC section 6) and "Food, animals + beverages, tobacco" (SITC section 0+1) were the largest commodity groups for imports in 2013, representing respectively 43.4, 18.3 and 13.7 percent of imported goods (see table 3). From 2011 to 2013, the largest import commodity was "Motor cars and other motor vehicles principally designed for the transport" (HS code 8703) (see table 4). The top three partners for merchandise imports were the United States, China and Germany, accounting for respectively 12.9, 12.8 and 7.0 percent of total imports. "Government services, n.i.e." (EBOPS code 291) accounted for the largest share of imports of services in 2013 at 24.9 bln US$, followed by "Transportation" (EBOPS code 205) at 19.2 bln US$ and "Travel" (EBOPS code 236) at 17.7 bln US$ (see graph 6).

Table 4: Top 10 import commodities 2011 to 2013

HS code	4-digit heading of Harmonized System 2007	2011	2012	2013	2011	2012	2013	Unit	SITC code
	All Commodities	131 586.6	155 593.0	163 712.8					
8703	Motor cars and other motor vehicles principally designed for the transport	11 246.3	15 987.2	16 089.8		21.9	22.4	thsd US$/unit	781
8517	Electrical apparatus for line telephony or line telegraphy	5 641.5	6 191.9	6 951.3					764
8704	Motor vehicles for the transport of goods	2 143.5	3 321.3	3 653.6					782
3004	Medicaments (excluding goods of heading 30.02, 30.05 or 30.06)	1 959.7	3 192.9	3 760.2	81.8	92.3	94.9	US$/kg	542
7108	Gold (including gold plated with platinum)	1 810.6	2 260.4	4 472.7	49.5	53.2	42.9	thsd US$/kg	971
1003	Barley	1 958.7	2 514.1	3 249.6	0.3	0.3	0.3	US$/kg	043
8471	Automatic data processing machines and units thereof	1 907.7	2 062.2	2 188.2					752
0207	Meat and edible offal, of the poultry of heading 01.05	1 827.0	1 757.1	2 027.9	2.4	2.2	2.4	US$/kg	012
8708	Parts and accessories of the motor vehicles of headings 87.01 to 87.05	1 883.7	1 764.7	1 838.4	9.6	8.1	8.7	US$/kg	784
4011	New pneumatic tyres, of rubber	1 607.1	1 846.3	1 789.6					625

Senegal

Goods Imports: CIF, by origin **Goods Exports:** FOB, by last known destination **Trade System:** General

Overview:
In 2013, the value of merchandise exports of Senegal increased moderately by 5.3 percent to reach 2.7 bln US$, while its merchandise imports increased slightly by 3.5 percent to reach 6.7 bln US$ (see graph 1, table 2 and table 3). The merchandise trade balance recorded a large deficit of 4.0 bln US$ (see graph 1). The largest merchandise trade balance was with MDG Developed Europe at -2.2 bln US$ (see graph 4). Merchandise exports in Senegal were diversified amongst partners; imports were also diversified. The top 17 partners accounted for 80 percent or more of exports and 18 partners accounted for 80 percent or more of imports (see graph 5). In 2012, the value of exports of services of Senegal increased slightly by 4.2 percent, reaching 1.2 bln US$, while its imports of services increased slightly by 2.4 percent and reached 1.3 bln US$ (see graph 2). There was a relatively small trade in services deficit of 107.1 mln US$.

Graph 1: Total merchandise trade, by value
(Bln US$ by year)

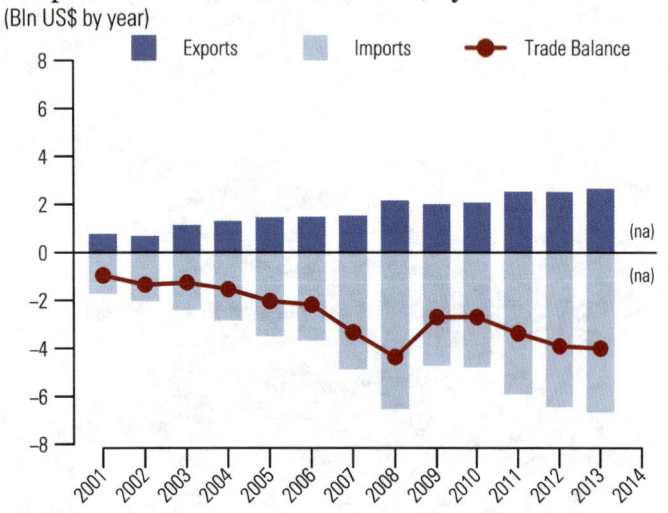

Graph 2: Total services trade, by value
(Bln US$ by year)

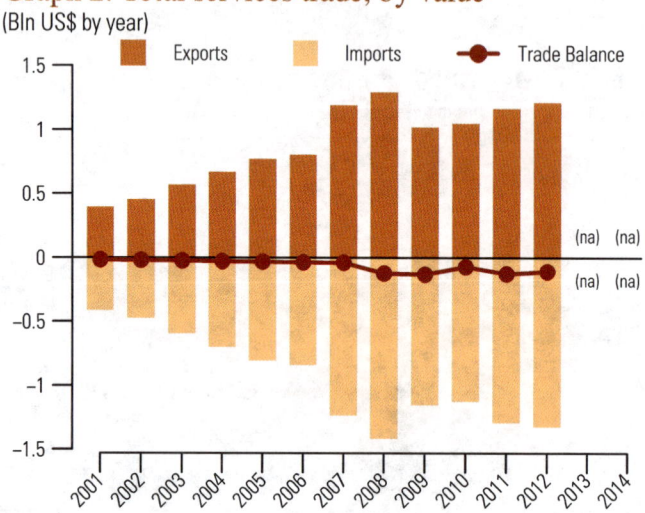

Exports Profile:
"Food, animals + beverages, tobacco" (SITC section 0+1), "Mineral fuels, lubricants" (SITC section 3) and "Goods classified chiefly by material" (SITC section 6) were the largest commodity groups for exports in 2013, representing respectively 30.1, 17.5 and 14.7 percent of exported goods (see table 2). From 2011 to 2013, the largest export commodity was "Petroleum oils, other than crude" (HS code 2710) (see table 1). The top three destinations for merchandise exports were Mali, India and Switzerland, accounting for respectively 16.3, 10.7 and 10.2 percent of total exports. "Travel" (EBOPS code 236) accounted for the largest share of exports of services in 2012 at 405.2 mln US$, followed by "Communications services" (EBOPS code 245) at 234.3 mln US$ and "Other business services" (EBOPS code 268) at 198.4 mln US$ (see graph 3).

Graph 3: Exports of services by EBOPS category
(% share in 2012)

- Communication (19.3 %)
- Other business (16.3 %)
- Gov. services, n.i.e. (11.6 %)
- Transportation (10.3 %)
- Construction (5.6 %)
- Remaining (3.6 %)
- Travel (33.3 %)

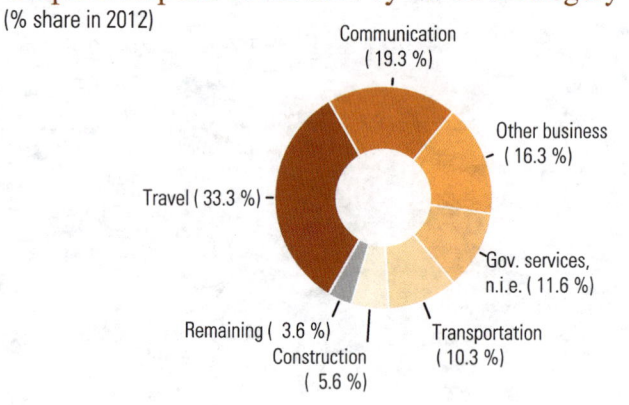

Table 1: Top 10 export commodities 2011 to 2013

HS code	4-digit heading of Harmonized System 2007	Value 2011	Value 2012	Value 2013	Unit value 2011	Unit value 2012	Unit value 2013	Unit	SITC code
	All Commodities	2 541.7	2 531.7	2 665.9					
2710	Petroleum oils, other than crude	364.9	351.3	431.2	1.0	1.0	1.0	US$/kg	334
7108	Gold (including gold plated with platinum)	247.7	351.0	329.0	32.3	44.5	36.1	thsd US$/kg	971
2809	Diphosphorus pentaoxide; phosphoric acid	340.8	274.9	165.2	0.9	0.8	0.6	US$/kg	522
2523	Portland cement, aluminous cement, slag cement	238.0	219.2	165.4	0.1	0.1	0.1	US$/kg	661
0303	Fish, frozen, excluding fish fillets and other fish meat of heading 03.04	99.1	107.2	151.0	1.3	1.3	1.3	US$/kg	034
2104	Soups and broths and preparations therefor	69.3	86.7	122.8	2.6	2.5	2.4	US$/kg	098
0302	Fish, fresh or chilled, excluding fish fillets	82.0	58.2	57.0	9.9	9.8	10.9	US$/kg	034
0307	Molluscs, whether in shell or not	81.8	65.7	31.3	5.8	5.4	4.0	US$/kg	036
2402	Cigars, cheroots, cigarillos and cigarettes	52.6	49.1	51.0	17.7	18.3	21.5	US$/kg	122
1508	Ground-nut oil and its fractions	79.4	27.2	36.9	1.4	2.0	2.2	US$/kg	421

Senegal

Services Imports and Exports: EBOPS 2002 categories

Table 2: Merchandise exports by SITC
(Value in million US$, growth and shares in percentage)

SITC	2013	Avg. Growth rates 2009-2013	Avg. Growth rates 2012-2013	2013 share
Total	2 665.9	7.2	5.3	100.0
0+1	802.1	12.5	27.3	30.1
2+4	202.9	15.6	14.8	7.6
3	465.4	1.4	29.0	17.5
5	297.6	2.7	-25.8	11.2
6	390.9	8.0	-6.6	14.7
7	108.7	-9.6	-25.6	4.1
8	67.5	1.2	44.6	2.5
9	330.9	16.2	-5.9	12.4

Table 3: Merchandise imports by SITC
(Value in million US$, growth and shares in percentage)

SITC	2013	Avg. Growth rates 2009-2013	Avg. Growth rates 2012-2013	2013 share
Total	6 659.4	9.0	3.5	100.0
0+1	1 409.4	8.6	6.0	21.2
2+4	316.9	10.2	-34.2	4.8
3	1 943.2	15.5	5.3	29.2
5	618.7	8.4	3.3	9.3
6	741.2	5.4	9.9	11.1
7	1 380.8	5.2	8.1	20.7
8	246.5	3.4	10.7	3.7
9	2.7	0.8	-24.0	0.0

SITC Legend

SITC Code	Description
Total	All commodities
0+1	Food, animals + beverages, tobacco
2+4	Crude materials + anim. & veg. oils
3	Mineral fuels, lubricants
5	Chemicals
6	Goods classified chiefly by material
7	Machinery and transport equipment
8	Miscellaneous manufactured articles
9	Not classified elsewhere in the SITC

Graph 4: Merchandise trade balance
(Bln US$ by MDG Regions in 2013)

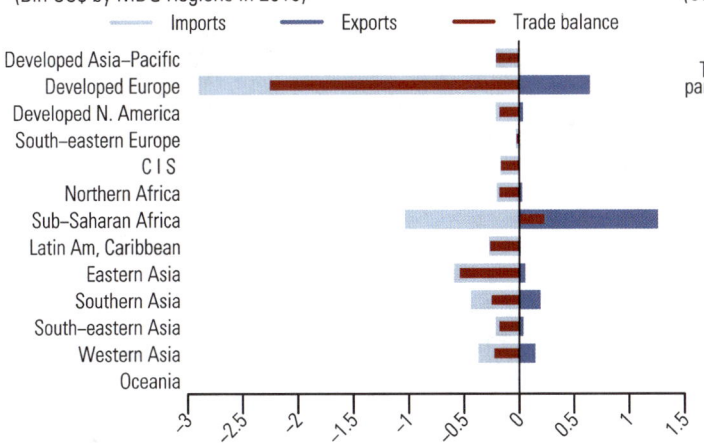

Graph 5: Partner concentration of merchandise trade
(Cumulative share by ranked partners in 2013)

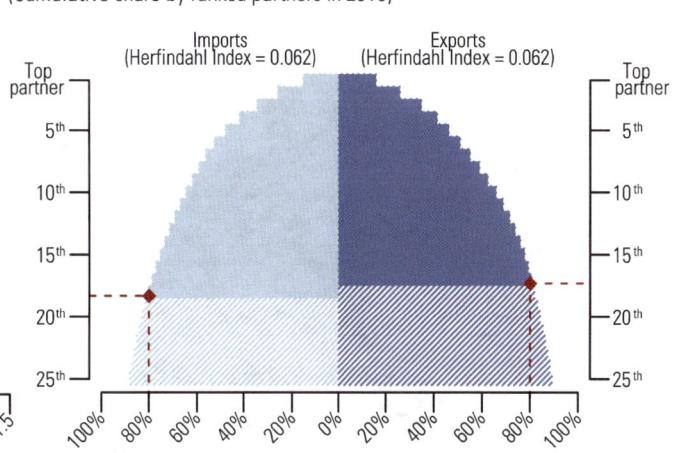

Graph 6: Imports of services by EBOPS category
(% share in 2012)

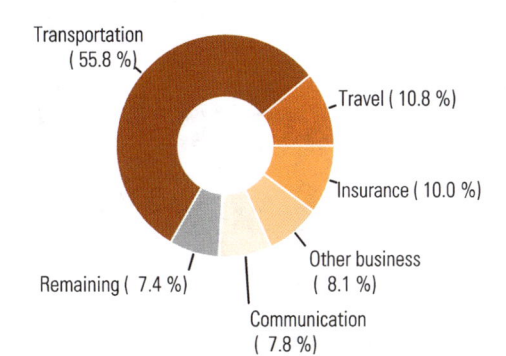

- Transportation (55.8 %)
- Travel (10.8 %)
- Insurance (10.0 %)
- Other business (8.1 %)
- Communication (7.8 %)
- Remaining (7.4 %)

Imports Profile:

"Mineral fuels, lubricants" (SITC section 3), "Food, animals + beverages, tobacco" (SITC section 0+1) and "Machinery and transport equipment" (SITC section 7) were the largest commodity groups for imports in 2013, representing respectively 29.2, 21.2 and 20.7 percent of imported goods (see table 3). From 2011 to 2013, the largest import commodity was "Petroleum oils, other than crude" (HS code 2710) (see table 4). The top three partners for merchandise imports were France, Nigeria and China, accounting for respectively 15.7, 10.5 and 6.7 percent of total imports. "Transportation" (EBOPS code 205) accounted for the largest share of imports of services in 2012 at 738.7 mln US$, followed by "Travel" (EBOPS code 236) at 143.4 mln US$ and "Insurance services" (EBOPS code 253) at 132.6 mln US$ (see graph 6).

Table 4: Top 10 import commodities 2011 to 2013

HS code	4-digit heading of Harmonized System 2007	2011	2012	2013	2011	2012	2013	Unit	SITC code
	All Commodities	5 908.9	6 434.2	6 659.4					
2710	Petroleum oils, other than crude	1 131.4	907.8	1 070.6	0.9	0.9	0.9	US$/kg	334
2709	Petroleum oils and oils obtained from bituminous minerals, crude	539.3	753.0	699.8	0.9	0.9	0.9	US$/kg	333
1006	Rice	376.4	449.6	461.6	0.5	0.4	0.4	US$/kg	042
1001	Wheat and meslin	170.6	189.1	191.7	0.4	0.4	0.4	US$/kg	041
3004	Medicaments (excluding goods of heading 30.02, 30.05 or 30.06)	157.4	165.4	171.3	23.9	20.2	20.0	US$/kg	542
8703	Motor cars and other motor vehicles principally designed for the transport	155.8	155.5	168.4		24.5	23.8	thsd US$/unit	781
7213	Bars and rods, hot-rolled, in irregularly wound coils	120.8	105.1	93.7	0.8	0.7	0.7	US$/kg	676
1511	Palm oil and its fractions	81.3	115.5	112.0	1.3	1.3	1.2	US$/kg	422
1701	Cane or beet sugar and chemically pure sucrose, in solid form	114.0	92.7	99.1	0.8	0.7	0.7	US$/kg	061
2711	Petroleum gases and other gaseous hydrocarbons	103.9	91.6	105.2	1.0	0.9	1.0	US$/kg	343

Source: UN Comtrade and UN ServiceTrade

Serbia

Goods Imports: CIF, by origin **Goods Exports:** FOB, by last known destination **Trade System:** General

Overview:

In 2014, the value of merchandise exports of Serbia increased slightly by 1.6 percent to reach 14.8 bln US$, while its merchandise imports increased slightly by 0.3 percent to reach 20.6 bln US$ (see graph 1, table 2 and table 3). The merchandise trade balance recorded a moderate deficit of 5.8 bln US$ (see graph 1). The largest merchandise trade balance was with MDG Developed Europe at -3.8 bln US$ (see graph 4). Merchandise exports in Serbia were diversified amongst partners; imports were also diversified. The top 15 partners accounted for 80 percent or more of exports and 18 partners accounted for 80 percent or more of imports (see graph 5). In 2012, the value of exports of services of Serbia decreased moderately by 6.7 percent, reaching 3.3 bln US$, while its imports of services decreased moderately by 5.7 percent and reached 3.0 bln US$ (see graph 2). There was a relatively small trade in services surplus of 240.8 mln US$. See footnote*.

Graph 1: Total merchandise trade, by value
(Bln US$ by year)

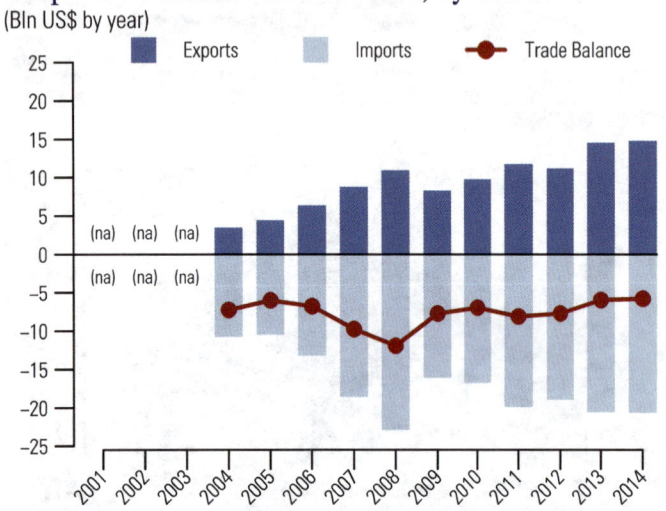

Graph 2: Total services trade, by value
(Bln US$ by year)

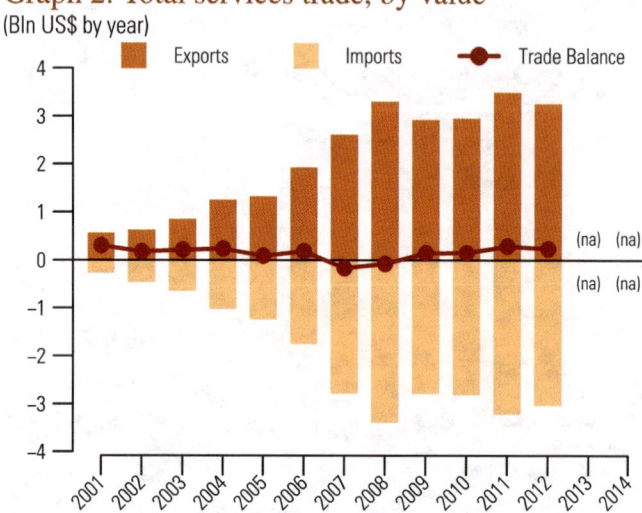

Exports Profile:

"Machinery and transport equipment" (SITC section 7), "Goods classified chiefly by material" (SITC section 6) and "Food, animals + beverages, tobacco" (SITC section 0+1) were the largest commodity groups for exports in 2014, representing respectively 30.1, 20.9 and 18.6 percent of exported goods (see table 2). From 2012 to 2014, the largest export commodity was "Motor cars and other motor vehicles principally designed for the transport" (HS code 8703) (see table 1). The top three destinations for merchandise exports were Italy, Germany and Bosnia and Herzegovina, accounting for respectively 15.1, 11.8 and 8.8 percent of total exports. "Other business services" (EBOPS code 268) accounted for the largest share of exports of services in 2012 at 1.2 bln US$, followed by "Travel" (EBOPS code 236) at 906.1 mln US$ and "Computer and information services" (EBOPS code 262) at 287.6 mln US$ (see graph 3).

Graph 3: Exports of services by EBOPS category
(% share in 2012)

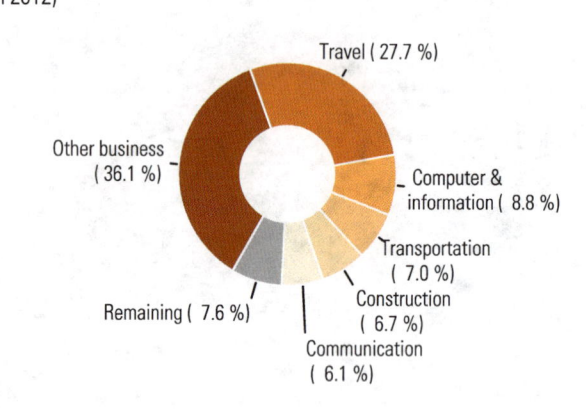

- Travel (27.7 %)
- Other business (36.1 %)
- Computer & information (8.8 %)
- Transportation (7.0 %)
- Construction (6.7 %)
- Communication (6.1 %)
- Remaining (7.6 %)

Table 1: Top 10 export commodities 2012 to 2014

HS code	4-digit heading of Harmonized System 2012	Value (million US$) 2012	2013	2014	Unit value 2012	2013	2014	Unit	SITC code
	All Commodities	11 229.0	14 610.8	14 843.3					
8703	Motor cars and other motor vehicles principally designed for the transport	397.9	1 946.6	1 780.3	11.5	12.1	12.9	thsd US$/unit	781
8544	Insulated (including enamelled or anodised) wire, cable	411.0	561.4	547.0	12.1	14.3	14.4	US$/kg	773
1005	Maize (corn)	567.7	210.7	507.2	0.3	0.3	0.2	US$/kg	044
4011	New pneumatic tyres, of rubber	305.2	394.0	398.8					625
0811	Fruit and nuts	258.0	318.9	363.3	1.9	2.3	2.2	US$/kg	058
2710	Petroleum oils, other than crude	202.5	268.2	321.3	0.9	0.8	0.8	US$/kg	334
6115	Panty hose, tights, stockings, socks and other hosiery	227.9	274.1	261.8	21.6	23.7	21.7	US$/kg	846
3004	Medicaments (excluding goods of heading 30.02, 30.05 or 30.06)	239.0	236.7	237.4	16.7	16.1	15.5	US$/kg	542
8503	Parts suitable for use principally with the machines of heading 85.01	159.5	222.2	258.6	8.1	8.1	8.2	US$/kg	716
7606	Aluminium plates, sheets and strip, of a thickness exceeding 0.2 mm	158.5	166.6	172.4	3.1	3.1	3.0	US$/kg	684

*Special trade system up to 2008.

Serbia

Services Imports and Exports: EBOPS 2002 categories

Table 2: Merchandise exports by SITC
(Value in million US$, growth and shares in percentage)

SITC	2014	Avg. Growth rates 2010-2014	Avg. Growth rates 2013-2014	2014 share
Total	14 843.3	11.0	1.6	100.0
0+1	2 764.2	8.4	14.3	18.6
2+4	697.5	3.4	-17.3	4.7
3	553.0	2.5	-21.5	3.7
5	1 191.5	8.0	-4.4	8.0
6	3 108.6	2.3	6.7	20.9
7	4 466.5	29.4	-1.6	30.1
8	1 940.8	12.1	6.2	13.1
9	121.3	-4.0	1.8	0.8

Table 3: Merchandise imports by SITC
(Value in million US$, growth and shares in percentage)

SITC	2014	Avg. Growth rates 2010-2014	Avg. Growth rates 2013-2014	2014 share
Total	20 608.6	5.3	0.3	100.0
0+1	1 452.8	13.0	3.0	7.0
2+4	690.9	0.1	-2.8	3.4
3	2 893.7	-0.7	-7.0	14.0
5	2 967.3	9.2	-6.1	14.4
6	3 626.7	4.5	2.1	17.6
7	5 151.9	14.5	-10.4	25.0
8	1 576.4	6.6	1.1	7.6
9	2 248.7	-5.7	73.6	10.9

SITC Legend

SITC Code	Description
Total	All commodities
0+1	Food, animals + beverages, tobacco
2+4	Crude materials + anim. & veg. oils
3	Mineral fuels, lubricants
5	Chemicals
6	Goods classified chiefly by material
7	Machinery and transport equipment
8	Miscellaneous manufactured articles
9	Not classified elsewhere in the SITC

Graph 4: Merchandise trade balance
(Bln US$ by MDG Regions in 2014)

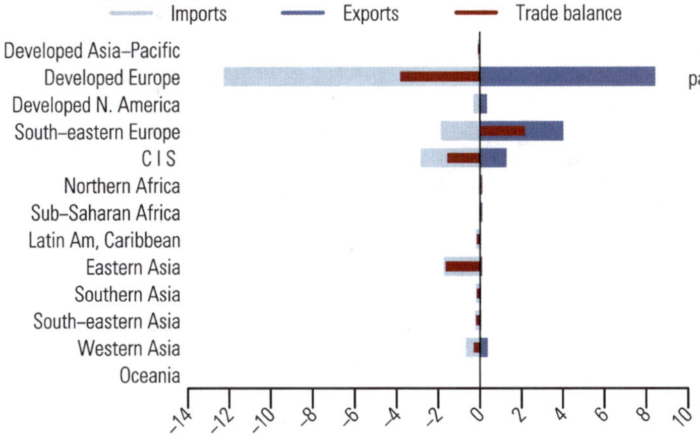

Graph 5: Partner concentration of merchandise trade
(Cumulative share by ranked partners in 2014)
Imports (Herfindahl Index = 0.059)
Exports (Herfindahl Index = 0.072)

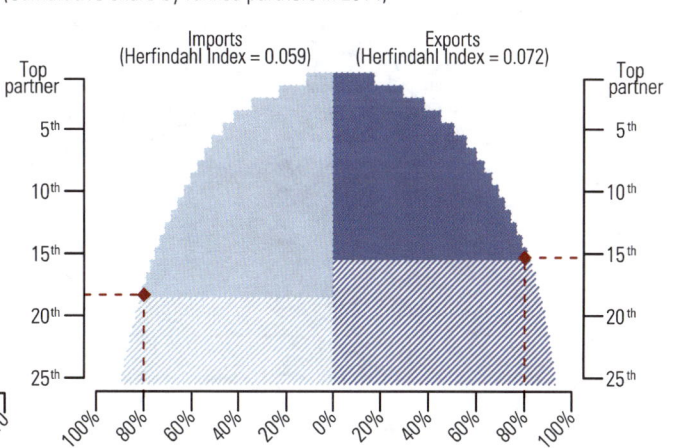

Graph 6: Imports of services by EBOPS category
(% share in 2012)

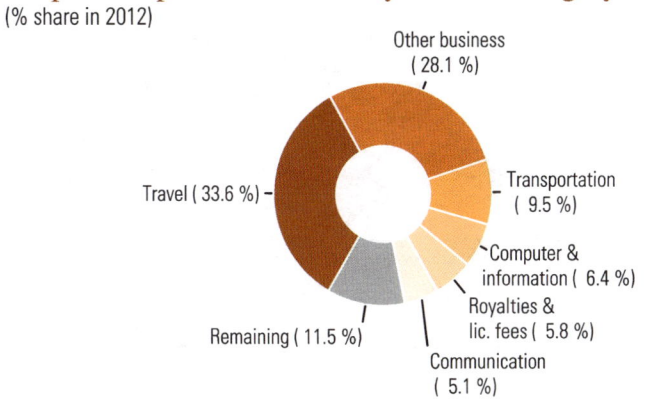

- Other business (28.1 %)
- Travel (33.6 %)
- Transportation (9.5 %)
- Computer & information (6.4 %)
- Royalties & lic. fees (5.8 %)
- Communication (5.1 %)
- Remaining (11.5 %)

Imports Profile:

"Machinery and transport equipment" (SITC section 7), "Goods classified chiefly by material" (SITC section 6) and "Chemicals" (SITC section 5) were the largest commodity groups for imports in 2014, representing respectively 25.0, 17.6 and 14.4 percent of imported goods (see table 3). From 2012 to 2014, the largest import commodity was "Commodities not specified according to kind" (HS code 9999) (see table 4). The top three partners for merchandise imports were Germany, Italy and the Russian Federation, accounting for respectively 11.2, 10.8 and 10.5 percent of total imports. "Travel" (EBOPS code 236) accounted for the largest share of imports of services in 2012 at 1.0 bln US$, followed by "Other business services" (EBOPS code 268) at 849.1 mln US$ and "Transportation" (EBOPS code 205) at 287.1 mln US$ (see graph 6).

Table 4: Top 10 import commodities 2012 to 2014

HS code	4-digit heading of Harmonized System 2012	Value 2012	Value 2013	Value 2014	Unit value 2012	Unit value 2013	Unit value 2014	Unit	SITC code
	All Commodities	18 924.9	20 551.0	20 608.6					
9999	Commodities not specified according to kind	1 238.7	1 295.4	2 248.5					931
8708	Parts and accessories of the motor vehicles of headings 87.01 to 87.05	394.6	1 646.3	1 425.9	6.8	7.9	7.6	US$/kg	784
2709	Petroleum oils and oils obtained from bituminous minerals, crude	900.5	1 321.6	1 105.7	0.8	0.8	0.8	US$/kg	333
2711	Petroleum gases and other gaseous hydrocarbons	1 089.8	923.8	807.5	0.7	0.6	0.6	US$/kg	343
2710	Petroleum oils, other than crude	936.4	586.0	666.5	1.1	1.0	0.9	US$/kg	334
3004	Medicaments (excluding goods of heading 30.02, 30.05 or 30.06)	591.6	636.0	569.2	57.7	63.9	58.5	US$/kg	542
8703	Motor cars and other motor vehicles principally designed for the transport	504.6	545.0	466.7	17.9	17.4	17.3	thsd US$/unit	781
8517	Electrical apparatus for line telephony or line telegraphy	296.6	311.0	281.2					764
8544	Insulated (including enamelled or anodised) wire, cable	218.1	281.4	221.1	12.6	13.5	13.0	US$/kg	773
2716	Electrical energy	228.4	159.9	150.0	66.1	66.1	60.6	US$/MWh	351

2014 International Trade Statistics Yearbook, Vol. I — Source: UN Comtrade and UN ServiceTrade

Singapore

Goods Imports: CIF, by origin **Goods Exports:** FOB, by last known destination **Trade System:** General

Overview:
In 2013, the value of merchandise exports of Singapore increased slightly by 0.5 percent to reach 410.2 bln US$, while its merchandise imports decreased slightly by 1.8 percent to reach 373.0 bln US$ (see graph 1, table 2 and table 3). The merchandise trade balance recorded a relatively small surplus of 37.2 bln US$ (see graph 1). The largest merchandise trade balance was with MDG South-eastern Asia at 50.8 bln US$ (see graph 4). Merchandise exports in Singapore were diversified amongst partners; imports were also diversified. The top 14 partners accounted for 80 percent or more of exports and 15 partners accounted for 80 percent or more of imports (see graph 5). In 2013, the value of exports of services of Singapore increased slightly by 3.7 percent, reaching 130.1 bln US$, while its imports of services increased slightly by 3.8 percent and reached 129.3 bln US$ (see graph 2). There was a relatively small trade in services surplus of 776.5 mln US$.

Graph 1: Total merchandise trade, by value
(Bln US$ by year)

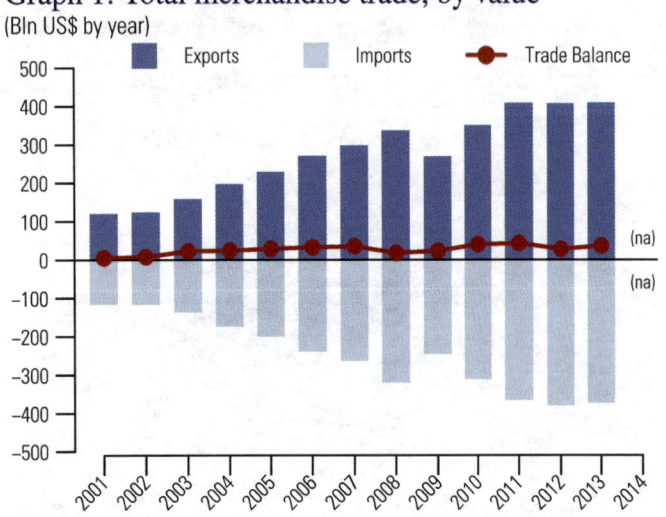

Graph 2: Total services trade, by value
(Bln US$ by year)

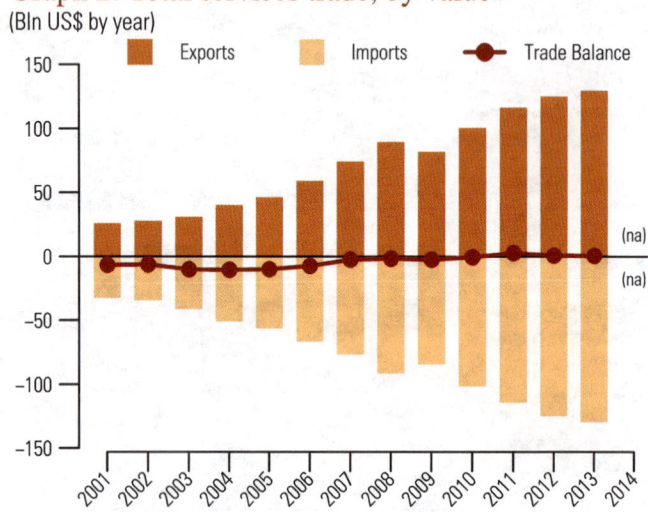

Exports Profile:
"Machinery and transport equipment" (SITC section 7), "Mineral fuels, lubricants" (SITC section 3) and "Chemicals" (SITC section 5) were the largest commodity groups for exports in 2013, representing respectively 46.4, 17.4 and 12.2 percent of exported goods (see table 2). From 2011 to 2013, the largest export commodity was "Electronic integrated circuits" (HS code 8542) (see table 1). The top three destinations for merchandise exports were Malaysia, China, Hong Kong SAR and China, accounting for respectively 12.2, 11.1 and 11.0 percent of total exports. "Transportation" (EBOPS code 205) accounted for the largest share of exports of services in 2013 at 44.1 bln US$, followed by "Other business services" (EBOPS code 268) at 27.9 bln US$ and "Travel" (EBOPS code 236) at 19.1 bln US$ (see graph 3).

Graph 3: Exports of services by EBOPS category
(% share in 2013)

- Other business (21.5 %)
- Travel (14.6 %)
- Transportation (33.9 %)
- Remaining (30.0 %)

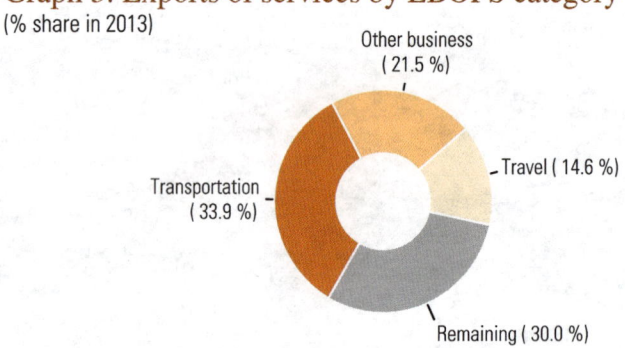

Table 1: Top 10 export commodities 2011 to 2013

HS code	4-digit heading of Harmonized System 2007	Value (million US$) 2011	2012	2013	Unit value 2011	2012	2013	Unit	SITC code
	All Commodities	409 503.6	408 393.0	410 249.7					
8542	Electronic integrated circuits	75 633.3	74 842.4	83 052.4					776
2710	Petroleum oils, other than crude	79 210.7	73 239.8	69 253.4	0.9		0.9	US$/kg	334
9999	Commodities not specified according to kind	32 103.6	33 425.3	33 134.5					931
8471	Automatic data processing machines and units thereof	8 450.9	9 411.7	9 723.5	72.1	126.4	126.8	US$/unit	752
8473	Parts and accessories for use with machines of heading 84.69 to 84.72	10 548.7	8 881.3	7 151.8					759
8517	Electrical apparatus for line telephony or line telegraphy	8 164.7	8 506.5	8 628.7					764
8443	Printing machinery used for printing by means of the printing type, blocks	8 168.1	7 526.6	6 874.8					726
8541	Diodes, transistors and similar semiconductor devices	7 471.0	6 626.8	6 830.9					776
8803	Parts of goods of heading 88.01 or 88.02	5 124.8	5 727.5	6 229.4					792
8431	Parts suitable for use principally with the machinery of headings 84.25	5 024.2	5 670.0	5 823.5	15.9		19.5	US$/kg	723

Singapore

Services Imports and Exports: EBOPS 2002 categories

Table 2: Merchandise exports by SITC
(Value in million US$, growth and shares in percentage)

SITC	2013	Avg. Growth rates 2009-2013	2012-2013	2013 share
Total	410 249.7	11.0	0.5	100.0
0+1	9 331.9	15.8	10.3	2.3
2+4	3 165.3	12.8	17.4	0.8
3	71 380.3	14.8	-5.5	17.4
5	50 084.4	13.5	-7.2	12.2
6	15 845.8	8.9	5.6	3.9
7	190 318.3	8.0	2.8	46.4
8	35 323.5	16.8	11.8	8.6
9	34 800.1	13.3	-3.1	8.5

Table 3: Merchandise imports by SITC
(Value in million US$, growth and shares in percentage)

SITC	2013	Avg. Growth rates 2009-2013	2012-2013	2013 share
Total	373 015.7	11.0	-1.8	100.0
0+1	11 927.9	12.5	7.2	3.2
2+4	4 271.1	9.5	-3.8	1.1
3	116 899.3	18.7	-5.6	31.3
5	25 209.4	14.6	-2.0	6.8
6	23 174.8	7.1	-0.8	6.2
7	155 168.6	7.3	0.2	41.6
8	28 542.9	13.6	5.2	7.7
9	7 821.6	-6.1	-15.1	2.1

SITC Legend

SITC Code	Description
Total	All commodities
0+1	Food, animals + beverages, tobacco
2+4	Crude materials + anim. & veg. oils
3	Mineral fuels, lubricants
5	Chemicals
6	Goods classified chiefly by material
7	Machinery and transport equipment
8	Miscellaneous manufactured articles
9	Not classified elsewhere in the SITC

Graph 4: Merchandise trade balance
(Bln US$ by MDG Regions in 2013)

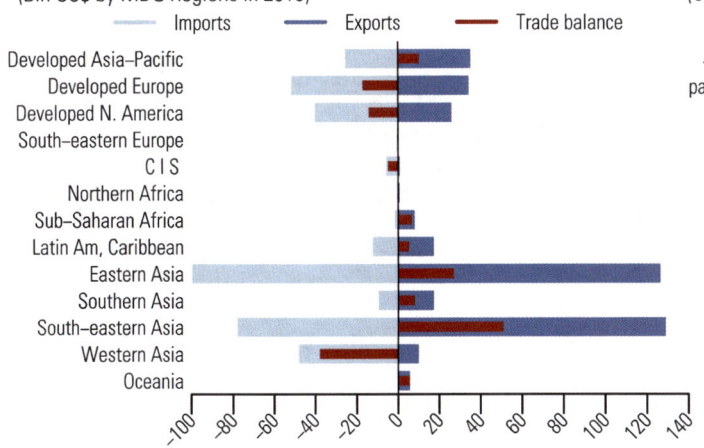

Graph 5: Partner concentration of merchandise trade
(Cumulative share by ranked partners in 2013)

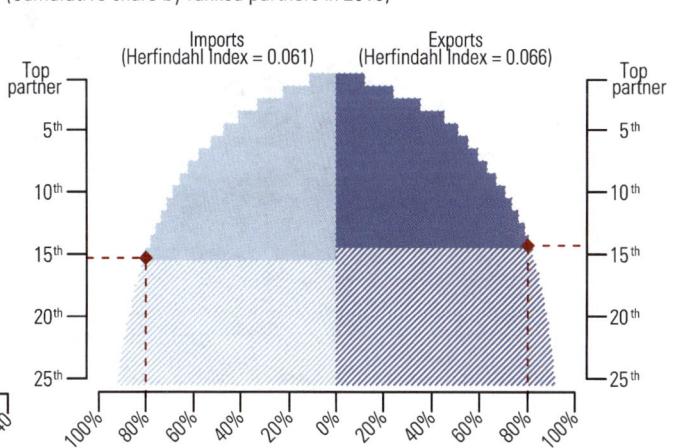

Imports (Herfindahl Index = 0.061)
Exports (Herfindahl Index = 0.066)

Graph 6: Imports of services by EBOPS category
(% share in 2013)

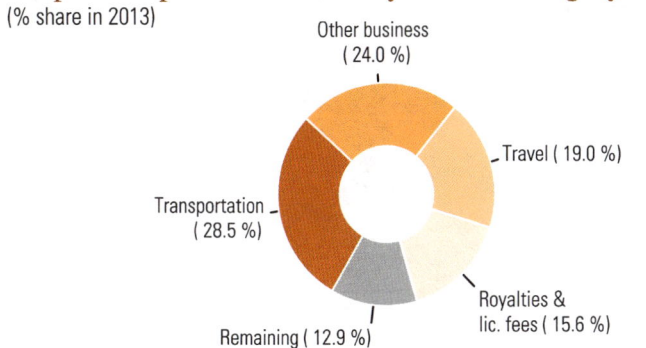

- Other business (24.0 %)
- Travel (19.0 %)
- Royalties & lic. fees (15.6 %)
- Remaining (12.9 %)
- Transportation (28.5 %)

Imports Profile:

"Machinery and transport equipment" (SITC section 7), "Mineral fuels, lubricants" (SITC section 3) and "Miscellaneous manufactured articles" (SITC section 8) were the largest commodity groups for imports in 2013, representing respectively 41.6, 31.3 and 7.7 percent of imported goods (see table 3). From 2011 to 2013, the largest import commodity was "Petroleum oils, other than crude" (HS code 2710) (see table 4). The top three partners for merchandise imports were China, Malaysia and the United States, accounting for respectively 10.8, 10.8 and 10.5 percent of total imports. "Transportation" (EBOPS code 205) accounted for the largest share of imports of services in 2013 at 36.9 bln US$, followed by "Other business services" (EBOPS code 268) at 31.1 bln US$ and "Travel" (EBOPS code 236) at 24.6 bln US$ (see graph 6).

Table 4: Top 10 import commodities 2011 to 2013

HS code	4-digit heading of Harmonized System 2007	2011	2012	2013	2011	2012	2013	Unit	SITC code
	All Commodities	365 770.5	379 722.9	373 015.7					
2710	Petroleum oils, other than crude	80 335.8	77 316.5	74 603.6	0.8		0.7	US$/kg	334
8542	Electronic integrated circuits	50 716.7	54 069.0	59 380.1					776
2709	Petroleum oils and oils obtained from bituminous minerals, crude	33 584.4	39 879.3	35 538.7	0.8	0.8	0.8	US$/kg	333
8517	Electrical apparatus for line telephony or line telegraphy	9 882.3	9 811.5	9 365.2					764
8471	Automatic data processing machines and units thereof	6 465.0	6 978.1	6 558.9	84.2	111.9	79.0	US$/unit	752
8411	Turbo-jets, turbo-propellers and other gas turbines	5 378.5	6 300.7	7 720.1					714
8473	Parts and accessories for use with machines of heading 84.69 to 84.72	6 805.0	6 239.7	5 716.7					759
2711	Petroleum gases and other gaseous hydrocarbons	4 888.0	6 122.0	6 532.0	0.8	0.8	0.7	US$/kg	343
9999	Commodities not specified according to kind	4 255.9	6 825.0	5 947.8					931
8431	Parts suitable for use principally with the machinery of headings 84.25	5 179.0	5 501.8	4 927.7	18.0		19.7	US$/kg	723

2014 International Trade Statistics Yearbook, Vol. I   Source: UN Comtrade and UN ServiceTrade

Slovakia

Goods Imports: CIF, by origin **Goods Exports: FOB, by last known destination** **Trade System: Special**

Overview:
In 2014, the value of merchandise exports of Slovakia increased slightly by 0.8 percent to reach 85.9 bln US$, while its merchandise imports decreased slightly by 4.6 percent to reach 77.6 bln US$ (see graph 1, table 2 and table 3). The merchandise trade balance recorded a relatively small surplus of 8.3 bln US$ (see graph 1). The largest merchandise trade balance was with MDG Developed Europe at 20.3 bln US$ (see graph 4). Merchandise exports in Slovakia were diversified amongst partners; imports were also diversified. The top 13 partners accounted for 80 percent or more of exports and the same number of partners accounted for 80 percent or more of imports (see graph 5). In 2013, the value of exports of services of Slovakia increased slightly by 3.9 percent, reaching 7.4 bln US$, while its imports of services increased moderately by 7.1 percent and reached 7.2 bln US$ (see graph 2). There was a relatively small trade in services surplus of 197.9 mln US$.

Graph 1: Total merchandise trade, by value
(Bln US$ by year)

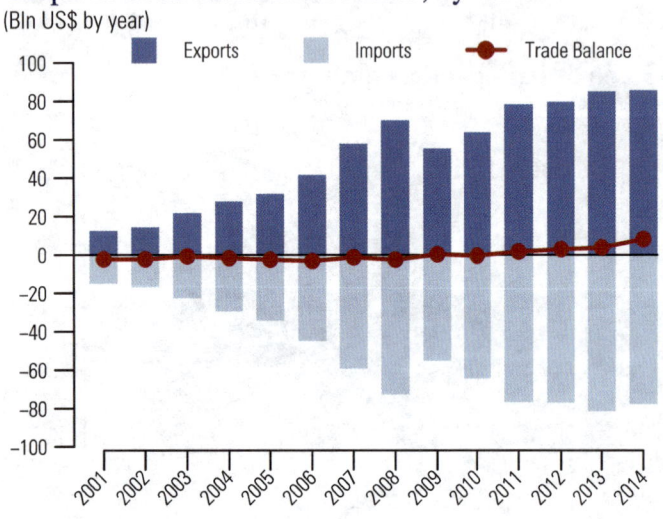

Graph 2: Total services trade, by value
(Bln US$ by year)

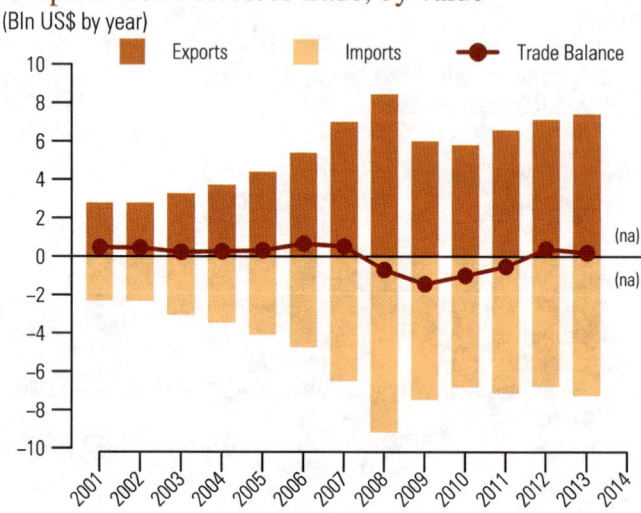

Exports Profile:
"Machinery and transport equipment" (SITC section 7), "Goods classified chiefly by material" (SITC section 6) and "Miscellaneous manufactured articles" (SITC section 8) were the largest commodity groups for exports in 2014, representing respectively 57.9, 16.9 and 9.7 percent of exported goods (see table 2). From 2012 to 2014, the largest export commodity was "Motor cars and other motor vehicles principally designed for the transport" (HS code 8703) (see table 1). The top three destinations for merchandise exports were Germany, the Czech Republic and Poland, accounting for respectively 21.4, 13.4 and 8.1 percent of total exports. "Travel" (EBOPS code 236) accounted for the largest share of exports of services in 2013 at 2.5 bln US$, followed by "Transportation" (EBOPS code 205) at 2.1 bln US$ and "Other business services" (EBOPS code 268) at 1.6 bln US$ (see graph 3).

Graph 3: Exports of services by EBOPS category
(% share in 2013)

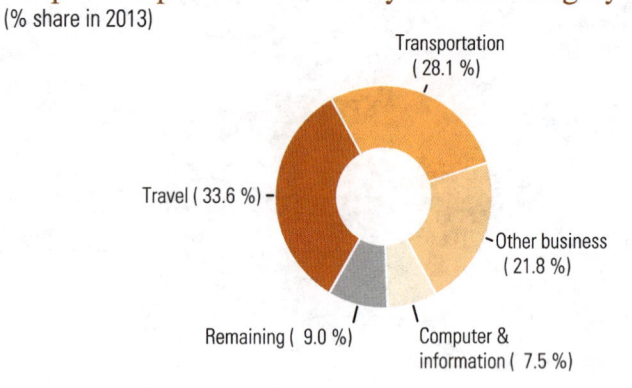

- Transportation (28.1 %)
- Travel (33.6 %)
- Other business (21.8 %)
- Computer & information (7.5 %)
- Remaining (9.0 %)

Table 1: Top 10 export commodities 2012 to 2014

HS code	4-digit heading of Harmonized System 2012	Value (million US$) 2012	2013	2014	Unit value 2012	2013	2014	Unit	SITC code
	All Commodities	79 867.0	85 184.2	85 874.0					
8703	Motor cars and other motor vehicles principally designed for the transport	13 222.7	14 446.9	14 950.4	15.5	14.5	14.9	thsd US$/unit	781
8528	Reception apparatus for television	6 558.0	7 034.9	7 261.9	422.9	381.0	382.5	US$/unit	761
8517	Electrical apparatus for line telephony or line telegraphy	2 934.6	4 082.9	4 084.3					764
2710	Petroleum oils, other than crude	3 685.6	3 878.6	3 091.3		0.9	0.8	US$/kg	334
8708	Parts and accessories of the motor vehicles of headings 87.01 to 87.05	2 914.3	3 597.1	3 899.7	9.4	9.0	8.8	US$/kg	784
8707	Bodies (including cabs), for the motor vehicles of headings 87.01 to 87.05	2 168.4	2 252.9	1 988.5	2.9	1.8	1.4	thsd US$/unit	784
4011	New pneumatic tyres, of rubber	1 459.1	1 716.0	1 689.9	94.8	98.6	96.9	US$/unit	625
8544	Insulated (including enamelled or anodised) wire, cable	1 354.5	1 312.0	1 367.5	13.8	13.4	15.9	US$/kg	773
7208	Flat-rolled products of iron or non-alloy steel	1 086.8	1 239.8	1 176.5	0.7	0.7	0.6	US$/kg	673
8471	Automatic data processing machines and units thereof	778.7	1 313.1	1 296.3	210.0	213.1	207.7	US$/unit	752

Slovakia

Services Imports and Exports: EBOPS 2002 categories

Table 2: Merchandise exports by SITC
(Value in million US$, growth and shares in percentage)

SITC	2014	Avg. Growth rates 2010-2014	Avg. Growth rates 2013-2014	2014 share
Total	85874.0	7.6	0.8	100.0
0+1	3068.5	6.5	-7.0	3.6
2+4	1891.2	0.4	-19.5	2.2
3	4076.6	7.2	-14.4	4.7
5	4102.8	8.3	3.5	4.8
6	14516.8	4.4	0.9	16.9
7	49726.7	9.2	2.5	57.9
8	8329.4	7.1	7.7	9.7
9	162.1	-1.6	2.3	0.2

Table 3: Merchandise imports by SITC
(Value in million US$, growth and shares in percentage)

SITC	2014	Avg. Growth rates 2010-2014	Avg. Growth rates 2013-2014	2014 share
Total	77596.0	4.8	-4.6	100.0
0+1	4498.5	4.5	-2.7	5.8
2+4	2472.9	-1.0	-14.2	3.2
3	4697.8	-13.0	-55.6	6.1
5	7207.2	7.2	4.3	9.3
6	12579.6	6.5	3.8	16.2
7	35928.3	6.8	4.1	46.3
8	9936.7	10.3	5.7	12.8
9	274.8	2.9	-0.6	0.4

SITC Legend

SITC Code	Description
Total	All commodities
0+1	Food, animals + beverages, tobacco
2+4	Crude materials + anim. & veg. oils
3	Mineral fuels, lubricants
5	Chemicals
6	Goods classified chiefly by material
7	Machinery and transport equipment
8	Miscellaneous manufactured articles
9	Not classified elsewhere in the SITC

Graph 4: Merchandise trade balance
(Bln US$ by MDG Regions in 2014)

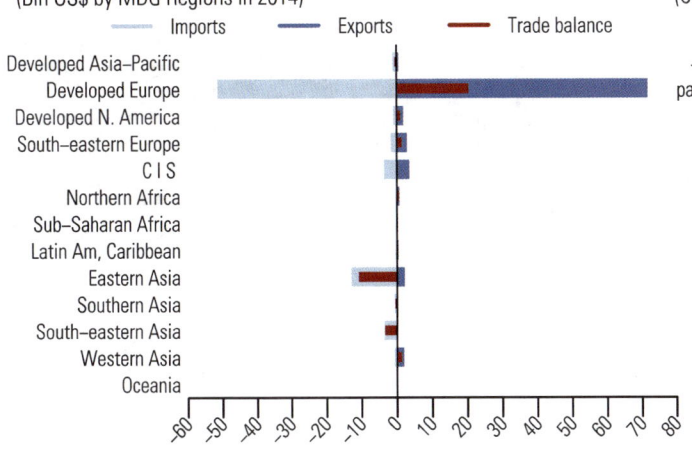

Graph 5: Partner concentration of merchandise trade
(Cumulative share by ranked partners in 2014)

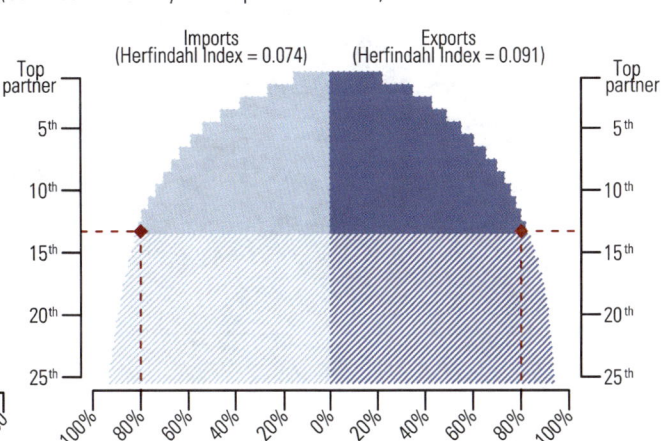

Imports (Herfindahl Index = 0.074)
Exports (Herfindahl Index = 0.091)

Graph 6: Imports of services by EBOPS category
(% share in 2013)

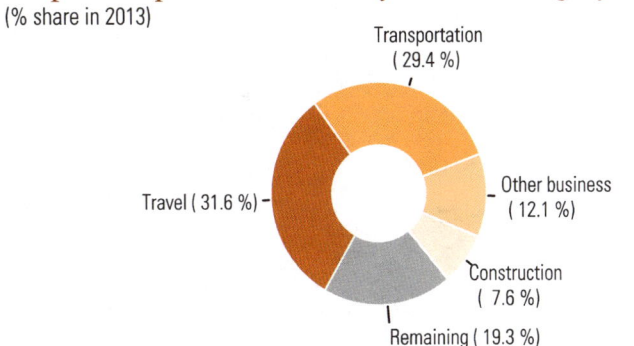

- Transportation (29.4%)
- Travel (31.6%)
- Other business (12.1%)
- Construction (7.6%)
- Remaining (19.3%)

Imports Profile:

"Machinery and transport equipment" (SITC section 7), "Goods classified chiefly by material" (SITC section 6) and "Miscellaneous manufactured articles" (SITC section 8) were the largest commodity groups for imports in 2014, representing respectively 46.3, 16.2 and 12.8 percent of imported goods (see table 3). From 2012 to 2014, the largest import commodity was "Parts and accessories of the motor vehicles of headings 87.01 to 87.05" (HS code 8708) (see table 4). The top three partners for merchandise imports were Germany, Rest of Europe nes and the Czech Republic, accounting for respectively 16.3, 10.8 and 10.7 percent of total imports. "Travel" (EBOPS code 236) accounted for the largest share of imports of services in 2013 at 2.3 bln US$, followed by "Transportation" (EBOPS code 205) at 2.1 bln US$ and "Other business services" (EBOPS code 268) at 876.5 mln US$ (see graph 6).

Table 4: Top 10 import commodities 2012 to 2014

HS code	4-digit heading of Harmonized System 2012	Value (million US$) 2012	2013	2014	Unit value 2012	2013	2014	Unit	SITC code
	All Commodities	76859.4	81295.1	77596.0					
8708	Parts and accessories of the motor vehicles of headings 87.01 to 87.05	6870.2	7306.2	7372.9	4.4	3.7	3.2	US$/kg	784
8517	Electrical apparatus for line telephony or line telegraphy	3496.3	4876.9	4856.9					764
2711	Petroleum gases and other gaseous hydrocarbons	3441.7	3473.6	2356.3	0.6	0.6	2.0	US$/kg	343
2709	Petroleum oils and oils obtained from bituminous minerals, crude	4231.7	4529.0	104.6	0.8	0.8	0.5	US$/kg	333
9013	Liquid crystal devices	1952.8	1880.3	1779.3					871
8703	Motor cars and other motor vehicles principally designed for the transport	1462.0	1601.8	2182.1	12.5	5.7	9.3	thsd US$/unit	781
8529	Parts suitable for use with the apparatus of headings 85.25 to 85.28	1516.2	1747.5	1804.6	14.7	34.5	35.0	US$/kg	764
2710	Petroleum oils, other than crude	1546.6	1781.1	1457.2		1.3	1.0	US$/kg	334
3004	Medicaments (excluding goods of heading 30.02, 30.05 or 30.06)	1482.9	1642.3	1630.9	101.7	90.3	103.9	US$/kg	542
8471	Automatic data processing machines and units thereof	989.7	1468.2	1471.4	172.0	135.0	132.1	US$/unit	752

2014 International Trade Statistics Yearbook, Vol. I   Source: UN Comtrade and UN ServiceTrade

Slovenia

Goods Imports: CIF, by origin **Goods Exports:** FOB, by last known destination **Trade System:** Special

Overview:
In 2014, the value of merchandise exports of Slovenia increased moderately by 7.1 percent to reach 30.7 bln US$, while its merchandise imports increased slightly by 2.8 percent to reach 30.2 bln US$ (see graph 1, table 2 and table 3). The merchandise trade balance recorded a relatively small surplus of 485.1 mln US$ (see graph 1). The largest merchandise trade balance was with MDG Eastern Asia at -2.5 bln US$ (see graph 4). Merchandise exports in Slovenia were diversified amongst partners; imports were also diversified. The top 16 partners accounted for 80 percent or more of exports and 18 partners accounted for 80 percent or more of imports (see graph 5). In 2013, the value of exports of services of Slovenia increased moderately by 8.4 percent, reaching 7.2 bln US$, while its imports of services increased substantially by 10.4 percent and reached 4.8 bln US$ (see graph 2). There was a moderate trade in services surplus of 2.4 bln US$.

Graph 1: Total merchandise trade, by value
(Bln US$ by year)

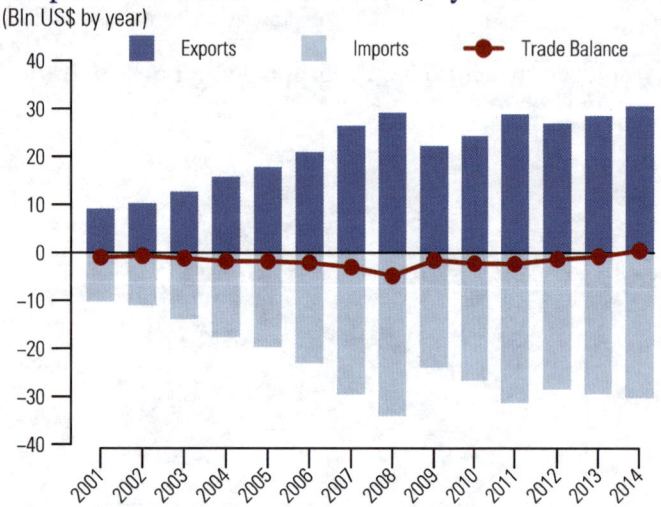

Graph 2: Total services trade, by value
(Bln US$ by year)

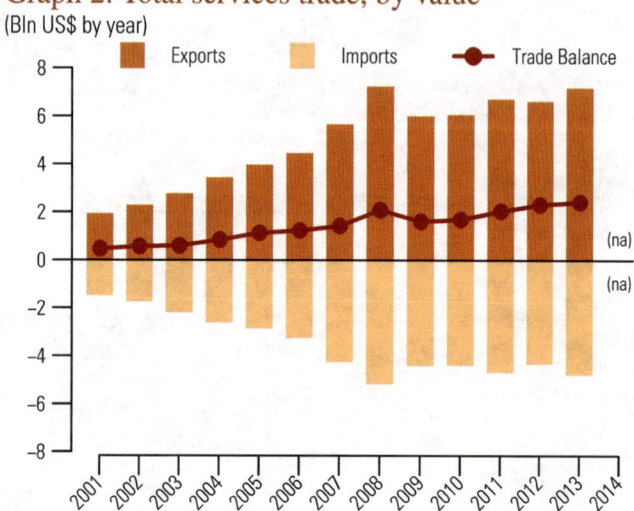

Exports Profile:
"Machinery and transport equipment" (SITC section 7), "Goods classified chiefly by material" (SITC section 6) and "Chemicals" (SITC section 5) were the largest commodity groups for exports in 2014, representing respectively 36.2, 20.7 and 18.0 percent of exported goods (see table 2). From 2012 to 2014, the largest export commodity was "Medicaments (excluding goods of heading 30.02, 30.05 or 30.06)" (HS code 3004) (see table 1). The top three destinations for merchandise exports were Germany, Italy and Austria, accounting for respectively 20.5, 11.6 and 8.6 percent of total exports. "Travel" (EBOPS code 236) accounted for the largest share of exports of services in 2013 at 2.8 bln US$, followed by "Transportation" (EBOPS code 205) at 1.9 bln US$ and "Other business services" (EBOPS code 268) at 988.8 mln US$ (see graph 3).

Graph 3: Exports of services by EBOPS category
(% share in 2013)

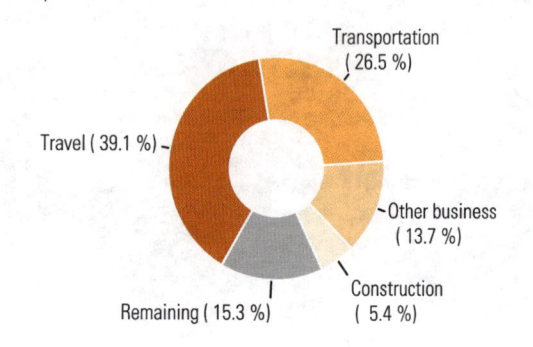

- Transportation (26.5 %)
- Travel (39.1 %)
- Other business (13.7 %)
- Construction (5.4 %)
- Remaining (15.3 %)

Table 1: Top 10 export commodities 2012 to 2014

HS code	4-digit heading of Harmonized System 2012	Value (million US$) 2012	2013	2014	Unit value 2012	2013	2014	Unit	SITC code
	All Commodities	27080.0	28628.7	30671.7					
3004	Medicaments (excluding goods of heading 30.02, 30.05 or 30.06)	2366.1	2723.1	2874.5	90.3	94.4	90.7	US$/kg	542
8703	Motor cars and other motor vehicles principally designed for the transport	2075.4	2064.6	2610.0	10.8	11.5	11.3	thsd US$/unit	781
2710	Petroleum oils, other than crude	944.7	1165.1	1184.8	1.1	1.1	1.0	US$/kg	334
8708	Parts and accessories of the motor vehicles of headings 87.01 to 87.05	694.4	778.5	843.5	7.3	7.4	7.3	US$/kg	784
2716	Electrical energy	791.7	677.9	676.7	64.1	58.2	52.6	US$/MWh	351
8512	Electrical lighting or signalling equipment	463.7	446.2	494.4					778
8516	Electric instantaneous or storage water heaters and immersion heaters	440.8	486.1	412.2					775
4011	New pneumatic tyres, of rubber	443.7	421.1	413.6	55.8	53.3	46.9	US$/unit	625
9401	Seats (other than those of heading 94.02)	382.8	401.0	413.4					821
8503	Parts suitable for use principally with the machines of heading 85.01	360.8	370.0	345.4	7.9	7.9	8.6	US$/kg	716

Source: UN Comtrade and UN ServiceTrade

Slovenia

Services Imports and Exports: EBOPS 2002 categories

Table 2: Merchandise exports by SITC
(Value in million US$, growth and shares in percentage)

SITC	2014	Avg. Growth rates 2010-2014	Avg. Growth rates 2013-2014	2014 share
Total	30 671.7	5.8	7.1	100.0
0+1	1 209.8	8.1	10.0	3.9
2+4	1 206.1	5.2	6.4	3.9
3	2 039.2	18.5	7.3	6.6
5	5 534.5	8.4	4.7	18.0
6	6 338.3	4.2	5.4	20.7
7	11 090.4	4.1	8.9	36.2
8	3 134.6	4.5	8.9	10.2
9	118.9	25.6	-10.2	0.4

Table 3: Merchandise imports by SITC
(Value in million US$, growth and shares in percentage)

SITC	2014	Avg. Growth rates 2010-2014	Avg. Growth rates 2013-2014	2014 share
Total	30 186.6	3.2	2.8	100.0
0+1	2 434.9	5.8	3.9	8.1
2+4	1 819.4	1.1	1.3	6.0
3	4 048.9	4.3	-8.5	13.4
5	4 451.0	5.2	4.8	14.7
6	5 515.9	1.9	4.1	18.3
7	9 035.0	3.0	5.4	29.9
8	2 791.9	1.7	8.4	9.2
9	89.6	-5.1	-22.0	0.3

SITC Legend

SITC Code	Description
Total	All commodities
0+1	Food, animals + beverages, tobacco
2+4	Crude materials + anim. & veg. oils
3	Mineral fuels, lubricants
5	Chemicals
6	Goods classified chiefly by material
7	Machinery and transport equipment
8	Miscellaneous manufactured articles
9	Not classified elsewhere in the SITC

Graph 4: Merchandise trade balance
(Bln US$ by MDG Regions in 2014)

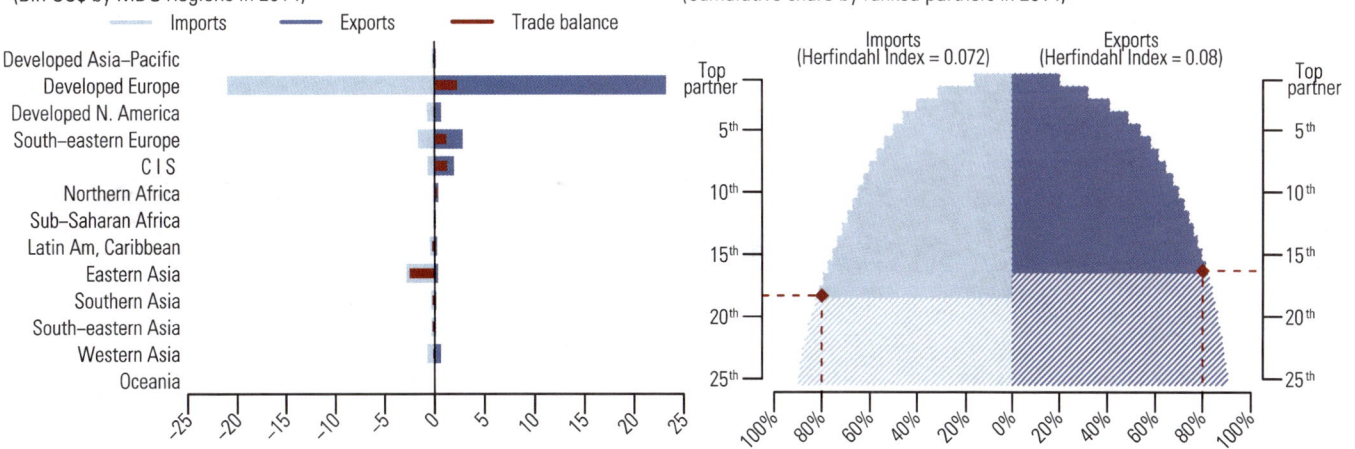

Graph 5: Partner concentration of merchandise trade
(Cumulative share by ranked partners in 2014)

Imports (Herfindahl Index = 0.072)
Exports (Herfindahl Index = 0.08)

Graph 6: Imports of services by EBOPS category
(% share in 2013)

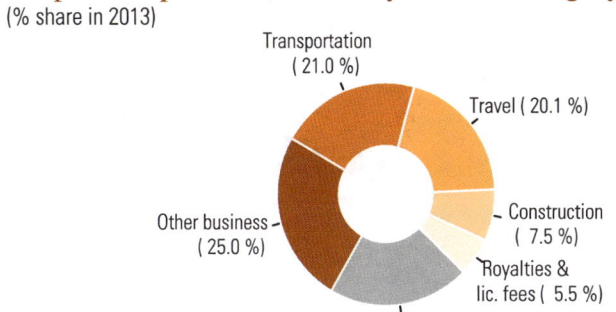

- Transportation (21.0 %)
- Travel (20.1 %)
- Construction (7.5 %)
- Royalties & lic. fees (5.5 %)
- Remaining (21.0 %)
- Other business (25.0 %)

Imports Profile:

"Machinery and transport equipment" (SITC section 7), "Goods classified chiefly by material" (SITC section 6) and "Chemicals" (SITC section 5) were the largest commodity groups for imports in 2014, representing respectively 29.9, 18.3 and 14.7 percent of imported goods (see table 3). From 2012 to 2014, the largest import commodity was "Petroleum oils, other than crude" (HS code 2710) (see table 4). The top three partners for merchandise imports were Germany, Italy and Austria, accounting for respectively 16.6, 15.8 and 8.5 percent of total imports. "Other business services" (EBOPS code 268) accounted for the largest share of imports of services in 2013 at 1.2 bln US$, followed by "Transportation" (EBOPS code 205) at 999.8 mln US$ and "Travel" (EBOPS code 236) at 958.5 mln US$ (see graph 6).

Table 4: Top 10 import commodities 2012 to 2014

HS code	4-digit heading of Harmonized System 2012	Value 2012	Value 2013	Value 2014	Unit value 2012	Unit value 2013	Unit value 2014	Unit	SITC code
	All Commodities	28 382.6	29 375.4	30 186.6					
2710	Petroleum oils, other than crude	3 433.9	3 220.0	2 950.1	1.0	1.0	0.9	US$/kg	334
8703	Motor cars and other motor vehicles principally designed for the transport	1 215.1	1 533.3	1 893.4	14.3	15.0	15.8	thsd US$/unit	781
3004	Medicaments (excluding goods of heading 30.02, 30.05 or 30.06)	773.5	926.7	987.2	77.3	84.2	88.5	US$/kg	542
8708	Parts and accessories of the motor vehicles of headings 87.01 to 87.05	696.8	614.2	683.9	6.8	6.8	7.1	US$/kg	784
2711	Petroleum gases and other gaseous hydrocarbons	559.0	515.5	529.5	0.7	0.6	0.6	US$/kg	343
2716	Electrical energy	663.4	523.9	405.2	65.0	59.7	56.5	US$/MWh	351
8517	Electrical apparatus for line telephony or line telegraphy	319.4	363.6	439.5					764
7204	Ferrous waste and scrap; remelting scrap ingots of iron or steel	342.6	296.1	326.5	0.6	0.5	0.6	US$/kg	282
8544	Insulated (including enamelled or anodised) wire, cable	308.8	300.7	295.0	8.3	9.4	8.7	US$/kg	773
8704	Motor vehicles for the transport of goods	265.8	293.2	336.2	22.3	23.4	23.5	thsd US$/unit	782

2014 International Trade Statistics Yearbook, Vol. I   Source: UN Comtrade and UN ServiceTrade

Solomon Islands

Goods Imports: CIF, by origin **Goods Exports:** FOB, by last known destination **Trade System:** Special

Overview:
In 2014, the value of merchandise exports of Solomon Islands decreased moderately by 6.3 percent to reach 458.5 mln US$, while its merchandise imports decreased substantially by 13.9 percent to reach 499.6 mln US$ (see graph 1, table 2 and table 3). The merchandise trade balance recorded a relatively small deficit of 41.1 mln US$ (see graph 1). The largest merchandise trade balance was with MDG Eastern Asia at 205.2 mln US$ (see graph 4). Merchandise exports in Solomon Islands were highly concentrated amongst partners; imports were moderately concentrated. The top 4 partners accounted for 80 percent or more of exports and 6 partners accounted for 80 percent or more of imports (see graph 5). In 2013, the value of exports of services of Solomon Islands increased slightly by 4.8 percent, reaching 124.8 mln US$, while its imports of services increased substantially by 30.8 percent and reached 265.8 mln US$ (see graph 2). There was a relatively large trade in services deficit of 141.0 mln US$.

Graph 1: Total merchandise trade, by value
(Mln US$ by year)

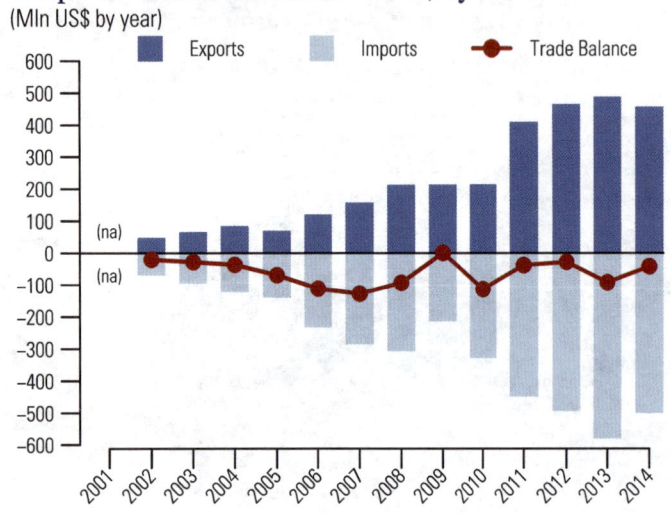

Graph 2: Total services trade, by value
(Mln US$ by year)

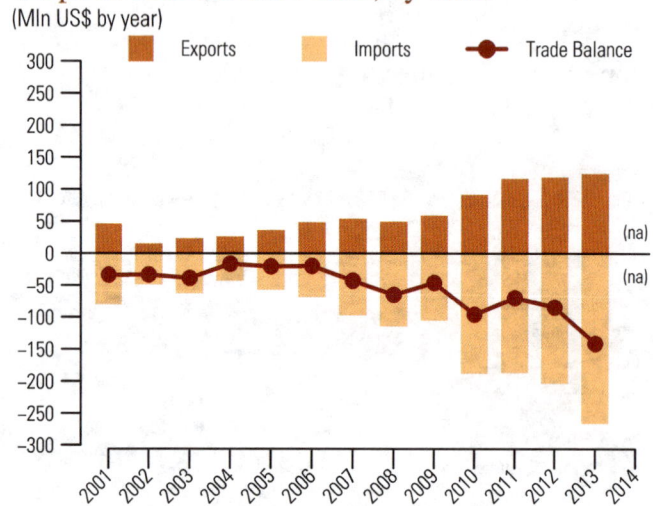

Exports Profile:
"Not classified elsewhere in the SITC" (SITC section 9), "Crude materials + anim. & veg. oils" (SITC section 2+4) and "Food, animals + beverages, tobacco" (SITC section 0+1) were the largest commodity groups for exports in 2014, representing respectively 84.8, 11.0 and 3.5 percent of exported goods (see table 2). From 2013 to 2014, the largest export commodity was "Commodities not elsewhere specified" (HS code 9999) (see table 1). The top three destinations for merchandise exports were China, Australia and the United Kingdom, accounting for respectively 46.9, 19.6 and 7.0 percent of total exports. "Travel" (EBOPS code 236) accounted for the largest share of exports of services in 2013 at 60.6 mln US$, followed by "Transportation" (EBOPS code 205) at 28.6 mln US$ and "Other business services" (EBOPS code 268) at 25.0 mln US$ (see graph 3).

Graph 3: Exports of services by EBOPS category
(% share in 2013)

- Travel (48.6 %)
- Transportation (22.9 %)
- Other business (20.0 %)
- Remaining (8.4 %)

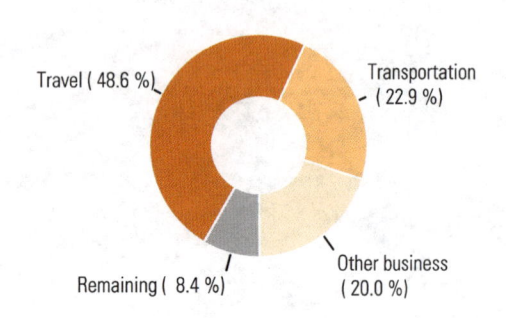

Table 1: Top 10 export commodities 2012 to 2014

HS code	4-digit heading of Harmonized System 1996	Value (million US$) 2012	2013	2014	Unit value 2012	2013	2014	Unit	SITC code
	All Commodities	466.3	489.2	458.5					
9999	Commodities not elsewhere specified	...	198.3	388.7					931
4403	Wood in the rough or roughly squared	195.2	234.4	...	117.4			US$/m³	247
7108	Gold, unwrought, semi-manufactured, powder form	112.6	...	...					971
1511	Palm oil and its fractions, not chemically modified	37.7	26.4	25.4	1.0	0.8		US$/kg	422
1203	Copra	23.5	5.8	9.9	0.6	0.0		US$/kg	223
1801	Cocoa beans, whole or broken, raw or roasted	8.9	9.2	12.9	2.2	2.6		US$/kg	072
1513	Coconut, palm kernel, babassu oil, fractions, refined	8.4	5.4	10.3					422
0303	Fish, frozen, whole	22.9	...	...					034
0305	Fish, cured, smoked, fish meal for human consumption	21.6	...	...					035
4407	Wood sawn, chipped lengthwise, sliced or peeled	9.9	0.0	0.0	972.4	832.8		US$/m³	248

Solomon Islands

Services Imports and Exports: EBOPS 2002 categories

Table 2: Merchandise exports by SITC
(Value in million US$, growth and shares in percentage)

SITC	2014	Avg. Growth rates 2010-2014	Avg. Growth rates 2013-2014	2014 share
Total	458.5	20.8	-6.3	100.0
0+1	16.1	-18.8	41.3	3.5
2+4	50.4	-25.9	-81.8	11.0
3	0.0	-8.3	-90.6	0.0
5	0.3	37.4	361.2	0.1
6	0.2	-14.9	128.9	0.0
7	2.7	-21.0	195.0	0.6
8	0.1	-41.3	-97.3	0.0
9	388.7	229.9	96.0	84.8

Table 3: Merchandise imports by SITC
(Value in million US$, growth and shares in percentage)

SITC	2014	Avg. Growth rates 2010-2014	Avg. Growth rates 2013-2014	2014 share
Total	499.6	11.1	-13.9	100.0
0+1	99.8	4.6	0.1	20.0
2+4	7.5	13.0	15.2	1.5
3	117.9	13.5	-31.9	23.6
5	7.7	-23.7	-27.3	1.5
6	18.7	-23.3	-8.1	3.7
7	41.4	-12.4	-25.0	8.3
8	17.5	-4.4	-17.9	3.5
9	189.0	404.4	-2.2	37.8

SITC Legend

SITC Code	Description
Total	All commodities
0+1	Food, animals + beverages, tobacco
2+4	Crude materials + anim. & veg. oils
3	Mineral fuels, lubricants
5	Chemicals
6	Goods classified chiefly by material
7	Machinery and transport equipment
8	Miscellaneous manufactured articles
9	Not classified elsewhere in the SITC

Graph 4: Merchandise trade balance
(Mln US$ by MDG Regions in 2014)

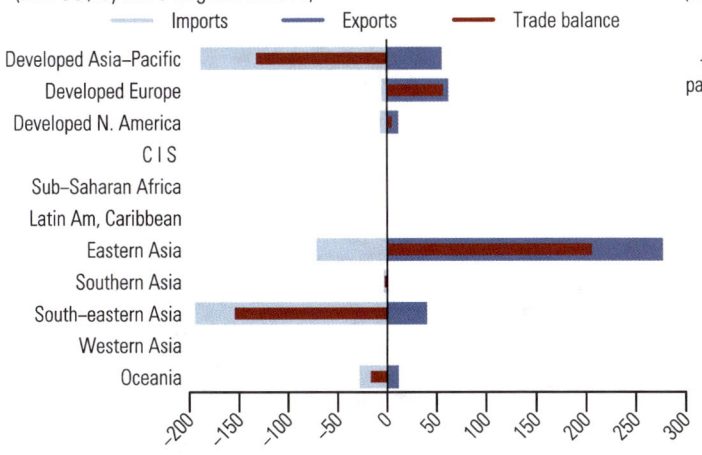

Graph 5: Partner concentration of merchandise trade
(Cumulative share by ranked partners in 2014)

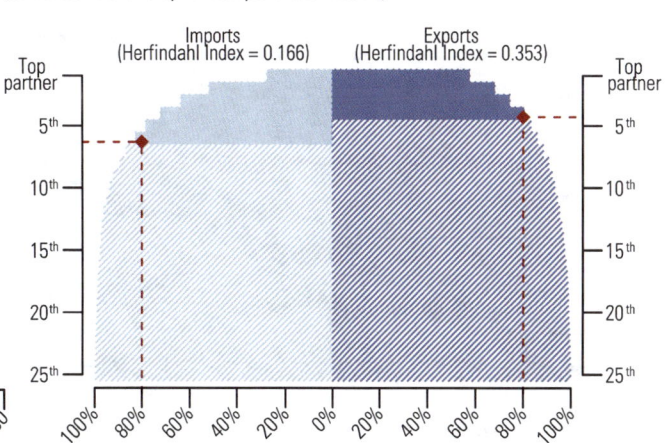

Imports (Herfindahl Index = 0.166)
Exports (Herfindahl Index = 0.353)

Graph 6: Imports of services by EBOPS category
(% share in 2013)

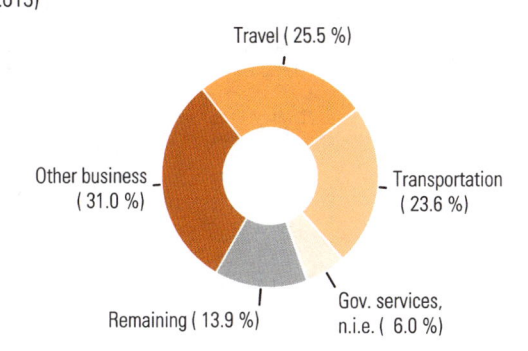

- Travel (25.5 %)
- Transportation (23.6 %)
- Gov. services, n.i.e. (6.0 %)
- Remaining (13.9 %)
- Other business (31.0 %)

Imports Profile:

"Not classified elsewhere in the SITC" (SITC section 9), "Mineral fuels, lubricants" (SITC section 3) and "Food, animals + beverages, tobacco" (SITC section 0+1) were the largest commodity groups for imports in 2014, representing respectively 37.8, 23.6 and 20.0 percent of imported goods (see table 3). From 2012 to 2014, the largest import commodity was "Oils petroleum, bituminous, distillates, except crude" (HS code 2710) (see table 4). The top three partners for merchandise imports were Australia, Singapore and China, accounting for respectively 28.8, 28.0 and 9.5 percent of total imports. "Other business services" (EBOPS code 268) accounted for the largest share of imports of services in 2013 at 82.3 mln US$, followed by "Travel" (EBOPS code 236) at 67.8 mln US$ and "Transportation" (EBOPS code 205) at 62.7 mln US$ (see graph 6).

Table 4: Top 10 import commodities 2012 to 2014

HS code	4-digit heading of Harmonized System 1996	2012	2013	2014	2012	2013	2014	Unit	SITC code
	All Commodities	493.4	580.2	499.6					
2710	Oils petroleum, bituminous, distillates, except crude	130.7	171.1	114.8		1.3	0.9	US$/kg	334
9999	Commodities not elsewhere specified	0.3	193.2	188.2					931
1006	Rice	41.3	42.1	43.2	5.3	1.0		US$/kg	042
1902	Pasta, couscous, etc.	5.9	7.1	7.4	4.1	3.9		US$/kg	048
0207	Meat, edible offal of domestic poultry	4.3	6.1	6.7	4.0	3.6		US$/kg	012
1001	Wheat and meslin	4.0	5.5	6.7	0.4	0.5		US$/kg	041
4907	Documents of title (bonds etc), unused stamps etc.	1.7	6.6	6.4					892
8517	Electric apparatus for line telephony, telegraphy	5.4	6.1	3.0					764
2202	Waters, non-alcoholic sweetened or flavoured beverages	3.4	4.0	4.2	2.7	1.9		US$/litre	111
8471	Automatic data processing machines (computers)	3.2	4.0	3.0	32.0	95.8		US$/unit	752

South Africa

Goods Imports: FOB, by origin **Goods Exports:** FOB, by last known destination **Trade System:** General

Overview:
In 2014, the value of merchandise exports of South Africa decreased slightly by 4.7 percent to reach 90.6 bln US$, while its merchandise imports decreased slightly by 3.4 percent to reach 99.9 bln US$ (see graph 1, table 2 and table 3). The merchandise trade balance recorded a relatively small deficit of 9.3 bln US$ (see graph 1). The largest merchandise trade balance was with MDG Sub-Saharan Africa at 14.1 bln US$ (see graph 4). Merchandise exports in South Africa were diversified amongst partners; imports were also diversified. The top 24 partners accounted for 80 percent or more of exports and 23 partners accounted for 80 percent or more of imports (see graph 5). In 2013, the value of exports of services of South Africa decreased moderately by 6.5 percent, reaching 14.2 bln US$, while its imports of services decreased moderately by 7.2 percent and reached 16.4 bln US$ (see graph 2). There was a relatively small trade in services deficit of 2.2 bln US$.

Graph 1: Total merchandise trade, by value
(Bln US$ by year)

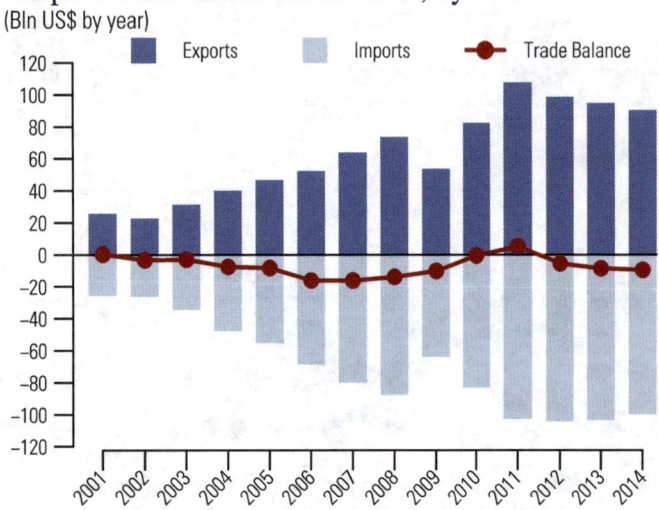

Graph 2: Total services trade, by value
(Bln US$ by year)

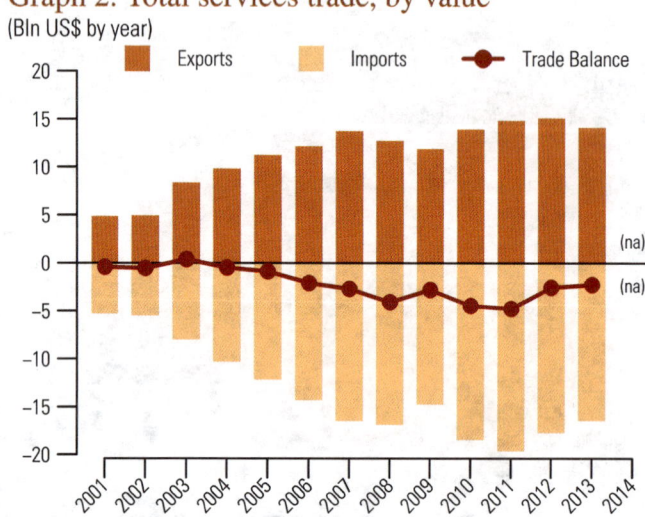

Exports Profile:
"Goods classified chiefly by material" (SITC section 6), "Machinery and transport equipment" (SITC section 7) and "Crude materials + anim. & veg. oils" (SITC section 2+4) were the largest commodity groups for exports in 2014, representing respectively 25.0, 20.6 and 16.9 percent of exported goods (see table 2). From 2012 to 2014, the largest export commodity was "Iron ores and concentrates, including roasted iron pyrites" (HS code 2601) (see table 1). The top three destinations for merchandise exports were China, Areas nes and the United States, accounting for respectively 10.9, 7.8 and 7.4 percent of total exports. "Travel" (EBOPS code 236) accounted for the largest share of exports of services in 2013 at 9.2 bln US$, followed by "Other business services" (EBOPS code 268) at 3.2 bln US$ and "Transportation" (EBOPS code 205) at 1.7 bln US$ (see graph 3).

Graph 3: Exports of services by EBOPS category
(% share in 2013)

- Travel (65.2 %)
- Other business (22.6 %)
- Transportation (12.2 %)

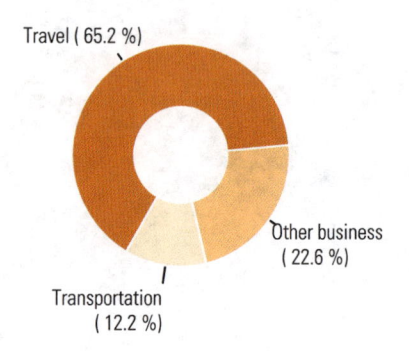

Table 1: Top 10 export commodities 2012 to 2014

HS code	4-digit heading of Harmonized System 2012	Value (million US$) 2012	2013	2014	Unit value 2012	2013	2014	Unit	SITC code
	All Commodities	98 872.2	95 111.5	90 612.1					
2601	Iron ores and concentrates, including roasted iron pyrites	7 750.7	8 458.4	6 738.7	0.1	0.1	0.1	US$/kg	281
7110	Platinum, unwrought or in semi-manufactured forms, or in powder form	7 925.9	8 412.7	6 504.4	25.6	32.2	29.3	thsd US$/kg	681
7108	Gold (including gold plated with platinum)	8 657.8	6 614.0	4 726.9	52.9	44.6	40.3	thsd US$/kg	971
2701	Coal; briquettes, ovoids and similar solid fuels manufactured from coal	6 785.5	5 826.5	5 192.9	0.1	0.1	0.1	US$/kg	321
8703	Motor cars and other motor vehicles principally designed for the transport	4 028.0	3 666.8	4 372.0	14.9	14.7	23.3	thsd US$/unit	781
7202	Ferro-alloys	3 581.6	3 663.0	4 099.3	1.0	1.0	0.9	US$/kg	671
2710	Petroleum oils, other than crude	3 497.6	3 206.4	3 081.3	0.9	0.9	1.1	US$/kg	334
8704	Motor vehicles for the transport of goods	3 038.3	2 973.2	3 024.5			21.1	thsd US$/unit	782
7102	Diamonds, whether or not worked, but not mounted or set	2 038.5	2 115.0	2 423.3					667
8421	Centrifuges, including centrifugal dryers	2 191.8	2 089.4	1 975.6					743

Source: UN Comtrade and UN ServiceTrade

South Africa

Services Imports and Exports: EBOPS 2002 categories

Table 2: Merchandise exports by SITC
(Value in million US$, growth and shares in percentage)

SITC	2014	Avg. Growth rates 2010-2014	2013-2014	2014 share
Total	90612.1	2.3	-4.7	100.0
0+1	9171.5	3.8	1.9	10.1
2+4	15296.5	3.3	-12.8	16.9
3	9507.4	1.8	-5.9	10.5
5	7042.4	3.6	2.7	7.8
6	22679.5	-3.7	-4.1	25.0
7	18692.5	3.5	4.6	20.6
8	3032.7	-2.1	-0.2	3.3
9	5189.6	90.9	-26.4	5.7

Table 3: Merchandise imports by SITC
(Value in million US$, growth and shares in percentage)

SITC	2014	Avg. Growth rates 2010-2014	2013-2014	2014 share
Total	99892.7	4.8	-3.4	100.0
0+1	5328.6	3.9	-9.1	5.3
2+4	2741.6	-0.2	-9.3	2.7
3	23256.3	10.3	4.4	23.3
5	10841.5	4.1	-1.3	10.9
6	10442.9	4.3	-4.5	10.5
7	32416.2	2.8	-8.5	32.5
8	8255.9	2.6	-5.0	8.3
9	6609.8	5.5	6.0	6.6

SITC Legend

SITC Code	Description
	Total All commodities
0+1	Food, animals + beverages, tobacco
2+4	Crude materials + anim. & veg. oils
3	Mineral fuels, lubricants
5	Chemicals
6	Goods classified chiefly by material
7	Machinery and transport equipment
8	Miscellaneous manufactured articles
9	Not classified elsewhere in the SITC

Graph 4: Merchandise trade balance
(Bln US$ by MDG Regions in 2014)

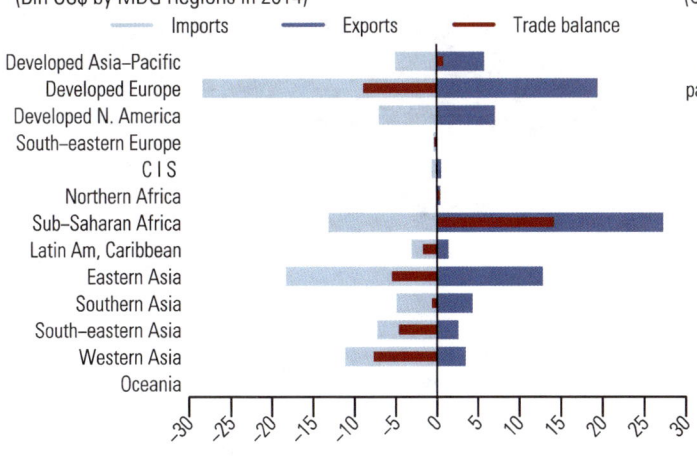

Graph 5: Partner concentration of merchandise trade
(Cumulative share by ranked partners in 2014)

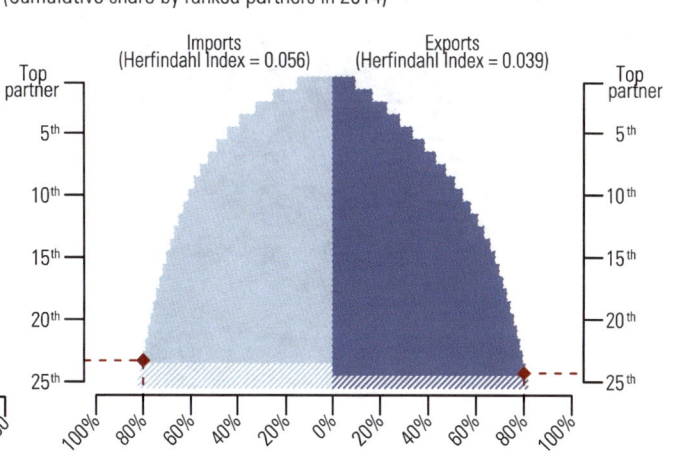

Imports (Herfindahl Index = 0.056)
Exports (Herfindahl Index = 0.039)

Graph 6: Imports of services by EBOPS category
(% share in 2013)

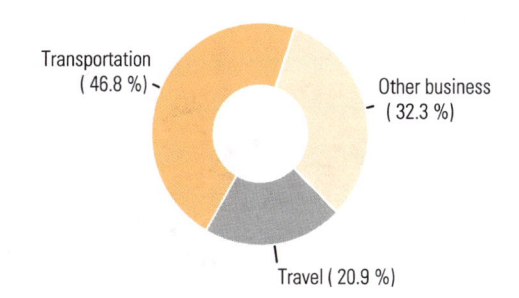

- Transportation (46.8%)
- Other business (32.3%)
- Travel (20.9%)

Imports Profile:
"Machinery and transport equipment" (SITC section 7), "Mineral fuels, lubricants" (SITC section 3) and "Chemicals" (SITC section 5) were the largest commodity groups for imports in 2014, representing respectively 32.5, 23.3 and 10.9 percent of imported goods (see table 3). From 2012 to 2014, the largest import commodity was "Petroleum oils and oils obtained from bituminous minerals, crude" (HS code 2709) (see table 4). The top three partners for merchandise imports were China, Germany and Saudi Arabia, accounting for respectively 15.0, 10.1 and 7.5 percent of total imports. "Transportation" (EBOPS code 205) accounted for the largest share of imports of services in 2013 at 7.7 bln US$, followed by "Other business services" (EBOPS code 268) at 5.3 bln US$ and "Travel" (EBOPS code 236) at 3.4 bln US$ (see graph 6).

Table 4: Top 10 import commodities 2012 to 2014

HS code	4-digit heading of Harmonized System 2012	2012	2013	2014	2012	2013	2014	Unit	SITC code
	All Commodities	104144.3	103441.3	99892.7					
2709	Petroleum oils and oils obtained from bituminous minerals, crude	15787.5	14721.8	16212.1	0.8	0.8	0.8	US$/kg	333
9999	Commodities not specified according to kind	6390.7	6234.2	6607.9					931
2710	Petroleum oils, other than crude	5856.1	6433.1	5805.7	1.1	1.0	1.1	US$/kg	334
8703	Motor cars and other motor vehicles principally designed for the transport	5168.0	5494.3	4706.2	18.2	17.5	14.8	thsd US$/unit	781
8517	Electrical apparatus for line telephony or line telegraphy	3066.1	3404.3	3165.0					764
8471	Automatic data processing machines and units thereof	1999.6	2054.4	1978.9			156.0	US$/unit	752
3004	Medicaments (excluding goods of heading 30.02, 30.05 or 30.06)	1861.8	1812.0	1569.4	61.6	55.7	66.0	US$/kg	542
8704	Motor vehicles for the transport of goods	1625.9	1241.0	1051.2			29.7	thsd US$/unit	782
8708	Parts and accessories of the motor vehicles of headings 87.01 to 87.05	1281.1	1263.4	1300.3	9.6	9.1	8.8	US$/kg	784
8429	Self-propelled bulldozers, angledozers, graders, levellers, scrapers	1218.7	1005.6	906.0			34.8	thsd US$/unit	723

Source: UN Comtrade and UN ServiceTrade

Spain

Goods Imports: CIF, by origin/consignment for intra-eu   **Goods Exports:** FOB, by last known destination   **Trade System:** Special

Overview:
In 2014, the value of merchandise exports of Spain increased slightly by 2.5 percent to reach 318.6 bln US$, while its merchandise imports increased moderately by 5.6 percent to reach 351.0 bln US$ (see graph 1, table 2 and table 3). The merchandise trade balance recorded a relatively small deficit of 32.3 bln US$ (see graph 1), which reversed positive growth trends in net exports in recent years. The largest merchandise trade balance was with MDG Eastern Asia at -19.4 bln US$ (see graph 4), consisting mostly electrical equipment, machineries, and articles of apparel. Merchandise exports in Spain were diversified amongst partners; imports were also diversified. The top 23 partners accounted for 80 percent or more of exports and 26 partners accounted for 80 percent or more of imports (see graph 5). In 2013, the value of exports of services of Spain increased moderately by 5.4 percent, reaching 145.2 bln US$, while its imports of services increased slightly by 0.7 percent and reached 90.9 bln US$ (see graph 2). There was a moderate trade in services surplus of 54.3 bln US$.

Graph 1: Total merchandise trade, by value
(Bln US$ by year)

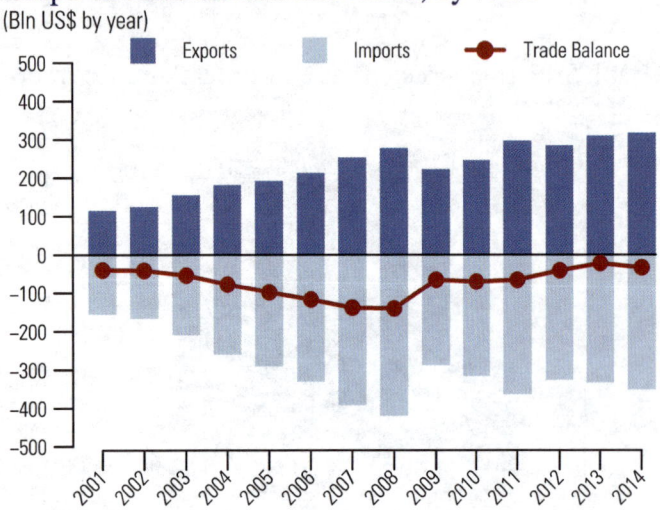

Graph 2: Total services trade, by value
(Bln US$ by year)

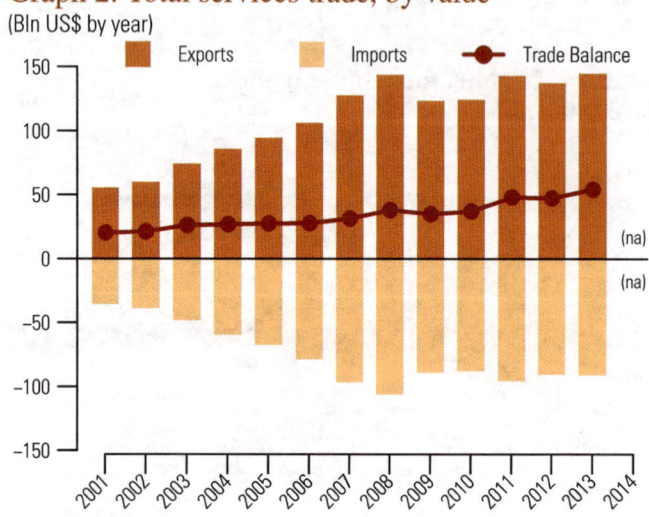

Exports Profile:
"Machinery and transport equipment" (SITC section 7), "Goods classified chiefly by material" (SITC section 6) and "Food, animals + beverages, tobacco" (SITC section 0+1) were the largest commodity groups for exports in 2014, representing respectively 31.9, 15.5 and 13.9 percent of exported goods (see table 2). From 2012 to 2014, the largest export commodity was "Motor cars and other motor vehicles principally designed for the transport" (HS code 8703) (see table 1). The top three destinations for merchandise exports (amounted of 107.0 bln US$) were France, Germany and Portugal, accounting for respectively 16.0, 10.3 and 7.3 percent of total exports. "Travel" (EBOPS code 236) accounted for the largest share of exports of services in 2013 at 60.4 bln US$, followed by "Other business services" (EBOPS code 268) at 36.4 bln US$ and "Transportation" (EBOPS code 205) at 23.3 bln US$ (see graph 3).

Graph 3: Exports of services by EBOPS category
(% share in 2013)

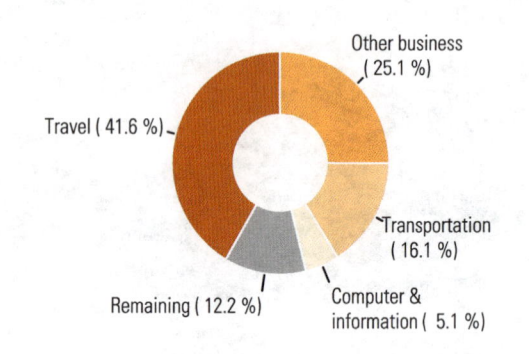

- Travel (41.6 %)
- Other business (25.1 %)
- Transportation (16.1 %)
- Computer & information (5.1 %)
- Remaining (12.2 %)

Table 1: Top 10 export commodities 2012 to 2014

HS code	4-digit heading of Harmonized System 2012	Value (million US$) 2012	2013	2014	Unit value 2012	2013	2014	Unit	SITC code
	All Commodities	285 936.4	310 963.6	318 649.3					
8703	Motor cars and other motor vehicles principally designed for the transport	25 120.2	29 175.6	31 932.0		13.5	16.2	thsd US$/unit	781
2710	Petroleum oils, other than crude	17 097.9	16 541.9	14 186.1	0.9	0.9	0.8	US$/kg	334
9999	Commodities not specified according to kind	12 659.1	13 109.6	12 566.0					931
8708	Parts and accessories of the motor vehicles of headings 87.01 to 87.05	10 177.3	10 909.7	10 712.3	5.7	6.6	6.2	US$/kg	784
3004	Medicaments (excluding goods of heading 30.02, 30.05 or 30.06)	8 936.5	9 555.2	8 945.6	43.9	51.3	49.1	US$/kg	542
8704	Motor vehicles for the transport of goods	4 635.6	5 289.5	6 113.7	17.1	16.1	20.2	thsd US$/unit	782
0805	Citrus fruit, fresh or dried	3 494.6	3 848.9	3 820.3	0.9	1.0	1.0	US$/kg	057
2204	Wine of fresh grapes, including fortified wines	3 300.5	3 430.0	3 401.3					112
0203	Meat of swine, fresh, chilled or frozen	2 999.1	3 170.6	3 382.4	2.9	3.2	3.1	US$/kg	012
8803	Parts of goods of heading 88.01 or 88.02	2 941.3	2 827.2	3 185.7	662.6	590.7	457.0	US$/kg	792

Source: UN Comtrade and UN ServiceTrade

Spain

Services Imports and Exports: EBOPS 2002 categories

Table 2: Merchandise exports by SITC
(Value in million US$, growth and shares in percentage)

SITC	2014	Avg. Growth rates 2010-2014	Avg. Growth rates 2013-2014	2014 share
Total	318 649.3	6.7	2.5	100.0
0+1	44 345.4	7.1	3.0	13.9
2+4	13 088.4	8.5	5.3	4.1
3	22 988.6	16.4	7.1	7.2
5	42 674.0	4.7	2.6	13.4
6	49 485.1	4.1	2.3	15.5
7	101 664.2	5.1	1.3	31.9
8	30 471.9	8.8	8.4	9.6
9	13 931.7	14.1	-10.9	4.4

Table 3: Merchandise imports by SITC
(Value in million US$, growth and shares in percentage)

SITC	2014	Avg. Growth rates 2010-2014	Avg. Growth rates 2013-2014	2014 share
Total	350 977.8	2.7	5.6	100.0
0+1	33 093.5	2.8	3.2	9.4
2+4	17 961.8	3.3	0.5	5.1
3	73 495.4	6.0	-3.2	20.9
5	49 094.2	2.5	3.1	14.0
6	36 848.2	1.2	6.7	10.5
7	96 143.9	1.4	13.3	27.4
8	43 390.4	2.3	13.7	12.4
9	950.3	-11.9	-26.5	0.3

SITC Legend

SITC Code	Description
Total	All commodities
0+1	Food, animals + beverages, tobacco
2+4	Crude materials + anim. & veg. oils
3	Mineral fuels, lubricants
5	Chemicals
6	Goods classified chiefly by material
7	Machinery and transport equipment
8	Miscellaneous manufactured articles
9	Not classified elsewhere in the SITC

Graph 4: Merchandise trade balance
(Bln US$ by MDG Regions in 2014)

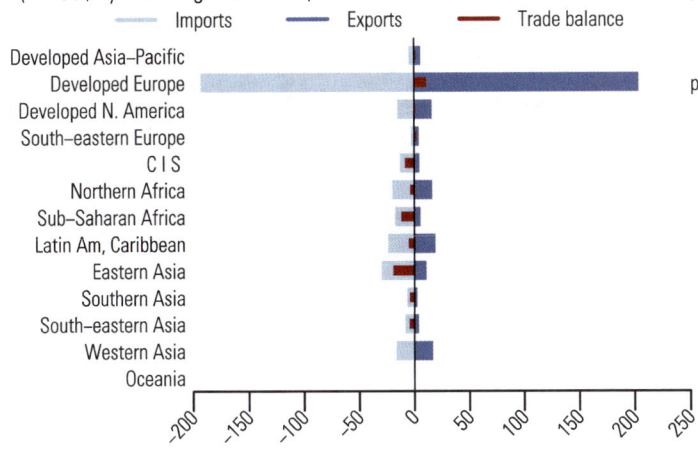

Graph 5: Partner concentration of merchandise trade
(Cumulative share by ranked partners in 2014)

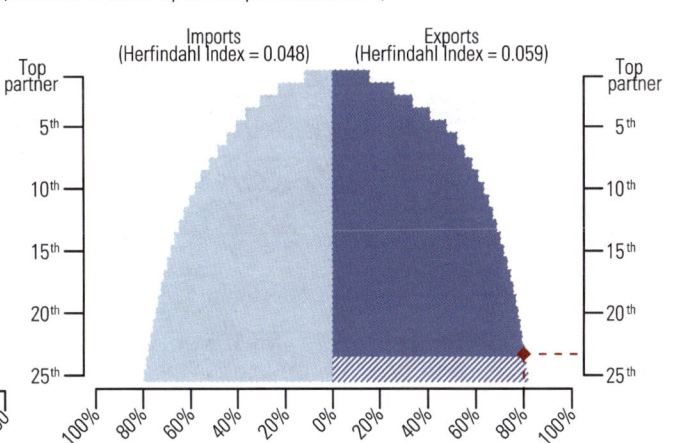

Imports (Herfindahl Index = 0.048)
Exports (Herfindahl Index = 0.059)

Graph 6: Imports of services by EBOPS category
(% share in 2013)

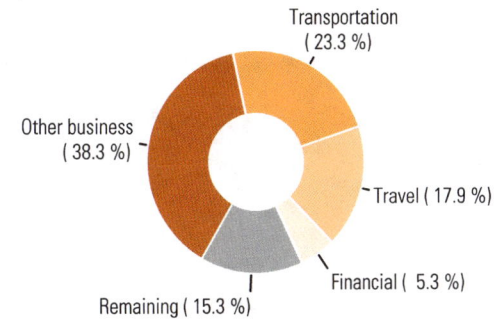

- Transportation (23.3 %)
- Other business (38.3 %)
- Travel (17.9 %)
- Financial (5.3 %)
- Remaining (15.3 %)

Imports Profile:

"Machinery and transport equipment" (SITC section 7), "Mineral fuels, lubricants" (SITC section 3) and "Chemicals" (SITC section 5) were the largest commodity groups for imports in 2014, representing respectively 27.4, 20.9 and 14.0 percent of imported goods (see table 3). From 2012 to 2014, the largest import commodity was "Petroleum oils and oils obtained from bituminous minerals, crude" (HS code 2709) (see table 4), originated mostly from Nigeria, Mexico, Saudi Arabia, Angola and Russian Federation. The top three partners for merchandise imports were Germany, France and China, accounting for respectively 11.3, 10.8 and 7.1 percent of total imports. "Other business services" (EBOPS code 268) accounted for the largest share of imports of services in 2013 at 34.8 bln US$, followed by "Transportation" (EBOPS code 205) at 21.1 bln US$ and "Travel" (EBOPS code 236) at 16.3 bln US$ (see graph 6).

Table 4: Top 10 import commodities 2012 to 2014

HS code	4-digit heading of Harmonized System 2012	Value 2012	Value 2013	Value 2014	Unit value 2012	Unit value 2013	Unit value 2014	Unit	SITC code
	All Commodities	325 835.2	332 266.8	350 977.8					
2709	Petroleum oils and oils obtained from bituminous minerals, crude	46 232.3	45 308.1	44 262.0	0.8	0.8	0.7	US$/kg	333
8708	Parts and accessories of the motor vehicles of headings 87.01 to 87.05	14 822.9	17 275.3	19 697.4	7.8	5.9	8.8	US$/kg	784
2711	Petroleum gases and other gaseous hydrocarbons	14 515.7	14 268.5	14 081.2	0.5	0.5	0.5	US$/kg	343
2710	Petroleum oils, other than crude	15 559.8	13 948.4	12 481.5	1.0	0.8	0.7	US$/kg	334
8703	Motor cars and other motor vehicles principally designed for the transport	10 072.3	11 325.3	14 966.0		14.2	*5.3*	thsd US$/unit	781
3004	Medicaments (excluding goods of heading 30.02, 30.05 or 30.06)	10 962.1	11 153.6	11 445.3	84.8	90.3	91.2	US$/kg	542
8517	Electrical apparatus for line telephony or line telegraphy	4 890.3	5 320.9	5 752.2					764
8471	Automatic data processing machines and units thereof	3 574.5	3 669.3	3 699.9	*171.8*	*127.5*	*130.0*	US$/unit	752
2603	Copper ores and concentrates	3 179.8	3 076.7	3 245.8	2.1	2.0	1.8	US$/kg	283
6204	Women's or girls' suits, ensembles, jackets, blazers, dresses, skirts	2 312.5	2 524.1	2 784.2		8.9	*14.7*	US$/unit	842

2014 International Trade Statistics Yearbook, Vol. I
Source: UN Comtrade and UN ServiceTrade

Sri Lanka

Goods Imports: CIF, by origin **Goods Exports: FOB, by last known destination** **Trade System: General**

Overview:
In 2014, the value of merchandise exports of Sri Lanka increased substantially by 12.9 percent to reach 11.3 bln US$, while its merchandise imports increased moderately by 7.3 percent to reach 19.2 bln US$ (see graph 1, table 2 and table 3). The merchandise trade balance recorded a moderate deficit of 7.9 bln US$ (see graph 1). The largest merchandise trade balance was with MDG Eastern Asia at -4.2 bln US$ (see graph 4). Merchandise exports in Sri Lanka were diversified amongst partners; imports were also diversified. The top 21 partners accounted for 80 percent or more of exports and 14 partners accounted for 80 percent or more of imports (see graph 5). In 2013, the value of exports of services of Sri Lanka increased substantially by 23.3 percent, reaching 4.7 bln US$, while its imports of services increased substantially by 38.1 percent and reached 3.5 bln US$ (see graph 2). There was a moderate trade in services surplus of 1.2 bln US$.

Graph 1: Total merchandise trade, by value
(Bln US$ by year)

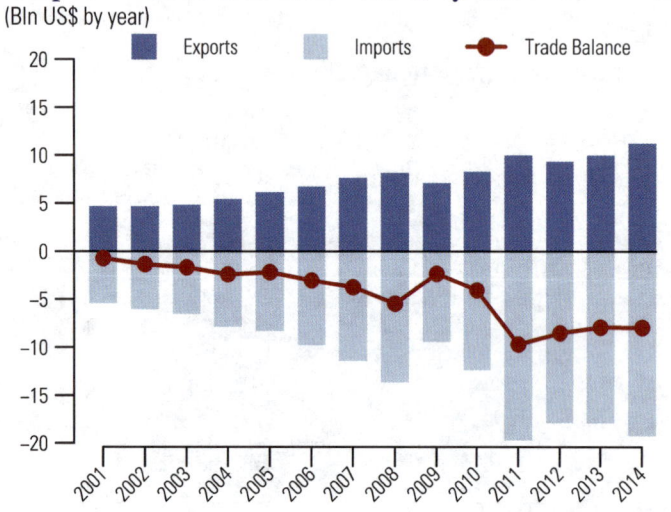

Graph 2: Total services trade, by value
(Bln US$ by year)

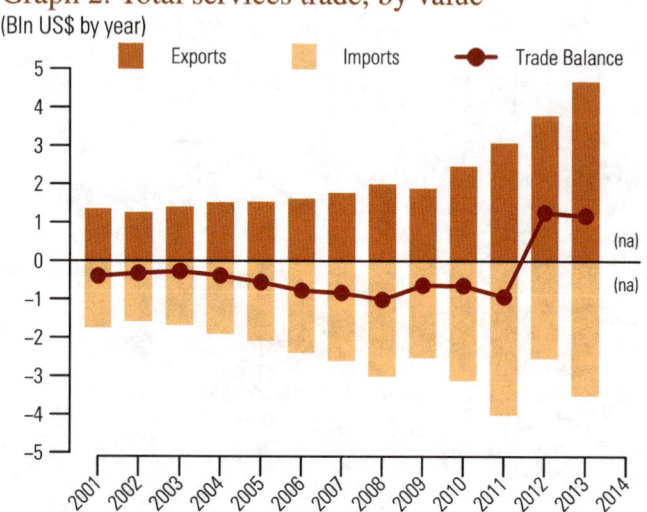

Exports Profile:
"Miscellaneous manufactured articles" (SITC section 8), "Food, animals + beverages, tobacco" (SITC section 0+1) and "Goods classified chiefly by material" (SITC section 6) were the largest commodity groups for exports in 2014, representing respectively 47.6, 25.1 and 13.8 percent of exported goods (see table 2). From 2012 to 2014, the largest export commodity was "Tea, whether or not flavoured" (HS code 0902) (see table 1). The top three destinations for merchandise exports were the United States, the United Kingdom and India, accounting for respectively 23.9, 10.6 and 6.1 percent of total exports. "Transportation" (EBOPS code 205) accounted for the largest share of exports of services in 2013 at 1.8 bln US$, followed by "Travel" (EBOPS code 236) at 1.7 bln US$ and "Computer and information services" (EBOPS code 262) at 604.3 mln US$ (see graph 3).

Graph 3: Exports of services by EBOPS category
(% share in 2013)

- Travel (36.6 %)
- Transportation (38.1 %)
- Computer & information (12.9 %)
- Remaining (12.4 %)

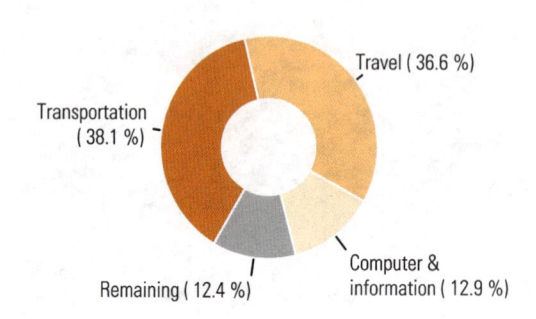

Table 1: Top 10 export commodities 2012 to 2014

HS code	4-digit heading of Harmonized System 2007	Value (million US$) 2012	2013	2014	Unit value 2012	2013	2014	Unit	SITC code
	All Commodities	9 369.8	10 004.9	11 295.5					
0902	Tea, whether or not flavoured	1 403.2	1 528.5	1 609.3	4.4	4.3	4.9	US$/kg	074
6204	Women's or girls' suits, ensembles, jackets, blazers, dresses, skirts	585.5	550.0	552.8	7.2		8.0	US$/unit	842
6108	Women's or girls' slips, petticoats, briefs, panties, knitted or crocheted	440.3	512.2	539.7	1.6		1.6	US$/unit	844
6212	Brassieres, girdles, corsets, braces, suspenders, garters	422.0	489.2	527.6	58.3	83.1	53.8	US$/kg	845
6109	T-shirts, singlets and other vests, knitted or crocheted	351.5	403.0	497.2	3.7	6.2	4.0	US$/unit	845
6203	Men's or boys' suits, ensembles, jackets, blazers, trousers	388.9	400.9	434.2	8.7		8.9	US$/unit	841
6104	Women's or girls' suits, ensembles, jackets, blazers, dresses, skirts	324.4	430.3	449.7	6.1		5.5	US$/unit	844
4012	Retreaded or used pneumatic tyres of rubber	331.1	347.8	356.6					625
7102	Diamonds, whether or not worked, but not mounted or set	330.3	313.3	197.0					667
6116	Gloves, mittens and mitts, knitted or crocheted	193.8	222.7	232.9	20.0	18.8	20.6	US$/kg	846

Sri Lanka

Services Imports and Exports: EBOPS 2002 categories

Table 2: Merchandise exports by SITC
(Value in million US$, growth and shares in percentage)

SITC	2014	Avg. Growth rates 2010-2014	Avg. Growth rates 2013-2014	2014 share
Total	11 295.5	8.0	12.9	100.0
0+1	2 836.3	6.4	8.2	25.1
2+4	401.0	0.9	25.5	3.6
3	295.4	117.9	833.1	2.6
5	170.2	14.8	15.6	1.5
6	1 561.0	6.6	-0.8	13.8
7	627.2	9.2	38.7	5.6
8	5 373.0	9.0	11.2	47.6
9	31.3	-30.3	9.1	0.3

Table 3: Merchandise imports by SITC
(Value in million US$, growth and shares in percentage)

SITC	2014	Avg. Growth rates 2010-2014	Avg. Growth rates 2013-2014	2014 share
Total	19 244.5	11.7	7.3	100.0
0+1	2 339.1	7.4	20.3	12.2
2+4	594.9	12.7	18.2	3.1
3	4 397.3	20.8	4.7	22.8
5	2 020.9	10.0	11.0	10.5
6	4 925.4	8.8	6.6	25.6
7	4 061.8	11.3	7.2	21.1
8	884.3	13.8	10.6	4.6
9	20.9	-30.3	-91.9	0.1

SITC Legend

SITC Code	Description
Total	All commodities
0+1	Food, animals + beverages, tobacco
2+4	Crude materials + anim. & veg. oils
3	Mineral fuels, lubricants
5	Chemicals
6	Goods classified chiefly by material
7	Machinery and transport equipment
8	Miscellaneous manufactured articles
9	Not classified elsewhere in the SITC

Graph 4: Merchandise trade balance
(Bln US$ by MDG Regions in 2014)

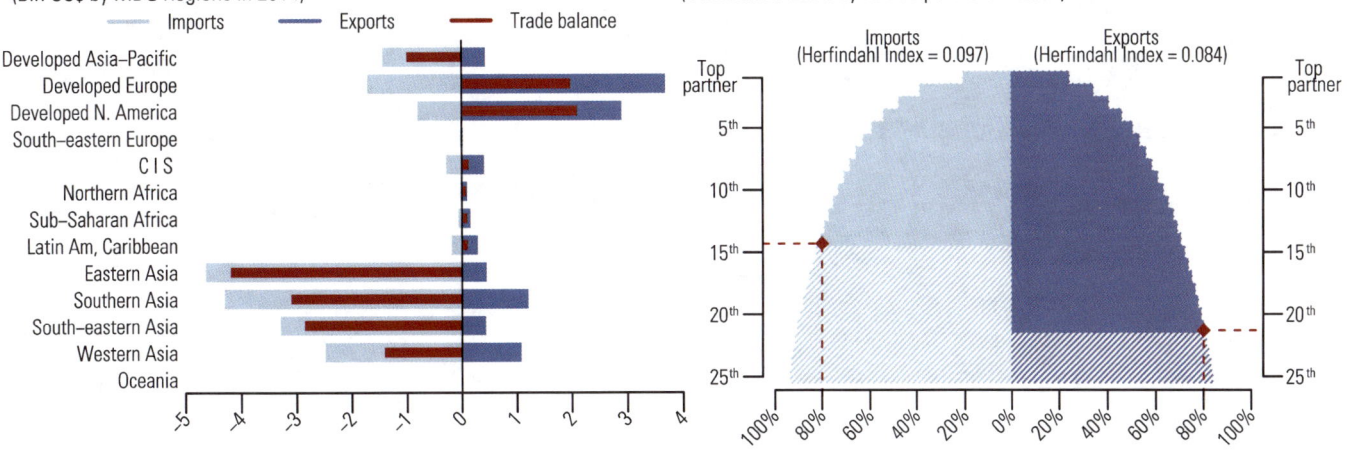

Graph 5: Partner concentration of merchandise trade
(Cumulative share by ranked partners in 2014)

Imports (Herfindahl Index = 0.097)
Exports (Herfindahl Index = 0.084)

Graph 6: Imports of services by EBOPS category
(% share in 2013)

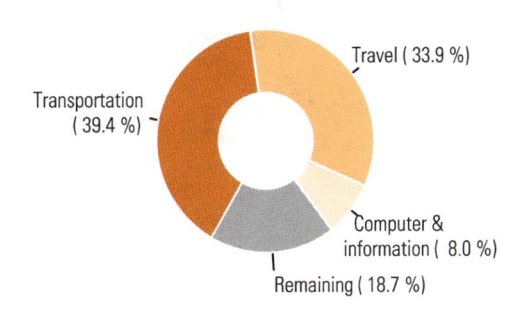

- Transportation (39.4 %)
- Travel (33.9 %)
- Computer & information (8.0 %)
- Remaining (18.7 %)

Imports Profile:

"Goods classified chiefly by material" (SITC section 6), "Mineral fuels, lubricants" (SITC section 3) and "Machinery and transport equipment" (SITC section 7) were the largest commodity groups for imports in 2014, representing respectively 25.6, 22.8 and 21.1 percent of imported goods (see table 3). From 2012 to 2014, the largest import commodity was "Petroleum oils, other than crude" (HS code 2710) (see table 4). The top three partners for merchandise imports were India, China and Singapore, accounting for respectively 19.3, 16.2 and 7.9 percent of total imports. "Transportation" (EBOPS code 205) accounted for the largest share of imports of services in 2013 at 1.4 bln US$, followed by "Travel" (EBOPS code 236) at 1.2 bln US$ and "Computer and information services" (EBOPS code 262) at 281.0 mln US$ (see graph 6).

Table 4: Top 10 import commodities 2012 to 2014

HS code	4-digit heading of Harmonized System 2007	2012	2013	2014	2012	2013	2014	Unit	SITC code
	All Commodities...	17 884.9	17 930.8	19 244.5					
2710	Petroleum oils, other than crude...	2 102.6	2 396.3	2 592.0	0.9		0.9	US$/kg	334
2709	Petroleum oils and oils obtained from bituminous minerals, crude...	1 289.3	1 344.2	1 337.7	0.8		0.8	US$/kg	333
8703	Motor cars and other motor vehicles principally designed for the transport...	504.2	593.1	800.7	4.2	12.7	6.5	thsd US$/unit	781
6006	Other knitted or crocheted fabrics...	511.9	499.8	566.6	9.0	10.5	9.0	US$/kg	655
2523	Portland cement, aluminous cement, slag cement...	398.6	520.7	511.7	0.1		0.1	US$/kg	661
1001	Wheat and meslin...	327.9	324.2	370.9	0.3	0.3	0.3	US$/kg	041
0402	Milk and cream, concentrated or containing added sugar...	290.8	277.2	324.7	3.7	3.7	4.8	US$/kg	022
3004	Medicaments (excluding goods of heading 30.02, 30.05 or 30.06)...	290.5	294.2	295.9	10.0		16.6	US$/kg	542
1701	Cane or beet sugar and chemically pure sucrose, in solid form...	332.2	281.2	247.7	0.6	0.8	0.5	US$/kg	061
5209	Woven fabrics of cotton, containing 85 % or more by weight of cotton...	330.2	267.1	259.7	7.3	10.6	8.0	US$/kg	652

State of Palestine

Goods Imports: CIF, by origin   **Goods Exports:** FOB, by last known destination   **Trade System:** General

Overview:
In 2013, the value of merchandise exports of the State of Palestine increased substantially by 15.1 percent to reach 900.6 mln US$, while its merchandise imports increased moderately by 9.9 percent to reach 5.2 bln US$ (see graph 1, table 2 and table 3). The merchandise trade balance recorded a large deficit of 4.3 bln US$ (see graph 1). The largest merchandise trade balance was with MDG Western Asia at -3.3 bln US$ (see graph 4). Merchandise exports in the State of Palestine were highly concentrated amongst partners; imports were also highly concentrated. The top 1 partner accounted for 80 percent or more of exports and 3 partners accounted for 80 percent or more of imports (see graph 5). In 2012, the value of exports of services of the State of Palestine decreased slightly by 1.9 percent, reaching 936.1 mln US$, while its imports of services increased substantially by 13.1 percent and reached 1.2 bln US$ (see graph 2). There was a moderate trade in services deficit of 260.3 mln US$.

Graph 1: Total merchandise trade, by value
(Bln US$ by year)

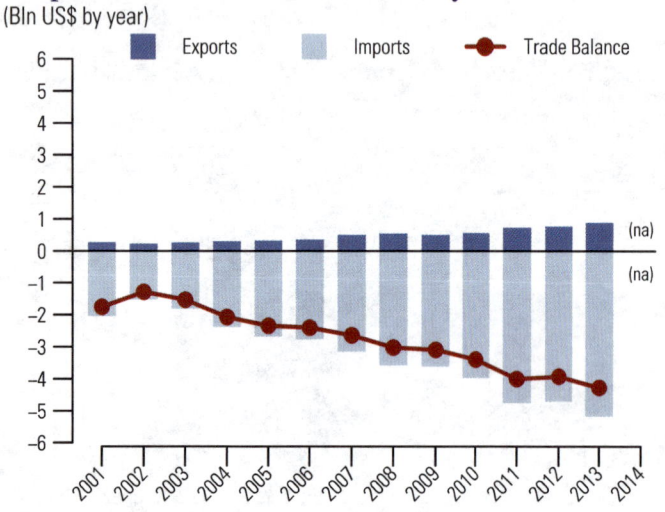

Graph 2: Total services trade, by value
(Bln US$ by year)

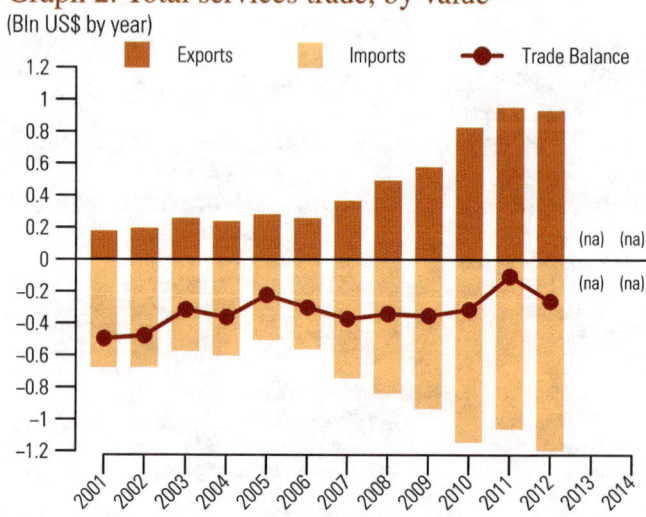

Exports Profile:
"Goods classified chiefly by material" (SITC section 6), "Miscellaneous manufactured articles" (SITC section 8) and "Food, animals + beverages, tobacco" (SITC section 0+1) were the largest commodity groups for exports in 2013, representing respectively 31.1, 21.2 and 20.6 percent of exported goods (see table 2). From 2011 to 2013, the largest export commodity was "Worked monumental or building stone (except slate) and articles thereof" (HS code 6802) (see table 1). The top three destinations for merchandise exports were Israel, Jordan and the United States, accounting for respectively 85.2, 6.3 and 1.3 percent of total exports. "Travel" (EBOPS code 236) accounted for the largest share of exports of services in 2012 at 755.1 mln US$, followed by "Government services, n.i.e." (EBOPS code 291) at 59.9 mln US$ and "Communications services" (EBOPS code 245) at 47.3 mln US$ (see graph 3).

Graph 3: Exports of services by EBOPS category
(% share in 2012)

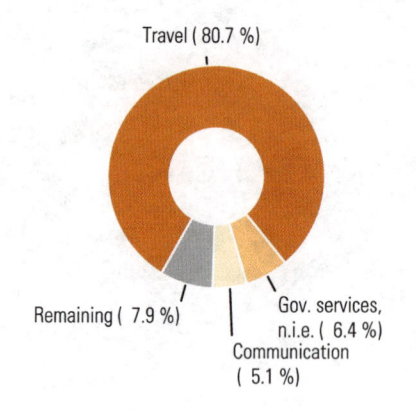

- Travel (80.7 %)
- Remaining (7.9 %)
- Gov. services, n.i.e. (6.4 %)
- Communication (5.1 %)

Table 1: Top 10 export commodities 2011 to 2013

HS code	4-digit heading of Harmonized System 2007	2011	2012	2013	2011	2012	2013	Unit	SITC code
	All Commodities	745.7	782.4	900.6					
6802	Worked monumental or building stone (except slate) and articles thereof	134.9	124.0	131.8	0.7	0.8	0.8	US$/kg	661
7204	Ferrous waste and scrap; remelting scrap ingots of iron or steel	57.7	49.9	41.8		0.4	0.4	US$/kg	282
3923	Articles for the conveyance or packing of goods, of plastics	26.8	32.3	40.1	3.4	3.8	3.6	US$/kg	893
9403	Other furniture and parts thereof	27.2	30.6	40.7					821
2402	Cigars, cheroots, cigarillos and cigarettes	22.4	28.8	35.4	12.9		14.4	US$/kg	122
6401	Waterproof footwear with outer soles and uppers of rubber or of plastics	24.3	21.9	26.3					851
1211	Plants and parts of plants (including seeds and fruits)	1.3	8.1	52.4	4.0	4.4	4.1	US$/kg	292
9404	Mattress supports; articles of bedding and similar furnishing	17.5	17.2	20.0					821
9401	Seats (other than those of heading 94.02)	14.6	15.8	21.3					821
1509	Olive oil and its fractions	16.4	23.0	8.8	4.3	4.2	4.0	US$/kg	421

State of Palestine

Services Imports and Exports: EBOPS 2002 categories

Table 2: Merchandise exports by SITC
(Value in million US$, growth and shares in percentage)

SITC	2013	Avg. Growth rates 2009-2013	Avg. Growth rates 2012-2013	2013 share
Total	900.6	14.8	15.1	100.0
0+1	185.3	22.3	20.8	20.6
2+4	152.6	36.3	20.0	16.9
3	2.1	0.8	-14.9	0.2
5	49.6	4.7	-2.3	5.5
6	280.0	10.0	10.4	31.1
7	40.1	8.6	16.7	4.5
8	190.8	11.2	25.4	21.2

Table 3: Merchandise imports by SITC
(Value in million US$, growth and shares in percentage)

SITC	2013	Avg. Growth rates 2009-2013	Avg. Growth rates 2012-2013	2013 share
Total	5163.9	9.4	9.9	100.0
0+1	1244.4	13.9	15.1	24.1
2+4	93.9	7.4	13.6	1.8
3	1611.0	9.1	11.9	31.2
5	450.2	13.6	16.2	8.7
6	893.9	12.7	5.9	17.3
7	630.1	2.6	7.9	12.2
8	240.4	6.6	-5.5	4.7
9	0.0	-87.9	-99.9	0.0

SITC Legend

SITC Code	Description
Total	All commodities
0+1	Food, animals + beverages, tobacco
2+4	Crude materials + anim. & veg. oils
3	Mineral fuels, lubricants
5	Chemicals
6	Goods classified chiefly by material
7	Machinery and transport equipment
8	Miscellaneous manufactured articles
9	Not classified elsewhere in the SITC

Graph 4: Merchandise trade balance
(Bln US$ by MDG Regions in 2013)

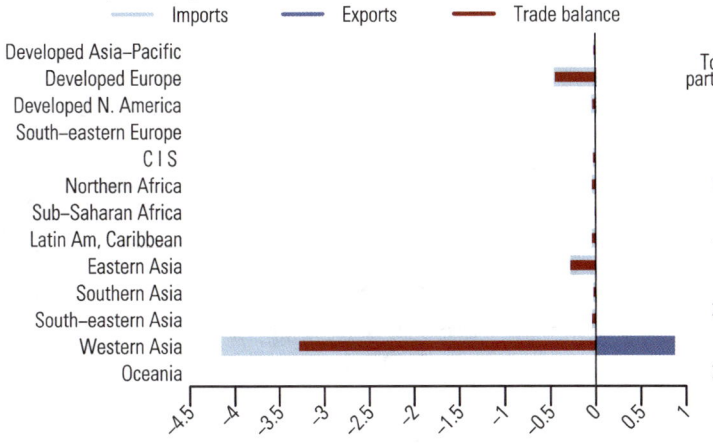

Graph 5: Partner concentration of merchandise trade
(Cumulative share by ranked partners in 2013)

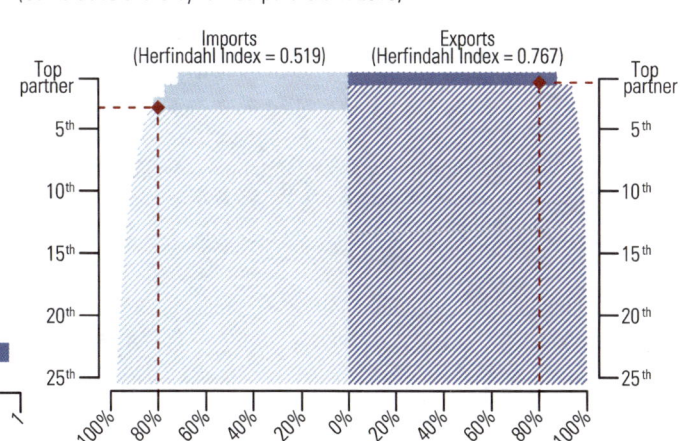

Imports (Herfindahl Index = 0.519)
Exports (Herfindahl Index = 0.767)

Graph 6: Imports of services by EBOPS category
(% share in 2012)

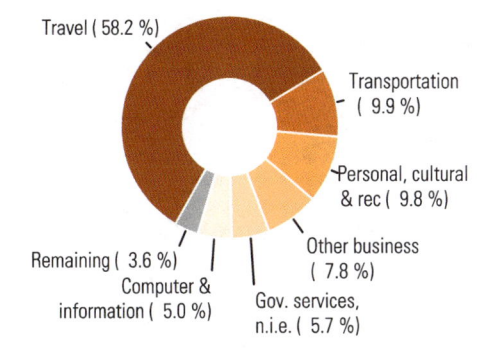

- Travel (58.2 %)
- Transportation (9.9 %)
- Personal, cultural & rec (9.8 %)
- Other business (7.8 %)
- Gov. services, n.i.e. (5.7 %)
- Computer & information (5.0 %)
- Remaining (3.6 %)

Imports Profile:

"Mineral fuels, lubricants" (SITC section 3), "Food, animals + beverages, tobacco" (SITC section 0+1) and "Goods classified chiefly by material" (SITC section 6) were the largest commodity groups for imports in 2013, representing respectively 31.2, 24.1 and 17.3 percent of imported goods (see table 3). From 2011 to 2013, the largest import commodity was "Petroleum oils, other than crude" (HS code 2710) (see table 4). The top three partners for merchandise imports were Israel, Turkey and China, accounting for respectively 71.2, 5.2 and 4.4 percent of total imports. "Travel" (EBOPS code 236) accounted for the largest share of imports of services in 2012 at 696.3 mln US$, followed by "Transportation" (EBOPS code 205) at 117.9 mln US$ and "Personal, cultural, and recreational services" (EBOPS code 287) at 117.7 mln US$ (see graph 6).

Table 4: Top 10 import commodities 2011 to 2013

HS code	4-digit heading of Harmonized System 2007	2011	2012	2013	2011	2012	2013	Unit	SITC code
	All Commodities	4737.6	4697.4	5163.9					
2710	Petroleum oils, other than crude	798.8	805.7	874.7	1.1			US$/kg	334
2716	Electrical energy	461.0	464.0	504.6	60.4	70.2	66.1	US$/MWh	351
2711	Petroleum gases and other gaseous hydrocarbons	213.1	155.0	202.3	0.4	0.5		US$/kg	343
2523	Portland cement, aluminous cement, slag cement	128.7	161.4	134.6					661
8703	Motor cars and other motor vehicles principally designed for the transport	127.7	102.4	96.2		15.0	13.4	thsd US$/unit	781
3004	Medicaments (excluding goods of heading 30.02, 30.05 or 30.06)	86.1	83.7	96.6					542
2309	Preparations of a kind used in animal feeding	79.9	86.8	92.5	1.5	1.7	1.6	US$/kg	081
6802	Worked monumental or building stone (except slate) and articles thereof	85.8	79.3	79.8	0.8	0.8	0.9	US$/kg	661
0102	Live bovine animals	66.4	77.0	72.0	1.2	1.0	1.1	thsd US$/unit	001
2202	Waters with added sugar	64.8	59.7	72.7	1.1	1.2	1.2	US$/litre	111

2014 International Trade Statistics Yearbook, Vol. I — Source: UN Comtrade and UN ServiceTrade

Sudan

Goods Imports: CIF, by origin **Goods Exports:** FOB, by last known destination **Trade System:** General

Overview:
In 2012, the value of merchandise exports of the Sudan decreased substantially by 62.3 percent to reach 3.4 bln US$, while its merchandise imports decreased substantially by 31.1 percent to reach 6.6 bln US$ (see graph 1, table 2 and table 3). The merchandise trade balance recorded a large deficit of 3.2 bln US$ (see graph 1). The largest merchandise trade balance was with MDG Eastern Asia at -1.2 bln US$ (see graph 4). Merchandise exports in the Sudan were highly concentrated amongst partners; imports were diversified. The top 3 partners accounted for 80 percent or more of exports and 19 partners accounted for 80 percent or more of imports (see graph 5). In 2013, the value of exports of services of the Sudan increased substantially by 19.2 percent, reaching 1.3 bln US$, while its imports of services decreased moderately by 9.2 percent and reached 1.8 bln US$ (see graph 2). There was a moderate trade in services deficit of 542.7 mln US$. See footnote*.

Graph 1: Total merchandise trade, by value
(Bln US$ by year)

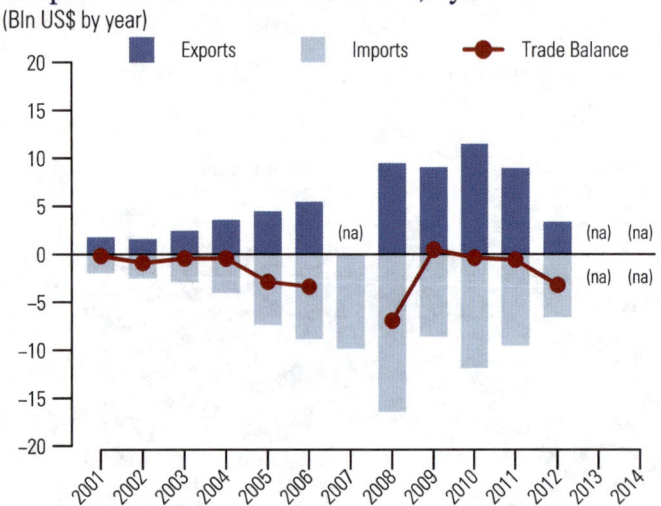

Graph 2: Total services trade, by value
(Bln US$ by year)

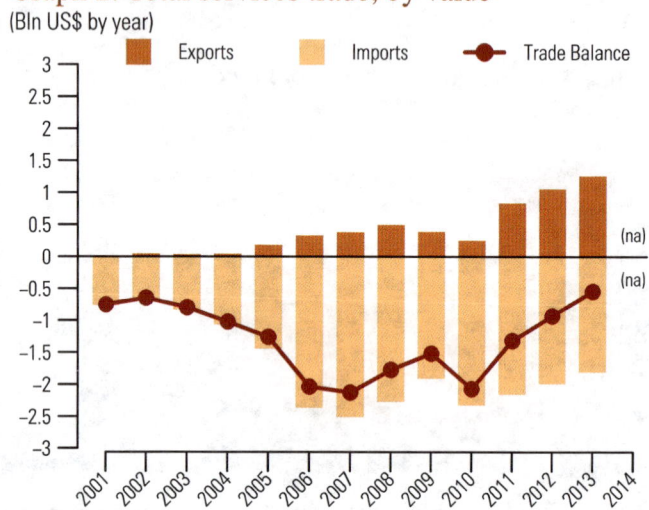

Exports Profile:
"Not classified elsewhere in the SITC" (SITC section 9), "Food, animals + beverages, tobacco" (SITC section 0+1) and "Crude materials + anim. & veg. oils" (SITC section 2+4) were the largest commodity groups for exports in 2012, representing respectively 64.1, 15.3 and 9.3 percent of exported goods (see table 2). From 2010 to 2012, the largest export commodity was "Petroleum oils and oils obtained from bituminous minerals, crude" (HS code 2709) (see table 1). The top three destinations for merchandise exports were China, the United Arab Emirates and Areas nes, accounting for respectively 62.0, 17.0 and 5.0 percent of total exports. "Travel" (EBOPS code 236) accounted for the largest share of exports of services in 2013 at 773.0 mln US$, followed by "Government services, n.i.e." (EBOPS code 291) at 238.9 mln US$ and "Transportation" (EBOPS code 205) at 141.1 mln US$ (see graph 3).

Graph 3: Exports of services by EBOPS category
(% share in 2013)

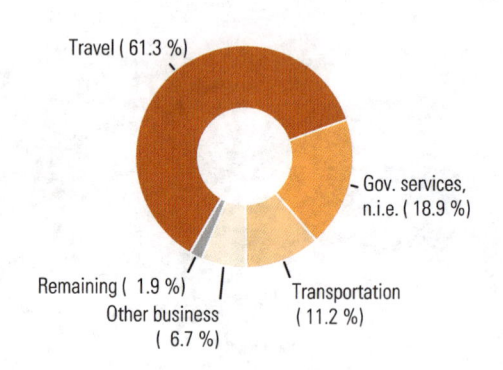

- Travel (61.3 %)
- Gov. services, n.i.e. (18.9 %)
- Transportation (11.2 %)
- Other business (6.7 %)
- Remaining (1.9 %)

Table 1: Top 10 export commodities 2010 to 2012

HS code	4-digit heading of Harmonized System 2007	Value (million US$) 2010	2011	2012	Unit value 2010	2011	2012	Unit	SITC code
	All Commodities	11529.3	8981.7	3383.9					
2709	Petroleum oils and oils obtained from bituminous minerals, crude	9683.5	7200.6	145.2	0.9	1.6	0.5	US$/kg	333
7108	Gold (including gold plated with platinum)	1160.3	827.9	2167.4	39.1	61.8	49.6	thsd US$/kg	971
0104	Live sheep and goats	130.6	257.6	284.1	228.1			US$/unit	001
1207	Other oil seeds and oleaginous fruits, whether or not broken	199.8	193.6	191.9	1.1	1.0	1.0	US$/kg	222
2710	Petroleum oils, other than crude	98.6	205.6	0.1	0.5	1.0	0.2	US$/kg	334
1301	Lac; natural gums, resins, gum-resins and oleoresins (for example, balsams)	67.8	69.8	65.4	1.3	1.4		US$/kg	292
2707	Oils and other products of high temperature coal tar	...	0.1	110.8		0.1	1.2	US$/kg	335
0102	Live bovine animals	2.1	4.1	85.8					001
5201	Cotton, not carded or combed	39.5	26.0	21.1	1.6	3.7	6.5	US$/kg	263
0204	Meat of sheep or goats, fresh, chilled or frozen	29.6	18.0	27.8	6.7	3.9	6.0	US$/kg	012

*Data up to 2011 refer to former Sudan (including South Sudan) and data beginning 2012 is attributed to Sudan without including South Sudan.

Sudan

Services Imports and Exports: EBOPS 2002 categories

Table 2: Merchandise exports by SITC
(Value in million US$, growth and shares in percentage)

SITC	2012	Avg. Growth rates 2008-2012	Avg. Growth rates 2011-2012	2012 share
Total	3383.9	-22.7	-62.3	100.0
0+1	519.1	42.4	41.4	15.3
2+4	314.4	-4.1	-6.2	9.3
3	256.1	-58.9	-96.5	7.6
5	78.5	190.9	653.0	2.3
6	36.0	6.7	24.4	1.1
7	5.9	-35.1	27.3	0.2
8	4.5	10.4	504.4	0.1
9	2169.3	409.4	161.9	64.1

Table 3: Merchandise imports by SITC
(Value in million US$, growth and shares in percentage)

SITC	2012	Avg. Growth rates 2008-2012	Avg. Growth rates 2011-2012	2012 share
Total	6580.6	-20.4	-31.1	100.0
0+1	940.7	-5.7	-40.9	14.3
2+4	269.0	35.0	-46.2	4.1
3	563.4	150.5	-40.4	8.6
5	797.6	19.2	-34.9	12.1
6	1152.5	-3.9	-21.1	17.5
7	1873.6	-32.0	-39.7	28.5
8	622.5	-1.2	-9.4	9.5
9	361.4	-45.0	1226.2	5.5

SITC Legend

SITC Code	Description
Total	All commodities
0+1	Food, animals + beverages, tobacco
2+4	Crude materials + anim. & veg. oils
3	Mineral fuels, lubricants
5	Chemicals
6	Goods classified chiefly by material
7	Machinery and transport equipment
8	Miscellaneous manufactured articles
9	Not classified elsewhere in the SITC

Graph 4: Merchandise trade balance
(Bln US$ by MDG Regions in 2012)

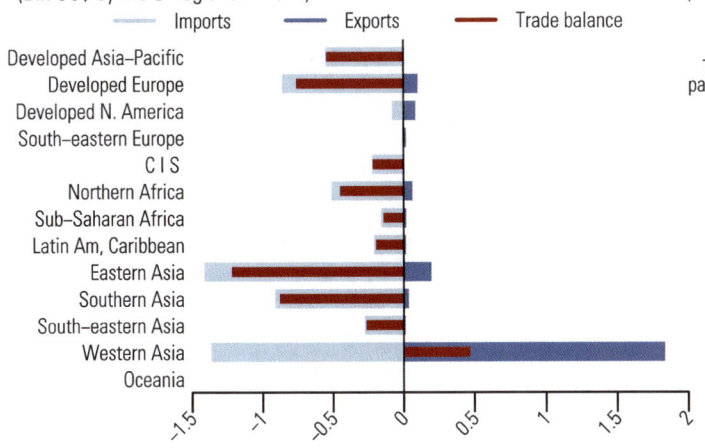

Graph 5: Partner concentration of merchandise trade
(Cumulative share by ranked partners in 2012)

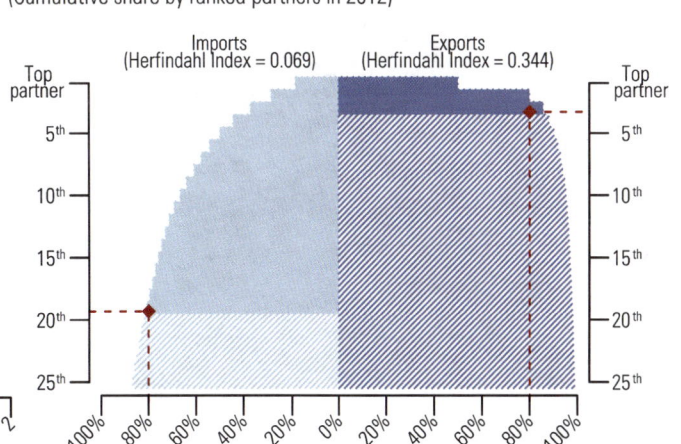

Imports (Herfindahl Index = 0.069)
Exports (Herfindahl Index = 0.344)

Graph 6: Imports of services by EBOPS category
(% share in 2013)

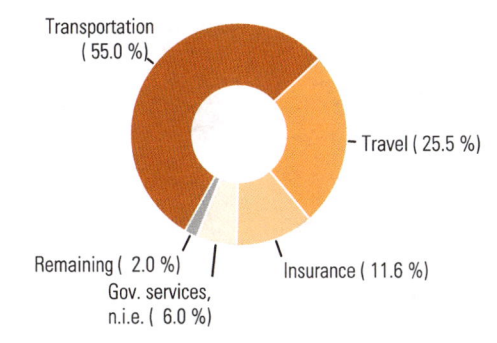

- Transportation (55.0 %)
- Travel (25.5 %)
- Insurance (11.6 %)
- Gov. services, n.i.e. (6.0 %)
- Remaining (2.0 %)

Imports Profile:

"Machinery and transport equipment" (SITC section 7), "Goods classified chiefly by material" (SITC section 6) and "Food, animals + beverages, tobacco" (SITC section 0+1) were the largest commodity groups for imports in 2012, representing respectively 28.5, 17.5 and 14.3 percent of imported goods (see table 3). From 2010 to 2012, the largest import commodity was "Petroleum oils, other than crude" (HS code 2710) (see table 4). The top three partners for merchandise imports were China, the United Arab Emirates and Saudi Arabia, accounting for respectively 19.2, 9.2 and 7.1 percent of total imports. "Transportation" (EBOPS code 205) accounted for the largest share of imports of services in 2013 at 991.8 mln US$, followed by "Travel" (EBOPS code 236) at 459.6 mln US$ and "Insurance services" (EBOPS code 253) at 209.7 mln US$ (see graph 6).

Table 4: Top 10 import commodities 2010 to 2012

HS code	4-digit heading of Harmonized System 2007	2010	2011	2012	2010	2011	2012	Unit	SITC code
	All Commodities	11874.8	9546.3	6580.6					
2710	Petroleum oils, other than crude	697.4	821.7	378.9	1.2	1.1	1.0	US$/kg	334
1001	Wheat and meslin	1290.1	580.1	0.0	1.0	0.4	0.3	US$/kg	041
1701	Cane or beet sugar and chemically pure sucrose, in solid form	388.4	409.3	443.6	0.5	0.9	0.8	US$/kg	061
8703	Motor cars and other motor vehicles principally designed for the transport	371.3	308.6	197.5	1.8	0.5	9.6	thsd US$/unit	781
8704	Motor vehicles for the transport of goods	393.7	331.6	121.8	2.0	2.3		thsd US$/unit	782
8517	Electrical apparatus for line telephony or line telegraphy	244.6	228.0	166.6					764
8708	Parts and accessories of the motor vehicles of headings 87.01 to 87.05	365.9	162.4	95.7	9.9	4.3	2.4	US$/kg	784
3003	Medicaments (excluding goods of heading 30.02, 30.05 or 30.06)	239.6	157.6	177.1	15.1	9.6	52.6	US$/kg	542
1513	Coconut (copra), palm kernel or babassu oil	509.6	7.2	2.8		0.9	1.1	US$/kg	422
2714	Bitumen and asphalt, natural	10.5	323.9	171.0	0.4	5.9	1.0	US$/kg	278

Suriname

Goods Imports: CIF, by origin   **Goods Exports:** FOB, by last known destination   **Trade System:** General

Overview:

In 2011, the value of merchandise exports of Suriname increased substantially by 21.8 percent to reach 2.5 bln US$, while its merchandise imports increased substantially by 17.2 percent to reach 1.6 bln US$ (see graph 1, table 2 and table 3). The merchandise trade balance recorded a moderate surplus of 829.0 mln US$ (see graph 1). The largest merchandise trade balance was with MDG Western Asia at 638.1 mln US$ (see graph 4). Merchandise exports in Suriname were diversified amongst partners; imports were moderately concentrated. The top 6 partners accounted for 80 percent or more of exports and 6 partners accounted for 80 percent or more of imports (see graph 5). In 2013, the value of exports of services of Suriname increased slightly by 1.8 percent, reaching 178.5 mln US$, while its imports of services decreased moderately by 8.9 percent and reached 541.5 mln US$ (see graph 2). There was a large trade in services deficit of 363.0 mln US$.

Graph 1: Total merchandise trade, by value
(Bln US$ by year)

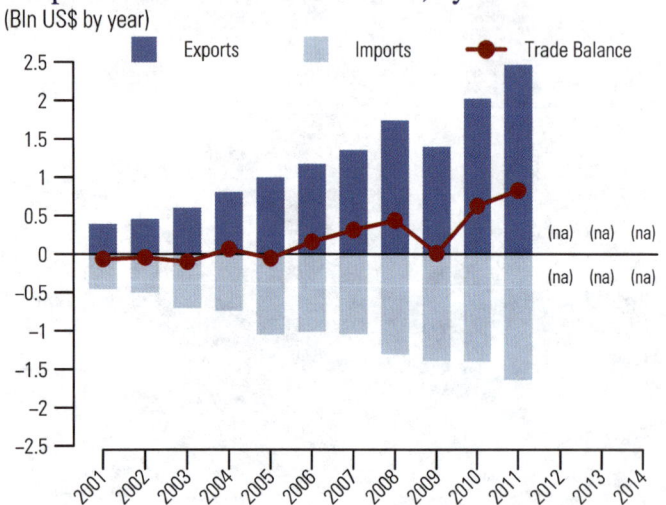

Graph 2: Total services trade, by value
(Mln US$ by year)

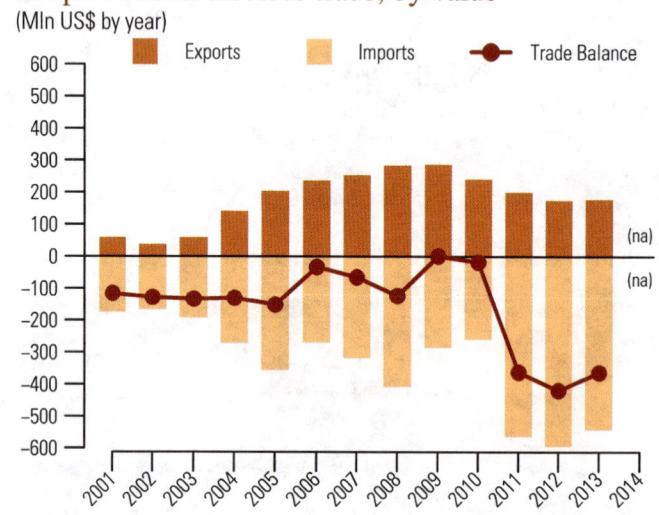

Exports Profile:

"Not classified elsewhere in the SITC" (SITC section 9), "Mineral fuels, lubricants" (SITC section 3) and "Food, animals + beverages, tobacco" (SITC section 0+1) were the largest commodity groups for exports in 2011, representing respectively 82.1, 9.0 and 3.6 percent of exported goods (see table 2). From 2009 to 2011, the largest export commodity was "Commodities not elsewhere specified" (HS code 9999) (see table 1). The top three destinations for merchandise exports were Canada, the United Arab Emirates and Belgium, accounting for respectively 23.9, 17.5 and 11.5 percent of total exports. "Travel" (EBOPS code 236) accounted for the largest share of exports of services in 2013 at 84.1 mln US$, followed by "Other business services" (EBOPS code 268) at 35.2 mln US$ and "Transportation" (EBOPS code 205) at 30.5 mln US$ (see graph 3).

Graph 3: Exports of services by EBOPS category
(% share in 2013)

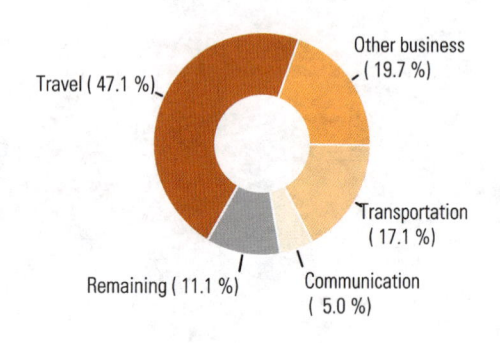

- Travel (47.1 %)
- Other business (19.7 %)
- Transportation (17.1 %)
- Communication (5.0 %)
- Remaining (11.1 %)

Table 1: Top 10 export commodities 2009 to 2011

HS code	4-digit heading of Harmonized System 1996	Value (million US$) 2009	2010	2011	Unit value 2009	2010	2011	Unit	SITC code
	All Commodities	1 401.8	2 025.6	2 466.9					
9999	Commodities not elsewhere specified	1 222.8	1 659.3	2 026.4					931
2710	Oils petroleum, bituminous, distillates, except crude	64.4	263.0	219.2	0.3	0.5	0.7	US$/kg	334
1006	Rice	21.2	37.8	33.7	0.4	0.4	0.7	US$/kg	042
8431	Parts for use with lifting, moving machinery	2.3	5.5	31.3	5.5	10.7	29.7	US$/kg	723
2202	Waters, non-alcoholic sweetened or flavoured beverages	5.4	4.6	21.7	0.6	0.4	1.5	US$/litre	111
2208	Liqueur, spirits and undenatured ethyl alcohol <80%	8.6	0.1	11.9	4.1	2.8	2.0	US$/litre	112
4403	Wood in the rough or roughly squared	0.9	3.6	8.9		368.9	390.0	US$/m^3	247
1507	Soya-bean oil, fractions, not chemically modified	5.1	0.0	6.4	1.2	0.9	1.5	US$/kg	421
7204	Ferrous waste or scrap, ingots or iron or steel	2.0	1.9	4.2	0.1	0.1	0.1	US$/kg	282
7304	Tube or hollow profile, seamless iron/steel not cast	0.0	0.1	7.8	1.2	3.9	2.5	US$/kg	679

Source: UN Comtrade and UN ServiceTrade

Suriname

Services Imports and Exports: EBOPS 2002 categories

Table 2: Merchandise exports by SITC
(Value in million US$, growth and shares in percentage)

SITC	2011	Avg. Growth rates 2007-2011	Avg. Growth rates 2010-2011	2011 share
Total	2 466.9	16.1	21.8	100.0
0+1	89.3	22.3	83.6	3.6
2+4	32.3	30.8	117.9	1.3
3	220.9	39.2	-16.2	9.0
5	7.0	15.4	89.5	0.3
6	18.6	43.9	262.2	0.8
7	58.9	25.7	176.5	2.4
8	13.5	33.6	48.7	0.5
9	2 026.4	13.7	22.1	82.1

Table 3: Merchandise imports by SITC
(Value in million US$, growth and shares in percentage)

SITC	2011	Avg. Growth rates 2007-2011	Avg. Growth rates 2010-2011	2011 share
Total	1 637.8	11.9	17.2	100.0
0+1	213.8	19.9	10.0	13.1
2+4	35.2	22.3	-4.3	2.2
3	382.9	23.1	45.0	23.4
5	231.3	49.1	42.3	14.1
6	230.6	21.3	4.9	14.1
7	411.1	10.7	5.2	25.1
8	124.8	15.8	2.0	7.6
9	8.2	-58.0	20.9	0.5

SITC Legend

SITC Code	Description
Total	All commodities
0+1	Food, animals + beverages, tobacco
2+4	Crude materials + anim. & veg. oils
3	Mineral fuels, lubricants
5	Chemicals
6	Goods classified chiefly by material
7	Machinery and transport equipment
8	Miscellaneous manufactured articles
9	Not classified elsewhere in the SITC

Graph 4: Merchandise trade balance
(Mln US$ by MDG Regions in 2011)

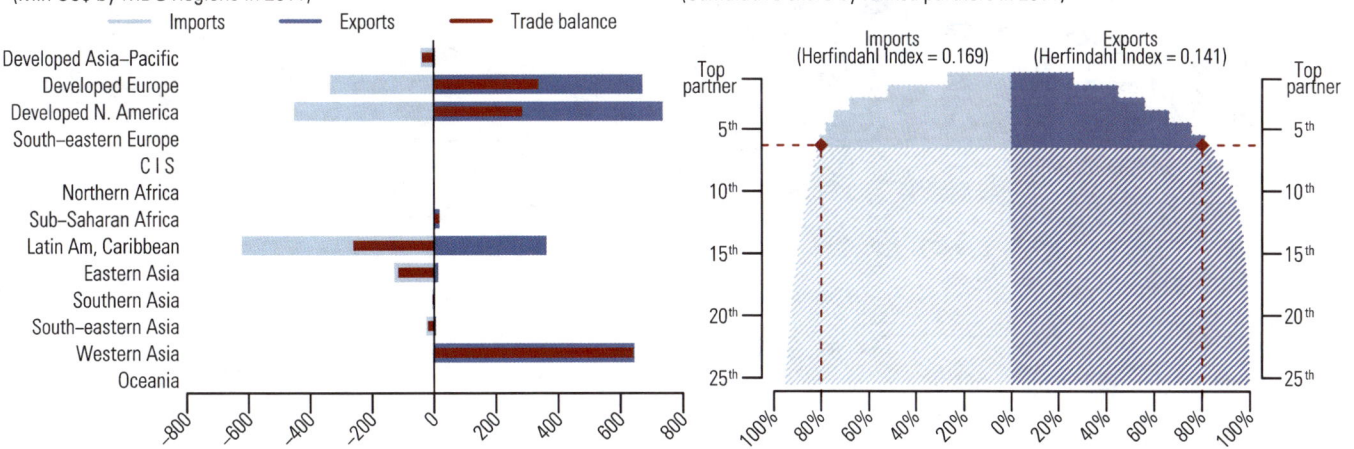

Graph 5: Partner concentration of merchandise trade
(Cumulative share by ranked partners in 2011)

Imports (Herfindahl Index = 0.169)
Exports (Herfindahl Index = 0.141)

Graph 6: Imports of services by EBOPS category
(% share in 2013)

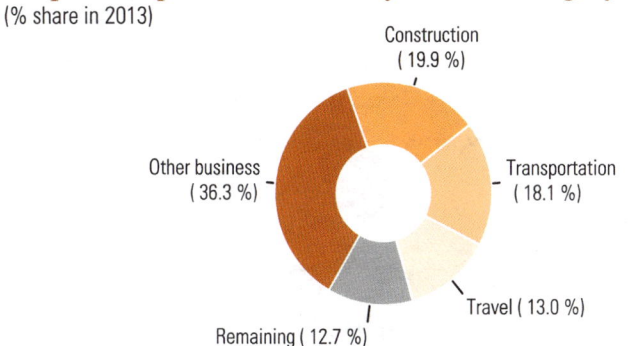

- Construction (19.9 %)
- Transportation (18.1 %)
- Travel (13.0 %)
- Remaining (12.7 %)
- Other business (36.3 %)

Imports Profile:

"Machinery and transport equipment" (SITC section 7), "Mineral fuels, lubricants" (SITC section 3) and "Chemicals" (SITC section 5) were the largest commodity groups for imports in 2011, representing respectively 25.1, 23.4 and 14.1 percent of imported goods (see table 3). From 2009 to 2011, the largest import commodity was "Oils petroleum, bituminous, distillates, except crude" (HS code 2710) (see table 4). The top three partners for merchandise imports were the United States, Trinidad and Tobago and the Netherlands, accounting for respectively 26.4, 23.1 and 17.4 percent of total imports. "Other business services" (EBOPS code 268) accounted for the largest share of imports of services in 2013 at 196.5 mln US$, followed by "Construction services" (EBOPS code 249) at 107.9 mln US$ and "Transportation" (EBOPS code 205) at 98.1 mln US$ (see graph 6).

Table 4: Top 10 import commodities 2009 to 2011

HS code	4-digit heading of Harmonized System 1996	2009	2010	2011	2009	2010	2011	Unit	SITC code
	All Commodities	1 390.1	1 397.5	1 637.8					
2710	Oils petroleum, bituminous, distillates, except crude	208.4	255.5	370.1	0.7	0.7	0.8	US$/kg	334
2815	Hydroxides and peroxides of sodium and potassium	56.9	23.4	78.7	0.2	0.1	0.2	US$/kg	522
8703	Motor vehicles for transport of persons (except buses)	44.0	46.2	53.9		17.0		thsd US$/unit	781
8429	Self-propelled earth moving, road making, etc machines	31.9	27.1	52.6		62.3	69.2	thsd US$/unit	723
8704	Motor vehicles for the transport of goods	41.3	29.8	25.1					782
8431	Parts for use with lifting, moving machinery	51.2	19.9	19.1	23.7	8.3	6.8	US$/kg	723
2523	Cement (portland, aluminous, slag or hydraulic)	27.5	23.5	22.4	0.1	0.1	0.1	US$/kg	661
2402	Cigars, cigarettes etc, tobacco or tobacco substitute	18.3	21.6	20.8	19.0	25.7	28.5	US$/kg	122
8413	Pumps for liquids	22.2	16.4	16.9					742
0207	Meat, edible offal of domestic poultry	16.1	17.4	21.4	1.0	1.0	1.2	US$/kg	012

Source: UN Comtrade and UN ServiceTrade

Sweden

Goods Imports: CIF, by origin/consignment for intra-eu   **Goods Exports:** FOB, by last known destination   **Trade System:** Special

Overview:
In 2014, the value of merchandise exports of Sweden decreased slightly by 1.8 percent to reach 164.5 bln US$, while its merchandise imports increased slightly by 1.2 percent to reach 162.6 bln US$ (see graph 1, table 2 and table 3). The merchandise trade balance recorded a relatively small surplus of 1.9 bln US$ (see graph 1). The largest merchandise trade balance was with MDG Developed Europe at -13.8 bln US$ (see graph 4). Merchandise exports in Sweden were diversified amongst partners; imports were also diversified. The top 20 partners accounted for 80 percent or more of exports and 14 partners accounted for 80 percent or more of imports (see graph 5). In 2012, the value of exports of services of Sweden increased slightly by 0.1 percent, reaching 71.0 bln US$, while its imports of services increased slightly by 0.2 percent and reached 54.4 bln US$ (see graph 2). There was a moderate trade in services surplus of 16.6 bln US$.

Graph 1: Total merchandise trade, by value
(Bln US$ by year)

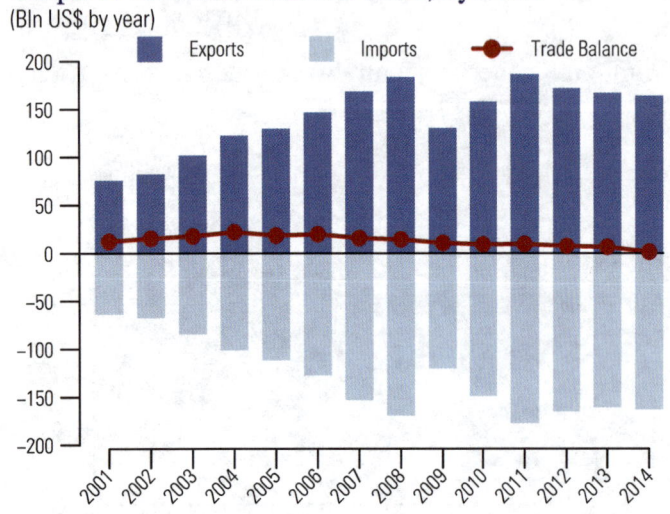

Graph 2: Total services trade, by value
(Bln US$ by year)

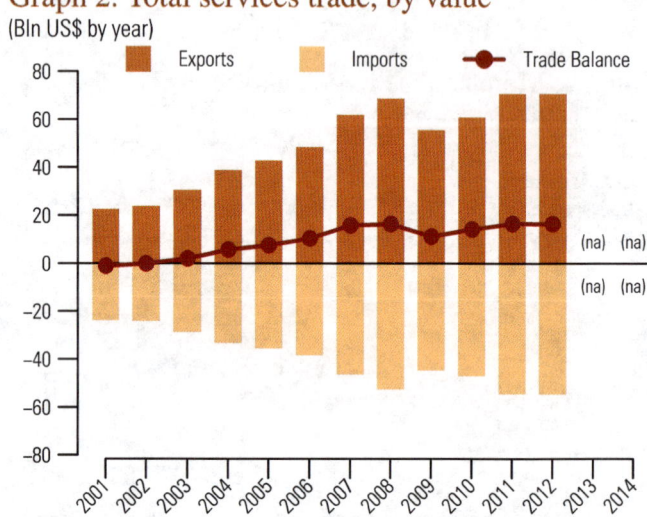

Exports Profile:
"Machinery and transport equipment" (SITC section 7), "Goods classified chiefly by material" (SITC section 6) and "Chemicals" (SITC section 5) were the largest commodity groups for exports in 2014, representing respectively 36.4, 17.9 and 11.4 percent of exported goods (see table 2). From 2012 to 2014, the largest export commodity was "Petroleum oils, other than crude" (HS code 2710) (see table 1). The top three destinations for merchandise exports were Norway, Germany and the United Kingdom, accounting for respectively 10.4, 9.6 and 7.0 percent of total exports. "Other business services" (EBOPS code 268) accounted for the largest share of exports of services in 2012 at 29.0 bln US$, followed by "Transportation" (EBOPS code 205) at 11.0 bln US$ and "Travel" (EBOPS code 236) at 10.4 bln US$ (see graph 3).

Graph 3: Exports of services by EBOPS category
(% share in 2012)

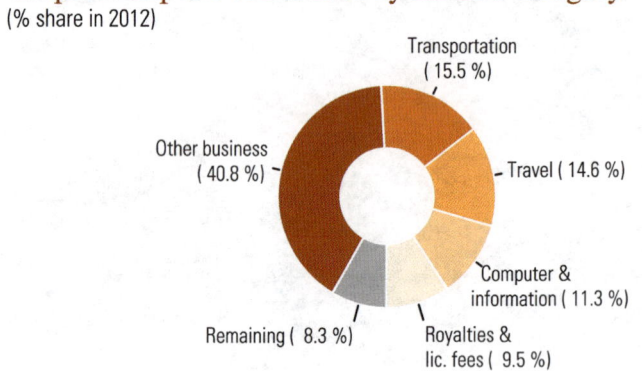

- Transportation (15.5 %)
- Travel (14.6 %)
- Computer & information (11.3 %)
- Royalties & lic. fees (9.5 %)
- Remaining (8.3 %)
- Other business (40.8 %)

Table 1: Top 10 export commodities 2012 to 2014

HS code	4-digit heading of Harmonized System 2012	Value (million US$) 2012	2013	2014	Unit value 2012	2013	2014	Unit	SITC code
	All Commodities	172 439.2	167 494.7	164 460.5					
2710	Petroleum oils, other than crude	13 558.0	10 836.5	10 968.0		0.9	0.8	US$/kg	334
9999	Commodities not specified according to kind	8 086.5	8 226.0	7 286.4					931
8517	Electrical apparatus for line telephony or line telegraphy	6 621.5	6 381.7	6 688.7					764
3004	Medicaments (excluding goods of heading 30.02, 30.05 or 30.06)	6 254.9	6 297.6	6 354.4	120.1	130.6		US$/kg	542
8708	Parts and accessories of the motor vehicles of headings 87.01 to 87.05	5 182.9	5 597.0	5 210.4	9.0	9.3	9.4	US$/kg	784
8703	Motor cars and other motor vehicles principally designed for the transport	5 338.3	5 204.8	4 927.1	29.2	26.3	25.1	thsd US$/unit	781
4407	Wood sawn or chipped lengthwise, sliced or peeled	3 173.9	3 288.5	3 513.7	271.5	285.6	289.3	US$/m³	248
4810	Paper and paperboard, coated on one or both sides with kaolin	3 160.5	3 312.8	3 193.7	1.0	1.1	1.0	US$/kg	641
2601	Iron ores and concentrates, including roasted iron pyrites	3 357.5	2 942.3	2 792.3	0.1	0.1	0.1	US$/kg	281
0302	Fish, fresh or chilled, excluding fish fillets	1 908.7	2 608.2	2 919.3					034

Sweden

Services Imports and Exports: EBOPS 2002 categories

Table 2: Merchandise exports by SITC
(Value in million US$, growth and shares in percentage)

SITC	2014	Avg. Growth rates 2010-2014	2013-2014	2014 share
Total	164 460.5	0.9	-1.8	100.0
0+1	9 679.9	7.9	4.4	5.9
2+4	11 592.9	1.6	2.9	7.0
3	13 295.1	4.7	1.1	8.1
5	18 712.2	0.9	-1.3	11.4
6	29 499.9	-0.8	-1.9	17.9
7	59 812.5	0.2	-2.8	36.4
8	13 899.0	0.3	-2.4	8.5
9	7 969.0	0.5	-11.8	4.8

Table 3: Merchandise imports by SITC
(Value in million US$, growth and shares in percentage)

SITC	2014	Avg. Growth rates 2010-2014	2013-2014	2014 share
Total	162 583.7	2.2	1.2	100.0
0+1	16 208.4	7.2	2.8	10.0
2+4	5 290.5	-0.4	-5.2	3.3
3	22 248.7	2.8	-3.2	13.7
5	18 147.2	2.9	3.3	11.2
6	19 785.7	-0.4	1.2	12.2
7	56 629.7	1.4	2.1	34.8
8	18 098.0	2.7	1.5	11.1
9	6 175.5	4.4	5.2	3.8

SITC Legend

SITC Code	Description
Total	All commodities
0+1	Food, animals + beverages, tobacco
2+4	Crude materials + anim. & veg. oils
3	Mineral fuels, lubricants
5	Chemicals
6	Goods classified chiefly by material
7	Machinery and transport equipment
8	Miscellaneous manufactured articles
9	Not classified elsewhere in the SITC

Graph 4: Merchandise trade balance
(Bln US$ by MDG Regions in 2014)

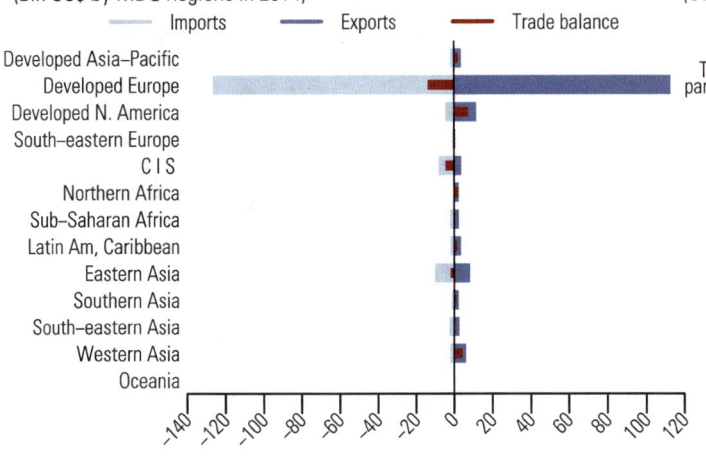

Graph 5: Partner concentration of merchandise trade
(Cumulative share by ranked partners in 2014)

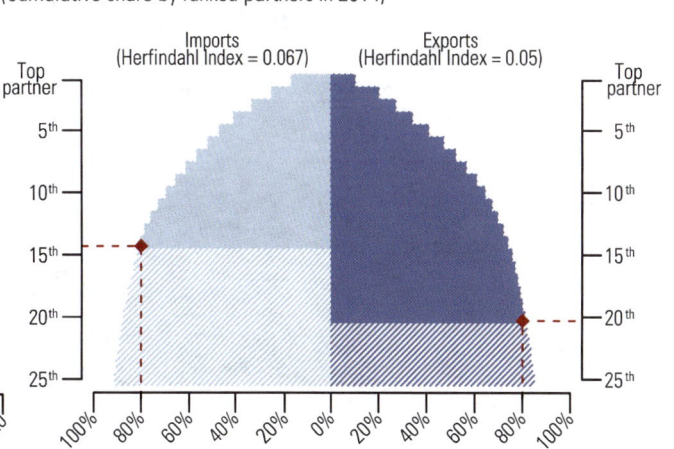

Imports (Herfindahl Index = 0.067)
Exports (Herfindahl Index = 0.05)

Graph 6: Imports of services by EBOPS category
(% share in 2012)

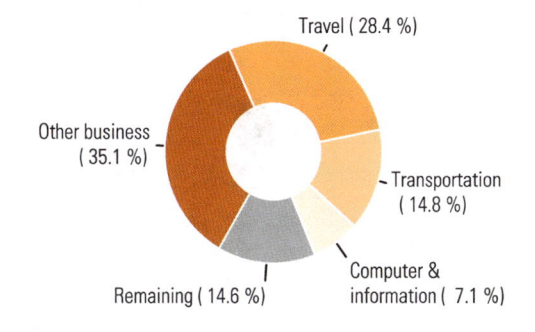

- Travel (28.4 %)
- Other business (35.1 %)
- Remaining (14.6 %)
- Computer & information (7.1 %)
- Transportation (14.8 %)

Imports Profile:

"Machinery and transport equipment" (SITC section 7), "Mineral fuels, lubricants" (SITC section 3) and "Goods classified chiefly by material" (SITC section 6) were the largest commodity groups for imports in 2014, representing respectively 34.8, 13.7 and 12.2 percent of imported goods (see table 3). From 2012 to 2014, the largest import commodity was "Petroleum oils and oils obtained from bituminous minerals, crude" (HS code 2709) (see table 4). The top three partners for merchandise imports were Germany, Norway and Denmark, accounting for respectively 17.3, 8.7 and 8.0 percent of total imports. "Other business services" (EBOPS code 268) accounted for the largest share of imports of services in 2012 at 19.1 bln US$, followed by "Travel" (EBOPS code 236) at 15.5 bln US$ and "Transportation" (EBOPS code 205) at 8.0 bln US$ (see graph 6).

Table 4: Top 10 import commodities 2012 to 2014

HS code	4-digit heading of Harmonized System 2012	Value (million US$) 2012	2013	2014	Unit value 2012	2013	2014	Unit	SITC code
	All Commodities	164 542.4	160 588.8	162 583.7					
2709	Petroleum oils and oils obtained from bituminous minerals, crude	17 026.8	12 751.8	12 491.9	0.8	0.8	0.7	US$/kg	333
8703	Motor cars and other motor vehicles principally designed for the transport	6 906.0	7 364.9	8 002.6	22.7	22.2	20.5	thsd US$/unit	781
2710	Petroleum oils, other than crude	6 898.4	7 701.9	7 435.2		1.0	0.9	US$/kg	334
8517	Electrical apparatus for line telephony or line telegraphy	6 063.9	6 286.7	6 763.8					764
9999	Commodities not specified according to kind	5 252.2	5 819.3	6 125.0					931
8708	Parts and accessories of the motor vehicles of headings 87.01 to 87.05	4 922.2	5 065.0	5 202.6	8.0	8.0	8.8	US$/kg	784
8471	Automatic data processing machines and units thereof	3 814.6	4 039.4	4 018.1	226.9	258.1	243.0	US$/unit	752
3004	Medicaments (excluding goods of heading 30.02, 30.05 or 30.06)	3 047.4	3 163.7	3 025.1	85.3	82.9		US$/kg	542
0302	Fish, fresh or chilled, excluding fish fillets	2 007.4	2 766.6	3 006.1					034
8528	Reception apparatus for television	1 487.4	1 404.1	1 467.6	320.3	337.6	322.5	US$/unit	761

2014 International Trade Statistics Yearbook, Vol. I — Source: UN Comtrade and UN ServiceTrade

Switzerland-Liechtenstein

Goods Imports: CIF, by origin **Goods Exports:** FOB, by last known destination **Trade System:** Special

Overview:
In 2014, the value of merchandise exports of Switzerland increased slightly by 4.2 percent to reach 238.8 bln US$, while its merchandise imports increased slightly by 0.9 percent to reach 202.7 bln US$ (see graph 1, table 2 and table 3). The merchandise trade balance recorded a relatively small surplus of 36.1 bln US$ (see graph 1). The largest merchandise trade balance was with MDG Developed North America at 20.6 bln US$ (see graph 4). Merchandise exports in Switzerland were diversified amongst partners; imports were also diversified. The top 18 partners accounted for 80 percent or more of exports and 12 partners accounted for 80 percent or more of imports (see graph 5). In 2012, the value of exports of services of Switzerland decreased slightly by 4.4 percent, reaching 90.8 bln US$, while its imports of services increased slightly by 3.6 percent and reached 46.9 bln US$ (see graph 2). There was a large trade in services surplus of 43.9 bln US$.

Graph 1: Total merchandise trade, by value
(Bln US$ by year)

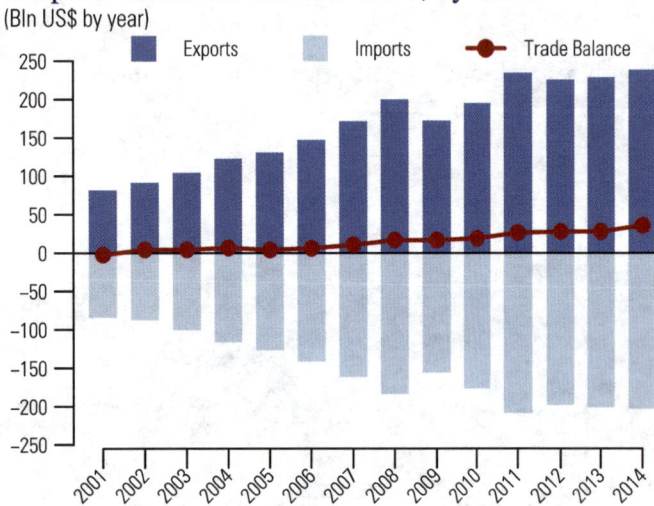

Graph 2: Total services trade, by value
(Bln US$ by year)

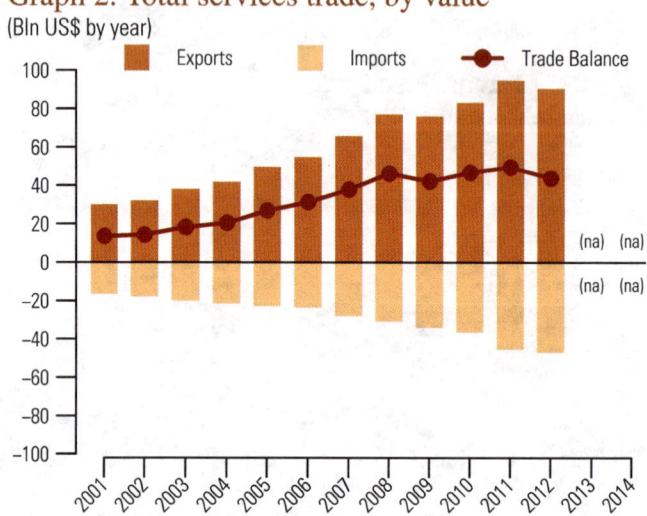

Exports Profile:
"Chemicals" (SITC section 5), "Miscellaneous manufactured articles" (SITC section 8) and "Machinery and transport equipment" (SITC section 7) were the largest commodity groups for exports in 2014, representing respectively 38.8, 25.3 and 18.9 percent of exported goods (see table 2). From 2012 to 2014, the largest export commodity was "Medicaments (excluding goods of heading 30.02, 30.05 or 30.06)" (HS code 3004) (see table 1). The top three destinations for merchandise exports were Germany, the United States and France, accounting for respectively 18.8, 12.0 and 7.1 percent of total exports. "Other business services" (EBOPS code 268) accounted for the largest share of exports of services in 2012 at 23.4 bln US$, followed by "Royalties and license fees" (EBOPS code 266) at 20.5 bln US$ and "Financial services" (EBOPS code 260) at 16.1 bln US$ (see graph 3).

Graph 3: Exports of services by EBOPS category
(% share in 2012)

- Royalties & lic. fees (22.5 %)
- Financial (17.7 %)
- Travel (17.6 %)
- Transportation (6.9 %)
- Insurance (6.5 %)
- Remaining (3.0 %)
- Other business (25.8 %)

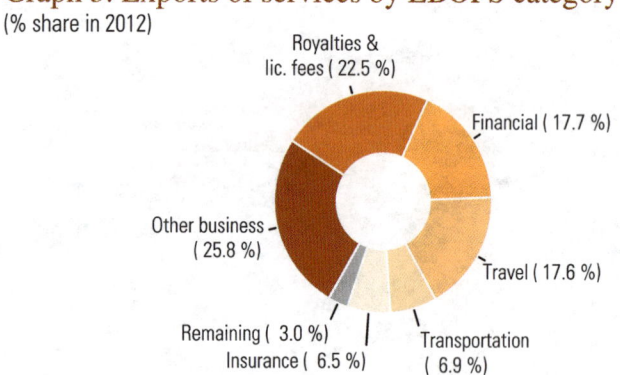

Table 1: Top 10 export commodities 2012 to 2014

HS code	4-digit heading of Harmonized System 2012	Value (million US$) 2012	2013	2014	Unit value 2012	2013	2014	Unit	SITC code
	All Commodities	225 942.6	229 156.6	238 809.5					
3004	Medicaments (excluding goods of heading 30.02, 30.05 or 30.06)	31 466.0	32 379.5	35 460.4	334.2	338.1	359.8	US$/kg	542
3002	Human blood; animal blood prepared for therapeutic uses	21 651.7	23 919.2	25 890.5	4.3	3.8	3.9	thsd US$/kg	541
9102	Wrist-watches, pocket-watches and other watches, of base metal	13 214.8	13 842.9	14 251.9	460.5	499.8	505.5	US$/unit	885
7113	Articles of jewellery and parts thereof, of precious metal	7 887.6	9 024.4	10 769.6	170.1	172.2	205.7	thsd US$/kg	897
9101	Wrist-watches, pocket-watches and other watches, precious metal	8 374.6	8 441.1	8 693.7	14.2	15.0	15.8	thsd US$/unit	885
9021	Orthopaedic appliances, including crutches, surgical belts and trusses	6 041.5	6 302.9	6 407.0					899
2933	Heterocyclic compounds with nitrogen hetero-atom(s) only	5 647.6	5 675.9	6 377.8			341.9	US$/kg	515
9999	Commodities not specified according to kind	3 954.6	4 384.1	4 103.6					931
2716	Electrical energy	6 428.4	2 528.1	2 445.2	72.4	66.1	58.1	US$/MWh	351
7110	Platinum, unwrought or in semi-manufactured forms, or in powder form	4 342.7	3 711.1	2 296.0	35.6	35.6	30.9	thsd US$/kg	681

Source: UN Comtrade and UN ServiceTrade

Switzerland-Liechtenstein

Services Imports and Exports: EBOPS 2002 categories

Table 2: Merchandise exports by SITC
(Value in million US$, growth and shares in percentage)

SITC	2014	Avg. Growth rates 2010-2014	Avg. Growth rates 2013-2014	2014 share
Total	238 809.5	5.1	4.2	100.0
0+1	9 395.9	6.6	3.5	3.9
2+4	2 043.9	-0.5	7.4	0.9
3	3 434.3	-11.2	-4.7	1.4
5	92 567.3	6.4	6.7	38.8
6	18 464.5	-1.5	-3.9	7.7
7	45 037.7	2.7	2.6	18.9
8	60 427.4	8.9	6.2	25.3
9	7 438.5	8.5	-5.1	3.1

Table 3: Merchandise imports by SITC
(Value in million US$, growth and shares in percentage)

SITC	2014	Avg. Growth rates 2010-2014	Avg. Growth rates 2013-2014	2014 share
Total	202 663.2	3.5	0.9	100.0
0+1	11 800.7	4.6	2.0	5.8
2+4	2 924.3	-1.2	-0.1	1.4
3	13 259.2	0.3	-15.3	6.5
5	48 769.4	6.8	4.7	24.1
6	28 706.4	2.7	0.6	14.2
7	52 471.9	2.7	2.5	25.9
8	43 725.8	4.4	3.3	21.6
9	1 005.6	-23.5	-53.1	0.5

SITC Legend

SITC Code	Description
Total	All commodities
0+1	Food, animals + beverages, tobacco
2+4	Crude materials + anim. & veg. oils
3	Mineral fuels, lubricants
5	Chemicals
6	Goods classified chiefly by material
7	Machinery and transport equipment
8	Miscellaneous manufactured articles
9	Not classified elsewhere in the SITC

Graph 4: Merchandise trade balance
(Bln US$ by MDG Regions in 2014)

Graph 5: Partner concentration of merchandise trade
(Cumulative share by ranked partners in 2014)

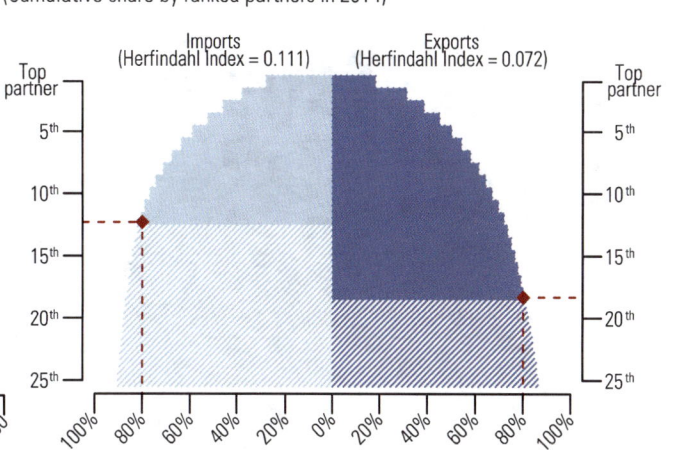

Imports (Herfindahl Index = 0.111)
Exports (Herfindahl Index = 0.072)

Graph 6: Imports of services by EBOPS category
(% share in 2012)

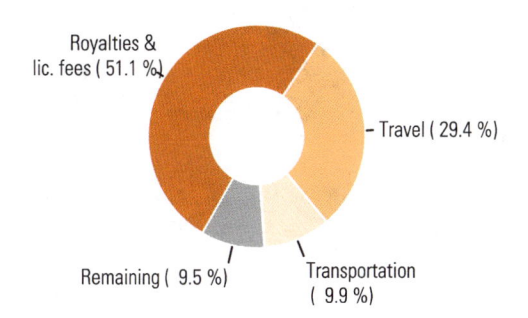

- Royalties & lic. fees (51.1 %)
- Travel (29.4 %)
- Transportation (9.9 %)
- Remaining (9.5 %)

Imports Profile:

"Machinery and transport equipment" (SITC section 7), "Chemicals" (SITC section 5) and "Miscellaneous manufactured articles" (SITC section 8) were the largest commodity groups for imports in 2014, representing respectively 25.9, 24.1 and 21.6 percent of imported goods (see table 3). From 2012 to 2014, the largest import commodity was "Medicaments (excluding goods of heading 30.02, 30.05 or 30.06)" (HS code 3004) (see table 4). The top three partners for merchandise imports were Germany, Italy and France, accounting for respectively 28.6, 10.0 and 8.3 percent of total imports. "Royalties and license fees" (EBOPS code 266) accounted for the largest share of imports of services in 2012 at 24.0 bln US$, followed by "Travel" (EBOPS code 236) at 13.8 bln US$ and "Transportation" (EBOPS code 205) at 4.7 bln US$ (see graph 6).

Table 4: Top 10 import commodities 2012 to 2014

HS code	4-digit heading of Harmonized System 2012	2012	2013	2014	2012	2013	2014	Unit	SITC code
	All Commodities	197 835.2	200 933.9	202 663.2					
3004	Medicaments (excluding goods of heading 30.02, 30.05 or 30.06)	14 586.4	15 364.2	15 839.0	*244.7*	*250.3*	*248.1*	US$/kg	542
8703	Motor cars and other motor vehicles principally designed for the transport	11 004.0	10 184.2	10 497.8	*29.4*	*29.7*	*31.1*	thsd US$/unit	781
7113	Articles of jewellery and parts thereof, of precious metal	8 978.8	8 731.5	9 131.5	*62.7*	*68.7*	*78.6*	thsd US$/kg	897
2710	Petroleum oils, other than crude	8 156.0	7 156.5	5 588.0	*1.0*	*1.0*	*1.0*	US$/kg	334
2933	Heterocyclic compounds with nitrogen hetero-atom(s) only	6 943.7	6 724.1	6 914.7			*188.3*	US$/kg	515
3002	Human blood; animal blood prepared for therapeutic uses	5 238.6	6 235.3	7 158.4	*886.1*	*847.8*	*936.1*	US$/kg	541
2709	Petroleum oils and oils obtained from bituminous minerals, crude	2 815.8	4 099.6	3 867.0	0.9	0.8	0.8	US$/kg	333
8471	Automatic data processing machines and units thereof	3 198.7	3 413.1	3 405.5	331.5	331.9	*326.5*	US$/unit	752
2716	Electrical energy	5 607.4	2 178.2	1 979.0	64.7	60.7	53.5	US$/MWh	351
8517	Electrical apparatus for line telephony or line telegraphy	2 911.3	3 174.8	3 179.0					764

Syrian Arab Republic

Goods Imports: CIF, by consignment **Goods Exports: FOB, by last known destination** **Trade System: Special**

Overview:
In 2010, the value of merchandise exports of the Syrian Arab Republic increased substantially by 17.1 percent to reach 11.4 bln US$, while its merchandise imports increased substantially by 13.7 percent to reach 17.6 bln US$ (see graph 1, table 2 and table 3). The merchandise trade balance recorded a moderate deficit of 6.2 bln US$ (see graph 1). The largest merchandise trade balance was with MDG Eastern Asia at -2.3 bln US$ (see graph 4). Merchandise exports in the Syrian Arab Republic were diversified amongst partners; imports were also diversified. The top 12 partners accounted for 80 percent or more of exports and 22 partners accounted for 80 percent or more of imports (see graph 5). In 2010, the value of exports of services of the Syrian Arab Republic increased substantially by 52.8 percent, reaching 7.3 bln US$, while its imports of services increased substantially by 23.2 percent and reached 3.5 bln US$ (see graph 2). There was a large trade in services surplus of 3.8 bln US$.

Graph 1: Total merchandise trade, by value
(Bln US$ by year)

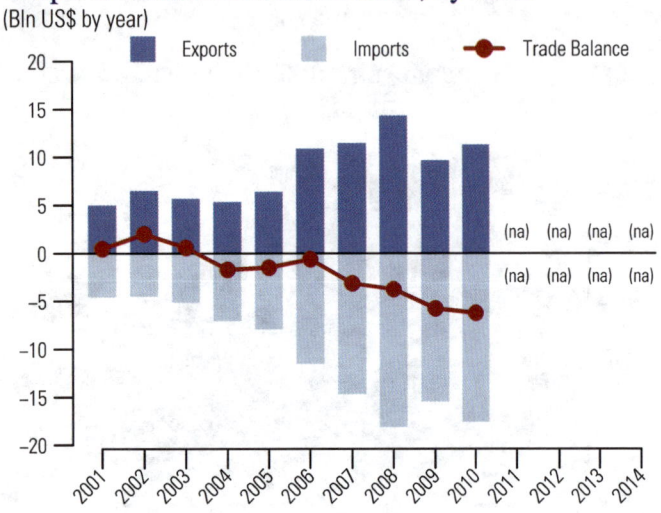

Graph 2: Total services trade, by value
(Bln US$ by year)

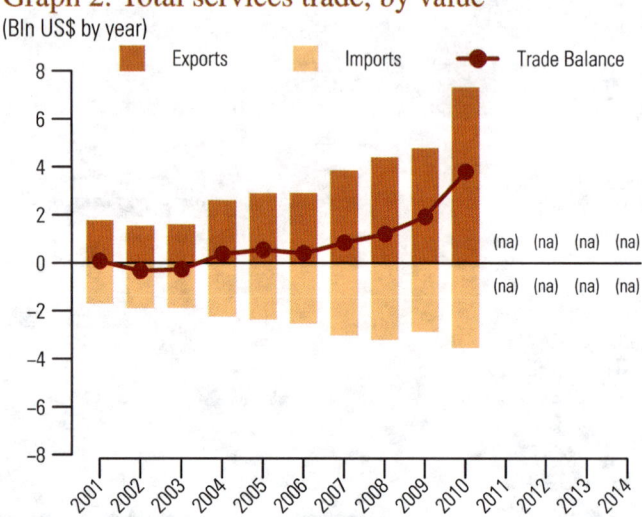

Exports Profile:
"Mineral fuels, lubricants" (SITC section 3), "Food, animals + beverages, tobacco" (SITC section 0+1) and "Goods classified chiefly by material" (SITC section 6) were the largest commodity groups for exports in 2010, representing respectively 49.9, 19.9 and 10.0 percent of exported goods (see table 2). From 2008 to 2010, the largest export commodity was "Petroleum oils and oils obtained from bituminous minerals, crude" (HS code 2709) (see table 1). The top three destinations for merchandise exports were Iraq, Germany and Italy, accounting for respectively 21.4, 11.5 and 9.3 percent of total exports. "Travel" (EBOPS code 236) accounted for the largest share of exports of services in 2010 at 6.2 bln US$, followed by "Transportation" (EBOPS code 205) at 529.2 mln US$ (see graph 3).

Graph 3: Exports of services by EBOPS category
(% share in 2010)

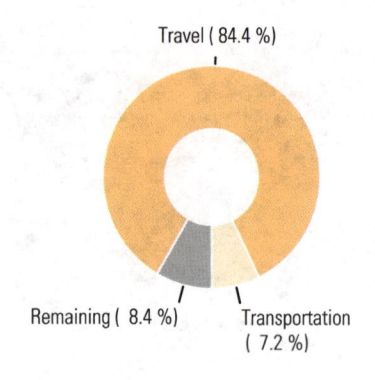

- Travel (84.4 %)
- Remaining (8.4 %)
- Transportation (7.2 %)

Table 1: Top 10 export commodities 2008 to 2010

HS code	4-digit heading of Harmonized System 2007	Value (million US$) 2008	2009	2010	Unit value 2008	2009	2010	Unit	SITC code
	All Commodities	14380.0	9693.8	11352.9					
2709	Petroleum oils and oils obtained from bituminous minerals, crude	4708.8	2865.5	4325.8	0.6	0.4	0.5	US$/kg	333
2710	Petroleum oils, other than crude	836.7	715.8	1160.8	0.7	0.5	0.7	US$/kg	334
2202	Waters with added sugar	843.5	159.0	105.5	0.5	0.3	0.2	US$/litre	111
5205	Cotton yarn (other than sewing thread), containing 85 % or more	608.2	137.6	191.2	3.2	2.1	2.9	US$/kg	651
5407	Woven fabrics of synthetic filament yarn	447.8	206.4	169.1	2.9	3.2	3.3	US$/kg	653
3402	Organic surface-active agents (other than soap)	292.7	188.6	328.0	1.2	0.8	0.9	US$/kg	554
2510	Natural calcium phosphates	388.9	139.7	202.5	0.2	0.1	0.1	US$/kg	272
8544	Insulated (including enamelled or anodised) wire, cable	350.0	232.3	37.6	5.6	5.6	4.4	US$/kg	773
0104	Live sheep and goats	236.2	137.4	216.1					001
0407	Birds' eggs, in shell, fresh, preserved or cooked	72.2	316.3	131.7	1.5	3.4	1.7	US$/kg	025

Syrian Arab Republic

Services Imports and Exports: EBOPS 2002 categories

Table 2: Merchandise exports by SITC
(Value in million US$, growth and shares in percentage)

SITC	2010	Avg. Growth rates 2006-2010	Avg. Growth rates 2009-2010	2010 share
Total	11 352.9	1.0	17.1	100.0
0+1	2 263.4	7.4	-10.9	19.9
2+4	527.7	0.0	35.9	4.6
3	5 663.5	6.5	54.5	49.9
5	703.1	7.0	2.3	6.2
6	1 140.0	-1.6	-3.9	10.0
7	243.4	-17.0	-37.7	2.1
8	808.3	-10.6	-0.2	7.1
9	3.5	-73.9	-85.5	0.0

Table 3: Merchandise imports by SITC
(Value in million US$, growth and shares in percentage)

SITC	2010	Avg. Growth rates 2006-2010	Avg. Growth rates 2009-2010	2010 share
Total	17 561.6	11.2	13.7	100.0
0+1	3 205.7	24.6	11.5	18.3
2+4	994.4	16.3	-15.2	5.7
3	3 451.1	2.6	74.4	19.7
5	2 290.1	16.8	7.1	13.0
6	3 686.3	11.2	-14.8	21.0
7	3 611.7	10.4	39.4	20.6
8	317.6	12.2	23.2	1.8
9	4.7	-62.0	-95.3	0.0

SITC Legend

SITC Code	Description
Total	All commodities
0+1	Food, animals + beverages, tobacco
2+4	Crude materials + anim. & veg. oils
3	Mineral fuels, lubricants
5	Chemicals
6	Goods classified chiefly by material
7	Machinery and transport equipment
8	Miscellaneous manufactured articles
9	Not classified elsewhere in the SITC

Graph 4: Merchandise trade balance
(Bln US$ by MDG Regions in 2010)

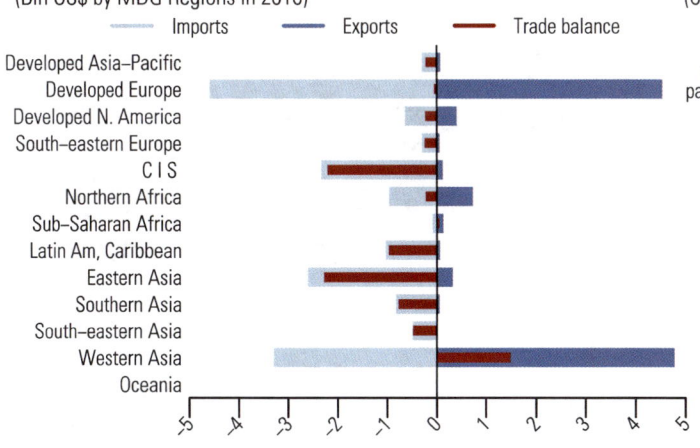

Graph 5: Partner concentration of merchandise trade
(Cumulative share by ranked partners in 2010)

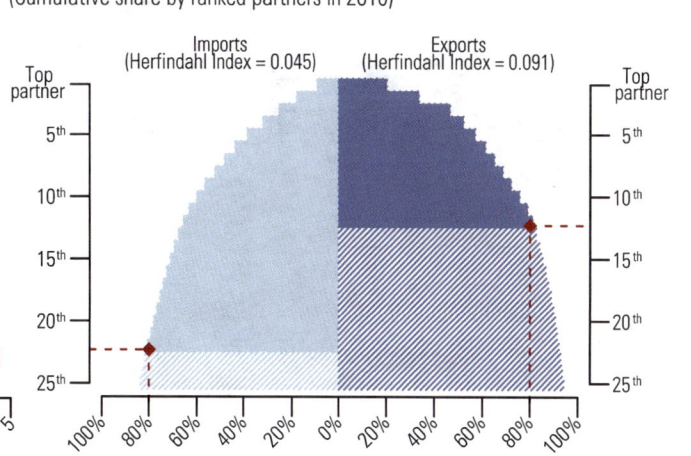

Imports (Herfindahl Index = 0.045)
Exports (Herfindahl Index = 0.091)

Graph 6: Imports of services by EBOPS category
(% share in 2010)

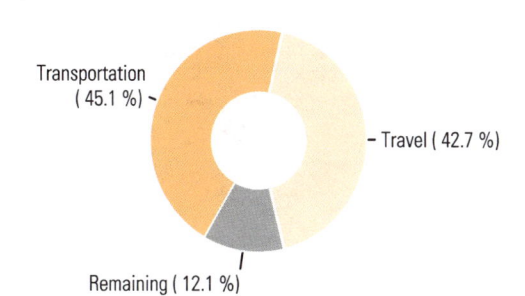

- Transportation (45.1 %)
- Travel (42.7 %)
- Remaining (12.1 %)

Imports Profile:
"Goods classified chiefly by material" (SITC section 6), "Machinery and transport equipment" (SITC section 7) and "Mineral fuels, lubricants" (SITC section 3) were the largest commodity groups for imports in 2010, representing respectively 21.0, 20.6 and 19.7 percent of imported goods (see table 3). From 2008 to 2010, the largest import commodity was "Petroleum oils, other than crude" (HS code 2710) (see table 4). The top three partners for merchandise imports were China, Ukraine and the Russian Federation, accounting for respectively 9.5, 8.9 and 8.6 percent of total imports. "Transportation" (EBOPS code 205) accounted for the largest share of imports of services in 2010 at 1.6 bln US$, followed by "Travel" (EBOPS code 236) at 1.5 bln US$ (see graph 6).

Table 4: Top 10 import commodities 2008 to 2010

HS code	4-digit heading of Harmonized System 2007	2008	2009	2010	2008	2009	2010	Unit	SITC code
	All Commodities	18 104.7	15 442.8	17 561.6					
2710	Petroleum oils, other than crude	5 363.2	1 638.5	3 002.9	0.8	0.5	0.7	US$/kg	334
7207	Semi-finished products of iron or non-alloy steel	1 128.3	855.3	552.2	0.6	0.4	0.5	US$/kg	672
8703	Motor cars and other motor vehicles principally designed for the transport	541.5	516.1	718.0	*13.6*		*15.6*	thsd US$/unit	781
1701	Cane or beet sugar and chemically pure sucrose, in solid form	314.6	530.0	740.6	0.4	0.4	0.6	US$/kg	061
1005	Maize (corn)	258.2	360.1	420.8	0.3	0.2	0.2	US$/kg	044
3901	Polymers of ethylene, in primary forms	343.1	323.0	353.6	1.6	1.1	1.3	US$/kg	571
7208	Flat-rolled products of iron or non-alloy steel	325.3	408.8	249.6	0.7	0.5	0.6	US$/kg	673
2711	Petroleum gases and other gaseous hydrocarbons	322.6	265.9	339.5	*0.8*	0.6	0.8	US$/kg	343
7210	Flat-rolled products of iron or non-alloy steel	246.0	348.8	188.7	0.9	0.7	0.8	US$/kg	674
1201	Soya beans, whether or not broken	166.9	340.0	222.5	0.3	0.4	0.4	US$/kg	222

Thailand

Goods Imports: CIF, by origin   **Goods Exports:** FOB, by last known destination   **Trade System:** Special

Overview:
In 2014, the value of merchandise exports of Thailand decreased slightly by 0.4 percent to reach 227.6 bln US$, while its merchandise imports decreased moderately by 9.1 percent to reach 227.9 bln US$ (see graph 1, table 2 and table 3). The merchandise trade balance recorded a relatively small deficit of 358.7 mln US$ (see graph 1). The largest merchandise trade balance was with MDG Western Asia at -18.1 bln US$ (see graph 4). Merchandise exports in Thailand were diversified amongst partners; imports were also diversified. The top 20 partners accounted for 80 percent or more of exports and 17 partners accounted for 80 percent or more of imports (see graph 5). In 2013, the value of exports of services of Thailand increased substantially by 19.1 percent, reaching 59.1 bln US$, while its imports of services increased slightly by 4.2 percent and reached 55.3 bln US$ (see graph 2). There was a relatively small trade in services surplus of 3.8 bln US$.

Graph 1: Total merchandise trade, by value
(Bln US$ by year)

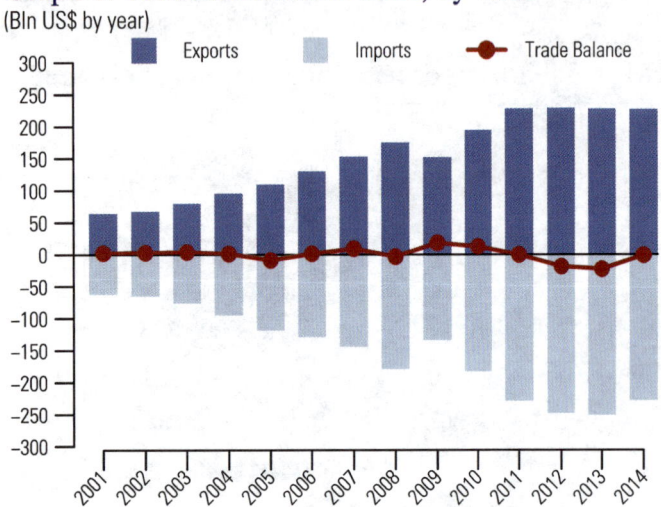

Graph 2: Total services trade, by value
(Bln US$ by year)

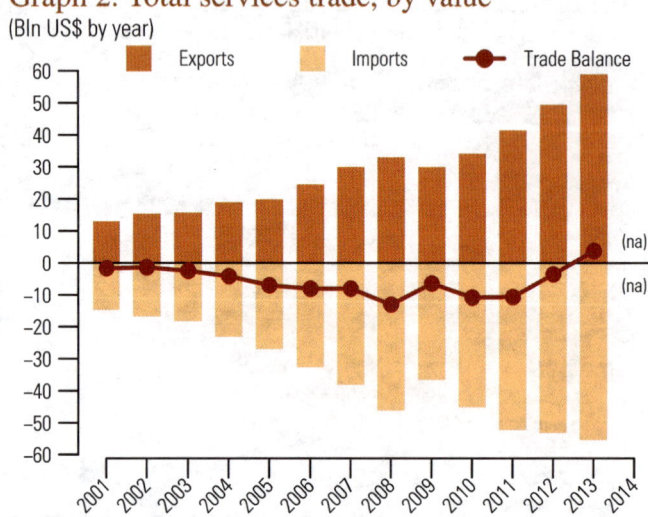

Exports Profile:
"Machinery and transport equipment" (SITC section 7), "Food, animals + beverages, tobacco" (SITC section 0+1) and "Goods classified chiefly by material" (SITC section 6) were the largest commodity groups for exports in 2014, representing respectively 43.0, 13.3 and 12.6 percent of exported goods (see table 2). From 2012 to 2014, the largest export commodity was "Automatic data processing machines and units thereof" (HS code 8471) (see table 1). The top three destinations for merchandise exports were China, the United States and Japan, accounting for respectively 11.6, 10.2 and 9.9 percent of total exports. "Travel" (EBOPS code 236) accounted for the largest share of exports of services in 2013 at 42.1 bln US$, followed by "Other business services" (EBOPS code 268) at 8.1 bln US$ and "Transportation" (EBOPS code 205) at 6.2 bln US$ (see graph 3).

Graph 3: Exports of services by EBOPS category
(% share in 2013)

- Travel (71.3 %)
- Other business (13.6 %)
- Transportation (10.4 %)
- Remaining (4.6 %)

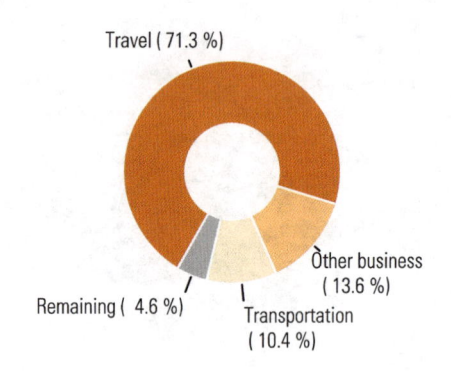

Table 1: Top 10 export commodities 2012 to 2014

HS code	4-digit heading of Harmonized System 2012	Value (million US$) 2012	2013	2014	Unit value 2012	2013	2014	Unit	SITC code
	All Commodities	229 544.5	228 527.4	227 572.8					
8471	Automatic data processing machines and units thereof	13 711.6	12 182.0	12 115.7					752
2710	Petroleum oils, other than crude	11 388.5	11 472.6	9 811.1					334
8704	Motor vehicles for the transport of goods	10 519.8	10 590.5	10 347.3					782
4001	Natural rubber, balata, gutta-percha, guayule, chicle	8 745.8	8 233.5	6 021.5	2.9	2.4	1.8	US$/kg	231
8542	Electronic integrated circuits	6 689.0	7 214.2	7 502.6					776
8708	Parts and accessories of the motor vehicles of headings 87.01 to 87.05	5 861.3	6 352.0	6 789.5	8.6	8.6	8.5	US$/kg	784
8703	Motor cars and other motor vehicles principally designed for the transport	5 680.4	6 625.3	6 524.5	14.1	14.1	13.8	thsd US$/unit	781
1006	Rice	4 632.3	4 420.4	5 438.8	0.7	0.7	0.5	US$/kg	042
8415	Air conditioning machines, comprising a motor-driven fan	4 081.0	4 506.8	4 609.8					741
7108	Gold (including gold plated with platinum)	6 637.6	3 272.5	2 779.7	17.9	29.4	27.2	thsd US$/kg	971

Thailand

Services Imports and Exports: EBOPS 2002 categories

Table 2: Merchandise exports by SITC
(Value in million US$, growth and shares in percentage)

SITC	2014	Avg. Growth rates 2010-2014	2013-2014	2014 share
Total	227 572.8	3.9	-0.4	100.0
0+1	30 228.9	5.3	6.0	13.3
2+4	10 822.6	-1.6	-16.9	4.8
3	11 984.2	5.6	-16.3	5.3
5	24 715.9	9.9	1.4	10.9
6	28 692.4	4.8	-3.0	12.6
7	97 868.3	4.4	2.6	43.0
8	20 441.5	0.7	2.3	9.0
9	2 818.9	-18.9	-15.6	1.2

Table 3: Merchandise imports by SITC
(Value in million US$, growth and shares in percentage)

SITC	2014	Avg. Growth rates 2010-2014	2013-2014	2014 share
Total	227 931.5	5.7	-9.1	100.0
0+1	11 060.1	10.3	-3.1	4.9
2+4	6 561.0	2.7	2.8	2.9
3	48 079.3	11.0	-7.9	21.1
5	23 455.3	4.2	-0.6	10.3
6	37 697.1	3.3	-7.4	16.5
7	79 708.7	5.5	-7.8	35.0
8	14 757.2	4.9	-1.7	6.5
9	6 612.8	-4.2	-55.9	2.9

SITC Legend

SITC Code	Description
Total	All commodities
0+1	Food, animals + beverages, tobacco
2+4	Crude materials + anim. & veg. oils
3	Mineral fuels, lubricants
5	Chemicals
6	Goods classified chiefly by material
7	Machinery and transport equipment
8	Miscellaneous manufactured articles
9	Not classified elsewhere in the SITC

Graph 4: Merchandise trade balance
(Bln US$ by MDG Regions in 2014)

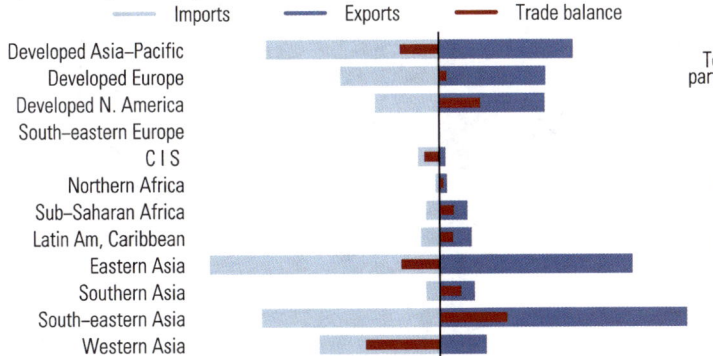

Graph 5: Partner concentration of merchandise trade
(Cumulative share by ranked partners in 2014)

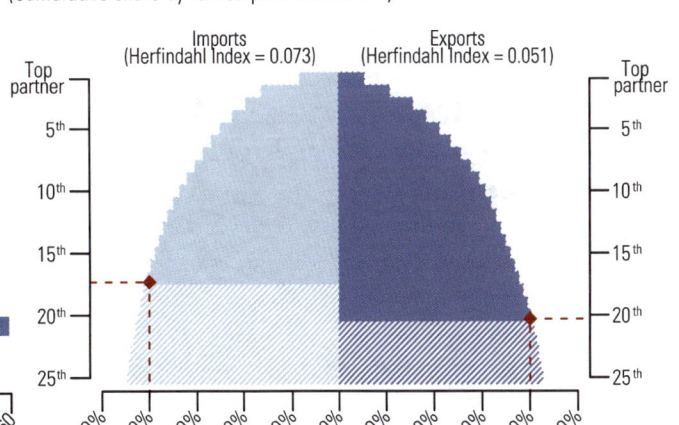

Imports (Herfindahl Index = 0.073)
Exports (Herfindahl Index = 0.051)

Graph 6: Imports of services by EBOPS category
(% share in 2013)

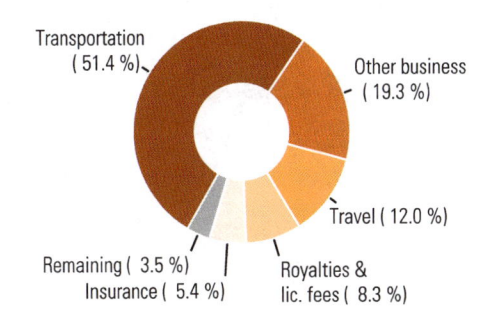

- Transportation (51.4 %)
- Other business (19.3 %)
- Travel (12.0 %)
- Royalties & lic. fees (8.3 %)
- Insurance (5.4 %)
- Remaining (3.5 %)

Imports Profile:
"Machinery and transport equipment" (SITC section 7), "Mineral fuels, lubricants" (SITC section 3) and "Goods classified chiefly by material" (SITC section 6) were the largest commodity groups for imports in 2014, representing respectively 35.0, 21.1 and 16.5 percent of imported goods (see table 3). From 2012 to 2014, the largest import commodity was "Petroleum oils and oils obtained from bituminous minerals, crude" (HS code 2709) (see table 4). The top three partners for merchandise imports were Japan, China and the United Arab Emirates, accounting for respectively 17.4, 15.6 and 6.3 percent of total imports. "Transportation" (EBOPS code 205) accounted for the largest share of imports of services in 2013 at 28.4 bln US$, followed by "Other business services" (EBOPS code 268) at 10.7 bln US$ and "Travel" (EBOPS code 236) at 6.7 bln US$ (see graph 6).

Table 4: Top 10 import commodities 2012 to 2014

HS code	4-digit heading of Harmonized System 2012	2012	2013	2014	2012	2013	2014	Unit	SITC code
	All Commodities	247 575.9	250 708.2	227 931.5					
2709	Petroleum oils and oils obtained from bituminous minerals, crude	35 843.2	38 916.9	33 216.5	0.9	0.9	0.8	US$/kg	333
7108	Gold (including gold plated with platinum)	10 742.3	14 981.2	6 612.5	35.2	44.2	39.9	thsd US$/kg	971
8542	Electronic integrated circuits	9 166.1	9 206.2	9 680.8					776
8708	Parts and accessories of the motor vehicles of headings 87.01 to 87.05	8 359.7	7 877.0	5 313.0	11.2	10.7	10.3	US$/kg	784
2711	Petroleum gases and other gaseous hydrocarbons	5 729.4	6 890.7	6 585.9	0.5	0.6	0.5	US$/kg	343
8517	Electrical apparatus for line telephony or line telegraphy	4 087.0	4 794.0	5 454.3					764
2710	Petroleum oils, other than crude	3 441.6	3 676.2	5 573.1					334
8471	Automatic data processing machines and units thereof	4 369.9	3 888.1	3 560.7					752
8473	Parts and accessories for use with machines of heading 84.69 to 84.72	3 802.0	3 146.5	3 004.3			53.8	US$/kg	759
8802	Other aircraft (for example, helicopters, aeroplanes); spacecraft	2 167.5	4 417.5	3 009.6	1.0	24.4	0.6	mln US$/unit	792

2014 International Trade Statistics Yearbook, Vol. I — Source: UN Comtrade and UN ServiceTrade

The former Yugoslav Republic of Macedonia

Goods Imports: CIF, by origin **Goods Exports:** FOB, by last known destination **Trade System:** Special

Overview:

In 2014, the value of merchandise exports of the former Yugoslav Republic of Macedonia increased substantially by 15.6 percent to reach 4.9 bln US$, while its merchandise imports increased substantially by 10.3 percent to reach 7.3 bln US$ (see graph 1, table 2 and table 3). The merchandise trade balance recorded a moderate deficit of 2.3 bln US$ (see graph 1). The largest merchandise trade balance was with MDG Developed Europe at -697.9 mln US$ (see graph 4). Merchandise exports in the former Yugoslav Republic of Macedonia were moderately concentrated amongst partners; imports were diversified. The top 11 partners accounted for 80 percent or more of exports and 17 partners accounted for 80 percent or more of imports (see graph 5). In 2013, the value of exports of services of the former Yugoslav Republic of Macedonia increased substantially by 10.5 percent, reaching 1.2 bln US$, while its imports of services increased moderately by 6.4 percent and reached 1.1 bln US$ (see graph 2). There was a relatively small trade in services surplus of 103.0 mln US$.

Graph 1: Total merchandise trade, by value
(Bln US$ by year)

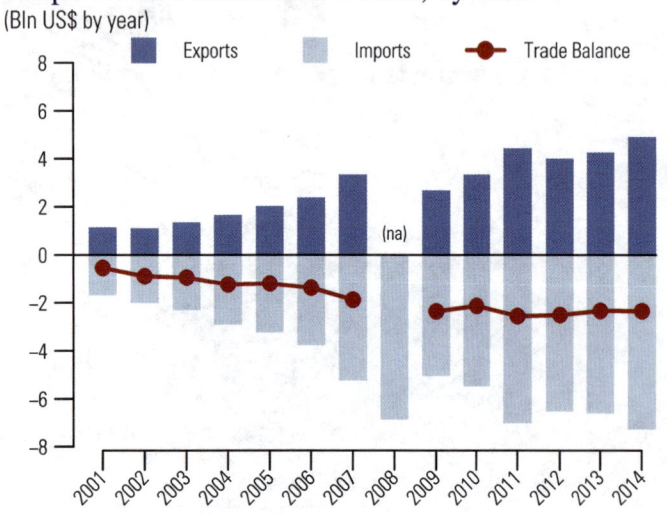

Graph 2: Total services trade, by value
(Bln US$ by year)

Exports Profile:

"Chemicals" (SITC section 5), "Machinery and transport equipment" (SITC section 7) and "Goods classified chiefly by material" (SITC section 6) were the largest commodity groups for exports in 2014, representing respectively 21.3, 21.1 and 19.4 percent of exported goods (see table 2). From 2012 to 2014, the largest export commodity was "Reaction initiators, reaction accelerators and catalytic preparations" (HS code 3815) (see table 1). The top three destinations for merchandise exports were Germany, Serbia and Bulgaria, accounting for respectively 36.0, 13.1 and 7.1 percent of total exports. "Transportation" (EBOPS code 205) accounted for the largest share of exports of services in 2013 at 363.0 mln US$, followed by "Travel" (EBOPS code 236) at 267.0 mln US$ and "Other business services" (EBOPS code 268) at 244.0 mln US$ (see graph 3).

Graph 3: Exports of services by EBOPS category
(% share in 2013)

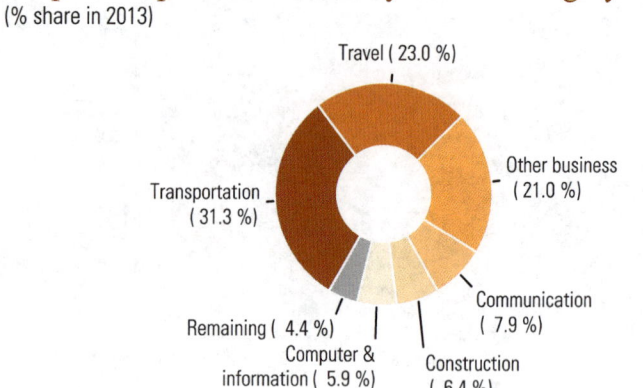

- Travel (23.0 %)
- Other business (21.0 %)
- Transportation (31.3 %)
- Communication (7.9 %)
- Construction (6.4 %)
- Computer & information (5.9 %)
- Remaining (4.4 %)

Table 1: Top 10 export commodities 2012 to 2014

HS code	4-digit heading of Harmonized System 2012	Value (million US$) 2012	2013	2014	Unit value 2012	2013	2014	Unit	SITC code
	All Commodities	4015.4	4266.9	4933.8					
3815	Reaction initiators, reaction accelerators and catalytic preparations	493.9	638.3	860.1	151.6	140.7	117.9	US$/kg	598
7202	Ferro-alloys	460.6	424.6	382.7	3.0	2.5	2.4	US$/kg	671
8421	Centrifuges, including centrifugal dryers	176.0	267.7	424.4					743
6204	Women's or girls'suits, ensembles, jackets, blazers, dresses, skirts	146.0	157.2	150.5	17.6	17.9	17.5	US$/unit	842
2401	Unmanufactured tobacco; tobacco refuse	121.3	153.2	127.9	5.3	5.9	5.3	US$/kg	121
7208	Flat-rolled products of iron or non-alloy steel	134.1	99.2	123.1	0.6	0.7	0.7	US$/kg	673
8544	Insulated (including enamelled or anodised) wire, cable	24.3	62.1	265.2	4.1	10.3	20.7	US$/kg	773
6203	Men's or boys'suits, ensembles, jackets, blazers, trousers	101.9	99.6	136.7	26.4	26.5	30.0	US$/unit	841
2710	Petroleum oils, other than crude	197.2	81.5	53.2	1.0		1.0	US$/kg	334
7210	Flat-rolled products of iron or non-alloy steel	88.7	121.2	102.2	0.9	1.2	1.1	US$/kg	674

The former Yugoslav Republic of Macedonia

Services Imports and Exports: EBOPS 2002 categories

Table 2: Merchandise exports by SITC
(Value in million US$, growth and shares in percentage)

SITC	2014	Avg. Growth rates 2010-2014	2013-2014	2014 share
Total	4 933.8	10.2	15.6	100.0
0+1	611.4	3.6	-3.7	12.4
2+4	279.7	0.8	-3.0	5.7
3	86.8	-23.8	-18.4	1.8
5	1 053.4	28.9	26.0	21.3
6	954.9	-0.9	-5.7	19.4
7	1 042.5	51.3	82.6	21.1
8	901.0	5.8	10.7	18.3
9	4.2	15.2	25.6	0.1

Table 3: Merchandise imports by SITC
(Value in million US$, growth and shares in percentage)

SITC	2014	Avg. Growth rates 2010-2014	2013-2014	2014 share
Total	7 276.7	7.4	10.3	100.0
0+1	756.3	5.2	-0.4	10.4
2+4	316.8	-1.8	11.8	4.4
3	1 048.6	2.0	-2.2	14.4
5	822.3	5.5	-4.4	11.3
6	2 487.2	15.8	22.1	34.2
7	1 368.8	5.5	17.7	18.8
8	466.1	4.7	10.8	6.4
9	10.5	9.2	91.9	0.1

SITC Legend

SITC Code	Description
Total	All commodities
0+1	Food, animals + beverages, tobacco
2+4	Crude materials + anim. & veg. oils
3	Mineral fuels, lubricants
5	Chemicals
6	Goods classified chiefly by material
7	Machinery and transport equipment
8	Miscellaneous manufactured articles
9	Not classified elsewhere in the SITC

Graph 4: Merchandise trade balance
(Bln US$ by MDG Regions in 2014)

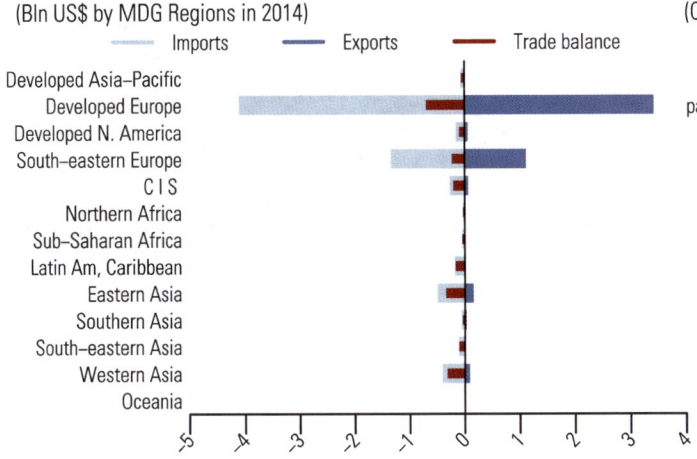

Graph 5: Partner concentration of merchandise trade
(Cumulative share by ranked partners in 2014)

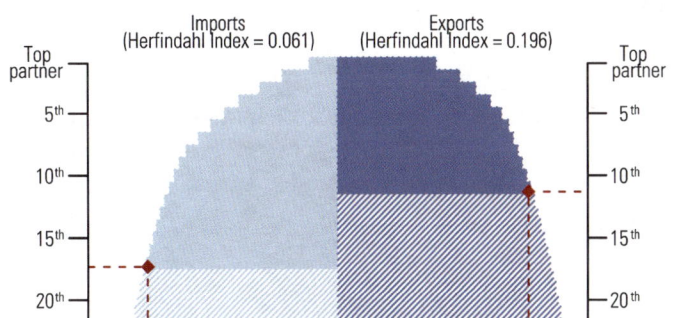

Imports (Herfindahl Index = 0.061)
Exports (Herfindahl Index = 0.196)

Graph 6: Imports of services by EBOPS category
(% share in 2013)

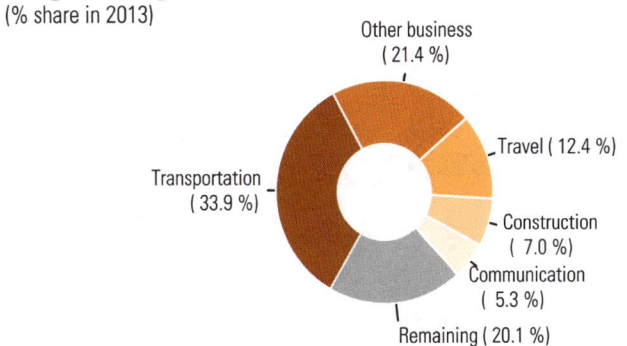

- Other business (21.4 %)
- Travel (12.4 %)
- Construction (7.0 %)
- Communication (5.3 %)
- Remaining (20.1 %)
- Transportation (33.9 %)

Imports Profile:

"Goods classified chiefly by material" (SITC section 6), "Machinery and transport equipment" (SITC section 7) and "Mineral fuels, lubricants" (SITC section 3) were the largest commodity groups for imports in 2014, representing respectively 34.2, 18.8 and 14.4 percent of imported goods (see table 3). From 2012 to 2014, the largest import commodity was "Petroleum oils, other than crude" (HS code 2710) (see table 4). The top three partners for merchandise imports were the United Kingdom, Greece and Germany, accounting for respectively 10.7, 10.6 and 10.5 percent of total imports. "Transportation" (EBOPS code 205) accounted for the largest share of imports of services in 2013 at 358.0 mln US$, followed by "Other business services" (EBOPS code 268) at 226.0 mln US$ and "Travel" (EBOPS code 236) at 131.0 mln US$ (see graph 6).

Table 4: Top 10 import commodities 2012 to 2014

HS code	4-digit heading of Harmonized System 2012	Value (million US$) 2012	2013	2014	Unit value 2012	2013	2014	Unit	SITC code
	All Commodities	6 522.4	6 599.8	7 276.7					
2710	Petroleum oils, other than crude	703.1	663.9	672.7	1.0		0.9	US$/kg	334
7110	Platinum, unwrought or in semi-manufactured forms, or in powder form	406.8	522.6	835.0	41.0	38.9	39.4	thsd US$/kg	681
2716	Electrical energy	253.2	170.1	187.5	2.7	66.5	5.3	US$/MWh	351
7208	Flat-rolled products of iron or non-alloy steel	175.5	170.4	148.8	0.6	0.6	0.6	US$/kg	673
8703	Motor cars and other motor vehicles principally designed for the transport	139.2	136.7	139.3	4.3	4.2	4.3	thsd US$/unit	781
3004	Medicaments (excluding goods of heading 30.02, 30.05 or 30.06)	120.2	127.7	136.7	33.9	36.1	37.9	US$/kg	542
2604	Nickel ores and concentrates	146.1	100.0	101.7	0.1	0.1	0.1	US$/kg	284
2711	Petroleum gases and other gaseous hydrocarbons	120.7	110.1	114.5	0.8	0.7	0.7	US$/kg	343
2709	Petroleum oils and oils obtained from bituminous minerals, crude	230.5	45.8	0.0	0.9	0.9	2.6	US$/kg	333
8517	Electrical apparatus for line telephony or line telegraphy	88.9	84.1	99.9					764

Source: UN Comtrade and UN ServiceTrade

Togo

Goods Imports: CIF, by origin **Goods Exports:** FOB, by last known destination **Trade System:** Special

Overview:

In 2013, the value of merchandise exports of Togo increased substantially by 11.3 percent to reach 1.0 bln US$, while its merchandise imports increased substantially by 20.2 percent to reach 2.0 bln US$ (see graph 1, table 2 and table 3). The merchandise trade balance recorded a large deficit of 999.9 mln US$ (see graph 1). The largest merchandise trade balance was with MDG Developed Europe at -552.5 mln US$ (see graph 4). Merchandise exports in Togo were diversified amongst partners; imports were also diversified. The top 10 partners accounted for 80 percent or more of exports and 22 partners accounted for 80 percent or more of imports (see graph 5). In 2012, the value of exports of services of Togo decreased substantially by 15.9 percent, reaching 428.0 mln US$, while its imports of services decreased moderately by 7.1 percent and reached 440.0 mln US$ (see graph 2). There was a relatively small trade in services deficit of 12.0 mln US$.

Graph 1: Total merchandise trade, by value
(Bln US$ by year)

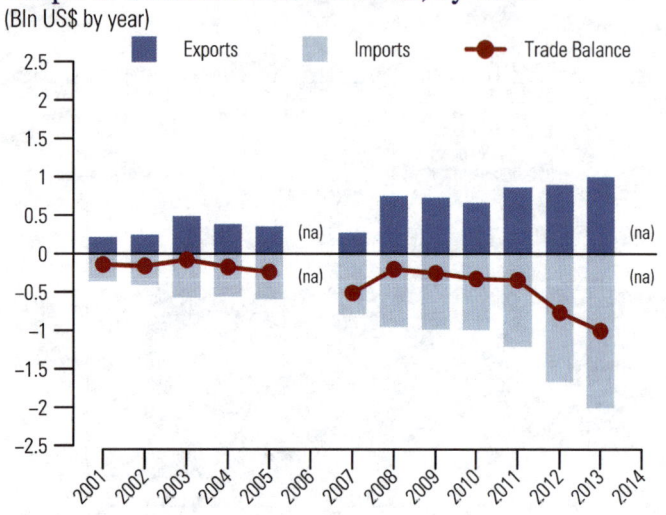

Graph 2: Total services trade, by value
(Mln US$ by year)

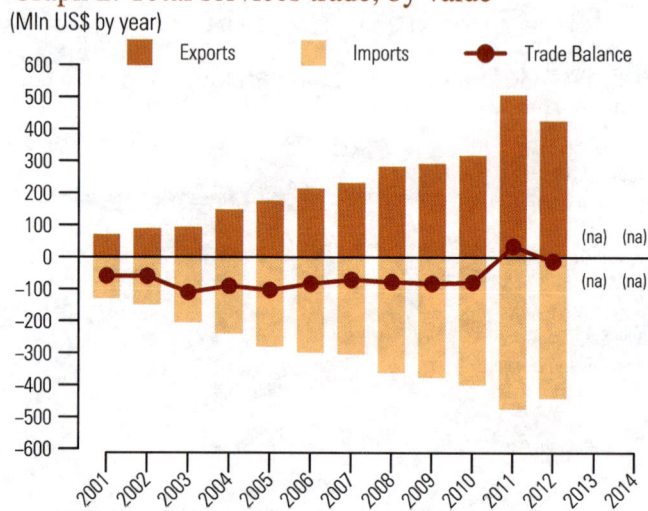

Exports Profile:

"Goods classified chiefly by material" (SITC section 6), "Machinery and transport equipment" (SITC section 7) and "Crude materials + anim. & veg. oils" (SITC section 2+4) were the largest commodity groups for exports in 2013, representing respectively 29.4, 15.0 and 14.4 percent of exported goods (see table 2). From 2011 to 2013, the largest export commodity was "Portland cement, aluminous cement, slag cement" (HS code 2523) (see table 1). The top three destinations for merchandise exports were Burkina Faso, Benin and the Niger, accounting for respectively 15.9, 11.8 and 9.8 percent of total exports. "Transportation" (EBOPS code 205) accounted for the largest share of exports of services in 2012 at 175.1 mln US$, followed by "Travel" (EBOPS code 236) at 88.3 mln US$ and "Communications services" (EBOPS code 245) at 65.0 mln US$ (see graph 3).

Graph 3: Exports of services by EBOPS category
(% share in 2012)

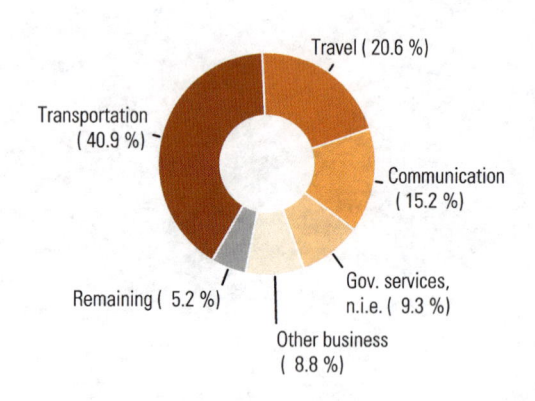

- Transportation (40.9 %)
- Travel (20.6 %)
- Communication (15.2 %)
- Gov. services, n.i.e. (9.3 %)
- Other business (8.8 %)
- Remaining (5.2 %)

Table 1: Top 10 export commodities 2011 to 2013

HS code	4-digit heading of Harmonized System 2007	Value (million US$) 2011	2012	2013	Unit value 2011	2012	2013	Unit	SITC code
	All Commodities	865.5	900.4	1 002.3					
2523	Portland cement, aluminous cement, slag cement	121.7	141.9	165.8	0.1	0.1	0.1	US$/kg	661
5201	Cotton, not carded or combed	268.2	63.3	57.3	1.9	1.9	1.7	US$/kg	263
3923	Articles for the conveyance or packing of goods, of plastics	47.8	55.2	53.3	1.7	1.7	2.0	US$/kg	893
2510	Natural calcium phosphates	42.5	95.2	...	0.3	1.1		US$/kg	272
8905	Light-vessels, fire-floats, dredgers, floating cranes and other vessels	0.2	47.3	76.5					793
3304	Beauty or make-up preparations	34.4	34.5	44.3	3.5	3.3	3.1	US$/kg	553
7108	Gold (including gold plated with platinum)	33.3	35.4	43.4	2.1	2.0	2.0	thsd US$/kg	971
2713	Petroleum coke and other residues	...	51.3	51.4		0.6	0.6	US$/kg	335
3105	Mineral or chemical fertilisers	45.8	22.6	9.7	0.6	0.7	0.6	US$/kg	562
2202	Waters with added sugar	14.8	15.7	31.6	*0.7*	*0.7*	*1.0*	US$/litre	111

Togo

Services Imports and Exports: EBOPS 2002 categories

Table 2: Merchandise exports by SITC
(Value in million US$, growth and shares in percentage)

SITC	2013	Avg. Growth rates 2009-2013	Avg. Growth rates 2012-2013	2013 share
Total	1 002.3	8.1	11.3	100.0
0+1	99.2	6.0	10.8	9.9
2+4	144.2	-17.7	-27.7	14.4
3	59.8	196.5	-8.2	6.0
5	96.6	6.8	14.5	9.6
6	294.3	14.5	33.4	29.4
7	150.6	62.3	45.3	15.0
8	114.1	13.7	11.6	11.4
9	43.4	69.8	22.8	4.3

Table 3: Merchandise imports by SITC
(Value in million US$, growth and shares in percentage)

SITC	2013	Avg. Growth rates 2009-2013	Avg. Growth rates 2012-2013	2013 share
Total	2 002.2	19.4	20.2	100.0
0+1	234.7	15.2	10.4	11.7
2+4	81.6	23.4	9.2	4.1
3	434.4	31.0	19.9	21.7
5	330.3	34.5	23.9	16.5
6	446.9	19.1	39.8	22.3
7	392.8	9.6	14.2	19.6
8	81.4	2.8	-4.5	4.1

SITC Legend

SITC Code	Description
Total	All commodities
0+1	Food, animals + beverages, tobacco
2+4	Crude materials + anim. & veg. oils
3	Mineral fuels, lubricants
5	Chemicals
6	Goods classified chiefly by material
7	Machinery and transport equipment
8	Miscellaneous manufactured articles
9	Not classified elsewhere in the SITC

Graph 4: Merchandise trade balance
(Mln US$ by MDG Regions in 2013)

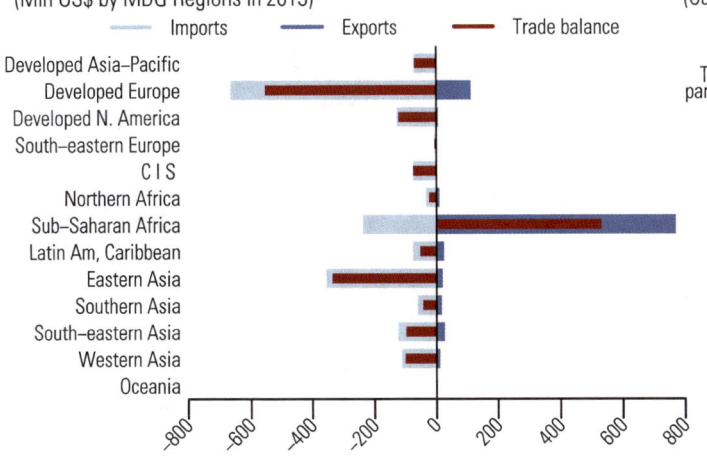

Graph 5: Partner concentration of merchandise trade
(Cumulative share by ranked partners in 2013)

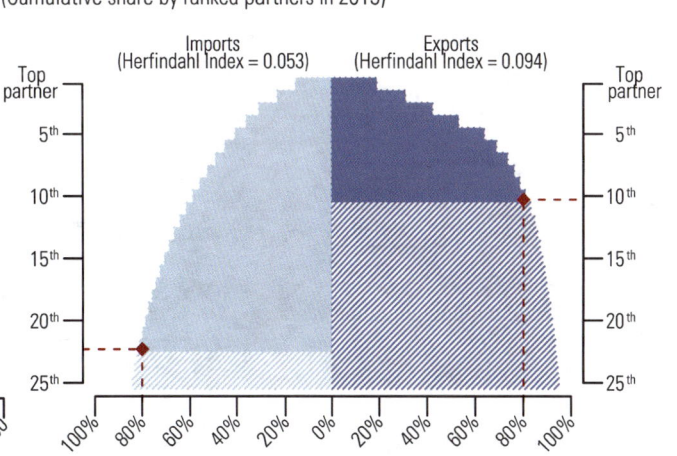

Imports (Herfindahl Index = 0.053)
Exports (Herfindahl Index = 0.094)

Graph 6: Imports of services by EBOPS category
(% share in 2012)

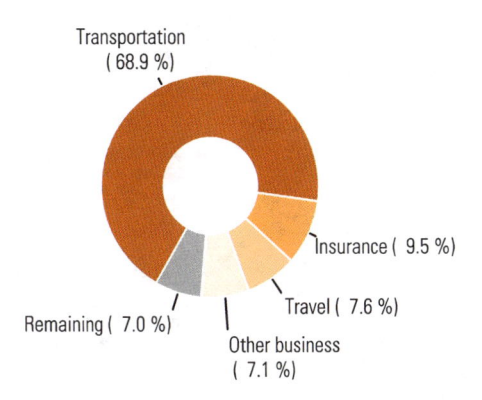

- Transportation (68.9 %)
- Insurance (9.5 %)
- Travel (7.6 %)
- Other business (7.1 %)
- Remaining (7.0 %)

Imports Profile:

"Goods classified chiefly by material" (SITC section 6), "Mineral fuels, lubricants" (SITC section 3) and "Machinery and transport equipment" (SITC section 7) were the largest commodity groups for imports in 2013, representing respectively 22.3, 21.7 and 19.6 percent of imported goods (see table 3). From 2011 to 2013, the largest import commodity was "Petroleum oils, other than crude" (HS code 2710) (see table 4). The top three partners for merchandise imports were China, France and the United States, accounting for respectively 15.6, 9.7 and 5.5 percent of total imports. "Transportation" (EBOPS code 205) accounted for the largest share of imports of services in 2012 at 303.0 mln US$, followed by "Insurance services" (EBOPS code 253) at 41.8 mln US$ and "Travel" (EBOPS code 236) at 33.4 mln US$ (see graph 6).

Table 4: Top 10 import commodities 2011 to 2013

HS code	4-digit heading of Harmonized System 2007	2011	2012	2013	2011	2012	2013	Unit	SITC code
	All Commodities	1 207.7	1 665.1	2 002.2					
2710	Petroleum oils, other than crude	174.6	268.2	341.1	0.9	1.0	1.0	US$/kg	334
2523	Portland cement, aluminous cement, slag cement	93.3	87.8	108.9	0.1	0.1	0.1	US$/kg	661
3004	Medicaments (excluding goods of heading 30.02, 30.05 or 30.06)	48.8	68.0	80.7	13.8	17.2	21.5	US$/kg	542
8905	Light-vessels, fire-floats, dredgers, floating cranes and other vessels	...	90.6	36.5					793
8703	Motor cars and other motor vehicles principally designed for the transport	46.2	37.4	35.8		25.5	22.5	thsd US$/unit	781
2713	Petroleum coke and other residues	3.2	57.6	56.9	0.7	0.7	0.6	US$/kg	335
3901	Polymers of ethylene, in primary forms	0.0	53.5	63.5	0.5	1.6	1.7	US$/kg	571
5208	Woven fabrics of cotton, containing 85 % or more by weight of cotton	24.2	33.6	40.1	1.6	1.4	1.4	US$/kg	652
1001	Wheat and meslin	29.5	28.2	38.8	0.4	0.4	0.5	US$/kg	041
0303	Fish, frozen, excluding fish fillets and other fish meat of heading 03.04	28.3	27.9	28.4	0.6	0.6	0.6	US$/kg	034

Source: UN Comtrade and UN ServiceTrade

Tonga

Goods Imports: CIF, by origin **Goods Exports:** FOB, by last known destination **Trade System:** General

Overview:
In 2012, the value of merchandise exports of Tonga increased moderately by 8.3 percent to reach 15.6 mln US$, while its merchandise imports increased slightly by 3.2 percent to reach 199.2 mln US$ (see graph 1, table 2 and table 3). The merchandise trade balance recorded a large deficit of 183.6 mln US$ (see graph 1). The largest merchandise trade balance was with MDG Developed Asia-Pacific at -73.6 mln US$ (see graph 4). Merchandise exports in Tonga were diversified amongst partners; imports were moderately concentrated. The top 6 partners accounted for 80 percent or more of exports and 5 partners accounted for 80 percent or more of imports (see graph 5). In 2009, the value of exports of services of Tonga decreased slightly by 2.2 percent, reaching 34.8 mln US$, while its imports of services decreased substantially by 13.2 percent and reached 47.0 mln US$ (see graph 2). There was a moderate trade in services deficit of 12.1 mln US$.

Graph 1: Total merchandise trade, by value
(Mln US$ by year)

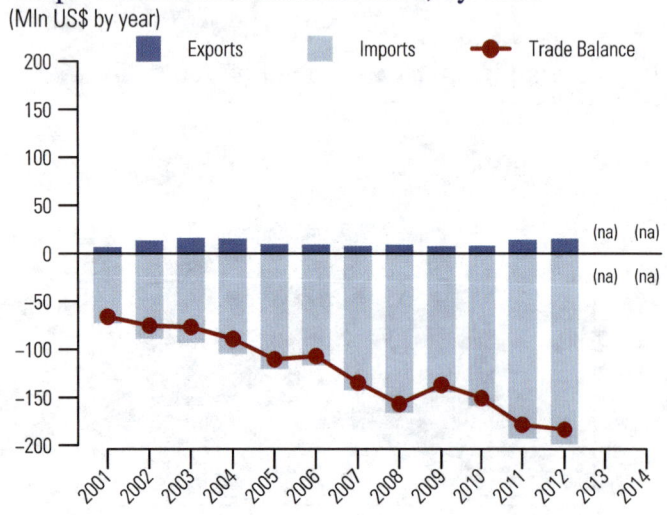

Graph 2: Total services trade, by value
(Mln US$ by year)

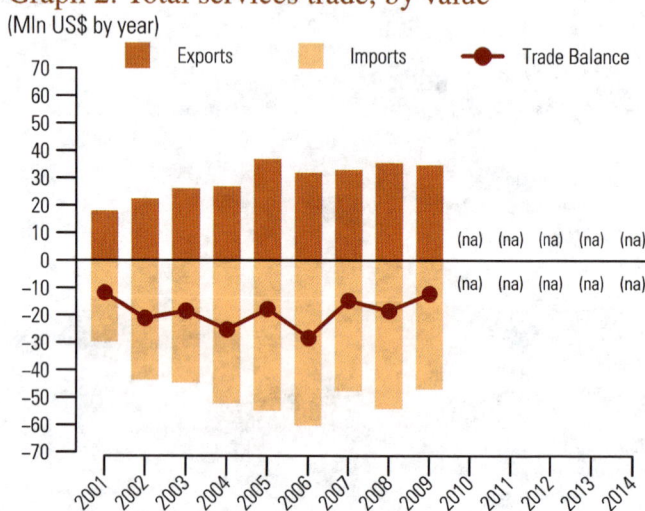

Exports Profile:
"Food, animals + beverages, tobacco" (SITC section 0+1), "Miscellaneous manufactured articles" (SITC section 8) and "Machinery and transport equipment" (SITC section 7) were the largest commodity groups for exports in 2012, representing respectively 67.6, 12.2 and 11.3 percent of exported goods (see table 2). From 2010 to 2012, the largest export commodity was "Fish, fresh or chilled, excluding fish fillets" (HS code 0302) (see table 1). The top three destinations for merchandise exports were New Zealand, China, Hong Kong SAR and Japan, accounting for respectively 21.3, 21.3 and 15.7 percent of total exports. "Travel" (EBOPS code 236) accounted for the largest share of exports of services in 2009 at 16.0 mln US$, followed by "Government services, n.i.e." (EBOPS code 291) at 6.8 mln US$ and "Transportation" (EBOPS code 205) at 5.3 mln US$ (see graph 3).

Graph 3: Exports of services by EBOPS category
(% share in 2009)

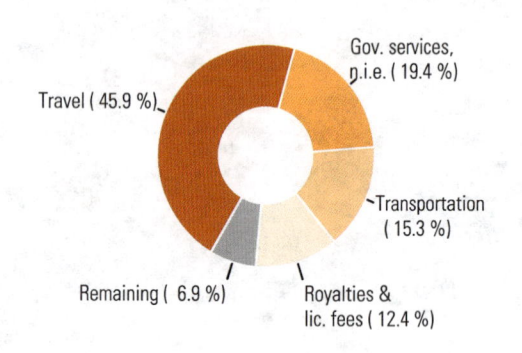

- Travel (45.9 %)
- Gov. services, n.i.e. (19.4 %)
- Transportation (15.3 %)
- Royalties & lic. fees (12.4 %)
- Remaining (6.9 %)

Table 1: Top 10 export commodities 2010 to 2012

HS code	4-digit heading of Harmonized System 2007	Value (million US$) 2010	2011	2012	Unit value 2010	2011	2012	Unit	SITC code
	All Commodities	8.3	14.4	15.6					
0302	Fish, fresh or chilled, excluding fish fillets	1.7	3.2	2.1	8.1	8.0	7.6	US$/kg	034
0307	Molluscs, whether in shell or not	2.5	0.7	2.1	12.0	16.2	15.7	US$/kg	036
0714	Manioc, arrowroot, sweet potatoes and similar roots	0.5	1.4	1.7	0.4	0.5	1.0	US$/kg	054
1212	Locust beans, seaweeds and other algae	0.5	1.1	1.9	7.5	4.3	4.1	US$/kg	292
1211	Plants and parts of plants (including seeds and fruits)	0.0	2.9	0.1		25.3	6.3	US$/kg	292
0709	Other vegetables, fresh or chilled	0.3	1.2	1.5	0.4	0.4	0.4	US$/kg	054
4907	Unused postage, revenue or similar stamps of current or new issue	0.0	0.8	1.1					892
0305	Fish, dried, salted or in brine	0.9	0.7	0.0	8.7	24.1	18.7	US$/kg	035
0801	Coconuts, Brazil nuts and cashew nuts, fresh or dried	0.4	0.5	0.6	1.2	0.9	0.6	US$/kg	057
3208	Paints and varnishes	0.3	0.3	0.2	4.7	4.3	4.7	US$/kg	533

Tonga

Services Imports and Exports: EBOPS 2002 categories

Table 2: Merchandise exports by SITC
(Value in million US$, growth and shares in percentage)

SITC	2012	Avg. Growth rates 2008-2012	Avg. Growth rates 2011-2012	2012 share
Total	15.6	13.8	8.3	100.0
0+1	10.5	15.1	14.0	67.6
2+4	1.0	-18.2	-70.3	6.6
3	0.0	-8.4	...	0.0
5	0.2	-15.7	-24.5	1.4
6	0.1	-5.6	-38.1	0.8
7	1.8	77.5	4063.0	11.3
8	1.9	108.8	74.1	12.2
9	0.0	-42.4	-76.5	0.1

Table 3: Merchandise imports by SITC
(Value in million US$, growth and shares in percentage)

SITC	2012	Avg. Growth rates 2008-2012	Avg. Growth rates 2011-2012	2012 share
Total	199.2	4.7	3.2	100.0
0+1	56.9	5.0	0.5	28.6
2+4	4.5	2.1	-11.0	2.2
3	47.2	2.3	4.0	23.7
5	9.2	6.2	-3.2	4.6
6	22.7	7.1	-20.0	11.4
7	38.2	6.4	20.6	19.2
8	20.3	17.6	27.6	10.2
9	0.1	-65.2	-73.4	0.1

SITC Legend

SITC Code	Description
Total	All commodities
0+1	Food, animals + beverages, tobacco
2+4	Crude materials + anim. & veg. oils
3	Mineral fuels, lubricants
5	Chemicals
6	Goods classified chiefly by material
7	Machinery and transport equipment
8	Miscellaneous manufactured articles
9	Not classified elsewhere in the SITC

Graph 4: Merchandise trade balance
(Mln US$ by MDG Regions in 2012)

Graph 5: Partner concentration of merchandise trade
(Cumulative share by ranked partners in 2012)
Imports (Herfindahl Index = 0.176)
Exports (Herfindahl Index = 0.144)

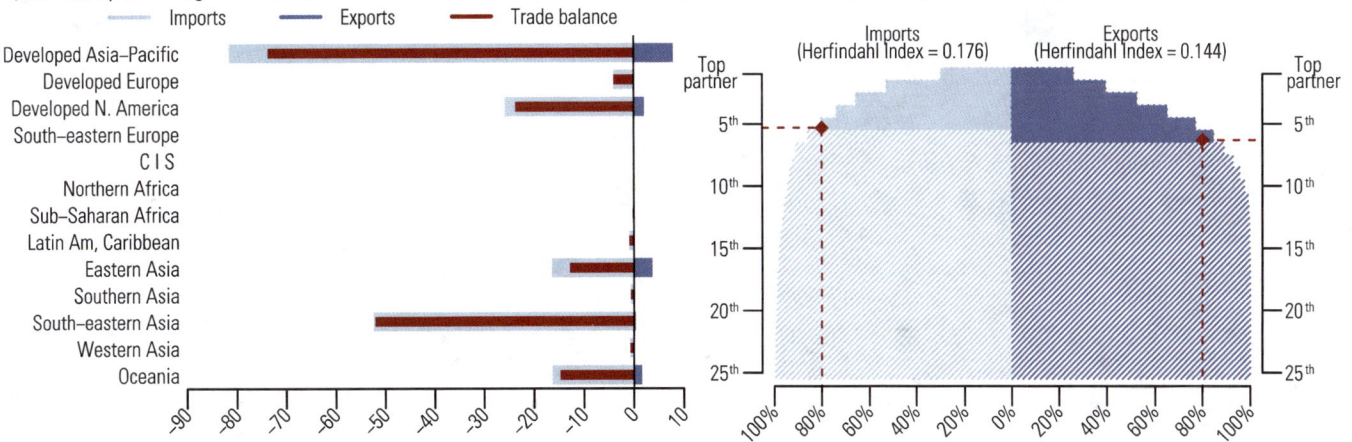

Graph 6: Imports of services by EBOPS category
(% share in 2009)

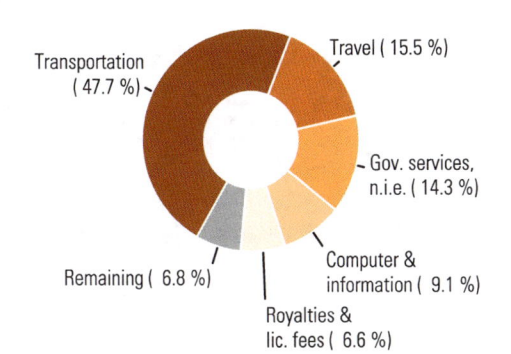

- Transportation (47.7 %)
- Travel (15.5 %)
- Gov. services, n.i.e. (14.3 %)
- Computer & information (9.1 %)
- Royalties & lic. fees (6.6 %)
- Remaining (6.8 %)

Imports Profile:

"Food, animals + beverages, tobacco" (SITC section 0+1), "Mineral fuels, lubricants" (SITC section 3) and "Machinery and transport equipment" (SITC section 7) were the largest commodity groups for imports in 2012, representing respectively 28.6, 23.7 and 19.2 percent of imported goods (see table 3). From 2010 to 2012, the largest import commodity was "Petroleum oils, other than crude" (HS code 2710) (see table 4). The top three partners for merchandise imports were New Zealand, Singapore and the United States, accounting for respectively 30.6, 22.0 and 12.6 percent of total imports. "Transportation" (EBOPS code 205) accounted for the largest share of imports of services in 2009 at 22.4 mln US$, followed by "Travel" (EBOPS code 236) at 7.3 mln US$ and "Government services, n.i.e." (EBOPS code 291) at 6.7 mln US$ (see graph 6).

Table 4: Top 10 import commodities 2010 to 2012

HS code	4-digit heading of Harmonized System 2007	2010	2011	2012	2010	2011	2012	Unit	SITC code
	All Commodities	158.8	192.9	199.2					
2710	Petroleum oils, other than crude	34.2	42.5	44.6					334
0207	Meat and edible offal, of the poultry of heading 01.05	8.9	11.5	12.4	1.2	1.4	1.6	US$/kg	012
8703	Motor cars and other motor vehicles principally designed for the transport	3.1	3.6	5.1	1.3	0.5	5.1	thsd US$/unit	781
1101	Wheat or meslin flour	3.1	3.9	3.8	0.6	0.7	0.7	US$/kg	046
0204	Meat of sheep or goats, fresh, chilled or frozen	3.2	3.5	4.0	3.1	4.1	4.3	US$/kg	012
8517	Electrical apparatus for line telephony or line telegraphy	5.0	3.0	2.6					764
1602	Other prepared or preserved meat, meat offal or blood	3.1	3.1	3.7	3.9	5.6	5.6	US$/kg	017
2202	Waters with added sugar	2.3	2.7	2.8	0.6	0.9	0.8	US$/litre	111
4818	Toilet paper and similar paper	2.2	2.8	2.5	3.1	3.0	3.1	US$/kg	642
0202	Meat of bovine animals, frozen	1.9	2.0	2.7	3.1	3.7	3.8	US$/kg	011

Trinidad and Tobago

Goods Imports: CIF, by origin **Goods Exports: FOB, by last known destination** **Trade System: Special**

Overview:
In 2010, the value of merchandise exports of Trinidad and Tobago increased substantially by 20.3 percent to reach 11.0 bln US$, while its merchandise imports decreased moderately by 6.8 percent to reach 6.5 bln US$ (see graph 1, table 2 and table 3). The merchandise trade balance recorded a moderate surplus of 4.5 bln US$ (see graph 1). The largest merchandise trade balance was with MDG Developed North America at 3.5 bln US$ (see graph 4). Merchandise exports in Trinidad and Tobago were moderately concentrated amongst partners; imports were diversified. The top 15 partners accounted for 80 percent or more of exports and 12 partners accounted for 80 percent or more of imports (see graph 5). In 2010, the value of exports of services of Trinidad and Tobago increased substantially by 14.3 percent, reaching 874.2 mln US$, while its imports of services increased slightly by 0.9 percent and reached 386.6 mln US$ (see graph 2). There was a large trade in services surplus of 487.6 mln US$.

Graph 1: Total merchandise trade, by value
(Bln US$ by year)

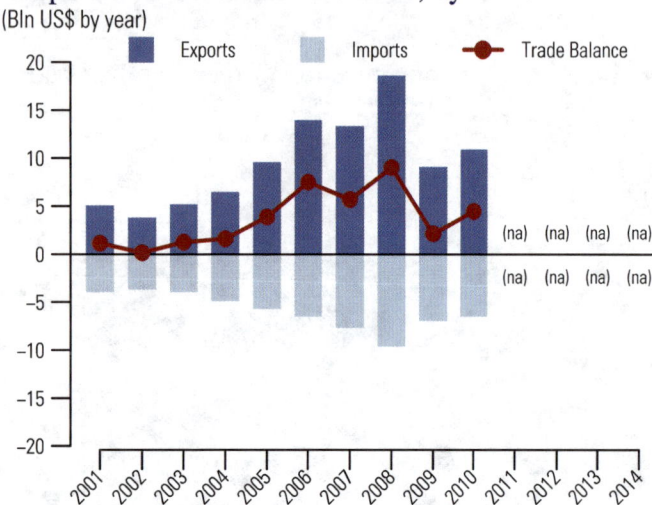

Graph 2: Total services trade, by value
(Mln US$ by year)

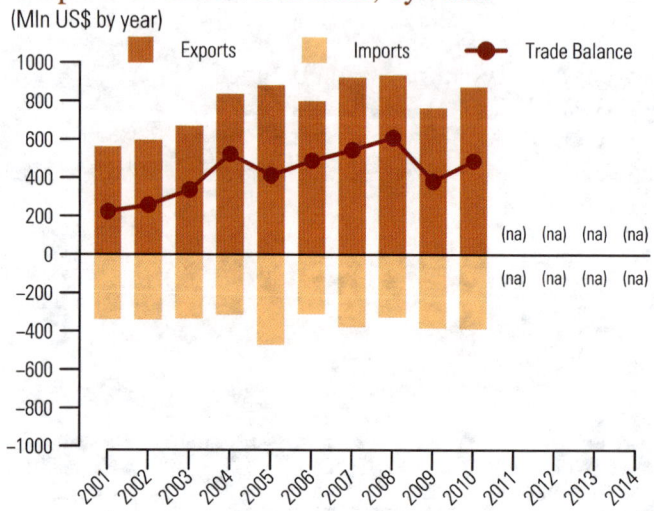

Exports Profile:
"Mineral fuels, lubricants" (SITC section 3), "Chemicals" (SITC section 5) and "Goods classified chiefly by material" (SITC section 6) were the largest commodity groups for exports in 2010, representing respectively 60.9, 21.7 and 6.0 percent of exported goods (see table 2). From 2008 to 2010, the largest export commodity was "Petroleum gases and other gaseous hydrocarbons" (HS code 2711) (see table 1). The top three destinations for merchandise exports were the United States, Jamaica and Spain, accounting for respectively 48.6, 6.3 and 4.8 percent of total exports. "Travel" (EBOPS code 236) accounted for the largest share of exports of services in 2010 at 449.6 mln US$, followed by "Transportation" (EBOPS code 205) at 223.2 mln US$ and "Insurance services" (EBOPS code 253) at 139.4 mln US$ (see graph 3).

Graph 3: Exports of services by EBOPS category
(% share in 2010)

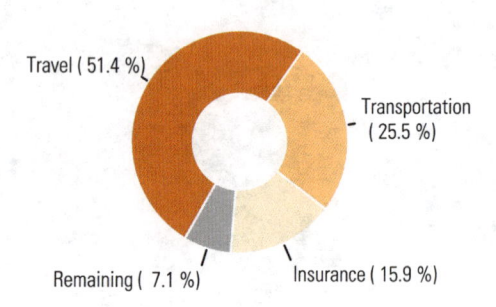

Travel (51.4 %)
Transportation (25.5 %)
Insurance (15.9 %)
Remaining (7.1 %)

Table 1: Top 10 export commodities 2008 to 2010

HS code	4-digit heading of Harmonized System 2007	Value (million US$) 2008	2009	2010	Unit value 2008	2009	2010	Unit	SITC code
	All Commodities	18650.4	9126.0	10981.7					
2711	Petroleum gases and other gaseous hydrocarbons	5846.0	3830.0	1885.0	0.5	0.3	0.4	US$/kg	343
2710	Petroleum oils, other than crude	5132.9	1985.9	3430.9	0.8	0.5	0.6	US$/kg	334
2709	Petroleum oils and oils obtained from bituminous minerals, crude	2067.6	1101.5	1367.5	1.0	0.5	0.6	US$/kg	333
2814	Ammonia, anhydrous or in aqueous solution	1775.2	336.6	1376.7	0.7	0.2	0.3	US$/kg	522
2905	Acyclic alcohols and their derivatives	1058.9	299.8	616.5		0.2	0.2	US$/kg	512
2601	Iron ores and concentrates, including roasted iron pyrites	484.6	236.1	522.0	0.4	0.3	0.4	US$/kg	281
7203	Ferrous products obtained by direct reduction of iron ore	307.7	150.6	303.2	0.3	0.2	0.3	US$/kg	671
3102	Mineral or chemical fertilisers, nitrogenous	364.1	152.9	218.5	0.6	0.3	0.3	US$/kg	562
7213	Bars and rods, hot-rolled, in irregularly wound coils	245.3	81.1	176.0	0.8	0.4	0.2	US$/kg	676
8905	Light-vessels, fire-floats, dredgers, floating cranes and other vessels	61.4	129.4	226.3	15.4	25.9	37.7	mln US$/unit	793

Source: UN Comtrade and UN ServiceTrade

Trinidad and Tobago

Services Imports and Exports: EBOPS 2002 categories

Table 2: Merchandise exports by SITC
(Value in million US$, growth and shares in percentage)

SITC	2010	Avg. Growth rates 2006-2010	Avg. Growth rates 2009-2010	2010 share
Total	10981.7	-5.9	20.3	100.0
0+1	261.5	-5.1	-10.4	2.4
2+4	577.3	86.9	106.6	5.3
3	6683.7	-11.1	-3.4	60.9
5	2382.1	3.9	171.8	21.7
6	658.1	0.0	54.0	6.0
7	354.3	24.1	34.9	3.2
8	64.2	-5.2	-8.1	0.6
9	0.5	7.2	19.6	0.0

Table 3: Merchandise imports by SITC
(Value in million US$, growth and shares in percentage)

SITC	2010	Avg. Growth rates 2006-2010	Avg. Growth rates 2009-2010	2010 share
Total	6479.6	0.0	-6.8	100.0
0+1	677.0	9.2	3.0	10.4
2+4	363.4	3.4	47.0	5.6
3	2157.6	-1.3	-5.8	33.3
5	495.0	-1.5	-9.1	7.6
6	743.4	-1.7	-18.3	11.5
7	1680.3	-0.7	-12.5	25.9
8	357.9	0.2	-4.9	5.5
9	5.0	-9.4	-44.3	0.1

SITC Legend

SITC Code	Description
Total	All commodities
0+1	Food, animals + beverages, tobacco
2+4	Crude materials + anim. & veg. oils
3	Mineral fuels, lubricants
5	Chemicals
6	Goods classified chiefly by material
7	Machinery and transport equipment
8	Miscellaneous manufactured articles
9	Not classified elsewhere in the SITC

Graph 4: Merchandise trade balance
(Bln US$ by MDG Regions in 2010)

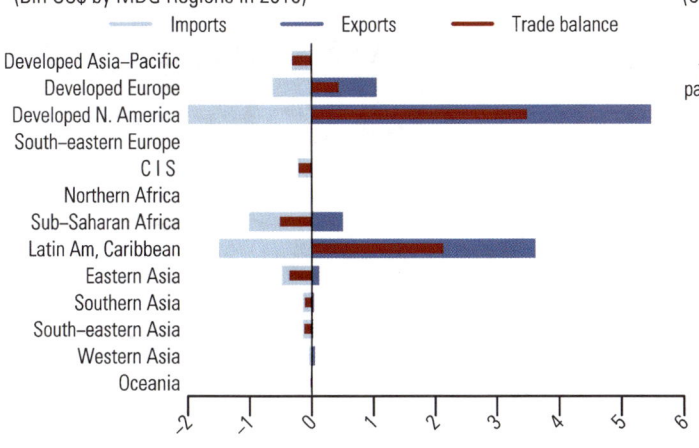

Graph 5: Partner concentration of merchandise trade
(Cumulative share by ranked partners in 2010)

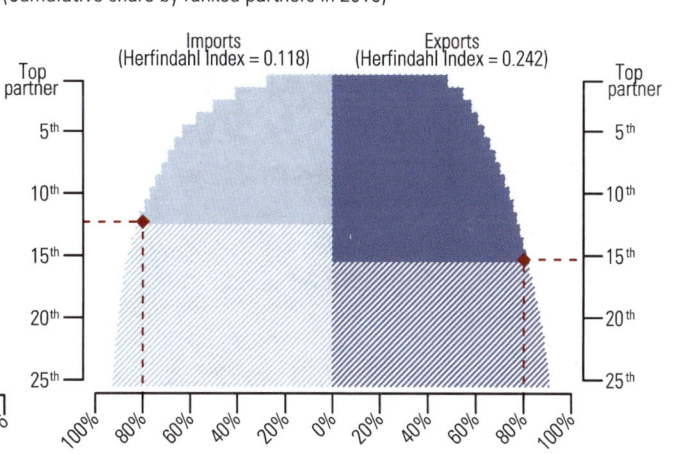

Graph 6: Imports of services by EBOPS category
(% share in 2010)

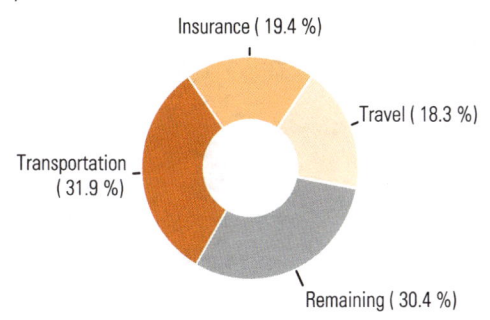

- Insurance (19.4%)
- Travel (18.3%)
- Transportation (31.9%)
- Remaining (30.4%)

Imports Profile:

"Mineral fuels, lubricants" (SITC section 3), "Machinery and transport equipment" (SITC section 7) and "Goods classified chiefly by material" (SITC section 6) were the largest commodity groups for imports in 2010, representing respectively 33.3, 25.9 and 11.5 percent of imported goods (see table 3). From 2008 to 2010, the largest import commodity was "Petroleum oils and oils obtained from bituminous minerals, crude" (HS code 2709) (see table 4). The top three partners for merchandise imports were the United States, Colombia and Brazil, accounting for respectively 27.2, 9.0 and 8.4 percent of total imports. "Transportation" (EBOPS code 205) accounted for the largest share of imports of services in 2010 at 123.4 mln US$, followed by "Insurance services" (EBOPS code 253) at 75.0 mln US$ and "Travel" (EBOPS code 236) at 70.6 mln US$ (see graph 6).

Table 4: Top 10 import commodities 2008 to 2010

HS code	4-digit heading of Harmonized System 2007	Value 2008	Value 2009	Value 2010	Unit value 2008	Unit value 2009	Unit value 2010	Unit	SITC code
	All Commodities	9591.4	6955.4	6479.6					
2709	Petroleum oils and oils obtained from bituminous minerals, crude	3145.6	2135.6	2035.7	0.7	0.4	0.6	US$/kg	333
2601	Iron ores and concentrates, including roasted iron pyrites	469.0	141.6	254.3	0.2	0.1	0.2	US$/kg	281
8419	Machinery, plant or laboratory equipment	411.1	360.6	34.9					741
8703	Motor cars and other motor vehicles principally designed for the transport	230.5	122.1	152.8	1.8	0.6	1.3	thsd US$/unit	781
2710	Petroleum oils, other than crude	212.7	150.6	115.6	0.9	0.6	1.1	US$/kg	334
8704	Motor vehicles for the transport of goods	136.8	85.3	105.9	0.6	0.7	2.0	thsd US$/unit	782
7304	Tubes, pipes and hollow profiles, seamless, of iron (other than cast iron)	104.1	178.8	38.3	2.3	6.4	5.8	US$/kg	679
3004	Medicaments (excluding goods of heading 30.02, 30.05 or 30.06)	99.4	101.9	90.4	3.0	8.2	13.4	US$/kg	542
7308	Structures (excluding prefabricated buildings of heading 94.06)	195.1	57.3	34.8	2.8	3.0	1.1	US$/kg	691
8517	Electrical apparatus for line telephony or line telegraphy	91.1	84.9	98.6					764

Source: UN Comtrade and UN ServiceTrade

Tunisia

Goods Imports: CIF, by origin   **Goods Exports: FOB, by last known destination**   **Trade System: General**

Overview:
In 2013, the value of merchandise exports of Tunisia increased slightly by 0.3 percent to reach 17.1 bln US$, while its merchandise imports decreased slightly by 0.8 percent to reach 24.3 bln US$ (see graph 1, table 2 and table 3). The merchandise trade balance recorded a moderate deficit of 7.2 bln US$ (see graph 1). The largest merchandise trade balance was with MDG Eastern Asia at -1.8 bln US$ (see graph 4). Merchandise exports in Tunisia were diversified amongst partners; imports were also diversified. The top 10 partners accounted for 80 percent or more of exports and 18 partners accounted for 80 percent or more of imports (see graph 5). In 2012, the value of exports of services of Tunisia increased moderately by 9.9 percent, reaching 5.3 bln US$, while its imports of services increased slightly by 0.4 percent and reached 3.3 bln US$ (see graph 2). There was a moderate trade in services surplus of 2.0 bln US$.

Graph 1: Total merchandise trade, by value
(Bln US$ by year)

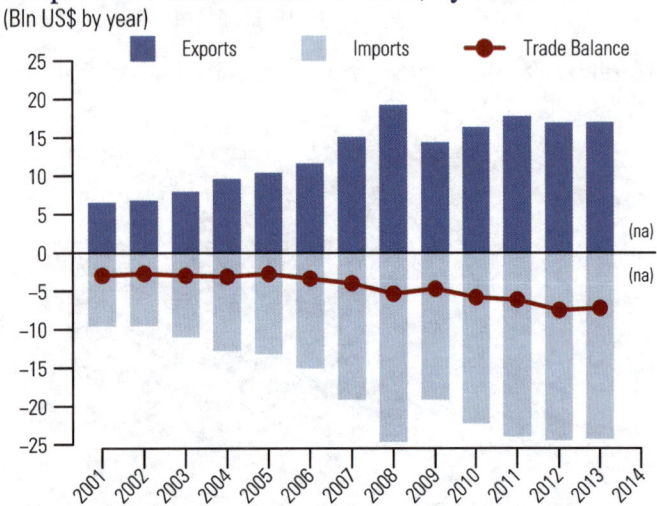

Graph 2: Total services trade, by value
(Bln US$ by year)

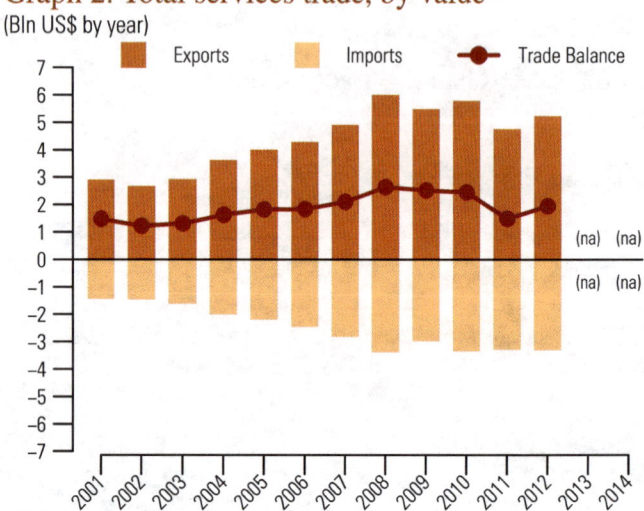

Exports Profile:
"Machinery and transport equipment" (SITC section 7), "Miscellaneous manufactured articles" (SITC section 8) and "Mineral fuels, lubricants" (SITC section 3) were the largest commodity groups for exports in 2013, representing respectively 31.3, 24.6 and 15.2 percent of exported goods (see table 2). From 2011 to 2013, the largest export commodity was "Petroleum oils and oils obtained from bituminous minerals, crude" (HS code 2709) (see table 1). The top three destinations for merchandise exports were France, Italy and Germany, accounting for respectively 28.1, 19.7 and 8.8 percent of total exports. "Travel" (EBOPS code 236) accounted for the largest share of exports of services in 2012 at 2.2 bln US$, followed by "Transportation" (EBOPS code 205) at 1.5 bln US$ and "Construction services" (EBOPS code 249) at 406.8 mln US$ (see graph 3).

Graph 3: Exports of services by EBOPS category
(% share in 2012)

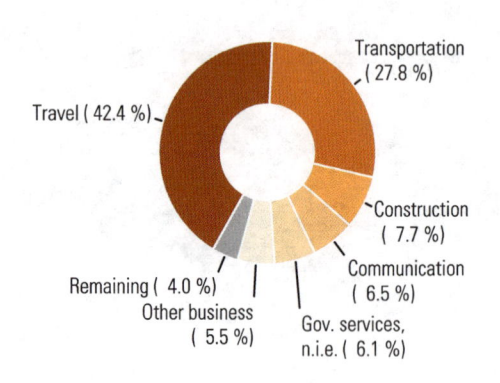

- Travel (42.4 %)
- Transportation (27.8 %)
- Construction (7.7 %)
- Communication (6.5 %)
- Gov. services, n.i.e. (6.1 %)
- Other business (5.5 %)
- Remaining (4.0 %)

Table 1: Top 10 export commodities 2011 to 2013

HS code	4-digit heading of Harmonized System 2007	Value (million US$) 2011	2012	2013	Unit value 2011	2012	2013	Unit	SITC code
	All Commodities	17 847.0	17 007.4	17 060.5					
2709	Petroleum oils and oils obtained from bituminous minerals, crude	2 288.9	1 875.9	1 748.1	0.8	0.8	0.8	US$/kg	333
8544	Insulated (including enamelled or anodised) wire, cable	1 751.6	1 633.7	1 678.2	14.5	14.2	14.7	US$/kg	773
6203	Men's or boys' suits, ensembles, jackets, blazers, trousers	753.7	614.6	676.2	19.8		20.1	US$/unit	841
2710	Petroleum oils, other than crude	288.4	948.8	802.9	0.9	0.9	0.8	US$/kg	334
6211	Track suits, ski suits and swimwear; other garments	678.4	625.5	634.3					845
8528	Reception apparatus for television	572.3	492.6	487.0	101.4	89.0	99.9	US$/unit	761
8536	Electrical apparatus for switching or protecting electrical circuits	414.3	368.6	440.6	28.0	26.2	28.8	US$/kg	772
1509	Olive oil and its fractions	286.1	375.2	504.6	2.9	2.4	3.3	US$/kg	421
6109	T-shirts, singlets and other vests, knitted or crocheted	406.1	324.6	316.4	6.5		5.9	US$/unit	845
3105	Mineral or chemical fertilisers	237.3	331.5	378.4	0.6	0.6	0.5	US$/kg	562

Source: UN Comtrade and UN ServiceTrade

Tunisia

Services Imports and Exports: EBOPS 2002 categories

Table 2: Merchandise exports by SITC
(Value in million US$, growth and shares in percentage)

SITC	2013	Avg. Growth rates 2009-2013	Avg. Growth rates 2012-2013	2013 share
Total	17 060.5	4.2	0.3	100.0
0+1	1 035.5	5.5	6.7	6.1
2+4	861.8	5.4	-3.2	5.1
3	2 595.5	7.1	-9.1	15.2
5	1 505.1	-0.3	2.0	8.8
6	1 512.1	0.6	3.7	8.9
7	5 348.1	10.2	3.1	31.3
8	4 200.9	-0.7	2.3	24.6
9	1.4	-17.6	-97.8	0.0

Table 3: Merchandise imports by SITC
(Value in million US$, growth and shares in percentage)

SITC	2013	Avg. Growth rates 2009-2013	Avg. Growth rates 2012-2013	2013 share
Total	24 266.4	6.2	-0.8	100.0
0+1	1 965.5	11.5	19.6	8.1
2+4	1 287.1	7.8	-5.1	5.3
3	4 318.4	18.7	1.4	17.8
5	2 859.7	8.5	6.0	11.8
6	4 628.3	1.7	1.1	19.1
7	7 416.0	2.9	-5.0	30.6
8	1 783.5	1.4	6.3	7.3
9	7.8	4.5	-98.3	0.0

SITC Legend

SITC Code	Description
Total	All commodities
0+1	Food, animals + beverages, tobacco
2+4	Crude materials + anim. & veg. oils
3	Mineral fuels, lubricants
5	Chemicals
6	Goods classified chiefly by material
7	Machinery and transport equipment
8	Miscellaneous manufactured articles
9	Not classified elsewhere in the SITC

Graph 4: Merchandise trade balance
(Bln US$ by MDG Regions in 2013)

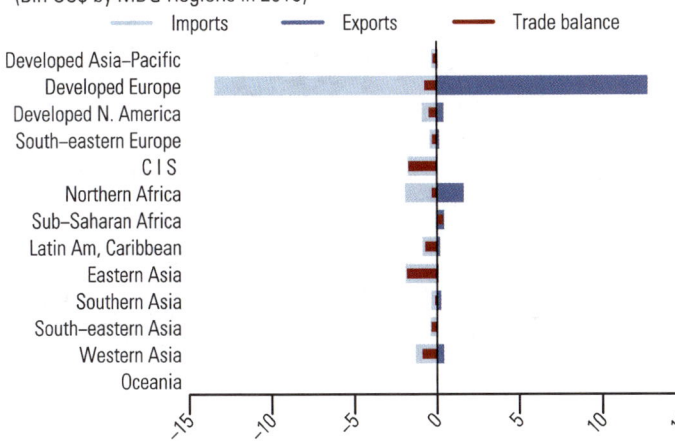

Graph 5: Partner concentration of merchandise trade
(Cumulative share by ranked partners in 2013)

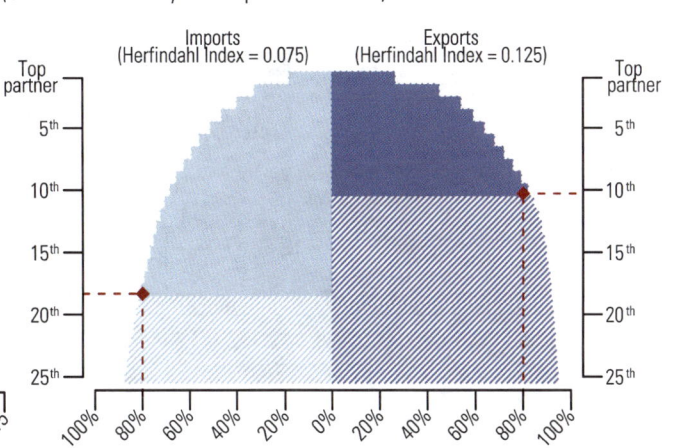

Imports (Herfindahl Index = 0.075)
Exports (Herfindahl Index = 0.125)

Graph 6: Imports of services by EBOPS category
(% share in 2012)

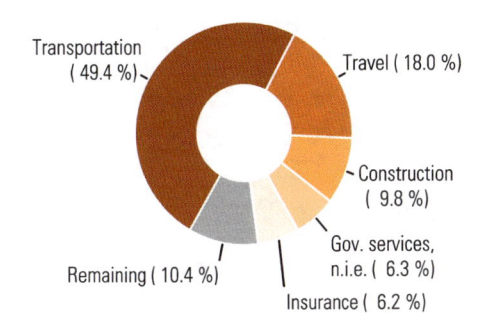

- Transportation (49.4 %)
- Travel (18.0 %)
- Construction (9.8 %)
- Gov. services, n.i.e. (6.3 %)
- Insurance (6.2 %)
- Remaining (10.4 %)

Imports Profile:

"Machinery and transport equipment" (SITC section 7), "Goods classified chiefly by material" (SITC section 6) and "Mineral fuels, lubricants" (SITC section 3) were the largest commodity groups for imports in 2013, representing respectively 30.6, 19.1 and 17.8 percent of imported goods (see table 3). From 2011 to 2013, the largest import commodity was "Petroleum oils, other than crude" (HS code 2710) (see table 4). The top three partners for merchandise imports were France, Italy and Germany, accounting for respectively 17.7, 14.8 and 7.1 percent of total imports. "Transportation" (EBOPS code 205) accounted for the largest share of imports of services in 2012 at 1.6 bln US$, followed by "Travel" (EBOPS code 236) at 593.1 mln US$ and "Construction services" (EBOPS code 249) at 321.7 mln US$ (see graph 6).

Table 4: Top 10 import commodities 2011 to 2013

HS code	4-digit heading of Harmonized System 2007	2011	2012	2013	2011	2012	2013	Unit	SITC code
	All Commodities	23 952.1	24 470.6	24 266.4					
2710	Petroleum oils, other than crude	2 342.0	2 007.7	1 916.9	0.9	1.0	0.9	US$/kg	334
2711	Petroleum gases and other gaseous hydrocarbons	810.7	1 251.8	1 312.0	0.6	0.6	0.6	US$/kg	343
8703	Motor cars and other motor vehicles principally designed for the transport	622.6	801.5	820.0	14.3	14.1	13.8	thsd US$/unit	781
2709	Petroleum oils and oils obtained from bituminous minerals, crude	274.0	859.5	957.2	0.9	0.9	0.8	US$/kg	333
1001	Wheat and meslin	553.0	281.6	508.9	0.4	0.3	0.3	US$/kg	041
5209	Woven fabrics of cotton, containing 85 % or more by weight of cotton	506.8	380.4	376.6	14.4	13.0	12.9	US$/kg	652
8704	Motor vehicles for the transport of goods	347.2	466.7	441.8	18.8	20.5	19.3	thsd US$/unit	782
8536	Electrical apparatus for switching or protecting electrical circuits	445.2	381.5	404.1	28.6	25.6	25.9	US$/kg	772
7408	Copper wire	447.7	363.4	338.6	9.1	8.0	7.8	US$/kg	682
8544	Insulated (including enamelled or anodised) wire, cable	401.5	340.6	366.5	14.8	13.8	14.7	US$/kg	773

2014 International Trade Statistics Yearbook, Vol. I   Source: UN Comtrade and UN ServiceTrade

Turkey

Goods Imports: CIF, by origin **Goods Exports:** FOB, by last known destination **Trade System:** Special

Overview:
In 2014, the value of merchandise exports of Turkey increased slightly by 3.9 percent to reach 157.7 bln US$, while its merchandise imports decreased slightly by 3.7 percent to reach 242.2 bln US$ (see graph 1, table 2 and table 3). The merchandise trade balance recorded a moderate deficit of 84.5 bln US$ (see graph 1). The largest merchandise trade balance was with MDG Eastern Asia at -30.6 bln US$ (see graph 4). Merchandise exports in Turkey were diversified amongst partners; imports were also diversified. The top 31 partners accounted for 80 percent or more of exports and 23 partners accounted for 80 percent or more of imports (see graph 5). In 2012, the value of exports of services of Turkey increased moderately by 6.6 percent, reaching 43.8 bln US$, while its imports of services decreased slightly by 0.3 percent and reached 20.9 bln US$ (see graph 2). There was a large trade in services surplus of 22.9 bln US$.

Graph 1: Total merchandise trade, by value
(Bln US$ by year)

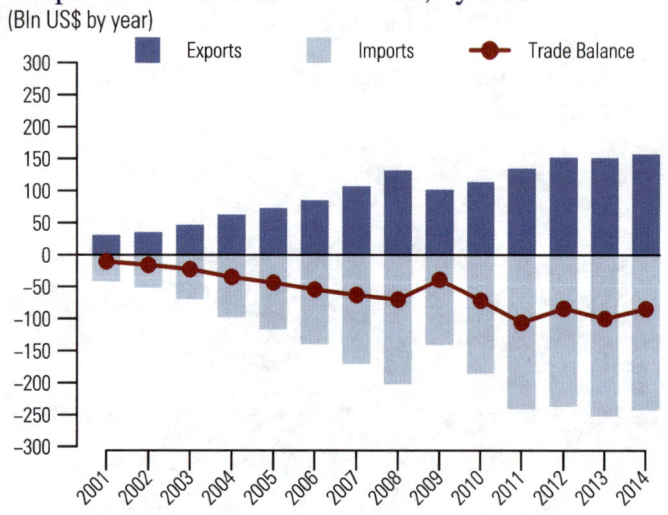

Graph 2: Total services trade, by value
(Bln US$ by year)

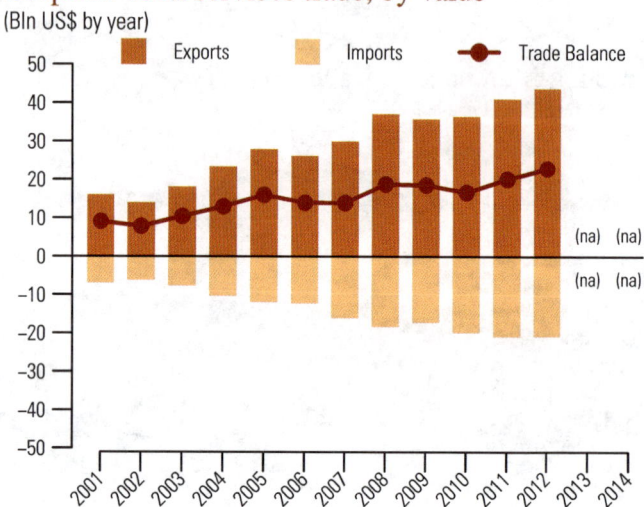

Exports Profile:
"Machinery and transport equipment" (SITC section 7), "Goods classified chiefly by material" (SITC section 6) and "Miscellaneous manufactured articles" (SITC section 8) were the largest commodity groups for exports in 2014, representing respectively 27.1, 26.8 and 18.8 percent of exported goods (see table 2). From 2012 to 2014, the largest export commodity was "Motor cars and other motor vehicles principally designed for the transport" (HS code 8703) (see table 1). The top three destinations for merchandise exports were Germany, Iraq and the United Kingdom, accounting for respectively 9.1, 7.3 and 5.9 percent of total exports. "Travel" (EBOPS code 236) accounted for the largest share of exports of services in 2012 at 25.7 bln US$, followed by "Transportation" (EBOPS code 205) at 12.5 bln US$ (see graph 3).

Graph 3: Exports of services by EBOPS category
(% share in 2012)

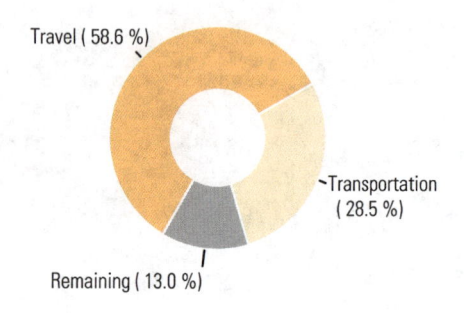

- Travel (58.6 %)
- Transportation (28.5 %)
- Remaining (13.0 %)

Table 1: Top 10 export commodities 2012 to 2014

HS code	4-digit heading of Harmonized System 2012	Value (million US$) 2012	2013	2014	Unit value 2012	2013	2014	Unit	SITC code
	All Commodities..	152 536.7	151 802.6	157 714.9					
8703	Motor cars and other motor vehicles principally designed for the transport........	6 069.1	6 856.5	7 256.1	12.5	12.4	11.8	thsd US$/unit	781
7108	Gold (including gold plated with platinum)...........................	13 344.6	3 349.0	3 211.8	52.8	46.5	41.3	thsd US$/kg	971
2710	Petroleum oils, other than crude..	6 782.6	5 963.3	5 494.7	0.9	0.9	0.8	US$/kg	334
7214	Other bars and rods of iron or non-alloy steel.....................	5 402.3	4 849.1	4 351.8	0.6	0.6	0.6	US$/kg	676
8708	Parts and accessories of the motor vehicles of headings 87.01 to 87.05........	3 403.7	3 905.2	4 134.9	4.9	5.1	4.9	US$/kg	784
8704	Motor vehicles for the transport of goods..........................	3 385.7	3 850.7	4 139.0	14.2	14.8	13.2	thsd US$/unit	782
7113	Articles of jewellery and parts thereof, of precious metal.......	2 675.8	3 411.3	4 347.5	19.4	18.7	17.8	thsd US$/kg	897
6109	T-shirts, singlets and other vests, knitted or crocheted........	3 090.1	3 276.0	3 569.5	4.1	4.3	4.2	US$/unit	845
8544	Insulated (including enamelled or anodised) wire, cable.......	2 382.6	2 499.7	2 422.2	6.4	6.2	5.8	US$/kg	773
6204	Women's or girls' suits, ensembles, jackets, blazers, dresses, skirts.........	2 204.5	2 283.1	2 418.8	13.2	13.7	13.3	US$/unit	842

Source: UN Comtrade and UN ServiceTrade

Turkey

Services Imports and Exports: EBOPS 2002 categories

Table 2: Merchandise exports by SITC
(Value in million US$, growth and shares in percentage)

SITC	2014	Avg. Growth rates 2010-2014	Avg. Growth rates 2013-2014	2014 share
Total	157 714.9	8.5	3.9	100.0
0+1	16 557.8	9.8	8.2	10.5
2+4	5 599.4	10.6	-10.1	3.6
3	5 899.8	7.6	-8.9	3.7
5	9 160.5	10.7	7.1	5.8
6	42 290.7	6.2	1.2	26.8
7	42 714.9	7.6	4.1	27.1
8	29 703.3	10.9	10.0	18.8
9	5 788.5	12.0	6.1	3.7

Table 3: Merchandise imports by SITC
(Value in million US$, growth and shares in percentage)

SITC	2014	Avg. Growth rates 2010-2014	Avg. Growth rates 2013-2014	2014 share
Total	242 224.0	6.9	-3.7	100.0
0+1	7 760.9	11.9	3.7	3.2
2+4	19 161.9	3.9	2.6	7.9
3	20 140.1	-6.8	-0.5	8.3
5	32 789.4	6.9	4.2	13.5
6	38 477.6	4.9	-0.6	15.9
7	65 813.6	5.1	-3.8	27.2
8	15 404.4	7.6	2.8	6.4
9	42 676.2	29.5	-17.4	17.6

SITC Legend

SITC Code	Description
Total	All commodities
0+1	Food, animals + beverages, tobacco
2+4	Crude materials + anim. & veg. oils
3	Mineral fuels, lubricants
5	Chemicals
6	Goods classified chiefly by material
7	Machinery and transport equipment
8	Miscellaneous manufactured articles
9	Not classified elsewhere in the SITC

Graph 4: Merchandise trade balance
(Bln US$ by MDG Regions in 2014)

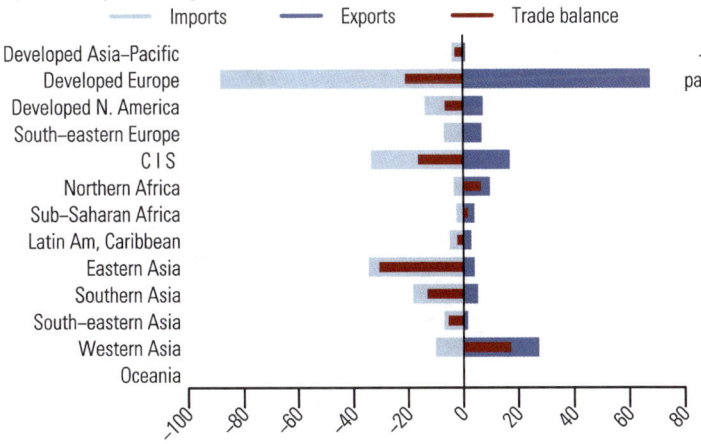

Graph 5: Partner concentration of merchandise trade
(Cumulative share by ranked partners in 2014)

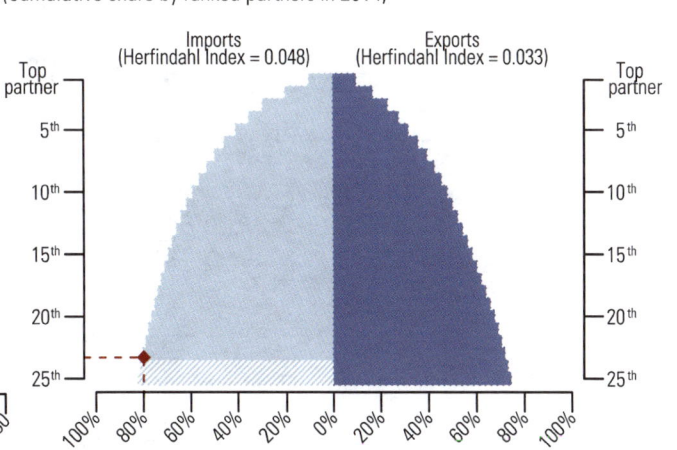

Imports (Herfindahl Index = 0.048)
Exports (Herfindahl Index = 0.033)

Graph 6: Imports of services by EBOPS category
(% share in 2012)

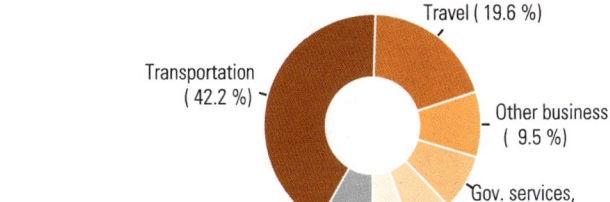

- Transportation (42.2 %)
- Travel (19.6 %)
- Other business (9.5 %)
- Gov. services, n.i.e. (8.2 %)
- Insurance (6.5 %)
- Financial (5.6 %)
- Remaining (8.4 %)

Imports Profile:

"Machinery and transport equipment" (SITC section 7), "Not classified elsewhere in the SITC" (SITC section 9) and "Goods classified chiefly by material" (SITC section 6) were the largest commodity groups for imports in 2014, representing respectively 27.2, 17.6 and 15.9 percent of imported goods (see table 3). From 2012 to 2014, the largest import commodity was "Commodities not specified according to kind" (HS code 9999) (see table 4). The top three partners for merchandise imports were the Russian Federation, China and Germany, accounting for respectively 10.5, 9.7 and 9.3 percent of total imports. "Transportation" (EBOPS code 205) accounted for the largest share of imports of services in 2012 at 8.8 bln US$, followed by "Travel" (EBOPS code 236) at 4.1 bln US$ and "Other business services" (EBOPS code 268) at 2.0 bln US$ (see graph 6).

Table 4: Top 10 import commodities 2012 to 2014

HS code	4-digit heading of Harmonized System 2012	Value (million US$) 2012	2013	2014	Unit value 2012	2013	2014	Unit	SITC code
	All Commodities	236 544.5	251 661.3	242 224.0					
9999	Commodities not specified according to kind	40 729.7	36 542.2	35 565.4					931
2710	Petroleum oils, other than crude	15 619.2	15 439.0	15 386.0	1.0	1.0	0.9	US$/kg	334
7108	Gold (including gold plated with platinum)	7 636.7	15 127.2	7 106.9	48.4	43.2	37.0	thsd US$/kg	971
8703	Motor cars and other motor vehicles principally designed for the transport	7 251.4	9 130.1	7 721.0	15.9	16.2	16.7	thsd US$/unit	781
7204	Ferrous waste and scrap; remelting scrap ingots of iron or steel	9 419.0	7 511.2	7 150.5	0.4	0.4	0.4	US$/kg	282
8708	Parts and accessories of the motor vehicles of headings 87.01 to 87.05	4 491.0	4 894.1	4 950.8	9.5	10.0	10.1	US$/kg	784
8517	Electrical apparatus for line telephony or line telegraphy	2 830.6	3 950.7	4 420.1					764
3902	Polymers of propylene or of other olefins, in primary forms	2 776.7	2 973.6	3 314.2	1.6	1.7	1.7	US$/kg	575
3004	Medicaments (excluding goods of heading 30.02, 30.05 or 30.06)	2 738.9	2 822.9	2 875.2	71.3	77.0	76.5	US$/kg	542
2711	Petroleum gases and other gaseous hydrocarbons	2 945.7	2 734.5	2 677.4	1.0	0.9	0.8	US$/kg	343

Turks and Caicos Islands

Goods Imports: CIF, by origin   **Goods Exports: FOB, by last known destination**   **Trade System: General**

Overview:
In 2012, the value of merchandise exports of the Turks and Caicos Islands increased substantially by 38.6 percent to reach 11.8 mln US$, while its merchandise imports increased slightly by 3.2 percent to reach 268.5 mln US$ (see graph 1, table 2 and table 3). The merchandise trade balance recorded a large deficit of 256.7 mln US$ (see graph 1). The largest merchandise trade balance was with MDG Developed North America at -191.5 mln US$ (see graph 4). Merchandise exports in the Turks and Caicos Islands were highly concentrated amongst partners; imports were also highly concentrated. The top 1 partner accounted for 80 percent or more of exports and 2 partners accounted for 80 percent or more of imports (see graph 5). No trade in services data is available.

Graph 1: Total merchandise trade, by value
(Mln US$ by year)

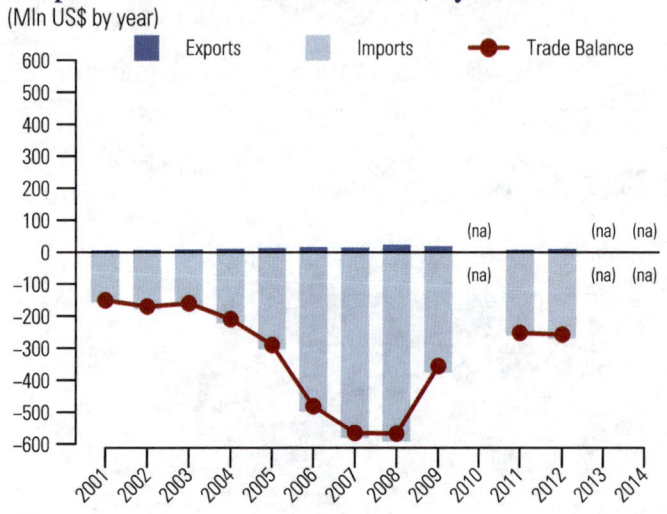

Graph 2: No Data Available

Exports Profile:
"Miscellaneous manufactured articles" (SITC section 8), "Food, animals + beverages, tobacco" (SITC section 0+1) and "Machinery and transport equipment" (SITC section 7) were the largest commodity groups for exports in 2012, representing respectively 65.7, 15.9 and 11.6 percent of exported goods (see table 2). From 2010 to 2012, the largest export commodity was "Unused postage, revenue or similar stamps of current or new issue" (HS code 4907) (see table 1). The top three destinations for merchandise exports were the United States, Areas nes and Haiti, accounting for respectively 83.3, 16.7 and 0.0 percent of total exports. Services data by detailed EBOPS category is not available for exports.

Graph 3: No Data Available

Table 1: Top 10 export commodities 2010 to 2012

HS code	4-digit heading of Harmonized System 2007	Value (million US$) 2010	2011	2012	Unit value 2010	2011	2012	Unit	SITC code
	All Commodities	...	8.5	11.8					
4907	Unused postage, revenue or similar stamps of current or new issue	...	4.9	7.3		3.5	6.2	thsd US$/kg	892
0306	Crustaceans, whether in shell or not	...	1.0	1.1		13.1	12.2	US$/kg	036
0307	Molluscs, whether in shell or not	...	0.2	0.8		4.7	4.2	US$/kg	036
9999	Commodities not specified according to kind	...	0.3	0.3					931
8429	Self-propelled bulldozers, angledozers, graders, levellers, scrapers	...	0.4	0.0		38.0	6.0	thsd US$/unit	723
8704	Motor vehicles for the transport of goods	...	0.1	0.2		41.8	5.5	thsd US$/unit	782
8502	Electric generating sets and rotary converters	...	0.1	0.2		30.8	122.5	thsd US$/unit	716
8903	Yachts and other vessels for pleasure or sports; rowing boats and canoes	...	0.2	0.1		97.2	37.5	thsd US$/unit	793
7113	Articles of jewellery and parts thereof, of precious metal	...	...	0.3			2.8	thsd US$/kg	897
8702	Motor vehicles for the transport of ten or more persons, including the driver	...	0.1	0.1		7.1	2.4	thsd US$/unit	783

Source: UN Comtrade and UN ServiceTrade

Turks and Caicos Islands

Services Imports and Exports: EBOPS 2002 categories

Table 2: Merchandise exports by SITC
(Value in million US$, growth and shares in percentage)

SITC	2012	Avg. Growth rates 2008-2012	Avg. Growth rates 2011-2012	2012 share
Total	11.8	-16.9	38.6	100.0
0+1	1.9	-20.2	48.8	15.9
2+4	0.2	-0.6	31.0	1.8
3	0.0	-77.4	-33.3	0.0
5	0.0	-48.8	314.6	0.1
6	0.3	-29.2	13.5	2.8
7	1.4	-44.5	-2.6	11.6
8	7.8	79.8	53.1	65.7
9	0.3	-45.2	-23.3	2.1

Table 3: Merchandise imports by SITC
(Value in million US$, growth and shares in percentage)

SITC	2012	Avg. Growth rates 2008-2012	Avg. Growth rates 2011-2012	2012 share
Total	268.5	-17.9	3.2	100.0
0+1	66.9	-4.7	1.2	24.9
2+4	5.0	-28.6	-19.4	1.8
3	75.9	1.5	1.1	28.3
5	13.4	-22.1	-8.5	5.0
6	26.0	-30.9	-5.0	9.7
7	41.1	-26.9	24.7	15.3
8	36.8	-23.6	7.0	13.7
9	3.6	-33.2	-0.5	1.3

SITC Legend

SITC Code	Description
Total	All commodities
0+1	Food, animals + beverages, tobacco
2+4	Crude materials + anim. & veg. oils
3	Mineral fuels, lubricants
5	Chemicals
6	Goods classified chiefly by material
7	Machinery and transport equipment
8	Miscellaneous manufactured articles
9	Not classified elsewhere in the SITC

Graph 4: Merchandise trade balance
(Mln US$ by MDG Regions in 2012)

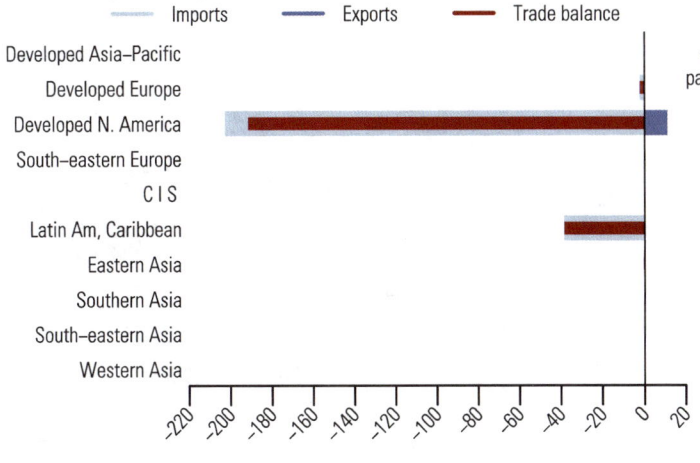

Graph 5: Partner concentration of merchandise trade
(Cumulative share by ranked partners in 2012)

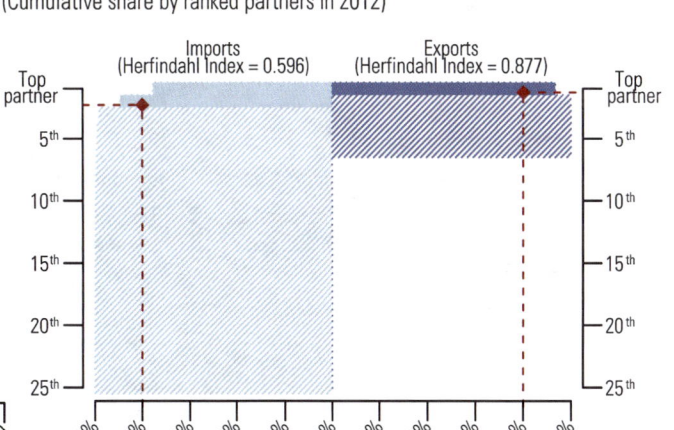

Imports (Herfindahl Index = 0.596)
Exports (Herfindahl Index = 0.877)

Graph 6: No Data Available

Imports Profile:

"Mineral fuels, lubricants" (SITC section 3), "Food, animals + beverages, tobacco" (SITC section 0+1) and "Machinery and transport equipment" (SITC section 7) were the largest commodity groups for imports in 2012, representing respectively 28.3, 24.9 and 15.3 percent of imported goods (see table 3). From 2010 to 2012, the largest import commodity was "Petroleum oils, other than crude" (HS code 2710) (see table 4). The top three partners for merchandise imports were the United States, the Bahamas and Areas nes, accounting for respectively 77.6, 13.9 and 7.0 percent of total imports. Services data by detailed EBOPS category is not available for imports.

Table 4: Top 10 import commodities 2010 to 2012

HS code	4-digit heading of Harmonized System 2007	2010	2011	2012	2010	2011	2012	Unit	SITC code
	All Commodities	...	260.2	268.5					
2710	Petroleum oils, other than crude	...	72.2	73.5		0.6	0.7	US$/kg	334
8703	Motor cars and other motor vehicles principally designed for the transport	...	4.8	7.8		10.4	8.5	thsd US$/unit	781
7113	Articles of jewellery and parts thereof, of precious metal	...	5.7	5.8		855.3	899.1	US$/kg	897
0207	Meat and edible offal, of the poultry of heading 01.05	...	3.8	4.5		0.9	1.1	US$/kg	012
9403	Other furniture and parts thereof	...	3.7	4.1					821
2208	Alcohol of a strength by volume of less than 80 % vol	...	4.2	3.2		12.3	8.3	US$/litre	112
2009	Fruit juices (including grape must) and vegetable juices	...	3.7	3.6		0.5	0.6	US$/kg	059
9999	Commodities not specified according to kind	...	3.6	3.6					931
2203	Beer made from malt	...	3.8	2.8		1.9	1.3	US$/litre	112
1905	Bread, pastry, cakes, biscuits and other bakers' wares	...	3.0	3.3		0.9	1.1	US$/kg	048

Uganda

Goods Imports: CIF, by origin **Goods Exports:** FOB, by last known destination **Trade System:** General

Overview:
In 2014, the value of merchandise exports of Uganda decreased moderately by 6.1 percent to reach 2.3 bln US$, while its merchandise imports increased slightly by 4.4 percent to reach 6.1 bln US$ (see graph 1, table 2 and table 3). The merchandise trade balance recorded a large deficit of 3.8 bln US$ (see graph 1). The largest merchandise trade balance was with MDG Southern Asia at -1.6 bln US$ (see graph 4). Merchandise exports in Uganda were diversified amongst partners; imports were also diversified. The top 14 partners accounted for 80 percent or more of exports and 15 partners accounted for 80 percent or more of imports (see graph 5). In 2013, the value of exports of services of Uganda increased slightly by 2.2 percent, reaching 2.2 bln US$, while its imports of services increased moderately by 8.7 percent and reached 2.7 bln US$ (see graph 2). There was a moderate trade in services deficit of 501.7 mln US$.

Graph 1: Total merchandise trade, by value
(Bln US$ by year)

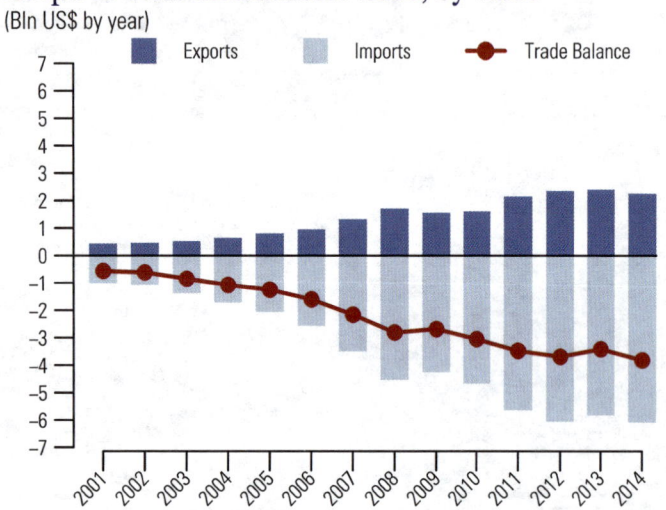

Graph 2: Total services trade, by value
(Bln US$ by year)

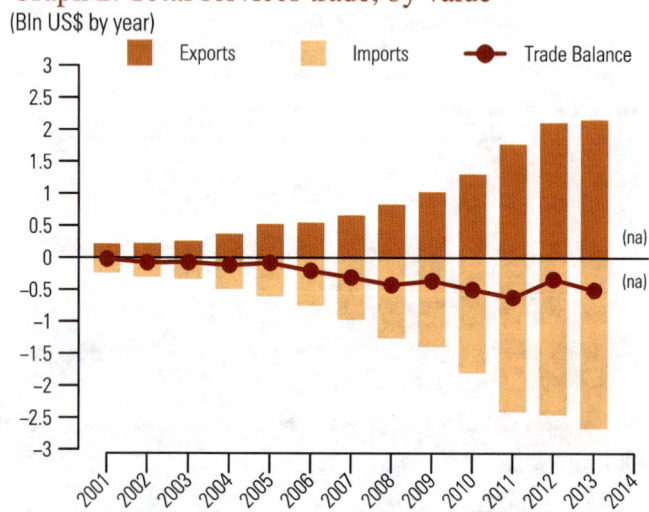

Exports Profile:
"Food, animals + beverages, tobacco" (SITC section 0+1), "Goods classified chiefly by material" (SITC section 6) and "Crude materials + anim. & veg. oils" (SITC section 2+4) were the largest commodity groups for exports in 2014, representing respectively 48.6, 15.4 and 11.9 percent of exported goods (see table 2). From 2012 to 2014, the largest export commodity was "Coffee, whether or not roasted or decaffeinated" (HS code 0901) (see table 1). The top three destinations for merchandise exports were Kenya, the Sudan and Democratic Republic of the Congo, accounting for respectively 12.3, 10.7 and 9.8 percent of total exports. "Travel" (EBOPS code 236) accounted for the largest share of exports of services in 2013 at 1.2 bln US$, followed by "Other business services" (EBOPS code 268) at 297.3 mln US$ and "Construction services" (EBOPS code 249) at 240.4 mln US$ (see graph 3).

Graph 3: Exports of services by EBOPS category
(% share in 2013)

- Travel (54.7 %)
- Other business (13.7 %)
- Construction (11.1 %)
- Transportation (10.3 %)
- Remaining (10.2 %)

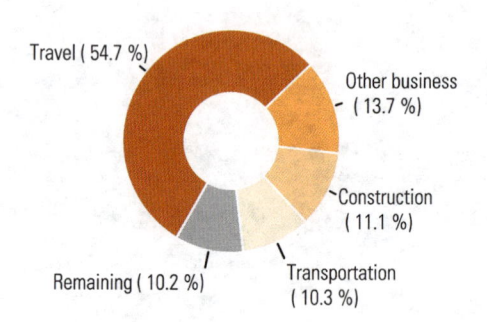

Table 1: Top 10 export commodities 2012 to 2014

HS code	4-digit heading of Harmonized System 2012	Value (million US$) 2012	2013	2014	Unit value 2012	2013	2014	Unit	SITC code
	All Commodities	2357.5	2407.7	2262.0					
0901	Coffee, whether or not roasted or decaffeinated	372.2	425.4	410.1	2.2	1.8	1.9	US$/kg	071
2710	Petroleum oils, other than crude	138.3	135.3	149.0		1.1	1.1	US$/kg	334
2523	Portland cement, aluminous cement, slag cement	107.2	103.0	89.1	0.2	0.2	0.2	US$/kg	661
0304	Fish fillets and other fish meat (whether or not minced)	50.0	104.6	98.0	4.9	5.6	6.1	US$/kg	034
0902	Tea, whether or not flavoured	73.9	85.6	84.7	1.3	1.4	1.4	US$/kg	074
2401	Unmanufactured tobacco; tobacco refuse	58.3	115.0	61.9	3.3	3.5	2.6	US$/kg	121
1701	Cane or beet sugar and chemically pure sucrose, in solid form	76.4	79.8	64.6	0.8	0.7	0.6	US$/kg	061
8517	Electrical apparatus for line telephony or line telegraphy	148.0	49.3	8.2					764
9999	Commodities not specified according to kind	119.4	31.9	37.5					931
0602	Other live plants (including their roots), cuttings and slips; mushroom spawn	52.4	54.5	56.4					292

Source: UN Comtrade and UN ServiceTrade

Uganda

Services Imports and Exports: EBOPS 2002 categories

Table 2: Merchandise exports by SITC
(Value in million US$, growth and shares in percentage)

SITC	2014	Avg. Growth rates 2010-2014	Avg. Growth rates 2013-2014	2014 share
Total	2262.0	8.7	-6.1	100.0
0+1	1098.4	7.6	-8.7	48.6
2+4	269.9	13.3	11.6	11.9
3	184.0	20.2	19.7	8.1
5	94.9	15.5	-1.4	4.2
6	349.4	11.8	-6.3	15.4
7	157.5	-5.5	-32.3	7.0
8	70.1	13.6	-3.9	3.1
9	37.7	4.9	7.6	1.7

Table 3: Merchandise imports by SITC
(Value in million US$, growth and shares in percentage)

SITC	2014	Avg. Growth rates 2010-2014	Avg. Growth rates 2013-2014	2014 share
Total	6073.5	6.8	4.4	100.0
0+1	551.7	9.7	30.3	9.1
2+4	421.7	10.4	18.3	6.9
3	1440.6	11.5	7.5	23.7
5	936.1	13.0	2.0	15.4
6	886.7	3.6	4.0	14.6
7	1460.9	0.9	3.8	24.1
8	374.0	4.6	-10.0	6.2
9	1.8	23.2	-98.3	0.0

SITC Legend

SITC Code	Description
Total	All commodities
0+1	Food, animals + beverages, tobacco
2+4	Crude materials + anim. & veg. oils
3	Mineral fuels, lubricants
5	Chemicals
6	Goods classified chiefly by material
7	Machinery and transport equipment
8	Miscellaneous manufactured articles
9	Not classified elsewhere in the SITC

Graph 4: Merchandise trade balance
(Bln US$ by MDG Regions in 2014)

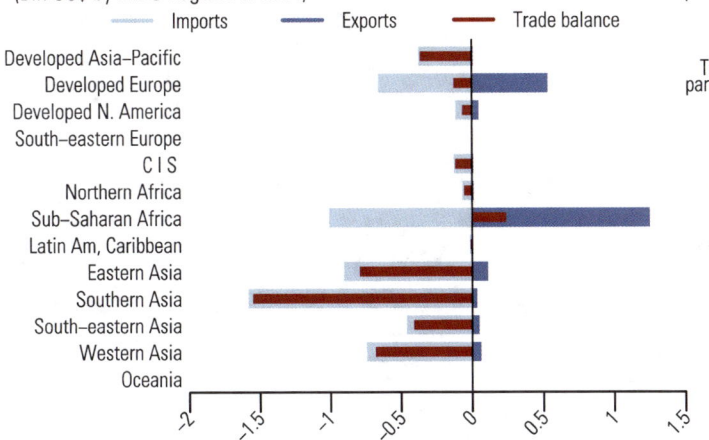

Graph 5: Partner concentration of merchandise trade
(Cumulative share by ranked partners in 2014)

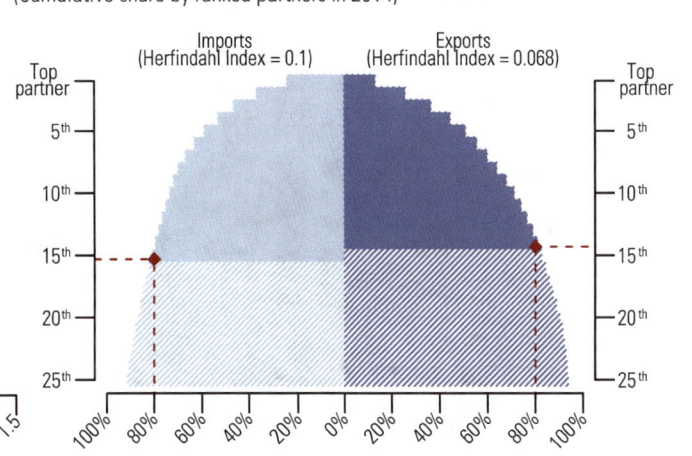

Imports (Herfindahl Index = 0.1)
Exports (Herfindahl Index = 0.068)

Graph 6: Imports of services by EBOPS category
(% share in 2013)

- Transportation (45.0 %)
- Other business (21.2 %)
- Travel (17.0 %)
- Construction (6.7 %)
- Remaining (9.9 %)

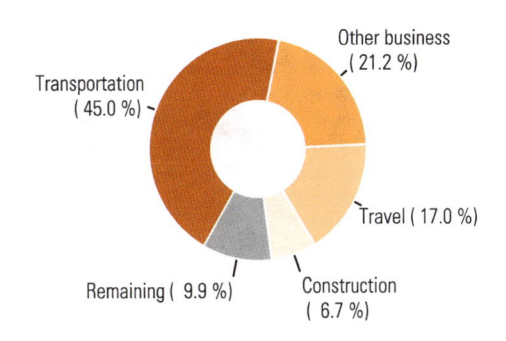

Imports Profile:
"Machinery and transport equipment" (SITC section 7), "Mineral fuels, lubricants" (SITC section 3) and "Chemicals" (SITC section 5) were the largest commodity groups for imports in 2014, representing respectively 24.1, 23.7 and 15.4 percent of imported goods (see table 3). From 2012 to 2014, the largest import commodity was "Petroleum oils, other than crude" (HS code 2710) (see table 4). The top three partners for merchandise imports were India, China and Kenya, accounting for respectively 24.1, 11.4 and 9.7 percent of total imports. "Transportation" (EBOPS code 205) accounted for the largest share of imports of services in 2013 at 1.2 bln US$, followed by "Other business services" (EBOPS code 268) at 566.3 mln US$ and "Travel" (EBOPS code 236) at 452.7 mln US$ (see graph 6).

Table 4: Top 10 import commodities 2012 to 2014

HS code	4-digit heading of Harmonized System 2012	2012	2013	2014	2012	2013	2014	Unit	SITC code
	All Commodities	6044.1	5817.5	6073.5					
2710	Petroleum oils, other than crude	1309.0	1281.1	1392.0		1.0	1.0	US$/kg	334
3004	Medicaments (excluding goods of heading 30.02, 30.05 or 30.06)	203.2	290.8	297.7	13.7	19.2	17.8	US$/kg	542
1511	Palm oil and its fractions	229.5	209.9	247.7	1.1	0.9	0.9	US$/kg	422
8703	Motor cars and other motor vehicles principally designed for the transport	213.4	209.0	220.9	5.3	5.2	5.8	thsd US$/unit	781
8517	Electrical apparatus for line telephony or line telegraphy	249.4	165.9	100.1					764
8704	Motor vehicles for the transport of goods	144.8	112.4	134.5	11.7	11.1	12.2	thsd US$/unit	782
1701	Cane or beet sugar and chemically pure sucrose, in solid form	130.5	127.9	87.8	0.8	0.7	0.6	US$/kg	061
9999	Commodities not specified according to kind	235.4	104.5	1.8					931
2523	Portland cement, aluminous cement, slag cement	106.6	84.8	96.5	0.1	0.1	0.1	US$/kg	661
1001	Wheat and meslin	16.5	61.7	165.4	0.4	0.3	0.3	US$/kg	041

Source: UN Comtrade and UN ServiceTrade

Ukraine

Goods Imports: CIF, by origin   **Goods Exports: FOB, by last known destination**   **Trade System: General**

Overview:

In 2014, the value of merchandise exports of Ukraine decreased substantially by 14.9 percent to reach 53.9 bln US$, while its merchandise imports decreased substantially by 29.4 percent to reach 54.4 bln US$ (see graph 1, table 2 and table 3). The merchandise trade balance recorded a relatively small deficit of 468.1 mln US$ (see graph 1). The largest merchandise trade balance was with MDG Western Asia at 5.4 bln US$ (see graph 4). Merchandise exports in Ukraine were diversified amongst partners; imports were also diversified. The top 27 partners accounted for 80 percent or more of exports and 18 partners accounted for 80 percent or more of imports (see graph 5). In 2013, the value of exports of services of Ukraine increased moderately by 9.1 percent, reaching 14.8 bln US$, while its imports of services increased substantially by 13.0 percent and reached 7.6 bln US$ (see graph 2). There was a large trade in services surplus of 7.2 bln US$.

Graph 1: Total merchandise trade, by value
(Bln US$ by year)

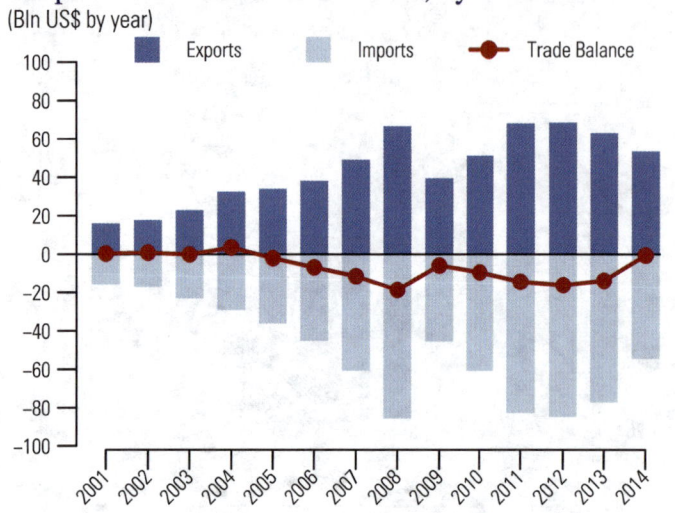

Graph 2: Total services trade, by value
(Bln US$ by year)

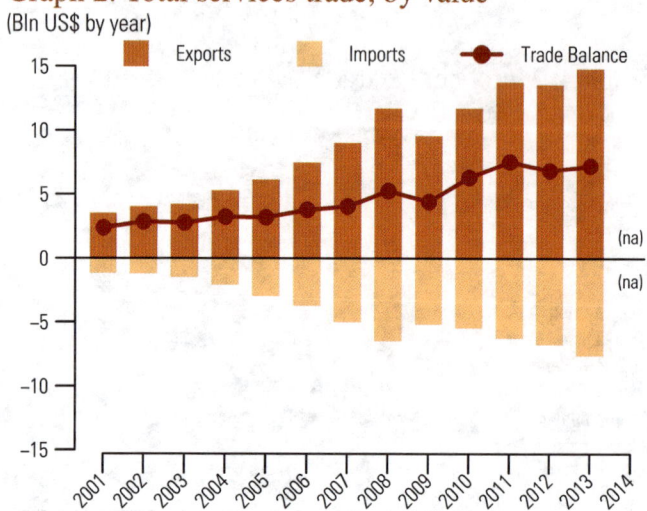

Exports Profile:

"Goods classified chiefly by material" (SITC section 6), "Crude materials + anim. & veg. oils" (SITC section 2+4) and "Food, animals + beverages, tobacco" (SITC section 0+1) were the largest commodity groups for exports in 2014, representing respectively 32.0, 20.8 and 20.6 percent of exported goods (see table 2). From 2012 to 2014, the largest export commodity was "Semi-finished products of iron or non-alloy steel" (HS code 7207) (see table 1). The top three destinations for merchandise exports were the Russian Federation, Turkey and Egypt, accounting for respectively 22.9, 5.9 and 4.6 percent of total exports. "Transportation" (EBOPS code 205) accounted for the largest share of exports of services in 2013 at 8.3 bln US$, followed by "Other business services" (EBOPS code 268) at 1.6 bln US$ and "Computer and information services" (EBOPS code 262) at 1.1 bln US$ (see graph 3).

Graph 3: Exports of services by EBOPS category
(% share in 2013)

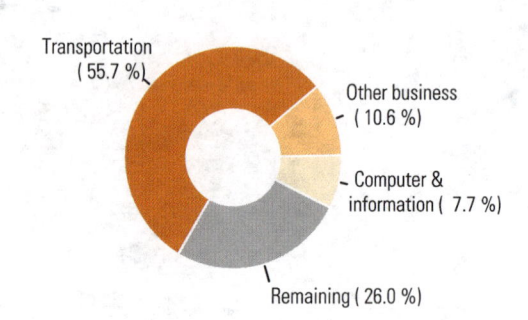

- Transportation (55.7 %)
- Other business (10.6 %)
- Computer & information (7.7 %)
- Remaining (26.0 %)

Table 1: Top 10 export commodities 2012 to 2014

HS code	4-digit heading of Harmonized System 2007	Value (million US$) 2012	2013	2014	Unit value 2012	2013	2014	Unit	SITC code
	All Commodities	68 694.5	63 320.5	53 913.3					
7207	Semi-finished products of iron or non-alloy steel	5 423.1	5 254.8	4 342.1	0.5	0.5	0.5	US$/kg	672
1005	Maize (corn)	3 893.0	3 833.3	3 350.7	0.2	0.2	0.2	US$/kg	044
1512	Sunflower-seed, safflower or cotton-seed oil	3 934.0	3 281.3	3 554.3	1.1	1.0	0.8	US$/kg	421
2601	Iron ores and concentrates, including roasted iron pyrites	3 131.7	3 739.1	3 315.4	0.1	0.1	0.1	US$/kg	281
7208	Flat-rolled products of iron or non-alloy steel	2 971.8	2 763.0	2 533.0	0.6	0.5	0.5	US$/kg	673
1001	Wheat and meslin	2 330.5	1 891.5	2 290.8	0.3	0.2	0.2	US$/kg	041
8606	Railway or tramway goods vans and wagons, not self-propelled	2 908.4	1 330.9	234.4	71.1	64.4	46.9	thsd US$/unit	791
7214	Other bars and rods of iron or non-alloy steel	1 605.2	1 519.9	1 322.4	0.6	0.6	0.5	US$/kg	676
3102	Mineral or chemical fertilisers, nitrogenous	1 690.0	1 133.5	646.1	0.3	0.3	0.3	US$/kg	562
8544	Insulated (including enamelled or anodised) wire, cable	945.8	1 081.6	1 170.2	15.2	17.8	18.2	US$/kg	773

Ukraine

Services Imports and Exports: EBOPS 2002 categories

Table 2: Merchandise exports by SITC
(Value in million US$, growth and shares in percentage)

SITC	2014	Avg. Growth rates 2010-2014	Avg. Growth rates 2013-2014	2014 share
Total	53 913.3	1.2	-14.9	100.0
0+1	11 122.2	15.3	-3.3	20.6
2+4	11 220.4	9.2	-3.0	20.8
3	2 012.7	-13.9	-29.8	3.7
5	2 824.4	-4.7	-30.8	5.2
6	17 251.7	-2.5	-14.1	32.0
7	7 095.5	-5.5	-30.9	13.2
8	2 110.3	4.2	-8.8	3.9
9	276.2	-6.8	-56.9	0.5

Table 3: Merchandise imports by SITC
(Value in million US$, growth and shares in percentage)

SITC	2014	Avg. Growth rates 2010-2014	Avg. Growth rates 2013-2014	2014 share
Total	54 381.4	-2.7	-29.4	100.0
0+1	5 309.5	1.2	-26.5	9.8
2+4	2 049.1	-5.9	-20.8	3.8
3	15 116.4	-6.3	-28.8	27.8
5	9 081.2	1.3	-18.7	16.7
6	7 674.7	-3.2	-27.4	14.1
7	11 314.2	-1.2	-38.5	20.8
8	3 247.3	-2.8	-33.0	6.0
9	589.2	-0.5	-37.7	1.1

SITC Legend

SITC Code	Description
Total	All commodities
0+1	Food, animals + beverages, tobacco
2+4	Crude materials + anim. & veg. oils
3	Mineral fuels, lubricants
5	Chemicals
6	Goods classified chiefly by material
7	Machinery and transport equipment
8	Miscellaneous manufactured articles
9	Not classified elsewhere in the SITC

Graph 4: Merchandise trade balance
(Bln US$ by MDG Regions in 2014)

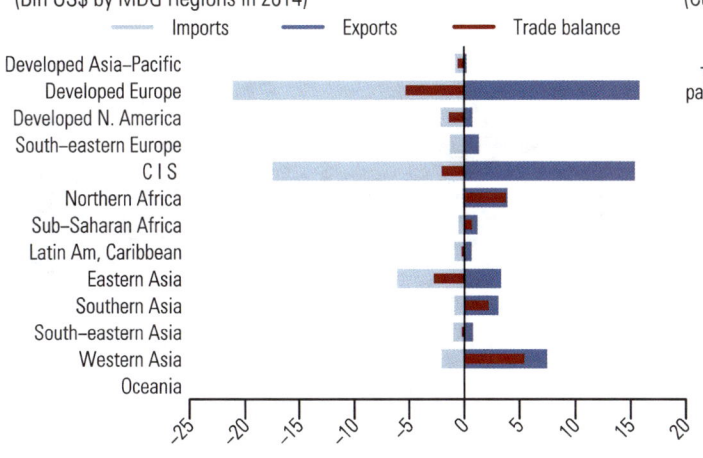

Graph 5: Partner concentration of merchandise trade
(Cumulative share by ranked partners in 2014)

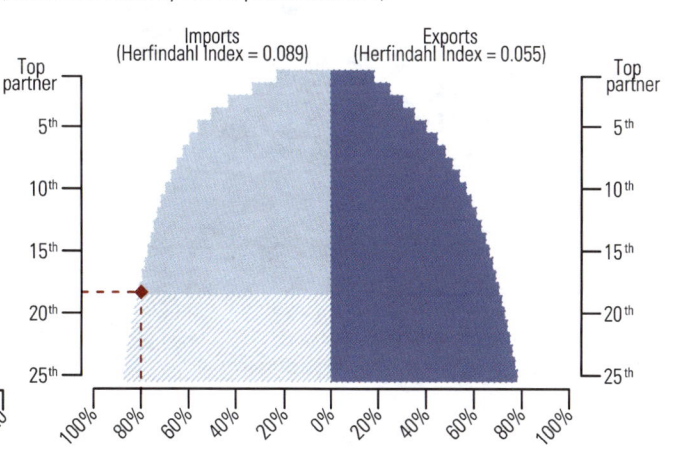

Imports (Herfindahl Index = 0.089)
Exports (Herfindahl Index = 0.055)

Graph 6: Imports of services by EBOPS category
(% share in 2013)

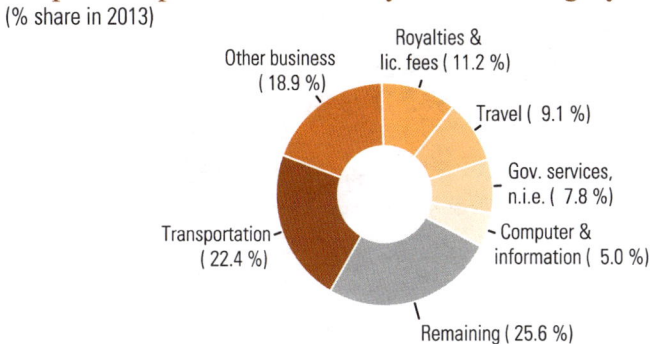

- Other business (18.9 %)
- Royalties & lic. fees (11.2 %)
- Travel (9.1 %)
- Gov. services, n.i.e. (7.8 %)
- Computer & information (5.0 %)
- Remaining (25.6 %)
- Transportation (22.4 %)

Imports Profile:

"Mineral fuels, lubricants" (SITC section 3), "Machinery and transport equipment" (SITC section 7) and "Chemicals" (SITC section 5) were the largest commodity groups for imports in 2014, representing respectively 27.8, 20.8 and 16.7 percent of imported goods (see table 3). From 2012 to 2014, the largest import commodity was "Petroleum gases and other gaseous hydrocarbons" (HS code 2711) (see table 4). The top three partners for merchandise imports were the Russian Federation, China and Germany, accounting for respectively 29.3, 9.8 and 8.8 percent of total imports. "Transportation" (EBOPS code 205) accounted for the largest share of imports of services in 2013 at 1.7 bln US$, followed by "Other business services" (EBOPS code 268) at 1.4 bln US$ and "Royalties and license fees" (EBOPS code 266) at 854.2 mln US$ (see graph 6).

Table 4: Top 10 import commodities 2012 to 2014

HS code	4-digit heading of Harmonized System 2007	Value 2012	Value 2013	Value 2014	Unit value 2012	Unit value 2013	Unit value 2014	Unit	SITC code
	All Commodities	84 656.7	76 986.0	54 381.4					
2711	Petroleum gases and other gaseous hydrocarbons	14 289.0	11 822.0	6 018.3	0.6	0.6	0.4	US$/kg	343
2710	Petroleum oils, other than crude	7 606.7	6 418.3	6 685.2	1.0	1.0	0.9	US$/kg	334
3004	Medicaments (excluding goods of heading 30.02, 30.05 or 30.06)	2 881.2	2 597.9	2 091.8	81.6	91.1	87.2	US$/kg	542
8703	Motor cars and other motor vehicles principally designed for the transport	3 247.1	2 995.5	1 209.9	15.8	17.3	19.3	thsd US$/unit	781
2701	Coal; briquettes, ovoids and similar solid fuels manufactured from coal	2 637.0	1 980.9	1 768.7	0.2	0.1	0.1	US$/kg	321
8517	Electrical apparatus for line telephony or line telegraphy	740.0	810.7	654.6					764
3808	Insecticides, rodenticides, fungicides, herbicides	754.6	769.5	608.4	8.3	9.0	8.2	US$/kg	591
2709	Petroleum oils and oils obtained from bituminous minerals, crude	1 235.9	630.3	146.5	0.8	0.8	0.8	US$/kg	333
8704	Motor vehicles for the transport of goods	846.6	755.1	359.6	5.8	6.0	4.4	thsd US$/unit	782
8401	Nuclear reactors; fuel elements (cartridges), non-irradiated	623.5	619.7	652.5	1.6	1.5	1.6	thsd US$/kg	718

Source: UN Comtrade and UN ServiceTrade

United Arab Emirates

Goods Imports: CIF, by origin **Goods Exports: FOB, by last known destination** **Trade System: Special**

Overview:
In 2011, the value of merchandise exports of the United Arab Emirates increased substantially by 27.3 percent to reach 252.6 bln US$, while its merchandise imports increased substantially by 16.7 percent to reach 210.9 bln US$ (see graph 1, table 2 and table 3). The merchandise trade balance recorded a relatively small surplus of 41.6 bln US$ (see graph 1). The largest merchandise trade balance was with MDG Eastern Asia at 76.0 bln US$ (see graph 4). Merchandise exports in the United Arab Emirates were moderately concentrated amongst partners; imports were diversified. The top 5 partners accounted for 80 percent or more of exports and 17 partners accounted for 80 percent or more of imports (see graph 5). In 2012, the value of exports of services of the United Arab Emirates increased substantially by 17.7 percent, reaching 15.1 bln US$, while its imports of services increased substantially by 13.1 percent and reached 63.9 bln US$ (see graph 2). There was a large trade in services deficit of 48.9 bln US$.

Graph 1: Total merchandise trade, by value
(Bln US$ by year)

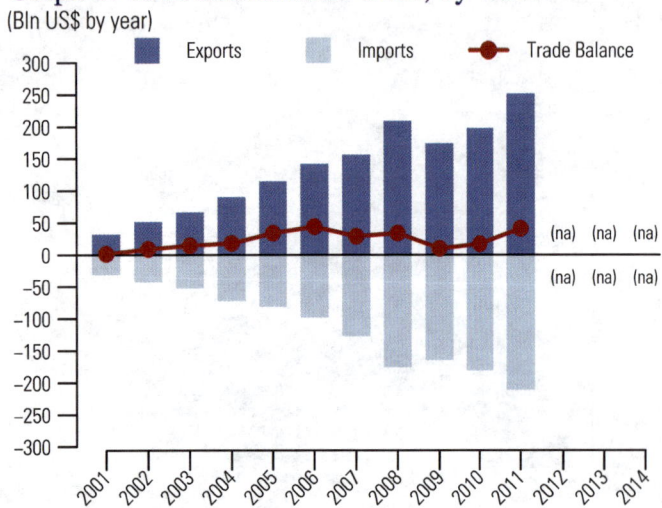

Graph 2: Total services trade, by value
(Bln US$ by year)

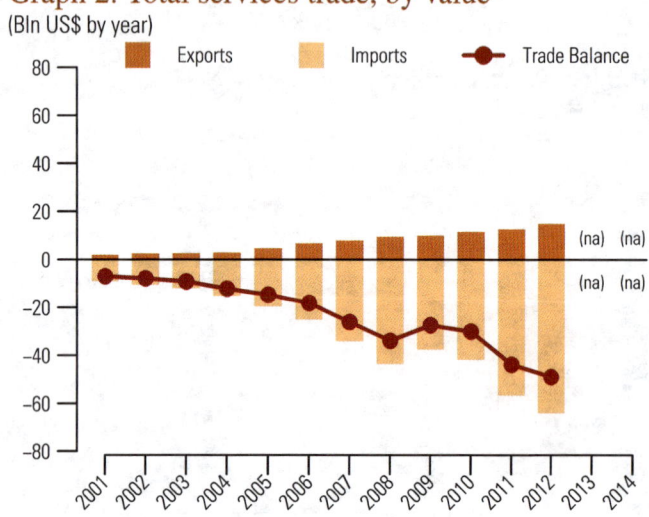

Exports Profile:
"Mineral fuels, lubricants" (SITC section 3), "Not classified elsewhere in the SITC" (SITC section 9) and "Goods classified chiefly by material" (SITC section 6) were the largest commodity groups for exports in 2011, representing respectively 41.4, 31.4 and 10.8 percent of exported goods (see table 2). From 2009 to 2011, the largest export commodity was "Petroleum oils, crude" (HS code 2709) (see table 1). The top three destinations for merchandise exports were Other Asia nes, Areas nes and India, accounting for respectively 32.8, 31.2 and 9.4 percent of total exports. "Travel" (EBOPS code 236) accounted for the largest share of exports of services in 2012 at 10.4 bln US$, followed by "Transportation" (EBOPS code 205) at 3.9 bln US$ and "Government services, n.i.e." (EBOPS code 291) at 789.7 mln US$ (see graph 3).

Graph 3: Exports of services by EBOPS category
(% share in 2012)

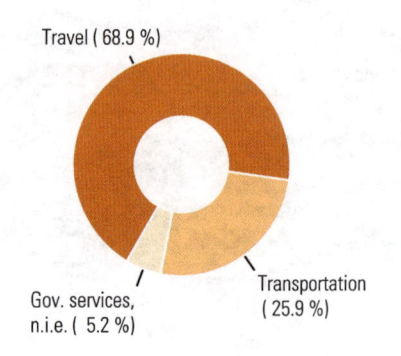

- Travel (68.9 %)
- Transportation (25.9 %)
- Gov. services, n.i.e. (5.2 %)

Table 1: Top 10 export commodities 2009 to 2011

HS code	4-digit heading of Harmonized System 2002	Value (million US$) 2009	2010	2011	Unit value 2009	2010	2011	Unit	SITC code
	All Commodities	174725.0	198362.0	252556.0					
2709	Petroleum oils, crude	43535.4	65482.1	91935.8					333
9999	Commodities not specified according to kind	53154.1	51994.9	60902.6					931
7108	Gold (including gold plated with platinum)	10520.8	11508.4	18201.4					971
7102	Diamonds, whether or not worked, but not mounted or set	7692.7	15193.9	17087.8					667
2710	Petroleum oils, other than crude	15852.0	6514.1	10087.3					334
7113	Articles of jewellery and parts thereof, of precious metal	3046.3	3689.2	5458.6					897
8703	Motor cars and other motor vehicles principally designed for the transport	3283.5	3237.1	3467.9					781
2711	Petroleum gases and other gaseous hydrocarbons	5157.5	2030.7	2519.9					343
8517	Electrical apparatus for line telephony or line telegraphy	1791.7	2352.2	2840.7					764
8803	Parts of goods of heading 88.01 or 88.02	1268.2	1732.5	1111.2					792

United Arab Emirates

Services Imports and Exports: EBOPS 2002 categories

Table 2: Merchandise exports by SITC
(Value in million US$, growth and shares in percentage)

SITC	2011	Avg. Growth rates 2007-2011	Avg. Growth rates 2010-2011	2011 share
Total	252 556.0	12.7	27.3	100.0
0+1	4 797.8	17.4	6.9	1.9
2+4	1 963.9	5.7	38.9	0.8
3	104 579.5	7.7	41.2	41.4
5	4 139.2	14.4	26.5	1.6
6	27 334.2	21.0	20.2	10.8
7	21 202.3	11.1	5.4	8.4
8	9 281.1	15.4	21.8	3.7
9	79 257.9	18.2	22.6	31.4

Table 3: Merchandise imports by SITC
(Value in million US$, growth and shares in percentage)

SITC	2011	Avg. Growth rates 2007-2011	Avg. Growth rates 2010-2011	2011 share
Total	210 945.0	13.5	16.7	100.0
0+1	12 074.1	14.4	16.1	5.7
2+4	4 861.0	17.2	54.8	2.3
3	2 808.0	27.2	38.4	1.3
5	10 102.3	8.8	20.1	4.8
6	39 947.8	10.5	26.3	18.9
7	48 328.5	6.1	15.3	22.9
8	18 101.2	7.2	11.8	8.6
9	74 722.1	25.1	11.5	35.4

SITC Legend

SITC Code	Description
Total	All commodities
0+1	Food, animals + beverages, tobacco
2+4	Crude materials + anim. & veg. oils
3	Mineral fuels, lubricants
5	Chemicals
6	Goods classified chiefly by material
7	Machinery and transport equipment
8	Miscellaneous manufactured articles
9	Not classified elsewhere in the SITC

Graph 4: Merchandise trade balance
(Bln US$ by MDG Regions in 2011)

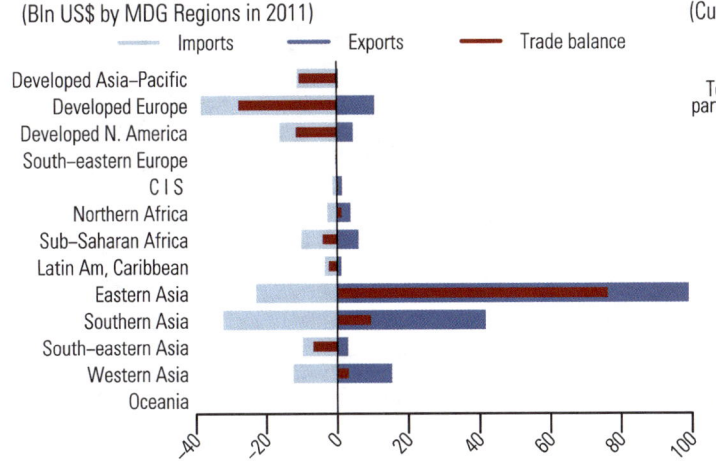

Graph 5: Partner concentration of merchandise trade
(Cumulative share by ranked partners in 2011)

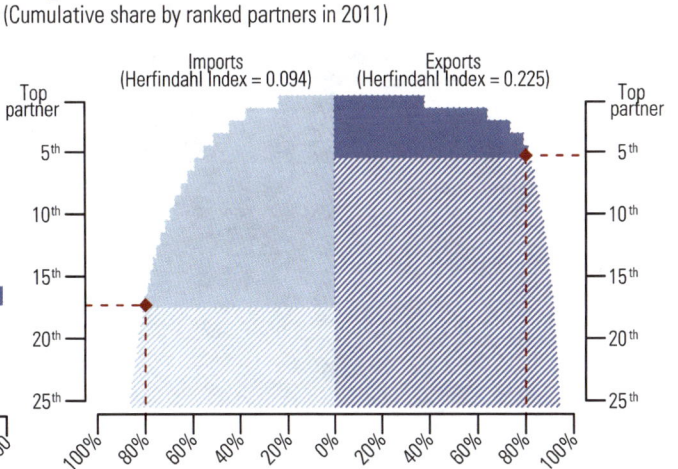

Imports (Herfindahl Index = 0.094)
Exports (Herfindahl Index = 0.225)

Graph 6: Imports of services by EBOPS category
(% share in 2012)

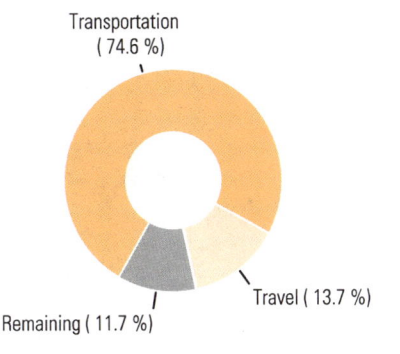

- Transportation (74.6 %)
- Travel (13.7 %)
- Remaining (11.7 %)

Imports Profile:

"Not classified elsewhere in the SITC" (SITC section 9), "Machinery and transport equipment" (SITC section 7) and "Goods classified chiefly by material" (SITC section 6) were the largest commodity groups for imports in 2011, representing respectively 35.4, 22.9 and 18.9 percent of imported goods (see table 3). From 2009 to 2011, the largest import commodity was "Commodities not specified according to kind" (HS code 9999) (see table 4). The top three partners for merchandise imports were Areas nes, India and China, accounting for respectively 26.1, 12.2 and 7.5 percent of total imports. "Transportation" (EBOPS code 205) accounted for the largest share of imports of services in 2012 at 47.7 bln US$, followed by "Travel" (EBOPS code 236) at 8.7 bln US$ (see graph 6).

Table 4: Top 10 import commodities 2009 to 2011

HS code	4-digit heading of Harmonized System 2002	Value (million US$) 2009	2010	2011	Unit value 2009	2010	2011	Unit	SITC code
	All Commodities	164 251.0	180 726.0	210 945.0					
9999	Commodities not specified according to kind	42 663.7	48 773.7	47 038.0					931
7108	Gold (including gold plated with platinum)	14 513.0	18 051.1	27 210.9					971
7102	Diamonds, whether or not worked, but not mounted or set	7 223.5	13 108.0	16 144.0					667
8703	Motor cars and other motor vehicles principally designed for the transport	5 203.5	7 324.5	7 645.1					781
7113	Articles of jewellery and parts thereof, of precious metal	5 172.2	6 150.9	6 352.9					897
8803	Parts of goods of heading 88.01 or 88.02	3 462.4	2 807.1	3 354.2					792
8517	Electrical apparatus for line telephony or line telegraphy	2 901.5	2 843.5	2 602.2					764
8802	Other aircraft (for example, helicopters, aeroplanes); spacecraft	1 603.8	2 191.6	3 799.8					792
8411	Turbo-jets, turbo-propellers and other gas turbines	2 166.9	2 161.1	2 515.8					714
8708	Parts and accessories of the motor vehicles of headings 87.01 to 87.05	1 603.2	1 833.3	1 978.9					784

United Kingdom

Goods Imports: CIF, by origin/consignment for intra-eu   **Goods Exports:** FOB, by last known destination   **Trade System:** General

Overview:

In 2014, the value of merchandise exports of the United Kingdom decreased moderately by 6.7 percent to reach 511.3 bln US$, while its merchandise imports increased slightly by 4.6 percent to reach 687.3 bln US$ (see graph 1, table 2 and table 3). After a reduction in the merchandise trade deficit in 2013, the deficit increased to 176.0 bln US$ in 2014, as a result of decreased exports and increased imports (see graph 1). The largest merchandise trade balance was with MDG Developed Europe at -128.3 bln US$ (see graph 4). Merchandise exports in the United Kingdom were diversified amongst partners; imports were also diversified. The top 21 partners accounted for 80 percent or more of exports and 20 partners accounted for 80 percent or more of imports (see graph 5). In 2013, the value of exports of services of the United Kingdom increased substantially by 13.8 percent, reaching 332.0 bln US$, while its imports of services increased substantially by 13.1 percent and reached 205.2 bln US$ (see graph 2). There was a moderate trade in services surplus of 126.8 bln US$.

Graph 1: Total merchandise trade, by value
(Bln US$ by year)

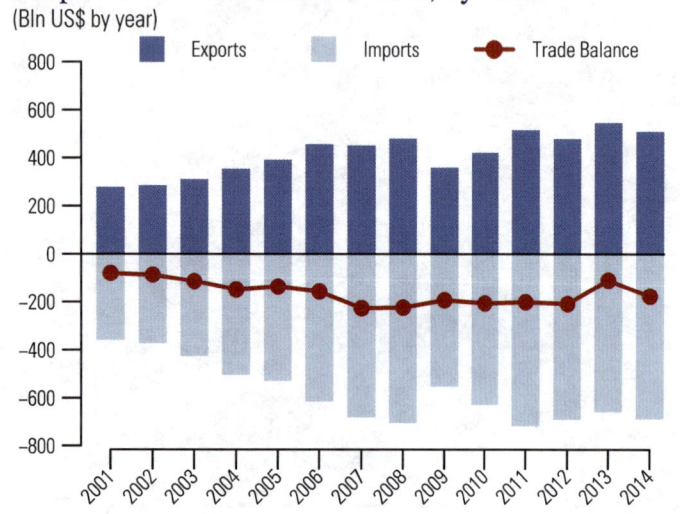

Graph 2: Total services trade, by value
(Bln US$ by year)

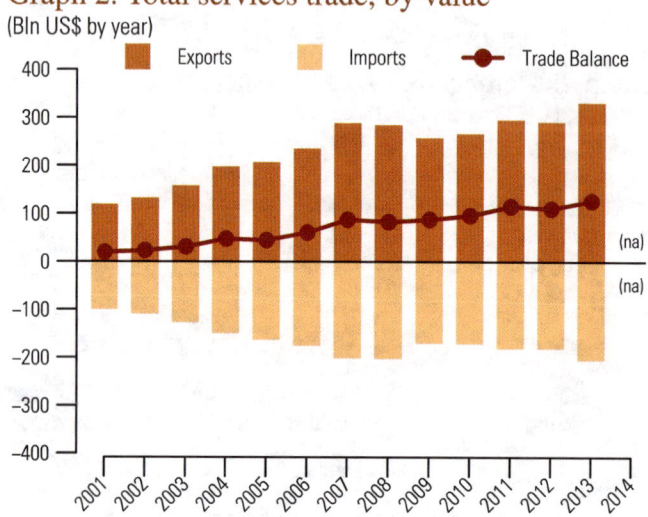

Exports Profile:

"Machinery and transport equipment" (SITC section 7), "Chemicals" (SITC section 5) and "Miscellaneous manufactured articles" (SITC section 8) were the largest commodity groups for exports in 2014, representing respectively 34.5, 14.8 and 12.3 percent of exported goods (see table 2). In particular, SITC section 7, the largest SITC section, registered a strong growth of 14.7 percent in 2014. From 2012 to 2014, the largest export commodity was "Gold (including gold plated with platinum)" (HS code 7108) (see table 1). The top three destinations for merchandise exports were the United States, Germany and Switzerland, accounting for respectively 12.4, 9.9 and 7.9 percent of total exports. "Other business services" (EBOPS code 268) accounted for the largest share of exports of services in 2013 at 81.1 bln US$, followed by "Insurance services" (EBOPS code 253) at 35.4 bln US$ (see graph 3).

Graph 3: Exports of services by EBOPS category
(% share in 2013)

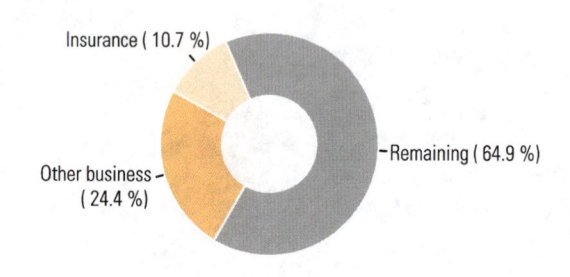

- Insurance (10.7 %)
- Other business (24.4 %)
- Remaining (64.9 %)

Table 1: Top 10 export commodities 2012 to 2014

HS code	4-digit heading of Harmonized System 2012	Value (million US$) 2012	2013	2014	Unit value 2012	2013	2014	Unit	SITC code
	All Commodities...	481 225.8	548 041.9	511 283.3					
7108	Gold (including gold plated with platinum).........................	2 314.9	79 120.8	37 574.1	46.8	45.4	39.8	thsd US$/kg	971
8703	Motor cars and other motor vehicles principally designed for the transport..............	33 990.0	38 228.3	42 363.5	22.5	25.1	29.6	thsd US$/unit	781
2709	Petroleum oils and oils obtained from bituminous minerals, crude............................	30 654.3	29 793.9	29 717.6	0.8	0.8	0.8	US$/kg	333
9999	Commodities not specified according to kind.........................	41 959.4	31 381.6	13 537.9					931
2710	Petroleum oils, other than crude...	27 886.1	25 963.0	20 187.1	0.9	0.9	0.8	US$/kg	334
3004	Medicaments (excluding goods of heading 30.02, 30.05 or 30.06)............................	23 226.5	20 885.9	23 302.7	122.0	111.7	128.9	US$/kg	542
8411	Turbo-jets, turbo-propellers and other gas turbines.............	20 068.9	22 130.9	21 427.3					714
2208	Alcohol of a strength by volume of less than 80 % vol.........	8 514.6	8 447.9	8 348.7	20.0	19.5	19.6	US$/litre	112
3002	Human blood; animal blood prepared for therapeutic uses...	6 291.8	7 191.2	8 089.9	367.8	342.9	343.0	US$/kg	541
8708	Parts and accessories of the motor vehicles of headings 87.01 to 87.05.............	6 642.9	6 463.4	6 488.6	9.4	9.5	10.0	US$/kg	784

United Kingdom

Services Imports and Exports: EBOPS 2002 categories

Table 2: Merchandise exports by SITC
(Value in million US$, growth and shares in percentage)

SITC	2014	Avg. Growth rates 2010-2014	2013-2014	2014 share
Total	511 283.3	4.9	-6.7	100.0
0+1	31 040.6	5.6	5.3	6.1
2+4	10 819.8	0.3	-2.2	2.1
3	55 867.9	1.7	-9.9	10.9
5	75 536.2	0.8	3.3	14.8
6	46 902.7	1.1	-5.6	9.2
7	176 371.8	8.1	14.7	34.5
8	62 830.9	6.6	9.8	12.3
9	51 913.3	7.6	-53.5	10.2

Table 3: Merchandise imports by SITC
(Value in million US$, growth and shares in percentage)

SITC	2014	Avg. Growth rates 2010-2014	2013-2014	2014 share
Total	687 269.9	2.3	4.6	100.0
0+1	63 624.7	4.3	3.8	9.3
2+4	18 515.6	1.7	0.6	2.7
3	77 333.4	5.1	-12.3	11.3
5	78 651.3	3.2	6.2	11.4
6	73 374.6	-0.6	-1.1	10.7
7	239 882.4	5.6	18.1	34.9
8	105 533.7	3.1	9.4	15.4
9	30 354.2	-16.4	-26.8	4.4

SITC Legend

SITC Code	Description
Total	All commodities
0+1	Food, animals + beverages, tobacco
2+4	Crude materials + anim. & veg. oils
3	Mineral fuels, lubricants
5	Chemicals
6	Goods classified chiefly by material
7	Machinery and transport equipment
8	Miscellaneous manufactured articles
9	Not classified elsewhere in the SITC

Graph 4: Merchandise trade balance
(Bln US$ by MDG Regions in 2014)

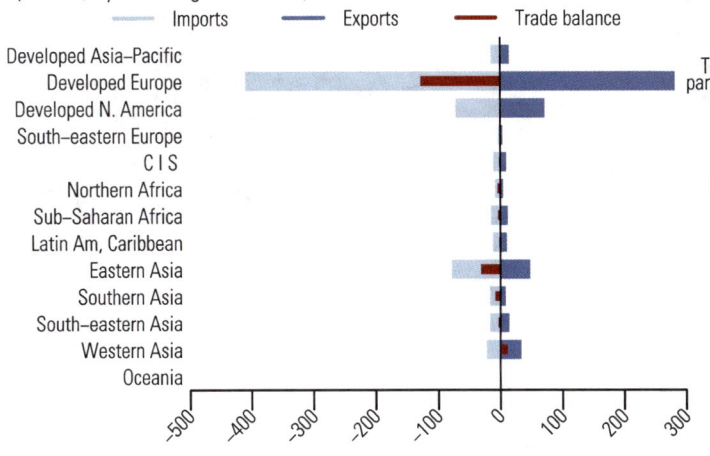

Graph 5: Partner concentration of merchandise trade
(Cumulative share by ranked partners in 2014)

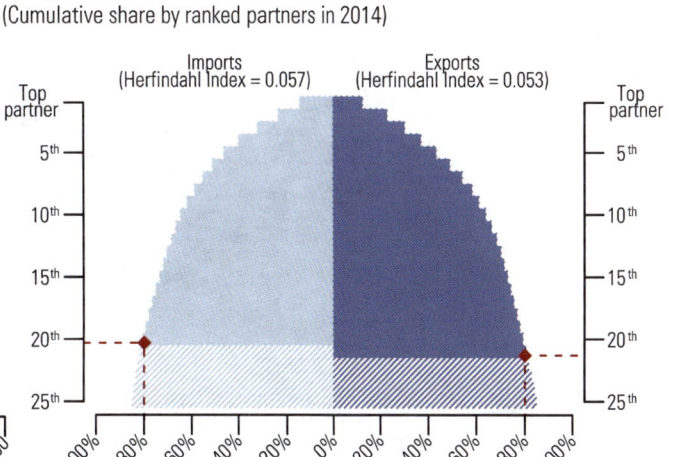

Imports (Herfindahl Index = 0.057)
Exports (Herfindahl Index = 0.053)

Graph 6: Imports of services by EBOPS category
(% share in 2013)

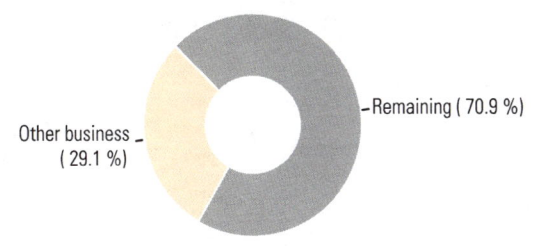

Other business (29.1 %)
Remaining (70.9 %)

Imports Profile:

"Machinery and transport equipment" (SITC section 7), "Miscellaneous manufactured articles" (SITC section 8) and "Chemicals" (SITC section 5) were the largest commodity groups for imports in 2014, representing respectively 34.9, 15.4 and 11.4 percent of imported goods (see table 3). From 2012 to 2014, the largest import commodity was "Petroleum oils and oils obtained from bituminous minerals, crude" (HS code 2709) (see table 4). The top three partners for merchandise imports were Germany, China and the United States, accounting for respectively 13.4, 8.8 and 8.6 percent of total imports. "Other business services" (EBOPS code 268) accounted for the largest share of imports of services in 2013 at 59.8 bln US$ (see graph 6).

Table 4: Top 10 import commodities 2012 to 2014

HS code	4-digit heading of Harmonized System 2012	2012	2013	2014	2012	2013	2014	Unit	SITC code
	All Commodities	689 137.0	657 222.5	687 269.9					
2709	Petroleum oils and oils obtained from bituminous minerals, crude	47 915.4	40 092.0	35 971.9	0.9	0.8	0.8	US$/kg	333
8703	Motor cars and other motor vehicles principally designed for the transport	34 504.5	38 762.8	46 331.9	18.1	18.0	19.6	thsd US$/unit	781
9999	Commodities not specified according to kind	75 805.0	25 962.9	9 483.4					931
2710	Petroleum oils, other than crude	28 072.4	27 621.7	25 809.9	1.0	1.0	0.9	US$/kg	334
3004	Medicaments (excluding goods of heading 30.02, 30.05 or 30.06)	16 514.1	17 619.4	21 012.0	89.7	103.3	109.0	US$/kg	542
8517	Electrical apparatus for line telephony or line telegraphy	15 887.1	17 507.7	16 635.6					764
8411	Turbo-jets, turbo-propellers and other gas turbines	14 951.5	16 393.3	16 261.9					714
8708	Parts and accessories of the motor vehicles of headings 87.01 to 87.05	14 714.5	15 388.3	16 480.4	9.3	9.6	10.4	US$/kg	784
8471	Automatic data processing machines and units thereof	14 308.8	14 406.8	14 910.3	164.6	152.8	171.3	US$/unit	752
7108	Gold (including gold plated with platinum)	5 555.4	15 197.5	20 296.2	43.3	44.7	40.8	thsd US$/kg	971

United Republic of Tanzania

Goods Imports: CIF, by origin **Goods Exports:** FOB, by last known destination **Trade System:** General

Overview:
In 2014, the value of merchandise exports of the United Republic of Tanzania increased substantially by 29.3 percent to reach 5.7 bln US$, while its merchandise imports increased slightly by 1.3 percent to reach 12.7 bln US$ (see graph 1, table 2 and table 3). The merchandise trade balance recorded a large deficit of 7.0 bln US$ (see graph 1). The largest merchandise trade balance was with MDG Developed Europe at -1.8 bln US$ (see graph 4). Merchandise exports in the United Republic of Tanzania were diversified amongst partners; imports were also diversified. The top 12 partners accounted for 80 percent or more of exports and 13 partners accounted for 80 percent or more of imports (see graph 5). In 2013, the value of exports of services of the United Republic of Tanzania increased substantially by 14.6 percent, reaching 3.0 bln US$, while its imports of services increased moderately by 5.8 percent and reached 2.5 bln US$ (see graph 2). There was a relatively small trade in services surplus of 520.7 mln US$.

Graph 1: Total merchandise trade, by value
(Bln US$ by year)

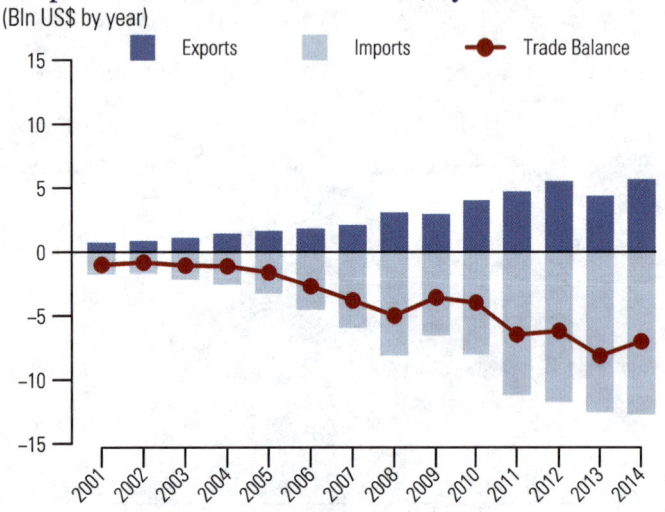

Graph 2: Total services trade, by value
(Bln US$ by year)

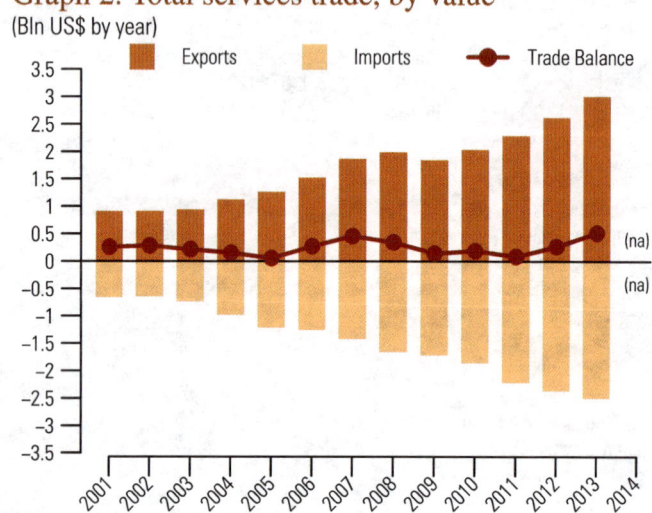

Exports Profile:
"Food, animals + beverages, tobacco" (SITC section 0+1), "Crude materials + anim. & veg. oils" (SITC section 2+4) and "Not classified elsewhere in the SITC" (SITC section 9) were the largest commodity groups for exports in 2014, representing respectively 33.5, 26.8 and 23.2 percent of exported goods (see table 2). From 2012 to 2014, the largest export commodity was "Gold (including gold plated with platinum)" (HS code 7108) (see table 1). The top three destinations for merchandise exports were India, South Africa and China, accounting for respectively 15.9, 15.6 and 9.7 percent of total exports. "Travel" (EBOPS code 236) accounted for the largest share of exports of services in 2013 at 1.7 bln US$, followed by "Transportation" (EBOPS code 205) at 785.1 mln US$ (see graph 3).

Graph 3: Exports of services by EBOPS category
(% share in 2013)

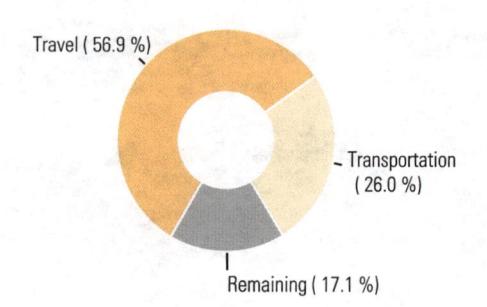

- Travel (56.9 %)
- Transportation (26.0 %)
- Remaining (17.1 %)

Table 1: Top 10 export commodities 2012 to 2014

HS code	4-digit heading of Harmonized System 2007	Value (million US$) 2012	2013	2014	Unit value 2012	2013	2014	Unit	SITC code
	All Commodities	5547.2	4412.5	5704.7					
7108	Gold (including gold plated with platinum)	1863.3	1549.6	1322.0	5.8	11.1	4.7	thsd US$/kg	971
2616	Precious metal ores and concentrates	421.3	301.6	566.5	10.0	7.8	7.1	US$/kg	289
0801	Coconuts, Brazil nuts and cashew nuts, fresh or dried	163.1	189.5	394.2	1.2	1.2	2.0	US$/kg	057
1207	Other oil seeds and oleaginous fruits, whether or not broken	94.4	140.4	337.8	1.1	1.3	2.5	US$/kg	222
2603	Copper ores and concentrates	324.3	90.9	145.6	8.7	7.0		US$/kg	283
2401	Unmanufactured tobacco; tobacco refuse	188.4	97.0	193.2	1.8	1.4	2.5	US$/kg	121
0901	Coffee, whether or not roasted or decaffeinated	187.7	163.1	123.6	3.5	2.6	2.6	US$/kg	071
0713	Dried leguminous vegetables, shelled, whether or not skinned or split	101.0	86.0	177.7	0.6	0.5	0.8	US$/kg	054
0304	Fish fillets and other fish meat (whether or not minced)	99.7	113.8	149.2	5.4	5.2	6.2	US$/kg	034
5201	Cotton, not carded or combed	126.4	86.6	38.7	1.4	1.3	1.1	US$/kg	263

United Republic of Tanzania

Services Imports and Exports: EBOPS 2002 categories

Table 2: Merchandise exports by SITC
(Value in million US$, growth and shares in percentage)

SITC	2014	Avg. Growth rates 2010-2014	Avg. Growth rates 2013-2014	2014 share
Total	5704.7	8.9	29.3	100.0
0+1	1911.5	22.8	71.5	33.5
2+4	1529.2	3.7	86.1	26.8
3	95.5	5.5	-3.9	1.7
5	142.1	-5.2	57.3	2.5
6	405.1	3.6	5.0	7.1
7	156.9	-3.3	-35.8	2.8
8	142.3	3.2	37.9	2.5
9	1322.0	7.9	-14.9	23.2

Table 3: Merchandise imports by SITC
(Value in million US$, growth and shares in percentage)

SITC	2014	Avg. Growth rates 2010-2014	Avg. Growth rates 2013-2014	2014 share
Total	12691.1	12.2	1.3	100.0
0+1	750.8	6.7	0.4	5.9
2+4	627.5	19.3	68.3	4.9
3	3559.1	12.6	-26.6	28.0
5	1839.7	15.1	31.4	14.5
6	1876.1	13.0	0.9	14.8
7	3422.7	9.5	22.3	27.0
8	614.2	17.0	26.5	4.8
9	1.0	-33.2	-91.4	0.0

SITC Legend

SITC Code	Description
Total	All commodities
0+1	Food, animals + beverages, tobacco
2+4	Crude materials + anim. & veg. oils
3	Mineral fuels, lubricants
5	Chemicals
6	Goods classified chiefly by material
7	Machinery and transport equipment
8	Miscellaneous manufactured articles
9	Not classified elsewhere in the SITC

Graph 4: Merchandise trade balance
(Bln US$ by MDG Regions in 2014)

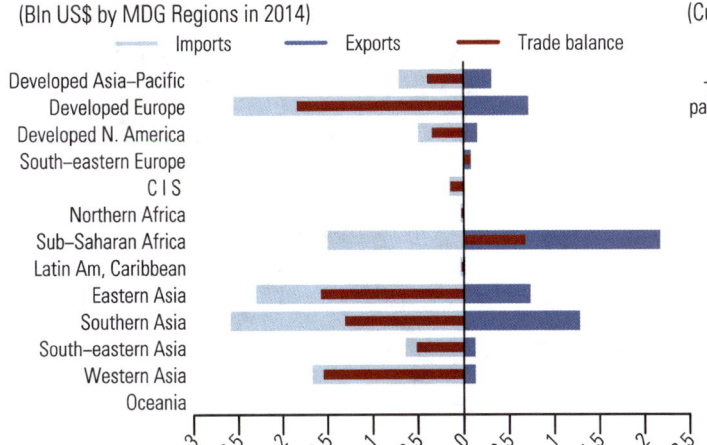

Graph 5: Partner concentration of merchandise trade
(Cumulative share by ranked partners in 2014)

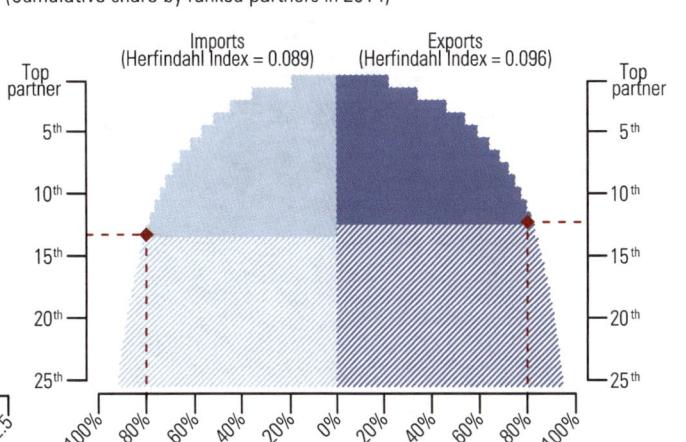

Imports (Herfindahl Index = 0.089)
Exports (Herfindahl Index = 0.096)

Graph 6: Imports of services by EBOPS category
(% share in 2013)

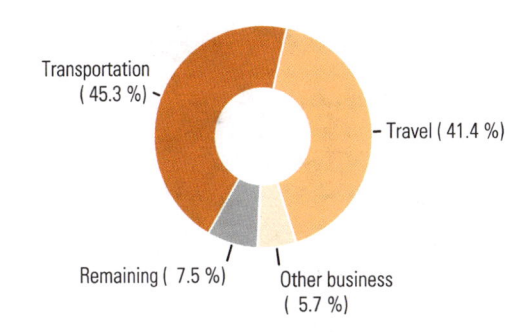

- Transportation (45.3 %)
- Travel (41.4 %)
- Other business (5.7 %)
- Remaining (7.5 %)

Imports Profile:

"Mineral fuels, lubricants" (SITC section 3), "Machinery and transport equipment" (SITC section 7) and "Goods classified chiefly by material" (SITC section 6) were the largest commodity groups for imports in 2014, representing respectively 28.0, 27.0 and 14.8 percent of imported goods (see table 3). From 2012 to 2014, the largest import commodity was "Petroleum oils, other than crude" (HS code 2710) (see table 4). The top three partners for merchandise imports were India, China and Switzerland, accounting for respectively 15.3, 13.0 and 11.1 percent of total imports. "Transportation" (EBOPS code 205) accounted for the largest share of imports of services in 2013 at 1.1 bln US$, followed by "Travel" (EBOPS code 236) at 1.0 bln US$ and "Other business services" (EBOPS code 268) at 143.4 mln US$ (see graph 6).

Table 4: Top 10 import commodities 2012 to 2014

HS code	4-digit heading of Harmonized System 2007	Value (million US$) 2012	2013	2014	Unit value 2012	2013	2014	Unit	SITC code
	All Commodities	11715.6	12525.4	12691.1					
2710	Petroleum oils, other than crude	3636.5	4665.4	3407.5	1.1	1.0	0.9	US$/kg	334
8703	Motor cars and other motor vehicles principally designed for the transport	302.4	311.4	327.1	21.5	20.3	19.3	thsd US$/unit	781
1001	Wheat and meslin	244.1	307.1	319.3	0.4	0.4	0.4	US$/kg	041
1511	Palm oil and its fractions	247.7	192.7	367.6	1.0	0.8	0.9	US$/kg	422
8704	Motor vehicles for the transport of goods	252.7	264.5	234.1					782
7208	Flat-rolled products of iron or non-alloy steel	214.2	237.1	189.2	0.8	0.7	0.6	US$/kg	673
3004	Medicaments (excluding goods of heading 30.02, 30.05 or 30.06)	132.6	163.7	337.7	10.3	13.0	13.5	US$/kg	542
8701	Tractors (other than tractors of heading 87.09)	226.2	193.5	199.9					722
8431	Parts suitable for use principally with the machinery of headings 84.25	240.0	141.4	139.1		16.5	13.7	US$/kg	723
4011	New pneumatic tyres, of rubber	166.8	163.8	147.7					625

2014 International Trade Statistics Yearbook, Vol. I — Source: UN Comtrade and UN ServiceTrade

United States of America, including Puerto Rico and U.S.V.I.

Goods Imports: CIF, by origin **Goods Exports:** FOB, by last known destination **Trade System:** General

Overview:
In 2014, the value of merchandise exports of the United States increased slightly by 2.8 percent to reach 1622.7 bln US$, while its merchandise imports increased slightly by 3.4 percent to reach 2408.1 bln US$ (see graph 1, table 2 and table 3). Despite being overtaken by China in 2007 as the largest exporter of merchandise, the United States is still the world's largest importer. The merchandise trade balance recorded a moderate deficit of 785.4 bln US$ (see graph 1). The largest merchandise trade balance was with MDG Eastern Asia at -369.2 bln US$ (see graph 4). Merchandise exports in the United States were diversified amongst partners; imports were also diversified. The top 22 partners accounted for 80 percent or more of exports and 18 partners accounted for 80 percent or more of imports (see graph 5). In 2013, the value of exports of services of the United States increased slightly by 4.8 percent, reaching 671.1 bln US$, while its imports of services increased slightly by 2.7 percent and reached 454.5 bln US$ (see graph 2). In recent years, the United States has been the world's largest exporter and importer of services. There was a trade in services surplus of 216.6 bln US$, which is the largest trade in services surplus recorded.

Graph 1: Total merchandise trade, by value
(Bln US$ by year)

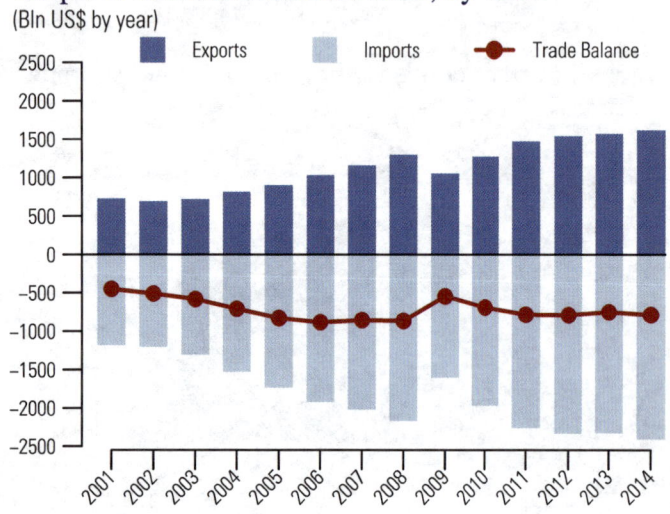

Graph 2: Total services trade, by value
(Bln US$ by year)

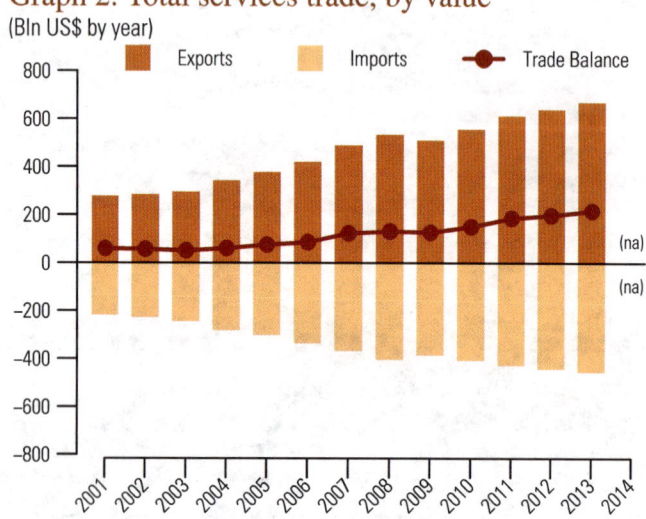

Exports Profile:
"Machinery and transport equipment" (SITC section 7), "Chemicals" (SITC section 5) and "Not classified elsewhere in the SITC" (SITC section 9) were the largest commodity groups for exports in 2014, representing respectively 34.0, 13.1 and 11.1 percent of exported goods (see table 2). From 2012 to 2014, the largest export commodity was "Commodities not specified according to kind" (HS code 9999) (see table 1). The top three destinations for merchandise exports were Canada, Mexico and China, accounting for respectively 19.0, 14.4 and 7.5 percent of total exports. "Travel" (EBOPS code 236) accounted for the largest share of exports of services in 2013 at 173.1 bln US$, followed by "Royalties and license fees" (EBOPS code 266) at 129.2 bln US$ and "Other business services" (EBOPS code 268) at 120.1 bln US$ (see graph 3).

Graph 3: Exports of services by EBOPS category
(% share in 2013)

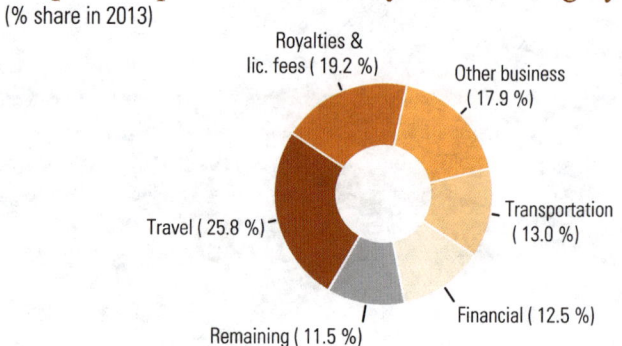

- Royalties & lic. fees (19.2 %)
- Other business (17.9 %)
- Transportation (13.0 %)
- Financial (12.5 %)
- Remaining (11.5 %)
- Travel (25.8 %)

Table 1: Top 10 export commodities 2012 to 2014

HS code	4-digit heading of Harmonized System 2012	Value (billion US$) 2012	2013	2014	Unit value 2012	2013	2014	Unit	SITC code
	All Commodities	1545.6	1578.0	1622.7					
9999	Commodities not specified according to kind	136.7	149.4	157.6					931
2710	Petroleum oils, other than crude	102.7	111.8	111.6					334
8703	Motor cars and other motor vehicles principally designed for the transport	54.5	57.1	61.7	20.0	20.3	21.5	thsd US$/unit	781
8708	Parts and accessories of the motor vehicles of headings 87.01 to 87.05	41.8	42.9	42.6	10.9	11.0	10.8	US$/kg	784
8542	Electronic integrated circuits	34.4	34.5	34.5					776
8517	Electrical apparatus for line telephony or line telegraphy	28.7	31.2	33.8					764
7108	Gold (including gold plated with platinum)	33.7	32.1	21.5	48.0	45.2	39.8	thsd US$/kg	971
8471	Automatic data processing machines and units thereof	27.8	26.5	26.8	255.0	275.2	285.0	US$/unit	752
9018	Instruments and appliances used in medical, surgical, dental or veterinary	24.6	25.2	26.2					872
3004	Medicaments (excluding goods of heading 30.02, 30.05 or 30.06)	24.7	23.1	24.4	182.9	187.4	217.2	US$/kg	542

United States of America, including Puerto Rico and U.S.V.I.

Services Imports and Exports: EBOPS 2002 categories

Table 2: Merchandise exports by SITC
(Value in million US$, growth and shares in percentage)

SITC	2014	Avg. Growth rates 2010-2014	Avg. Growth rates 2013-2014	2014 share
Total	1 622 657.5	6.2	2.8	100.0
0+1	119 864.0	8.0	5.0	7.4
2+4	90 635.6	1.5	0.4	5.6
3	157 023.7	18.1	5.9	9.7
5	211 761.7	2.9	1.5	13.1
6	150 282.7	5.9	3.8	9.3
7	551 298.0	5.3	3.5	34.0
8	161 583.8	4.8	3.5	10.0
9	180 208.0	8.2	-1.5	11.1

Table 3: Merchandise imports by SITC
(Value in million US$, growth and shares in percentage)

SITC	2014	Avg. Growth rates 2010-2014	Avg. Growth rates 2013-2014	2014 share
Total	2 408 098.7	5.2	3.4	100.0
0+1	124 500.9	7.9	8.2	5.2
2+4	44 960.2	6.6	4.2	1.9
3	356 084.4	-0.5	-8.5	14.8
5	211 879.6	4.6	6.0	8.8
6	265 563.1	6.9	8.1	11.0
7	956 173.6	7.0	5.9	39.7
8	361 330.9	4.8	4.4	15.0
9	87 605.9	6.3	1.3	3.6

SITC Legend

SITC Code	Description
Total	All commodities
0+1	Food, animals + beverages, tobacco
2+4	Crude materials + anim. & veg. oils
3	Mineral fuels, lubricants
5	Chemicals
6	Goods classified chiefly by material
7	Machinery and transport equipment
8	Miscellaneous manufactured articles
9	Not classified elsewhere in the SITC

Graph 4: Merchandise trade balance
(Bln US$ by MDG Regions in 2014)

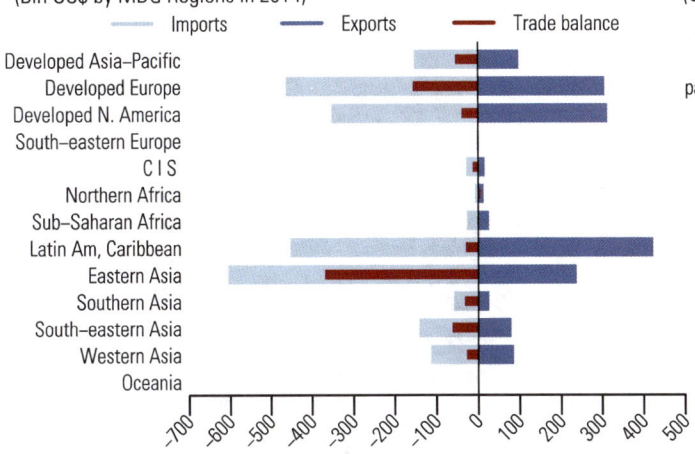

Graph 5: Partner concentration of merchandise trade
(Cumulative share by ranked partners in 2014)

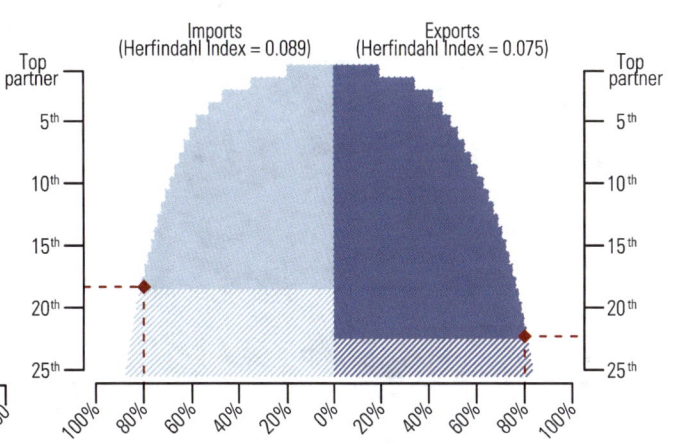

Imports (Herfindahl Index = 0.089)
Exports (Herfindahl Index = 0.075)

Graph 6: Imports of services by EBOPS category
(% share in 2013)

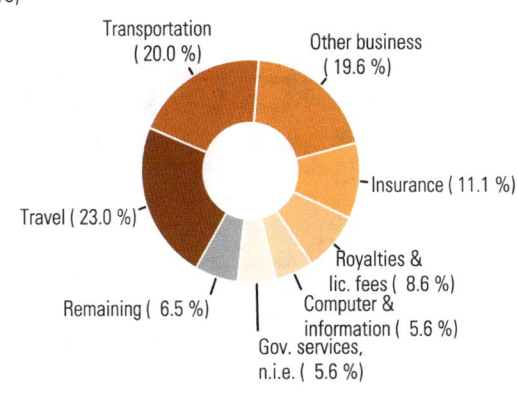

- Transportation (20.0 %)
- Other business (19.6 %)
- Insurance (11.1 %)
- Royalties & lic. fees (8.6 %)
- Computer & information (5.6 %)
- Gov. services, n.i.e. (5.6 %)
- Remaining (6.5 %)
- Travel (23.0 %)

Imports Profile:

"Machinery and transport equipment" (SITC section 7), "Miscellaneous manufactured articles" (SITC section 8) and "Mineral fuels, lubricants" (SITC section 3) were the largest commodity groups for imports in 2014, representing respectively 39.7, 15.0 and 14.8 percent of imported goods (see table 3). From 2012 to 2014, the largest import commodity was "Petroleum oils and oils obtained from bituminous minerals, crude" (HS code 2709), despite a decrease of 9.3 percent in 2014 (see table 4). The top three partners for merchandise imports were China, Canada and Mexico, accounting for respectively 19.7, 14.4 and 12.2 percent of total imports. "Travel" (EBOPS code 236) accounted for the largest share of imports of services in 2013 at 104.7 bln US$, followed by "Transportation" (EBOPS code 205) at 90.8 bln US$ and "Other business services" (EBOPS code 268) at 89.1 bln US$ (see graph 6).

Table 4: Top 10 import commodities 2012 to 2014

HS code	4-digit heading of Harmonized System 2012	Value (billion US$) 2012	2013	2014	Unit value 2012	2013	2014	Unit	SITC code
	All Commodities	2 333.8	2 328.3	2 408.1					
2709	Petroleum oils and oils obtained from bituminous minerals, crude	321.9	279.1	253.2			0.7	US$/kg	333
8703	Motor cars and other motor vehicles principally designed for the transport	149.6	155.7	156.5	21.9	22.5	22.2	thsd US$/unit	781
8517	Electrical apparatus for line telephony or line telegraphy	81.4	89.9	96.1					764
2710	Petroleum oils, other than crude	92.4	88.8	79.1					334
8471	Automatic data processing machines and units thereof	85.7	83.1	82.1	145.8	141.2	142.9	US$/unit	752
9999	Commodities not specified according to kind	66.4	70.5	73.1					931
8708	Parts and accessories of the motor vehicles of headings 87.01 to 87.05	58.1	58.9	63.7	11.5	11.4	11.6	US$/kg	784
3004	Medicaments (excluding goods of heading 30.02, 30.05 or 30.06)	47.3	47.1	55.3	220.2	198.2	206.4	US$/kg	542
8542	Electronic integrated circuits	27.5	29.5	29.9					776
8528	Reception apparatus for television	30.9	27.5	27.2	218.1	201.3	194.0	US$/unit	761

Source: UN Comtrade and UN ServiceTrade

Uruguay

Goods Imports: CIF, by origin **Goods Exports:** FOB, by last known destination **Trade System:** Special

Overview:
In 2013, the value of merchandise exports of Uruguay increased slightly by 4.1 percent to reach 9.1 bln US$, while its merchandise imports decreased slightly by 0.1 percent to reach 11.6 bln US$ (see graph 1, table 2 and table 3). The merchandise trade balance recorded a moderate deficit of 2.6 bln US$ (see graph 1). The largest merchandise trade balance was with MDG Latin America and the Caribbean at -1.3 bln US$ (see graph 4). Merchandise exports in Uruguay were diversified amongst partners; imports were also diversified. The top 14 partners accounted for 80 percent or more of exports and 14 partners accounted for 80 percent or more of imports (see graph 5). In 2013, the value of exports of services of Uruguay decreased moderately by 5.6 percent, reaching 3.3 bln US$, while its imports of services increased substantially by 39.9 percent and reached 3.4 bln US$ (see graph 2). There was a relatively small trade in services deficit of 83.6 mln US$.

Graph 1: Total merchandise trade, by value
(Bln US$ by year)

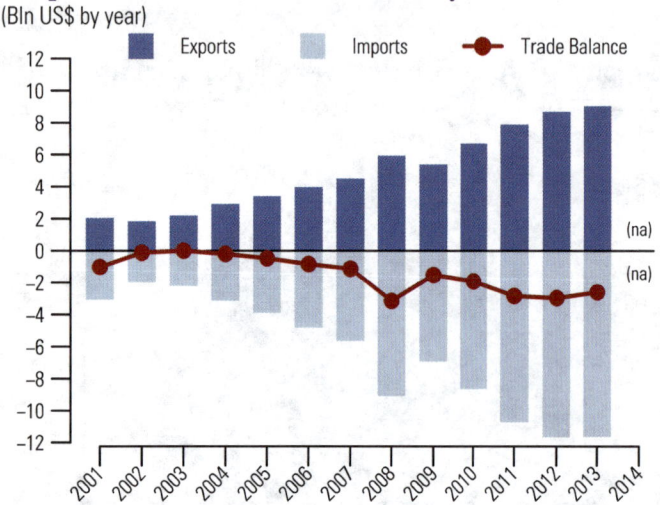

Graph 2: Total services trade, by value
(Bln US$ by year)

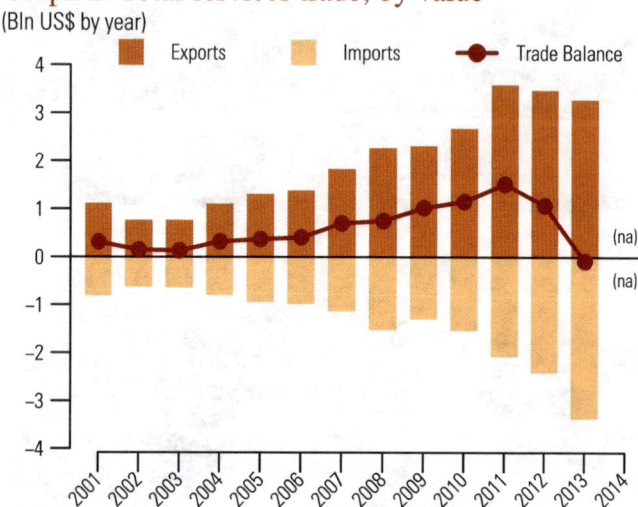

Exports Profile:
"Food, animals + beverages, tobacco" (SITC section 0+1), "Crude materials + anim. & veg. oils" (SITC section 2+4) and "Goods classified chiefly by material" (SITC section 6) were the largest commodity groups for exports in 2013, representing respectively 44.8, 30.4 and 8.2 percent of exported goods (see table 2). From 2011 to 2013, the largest export commodity was "Soya beans, whether or not broken" (HS code 1201) (see table 1). The top three destinations for merchandise exports were Brazil, Free zones and China, accounting for respectively 19.6, 15.0 and 10.2 percent of total exports. "Travel" (EBOPS code 236) accounted for the largest share of exports of services in 2013 at 1.9 bln US$, followed by "Transportation" (EBOPS code 205) at 599.3 mln US$ and "Other business services" (EBOPS code 268) at 345.2 mln US$ (see graph 3).

Graph 3: Exports of services by EBOPS category
(% share in 2013)

- Travel (58.4 %)
- Transportation (18.2 %)
- Other business (10.5 %)
- Computer & information (5.5 %)
- Remaining (7.4 %)

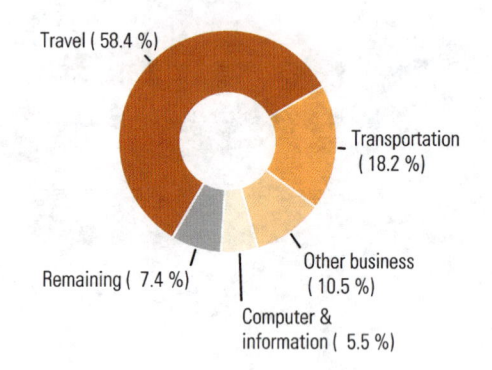

Table 1: Top 10 export commodities 2011 to 2013

HS code	4-digit heading of Harmonized System 2007	Value (million US$) 2011	2012	2013	Unit value 2011	2012	2013	Unit	SITC code
	All Commodities	7911.7	8709.2	9065.8					
1201	Soya beans, whether or not broken	805.6	1379.7	1874.5	0.5	0.5	0.5	US$/kg	222
0202	Meat of bovine animals, frozen	971.3	1017.6	939.7	5.2	4.9	4.8	US$/kg	011
1006	Rice	472.1	560.1	508.0	0.5	0.5	0.6	US$/kg	042
0402	Milk and cream, concentrated or containing added sugar	307.4	333.9	458.8	4.0	3.6	4.4	US$/kg	022
0201	Meat of bovine animals, fresh or chilled	320.0	384.7	361.0	9.4	8.7	9.0	US$/kg	011
1001	Wheat and meslin	309.4	379.2	282.8	0.3	0.3	0.3	US$/kg	041
4403	Wood in the rough, whether or not stripped of bark or sapwood	256.4	269.6	298.2	3.7	5.2	13.5	US$/m^3	247
0406	Cheese and curd	235.7	264.3	251.5	5.5	5.6	5.6	US$/kg	024
1107	Malt, whether or not roasted	209.1	204.7	208.5	0.7	0.7	0.7	US$/kg	048
3923	Articles for the conveyance or packing of goods, of plastics	195.3	202.4	191.1	2.5	2.4	2.4	US$/kg	893

Uruguay

Services Imports and Exports: EBOPS 2002 categories

Table 2: Merchandise exports by SITC
(Value in million US$, growth and shares in percentage)

SITC	2013	Avg. Growth rates 2009-2013	2012-2013	2013 share
Total	9 065.8	13.8	4.1	100.0
0+1	4 057.2	8.5	-4.0	44.8
2+4	2 752.9	27.6	24.4	30.4
3	44.6	-13.4	-53.2	0.5
5	570.7	13.3	-2.4	6.3
6	745.9	12.3	1.2	8.2
7	402.5	21.8	50.9	4.4
8	398.7	7.7	-6.6	4.4
9	93.2	9.3	-42.4	1.0

Table 3: Merchandise imports by SITC
(Value in million US$, growth and shares in percentage)

SITC	2013	Avg. Growth rates 2009-2013	2012-2013	2013 share
Total	11 642.4	13.9	-0.1	100.0
0+1	1 187.4	17.4	20.7	10.2
2+4	427.1	15.1	10.6	3.7
3	2 144.1	6.2	-31.6	18.4
5	2 032.1	16.3	5.1	17.5
6	1 266.1	14.0	4.5	10.9
7	3 542.1	16.1	16.9	30.4
8	1 043.6	17.6	7.5	9.0
9	0.0	-36.3	18.5	0.0

SITC Legend

SITC Code	Description
Total	All commodities
0+1	Food, animals + beverages, tobacco
2+4	Crude materials + anim. & veg. oils
3	Mineral fuels, lubricants
5	Chemicals
6	Goods classified chiefly by material
7	Machinery and transport equipment
8	Miscellaneous manufactured articles
9	Not classified elsewhere in the SITC

Graph 4: Merchandise trade balance
(Bln US$ by MDG Regions in 2013)

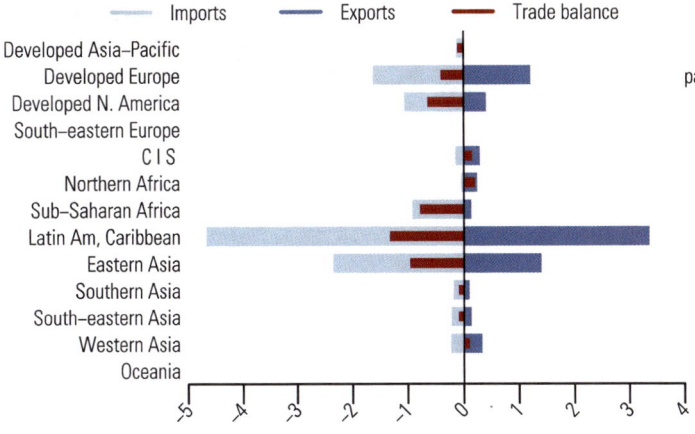

Graph 5: Partner concentration of merchandise trade
(Cumulative share by ranked partners in 2013)

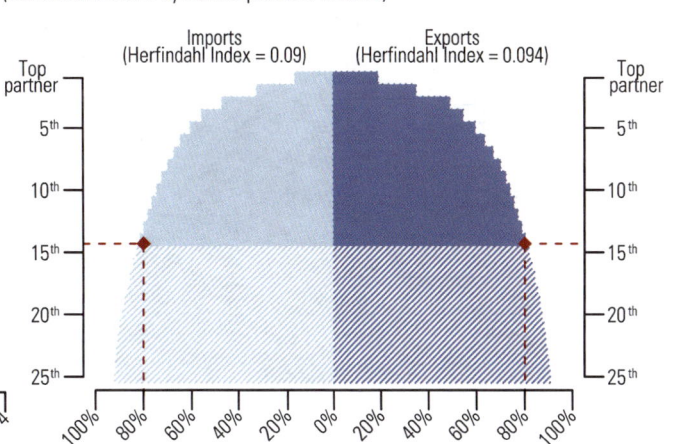

Imports (Herfindahl Index = 0.09)
Exports (Herfindahl Index = 0.094)

Graph 6: Imports of services by EBOPS category
(% share in 2013)

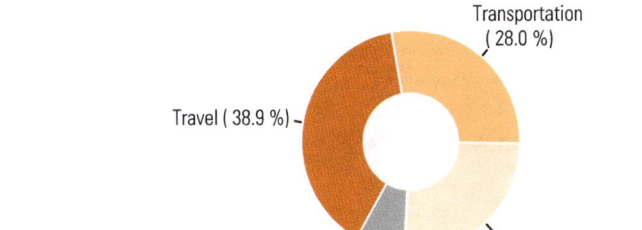

- Transportation (28.0 %)
- Travel (38.9 %)
- Other business (25.6 %)
- Remaining (7.5 %)

Imports Profile:

"Machinery and transport equipment" (SITC section 7), "Mineral fuels, lubricants" (SITC section 3) and "Chemicals" (SITC section 5) were the largest commodity groups for imports in 2013, representing respectively 30.4, 18.4 and 17.5 percent of imported goods (see table 3). From 2011 to 2013, the largest import commodity was "Petroleum oils and oils obtained from bituminous minerals, crude" (HS code 2709) (see table 4). The top three partners for merchandise imports were Brazil, Argentina and China, accounting for respectively 17.7, 15.9 and 14.9 percent of total imports. "Travel" (EBOPS code 236) accounted for the largest share of imports of services in 2013 at 1.3 bln US$, followed by "Transportation" (EBOPS code 205) at 943.5 mln US$ and "Other business services" (EBOPS code 268) at 862.7 mln US$ (see graph 6).

Table 4: Top 10 import commodities 2011 to 2013

HS code	4-digit heading of Harmonized System 2007	Value (million US$) 2011	2012	2013	Unit value 2011	2012	2013	Unit	SITC code
	All Commodities	10 726.4	11 652.1	11 642.4					
2709	Petroleum oils and oils obtained from bituminous minerals, crude	948.2	1 685.1	1 564.1	0.8	0.8	0.8	US$/kg	333
2710	Petroleum oils, other than crude	1 039.6	1 172.1	494.8	0.9	1.0	1.0	US$/kg	334
8703	Motor cars and other motor vehicles principally designed for the transport	391.8	405.3	414.7	9.0	9.5	9.4	thsd US$/unit	781
8517	Electrical apparatus for line telephony or line telegraphy	216.6	244.2	298.2					764
8704	Motor vehicles for the transport of goods	212.3	253.6	280.3	15.4	15.0	15.4	thsd US$/unit	782
8708	Parts and accessories of the motor vehicles of headings 87.01 to 87.05	266.6	144.9	256.6	7.3	8.1	8.0	US$/kg	784
3808	Insecticides, rodenticides, fungicides, herbicides	159.7	189.5	222.7	4.7	5.0	5.8	US$/kg	591
3907	Polyacetals, other polyethers and epoxide resins, in primary forms	168.5	164.2	160.6	1.8	1.6	1.6	US$/kg	574
8471	Automatic data processing machines and units thereof	126.4	161.7	172.2	88.6	92.9	84.1	US$/unit	752
3105	Mineral or chemical fertilisers	160.6	145.9	136.6	0.6	0.6	0.5	US$/kg	562

2014 International Trade Statistics Yearbook, Vol. I — Source: UN Comtrade and UN ServiceTrade

Vanuatu

Goods Imports: CIF, by origin   **Goods Exports:** FOB, by last known destination   **Trade System:** General

Overview:

In 2011, the value of merchandise exports of Vanuatu increased substantially by 37.6 percent to reach 63.5 mln US$, while its merchandise imports increased slightly by 1.7 percent to reach 280.6 mln US$ (see graph 1, table 2 and table 3). The merchandise trade balance recorded a large deficit of 217.1 mln US$ (see graph 1). The largest merchandise trade balance was with MDG Developed Asia-Pacific at -108.4 mln US$ (see graph 4). Merchandise exports in Vanuatu were diversified amongst partners; imports were moderately concentrated. The top 7 partners accounted for 80 percent or more of exports and 7 partners accounted for 80 percent or more of imports (see graph 5). In 2013, the value of exports of services of Vanuatu increased substantially by 10.3 percent, reaching 331.5 mln US$, while its imports of services decreased slightly by 0.3 percent and reached 145.5 mln US$ (see graph 2). There was a large trade in services surplus of 185.9 mln US$.

Graph 1: Total merchandise trade, by value
(Mln US$ by year)

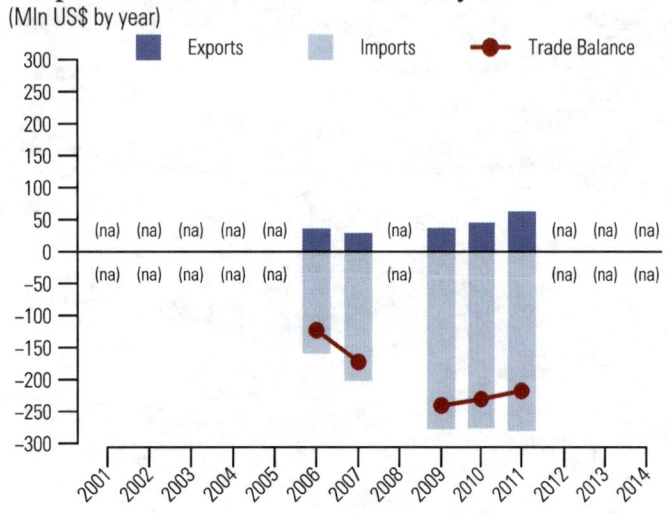

Graph 2: Total services trade, by value
(Mln US$ by year)

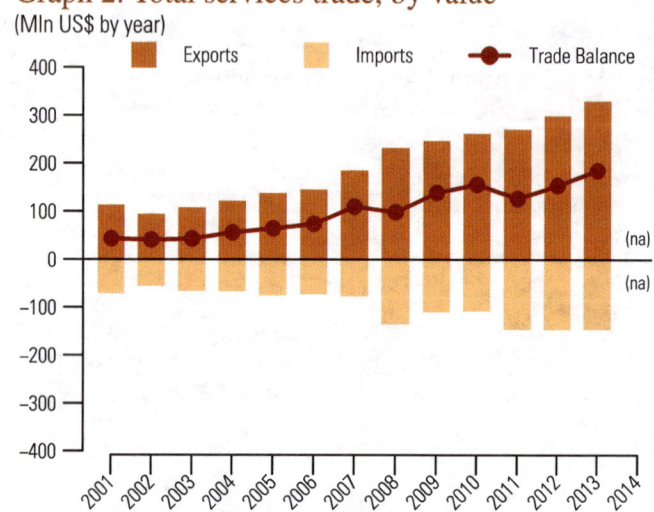

Exports Profile:

"Crude materials + anim. & veg. oils" (SITC section 2+4), "Food, animals + beverages, tobacco" (SITC section 0+1) and "Chemicals" (SITC section 5) were the largest commodity groups for exports in 2011, representing respectively 49.4, 40.3 and 5.4 percent of exported goods (see table 2). From 2009 to 2011, the largest export commodity was "Coconut (copra), palm kernel or babassu oil" (HS code 1513) (see table 1). The top three destinations for merchandise exports were the Philippines, Australia and Malaysia, accounting for respectively 14.8, 10.0 and 10.0 percent of total exports. "Travel" (EBOPS code 236) accounted for the largest share of exports of services in 2013 at 265.9 mln US$, followed by "Transportation" (EBOPS code 205) at 33.5 mln US$ (see graph 3).

Graph 3: Exports of services by EBOPS category
(% share in 2013)

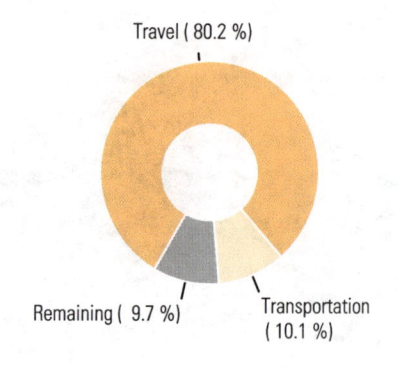

- Travel (80.2 %)
- Transportation (10.1 %)
- Remaining (9.7 %)

Table 1: Top 10 export commodities 2009 to 2011

HS code	4-digit heading of Harmonized System 2002	Value (million US$) 2009	2010	2011	Unit value 2009	2010	2011	Unit	SITC code
	All Commodities	37.7	46.2	63.5					
1513	Coconut (copra), palm kernel or babassu oil	2.5	9.3	16.8	*1.4*	*0.9*	*1.1*	US$/kg	422
1203	Copra	5.3	6.0	11.3	0.4	0.5	0.8	US$/kg	223
1212	Locust beans, seaweeds and other algae	6.0	5.3	7.4	12.3	10.5	10.9	US$/kg	292
0202	Meat of bovine animals, frozen	3.3	4.6	5.1	4.1	4.5	4.9	US$/kg	011
1801	Cocoa beans, whole or broken, raw or roasted	3.2	4.0	2.6	2.2	2.6	2.4	US$/kg	072
0301	Live fish	1.4	3.3	1.8	13.9	14.0	8.5	US$/kg	034
0302	Fish, fresh or chilled, excluding fish fillets	1.9	0.9	2.3	4.1	2.5	2.6	US$/kg	034
9999	Commodities not specified according to kind	1.2	1.5	1.3					931
2203	Beer made from malt	0.9	1.1	1.1	0.6	0.7	0.6	US$/litre	112
3205	Colour lakes; preparations	...	0.4	2.7		3.0	0.0	thsd US$/kg	531

Source: UN Comtrade and UN ServiceTrade

Vanuatu

Services Imports and Exports: EBOPS 2002 categories

Table 2: Merchandise exports by SITC
(Value in million US$, growth and shares in percentage)

SITC	2011	Avg. Growth rates 2007-2011	Avg. Growth rates 2010-2011	2011 share
Total	63.5	20.7	37.6	100.0
0+1	25.6	30.8	16.5	40.3
2+4	31.4	32.1	78.3	49.4
3	0.0	-25.0	-57.5	0.1
5	3.4	81.1	61.8	5.4
6	0.3	-13.3	-13.3	0.5
7	1.0	4.7	-38.9	1.6
8	0.5	-10.6	-42.5	0.8
9	1.3	-37.5	-14.8	2.0

Table 3: Merchandise imports by SITC
(Value in million US$, growth and shares in percentage)

SITC	2011	Avg. Growth rates 2007-2011	Avg. Growth rates 2010-2011	2011 share
Total	280.6	8.6	1.7	100.0
0+1	68.7	13.8	9.8	24.5
2+4	5.0	3.7	-5.5	1.8
3	51.1	8.8	37.3	18.2
5	29.6	21.2	0.5	10.5
6	36.8	3.5	-3.5	13.1
7	53.1	1.8	-22.5	18.9
8	28.7	10.6	5.5	10.2
9	7.7	8.4	-0.1	2.7

SITC Legend

SITC Code	Description
Total	All commodities
0+1	Food, animals + beverages, tobacco
2+4	Crude materials + anim. & veg. oils
3	Mineral fuels, lubricants
5	Chemicals
6	Goods classified chiefly by material
7	Machinery and transport equipment
8	Miscellaneous manufactured articles
9	Not classified elsewhere in the SITC

Graph 4: Merchandise trade balance
(Mln US$ by MDG Regions in 2011)

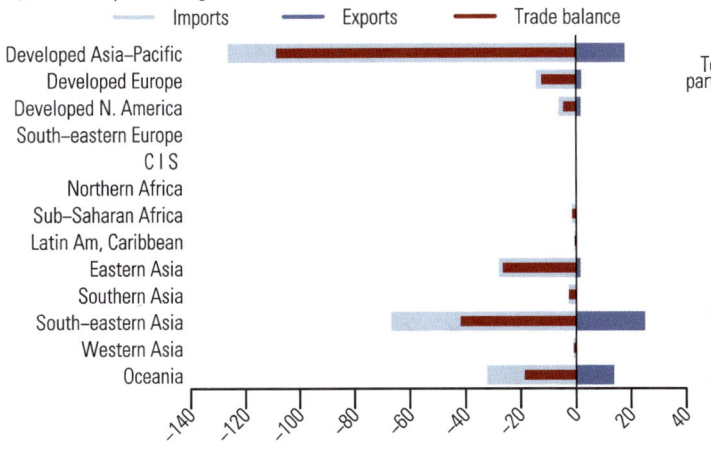

Graph 5: Partner concentration of merchandise trade
(Cumulative share by ranked partners in 2011)

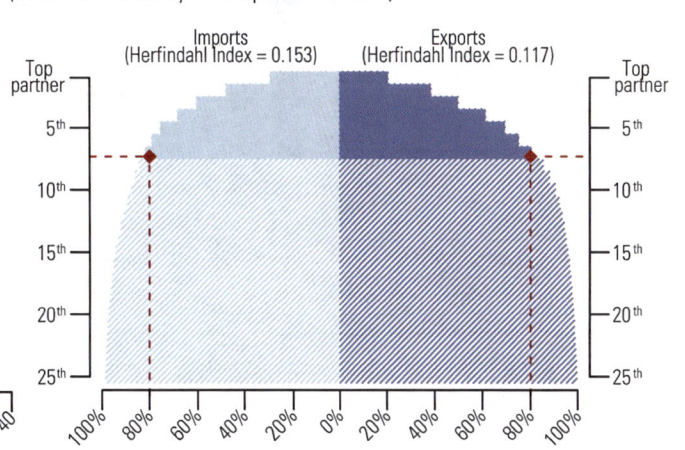

Imports (Herfindahl Index = 0.153)
Exports (Herfindahl Index = 0.117)

Graph 6: Imports of services by EBOPS category
(% share in 2013)

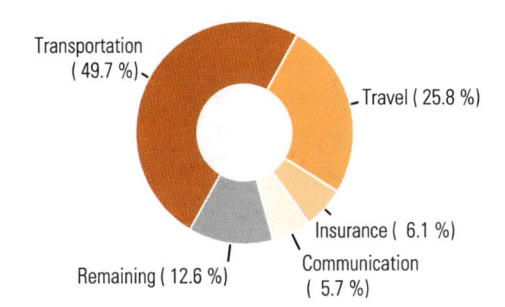

- Transportation (49.7%)
- Travel (25.8%)
- Insurance (6.1%)
- Communication (5.7%)
- Remaining (12.6%)

Imports Profile:

"Food, animals + beverages, tobacco" (SITC section 0+1), "Machinery and transport equipment" (SITC section 7) and "Mineral fuels, lubricants" (SITC section 3) were the largest commodity groups for imports in 2011, representing respectively 24.5, 18.9 and 18.2 percent of imported goods (see table 3). From 2009 to 2011, the largest import commodity was "Petroleum oils, other than crude" (HS code 2710) (see table 4). The top three partners for merchandise imports were Australia, Singapore and New Zealand, accounting for respectively 30.0, 13.7 and 13.3 percent of total imports. "Transportation" (EBOPS code 205) accounted for the largest share of imports of services in 2013 at 72.4 mln US$, followed by "Travel" (EBOPS code 236) at 37.6 mln US$ and "Insurance services" (EBOPS code 253) at 8.9 mln US$ (see graph 6).

Table 4: Top 10 import commodities 2009 to 2011

HS code	4-digit heading of Harmonized System 2002	Value (million US$) 2009	2010	2011	Unit value 2009	2010	2011	Unit	SITC code
	All Commodities	277.5	276.0	280.6					
2710	Petroleum oils, other than crude	32.6	34.3	48.2	0.8	1.0	1.2	US$/kg	334
3004	Medicaments (excluding goods of heading 30.02, 30.05 or 30.06)	15.5	15.3	15.5	100.0	113.9	13.3	US$/kg	542
1006	Rice	12.3	11.6	10.8	1.0	0.9	0.9	US$/kg	042
9999	Commodities not specified according to kind	7.5	7.7	7.7					931
8703	Motor cars and other motor vehicles principally designed for the transport	3.9	11.1	7.0	9.1	16.8	11.4	thsd US$/unit	781
8704	Motor vehicles for the transport of goods	11.9	3.9	3.2	17.6	16.8	16.6	thsd US$/unit	782
2523	Portland cement, aluminous cement, slag cement	4.4	5.1	4.3	0.2	0.3	0.4	US$/kg	661
1905	Bread, pastry, cakes, biscuits and other bakers' wares	3.1	4.5	5.5	2.0	2.2	2.0	US$/kg	048
0207	Meat and edible offal, of the poultry of heading 01.05	2.9	4.2	5.2	2.1	2.4	2.7	US$/kg	012
1101	Wheat or meslin flour	2.9	3.6	4.4	0.6	0.7	0.9	US$/kg	046

Venezuela (Bolivarian Republic of)

Goods Imports: CIF, by origin **Goods Exports: FOB, by last known destination** **Trade System: General**

Overview:
In 2013, the value of merchandise exports of the Bolivarian Republic of Venezuela decreased moderately by 7.4 percent to reach 88.0 bln US$, while its merchandise imports decreased substantially by 23.9 percent to reach 45.0 bln US$ (see graph 1, table 2 and table 3). The merchandise trade balance recorded a large surplus of 43.0 bln US$ (see graph 1). The largest merchandise trade balance was with MDG Eastern Asia at 19.8 bln US$ (see graph 4). Merchandise exports in the Bolivarian Republic of Venezuela were highly concentrated amongst partners; imports were diversified. The top 3 partners accounted for 80 percent or more of exports and 14 partners accounted for 80 percent or more of imports (see graph 5). In 2012, the value of exports of services of the Bolivarian Republic of Venezuela increased substantially by 10.6 percent, reaching 2.2 bln US$, while its imports of services increased substantially by 15.8 percent and reached 18.2 bln US$ (see graph 2). There was a large trade in services deficit of 16.0 bln US$. See footnote*.

Graph 1: Total merchandise trade, by value
(Bln US$ by year)

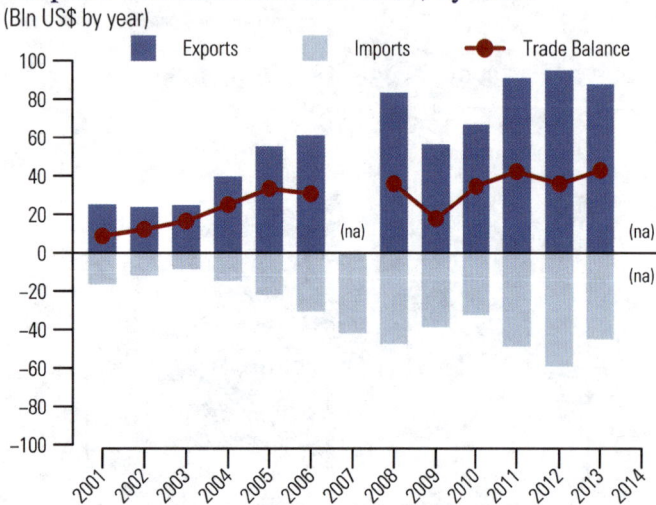

Graph 2: Total services trade, by value
(Bln US$ by year)

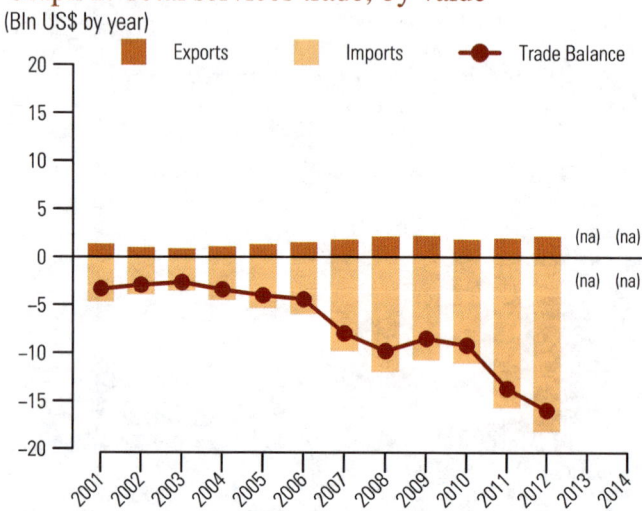

Exports Profile:
"Mineral fuels, lubricants" (SITC section 3), "Chemicals" (SITC section 5) and "Goods classified chiefly by material" (SITC section 6) were the largest commodity groups for exports in 2013, representing respectively 97.7, 1.1 and 0.6 percent of exported goods (see table 2). From 2011 to 2013, the largest export commodity was "Petroleum oils, crude" (HS code 2709) (see table 1). The top three destinations for merchandise exports were LAIA nes, North and Central America, Caribbean nes and Areas nes, accounting for respectively 24.4, 23.9 and 22.9 percent of total exports. "Travel" (EBOPS code 236) accounted for the largest share of exports of services in 2012 at 844.0 mln US$, followed by "Transportation" (EBOPS code 205) at 656.0 mln US$ and "Government services, n.i.e." (EBOPS code 291) at 354.0 mln US$ (see graph 3).

Graph 3: Exports of services by EBOPS category
(% share in 2012)

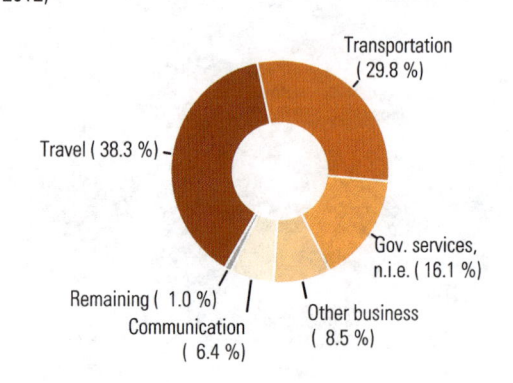

- Transportation (29.8 %)
- Travel (38.3 %)
- Gov. services, n.i.e. (16.1 %)
- Other business (8.5 %)
- Communication (6.4 %)
- Remaining (1.0 %)

Table 1: Top 10 export commodities 2011 to 2013

HS code	4-digit heading of Harmonized System 2002	Value (million US$) 2011	2012	2013	Unit value 2011	2012	2013	Unit	SITC code
	All Commodities	91 094.2	95 034.9	87 961.2					
2709	Petroleum oils, crude	60 913.2	68 912.5	74 850.6	0.8	0.8	0.8	US$/kg	333
2710	Petroleum oils, other than crude	...	24 656.5	11 010.4		1.1		US$/kg	334
9999	Commodities not specified according to kind	27 217.8	...	17.0					931
2905	Acyclic alcohols and their derivatives	53.1	401.1	597.4	0.5	0.3	0.4	US$/kg	512
7203	Ferrous products obtained by direct reduction of iron ore	447.6	304.5	204.5	0.2	0.2	0.2	US$/kg	671
2601	Iron ores and concentrates	567.3	...	262.3	0.1		0.1	US$/kg	281
3102	Mineral or chemical fertilisers, nitrogenous	128.3	250.6	152.8	0.4	0.4	0.3	US$/kg	562
7208	Flat-rolled products of iron or non-alloy steel	292.7	...	43.3	0.7		0.6	US$/kg	673
2814	Ammonia, anhydrous or in aqueous solution	73.0	131.6	83.3	0.5	0.5	0.4	US$/kg	522
7601	Unwrought aluminium	146.3	90.3	28.1	1.6	2.0	2.0	US$/kg	684

*Major export partners were defined as regions only and resulted in high partner concentration for exports in graph 5.

Source: UN Comtrade and UN ServiceTrade

Venezuela (Bolivarian Republic of)

Services Imports and Exports: EBOPS 2002 categories

Table 2: Merchandise exports by SITC
(Value in million US$, growth and shares in percentage)

SITC	2013	Avg. Growth rates 2009-2013	Avg. Growth rates 2012-2013	2013 share
Total	87 961.2	11.7	-7.4	100.0
0+1	29.0	-18.6	5711.9	0.0
2+4	299.9	2.8	766.6	0.3
3	85 918.6	12.2	-8.2	97.7
5	998.1	37.1	20.5	1.1
6	488.1	-23.8	-0.9	0.6
7	171.8	-7.6	64.2	0.2
8	38.7	-7.1	1078.6	0.0
9	17.0	...	...	0.0

Table 3: Merchandise imports by SITC
(Value in million US$, growth and shares in percentage)

SITC	2013	Avg. Growth rates 2009-2013	Avg. Growth rates 2012-2013	2013 share
Total	44 951.8	3.8	-23.9	100.0
0+1	7 368.9	6.4	-12.8	16.4
2+4	1 386.6	5.9	-29.2	3.1
3	373.6	-28.7	-34.5	0.8
5	8 550.6	6.6	-20.5	19.0
6	6 739.7	4.1	-18.4	15.0
7	13 003.2	-0.6	-36.7	28.9
8	3 889.9	-2.4	-35.0	8.7
9	3 639.4	72.2	43.1	8.1

SITC Legend

SITC Code	Description
Total	All commodities
0+1	Food, animals + beverages, tobacco
2+4	Crude materials + anim. & veg. oils
3	Mineral fuels, lubricants
5	Chemicals
6	Goods classified chiefly by material
7	Machinery and transport equipment
8	Miscellaneous manufactured articles
9	Not classified elsewhere in the SITC

Graph 4: Merchandise trade balance
(Bln US$ by MDG Regions in 2013)

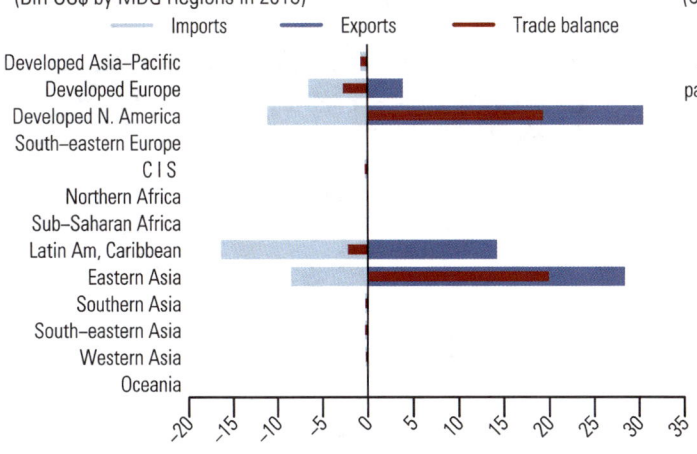

Graph 5: Partner concentration of merchandise trade
(Cumulative share by ranked partners in 2013)

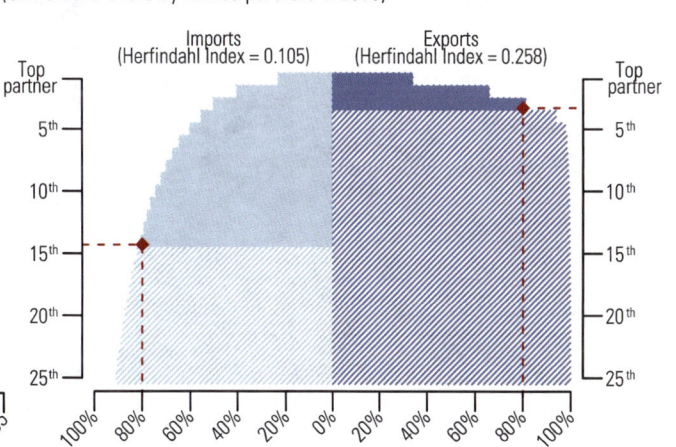

Imports (Herfindahl Index = 0.105)
Exports (Herfindahl Index = 0.258)

Graph 6: Imports of services by EBOPS category
(% share in 2012)

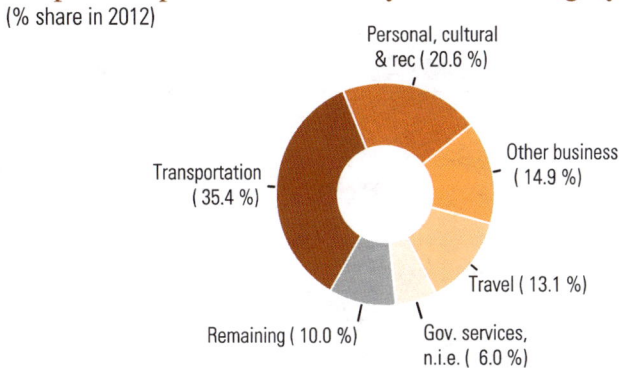

- Transportation (35.4 %)
- Personal, cultural & rec (20.6 %)
- Other business (14.9 %)
- Travel (13.1 %)
- Gov. services, n.i.e. (6.0 %)
- Remaining (10.0 %)

Imports Profile:

"Machinery and transport equipment" (SITC section 7), "Chemicals" (SITC section 5) and "Food, animals + beverages, tobacco" (SITC section 0+1) were the largest commodity groups for imports in 2013, representing respectively 28.9, 19.0 and 16.4 percent of imported goods (see table 3). From 2011 to 2013, the largest import commodity was "Commodities not specified according to kind" (HS code 9999) (see table 4). The top three partners for merchandise imports were the United States, China and Brazil, accounting for respectively 25.0, 15.9 and 9.4 percent of total imports. "Transportation" (EBOPS code 205) accounted for the largest share of imports of services in 2012 at 6.4 bln US$, followed by "Personal, cultural, and recreational services" (EBOPS code 287) at 3.7 bln US$ and "Other business services" (EBOPS code 268) at 2.7 bln US$ (see graph 6).

Table 4: Top 10 import commodities 2011 to 2013

HS code	4-digit heading of Harmonized System 2002	2011	2012	2013	2011	2012	2013	Unit	SITC code
	All Commodities	48 725.7	59 073.2	44 951.8					
9999	Commodities not specified according to kind	2 148.8	2 542.5	3 638.8					931
3004	Medicaments (excluding goods of heading 30.02, 30.05 or 30.06)	2 309.7	2 800.9	2 566.3	49.0	55.7	51.0	US$/kg	542
8525	Transmission apparatus for radio-telephony, radio-broadcasting	1 010.7	999.0	724.2					764
9018	Instruments and appliances used in medical, surgical, dental or veterinary	1 040.0	852.2	486.2					872
0102	Live bovine animals	603.2	1 118.8	633.9	925.0	960.4	971.4	US$/unit	001
0402	Milk and cream, concentrated or containing added sugar	682.8	869.4	729.5	4.2	4.1	4.0	US$/kg	022
0202	Meat of bovine animals, frozen	602.0	776.8	865.4	5.8	5.7	5.7	US$/kg	011
7304	Tubes, pipes and hollow profiles, seamless, of iron (other than cast iron)	489.1	663.5	918.8	2.2	2.3	3.0	US$/kg	679
2304	Oil-cake and other solid residues	592.7	618.7	747.2	0.5	0.6	0.7	US$/kg	081
8471	Automatic data processing machines and units thereof	624.4	728.3	480.3					752

Source: UN Comtrade and UN ServiceTrade

Viet Nam

Goods Imports: CIF, by origin **Goods Exports:** FOB, by last known destination **Trade System:** General

Overview:
In 2013, the value of merchandise exports of Viet Nam increased substantially by 15.3 percent to reach 132.0 bln US$, while its merchandise imports increased substantially by 16.0 percent to reach 132.0 bln US$ (see graph 1, table 2 and table 3). The merchandise trade balance recorded a relatively small surplus of 0.3 mln US$ (see graph 1). The largest merchandise trade balance was with MDG Eastern Asia at -41.8 bln US$ (see graph 4). Merchandise exports in Viet Nam were diversified amongst partners; imports were also diversified. The top 19 partners accounted for 80 percent or more of exports and 10 partners accounted for 80 percent or more of imports (see graph 5). In 2012, the value of exports of services of Viet Nam increased substantially by 10.5 percent, reaching 9.6 bln US$, while its imports of services increased moderately by 5.6 percent and reached 12.5 bln US$ (see graph 2). There was a moderate trade in services deficit of 2.9 bln US$.

Graph 1: Total merchandise trade, by value
(Bln US$ by year)

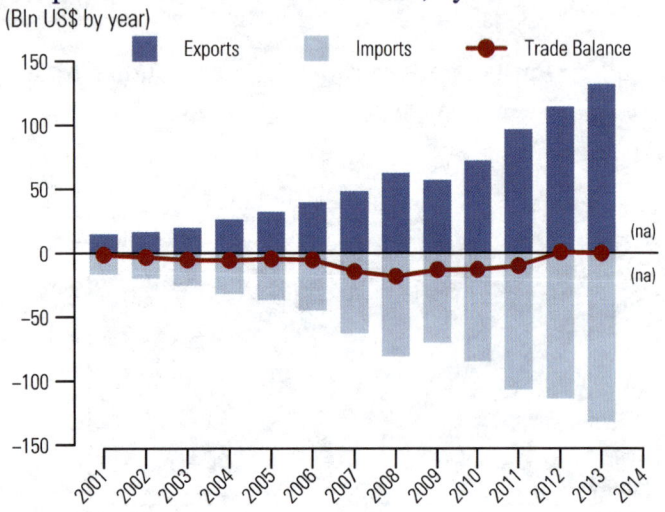

Graph 2: Total services trade, by value
(Bln US$ by year)

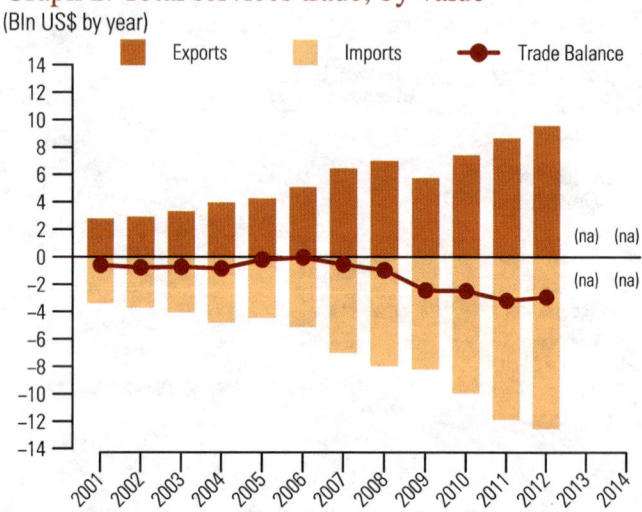

Exports Profile:
"Machinery and transport equipment" (SITC section 7), "Miscellaneous manufactured articles" (SITC section 8) and "Food, animals + beverages, tobacco" (SITC section 0+1) were the largest commodity groups for exports in 2013, representing respectively 32.6, 28.3 and 14.2 percent of exported goods (see table 2). From 2011 to 2013, the largest export commodity was "Electrical apparatus for line telephony or line telegraphy" (HS code 8517) (see table 1). The top three destinations for merchandise exports were the United States, Japan and China, accounting for respectively 17.6, 11.0 and 11.0 percent of total exports. "Travel" (EBOPS code 236) accounted for the largest share of exports of services in 2012 at 6.8 bln US$, followed by "Transportation" (EBOPS code 205) at 2.1 bln US$ (see graph 3).

Graph 3: Exports of services by EBOPS category
(% share in 2012)

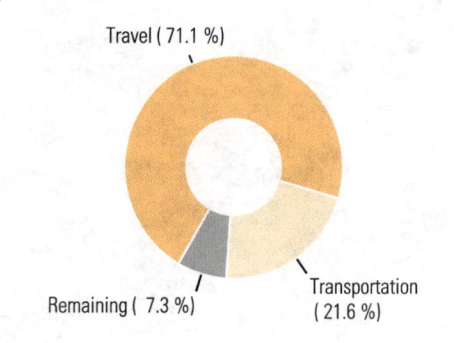

Travel (71.1 %)
Transportation (21.6 %)
Remaining (7.3 %)

Table 1: Top 10 export commodities 2011 to 2013

HS code	4-digit heading of Harmonized System 2007	Value (million US$) 2011	2012	2013	Unit value 2011	2012	2013	Unit	SITC code
	All Commodities	96 905.7	114 529.2	132 032.9					
8517	Electrical apparatus for line telephony or line telegraphy	6 676.5	13 157.0	21 853.0					764
2709	Petroleum oils and oils obtained from bituminous minerals, crude	7 241.5	8 398.0	7 375.4	0.9	0.9	0.9	US$/kg	333
1006	Rice	3 659.2	3 677.9	2 926.3	0.5		0.4	US$/kg	042
6403	Footwear with outer soles of rubber, plastics, leather	2 917.9	3 245.1	3 639.2	31.1		32.7	US$/pair	851
0901	Coffee, whether or not roasted or decaffeinated	2 761.1	3 545.3	2 551.4	2.2	2.1	2.0	US$/kg	071
9403	Other furniture and parts thereof	2 258.1	2 655.1	2 961.8					821
4001	Natural rubber, balata, gutta-percha, guayule, chicle	2 989.2	2 496.2	2 378.7	4.2	2.9	2.4	US$/kg	231
0304	Fish fillets and other fish meat (whether or not minced)	2 348.7	2 415.7	2 262.1					034
6404	Footwear with outer soles of rubber, plastics, leather	1 812.4	2 152.9	2 865.1					851
8443	Printing machinery used for printing by means of the printing type, blocks	1 912.2	2 330.6	2 518.8					726

Viet Nam

Services Imports and Exports: EBOPS 2002 categories

Table 2: Merchandise exports by SITC
(Value in million US$, growth and shares in percentage)

SITC	2013	Avg. Growth rates 2009-2013	2012-2013	2013 share
Total	132 032.9	23.3	15.3	100.0
0+1	18 786.7	12.6	-2.0	14.2
2+4	4 994.5	26.1	9.3	3.8
3	9 685.2	3.3	-14.7	7.3
5	3 829.2	31.9	2.2	2.9
6	13 787.7	27.8	13.6	10.4
7	43 030.4	55.3	40.1	32.6
8	37 313.5	17.0	15.2	28.3
9	605.6	-15.6	32.7	0.5

Table 3: Merchandise imports by SITC
(Value in million US$, growth and shares in percentage)

SITC	2013	Avg. Growth rates 2009-2013	2012-2013	2013 share
Total	132 032.5	17.2	16.0	100.0
0+1	9 402.3	17.6	18.5	7.1
2+4	7 690.8	19.9	5.4	5.8
3	10 118.8	7.8	-11.6	7.7
5	18 178.5	15.5	12.6	13.8
6	29 977.5	14.0	14.7	22.7
7	49 415.5	22.5	27.0	37.4
8	6 474.7	18.6	18.9	4.9
9	774.6	5.2	70.9	0.6

SITC Legend

SITC Code	Description
Total	All commodities
0+1	Food, animals + beverages, tobacco
2+4	Crude materials + anim. & veg. oils
3	Mineral fuels, lubricants
5	Chemicals
6	Goods classified chiefly by material
7	Machinery and transport equipment
8	Miscellaneous manufactured articles
9	Not classified elsewhere in the SITC

Graph 4: Merchandise trade balance
(Bln US$ by MDG Regions in 2013)

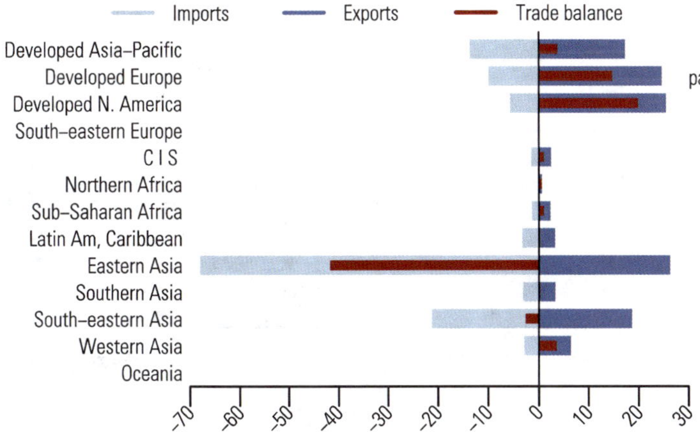

Graph 5: Partner concentration of merchandise trade
(Cumulative share by ranked partners in 2013)

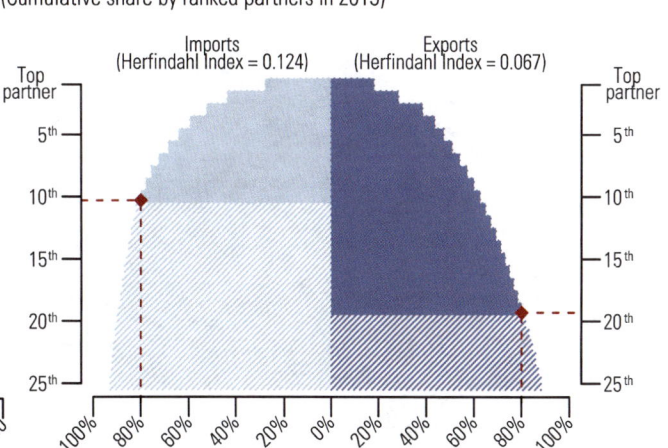

Imports (Herfindahl Index = 0.124)
Exports (Herfindahl Index = 0.067)

Graph 6: Imports of services by EBOPS category
(% share in 2012)

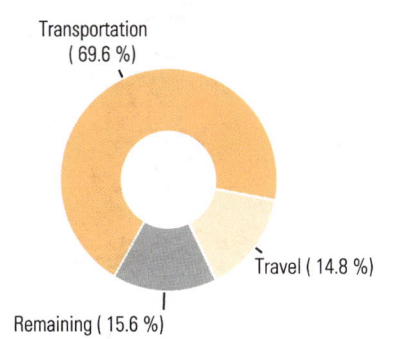

- Transportation (69.6 %)
- Travel (14.8 %)
- Remaining (15.6 %)

Imports Profile:

"Machinery and transport equipment" (SITC section 7), "Goods classified chiefly by material" (SITC section 6) and "Chemicals" (SITC section 5) were the largest commodity groups for imports in 2013, representing respectively 37.4, 22.7 and 13.8 percent of imported goods (see table 3). From 2011 to 2013, the largest import commodity was "Petroleum oils, other than crude" (HS code 2710) (see table 4). The top three partners for merchandise imports were China, the Republic of Korea and Japan, accounting for respectively 25.8, 14.0 and 9.5 percent of total imports. "Transportation" (EBOPS code 205) accounted for the largest share of imports of services in 2012 at 8.7 bln US$, followed by "Travel" (EBOPS code 236) at 1.9 bln US$ (see graph 6).

Table 4: Top 10 import commodities 2011 to 2013

HS code	4-digit heading of Harmonized System 2007	2011	2012	2013	2011	2012	2013	Unit	SITC code
	All Commodities	106 749.9	113 780.4	132 032.5					
2710	Petroleum oils, other than crude	10 341.8	9 356.3	7 392.7					334
8542	Electronic integrated circuits	3 327.6	7 313.5	10 152.8					776
8517	Electrical apparatus for line telephony or line telegraphy	3 233.8	5 314.1	8 559.3					764
7208	Flat-rolled products of iron or non-alloy steel	2 520.6	2 341.3	2 607.7	0.7	0.6	0.6	US$/kg	673
3004	Medicaments (excluding goods of heading 30.02, 30.05 or 30.06)	1 401.8	1 642.8	1 725.4					542
3901	Polymers of ethylene, in primary forms	1 359.9	1 394.2	1 674.5	1.6	1.5	1.6	US$/kg	571
2304	Oil-cake and other solid residues	1 286.9	1 269.8	1 743.3	0.4		0.6	US$/kg	081
6006	Other knitted or crocheted fabrics	1 161.7	1 307.6	1 675.2	9.7		9.5	US$/kg	655
7204	Ferrous waste and scrap; remelting scrap ingots of iron or steel	1 147.3	1 415.4	1 247.1		0.4	0.4	US$/kg	282
3902	Polymers of propylene or of other olefins, in primary forms	1 048.2	1 000.8	1 289.4	1.6	1.5	1.6	US$/kg	575

Source: UN Comtrade and UN ServiceTrade

Yemen

Goods Imports: CIF, by origin **Goods Exports:** FOB, by last known destination **Trade System:** Special

Overview:
In 2013, the value of merchandise exports of Yemen increased slightly by 1.0 percent to reach 7.1 bln US$, while its merchandise imports increased substantially by 17.9 percent to reach 13.3 bln US$ (see graph 1, table 2 and table 3). The merchandise trade balance recorded a large deficit of 6.1 bln US$ (see graph 1). The largest merchandise trade balance was with MDG Western Asia at -3.2 bln US$ (see graph 4). Merchandise exports in Yemen were diversified amongst partners; imports were also diversified. The top 9 partners accounted for 80 percent or more of exports and 17 partners accounted for 80 percent or more of imports (see graph 5). In 2012, the value of exports of services of Yemen increased substantially by 24.4 percent, reaching 1.6 bln US$, while its imports of services increased moderately by 8.1 percent and reached 2.3 bln US$ (see graph 2). There was a moderate trade in services deficit of 764.2 mln US$.

Graph 1: Total merchandise trade, by value
(Bln US$ by year)

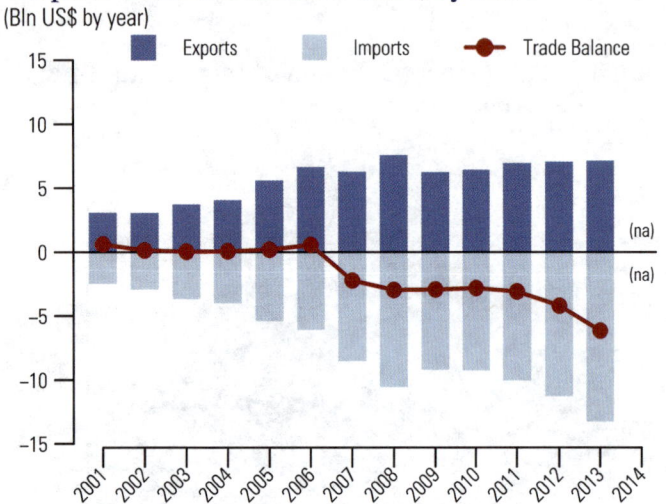

Graph 2: Total services trade, by value
(Bln US$ by year)

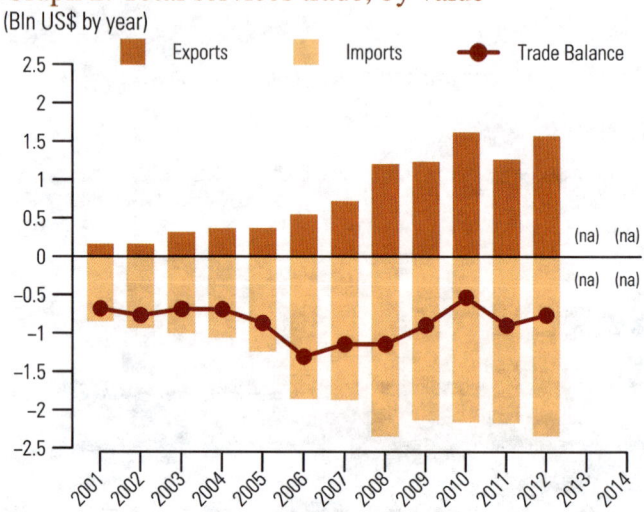

Exports Profile:
"Mineral fuels, lubricants" (SITC section 3), "Not classified elsewhere in the SITC" (SITC section 9) and "Food, animals + beverages, tobacco" (SITC section 0+1) were the largest commodity groups for exports in 2013, representing respectively 83.7, 7.0 and 6.1 percent of exported goods (see table 2). From 2011 to 2013, the largest export commodity was "Petroleum oils and oils obtained from bituminous minerals, crude" (HS code 2709) (see table 1). The top three destinations for merchandise exports were China, Thailand and India, accounting for respectively 32.5, 18.9 and 10.9 percent of total exports. "Travel" (EBOPS code 236) accounted for the largest share of exports of services in 2012 at 848.0 mln US$, followed by "Communications services" (EBOPS code 245) at 325.1 mln US$ and "Transportation" (EBOPS code 205) at 236.5 mln US$ (see graph 3).

Graph 3: Exports of services by EBOPS category
(% share in 2012)

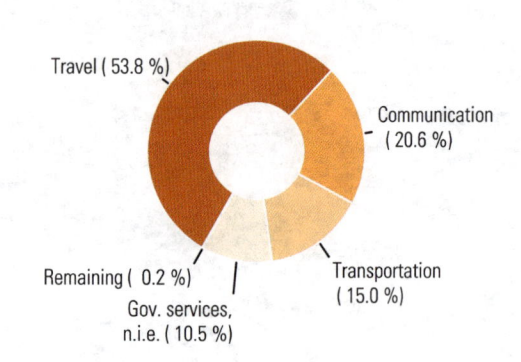

- Travel (53.8 %)
- Communication (20.6 %)
- Transportation (15.0 %)
- Gov. services, n.i.e. (10.5 %)
- Remaining (0.2 %)

Table 1: Top 10 export commodities 2011 to 2013

HS code	4-digit heading of Harmonized System 2007	Value (million US$) 2011	2012	2013	Unit value 2011	2012	2013	Unit	SITC code
	All Commodities	6 947.7	7 062.1	7 129.8					
2709	Petroleum oils and oils obtained from bituminous minerals, crude	4 480.4	5 335.2	3 248.7	0.8	0.8	0.8	US$/kg	333
2711	Petroleum gases and other gaseous hydrocarbons	1 254.3	555.5	2 053.7	0.2	0.2	0.3	US$/kg	343
2707	Oils and other products of high temperature coal tar	112.5	184.2	642.3	0.9	1.0	0.9	US$/kg	335
2710	Petroleum oils, other than crude	282.2	250.5	20.8	0.8	0.8	0.6	US$/kg	334
9999	Commodities not specified according to kind	0.1	1.5	483.6					931
0302	Fish, fresh or chilled, excluding fish fillets	115.8	101.1	121.3	1.8	1.9	2.0	US$/kg	034
0307	Molluscs, whether in shell or not	77.5	49.6	43.1	3.7	3.5	2.5	US$/kg	036
0303	Fish, frozen, excluding fish fillets and other fish meat of heading 03.04	35.0	37.4	27.4	1.1	1.0	1.0	US$/kg	034
8708	Parts and accessories of the motor vehicles of headings 87.01 to 87.05	33.7	44.3	11.3	11.3	14.4	11.4	US$/kg	784
1103	Cereal groats, meal and pellets	15.0	24.3	23.8	0.2	0.2	0.2	US$/kg	04

Source: UN Comtrade and UN ServiceTrade

Yemen

Services Imports and Exports: EBOPS 2002 categories

Table 2: Merchandise exports by SITC
(Value in million US$, growth and shares in percentage)

SITC	2013	Avg. Growth rates 2009-2013	Avg. Growth rates 2012-2013	2013 share
Total	7129.8	3.3	1.0	100.0
0+1	433.5	4.3	-0.9	6.1
2+4	51.3	19.0	83.8	0.7
3	5965.4	1.6	-5.7	83.7
5	39.1	0.9	-14.8	0.5
6	41.9	-5.9	-35.8	0.6
7	90.8	-11.1	-37.9	1.3
8	10.6	-16.0	3.6	0.1
9	497.4	162.9	13503.9	7.0

Table 3: Merchandise imports by SITC
(Value in million US$, growth and shares in percentage)

SITC	2013	Avg. Growth rates 2009-2013	Avg. Growth rates 2012-2013	2013 share
Total	13272.9	9.6	17.9	100.0
0+1	3539.4	9.8	5.0	26.7
2+4	387.4	16.6	10.3	2.9
3	203.1	-43.0	-93.4	1.5
5	960.7	10.9	11.0	7.2
6	1436.8	3.9	19.0	10.8
7	2097.5	-0.6	26.3	15.8
8	430.9	-7.4	25.8	3.2
9	4217.3	308.6	940.0	31.8

SITC Legend

SITC Code	Description
Total	All commodities
0+1	Food, animals + beverages, tobacco
2+4	Crude materials + anim. & veg. oils
3	Mineral fuels, lubricants
5	Chemicals
6	Goods classified chiefly by material
7	Machinery and transport equipment
8	Miscellaneous manufactured articles
9	Not classified elsewhere in the SITC

Graph 4: Merchandise trade balance
(Bln US$ by MDG Regions in 2013)

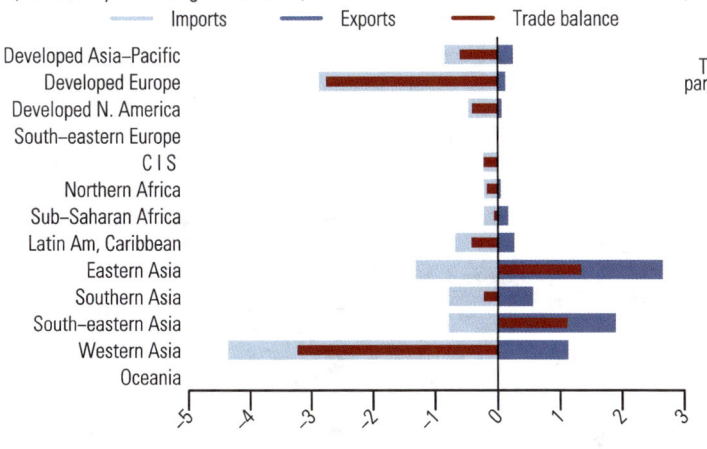

Graph 5: Partner concentration of merchandise trade
(Cumulative share by ranked partners in 2013)

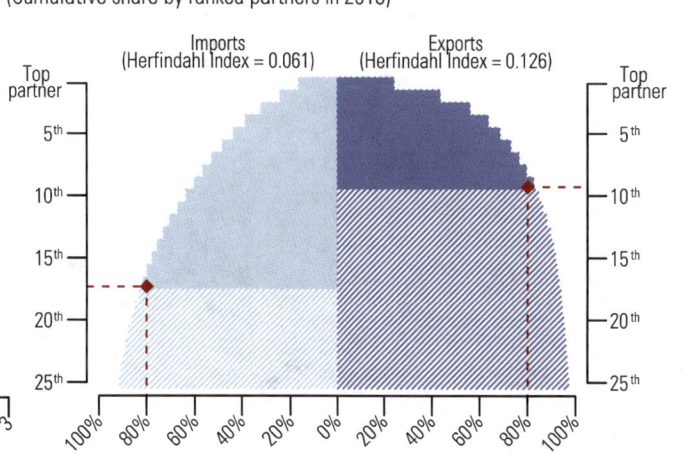

Imports (Herfindahl Index = 0.061)
Exports (Herfindahl Index = 0.126)

Graph 6: Imports of services by EBOPS category
(% share in 2012)

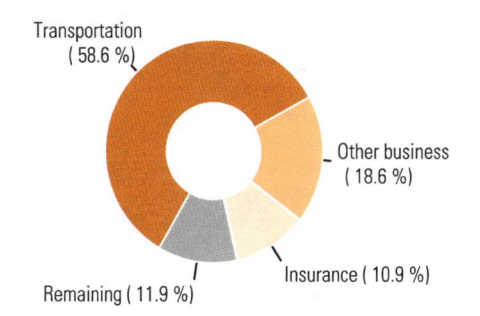

- Transportation (58.6%)
- Other business (18.6%)
- Insurance (10.9%)
- Remaining (11.9%)

Imports Profile:
"Not classified elsewhere in the SITC" (SITC section 9), "Food, animals + beverages, tobacco" (SITC section 0+1) and "Machinery and transport equipment" (SITC section 7) were the largest commodity groups for imports in 2013, representing respectively 31.8, 26.7 and 15.8 percent of imported goods (see table 3). From 2011 to 2013, the largest import commodity was "Petroleum oils, other than crude" (HS code 2710) (see table 4). The top three partners for merchandise imports were the United Arab Emirates, the Netherlands and China, accounting for respectively 12.7, 7.4 and 7.3 percent of total imports. "Transportation" (EBOPS code 205) accounted for the largest share of imports of services in 2012 at 1.4 bln US$, followed by "Other business services" (EBOPS code 268) at 436.1 mln US$ and "Insurance services" (EBOPS code 253) at 255.1 mln US$ (see graph 6).

Table 4: Top 10 import commodities 2011 to 2013

HS code	4-digit heading of Harmonized System 2007	2011	2012	2013	2011	2012	2013	Unit	SITC code
	All Commodities	10033.6	11259.6	13272.9					
2710	Petroleum oils, other than crude	2959.2	3024.2	138.6	0.9	1.0	1.7	US$/kg	334
9999	Commodities not specified according to kind	1.4	354.7	4173.4					931
1001	Wheat and meslin	961.9	983.8	1048.4	0.4	0.3	0.3	US$/kg	041
8703	Motor cars and other motor vehicles principally designed for the transport	414.7	516.9	523.8	11.9	10.9	8.4	thsd US$/unit	781
1701	Cane or beet sugar and chemically pure sucrose, in solid form	513.0	444.7	342.1	0.8	0.7	0.6	US$/kg	061
1006	Rice	239.2	346.3	363.1	0.7	0.8	0.8	US$/kg	042
3004	Medicaments (excluding goods of heading 30.02, 30.05 or 30.06)	191.7	287.2	330.9	11.4	17.5	5.2	US$/kg	542
0207	Meat and edible offal, of the poultry of heading 01.05	166.3	207.0	244.7	2.0	1.8	2.3	US$/kg	012
0402	Milk and cream, concentrated or containing added sugar	156.7	221.6	222.4	3.6	3.5	3.9	US$/kg	022
1511	Palm oil and its fractions	155.7	190.7	211.3	1.0	1.1	1.0	US$/kg	422

Zambia

Goods Imports: CIF, by origin   **Goods Exports: FOB, by last known destination**   **Trade System: General**

Overview:

In 2014, the value of merchandise exports of Zambia decreased moderately by 8.6 percent to reach 9.7 bln US$, while its merchandise imports decreased moderately by 6.1 percent to reach 9.5 bln US$ (see graph 1, table 2 and table 3). The merchandise trade balance recorded a relatively small surplus of 148.9 mln US$ (see graph 1). The largest merchandise trade balance was with MDG Developed Europe at 3.7 bln US$ (see graph 4). Merchandise exports in Zambia were highly concentrated amongst partners; imports were diversified. The top 5 partners accounted for 80 percent or more of exports and 10 partners accounted for 80 percent or more of imports (see graph 5). In 2013, the value of exports of services of Zambia increased substantially by 25.5 percent, reaching 585.4 mln US$, while its imports of services increased substantially by 16.7 percent and reached 1.5 bln US$ (see graph 2). There was a large trade in services deficit of 880.2 mln US$.

Graph 1: Total merchandise trade, by value
(Bln US$ by year)

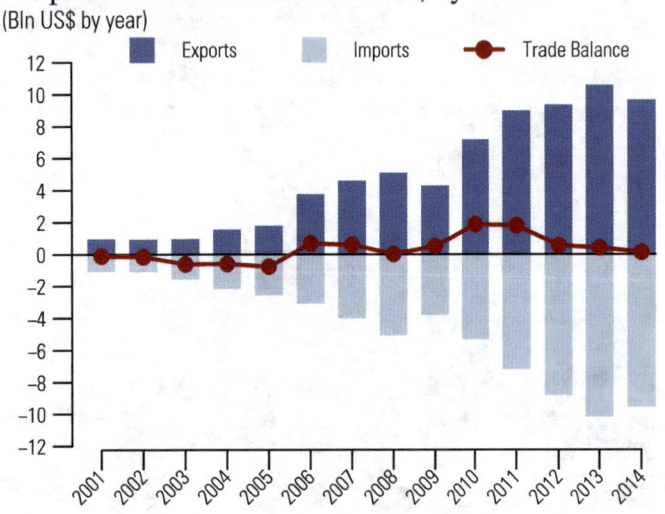

Graph 2: Total services trade, by value
(Bln US$ by year)

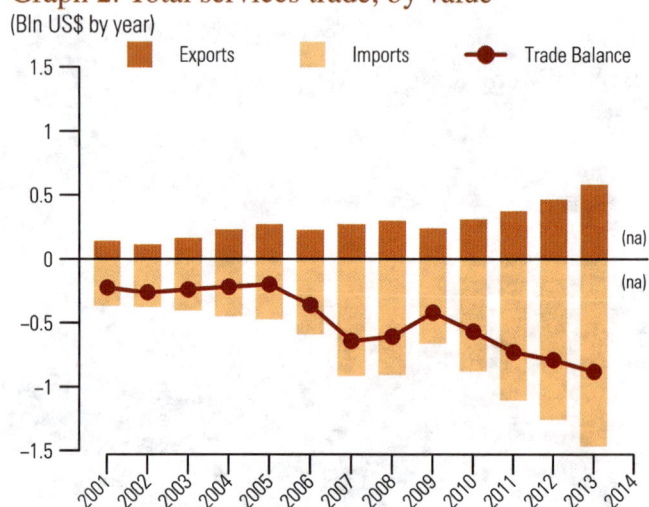

Exports Profile:

"Goods classified chiefly by material" (SITC section 6), "Food, animals + beverages, tobacco" (SITC section 0+1) and "Chemicals" (SITC section 5) were the largest commodity groups for exports in 2014, representing respectively 79.3, 6.6 and 4.0 percent of exported goods (see table 2). From 2012 to 2014, the largest export commodity was "Refined copper and copper alloys, unwrought" (HS code 7403) (see table 1). The top three destinations for merchandise exports were Switzerland, China and Democratic Republic of the Congo, accounting for respectively 41.2, 19.7 and 9.1 percent of total exports. "Transportation" (EBOPS code 205) accounted for the largest share of exports of services in 2013 at 285.8 mln US$, followed by "Travel" (EBOPS code 236) at 224.5 mln US$ and "Personal, cultural, and recreational services" (EBOPS code 287) at 32.6 mln US$ (see graph 3).

Graph 3: Exports of services by EBOPS category
(% share in 2013)

- Transportation (48.8 %)
- Travel (38.4 %)
- Personal, cultural & rec (5.6 %)
- Remaining (7.3 %)

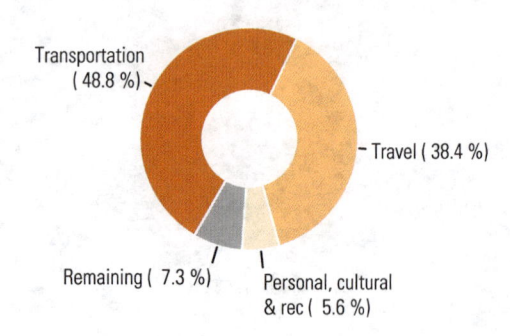

Table 1: Top 10 export commodities 2012 to 2014

HS code	4-digit heading of Harmonized System 2012	Value (million US$) 2012	2013	2014	Unit value 2012	2013	2014	Unit	SITC code
	All Commodities	9364.7	10594.1	9687.9					
7403	Refined copper and copper alloys, unwrought	5936.2	6607.4	7104.5	7.4	7.1	7.5	US$/kg	682
1005	Maize (corn)	414.2	154.8	65.4	0.6	0.9	0.7	US$/kg	044
2807	Sulphuric acid; oleum	76.4	254.0	217.7	0.2	0.7	0.5	US$/kg	522
2401	Unmanufactured tobacco; tobacco refuse	156.7	180.3	143.1	4.1	4.3	4.5	US$/kg	121
8105	Cobalt mattes and other intermediate products of cobalt metallurgy	214.5	132.5	122.7	13.0	24.2	24.9	US$/kg	689
7108	Gold (including gold plated with platinum)	138.5	162.9	117.7	0.1	43.3	41.9	thsd US$/kg	971
1701	Cane or beet sugar and chemically pure sucrose, in solid form	123.5	122.0	132.4	0.6	0.6	0.6	US$/kg	061
7409	Copper plates, sheets and strip, of a thickness exceeding 0.15 mm	276.0	79.0	10.7	9.6	7.9	8.0	US$/kg	682
7408	Copper wire	150.3	127.7	84.5	10.1	9.7	7.6	US$/kg	682
2523	Portland cement, aluminous cement, slag cement	65.8	209.8	68.5	0.2	0.8	0.3	US$/kg	661

Zambia

Services Imports and Exports: EBOPS 2002 categories

Table 2: Merchandise exports by SITC
(Value in million US$, growth and shares in percentage)

SITC	2014	Avg. Growth rates 2010-2014	Avg. Growth rates 2013-2014	2014 share
Total	9687.9	7.7	-8.6	100.0
0+1	637.4	11.8	-38.7	6.6
2+4	354.8	-13.1	-22.9	3.7
3	106.5	30.7	-46.4	1.1
5	391.7	29.8	-39.3	4.0
6	7686.0	7.5	2.1	79.3
7	307.0	22.4	-27.9	3.2
8	74.1	31.8	-22.6	0.8
9	130.5	16.3	-35.6	1.3

Table 3: Merchandise imports by SITC
(Value in million US$, growth and shares in percentage)

SITC	2014	Avg. Growth rates 2010-2014	Avg. Growth rates 2013-2014	2014 share
Total	9539.0	15.7	-6.1	100.0
0+1	361.7	21.5	7.0	3.8
2+4	1763.1	15.8	-2.7	18.5
3	1337.8	21.3	24.2	14.0
5	1292.1	8.7	-18.0	13.5
6	1372.4	12.1	-10.2	14.4
7	3026.2	18.6	-9.9	31.7
8	374.6	15.8	-17.5	3.9
9	11.1	-16.2	-36.2	0.1

SITC Legend

SITC Code	Description
Total	All commodities
0+1	Food, animals + beverages, tobacco
2+4	Crude materials + anim. & veg. oils
3	Mineral fuels, lubricants
5	Chemicals
6	Goods classified chiefly by material
7	Machinery and transport equipment
8	Miscellaneous manufactured articles
9	Not classified elsewhere in the SITC

Graph 4: Merchandise trade balance
(Bln US$ by MDG Regions in 2014)

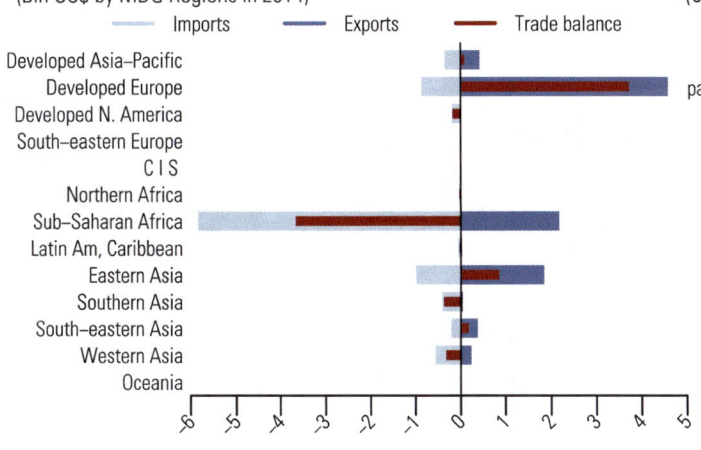

Graph 5: Partner concentration of merchandise trade
(Cumulative share by ranked partners in 2014)

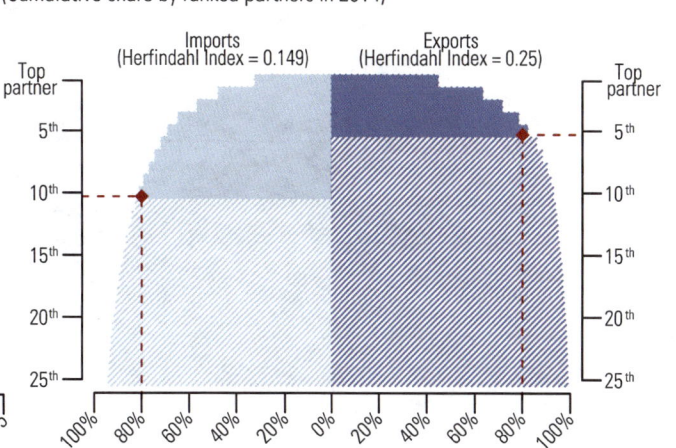

Imports (Herfindahl Index = 0.149)
Exports (Herfindahl Index = 0.25)

Graph 6: Imports of services by EBOPS category
(% share in 2013)

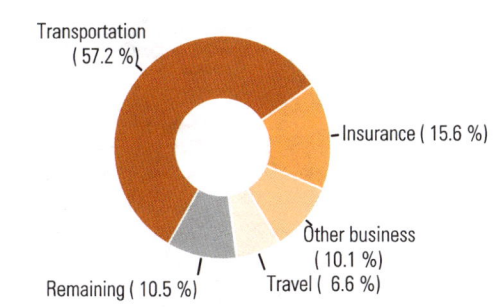

- Transportation (57.2%)
- Insurance (15.6%)
- Other business (10.1%)
- Travel (6.6%)
- Remaining (10.5%)

Imports Profile:

"Machinery and transport equipment" (SITC section 7), "Crude materials + anim. & veg. oils" (SITC section 2+4) and "Goods classified chiefly by material" (SITC section 6) were the largest commodity groups for imports in 2014, representing respectively 31.7, 18.5 and 14.4 percent of imported goods (see table 3). From 2012 to 2014, the largest import commodity was "Copper ores and concentrates" (HS code 2603) (see table 4). The top three partners for merchandise imports were South Africa, Democratic Republic of the Congo and China, accounting for respectively 32.1, 16.0 and 9.4 percent of total imports. "Transportation" (EBOPS code 205) accounted for the largest share of imports of services in 2013 at 838.4 mln US$, followed by "Insurance services" (EBOPS code 253) at 228.9 mln US$ and "Other business services" (EBOPS code 268) at 147.5 mln US$ (see graph 6).

Table 4: Top 10 import commodities 2012 to 2014

HS code	4-digit heading of Harmonized System 2012	Value 2012	Value 2013	Value 2014	Unit value 2012	Unit value 2013	Unit value 2014	Unit	SITC code
	All Commodities	8805.2	10161.8	9539.0					
2603	Copper ores and concentrates	847.1	1389.4	1220.2	3.3	2.9	4.3	US$/kg	283
2710	Petroleum oils, other than crude	315.3	919.7	1075.8	1.5	0.9	1.6	US$/kg	334
8704	Motor vehicles for the transport of goods	366.8	341.0	348.1					782
2709	Petroleum oils and oils obtained from bituminous minerals, crude	543.9	89.1	179.5	0.8	0.2	0.7	US$/kg	333
7308	Structures (excluding prefabricated buildings of heading 94.06)	130.7	325.2	316.2	3.3	2.8	2.9	US$/kg	691
8429	Self-propelled bulldozers, angledozers, graders, levellers, scrapers	219.5	252.4	228.0					723
8474	Machinery for sorting, screening, separating, washing, crushing, grinding	140.5	295.5	208.7					728
8703	Motor cars and other motor vehicles principally designed for the transport	186.7	238.6	213.1	18.5	17.4	17.5	thsd US$/unit	781
3102	Mineral or chemical fertilisers, nitrogenous	158.5	254.3	203.5	0.7	0.7	0.6	US$/kg	562
2605	Cobalt ores and concentrates	190.5	167.4	203.4	2.5	2.7	2.4	US$/kg	287

2014 International Trade Statistics Yearbook, Vol. I
Source: UN Comtrade and UN ServiceTrade

Zimbabwe

Goods Imports: CIF, by origin **Goods Exports:** FOB, by last known destination **Trade System:** General

Overview:
In 2014, the value of merchandise exports of Zimbabwe decreased substantially by 12.6 percent to reach 3.1 bln US$, while its merchandise imports decreased substantially by 17.2 percent to reach 6.4 bln US$ (see graph 1, table 2 and table 3). The merchandise trade balance recorded a large deficit of 3.3 bln US$ (see graph 1). The largest merchandise trade balance was with MDG South-eastern Asia at -1.2 bln US$ (see graph 4). Merchandise exports in Zimbabwe were highly concentrated amongst partners; imports were moderately concentrated. The top 2 partners accounted for 80 percent or more of exports and 8 partners accounted for 80 percent or more of imports (see graph 5). In 2013, the value of exports of services of Zimbabwe increased substantially by 13.7 percent, reaching 439.9 mln US$, while its imports of services increased substantially by 20.4 percent and reached 1.2 bln US$ (see graph 2). There was a large trade in services deficit of 724.9 mln US$.

Graph 1: Total merchandise trade, by value
(Bln US$ by year)

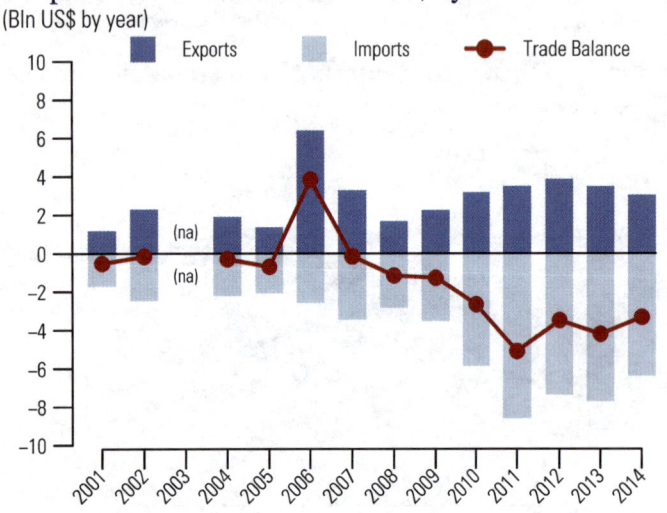

Graph 2: Total services trade, by value
(Bln US$ by year)

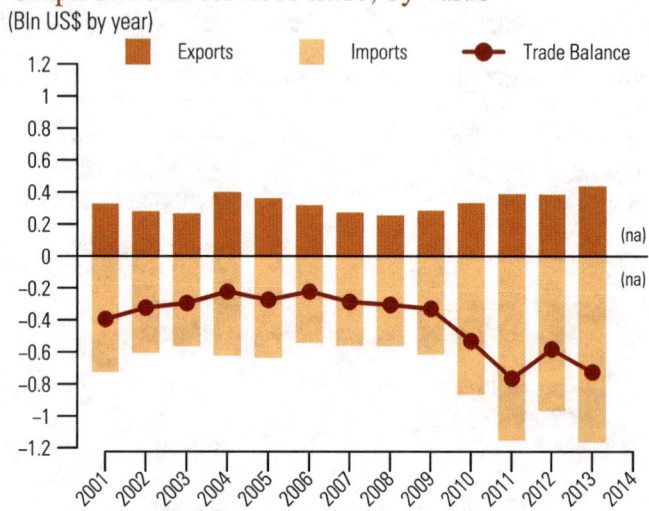

Exports Profile:
"Food, animals + beverages, tobacco" (SITC section 0+1), "Goods classified chiefly by material" (SITC section 6) and "Crude materials + anim. & veg. oils" (SITC section 2+4) were the largest commodity groups for exports in 2014, representing respectively 35.2, 24.2 and 18.9 percent of exported goods (see table 2). From 2012 to 2014, the largest export commodity was "Unmanufactured tobacco; tobacco refuse" (HS code 2401) (see table 1). The top three destinations for merchandise exports were South Africa, Mozambique and the United Arab Emirates, accounting for respectively 70.2, 11.8 and 7.7 percent of total exports. "Travel" (EBOPS code 236) accounted for the largest share of exports of services in 2013 at 198.4 mln US$, followed by "Transportation" (EBOPS code 205) at 164.4 mln US$ and "Government services, n.i.e." (EBOPS code 291) at 41.3 mln US$ (see graph 3).

Graph 3: Exports of services by EBOPS category
(% share in 2013)

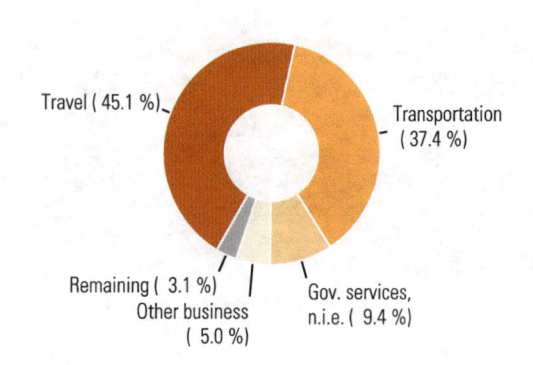

- Travel (45.1 %)
- Transportation (37.4 %)
- Gov. services, n.i.e. (9.4 %)
- Other business (5.0 %)
- Remaining (3.1 %)

Table 1: Top 10 export commodities 2012 to 2014

HS code	4-digit heading of Harmonized System 2007	Value (million US$) 2012	2013	2014	Unit value 2012	2013	2014	Unit	SITC code
	All Commodities	3882.4	3507.3	3063.7					
2401	Unmanufactured tobacco; tobacco refuse	777.9	869.9	807.6	5.9	5.9	5.7	US$/kg	121
7108	Gold (including gold plated with platinum)	624.9	502.5	532.9	39.2		40.5	thsd US$/kg	971
7102	Diamonds, whether or not worked, but not mounted or set	665.7	326.6	233.6	7.1			US$/carat	667
2604	Nickel ores and concentrates	358.2	326.7	354.4	3.3	2.1	1.9	US$/kg	284
7501	Nickel mattes, nickel oxide sinters and other intermediate products	352.5	411.2	4.1	56.4	55.8	50.5	US$/kg	284
7202	Ferro-alloys	127.6	148.4	271.4	1.2	1.0	0.9	US$/kg	671
7110	Platinum, unwrought or in semi-manufactured forms, or in powder form	144.8	140.2	136.9	2.0	2.1	2.1	US$/kg	681
5201	Cotton, not carded or combed	215.2	97.2	66.2	1.6	1.7	1.7	US$/kg	263
1701	Cane or beet sugar and chemically pure sucrose, in solid form	102.7	90.6	150.3	0.7	0.6	0.6	US$/kg	061
2402	Cigars, cheroots, cigarillos and cigarettes	38.1	29.1	22.4	8.4	8.5	7.2	US$/kg	122

Zimbabwe

Services Imports and Exports: EBOPS 2002 categories

Table 2: Merchandise exports by SITC
(Value in million US$, growth and shares in percentage)

SITC	2014	Avg. Growth rates 2010-2014	Avg. Growth rates 2013-2014	2014 share
Total	3063.7	-1.1	-12.6	100.0
0+1	1079.4	16.9	0.2	35.2
2+4	579.2	-16.7	-49.7	18.9
3	14.1	-25.9	-58.0	0.5
5	20.6	-1.3	-36.6	0.7
6	742.4	15.6	23.8	24.2
7	51.2	5.4	-6.6	1.7
8	43.7	-48.2	-5.1	1.4
9	533.2	16.7	4.3	17.4

Table 3: Merchandise imports by SITC
(Value in million US$, growth and shares in percentage)

SITC	2014	Avg. Growth rates 2010-2014	Avg. Growth rates 2013-2014	2014 share
Total	6379.8	2.2	-17.2	100.0
0+1	849.0	-1.7	-13.3	13.3
2+4	240.0	-8.9	-18.2	3.8
3	1566.1	13.7	-3.2	24.5
5	1107.4	13.6	-41.3	17.4
6	708.0	3.9	0.8	11.1
7	1490.6	-7.6	-16.8	23.4
8	372.0	14.5	4.2	5.8
9	46.7	-21.0	-39.3	0.7

SITC Legend

SITC Code	Description
Total	All commodities
0+1	Food, animals + beverages, tobacco
2+4	Crude materials + anim. & veg. oils
3	Mineral fuels, lubricants
5	Chemicals
6	Goods classified chiefly by material
7	Machinery and transport equipment
8	Miscellaneous manufactured articles
9	Not classified elsewhere in the SITC

Graph 4: Merchandise trade balance
(Bln US$ by MDG Regions in 2014)

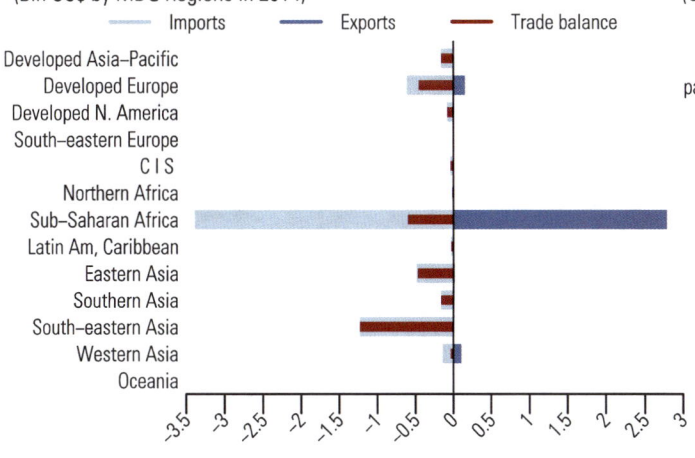

Graph 5: Partner concentration of merchandise trade
(Cumulative share by ranked partners in 2014)

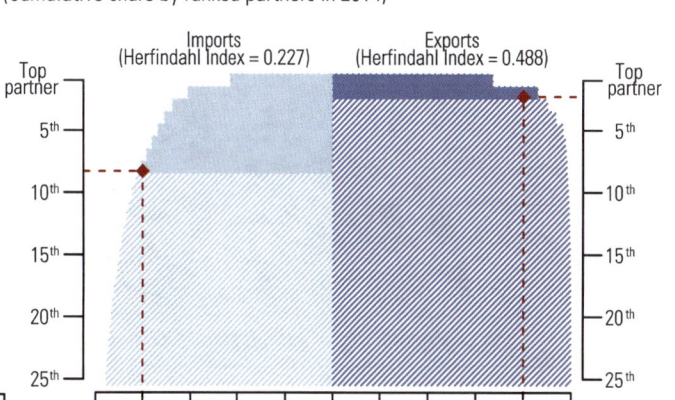

Imports (Herfindahl Index = 0.227)
Exports (Herfindahl Index = 0.488)

Graph 6: Imports of services by EBOPS category
(% share in 2013)

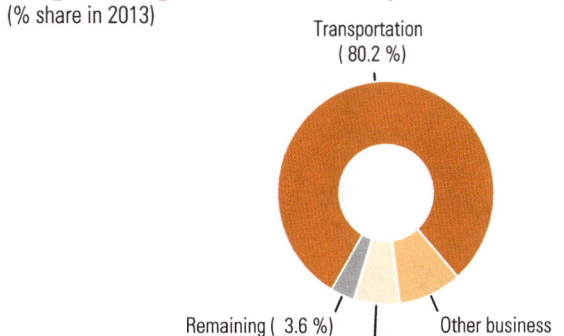

- Transportation (80.2 %)
- Other business (9.5 %)
- Travel (6.7 %)
- Remaining (3.6 %)

Imports Profile:

"Mineral fuels, lubricants" (SITC section 3), "Machinery and transport equipment" (SITC section 7) and "Chemicals" (SITC section 5) were the largest commodity groups for imports in 2014, representing respectively 24.5, 23.4 and 17.4 percent of imported goods (see table 3). From 2012 to 2014, the largest import commodity was "Petroleum oils, other than crude" (HS code 2710) (see table 4). The top three partners for merchandise imports were South Africa, the United Kingdom and Singapore, accounting for respectively 44.3, 13.5 and 5.9 percent of total imports. "Transportation" (EBOPS code 205) accounted for the largest share of imports of services in 2013 at 933.8 mln US$, followed by "Other business services" (EBOPS code 268) at 110.7 mln US$ and "Travel" (EBOPS code 236) at 78.4 mln US$ (see graph 6).

Table 4: Top 10 import commodities 2012 to 2014

HS code	4-digit heading of Harmonized System 2007	Value 2012	Value 2013	Value 2014	Unit value 2012	Unit value 2013	Unit value 2014	Unit	SITC code
	All Commodities	7362.5	7704.2	6379.8					
2710	Petroleum oils, other than crude	1442.7	1511.8	1478.9	1.2	1.2	1.2	US$/kg	334
3105	Mineral or chemical fertilisers	264.8	979.4	89.3	3.2	7.0	0.6	US$/kg	562
8703	Motor cars and other motor vehicles principally designed for the transport	533.3	257.7	197.0	8.9	3.0	1.8	thsd US$/unit	781
8704	Motor vehicles for the transport of goods	391.2	269.2	174.8	9.5	6.6	2.0	thsd US$/unit	782
3004	Medicaments (excluding goods of heading 30.02, 30.05 or 30.06)	148.6	165.5	203.8	46.6	20.8	46.8	US$/kg	542
1005	Maize (corn)	268.8	108.7	114.6	0.6	0.4	0.4	US$/kg	044
8517	Electrical apparatus for line telephony or line telegraphy	115.4	154.3	135.8					764
1006	Rice	102.5	106.5	115.1	0.7	0.7	0.7	US$/kg	042
3102	Mineral or chemical fertilisers, nitrogenous	51.8	80.3	160.8	0.7	0.6	0.8	US$/kg	562
2401	Unmanufactured tobacco; tobacco refuse	159.8	71.6	52.5	3.7	3.7	3.4	US$/kg	121

European Union

Goods Imports: CIF, by origin **Goods Exports:** FOB, by last known destination **Trade System:** Special

Overview:
In 2014, the value of merchandise exports of the EU decreased slightly by 2.5 percent to reach 2337.4 bln US$, while its merchandise imports decreased slightly by 0.4 percent to reach 2274.2 bln US$ (see graph 1, table 2 and table 3). The merchandise trade balance recorded a relatively small surplus of 63.2 bln US$ (see graph 1). The largest merchandise trade balance was with MDG Eastern Asia at -153.4 bln US$ (see graph 4). Merchandise exports in the EU were diversified amongst partners; imports were also diversified. The top 24 partners accounted for 80 percent or more of exports and 22 partners accounted for 80 percent or more of imports (see graph 5). In 2013, the value of exports of services of the EU increased moderately by 6.9 percent, reaching 908.9 bln US$, while its imports of services increased slightly by 3.9 percent and reached 679.0 bln US$ (see graph 2). There was a moderate trade in services surplus of 230.0 bln US$. See footnote*.

Graph 1: Total merchandise trade, by value
(Bln US$ by year)

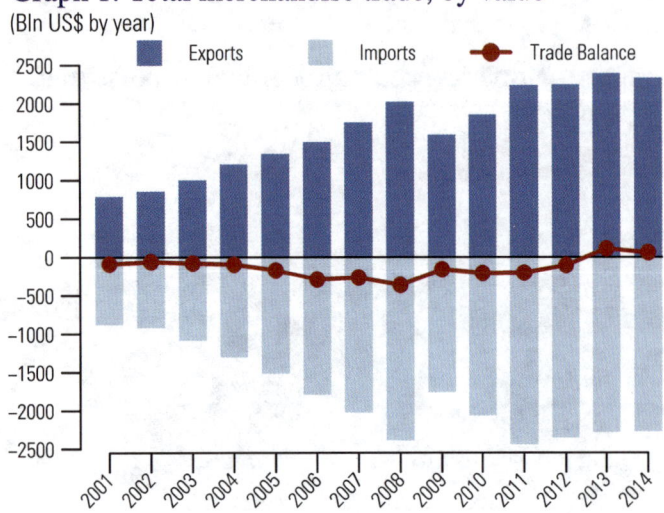

Graph 2: Total services trade, by value
(Bln US$ by year)

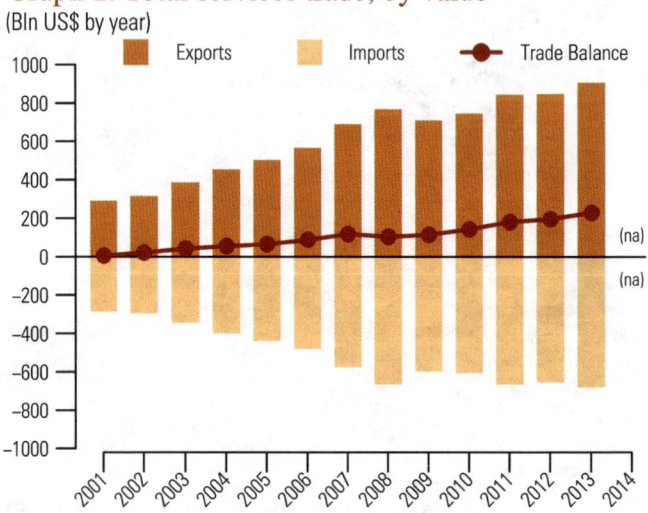

Exports Profile:
"Machinery and transport equipment" (SITC section 7), "Chemicals" (SITC section 5) and "Goods classified chiefly by material" (SITC section 6) were the largest commodity groups for exports in 2014, representing respectively 40.2, 15.5 and 11.2 percent of exported goods (see table 2). From 2012 to 2014, the largest export commodity was "Motor cars and other motor vehicles principally designed for the transport" (HS code 8703) (see table 1). The top three destinations for merchandise exports were the United States, China and Switzerland, accounting for respectively 16.8, 8.6 and 8.4 percent of total exports. "Other business services" (EBOPS code 268) accounted for the largest share of exports of services in 2013 at 291.1 bln US$, followed by "Transportation" (EBOPS code 205) at 186.2 bln US$ and "Travel" (EBOPS code 236) at 134.4 bln US$ (see graph 3).

Graph 3: Exports of services by EBOPS category
(% share in 2013)

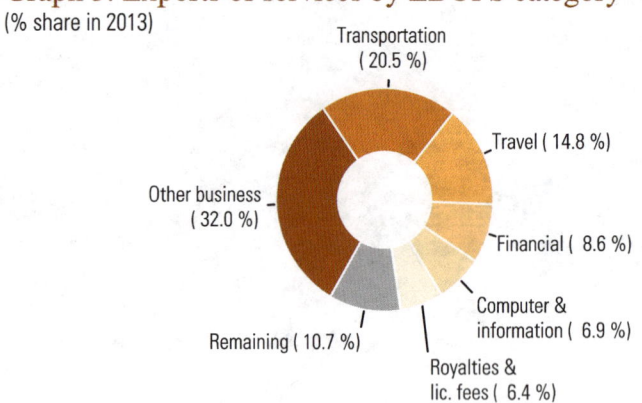

- Transportation (20.5 %)
- Travel (14.8 %)
- Financial (8.6 %)
- Computer & information (6.9 %)
- Royalties & lic. fees (6.4 %)
- Remaining (10.7 %)
- Other business (32.0 %)

Table 1: Top 10 export commodities 2012 to 2014

HS code	4-digit heading of Harmonized System 2012	Value (billion US$) 2012	2013	2014	Unit value 2012	2013	2014	Unit	SITC code
	All Commodities	2251.6	2396.2	2337.4					
8703	Motor cars and other motor vehicles principally designed for the transport	138.9	148.7	152.9	23.8	24.4	27.4	thsd US$/unit	781
9999	Commodities not specified according to kind	143.5	147.4	143.6					931
2710	Petroleum oils, other than crude	130.3	130.0	114.7	0.9	0.9	0.8	US$/kg	334
3004	Medicaments (excluding goods of heading 30.02, 30.05 or 30.06)	95.7	100.2	104.0	126.5	127.1	126.4	US$/kg	542
8802	Other aircraft (for example, helicopters, aeroplanes); spacecraft	52.0	57.9	55.6	14.0	0.4	12.4	mln US$/unit	792
7108	Gold (including gold plated with platinum)	23.9	90.5	46.4	46.6	44.5	38.9	thsd US$/kg	971
8708	Parts and accessories of the motor vehicles of headings 87.01 to 87.05	48.5	52.2	52.4	10.8	11.3	11.8	US$/kg	784
8411	Turbo-jets, turbo-propellers and other gas turbines	38.9	41.9	42.1					714
3002	Human blood; animal blood prepared for therapeutic uses	29.3	30.3	33.5	711.1	667.2	650.8	US$/kg	541
8517	Electrical apparatus for line telephony or line telegraphy	31.1	28.3	26.4					764

*Data beginning 2002 reporting EU-28. Trade in services reporting EU-15 for 2000-2002; EU-25 for 2003; EU-27 for 2004-2009; and EU-28 for 2010-2013.

European Union

Services Imports and Exports: EBOPS 2002 categories

Table 2: Merchandise exports by SITC
(Value in million US$, growth and shares in percentage)

SITC	2014	Avg. Growth rates 2010-2014	Avg. Growth rates 2013-2014	2014 share
Total	2 337 392.1	5.9	-2.5	100.0
0+1	143 011.8	9.2	3.0	6.1
2+4	56 464.1	3.6	-4.9	2.4
3	134 319.9	7.6	-11.4	5.7
5	361 614.5	4.7	1.3	15.5
6	262 384.0	4.0	-0.9	11.2
7	940 417.4	5.6	-0.4	40.2
8	248 034.1	8.0	3.2	10.6
9	191 146.1	7.2	-20.4	8.2

Table 3: Merchandise imports by SITC
(Value in million US$, growth and shares in percentage)

SITC	2014	Avg. Growth rates 2010-2014	Avg. Growth rates 2013-2014	2014 share
Total	2 274 200.5	2.4	-0.4	100.0
0+1	130 178.2	5.1	5.2	5.7
2+4	96 452.9	0.8	-4.4	4.2
3	555 520.9	3.7	-11.0	24.4
5	215 078.9	4.7	3.8	9.5
6	229 617.1	2.8	4.8	10.1
7	598 945.3	0.5	3.2	26.3
8	311 727.5	3.4	8.3	13.7
9	136 679.7	-0.5	-2.6	6.0

SITC Legend

SITC Code	Description
Total	All commodities
0+1	Food, animals + beverages, tobacco
2+4	Crude materials + anim. & veg. oils
3	Mineral fuels, lubricants
5	Chemicals
6	Goods classified chiefly by material
7	Machinery and transport equipment
8	Miscellaneous manufactured articles
9	Not classified elsewhere in the SITC

Graph 4: Merchandise trade balance
(Bln US$ by MDG Regions in 2014)

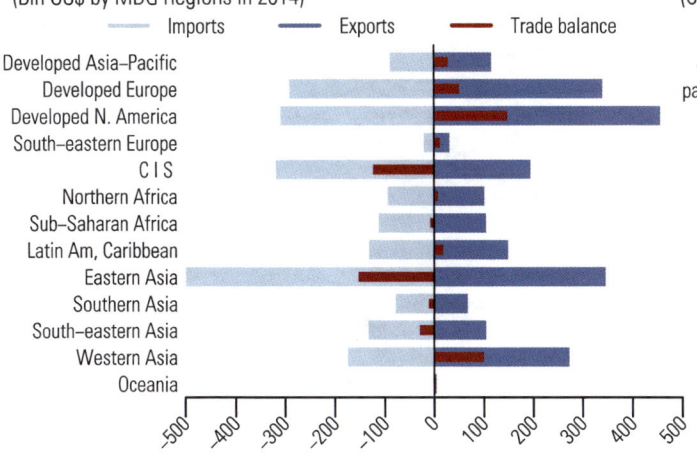

Graph 5: Partner concentration of merchandise trade
(Cumulative share by ranked partners in 2014)

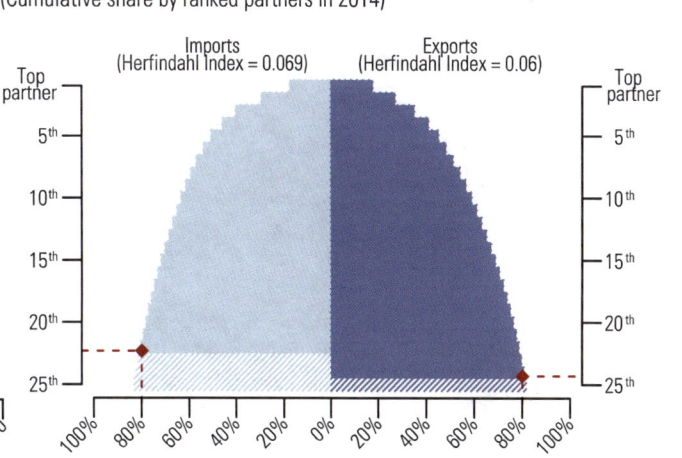

Imports (Herfindahl Index = 0.069)
Exports (Herfindahl Index = 0.06)

Graph 6: Imports of services by EBOPS category
(% share in 2013)

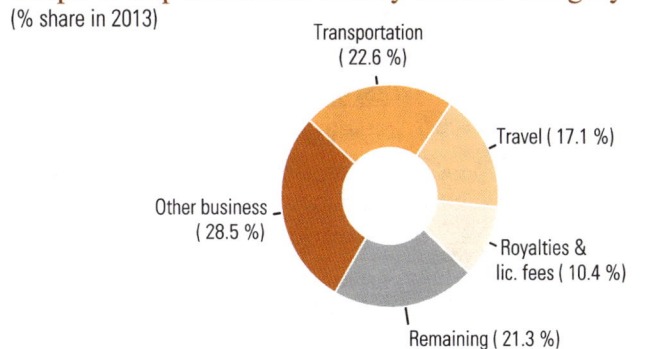

- Transportation (22.6 %)
- Travel (17.1 %)
- Royalties & lic. fees (10.4 %)
- Remaining (21.3 %)
- Other business (28.5 %)

Imports Profile:

"Machinery and transport equipment" (SITC section 7), "Mineral fuels, lubricants" (SITC section 3) and "Miscellaneous manufactured articles" (SITC section 8) were the largest commodity groups for imports in 2014, representing respectively 26.3, 24.4 and 13.7 percent of imported goods (see table 3). From 2012 to 2014, the largest import commodity was "Petroleum oils and oils obtained from bituminous minerals, crude" (HS code 2709) (see table 4). The top three partners for merchandise imports were China, the United States and the Russian Federation, accounting for respectively 16.6, 11.5 and 11.5 percent of total imports. "Other business services" (EBOPS code 268) accounted for the largest share of imports of services in 2013 at 193.8 bln US$, followed by "Transportation" (EBOPS code 205) at 153.8 bln US$ and "Travel" (EBOPS code 236) at 116.0 bln US$ (see graph 6).

Table 4: Top 10 import commodities 2012 to 2014

HS code	4-digit heading of Harmonized System 2012	2012	2013	2014	2012	2013	2014	Unit	SITC code
	All Commodities	2 354.2	2 283.8	2 274.2					
2709	Petroleum oils and oils obtained from bituminous minerals, crude	436.9	401.7	360.6	0.8	0.8	0.7	US$/kg	333
9999	Commodities not specified according to kind	118.4	115.5	107.6					931
2710	Petroleum oils, other than crude	105.1	112.8	101.9	0.9	0.9	0.8	US$/kg	334
2711	Petroleum gases and other gaseous hydrocarbons	85.1	82.3	66.7	0.6	0.6	0.5	US$/kg	343
8517	Electrical apparatus for line telephony or line telegraphy	61.1	65.6	65.1					764
8471	Automatic data processing machines and units thereof	57.1	58.2	58.4	133.0	132.6	110.6	US$/unit	752
3004	Medicaments (excluding goods of heading 30.02, 30.05 or 30.06)	39.3	38.8	41.8	247.6	234.0	246.3	US$/kg	542
7108	Gold (including gold plated with platinum)	62.8	23.9	28.0	51.1	41.1	39.8	thsd US$/kg	971
8411	Turbo-jets, turbo-propellers and other gas turbines	32.8	34.1	34.6					714
8703	Motor cars and other motor vehicles principally designed for the transport	31.5	31.6	32.4	14.7	14.5	14.5	thsd US$/unit	781

Source: UN Comtrade and UN ServiceTrade

Country Trade Profiles
Profils de pays de commerce

General notes:

For further information on Sources, Method of Estimation, Currency Conversion, Period, Country Nomenclature and Country Grouping of this table, as well as for a brief table description, please see the Introduction.

Remarque générale:

Pour plus d'information en ce qui concerne les sources, la méthode d'estimation, taux d'exchange, période, nomenclature des pays et groupement de pays, ainsi que pour une brève description de ce tableau, veuillez voir l'introduction.